Hans Moldenhauer and Arthur Vogel
Matterhorn (August 2, 1933)
Photograph taken by Fritz Kast

The Rosaleen Moldenhauer Memorial

Music History from Primary Sources

The Rosaleen Moldenhauer Memorial

Music History from Primary Sources

A Guide to the Moldenhauer Archives

Jon Newsom and Alfred Mann

Editors

Library of Congress   Washington 2000

Endpapers map:

Sheet 22 (printed 1917) from *Topographische Karte der Schweiz* (1/100,000) by G. H. Dufour.
Geography and Map Division, Library of Congress

Frontispiece:

A page from Beethoven's autograph copy of portions from the second act of Mozart's *Don Giovanni.* The text appears in German translation, and the Beethoven bibliographer George Kinsky assumed that Beethoven made the copy for study purposes in preparation for composing ensemble sections in *Fidelio.*

The Library of Congress plans to make a version of this publication available through the Internet. We will be grateful for information about any errors you discover in this book so that they can be corrected in future electronic editions. Please address comments to the editor at the following E-mail address: cwar@loc.gov; or at the following address: Jon Newsom, Chief, Music Division, Library of Congress, Washington, DC 20540-4710.

Library of Congress Cataloging-in-Publication Data

The Rosaleen Moldenhauer memorial : music history from primary sources
   : a guide to the Archives / Jon Newsom and Alfred Mann, editors.
      p.   cm.
   Essays relating to manuscripts in the Moldenhauer Archives at the
Library of Congress, founded by Hans Moldenhauer. Includes inventory.
   Includes bibliographical references.
   ISBN 0-8444-0987-1
  ------   Z663.37 .R67   1999
   1. Music—Manuscripts.   2. Music—History and criticism.
3. Library of Congress.   4. Moldenhauer Archives at the Library of
Congress.   I. Moldenhauer, Rosaleen.   II. Newsom, Jon, 1941– .   III. Mann,
Alfred, 1917–   .   IV. Moldenhauer, Hans.   V. Moldenhauer Archives
at the Library of Congress.   VI. Title: Music history from primary sources.
ML93.R67   2000   99-24281
016.78—dc21   CIP

DER BERG

Er ist der stolze Herr
der Wolken und des Sturms.
Und stößt mit heller Stirn
hoch an der Sterne Dach.

THE MOUNTAIN
He is the proud lord
of the clouds and the storm
And thrusts with bright brow
high up to the stars' roof.

Er ist der Erde Haupt.
Er ist das Ziel der Welt.
Und ist doch Brücke nur
in ein geträumtes Land.

HANS MOLDENHAUER

He is the earth's peak
He is the world's destination
And yet is only a bridge
into a dreamed land.

Contents

xiii Foreword
James H. Billington
The Librarian of Congress

xv Acknowledgments
Jon Newsom
Chief, Music Division

xix **Introduction**
Jon Newsom

1 **Music History from Primary Sources**
An Introductory Essay
Alfred Mann

3 The Art of Musical Notation
12 The Rise of Music Drama
27 Classicism and Romanticism
60 An Age of Personal Memory

79 **Essays on Selected Documents**
81 The Nathan Bequest: Payment Receipts in the Hand of Johann
Sebastian Bach, 1746 to 1748 (With a Fragment for the Year
1749 in the Hand of His Son)
Robert L. Marshall

86 Comments on Béla Bartók's Working Method in Dealing with
Proofs for His Violin Concerto (1937–1938)
Ferenc Bónis

102 A Sketch Leaf from Ludwig van Beethoven's Piano Sonata,
op. 28
Susan Clermont

109   A Beethoven Sketch for the Puzzle Canon "Das Schweigen,"
WoO 168
Susan Clermont

115   Two Sketches for Alban Berg's *Lulu*
Patricia Hall

121   Ernest Bloch's Conducting Score for *Schelomo*
Michael Nott

126   John Blow's "Arise, Great Monarch, and Ascend the Throne"
Watkins Shaw

134   Pierre Boulez's *Le Marteau sans maître*
Robert Piencikowski

142   Johannes Brahms's Autograph of "Die Kränze"
Jürgen Thym

147   Two Brahms Letters
Jürgen Thym

156   Some Autobiographical Overtones in Brahms's *Rinaldo*
Carol A. Hess

161   Two Letters by Anton Bruckner
Jürgen Thym

169   Dr. Burney, Samuel Wesley, and J. S. Bach's *Goldberg Variations*
Philip Olleson

176   John Cage's "The Wonderful Widow of Eighteen Springs"
Lauriejean Reinhardt

182   Pablo Casals: A Letter Written from Exile
Douglas W. Foard

190   Mario Castelnuovo-Tedesco's "Ozymandias"
Massimo Ossi

198   A Chopin Manuscript: Prelude in A-flat Major, op. posth.
Robin Rausch

201 Luigi Dallapiccola's Sketch for *Ulisse*
   Wayne Shirley

206 Frederick Delius's "Zwei Braune Augen"
   Don C. Gillespie

213 George Gershwin: A Sketch for *Porgy and Bess*
   Wayne Shirley

217 Excerpts from Gluck's *Alceste*, Copied and Revised by Hector
   Berlioz
   Joël-Marie Fauquet

228 George Frideric Handel's 1749 Letter to Charles Jennens
   William D. Gudger

239 Karl Amadeus Hartmann's *Miserae* (1933–1934)
   Lauriejean Reinhardt

249 Josef Matthias Hauer's *Melischer Entwurf*
   Lauriejean Reinhardt

258 Paul Hindemith's *Hérodiade*
   Jürgen Thym

266 Arthur Honegger's "Les Ombres": Fragment of a Lost Film Score
   Fred Steiner

272 Transformation and Adaptation: The Evolution of Charles Ives's
   Song "From 'Paracelsus'"
   Felix Meyer

283 The Kerver *Missale Romanum*
   Denise P. Gallo

288 Franz Liszt's *Psalm XVIII*
   Rena Charnin Mueller

297 Witold Lutosławski *Venetian Games*
   Michael O'Brien

301 Gustav Mahler Sketches in the Moldenhauer Archives
Edward R. Reilly

313 Felix Mendelssohn-Bartholdy: Overture to *Elijah*, Arrangement
for Piano Duet (1847)
R. Larry Todd

321 A Letter by Pietro Metastasio
Denise P. Gallo

327 Wolfgang Amadè Mozart's Allegro and Andante ("Fantasy")
in F Minor for Mechanical Organ, K. 608
Neal Zaslaw

341 The Coronation Scene from Modest Musorgsky's *Boris Godunov*
in Rimsky-Korsakov's Edition
Kevin LaVine

350 Krzysztof Penderecki's *Polymorphia* and *Fluorescences*
Peggy Monastra

358 A Fragment from Act II of Giacomo Puccini's *La Bohème*
Linda B. Fairtile

367 George Rochberg's *Fifth Symphony:* A Commentary by the
Composer

369 Gioachino Rossini's *Moïse*
Philip Gossett

375 Arnold Schoenberg's *Adagio for Strings and Harp*
Claudio Spies

385 Two Leaves of Sketches for Arnold Schoenberg's Concerto for
String Quartet and Orchestra
Claudio Spies

392 Of Songs and Cycles: A Franz Schubert Bifolio
Morten Solvik

400 Gunther Schuller on Edward Steuermann and Schuller's
Symphony for Brass
Interview with Jon Newsom

414 Robert Schumann's *Burla* in G Minor
John Daverio

420 Igor Stravinsky's *Threni*: Conducting Details
Claudio Spies

429 Germaine Tailleferre's *Concerto pour Piano et 12 Instruments*
Michael O'Brien

431 Aurelio de la Vega's *The Magic Labyrinth:* Reminiscences
of the Composer

436 Giuseppe Verdi's *Attila*
Philip Gossett

444 Anton Webern's Six Pieces for Orchestra, op. 6, Arrangement
for Chamber Ensemble
Felix Meyer

456 Anton Webern's "Mein Weg geht jetzt vorüber," op. 15, No. 4
Lauriejean Reinhardt

462 Anton Webern's *Zwei Lieder für gemischten Chor,* op. 19
Lauriejean Reinhardt

469 Anton Webern's Jone Poems
Lauriejean Reinhardt

475 Frank Wedekind: Stock Poster with His Autograph Prologue
to *Der Erdgeist*
Lauriejean Reinhardt

483 **Inventory**

729 Glossary

730 Repositories

731 Contributors

Foreword

IN 1987, A BEQUEST OF HANS MOLDENHAUER (1906-1987)
brought to the Library of Congress the greatest composite gift
of musical documents this institution has ever received.
Established as the Moldenhauer Archives at the Library of
Congress, it consisted of about 3,500 autograph music
manuscripts, letters, and other materials spanning the range
of musical genres from medieval chant to modern serialism,
with neumes inscribed with quill on vellum to innovative
notations for aleatoric orchestral effects written with colored
ball-point pen.

The donor also provided a generous fund to support his
directive that the Library publish a book about his fabulous
Archives as a memorial to his wife of nearly forty years,
Rosaleen, who had worked with him on his collection and had
been his coauthor in researching and writing a monumental
biography of Anton Webern. In October 1986, he wrote to Jon
Newsom of the Library's Music Division saying that "a
preliminary telephone conversation would serve the end of a
distinct opportunity for direct and close collaboration." That
letter initiated a working friendship through which, among
other things, the outlines of this volume were developed
during the last year of Dr. Moldenhauer's life. The relationship
has since been carried on by his wife, Mary, who has nobly
supported the project in the spirit of both Hans and Rosaleen
Moldenhauer.

The original plan grew in scope from a choice collection of
illustrated essays dealing with a selection of the Moldenhauers'
most prized manuscripts to a book that would include, besides
the essays, a comprehensive inventory of all holdings of the
Moldenhauer Archives at all nine institutions, including the
Library of Congress, to which over the years portions of the

Archives had been sent: the Paul Sacher Foundation (Paul Sacher Stiftung), Basel; the Bavarian State Library (Bayerische Staatsbibliothek), Munich; the Houghton Library of Harvard University, Cambridge, Massachusetts; Northwestern University, Evanston, Illinois; the Viennese Municipal and National Library (Wiener Stadt- und Landesbibliothek); the Central Library of Zürich (Zentralbibliothek Zürcher); the Washington State University, Pullman; and Whitworth College, Spokane. This undertaking, proposed at first by Dr. Moldenhauer when he hoped the completion of his memorial work to Rosaleen might fall within his lifetime, was initially abandoned as impractical but, after his death, was once again taken up as a way of fulfilling his dream that through the Library of Congress the fruits of his collecting could be described and gathered together in one volume.

James H. Billington
The Librarian of Congress

Acknowledgments

The Music Division has been blessed with donors, each of whom has shaped, through a personal vision, the course of our development. This volume is the first landmark in the work that Hans Moldenhauer envisioned when he bequeathed the greatest portion of his Archives to the Library of Congress. Dedicated to the memory of his wife Rosaleen, with whom he gathered the Moldenhauer Archives and who is the first author of the extensive inventory contained at the end of this book, it marks the beginning of a program of acquisitions, publications, commissions, performances, and other appropriate activities to be supported by the Moldenhauer Fund. After Rosaleen's death in 1982, Dr. Moldenhauer married Mary Moldenhauer, who has actively continued building the Archives and guiding this publication. Since his death in 1987, her deep and informed involvement with the publication of this book has been for its editors and other staff of the Library a source of inspiration and wisdom. She has united her understanding of the donor with a growing knowledge of the institution to whom he entrusted the greatest work of his lifetime. In so doing, she has become a trusted friend and benefactor to whom we owe the highest gratitude.

During his tenure as chief of the Music Division (1987–1995), James W. Pruett generously gave his advice and support for this publication. He was instrumental in bringing to the Music Division a former student, Carol Lynn Ward-Bamford, who became my editorial assistant for the last five years of the project, and she assumed a crucial role in coordinating all aspects of the work. Susannah C. Lyson served as my first editorial assistant during the initial planning of the inventory and essays. Building on the pioneering labors of Rosaleen Moldenhauer, whose comprehensive catalog forms the basis of the inventory published here, she produced the first draft of the inventory. Mrs. Jefferson Patterson, a benefactor to the Library, established the Junior Fellows Program to bring young scholars to work during the summers on processing special collections. Several of these Fellows worked on the Moldenhauer Archives and made valuable contributions to this book: Linda B. Fairtile, Gail Miller, Michael O'Brien, and Ann Silverberg. We were also greatly assisted in the processing of the Archives, the preparation of the inventory, and in many other ways by students from the Catholic University of America whom Prof. Cyrilla Barr graciously sent: Margaret Ball, Esperanza Barrocal, Christine Bisacco, Gregory Capaldini, Betsy Dean, Evelyn Donnelly, Dee Gallo, Marcelo Campos Hazan, Chun-Zen Huang, and Alejandro Muzio.

Library staff assisted through their expert knowledge of languages and subjects: Carol Armbruster (French), E. Paul Frank (Hungarian), Grant Harris (European languages), George Kovtun (Czech), Everette E. Larson (Hispanic Literature), Kevin LaVine (Russian), and David Skelly (Russian). Ron Grim, of the Geography and Map Division, found the map of the Swiss Alps used for the endpapers. Sam Brylawski, of the Motion Picture, Broadcasting, and Recorded Sound Division, enabled us to organize and describe the sound recordings. Wilda Heiss was instrumental in getting the inventory into a DOS database, and Jason Yasner's knowledge of the Apple Macintosh system saw us through several software and hardware problems. Portions of this book have been prepared for release by the Library on its web page through the Library's National Digital Library, and several of its staff members advised us on technical matters that contributed to the production of the book, including the digital scanning of items selected for illustration. For this assistance, we are grateful to: Carl Fleischauer, Morgan Cundiff, David Arbury, Jeni Dahmus, Debbie Fulmore, Susan Manus, and Ashley Short. During the organization of materials and their preparation for scanning, the staff of the Conservation Office—in particular, Ann Seibert, Jake Benson, and Yasmeen Khan—assured their safe handling and provided necessary conservation treatment and housing. My wife, Iris Newsom, senior editor of the Library's Publishing Office, helped to plan the book from the beginning, edited the typescript of the book at several stages of its preparation, and, along with Gloria Holmes, also of the Publishing Office, moved this unusually complex project through production. Our designer, Stephen Kraft, provided exceptional advice and support above, beyond, and even before the call of duty, since he joined the project at its outset to help us visualize and budget the volume when it was just a dream. While not on the Library's staff, his nearly ten years of patient dedication to this undertaking earn him honorary status as one of this institution's treasures.

Librarians from many other institutions corrected inventory entries for items in their collections: Ulrich Montag, Hartmut Schaeffer, and Renata Wagner (of the Bavarian Municipal Library); Barbara Wolff (of Harvard University Library); Don L. Roberts (of Northwestern University Library); Felix Meyer (of the Sacher Foundation); Otto Brusatti and Ludwig Neunlinger (of the Vienna State Library); John Guido, Mark Bolton, William Brandt, Robert N. Matuozzi, and John Mueter (of the Washington State University Library); and Christopher Walton (of the Zurich Central Library).

We received further generous advice in many ways from Anthony Beaumont (on Schoenberg), Manuel Barrueco (on Segovia), Suzanne Bloch (on her father, Ernest Bloch), David Cannata (on Russian manuscripts), Tom Denny (on Schubert), Mark Devoto (on Berg), Christopher Hogwood (on Handel and Haydn), Mary I. Ingraham (on Brahms), Robert Kimball (on Cole Porter), Hugh Macdonald (on Berlioz), Awadagin Pratt (on Franck), Fr. Alvaro Ribeiro (on Charles Burney), Susan T. Sommer (on the inventory), Ruth Steiner (on Gregorian Chant), Charles Sutoni (on Liszt), James Webster (on Schubert), and Victor Yuzefovich (on several Russian musicians). Gudula Fischer was a longtime assistant to Hans and Rosaleen Moldenhauer. Others who assisted the Moldenhauers were Enid Alger, Theresa Allen, Kelly Farris, Anne Marie Baker Fuhrmeister, Edwin Haugan, Elizabeth Kopzcynski Moore, Cynthia A. Prior, and Isabel d'Urbal. Ethel Louise Kelsy served as secretary to Alfred Mann. We are indebted to Henry Krotoschin for his photograph of Hans Moldenhauer on Mount Blanc. Furthermore, for their general interest and guidance, we wish to thank Dr. Moldenhauer's nephew, Henry Huttenbach, and Albi Rosenthal, a longtime friend and associate of the Moldenhauers.

We owe special thanks to Alfred Mann. He introduced Hans Moldenhauer to Rosaleen and remained their lifelong friend. His initial role as advisor and author of the book's opening section soon extended to work on all aspects of its development. I am deeply grateful that he accepted the responsibilities of co-editor in this ambitious undertaking, for without his collaboration the publication of this volume would not have been possible.

Jon Newsom
Chief, Music Division

Introduction

Jon Newsom

THIS BOOK, WHICH DOCUMENTS THE Moldenhauer Archives now in the Library of Congress and eight other institutions, is the realization of a project first envisioned by Hans Moldenhauer in 1982 as a memorial to Rosaleen, his wife of nearly four decades. He referred to it often as "my Taj Mahal." They collaborated throughout most of their long marriage in a working relationship that grew early out of their common interest in music—both were professional pianists—and, in later years, his increasing dependence on Rosaleen as his eyesight progressively weakened.

Although parts of his Archives became famous for their richness in manuscripts of such renowned composers as Brahms, Mahler, and Webern, his idea had always been to gather documents from the entire history of Western music, an ambitious undertaking that even a major library would find daunting. His enterprise was unusual, too, in another way, for not only had he the private collector's necessary passion for, and aesthetic appreciation of, the things he acquired, but he also saw their importance for research.

His motto for the Archives, "Music History from Primary Sources," might well have been the motto, beginning in the 1950s, of every music historian concerned with Western music, for there was then no authoritative body of scores of the works of the great masters consistently based on available primary sources. Musicologists had only just begun, after the disruptions of the Second World War, to address the need to make new critical editions. The nineteenth century, to be sure, had produced monumental editions of Bach, Beethoven, and Mozart. Even earlier music by such composers as Palestrina, Couperin, and Schütz had been carefully edited and published during that century when Europeans were rediscovering their great artistic heritage. After Mendelssohn's historic revival of Bach's *St. Matthew Passion* in 1829, Germans were particularly active in bringing to light forgotten masterpieces. But in the postwar years of our century, there were several important developments of which scholars could take advantage: a growing number of trained musicologists; improved methods of making inexpensive microfilms, which provided better access than before to original sources; and a widely available and reliable history of paper and watermarks which provided new tools for dating and authenticating works. With due acknowledgment to such pioneers as the Bach scholars Phillip Spitta and Wilhelm Rust, music historians undertook first a complete revision of the chronology of Bach's musical works and then a new edition based on holographs and other primary sources. Each volume was issued with a separate, detailed, measure-by-measure commentary documenting the editor's decisions. Similar projects for Handel, Mozart, Beethoven, and many others were soon to follow. This was the beginning of an era in which standard editions of familiar classics fell under the suspicion of infidelity to the intentions of the composer. Artur Schnabel's insightful but highly interpretive edition of Beethoven's piano sonatas was among the many well-worn tomes with which generations of musicians had grown up that were replaced by new scholarly editions that stripped away layers of all phrasings, dynamics, tempo indications, and other such markings added without the composer's authority. Henceforth, no respectable performer could fail to consult the so-called "Urtext" if it were published; and graduate seminars in musicology frequently relied on photocopies of manuscripts rather than printed scores. It was primarily for this new breed of researcher that Moldenhauer proudly built his collection.

Yet he had the connoisseur's sense of the intrinsic worth of a beautiful and rare page, and so, besides their research value, some of his manuscripts— and these were the ones he treasured most highly—represent, in his words, "tangible links with the esoteric efforts which produced them in the composer's hour of inspiration." We stand in awe before the pages on which Mozart or Brahms wrote down a memorable piece and wonder at the mysterious role that the composer's original notation plays in the relationship between his musical idea, its realization as sound by a performer, and the listener. The manuscript score serves, on the one hand, its essential and practical function of charting for singers and instrumentalists a succession of pitches in time. On the other hand, it has acquired, for the listener drawn to it out of reverence for the audible art it serves, a silent and numinous significance as a sacred relic of the act of musical conception, a tangible link with esoteric efforts. There is, moreover, the strong visual impact that many music manuscripts have as kinetic art, whether or not they can always be considered calligraphic in the truest sense. Whether or not they are written at the hour of inspiration, many listeners see in composers' manuscripts characteristics analogous to the music itself: Webern's precise expressivity, Beethoven's cerebral urgency. Whatever our subjective response may be to such things, Moldenhauer appreciated their visual beauty or graphic style as well as their associative and informative value, collected them passionately as his sight failed, and held them vividly in his mind's eye when he could no longer see them.

Aware that he could not afford to acquire representative documents from Gregorian chant to the present day in examples of only major composers and musicians, Moldenhauer took a great interest in subordinate figures with significant associations. In his own words, the scope of his Archives was to include "not only the bricks, but the mortar." For this he had a special genius for finding not only interesting items from lesser figures, but documents that show great ones occupied with matters other than the original work for which they are famous: Berlioz, for example, restoring Gluck's *Alceste*; or Beethoven copying, presumably for his own edification, ensembles from Mozart's *Don Giovanni*.

In his early days of collecting, Moldenhauer also successfully acquired manuscripts from younger contemporaries, adding to his Archives valuable sketches and complete scores of composers who were then just beginning to be recognized: Boulez, Lutosławski, Penderecki, Rochberg, Schuller, and Stockhausen, among others. Among musicians of the twentieth century, he was also particularly interested in those who, like himself, had been uprooted by the rise of Fascism: Mario Castelnuovo-Tedesco,

Wolfgang Fraenkel, Karl Weigl, and Jaromir Weinberger. They had escaped the concentration camps, but some were shattered. While the Italian Castelnuovo-Tedesco had the temperament and technical facility to adapt to life in America and enjoy a successful career in Hollywood, Weinberger was never able to resume his once brilliant career. In 1967, after putting his manuscripts in order, he committed suicide.

Hans Moldenhauer was born in Mainz in 1906. The two pillars of his education, beyond the traditionally rigorous Gymnasium, were music and mountain climbing. His musical training consisted of five years at the Mainz Municipal College of Music with the eminent Hans Rosbaud, best known to several generations of musicians as a conductor whose recordings made it possible to hear for the first time superbly realized performances of music by Schoenberg, Berg, and Webern, and also Stravinsky after his adoption of serial techniques. It was with Rosbaud that Moldenhauer must have developed his interest in contemporary music. The piano, however, was Moldenhauer's major interest, and his proficiency on it enabled him to establish himself professionally as a musician when he was finally forced to move with his family to America.

He emigrated to the United States in May 1938, arriving in New York, and was followed a few months later by his first wife, Margot, his mother-in-law, and his two children. As a German, his heritage of forests and, most important to him, mountains, was as much a part of him as music. One can only imagine how desolate the mountainless city skyline appeared to the man, leaving a home whose landscape of alps, far more than providing familiar and comforting scenery, was a way of life. His unpublished essay "Die Bergsteiger-Legende" (The Legend of the Mountaineer) is about the ethos of climbing in those mountains where he developed the characteristic tenacity and courage with which he met life's later challenges. In July 1939, encouraged by what he had learned of his new country's northwest, he bought a single round-trip bus fare to Spokane, Washington. Almost at once, he led a climbing party up Mt. Rainier, established himself as a piano teacher, and began a new life. In the last year of his life, he recalled that somewhere in his unsorted papers one might still find the unused part of his bus ticket.

Among his students was a young woman named Rosaleen Jackman. When he was drafted to serve, because of his alpine skills, as an instructor in the U. S. Army's newly formed 10th Mountain Division, Rosaleen took over his private teaching. Shortly after, she joined him as a Red Cross nurse where he was stationed at Camp Hale, Colorado, and they were married there in 1943. Camp Hale was a spectacular and rugged base situated on the Eagle River 100 miles west of Denver, surrounded by mountains and with winter temperatures of 30 degrees below zero. During training there, Moldenhauer suffered frostbite and was unable to join his Division when it was sent into combat in Italy.

After his honorable discharge from the Army in August 1943, he and Rosaleen returned to Spokane, where they resumed their musical activities. In 1946, the Spokane Conservatory, which he had founded in 1942, was incorporated as an educational institution. Having earned his bachelor's degree in music as Whitworth College's first student under the G.I. Bill in 1945, and receiving in the same year an honorary doctorate from Chicago's Boguslawski College of Music, he completed his doctoral dissertation, "Duo-Pianism," at Roosevelt University's Chicago Musical College. Published in 1950, it remains a unique and important study.

At about this time, with the onset of an illness diagnosed as retinitis pigmentosa—an hereditary disease that is incurable, progressive, and eventually leads to blindness—he started to build the great collection of musical documents for which he is best known. Albi Rosenthal, a longtime friend and an eminent dealer in music manuscripts, recalls that Moldenhauer began collecting in the early 1940s and recollects the story that, even as a boy, he was teased by his father for his preoccupation with his "little bits of paper." But he decided to embark on serious collecting after the prognosis that he might lose his sight completely within two years. By giving him an urgent incentive to make the most of his failing eyesight, it was, in his opinion, a fortuitous misprognosis without which he might neither have conceived the project of his Archive nor pursued it with such urgency. Happily, however, the process which was predicted to take two years took more than twenty.

The Moldenhauer Archives had become legendary in the 1960s with Moldenhauer's acquisition of the Anton Webern papers. After the death of Schoenberg in 1951, increasing interest in his music extended to the work of his two great pupils, Alban Berg and Webern. Webern had remained particularly obscure even for a twelve-tone composer of the time. Not only had the source of his few published works, as with other contemporaries, been cut off by the war, but being ethnically, if not musically, unobjectionable to the Nazis, he had chosen to remain in his native Austria where, his music banned, he earned a living as a proofreader. Then, the war over, at the age of sixty-one and at the peak of his creative powers, he stepped out of his house one evening to smoke a cigar and, apparently misunderstanding an order to identify himself—it was September 1945 at the beginning of the occupation—was shot and killed by an American soldier.

In 1959, on a visit to Webern's last home in the Austrian village of Mittersill, Moldenhauer began investigating the then still mysterious circumstances of Webern's tragic death. It marked the beginning of his long association with the Webern family, which began in 1961 to give him the composer's papers. His research led first to the publication of an article in the *New York Times*, then a book, *The Death of Anton Webern*, and, finally, to his and Rosaleen's major Webern biography in 1978. Speaking of this labor in 1987, he recalled his ambivalent feelings toward not Webern the artist but the man whose national loyalty and unshaken pride in his noble lineage during the Nazi regime—the Webern genealogy is among the manuscripts Moldenhauer acquired from Webern's heirs—he felt to be morally questionable. And he recalled the anger it caused him, which Rosaleen, who occasionally even suggested that he abandon the biography, could not fully share.

Raised a Christian by Christian parents, he was proud of his Jewish lineage. Among his last major acquisitions was the holograph score of *Schelomo*, the only major Bloch manuscript not already in the comprehensive Bloch collection at the Library of Congress. He dictated the following note in his catalog:

> The manuscript was acquired in tribute to Rabbi Solomon Weil, to his son Abraham Weil (first Jewish tax collector

in Royal Bavarian employ and honorary citizen of Leimersheim in the Palatinate) and to his eldest daughter, Thekla Weil. A Christian, she married Richard Moldenhauer and became the mother of Hans Moldenhauer.

In January 1987, Moldenhauer ruminated over the placement of his remaining Archives. He had given careful consideration to finding appropriate institutions for certain parts of the Archives. His Richard Strauss, Reger, Pfitzner, and Berg manuscripts were already in Munich. He had just offered his Loeffler and Castelnuovo-Tedesco materials to the Library of Congress, which has the virtually complete manuscripts of both composers, and an important group of Brahms manuscripts, in consideration of the Library's exceptional Brahms collection, was to follow.

Yet he was hesitant in settling on a home for certain other pieces. In 1984, most of his Webern manuscripts had already joined the significant twentieth-century collections at the Sacher Foundation in Basel, but he had set aside a portion of them, along with other jewels he had reserved as a memorial collection to Rosaleen, for the crown—his "Taj Mahal"—that he had planned for her, and these he finally decided to keep with the body of that memorial collection that is now at the Library of Congress.

But old conflicts continued to disturb him, and when he spoke of the "out and out contest between the old and new world" it seemed that he was referring not only to external pressures but to his continuing inner struggle to reconcile his love for the world that had rejected him with the loyalties he had developed in his adopted nation. He recounted a conversation of some ten years earlier with a former classmate who had said, regarding certain portions of his Archives still in Spokane: "Strictly speaking, those things belong in Germany," to which Moldenhauer had responded: "Strictly speaking, so do I."

Over the years during which Moldenhauer sold and donated parts of his Archives, various other items found homes away from the places in which, strictly speaking, one might expect them to be. Besides Brahms's, manuscripts of other German masters, including Bach, Beethoven, Mendelssohn, Schumann, and Wagner came to the Library of Congress, along with those of composers of virtually every other nation. Yet the sketches for Hindemith's *Hérodiade*, commissioned by the Coolidge Foundation in the Library of Congress, are in Basel. Important American pieces that complement the Library's holdings are at Harvard. It cannot be entirely without deliberation on Moldenhauer's part that at least some of these things occurred, and it is certain that at the end he foresaw the constructive possibilities of such distributions.

During his lifetime, he established the Moldenhauer Archives in nine institutions in the United States and Europe. While he probably never envisioned a single repository for his Archives, the matter of unification was of deep concern to him, as was the matter of continuity. He did not wish to have the fruits of his and Rosaleen's labors scattered in such a way that they would be inaccessible through a central institution, nor did he want the acquisition of new archival materials to cease when he could no longer personally direct the activities of the Moldenhauer Archives. It was his hope that the Library of Congress could provide not only a home for the very substantial remainder of his Archives not already in other institutions, but that it could continue in his name the role he had played for nearly four decades in acquiring, cataloging, and preserving archival materials that are the primary sources for musical research. This we are able to do, thanks to the bequest of a fund that came with the Archives and the continued generosity of Mary Moldenhauer. Above all, it was his hope that this volume, much of which we planned with him, would be the cornerstone of a cooperative program supported by all custodians of the Moldenhauer legacy.

Jon Newsom
Chief, Music Division

Music History
from Primary Sources
An Introductory
Essay

Alfred Mann

erat dragma den. O culpa nimiu[m] b[ea]ta. q[ue] t[a]-
cep... O[mne]s q[ui] c[re]ditur O x[pist]e p[at]ris unice.
Et quo[rum] p[ar]ticipe te f[ier]e dig. es ih[es]u
dignat. co[rum] l... p[re]c. O[mne]s ip[s]os d[i]ut. i. p[ro].
S[an]ctificami[n]i filie syon + c[...]
te quia die hodierna uid[ebitis] m[a]-
iestate[m] d[e]i i[n] uobis. Hodie sci[ti]s
quia ueniet dominus. + uide-
bitis gloriam eius i[n] uobis.

doro te raro do-
minica. que
sola digna fu-
isti tegere so-
le[m] iustitie. + di-
uitat[i]s radi-
os obu[m]bra[n]-
do occultare. Tu medicina sa-
lutifera. te gestauit p[r]ius salua

The Art of Musical Notation

I N ITS PRIMARY SOURCES, MUSIC MERGES with the representational arts. Oral tradition has played a fundamental role in all ages, but in its formal sense, history—and the history of music—begins with the visual record.

Musical notation, having emerged on a wide scale in all civilizations, produced in itself a highly individual record of artistic endeavor. The medieval monks who compiled the missals and other liturgical books for the service of worship rose from their function as scribes to artists in their own right; among the greatest documents of Baroque art are the holographs by Bach; and an entirely novel phase in artistic musical score design was initiated in the twentieth century. The primary sources of music reproduced in this volume rely on various aspects of the graphic arts, but foremost among them stands the representation of the musical sound itself, the art of musical notation.

Among the manifold forms the written image of music has taken are letters or syllables, to represent individual tones, and symbols to represent groups of them. But a more advanced approach is expressed in notation guided not only by the wish to fix the immediate impression of a given musical sound but by the attempt to render the act of musical performance in its continuity. The notational signs which were to prove of the most lasting influence were the highly expressive neumes; it was from them that the generally surviving style of musical script arose. The term was derived from the Greek word *neuma*—a nod or motion, and in this particular context the manual gesture or gestures to establish different pitch levels—and it suggests the melodic flow as indicated by the leader of an ensemble. Widely used in Eastern and Western music practice, the neumes were invariably connected with vocal

(Opposite page)
A vellum leaf, 22 by 17 cm., from a prayer book. The letter forms of early Gothic script suggest the twelfth century, or a period even earlier. Neumes (marked in red) are placed above the first four lines of the Latin text. The entire page is richly illuminated in black, red, and blue, with a heavy gold layer decorating the initial A for the phrase beginning "Adoro te." The leaf was obtained for the Moldenhauer Archives from the music dealer and publishing firm Schneider, Tutzing.

performance whose notation was also greatly aided by the joining of musical symbols with verbal text.

The decisive step in the evolution of a readily perceptible image for the musical sound was taken by the Benedictine monk Guido of Arezzo (circa 1000), the preceptor of the cathedral choir school at that northern Italian city and a theorist of unusual pedagogical gift. Guido's achievement was in placing the neumes on lines, for clearer orientation drawn in different colors and representing the interval of a third. With this invention he created the basis of a system that has remained alive in modern practice. So immediately successful was his method that Pope John XIX, "after brief instruction, and to his own surprise, was able to sight-read a melody not previously known to him, without any error," and in justified pride, Guido added "*musica sine linea est sicut puteus sine fune*" ("music without lines is like a well without a rope").[1]

Guido's refinements in the definition of pitch were followed by corresponding advances in graphically defining the musical sound's duration. The use of neumes gradually gave way to that of square-shaped notes and combinations of notes in so-called ligatures. While obviously emanating from the forms of neumes, these new symbols served their purpose with greater exactness of detail.

The need for such exactness had arisen with the evolution of polyphony, the decisive occidental contribution to the history of music. Influences from the south and east met with those from the north and west by which traditions of monophonic music—unaccompanied melody—merged with developments in probing the harmony of simultaneously sounding voices. They led to the work of the masters at Notre Dame in Paris and various other regions of northern France, the first figures in music history who stand out as individual composers of indigenous styles. In the early polyphonic settings of chant, long and short note values were distinguished by applying the rhythmic modes, inferred from the verse meters of antiquity, to groups of notes. But fourteenth-century theorists declared a categoric difference between old and new styles (*ars antiqua* and *ars nova*), the latter reflected by means of notation that departed from the modal system and adopted a system of strict

[1] Guido's text is given in vol. II of the series *Scriptores Ecclesiastici de Musica,* published in 1784 by the Benedictine scholar Martin Gerbert.

measuring, the so-called mensural notation. The differentiation of note values grew, adding to the horizontally placed square shapes more precisely placed diamond shapes; and the color of notes changed from black to white (i.e., a mere black outline of the note shape which, once again, ensured greater precision of notation).

The magnificent appearance of missals from the waning Middle Ages and early Renaissance, with their lavish illuminations, may make it at times difficult to decide which is the greater artistic achievement: the manuscript itself, or the art it represents. We are dealing with a period that was not yet fully conscious of the distinction between artist and artisan known in later ages. But the time was approaching when the work of the scribe was supplanted by that originating in centers of printing whose interest and influence reached beyond the sphere of the individual artifact. The process of music printing obviously grew in stages. In early phases, merely the lines were given in print, the neumes being entered by hand, or folios were produced by "double printing"—the lines in red and, in a second imprint, the notes in black. The first printer of mensural music, the Venetian Ottaviano Petrucci, was for a long time considered the inventor of the art of printing music with movable type, yet his excellent work (begun about 1500) was preceded by that of various print shops in the north.

The sixteenth century became a "golden age" that produced the classical summaries of the art of vocal polyphony in sacred and secular music as well as in treatises on music theory. Among the latter, *L'Istitutioni Harmoniche* (1555, reprinted 1562 and 1573) by Gioseffo Zarlino (1517–1590), Master of the Chapel at St. Mark's in Venice, assumed a preeminent place. As the title suggests, the work was dedicated to the age-old ideals of symmetry and proportion, the "harmony of all parts in relation to the whole," as described by the writers of antiquity. In his thorough discussion of the correlation of tones and melodies, Zarlino—like the early authors on perspective—saw himself obliged to create a completely new terminology. His concern with measurement and the concepts of division and inversion

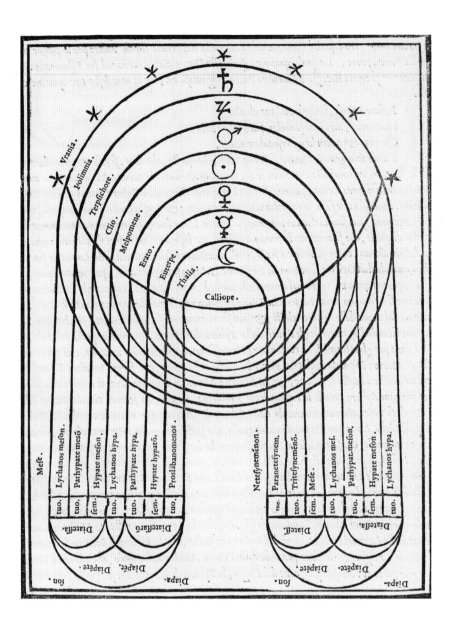

One of the typical illustrations from *L'Istitutioni Harmoniche,* linking the octave (diapason) and its divisions into fifth (diapente) and fourth (diatessaron) to the astrological signs for the days of the week and the names of the Muses. (The interval names appear at the bottom, printed upside-down.)

lends his work an authority extending to the fine arts as much as to music, and the numerous ornamental illustrations accompanying his text go far beyond the traditional embellishment of enhanced initial letters. They render scientific design that represents a true counterpart to the decorative music printing of the era.

The work is divided into four parts which the author joins in two larger sections. The first pair deals with the conceptual and physical properties of the musical sound, and the second with the technique of composition. What Zarlino recognizes

·6·

and, in fact, reconciles, is the time-honored distinction between *musica speculativa* and *musica activa*—theory and practice. In a rather robust way, Guido had referred to the two domains with the well-known verse:

Musicorum et cantorum magna est distantia
Isti dicunt, illi sciunt, quae componit musica

Between musicians and singers exists a wide gulf
The latter perform, the former know, the substance of music

His dichotomy led Guido into a bit of polemic comment on "those who do what they not know" which has remained alive through the centuries, though amply misconstrued. While Zarlino links an introductory chapter on the division of music into speculative and practical branches to "the difference between musician and singer," he significantly redefines the ideas and terms involved, because he speaks of the *musico* as the artist able to judge not only the sound but also the "reason contained in this science," whereas the *prattico* is considered, in his text, on equal terms with a "composer, singer, or player." He states categorically that "practical music is the art of counterpoint," and that the domains of theory and practice are, as in other arts, complementary rather than opposed.

What is of special interest is that he refers to the practice of playing as well as singing, for the rise of instrumental music had posed a fresh challenge to polyphony and to its notation. Zarlino's music examples are still arranged according to the old choir book notation in which the separate voices appear side by side; and the audition requirements for early sixteenth-century organists, which have been preserved, call for the ability to play a motet from the given number of individual part books. Such an astounding grasp of polyphonic texture, however, gradually became a rare achievement. A historic exception was Mozart's encounter with the choral music of Bach, kept in the library of St. Thomas's church in Leipzig only in separate parts. The account of an eyewitness reads: "and then it was for the silent observer a joy to see how eagerly Mozart sat himself down, with the parts all around him—in both hands, on his knees, and on the chairs next to him—and, forgetting everything else, did not get up again until he had looked

The floral arabesque cover design (seventeenth to eighteenth century, possibly Turkish) was created through a process known as paper marbling, an ancient art whose origins remain unclear. Many marble papers were collected by travelers to the East and used in "Alba Amicorum" (early autograph albums) or as wrappers for ephemeral documents. A systematic study of prevalent paper samples shows this particular piece to be exceedingly rare.

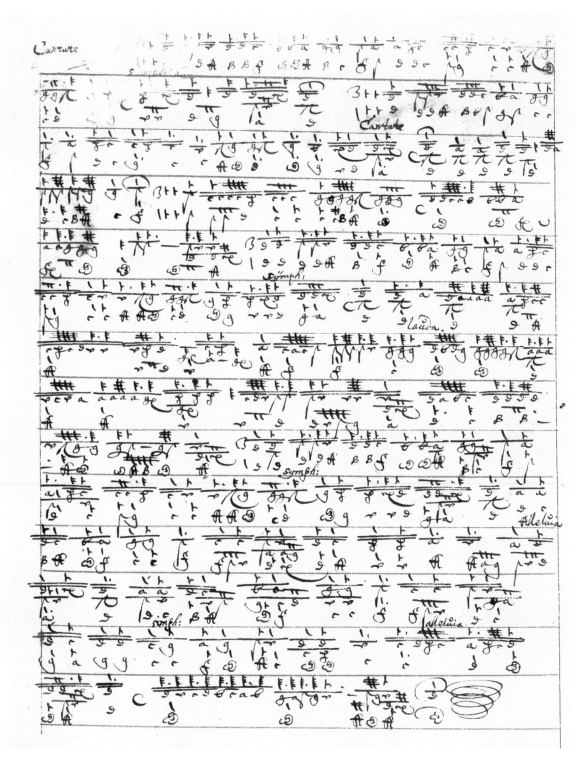

Excerpt from a manuscript written in German organ tablature. It is a keyboard score whose two voices display in their letter notation the flourishes that indicate sharping of a given tone. Apparent is its connection with a vocal work, whose sections are marked either by "Symphonia" (instrumental introduction or interlude), text beginning ("Cantate," "lauda," "Alleluia") or metric indication (C or 3/1).

[2] Quoted from H. T. David and A. Mendel, *The Bach Reader* (New York: Norton, 1945, 1966), p. 360. The work has since appeared as *The New Bach Reader*, ed. by Christoph Wolff (New York: Norton, 1998), where the quotation is given on page 488.

through everything."[2] The sixteenth-century organist, faced with the task of rendering all parts of a polyphonic composition on a single instrument, soon felt the need to tabulate them in a form in which their simultaneous sound could be readily recognized. The "tabulations" that resulted characterize the appearance of the early keyboard literature and herald the notation of the modern keyboard score.

Score arrangements were actually known as early as the *ars antiqua,* for the works of the Notre Dame school appear in parts written one under the other, though not necessarily in careful alignment. Older, too, was the device of intabulation itself, but it covered a wide range of notation applied to instrumental music of various kinds. In fact, the device of tablature goes back to the ancient world in the notation of music for instruments such as the flute or zither in systems that lived on in the lute tablatures of the Renaissance. Here, however, it was not a series of pitches that was tabulated, but rather the relative position of fingers or strings to be used in order to produce them, and the tradition has survived in examples of modern notation. Conversely, the tablatures of polyphonic keyboard music retained a direct connection with the early scores rendering vocal music, and they appeared on a number of staves representing the different voices of the composition, or merely on two staves, showing how these voices were to be combined in the right and left hands of the player.

A certain exception was the tablature notation used by German organists, in which the tones were not identified by notes but by the letters designating them. Since this was done in Gothic script, German organ tablature presents a particularly difficult picture, and this picture becomes doubly bewildering through the use of a number of special symbols. Nevertheless, the notation is precise. Measures and individual parts are neatly grouped; the rhythm is marked by strokes, dots, and flags; and the register is indicated by horizontal lines as well as by a distinction between the use of capital and small letters (among which, according to German custom, b stands for b-flat and h for b-natural).

Above all, the manuscripts in German organ tablature impress again upon the modern reader the fact that the scribe approached his task as an art. Perhaps the most conspicuous feature on a page of German organ tablature is the occasional elongation of a letter by which, for instance, "f" is changed to "fis" (the German note name for f-sharp). What was an abbreviation of the suffix "is" became a flourish, a very characteristic expression of the art of musical notation. In its particular form of German organ tablature this art was ultimately glorified in isolated cases appearing in the autographs of Handel and Bach.

The Rise of Music Drama

We speak of the intellectual life of the Renaissance as Humanism—the study of man—and the first writer to use the term Renaissance, the French historian Jules Michelet, referred to the reawakening or "rebirth" of ancient culture as both *la découverte du monde* and *la découverte de l'homme*—the discovery of the world and the discovery of man. It is indicative of the era that several documents in this collection, preserved from the waning sixteenth century, bear personal signatures. In documentary history the signature moves into focus, as the portrait moves into the focus of pictorial history. Western music had for centuries evolved primarily in the sacred service, but a new age of the art began to be oriented not by the relation of man to God so much as by his relation to man. Its prime expression was no longer the liturgy but human drama.

It is well known that a learned academy met in one of the Florentine palaces for discussions devoted to a revival of the dramatic art of antiquity and that these discussions led to the inception of music drama. The name Camerata, by which the group is remembered, signaled the fact that decisive developments in music had passed from the church to the *camera*, the princely chamber. Yet the scholars and artists of the Camerata were by no means the originators of dramatic music, nor did the influence of sacred music practice decline due to the evolution of dramatic music.

The two great Venetians of the period, Gioseffo Zarlino and Giovanni Gabrieli, who in this collection are represented by autograph signatures, were church musicians; they both served at St. Mark's. But the work of Gabrieli, whose fame outshone that of all other musicians of his era, announces a new age, a new style of music that is totally dramatic.

Unlike Palestrina's music, written for the Papal Chapel and borne by ideas of retrospection, the music of Gabrieli was of a progressive, in fact, revolutionary nature. It favored the dramatic contrasts of the "concerted" style, in which several choirs vied with one another in the unfolding of resonant splendor, and in which a "choir" of instruments began to assume an independent role. It is especially interesting that we find Gabrieli's signature paired with that of Heinrich Julius, Duke of Brunswick, one of the most eminent musical patrons of the new era and himself well trained as a musician. The names of Antonio Goretti, Giovanni Battista Buonamente, and Luigi Battiferri, however, lead us to a generation of church musicians already fully versed in the secular dramatic style, the greatest of whom was Claudio Monteverdi.

Here we encounter one of those towering figures whose work shaped an epoch in music history. Born in 1567 at Cremona, the city of the famed violin makers, Monteverdi was trained in the old contrapuntal art by Marco Antonio Ingegneri, the eminent master of the Cathedral Chapel, but it was as a violinist that in young years he was appointed to the ducal court of Mantua. Soon he was also to earn the more highly regarded title of *cantore,* and in time he took over the direction of all instrumental and vocal music at the court. By the turn of the century he had become the leading exponent of what in the works of one of his contemporaries, the Florentine lutenist and singer Giulio Caccini, was designated as *"nuove musiche"* and *"nuova maniera di scriverla"* ("new music" and "the new manner of writing it"), but what was attacked by another contemporary, the Bolognese theorist Giovanni Maria Artusi, as *"imperfettioni della moderna musica"* ("imperfections of modern music"). Monteverdi answered the latter charge with a famous statement in which he boldly asserted that the alleged imperfections were in reality perfections; that what was involved was a novel style with its own legitimacy; and that it represented a "Second Practice," postulated by the requirements of dramatic music, to which the principles of the "First Practice"—those codified by Zarlino—no longer applied. Just as the fourteenth century had declared an *ars nova* in music, the rising seventeenth century thus established a new style period that, in fact, figures as the beginning of many to follow.

In 1607 Monteverdi received a court commission to write a "musical fable," characteristically based on the legend of Orpheus, the mythical singer whose art moved the forces of nature and conquered the supernatural spirits. *Orfeo* became Monteverdi's most celebrated work. In it he drew on the wealth of musical expression the Renaissance had produced, placing it in the service of drama. It is indicative of a new age that in *Orfeo* it is no longer the voice alone that serves dramatic means but the instrument as well—an example is the expressive use of the violin, Monteverdi's own instrument, in introducing the climactic song of Orpheus. Monteverdi's achievement went beyond a fulfillment of the aims of the Camerata. It was music itself that triumphed through his work in the rebirth of ancient drama.

Yet the "new music" of the theater was immediately blended with the music of the church. In 1613, a year after Gabrieli had died, Monteverdi was appointed Master of the Chapel at St. Mark's Cathedral. The "sacred concerto" now took its place next to mass and motet; and from it was to arise the Protestant church cantata, for the greatest of the German church composers of the time, Heinrich Schütz, who had studied with both Gabrieli and Monteverdi, brought the new forms to the north.

Giovanni Battista Buonamente, less well known as one of the Monteverdi followers, may have shared with Schütz the latter's role as initiator of dramatic music beyond the Alps. Like Monteverdi, active at the court of the Gonzagas in Mantua as a violinist, he wrote works in which the element of instrumental virtuosity begins to come to the fore. They are characteristic of the rapidity with which the dramatic style had entered all aspects of musical practice. It found expression in the sonata which now arose in distinction to the cantata as the piece that was "sounded" rather than sung, and it led eventually to the instrumental concerto in which one or several soloists are singled out from the orchestra. But on a broader scale it continued to serve the music for the stage. At the occasion of the wedding of Princess Eleanora Gonzaga to the Emperor Ferdinand II, Buonamente took up service at the Viennese court. His preserved letters to Prince Cesare Gonzaga give a vivid account of the Imperial court music, and his description of a *Pastoral Comedia* suggests that it was he who composed the instrumental music for the dances in the work.

The term *Comedia* did not carry the connotation of the later "comic" play—rather, in accordance with the Greek origin of the word, it designated a festive entertainment that was presented through song. In his letter written in Parma on February 28, 1628, Antonio Goretti, a distinguished patron of music and friend of Monteverdi's, mentions his ardent wish (*"mi moro di voglia"*—"I die with desire") to return from Parma to Ferrara in order to attend the forthcoming Comedia there. The letter was apparently addressed to the Marchesa Bentivoglio who represented one of the aristocratic families of Ferrara and with whom Monteverdi and Goretti were visiting at the time.

Ever since his early years in the employ at the court of Mantua, Monteverdi had been connected in various ways with the neighboring court of Ferrara. Musical life in Ferrara, which flourished at the court, in churches, and in theaters, had received a particular impetus from various academies, learned and philanthropic societies which often maintained their own musical establishments. To one of them, the Accademia degli Intrepidi, Monteverdi had dedicated his Fourth Book of Madrigals, the earliest of the works that had touched off the controversy with Artusi. The most famous of the academies was the Accademia della Morte (originally a monastic order to aid those condemned to death), and among its eminent music directors was Luigi Battiferri, who, as late as the time of Bach, was praised as a master of the contrapuntal art.[1]

The Renaissance was an essentially Italian movement, though its roots stretched throughout Europe. In the north it was paralleled by the Reformation which was to lead the northern world into a war that lasted for an entire generation—the Thirty Years War. It profoundly affected all cultural life, and the work of such a composer as Schütz gives eloquent witness to the adversity of the age. In the highly interesting statements with which he prefaced the prints of his works, he referred to "the wretched times our dear homeland is still undergoing"

[1] Samples from his works are quoted in Friedrich Wilhelm Marpurg's *Abhandlung von der Fuge* (Berlin: A. Haide, and J. C. Spener, 1753/1754), a work intended to summarize the principles of Bach's fugal style.

and he gave suggestions to the performer as to how his compositions might be executed with more modest means than called for in the printed form.

Nevertheless, the early seventeenth century saw a significant turn to German texts in manuscripts and published editions of music. German had become an established literary language with Luther's Bible translation, and whereas in the documents of this collection we have dealt so far only with Latin and Italian, we now have before us an immense body of works in which texts in the northern languages predominate. The rise of music drama spread beyond the Alps, and it found its strongest expression in the Protestant liturgy.

The oldest piece of Protestant church music represented here introduces a little-known name, Johannes Wanning. One of the numerous musicians who had migrated from the Netherlands to Germany, this fertile and imaginative composer is a true representative of a well-developed art with which the new church had begun to assimilate the influences of music drama. Though Latin texts still prevail in his music, it suggests a genuinely northern style. He spent the major part of his life in Danzig, one of the Hanseatic seaports, whose new organ at St. Mary's Church had "caused a sensation in all of Europe."[2]

[2] Hermann Rauschning, *Geschichte der Musik und Musikpflege in Danzig* (Danzig, 1931), p. 50.

The Reformation had divided the continent into a Catholic south and a Protestant north. A dividing line was never sharply drawn, nor did it remain without various enclaves north and south. But there is no question that this division initiated a certain shift of weight. Padre Giambattista Martini, teacher of the young Mozart, was to open his famous treatise on counterpoint with the statement that in the art of music, the sixteenth century had made Italy "the mistress of the other nations." This hegemony gradually declined in subsequent centuries, though not without leaving an Italian legacy to the world. The Italian language became international in musical terminology. It was within the lands where the German language was spoken, however, that a certain dividing line between Catholic and Protestant music became recognizable. The works of Christoph Demantius and Christoph Bernhard mark the generations of German Protestantism before and after Schütz, whereas the name of Wolfgang Ebner reminds us of a different school of composers whose works initiated the style that was to become of enduring influence at the Catholic imperial court of Vienna.

The style element that characterized the rise of dramatic music everywhere was the *bassus generalis* or *basso continuo*, the thoroughbass that accompanied the vocal melody with harmonic support of keyboard or other chordal instruments as well as various bass instruments. As its designation implies, it ran through the entire composition; being executed by the conductor himself at the keyboard, with the support of bass instruments, it provided a sure foundation for a musical fabric largely dominated by the dramatic expression of the vocal or instrumental solo. Its rule arose in phases, and it is typical of the church music of Demantius that its polyphonic texture, though tending toward a polarity of the outer voices, is maintained without continuo accompaniment. His orientation was conservative, though in his most significant work, a St. John Passion for six-part choir, he heralded the form in which Protestant church music was to culminate.

Christoph Bernhard, foremost student of Schütz, was born in Danzig, the city where Wanning had been active, but he was trained in Italy as well as in Germany. In his important theoretical writings he acted as the catalyst who interpreted the old art of polyphony to a new generation. Through Schütz's tutelage he was thoroughly schooled in the a cappella style, the "Palestrinian manner," but in his sacred concertos, which again adopted the model of Schütz, the modern continuo style was firmly established. His works were of direct influence upon Dietrich Buxtehude, the mentor of the young Bach, into whose era the life of Bernhard was to extend.

The work of Ebner, while itself overshadowed by that of his greater contemporary Johann Jakob Froberger, guides us to the Viennese keyboard art of the seventeenth century. The dance suite, one of the oldest forms of instrumental ensemble music, now appears as a form of courtly keyboard music, merging French, German, and English style elements with genuine Viennese influences. Ebner's keyboard music remained in high esteem, as is shown by the fact that his own name is joined in the copy of the composition here preserved to those of

Christoph Bernhard, a receipt

Alessandro Poglietti and Giuseppe Antonio Paganelli, noted Italian keyboard composers, both of whose careers developed on German soil. Ebner served, together with Froberger, as imperial court organist, though during the latter's extensive travels, he often carried out the duties of this assignment alone. Eventually he combined his court position with that of Master of the Chapel at St. Stephen's Cathedral, where in later years Johann Pachelbel served for some time as organist.

It was Pachelbel who carried the South German keyboard style into the Protestant orbit, and it is indicative of his influence that the sample of his work contained in this collection, and as yet unpublished, has come down to us in a copy by Heinrich Nikolaus Gerber, one of Bach's pupils. The generations overlap. Pachelbel had moved to Eisenach, Bach's birthplace, where for a brief period he held the position of court organist, and he became a friend of Bach's father who was in charge of the town music. Bach's eldest brother, Johann Christoph, to whose household Bach moved when he lost his parents at an early age, was Pachelbel's student, and it was through him that the young Bach was introduced to the organist's profession.

As we approach the era of Bach and Handel, we enter into two realms of music that during the seventeenth and eighteenth centuries may seem to have grown far apart in purpose and style, though in reality they remained innately related to one another. It is more difficult to honor the height of an era than to trace its beginnings. Music history has borrowed the term *Baroque*, now commonly accepted, from the history of art, in order to describe characteristics that works of music from the seventeenth century and the first half of the eighteenth century have in common. Such epoch designations are always problematic because an afterglow of the past invariably merges with developments that foreshadow the future. As an alternate, more precise designation of what has come to be recognized as a particular era of music, historians formed the term *basso continuo* age. Though more cumbersome, it represents a more direct understanding of the style involved, for the technical criterion of thoroughbass accompaniment is by its very function inseparably connected with the emergence of the dramatic art forms that dominated the music of this era and that found their fulfillment in the works of Bach and Handel.

The names of the two great composers, both of whom were born in 1685, have been linked customarily, as have been those of Palestrina and Orlando di Lasso, who both died in 1594. But the attempt to derive a certain periodization from these dates remains in its ramifications inaccurate, as does the attempt to see any obvious parallel in the composers' artistic bequest and mission.

Bach and Handel were born in Saxon towns less than a hundred miles apart, and they entered their profession in the

Freü dich sehr ó meine Seele. Joh. Pachelbel.

environment of the Protestant church. The legacy of Protestant church music, however, was imparted in diverse ways to the lives of the two masters. Bach, born into a family of town and church musicians, was heir to a tradition which, ranging over more than a century before his time and extending for generations after his own, stands for a unique hereditary history. Handel appears in a genealogy of more than two centuries as the only musician. His was a well-to-do bourgeois family in which artistic and intellectual tendencies were represented rather through the goldsmith's trade and the ministry. His father, a court physician, had not looked with favor upon the son's studies for the musical profession.

This may help to explain the divergent course of the two careers. Bach was committed to an overwhelming artistic inheritance; Handel, throughout his life, was an artist of absolute independence. Bach's work unfolded entirely on German soil, whereas Handel's extended through Europe, became Italianized and eventually Anglicized to the astounding degree that English music became thoroughly shaped by the Handelian style. But in Bach's German church cantatas and Passion settings, and in Handel's English oratorios, the music drama of what we have come to call the age of the Baroque reached its final form.

It is also a final phase of the composers' lives with which the documents before us are concerned. Though merely provided as a formality, Bach's signatures are of particular historical significance because they are the last we have from his hand—the signature bearing the latest date had, in fact, to be supplied by his son Johann Christian because of the master's increasing blindness. And they verify the fact that Bach's duties had remained those of a church musician and official. Handel's autograph happens to be likewise written within a short period before the onset of blindness. But he was to resist the decline of his powers for yet another decade, in which his work remained devoted to English oratorio, the form which was his most original creation.

Opera, which all but absorbed musical life in Italy, had experienced a different fate in the countries north of the Alps. In France, it had risen to prime importance at the court

(Opposite page)
Johann Pachelbel, from a keyboard partita on a chorale

Copied by the Bach student, Heinrich Nikolaus Gerber

through the work of an Italian, Giovanni Battista Lulli, who, as Jean Baptiste Lully, gave opera its French guise and strengthened its nature by imparting to it a salient feature, the overture, which in turn came to be combined with operatic ballets to form the orchestral suite. In Germany, devastated by the war that raged in the first half of the seventeenth century, opera gained its place in society with much delay, and for a long time it survived essentially as an Italian import. In England, removed from the source of opera by a continent and the sea, it was considered totally alien—in the words of the satirist Samuel Johnson, "an exotic and irrational entertainment." Whereas in Germany music drama had found its way into the Protestant cantata and dramatic setting of the Gospel story, England had essentially resisted these developments. The very term *opera* appeared in English music first in the *The Beggar's Opera* (1728), written in open defiance of Handel's introduction of Italian opera to London audiences.

Handel's opera enterprise, desired and supported by the English aristocracy and a primary challenge of absorbing fascination to the composer, eventually failed. Relying on Italian singers whose fame and virtuosity was its principal attraction, opera was undeniably foreign to the wider English audience. Its Italian texts, dealing with intrigues from unfamiliar history, had no meaning for its listeners. And from a protracted struggle between the composer and his public emerged, as a solution, English oratorio, a new form in which English texts, chosen predominantly (though by no means exclusively) from the Old Testament, were presented by English singers (or foreign artists who had adapted their performance to the English language). It was the form that eventually raised the composer to the level of a national hero.

The Reformation had created a Church of the State in England; yet the Anglican rite, despite all violent reactions to "popish" tendencies, stayed closer to the Roman rite than German Protestantism. Henry Purcell, "true genius of the Restoration,"[3] was one of the first openly to embrace the new dramatic forms in England, and in his sacred and secular works English seventeenth-century music found its finest expression. It was through the tragically early death of Purcell that John Blow, an able composer, though of minor stature, emerged as

[3] See Manfred F. Bukofzer, *Music in the Baroque Era* (New York: Norton, 1947), pp. 203ff.

the leading English musician of the waning seventeenth century. He was a teacher and predecessor of Purcell as court composer and Master of the Chapel Royal, but in the end also his successor. In his anthems and odes we encounter what had become the predominant forms of English music, forms that were to contribute decisively to the genesis of English oratorio.

Unlike Bach, Handel was surrounded by musicians who, like himself, were immigrants and had sought their fortune in a country representing "a parliamentary state with free institutions alongside a Europe ruled by absolutism."[4] German musicians took a significant part in the Royal Band that, after 1714, served a German prince as ruler, and to German musicians was entrusted the musical instruction of the nobility. Handel's official court appointment was that of Royal Music Master, and his course of instruction for Anne, the eldest of the daughters of George I, is preserved.[5] A counterpart to this extraordinary didactic document is a theoretical discourse by John Christopher (Johann Christoph) Pepusch. Apparently written for the daughter of a prominent English official, and still unpublished, it reflects the authority this German musician enjoyed as a theorist and teacher. He was one of the

[4] Paul Henry Lang, *George Frideric Handel* (New York: Norton, 1966), p. 112.

[5] *Hallische Händel-Ausgabe*, suppl., vol. I (Kassel and Leipzig, 1978).

John Christopher Pepusch, didactic manuscript

Northwestern University Music Library Moldenhauer Archive

founders of the Academy of Ancient Music, a Fellow of the Royal Society, and a widely respected composer. Handel had entrusted his own student John Christopher Smith (later his assistant and successor as Royal Music Master) to the tutelage of Pepusch, and he was at times closely associated with Pepusch in his work, though the fact that Pepusch had composed music for *The Beggar's Opera* finally led to an estrangement.

As if to summarize the large chapter of music history we have considered in this section, the sequence of the collection's documents leads finally to the title most universally applied in the seventeenth and early eighteenth centuries to dramatic works of secular as well as sacred nature—*dramma per musica*. It appears in a work by Georg Philipp Telemann (who rearranged the letters of his name in his often preferred pseudonym Melante), Bach's and Handel's most celebrated and prolific contemporary. Telemann was originally given preference to Bach as a candidate for the office of Cantor at St. Thomas's in Leipzig, but he declined the position in favor of the musical directorship at the churches of the North German metropolis of Hamburg, a position in which he was to be succeeded by his godson, C. P. E. Bach. In fact, a lifelong friendship connected him with Bach and Handel, both of whom he outlived, though his name was ultimately overshadowed by theirs.

(Opposite page)
Georg Philipp Telemann, sketch for an overture

The composer's signature in the upper right-hand corner shows his pseudonym "Melante." Though crossed out, the customary pattern of a French overture, with its dotted rhythm of an opening section and a subsequent fugue in livelier rhythmic motion, can be recognized clearly. The theme for the latter, revised at the end of the last four staves, appears there in a more marked melodic contour than in the earlier version above.

> History is the most partial of the sciences. When it becomes enamored of a man, it loves him jealously; it will not even hear of others. Since the day when the greatness of Johann Sebastian Bach was admitted, all that was great in his lifetime has become less than nothing. The world has hardly been able to forgive Handel for the impertinence of having had as great a genius as Bach's and a much greater success. The rest have fallen into dust; and there is no dust so dry as that of Telemann, whom posterity has forced to pay for the insolent victory which he won over Bach in his lifetime.

These words by Romain Rolland, the French writer and music historian, were somewhat superseded in years closer to our time, and they characterize the varying approach posterity has taken to the climax of an epoch.[6] Telemann's greatest dramatic

6 "The Autobiography of a Forgotten Master: Telemann," in *A Musical Tour Through the Land of the Past* (New York: Holt & Co., 1922), pp. 97–144.

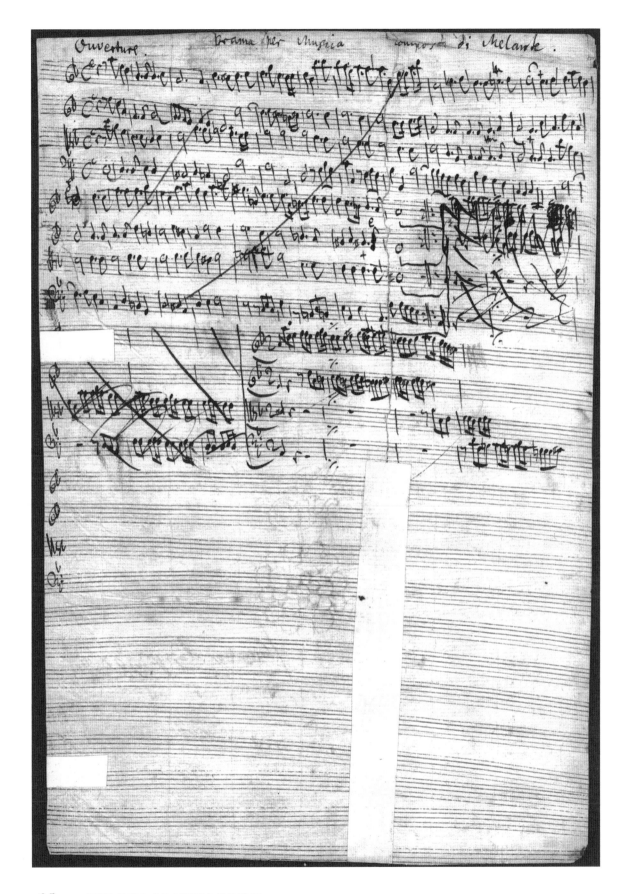

works were written at the time Mozart composed his first sonatas and symphonies, and whatever judgment is accorded his stature, he was the last illustrious master of the musical Baroque.

Classicism and Romanticism

I N A PENETRATING ESSAY, FRIEDRICH BLUME, the eminent music encyclopedist of the twentieth century, has convincingly argued that Classicism and Romanticism were not opposed but rather collateral and complementary tendencies which have guided the arts since the eighteenth century.[1] Both meant a certain return to the ideals of the past. The word classic, which ever since the days of the Roman Empire applied to that which was in a "class" by itself, and hence exemplary, was now applied to the art of antiquity as such, whereas the word romantic harkens back to the "roman," the medieval epic, and thus to a more recent past that had developed a folklore and art born from the mist of northern climates rather than the southern sun. In distinction to classic clarity, equilibrium, and remoteness, its spirit is that of varying immediacy, of emotional changes of mood, of that which is not deliberately measured but passionate and fantastic, dreamlike and mysterious—"romantic."

The juxtaposition of heterogeneous elements might be seen as the rightful bequest of dramatic art, and in ever new ways music was ruled by drama. Opera itself had developed into two contrasting forms: serious opera, *opera seria*, and comic opera, *opera buffa*. The latter had evolved especially in the south of Italy, in Naples, at the hands of Alessandro Scarlatti and his followers Leonardo Leo and Giovanni Battista Pergolesi. It dealt with contemporary types and situations, rather than subjects of history and mythology, and it contributed an enlivening element to opera: ensemble. That which in spoken drama is not possible, the simultaneous expression of different personages and moods, now gave polyphony a novel function which, as we shall see, also greatly influenced instrumental music.

[1] Friedrich Blume, *Classic and Romantic Music* (New York: Norton, 1970).

2 "Metastasio: The Forerunner of Gluck," op. cit., pp. 166ff.

Opera seria was dominated for a long time by its famed librettist, Pietro Metastasio, himself a gifted musician. But the vitality of the traditional form gradually declined, and Romain Rolland has shown that Metastasio's influence heralded much of the impending reform of opera.[2] As we know, it was brought about—in part through the encounter with the aged Handel— by the epochal works of Christoph Willibald von Gluck, whose first reform opera significantly returned to the subject of *Orfeo*.

The key figure in the rise of opera buffa was Pergolesi, who in his short life veritably changed operatic history. His famous miniature, *La Serva Padrona* (The Servant as Mistress), was designed, in the prevalent manner of early opera buffa, as intermezzo scenes to be presented between the acts of an opera seria. But its title was symbolic; the young subsidiary form was destined to assume a ruling role. We sense here the dawn of the Age of Revolution. And it was similarly reflected in another fundamental development of eighteenth-century music. The concerto which, in the works of such Italian masters as Arcangelo Corelli and Antonio Vivaldi as well as in the works of Bach and Handel, had risen to leadership in instrumental music, began to share this leadership with a new genre. Alessandro Scarlatti transformed the old opera overture of Lullian style, with its ceremoniously slow-paced beginning (often resumed for the ending), reversing its slow and fast sections. His overtures, for which he adopted the age-old term *sinfonia*, opened and closed in a lively (allegro) tempo, and the new form eventually gained independence in the Classical symphony. Its independence became complete. What the small introduction had assimilated from the drama acted out by the singers took on a new dramatic guise. It rose from the orchestra pit (or its equivalent) and conquered the stage. Its hero and heroine were themes and instrumental timbres, and, aided by the operatic ensemble technique, a new and purely instrumental form arose that dominated musical life for the era to come.

One of the first important symphonists was C. P. E. Bach, and in the legacy of J. S. Bach's work we recognize again the oscillating roles of classic and romantic orientation. Though Bach had close to a hundred students, his posthumous

(Opposite page)
C. P. E. Bach, autograph letter

er hat dies Unglück in der H. Schulze erzählt,
aber zu spät die Ursache dieses Str..., weil die
Sachen nicht in Augsten gestochen, sondern uns
in Unmuth freundschaftlichen würden.

Hier ist er schon Lebendig doch.

Um zu erfahren, was in der Sache Zeitung Ihrer
vermuthet hat, will ich mir alle Mühe geben, gesehen
habe ich es nicht, aber ich vermuthe daß der ...
oder ... ist, Sumwa mein Freund ...
nicht, weil dieser ... allen ... zu ge-
braucht, und ... schließt ... jemand
es ist gewiß gewiß uns uns freuen Leid
... hinter den unschuldigen Menschen zu
verstecken, ich werde Ihnen bei ... Gelegen-
heit ..., daß ich das ... entschuldige.

dießen Augenblick ... zu meiner Gnädigen
Herrschaft, ich muß also schließ, ob ich gleich noch
viel ... und Sachen würde.

Berlin d. 4 Sept. 1779.

L....berger

recognition grew slowly, but to those who recognized and understood his greatness, his work assumed the stature of an ideal model described in words that are born of the spirit of Classicism. Johann Philipp Kirnberger, court conductor in Berlin who had been Bach's foremost disciple in later years, published a two-volume treatise, *The Art of Composition* (*Die Kunst des reinen Satzes*, 1774/1779)—an art to be obtained by reducing, as he said, "the method of the late J. S. Bach to principles." And Kirnberger's Berlin colleague, Friedrich Wilhelm Marpurg, prompted by the appearance of Bach's *Art of Fugue* to issue a *Manual of Fugue* (*Abhandlung von der Fuge*, 1753/54), speaks of "principles of an art" in dedicating his work to Bach's two oldest sons.

Johann Friedrich Reichardt, Berlin court conductor in later years, extolled Bach's chorales as "the highest achievement of German art" and referred to Bach as "the greatest harmonist of all times and nations." This statement is all the more interesting because it came from one of the principal representatives of the modern form of singspiel, the German counterpart to opera buffa. But the new and old worlds of music met and crossed in many ways; Johann Adam Hiller, also active in Berlin as a singspiel composer, became one of the successors to Bach's Leipzig office.

Thus we are dealing with a greatly widened array of musical personalities and trends, and it is a characteristic phenomenon of eighteenth-century music that it produced the first music historians offering an overview of the development of different styles. The learned Padre Giambattista Martini, author of a three-volume history of the music of antiquity and teacher of Bach's youngest son, Johann Christian, and of Mozart, spoke again of "the world famous Bach." The English historian Charles Burney, whose *History of Music* (1776–1789) stands out among the similar works of the period, failed to deal with Bach's work, but his praise of Bach was reported by a contemporary. Samuel Wesley, the eminent organist who was the first to make Bach's works known in England and who in veneration of the Leipzig master had named his son Sebastian, related in a letter to a colleague that, in conversation, Burney "evinced the most cordial veneration for our Sacred Musician."

(Opposite page)
Johann Philipp Kirnberger, page from an autograph letter

In the end, the Romantics claimed Bach as their own and made his works known to the whole world. We know of Mendelssohn's epochal revival of the St. Matthew Passion, aided by his teacher Karl Friedrich Zelter who had revived Bach's motets with his Berlin *Singakademie,* and it was also Mendelssohn who gave the first recital entirely devoted to Bach's organ works. His influence brought about a decisive change, for while the name Bach had remained known to everyone throughout the eighteenth century, it had referred generally to one or the other of Bach's famous sons, and to works which were quite removed from the sphere of Johann Sebastian Bach. When Mozart said in a letter to his father from Paris in 1778 "Kapellmeister Bach is about to arrive . . . as you know, I love and revere him with all my heart," he spoke of Johann Christian Bach; and when Haydn acknowledged his great debt to Bach, he referred to Philipp Emanuel.

It was the domain of the sonata, the string quartet, and the symphony—the last amply paying back to its parent form what debt of origin it owed—that had taken over the music of the later eighteenth century. In the narrower sense, the classic era of music is understood to mean Viennese Classicism, the style that arose in the works of Haydn and Mozart. Yet the critical phase in the evolution of Haydn's symphonic work has become known as the "Romantic crisis" in his creative career.

Haydn's long life extended from the first third of the eighteenth to the beginning of the nineteenth century. He wrote his greatest compositions in old age. One might say that the secret of his art was his remarkable power of rejuvenation. One of the strongest influences upon his work was the encounter with Mozart who, in turn, was profoundly influenced by Haydn, almost a quarter of a century his senior. The work of both masters embraced all genres. While Haydn virtually created the string quartet, his church music goes back to strong roots of the Baroque, and his indebtedness in the oratorio unequivocally to Handel. In his operas he followed such Italian composers as Giovanni Paisiello and Domenico Cimarosa; in his piano works he was the disciple of C. P. E. Bach; but in his symphonies, taking their point of departure from such works as those by the Imperial court composer Georg Christoph Wagenseil, he was at his most Viennese. All of these forms he led to consummate heights. Yet posterity has almost forgotten that, like Bach's, Haydn's name held a dual meaning in its time. It is in the a cappella music of Michael Haydn, who served with Mozart at the court of Salzburg, and whose work has been overshadowed by that of his older brother, that the Classic image was most truly revealed to the young Schubert. As a student, Schubert noted after a vocal trio (preserved only in fragmentary form) "written in the manner of Haydn"—by which he meant the style of Michael Haydn—and in a letter he wrote in later years to his brother, Schubert described his thoughts in visiting a monument erected to Michael Haydn: "May your calm, clear spirit be imparted to me, cherished Haydn; though I can never be so calm and clear, no one on earth reveres you as dearly as I."

A similar sense of affection, absent from documents of earlier periods, is expressed in the letter of dedication to Joseph Haydn that accompanied the collection of Mozart's six string quartets subsequently published as Opus X, his masterwork in the genre. The wide range of Mozartiana in this collection attests to an equally wide range of close personal attachments. Mozart biography has given honored places to Leopold Mozart, the composer's father who provided the child prodigy with a uniquely rich education and who remained an important figure in later phases of his professional life; to his sister Maria Anna ("Nannerl") who shared his appearances in the early travels throughout Europe with their father; to Franz Xaver Süssmayr, Mozart's pupil who is believed to have finished his teacher's last work, the Requiem; and to Thomas Attwood, whose course of studies under Mozart represents the most extraordinary didactic document from the waning eighteenth century. It is indicative of these associations that Mozart's handwriting has been confused with his father's, with Süssmayer's, and with Attwood's, and that it has taken scholars a long time to establish clear texts in the instances concerned.

Elation and tragedy were intermingled in Mozart's short life—less than half the span of Haydn's. It has been difficult for posterity to understand fully that the ingratiating, romanticized rococo idol grew to a heroic figure, the classic master, in very young years, and that, in fact, utter seriousness permeated the life of the playful artist at all times. The Age of the Revolution here, too, cast its shadow over the career of the composer who failed to obtain the traditional supportive court or church position, and who was less suited to take on the lot of an independent position in society than Handel before and Beethoven after him.

Whereas he was the student of Haydn in his string quartets, his symphonies influenced the work of the older master, and the latter clearly admitted Mozart's superiority in the genre of opera. Yet the encounter with Haydn remained the turning point in his artistic orientation; it guided him to a new exploration of polyphony and an assimilation of styles of the past with which he became acquainted through the eminent music collection of Haydn's later oratorio librettist, the imperial court librarian Gottfried van Swieten.

Mozart's blending of Italian melody and German counterpoint, his power of synthesis and miraculously fertile imagination, and in particular his power of characterization raised opera buffa to a dramatic form that spoke to the audience in earnest. Mozart had the good fortune to find an accomplished librettist in the Vienna court poet Lorenzo da Ponte, who provided him with his most important opera buffa texts. With *Figaro*, the work in which Pergolesi's theme of the superiority of the servant is carried to new heights through the text of Beaumarchais that da Ponte adapted, opera buffa became a truly human drama, though this drama never denies the parentage of comic opera. The demonic story of Don Giovanni was entitled *dramma giocoso*. With the *The Magic Flute*, written for a lowly suburban theater of Vienna, Mozart transformed the buffoonery of the German singspiel to what became the foundation of German grand opera.

The three generations of the masters of Viennese Classicism overlap in striking manner. By the time Haydn wrote his last symphonies and quartets and Mozart wrote his last operas, the young Beethoven had journeyed to Vienna in order to study with Mozart. His early works had already reached the international market, but he still felt the need for a concentrated course of study. This fact, which found a parallel in Schubert's career, is indicative of the greatly widened perspective from which a modern generation of composers viewed the craft. Beethoven was called back to his hometown, Bonn, where he was in service at the Electoral court. When he was able to return to Vienna, several years later, Mozart had died; Beethoven turned to Haydn for instruction, and his studies have been preserved.

Impatient about his progress, he secretly supplemented his lessons in consultation with the Viennese singspiel composer Johann Schenk, a student of Wagenseil. But once again, the facts were romanticized by posterity. The document that combines the handwriting of Beethoven with that of Haydn shows a very deliberate survey of the technique of strict counterpoint. The exchange of the aged master and his student was anything but superficial or—as has often been asserted—a failure, and it is characteristic of the situation that when Haydn left on his second journey for engagements in England (a journey on which Beethoven originally was to accompany him), Beethoven embarked on further contrapuntal study with Haydn's friend Johann Georg Albrechtsberger, Master of the Cathedral Chapel in Vienna; at the same time he took up studies in the Italian vocal style with the Viennese court composer Antonio Salieri.

The enlarged scope of didactic commitment reflects the musical crosscurrents at the turn of the century. Salieri, whose role in music history has come down mainly (and unjustly) as that of Mozart's antagonist, represented a tradition that remained of great importance to a generation no longer readily conversant with it—Italian opera. His eminent pedagogical influence is reflected in the fact that it led from his training of the choirboys as Master of the Imperial Chapel to the establishment of the Vienna Conservatory. He was the teacher of the young Schubert and, in later years, of Meyerbeer and Liszt. Several of his contemporaries are remembered principally through their teaching manuals and collections of methodical studies. In the case of Stanislao Mattei, the student of Padre Martini, and that of Luigi Cherubini, *Inspecteur* and subsequently director of the Paris Conservatory, it was the contrapuntal legacy that was handed down in their works; in those of Ignaz Pleyel, Muzio Clementi, and Karl Czerny, it was

the new pianistic art; and in Rodolphe Kreutzer's famous
Etudes, that of classical violin virtuosity.

We tend to forget that these preceptors of compositional and
instrumental technique were composers in their own right and
of deserved recognition. Kreutzer's operas, though relegated to
oblivion, were not without influence upon the works of later
generations, and Cherubini's sacred and dramatic works were
highly regarded by Beethoven (who also honored Kreutzer
with the dedication of his Sonata Opus 47). Clementi was
ranked next to Mozart in his time; Pleyel next to Haydn
(whose devoted student he was). But the fame of Czerny,
whom Beethoven had singled out as a piano pupil and whose
guidance as a teacher became decisive upon the young Liszt,
rested solely, as it does now, on his genius of piano pedagogy.

A new situation arose in music history by which the domains of
creative and interpretive arts were beginning to be separated.
Nor did performance remain limited to interpretation; more
than ever before, it now took on a role of its own. It is
epitomized in the thoroughly Romantic figure of the travelling
virtuoso, for which Niccolò Paganini, the demonic violinist,
stands as a symbol for all times. And it extended into all
spheres of performance. A particularly arresting example is the
career of Domenico Dragonetti, the "Paganini of the double
bass," whose stupendous proficiency on his instrument
evidently influenced the design of passages in the fifth and
ninth symphonies of Beethoven, with whom he was on
friendly terms.

A counterpart to the specialized performer became the
specialized teacher. The theorists of past ages, such as Zarlino,
Artusi, or Kirnberger, were active and appreciated as composers
and performers in the first place. But Simon Sechter, the
leading Viennese theorist in the first half of the nineteenth
century, to whom Schubert still turned for advice in his last
days, represented a new profession, that of "Professor of
Thoroughbass and Composition," at the Vienna Conservatory,
while his allegedly more than 8,000 compositions remained
unknown. But the pervading influence he exerted in his time
is characterized by the fact that toward the end of his long
tenure he became the trusted mentor of Anton Bruckner who,

(Opposite page)
Letter from Niccolò Paganini to Francesco
Morlacchi, Kapellmeister in Dresden,
February 19, 1830

·36·

Amico Carissimo

Francfort sul meno li 19. Febbraro 1830

L'amore col quale mi hai sempre favorito m'invita a chiedervi le notizie intorno la tua salute, e quella dell'adorabile nostro ... Barone De Guaggivini quali spero saranno Consolanti. Lusingato da ... vorrei sperare l'amabile Compagnia del ... Scatiggi nei miei viaggi, onde avere un amico capace al carteggio, e al buon ordine nei miei affari, mescolati a dividere meco i piaceri della vita, ed è perciò che ti prego d'interrogar lo stesso affine di sapere se posso lusingarmi di possederlo per i primi dell'entrante mese, e condurlo a Parigi, a Londra, in Russia &c &c ... Circa alle Condizioni, per premio alla sua opera, se le spieghi; io farò ogni sforzo per attestargli quella Stima che le sue eccellenti prerogative mi hanno inspirato: quindi favorisci parteciparmi al più presto possibile le sue intenzioni e pretese che trovandole ragionevoli mi farò un piacere di avvertirvi bramando di avere accanto un Compatriota che mi tratti non come mercenario, ma come amico di cuore ——. Rammentami al ... colla amabile sua famiglia, e a tutti gli amici. Bramoso da tuoi amati caratteri ti abbraccio con tutta l'anima dal

Tuo ... amico, e servitore
Niccolò Paganini

3 Quoted from the obituary published by William Ayrton, Director of the London Philharmonic Society, in the *Gentleman's Magazine* (May 1838).

4 *Neue-Mozart-Ausgabe*, X/30/1 (Kassel and Leipzig: Bärenreiter, 1955).

(Opposite page)
Thomas Attwood, page from an autograph letter

Northwestern University Music Library
Moldenhauer Archive

in fact, succeeded him in his professorship at the Conservatory. Whereas Sechter is remembered as a famous teacher, the memory of the English composer Thomas Attwood lives on as that of a famous student. Son of a British court musician, the gifted young member of the Chapel Royal had received a stipend from the Prince of Wales to take up studies in Italy. Though pursued under two noted Neapolitan *maestri*, they proved in the end not satisfactory, and Attwood, "perceiving the decline of the Italian school and foreseeing the ascendancy of that of Germany . . . proceeded to Vienna and immediately became a pupil of Mozart."[3]

We owe it to the association with Attwood that Mozart's work as a teacher is fully documented. The course of studies he designed for the student, who became a close friend, covered the better part of two years; the manuscript was carefully preserved by Attwood and has been published.[4] Attwood, in later years organist at St. Paul's and composer-in-ordinary of the Chapel Royal, became the guardian of the legacy of Viennese Classicism. It was he who was principally responsible for introducing Mozart's and Beethoven's symphonic work in England. But in equal measure he became the advocate of the young German Romantics and of the nineteenth-century Bach renaissance. The year in which Mendelssohn gave his epochal performance of Bach's St. Matthew Passion also marked his first journey to England, on which he was warmly welcomed by the sixty-four-year-old Attwood. The two composers, though of unequal stature, found themselves devoted to some of the same ideals. Britain, as we know, became Mendelssohn's second homeland, and a remarkable association developed between the representatives of the old and young generations—of what we have to come to call the Classic and Romantic ages of music.

Nowhere are Classic form and Romantic expression more powerfully blended than in the work of Beethoven. Popular appellations have somewhat superficially attached the defiance of fate to his Fifth Symphony and the serene tranquillity of moonlight to his Piano Sonata op. 27, No. 2. But the designation *Grande Sonate Pathétique* for his Piano Sonata op. 13, written before his first quartets, concertos and symphonies, and that of *Sinfonia Eroica* for his Third Symphony, are his own.

Norwood Surrey
Sept.r 24. 1829 —

Dear Miss Susan —

  I hope by this time the promised
Music is arrived, & that I have redeemed my lost character,
which, from the verbal communication made by our friend
Mendelssohn, I had reason to apprehend was in some
danger. I trust however the accusation of forgetting my friends
will not be added to the many sins I have to answer for,
& though late, the delay may be deemed satisfactory,
since I have had the advantage of sending three pieces
instead of one.
 I have to apologize for not writing when I sent the
Music, but as at that time a black cloud was hanging
over me, which thank God is now dissipated, I felt
it would be a pity to cause any uneasiness without
the opportunity of affording immediate relief — the truth
is our friend Mendelssohn was then confined to his bed
from having been upset in a chaise by an unskilful driver,
but you will all be happy to hear, is now going on

One of his biographers called Beethoven the "man who freed music," a dictum which is again of flimsy nature. Yet Beethoven was totally a son of the Revolutionary Age. He tore up the dedication of his Third Symphony to Napoleon when Bonaparte declared himself emperor. He was devoted to the revolutionary ideas of *liberté* and *egalité;* and the ideal of *fraternité* is glorified in the ode that concludes his Ninth Symphony. It is the rebellion of the artist that placed Beethoven in his era. He wrote to Count Lichnowsky, soon after dedicating the *Sonate Pathétique* to him, "Prince, what you are you are by the accident of birth; what I am, I am of myself." But no artist ever wrestled more intensely with law and order, with classical discipline, than Beethoven. Whereas the Romantics were to claim him as theirs, his life work proceeded along the lines of the Classic forms. It is no mere accident that the Beethoveniana of this collection include, with samples from his sketches—his ubiquitous detailed working material—his copy from one of Mozart's works. Beyond the classical genres of sonata, quartet and symphony, he even turned to opera, though it represented a world essentially foreign to him, and his vocal works attest to some of the greatest triumphs of his symphonic language.

When Beethoven undertook the composition of *Fidelio* (originally *Leonore*), the genre of opera had undergone wide proliferation. We have seen that the two prototypes, opera seria and opera buffa, were interrelated from the beginning: the latter arose in intermezzo performances from the former. By and large, it was to opera buffa that the future belonged. But its original subject matter, the antagonism of master and servant, had lost its significance, or rather, the human and social implications had widened to the point where comic elements were intermingled with genuine drama and tragedy. Nevertheless, in Gioacchino Rossini's *Barber of Seville*, whose story came from the same literary source as Mozart's *Figaro*, the old opera buffa found a lasting monument whose quality remained unattained in any of the works by his contemporaries.

Opera seria was, one might say, buried with Mozart's last opera, *La Clemenza di Tito*, commissioned for the coronation of Emperor Leopold II. While the score contains some of

Mozart's finest writing, the work has suffered, from the outset and in the reception of posterity, because the genre itself was beginning to be superseded by what became *"Grand Opéra,"* the genre that, more than any other, reflected the Revolutionary Age. Thus we speak of "Heroic Opera" and the type of work based on the theme of liberation, "Rescue Opera," the latter owing its nature particularly to subjects favored in French literary models of the time. It was this type that caught Beethoven's interest. *Fidelio* is a genuine rescue opera, its text going back to a work by the French librettist Jean Nicolas Bouilly, but arranged for Beethoven by the Viennese opera manager Joseph von Sonnleithner, member of a prominent family to whose influence the development of Vienna's musical life in the activities of opera, concert stage, salon, and conservatory was indebted in many ways.

It is of significance that Beethoven's copy of portions from Mozart's *Don Giovanni* are adapted to German text. *Fidelio,* though of French origin, and though its plot is set in Spain, is a German opera, adhering even to the spoken dialogue of the singspiel tradition. After the delayed starts of its history, German opera developed rather slowly. The German-born Giacomo Meyerbeer experienced his first triumphs in Italy, where he became one of the foremost followers of Rossini. But his success carried him to France, and as a representative of *Grand Opéra,* he became the most celebrated French opera composer of his time. A national school of German opera found its beginning with the work of Carl Maria von Weber, a fellow student of Meyerbeer under Georg Joseph (Abbé) Vogler, court conductor in Darmstadt, whose adventuresome career developed under Italian and French, as well as German, influence.

Wagner was to call Weber "the most German of all musicians." In his masterpiece *Der Freischütz* (the title, difficult to translate, describes the figure of a marksman whose marksmanship is given free reign through a pact with the devil) Weber created what he himself called a "Romantic opera." The typical elements of German poetic Romanticism, the world of the German fairy tale, the folklore and superstitions of German forest country, the horn calls, peasant dances, village lyricism are all there, as well as demonic motifs of Romantic saga. They are merged into a musical language that was as fresh and sound in its dramatic originality as it was responsive to the trends of the time, and Weber's work had a large following. Heinrich Marschner, whose name is remembered, though his operas are all but forgotten, worked in close collaboration with Weber as conductor at the Dresden court opera. With Marschner, opera entered into a German middle class milieu characterized by the word *Biedermeier* (a type of honest but somewhat humdrum citizen). It represented a welcome reaction to the increasing shallowness and mannerism of heroic librettos. But the works it produced owed their place in history to popularity rather than vitality. Thus the slightly later operas by Albert Lortzing likewise remain mere names. Yet in the work of Lortzing, who returned with his *Undine* to the field of grand opera, we also find the seeds of Wagnerian music drama.

The German-born Friedrich von Flotow, whose works have retained a somewhat uneasy place in the repertory, partly because of their sentimental appeal, transplanted the *Biedermeier* opera to France; it was left to a later German-born French opera composer, Jacques Offenbach, to produce some lasting works derived from the genre. With Offenbach, however, the opera of bourgeois society was transformed to the entertaining and satirical operetta, though his great lyrical and dramatic gifts are revealed in the work that took its point of departure from the stories of the poet-artist-musician who was the embodiment of the German Romantic—*Tales of Hoffmann*.

While the opera of German Romanticism had surrendered, in the end, to styles of French entertainment, the genre of operetta was to be glorified in the work of a Viennese composer, Johann Strauss. His popular operettas, above all *Die Fledermaus* (The Bat) were born of dance. Like his father, Johann Strauss the elder, he was the master of the waltz that dominated the imperial court of Vienna—and Europe—as its ancestral dance form, the minuet, had dominated the royal French court—and Europe—in the Age of Absolutism.

Italian opera, unlike German opera, always had solid traditions on which to draw; and they are evident in the works of the two principal opera composers Italy produced next to Rossini, neither, however, reaching his greatness—Gaetano Donizetti and Vincenzo Bellini. Donizetti's comic operas are the last fine examples of opera buffa, and they outshine his works in the serious vein, whereas Bellini's operas are entirely devoted to the glories of the human voice, though they do not measure up to the glories of the old bel canto. But both composers eventually forsook the Italian stage, turning to France. It was in Verdi's work that Italy finally recovered its leading role in operatic tradition, while Wagner's work established a totally new one in Germany.

Almost completely obscured by the great and lesser names of Classic and Romantic music is that of Johann Rudolf Zumsteeg, Swabian court conductor at the turn of the eighteenth century. Yet it deserves to be singled out, as it stands for a genre that, despite its own relative obscurity, marked a fresh departure of significance—the ballad. In its original meaning, the "dancing song," the ballad had a long and distinguished history, and the song as such is obviously the oldest of musical forms. But in the merging of musical Classicism and Romanticism, the term song—in its German version lied—acquired a new meaning. Greatly influenced by the poetry of Goethe and Schiller, Classical figures of German literature, the decisive phase in the history of the art song was heralded in works of such composers as Reichardt and Zelter (as well as in isolated examples by Haydn, Mozart and Beethoven).

In the development leading to the Romantic lied, the special form of the ballad assumed an important role. The dancing character of the ballad had early receded to the choral refrain with which the narrative of a solo singer was rounded out. This narrative, dealing predominantly with ancient and medieval sagas and valiant stories of feudal times, turned in the works of Classic German poetry more and more to folklike renditions of adventuresome, mysterious, and not infrequently gruesome scenes. The new form of solo song whose accompaniment was determined by the ascendancy of the modern keyboard instrument, the piano, lent itself especially well to the ballad.

In its terse structure, it served the dramatic tendencies of the time more directly than the elaborate opera, and thus the ballad holds a key position in a transitional phase of vocal styles.

Zumsteeg, who had become a friend of Schiller's in school days, became the prime representative of the ballad, and the direct way in which his work influenced that of Schubert can be gathered from the fact that Schubert's first song, "Hagar's Lament" (*Hagars Klage*), was modeled on Zumsteeg's ballad bearing the same title. Schubert's ballad *Erlkönig*, on a poem by Goethe and published four years later as his Opus 1, opens the literature of the Romantic song, and Schubert's more than six hundred contributions to the genre remained the chief component of the nineteenth-century song literature. The ballad, however, retained its own life and reached a high point in the works of Karl Loewe, a student of Zelter's and strongly influenced by Reichardt. Through these two early lied composers, Loewe had become acquainted with the world of Goethe and Schiller, but it is most characteristic of his work that as his Opus 1 he published settings of *Erlkönig* and *Edward*, the latter on the text of an old Scottish ballad that had served Schubert for one of his last songs.

Schubert has always been seen as a Januslike figure, "at times called the classicist of romanticism, at others the romanticist of classicism."[5] While this observation, germane to our discussion, is so convincingly true to the facts of stylistic analysis, it does not provide a key to the understanding of Schubert's creative nature. The same duality (which we have observed earlier in connection with the work of Beethoven) can be and has been ascribed to Brahms. Yet the blending of stylistic bequests must in each case merely be understood as an element characterizing, in different ways, overwhelmingly individual artistic personalities. Similarly, the epithet "Father of the Song" is as unjustly applied to Schubert as it does an injustice to the genre itself: it is the individuality of the Schubertian lied that explains the inception of a new literature.

The house in which Schubert was born, unchanged over the centuries, offers the visitor a most touching impression—the tiny dwelling of a schoolmaster's family, in which Schubert

5 See Paul Henry Lang, *Music in Western Civilization* (New York: Norton, 1941), p. 776. Lang speaks of Schubert's D-Minor Quartet as the triumph of the reconciliation of Classicism with Romanticism.

grew up as one of nineteen children. Salieri discovered the talent of the boy and accepted him into the Imperial Chapel. But Schubert's existence moved with remarkable directness into circles far removed from his background. His deep sense of literary values determined his work from the beginning, and he spent his short life in the company of highly cultivated young artists and poets. In the immense wealth of his songs, he grew to maturity immediately. But though the form of the song remained his own until his last composition, one might say that he departed from it to an extent often not fully realized. His genius sought expression in the Classical forms of the symphony and string quartet, and while he labored consciously and with unabating discipline under the shadow of Beethoven, he rose to equal the stature of the giant as did no later composer. His symphonies in B Minor (the "Unfinished") and C Major (the "Great"), his quartets in A and D Minor, and his last chamber music work, the String Quintet in C Major, mark the end of Classic instrumental literature. It is characteristic of Schubert's earnestness and modesty that toward the end of his life he became conscious of the fact that he had not mastered one particular form, the fugue. And it is well known that, two weeks before his death, he turned to Sechter for the discussion of some sketches of fugal compositions—the last music manuscript we have from his hand.

The forms of Classical chamber music and symphony remained the challenge for composers throughout the nineteenth century. Yet the Romantic song, as the century's most original creation, dominated the era to the extent that Mendelssohn wrote his famous "Songs without Words." Though they inaugurated the Romantic symphony, both Mendelssohn's and Schumann's best known major instrumental compositions are their concertos in which classic form was united with Romantic virtuosity. But the lives of these two masters, tragically short like Schubert's, produced a broad spectrum of highly original works. Schumann, barely in his twenties, also founded the first modern journal of music criticism that heralded the careers of Chopin and later Brahms. His many-sided work, guided by a wide vision of the Romantic scene, favors the fantastic element yet shows genuine lyrical strength. He was the greatest exponent of the German lied after Schubert. In his songs, the brilliance of the accompaniment often rises to leadership, and in extended postludes he tends to develop the poet's text to a level not reached by the voice but reflecting the finesse of his pianistic art and his power of interpretation.

There is something admirably sound about the gentle and refined figure of Mendelssohn. His work burst into maturity with his Overture for *A Midsummer Night's Dream* when he was seventeen, but he harnessed his great gift with elegant assuredness, and his amiable music exhibits true mastery. An intellectual by background and upbringing, he was always earnest, sincere, and wholly artistic in his work. More clearly devoted to the bequest of past generations than any other composer of his time, he yet remained entirely original. The Protestant chorale and the Handelian oratorio became all-important models for him, and though it was not given to his era to recover their original strength, this era was ennobled by Mendelssohn's historical orientation. Yet there is none of the historian in his brilliant violin concerto, his octet, or the *First Walpurgis Night*. Later ages, in turn, were unable to recover his finely controlled expression. He fully shared the problems of a post-Classical age, but he mastered them with the grace of his art.

Schubert, Schumann and Mendelssohn were composers for

Felix Mendelssohn, a sketch from his travels to Italy

whom the range of Classic forms remained a natural working basis. But while their masterpieces were thus distributed over various genres, the emphasis of nineteenth-century music turned to composers devoted to a single form or medium—as if history were to acknowledge with a grand gesture that the opulence it had produced began to elude a comprehensive grasp. The career of the traveling virtuoso, writing works for his own appearances, was an isolated phenomenon in the time of Vivaldi; in the nineteenth century, however, it tended to dominate the musical scene. The triumphs of Paganini were paralleled in the appearances of the young Liszt, who became the greatest pianist of all times, and Liszt's activities as a composer were determined at first by his international success on the concert stage.

The most typical representative of the composer whose creative work was so closely focused on his own performance medium was Frédéric Chopin, whom Liszt hailed as his equal. Chopin's piano works mirror the world of the Romantic virtuoso to the extent that his concertos for piano and orchestra were almost completely neglected—by the composer who gave them the most sparsely developed accompaniment, as well as by posterity which knows the composer merely by his finely wrought preludes, polonaises, mazurkas, impromptus, nocturnes and waltzes. These compositions combine frail detail and intensely poetic expression with a passionate virtuosity that makes them a unique achievement in the keyboard literature, and Chopin's life work, once again prematurely ended, raised soloistic composition to a level unattained ever after.

The violin literature fared differently; and though the nineteenth century is studded with spectacular violin concertos, we are dealing here by and large with mere show pieces. The exceptions came from composers committed to the symphonic rather than the soloistic ideal, and it is characteristic of the merging of Romantic virtuosity and Classic form that one of the most popular violin concertos of the era bears the title symphony—the *Symphonie Espagnole* by Edouard Lalo, a French composer of Spanish ancestry.

* 🎜 *

A gigantic rapprochement took place, more or less curiously brought about, by which the genres of opera, symphony and song met in new forms. In the case of Hector Berlioz, it was not the single instrument but their sum total—the vastly enlarged and technically perfected orchestra—that was the adopted "specialty." His *Grand Traité d'instrumentation et d'orchestration* (1844) became the classic of orchestration manuals, and in his works he explored the resources of the Romantic orchestra to their fullest. He called his symphonies, headed by the *Symphonie Fantastique*, "instrumental dramas," and in them he raised the concept of program music—purely instrumental music based on a literary source—to a new ideal. They embraced, once again, the genre of the concerto—the solo part in *Harold in Italie* was written with Paganini in mind. The monumental works of Berlioz include church music (his Requiem Mass and Te Deum), oratorios and operas, but in all of them he remained at heart the orchestrator. Despite their originality, his sacred works, in their grandiose sonority, negate the essence of the spiritual element, while staged drama negated, in fact, the artistic creed of program music.

Liszt, in the end dissatisfied with the career of the virtuoso and with compositions determined solely by the scope (albeit greatly widened) of his instrument, was inspired by the concept of program music in the work of Berlioz. At the height of his fame, he took up this new challenge and, turning now entirely to his creative work, arrived at a new symphonic form that became the model for a "New German School" whose influence actually extended well beyond Germany, the Tone Poem. His mastery of the Romantic orchestra was entirely beholden to symphonic principles of elaboration, and rather than following a "program," his works arose from a total conception that did not rely on descriptive details. In later years he wrote sacred oratorios and liturgical compositions, and just as his symphonic language stands in contrast to that of Berlioz by a thoroughly poetic approach, these choral works differ from those of Berlioz by a genuinely religious attitude. Liszt was a devoted Roman Catholic and, in later years, took minor orders as an abbé. His interests in all aspects of the music of his time developed on a wide scale throughout his life, and a host of students followed him to his centers of activity in Germany, Italy and Hungary.

Liszt was closely associated, both through his work and family ties, with Wagner (who married his daughter Cosima), and the extensive literary work of both composers provides revealing commentary on the ideals which they shared and which dominated the musical scene of the waning nineteenth century. Nevertheless, the two great exponents of the New German School were worlds apart. Whereas Liszt solved the challenges of over-ripe Romanticism by blending symphony and poem, Wagner announced that the time had come for a blending of all the arts and, in no way hesitant to suggest that the total artistic effort of past generations led to his own work, inaugurated a new concept, the *Gesamtkunstwerk* or Universal Art Work. That he could maintain such a claim is, in the end, due to his musical genius that triumphed over the problems posed by his complex artistic personality.

Wagner, in whose family the theater governed professional life, grew up under the influence of Weber and the early Romantic opera of Germany, but soon reached for the grand opera of France. A revolutionary to the core, he found himself fleeing from one country to another between successes and failures. It was in Switzerland that he wrote the text for his most towering work, the *Ring of the Nibelung*, and it bespeaks the magnitude of his planning that this work, originally designed as a single drama, grew into a cycle of four, as each text required the preface of a new one. The vastness of his conception becomes fully evident when we consider that, in setting the finished libretto to music, he stopped in the middle and, over a number of years, interspersed two of his most decisive, yet totally unlike dramatic works—*Tristan und Isolde* and *Die Meistersinger*—before completing the *Ring*. The choice of his subject matter, ranging from romantic fairy tale and Nordic myth to the solid burgher milieu of the late medieval guild, was determined in different ways by a pervading idea of redemption, to which in his last work, *Parsifal*, he gave final form.

It is equally characteristic of Wagner's extraordinary career that he salvaged its perilously disintegrating fortunes by what had become an anachronism—princely subvention—and that this subvention came from a mentally ailing king, Ludwig II of Bavaria. The king, who built the fantastic castles in the

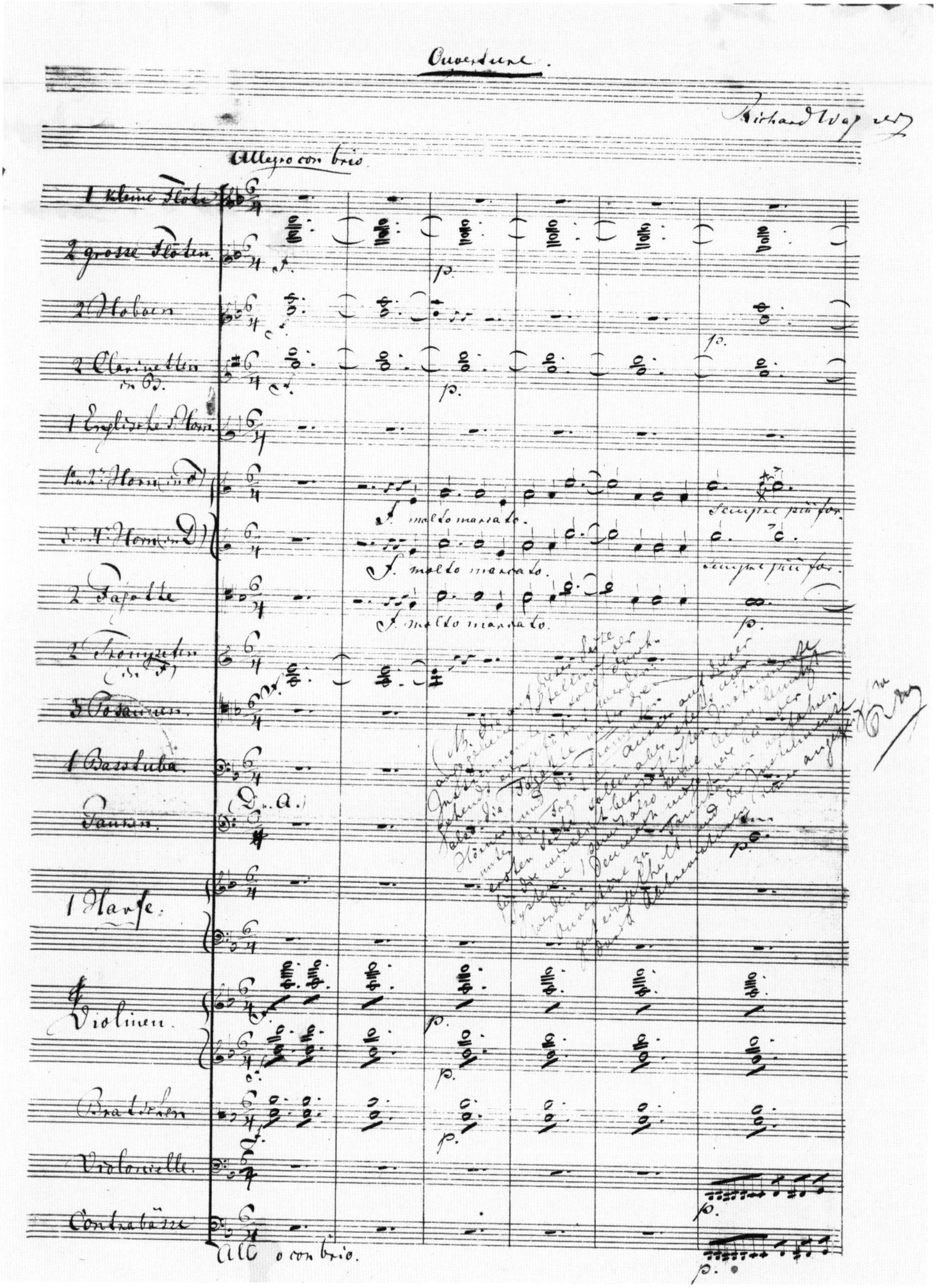
Ouverture.
Richard Wagner
Allegro con brio
1 kleine Flöte
2 grosse Flöten
2 Hoboen
2 Clarinetten in B.
1 Englisches Horn
1. u. 2. Horn in D
3. u. 4. Horn in D
2 Fagotte
2 Trompeten
3 Posaunen
1 Basstuba
Pauken
D. A.
1 Harfe
Violinen
Bratschen
Violoncelle
Contrabässe
p.
f. molto marcato.
sempre più for.
All^o con brio.

Bavarian Alps, enabled Wagner to establish a shrine for the Universal Art Work—for what Wagner had termed the "Music of the Future"—in Bayreuth, formerly the residence of the rulers of a Franconian principality, and a place of pilgrimage for an international opera audience ever since.

While Wagner appears as the most powerful figure of nineteenth-century music, he was destined to share this place with a composer whose work was the very antithesis of Wagner's *Gesamtkunstwerk*—Giuseppe Verdi. Born in the same year as Wagner, Verdi was, like Wagner, politically involved in his younger years, and his name became for a time the very symbol of the *risorgimento*, the rise of a free Italy. But unlike Wagner, he freed his own work in later years from national connotations. He became a national hero through the sheer power of his music, and the performance of *Aida*, commissioned to mark the historic opening of the Suez Canal, stands as the first truly international musical event.

It remains problematic to compare the two great representatives of nineteenth-century opera, the egocentric Wagner and the philanthropic Verdi: the creator of the new "music drama" who—mistakenly—considered himself first and foremost a literary figure, and the consummate master of traditional Italian opera which Wagner considered superseded. While the aims of their art were so diverse as virtually to defy comparison, their techniques show some surprising similarities. Wagner considered himself the heir of Beethoven, and the Beethovenian symphonic development of musical ideas assumed in Wagner's scores the role of the narrator who, like the ancient Greek chorus, interpreted dramatic continuity and meaning. His well-known orchestral device of using recurring and "guiding" melodies (leitmotives), however, was not his own invention. It appears in Verdi's works as well as those of other composers of the time. Yet while in Wagner's language the orchestral comment became the primary agent in conveying dramatic situations and philosophical concepts, in Verdi's works the human voice and human drama rule throughout. His roles eschew the supernatural and the saga; the brooding elements of Wagner's poetry and music were foreign to him. He was the supreme *operista*, and his last two works, *Otello* and *Falstaff*, written when the composer was at a

(Opposite page)
Richard Wagner, autograph note on the engraver's copy for *Der fliegende Holländer*

very advanced age, are lasting monuments to the old opera seria and opera buffa.

There is only one nineteenth-century opera that has equaled the stature and popularity of Wagner's and Verdi's works: Bizet's *Carmen*; in fact, this work has become the most popular opera in history. Georges Bizet, a highly educated musician, was by no means what history made of him: the composer of a single work. But *Carmen* became a world success because here the composer's great gifts merged with the tendencies of his time in a unique manner. The characterization of a heroine who is also the villain and murdered on stage in the final scene took unusual dramatic skill. It reflected the fin de siècle trend of Realism, a strong reaction to the gentleness of early Romanticism, and the choice of setting, drawing on Spanish and gypsy themes, was guided by another typical expression of the declining Romantic age, Exoticism. Bizet treated the subject with a surprisingly light hand, and his delicate and invariably interesting orchestration borders on the finesse of chamber music. He did not live to witness his triumph; the work was initially a failure that may have contributed to the composer's untimely death.

Bizet's *Carmen*, despite the enduring qualities of the work, signals a moribund epoch. Realism was met immediately with yet another reaction, Impressionism. The Romantic world withdrew into its most refined utterances, and in the last of the famous French operas, Claude Debussy's *Pelléas et Mélisande*, music no longer presents, it merely suggests the drama. Its frailty has a wonderful strength of its own, and its miraculously enriched palette of subtle colors heralds a new century and a new age.

As in all phases of history, what appears as a deltalike disintegration of a major era actually carries the seeds of significant rejuvenation and integration. A final reconstruction of Romantic expression and Classic form entered the music of the declining nineteenth century in the work of several major symphonists who, like the symphonists of Viennese Classicism, contributed to a large array of musical genres while being

(Opposite page)
Georges Bizet, piano arrangement of *Scènes de bal* by Jules Massenet

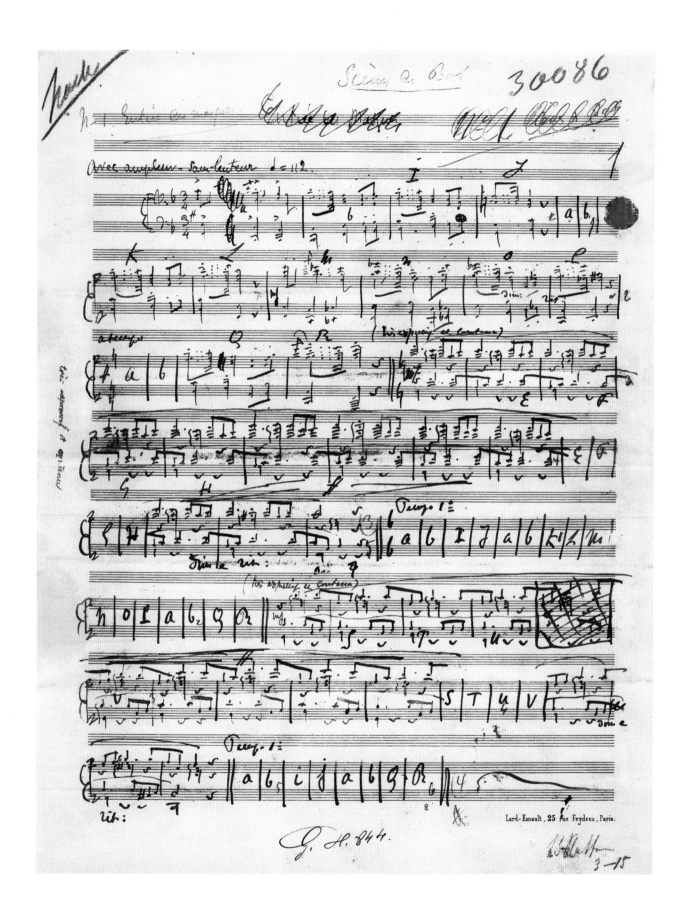

especially committed to the instrumental idiom. Vienna again claimed its place as a European musical capital in the works of Johannes Brahms and Anton Bruckner—as in the twentieth century it was to see the rise of a "Second Viennese School." The concept of a "School," however, would in no way fit the work of the two composers who dominated the Viennese musical scene in the last decades of the nineteenth century, because of the radical difference in their styles and because of a renewed emergence of the symphony at the hands of such entirely heterogeneous composers as Tchaikovsky, Dvořák, and César Franck. But that the traditional symphonic structure was by no means exhausted was amply borne out by their work and their influence that lasted well into the twentieth century.

The personalities of Brahms, the pianist, and Bruckner, the organist, strongly exemplify the contrast of Northern Protestantism and Southern Catholicism. They found their way early to choral works inspired by the new role of choral music in society—both of them conducted various amateur choral organizations. In Bruckner's work, however, the choral medium remained closely tied to the service of worship, and religious mysticism was to be carried into his symphonic work. The symphonic bequest of Brahms, on the other hand, is entirely Beethovenian, and the model of Beethoven remained a fundamental challenge throughout his life. As he embarked upon the large form, he found himself immediately in a crisis; what was to be his first symphony turned into a piano concerto. But from the young composer's crisis arose works marked both by overwhelming beauty and a conscientious working procedure that produced abundant, though always highly integrated, proportions. Like Beethoven, he returned to the piano concerto; but against Beethoven's five stand only two; against Beethoven's nine symphonies stand four. Like Beethoven, Brahms wrote one violin concerto that has remained a lasting work in the repertoire, as did Tchaikovsky (and as had Mendelssohn before him); and we might add to this list the G Minor Violin Concerto by Max Bruch, a composer close in orientation to Brahms, though he did not reach his stature.

Bruckner's symphonic work towers over the orchestral music of the late nineteenth century by its sheer monumentality. It is a monumentality seemingly inconsistent with the touching naiveté of a composer who dedicated one of his symphonies "to the dear Lord," and who pleaded with the emperor to call a halt to the bad reviews his works were receiving—but indeed only seemingly so. His simple soul was imbued with genius. His nine symphonies are related to one another in a vast cycle not unlike Wagner's tetralogy. Wagnerian is the language of his harmony and orchestration. But his work is the antithesis of Romantic music drama; it reaches back beyond the world of Schubertian lyricism to that of the great Catholic past, yet in epic dimensions that bring the history of the nineteenth-century symphony to a close.

The reconciliation of Romantic spirit and Classic tradition was a universal phenomenon that pervaded the music of Europe. When we speak of national "schools," in Russia, Bohemia and Scandinavia, we actually refer to individual expressions in the same process, although individuality defies such a generalization, as we are reminded in the cases of some bold innovations. Yet in a certain way even France, with its glorious legacy of music, developed a "school" that, on the whole departing from opera, reflected the age of Brahms and Bruckner. Like Bruckner, arriving at the symphonic form through his work as an organist, César Franck dealt in new ways with the old form. Like Brahms, Franck and his followers returned to a variety of classic genres which met with fresh interest and the support of a Societé Nationale de Musique established through the initiative of Camille Saint-Saëns, a composer versed and successful in veritably all musical forms. The most colorful of a group called the "Russian five," Nikolai Rimsky-Korsakov was also the first Russian composer to write a symphony. Standing apart from this group, Tchaikovsky, the single nineteenth-century Russian composer of truly European training and orientation, was essentially a traditionalist, though of eminent stature. But in the last of the "five"—Modest Petrovitch Musorgsky—Russia gave to nineteenth-century music a totally original and overpowering figure. A number of nineteenth-century composers such as Bruch, Saint-Saëns, and his student Gabriél Fauré, saw the Classic-Romantic tradition into the new century—Dvořák, significantly, into the New World.

Moderato Prélude 1

In concluding our survey of the epochs of musical Classicism and Romanticism, we must pay tribute once more to the role of the interpreter. As we have observed, composer and performer, creative and interpretive art, tended to claim individually defined domains at the rise of the nineteenth century. In the process, the role of the interpreter gained in originality and importance. A new key figure now took command of the concert stage and the opera pit: the professional conductor. Liszt and Wagner, like earlier composers, were professional conductors in their own right—the premiere of Wagner's *Lohengrin* was conducted by Liszt. But the premiere performances of *Tristan* and *Die Meistersinger* were in the hands of an acknowledged specialist, Hans von Bülow. A student of Liszt, whose daughter Cosima was espoused to him in first marriage, von Bülow became the chief interpreter of Wagner's and later of Brahms's work. He set the model for the modern career of the orchestral disciplinarian and virtuoso conductor. Public attendance at civic concerts had grown considerably, and the works of the masters, interpreted by professional conductors, became subject to further interpretation through daily reviews in which the public was served by professional critics.

Eduard Hanslick, prototype of the powerful and domineering critic, is known for his relentless attacks upon Wagner's and Bruckner's work (it was he who prompted Bruckner's plea for the emperor's protection) as well as for his loyal support of the work of Brahms. But posterity has unjustly judged this knowledgeable guardian of classic principles a belligerent misanthrope. Though seemingly conservative, he was ahead of his time in sensing in its musical grandeur the dangers of a decline.

Hanslick was the first to be appointed to the faculty of the University of Vienna to represent music as an integral part of the academic curriculum, and chairs of music had meanwhile been established also at other universities. The professorship at the University of Berlin was held in Hanslick's time by Heinrich Bellermann, a scholar whose influence was of a more broadly didactic, rather than polemic, kind. Devoted to the a cappella ideal that had been reawakened in the early part of the nineteenth century, he freshly interpreted the roots of its

(Opposite page)
César Franck, opening page of *Prélude, Chorale et Fugue,* dedicated to Mademoiselle Marie Poitevin

Joseph Joachim, letter to Hermann Levi
regarding a communication to Brahms

pedagogy and issued the first modern textbook of
counterpoint. It was of decisive influence on numerous
subsequent courses of instruction in a period in which
composer, performer, and audience alike began to obtain a
more clearly defined view of past musical styles.

When Liszt gave the first performance of *Lohengrin*, the
concertmaster of the orchestra was the nineteen-year-old
Joseph Joachim. One of the finest interpreters of the era,
Joachim was a musician of comprehensive command. It was he

who called Schumann's attention to the young Brahms. His
artistry inspired the violin concertos of Mendelssohn, Brahms,
and Bruch. He was the first to free Bach's solo violin works
from contemporaneous arrangements; and over a period of
forty years, as director of the newly founded Berlin Academy of
Music, he led the string quartet that established the classic
works of chamber music in the modern concert repertoire.
Like that from Liszt, a direct line of descent leads from
Joachim to yesterday's and today's great performers on the
concert stage.

An Age of Personal Memory

As the perspective of time diminishes and the historian becomes witness, the image of personages and events is apt to lose rather than gain in clarity. Figures and events that seem to "make history" may quickly fade; their significance is in danger of being blurred rather than being authoritatively defined. The heir apparent to the "New German" tradition of the era of Liszt and Wagner, Richard Strauss, wrote his last works as the new century that is now drawing to its close had reached the halfway mark. The past mingles with the present. It was with a shock of immediacy that the writer of these lines received, by curious circumstances, from the hand of the aged master what he had designated as his Artistic Testament, to be handed to the proper authorities in the turmoil of war. Yet the remarkable document, which now forms part of this collection, in the end gives witness only to the fact that the great symphonist and composer of dramatic works, while still in command of his extraordinary powers, began to outlive his own times. It deals with a future of opera that can no longer be realized.[1]

Opera, like symphony and art song, had lived into the twentieth century, continuing to glorify the spirit of the nineteenth century despite all the radical reactions of a new age. There is no opera composer who has remained in more general demand than Giacomo Puccini, whose often drastic style is undeniably derived from nineteenth-century Realism ("verismo") and its frequently favored Exoticism.

It is characteristic of our unvarying indebtedness to the past as well that Vienna never ceased to be the musical metropolis of immediate memory. It was in Vienna that Hugo Wolf, who barely lived into the twentieth century, spent his tragically brief life. The only song composer who could fully measure up

[1] See "The Artistic Testament of Richard Strauss," *The Musical Quarterly*, vol. XXXVI, no. 1 (January 1950).

Richard Strauss, Artistic Testament

Moldenhauer-Sammlungen in der
Bayerischen Staatsbibliothek München
Ana 330

to Schubert's stature, he gave the Romantic lied its final form.
Yet it is no longer the song composed for the private and
intimate setting that lives in his oeuvre, but the song for the
modern concert hall, the work in which the "accompaniment,"
designed for the modern concert piano, dominates and
penetrates the poetic meaning to an extent unknown to earlier
composers of the genre.

The powerful interpretation of Romantic lyricism proved to be
more problematic in the Viennese symphony of the turn of the
century. Gustav Mahler, the key figure in upholding the
Bruckner tradition, introduced the song as an essential

AN AGE OF PERSONAL MEMORY

Gustav Mahler, page from the autograph of
Symphony No. 4, third movement

component into the symphony; in fact, he gave the designation
"Symphonie" to his *Lied von der Erde*, a cycle of orchestral
songs. It is the lyrical element that rules his symphonic work,
yet its permeating influence stands in contrast to the grandiose
gestures with which the symphonic genre overreached itself.
Mahler's Eighth Symphony, the "Symphony of the Thousand,"
is the largest vocal work ever written.

Nevertheless, paired with such abandon to post-Wagnerian
dimensions, there is prophetic strength in the composer's work,
and in his frequent returns to smaller forms he anticipated the
rise of a "Second Viennese School." In later years he was
closely connected with the work of Alexander von Zemlinsky

and Zemlinsky's student and brother-in-law, Arnold Schoenberg. A new spirit of chamber music entered the orchestral world; but the most pronounced reaction to post-Romanticism became a new theory that renounced the fin de siècle language of overwrought chromaticism.

Schoenberg introduced the concept of twelve-tone music, a melodic idiom that dismissed all harmonic implications; and, constructed over predetermined series or rows, all tones of the chromatic scale were now declared as equals in musical importance. It was a theory of "atonality" which swept away all past traditions and to which the gifted followers of the Schoenberg school, Alban Berg and Anton von Webern, and in later years even the aged Igor Stravinsky, succumbed.

This revolutionary step has to be seen against the background of the dawn of an agitated century, and through the disasters of two global wars the new musical language experienced both setbacks and expansion. Leading twentieth-century composers, including Paul Hindemith and a host of others, distanced themselves from it; under political suppression it temporarily all but vanished, only to reawaken to a late bloom especially in postwar America; and it eventually gave way to more radical developments that changed, technologically expanded, and veritably obliterated the nature of musical sound. It gave way to aleatory tendencies, and to such extremes as the American John Cage's *4'33"*—a gesture that seems to raise the question: What *is* music?

The immediacy of events—remembered or known to have been witnessed—makes it problematic for the observer to chart a course through the music of our century. Hand in hand with the twentieth-century world conflicts went a new international understanding and interpenetration. Ever since the days of Dvořák and Tchaikovsky, European composers and performers spent a significant part of their careers in America. In totally new dimensions, an international musical language took form, shaped by components from many cultures. The so-called domains of "popular" and "serious" music merged, while they continued to claim individual, growing and

shrinking, territories. With George Gershwin's *Rhapsody in Blue*, American jazz had obtained legitimacy on the international concert stage; yet for a young generation at the end of the twentieth century, the word "concert" has taken on a new meaning of vast demonstrations, often out-of-doors, of musical entertainment entirely oblivious to the old "concert repertoire."

Nevertheless, demarcation lines remain. During the First World War, a German composer died whose work, while of recognized stature, has been genuinely appreciated only in Germany—Max Reger. His role in this respect is not unlike that of his American contemporary, Edward MacDowell, and a "school" of American composers began to form whose most widely acclaimed exponent became Charles Ives. Universally admired, his originality and keen sense of independence have recently become a matter of dispute, because evidence has come to light to suggest that he consciously altered dates of his compositions, so that they would have preceded such revolutionary works as Stravinsky's *Sacre du Printemps*.[2] If so, he cast a tragic shadow over works that in no way would be in need of such defense—doubly tragic, for the situation would reflect the agonies of twentieth-century innovations of so-called serious music. The composer's ideal of freedom from the European heritage was doubtless served in his novel creations; yet the popular works of his contemporary, Cole Porter, steeped in the folklore of the Western Hemisphere, were recognized as being free of any other derivation—without argument or lack of ease.

Ironically, it was at the hands of the European-born that some of the most important developments in modern American experimentalism grew. An outstanding case is that of Edgar Varèse, a Parisian who was trained by some of the leading French composers of the early twentieth century, after having studied mathematics and sciences at the École Polytechnique. Having come to America during the First World War, he inspired generations of American composers with his novelties in sound and rhythm, novelties which remain "somewhat abstruse to those of us who have not studied in polytechnical schools."[3]

(Opposite page)
Opening page of Max Reger's piano-vocal score for *Requiem*, op. 144b on a text by Friedrich Hebbel

At the upper right margin appears the composer's dedication of the piece to the German soldiers killed during the first year of World War I.

Moldenhauer-Sammlungen in der Bayerischen Staatsbibliothek München Mus. ms. 17495

2 See Donal Henahan, "Did Ives Fiddle with the Truth?" *New York Times*, February 21, 1988.

3 Adolfo Salazar, *Music in Our Time* (New York, 1946), p. 318.

Carl Fischer, New York.
No. 34—16 lines.

The impact of such influences, however, can be no more subject to question than their sincerity. At the same time, the traditional European influence has remained an integral part of the American musical scene. This is in part due to the fact that leading European composers, such as Schoenberg, Stravinsky, and Hindemith, who left Europe under the threat of the approaching Second World War, became the mentors of young Americans. A far-reaching didactic influence was exerted by Ernest Bloch, who had come to this country earlier. Yet the pedagogical role of the European composer in America varied. Bloch, a Swiss by birth, who with his widely recognized works served an independent ideal of establishing a new Jewish idiom in music, became, as director of the Cleveland Institute of Music and of the San Francisco Conservatory, the admired teacher of a host of American composers who were to pursue their own independent paths of success. His somewhat younger contemporary, Ernst Křenek, a Viennese who had gained an international reputation early in life, received an appointment at an American college that dismissed him when he introduced twelve-tone music in his theory curriculum. A highly respected, though more or less intentionally isolated career was to carry his life almost to the end of the century at whose beginning he was born.

It is with dismay that the chronicler makes mention of the American phase that concluded the life of Béla Bartók, in the opinion of many destined to become the century's most enduring composer. Bartók gave new meaning to creative impulse guided by a commitment to national heritage. What achieved world fame in the work of this modest and withdrawn artist was due to the dual attributes of scrupulous scholarship and a most original gift. He had recognized early that the wealth of indigenous Slavic music was in danger of being forever lost, and in painstaking exploration he set out to uncover its roots. He was neither a folklorist nor a curator. But in exacting field work that would put many a social scientist to shame, he rescued treasures whose preservation would represent a life work in itself. From the achievement of the researcher, however, departed that of the composer, and while the culture of the land formed a nurturing element in his music, the style of his works became entirely his own. His last compositions were written in the United States, but the ailing

(Opposite page)
Edgard Varèse, score of *Intégrales*, fair copy with corrections

Moldenhauer Archives, Paul Sacher Foundation, Basel

Varèse INTÉGRALES

© Copyright 1926 by Colfranc Music Publishing Corporation; Copyright Renewed. Reprinted by permission of Hendon Music, Inc., Agents for G. Ricordi & C., Milan

composer remained a stranger in the country, and he died in relative obscurity and poverty.

In curious contrast to the fate of Bartók stands that of Kurt Weill. Like Křenek born with the century, this highly gifted and successful composer wrote music that, in the best sense of the word, was popular. As a young man he came to America, leaving Germany at the time the National Socialists came into power, but he did not remain a mere immigrant. More readily than any of the other Europeans who had crossed the Atlantic, he embraced the art of American twentieth-century music and, with an innate sense for its dramatic potential, added his own impulse to it. His posthumous fame, which has markedly grown toward the end of the century, attests to a singularly gratifying career.

* *

Yet the survey of twentieth-century developments in music directs our attention to the fact that, in very different manners, the age that has seen an unparalleled widening and integration of the international scene remains, despite all fertile exchange, beholden to national domains.

Sergei Prokofieff, the greatest among the older generation of Russian twentieth-century composers, wrote after an extended stay abroad, "A foreign atmosphere does not provide me with any foreign inspiration, I am a Russian." The spell of their country's fate looms over the career of this eminent composer as well as over that of his younger contemporary Dimitri Shostakovitch. Unlike Prokofieff, the latter identified his work clearly with Soviet ideals. In contrasting ways, their art was committed to their homeland and its sad lot in twentieth-century history. In contrasting ways, too, it was committed to the symphony and its Western heritage. Prokofieff approached the latter early in life with his famous "Classical Symphony," but his work was distributed over many genres, notably those of opera and ballet. In the oeuvre of Shostakovitch the symphony took on a central role, and especially in his later periods one senses the influence of Bruckner and Mahler.

What is totally absent from his work is the influence of French

Impressionism, and this seems to suggest an enforced separation between the European East and West. Yet the palette of the twentieth century had grown too complex for categoric distinctions. While no twentieth-century composer seems more markedly French than Maurice Ravel, this foremost twentieth-century representative of the music of his country was drawn to the work of Mussorgsky, Rimsky-Korsakov, and Stravinsky (with whom he shares a penchant for articulate clarity), and his famous *Daphnis and Chloé* was written for Sergei Diaghilev's Russian Ballet. Ravel was at heart an instrumental composer, inspired by the dance and apt to treat even the voice with instrumental precision. The style of his piano music, chamber music, and orchestral works may border on the brittle, but it never lacks a characteristic French grace.

The indebtedness to a national character comes to the fore even in the music of Arthur Honegger, although here we are dealing with composite nationality. This Swiss composer was born in France; he settled eventually in Paris, and a French orientation is predominant in his music. But it is the French orientation of an artist in whose home country French is one of several native languages. He received his early training in Zurich and returned to Switzerland throughout his life. The German-Swiss Alemanic heritage remained strongly present in his many-sided oeuvre. He is "one of the least dogmatic composers of the recent past, whose work is governed by synthesis rather than eclecticism."[4]

4 Wiley Tappolet in *Die Musik in Geschichte und Gegenwart*.

Like Honegger, Germaine Tailleferre, the composer of fine orchestral scores that are remembered, belonged to the group *Les Six*, whose work she propagated throughout Europe. Its members, however, were connected in friendly association rather than a set program of French modern music.

More directly felt is the national influence of the most prominent twentieth-century composers in Spain and Latin America, Manuel de Falla and the slightly younger Heitor Villa-Lobos. De Falla raised Spanish music, after a long period of relative obscurity, to international importance again. A friend of Debussy and Ravel, he spent his formative years in Paris, yet a fundamental direction to his creative work was given by Felipe Pedrell, Spain's most eminent music historian whose research in the treasures of indigenous music is comparable to Bartók's. The folk music of Andalusia, the region where he was born, gave de Falla's work inspiration—the work of a highly sensitive and disciplined artist whose historic role it was to deliver Spanish music from its Romantic stigma of Exoticism. In contrast with de Falla's work stands that of the lesser known Federico Mompou whose predominantly pianistic work is not without reference to folkloristic themes. But the style of this Spanish composer was more clearly guided by his interest in the group *Les Six* and his devotion to Debussy.

The music of Villa-Lobos is not so much indebted to scholarly discovery as to technical brilliance which, however, is obviously founded in the composer's interest in Brazilian folk traditions. Trained as a violoncellist, he turned to the study of the guitar and popular improvisations; and while his life work embraced the symphonic and dramatic genres, chamber and piano music, his most successful works were written for his own instruments. In later years he explored the classical heritage of music, largely in his role as his country's most acknowledged musical educator, and the pieces involving an ensemble of eight cellos in his *Bachianas Brasileiras* are among his best known.

The tendency to draw fresh strength from the roots of folk music might be understood in a larger sense as a reaction against the over-refined and intellectualized twentieth-century musical language. Nevertheless, the incentives varied. In Poland, as in Russia, it was the regime that urged composers to concern themselves with the national heritage, and this pressure obscured many an artist's life. Yet it was only until about a decade after the end of the Second World War that Polish music was virtually closed off from the West; by 1956, international music festivals were being held in that country. This may have been the reason why the folk element in the music of Witold Lutosławski, the foremost Polish composer in the first half of the century, was in evidence only in those years. But it was doubtless also prompted by genuine interest. Lutosławski's *Concerto for Orchestra*, possibly his most eminent work, was inspired by folk music, yet as a matter of course he would treat folk motifs with atonality. Thus his *Funeral Music* honoring the memory of Bartók, whose work was venerated in Poland, is based on a twelve-tone row.

(Opposite page)
Manuel de Falla, detail from a draft for his Concerto for Harpsichord

By permission of
Manuel de Falla Ediciones
Mrs. Isabel de Falla

2

moins

·72·

Poland produced another internationally recognized composer who, in fact, stands out as the most vigorous and the most successful of the waning twentieth century. Freed from the nineteenth-century and twentieth-century commitment to folk music, Krysztof Penderecki rose to universal fame overnight with his St. Luke Passion. In full command of all the means of a new age, he has embraced the major orchestral and choral forms and has proved himself a master of the music drama. Trained as a violinist, he developed a keen sense for all colors of sound and harmony. In view of the complexity of his work, his mastery of the a cappella medium is remarkable, and in such works as his Agnus Dei for eight-part unaccompanied chorus, or his *Stabat Mater* for three unaccompanied choirs, the listener is immediately under the spell of his sense of form and expression.

Trends of twentieth-century music have curiously overlapped in the work of some of its central figures. Whereas the "Second Viennese School," led by Schoenberg, was unequivocal in its adherence to serialism, its post-Romantic heritage nevertheless was undeniable. It merged in Alban Berg's music with an individual interpretation of atonality, and even the bold language of *Wozzeck*, the opera that established his reputation, is beholden to Romantic ideals. But the sensitive art of Anton von Webern, whose posthumous recognition is decisively indebted to the collector of these source documents,[5] severed its Romantic roots with a radically new approach to form. He became the celebrated "miniaturist" of the twentieth century, an aspect of his creative career that by no means exhausts a characterization of his strikingly original oeuvre. In Stravinsky's work, Russian heritage met with a pervading Western orientation of the composer who settled in Paris and later in the United States, with "Neo-Classicism," and eventually with the undeniable influence of the Schoenberg circle, especially Anton von Webern. By contrast, Hindemith, who had dominated the scene of German music in the second and third decades of the century, remained inherently German. Having made America his home at the height of his creative powers, he returned to Europe in later years to take a professorship in Zurich. His innate gift of instrumental performance and a wide artistic perspective always guided his course; he was a traditional guild musician as well as a historian and mystic.

5 See Hans Moldenhauer, *Anton von Webern; Perspectives* and "A Webern Archive in America" (Seattle and London: University of Washington Press, 1966).

(*Opposite page*)
Page from Heitor Villa-Lobos, *Estudio No. 7*, for Guitar, with pencil fingerings entered by Segovia

The Moldenhauer Archives at Harvard University. By permission of the Houghton Library, Harvard University

Reprinted by permission of the Publisher Sole representative U.S.A. Theodore Presser Company

There is a further aspect of Hindemith's work which was to become an important bequest to the later German and international scene, that of organizer for the promotion of modern music. Under his leadership the gathering place for young composers developed in Donaueschingen, center of a former German principality, which after the Second World War found a parallel in the Darmstadt music festivals.

The countries freed from Fascism reawakened with a certain shock to contemporary music, and the prototype of the composer-performer found greatly varying new challenges in experimentation. While Luigi Dallapiccola, the Italian, remained indebted to the brilliant dualistic career of Ferruccio Busoni and later to Schoenberg and Alban Berg, the most conspicuous figure among the young Germans, Karlheinz Stockhausen, extended serialism in ways that relied upon the whim of the performer as much as upon the precision provided by the means of the electronic age. His work had received primary impulse from latter-day French music, and his partner at Darmstadt became the composer-conductor Pierre Boulez, one of the foremost avant-gardists. But throughout the twentieth century the avant-garde wrestled with the problem of becoming the old guard. A telling epithet for the music of the declining century has become "Post-modernism," and composers such as the American George Rochberg renounced the advances of technology and looked to past ages for inspiration.

The latter orientation has led to especially stimulating results in the music of Elliott Carter, one of the most highly honored American composers of the century. New interpretations of polyphony and the *concertante* element are determining factors in his far-flung oeuvre, in which what one might call the counterpoint of rhythm and meter has assumed a major role; and the classical genre of the string quartet has occupied a key position in his work.

The old and the ever new developed the greatest contrasts in the world of twentieth-century performance. The autonomous composer who became his own conductor with the aid of the synthesizer worked next to such a widely versed musician as Boulez who, for a time, was the conductor of the New York

AN AGE OF PERSONAL MEMORY

Philharmonic. But the image of the orchestral sovereign such as the erstwhile conductor of the Boston Symphony, Karl Muck, whose imposing career lasted well into the twentieth century, lives on. The era of the Romantic performer stayed with us in such supreme figures as Andrés Segovia and Pablo Casals, and the legacy of the nineteenth-century pedagogue remained alive in the famous twentieth-century violinists who studied with Leopold Auer, himself a student of Joachim.

Personal recollection rather than the detached sifting process granted by the passage of time increasingly influences the sorting out of names from the twentieth century, and while the collectors' views continue to be guided by critical observation, their numbers become legion. Hans Moldenhauer, himself an active musician, retained through direct encounters of his long life an unusually vivid impression of the unfolding European and American musical scene. As a friend, he witnessed the essentially tragic career of Mario Castelnuovo-Tedesco whose great gift suffered in emigration—the young avant-gardist was destined to become a respected conservative. Moldenhauer's teacher in young years was the prominent conductor Hans Rosbaud, the early interpreter of Schoenberg who in later years became the champion of contemporary music in Donaueschingen. In America it was Rudolph Ganz, President of the Chicago Musical College, under whose guidance Moldenhauer continued and completed his formal education. He was connected, often in close association, with such heterogeneous musical personalities as Karl Amadeus Hartmann, proponent of avant-garde performance and eminent symphonist; Paul A. Pisk, Schoenberg student, able composer, critic, and scholar; Eduard Steuermann, student of Busoni and Schoenberg, to whom many of the latter's premiere performances were entrusted; Nicolas Slonimsky, pianist, conductor and spirited lexicographer; Aurelio de la Vega, Cuban-American composer and musicographer; and Wolfgang Fraenkel, whom the escape from Germany had driven to new educational challenges in China before he settled in the United States.

The documents brought together in this collection obviously vary in importance, and the record of history they offer remains in constant need of revision. Will continuing currency or growing obscurity be accorded to figures of the recent past? To what extent will a new century rearrange the phalanx of the old? History has its own ways of being selective, and a name seemingly lost may acquire a new ring after a good deal more than a century. At any given age, critical evaluation can do no more than attempt to point the way. The only reliable guide into the future will always be the primary source.

Essays on Selected Documents

☐ *Explanatory Note*
The essays are presented in alphabetical order by composer.

Obermaße hat der H. Inspector
Eulenberg vor d. Jahr 1746, weg.
des Nathanischen Legati, so den 26.
Octobr. vermittelst kund Oberlieder
als am Tage Sabina in der Thoma..
abgesungen worden, ein genüge gethan,
indem die fünf gülden Meißn.
mir auch benandt richtig gezahlet,
so auch laut des Testaments nach die
selbigen Tages im Chore befindlich Schüler richtig und egal ausgetheilet
worden sollen. Leipzig d. 26. October.
1746.   Joh. Seb: Bach

Obgedrum hat der heilige Inspector
H. Paul Francke vor d. Jahr 1747.
wegen des Nathanischen Legati, so den
26. Octobr. vermittelst kind Noth lieder,
so ihr am Sabinen tag in der Thoma,
kirche abgesungen worden, ein richtig genüge
gethan, indem die fünf Gulden Meißner
mir auch benandt richtig gezahlet, so
auch laut Testamenti unter die selbigen
Tages im Chore befindliche Schüler richtig und
egal ausgetheilet werd soll. Leipzig d. 26.
Octobr. 1747.   Joh: Sebast: Bach.

Daß der Inspector des Natha-
nisch Legati, Herr Eulenberg
auch vor des 1748. Jahr, weg.
und auf d. Sabina Tag in Monat
Octobris abgesungenen Oberlieder,
mir dieselben mit ein genüge gethan
sindemaße derselbe heute dato fünf
Gulden, Meißn. nauch. zu vor d. Sachr.
..en, satz vor die Schüler mir auch
benandt ausgezahlet, solches wird
hierdurch daten Carlich quittiret,
Leipzig d. 27. Octobr. 1748.
                   Joh: Sebast: Bach
                          C.

Daß der Inspector des Nathanischen
Legati, Herr Eulenberg auch vor des
1749 Jahr, wegen eines theil der
Sabinen Tag in Monath Octobris
abgesungenen Oberlieder, vor die
Bes Maße ein genüge gethan, heute

The Nathan Bequest: Payment Receipts in the Hand of Johann Sebastian Bach, 1746 to 1748 (With a Fragment for the Year 1749 in the Hand of His Son)

Robert L. Marshall

AMONG JOHANN SEBASTIAN BACH'S duties as Thomas Cantor in Leipzig was the obligation to lead the choirboys of the Thomasschule in annual renditions of motets or chorales offered in memory of benefactors of the school. In some twenty instances the terms of the bequest governing these performances entailed an honorarium for the cantor, who dutifully prepared and signed a receipt confirming its payment.[1]

The most copiously documented of these obligations was the so-called Nathan Bequest (Nathanisches Legat). Sabine Nathan, evidently the wealthy widow of a Leipzig master cabinetmaker, died in 1612. Her last will and testament provided that each year, on or about Sabina's Day (i.e., October 26), funeral motets were to be performed before and after the weekly sermon in the appropriate church: either St. Thomas or St. Nikolai. For this purpose the widow earmarked the sum of 1000 gulden, from whose annual interest five gulden were to be shared by the cantor (two gulden) and the participating choirboys (three gulden). The bequest was to be administered by the Leipzig cabinetmakers' guild.[2]

Between 1686 and 1821 receipts for these payments were entered into a leather-backed, bound receipt book belonging to the guild. Since Bach assumed the post of Thomas Cantor in May 1723 and retained it until his death in July 1750, we may presume that (whenever possible) he personally drafted and signed all the receipts for the Nathan bequest falling within that twenty-seven-year period. In fact, sixteen-and-a-half annual receipts survive, as does the receipt

[1] See Hans-Joachim Schulze, "Marginalien zu einigen Bach-Dokumenten," *Bach-Jahrbuch 1961* (Leipzig: Breitkopf und Härtel), especially pp. 88ff.

[2] This paragraph is based on the discussion in Werner Neumann and Hans-Joachim Schulze, eds., *Bach-Dokumente, Band I: Schriftstücke von der Hand Johann Sebastian Bachs* (hereafter *Bach-Dokumente I*) (Kassel: Bärenreiter, 1963), p. 192.

3 From 1951 until 1993 the volume was in the possession of Dr. Otto Kallir. See Gerhard Herz, *Bach Sources in America* (Kassel: Bärenreiter, 1984), p. 161. In 1993 it was acquired at auction from Sotheby's, London, by the Bach-Archiv, Leipzig. See Hans-Joachim Schulze, "Johann Sebastian Bach und das 'Nathanische Legat'" in Bach-Archiv Leipzig, *Das Quittungsbuch des Nathanischen Legats* (Berlin: Kulturstiftung der Länder, n.d. [1995]), pp. 11–12.

4 The receipts for the years 1723 to 1726 are published in Hans-Joachim Schulze, "Vier unbekannte Quittungen J. S. Bachs und ein Briefauszug Jacob von Stählins," *Bach-Jahrbuch 1973*, pp. 88–89; the receipt for the year 1748, along with an English translation is published in Herz, op. cit., pp. 164–65; the receipts for the years 1746, 1747, and 1749, along with English translations, are published below. The receipts for the remaining years are published in *Bach-Dokumente I*, pp. 192–93, 196–97, 200–203.

5 *Bach-Dokumente I*, p. 202.

6 Herz op. cit., pp. 163–64.

7 During the period that the leaf was in the possession of Georg Floersheim until its acquisition by the Moldenhauer Archives it was unavailable for scholarly examination or reproduction—hence the absence of the texts for the years 1747 to 1749 from the definitive *Bach-Dokumente I*. See the discussion there of documents 133, 139, 143 (pp. 205, 208–9); also Herz, op. cit., pp. 163–64.

8 *Bach-Dokumente I*, p. 209.

book itself.[3] The book proper contains Bach's entries only for the years 1727–1729; the other pertinent leaves were removed from the volume—in order, no doubt, to be sold (or perhaps given away) to collectors.

A single leaf typically contains three or, space permitting, four annual entries. In the latter case, two successive years are entered on each side, one above the other and separated from one another by a freely drawn horizontal line. In all, surviving single leaves from the receipt book include Bach's entries for the years 1723–1726, 1735, 1737, 1742–1748, along with the nonautograph fragmentary entry for the year 1749 (see below).[4]

The last four receipts from Bach's Leipzig tenure, for the years 1746 to 1749, are contained on the single leaf now preserved in the Library of Congress. In all four Bach acknowledges receiving the sum of five gulden from the designated inspector of the cabinet makers' guild. Beginning with the payment for the year 1744 this function was usually carried out by the master cabinetmaker, Christoph Eulenberg (1692–1755).[5] In the year 1745, however, the inspector was one Johann Bode and in 1747 a certain Paul Francke.

The Library of Congress leaf measures approximately 15.6 by 9.6 cm. and is in good condition. Its provenance has been traced by Gerhard Herz.[6] The leaf was purchased by the Frankfurt collector Louis Koch (1862–1930), directly or indirectly from the original owner, the Leipzig cabinetmakers' guild. As part of the Koch collection it was bequeathed by Koch's daughter, Maria Floersheim-Koch, to her son, Georg Floersheim. The leaf was purchased from the Floersheim Collection by the Moldenhauer Archives, in December 1976.[7]

Bach's receipts for 1746 and 1747 are on the recto of the leaf, his entry for 1748 on the top of the verso. Below it is the beginning of the receipt for the year 1749; it is in the hand of his son, Johann Christian Bach, who was fourteen years old at the time.[8] Bach was evidently unable, owing to his failing health and eyesight, to write the entry himself. Indeed, Bach's handwriting had already deteriorated considerably at the time of the 1748 receipt. With the exception of the date, Christian set out to copy the 1748 receipt literally. It was almost certainly completed on the following leaf. Whether or not Johann Sebastian Bach signed it himself is not known.

Two of the four entries on the Library of Congress leaf have been published previously. A transcription of the receipt for 1746 appears in *Bach-Dokumente I*; the receipt for 1748 has been transcribed and translated into English by Gerhard Herz in *Bach Sources in America*. The 1747 version, along with the portion of the receipt for 1749, copied by Johann Christian Bach, have not been transcribed or translated before. The texts for all four years, in transcription and English translation, follow herewith.

Receipt for the Year 1746 (recto, top).[9]

9 Transcribed in *Bach-Dokumente I* as document 129 (p. 203).

> Abermahln hat der Herr *Inspector* Eülenberg vor das Jahr 1746., wegen des *Nathan*ischen *Legati*, so den 26. *Octobr.* vermittelst eines Sterbe Liedes als am Tage *Sabinæ* in der Kirche abgesungen worden, eine Genüge gethan, indem Er fünff Gulden Meißnisch mir endes benandten richtig gezahlet; so auch laut des *Testaments* unter die selbigen Tages im *Chore* befindlichen Schüler richtig und *egal* ausgetheilet werden sollen. Leipzig. den 26. *Octobr.* 1746.
>
> > *Joh: Seb: Bach*

Once again Inspector Eülenberg has fulfilled the obligation of the Nathan bequest, [this time] for the year 1746, insofar as he has properly paid to the undersigned five Meissen gulden in compensation for the singing of a dirge in the church on the 26th of October, i.e., on Sabina Day, which payment, in accordance with the will, is to be equally and properly divided among the pupils who were present in the choir on that day. Leipzig, the 26th of October 1746.

> Joh: Seb: Bach

Receipt for the Year 1747 (recto, bottom).

> Wiederum hat der heurige *Inspector* Herr Paul Francke vor das Jahr 1747, wegen des *Nathan*ischen *Legati*, so den 26. Octobr. vermittelst eines Sterbe Liedes, als am *Sabinen* Tag in der *Thomas* Kirche abgesungen worden, eine völlige Genüge gethan, indem Er fünff Gülden Meißnisch mir endes benandten richtig gezahlet, so auch laut *Testamenti* unter die selbigen Tages im *Chore* befindliche[n] Schüler

richig und *egal* ausgetheilet werden soll[en]. Leipzig. den
25. *Octobr.* 1747.

Joh: Sebast: Bach.

Once again, the current inspector, Mr. Paul Francke, has completely fulfilled the
obligation of the Nathan bequest [this time] for the year 1747, insofar as he has
properly paid to the undersigned five Meissen gulden in compensation for the
singing of a dirge in the Thomas Church on the 26th of October, i.e., on Sabina
Day, which payment, in accordance with the will is to be equally and properly
divided among the pupils who were present in the choir on that day. Leipzig, the
25th of October 1747.

Joh: Sebast: Bach.

¹⁰ As transcribed and translated in Herz op.
cit., p. 164. A facsimile of the verso appears
in Herz, op. cit., p. 376, illus. 62.

Receipt for the Year 1748 (verso, top).[10]

Daß der *Inspector* des *Nathan*ischen *Legati,* Herr Eülenberg auch
vor das 1748. Jahr., wegen eines auf den Sabinen Tag in *Monat
Octobris* abgesungenen Sterbe Liedes, vor dießes mahl ein
Genüge gethan, sindemahln derselbe heüte *dato* fünff Gülden
Meißn[isch], nämlich. 2 vor den *Cantorem,* und 3 vor die Schüler
mir endes benandten ausgezahlet; solches wird hiedurch
danckbarlich *quittiret.* Leipzig. den 27. *Octobr.* 1748.

*Joh: Sebast: Bach
C.*

That the Inspector of the Nathan bequest, Mr. Eülenberg, in compensation for the
singing of a dirge on Sabina Day in the month of October, has once again fulfilled
the obligation, this time for the year 1748, insofar as he has paid to the undersigned
on this day five Meissen gulden—namely, 2 for the Cantor and 3 for the pupils—
such is hereby gratefully acknowledged. Leipzig, the 27th of October 1748.

Joh: Sebast: Bach
C. [=Cantor]

Receipt for the Year 1749: Fragment in the Hand of Johann Christian
Bach (verso, bottom).

Daß der *Inspector* des *Nathan*ischen *Legati,* Herr Eülenberg auch
vor das 1749 Jahr, wegen eines auf den Sabinen Tag in Monath

Octobris abgesungenen Sterbelieder [sic], vor dießes Mahl ein Genüge gethan, sinde[mahln]

That the Inspector of the Nathan bequest, Mr. Eülenberg, in compensation for the singing of a dirges [sic] on Sabina Day in the month of October, has once again fulfilled the obligation, this time for the year 1749, insofar

[End of fragment]

Comments on Béla Bartók's Working Method in Dealing with Proofs for His Violin Concerto (1937–1938)

Ferenc Bónis

Bartók himself once said to the writer of these lines that his artistic development might be likened to a spiral: to deal with the same problems on an ever rising level, with correspondingly rising success—this seemed to him the guiding principle of his development.[1]

BENCE SZABOLCSI

THE VALIDITY OF BÉLA BARTÓK'S quoted statement—"to deal with the same problems on an ever rising level, with correspondingly rising success"—becomes evident in a particularly convincing manner from the structural affinity of his two violin concertos: the one composed in 1907–1908 (not performed or published during the composer's life), and the accomplished masterpiece written thirty years later, 1937–1938.[2]

Totally different in quality, these two works are related in kind through the determining role of the variation principle. Bartók composed the concerto from his early years for Stefi Geyer (1888–1956), the beautiful and gifted violinist, with whom he had fallen in love. His original concept of the work called for three movements using variants of a "love chord of four notes": character variations reflecting the nature of the beloved. Next to that of the "heavenly" ideal image, Bartók wanted to sketch the "humorous" portrait of a "tempestuous" and an "indifferent, cool and silent" Stefi Geyer.[3]

In the end, only the "ideal image" within this total concept was realized in the opening movement of a concerto. It was subsequently published as the first part of the orchestral work *Deux Portraits,* op. 5. Supposed rests of the planned remaining movements, in the form of variants of upon the "love motif,"

[1] Bence Szabolcsi, "Das Leben Béla Bartóks" in *Béla Bartók. Weg und Werk, Schriften und Briefe,* comp. Bence Szabolcsi (Budapest: Corvina, 1957), p. 45.

[2] Ever since 1957, the date of publication for the earlier work, Boosey & Hawkes distinguished the two concertos by the titles Violin Concerto No. 1, op. posth. and Violin Concerto No. 2. The composer himself, for various reasons not having wanted to publish the earlier work in its entirety, nor having issued it in print, deemed it unnecessary to add a number to the later work and referred to it simply as Violin Concerto.

[3] Ferenc Bónis, "Első hegedűverseny, első vonósnégyes. Bartók zeneszerzői pályájának fordulópontja" ("First Violin Concerto, First String Quartet. A Turning Point in Béla Bartók's Creative Career") contained in the author's volume *Hódolat Bartóknak és Kodálynak* ("Homage to Bartók and Kodály") (Budapest: Püski, 1992), p. 37.

can be traced in Bartók's works ranging from *Fourteen Bagatelles, Ten Easy Piano Pieces, Two Elegies, String Quartet No. 1* to the opera *A kékszakállú herceg vára* (Duke Bluebeard's Castle) and a number of others.

This, however, does not mean that he had given up his early violin concerto. Rather, he fundamentally altered the structural design of the work. He rejected the traditional three-movement pattern and supplanted it by a pattern of paired movements. "One day this week," he wrote to Stefi Geyer on December 21, 1907, "I was impressed, as if by a sudden inspiration, with the seemingly unarguable fact that your piece must consist only of two movements, two contrasting images— that is all. Now I am surprised that I did not discover this truth earlier."[4]

The change in Bartók's conception suggests the influence of Franz Liszt and his "Faustian dramaturgy." This dramaturgical scheme, whose most striking expression can be observed in Liszt's "Faust" Symphony, opens a new chapter in the history of variation. The outer movements of this work—"Faust" and "Mephisto"—represent the portraits of two *contrasting characters*, drawn with *the same musical material*. The artistic intent was clear: it was a matter of showing the simultaneous existence of Good and Evil within ourselves, pointing out that a struggle of the two principles remains essentially a constant incentive. (We might add here that the "Faust" Symphony opens with the first dodecaphonic theme in history.)

Bartók discovered in the Faustian dramaturgy—applying the term subsequently in order to point out the idea of unity within contrasts—new form-giving elements. The first work generated by this discovery was thus the two-movement violin concerto. And when, for various reasons, he decided against publication of the two concerto movements, he completed the first movement, on the basis of the same dramaturgical considerations, with the orchestrated version of a piano work composed on the same love motif as a second movement— resulting in the *Deux Portraits,* op. 5. In his *Second Piano Concerto* (1930–1931), Bartók combined the principle of unity in the outer movements with those of inversion of themes and symmetry of the whole form. The finale is in this case a quasi

4 E hét valamelyik napján mintha felsőbb sugallatra, oly hirtelen ötlött eszembe az az elvitázhatatlannak látszó kényszerűség, hogy a maga darabja nem is állhat csak 2 tételből. 2 ellentétes kép: ez az egész. Most csak azt csodálom, hogy ezt az igazságot nem láttam meg előbb. Ibid., p. 38.

recapitulation of the opening movement, with its themes recurring inverted; the first and third sections of the slow movement surround a Presto (thus the form of the entire work may be described as A B C B A'). In the great *Violin concerto* the principle of variation encompasses the total composition. The "Faustian" linking of the first and third movements (pairing of contrasted characters through the same thematic material) is here rounded out by an independent variation movement (the second) to form an organic entity.

Brief mention should be made of another principle by which the two violin concertos are related: the principle of synthesis. In the earlier work, a deeper identity of "heavenly" and "terrestrial" characters is suggested through the same "Ur-motif," whereas musical spheres more distant from one another are united in the later violin concerto. The totally integrated language of its first movement arises from the joining of a stylized *Verbunkos* melody (a derivative of Hungarian Romanticism) with a tonal twelve-tone theme.

According to annotations in the score, Bartók composed his "great" violin concerto between August 1937 and December 31, 1938, on commission from the violinist Zoltán Székely, Bartók's chamber music partner who at that time was living in Holland. Though given by the composer himself, these dates can only be accepted with a certain reservation. The first musical idea for the violin concerto dates back to 1936 or even earlier. Conversely, Bartók would not have been able to begin the actual composition of the work by August of 1937: apparently only the known sketches for the first and second themes of the opening movement were written down at that time.

No plan for a work of concerto dimensions seems to have been connected with the "Ur-idea," sketched in 1936 or earlier. Rather, it was the request coming from the performer which apparently gave the composer the thought of applying the existing idea to the form of a work for violin and orchestra.

György Kroó was the first to give an account of Bartók's intention to add, during the summer of 1936, to his *Music for Strings, Percussion and Celesta* a further orchestral work, made up of shorter movements.[5] It was a plan the composer never

5 György Kroó, "Unrealized Plans and Ideas for Projects by Bartók" in *Studia Musicologica* XII/1–4 (Budapest, 1970), p. 17.

realized, despite existing sketches; Kroó conjectured, rightly so, that these sketches were subsequently applied to the violin concerto.[6]

6 Ibid, p. 18.

The preserved documentation, though still dispersed and published only in fragmentary form, nevertheless makes it possible to construct an outline chronology for the genesis of the entire work. On July 14, 1936, Bartók gave a provisional promise of a new work for a first performance in Baden-Baden. A letter of July 24 to Universal Edition of Vienna, mentioning concrete details with regard to scoring and form, could refer only to this Baden-Baden work: "I am planning also another orchestral piece (normal orchestration in pairs of instruments, a series of shorter movements)." From a letter of September 1, 1936, again to Universal, we gather that "sketches have likewise been made"[7] for the mentioned further orchestral work. But this evidently was Bartók's last statement concerning the plan of this composition; it was not to be mentioned in any later correspondence. What event was it that intervened?

7 The quotations from Bartók's correspondence (conducted in German) were published in László Somfai's "Strategics of Variation in the Second Movement of Bartók's Violin Concerto, 1937–1938" in *Studia Musicologica* XIX/1–4 (Budapest, 1977), p. 162.

The event, doubtless, was the receipt of Zoltán Székely's letter of August 10, 1936, in which he asked Bartók to write a violin concerto for him as a commissioned work.[8] This commission evidently guided Bartók's interest, after the passing of three decades, again to the genre of the violin concerto. On September 26, 1936, in complying with his wishes, Universal sent him a copy each of Alban Berg's, Kurt Weill's, and Karol Szymanowski's violin concertos for study purposes.[9] Bartók's consent—to compose a new work without nearer determination—is to be read in his letter of October 17, 1936 to the violinist.[9a] The composer's initial suggestion of a one-movement concert piece in the form of variations was declined by the violinist, who desired a concerto in the customary form of three movements.[10] In his two studies, László Somfai showed convincingly that Bartók's conjectured one-movement work essentially would have been an enlarged version of the one planned for Baden-Baden; and that, on the other hand, the conjectured work could be identified only with the middle movement of the later violin concerto.[11] When Bartók decided to carry out the scheme desired by Székely, he extended the variation principle—the primary form-giving element in the early violin concerto—to the entire new composition. The

8 Székely's wording (in Hungarian) was published again by László Somfai, op. cit.

9 Ibid.

9a Claude Kenneson, *Székely and Bartók, The Story of a Friendship* (Portland: Oregon, 1994), p. 382–383.

10 Personal communication from Székely to László Somfai, op. cit., p. 161, see also his "Drei Themenentwürfe zu dem Violinkonzert aus den Jahren 1936/37" in *Documenta Bartókiana*, no. 6 (Budapest and Mainz, 1981), p. 248.

11 See notes 7 and 10.

[12] The sketches mentioned here were presented by Bartók to Tossy Spivakovsky, soloist for the American premiere, in 1943. A photographic copy went to the Bartók Archives of the Hungarian Academy of Sciences, Budapest, in 1965. They were published in Somfai's study, see note 7.

sketch of 1936 (or earlier) became the theme for the slow middle movement. The additional preserved sketches—to which we will return below—were used for the fast opening movement (and thus also the finale serving as a recapitulation).[12]

Bartók's original intention was to work on two commissions during the summer of 1937. The first was the *Sonata for Two Pianos and Percussion*, the premiere of which had been scheduled for January 16, 1938, for an anniversary concert planned by the Basel section of the International Society for New Music. The other one was the violin concerto, whose elaboration the composer could not take on until after the completion of the sonata. The Basel commission reached him relatively late, in the spring of 1937; Bartók's provisional confirming answer went to Paul Sacher on May 24. After the summer vacation, leaving his family in Austria, Bartók returned to Budapest alone on July 17, in order to work there in complete isolation. He sketched on the two sides of a leaf themes for both the sonata and the violin concerto, a fact which makes it likely that the sketches were made at about the same time. It was for this reason that Bartók could subsequently note July 1937 as a date for the inception of the sonata and August 1937 for that of the concerto. The problem was that, in August 1937, he could not turn to the actual composition of the violin concerto because he had not completed the sonata.

[13] most megint "megrendelés"-en dolgozom és megint Basel-nek (de most kamarazenéről van szó). Remélhetőleg elkészülök vele. Még egy másik megrendelésem is volna (hegedűkoncert), hát ezzel aztán nem tudom, hogyan készülök el, mert ez már az őszi hónapokra marad. *Bartók Béla családi levelei*, ed. Béla Bartók, Jr. (Budapest: Zeneműkiadó, 1981), p. 576.

On August 21 the composer wrote to his elder son Béla: "I am working now again on a 'commission,' and again for Basel (involved, this time, is a piece of chamber music). I hope I can finish it. There is another commissioned work (a violin concerto), but I really don't know how I can finish that one; it will have to go into the fall."[13]

[14] Willi Schuh, "Kompositionsaufträge" in *Alte und neue Musik* (Zurich: Atlantis Verlag, 1952), p. 73.

By September 2, the sonata was still not quite completed, as is documented in Bartók's letter to Sacher: "I am glad to be able to report that the planned work—my choice became a quartet for two pianos and two groups of percussion instruments—is almost ready..."[14] Another letter, however, written on September 6 by the composer to his former student Sándor Albrecht in Bratislava, refers to the sonata as a work still in progress: "The new piece, on which I am now working, is a

'Quartet' for two pianos and two groups of percussion instruments. Aside from this, I should write a violin concerto."[15]

Zoltán Székely's September 20, 1937,[16] visit to the composer in Budapest evidently resulted in a fresh impulse for the work on the violin concerto. And, though from September to the beginning of the year 1938 Bartók could not concentrate upon his work without disturbance, he was at least spared from concertizing abroad. Bartók's October 9, 1938, letter to Annie Müller-Widman, a devotee of his in Basel, shows that the major part of the composition remained for the summer of 1938. During the summer, wrote Bartók, he had worked hard in order to finish the violin concerto and to write *Contrasts*, a trio promised to Joseph Szigeti and Benny Goodman.[17] The score of *Contrasts* shows September 24, 1938, as the finishing date of composition. On September 5, 1938, Bartók sent to the "King of Swing" his firm promise to compose a new work for him. It is to be assumed that this promise was given only after completion of the sketch for the violin concerto.

The concerto's instrumentation covered several months, interrupted in November by a concert tour through Holland and Belgium. During this tour, Bartók apparently made changes in the composition. The composer and pianist Géza Frid, a former Bartók student living in Holland (who assisted Székely in his study of the work before the first performance) supplied important details about Bartók's last-minute decisions: "The final measures of the violin concerto, incidentally, were completed by Bartók here in Amsterdam, at my Bechstein piano. This finishing and not only this one, had troubled the composer. He chose then from among various possibilities the one known today. I thereupon made bold to suggest a two-note upbeat to be added to the beginning of the first theme. Bartók only smiled; several years later, however, after the work's appearance, I looked at the score and saw that he had accepted my suggestion."[18]

Bartók returned to Budapest from this concert tour on November 21. The score of the violin concerto was completed on the last day of the year. At the beginning of March 1939, he had the opportunity to go through the whole work with

[15] Az az új mű, amin most dolgozom, egy "kvartett" 2 zongorára és 2 ütőhangszercsoportra. De ezen kívül még egy hegedűkoncertet is kellene írnom. *Bartók Béla levelei*, (B. Bartók's letters, ed. János Demény (Budapest: Zeneműkiadó, 1976), p. 559.

[16] See Béla Bartók, Jr., *Apám féletének krónikája* (My Father's Life Story) (Budapest: Zeneműkiadó, 1981), p. 385.

[17] *Bartók Béla levelei*, ed. János Demény (Budapest: Zeneműkiadó, 1976), p. 605.

[18] A Hegedűverseny utolsó taktusait egyébként Amszterdamban, minálunk, az én Bechstein zongorámon fejezte be Bartók. E befejezés, nem egyedülálló módon, gondot okozott a zeneszerzőnek. Több lehetőség közül végül is a ma ismert változatot hagyta jóvá. Felbátorodva azt javasoltam neki, hogy az első tétel témája elé írjon két ütemelőző hangot. Bartók erre csak mosolygott; de amikor a darab megjelenése után, évekkel később, megláttam a partitúrát: kioerült, hogy megfogadta tanácsomat. See *Így lattuk Bartókot*, ed. Ferenc Bónis (Budapest: Zeneműkiadó, 1981), p. 107.

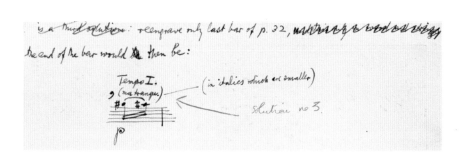

B. & H. 9003

VIOLIN CONCERTO NO. 2
© Copyright 1946 by Hawkes & Son
(London) Ltd.
Copyright renewed
Reprinted by permission of Boosey &
Hawkes, Inc.

Székely in Paris. Bartók was unable to attend the premiere of March 23 in Amsterdam, by the Concertgebouw Orchestra under Willem Mengelberg with Zoltán Székely as soloist. He did not hear an orchestral rendition of his work until four years later when Tossy Spivakovsky, the soloist for the American premiere in Cleveland on January 21, 1943, with a repeat on January 23, performed the work on October 14, 15, and 17 in the same year with the New York Philharmonic Orchestra under the direction of Artur Rodzinsky.

The Violin Concerto was to become the one among Bartók's symphonic works in his lifetime that was most frequently performed in the United States. Between January 21, 1943, and August 11, 1945, it saw twelve performances in such cities as Cleveland, New York, Minneapolis, Baltimore, Pittsburgh, Chicago, and Hollywood. What doubtless contributed to this popularity was Yehudi Menuhin's decision, after Spivakovsky's success, to take the work into his repertoire. Among the conductors who, after Rodzinsky, took a special interest in the work were Dimitri Mitropoulos, Antal Dorati, Fritz Reiner, and Desiré Defauw.[19]

[19] There are eleven performances listed in Tibor Tallián's book *Bartók fogadtatása Amerikában 1940–1945* (The Bartók Reception in America 1940–1945) (Budapest: Zeneműkiadó, 1988), pp. 197–98. A twelfth performance on February 14, 1943, in Pittsburgh is mentioned in the letter to Bartók from H. W. Heinsheimer of Boosey & Hawkes/Belwin Inc. dated February 10, 1943. Having remained unpublished, this letter was placed at the disposal of the writer by Mr. Peter Bartók, Homosassa, Florida.

The scores for these performances were photographic copies made from Bartók's autograph, added to which were handwritten errata sheets. Bartók's new publisher after 1939, Boosey & Hawkes, London, placed the work on the list of forthcoming publications immediately after the Amsterdam premiere. But the outbreak of the Second World War delayed the production for years. The piano reduction did not appear until April of 1941, and the full score not until 1946. Bartók was still able to read proofs for both, but he did not live to see the publication of the printed orchestral score. In the long chain of sources for the Violin Concerto—from the first thematic sketch to the printing of the orchestral score—the proofs for the latter form the penultimate link. At the same time they represent the last musical document in which the composer himself was involved within the genesis of the work and in which his handwriting is to be found. This fact and the fact that the hand-corrected proofs for Bartók's later works are for the most part lost assign special historical value to the complete corrected proofs for the Violin Concerto, which were located and acquired by Hans Moldenhauer and bequeathed by him to the Library of Congress in Washington, D.C.

In order to obtain a clear picture of Bartók's corrections, we have compared the proof sheets which he himself reviewed with the copy submitted for production—a copy of the autograph score—as well as with the printed orchestral score (Boosey & Hawkes 9003).

What insights do these comparisons afford us?

—By reference to other documents, we are able to reconstruct phases of the process by which the orchestral score was published.

—They also provide a glance into Bartók's workshop and give witness to its perfect order and high degree of organization. Without exaggeration, we venture the claim that even Bartók's style of correction reflects his uncompromising character.

The proof of the engraved orchestral score, of which Bartók received a copy, was based upon a copy of the photographic reproduction of his autograph score, revised by him, as well as upon certain written instructions which Boosey & Hawkes had transmitted to the engraver. On May 29, 1939, Bartók had sent a copy each of the photographic reproduction of the piano score and orchestral score from Budapest to the publishers in London.[20] As early as November 5, 1939, the composer could return the revised proofs of the piano score and of the solo violin part to London. These were followed two days later by the return of "printer's copies" for both piano and full score.[21]

No correspondence between publisher and composer with regard to the Violin Concerto has survived from the year 1940—the time of Bartók's two journeys from Europe to America with all its complications of preparation for his relocation in New York. As late as February 5, 1941, Ralph Hawkes wrote to Bartók:

VIOLIN CONCERTO. The Piano reduction of this work is now being printed and I hope to get copies away some time of this month. My idea with regard to the Full Score of this work is that we should engrave it, so that it could be submitted to various Conductors and I think this is really necessary. It will cost a lot of money to do but I think it could be managed during the next six months. I shall be glad to know your views on this but, of course, much will depend upon the arrangement of any First Performance.[22]

[20] Bartók's unpublished letter to Ralph Hawkes, May 29, 1939. It contains the composer's first instructions for the engraver.

[21] Unpublished letter by Bartók to Erwin Stein of Boosey & Hawkes in London, December 7, 1939, quoted from a typewritten copy.

[22] Copies of typed letters from Ralph Hawkes to Béla Bartók in the possession of Peter Bartók.

On April 30, 1941, Hawkes wrote further to Bartók:

VIOLIN CONCERTO. I am sure you will be glad to see the copies of the Violin and Piano Reduction of this work; I received them from the printer yesterday and they have gone forward to you via our Office. I shall be interested to hear from you that they have arrived safely and that you are pleased with the publication. I am taking no steps here to arrange a performance until I hear from you.[23]

It took some time before the first copies of the published piano score reached New York from London, the mails having been slowed by war conditions. Dr. Heinsheimer, representative of Boosey & Hawkes in New York, was able to inform Bartók of getting ten copies only on June 17, 1941.[24] In this form the work made its way through preparations for the first performance. The prospect of an American premiere—Spivakovsky's Cleveland performance in January of 1943—emerged by the end of the year 1941. On January 9, 1942, Heinsheimer wrote Bartók about the Violin Concerto: "The parts and score have been sent to Cleveland this morning."[25] Chances are that the publisher was not ready to face the considerable expense for the production of the large orchestral score until after a successful performance in Cleveland. The engraving process—the copyright year in the proof is given as 1945—could not have been completed earlier than 1944 (more likely, however, 1945). Since the proofs for the engraving contain entries reflecting the composer's rehearsal, or rather direct listening impressions, it may be assumed that his revisions were not made until 1944 (more likely again 1945). Two such entries, emanating from rehearsal or performance experience, might be mentioned here. In the second movement, measure 35, Bartók added to the last bottom note of the harp: "(sic)." What is involved is an extended unison passage, in which this note appears as B rather than A. Bartók's comment reads:

> I have the experience that (good) musicians believed this B to be a misprint for "A". It would be advisable (though unusual) to add a (sic).

We find an earlier suggestion of this point in the autograph (page 43) in what obviously reflects an exchange between a performer or editor and the composer. The former apparently marked the pitch B and placed at the margin: "A?", and Bartók

[23] See note 22.

[24] See note 22.

[25] Original in the possession of Peter Bartók.

added : "no!" The other entry occurs in the first movement, page 25, measures 179–184. Here Bartók changed twelve dynamic indications with the commentary: "(these are later changes made after I heard the performance)."

Several other changes in the proofs similarly correspond with entries added in the autograph:

TABLE I

Page	Measure	
		Movement 1
4	31	Vln Solo: *sf*
4	31	Ob I: ♮
26	187	Dbl Bass: three tenuto signs
34	224	Horn II: instead of a dotted half note G with following quarter rest, correctly: a whole note G
38	270	Clar I: ♮ before the first note
42	293	Vln Solo: second trill-group ("Triller-Welle") marked with ♮
43	294	Bassoons I, II: *f* added to the first note
43	294	Dbl Bass: a superfluous staccato dot removed above the third note
		Movement 2
58	34	Flute II: ♮ before the first note
		Movement 3
103	320	Cellos: ♮
105	344	Violas: *mf*
105	346–348	Dbl Bass: - - - - *f*
106	353	Violas: first note not D♯ but C♯
111	413	Violas: the natural sign before the A in the thirty-second-note tremolo subsequently added
112	417	Vln II: tutti (senza sord.) added
112	417	Violas: tutti [sic] (senza sord.) added

Other changes that the composer made are concerned with corrections of errors in the autograph:

TABLE II

Page	Measure	
		Movement 1
15	97	Violas: instead of D♭ correctly E♭
15	98	Violas: instead of F♯ correctly E♮
		In the above cases the notation in the autograph seems uncertain: the note heads are correctly rendered but the accidentals appear lower.
35	235	Clar I, II: instead of concert E, correctly concert F♯
48	360	Vln I: the second note changed from A to G with the following comment: "This deviation has not much sense. seems to be a slip of the pen in MS. (cf. 1st Horn); should evidently be G."
		Movement 2
60	50	Clar I: ♭ added to the second note with the comment "this is a fault in MS."
62	before 69	Vln II: Bartók's comment on the rubato-like passage: "I omitted by mistake to indicate the score that these hemisemidemiquaver groups should have small heads (as in the piano score). What can be done? perhaps leave it unchanged; for the reduced pocket score it would be too small anyway." Bartók's remark was crossed out afterwards, and the passage remained unchanged.
		Movement 3
103	319	Timp: the correct rhythm: three even quarter notes instead of quarter note, dotted quarter note, eighth note. Bartók comments: "mistake in MS!"

*Two errors not discovered by Bartók in the proof, and thus remaining uncorrected in the printed score, are: movement 2, p54/m8, cellos (the autograph shows correctly that the second note should be a quarter note instead of an eighth note); and p55/m9, bassoons I, II (instead of alto clef, tenor clef).

The annotations with which Bartók explained his specific performance directions to the engraver are important.

TABLE III

Page	Measure	
		Movement 1
2	10	Vln Solo: the triplet groups should not be marked by brackets but by slurs.
2	13	Vln Solo: the waves serving as trill marks should be lengthened (or shortened) to correspond with the duration of the trill. (The same principle applies to crescendo and decrescendo marks.)
5	36–38	Vln II, Violas: the glissando marks must lead directly from and to the notes involved:

sul pont.

Bartók's words: "gliss. marks quite wrong. (from head to head)."

The composer placed particular emphasis upon the combination of slurs and staccato dots. Rather than a number of corrections in the proofs, we cite here Bartók's letter of December 7, 1939 to the editor Erwin Stein (see note 21):

> In string (bow-) instruments [group a: three eighth-note triplets, the first two joined by a slur, the third separated with a staccato dot;] and [group b: three eighth-note triplets under one slur, the third note also marked with a staccato dot;] (or [the same figures as above but marked beneath the notes rather than above] have a different meaning [:] a) means an interruption before the last quaver, b) means a shorter sound of the last note, without any interruption.

Bartók also attributed great importance to the clear marking of the strong pizzicato, which he was the first to use, with the explanation "the string rebounds off the fingerboard."[26] The engraver, not familiar with Bartók's symbol ⬯ (a circle bisected by a vertical stroke) and its interpretation attempted to render it by an ó (ellipsis with a vertical stroke placed above it). The composer responded with an extensive explanation:

> These signs [ó] will not do: they mean "use of the thumb" (Daumenaufsatz) in Cello. My sign is this: ⬯ which is not yet used in music as far as I know. (See 4th String Quartet, Music for strings etc.) (◯) (this is a regular circle, not ó oblong). However, I am inclined to a compromise: it would perhaps do, if the ó signs on this page are transformed into i.e. into signs similar to those on p. 66.[27]

As shown in the printed score, Bartók's wish was in this case followed without compromise.

[26] See p. 51 of the printed full score.

[27] See p. 51 of the proof of the full score.

Bartók's most thorough change in the engraver's layout applies to pages 32–33. The upbeat to measure 213 signals a new section within the first movement, with a new tempo indication. This upbeat was engraved at the end of page 32, while the first full measure of the new section with the new tempo indication appeared on page 33. Bartók formulated his objection as follows:

> This is a bad situation indeed. The Tempo I. (ma tranquillo) begins on the upbeat, this I cannot help and change. Every different placement would be incorrect. It is too bad that the piano score has this inexactitude! As I see the [crossed out: only] two possible solutions are: (1) As in the MS, which looks queer yet I would not mend it; (2) to re-engrave pp. 32, 33, and bring over the two following bars from p. 33 to p. 32 which is costly. Decide please! - I just discovered that there [crossed out: is a third solution]: re-engrave only last bar of p. 32, the end of the bar would then be:

Nevertheless, a solution was found and used, namely to engrave pages 32 and 33 over again. In the new engraving,

measure 213 was transferred from page 33 to page 32. In the printed score page 33 has one measure less and page 32 one measure more than in the proofs.

The unity of the notational image—marking like effects and phenomena with like means or symbols—mattered greatly to Bartók. A few examples of his comments in this connection:

TABLE IV

Page	Measure	
		Movement 1
1	—	General remark:
		1) I, II (etc.) or I. II (etc.)?
		2) Ca. has a period in duration marks but no period in M.M. indications! Now. Anglosaxons are very touchy about abbreviation-periods! Better put everywhere period after ca. Check up.
9	56–57	Vln Solo: why a difference in type (size) of 5 and 3?!
36	249–251	Vln Solo: decision about equal size of 5 and 3?
47	346,348	Bassoons I, II: Bartók added "senza sordino" for Bassoon I and "(senza sordino)" for Bassoon II. His explanation: "an embarassing situation: senza sord. applies, of course, only to I because II is and was senza! But if we put here senza sord., then it will look as if II in the previous bars is meant con sord.! Perhaps my suggested solution will do and is not to[o] illogical."

Page	Measure	
86	135	Movement 3 (TABLE IV *continued*) 135ff., Strings: "NB. string tremolos: for no apparent reason I marked tremolos by 4 beams ♫ from here on (until p. 112) instead of 3 beams ♫ [My method is in slow tempo 4, in fast 3 beams]. Mea culpa! this inconsistency which to help would mean to[o] much trouble, probably!"

*There was one instance, however, where Bartók's wish with respect to beams was not honored. In measures 555ff., third movement, the repeated figures in the part of the solo violin were partly written out and partly abbreviated. In response to Bartók's comment about the inconsistency, Erwin Stein, editor for Boosey & Hawkes, London, appealed to the engraver "to satisfy the composer," but Bartók's objection seemed in this case not sufficiently founded.

Another category of Bartók's corrections was concerned with the matter of language. Verbal clarity and precision were as important to the composer as corresponding aspects of the musical text. In the autograph score, completed in 1938 in Budapest, instrument names and most of the interpretative indications and instructions were given in Italian, annotations in Hungarian or Hungarian and English, and the performance duration in French. In the printed score, Bartók intended to indicate the instrument names and performance duration in English and the annotations in English or French, and he abandoned Hungarian comments.

Some details dealing with these matters in the proofs follow:

TABLE V

Page	Measure	
		Movement 1
12	74	Harp: Bartók says regarding the instruction *près de la table*. "(Question of principle) Should this not be in English? How is is [sic] it in 'Concerto' (1st Mov.)?" The remark was crossed out and the French instruction kept.
45	305–308	Vln Solo, Footnote: "Hungarian better omit. Remain two languages. In case of bi-lingual remarks one would be italicized. Which one? The whole should be re-engraved, thus: *↑ means a quarter [tone] higher. ↓ quarter tone lower (no period!) *↑ indique un quart de ton etc. As for the French footnote I don't know if "indique" will do: perhaps indique une intonation d'un quart de ton? (check this please!)"
51	373–375	Strings: Bartók's commentary regarding the footnote dealing with the strong pizzicato: "Some remarks as to p. 45. It would be nicer to have the word pizzicato in a 'contrary' type, i.e.: 1) if English is Roman, then there in italics, and in the italicized French the word in Roman, 2) or vice versa. Then no parenth. are needed. [parenth. always mean something strange, unusual, something 'so to speak': italics (in Roman typed text) mean a foreign word (which may be very well known and much in use)] or vice versa."
		Movement 2
59	41	Viola: "2 a 3 Soli" was corrected to read: "2 o 3 Sole." Bartók's comment: "(Letter 'o' which means in Italian or.)"
63	83	Vln Solo: "leggiero" corrected to "leggero." Bartók, adding "see MS," claims parenthetically: "leggero is the correct form of this Italian word"
69	last	Comment regarding the French term "Dureé": "not English?"
		Movement 3
87	260	Viola: "3 Soli" corrected to read "3 Sole." Bartók's comment: "(sorry, but Viola is feminine in Italian) in English too if it is a girl"
99	267	Vln Solo: "sonore" corrected to read "sonoro". Bartók's comment: "sorry, but in Italian it must be sonoro"

It was not the intention of this study to discuss Bartók's corrections of the engraver's proofs for his great violin concerto in thorough detail; rather we have been concerned with the *types* of Bartók's corrections (corrections of routine errors or engraving flaws not having been taken into account). Yet such an identification of the principles guiding Bartók's corrections will make it possible to recognize Bartók's methodical working procedure and afford the observer impressions of Bartók the man and creative artist.

For a composer of Bartók's importance it would have sufficed in the years 1944–1945 to enter his proof corrections without any comment. But he considered it necessary to offer reasons and even defense of them, to explain his changes and clarifications to the publisher and engraver, and thus to stand for an unmistakable expression of his ideas down to the smallest point. The several layers of his revisions, in pencil, ink, and other graphic tools, both in autograph and proof, are reminiscent of his multiple revisions in his written record of folk songs,[28] where, to quote Zoltán Kodály, "a growing sense of responsibility is also evident."[29] This same "growing sense of responsibility" is found in the notation and correction of his works.

Zoltán Kodály wrote:

For the roots of science and of art are the same. Each, in its own way, reflects the world. The basic conditions: sharp powers of observation, precise expression of the life observed, and raising it to a higher synthesis. And the foundation of scientific and artistic greatness is also the same: just man, *vir justus*. And Bartók, who left Europe because he was unable to bear the injustice raging here any longer, followed Rousseau's slogan: *vitam impendere vero* (stake one's life on justice).[30]

[28] A sample of this procedure was issued as a colorprint reproduction in Ferenc Bónis, *Béla Bartók: His Life in Pictures and Documents* (Budapest: Corvina, 1981), p. 92.

[29] Zoltán Kodály, "A folklorista Bartók" in his collected writings *Visszatekintés* (In Retrospect), ed. Ferenc Bónis (Budapest: Zeneműkiadó, 1964), 2, p. 454. English translation "Bartók the Folklorist" in *The Selected Writings of Zoltán Kodály* (Budapest: Corvina, 1974), p. 107.

[30] Op. cit., p. 456 (1964 edition), p. 106 (1974 edition).

A Sketch Leaf from Ludwig van Beethoven's Piano Sonata, op. 28

Susan Clermont

[1] See the introductory paragraph from Douglas Johnson and Alan Tyson's article, "Reconstructing Beethoven's Sketchbooks," *Journal of the American Musicological Society* XXV (Summer 1972, no. 2), 137.

[2] Previously referred to as the "Virneisel" sketchbook.

[3] Richard Kramer, *The Sketches for Beethoven's Violin Sonatas, opus 30: History, Transcription, Analysis* (Ph.D. diss., Princeton University, 1974), vol. 1, p. 35.

[4] Douglas Johnson, Alan Tyson, and Robert Winter, *The Beethoven Sketchbooks: History, Reconstruction, Inventory* (Berkeley and Los Angeles: University of California Press, 1985), p. 113.

ONE OF THE MORE POIGNANT ASSERTIONS MADE on the subject of the history of Beethoven's sketchbooks is that the day of his death marked the beginning of the history of their destruction.[1] This statement is particularly apropos with regard to a single-leaf manuscript from the Moldenhauer Archives, which contains music from the second movement of the Piano Sonata, op. 28, and which is one of the twenty-two identified extant leaves from the "SAUER" sketchbook, perhaps the most ill-fated of Beethoven manuscripts.[2]

This sketchbook was purchased on November 5, 1827, at the auction of Beethoven's estate by the Viennese art and music dealer Ignaz Sauer. Information contained among the five extant auction catalogs identifies it, Sauer's sole acquisition at the sale, as *Notirbuch #17;* catalog annotations also indicate that this item commanded a substantially higher sum than the average sketchbook, selling at *2 florins 50 kreutzers.* Two possible explanations have been proposed for this unusually steep price: first, that the contents, which included the popular Piano Sonata in C-sharp Minor, the second work of op. 27 ("Moonlight"), may have been identified before the auction; second, that the original sketchbook was substantial in size, having been classified with others consisting of about 100 leaves.[3]

Sauer's motive for purchasing the sketchbook was purely that of profit, with no perceptible concern to preserving its integrity. Soon after the auction, he dismembered either a significant portion of it, or possibly the entire book, and sold the individual leaves as souvenirs to friends and private collectors at prices ranging from 20 to 36 kreutzer.[4] Sauer furnished the individual manuscripts with covers, upon which he had inscribed his personal attestation of authenticity as well as documentation regarding the legality of his procurement of the sketchbook itself. The inscription, which also cites the date of the auction and the lot number, appears to be virtually the same on each coverleaf. Today, several of the twenty-two extant leaves, including the leaf preserved in the Moldenhauer Archives,[5] are still attached to their coverleaves which read:

[5] This is contrary to information stated by Johnson et al., op. cit., p. 120.

Musikalisches Andenken
aus
Ludwig van Beethoven's
eigenhändigem
Notirbuche,

welches aus seiner Verlassenschaft in der am 5. Nov. 827 abgehaltenen wiener magistratischen Lizitation laut gerichtlichem Protokoll No. 17 erstand

Ignaz Sauer
beeideter Schätzungskommissär
in Kunstsachen
20+ C.M.

Musical Souvenir
from
Ludwig van Beethoven's
Manuscript
Notebook

which has been obtained from his estate, as recorded in No. 17, meeting minutes of the Vienna Municipal license Bureau, Nov. 5, 1827

by Ignaz Sauer
certified Appraiser
of *objects d'art*
20+ C.M.

(The sale price of the leaf is an abbreviation for 20 kreutzer, Conventionsmünze [normal currency].)

The provenance of the Moldenhauer leaf, identified by Kramer as item "j" and by Johnson et al., as leaf no. 10[6,7] is both colorful and unique. Its date is likely to be 1801, based

[6] Kramer, op. cit., p. 39.
[7] Johnson et al., pp. 120–121.

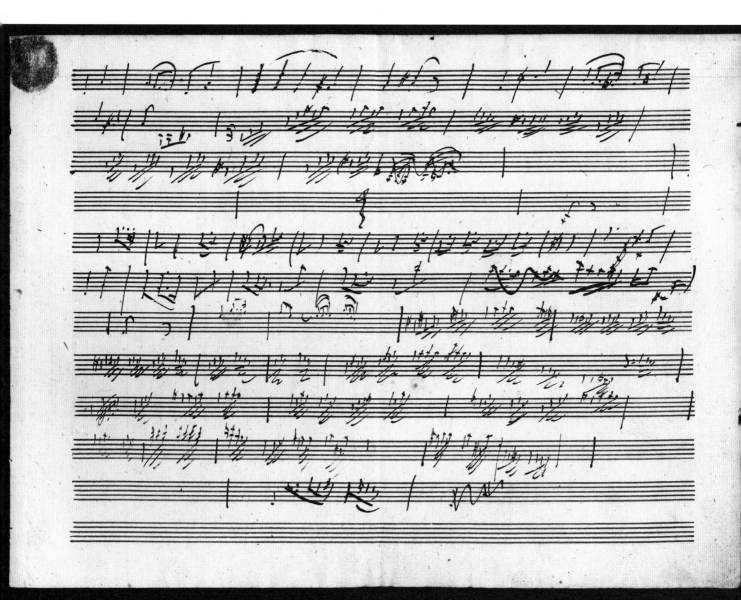

(recto)

on two considerations: the complete autograph, located in
Bonn at the Beethoven-Haus, bears the inscription *"gran
Sonata op: 28 1801 da L v. Beethoven.,"* and Beethoven
apparently made use of the SAUER sketchbook between
March of 1801, and November or December of the
same year.[8]

Severed from the sketchbook, trimmed on all four sides, and
inserted into its coverleaf, the manuscript was sold to the
Mödlinger merchant Ignaz Arlet. He and Beethoven most

[8] Ibid., p. 116.

·104·

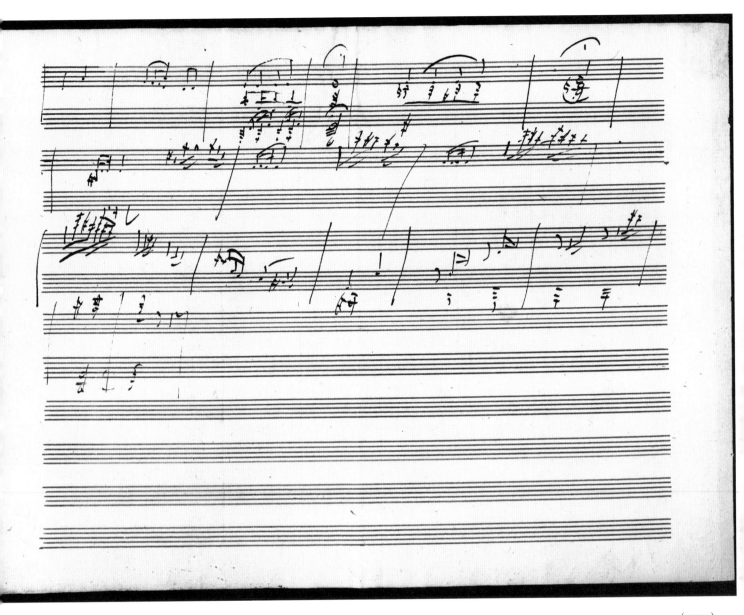

(verso)

likely became acquainted during the summer of 1818, when
Arlet assumed co-ownership of the well-established tavern
known as *Zum schwarzen Kamel*, located in Mödling. This was
the first of three consecutive summers that Beethoven spent in
Mödling, then a quiet country resort recommended by his
doctor for its baths; it was here that Beethoven took his
legendary walks in the woods with sketchbook in hand,
gathering ideas for such works as the *Missa solemnis*, the Ninth
Symphony, and the Piano Sonatas, op. 109–111. During these
summers Beethoven became a regular patron of the *Schwarze*

·105·

9 See Emily Anderson, *The Letters of Beethoven*, II (New York: St. Martin's Press Inc., 1961), no. 1047, p. 911.

10 Theodor von Frimmel, "Neue Beethovenstudien," *Deutsche Kunst- und Musik-Zeitung XVIII* (January 1, 1891), p. 2. Additional documentation of Beethoven's patronage at the "Kamel" appears in *Ludwig van Beethovens Konversationshefte*, ed. Georg Schünemann (Berlin: Max Hesses Verlag, 1941). See Band I, heft 8, fol. 31b, 49a, 68b and 89a.

11 Walter Szmolyan, "Beethoven-Funde in Mödling," *Österreichische Musikzeitschrift* XXVI (1971), p. 10. Szmolyan points out that the Moldenhauer leaf was one of three autographs to be rediscovered while preparations were being made for Mödling's commemoratory celebration of Beethoven's 200th birthday; despite the fact that Frimmel made the existence of this leaf public in his 1891 article (see previous note), it was not cited in the literature (e.g., it is not included in Hans Schmidt's "Verzeichnis die Skizzen Beethovens" of 1969) until 1971. One exception is a note included in Jacques-Gabriel Prod'homme's 1948 book *Die Klaviersonaten Beethovens*, p. 134, where he incorrectly cites the 1891 article by Frimmel.

12 Kramer, op cit., p. 39.

13 According to Johnson et al., op cit., p. 114, these measurements are consistent with those of the other extant leaves from SAUER.

14 Ibid., p. 114; Kramer, op cit., p. 36. When comparing Kramer's rough drawing of staff twelve's profile with the same on the Moldenhauer leaf, the resemblance becomes tenuous because of a slight variation in the G line (assuming a treble clef).

15 Johnson et al., op. cit., p. 545.

Kamel, where he purchased supplies from the Arlet family,[9] and enjoyed sitting at his usual window seat.[10]

In 1832, Arlet retired and sold his share of the business; upon his death in 1850, his daughter-in-law, Anna Neubauer Arlet, assumed ownership of the manuscript. It remained in the Arlet family for approximately 120 years. Finally, in 1970, the manuscript was acquired by the Viennese antiquarian Wolfdietrich Hassfurther,[11] who sold it soon thereafter to Moldenhauer.[12]

Besides Sauer's cover of authentication, a number of physical characteristics function as confirming references that link the Moldenhauer leaf to SAUER. The manuscript of oblong format measures 22 cm. high by 30 cm. wide and is ruled with twelve staves on both recto and verso. The total span of the staves from the topmost to bottommost lines measures 187.5 mm.; the width varies between 255 mm. to 258 mm.[13]

The slightly irregular staff-ruling pattern that makes up the left margin profile, particularly the imperfections involving staves eleven and twelve, has been cited as an important identifying element among all twenty-two extant leaves. This common trait, which is evident on the Moldenhauer leaf,[14] suggests that the staves were ruled mechanically with a machine-operated rastrum, a kind frequently used in the production of late-eighteenth-century manuscript paper. The rulers or rastra used on these devices often created recurrent and, therefore, distinguishing characteristics at the left or right margins, wherever the pen nibs would lift from the page. The original dark grey ink used to rule the staves has, in the case of the Moldenhauer leaf, taken on a brownish appearance. The ink used for the musical notation varies somewhat in color, ranging from dark brown to black.

There is a watermark, which consists of a seven-pronged starfish measuring 46 mm. long by 53 mm. wide and 56 mm. in diameter, centered approximately along the top edge of the leaf. Also evident across the page are nine evenly spaced, vertical chain lines, appearing at 32-mm. intervals. In Appendix A of Johnson et al., the leaf's watermark is classified as number 6, quadrant 2a.[15]

The uniformity of the physical characteristics that exists among the extant leaves of the original sketchbook leads one to conclude that SAUER was a preassembled or *integral* sketchbook. Experts speculate that it originally contained ninety-six leaves, the same size as LANDSBERG 7, a homemade book that directly preceded it, as well as the three professionally made books that directly followed SAUER; besides the Piano Sonata, op. 28, the extant leaves include music from the Piano Sonata in C-sharp Minor, op. 27, the String Quintet in C Major, op. 29, and a single sketch for the Bagatelle No. 5, op. 33.[16]

Like many of Beethoven's sketchbook entries, this manuscript of the second half of the Andante in D Minor from op. 28—often called the "Pastoral" or "Sonnenfels" sonata—may be categorized as a continuity draft.[17] It includes approximately fifty-seven measures of music: staves one through ten recto contain measures 39–50 (in the finished work) with an interruption of three empty measures, followed by measures 54–82. There is one measure of unidentified music located on staff 11. Measures 83–93 and 95–99 occupy the top eight staves of the leaf's verso. The draft confirms that Beethoven had already negotiated both the thematic content as well as the overall harmonic direction of the movement; in fact, relative to the published version, there are only occasional, minor variations of pitch or rhythm. One such example occurs on beat two of measure 92 through the beginning of measure 95, where the flourish outlining the diminished seventh approximates the appearance of a sketch, although the registral parameters of the descending gesture (from e^3 in measure 92 to C-sharp–A in measure 95) are established; measure 94 of the published work does not appear.

An explanation for the single-staff format of this draft emerges when we consider some of Beethoven's sketching techniques and assess the leaf's content and purpose. As is well known, Beethoven developed a highly abbreviated notation in both his fragmentary and extended sketches, reflecting his desire for economy of time, space, and effort.

The Andante, then, consists of an opening section (A) in D minor (measures 1–22) followed by a contrasting section (B) in

[16] Ibid., pp. 115–18; Kramer, op. cit., pp. 35, 41.

[17] The latter title alludes to the dedicatee, Monsieur Joseph Noble de Sonnenfels. See Alexander Wheelock Thayer, *The Life of Beethoven*, ed. and rev. Henry Edward Krehbiel, vol. 1 (New York: The Beethoven Association, 1921), pp. 292–93.

[18] There are sketches containing both the treble and bass lines from selected measures of the first half of the Andante located on another extant leaf from SAUER, identified as SV 163, fol. I^v; Bonn Bsk 10 (SBH 613). A third leaf with music from the Andante, located at the Vienna Stadtbibliothek (SV 394; MH4169), was not consulted for this essay.

[19] Thayer, op. cit., p. 289.

[20] In Beethoven: Impressions of Contemporaries (New York: G. Schirmer, Inc., 1926), p. 31.

[21] Frimmel, op. cit., pp. 2–3.

[22] Theodor von Frimmel, Beethoven-Jahrbuch, I (1908): 112–13, 185–86.

[23] Wilhelm Virneisel, "Aus Beethovens Skizzenbuch zum Streichquintett op. 29," Zeitschrift für Musik, CXIII (1952): 142–46.

[24] Kramer, op. cit.

[25] Johnson et al., op cit.

[26] Szmolyan, op cit., pp. 9–16.

the parallel major (measures 23–38); measure 39 marks the return (A1) of the introductory A section in D minor. The movement concludes with a brief reiteration of the opening thematic material (measures 83–88), revoiced and modified to serve as predominant preparation for the closing cadential flourish. A comparison of sections A and A1 reveals that the bass line from measures 39–82 virtually duplicates that from the initial 44 measures of the A section, whereas the treble from A1 introduces new material in the form of melodic variations located in measures 47–54 and measures 69–82. Without access to SAUER in its original format, we can only speculate that Beethoven had worked out both treble and bass lines for sections A and B, and that the primary purpose of this draft of section A1 was to set the final proportions of the movement and provide a work space for the melodic variations in the treble.[18] To rewrite the bass line would have been redundant.

According to Czerny, this Andante "was long [Beethoven's] favorite and he played it often for his own pleasure."[19] Czerny later referred to this work as one of the final pieces to be completed before Beethoven's self-proclaimed "new way."[20]

Frimmel was the first Beethoven scholar to mention the leaf in the musicological literature in 1891, when he offered a fairly accurate annotated transcription;[21] he was also the first to draw attention to the SAUER sketchbook, in 1908, when he quoted the cover inscription and included a facsimile of one leaf containing sketches of the String Quintet, op. 29.[22] It was only much later, in 1952, that an attempt was made by Wilhelm Virneisel to compile a list of the then-known extant leaves from SAUER; the Moldenhauer leaf, however, does not appear to be among the eight items cited in this discussion.[23] A proposed inventory and discussion of the twenty-two identified leaves was published in 1974 by Richard Kramer;[24] subsequent and more substantial treatment of SAUER was presented by Douglas Johnson et al.[25] The most comprehensive commentary on the Moldenhauer leaf, accompanied by a facsimile reproduction, was published by Walter Szmolyan in 1971.[26]

A Beethoven Sketch for the Puzzle Canon "Das Schweigen," WoO 168

Susan Clermont

IN HIS ESSAY ON "Beethoven's Sketches for *Sehnsucht* (WoO 146)," Lewis Lockwood cites Gustav Nottebohm's pioneering essays on the subject of Beethoven's sketchbooks as primary sources for what he calls the prevailing view of the composer's creative approach to composition. Defined as a process of assiduous labor by which initial musical ideas were transformed by gradual stages into artistic substance, this view is admonished in some cases for its over-generalization and lack of accurate perspective, depth, and substance; in many cases, however, it is endorsed.[1] One example in support of the prevailing view is a manuscript leaf from the Moldenhauer Archives at the Library of Congress, containing fragmentary sketches for Beethoven's WoO 168, "Das Schweigen," the final movement of the Piano Sonata opus 101, as well as unidentified sketches in D minor.

The sketch leaf was originally part of the sketchbook, acquired long since the leaf's removal and now owned by William Scheide. Beethoven used it from about March 1815 through about May 1816.[2] The composer's proclivity for intensive and quantitative preliminary work on his compositions is the quintessence of the Scheide sketchbook (SCHEIDE) as a whole. Portrayed as a reflection of a complex period in Beethoven's life and of a critical phase of transition for him as a composer, SCHEIDE has also been characterized as having the "function of a workshop for ideas that had run into trouble elsewhere, a place particularly suited for work on difficult problems but not to write out full compositional drafts in detail."[3]

SCHEIDE was purchased at the 1827 auction of Beethoven's estate by the music publisher and dealer Domenico Artaria,

[1] See Lockwood's article in *Beethoven Studies*, ed. Alan Tyson (New York: W.W. Norton & Company, Inc., 1973), pp. 97–98.

[2] Douglas Johnson, Alan Tyson, and Robert Winter, *The Beethoven Sketchbooks: History, Reconstruction, Inventory* (Berkeley and Los Angeles: University of California Press, 1985), p. 241.

[3] Lewis Lockwood, "The Beethoven Sketchbook in the Scheide Library," *The Princeton University Library Chronicle*, XXXVII, Winter 1976, no. 2. p. 149.

[4] Ibid., p. 142; see also Johnson et al., *The Beethoven Sketchbooks...*, p. 241.

[5] Gustav Nottebohm, "Neue Beethoveniana: Ein Skizzenbuch aus den Jahren 1815 und 1816," *Musikalisches Wochenblatt*, VII, 1876, pp. 609–11, 625–27, 637–39, 653–55, 669–70; and Gustav Nottebohm, *Zweite Beethoveniana*, E. Mandyczewski, ed. (Leipzig: Verlag von C.F. Peters, 1887), pp. 321–48.

[6] According to Johnson et al., this inventory was probably completed not long after auction, but certainly before the spring of 1835. See *The Beethoven Sketchbooks...*, p. 20.

[7] Classified as paper type 42, quadrant 4a in Johnson et al., *The Beethoven Sketchbooks...*, p. 558.

whose son, August Artaria, sold it to the Viennese collector Eugen von Miller in 1871. From von Miller, it passed on to G. B. Davy of Kingussie, Scotland; Louis Koch of Frankfurt-am-Main then acquired it for his collections; his heirs incorporated it into the Flörsheim collection, from which William Scheide procured it in 1965. [4]

Gustav Nottebohm provided the first extensive description of the sketchbook in an 1876 essay published in the periodical *Musikalisches Wochenblatt* and subsequently reprinted with minor modifications in *Zweite Beethoveniana*. [5] Here he identifies the most striking physical characteristic of SCHEIDE, the loss of seventeen and three-quarters consecutive leaves between pages 32 and 33. These leaves, which include the Moldenhauer sketch leaf, were severed from the sketchbook sometime before the initial inventory of Artaria's auction purchases was compiled.[6]

The manuscript in the Moldenhauer Archives consists of a single leaf of oblong format measuring approximately 225 millimeters by 287/295 millimeters, and is ruled on both sides with sixteen staves approximately 196 millimeters long. There are three stitch holes [?] located 6 millimeters to 10 millimeters from the left edge. Measuring from the top downwards, the first hole is at 28 millimeters (slightly above staff two), the second at 107 millimeters (adjacent to staff eight), and the third at 190 millimeters (directly below staff fourteen). The watermark consists of the letters [S]LING located along the upper left corner and the letters JJ along the lower right edge of staves twelve and thirteen;[7] nine vertical chain lines, positioned approximately 32-millimeter to 35-millimeter intervals apart, are also discernible. Sometime after its extraction from the sketchbook, the manuscript was folded in half in the middle. Additional idiosyncrasies include the following: on the recto, an inscription in black ink positioned vertically along the right edge that reads "(Beethoven's own holograph)"; the numbers 2-92-243,35 in pencil along the bottom, slightly to the right of the fold; also in pencil, a partially erased number fifteen located to the right of staves fourteen and fifteen. On the verso, the inscription B5 appears in pencil along the top center.

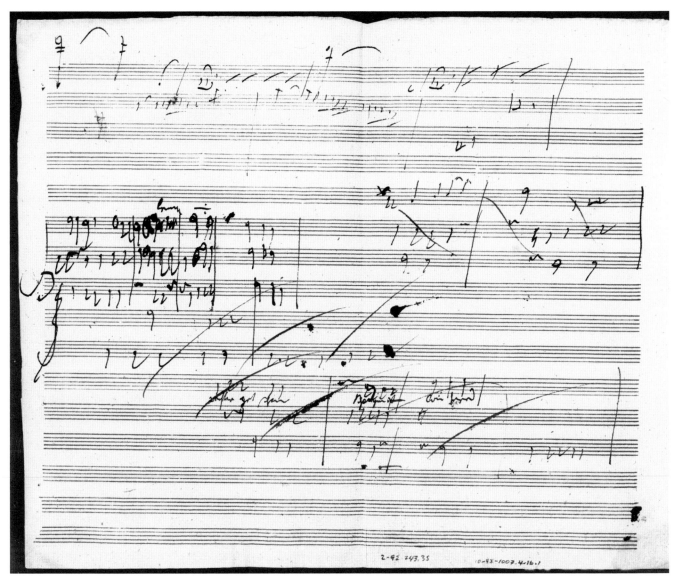

Following four staves of unidentified music in D minor, are sketches for the puzzle canon "Das Schweigen," WoO 168 no.1, located on staves five through thirteen (recto). Beethoven's long-term attraction to the poem by Johann Gottfried Herder is substantiated by the fact that he copied the extract on at least two known occasions: first, in an 1813 entry in his Tagebuch, and again in 1815 on the inner cover (verso) of MENDELSSOHN 1.[8]

> "Lerne schweigen, o Freund. Dem Silber gleichet die Rede, aber zu rechter Zeit schweigen is lauteres Gold."

> "Learn to keep silent, O friend. Speech is like silver, but to be silent at the right moment is pure gold."[9]

[8] On the Tagebuch, see Maynard Solomon's essay "Beethoven's Tagebuch" in *Beethoven Essays* (Cambridge, Mass.: Harvard University Press, 1988), pp. 235–36 and 247–48. A third, albeit illegible, transcription of this extract, or portions thereof, might be located on folio 10 of Add. Ms 29997.

[9] According to Solomon, "Das Schweigen" is one of Johann Gottfried Herder's free renderings of didactic, aphoristic poetry from the *Bustan* and *Gulistan* by the Persian poet Sa'di (ca. 1184–1291) and was first published as part of the *Blumen aus morgenländischen Dichtern gesammlet in Zerstreute Blätter, vierte Sammlung* in 1792. It was reprinted in *Herders poetische Werke*, ed. Carl Redlich, *Sämmtliche Werke*, vol. 26/2 (Berlin, 1882), p. 374.

[10] One of Neate's obligations on this Viennese expedition was to present a proposal to Beethoven from the Philharmonic Society, requesting three new concert overtures to be performed by the London orchestra. Instead of composing new works, however, Beethoven gave Neate manuscript copies of the overtures "Die Ruinen von Athen," opus 113, "Zur Namensfeier," opus 115, and "König Stephan," opus 117. Unfortunately, with the Eroica Symphony still fresh in their minds, these works did not meet the Philharmonic's expectations. See Emily Anderson, "Charles Neate: A Beethoven Friendship," in *Festschrift Otto Erich Deutsch zum 80. Geburtstag am 5. September 1963* (Kassel: Bärenreiter, 1963), p. 198.

[11] Alexander Wheelock Thayer, *Ludwig van Beethovens Leben* (Leipzig: Breitkopf & Härtel, 1923), Dritter Band, p. 505. Ibid., pp. 197–99.

[12] Unfortunately, Neate's souvenir album was lost, but not before he showed it to Thayer in 1861, who copied and published the canons in 1865.

[13] Alexander W. Thayer, *Chronologisches Verzeichniss der Werke Ludwig van Beethovens* (Berlin: Ferdinand Schneider, 1865), entry 202, p. 131.

[14] *43. Autographen-Sammlung: Versteigerung vom 21. bis 22. November 1913 bei Leo Liepmannssohn. Antiquariat*, entry 578, p. 77.

Beethoven dedicated "Das Schweigen" along with a second canon on Herder's subsequent verse, "Das Reden," to Englishman Charles Neate, a well-known musician of the time who was a proficient pianist, cellist, teacher, and composer and whose great ambition in life was to meet and study with Beethoven. To this purpose, he traveled to Vienna in May of 1815 and arranged to be introduced to his idol.[10] Not long afterwards, when Beethoven moved to Unter-Döbling that July through October, Neate followed him there and took up residence nearby. Even though the two became friends over the ensuing months, Neate's hopes to have private instruction in composition did not materialize; rather it was recommended that he study with Beethoven's former teacher Emanuel Aloys Förster.[11]

Neate remained in Vienna from October 1815 until early February of 1816; on 24 January, a fortnight before his return to London, Beethoven inscribed the two canons, "Das Schweigen" and "Das Reden" into his *Stammbuch* with the following dedication: "Mein lieber englisher Landsmann, gedenken Sie beim Schweigen und Reden Ihres aufrichtigen Freundes Ludwig van Beethoven."[12]

Published research concerning the canon's autographs, sketches, and solutions is as disperse as it is nebulous. Although five autograph manuscripts of WoO 168 have been cited in the literature, only one has been manifested as being both authentic and extant. Neate's *Stammbuch*, mentioned above, described by Thayer in his *Chronologisches Verzeichniss* of 1865 is no longer extant.[13] Kinsky-Halm mentions a second autograph dating from ca. 1815 and cited in Berlin antiquarian Leo Liepmannssohn's auction catalog 43, entry 578. According to this source, page one of the oblong Skizzenblatt contained music for the complete canon with text, while the opposite (fourth) side included short sketches from the same work.[14] The whereabouts of this source are also unknown.

Otto E. Albrecht cites the Moldenhauer sketch leaf in his publication on Beethoven manuscripts in the United States (Census 231D); the citation, however, may be (and has been) misconstrued as it specifically identifies the music for the Piano Sonata in A Major as "sketches for the third movement," but then concludes by reporting that the manuscript "Contains also WoO 168, 'Das Schweigen.'"[15] Based on this information, Kurt Dorfmüller, in his supplement to Kinsky-Halm's *Thematisch-Bibliographischen Verzeichnis*, classifies the music for WoO 168 on the Moldenhauer leaf as an autograph, rather than as a sketch.[16] The authenticity of the fourth autograph manuscript (cited in Dorfmüller's Supplement as London, Royal College of Music, MS 2174) is dubious at best.[17] Finally, the Gesellschaft der Musikfreunde in Vienna holds the only extant autograph manuscript, identified as A 18.[18]

A brief survey of five identified sketches for "Das Schweigen" raises the issue of two separate musical renditions based on the same text. Of the four manuscripts cited in the Schmidt *Verzeichnis*, two appear to contain music unrelated to WoO 168: the first of these in E Major, SV70, is located on page 22 of MENDELSSOHN I;[19] both Schmidt and Dorfmüller indicate that a second sketch in B Major, identified as SV187 (not 185) and found on folio 39 of London, British Museum Library Add. 29997, is also independent of WoO 168.[20] A third manuscript, SV389, was unavailable for consultation at this writing.[21]

Thus, only the two remaining sources, SV364 and the Moldenhauer leaf (not in SV, Albrecht Census 231D), contain sketches for the puzzle canon WoO 168, which together offer a small but significant contribution toward our understanding of its solution.[22] Immediately striking upon comparison is the close parallel in musical content between the two manuscripts; overall, they disclose a combination of voices, especially in measures 11 through 16 of the published solution (see below), that were obviously troublesome for Beethoven at this early stage of composition. Four separate fragments on the Moldenhauer leaf reiterate elements from measures 9 through 16; Beethoven included the text, "rechter Zeit schweigen - Schweigen ist lauteres," in the final four-measure segment (staves 11–13).

The first edition of the canon was published in the Vienna *Allgemeine musikalische Zeitung* on March 6, 1817.[23] Apparently, the inclusion of entry signs was recommended, perhaps due to

[15] Otto E. Albrecht, "Beethoven Autographs in the United States," in *Beiträge zur Beethoven-Bibliographie: Studien und Materialien zum Werkverzeichnis von Kinsky-Halm*, ed. Kurt Dorfmüller (München: G. Henle Verlag, 1978), p. 6.

[16] Kurt Dorfmüller, "Supplement zum Thematisch-Bibliographischen Verzeichnis von Kinsky-Halm," in *Beiträge zur Beethoven-Bibliographie: Studien und Materialien zum Werkverzeichnis von Kinsky-Halm*, ed. Kurt Dorfmüller (München: G. Henle Verlag, 1978), p. 384.

[17] Ibid., pp. 364–65. Under the entry for WoO 60 is a brief discussion of a single-leaf manuscript originating from one of Beethoven's pocket sketchbooks, which dates from 1818 according to Nottebohm, and containing music for opus 106 (SV275). According to Nottebohm, an autograph of WoO 168, dated "24 January 1816" is written "without dedication." Dorfmüller adds the disclaimer that the authenticity of this source is yet to be proven. See also Nottebohm, *Zweite Beethoveniana*, p. 137.

[18] Dr. Otto Biba of the Gesellschaft der Musikfreunde has confirmed this holding; the manuscript was included in the 1927 Beethoven Centenary Exhibition in Vienna.

[19] Hans Schmidt, "Verzeichnis der Skizzen Beethovens," in *Beethoven-Jahrbuch*, Jahrgang 1965/68 (Bonn: Beethovenhaus, 1969), p. 46; Nottebohm, *Zweite Beethoveniana*, p. 317. The transcription for approximately five measures of music in E Major (key signature included) are accompanied with Nottebohm's comment that this canon was never published in this form.

[20] Schmidt, *Verzeichnis...*, p. 74; Dorfmüller, *Supplement...*, p. 384. Reported in Augustus Hughes-Hughes, *Catalogue of Manuscript Music in the British Museum*, vol. II (London: Trustees of the British Museum, 1909), p. 9.

[21] According to Schmidt, SV389 is held in Weimar's Nationale Forschungs- und Gedenkstätten der klassichen deutschen Literatur; recent correspondence with the music reference staff at the Stiftung Weimarer Klassik of Weimar's Herzogin Anna Amalia Bibliothek contends that the manuscript is not part of their collections.

[22] SV364 refers to page 55 of the SCHEIDE sketchbook; see Nottebohm, *Zweite Beethoveniana*, pp. 330–31.

23 (Weiner) *Allgemeine musikalische Zeitung, mit besonderer Rücksicht aft den österreichischen Kaiserstaat,* Erster Jahrgang Nr. 10, Beylage No. 3 (6 März 1817), 80/81.

24 (Weiner) *Allgemeine musikalische Zeitung, mit besonderer Rücksicht aft den österreichischen Kaiserstaat,* Erster Jahrgang Nr. 23, Beylage No. 6 (5 Juny 1817), 192/93. This edition is cited by Thayer in the *Chronologisches Verzeichniss...,* p. 131.

the imitations' irregular entry periods: one voice at the lower fifth entering in measure 2 and the third voice at the octave below entering in measure 4. On June 5, 1817, the same journal published a solution, now in score form, submitted by Hyronimus Payer under the slightly inflated title: "Auflösung des Räthsels Canons von Herrn L. van Beethoven/Siehe No. 10 dieses Blättes Beylage No. 3/und zwar ganz richtig durch Herrn Hyronimus Payer."[24] There is no evidence in the literature that Beethoven ever objected to the content of this publication. Here is a reproduction of Payer's score.

25 Thayer, *Ludwig van Beethovens Leben,* p. 533. On this subject see Ludwig Misch, *Beethoven Studies,* (Norman, Okla.: University of Oklahoma Press, 1953), pp. 124–25.

The third published solution to the canon in volume three of the German edition of Thayer's biography of Beethoven interjects a puzzle of its own by replacing the signature of F Major with B-flat Major, without transposing the melody.[25] This would ensure that strict imitation at the lower fifth (D, C, B-flat - G, F, E-flat) is accomplished, but at the same time discredits the integrity of the work as the composer intended it. Both the Moldenhauer manuscript and SV364 verify Beethoven's resolution to the issue of precise imitation, showing a notated E-flat in the inner voice at measure 15; the note E remains natural, however, in the remainder of both sketches.

Two Sketches for Alban Berg's *Lulu*

Patricia Hall

BOTH SKETCHES for *Lulu* preserved in the Bayerische Staatsbibliothek contain material from Act I, scene 3, and originate from the same collection of autographs in the Austrian National Library.[1] Mus. ms. 17489 is a single leaf containing a draft of the ragtime music of Act I, scene 3, measures 1007–1021, and a rhythmic sketch of the opening of the ragtime music, measures 991–993. Berg cut the leaf by hand from the middle third of a bifolium of fourteen-stave paper (J. E. and Co., *Protokoll Schutzmarke* No. 3), leaving dull, somewhat jagged edges along its top, bottom, and right sides (recto). The cut along the fold side, in contrast, is very precise and apparently made at a different time. The dimensions of the sketch are 25 cm. (length), 10.5 cm. (left edge, recto), 10.1 cm. (right edge, recto). The sketch is completed almost entirely in pencil and has a very smudged appearance. There are four small strokes of black ink on the recto side, and four overlaid notes on the verso side. The ink is the same type Berg used in his autograph *Particell*, and the strokes on the recto side in particular suggest that Berg was simply priming his pen as he copied the finished sketch.[2]

The oblong format of the sketch, the precise cut along the fold side, and the fragmentary nature of the draft itself suggest that this leaf was removed from a sketchbook. It proves to be, in fact, the sketchbook F 21 Berg 80/V folios 1–17 in the Austrian National Library which Berg constructed from the upper, middle, and lower third of four overlaid bifolia of fourteen-stave paper. An additional leaf has been removed from the middle set of bifolia; the six remaining leaves have the same profile and stave placement as Mus. ms. 17489.[3] The sketchbook contains initial thematic material for the Sonata of Act I, as well as preliminary sketches of the sextet of Act I, scene 3. Because Berg was composing the development and

[1] See Rosemary Hilmar, *Katalog der Musikhandschriften, Schriften und Studien Alban Bergs im Fond Alban Berg und der weiteren handschriftlichen Quellen im Besitz der Österreichischen Nationalbibliothek, Alban Berg Studien, Band 1* (Vienna: Universal Edition, 1980).

[2] The call number of the *Particell* is ÖNB Musiksammlung F 21 Berg 29.

[3] This leaf presumably is lost.

4 See the excerpt of Berg's letter to Webern of July 23, 1931, in Ernst Hilmar, "Alban Bergs Selbstzeugnisse zu Entstehung und Aufführbarkeit der Oper *Lulu*," in *Alban Berg "Lied der Lulu": Faksimile-Ausgabe der Anton v. Webern gewidmeten autographen Partitur* (Vienna: Wiener Stadt- und Landesbibliothek, 1985), p. 14.

5 For a more detailed discussion of Berg's compositional process on *Lulu*, see Patricia Hall, "The Sketches for *Lulu*," in *The Berg Companion*, ed. Douglas Jarman (Great Britain: Macmillan, 1989), pp. 235–59.

6 Ernst Hilmar, "Die verschiedenen Entwicklungsstadien in den Kompositionsskizzen," in *50 Jahre "Wozzeck" von Alban Berg*, ed. Otto Kolleritsch (Graz: Universal Edition, 1978), p. 24.

7 ÖNB Musiksammlung F 21 Berg 80/II fols. 12r–35v.

reprise of the Sonata—the music immediately following the sextet—during the summer of 1931, this sketchbook, together with Mus. ms. 17489, almost certainly date from the summer of 1930.[4] It has a total of six stubs in its binding, implying that it was, unfortunately, a favorite source of souvenir material for the donor of the Munich sketch, Helene Berg.

There are many types of evidence to match Mus. ms. 17489 with its corresponding stub, the most convincing of which are the internal content and continuation marks. Folio 7 verso of the Vienna sketchbook contains a draft of measures 992–993 of the ragtime music, using the same two-stave format as the opening of Mus. ms. 17489. The draft is followed by two stubs and folio 8 recto, which begins with the final note of Mus. ms. 17489. In addition, the second stub has two continuation marks which match with those on the left recto edge of Mus. ms. 17489. Thus, the Munich sketch was not only attached to this second stub, but the earlier stub originally contained the remaining section of the draft, measures 994–1006. Berg numbered the two measures on folio 7 verso, 1–2. Mus. ms. 17489, correspondingly, is numbered 16–30, and the missing leaf undoubtedly bears the measure numbers 3–15.

Even in isolation, Mus. ms. 17489 is a beautiful sample of Berg's compositional process.[5] In contrast to a typical Beethoven sketch, this draft shows very little revision. We can attribute this to Berg's "additive" approach to composition— that is, he usually adds progressively defined pitch material, rather than rejecting and revising earlier versions. For instance, on the verso side, stave two, appear stems without noteheads— a type of rhythmic notation or shorthand first noted by Ernst Hilmar in Berg's sketches for *Wozzeck*.[6] At a later time, Berg superimposed pitches on these stems, completing the passage. Berg was thus able to progress essentially from a rhythmic skeleton to a compositional draft which differed very little from the published score. Yet composing ragtime music did not come entirely second nature to Berg; his autographs show that he resorted to using a "self-help" booklet entitled, *Das Jazzbuch*. Moreover, its annotations include careful underlinings in sections such as "How to orchestrate a jazz band."[7]

The sketch also offers significant insights about the role of orchestration in Berg's compositional process. Although, according to one of Berg's letters to Webern, he orchestrated the opera after he had completed it, he made various initial decisions about orchestration during his earliest stages of composing.[8] Indeed, it appears that choices in instrumentation even generated some of the passages. For instance, folio 1r shows Berg's annotation, "Gg" (*Geige*) in measures 1007 and 1010, and "Sax" (*Saxophon*) in measures 1008 and 1012. In the final version, Berg retains the saxophones, but substitutes the more jazzlike trumpet for the violins.

The second sketch, Mus. ms. 17488, is written entirely in pencil, again on a bifolium of fourteen-stave paper, J. E. and Co., *Protokoll Schutzmarke* No. 3. According to Berg's correspondence, he probably wrote this sketch during the summer of 1931.[9] Folio 1r consists of compositional drafts for Act I, scene 3, measures 1278–1283, folio 1v measures 1289–1299, and folio 2r measures 1300–1309; folio 2v is blank. The bottom of folio 1r bears a typical, enigmatic Bergian dedication written in red pencil: "Lieber Schloss, Auch eine 'Briefarie' aber leider nur von Alban Berg. Oktober [19]31." ("Dear Schloss, Also a 'letter aria,' but unfortunately only by Alban Berg. October [19]31.")

Julius Schloss was Berg's composition student from 1925 to 1935.[10] Berg entrusted him with collating the scores of *Wozzeck*, *Der Wein*, and the *Lulu Suite*, and to this end he was employed by Universal Edition. Although Adorno claims that Schloss was often the butt of Berg's jokes, Berg's and Schloss's mutual correspondence reveals Schloss to be a loyal and assiduously dedicated student and friend.[11] Berg frequently relied on Schloss to attend to personal and musical errands in Vienna while he composed at his summer home in Carinthia. The personal errands ranged from picking up a mended blue sock (for which Schloss expended an enormous amount of effort due to a missing claim slip) to facilitating an affair while Helene Berg was briefly away from Vienna.[12] In contrast, one of Schloss's musical errands was to complete a row chart for *Lulu*, listing the twelve prime and inverted forms of Countess Geschwitz's row.[13] Schloss quickly completed the chart in September of 1931, and Mus. ms. 17488, presented to Schloss

[8] See the excerpt of Berg's letter to Webern of May 6, 1934, op. cit., in Ernst Hilmar, p. 17.

[9] See note 4. In this excerpt, Berg reports to Webern that he is working on the development and reprise of the Sonata. On August 6th he reports that he has essentially finished the first act.

[10] Schloss's letters to Berg are in the Musiksammlung of the Österreichische Nationalbibliothek under the call number F 21 Berg 1309. Berg's letters to Schloss are in the Bayerische Staatsbibliothek under the call number Ana 500, B, Schloß, Julius, I.

[11] *Theodor Adorno Gesammelte Schriften Band 18, Musikalische Schriften V* (Frankfurt am Main: Suhrkamp Verlag, 1984), p. 489.

[12] See Schloss's letter to Berg of January 26, 1932 (ÖNB Musiksammlung F 21 Berg 1309/90) and Berg's letter to Schloss of November 9, 1932 (Ana 500, B, Schloß, Julius, I/116). The woman Berg refers to, cryptically notated with the musical notes E-D-A, is probably the actress Edyth Edwards, the recipient of several effusive love letters. I thank Janet Naudé for suggesting the name and supplying me with copies of Berg's letter to her.

[13] See Berg's letter to Schloss of August 27, 1931 (Ana 500, B, Schloß, Julius, I/86) and Schloss's responses to Berg's letter (ÖNB Musiksammlung F 21 Berg 1309/82–83).

the following month, could conceivably have been Berg's expression of thanks. Whether Berg presented it in person (he was in Vienna for approximately a week during October 1931), or whether it arrived by mail, is unclear.[14] If the latter, then this "letter aria" as Berg refers to it, would have been an interesting double entendre: an aria in which the featured character, Dr. Schoen, is writing a letter, sent to Schloss via mail.

[14] See Berg's letter to Schloss (Ana 500, B, Schloß, Julius, I/87).

Figure 1. Moldenhauer Archives Bayerische Staatsbibliothek
Mus. ms. 17489, recto

Each act of *Lulu* is structured around a central musical form, and the sonata is the predominant form of Act I. Dramatically, it is the epic of Dr. Schoen's struggle finally to break his ties with Lulu by marrying the woman to whom he has been engaged for three years. Like a typical sonata, it has a main theme, bridge theme, second theme, and coda. Berg indicates three of these themes with letters in the margins of folio 1r, staves 1–5: "S" (*Seitenthema*), "C" (*Coda*) and "H" (*Hauptthema*). The section of the sonata featured in this sketch, the music surrounding the recapitulation, is where Schoen realizes that he is powerless to end his relationship with Lulu and writes a letter to his fiancée, breaking off their engagement. In addition to being an emotional climax, it is also a highly complex, notey moment of the opera. We are in the eye of the hurricane, so to speak.

The format of the sketch is in itself striking; instead of the

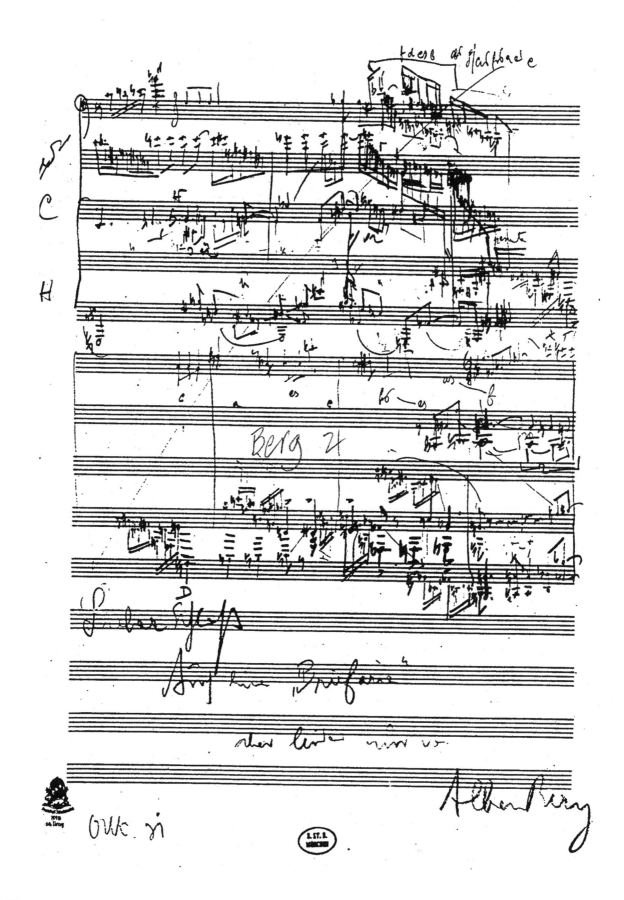

[15] ÖNB Musiksammlung F 21 Berg 29/I fol.
127.

two- to three-stave format of Mus. ms. 17489, Berg uses a four- to five-stave format similar to that in his *Particell*. The sketch also has a more unfinished appearance: there are many notes missing from the manuscript on folio 2r, and Berg frequently erases, revises, or uses shorthand and letters to indicate pitches. And further, the content of the sketch itself is sporadic; folio 1r ends with measure 1283, but then skips to measure 1289 for folio 1v. Unlike the case of the previous sketch, however, this is obviously not the result of a missing leaf. Rather, folio 1r replaced an earlier version of the passage which Berg simply abandoned. This earlier sketch is again in the Austrian National Library.

Österreichische Nationalbibliothek Musiksammlung F 21 Berg XXX folio 12v–13r shows measures 1277–1279 tentatively sketched, using shorthand to indicate the rhythms and general contours, and letters to identify the accompanying sonata theme (U, S, etc.). For the remainder of the sketch (measures 1280–1283), Berg writes a less dramatic version of the Munich sketch Mus. ms. 17488, with the vocal line ("Aber wohin...zu meiner Braut...nach Hause...") beginning one beat earlier and a semitone lower. This results in an unconvincing setting of the vocal line, with the naturally stressed "hin" of the first gesture occurring on a metrically weak beat. Moreover, the ascending sixth that signals the beginning of each of the three gestures in the finished score appear as an ascending diminished fourth, a descending minor third, and an ascending major sixth. Perhaps Berg was simply experimenting with this initial version, and considered it to be as preliminary as the sketched—in measures at the beginning of the passage.

Given the rough appearance of Mus. ms. 17488, did Berg complete a more finished draft which he then copied into his *Particell*? Surprisingly, no. The autograph *Particell* for this section is replete with erasures, revisions, and many additions in colored pencil.[15] This revises the common view that the *Particell* is a "finished product." On the contrary, it too is an evolving composition, worthy of individual study.

I would like to thank Dr. Hartmut Schaefer of the Bayerische Staatsbibliothek and Dr. Joseph Gmeiner of the Österreichische Nationalbibliothek for their extremely helpful assistance during my research at their respective music divisions.

Ernest Bloch's Conducting Score for *Schelomo*

Michael Nott

…For years I had a number of sketches for the book of Ecclesiastes which I had wanted to set to music, but the French language was not adaptable to my rhythmic patterns. Nor was German or English, and I hadn't a good enough command of Hebrew. Thus the sketches accumulated and…lay dormant.

One day I met the cellist Alexander Barjansky and his wife. I heard Barjansky play….Why shouldn't I use for my Ecclesiastes—instead of a singer limited in range, a voice vaster and deeper than any spoken language—his cello?

Thus I took my sketches and without a plan, without a program, almost without knowing where I was headed, worked day after day on my Rhapsody. The Ecclesiastes was completed in a few weeks, and since legend attributes this book to King Solomon, I named it Schelomo…[1]

[1] Sam Morgenstern, "Ernest Bloch," in *Composers on Music* (New York: Pantheon Books, 1956), p. 413.

ONE CAN DETECT IN THIS ACCOUNT of the origins of *Schelomo* something of a spiritual force which inspired it and which it has conveyed so compellingly to generation after generation of listeners. The entry for the manuscript in Moldenhauer's own listing reads: "Full score. 63 pages . . . notated in blue ink, with many corrections, alterations and erasures, additional notes in pencil, others in black, brown and blue crayon." To round out the picture, one might mention that the musical notation offers a characteristic example of Bloch's small and fastidious hand. The presence of markings in a range of colors is also more or less characteristic, as the composer made it a career-long practice to use different pencils, crayons, and inks in his work. Though to a lesser extent with the *Schelomo* manuscript than with some others, this imparts a visual impression that forms an apt, if wholly incidental, counterpart to the vividness of the musical ideas.

The numerous markings to which the description refers tell a story different from what one might expect, for careful review of the manuscript suggests that it was actually undertaken as a clean copy of a work essentially in its final form. To be sure, one encounters erasures in the manuscript, suggesting that Bloch was still changing his mind about certain aspects of the writing; the most extensive series of these appears in the passage extending roughly through rehearsal numbers 28 to 30 (the rehearsal numbers in the manuscript were carried over into the published score)—it seems here he was unsure about the exact figuration of the solo cello line. Yet, as in all such cases, the erasures, appearing only at very isolated points in the manuscript to begin with, come to bear solely on minute details of the writing—certainly, never on any aspect that we might consider fundamental. Indeed, a number clearly were made merely to correct minor errors that probably resulted from copying out the clean score from some prior source. In short, the *Schelomo* manuscript itself documents little of the creative process that had proceeded "without a plan."

Rather, the various markings seem to belong to later stages in the history of the manuscript, and we can recognize two distinct categories of entries in its pages. The first consists of markings that are most reasonably explained as having arisen in the course of preparation for the publication of *Schelomo*. For example, appearing intermittently throughout the manuscript are miscellaneous detailed notations from Bloch—a dynamic marking here, an additional slur there—in pencil, in ink, or in ink copied over pencil. Mostly, these serve only to bring various orchestral lines into exact concordance.

The markings comprising a second category are the most numerous and by far the most prominent. One encounters these—typically large, bold notations in pencil or black crayon—on every page. They impart no new information but only duplicate indications that had already appeared in the blue ink with which Bloch had notated the score itself. Original matters pertaining to changes in tempo, dynamics, and orchestration are among those that are frequently underscored by these bold markings, changes of meter being invariably thus emphasized. The obvious explanation is that the *Schelomo* manuscript served for a time as a performing score: these markings were made to put various indications in more readily visible form, to benefit a conductor in the course of rehearsing or performing the work.

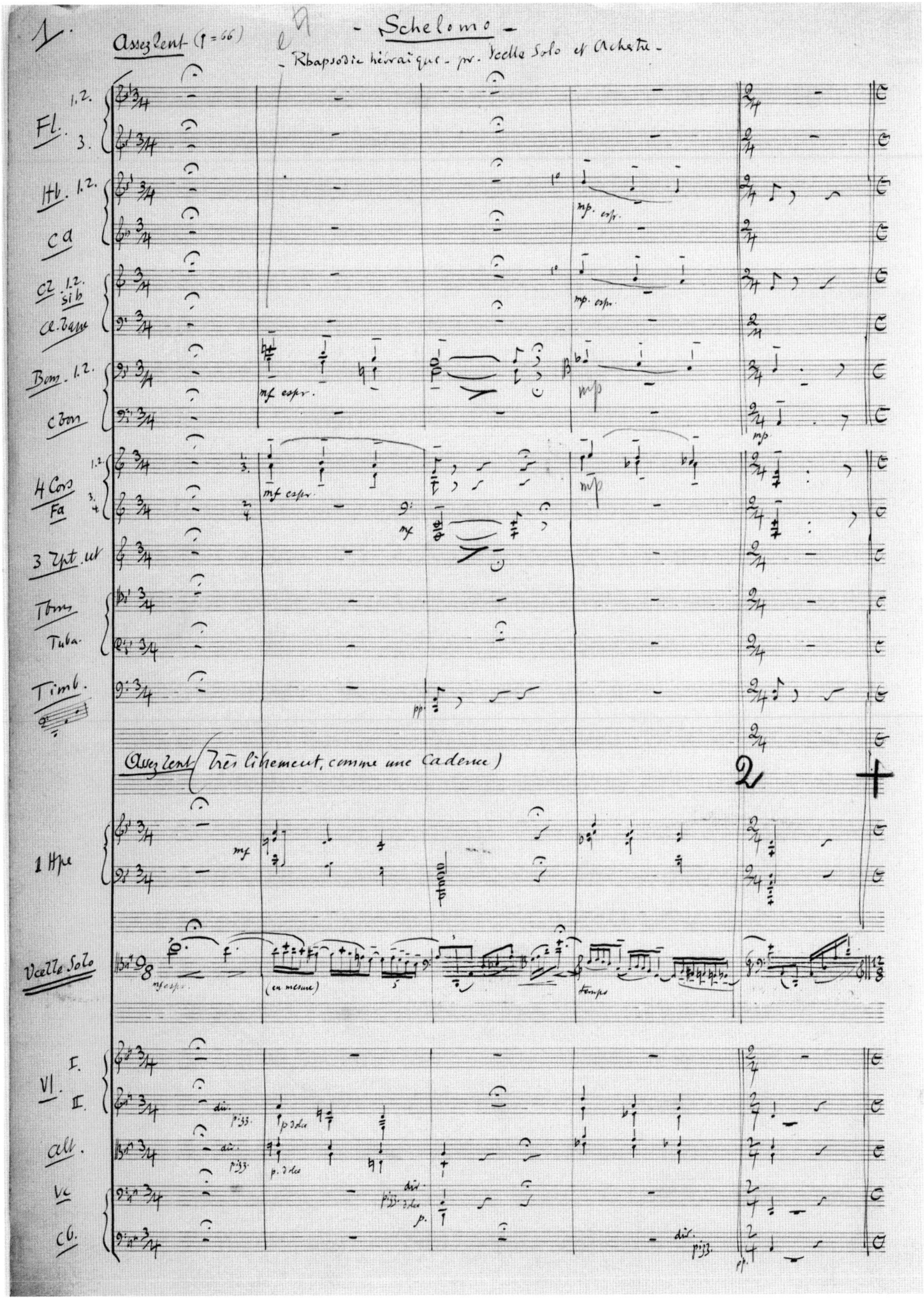
1.
- Schelomo -
- Rhapsodie hébraïque - pr. Vcelle Solo et Orchestre -
Assez lent (♩= 66)
Fl. 1.2. 3.
Htb. 1.2.
C.A
Cl. 1.2. sib
Cl. basse
Bon. 1.2.
C. Bon
4 Cors Fa
3 Tpt. ut
Tbns
Tuba
Timb.
Assez lent (Très librement, comme une Cadence)
2
1 Hpe
Vcelle Solo
(en mesure)
Vl. I. II.
Alt.
Vc
Cb.

This is consistent with the early history of *Schelomo;* for, indeed, it was only in the wake of acclaim accorded to the piece at its initial performances, in New York (1917) and Philadelphia (1918), that the publisher G. Schirmer decided to issue this and other works by Bloch. The score appeared in published form later in 1918, and thus it was the manuscript score that was pressed into service on the earlier performance dates. Bloch himself was on the podium for the Philadelphia performance, and, correspondingly, many of these "conductor's markings" have the look of having come from Bloch's hand. Yet on the occasion of the premiere in New York, the performance was led by Arthur Bodansky, and conceivably he added entries of his own.

In a very few instances, the "conductor's markings" do more than merely duplicate a parallel notation in ink; they either supplement it or introduce an entirely new idea. For example, at rehearsal number 43 the indication (in ink) "Più animato" is followed by the entry (in crayon) "non troppo." As is true in almost all such cases, both the original and supplementary indications are included in the published score. There are, however, a mere two or three instances where one encounters a marking that does not appear in the published score. An entry (almost certainly in Bloch's hand) at rehearsal number 4, for instance, reads "Langoureux (non troppo vivo)," whereas the published score has no interpretive marking at this point. Thus we are evidently dealing with a notation made after the score had been published, suggesting that Bloch continued to make some practical use of the manuscript even after the work's publication.

The page of the *Schelomo* manuscript here reproduced offers examples of most of the various kinds of entries that were made in the score. The slur that appears in both the bassoon part and the horn part in the fourth measure of the page is in pencil; it would seem the intention here was to bring these parts into line—probably as a step in the process leading to publication—with what had been previously notated in ink in the oboe and clarinet parts. In the third measure, erasures appear in the solo cello line, and a corrected or slightly revised melodic figure is written in pencil on top of the erasures. "Conductor's markings" were added, in typically bold manner, toward the middle of the page to emphasize the change to duple meter in the fifth measure and the change to common time in the measure to follow. A pencil marking in the page's second measure, curiously, calls attention to an accidental in the first bassoon part that had already been clearly notated in ink. Perhaps Bloch chose this way of making note of an error on the bassoonist's part so as to avoid interrupting an initial reading of the piece. In the case of the decrescendo marked in the bassoon and horn parts in the third measure and the dynamic marking "mp" added to these parts in the succeeding measure, we are dealing with rare instances in which additions (here in pencil) are not included in the published score.

Bloch was not, in fact, the last conductor to ponder the manuscript score of *Schelomo*. In the late 1920s, Bloch made a gift of the manuscript to Willem Mengelberg, who was to undertake several performances of *Schelomo* with the Concertgebouw Orchestra in January 1930. It remained in Mengelberg's possession until the time of the Nazi invasion of Holland, at which point it was hidden in a bank vault, filed under a false name for its protection.[2] After Mengelberg's death, in 1951, possession of the manuscript remained unsettled for a time, until it was purchased at auction in 1986, in The Hague, by Hans Moldenhauer.

[2] A letter of December 4, 1992, from Bloch's daughter Suzanne to the editor of this volume reads: "the *Schelomo* score had been hidden from the Nazis in Holland—we thought it had just disappeared—possibly destroyed with the invasion in Holland. My father who sent it to Mengelberg died not knowing what had happened. Well, it found its right place!"

John Blow's "Arise, Great Monarch, and Ascend the Throne"

Watkins Shaw

FOLLOWING RESTORATION TO HIS THRONE in 1660, King Charles II initiated the regular practice of having a specially written ode set to music for performance at the English Court in celebration of New Year's Day and royal birthdays. It was maintained until 1820, but its heyday lies in the last twenty-five years of the seventeenth century during which it was responsible for such fine works as Purcell's six Birthday Odes for Queen Mary, 1689–1694. After some rather inchoate efforts during its first ten years, definition was given to the genre by Pelham Humfrey. On his premature death in 1674 his post as one of the royal composers fell to John Blow (1649–1708) who was to become the doyen of the late-seventeenth-century English school, combining in plurality all the leading musical appointments save that of Master of the King's Music. From 1680 he was joined in the duty by his former pupil and younger colleague in royal service, Henry Purcell, the greatest ornament of that school. Blow is known to have written at least twenty-five court odes, those still extant, nineteen in number, running from 1678 to 1700. His contributions certainly represent a gradual development in organization and idiom from where Humfrey left off; nevertheless it must be recognized that these odes are very far from representing his best work as a composer of secular music. In this connection it seems significant that whenever one comes across a good movement in them, it is an instrumental one. Perhaps, unlike Purcell, whose genius was able to transcend the all too feeble verbal texts, he could make little or no response to the words.

Blow attempts nothing sophisticated in his musical setting of "Arise, Great Monarch," which is cheerful, not a little superficial, eschewing counterpoint but with plenty of the straightforward rhythm the king is known to have liked, including a brisk alla breve trio ("See how our troubles vanish") and a final chorus. All the choral movements are brief, bright, and homophonic, but the main burden of the nine short vocal sections is carried by a bass soloist and solo ensembles. The pervasive, all too predictable lilt of the greater part of the work is relieved by a rhetorical declamation for the bass, culminating in a fine flourish from E above middle C to D two octaves and a tone below at the words "Nor lagg'd ingloriously behind." Presumably this was brought off with éclat by John Gostling, the redoubtable Court and Chapel Royal bass. Strings contribute a competent opening "symphony" and keep spirits up with five ritornelli between vocal movements.

It is somewhat curious that each of Blow's court odes was the subject of one or more contemporary transcripts (sometimes as many as four and five) such as the present manuscript. These involve some dozen scribes, and most are contained in albums of mixed contents, one such anthology (British Library, Add. MS 33287) including no fewer than ten court odes by Blow together with one more transcribed by a later copyist. Humfrey's and Purcell's court odes, too, were the subject of such transcripts, the purpose of which is not readily explicable at present. Private study is by no means an adequate explanation covering all instances. And yet the possibility of repeat performances outside the court is in the highest degree unlikely.

In the first place, the words of such works were for the most part all too intimately connected with the single occasion and the audience for which they were written. Again, beyond the regularly constituted body of musicians at court, only Oxford (and then but fitfully) could command the resources needed for their performance: solo voices (particularly a good countertenor and bass), a small chorus, and an instrumental ensemble basically of four-part strings. Sporadic occasions outside Court, in celebration of St. Cecilia's Day, for example, must have required special arrangements, probably making use of royal musicians. Thus, at a time when public concerts were yet unknown, it is hard to understand why anyone should have troubled to make copies. As it is, we must accept the fact of these transcripts, among which the present manuscript is more than usually interesting.

For one thing, it is uncommon to find a transcript of an ode by Blow in the form, as here, of a single physical entity. The sole parallel exemplar is a copy of his New Year Ode, "My Trembling Song, Awake," now item 107 in the Memorial Library of Music at Stanford University, California. As we have seen, all other transcripts are contained in albums together with other material.

Furthermore, it is unusual in that, apart from William Croft (1678–1727, who, as a pupil-apprentice of Blow, may well have wanted to make a close study of his elder's work), its scribe is the only one to make these copies who has so far been identified. Comparison of its script with a well-authenticated specimen forming part of a music manuscript (Cap. VI/1/1) now in the Chichester Diocesan Record Office, West Sussex, reveals it as the work of John Walter (Walters/Water(s)), who became organist of Eton College in 1681. Allowing for the prevalent instability of surnames often phonetically transcribed, he is quite plainly to be identified as the "John Waters" who was a chorister of the Chapel Royal under Blow (in his capacity as Master of the Children, as the boys were known) from some time before 1674 and whose voice was certified as changed by February 1677.[1] He remained organist of Eton College until 1705, and then received what must be regarded as a sort of pension until 1708 when, presumably, he died.[2]

Walter was a minor—very minor—composer, but is interesting now on account of his work as a music copyist. At Eton there are some organ scores of church music which he wrote out, payments for which, over and above his stipend as organist, are recorded in the college accounts. But these, of course, arise from his professional duties and are of little import. Far more interesting is evidence of his copying activity wholly outside those duties and of which, besides the present manuscript, there is abundant evidence. It certainly reveals a close connection with Blow, reinforcing the presumption that Walter had been a Chapel Royal chorister. If its purpose were more fully understood than at present it might well shed some light on the attitude of cultivated amateurs of the time and on music making beyond the Court and Chapel Royal. As it is, its nature is such as to justify some general account to place the present manuscript in context.

[1] Andrew Ashbee, *Records of English Court Music*, vol. 1, (Kent: Snodland, 1986), pp. 144 and 169.

[2] Watkins Shaw, *The Succession of Organists* (Oxford: Clarendon Press, 1991), p. 375.

of a new born year. Ritor:

of a new born year.

bers solus:

be y[e] sun y[e] in times fruitfull wombe was to thy noble Gimbassa desigh

to head y[e] golden troop of dayes to come, Nor lag'd Ingло——nously behind

First in scope and variety of contents stands British Library, Add. MS 22100, wholly in his hand. This is an extensive compendium of secular music ranging from solo songs, duets, and trios to larger-scale compositions. Apart from one minor item by Lully and a slight piece by Walter himself, it concentrates on music by composers associated with the court, circa 1676–1684. It includes Purcell's court ode "Welcome, Viceregent" of 1680, and Blow's "Great Sir, the Joy of All Our Hearts" (1681) and "The Birth of Jove" (doubtless 1678). Also found is Blow's Oxford "Act Music" of circa 1677, "Awake, Awake, My Lyre," in a transposed version, thus suggesting a relation to some practical purpose. But what gives the album primacy as a source of text is a fair copy of "A Masque for the Entertainment of the King," Blow's highly interesting miniature opera "Venus and Adonis," to be dated circa 1683 and not later than 1684. This forms the final item of the manuscript, which is perhaps best understood on the hypothesis that it may have been compiled gradually from 1682, on behalf of "Mr Dolbin" whose name as owner in that year is found on the flyleaf. Gilbert Dolbin (1658–1722), afterwards a baronet, was a distinguished lawyer known for his active interest in music, and on this supposition the contents represent the taste of a cognoscente.

Uncertain in its purpose is the album, again wholly in Walter's hand, now King's College, Cambridge, Rowe MS 22,[3] which contains no date or mark of ownership. This, too, may have been compiled for a patron; equally Walter may have made it for his own use, a quarry from further copies might be taken for potential patrons. Its contents are a mixture of contemporary secular music and specimens of the larger form of Chapel Royal anthem with string symphonies, together with some Italian cantatas. Blow is strongly represented, Walter supplying inter alia useful text of a number of his anthems, and the scores of three more court odes, "Arise, Great Monarch" (the present work: for date, see below), "Dread Sir, Father Janus" (doubtless 1683), and "My Trembling Song, Awake" (1684), in that order.

In 1683 he began to enter a copy of Blow's Morning Service in G into a thick volume, now British Library, Add. MS 17839, but did not quite complete it, leaving over two hundred leaves

[3] See Bruce Wood, "A Note on Two Cambridge Manuscripts and Their Copyists," *Music and Letters*, 61 (1975): 308–12.

blank which much later were filled up with Blow's church music by Philip Hayes of Oxford (1738–1797).

British Library, Add. MS 31453, which can hardly be thought of as written for a patron but rather as a means of record, is later than these. Nor is it wholly the work of Walters, being in part in the hand of William Isaack who copied a score of Purcell's Ode for St. Cecilia's Day, 1692. Isaack was an older man, a singer in the choir of Eton College whose son Bartholomew had been a contemporary of Walter's in the Chapel Royal.[4] Walter contributed a score (not quite complete) of Blow's "Venus and Adonis" which differs somewhat from that in Add. MS 22100 and contains additional amendments. Evidently, then, he was in close touch with the composer as the work evolved under his hand.

4 Ashbee, op. cit., pp. 144 and 166.

Finally, Isaack and Walter were jointly concerned in copying what Bruce Wood[5] considers to be the performing score of Purcell's Birthday Ode for Queen Mary, 1693, now Bodleian Library, Oxford, U.K., MS Mus. c. 28.

5 Personal information.

This may not prove to be the complete tally of Walter's extant music copying. But it is enough for us to discern something of a picture. After initial training, and perhaps an informal apprenticeship, in the Chapel Royal he settled in the relatively minor post of organist of Eton College which he was to retain throughout his life. Concurrently, he almost immediately began to undertake independent work as a music copyist, no doubt for a fee, perhaps stimulated by the example of Isaack, with whom he conferred and collaborated. He was in a favorable position for this, having for some reason access to the primary sources of recent music by his former master Blow and other court composers. Besides working for independent patrons, he was in some unexplained way closely involved in copying for both Blow and Purcell in connection with performances, and his activities extend well into the final decade of the seventeenth century.

Turning now to the present manuscript, not only has the top of its first leaf been cropped, but its right-hand corner has worn away, so that at the end of the first line of the heading the figures of the year date are now incomplete. Obviously the first three must be "168," and judging from the lower fragment remaining of the fourth that is very likely to have been "3," almost certainly not "2." This raises a problem about the exact date of this ode. Blow's original holograph score (Barber Institute of Fine Arts, University of Birmingham, MS 5001, pp. 53–91/ff. 52–31) bears no date. However, on an independent transcript (Royal College of Music, London, MS 1097, f. 119v) someone, closely contemporary but not the scribe of the music, has noted the year 1692. One is at first inclined to give the greater weight to what appears to be Walter's testimony, but on turning to the words it is impossible to find support for 1683. The final chorus reads:

> See how our troubles vanish...
> Propitious winds bear all our griefs away
> And peace clears up the troubled day.
> Not a wrinkle, not a scar
> Of faction or dishonest war...

Any idea that this might refer to some military or naval event must be dismissed, for there was none either in the year ending 1681 (appropriate for the Royal College of Music manuscript date) or 1682 (for Walter's date). Moreover, there is a different ode, "Dread Sir, Father Janus," which may be assigned to New Year 1683 as being apt for events of the year 1682. On the other hand, up to February 1681, when he summoned and quickly dismissed a Parliament, Charles II had long been beset by troubles about Whig proposals to exclude his brother James, the heir-presumptive, from the succession. But then, by adroit maneuvers, he circumvented the opposition and engineered a Tory reaction. Thus the political tide turned in his favor and the problem seemed laid to rest by late 1681. One hardly hesitates, then, before concurring with Rosamond McGuinness's view[6] that the words quoted refer to this, making Blow's ode apt for the New Year, 1682, and rejecting the putative 1683. In Rowe MS 22 Walter's other transcript bears no date. If, however, we make the assumption that, as a kind of file copy, it was the source of the present manuscript, then he may have mistakenly supplied the date from memory. From the point of view of the music, however, the difference of a single year is of no moment.

6 Rosamond McGuinness, *English Court Odes 1660–1820* (Oxford: Clarendon Press, 1971), p. 47.

Be that as it may, we have here an admirable specimen of his penmanship, with clearly formed, well-spaced musical notation and a good round hand for the words, speaking favorably of Walter's general education received as a boy in the Chapel Royal choir. The manuscript apparently remained unbound until the twentieth century, with the result that the first page has become a little discolored. But nothing is known of its history from the time it left Walter's hands until it belonged to Nathan van Patten in the midtwentieth century, from whom it was acquired by the Moldenhauer Archives. Unfortunately van Patten was misled into thinking it was in the composer's writing, hence its erroneous inclusion as item 310 of Otto E. Albrecht's census of autograph music manuscripts of European composers in American libraries (1953) in which it is unequivocally ascribed to the year 1683.

Pierre Boulez's
Le Marteau sans maître

Robert Piencikowski

PIERRE BOULEZ WROTE HIS *Le Marteau sans maître* (*The Hammer without a Master*) between the years 1952 and 1955. The work, whose title is borrowed from the collection of poems by René Char, consists of three intermingled cycles, each based on a specific musical setting of one of the three poems the composer has selected, surrounded by purely instrumental "commentaries." He has deliberately avoided the term "variations" to eliminate any confusion with traditional thematic development. The succession of the movements appears as follows:

1. Avant "L'Artisanat furieux"
2. Commentaire I de "Bourreaux de solitude"
3. "L'Artisanat furieux"
4. Commentaire II de "Bourreaux de solitude"
5. "Bel édifice et les pressentiments," version première
6. "Bourreaux de solitude"
7. Après "L'Artisanat furieux"
8. Commentaire III de "Bourreaux de solitude"
9. "Bel édifice et les pressentiments," double

The autograph manuscript of *Le Marteau sans maître* comprises three leaves of manuscript paper of two different types. The first two leaves consist of fragments cut from larger leaves originally measuring 34 by 56 centimeters and containing 56 staves. This paper is of a very thin weight, and printed with staves on only one side. Since it is so translucent that the staves printed on one side can easily be read on the reverse side, on several occasions Boulez has actually notated material on these sides using such "ghost" staves. The other paper type, thicker, is printed on both sides. Boulez used these types of papers throughout the 1950s, and he may have obtained a large quantity of both types at that time for use in his

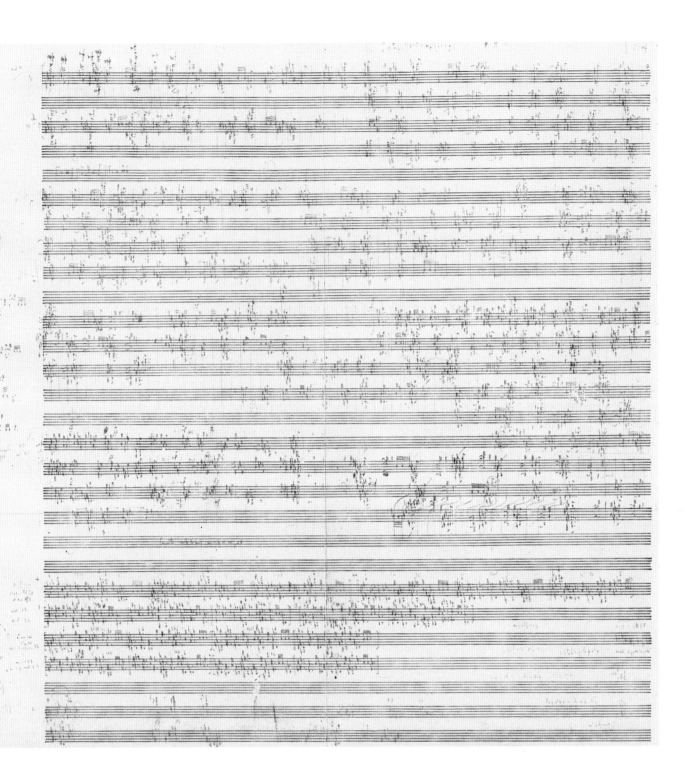

1948–1950 orchestral revision of *Le Visage nuptial* (originally composed in 1946). Boulez typically added to a leaf fragments of manuscript paper, cut from larger sheets, in order to accommodate the demands of denser musical ideas.

The manuscript papers used in the Moldenhauer sketches of *Le Marteau sans maître* are as follows:

One-sided: Two sheets, of 28 staves per sheet, obtained by cutting one whole sheet (of 56 staves) in half horizontally; both halves contain drafts of the first two "Bourreaux de solitude" movements (Commentaires I and II).

Two-sided: One sheet of 20 staves obtained by the asymmetrical division of a larger sheet of manuscript paper. The two sides of the sheet contain the final part after measure 88 of "Bel édifice et les pressentiments," double movement.

My observations of the musical material in these fragments are limited to the first document's single side, which comprises sketches for the second and third parts of "Commentaire I de 'Bourreaux de solitude,'" measures 54 to 102, and measures 103 to 114 of the complete score. (The staves on which these measures appear are designated in numerical order from the top to the bottom of the page.)

The printed staves contain, for the most part, sketches for the draft of measures 54 to 102. The margins are devoted to sketches for measures 74 to 102—which leads us to believe that the latter material preceded the former on the page. There is also a first sketch of material which will figure in measures 103 to 114, and which is more fully developed on the verso. The remaining areas of the page contain sparsely written indications regarding the use of register, as well as the vertical disposition of groupings of notes, deduced from the structure. Since Boulez was concerned in this movement with his technique of total serialization in which not only pitch but other musical components such as the duration of pitches and dynamics are involved, there are many evidences of this concern in this sketch. Detailed notes and instructions extend even into the margins of the page, which are filled with indications concerning the compression and/or extension of the

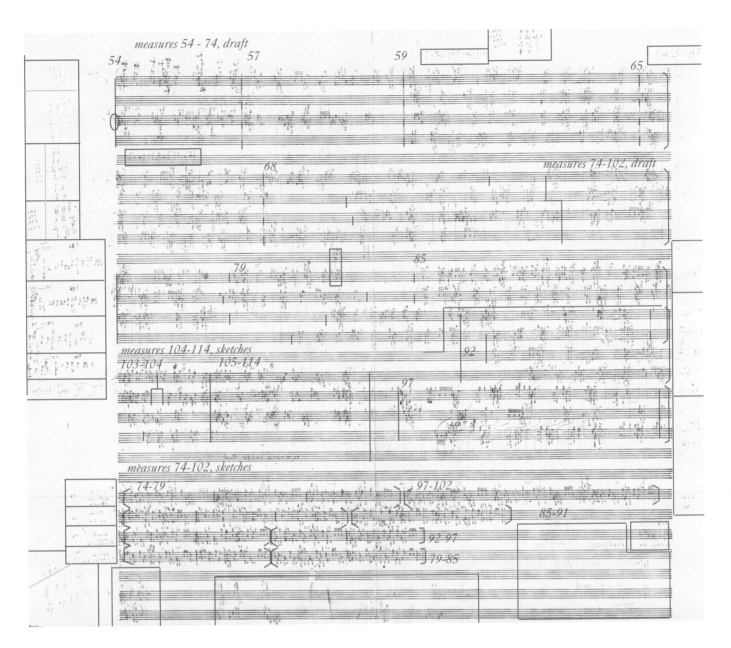

Staves 1–20: bars 54–102: draft

staves 1–4:	left :	bars 54–56; 57–58
	middle:	bars 59–64
	right:	bar 65
staves 6–9:	left:	bars 65–67
	middle:	bars 68–73
	right:	bars 74–76
staves 11–14:	left:	bars 77–78
	middle:	bars 79–84
	right:	bars 85–102 (staves 11–12)
staves 13–16:	right:	bars 92–96
staves 17–19:	right:	bars 97–102

Staves 16–19: bars 103–114: sketches

| staves 16–19: | left: | bars 103–104 and bars 105–114 |

Staves 22–25: bars 74–102: sketches

staff 22:	left:	bars 74–79; right: bars 97–102
staff 23:	left:	bars 85–91
staff 24:	left:	bars 92–97
staff 25:	left:	bars 79–85

scales of duration, as well as of dynamics and attacks which will be given to those durations.

The sketches for the draft of measures 54 to 102 are notated using five systems, generally consisting of four staves, each separated by a blank staff. To find space, Boulez drafts the two last systems tightly together on the right side of the page, the left side having been devoted to the structural sketching of measures 103 to 114, and puts them higher than usual, so that the fourth system overlaps the third and fourth staves of the third system, filling the blank staff between these systems. The same compression occurs between the fourth and fifth systems, resulting in a reduction in the size of the latter system from four staves to three.

This compression is due to the presence, on the left side, of the structural sketch for the material in measures 103 to 114. Appearing at this point as only the barest outline of the musical shapes they are eventually to assume, this material will be filled out by sound complexes produced by various combinations of intervals. In this way the composer amplifies the musical texture to give it the character of a coda. The instrumentation also contributes to this amplification: the reappearence of the alto flute, for example, which had been silent during measures 54 to 102. Boulez applies this procedure of structural amplification to the sketch on the verso of this page, indicated by the textual note in solfeggio notation at the bottom of this system (staff 20), evidently regarding the work's structure: "Ensuite mi-♭, do, mi-♮, sur ré-♮, et sur fa-♯" [Then E-flat, C, E-natural on D, and on F-sharp].

Staves 22 through 25 contain the structural sketches for measures 74 to 102, as follows:

staff number 22 mm. 74–79 and 97–102
staff number 23 mm. 85–91
staff number 24 mm. 92–97
staff number 25 mm. 79–85

Even more preliminary sketches for these structural sketches appear at the bottom of the page. We can hypothesize that this preparatory material was written as a continuation to a previous

page of even earlier sketches intended to be developed as measures 54 through 74, perhaps even as measures 1 through 53. This would explain the appearance of these sketches at the bottom of the page, which seem to be the reason why Boulez was obliged to compress the system on staves 13 through 16 and 17 through 19.

As stated above, a large part of the rest of the page contains sparse annotations concerning registration. However, on staves 26 through 28, at the lower left of the page, we can see the sound blocks from which Boulez derives the sonorities of measures 79 through 85. On staff 24, at the lower right of the page (adjacent to structural notation in solfeggio), is an array of seven notes (si-♭, ré-♮, la-♮, mi-♮, sol-♮, mi-♭, fa-♮) above which the composer has written their German solfeggio equilavents (B D A E G S F) and under which he has written *"Oubli, signal lapidé,"* the title of the composition whose structural elements were to be reemployed in *Le Marteau sans maître.* The earlier work, a setting of poems by the French poet and playwright Armand Gatti for a cappella chorus, has been withdrawn.

The technique on which Boulez bases the "Bourreaux de solitude" cycle was described by him on two different occasions. The first of these was in 1954 in the article "…auprès et au loin":

> If the interval is tied to a duration, and this duration is inserted into the order of the derived series, then a third type of generation occurs, much stricter than the others, because the pitches are ineluctably tied to a duration from the start; yet the wealth of possible combinations is just as great, since the order is modified with each derivation. Thus one gets different groupings, horizontally and vertically, in which one can vary the unit of duration since the relationship of serial order to duration is a function of a unit common to all the durations used. In this form of generation, therefore, time alone is the necessary and sufficient condition for the creation of a hierarchy, both in an absolute form not susceptible to variation (the serial order) and in a relative, variable form (duration, the unit of duration). Here again we have respected that duality which we defined as the principle of all musical action: the possibility of choice within a coherent system; the consequent avoidance of the arbitrary.[1,2]

This may eventually not be the place for a detailed discussion of Boulez's unique and original explorations of serialization, or of the very different techniques he used in other different movements of *Le Marteau sans maître*. Suffice it to say that, initially conceived for use in a section of *Oubli, signal lapidé* of 1952, the serial technique involving pitch and duration used in *Le Marteau sans maître* is intended to serve as a contrast to the "sound-blocs" of variable density of the "L'Artisanat furieux" cycle, as well as to the series of registers of the "Bel édifice et les pressentiments" cycle.

To sum up, this document details the three different stages involved in the compositional process, from the first sketches of the basic material used in this work, through the development of this material, and ultimately to the work's

[1] Pierre Boulez, *Relevés d'apprenti*, ed. Paule Thévenin (Paris: Éditions Le Seuil, Collection "Tel Quel," 1966), p. 198; trans. Stephen Walsh, in "Stocktakings from an Apprenticeship" (Oxford: Clarendon Press, 1991), pp. 153–54. For further reading, see Mary Breatnach, *Boulez and Mallarmé: A Study in Poetic Influence* (England: Scolar Press, 1996), esp. chap. 2, "Music and Mallarmé's Aesthetic," pp. 20–69; and Pierre Boulez, *Relevés d'apprenti*, trans. Stephen Walsh, "Sound and Word," pp. 38–43, esp. p. 40.

[2] The second of these may be found in Pierre Boulez, *Boulez on Music Today*, trans. Susan Bradshaw and Richard Rodney Bennett (Cambridge, Mass.: Harvard University Press, 1972), p. 40, ex. 4.

definitive version:

1. Measures 54 through 74:   draft
2. Measures 74 through 102:   sketches, draft
3. Measures 103 through 114: sketches; draft on the reverse
                              side

We are thus confronted with a sort of "snapshot," witnessing the composer grappling with the transformation of his sound material from an embryonic stage, where the sound structures are still not outlined, to the definitive state in which, through their formal placing, the structures will be shaped by way of musical craftsmanship.

Johannes Brahms's Autograph of "Die Kränze"

Jürgen Thym

MUSIC AUTOGRAPHS CAN BE elusive. After the composer puts finishing touches on a work, the manuscript may remain in the possession of the author for a while longer, or in the hands of the publisher to whom the work is sold, or it may be given as a present to a friend in gratitude for loyalty past or to ensure continuing goodwill or as a more straightforward act of generosity. Autographs are destroyed in wars or by accident, or they may simply disappear from sight, often for generations. They may emerge briefly in the form of items in an auction catalog (just to tease collectors and scholars), only to be submerged again in the anonymity of the private domain. Collectors invest in autographs in the hope of selling them at a later stage for profit or keeping them as a ready source of funds in time of need. Autographs listed as missing or lost (or even destroyed) reappear, mysteriously, often in unexpected corners of the world.

Our story about this Brahms manuscript begins on October 6, 1909. The Russian pianist and conductor Ossip Gabrilowitsch and Clara Clemens, daughter of Mark Twain (whose real name was Samuel Langhorne Clemens) and herself a contralto of considerable renown, are getting married in a small but lavish ceremony at the bride's rural residence of her father in Redding, Connecticut. They have known each other for quite some time, but they decided to join their lives only two weeks earlier after a benefit concert for the Redding Public Library. "My daughter has not attained the fame of these two gentlemen," Mark Twain reportedly said in reference to the other performers of the recital, Gabrilowitsch and the renowned baritone, David Bisham, "but I am sure you will all admit that she is much better-looking." And when his daughter confesses a little later that she has just gotten engaged to one of these gentlemen, the old man is delighted: "Any girl could

Example 1

be proud to marry him. He is a man—a real man." Clara
Clemens's husband-to-be had toured widely, both in Europe
and the United States, and on one of the European trips had
acquired a manuscript of the Brahms song "Die Kränze" (The
Garlands), the haunting setting of a love poem by Daumer, full
of melancholy tears, devotion, and a faint glimmer of hope.
The treasured autograph was kept in a hard-cover folder with a
gold-embossed descriptive label in a mixture of English and
German: "Johannes Brahms / Musical Manuscript / Die Kränze
/ Op. 46 No. 1 / Baden-Baden d. 26. Juni 1885 / aus Polydora

von Daumer" and presented by Gabrilowitsch to his bride as a gift on a gorgeous fall day when the leaves were revealing their autumnal splendor. The gift was a wonderful bond between the two musicians as they began their married life, signifying their love for each other and for music, especially for Brahms, whose compositions both had frequently performed. (Shortly after the wedding Clara and Ossip Gabrilowitsch left for Europe, not knowing that they would not meet Clara's sister Jean again and be cabled to return to the United States in April 1910 to witness the death of her father.)

The events just described form a likely scenario, embellished perhaps in a few details but, for the most part, true to the evidence accompanying the manuscript now in the Moldenhauer Collection of the Library of Congress.

For nearly ninety years the Brahms manuscript did remain elusive. Margit McCorkle, in her thematic catalog of Brahms's works (1984), described two autographs of "Die Kränze"

Example 2

(about whose existence she learned from various secondary sources) and reported them as missing. One of the manuscripts had briefly emerged in 1930 as an item offered for sale in Sotheby's catalog. Unlikely though it may sound, this seems to have been the treasured Gabrilowitsch wedding gift. Did they consider parting with it because of financial difficulties that they had perhaps incurred as a result of the stock market crash in 1929? Whatever their motivation, the sale did not materialize. The Gabrilowitsches's manuscript remained in their possession even after Ossip's death and Clara's remarriage and divorce in the mid-1940s. Upon Clara's death in 1962, Phyllis Harrington—housekeeper, secretary, and long-time confidante of the family—became the owner of the manuscript; after she died in 1985, Scriptorium, a Beverly Hills autograph dealer, sold it to Hans Moldenhauer.

While there is sufficient evidence to trace the provenance of the autograph from 1909 to the present, it is much more difficult to chart its sojourns before the Gabrilowitsch wedding; and some of the following is, admittedly, conjecture. McCorkle listed two autographs for "Die Kränze" as being lost. Her brief description of these items suggests that not one (the Sotheby) but both bear resemblances to the auto-graph under consideration here. The first, owned by the conductor Hermann Levi as early as 1873 and shown at the Meiningen Brahms exhibition in 1899, consisted of two oblong sheets (or four pages) and, according to Levi, contains some variants in measures 10–13; the Library of Congress manuscript indeed has the same format and shows an ossia in the vocal part with text underlay (not in Brahms's handwriting but perhaps preserving an authentic variant) concerning those very same measures (see example 1). The second, dated in the aforementioned Sotheby catalog of 1930 as "Baden-Baden, 26. Juni 1885," has a wording almost identical with the one given on the binding of our manuscript. In short, there is strong evidence that the two lost autographs are one and the same and have now been "found" in the Library of Congress. In this case, the manuscript of "Die Kränze" must have been passed on after the death of its first owner, Hermann Levi, to Ossip Gabrilowitsch and purchased by him in or before 1909.

One more problem can now be resolved; the date given on the binding (and in the Sotheby catalog) is wrong. Brahms's characteristically hasty handwriting caused a "6" at some point to be read as an "8": the actual date at the end of the manuscript is "1865" (see example 2). Presumably the mistake originated with Gabrilowitsch when he wrote out the information for the embosser preparing the binder before the wedding. The date of 1865, by the way, coincides closely with the Brahms biographer Kalbeck's statement that "Die Kränze" might have been composed as early as 1864 and with the fact that the song was published by Simrock in October 1868.

Two Brahms Letters

Jürgen Thym

[To Dr. Max Abraham at C.F. Peters, Leipzig]
[Wien, 3. Oktober 1881][1]

[1] Dates provided by Wilhelm Altmann in *Johannes Brahms: Briefwechsel*, 4 vols., ed. Max Kalbeck (Berlin, 1917–19, reprinted Tutzing: Schneider, 1974).

SEHR GEEHRTER HERR.

Ich glaubte täglich den Kopisten erwarten zu dürfen u. verschob deshalb den Dank für Ihre neuliche Sendung.

Diese aber war gar zu prompt denn Sie haben das Stück ja noch gar nicht! Und unsre hiesige Aufführung mußten wir leider vom Nov. bis in den Dec. oder Jan. verschieben! Der Tage sende ich jedenfalls Chor u. Violinstimmen.

Am 15. Oktober denke ich in Meiningen zu sein um ein Concert mit Bülow u. s. Kapelle zu versuchen. Nun wäre es hübsch wenn Sie zu der Zeit (einfach an Hrn v. B[ülow]) die Geigenstimmen schicken könnten! Etwa 5 erste und zweite Geigen, 3 Br. 3 V.C., 3 Bass.

Den Chor dazu werden wir nicht versuchen können denn in Norddeutschland singt man nicht wie hier vom Blatte.

Von den Händelschen Duetten bitte ich um 3 Ex. u. vielleicht haben Sie die Güte in m[einem] Namen eines an Stockhausen, eines an Adolf Schulze, Gesangs-Professor a. d. Hochschule in Berlin zu senden und eines an den Hofcapellm. Franz Wüllner in Dresden.

Verzeihen Sie, aber bei mir ist jedes Paquet u. Xband [Kreuzband] ein trauriges Ereignis.

Meine Bitte wegen Meiningen ist natürlich gar nicht wichtig und gilt nur falls Sie Ihnen gar keine Umstände macht.

Eine Correktur brauchte ich ja vorher nicht zu lesen.

Und so nächstens mehr von Ihrem sehr ergebenen Joh[annes] Brahms

DEAR SIR:

I thought that the copyist would be coming here any day and therefore postponed thanking you for what you recently sent me.

This, however, was all too prompt, because you do not have the piece as yet! And unfortunately we had to postpone our performance here from November to December or January. In any case, I will soon send chorus and string parts.

On October 15 I plan to be in Meiningen to try out a concerto with Bülow and his orchestra. It would be nice if around that time you could send (addressed simply to "Mr. v. Bülow") the string parts, say: 5 first and second violins, 3 violas, 3 violoncellos, and 3 basses.

It will not be possible to try the chorus because in North Germany people do not sight-sing as well as they do here.

May I ask for three copies of the Duets by Handel, and perhaps you would be kind enough to send, on my behalf, one to Stockhausen, one to Adolf Schulze, voice professor at the Hochschule in Berlin, and one to Court Conductor Franz Wüllner in Dresden.

I apologize for the imposition, but every time I wrap a package, the result is a sorry job.

My request for Meiningen, of course, is not important and applies only if it does not inconvenience you.

It would probably not be necessary for me to read the proofs ahead of time.

With more soon from yours sincerely,

Johannes Brahms

[2] Dates provided by Wilhelm Altmann (on the basis of context and postage stamp).

[20. November 1881][2]

GEEHRTESTER HR DR,

Unsere Lorbeeren sind wirklich übel gerathen, Feuerbach verdient bessere u. ich hoffe die Nänie auch ein wenig.

Mögen Sie trotzdem wohl die Güte haben an Fr. Hofrath F[euerbach] in Ansbach, Bayern zu senden u. kann es wohl ein gebundenes Ex. sein? G[egebener] Z[eit] schicken Sie vielleicht dito eine Partitur die sich dann etwas stattlicher ausnimmt.

In Zürich werde ich nicht säumen Ihnen zu schreiben ob auch Correkturen nöthig.

In Eile Ihr ergebenster

Joh Brahms

DEAR DOCTOR:

Our laurel decorations really turned out badly. Feuerbach deserves better ones and so, I hope, does *Nänie*.

Anyway, would you be so kind as to send a copy to the Frau Court Counselor Feuerbach in Ansbach, Bavaria? And could it perhaps be a bound copy? At the appropriate time you could perhaps send to the same a score, which in turn would look more substantial.

Once in Zürich, I will not hesitate to write you whether corrections are needed.

In a rush I remain yours sincerely,

Johannes Brahms

Geehrter Hr. D.

Unsere Verbrecher
sind wirklich übel
geworden, ...
verdient besser ...
ich hoffe die Miene auch
...

...

Commentary:

Brahms never had much trouble getting his compositions published. Introduced to the music world by Robert Schumann in the famous "Neue Bahnen" paean of 1853 as a genius "who, like Athena, sprang fully armed from the head of Zeus" (in other words: a second Beethoven and a new Messiah of music), Brahms offered his earliest works to Breitkopf & Härtel. And the Härtel brothers, informed by Schumann about the rising star, immediately accepted the music of the twenty-year-old for publication (the two piano sonatas, opp. 1 and 2; six songs, op. 3; and the Scherzo in E-flat Minor, op. 4). The Leipzig company, founded in 1719, was one of the most distinguished music-publishing firms in the German-speaking world, and Brahms probably would have continued entrusting his works to this firm, if there had not been a falling-out over the publication of his String Sextet, op. 36, in 1865. (Simrock finally got the piece.) Over the next three decades Brahms participated as editor or adviser in the publication of several Breitkopf & Härtel collected-works editions (e.g., Bach, Chopin, Mozart, Schumann), but never again did the composer give any new manuscript to the Leipzig firm.

Instead, two companies which until then had played a subordinate role to Breitkopf & Härtel in connection with Brahms emerged as the winners: the recently founded (1849) firm of Johann Rieter-Biedermann in Winterthur, Switzerland, and Simrock in Bonn, the latter being a house with a solid reputation acquired over several generations. (Nikolaus Simrock had been Beethoven's enthusiastic promoter despite the composer's frequent temper tantrums, and his son Peter had been able to lay claim to Mendelssohn's scores and gratitude.) Rieter succeeded in acquiring, among other Brahms works, the First Piano Concerto, op. 15 (certainly a courageous decision, since the piece was tainted by the poor reception at the Hannover premiere in 1859); the Magelone cycle, op. 33; the Piano Quintet, op. 34; the Paganini variations, op. 35; and—a real gem for the small company—the German Requiem, op. 45. While the income from these works may initially have been minimal, Rieter scored a hit with the publication of Brahms's waltzes, op. 39, which, in arrangements for all kinds of instruments and ensembles, including editions that took into account the limited skill of beginners at the keyboard, must have been a publisher's dream of a fast profit investment. After the premature death of Johann Rieter in 1876, the professional relations between the composer and the publishing house cooled somewhat, although personal exchanges with the widow and several business successors remained cordial.

The real victor in the struggle for Brahms manuscripts was Simrock. After the company's leadership had passed to the third generation in 1867 or 1868, Fritz Simrock, the founder's grandson, only four years younger than Brahms, wasted no time in combining business sense and artistic instinct for cornering the market on Brahms and acquiring a virtual monopoly. The company had moved from provincial Bonn to Berlin in 1871, shortly before the city became the capital of the Second German Empire. Inspired by the business fever of the *Gründerjahre*, Simrock was ready to become one of the major-league players in the music-publishing business with Brahms as its chief icon. The lion's share of Brahms's works in the following decades was indeed ultimately published by, or came into the hands of, the Simrock firm, including the lucrative Hungarian Dances (no opus number) of 1869 (first set) and 1880 (second set). Fritz Simrock even advanced to the status of Brahms's investment adviser and confidant. Despite enormous professional tensions between the businessman and the artist, the relationship and friendship survived to the end: Brahms even confirmed the latter by offering Simrock the familiar "Du" in 1895.

The only one who dared to challenge Simrock's Brahms monopoly in later years (if one disregards Albert Gutmann's rather public, and hence clumsy, attempt to outbid Simrock in acquiring the Third Symphony in 1883) was Dr. Max Abraham, the owner of the Leipzig music publishing firm of C.F. Peters (founded in 1800), which emerged in the late nineteenth century as a force to be reckoned with. No less inspired by the élan of the German Empire than Simrock, and directing his business zeal toward granting inexpensive access to musical artworks, Abraham had established "Edition Peters" in 1867, a subsidiary whose goal was to bring music to the masses. He may have hoped for another set of Hungarian Dances or waltzes (similar to op. 39), but Brahms, even though he was lured by generous honoraria and the prospects of Peters's affordable editions (which the socially conscious Brahms did not fail to hold up as a model to Fritz Simrock), only consented to give up some songs and vocal quartets (opp. 63 and 64) in 1874 and, after he felt personal gratitude toward Abraham mounting several years later, his arrangement of Handel duets (edited in collaboration with Friedrich Chrysander) and the choral-orchestral work *Nänie*, op. 82.

The immediate reason for setting Schiller's verses was the death of his friend, the artist Anselm Feuerbach (1829–1880). Brahms, who was quite fond of Feuerbach's canvasses with their idealized classical subjects, had been instrumental in attracting the painter to the Vienna Academy of Visual Arts in 1873 (a position which Feuerbach held with varying degrees of success until he resigned in 1877) and wanted to honor his memory. On a trip to Italy in the spring of 1881 the composer visited not only Venice, where Feuerbach had died, but also Rome, Southern Italy, and Sicily, where he could familiarize himself with many of the sites of classical antiquity so dear to his deceased friend. After returning from this trip, he was ready to approach the task of setting Schiller's lament "Auch das Schöne muß sterben!" (Even beauty must die!) with its evocation of classical mythology. The poem is laid out in alternating hexameter and pentameter lines (distichs)— certainly an apt choice for commemorating Feuerbach.

Even though Fritz Simrock helped Brahms acquire some photographic reproductions of Feuerbach's paintings during the summer of that year and even though he saw the composer at his summer residence in Preßbaum near Vienna during this time (no doubt learning about Brahms's composition of *Nänie* during his visit and urging Brahms to have it published with the Simrock house), ultimately the Feuerbach piece went to Peters. (Simrock's "consolation prize"—not a bad deal by any standards—was the Second Piano Concerto, which Brahms completed during the same summer.)

The two letters reproduced here in the original and in translation pertain to the publication process of Brahms's *Nänie*. Abraham, instinctively aware of Simrock's pressure on Brahms and perhaps fearing that the work might still go to his competitor, sent Brahms the honorarium even before the manuscript had reached his firm. Always reluctant to part with a new composition for publication before he had heard it in performance, Brahms instructed Abraham to forward, if possible, the freshly engraved string parts to Meiningen where he planned to try out his new piano concerto with Hans von Bülow and where he also hoped to squeeze in a rehearsal of *Nänie*, at least of the orchestral sections. Packing and preparing his manuscripts and scores for mailing seems to have been a dreaded chore for Brahms, but the prospect of having performance materials of the work available during his Meiningen visit would help to speed matters. Brahms managed to get the manuscript to Leipzig, decided on Henriette Feuerbach, the painter's stepmother, as a dedicatee of the work, and asked for laurel sprigs or wreaths as a decorative flourish on the title page. But the resulting proposed title page did not satisfy the composer, and, in the end, the first edition was published without such "vegetation." Brahms put pressure on Abraham to publish parts, piano reduction, and score as soon as possible, because in the meantime the premiere of *Nänie* had been scheduled in Zurich for early December of that year under the composer's baton, and Brahms also promised to inform Abraham immediately about any corrections to the score that might become apparent from the Zurich performance.

Nearly a year later Abraham reminded Brahms of the composer's informal promise to send more works, especially larger ones, to C.F. Peters. Despite his generosity in matters of honoraria and occasional urgings, Abraham was ultimately unable to break Simrock's monopoly. The only Brahms pieces that the Leipzig firm published in later years were the vocal quartets, op. 112, and canons, op. 113, of 1891, thereby making the setting of Schiller's *Nänie* the most substantial work that the company received from the composer's pen.

Some Autobiographical Overtones in Brahms's *Rinaldo*

Carol A. Hess

SINCE ITS EARLIEST PERFORMANCES Brahms's *Rinaldo* has met with challenge. The premiere (Vienna, February 28, 1869), at which Brahms conducted the Akademische Gesangverein and the Hofoper orchestra, was greeted by largely negative reviews.[1] With the exception of Theodor Billroth's qualified praise, commentary ranged from tepid to hostile, with critics emphasizing *Rinaldo*'s "endless shades of gray," "excessive Baroque conceits," and lack of sensuality.[2] Somewhat more favorable notices for performances outside Vienna (Jena, 1870; Koblenz, 1872; Munich, 1873; Leipzig, 1874; Darmstadt, 1878) failed to establish *Rinaldo* securely in the repertory.[3] Nor did the critical essays by Brahms's supporters Hermann Deiters (1870) and Hermann Kretzschmar (1874) enhance the cantata's standing in Vienna; a second performance there in 1883, reviewed by Eduard Hanslick, met with similar reservations.[4]

Yet recent scholars have begun to view *Rinaldo* more positively. In his discussion of the cantata's "stylistic relations to the world of opera," Michael Musgrave compares the "blurring" between aria and recitative in *Rinaldo* to that in Schubert's incompletely preserved oratorio *Lazarus*, while also finding parallels with *Fidelio*, *Der fliegende Holländer* and the "warmth of feeling" of Italian opera. John Daverio alludes to Brahms's "Mozartean ideal" as manifested in the formal disposition of Rinaldo's two "grand arias." He has also referred both to *Rinaldo* and the *Alto Rhapsody*, op. 53, as "profound embodiments of personal expression," while noting the strength of their "autobiographical overtones."[5]

What "autobiographical overtones" might the text have awakened in the composer? Goethe's free adaptation of the fourteenth canto in Tasso's *Gerusalemme liberata* would have presented significant challenges even to a highly experienced

[1] A trial performance with the Wiener Männergesangverein had originally been scheduled but was canceled. See Margit L. McCorkle, "The Role of Trial Performances for Brahms's Orchestral and Large Choral Works: Sources and Circumstances," in *Brahms Studies: Analytical and Historical Perspectives*, ed. George Bozarth (Oxford: Oxford University Press, 1990), pp. 309–10.

[2] See Theodor Billroth, "Über *Rinaldo* von Johannes Brahms," in *Theodor Billroth als Musikkritiker*, ed. Otto-Hans Kahler (Rockville, Maryland: Kabel Verlag, 1988), pp. 44–45. The quotations are taken from an anonymous reviewer writing in the *Signale für die musikalische Welt* 27 (1869): 375, and Leopold Alexander Zellner, "Rezensionen," *Blätter für Theater, Musik und bildende Kunst* 15 (1869): 70. Addressing the cantata's lack of sensuality is "Wiener Musikreminiscenzen III," *Neue Berliner Musikzeitung* 23 (1869): 117. All these reviews are cited in Katharina Hofmann, "Die Kantate *Rinaldo* von Johannes Brahms: Genese, Rezeption, Struktur" (M. A. thesis, Kiel: Christian-Albrechts Universität, 1992), pp. 64–77.

[3] In Koblenz only the final chorus, "Auf dem Meere," was performed; in Munich, only the solo numbers. For a survey of the first decade of the cantata's performance history, see Angelika Horstmann, *Untersuchungen zur Brahms-Rezeption der Jahre 1860–1880* (Hamburg: K. D. Wagner, 1986), pp. 179–85; see also Hofmann, op. cit., pp. 64–65.

[4] Hermann Deiters, "Anzeigen und Beurtheilungen: *Rinaldo*," *Allgemeine Musikalische Zeitung* 13–14 (1870): 98–101, 105–7; Hermann Kretzschmar, "Neue Werke von J. Brahms," *Musikalisches Wochenblatt* 5–7 (1874): 58–60, 70–73, 83–85.

dramatist. The poem's most salient feature is its unabated emphasis on the protagonist's inner turmoil: Rinaldo vacillates between remaining with the siren Armida on her enchanted island or renouncing her. Goethe's protagonist is a far cry from the invulnerable masculine hero commonly portrayed in chivalric texts.

What factors in the composer's biographical circumstances might have drawn Brahms to Goethe's indecisive hero? It is not certain when Brahms first became acquainted with Goethe's text, although in 1855 he acquired a copy of *Gerusalemme liberata* in a translation by Dutenhofer.[6] During his last season at Detmold (fall 1859) Brahms conducted Mendelssohn's cantata *Die erste Walpurgisnacht*. The Brahms biographer Max Kalbeck suggests that at this time the composer may have browsed through Goethe's collected works, wherein *Rinaldo* follows *Die erste Walpurgisnacht*.[7] Whether or not he made a detailed study of Goethe's departures from Tasso's text, the differences between the two versions would have been obvious to one as sensitive to textual nuances as Brahms. The most significant of these is the treatment of the female role.

As Mary Ingraham points out, Goethe eliminates all female characters (such as the guide who leads the knights to the island) but Armida.[8] Indeed, even Armida's presence is minimized, despite her overwhelming power, for she has no singing part. The silencing of Armida is all the more paradoxical in light of the common literary trope of the siren: the sexually alluring and supremely powerful temptress who from the time of Odysseus has lured men to self-destruction through voluptuous cascades of virtuosic song.

This stifling of the female presence may well have struck a responsive chord in Brahms during the fall of 1859. During the previous January he had broken off his engagement to Agathe von Siebold, declaring that he loved her but could not "wear fetters." Given Agathe's exquisite singing voice (biographers often cite Joachim's comparison of her voice to an Amati violin), Goethe's treatment of the female voice may have struck Brahms on a perverse or quixotic level.[9] In fact, Kalbeck suggested that Brahms's conflicted feelings about Agathe were what attracted him to Goethe's hesitant protagonist.

Other commentaries include Carl Grabau, *Johannes Brahms. Rinaldo: Kantate von Goethe für Tenor-Solo, Männerchor und Orchester, op. 50, Der Musikführer*, no. 299 (Berlin: Schlesinger, R. Lienau [190?]); and Emil Krause, *Johannes Brahms in seinen Werken* (Hamburg: Lucas Gräfe & Sillem., 1892), pp. 20–21. Hanslick's review is published in *Concerte, Componisten und Virtuosen der letzten fünfzehn Jahre, 1870–1885, Kritiken von Eduard Hanslick* (Berlin: Allgemeiner Verein für Deutsche Literatur, 1896), p. 383–86.

5 Michael Musgrave, *The Music of Brahms* (London: Routledge & Kegan Paul, 1985), p. 78. Daverio's remarks are found in "Brahms's *Magelone-Romanzen* and the 'Romantic Imperative,'" *Journal of Musicology* 7 (1989): 357, 360, and "The *Wechsel der Töne* in Brahms's *Schicksalslied*," *Journal of the American Musicological Society* 46 (1993): 111.

6 According to Mary I. Ingraham, "Brahms's *Rinaldo*, op. 50: A Structural and Contextual Study" (Ph.D. diss., University of Nottingham, 1994), p. 134, it was not until January of 1862 that Brahms acquired the 1860 edition of Goethe he used while working on *Rinaldo*.

7 Max Kalbeck, *Johannes Brahms*, vol. 2, (Berlin: Deutsche Brahms-Gesellschaft, 1908), p. 64.

8 Ingraham, op. cit., p. 136. Another difference is that in Tasso's version Rinaldo can hardly be held accountable for his behavior since he falls in love with Armida under the influence of a magical spell, a point Deiters discusses in his op. cit., p. 99.

9 See, for example, Karl Geiringer, *Brahms: His Life and Work*, 2nd ed. rev. (New York: Oxford University Press, 1947), p. 57.

[10] *Johannes Brahms im Briefwechsel mit Karl Reinthaler, Max Bruch, Hermann Deiters,* Wilhelm Altman, ed. (Berlin: 1908), vol. 3, p. 21. Brahms's description of this chorus as "new" implies the existence of an earlier version, either lost or destroyed. In Brahms's handwritten catalog of his own works he writes: "Sommer 1863 (einen 2ten Schlußchor Sommer 68), Bonn. See Ingraham, op. cit., pp. 78–79. See also Margit L. McCorkle, *Johannes Brahms: Thematisch-Bibliographisches Werkverzeichnis* (Munich: G. Henle, 1984), p. 205.

[11] Geiringer cites a letter from Brahms to Clara, in which the composer writes about "a very pretty girl with whom I, God knows, would have made a fool of myself, if as luck would have it, someone had not snatched her up at Christmas." Geiringer, op. cit., p. 71.

[12] Ibid., p. 82; Malcolm MacDonald, *Brahms* (New York: Schirmer, 1990), p. 236.

[13] The first movement of op. 36 may have been written in 1858–1859. See MacDonald, op. cit., pp. 170–73. Geiringer reports that with the completion of the Sextet Brahms declared to Gänsbacher that with this gesture Brahms "freed himself from his last love." See Geiringer, op. cit., pp. 59–61, who also cites from Agathe's *Erinnerungen.*

This possibility is all the more plausible in light of *Rinaldo*'s protracted genesis. As is well known, Brahms often delayed the completion of works that posed psychological challenges. (Comparable examples include the Piano Quartet in C Minor, op. 60, the *German Requiem*, and the First Symphony.) He began the cantata in 1863 with the hope of entering it into a contest sponsored by the Aachener Liedertafel but failed to meet the October 1 deadline of that year because he did not complete the final chorus. It was not until August 1868 that he was finally able to realize Rinaldo's "victory" in a "great, new final chorus."[10]

Certainly during the early stages of *Rinaldo*'s composition Brahms experienced conflicts similar to those of Goethe's troubled protagonist. As his Wertherlike agitation over Clara Schumann settled into greater calm, he fell in love with and then spurned Agathe. Soon afterwards he embarked upon a friendship with the singer Ottilie Hauer, which developed to the point that her family fully expected Brahms to propose to her. When, however, on Christmas Day 1863 Ottilie became engaged to another man Brahms expressed relief that marriage had again eluded him.[11] From 1863 to 1864 Brahms gave piano lessons to the attractive and highly musical Elisabeth von Stockhausen. But as he later confessed to Julius Epstein, Brahms terminated this arrangement because he sensed danger in placing himself in such close proximity to Elisabeth's considerable charms.[12] Even Agathe continued to exercise a certain fascination upon the composer, for Brahms is reported to have referred nostalgically to her Göttingen home some five years after the episode had ended. He also included her cipher—the letters of her name expressed in respective notes—in the first movement of the G-Major Sextet, op. 36, completed in 1864–1865.[13]

What did the 1868 resurrection of *Rinaldo* indicate? Was the composer simply tying up loose ends? Or did the victorious final chorus, in which Rinaldo sails away from the seductress proclaiming that the past has "vanished," resonate on some level with Brahms's own experience? The facts of Brahms's biography suggest that fundamental changes had occurred from 1865 to 1868, several of which spelled greater equilibrium if not outright "victory." By 1868 his career prospects were more

secure, thanks to events like the hard-won triumph of the first Piano Concerto (Mannheim, 1865) and the enthusiastic reception to the *German Requiem* (Bremen, 1868). He was also becoming resigned to the fact that he would never find satisfactory employment in his native city (having been twice denied the directorship of the Hamburg Philharmonic) and by the spring of 1869 gave up his rooms in Hamburg to take an apartment in Vienna. Personal victories are harder to pinpoint. But the open demonstrations of romantic interest that characterized Brahms's behavior during the 1850s and early 1860s seem to play no part in this period. His feelings for Julie Schumann, who in 1869 married another man, were so well concealed that not even Clara was aware of them. Indeed, the first half of 1868 was an extremely tense period in his

14 Presumably the conflict occurred because Brahms tried to interfere in family decisions. MacDonald, op. cit., p. 138.

15 David Brodbeck, "Review: *The Music of Brahms* by Michael Musgrave," *Journal of Musicology* 7 (1989): 412. See also Brodbeck's *Brahms: Symphony No. 1* (Cambridge: Cambridge University Press, 1997). I discuss *Rinaldo's* autobiographical implications more fully in "'Als wahres volles Menschenbild:' Brahms's *Rinaldo* and Autobiographical Allusion," *Brahms Studies*, vol. 2, ed. David Brodbeck (Lincoln and London: University of Nebraska Press, 1998), pp. 63–89.

friendship with Clara.14 Although that summer he stayed away from her home in Lichtental, in September he sent her as a birthday greeting the Alphorn theme, which would appear in the introduction for the last movement of the First Symphony, still years away from completion. As David Brodbeck has suggested, the contrast between the Sturm und Drang character of the symphony's tumultuous first movement, composed when his feelings for Clara had been at their most intense, and the "idyllic tones of the horn" may well reflect an increasing stability of Brahms's feelings.15 The completion at the same time of *Rinaldo's* "victory" chorus, with its extolling of manly fortitude, might suggest something of a similar kind.

Two Letters by Anton Bruckner

Jürgen Thym

Bruckner ALS, 13.XI.1883

LIEBER FREUND!

Auf Gerathewohl schreibe ich; denn Ihr Brief ist versteckt.
Weiß weder Ihre Adresse noch sonstigen Charakter von Ihnen.
Danke sehr für Ihr liebes Schreiben. Omnes amici mei
dereliquerunt me! In diesen Worten haben Sie die ganze
Situation. Hans Richter nennt mich jetzt musik[alischen]
Narren weil ich zu wenig kürzen wollte; (wie *er* sagt;) führt
natürlich gar nichts auf; ich stehe gegenwärtig ganz allein da.
Wünsche, daß es Ihnen besser ergehen möge, und Sie bald
oben hinauf kommen mögen! Dann werden Sie gewiß meiner
nicht vergessen. Glück auf!

Ihr A. Bruckner

Wien, 13. Nov. 1883

DEAR FRIEND:

I take the risk or writing to you, even though I cannot find
your letter and know neither your address nor title. Thank you
very much for your nice letter. All my friends have abandoned
me! These words tell you the whole situation. Hans Richter
calls me now a musical fool, because I did not want to make
enough cuts (as *he* puts it). And, of course, he does not perform
anything at all; I stand alone at the moment. I hope that things
will be better for you and that you will soon succeed then you
will surely not forget me. Good luck!

Your A. Bruckner

Vienna, November 13, 1883

Lieber Freund!

Auch Ihnen [...] wohl schreibe ich,
denn Ihr Brief ist [...].
[...] wieder Ihre Adresse noch
[...] Charakter von Ihnen.
Danke sehr für Ihr liebes
Schreiben. Omnes amici mei
dereliquerunt me! Zu diesen
Worten haben Sie die ganze
Situation. Hans [...]
nennt mich jetzt [...]. Nennen
weil ich zu wenig [...] wollte,
(wie [...] sagt;)

Bruckner, ALS, 27.II.1885

Hochgeborener Herr Baron!

Schon wieder muß ich zur Last fallen. Da die Sinfonie am 10.
März aufgeführt wird, so komme ich schon *Sonntag den 8. März
früh* nach München und werde wieder bei den vier
Jahreszeiten Quartier nehmen. Ich bath Hl[*]
Hofkapellmeister um ein paar Vorproben, weil die *geheimen*
Schwierigkeiten in dem Werke sehr viele sind und dgl. Da
könnte dann Sonntag ganz gut eine Probe stattfinden, wenn es
Hl von Levi genehm wäre. Dürfte ich Hl Baron bitten,
dießfalls eine Fürbitte einlegen zu wollen!? Zudem sind in der
Partitur einige Verbesserungen gemacht worden.

Hl Landgraf befindet sich besser, und sendet herzliche Grüße;
auch vereinigt er seine Bitte mit der meinen. Hl Landgraf
sagte mir, ich soll Hl Baron aufmerksam machen, daß es sehr
gut wäre, mich vor dem Concerte in einer außerordentlichen
Versammlung des Wagnervereines mit den PT[**] Mitgliedern
desselben bekannt zu machen, was mir *viele Freunde* erwerben
würde. Eben so mit den Mitgliedern des H[eiligen] Gral. Ich
bitte daher recht innigst um Hochdero Hülfe in dieser so
wichtigen Angelegenheit. Gewiß würde ich die Herrschaften
nicht so belästigen, wenn ich nicht die Situation als so wichtig
erblicken würde. Mit dem Ausdrucke meines tiefsten
Respektes verbleibe ich meine innigsten Bitten wiederholend

Euer Hochgeboren Hl Baron

Dankschuldigster A. Bruckner

Wien, 27. Febr.1885

Illustrious Baron:

Again I have to burden you with something. Since the
symphony is going to be performed on *March 10*, I will arrive in
Munich on *Sunday morning (March 8)* and will again be staying
at the Vier Jahreszeiten Hotel. I asked Herr Hofkapellmeister
for a few rehearsals in advance, since there are many *hidden*
difficulties etc. in the work. Thus a rehearsal could very well

Hochgebornen Herrn
Baron!

Schon wieder muß ich zum Last.
fallen. Da die Sinfonie am
10. März aufgeführt wird
so komm ich schon Sonntag
den 8. März früh nach München,
und werde wieder bei den
mir Jahrszeiten Quartier
nehmen. Ich bath H. Hofka.
pellmeister mir ein paar
Tanzprobew, weil die geheimen
Schwierigkeiten in den Streich.
Stim̄en sind u dgl.

·164·

take place on Sunday, if it is convenient to Herr von Levi. Could I ask Herr Baron to intervene on my behalf!? Furthermore, there are several corrections in the score. Herr Landgraf feels better and sends cordial greetings; he also supports my request. Herr Landgraf asked me to let Herr Baron know that it might be very good to introduce me to the distinguished members of the Wagner Society, which might enable me to win *many friends*. Similarly, also with the members of the Holy Grail. Thus I beg for the help of your Highness in this very important matter. I would not burden the gentlemen if I did not consider the situation so very important. With the expression of my deepest respect, and repeating my heartfelt requests, I remain your Illustrious Baron's most grateful,

A. Bruckner

Vienna, February 27, 1885

[*]   Hl = Herr
[**] PT = praemisso titolo

THE TWO LETTERS PUBLISHED HERE for the first time were written during a crucial period in the life of Anton Bruckner (1824–1896): the midlife years in which he fought for recognition of his music, especially his symphonies, by the musical world at large. In fact, the letters may be considered representative of two different stages in the reception of Bruckner's work: neglect and misunderstanding, on the one hand, and a gradual turn toward acceptance of Bruckner as a symphonist, on the other.

After having served as an assistant teacher and organist in the Austrian province until his midforties, Bruckner moved to Vienna in 1868 to teach organ and music theory at the Conservatory. In 1875 he accepted an appointment, initially unsalaried, as lecturer of music theory at the University of Vienna in addition to his duties at the Conservatory. Bruckner, who retained the habits of mind of a simple man from the peasantry of Upper Austria, must have seemed odd indeed in the context of the brilliant intellectual and artistic circles of the Austrian capital. Little blessed with social and political skills, he was unable, even after he had caused a stir as an organist and improviser in Paris and London in 1869 and 1871, respectively, to transfer the success he gained internationally into recognition at home.

Vienna was, in the 1870s and 1880s, in the throes of an aesthetic controversy between the so-called *neudeutsche Schule* with Wagner and Liszt as protagonists and a more academically oriented school of composition, propagated especially by Eduard Hanslick, with Johannes Brahms as the undisputed figurehead. And the naive Bruckner unwittingly became a player in a gravitational field dominated by artistic and intellectual forces politically more adept than he. Bruckner's dedication of his Symphony No. 3, with musical quotations from *Die Walküre*, to Richard Wagner, his pilgrimages to Bayreuth to attend the premieres of *Der Ring des Nibelungen* in 1876 and of *Parsifal* in 1882, and his joining the Wagner Society in Vienna (honorary member after 1884) no doubt were interpreted by Hanslick and others as expressions of a partisan. The Wagner camp was only too eager to appropriate Bruckner as its "symphonist," setting Bruckner up against Brahms who established himself in the mid-1870s as a symphonic composer (and thereby as Beethoven's heir). In the hothouse climate of Vienna, aesthetic conflicts were fought with unrestrained vehemence and little tolerance; soon clichés of Bruckner as "provincial organist" and of his symphonies as "gigantic serpents"[1] made the rounds and spoiled his chances of having his works get a fair hearing in the Austrian capital. Moreover, the Gesellschaft der Musikfreunde, which determined access to the concert hall appropriate for performances of orchestral works in Vienna was firmly under the control of Brahms and his associates. The neglect—even harassment—that Bruckner suffered from the Viennese music establishment was indeed scandalous, especially since it was directed at "a man who, unlike Wagner, was largely unable to defend himself."[2]

This was the sorry state of affairs which provides the context for the first letter published here. The year 1883 early on had dealt a severe blow to Bruckner, both personally and professionally. Wagner's death was felt by Bruckner as a profound loss, especially since Wagner had promised him

[1] Hans Conrad Fischer, *Anton Bruckner: Sein Leben* (Salzburg: Residenz-Verlag, 1974), p. 183.

[2] Carl Dahlhaus, in *Nineteenth-Century Music*, tr. J. Bradford Robinson (Berkeley and Los Angeles: University of California Press, 1989), p. 271.

during their last meeting, which saw the *Parsifal* premiere in Bayreuth, to perform all his symphonies. Under the impact of the news of Wagner's demise, Bruckner composed much of his Symphony No. 7. The Adagio, especially the coda, was conceived as a grandiose lament for the master of Bayreuth. Invigorated by attending another *Parsifal* performance in Bayreuth and vacationing in his native Upper Austria during the summer, Bruckner completed the symphony in September. Hopes for an early performance of the work in Vienna, however, did not materialize. Hans Richter, who had premiered Bruckner's Symphony No. 4 in 1881, became cautiously shy. Even though convinced of the symphonic genius of Bruckner, he was reluctant to venture out again; at least, that is the way Bruckner saw it. When Bruckner showed the new work to Richter later in the fall, the conductor seems to have proposed drastic cuts. The composer did not take the suggestion in the positive spirit it may have been meant; on the contrary, he believed that Richter, whom he considered a supporter, was bowing to Hanslick and company. As the letter to an anonymous acquaintance shows, the year 1883 ended in depression, loneliness, and hopelessness for Bruckner. By that time, he was nearly sixty years old and still had not experienced recognition of his symphonic works by the music world at large or even, and more importantly, in his hometown.

In the next year, however, the tide turned in favor of Bruckner, not necessarily in Vienna but certainly in other musical centers. Through his teaching at the university, Bruckner had gathered a devoted coterie of acolytes who were tireless in supporting their teacher and, once they had reached leadership positions, actively performed and promoted his work: Felix Mottl, Joseph Schalk, Karl Muck, Hugo Wolf, Gustav Mahler, Franz Schalk, and Ferdinand Loewe. Joseph Schalk and Loewe performed the new symphony on two pianos at a concert of the Wagner Society early in the year, and Schalk took his piano arrangement of the work for four hands on a trip to Leipzig, where he introduced Arthur Nikisch to the score. Nikisch immediately decided to perform the symphony in Leipzig. After considerable delays the premiere took place on December 30, 1884, in the presence of the composer, albeit with horns replacing the Wagner tubas required for the Adagio and Finale. The symphony was a tremendous success with both the public and the critics. A month later the performance was repeated in the presence of the King of Saxony.

An even greater triumph for Bruckner was the performance of Symphony No. 7 under Hermann Levi in Munich on March 10, 1885, mentioned in the second letter. Bruckner had gotten to know Levi, the conductor handpicked by Wagner for *Parsifal*, during several trips to Bayreuth. The composer was invited, as had been the case for the Leipzig premiere, to attend the rehearsals a few days before the performance, and he gladly accepted. Pointing to the difficulties of the work, Bruckner even asked Levi for extra rehearsals and, aided by the mediation of Baron Karl von Perfall, was accommodated. Perfall, court-appointed music and opera director in Munich, was also instrumental in introducing the composer to the members of two private organizations devoted to the legacy of Wagner—the local Wagner Society and the Holy Grail—which no doubt had a beneficial effect on the reception of the work. (Bruckner biographers Göllerich and Auer probably knew the letter published here.)[3] The performance was indeed a great success. Bruckner was celebrated by the public and the artistic community of Munich. Friends collected money to have the symphony published, and Bruckner dedicated the work to King Ludwig II, Wagner's great patron. Levi elevated Bruckner in public to the rank of "greatest symphonist since Beethoven's death." Performances of Bruckner symphonies took place in the Hague, in Cologne, Karlsruhe, and New York that same year, confirming the breakthrough that had been achieved in Leipzig and Munich. Bruckner's reception in Vienna, however, remained poisoned by partisanship even in the last decade of Bruckner's life when successes in other musical centers might have suggested a corrective course.

[3] August Göllerich and Max Auer, *Anton Bruckner: Ein Lebens-und Schaffensbild* (Regensburg: Bosse, 1936), esp. vol. IV/2.

Dr. Burney, Samuel Wesley, and J. S. Bach's *Goldberg Variations*

Philip Olleson

DR. CHARLES BURNEY'S LETTER TO Samuel Wesley of around July 15, 1810, concerning arrangements for a private performance for Burney of J. S. Bach's *Goldberg Variations* by Wesley and Vincent Novello illustrates both the warm friendship between Burney and Wesley and the lively interest that Burney developed in the music of Bach in the last years of his life. It is one of over twenty extant letters between Burney and Wesley from what was evidently a far more extensive correspondence which began in late 1799 and lasted until shortly before Burney's death in April 1814.[1] Many of the later letters are concerned with the promotion of Bach's music by Wesley and a group of his friends and professional colleagues which included Benjamin Jacob, C. F. Horn, A. F. C. Kollmann, Vincent Novello, Johann Peter Salomon, and William Crotch. They are thus key documents in the history of Bach reception in England, and are of particular value for the light they shed on the nature and extent of Burney's own involvement in the English Bach movement.[2]

Although the Library of Congress Burney letter is not a new find, its whereabouts were for many years unknown, and it was only with its acquisition by Hans and Rosaleen Moldenhauer that it became available for consultation by scholars. Its subsequent acquisition by the Library of Congress as part of the Moldenhauer Bequest has made its existence more widely known and has further increased its accessibility.

It was originally owned by Novello, to whom (as Novello's annotation states), Wesley had presented it in token of his part in the performance. It was subsequently owned by the leading British collector of music Julian Marshall, whose interest in Wesley may have stemmed from having been as a boy a chorister under Wesley's son Samuel Sebastian at Leeds Parish

[1] Burney's letters to Wesley will appear in volumes 3 and 4 of *The Letters of Dr. Charles Burney*, 4 vols., ed. Alvaro Ribeiro, SJ (Oxford: Clarendon Press, 1991–), vols. 2–4 in preparation; Wesley's letters to Burney will be published in *The Letters of Samuel Wesley: Professional and Social Correspondence, 1792–1837*, ed. Philip Olleson (Oxford: Clarendon Press, in preparation).

[2] On the English Bach movement, see F. G. E[dwards], "Bach's Music in England," *Musical Times* 37 (1896): 585–87, 652–57, 722–26, 797–800; Robert Pascall, "Ein Überblick der frühen Bach-Rezeption in England bis zirka 1860," in *Johann Sebastian Bach: Beiträge zur Wirkungsgeschichte*, ed. Ingrid Fuchs (Vienna: Verband der wissenschaftlichen Gesellschaften Oesterreichs, 1992), pp. 147–65.

3 Arthur Searle, "Julian Marshall and the British Museum: Music Collecting in the Later Nineteenth Century," *British Library Journal*, Vol. 11, no. 1 (Spring 1985): 67–87. See also A. Hyatt King, *Some British Collectors of Music, c.1600–1960* (Cambridge: Cambridge University Press, 1963), pp. 64–66; Malcolm Turner and Arthur Searle, "The Music Collections of the British Library Reference Division," *MLA Notes* 39 (March 1982): 499–549, especially 524.

4 *Concordia: A Weekly Journal of Music and the Sister Arts* (November 20, 1875): 476–77. Published by Novello & Co. as a weekly companion to *The Musical Times* and edited by Joseph Bennett, it ran for fifty-two issues between May 1, 1875, and April 22, 1876.

5 *Concordia*, May 29, June 5, June 26, 1875; a further letter appeared in the December 18 issue. The appearance of the letters in print followed their recent purchase by Novello & Co. at Sterndale Bennett's first sale at Puttick and Simpson's on April 26, 1875. They are now at the Royal College of Music, MS 2130.

6 Eliza Wesley, ed., *Letters of Samuel Wesley to Mr. Jacobs, Organist of Surrey Chapel, Relating to the Introduction into This Country of the Works of John Sebastian Bach* (London: Partridge, 1875); facsimile edition with Introduction by Peter Williams, *The Wesley Bach Letters* (London: Novello, 1988) (hereafter *Bach Letters*).

7 The British Library, London (hereafter BL), Add. MS 31764.

8 James T. Lightwood, *Samuel Wesley, Musician: The Story of His Life* (London: Epworth Press, 1937), pp. 131–32.

9 Percy A. Scholes, *The Great Dr. Burney: His Life, His Travels, His Works, His Family and His Friends*, 2 vols. (London: Oxford University Press, 1948), vol. 2, pp. 217–18.

10 Joyce Hemlow with Jeanne M. Burgess and Althea Douglas, *A Catalogue of the Burney Family Correspondence 1749–1878* (New York: The New York Public Library; and Montreal and London: McGill-Queen's University Press, 1971).

11 See Burney to Christian Ignatius Latrobe

Church.[3] In November 1875 it appeared in print in a brief article by Marshall in *Concordia*,[4] a short-lived London music journal. Marshall's article was prompted by the interest aroused by the appearance earlier in the year in *Concordia* of a selection of Wesley's letters to Jacob concerning the promotion of Bach's music in England.[5] This was the first time any of these had been published; the complete collection appeared shortly afterwards in an edition by Wesley's daughter Eliza.[6] Marshall subsequently incorporated the *Concordia* transcripts in a handsome volume of Wesley materials[7] which was included with the over 450 volumes comprising the bulk of his collection of manuscript music which he sold to the British Museum in 1880–1881. The quotations of the letter in Lightwood's *Samuel Wesley, Musician*[8] and in Scholes's *The Great Dr. Burney*[9] presumably came from Marshall's *Concordia* article. The letter itself was sold along with other autograph letters from Marshall's collection at Sotheby's sale on June 26, 1884; the purchaser was W. H. Cummings, another leading British collector. It was not included in the sale of Cummings's own collection at Sotheby's on May 17–24, 1917, and it has not been possible to discover the identity of its later owners up to the time it was purchased by Hans and Rosaleen Moldenhauer. Its whereabouts were not known to Joyce Hemlow at the time of compilation of her *Catalogue of the Burney Family Correspondence*,[10] and as she did not include letters known only from printed sources, it does not appear there.

Burney's first meeting with Wesley had occurred during Wesley's childhood in the early 1770s, when he was one of the many distinguished musicians to whom Wesley had demonstrated his precocious talents. Thereafter, their paths did not cross again until early 1799, when a chance meeting at a dinner party led to the renewal of their acquaintance.[11] Contact between Burney and Wesley appears to have been initially sporadic, but the frequency of their letters and meetings increased dramatically following Wesley's discovery of the music of J. S. Bach some time in the spring or summer of 1807.[12] In the autumn of that year, in a letter now lost, Wesley wrote to Burney to inform him of his study of Bach and his almost religious enthusiasm for Bach's music;[13] he may also have taken the opportunity to voice his disagreement with the harsh criticisms of Bach that Burney had made in his *General History of Music* and in his more recent article on Bach in Rees's *Cyclopaedia*.[14]

Wesley's letter led to one of the most celebrated events in the history of the English Bach movement. At Burney's invitation, Wesley visited him at his apartments at Chelsea College to play to him from the "very curious & beautiful Copy" of *Das wohltemperirte Clavier* which J. S. Bach's son Carl Philipp Emanuel had presented to Burney on his visit to Hamburg in October 1772.[15] Wesley, who by this time was thoroughly familiar with *Das wohltemperirte Clavier* and had made his own manuscript copy from the Nägeli edition of around 1800,[16] was astonished to find that Burney's copy was only of Book I, and that it was so "full of *scriptural* Faults" as to make his performance from it difficult. Nonetheless, he was able by his playing to persuade Burney of the error of his former opinions and later reported to Jacob that Burney had "expressed his Wonder *how such abstruse harmony* and such perfect and enchanting Melody could have been so marvellously united."

This visit marked Burney's conversion to the Bach cause, and subsequent letters indicate Burney's continuing enthusiasm and the extent to which Wesley came to consult him for advice on how best to promote Bach's music by performances, lectures, and the publication of editions. By this time Burney rarely left his apartments, but Wesley kept him in touch with developments by letter, and he and his friends also took care to visit him and to give him private performances of their latest Bach discoveries. On one such occasion, in September 1809, Wesley (on the violin) and Jacob (on the piano) performed some or all of the violin sonatas, BWV 1014–1019, probably from a recently acquired copy of the Nägeli edition of around 1804.[17]

The Library of Congress letter relates to another such performance. This time it was of the *Goldberg Variations*, BWV 988, a work evidently completely new to Burney, and which Wesley himself had probably only recently acquired.[18] It is one

[ca. February 5, 1799] The James Marshall and Marie-Louise Osborn Collection, Yale University Library, New Haven, Connecticut (hereafter Osborn); Latrobe to Burney, February 7, 1799 (Osborn). I am grateful to Dr. Alvaro Ribeiro, SJ, for alerting me to the references to Wesley in these letters.

[12] In his manuscript *Reminiscences* of circa 1836 (BL, Add. MS 27593, quoted in Edwards, "Bach's Music in England," p. 653), Wesley states that he had first been introduced to Bach's music by the violinist and composer George Frederick Pinto, who lent him a copy of *Das wohltemperirte Clavier*. He gives no date for this event, but Pinto died on March 23, 1806. It would appear from Wesley's letters, however, that his effective conversion to the Bach cause did not take place until well into 1807.

[13] Details of the contents of this letter, of Burney's reply (also lost), and of Wesley's subsequent visit to Burney are given in Wesley's long letter to Jacob of September 17, 1808 (*Bach Letters*, 1–5), on which this and the following paragraph are based.

[14] *A General History of Music, from the Earliest Ages to the Present Period*, 4 vols. (London, 1776–89), vol. 3, p. 110, and vol. 4, pp. 594–95; modern ed., ed. Frank Mercer, 2 vols. (London: Foulis, 1935; repr. New York: Dover, 1957), vol. 2, pp. 96, 954–55; "Bach, Sebastian," in *Cyclopaedia: or, Universal Dictionary of Arts, Sciences and Literature*, ed. Abraham Rees, 39 vols. (1802–19), vol. 3, section 2, part 6, unpaginated (1804). For Burney's contributions to Rees's *Cyclopaedia*, see Roger Lonsdale, *Dr. Charles Burney: A Literary Biography* (Oxford: Clarendon Press, 1965), pp. 407–31, and his "Dr. Burney's 'Dictionary of Music'," *Musicology* 5 (1977): 159–71.

[15] See also Hans-Günter Ottenberg, trans. Philip J. Whitmore, *C. P. E. Bach* (Oxford: Oxford University Press, 1987), pp. 145–46; Lonsdale, op. cit., p. 118.

[16] BL, Add. MS 14330. See also Wesley to Crotch, November 25, 1808 (Norwich, Norfolk Record Office MS 11244, T 140A, quoted in Lightwood, op. cit., pp. 127–28):

"the Zurich edition, from which I made my MS. copy is *the only* one, on which any tolerable Dependence can be safely placed."

17 It was originally intended that Salomon should play the violin part, and Wesley the keyboard part. The change of plan was presumably because of Salomon's nonavailability: see Wesley to Jacob, September 4 [1809] (*Bach Letters*, pp. 31–32); Wesley to Burney, September 4, 1809 (Osborn); Wesley to Jacob, n.d. [September 1809] (*Bach Letters*, pp. 43–45).

18 There were two recent editions of the *Goldberg Variations: Trente Variations Fuguées pour Clavecin ou Pianoforte* (Zurich: Nägeli, [1800?]) and *Exercises pour le clavecin* (Vienna and Leipzig: Hoffmeister, [1803]). It would appear from Wesley's references to the "Thirty Variations" that it was the Nägeli edition that he knew. Wesley's own manuscript copy (BL, Add. MS 14334, ff. 59–81) was probably used at, and may have been made for, the performance in Burney's apartments.

19 BL, Add. MS 11730, f. 33, quoted in Scholes, op. cit., vol. 2, p. 217.

20 This was the six-octave instrument included in the sale of Burney's library on August 8, 1814, and described in the catalog as a "*very capital* grand piano-forte, *by Broadwood, with additional Keys, treble and bass, having 6 octaves*, in handsome mahogany case" (see *Catalogue of the Music Library of Charles Burney, sold in London, 8 August 1814* [BL annotated copy, Pressmark S.C. 1076(1)], facsimile ed. with an Introduction by A. Hyatt King (Amsterdam: Frits Knuf, 1973), p. 40). It was evidently a replacement for the instrument made for Burney in 1777 by John Joseph Merlin, for in his will of January 12, 1807, he described it as "my large Piano Forte with additional keys at the top and bottom, originally made by Merlin, with a Compass of six Octaves, the first that was ever constructed, expressly at my desire, for duets à Quatre Mains, in 1777," and later as the instrument made "by Broadwood in the Merlin case." Burney also included in his will his "small Piano Forte made by Broadwood, with additional keys in the Treble, an excellent instrument for a small

of four extant letters which discuss the arrangements which had to be made, and from them it is possible to reconstruct the sequence of events that led up to the performance in Burney's apartments on July 20, 1810.

By the time of the first letter, from Burney to Wesley of June 27, 1810,[19] it had been agreed that Wesley and Novello would visit Burney, and Burney had proposed a date in the following week. Wesley's reply is not extant, but it is evident from the subsequent correspondence that it contained the further suggestion that he and Novello should take the opportunity to give a performance of the *Goldberg Variations*. As Burney did not possess the requisite two-manual harpsichord, Wesley proposed that he and Novello should play the *Variations* as a duet on two pianos, using Burney's Broadwood grand[20] and another similar instrument which they would have specially transported to Chelsea for the purpose. Burney initially turned down this suggestion on the grounds of lack of space in his apartments and fear of the damage that might ensue, suggesting that Wesley and Novello might instead like to find a suitable piano shop where they could play the *Variations*.

The drawback to this arrangement, as Burney subsequently recognized, was that he himself would have no part in it, as he had made up his mind never again to go out "into the open air." On reflection, he decided that his desire to hear the *Variations* outweighed any worries about damage to his apartments, and that there would after all be enough room in his parlor, "when unbe-littered," for two grand pianos. The Library of Congress letter records this change of mind:

My dear Friend

Now my French Packet[21] is off my mind, I have time to think of your last plan of rehearsing the quips and q[u]iddities of the great S.B. to the best advantage, concerng wch I must have seemed very cold (in spite of the heat of the weather) by the enumeration of difficulties that, at first, occurred to me for want of Room sufficient for 2 large instruments of equal force & magnitude; & Time, in one day, to do justice to, and enjoy the effects of such learned and ingenious arcana—But, allowing the old adage, wch you

My dear Friend

Now my French Packet is off my mind, I have time to think of your last plan of rehearsing the quips and quiddities of the great S.B. to the best advantage, concerning wᶜʰ I must have seemed very cold (in spite of the heat of the weather) by the enumeration of difficulties that, at first, occurred to me for want of Room sufficient for 2 large instruments of equal force & magnitude; & Time, in one day, to do justice to, ~~[deleted]~~, and enjoy the effects of such learned and ingenious arcana —— But, allowing the old adage, wᶜʰ you have quoted, to be just: that "second thoughts are best"—— instead of sending you & Sigʳ Novello to a P.F. maker's to find 2 Instrumᵗ of equal magnitude, nicely tuned together; upon examining my little parlour, or keeping room, (in health & warm weather) I find, when unbe-littered, that there wᵈ be sufficient space for 2 such first-rate Giants to lie along side each other — & that when I thought of sending you & your Friend to a P.F. shop for trial of your 30 very Comical pieces (as the most learned, ingenious, & original productions of Haydn, Mozart, & Beethoven, are often said to be, by ignorant and vulgar hearers) I never once thought of my sweet & precious self, to whom your performance wᵈ be as inaudible as the music of the spheres — for I never intend going into the open air again —— But now, though I have caught a fresh cold, and have 2 decayed teeth in my upper jaws, that give me aᵒ acute twinge whenever I inhale fresh air; I beg, during the warm weather, your performance may be within my obtuse ear-shot, that I may acquaint the Large I shall meet wᵗʰ (post obit) how the wonderful wonders produced by the pen of the great S.B. have been played, as a game at all fours, by the zealous and indefatigable Messʳˢ Wesley and Novello. Therefore send your Instrument, name your day, or days, & your hours, before the end of the present month, & I hope nothing finister will occasion a new procrastination of our promised pleasure. C.B.

Suppose we decimate the 30 variations, & divide them into 3 Decads: performing 10 once or twice, if we like or dislike them much, each day? wᶜʰ will allow us time to breathe, digest, & judge.

---

have quoted, to be just: that "second thoughts are best"—instead of sending you & Sigʳ Novello to a P.F. maker's to find 2 Instrumᵗˢ of equal magnitude, nicely tuned together; upon examining my little parlour, or keeping room, (in heal[t]h & warm weather) I find, when unbe-littered, that there wᵈ be sufficient space for 2 such first-rate Giants to lie along side each other—& that when I thought of sending you & your Friend to a P.F. shop for trial of your 30 very *comical* pieces (as the most learned, ingenious, & original

room." This was presumably a square, and if he still possessed it in 1810, it would have been considered insufficiently powerful to balance his grand piano. For Burney and Merlin, and for Burney's will, see Scholes, op. cit., vol. 2, pp. 202–4, 260–73. Burney's grand is thought to be no longer extant: see Martha Novak Clinkscale, *Makers of the Piano 1700–1820* (Oxford: Oxford University Press, 1993), p. 46.

21 A letter from Burney to his daughter Mme. d'Arblay in Paris (Osborn: see Hemlow, *A Catalogue of the Burney Family Correspondence*, 58, where it is dated [*post* May 5, 1810]), the delayed despatch of which had evidently caused Burney problems because of wartime conditions. For Mme. d'Arblay's reply of September 16, 1810, see *The Journals and Letters of Fanny Burney (Madame d'Arblay)*, ed. Joyce Hemlow et al., 12 vols. (Oxford: Clarendon Press, 1975), vol. 6, pp. 58–90. I am grateful to Fr. Ribeiro for explaining this allusion.

productions of Haydn, Mozart, & Beethoven, are often said to be, by ignorant and vulgar hearers) I never once thought of my sweet & precious self, to whom your performance w⁴ be as inaudible as the music of the spheres—for I never intend going into the open air again—But now, though I have caught a fresh cold, and have 2 decayed teeth in my upper jaw, that give me a very acute twinge whenever I inhale fresh air; I beg, during the warm weather, your performance may be within my obtuse *ear-shot*, that I may acquaint the Larv[a]e I shall meet wᵗʰ (post obit.) how the wonderful wonders produced by the pen of the great S.B. have been played, as a game at *all fours*, by the zealous and indefatigable Messʳˢ Wesley and Novello.

Therefore send your Instrument, name your day, or days, & your hours, before the end of the present month, & I hope nothing sinister will occasion a new procrastination of our promised pleasure.

C. B.

Suppose we decimate the 30 variations, & divide them into 3 Decads; performing 10 once, or twice, if we like or dislike them much, each day? wᶜʰ will allow us time to breathe, digest, & judge.

Now that Burney had given his agreement, the arrangements for the transport of the piano could be put in train. In his reply,[22] Wesley readily accepted Burney's suggestion that he and Novello should visit Burney three times, while demurring at his plan for the "decimation" of the *Variations*:

With regard to your Plan of Decimation I cannot but think that as it is always a cruel one in the military Sense, so it would be partly, in our small musical Regiment of 30.—The whole Series will not employ much more than *one* Hour to pervade, & I must say, that I fear a considerable Degree of the immediate Contrast between the several Sections, would be diminished by a Chasm.—As the Variations are all upon *one* Theme, & that Theme is every where felt throughout, at least as strongly as the Characteristic Letter in a Greek Verb, there is no Probability of *your* letting any Part of them run to Waste.—However, the Permission to attend you *thrice*

[22] Wesley to Burney, July 17, 1810 (Osborn).

instead of once is a Temptation outweighing my Objections, & therefore you shall have just as few or as many of these queer *Chunes* (as we say at Bristol) as you may find palatable.

By the time of Burney's reply to Wesley and Novello two days later,[23] the delivery of the piano had been ordered for the following day, and all that was left was to make the final arrangements. Burney characteristically caps Wesley's representation of the accent of his native Bristol ("Chunes"), by adding his mimicry of the accent of his own native Shrewsbury ("*Waryations*," "gemmen") and an imitation of a German accent ("shtill petter auch coot"):

23 Burney to Wesley and Novello, July 19, 1810 (BL, Add. MS 11730, f. 35), quoted in Lightwood, op. cit., p. 133; and Scholes, op. cit., vol. 2, pp. 218–19.

If you c^d send your Lumber-d[a]y Instrum^t sooner than 10, to-morrow morn^g I sh^d be right glad; that it may be tuned in unison with mine: for if its pitch sh^d be altered, the *2 Giants* will not remain in perfect friend^p an hour. While the weather continues warm, I had rather wait on ye at 11, than 12 or 1— I am now entirely for the performance of the 30 *Waryations de suite*: as you two virtuous gemmen, doubtless, are so *parfet* in all these pretty *chunes*, that you'll go on as swimming from beginning to end, as if wind and tide were both strongly in your favour. I think the forti, i.e. *fortès*, may begin to storm these works of Engineer Bach, before 12. And if we have any time to spare, after being played over, we can *talk* them over—or (what wd be shtill petter auch coot) if little i were to say *bis* there might, may-hap, be time for a Da Capo. So *fin Dimani*, at least, God bless ye!

There are no retrospective references in the correspondence to the performance of the *Variations*. What in the end was evidently a single visit on July 20 appears to have been a great success: Novello's annotation to the letter refers to:

the very pleasant meeting we had together at the Doctor's apartments in Chelsea Hospital, when I played the whole of the "30 Variations" by Sebastian Bach, as Duetts with Sam Wesley, to the great delight of Burney, who acknowledged to us both, that he had formed a very inadequate opinion of Sebastian Bach's fertility of invention and versatility of style, till he had heard our performance of those extraordinary specimens of counterpoint, called the "30 Variations.["]

John Cage's "The Wonderful Widow of Eighteen Springs"

Lauriejean Reinhardt

JOHN CAGE'S SETTING OF "The Wonderful Widow of Eighteen Springs" signals the beginning of what would become a profound and enduring fascination with the writings of James Joyce. Subsequent to this setting, composed in the fall of 1942, Cage would return to Joyce repeatedly throughout his career, using Joyce's words as the basis not only for a variety of musical compositions,[1] but also a series of literary projects including the mesostichic[2] and chance-inspired "writings"[3] through *Finnegans Wake* and *Ulysses*.[3] It is *Finnegans Wake*, however, a novel Cage once described as "endless and attractive,"[4] that exerted the greatest influence on his work, and it is *Finnegans Wake* on which this early setting is based. The centrality of Joyce's novel to Cage's aesthetic outlook is captured in the composer's observation some forty years after his first encounter with the work that "we live, in a very deep sense, in the time of *Finnegans Wake*."[5]

Cage composed "The Wonderful Widow" in response to a commission from the soprano Janet Fairbank (1903–1947), whom he had met during his brief appointment at the Chicago Institute of Design in 1941–1942. Fairbank was an ambitious amateur singer from a wealthy family with close ties to the Chicago arts community. Her grandfather, the turn-of-the-century industrialist Nathaniel K. Fairbank, had been a trustee and major benefactor of the Art Institute of Chicago, the Chicago Symphony Orchestra and the Chicago Club. Her mother was the novelist and political activist Janet Ayer Fairbank; and her aunt, Margaret Ayer Barnes, was a popular, Pulitzer prize-winning author. While her own career included occasional appearances with the Chicago Symphony Orchestra, the Chicago Opera, the Grant Park Orchestra, and the San Carlo Opera Company, the younger Fairbank would eventually make her mark as a proponent of contemporary art song.

[1] These include: the *Concerto for Piano and Orchestra* (1958), which features a vocal solo that draws on *Finnegans Wake;* a choral project inspired by the celebrated Ten Thunderclaps from *Finnegans Wake,* conceived in 1967 but realized only in 1982 as *Atlas Borealis; Child of Tree* (1975) for piano and amplified plant material, inspired by a phrase used in "The Wonderful Widow"; the radio montage *Roaratorio, an Irish Circus on Finnegans Wake* (1979); "Nowth upon Nacht" (1984), a companion setting to "The Wonderful Widow"; and *ASLSP* (1985), a piano piece inspired by the final paragraph of *Finnegans Wake*.

[2] "Mesostic" is a coinage for one of Cage's writing techniques. As he explains in *I-VI* (Cambridge, Mass.: Harvard University Press, 1990), p. 1, "I write texts. Most of the time they're mesostics. It was Norman O. Brown who said mesostics describes what you are writing. Like acrostics, mesostics are written in the conventional way horizontally, but at the same time they follow a vertical rule, down the middle not down the edge as in an acrostic, a string which spells a word or name, not necessarily connected with what is being written, though it may be."

[3] These include: the series of five "writings" through *Finnegans Wake*, dating from 1976–1980; *James Joyce, Marcel Duchamp, Erik Satie: An Alphabet* (1980); and additional essays and lectures that Cage acknowledged as generally indebted to Joyce, many of which are collected in *M: Writings '67–'72* (Middletown, Conn.: Wesleyan University Press, 1973), *Empty Words: Writings '73–'78* (Middletown, Conn.: Wesleyan University Press, 1979) and *I-VI* (Cambridge, Mass.: Harvard University Press, 1990). Significantly, Joyce also provided the basis for one of Cage's final works, *Muoyce II (Writing through Ulysses,*

Throughout the 1940s, she commissioned and performed over one hundred songs by recognized and aspiring composers (including Virgil Thomson, David Diamond, Francis Poulenc, Benjamin Britten, Lou Harrison, Olivier Messiaen, Ned Rorem, and Gottfried von Einem), which she presented in Chicago and at an annual series of recitals at New York's Carnegie Chamber Music Hall. Endowed with modest vocal abilities, Fairbank nevertheless endeared herself to critics and advocates of modern music by her tasteful and intelligent performances and her tireless promotion of contemporary music. Her success in this regard can be measured by the fact that publishers came to purchase the songs she commissioned even before they had been premiered. Fairbank herself felt that her greatest achievement lay in acquainting American audiences with the wealth of serious vocal literature being written by contemporary American composers. Her interest in Cage proved prescient, for the Carnegie Hall recital that occasioned the setting of "The Wonderful Widow" coincided with the composer's now-famous concert at the Museum of Modern Art, an event that placed the young Cage at the vanguard of modern music.[6]

The choice of song text for the Fairbank commission was apparently left to Cage, for he later recalled scanning a copy of *Finnegans Wake* (purchased shortly after it appeared in book form in 1939, but left largely unread) in search of a lyrical passage to set. He eventually decided on a memorable vignette of the infant Isobel (556.1–22) who, among other names, is identified as "the wonderful widow of eighteen springs."[7] The melodious quality of the passage is indebted not only to its immediate context—a lullaby for a beautiful child—or the remarkable consonance, clarity, and fluidity of Joyce's language, but also to the novelist's admission that one of his chief inspirations for the passage was the traditional tune "The Woods So Wild."[8] Cage's song text, condensed and rearranged from Joyce's original, only intensifies the lyrical dimension of the passage, for it highlights both the sylvan imagery with which the child is described ("wildwood's eyes and primarose hair," "like some losthappy leaf," "like blowing flower stilled") and a number of key alliterative phrases ("in mauves of moss and daphnedews," "win me, woo me, wed me, ah weary me!") that give rise to the passage's lilting lyricism.

1992), the premiere of which was preempted by the composer's death in August 1992.

4 "About Roaratorio: An Irish Circus on Finnegans Wake," in *Dream Chamber/About Roaratorio*, ed. Robert O' Driscoll (Toronto: The Black Brick Press, 1982), p. 76.

5 See John Cage and Richard Kostelanetz, "Talking about Writings through Finnegans Wake," in *A John Cage Reader in Celebration of his 70th Birthday*, comp. and ed. Peter Gena and Jonathan Brent, suppl. ed. Don Gillespie (New York/London/Frankfurt: C.F. Peters Corporation, 1982), p. 146.

6 Fairbank's career and her role as a patron of modern music have yet to arouse serious interest among the scholarly community. The information above has been gleaned from miscellaneous sources, including: an article by Edith Borroff that briefly outlines Fairbank's career and inventories part of her creative estate, "The Fairbank Collection," *College Music Syposium* 16 (1976): 105–22; an unsigned article entitled "Song Plugger" found in *Time*, 48 (December 16, 1946): 50; various obituaries for Fairbank following her death on September 27, 1947; and reviews of her recitals, including those discussed below.

7 The details surrounding Cage's early familiarity with *Finnegans Wake* and the text chosen for the Fairbank commission are reported in: John Cage, introduction to *Writings through Finnegans Wake* (Tulsa, Oklahoma: University of Tulsa, 1978), n.p., and "Writing for the Second Time through Finnegans Wake," in *Empty Words*, p. 133; John Cage and Klaus Schöning, "Laughtears: Gespräch über 'Roaratorio. Ein irischer Circus über Finnegans Wake' Auszüge," in *John Cage: Kunst als Grenzbeschreitung: John Cage und die Moderne*, ed. Ulrich Bischoff (Düsseldorf: Richter-Verlag, 1991), p. 83; and David Revill, *The Roaring Silence: John Cage, A Life* (New York: Arcade Publishing, 1992), pp. 82, 254.

8 Richard Ellmann, ed., *Letters of James Joyce* (New York: Viking Press, 1966), vol. 3, pp. 138–39. Joyce's attribution of "The Woods So Wild" to William Byrd (1543–1623), which is reiterated throughout the literature, is misleading. Joyce's inspiration for the passage was probably one of

THE WONDERFUL WIDOW OF EIGHTEEN SPRINGS

John Cage

Cage the composer imprints his unique stamp on the setting in a number of ways. By deleting much of the original punctuation, he negates the ornate, clausal rhythms that underlie the structure and sense of Joyce's original passage. A further negational effect is created by placing all words in capital letters. What results is a depersonalization of Joyce's literary "voice," an early intimation perhaps of Cage's desire to release art from the constraints of individual taste and self-expression. Cage's approach to melodic style contributes likewise to the nonexpressive neutrality of the setting. The melody unfolds as a hypnotic incantation based on three pitches only. According to Cage, these pitches should be understood as delimiting a basic register rather than serving as fixed tones. He explains that the melodic line may be transposed to any pitch level, "in order to employ a low and comfortable range," and he further advises the vocalist to sing without the aid of vibrato, "as in folk-singing."[9] Despite the chantlike reserve of the vocal line, Cage maintains an emotional involvement with the text. Out of Joyce's fractured phrases, he has shaped a coherent, sensitively structured song text consisting of an opening section that lovingly describes the infant Isobel, a climactic section based on a series of action verbs and alliterative trochees ("win me, woo me, wed me") and a dénouement that contemplates additional names for the child ("Night Isobel, Sister Isobel, Saintette Isobel, Madame Isa Veuve La Belle"). On a musical level, Cage imbues the melody with a sense of psychological purpose and rhetorical continuity by the deliberate rise and fall of the vocal line. For example, he uses the lower, adjacent pair of notes for the basic functions of recitation and cadence, with the gap created by the third, upper note serving as an element of contrast. Indeed, Cage openly acknowledged that his musical ideas had been inspired by "impressions received from the text."[10]

The true hallmark of the setting is not Cage's approach to melodic style, however, but his innovative approach to the piano accompaniment. Doubtless guided by his recent experiments with the prepared piano in *Bacchanale* (1940), Cage created a percussive accompaniment based on various knocks and taps produced by the pianist's knuckles and fingers at different spots on the outside of the instrument. Instructions regarding the interpretation of Cage's notation are provided in

numerous turn-of-the-century arrangements of the Tudor court song "As I walked the Wode so wylde." The song is associated with Byrd, not by way of a song setting, but rather a set of keyboard variations that appeared in the seventeenth-century *Fitzwilliam Virginal Book*. Since Joyce disposed of much of his library, his direct source for the tune remains open to question. One possibility that unites all of the evidence cited above is Granville Bantock's vocal arrangement of the tune, entitled "The Woods So Wild" and published in his *One Hundred Songs of England* (Boston: Oliver Ditson Co., 1914), see esp. pp. xiv, 14.

[9] See his introductory notes to the score, *The Wonderful Widow of Eighteen Springs* (New York/London/Frankfurt: C.F. Peters Corporation, 1961), n.p.

[10] See Cage's notes to *The 25-Year Retrospective Concert of the Music of John Cage* (1959), private issue recording by George Avakian (K08Y 1499–1504), n.p.

the introductory comments to the score. Round note heads, for example, are to be played with the fingers, whereas x-shaped note heads are to be played with the knuckles. The lowest space on the staff indicates the underside of the piano. Note especially the lack of clefs on both of the piano's "percussion staves." The piano accompaniment proceeds largely independently of the vocal part; in fact, Cage maintained that he had "no rhythmic structure or method" in mind as he composed the piece.[11] What the voice and piano parts share in common is an emphasis on simple additive rhythmic patterns and indeterminate sounds rather than determinate pitches.

Cage's setting of "The Wonderful Widow" soon became one of his most frequently performed compositions,[12] yet the critical response to the song following its premiere by Fairbank was less than favorable. Writing for the journal *Modern Music*, Arthur Berger counted "The Wonderful Widow" among the works on Fairbank's program that were "less hackneyed and cheap," but in the same breath rejected the song as "juvenile and unfertile."[13] The critic for the *New York Herald Tribune*, identified only as J.D.B., exercised a certain impartiality by acknowledging that he had found "none of the [evening's] songs particularly worthwhile."[14] Writing for the *New York Times*, Nicholas Slonimsky reserved critical judgment on the evening's repertoire (which included selections by Virgil Thomson, David Diamond, David Van Vactor, Ernst Bacon, Béla Wilda, Harry K. Lamont, Paul Bowles, Paul Creston, Theodore Chanler, John Sacco, Mary Howe, and Charles Naginski), but he commended Fairbank for her effort and accomplishments.[15] A radio rebroadcast of "The Wonderful Widow" in 1944 also elicited an unfavorable response. Charles Mills found the song "disappointingly self-enclosed and eccentrically hopeless," adding "I hope this example is unrepresentative of [Cage's] talents."[16] One of the few favorably disposed toward the song was Susan Thiemann, who, in reviewing the published score in 1961, offered the following, perceptive observations:

> This essentially rhythmic speech set against a patterned percussive accompaniment cannot be considered a song in the usual sense. Cage, however, is such an innovator that one often loses sight of the fact that if one does not expect

[11] Ibid.

[12] Robert Dunn's catalogue of Cage's works, compiled in the early 1960s, lists eleven performances of the song, including four by the artistic duo of Cathy Berberian and Luciano Berio; see *John Cage* (New York: Henmar Press, Inc., 1962), p. 22.

[13] Arthur Berger, "Spring Season, 1943," *Modern Music* 20 (1943): 256.

[14] J.D.B., "Janet Fairbank Is Heard in American Song Recital," *New York Herald Tribune*, March 6, 1943, p. 8.

[15] N.[icholas] S.[lonimsky], "Janet Fairbanks [sic] Heard: Soprano Presents Elaborate List of Songs, with 12 Novelties," *New York Times*, March 6, 1943, p. 8. Additional reviews of a similar nature may be found in *Musical America* 63 (March 25, 1943): 18, and *The Musical Courier* 127 (March 20, 1943): p. 9.

[16] Charles Mills, "Over the Air," *Modern Music* 21 (March/April 1944): p. 191.

conventional sounds, his music is often very well constructed. Here, for example, the composer weaves a hypnotically compelling pattern of rhythmic tension and relaxation, akin to certain non-Western music, which is very appropriate for Joyce's moody prose. The climaxing syncopation on the alliterative passage "win me, woo me, wed me" is most effective.[17]

[17] Susan Thiemann, "Music Reviews," *Notes* 19 (March 1962): p. 346.

The document shown here, an autograph copy of the song prepared by the composer on a transparent sheet, speaks to both the publication history of Cage's compositions and the status of music publishing after World War II. Cage later recalled that, until the early 1960s, the performance of his music was problematic due to the fact that he had not secured a publisher. (For Fairbank's performance of "The Wonderful Widow," he had had to prepare separate autograph copies of the song; Fairbank's copy is currently preserved with her estate as deposited at the Newberry Library in Chicago.) As Cage tells it, he chose the firm of C.F. Peters one day in 1960, while browsing through a New York telephone book. His inquiries over the phone were met with enthusiasm by Walter Hinrichsen, founder of the firm's American branch and an aficionado of contemporary American music; Cage signed an exclusive contract with Peters over lunch that very day.[18]

[18] See John Cage and Richard Kostelanetz, "Autobiography," in *Conversing with Cage* (New York: Limelight Editions, 1988), p. 21; and the composer's "Statement by John Cage," in *An Introduction to Music Publishing*, ed. Carolyn Sachs (New York: C.F. Peters Corporation, 1981), p. 17.

One of the composer's first works to be offered by Peters, "The Wonderful Widow" was printed by means of a process known alternately as diazotype, ozalid, or whiteprint. Popular during the years immediately following World War II, this photographic process allowed for the facsimile reproduction of a composer's manuscript, a method that was considerably cheaper and more efficient than engraving. The copy-ready manuscript shown herein was used for the Peters edition; note especially the indications for the size of reduction and the places on the sheet that have been cut out with a razor to eliminate signs of smudging.

Pablo Casals: A Letter Written from Exile

Douglas W. Foard

THERE IS A REMARKABLE POIGNANCY to this document written by Pablo Casals on May 6, 1940. Penned in the village of Prades, France, only a few miles from the Spanish border, it breathes the anguish of exile, the pain of shattered dreams, and a prophetic foreboding about the future.

Casals had moved to Prades not long after the sagging fortunes of the Spanish Republic had persuaded him in 1938 to abandon his native land and return to the relative safety of France. He had been a conspicuous champion of the Republican cause in Spain, but as one provincial capital after another succumbed to General Franco's forces in the year of the Munich Pact, the great cellist had been obliged to chose between exile or the notorious proceedings of a Nationalist military tribunal. Casals had prudently chosen the former course.[1]

Events had demonstrated the wisdom of his decision. The last Republican hopes for a military victory that might have produced a negotiated settlement to the Spanish Civil War evaporated in November 1938, as General Franco's armies beat back a desperate Republican offensive on the Ebro River and stood poised to invade Catalonia, Casals's native province and a former bastion of the Second Republic. Twenty thousand Republican soldiers had perished in the operation and perhaps another fifty-five thousand were wounded or captured. Christmas 1938 brought a Nationalist counter-offensive, which within a month captured the Catalan capital, Barcelona, and on February 18, 1939, carried the Generalísimo's forces to the French border.

Pablo Casals's bitter trip into exile in 1938 had been the harbinger of a tragic tide that would follow the next year. The

[1] Albert E. Kahn, *Joys and Sorrows: Reflections by Pablo Casals* (New York: Simon and Schuster, 1970), pp. 224–29.

exhausted Republican armies disintegrated as the Nationalist forces poured into Catalonia and tens of thousands fled northward seeking safety from reprisals in the French Republic. According to one authoritative source, "The number of refugees who crossed into France from January to March 1939 ranges from a total of 400,000 to 527,000, of which approximately 220,000 were members of the military."[2]

Only three years earlier, at the beginning of the civil war in Spain, the French government had been in the hands of Léon Blum, a socialist, who had evidenced much sympathy but little tangible support for the Republican regime in Madrid. In 1939, it was Edouard Daladier, a signatory of the Munich Pact, who ruled in Paris. While he opened the Pyrenean border to the humbled Spanish Republicans, Daladier offered them a meager welcome. "They were received as though they were tramps," one eye-witness grumbled. "I have never seen eyes of such anger and helplessness as those of the Spaniards," he continued. "They stood as turned to stone, and they did not understand."[3]

Other sources recall a much friendlier reception; yet it cannot be doubted that the sudden arrival of nearly half a million hungry refugees constituted a considerable drain on the French Republic's available resources. The president of the former Basque government, José Antonio de Aguirre, personally observed the migration and commented, "For this immense caravan of people without country and without homes there was no hope of hospitality other than the concentration camp."[4]

Fifteen of these camps were established in France during the course of 1939. To be near them and to his own beloved Catalonia, Pablo Casals had moved from Paris to Prades to observe conditions for himself and to offer whatever assistance he could to his fellow countrymen. His letter of May 6, 1940, begins by thanking two acquaintances for their thirty-dollar contribution to the refugees' cause.

Although the term *concentration camp* had not yet acquired the murderous connotations that Hitler's Third Reich would add to it, the French versions of 1939 were clearly not intended to

[2] James E. Cortada, "Republican Refugees" in *Historical Dictionary of the Spanish Civil War*, James W. Cortada, ed. (Westport, Conn.: Greenwood Press, 1982), pp. 414–15.

[3] Paul Preston, *The Spanish Civil War* (New York: Grove Press, 1986), p. 166.

[4] José Antonio de Aguirre, *Escape vía Berlín*, intro. Robert P. Clark (Reno: University of Nevada Press, 1991), p. 105.

Prades 6 mai 1940

Cher ami,

Je reçois avec tant de plaisir votre lettre, si bonne, et j'apprécie profondément votre chèque de 30 Dollars — Recevez mes remerciements de cœur et je vous prie de remercier pour moi Messieurs Zalkanes et Sauroma — Aujourd'hui même j'ai visité la Maternité d'Elne (Pyr. Or.) et j'ai pu distribuer l'équivalent de votre don — Je m'occupe beaucoup de cette Maternité suisse d'Elne — Les femmes, Toutes espagnoles, et les bébés y sont admirablement soignées — mais ces femmes entrent et sortent sans un sou et c'est bon de leur faire de temps à temps un petit cadeau en argent pour se procurer de petites choses nécessaires —

Les camps sont plus dégagés maintenant à cause de la formation de Compagnies de Travail, mais étant militarisés [...] ne gagnent que 50 centimes par jour —. Les hommes non valides — les femmes et les enfants partout dans les camps de concentration. Il faut aider tout cela et je peux encore le faire quoique j'épuise tout ce que je possède — En Espagne on a confisqué Tous mes biens — même ma maison. Tant que je demeurerai pour la tâche que je me suis imposée je resterai ici —

Je ne sais pas si l'Amérique se rend assez compte de ce qui se passe ici — Il y a une bête féroce qui ravage tout et qui par le crime et la terreur grandit et asservit une nation après l'autre — L'indignation que cet état de choses peut provoquer chez vous ou partout ailleurs n'a plus de valeur — même valeur morale — La seule attitude digne est l'action — car il faut tuer la bête qui, après Tout, menace Tout le monde — L'Angleterre et la France, en se défendant, elles défendent Toutes les autres Nations et celles-ci ne peuvent pas se croiser les bras et laisser que les Alliés se Tuent en attendant.

Saluez les amis.
En sincère affection
votre

Pablo Casals

encourage long-term occupancy. In 1970, Casals still had the following bitter recollections of the accommodations accorded to his countrymen:

> The scenes I witnessed might have been from Dante's *Inferno*. Tens of thousands of men and women and children were herded together like animals, penned in by barbed wire, housed—if one can call it that—in tents and crumbling shacks. There were not sanitation facilities or provisions for medical care. There was little water and barely enough food to keep the inmates from starvation. The camp at Argelès was typical. Here more than one hundred thousand refugees had been massed in open areas among sand dunes along the seashore. Though it was winter, they had been provided with no shelter whatsoever—many had burrowed holes in the wet sand to protect themselves from the pelting rains and bitter winds. The driftwood they gathered for fires to warm themselves was soon exhausted. Scores had perished from exposure, hunger, and disease.[5]

5 Kahn, op. cit., p. 233.

As shocking as conditions proved to be for the Spanish Republicans at Argelès, Barcerès (70,000 residents), and Saint Cyprien (30,000 residents), those who found refuge in them "were among the lucky ones," writes Paul Preston in his *Spanish Civil War.* Across the border, he claims, General Franco's contempt for the Republic's defenders revealed itself, "in the labor camps, the two million prisoners, and the 200,000 executions on which his dictatorship was built."[6] Stanley Payne, another student of the Franco regime, disputes these figures and reminds his readers that:

6 Preston, op. cit., p. 166.

> Republican exiles who escaped to France were not free from imprisonment or death. Many were held in camps by French authorities for months under harsh conditions little or no better than those of some of the imprisoned in Spain, and German occupation forces later deported thousands to imprisonment or slave labor in Germany.[7]

7 Stanley G. Payne, *The Franco Regime* (Madison: University of Wisconsin Press, 1987), p. 224n.

While he could do little for the Republican veterans who labored in Franco's prison camps, Casals made the plight of the Spanish refugees in France his own. For the next several months, he embarked upon a furious schedule of fund-raising and benefit concerts whose proceeds were devoted to feeding and housing the residents of Argelès and its counterparts in Pyrenean France.[8] His letter of May 6 is a testimonial to the passion which targeted his genius to that enterprise. One factor which had prolonged the Spanish Civil War had been the hopes of the Republic's leadership that the violence which had been inflicted on their homeland would spill over into a general European conflict, obliging England and France at last to support the Second Republic against Franco and his German and Italian allies. Ironically, only six months after the Nationalist armies marched into Madrid and the Franco regime was accorded diplomatic recognition by the Western democracies, Nazi Germany invaded Poland and the second great European war of the century had begun.

[8] Kahn, pp. 234–35.

Hitler's armies had sliced through Poland at breathtaking speed. The same aircraft which previously had battered Madrid and flattened Guernica now screamed down at Warsaw and shattered Polish defenses. Reflecting on these events, small wonder that Casals would write, "A ferocious beast is abroad that ravages everything and through crime and terror enslaves one nation after another."

He and thousands like him had understood the Spanish Civil War as a struggle against the beast called "Fascism." That it lurked in Spain there could be no doubt. The Fascist movement there had styled itself the "Falange" and like its counterparts elsewhere in Europe had extolled political violence, imperialism, militarism, dictatorship, and totalitarianism. With Franco's victory, the Falange had become a part of the nation's political establishment and the regime borrowed freely from its symbols and slogans. Falangists occupied key posts in the Franco government and the movement's adherents were not at all shy about urging in great public demonstrations that Spain now join its former German allies and enter the war against France. "Death to France," they shouted noisily from the plazas in Madrid.[9]

[9] Stanley G. Payne, *Falange: A History of Spanish Fascism* (Stanford: Stanford University Press, 1961), pp. 206–211; see also, Benjamin Welles, *Spain: The Gentle Anarchy* (New York: Praeger, Inc., 1965), p. 217.

Across the border at Prades, Casals was writing his friends that, "England and France in defending themselves are defending humanity as well." On May 6, 1940, however, it was not proving a very spirited defense. Allied bombs had not rained down on Berlin in retaliation for German depredations against Warsaw nor had Allied armies sallied forth from the protection of the Maginot defenses to capture German cities in the West. So far, this newest European conflict had proved to be a desultory affair marked primarily by angry speeches, isolated actions, and Polish suffering.

In the concentration camps in southern France, the onset of the war had actually brought some improvements for the resident Spaniards. As former Basque President Aguirre recalled, "The Basques…felt the cause of France to be their own, and 50,000 Basque immigrants signed the pledge offering to serve either at the front or in the factories, in this new battle for freedom."[10] Casals's May 6 letter also notes that, "The mood at the camps has improved since the creation of the Labor Battalions." At the very moment that the Falangists in Madrid were calling for the destruction of France, thousands of former Spanish Republicans rallied to its defense.

In spite of Casals's characterization of the enemy of that springtime as "the beast that threatens the world," it was clear that the animal had changed its spots in the year that had elapsed since the end of the Spanish conflict and the onset of this new Great War. "Madrid shall be the Graveyard of Fascism," the proud banners of the Republic had proclaimed in the autumn of 1936 as the Spanish capital successfully resisted bombardment by German planes, Italian tanks, and Franco's legions. Across the globe, the conflict was portrayed by those who sympathized with the Spanish Republic as an epic duel between the force of democracy (the "Popular Front") and the proponents of Fascism. This Manichaean appreciation of the civil war in Spain was abetted by Soviet propaganda since the USSR was the only great power openly to support the Republic. The fact that General Franco's cause was sustained by German aviation and Italian armor seemed only to validate the view that for some reason Spain had been chosen as the battlefield between two of the twentieth century's most powerful ideas.

The Hitler-Stalin Pact of August 1939 shattered that simplistic interpretation of events. By that instrument, the Soviet Union joined Nazi Germany in partitioning Poland and in echoing

[10] Aguirre, op. cit., p. 105.

Hitler's propaganda against the "plutocratic democracies." The Popular Front ideal had perished and now England and France stood alone against "the beast."

Four days after Casals wrote to his friends from Prades, the beast struck again—this time against France itself. On May 10, 1940, the German armored movements were set in motion which would flank the Maginot line and bring the Third French Republic to its knees. By the terms of a humiliating peace treaty signed only six weeks after the onset of the German attack, what remained of France had become a German satellite nation with its capital as Vichy. Prades and the nearby Spanish concentration camps were at its mercy.

"With the surrender of France and the establishment of the Vichy regime under the aging Marshall Pétain," Casals would later recall, "our situation at Prades became increasingly precarious." After one failed effort to escape to the United States, this internationally celebrated champion of the Spanish Republic endured the next several years under the watchful eye of Vichy security forces, haunted all the while by the prospect of sudden arrest and increasing privation. His liberation came only with the collapse of the French collaborationist regime.

"Throughout the dark years of the war," he later confessed, "I had longed for that day when victory would mean the end of fascism and the liberation of the nations enslaved by it." The events of 1945 would disappoint him. Casals observed, "Though Hitler and Mussolini had been crushed, the fascist dictatorship they had fostered in Spain remained in power." When the victorious Western democracies eschewed intervention in his homeland to bring down the Franco dictatorship, Pablo Casals cancelled future concert performances, returned to exile in Prades, and refused all efforts to entice him back to Spain while the despised "Caudillo" ruled from Madrid.[11] Franco survived Casals by two years. The cellist's exile, which seemed so circumstantial in May 1940, proved to be permanent.

[11] Kahn, op. cit., pp. 236–38 and 256–58.

Mario Castelnuovo-Tedesco's "Ozymandias"

Massimo Ossi

IN THE LATE 1950s Hans Moldenhauer began an extensive correspondence with Mario Castelnuovo-Tedesco that continued until the composer's death in 1968. In addition to some 134 letters to the collector, the Archives include a wealth of scores that the composer sent to Moldenhauer, the result of what the composer, writing in 1959, called his "library cleaning." Among the musical items are sketches and preparatory materials, including those for several of the Shakespeare overtures and for the cycle for guitar and narrator setting selections from Juan Ramón Jiménez's collection of prose poems *Platero y yo,* as well as autograph scores for major works such as the Concerto for Guitar and Orchestra, op. 99, composed for Andrés Segovia in 1938–1939, just before the composer's move to America.

Castelnuovo-Tedesco left his native Italy for the United States in 1939; of Jewish descent, he sought to escape the anti-Semitic atmosphere of Benito Mussolini's rule. By 1940, after a brief period in New York, he settled in Beverly Hills, California, where he remained until his death. A student of Ildebrando Pizzetti, Castelnuovo-Tedesco had been composing actively since the first decade of the century, and his reputation was well established by the time he left Italy: several major orchestral works had received premieres in Europe and the United States under the direction of Arturo Toscanini and Sir John Barbirolli and with such soloists as Jascha Heifetz and Gregor Piatigorsky. His arrival in California coincided with the beginning of a long period of great productivity. In the early 1940s he began composing film scores (his earliest was *Tortilla Flat* in 1942, and he went on to write over one hundred more between 1942 and 1956). He also produced a variety of solo and chamber compositions, ranging from songs with piano and other accompaniment to pieces for guitar, for which Castelnuovo-Tedesco is perhaps best known, as well as a number of large-scale works, including four operas, two ballets, five oratorios and other choral pieces, six symphonic Shakespeare overtures, several orchestral works, and concertos for guitar, violin, and other solo instruments.

The letter of February 6, 1959, stands as an example of the range of musical matters included in Castelnuovo-Tedesco's "library cleaning." It introduces a group of eighteen items, (see Table of Works), including, as the composer wrote to Moldenhauer,

> 1) old music, "middle-aged" music, recent music; 2) published music, unpublished music, music which will never be published!; 3) good music, mediocre music, bad music (I don't want you to think that I always write good music!).

As the last comment suggests, Castelnuovo-Tedesco was disarmingly and charmingly candid in assessing the works he was sending to Moldenhauer. The fantasy on Donizetti's *Daughter of the Regiment* was "an amusing pastiche" but "too long"; *Liberty, Mother of the Exiles* he characterized as "another of my choral songs, and *a bad one*!"; the Chopin transcriptions were "another of my *sins*!" done because "the American publishers, who refused to publish my original music, were asking for transcriptions."

Not all was bad, of course, and the composer singled out *The Fiery Furnace*, the *Six Proverbs of Solomon*, and the *Sacred Service* as works he particularly liked. The last held a great deal of personal significance: written in 1943, it marked the end of what Castelnuovo-Tedesco regarded as his "bad years" of 1939–1942, his first as an expatriate, and the composer wrote that "with this work my 'recovery' started." It was dedicated to the memory of his mother, who had died the year after he had arrived in America, and, he wrote to Moldenhauer, "[it] contains some of my most moving pages."

Among the pieces listed in the letter was also "Ozymandias." It dates from 1944, and according to the composer's account it, too, records a personal reaction, in this case to the news that on July 24–25, 1943, the Fascist Grand Council had deposed and

Table of Works
Items listed in the letter of February 6, 1959

1) *Due Canti Greci* (1916, for mixed chorus, unpublished, no op. number)
2) Stars, "four sketches for piano" (1940, unpublished)
3) *Nocturne in Hollywood* (1941, for piano, unpublished, no op. number)
4) *The Daughter of the Regiment*, "a phantasy for violin and piano on themes of Donizetti" (1941, op. 110; only two movements, "Valse" and "Romance," published)
5) *The Mermaid Tavern* (1962, unpublished, op. 113, No. 1; versions for solo voice and for chorus)
6) *Sacred Service (for the Sabbath eve)* (1943, op. 122; only the organ interludes were published)
7) *Ozymandias* (1944, for solo voice and piano, unpublished, op. 124, No.1)
8) *Candide*, "six illustrations for a novel by Voltaire for piano" (1944, published as op. 123)
9) *Liberty, Mother of the Exiles*, choral song (1944, unpublished, no op. number)
10 and 11) Transcriptions for violin and piano of Chopin's *11 Preludes* (1946) and *Fantasie-Impromptu* (no date; neither was published)
12) *Psyche* (1951, song, published as op. 113, No. 5)
13) *Six Proverbs of Solomon* (1953, for male chorus a cappella, unpublished, op. 168)
14) *Songs of Oceanides* (from Aeschylus, *Prometheus Bound*; 1954, op. 171; versions for women's chorus, two flutes, and harp, and for chorus and piano; the version for chorus and piano was published)
15) *Two sonatas for trumpet and piano* (1955, unpublished, op. 179; the packet included a separate trumpet part, not in the composer's hand)
16) *Cherry-Ripe*, "a Madrigal for Mixed Chorus" (1955, unpublished, no op. number)
17) *The Fiery Furnace* (cantata for baritone, children—or women's—chorus, and piano, originally scored with an accompaniment of organ and percussion; 1958, to be published as op. 183)
18) *Pastorale and Rondo* (1958, for clarinet, violin, cello, and piano, unpublished, op. 185)

arrested Mussolini. Although Mussolini was freed from prison by German commandos in September 1943 and managed to assemble a rogue government in the small town of Salò on the shores of Lake Garda until April 1945 when he was finally captured on his way to Switzerland and shot, the events of July 1943 represented the turning point in the war, preparing the way for the Italian government's capitulation to the invading Allied forces.

It was presumably to the first wave of optimism following the fall of the Fascist dictatorship that "Ozymandias" belongs, although the historical circumstances surrounding the genesis of this song suggest either that the composer, writing some fifteen years later, may have misremembered the date of its composition as having been later than it actually was, or that he waited at least several months—into 1944—before setting the text to music. As he wrote to Moldenhauer:

> *Ozymandias*. A song on a poem by Shelley (1944, unpublished, which should be op. 124, Nr. 1). Raymond Gram Swing, the commentator, read this poem at the radio the evening of Mussolini's downfall, and I set it to music…; but no publisher ever wanted to publish this "gloomy song" (although it was sung in concert). Anyway this is the first *autograph*.

The association of "Ozymandias," Shelley, Mussolini and Castelnuovo-Tedesco draws a neat historical rectangle. According to the Greek historian Diodorus Siculus, the "Tomb of Osymandias" was the remains of the Theban *Ramesseum*, the funerary temple of Ramses II (1279–13 BC) which was famous for its fifty-seven-foot statue of the Pharaoh ("Osymandyas" was a corruption of Ramses's prenomen, Usima re). In Diodorus's account, the temple carried this inscription:

> King of Kings am I, Osymandyas. If anyone would know how great I am and where I lie, let him surpass one of my works.[1]

Interest in Egyptian antiquity ran high in the late eighteenth and early nineteenth centuries, following the discovery of the Rosetta stone in 1799 and its subsequent decipherment,

[1] See *Diodorus of Sicily, with an English Translation* by C. H. Oldfather (London: William Heinemann, 1933), vol. 1, pp. 166–69, and also Anne Burton, *Diodorus Siculus: Book I, A Commentary* (Leiden: E. J. Brill, 1972), pp. 147–48.

269 So. Clark Drive   Feb. 6, 1959
Beverly Hills, Calif.

Dear Hans,

The results of some more „library cleaning",
which I am going to send you one of these days...
In the meantime some „explanations"... There is a little
of everything: 1) old music, „middle-aged" music, recent
music; 2) published music, unpublished music, music... which
will never be published!; 3) good music, mediocre music,
bad music (I don't want you to think that I always
write good music!).

    And here is the list (in chronological order):
1) 2 Canti greci for Mixed Chorus (1916, unpublished, no
opus number). They belong to my „school years" (I was still
studying with Pizzetti; they were performed at the Conservatory
of Florence... my wife was singing in the chorus!); I believe
they are still good...; and at least they may prove you how
„well trained" we were in choral writing at that time....
(I made the copy and the English translation here in Beverly Hills).
2) Stars. 4 Sketches for Piano (1940, unpublished). Here... we
jump many years! and we come to the first year I was in
America. These were written before I came to Hollywood,
and are an indication of the style „I would have liked
to use in motion-pictures (but I never could!). They were
never published; because all publishers objected. „Movie-
stars become old! and then who remembers them?". Anyway
here you have Greta Garbo in a romantic scene, Deanna
Durbin vocalizing, Marlene Dietrich in a cabaret-scene,

published first by Thomas Young in 1814 and then by Jean-François Champollion in 1821–1822. The English poet Percy Bysshe Shelley (1792–1822) probably encountered Diodorus's account in his readings of classical Greek and Roman letters, which he pursued with his friend Thomas Love Peacock (1785–1866), whom the classical scholar Thomas Taylor dubbed "Greeky-Peeky" for his interest in ancient Greece.[2] Shelley interpreted the image of the great Pharaoh's shattered statue in light of his lifelong concerns with social justice and revolutionary political movements in Europe: in the sonnet "Ozymandias" (1817) he drew from it an ironic parable of the transitory nature of absolute political power and ambition.

I met a traveler from an antique land
Who said: "Two vast and trunkless legs of stone
Stand in the desert…Near them, on the sand,
Half sunk, a shattered visage lies, whose frown,
And wrinkled lip, and sneer of cold command,
Tell that its sculptor well those passions read
Which yet survive, stamped on these lifeless things,
The hand that mocked them, and the heart that fed;
And on the pedestal these words appear:
"My name is Ozymandias, king of kings:
Look on my works, ye Mighty, and despair!"
Nothing beside remains. Round the decay
Of that colossal wreck, boundless and bare,
The lone and level sands stretch far away."[3]

Unlike Shelley, Castelnuovo-Tedesco was no political activist, but Swing's association of Shelley's commentary on Ramses II's fallen colossus with Mussolini's larger-than-life figure and his ouster from power obviously touched a chord in the émigré composer just as he was emerging from a difficult period. Indeed, the origins of Castelnuovo-Tedesco's interest in composing works on Jewish themes, most of them sacred, appear to have coincided with the decline of the Fascist government: his first essay in this new genre, the highly personal Sacred Service, was written in the year of Mussolini's downfall (1943, op. 122), and a setting of the *Kol Nidrei* follows shortly thereafter (1944). Religious themes recur with frequency throughout Castelnuovo-Tedesco's output after this point: to cite but one example, *The Fiery Furnace* (1958, based

[2] On Shelley's sonnet and his pursuit of Greek literature, see Desmond King-Hele, *Shelley, His Thought and Work*, 3rd ed. (London: Macmillan, 1984), pp. 93–95. In the notebook that contains the drafts and fair copy of this poem, "Ozymandias" is partially written over notes taken from Cicero's *De Natura Deorum*. See *Bodleian MS. Shelley e. 4*, ed. P. M. S. Dawson, vol. 3 in the series *The Bodleian Shelley Manuscripts: A Facsimile Edition, with Full Transcriptions and Scholarly Apparatus*, ed. Donald H. Reiman (New York and London: Garland, 1987), f. 85r–v, and p. xiii.

[3] *The Complete Poetical Works of Percy Bysshe Shelley*, ed. Neville Rogers (Oxford: Clarendon, 1975), vol. 2, pp. 319–20. The poem dates from 1817 and was published in 1818, just before Shelley left for his final move to Italy, where he drowned in 1822, when his boat sank in a storm off the coast of Liguria.

on the *The Book of Daniel*), the cantata listed in the letter that accompanies "Ozymandias," was the third in a series of biblical works that included *Naomi and Ruth* (1947, based on *The Book of Ruth*) and *The Queen of Sheba* (1953). "Ozymandias" can perhaps be counted as a secular counterpart to works of this sacred vein, since it responds to those historical and political events that most upset the core of the composer's personal identity—his nationality, both old and new, his Jewishness, and his family, divided by exile.

The choice of an English Romantic poet also fits with Castelnuovo-Tedesco's highly refined literary tastes, which ranged from Medieval Italian and Provençal poetry to modern Spanish poets such as Jiménez and García Lorca. It was English lyric poetry and drama, however, that were central to his production. He had begun composing the series of Shakespeare overtures in 1940 (the first was *A Midsummer Night's Dream Overture to a Fairy Tale*, op. 108), and in 1944–1947 he set twenty-eight of the poet's sonnets (op. 125); subsequently, two of his operas, *The Merchant of Venice* and *All's Well that Ends Well*, were also based on Shakespeare. In the 1960s he turned to Keats, setting a number of his works (the first of these settings is "The Mermaid Tavern," from 1962, also included in the group of manuscripts sent to Moldenhauer together with "Ozymandias"); and a chamber opera deals with a libretto based on Oscar Wilde's *The Importance of Being Earnest* (1961–1962).

Castelnuovo-Tedesco rendered the ironic remove of Shelley's poem with an austere syllabic setting whose severity, as much as its subject, may have led to its characterization as a "gloomy song" (the opening of the Andante lento section is marked "quiet and cold"). The overall tonality centers on a somber D Minor, although the introductory phrase momentarily highlights D Major; throughout, however, Castelnuovo-Tedesco makes use of richly chromatic and at times quite dissonant harmonies.

The song's form and prosody follow closely Shelley's sonnet, resulting in a balanced song of three sections with a brief recitative introduction. The main narrative (Andante lento, starting at measure 7) falls into three parts: two outer sections (of fourteen and seven measures each) balanced around the central quotation (six measures). The freely declamatory style of the introductory verse places it apart from the more melodic Andante lento of the narrative, and the climactic internal quote, "My name is Ozymandias…" is set off by brief piano interludes, as is the closing commentary, "Nothing besides remains…"

The opening piano phrase (measures 1–2), with its emphasis on parallel open fifths, establishes the sonority for both the beginning of the traveler's narrative (measures 7–8) and the central inscription from the base of the statue (measures 22–27), and evokes—without specific reference to Arabic music—a sense of the exotic associated both with the report from a distant land and with the self-aggrandizing words of a remote ruler.

In the outer sections, the sparse piano accompaniment juxtaposes a pulsating syncopated rhythmic figure in the left hand, which functions almost like a tolling bell, with, in the right hand, full chords that support the voice, moving generally in a slow harmonic rhythm of half-notes. For the climactic quotation, Castelnuovo-Tedesco exploits the wide range of the piano, spanning a full four octaves at "king of kings," and then continuing to emphasize low sonorities into the closing section, with its somber commentary on the unwitting irony of Ozymandias's (and Mussolini's) hubris.

A Chopin Manuscript: Prelude in A-flat Major, op. posth.

Robin Rausch

CHOPIN'S PRELUDE IN A-FLAT MAJOR, without opus number, was first published in Geneva in the August 1918 issue of the art journal *Pages d'Art*. Untitled by Chopin, the forty-one-measure piece appeared under the title *Prélude inédit*. The work was first performed in public on April 9, 1919, by E. R. Blanchet and was subsequently reissued in an edition by the music publisher Henn. French and English editions were planned but were never carried out. Today the piece is regarded as a posthumous prelude and is frequently published appended to the Preludes, op. 28 along with the Prelude in C-sharp Minor, op. 45.

Compared to the rest of Chopin's oeuvre the piece is a trifle, having caused some to question its authenticity.[1] Chopin, however, never actually submitted the work for publication, intending it instead as a gift for a friend. There is no reason to doubt its authorship, though Chopin himself did not consider it a work suited for inclusion among his published work.

The Prelude carries the dateline "Paris 10 [18?] Juillet 1834," but the actual day of the month is unclear and has been interpreted as both the 10th[2] and the 18th[3]. The dedication, "A mon ami P. Wolff," is to Pierre Wolff, a professor of piano at the Geneva Conservatory. Chopin and Wolff met through their mutual friendship with Anton Wodzinski who was living in Geneva at the time. The manuscript was apparently presented to Wolff as a gift and was passed on to his student Aline Forget. It was discovered among family papers by Pierre Forget and remained in the family's possession until 1962 when Edouard Forget sold it to the Spokane Conservatory, where it became part of the Moldenhauer Archives.

The manuscript consists of two leaves, 15.5 cm. by 24 cm. in

[1] Edouard Ganche, *Dans le Souvenir de Frédéric Chopin* (Paris: Mercure de France, 1925), pp. 96–97.

[2] Maurice J. E. Brown, *Chopin: An Index...* (London: Macmillan, 1960), p. 84.

[3] Józef Michał Chomiński and Teresa Dalila Turło, *Katalog Dziel Fryderyka Chopina* (Kraków, Poland: Polskie Wydawnictwo Muzyczne, 1990), p. 187.

size. There are eight staves per page, each approximately 19.5 cm. long. A partial unidentified watermark appears on the bottom right-hand corner of the second page.

A copy of a letter from the Chopin scholar Arthur Hedley accompanies the manuscript and attests to its authenticity. Due to Chopin's practice of using copyists, as well as to his tendency to submit differing copies of the same work to his French, German, and English publishers, the process of determining a manuscript to be in Chopin's hand is no easy task. In particular, the copies made by Julian Fontana are notoriously similar to Chopin's own hand and have been erroneously identified as originals in the past.[4] As an authentic Chopin manuscript, the Prelude in A-flat Major provides a noteworthy standard of comparison by which to judge other such documents and, we hope, will help in the process of distinguishing original Chopin manuscripts from those of his copyists.

4 See Emanuel Winternitz, *Musical Autographs, from Monteverdi to Hindemith* (Princeton University Press, 1955), vol. II, plates 110–11, where two alleged Chopin manuscripts, the Allegro de Concert, op. 46 and the Polonaise in A-flat Major, are reproduced on facing pages. In his letter of authentication, October 13, 1960, Hedley notes the Allegro, op. 46 was later discovered to be a Fontana copy.

Luigi Dallapiccola's Sketch for *Ulisse*

Wayne Shirley

ULISSE, AN OPERA IN A PROLOGUE and two acts, is the only full-length opera of Luigi Dallapiccola. It was preceded by two one-act pieces, *Volo di Notte* (1940) and *Il Prigioniero* (1950); by *Job*, a "sacra rappresentazione" in one act (1950); and by an edition of Monteverdi's *Il Ritorno d'Ulisse in Patria* (1941–1942). Like Monteverdi's opera, *Ulisse* is based on the *Odyssey* (Dallapiccola was annoyed during his work on the opera by frequent statements that the opera was to be "based on James Joyce's *Ulysses*," a work he was known to admire). Unlike Monteverdi's work, Dallapiccola's opera draws on traditions, beginning with Dante, which see Ulysses's quest as not ending with his homecoming to Ithaca. The work received its premiere on September 29, 1968, by the Deutsche Oper Berlin under the direction of Loren Maazel. Annabelle Bernard sang the dual roles of Calypso—whose music is sketched in the Moldenhauer manuscript—and Penelope.

The Moldenhauer manuscript is a sketch for the opening scene. In fact, it is the sketch for the opening words of the opera: the start of Calypso's monologue, which forms the first scene of the Prologue. Calypso speaks in apostrophe to the departed Ulysses.

> Son soli, un'altra volta, il tou cuore e il mare.
> Desolata ti piange Calypso, la Dea senz'amore.
> Ti rivelasti a me, mormorando in profondo sopore:
> "Guardare, meravigliarsi, e tornar a guardare."
> Compresi. Era menzogna la nostalgia del figlio, della
>   patria,
> del vecchio padre, della tua sposa...

> Once again you are alone, your heart and the sea.
> Desolate, Calypso, the goddess without love, weeps for you.

You revealed yourself to me, murmuring in deep sleep:
"To look, to marvel, and to look again."
I understand: it was all a lie,
Your longing for your son, for your homeland,
For your old father, for your wife…

The verbal text of the monologue is identical in the sketch to that of the final version; the musical text of the sketch differs, sometimes profoundly, from that of the opera as it was published. Sketch and opera are closest together on the first page of the sketch, which is reproduced here; by the final page, which contains the setting of the original of the last three lines above, sketch and opera represent essentially two quite different approaches to the same set of words.

Calypso's monologue, sketch and score, begins (through the words "tornar a guardare"—"to look again") by presenting the basic tone row in its four main forms: original, retrograde (starting with "desolata," final measure of the facsimile), retrograde inversion (starting with "Ti rivelasti"—"You revealed yourself", and inversion (starting with "Guardare"—"To look".) This kind of exposition of the row in its four principal forms—the Grand Row Tune[1]—occurs at the beginning of many large-scale serial works: one can almost depend on it at the start of a late Schoenberg serial piece.

[1] "Grand Row Tune" is my own term, a nontechnical phrase I have found useful. (A "Row Tune"—nonGrand—is a melody presenting one full version of the row and one only.)

The vocal line of the first four measures in the sketch—first sentence of the text, exposition of the original form of the row—is the closest to the final score at any given spot. Pitches and the octaves in which they appear are identical to those in the published score: though the rhythms have been changed, the general rhythmic profile is similar.

The general profile of the vocal part in the opera through the words "tornar a guardare"—that is, through the end of the Grand Row Tune—continues to show similarities, in rhythm and general melodic profile, to the voice part of the sketch. But the row-forms are at transposition levels different from those in the sketch—a change which itself has caused several octave shifts in order to keep the voice within a good singing range—and the rhythmic changes are more considerable than in the opening four measures. The changes in pitch level of the row all seem to have been done for the purpose of getting the voice in a more graceful range. In particular, Dallapiccola wants the phrase "Guardare, meravigliarsi, e tornar a guardare" to be at a pitch higher than in the sketch. This is one of the key phrases in the opera—Calypso repeats it towards the end of her monologue, and Ulysses sings it at a critical moment in the final scene—and Dallapiccola wants it, at its first appearance, to lie somewhat higher than the pleasant midrange of the voice at which it appears in the sketch.

The accompaniment to the voice is much changed in the final score, yet its basic pitch content (duly transposed) and shape are already present in the sketch. In particular, the two most distinctive textures are established: a set of static six-note chords in elaborate slowing-down rhythm (on page 3 of the sketch; thus not visible in the facsimile) and the complex single- and double-note texture immediately after the words "il mare" (bottom of page 1). This latter texture, which occurs often in the opera, seems to represent the undifferentiated flux of the tranquil sea. This fact is more evident in this sketch than in the final score, where its appearances are slightly more sophisticated in texture: a sketch can sometimes reveal the composer's intentions more clearly than the final work.

The last page of the sketch corresponds to the final version only in Calypso's words; the music is completely rewritten. In the sketch Calypso begins her new text immediately after the static six-note chords in elaborate slowing-down rhythm. In the opera these lines are preceded by the first appearance of a new motif. It will be associated with the word "nessuno"— "nobody." In the *Odyssey* "nobody" is the reply which Odysseus gives when the Cyclops asks him for his name. In Dallapiccola's opera it serves as a symbol of Ulysses's quest for a meaning to his adventures: has he really become "nobody"? This motif will be extremely important in Acts I and II of *Ulisse*; it is essential that it appear as well in the Prologue.

Dallapiccola thus adds an important element which is not present in the sketch. He also alters the emphasis of Calypso's outburst. As set in the sketch, the key word is "Compresi"—"I understand." The emphasis is on the fact of realizing, not what she realizes, which is what is in the final version: "It was a lie."

Lies, all lies—as Calypso cries at the departed Ulysses—are all the longing for his home and family which seem to motivate Ulysses through the remainder of the opera until the final scene. We need this passionate cry at the opening to remind us that beneath the outer action of the opera is an inner action, a searching for the truths beneath the adventures.

Frederick Delius's
"Zwei Braune Augen"

Don C. Gillespie

ON MARCH 2, 1884, twenty-two-year-old Fritz Delius—he
did not change his name to Frederick until 1902—set sail from
Liverpool for America with the intention of managing a large
orange plantation in the then primitive State of Florida.
Disembarking in Jacksonville, a backward but booming city of
around 17,000 inhabitants, he traveled by river steamer to his
lush plantation, Solano Grove, forty miles south up the St.
Johns River, then the gateway to America's southern
wilderness frontier. The "mighty river," as he would later
allude to it in his tone poem *Appalachia*, was almost four miles
wide at the point where his farm house was located. His
African-American helpers, descended from slaves, were waiting
on the river bank to assist the novice orange grower. From
Bradford, England, Delius's father, a prosperous native-born
German wool merchant, had sent his wayward son to the
United States in the expectation that the young man would
abandon his passion to follow music as a career and turn to the
sensible business of making more money for the growing
family fortune. Surely the headstrong young man would be too
busy with his oranges to think about musical improvisation and
his urge to abandon the family business.

Neglecting the oranges, Delius spent many evenings listening
to the singing on his plantation and on the riverboats passing
during the night on their voyages back and forth from
Jacksonville to Palatka, an old river town ten miles farther up
river. Delius later described the special ambiance that
convinced him that he *must* become a composer: "I used to get
up early and be spellbound watching the silent break of dawn
over the river; Nature awakening—it was wonderful! At night
the sunsets were all aglow—spectacular. Then the coloured
folk on neighbouring plantations would start singing
instinctively in parts as I smoked a cigar on my verandah."[1] For

[1] Eric Fenby, "On Delius in Florida."
Program note of the Twenty-fourth Annual
Delius Festival, Jacksonville, Florida,
March 7–10, 1984, p. 5.

the rest of his life he would attempt to recreate this unforgettable union of nature and music. But there was a problem. He lacked the training to fulfill his ambition.

Fate soon intervened in the form of an unusually gifted Catholic church organist, Thomas F. Ward (1856–1912), a consumptive who had recently moved from Brooklyn to Jacksonville in the hope of improving his health. Meeting Delius by chance in a Jacksonville music store, Ward, a pianist and composer versed in the music of the masters—Bach, Mendelssohn, Chopin—and in the American salon tradition, immediately sensed the young man's remarkable talent for harmonic improvisation. Delius hired him on the spot to move to Solano Grove and teach him the rudiments of music theory, which he accomplished during the next six months.

Ward, an orphan raised by the Catholic church in Brooklyn, is perhaps the most mysterious personality in the Delius biography, a man about whom very little has been known until recently.[2] Intellectual, devoutly religious, demanding from his students the highest standards of learning and conduct, Ward was nevertheless tormented by his own past. The son of a priest and an Irish kitchenmaid, he had been abandoned by his father and given over to the Sisters of St. Joseph in Brooklyn, who instilled in him a lifelong faith in the Church and a determination to pursue disciplined and purposeful activity. But his moral character had been shaped at a high price. Plagued by guilt about his concealed past, he wandered restlessly throughout the South in search of a cure for his tuberculosis and for spiritual peace. After a failed attempt to become a priest in a Benedictine monastery in central Florida, he eventually settled in Houston, Texas, where he died in 1912 and was buried in a pauper's grave.

Throughout his life, Delius acknowledged the profound influence of Ward's training, claiming repeatedly that Ward's course had been far more important than his subsequent studies at the Leipzig Conservatory in 1886–1887. The relationship between Delius and Ward was complicated, however, by the fact that Ward was a devout Christian, while Delius was already on the way to becoming the hater of organized religion and admirer of Nietzsche that he remained

[2] For a full account of Ward's life, see Don Gillespie, *The Search for Thomas F. Ward, Teacher of Frederick Delius* (Gainesville: University Press of Florida, 1996).

until the end of his life. Whatever the case, as Delius's invaluable amanuensis Eric Fenby later noted, Ward "had known his pupil for what he was—a headstrong, boisterous, hot-blooded young fellow with more than a streak of the adventurer in him—and he had taken him well in hand."[3] The essence of Ward's message to Delius can be found in the following lines of Lord Byron, which Ward had underlined in a volume of Byron's verses he later sent to Delius in Leipzig:

> The youth who trains, or runs a race,
> Must bear privations with unruffled face
> Be call'd to labour when he thinks to dine,
> And, harder still, leave wenching, and his wine.

3 Eric Fenby, *Delius As I Knew Him* (London: G. Bell and Sons, 1936), p. 168.

Several bits of Florida juvenilia have survived from the period of Delius's study with Ward and his short sojourn in Jacksonville thereafter. Among them may be cited the piano pieces "Pensées Mélodieuses," "Zum Carnival" (the latter published in Jacksonville in 1885), and the songs "Over the Mountains High" and "Zwei braune Augen," the composition under discussion here.[4] The brief song is set to a poem by Hans Christian Andersen ("To brune Øjne" from *Hjertets Melodier*) in a German version by Wilhelm Henzen. The two-page ink manuscript, like its companion song "Over the Mountains High" (text by Bjørnstjerne Bjørnson), is signed "Fritz Delius 1885."[5]

4 The authoritative study of the sources of Delius's early music is Robert Threlfall's *Delius' Musical Apprenticeship, Incorporating a Survey of the Leipzig Notebooks* (London: The Delius Trust, 1994).

5 The song, edited by Robert Threlfall and Allen Percival, appears in *The Complete Works of Frederick Delius*, vol. 18a (London: Stainer & Bell, 1987), pp. 6–7.

Significantly, from Delius's American period (1884–1886), only "Zwei braune Augen" is to be found in a list of Delius's compositions published in the first substantial study of his life and music, that of his friend and protégé Philip Heseltine (1894–1930). The brilliant songwriter and critic, who often used the pseudonym Peter Warlock, was a worshipper of the music of Delius. Delius became almost a father substitute and confided in him a wealth of previously unknown details about both his music and his past cosmopolitan adventures. He not only saved the manuscript of his fledgling song—he later destroyed many other scores—but permitted it to be placed as the first on the listing which Heseltine (with Delius's approval) described as "not altogether complete but including every work of any importance."[6] (It is followed by the now popular *Florida Suite* of 1887.) Andersen's short love lyric must have

6 Philip Heseltine, *Frederick Delius* (London: John Lane, Bodley Head, 1923), p. 158.

appealed to Delius, a romantically inclined youth whose cultured family appreciated the German romantic literary tradition:

Hab' jüngst gesehen zwei Augen braun,
d'rin war mein Heil, mein' Welt zu schau'n.
O Blick so liebreich und kindlich rein,
nein nie und nimmer vergess' ich dein![7]

I recently saw two brown eyes,
Therein were my well-being and my world to be seen.
What a look, as loving and pure as a child's,
No, I shall never ever forget you!
(Translated by Sabine Feisst)

There is no evidence of African-American influence in the song, although a suggestion of the American sentimental parlor tradition—the tradition of Gottschalk, Richard Hofmann, George William Warren, and their followers—can be detected. But the text itself might lend some credence to Delius's later confession to Percy Grainger that he had had a black sweetheart in Florida, a "lost love" whom he never forgot. According to Grainger, Delius returned to Florida in 1897 for the purpose of locating his mistress and their child.[8] If true, this woman (with two brown eyes and an unforgettable look?) could have partly inspired much of his music ("my world") and particularly those later works whose theme is lost love or the purity of youthful love—"Sea Drift," "Songs of Sunset," and "Idyll," to name only a few. However, aside from the inferences of his music and Grainger's account—Delius sometimes invented stories on the spot and Grainger tended to take people at their word—there is no proof that these romantic events ever occurred. The frequent assertion that in Florida Delius contracted the syphilis that would eventually cause his paralysis, blindness and, in 1934, his death in Grez-sur-Loing in France has been thoroughly discredited.[9]

Delius could take pride in a youthful creation which takes its place among the other Scandinavian settings that followed in the 1880s and 1890s—*Five Songs from the Norwegian*, *Seven Songs from the Norwegian*, and *Seven Danish Songs*. In ternary form, "Zwei braune Augen" moves briefly from G Major

[7] In the German translation, the word *dein* has untranslatable nuances. It can denote either the "look" or the girl herself.

[8] Percy Grainger, "The Personality of Frederick Delius," in *A Delius Companion*, ed. Christopher Redwood (London: John Calder, 1976), p. 122. See also letter from Percy Grainger to Richard Muller, October 5, 1941 (Library of Congress).

[9] Lionel Carley, ed., *Delius: A Life in Letters*, I, 1862–1908 (London: Scolar, 1983), pp. 92–94.

towards E Major before returning to the tonic. Interestingly, its thirty-four measures reveal primitive elements of Delius's later mature style. Although its harmony is diatonic, it contains chromatic inflections suggesting the influence of Chopin and Grieg and reflecting the richer chromatic palette of his first two operas *Irmelin* (1892) and *Koanga* (1897). The barcarollelike anapest rhythm of its 3/8 meter points towards Delius's later constant use of this device over long harmonic stretches. This Delian feature is to be found in works both lyrical and extrovert, from the tone poem *Over the Hills and Far Away* (1897) to *Eine Messe des Lebens* (1905)—(conclusion of Part I: "Nacht ist es")—to the *Cello Concerto* (1921). The listener will immediately recognize the rhythm in the famous "Serenade" (1920) from the incidental music for *Hassan*, where it is employed from beginning to end.

It is instructive to compare Delius's song with Grieg's setting of the same poem from his *Melodies of the Heart*, op. 5, No. 1, originally set in Danish in 1864, when Grieg was twenty-one, but later published by C.F. Peters, Leipzig, in Henzen's German translation.[10] Delius probably became acquainted with Grieg's German setting of "To brune Øjne" and other of the Norwegian's songs through his friendship with his Solano Grove neighbor, Jutta Belle, an amateur singer who was distantly related to Grieg. He might also have learned much of Grieg's music from Ward, whose repertoire doubtless included the popular *Lyric Pieces*. Delius's piece can easily bear comparison with Grieg's. Grieg's setting is also in G Major, but its mood is more playful and less wistful. Its dancelike "allegretto con grazia," in contrast to Delius's "nicht schnell," supports a straightforward love song without emotional complications. It moves fleetingly towards E Minor (in contrast to Delius's E Major) before returning to G Major and a conventional final cadence. Delius, however, chooses to repeat the words "nein nie und nimmer" with a quiet fadeout (ppp) that would become one of his stylistic trademarks. In its combined harmony and melody, Delius's four-measure ending reveals (with some infelicities in voice-leading) the stylistic feature of the "added sixth chord," a device later overused by both Delius and his imitators.

Throughout his creative life Delius retained his interest in

[10] Grieg's *Melodies of the Heart* also contains his most famous song "Jeg elsker dig" ("I Love Thee"). Henzen's German version first appeared in 1879 in Peters's *Grieg Album*, vol. III (Edition Peters 466c, pp. 26–27). Writing on December 15, 1884, to Dr. Hans Abraham of C.F. Peters about the publication of other German versions of his songs (including the famous "Solvejg's Cradle Song"), Grieg expressed his opinion about Wilhelm Henzen, a translator frequently employed by Peters. "[Please use] Mr. Henzen to translate the poems and not a lady, even if she were Sappho herself. Henzen was once a musician and this plays a main role. A translation that's merely good poetically is only a little useful to me, or not at all." See Elsa von Zschinsky-Troxler, ed., *Edvard Grieg, Briefe an die Verleger der Edition Peters 1866–1907* (Leipzig: C.F. Peters, 1932), p. 13.

song, and indeed his finest efforts are those works which combine vocal, choral, and orchestral forces. His first hesitating experiments would eventually lead to such masterpieces as *Sea Drift* (1904, to verses of Walt Whitman) and to the work which, in the present author's opinion, is Delius's finest achievement in song: "An Arabesk" (1911), for baritone solo, chorus, and orchestra, set to a text of the Danish poet Jens Peter Jacobsen. Here Delius's intense chromatic style with its accompanying restless romantic longing reaches perfection in a personal harmonic language braced with new stronger dissonances, perhaps unconsciously assimilated from the impressionists, and even from the European modernists whose music he had scorned. The formal structure is firm. Lyricism and passion are carefully controlled by the German text (in Delius's translation) and by balances of mood and texture. Almost thirty years after his Florida experience, the fifty-year-old composer expressed with intensity and conciseness one of his principal themes: the longing for lost youthful love combined with a heightened sensitivity to the beauty of nature, accepted as benevolent but indifferent to one's own swiftly passing existence. Admittedly, it is a limited message, but in "An Arabesk" the composer presents it with focused artistic vision.[11] Perhaps Delius's accomplishment in his finest song had its origin in the brief "Zwei braune Augen" sketched on the banks of the St. Johns River.

[11] In Europe "An Arabesk" is usually performed in Philip Heseltine's English translation. To date the author has discovered no evidence of an American performance of either version.

George Gershwin: A Sketch for *Porgy and Bess*

Wayne Shirley

GEORGE GERSHWIN'S SKETCHES FOR *Porgy and Bess* come
in many varieties. Most important—less a "sketch" than a step
in the creation of the work—is the manuscript short score, four
large oblong volumes, bound by Gershwin and containing the
entire score (save for the prelude) in its unorchestrated form.
This is the score from which the published vocal score was
prepared; one suspects that Gershwin thought of it as "the
score of *Porgy and Bess*" and that he thought of the score the
Library of Congress now exhibits as "the orchestration."

Other sketches range from those which present the fully
established (unorchestrated) text of a spot in *Porgy and Bess* as
we know it (the sketch of the prelude, essentially part of the
sketch-score but not bound with it, probably because it was
written after Act I, scene 1 was bound), through preliminary
sketches for music now in the score, to jottings of material not
used and schematic diagrams of ways to use material. Some
sketches are on the typescript libretto; some are in
sketchbooks (the melody line of "I Got Plenty o' Nuttin'" in
nearly final form appears in one of the notebooks containing
Gershwin's studies with Schillinger); many are on individual
sheets of music paper. Gershwin was neither a destroyer of
sketches (as was Brahms) nor a hoarder of sketches (as was
Beethoven); he was a "giver-away" of sketches—to friends, to
performers in his shows, to acquaintances. Thus we know only
a fraction of the *Porgy* sketches which may be extant.

Of those we do know, the "Robbins–page 3" sketch in the
Moldenhauer Archives is unique in being a detailed,
performable sketch for a rejected setting of an identifiable spot
in the current score. The spot occurs early in Act 1, scene 1—
cue numbers 40–42 in the vocal score. It contains the first
words we hear from Robbins—and almost the last, since by the

end of the scene he will lie on the stones of Catfish Row, brutally slain by Crown in an argument stemming from the crap game he was so eager to play. The final version of this spot is identical as to words and completely different as to music—key (F Major in the score), time signature (mixed 3/4 and 2/4 in the score), and thematic material (the score uses the "Robbins motive" which we will hear again briefly at cue numbers 123–124, as Robbins makes his fatal crap shoot). This is a page from a Porgy that "isn't": but unlike other such pages among the Gershwin sketches, it is complete enough for us to know both where it would have gone and how it would have sounded.

Some details of the sketch can be explained by reference to other manuscripts. "Page 3," for example, should not cause wonder about what is on the missing pages one and two: this is a setting of material from page three of the typescript libretto. In fact, the words—both of the sketch and of the final version—are from a separate typed revision at the top of the original page three in the libretto, which read:

ROBBINS
(Comes down to the floor—turns and looks back at her)
Now, for Gawd's sake, don't start that again. I goin' to play—Get
that!

SERENA
If you didn't have licker in you right now, you wouldn't talk
like that. You know what you done promised me last week.

ROBBINS
All right then, I wouldn't shoot more that fifty cent.

The text of the revised version runs as follows:

JAKE
(Seeing Robbins at head of stairs)
Come on down Robbins, we're waitin' for you.

SERENA
(to Robbins)
Honey, don't play tonight. Do like I say.

ROBBINS
(descending several steps and turning back to her)
I been sweatin' all day. Night time is a man's time. He got a
right to forget his trouble. He got a right to play.

SERENA
If you hadn't been drinkin' you wouldn't talk to me dat way.
You ain't nebber hear Lord Jesus say nuttin' 'bout got to play.

ROBBINS
(He has descended the steps and turns back from the court
speaking over his shoulder to her)
Dere you go again. Lissen what I say. I work all de week;
Sunday got to pray. But Saturday night a man's got a right to play.
(He saunters over to crap circle and continues)
That ole lady of mine [etc.]

("That ole lady..." marks the return to the original text of page three of the libretto.)

This change in the libretto seems to have been made to give Robbins a slightly larger part and to make him a more sympathetic figure. (For all that, Robbins remains the least rewarding male role in *Porgy and Bess*: twenty-five measures of singing, a strenuous onstage fight, and thirty minutes of lying still as an onstage corpse.)

As the new version of the libretto gives Robbins a slightly longer and more sympathetic part, so the music for Robbins in the score as we know it gives us a picture of Robbins more vivid than we get in this sketch. The sketch starts well enough—indeed it flows from the preceding material more naturally than the present music. But the F-Minor chord in the fifth measure seems abrupt and unmotivated, and the bluesy declamation of the last two lines suggests a man who is merely weary, not one who is looking forward to a night of excitement. In the final version of the opera those lines dance and crackle: Robbins may be the smallest named adult role in *Porgy and Bess*, but in the score as we now know it he leaps immediately to musical life.

Excerpts from Gluck's *Alceste*, Copied and Revised by Hector Berlioz

Joël-Marie Fauquet

THE SURVIVAL OF GLUCK'S OPERAS owes much to the efforts of Hector Berlioz. The present manuscript is an important document of some of those efforts, the culmination of a lifetime of experience and thought, to preserve *Alceste*.

In this work, the problems were different from those in the now more famous *Orphée*, where the role of Orpheus, originally intended for an alto castrato, has, since its revival in 1859 under Berlioz, usually been sung by a female contralto. The role of Alceste was originally intended for a soprano, but the great mezzo-soprano, Pauline Viardot,[1] whose voice Berlioz considered ideal for the part, required transposition—a procedure which Berlioz, a purist in the matter of honoring Gluck's intentions, accepted as a necessity and, in his adaptation of the part, took great pains to carry out with fidelity to the original.

In a letter of May 7, 1943, to Adolphe Boschot, Alfred Cortot mentioned "a manuscript of airs from the two *Alceste* versions written for Pauline Viardot" as among the collection of autograph documents of Hector Berlioz in his possession. The origin of the manuscript is clear, since at the foot of the first page Cortot has written: "This version of scenes from Gluck's *Alceste* combining the Italian *Alceste* with the French *Alceste* was probably undertaken for Pauline Viardot. This manuscript was sold by Paul Viardot[2] to the person from whom I had it. A. C."[3]

The seventy-five-page manuscript is in Berlioz's hand throughout, apart from the pagination and certain annotations.[4] It contains a coherent sequence of six movements from *Alceste* in orchestral score on fourteen-stave paper. The movements appear in the following order:

[1] A. Cortot to A. Boschot, A.L.S., May 7, 1943, Thierry Bodin, "Les Autographes, catalogue No. 52, November 1992, lot No. 55." We shall refer to the manuscript hereafter as the "Viardot manuscript."

Pauline Viardot (Paris 1821–1910), mezzo-soprano, composer, and singing teacher; daughter of Manuel García and sister of María Malibran. She studied the piano with Meysemberg and Liszt and composition with Reicha; she married Louis Viardot in 1840. She was interested in Gluck from an early age since in one of her first Paris concerts in 1839 she sang some extracts from the role of Euridice in *Orphée* and received an unfavorable notice from Berlioz. Her singing career reached its peak in 1859 at the Théâtre-Lyrique with her interpretation of the role of Orphée revised especially for her by Berlioz. See Joël-Marie Fauquet, "Berlioz's Version of Gluck's *Orphée*," *Berlioz Studies*, ed. Peter Bloom (Cambridge: Cambridge University Press, 1992), pp. 189–253.

[2] Paul Viardot (1857–1941), son of Pauline Viardot, violinist, conductor, and writer on music.

[3] I wish to express my sincere thanks to Dr. Hugh Macdonald for his support and collaboration with the present work and to Dr. Marie Rolf Lehman for her invaluable help in tracing the manuscript.

[4] The pagination duplicates the number 18. Pages 76, 77, 78 (numbered 79), and 79 are blank. The signature "H. Berlioz" appears at the foot of page 79 on the right.

5 By "Italian version" and, in the notes, "1769 edition," we refer to the original version composed by Christoph Willibald Gluck to a libretto by Ranieri de' Calzabigi, first performed in Vienna on December 26, 1767 (full score Vienna: G. T. Trattnern, 1769); by "French version" and, in the notes, "1776 edition," we refer to Gluck's revised version of a libretto by Louis Leblanc, bailli du Roullet, first performed in Paris on April 23, 1776 (full score Paris: Au Bureau d'Abonnement musical, [1776]). Alceste's recitative "Grand dieux soutenez mon courage" is in the 1776 edition, p. 200.

6 1769 edition, p. 91.

7 Berlioz translated the title of the movement from that of the 1769 edition: "Coro de Numi Infernali non veduto."

8 1776 edition, p. 208.

9 1776 edition, p. 210.

10 1776 edition, p. 230.

11 1769 edition, p. 66; 1776 edition, p. 84.

12 Seule Edition conforme à la représentation /ALCESTE/ Opéra en trois Actes/Musique de/Gluck/ accompagnement de Piano/ par/ E. Vauthrot [...] Paris, Editeur, Léon Escudier. Plate number L.E.2047.

13 H. Berlioz, "Gluck," Gazette musicale de Paris [G.M.P,] no. 22 (June 1, 1834): 173–76; no. 23 (June 8, 1834): 181–85.

14 H. Berlioz, "L'Alceste d'Euripide, celles de Quinault et de Calsabigi; les partitions de Lulli, de Gluck, de Schweizer et de Guglielmi sur ce sujet" [six articles], Journal des Débats [J.D.] (October 12, 16, 20, November 6, 24, December 8, 1861).

15 H. Berlioz, A travers chants, ed. L. Guichard (Paris: Gründ, 1971), pp. 155–222.

No. 1 [Récitatif d'Alceste] "Grands dieux soutenez mon courage" [Act III, scene 3, French version5], pp. 1–11.

No. 2 [Aria d'Alceste] "Qui me parle?" [Act II, scene 1, Italian version translated into French6].

No. 3 Choeur de dieux infernaux invisibles7 [Act II, scene 3, "Choeur des dieux infernaux," French version8], pp. 30–32.

No. 4 Air [Alceste] "Ah! divinités implacables" [Act III, scene 3, French version9], pp. 33–41.

No. 5 Air [Un dieu infernal] "Caron t'appelle" [Act III, scene 4, French version10], pp. 42–52.

No. 6 Air [Alceste] "Divinités du Styx"/"Ombres, larves" [Act 1, scene 7, French version superimposed on the Italian version translated11], pp. 53–75.

It is striking that two of the six movements which make up the Viardot manuscript show borrowings from the Italian version translated into French by Berlioz. Three of the six, furthermore, have been transposed down a minor third: No. 3 (D Minor, from the original F Minor), No. 4 (D Major, from the original F Major), and No. 6 (G Major, from the original B-flat Major). These details immediately suggest a direct relationship between the manuscript and the edition of Alceste published for the revival of the work at the Paris Opéra on October 21, 1861, with Pauline Viardot in the title role. That edition in fact contains most of the distinctive elements of the Viardot manuscript.12 But if the manuscript was used in preparing that revival, why did Berlioz only recopy scenes 3 and 4 of Act III and the final air of Act I? The question of the precise purpose of the manuscript remains open. When and for what occasion was it prepared? What light does it shed on Berlioz's lifelong opposition to those who treated what Gluck wrote with anything short of the most scrupulous respect?

To answer these questions we must examine the manuscript in the light of Berlioz's writings on Gluck. Concerning Alceste in particular, these writings extend from the article in the Gazette musicale de Paris in 1834[13] to the series of articles in the Journal des Débats in 1861,[14] reprinted in the volume A travers chants.[15]

These last articles partly reproduce a comparative study of the two versions of the opera which Berlioz had written in the same newspaper in 1835.[16] In addition there is information to be found in his correspondence, his *Traité d'instrumentation et d'orchestration modernes* and his *Mémoires*.

Before pursuing the analysis of the Viardot manuscript, we should note that the last complete performance of *Alceste* at the Paris Opéra was given on September 20, 1826.[17] Thereafter only *Orphée*, performed incomplete at long intervals, kept Gluck's name in the repertory of the Académie Royale de Musique. In 1835 the almost total disappearance of Gluck's operas caused Berlioz to wonder which voices would be most appropriate for the principal roles of these operas. He evoked traditions "which are vanishing daily, without which this music is almost incomprehensible."[18] Through his activities as conductor and concert promoter Berlioz set out to preserve Gluck's dramatic style himself.

On November 25, 1838, he gave a "Grand vocal and instrumental concert" in the Grande Salle des Menus Plaisirs, in which a revised fragment from *Alceste* was played. The program lists it as "Grand scene from Act III of Gluck's *Alceste* sung by M. Alizard, Mlle. d'Hernin and the chorus, and concluding with the final air of Act I." The extracts are shown in the following order:

> Récit
> Chorus: "Malheureuse où vas-tu?"
> Air: "Ah Divinités implacables"
> Air: "Où fuir! Où me cacher"[19]
> Air: "Caron t'appelle!"
> Air: "Ombres! Larves!"[20]

The program offers a note on the air "Où fuir! Où me cacher": "This piece belongs to the Italian *Alceste* and has never been heard in Paris."[21] The air of the God of Hades "Caron t'appelle!" and the air "Ombres!, larves!," on the other hand, were not commented upon. Yet the incipit in French ("Ombres!, larves!") proves that Berlioz had by this time adapted the Italian version of the air "Divinités du Styx" ("Ombre!, larve!") from the French version.[22] It is important to observe that the movements of this "grand scene" are in the

[16] H. Berlioz, "Des deux Alcestes de Gluck," *J.D.* (October 16 and 23, 1835).

[17] Théâtre de l'Opéra, *Journal*, vol. VIII (1811–1850): unpaginated. First and only performance of the eighth revival of the work.

[18] H. Berlioz, "Du répertoire de Gluck à l'Académie royale de musique," *Le Monde dramatique* (July 18, 1835): 180–81.

[19] The incipit given in the program is the third line of Alceste's aria which begins Chi mi parla? Che rispondo? Ah, che veggo? Ah, che spavento! Ove fuggo, ove m'ascondo [etc].

[20] The concert program is given in H. Berlioz, *Correspondance générale*, II (Paris: Flammarion, 1975), p. 471, note 1 to letter no. 582 to François Réty dated November between 20 and 23, 1838.

[21] The indisposition of Mlle. d'Hennin caused this extract from *Alceste* to be postponed until Berlioz's concert of December 16, when it was sung by Mme. Stoltz. Nevertheless in his notice of the Société des Concerts' concert of March 10, 1861, in which extracts from *Alceste* were sung by Mme. Viardot and Cazaux, Berlioz wrote that "a fragment of the Italian *Alceste*, which was sung in this memorable matinée, was being performed in Paris for the first time." *J.D.* (March 26, 1861).

[22] See below, no. 6. The programs for both concerts on November 25 and December 16 indicate as follows: "Nota. This air is the one performed in French as 'Divinités du Styx.' Since the translator disfigured the opening phrase, the first line has been changed in order to restore the beautiful vocal line which Gluck originally conceived." F-Pn, Fonds Montpensier, Berlioz IV, A529.

order found in the Viardot manuscript, with the famous air from Act I to close. Berlioz had already, no doubt, assembled a score of this sequence of pieces.

The "grand scene from Act III of *Alceste*" appeared again on the program of Berlioz's concert announced for February 3, 1844, in the Salle Herz with Mme. Nathan-Treillet and M. Bouché taking part. But this item was not performed, owing to the soprano's illness.[23] On January 19 of the following year, in a "grande fête musicale" presented at the Cirque Olympique, Berlioz conducted a "grand scene from the Italian *Alceste*," sung by Eugénie García (Pauline Viardot's sister-in-law). This was probably the piece later to be No. 2 in the Viardot manuscript. In the following years, no doubt discouraged by the failure of all the singers he had engaged to sing Alceste, Berlioz seems to have reverted to the French version of the opera. Thus on March 19, 1850, in the second concert given by the Société Philarmonique (which he founded and conducted), a large portion of Act I was heard with Mlle. Julienne, Arnoldi, and a chorus. The movements were listed in the following order:

1 Chorus, "O ciel! qu'allons-nous devenir!"
2 Chorus, "Dieu puissant!"
3 Religious march
4 Oracle scene, "Apollon est sensible à nos gémissements"
5 Air (soprano), "Non! ce n'est point un sacrifice!"
6 Air (bass), "Déjà la mort s'apprête"
7 Air (soprano), "Divinités du Styx!"[24]

Berlioz conducted an orchestra of 100, while Pierre-Louis Dietsch, later to conduct the revival of *Alceste* at the Opéra in 1861, was in charge of a chorus of 120. It was for this occasion that the *Revue et gazette musicale* reprinted a long extract on Act I of *Alceste*, slightly revised from Berlioz's feuilleton in the *Journal des Débats* of 1835.[25] The notice of the concert in the *Revue et gazette musicale* drew attention to the vocal problems posed by the title role. Allowing Mlle. Julienne her "flights of real passion and flashes of inspiration" the critic observed that her voice was "very strong in the top range but lacking in tone in the middle." On Berlioz's conducting he wrote: "You have to have Berlioz's profound grasp of this music to be able to conduct with such precision, assurance and lucid intelligence."[26]

[23] See "Concert de M. H. Berlioz," *R.G.M.P.*, no. 6 (February 11, 1844): 43.

[24] *R.G.M.P.*, no. 10 (March 10, 1850): 84.

[25] See above note 16. Partially reproduced, with revisions in the *R.G.M.P.*, no. 11 (March 17, 1850): 92 and 93. The most important change with regard to the present article is the following: in 1835 Berlioz had written "I believe this prodigious piece [*Divinités du Styx*] to be the most complete demonstration of Gluck's powers." In 1850 "prodigious piece" was changed to "Act I."

[26] "Société philarmonique. Deuxième concert […]," *R.G.M.P.*, no. 12 (March 24, 1850): 99.

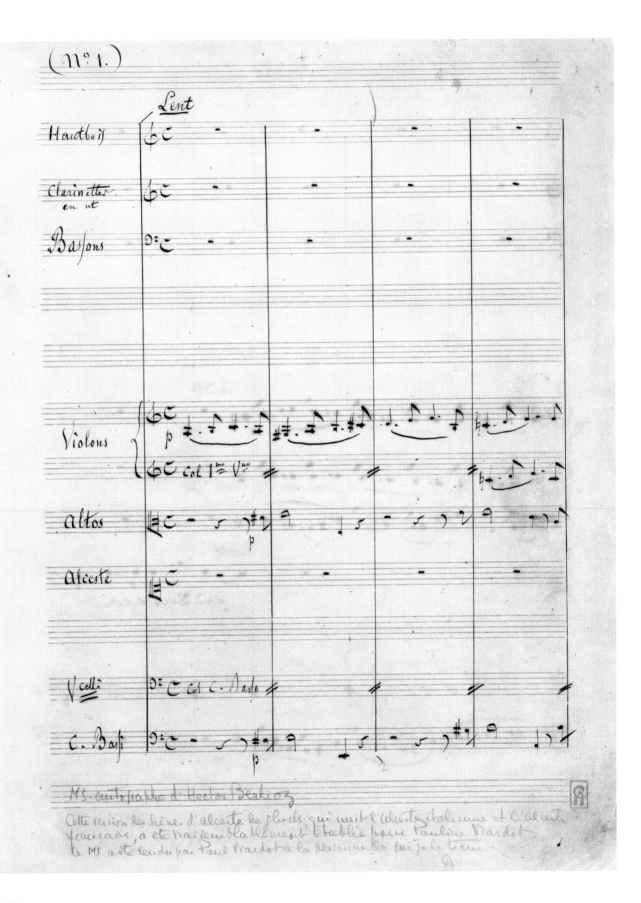

To turn to details of the manuscript:

No. 1 [Récitatif d'Alceste] "Grands dieux soutenez mon courage" [Act III, scene 3, French version].
No. 2 [Récitatif d'Alceste] "Qui me parle?" [Act II, scene 2, Italian version, translated into French].

The adaptation of this scene represents the most substantial revision Berlioz made to the score of *Alceste*. The idea for this change goes back to at least 1834, since in the second part of the article on Gluck which he published in the *Gazette musicale de Paris* on June 8 of that year Berlioz deplored the omission, in the French version, of the aria "Chi mi parla?". This is the piece to be found in Act II, scene 2 of the Italian version.[27] Not only did Berlioz praise the quality of this aria but he also quoted the opening words with a proposed translation: "Qui me parle!… que vois-je!…où fuir!…je brûle…je gèle…je meurs…etc."[28] The insertion of this piece in the French version had the further advantage of strengthening the dramatic character of Act III, which Gluck's contemporaries, chief among them Rousseau, regarded (as Berlioz well knew) as the weakest.[29] A few years later, in the article "De l'instrumentation" which he devoted to the violins, Berlioz gave, as an example of the sensible use of mutes "for light and rapid passages or for accompaniments in headlong rhythm," the "sublime monologue" from the Italian *Alceste* "Chi mi parla?".[30]

Some annotations made by Berlioz in two copies of *Alceste* in the Bibliothèque du Conservatoire, Paris, first remarked upon by Julien Tiersot,[31] are probably later than 1834–1835. In the copy of the Italian version Berlioz's markings relate only to the aria "Chi mi parla?," which was to be transferred to the French version.[32]

No. 3 Choeur de dieux infernaux invisibles [Act III, scene 3, French version].

In addition to wanting to transpose the "Choeur de dieux infernaux invisibles" down a minor third, as already mentioned, Berlioz had a further reason to recopy this movement. This is revealed by the brief correspondence with

[27] See above, note 5.

[28] *G.M.P.*, no. 23, June 8, 1834.

[29] Jean-Jacques Rousseau, "Fragments d'observation sur l'Alceste italien de M. le chevalier Gluck," *Ecrits sur la musique*, ed. Catherine Kintzler (Paris: Stock, 1979), p. 386.

[30] H. Berlioz, "De l'instrumentation" (second article), *R.G.M.P.*, November 28, 1841, p. 529. See H. Berlioz, *De l'instrumentation*, ed. J.-M. Fauquet (Bègles: Le Castor Astral, 1994), p. 35. Included in the *Grand traité d'instrumentation et d'orchestration modernes* (Paris: Schonenberger, [1844]), p. 24.

[31] Julien Tiersot, "Berlioziana," *Le Ménestrel*, (February 11, 1906): 44. These copies of the 1769 and 1776 editions annotated by Berlioz, referred to by Tiersot by their earlier call numbers, are now in F-Pn with the call numbers D.4706 (the 1769 edition) and Rés. F 1107 (the 1776 edition).

[32] 1769 edition, p. 95. A pencilled cross at the end of the aria and in the margin before the chorus (in Berlioz's hand): "Française X" "Allez à B = Française." Then at the reprise of the "Coro di Numi infernali" ("Altro non puoi raccogliere"): "B=."

François Delsarte from 1857 on the subject of the trombone parts of this chorus.[33] Delsarte had just published the chorus in question in his *Archives du chant*,[34] scrupulously preserving the incorrectly engraved trombone parts as he found them in the French version.[35] In his letter of April 30, 1857, in which he provided Delsarte with the proof of his mistake, Berlioz also revealed that in his curiosity concerning the difference between what he heard on stage and what he read in the score he had made an enquiry of Lefebvre, head of the Opéra's copying bureau (this was probably in 1825 or 1826) which confirmed that the trombone parts then in use were correctly copied.

The air for Alceste "Grand dieux soutenez mon courage," which follows the chorus "Malheureuse où vas-tu?," was published by Delsarte transposed down a third. This chorus is thus in D minor, as in the Viardot manuscript. The transposition may perhaps be explained by the fact that Pauline Viardot was at this time taking part in concerts organized by Delsarte.[36]

> No. 4 Air [Alceste] "Ah! divinités implacables" [Act III, scene 3, French version].
> Berlioz's interest in this air springs from the match of vocal expression and instrumental support, as he explained in his chapter on clarinets in his series of articles "De l'instrumentation": "Here again, in this deeply sorrowful and resigned air for Alceste, 'Ah! Divinités implacables', it is the clarinets who sing with the voice."[37]

> No. 5 Air [Un dieu infernal] "Caron t'appelle" [Act III, scene 4, French version].

The inclusion of an air for the God of Hades in this manuscript, which is otherwise devoted to the role of Alceste, is explained by the orchestral effect of placing the bells of two horns against each other. This effect, which is not found in any source before Berlioz, is certainly one of the earliest to have fired the composer's imagination. In his *Mémoires* Berlioz tells us that the lives of Gluck and Haydn which he read at the age of fourteen in Michaud's *Biographie universelle* "threw him into a state of feverish agitation."[38] In a footnote in the article on

[33] Delsarte to Berlioz, April 28, 1857, in H. Berlioz, *Correspondance générale*, V (Paris: Flammarion, 1989), letter no. 2226, pp. 457 ff.; Berlioz to Delsarte, April 30, 1857, op. cit., letter no. 2228, pp. 460 ff. The letter from Berlioz which prompted this exchange has not been traced.

[34] *Archives du chant* recueillies et publiées par François Delsarte, VIIe livraison, no. 12.

[35] 1776 edition, pp. 208–9.

[36] Mme. Viardot sang in Delsarte's concerts many times from 1856 on, and also in the classical and historical concerts put on by Lebouc and Paulin.

[37] H. Berlioz, "De l'instrumentation" (fifth article), *R.G.M.P.* (December 19, 1841): 568. See H. Berlioz *De l'instrumentation*, ed. cit. (1994), p. 58, and *Grand traité d'instrumentation et orchestration modernes* (1844), p. 147.

[38] H. Berlioz, *Mémoires*, ed. Citron (Paris: Flammarion, 1991), p. 52.

39 Delaulnaye, article "Gluck" in C. G. Michaud, *Biographie universelle ancienne et moderne* [...], XVII (Paris: Michaud, 1816), p. 519, col 1.

40 H. Berlioz, "Des deux Alcestes de Gluck (Deuxième et dernier article)," *J.D.* (October 23, 1835): 2, col. 3.

41 H. Berlioz, "De l'instrumentation" (seventh article), *R.G.M.P.* (January 9, 1842): 11. See H. Berlioz, *De l'instrumentation*, ed. cit. (1994), p. 73, and *Grand traité d'instrumentation et orchestration modernes* (1844), p. 183.

42 *J.D.*, fifth article (November 23, 1861). *A travers chants* (1971), p. 210.

43 H. Berlioz, "Gluck," *G.M.P.*, no. 23 (June 8, 1834): 182.

Gluck, Delaulnaye, its author, wrote: "When, for the accompaniment of this air, he could not get sufficiently muffled and lugubrious sounds from the instruments by the usual means, it is said that in rehearsal he thought up the idea of aligning pairs of horns in such a way that the sound of both instruments would collide in the bell and produce the terrifying effect he wanted."[39] Berlioz recalled the application of this effect in his study of *Alceste* in the *Journal des Débats* in 1835.[40] When he came to discuss the use of horns in his articles on instrumentation, Berlioz naturally cited the three horn notes imitating Charon's conch in the air from *Alceste* "Caron t'appelle" as "a stroke of genius," referring to the effect of two horns lined up against each other.[41] He came back to this effect in his extended analysis of *Alceste* in 1861.[42] In the Viardot manuscript Berlioz clung to a tradition which he believed was lost and of which no trace is to be found in the orchestral material preserved at the Opéra.

No. 6 Air [Alceste] "Divinités du Styx"/ "Ombres, larves" [Act I, scene 7, Italian version translated and superimposed on the French version].
On the first beat of measures 1, 3, 10, 12, and 14 Berlioz has carefully inserted "p." In measure 33 he changed the "andante un poco" of the French version to "un poco meno mosso." In measure 48 he added "ff" and in measure 51 "1r mouvement un peu animé."

This air, in the French version, was the subject of a critical discussion by Berlioz. It concerns the alteration of dramatic emphasis caused by Du Roullet's clumsy adaptation of Calzabigi's libretto. The effect of the declamatory note in the trombone parts of the Italian version is destroyed by this alteration, a criticism Berlioz articulated for the first time in his article in the *Gazette musicale de Paris* on June 8, 1834. In support of what turns out to be a veritable lesson in dramatic composition he inserted a musical example which combines the texts of the Italian and French versions.[43] In 1838, as we have seen, he replaced the words "Divinités du Styx, ministres de la mort" with a French translation of the Italian words: "Ombres, larves, compagnes de la mort," a solution he advocated until 1861 and which was adopted by Pauline Viardot.

While Berlioz devoted many years to the problems of restoring the works of the composer who for him equalled Beethoven in importance, we should also recognize Pauline Viardot's lifelong interest in Gluck. A plan to revive *Alceste* was mooted by the management of the Opéra at the same time that it was decided to revive *Orphée* at the Théâtre Lyrique in 1859, perhaps before. This is the conclusion we may draw from a letter of June 20, 1859, in which Berlioz noted that there was "talk of unstaging (*démonter*) Gluck's *Alceste*."[44] The ironical use of the word *démonter* implies that there was already a plan afoot to revise the score. Pauline Viardot probably began this work herself before the first performance of *Orphée* at the Théâtre Lyrique on November 19, 1859. In a letter which can be dated to the end of October 1859[45] Saint-Saëns wrote to the singer: "Don't forget to consult the Italian score of *Alceste*; you might find some valuable changes there since the role is lower than in the French score." Saint-Saëns seems to have been steering Pauline Viardot towards a solution which Berlioz had adopted for *Orphée*: adapt the role of Orpheus for the singer's voice by combining the Italian and French versions. In the case of *Alceste* such a solution could not be justified. In the two versions of *Orphée* the title role is written for voices which were obsolete in the nineteenth century, namely the alto castrato and the haute-contre. The same problem did not arise with *Alceste* despite the differences between the two versions of the title role, both conceived for a soprano. In this case it was simply the limitations of a low voice, that of Pauline Viardot, which made transposition necessary. The adaptation was therefore done for a special occasion and was not motivated by an original tessitura no longer practicable. Nonetheless, a few months after the revival of *Orphée* in which Berlioz took a more central part than he was prepared to admit, he was ready to get to work on *Alceste*. This emerges from a letter to Pauline Viardot of March 12, 1860. Grumbling at having to write a notice of Poniatowski's *Pierre de Médicis*, first heard at the Opéra three days before, he admits: "One thing would have appealed to me to do today, and that is the copying and transposing of the pieces from *Alceste*; and I can't do it."[46]

Then a year later, on March 10, 1861, Pauline Viardot and the bass Félix Cazaux sang some extracts from *Alceste* in a memorable concert given by the Société des Concerts du

44 Berlioz to the Princess Sayn-Wittgenstein, *Correspondance générale*, V, letter no. 2380, p. 693.

45 F-Pn, Manuscrits N.a.fr. 16273 (19). In the same letter Saint-Saëns followed Berlioz in refusing Pauline Viardot's invitation to "orchestrate the air from *Orphée*." Since the letter in which Berlioz refused the same invitation was dated by Lesure and Macdonald October 20, 1859 (*Correspondance générale*, VI (Paris: Flammarion, 1995), letter no. 2417) Saint-Saëns's letter must have been written soon thereafter.

46 H. Berlioz, *Correspondance générale*, VI, letter no. 2490.

Conservatoire. The order of the program was:

1   Religious march and High Priest's air "Dieu puissant, écarte du trône" (Act I, scene 3)

2   Alceste's air "Immortel Apollon," mime scene for the sacrifice, High Priest's recitative "Apollon est sensible," oracle and chorus (Act I, scene 4)

3   Alceste's recitative "Où suis-je" and air "Non! ce n'est point un sacrifice" (Act I, scene 5)

4   Chorus "Tant de grâces," recitative "Dérobez-moi vos pleurs," and Alceste's air "Ah! malgré moi" (Act II, scene 4)

5   Alceste's recitative "Grands dieux! soutenez mon courage" and the aria "Qui me parle? que répondre?" adapted from the Italian version, chorus of the Gods of Hades "Malheureuse où vas-tu?" and air "Ah, divinités implacables!" (Act III, scene 3)

6   "Caron t'appelle" (Act III, scene 4)

7   Alceste's air "Divinités du Styx" (Act I, scene 7)

[47] H. Berlioz, "Concert du Conservatoire," *J.D.* (March 26, 1861).

[48] *J.D.* (March 26, 1861): 2, col. 1.

Berlioz's notice of the concert[47] deserves close attention. His principal criticism was directed at Cazaux's transposition of the role of the High Priest. As Hugh Macdonald has observed, Berlioz does not actually condemn the transposition. He simply considers that once it became inevitable it could have been done more skillfully. This supports the notion that Berlioz was not against transposition in principle, if this was the price of reviving a work which had been ignored since 1826. At the same time the inclusion of the aria "Chi mi parla?" from the Italian version placed within Act III of the French version, the final air of Act I in the French version closing the concert, and Berlioz's precise and enthusiastic evocation of Pauline Viardot's voice ("full and spacious singing, intense, powerful and faithful")[48] are sufficient indication that the interpretation was already in line with Berlioz's work on the opera as in the Viardot manuscript. An argument against this hypothesis lies in the fact that in the same concert Pauline Viardot sang some parts of *Alceste* that are not found in the manuscript Berlioz prepared for her, but which were to be subject to transposition when the work was revived at the Opéra, as we can see from Escudier's edition. In other words, if the Viardot manuscript was written for the Société des Concerts occasion, why does it include only scenes 3 and 4 of Act III and scene 7 of Act I? The answer is clear: it is because the main revisions and rectifications which Berlioz had wanted to introduce since 1834 and which we have noted in our examination of the Viardot manuscript are concerned with these movements only, namely the insertion of the aria "Chi mi parla?," translated, in the French version; the correction of the trombone parts in the chorus of Gods of Hades "Malheureuse où vas-tu?"; the acoustic effect of placing two horns bell-to-bell in the air of the God of Hades "Caron t'appelle"; and finally the restoration of the Italian version of the air "Ombres, larves" adapted at the beginning of the air "Divinités du Styx" in the French version.

Another source supports this argument: a volume found in the Bibliothèque de l'Opéra, Paris, entitled "Alceste/Remise à la Scène pour/Me Viardot/le Lundi 21 octobre/1861."[49] This copyist's score includes the ballet music from Act II in a revised order and all the same changes in Alceste's part in Act III as are found in the Viardot manuscript.[50]

All this reflects on the importance of the Viardot manuscript as a synthesis of Berlioz's thoughts on *Alceste* over some forty years. This manuscript not only reveals Berlioz's efforts to safeguard Gluck's intentions but it was also the means whereby one of the greatest dramatic mezzo-sopranos of the nineteenth century was able to shine in a role which still remains one of the finest in the repertoire.

[49] F-Po, A 237 h.

[50] These are: No. 1, "Grands dieux, soutenez mon courage"; No. 2, Qui me parle? que répondre?"; No. 3, chorus "Malheureuse où vas-tu"; No. 4, "Ah! divinités implacables"; recitative and duetto, etc.

George Frideric Handel's 1749 Letter to Charles Jennens

William D. Gudger

A GOOD DEAL OF TWENTIETH-CENTURY musical research about George Frideric Handel's great contemporary Johann Sebastian Bach has been occupied with the search for the "Bach organ." Since Bach's some 250 surviving compositions for organ are central to that instrument's repertory, modern performers and organ builders have been anxious to find out what sort of organ Bach preferred for his music. This is particularly crucial to the art of "registration," all the more so since Bach left few directions about choices of stops or changes of keyboard in his scores. About a third of the essays in the recent book *J.S. Bach as Organist*[1] are devoted to the interrelated areas of organs known and played by Bach, their survival and restoration, and questions of registration.

Had Handel remained in his native Germany with a career centered, like Bach's, in the organ loft, similar questions would have been more critical in Handel research. The principal role played by the organ in Handel's music came in his adopted Great Britain, where his introduction of the oratorio required the presence of an organ as a support for the choral sound. As Newburgh Hamilton put it in the preface to his word-book for Handel's oratorio *Samson*, Handel "so happily introduc'd here *Oratorios*, a musical Drama, whose Subject must be Scriptural, and in which the Solemnity of Church-Musick is agreeably united with the most pleasing Airs of the Stage."[2] The solemn sound of church music consisted of that peculiarly English choral sound combining a choir of boy sopranos, countertenors (male altos), tenors, and basses, with the support of an organ. Handel hired his choral singers from the professional London church musicians active at the Chapel Royal, Westminster Abbey, and St. Paul's Cathedral, and the organ support to which they were accustomed came along as part and parcel of "the Solemnity of Church-Musick." With Handel presiding at

[1] George Stauffer and Ernest May, eds., *J. S. Bach as Organist: His Instruments, Music, and Performance Practices* (Bloomington: Indiana University Press, 1986).

[2] Cited in a number of Handel biographies and studies; the standard reference is Otto Erich Deutsch, *Handel: A Documentary Biography* (New York: 1955, R/1974), p. 559.

Sir

      Yesterday I received Your Letter,
in answer to which I hereunder specify
my Opinion of an Organ which I think
will answer the Ends You propose, being
every thing that is necessary for a good and
grand Organ, without Reed Stops, which I have
omitted, because they are continually wanting
to be tuned, which in the Country is very
inconvenient, and should it remain useless

on that Account, it wou'd still be very expensive,
altho' that may not be Your Consideration,
I very well approve of Mr Bridge who
without any Objection is a very good
Organ Builder, and I shall willingly (when
He has finish'd it) give You my Opinion of it.
I have referr'd You to the Flute stop in
Mr. Freemans Organ being excellent in
its Kind, but as I do not referr You
in that Organ, The System of the
Organ I advise is, (Viz.)

The Compass to be up to D and down to Gamut,
    full Octave, Church Work,
One Row of Keys, whole stops and none in halves.

Stops

An Open Diapason —— of Metal throughout to be in Front.

a Stopt Diapason —— the Treble Metal and the Bass Wood.

a Principal —— of Metal throughout.

a Twelfth —— of Metal throughout.

a Fifteenth —— of Metal throughout.

a Great Tierce —— of Metal throughout.

a Flute Stop —— such a one as in Freemans Organ.

I am glad of the Opportunity to show you my attention, wishing you all Health and Happiness, I remain with great Sincerity and Respect
Sir
    Your

London. Sept. 30.
    1749.

most obedient and most humble
    Servant
George Frideric Handel

·231·

3 Charles Burney, *An Account of the Musical Performances in Westminster-Abbey … in Commemoration of Handel* (London: 1785, R/1964), Introduction, p. 8.

4 Ibid., "Sketch of the Life of Handel," p. 23.

5 Sir John Hawkins, *A General History of the Science and Practice of Music* (London: Novello, 1776; page references to the 1853 edition, R/1963), p. 912.

6 See William D. Gudger, "Registration in the Handel Organ Concertos," *The American Organist*, xix/2 (February 1985): 71–73.

7 "Sketch of the Life of Handel," p. 23.

8 For more on the Handel organ concertos, see Gudger, "Handel and the Organ Concerto," in Stanley Sadie and Anthony Hicks, eds., *Handel: Tercentenary Collection* (London: Macmillan, 1987), pp. 271–78.

the organ—or at times from a combined harpsichord and organ controlled from one keyboard[3]—it was natural that he would improvise on the organ, a time-honored part of the organist's art.

The historian Charles Burney cites two musicians—Michael Christian Festing and Thomas Augustine Arne—who heard Handel improvise during a performance of the oratorio *Athalia* in Oxford in 1733: they "both assured me, that neither themselves, nor anyone else of their acquaintance, had ever before heard such extempore, or such premeditated playing, on that or any other instrument."[4] The other great eighteenth-century British music historian, John Hawkins, says that Handel's practice was "to introduce [an organ concerto] with a voluntary movement on the Diapasons, which stole on the ear in a slow and solemn progression."[5] Following the practice of British organists, Handel drew the two Diapason stops—Open Diapason and Stopped Diapason—as the foundation of organ sound, improvising on this combination before he played the concerto itself, often registered as "full organ," i.e., all of the stops of the one-manual organ at his disposal.[6] Burney also mentions the improvisation of movements within the concertos, "an extempore fugue, a diapason-piece, or an adagio."[7] After the publication of complete four-movement organ concertos as Opus 4 in 1738, Handel's later concertos invariably called for improvised movements, and even improvised continuations of the solo organ part within a movement. (These concertos were posthumously published as his "Opus 7.")

Thus Handel's acclaimed improvisations had led him to create the genre of organ concerto in order to combine his art as a keyboard virtuoso with the orchestra present in the London theaters. These works were heard in the intervals between the acts of the oratorios or sometimes integrated with them.[8] Handel created the organ concerto in London much as Bach was inventing the harpsichord concerto about the same time in Leipzig, at first transcribing preexistent music for the new combination and then later writing original keyboard concertos.

The search for the sort of organ which Handel used in Britain reveals few surviving instruments which he played. The organ he used for his oratorio performances at the Theatre Royal, Covent Garden—donated to the theater at his death—perished in a building fire in 1808.[9] Its specification was the same as what he recommended in the letter to Charles Jennens, though it had a trumpet stop rather than a flute. The organ Handel left to the Foundling Hospital Chapel was replaced shortly after his death, and the surviving keyboard from this latter organ was never touched by Handel, despite frequent claims to the contrary.[10] Likewise many instruments surviving nowadays at stately homes Handel visited rarely turn out to be instruments he actually played. Bach often assumed the role of consultant to advise on changes or restorations of organs or to test new instruments. Handel did the same on a lesser scale, and his letter to Charles Jennens gives us a picture of Handel the consultant, recommending the specification of an organ to an avid devotee of his music. Fortunately not only does the letter survive, but so does the organ built to Handel's design, little altered except for a controversial retuning about forty years ago.

Charles Jennens (1700–1773) was the well-to-do son of a country squire from Leicestershire who attended Oxford, where he formed his lifelong interests in music and literature and became a devout Anglican and Nonjuror (those who could not take an oath to the monarchs after the accession of William and Mary as long as James II and his successors were alive). Jennens collaborated with Handel during the period 1738 to 1745, selecting for the composer the words of *Messiah*, likely also helping him with *Israel in Egypt*, arranging the text of Parts I and II of the ode *L'Allegro, il Penseroso ed il Moderato* from Milton with his own text as Part III, and writing the masterful texts for the oratorios *Saul* and *Belshazzar*. This collaboration is certainly comparable to such teams as Da Ponte and Mozart or Hofmannsthal and Richard Strauss. Late in life Jennens turned to editing Shakespeare, producing what were in essence the first variorum editions of five of the plays. Much of the criticism unfairly thrown at Jennens after his death by George Steevens (and taken over into such standard sources as the *Dictionary of National Biography*) has been refuted in a recent article by Ruth Smith,[11] who admirably discusses Jennens's life and achievements. Handel's letters to Jennens constitute the composer's largest surviving correspondence with any

9 The most thorough survey of organs known and played by Handel is still W. L. Sumner, "George Frederick Handel and the Organ," *The Organ*, xxxviii (April 1959): 171–79; xxxix (July 1959): 37–44.

10 On the complicated history of organs in the Foundling Hospital, see James Boeringer, *Organa Britannica: Organs in Great Britain 1660–1860* (Lewisburg: Bucknell University Press, 1983–1989), vol. 2, pp. 261–65.

11 Ruth Smith, "The Achievements of Charles Jennens (1700–1773)," *Music and Letters*, lxx (May 1989): 161–90.

individual and, together with the recently available correspondence between Jennens and Edward Holdsworth, give a rare glimpse into Handel's working methods and professional relationships.

Jennens's father died in 1747 and Jennens set about immediately to alter Gopsall, the family house in Jacobean style, "into a splendid Palladian mansion."[12] Unfortunately the house was demolished in 1951, but a painting of it survives as do some eighty-nine drawings of the interior design (the painting is reproduced in Smith's article along with a discussion of Jennens's tastes in remodeling). Among the contents of the house would have been Jennens's library of musical manuscripts, including many volumes containing almost every note which Handel had composed (the so-called "Aylesford Collection," comprising both full scores and separate vocal and instrumental parts) and also many volumes of Italian music acquired for Jennens by his friend Edward Holdsworth during tours of Italy.[13] Jennens was capable of playing this music, for which purpose he often entered meticulous figured basses into his Handel manuscripts. He owned at least one harpsichord, another of his acquisitions from Italy, and like many other country house owners of the time he wanted an organ for Gopsall. Thus he wrote to Handel for advice, especially with regard to Richard Bridge as an organ builder, in September 1749. Handel's prompt reply of September 30 refers to the arrival of Jennens's letter "yesterday."

Handel begins by noting that he has omitted reed stops which require frequent tuning, inconvenient out of the city. Richard Bridge (fl. 1730–d.1758) is the organ builder Jennens apparently had planned to use. Handel approves of his work and adds that the sort of flute stop found in the organ belonging to Mr. Freeman[14] is to be recommended, though Handel would not recommend the builder of that organ. Handel's specifications follow the general design of British organs of the period. The compass up to D (i.e. the D on two leger lines above the treble clef) was common at this time; all of Handel's organ concertos require this note (German organs of this period usually go only to C). The bottom note is "Gamut," that is, low G below three leger lines under the bass

[12] Ibid., p. 166.

[13] Described in detail by John H. Roberts, "The Aylesford Collection," in Terence Best, ed., *Handel Collections and Their History* (Oxford: Clarendon Press, 1993), pp. 39–85.

[14] Identified by Deutsch, op. cit., p. 676, as William Freeman, an admirer of Handel, who lived in Hamels, Herfordshire.

clef. The lack of a pedal division in British organs was partly compensated by this extended bass range, allowing a good deal of octave doubling of the bass both in solo organ playing and continuo work. By "full octave" Handel meant a compass chromatically complete from low G—G-sharp, A, B-flat, B, C, etc. Many organs of this period had a "short octave" omitting some of the less-needed low notes; since these were the largest pipes of the organ they were the most expensive to build. The inclusion of low G-sharp is rather unusual, and it was in fact included in the organ. "Church Work" refers to the scaling of the organ, Handel opting here for a rather more full sound and not the sort of chamber organ tone (with narrow pipes) found in most domestic organs. Even though a second keyboard controlling three stops was added to the organ early in its life, Handel's design called for a complete chorus on the main keyboard, rather than using some of the echo effects found in many small organs. Handel's interest in a complete chorus without special effects stops is seen in the requirement that there be "whole stops and none in halves," like the cornet and trumpet stops common in Britain in this period, which sounded only in the treble and thus were used for solo melodies but not in the building of the chorus sound.

The list of stops specified by Handel follows the British usage and terminology of the time. The two Diapasons constituted the basis of the organ sound; drawn together they produced what was usually called "soft organ." Both sounded at what we now refer to as 8-foot pitch. (This nomenclature was not used in eighteenth-century Britain since a pipe which plays low C which is about 8 feet in height, but the tallest pipe in a G-compass organ would be 10 to 12 feet in height, depending on the pitch.) The metal Open Diapason is placed "in Front" forming the visible facade of the organ. It produces characteristic organ tone, while the quicker speaking Stop Diapason gives a wooden flutey sound. Handel then adds the other stops typical of the British organ chorus, all metal pipes of the Diapason family: a Principal (sounds at 4-foot range), Twelfth (2 and 2/3-foot), Fifteenth (2-foot), and Tierce (1 and 3/5-foot).

Jennens having never married, at his death in 1773 the bulk of his music library and the organ passed to Heneage Finch, the son of Jennens's first cousin Mary Fisher. Finch was a friend of both Jennens and Handel, who sent greetings to him (he was Lord Guernsey at the time) via Jennens. By the time of Jennens's death Finch had become Third Earl of Aylesford. Thus the music manuscripts (later sold) came to Packington Hall as did Jennens's organ, which was (late in the nineteenth century?) moved into the parish church of Great Packington, St. James', which lies within the grounds of the estate, inherited by succeeding generations of Finches, Earls of Aylesford (whose eldest sons are styled Lord Guernsey). At some unknown time the organ acquired a second manual with three stops, perhaps by John Snetzler (1710–1785). The main part of the organ (the "great" division), as originally built for Jennens, is now attributed to Thomas Parker (fl. 1740s–1770s), according to a pencil note left in the organ by Michael Woodward of Birmingham. Woodward "repaired" it in 1792 at the time of its removal from Gopsall. Another source suggests that the Tierce was replaced,[15] and if this is so, 1792 is the likely date, as mutations fell into disfavor around this time. (It is of course possible that the original Tierce pipes were left behind and are now once again in the organ; the origins of the present Tierce rank are unclear.) Much remains to be done on attribution of organs in this period, made difficult by the survival of so few unaltered examples. James Boeringer's three-volume *Organa Britannica*[16] is the most comprehensive study, based on the so-called Sperling Notebooks, a list of about 1300 British organs and their specifications compiled around 1850. The Jennens organ, at that time probably in Packington Hall, is not included as it was not in a public location.

Modern interest in hearing music on surviving instruments got a bit ahead of scholarship in the 1950s. British-born organist E. Power Biggs (1906–1977) was a leader in the performance of historical organ repertory, which he popularized during weekly radio broadcasts from Harvard University. As a recording artist for Columbia Records he set about to record organ music in its original settings—Buxtehude at Lüneburg; Mendelssohn in St. Paul's Cathedral, London; Haydn at Eisenstadt; Mozart on the Dutch organ he played while in Haarlem; and so on. Bach was at first not a large component of this series, due to many of the Bach instruments being in Communist East Germany. But the search for an instrument appropriate for the Handel concertos

[15] See Stanley Webb, "A Handel Organ Restored," *The Musical Times*, cix (December 1968): 1154.

[16] See above, note 10.

(to be recorded in conjunction with the two-hundredth anniversary of his death in 1959) with little difficulty netted the Great Packington organ. It had been heard in some BBC broadcasts, but attempts to play concertos with orchestra were difficult—the organ was lower than standard modern orchestral pitch. Transposing the organ part up a half-step still did not produce good results. So the decision was made to raise the pitch of the organ to modern standards, fitting the pipes with tuning sliders which could lengthen the pipes back to their original pitch if desired. The organ-building firm of N.P. Mander took this on, about the only British firm with any experience at the time with historical instruments.[17] To her credit organist Lady Susi Jeans (1911–1993) criticized this move, and in retrospect she was right—by the 1980s and 1990s there were many "original instrument" or "authentic" instrument groups which could play at the lower (Baroque) pitch level. The entire controversy has not been adequately documented, but the main points were raised in articles and letters which appeared in *The Musical Times*.[18] Early in the period of growing interest in historic instruments the problem was raised: do we leave surviving instruments untouched or do we effect enough restoration to make them usable? In the case of the Jennens organ, little had changed, and the organ was playable, being used by the parish church in Great Packington on a regular basis. Of course, the approach is now more scientific and the number of organ builders with experience in historic building methods and consequently historic restoration methods is much greater than in the 1950s.

But as distinct from large church organs known by Bach which have been repaired and rebuilt due to necessity as well as changing taste, the Great Packington organ still produces sounds close to what Handel approved (there is no evidence he visited the organ at Gopsall, though he may well have inspected and played it in London when it was finished at the builder's shop). Sitting in the BBC archives probably are recordings made before the alteration of the tunings. The Biggs recording of the concertos, with Adrian Boult conducting, has been issued several times on long-playing records by Columbia and recently remastered onto compact disc.[19] One record in a series of the Handel concertos by Simon Preston, organist, with Yehudi Menuhin conducting was made

[17] Biggs himself wrote about the controversy stirred by this decision in the article "Organ Designed by Handel Stirs a Teapot Tempest," *The Diapason*, 1 (January 1959): 8.

[18] See Stanley Webb's aricle, cited above in note 12, then Susi Jeans's letter (cx [February 1969]: 154; further letters (cx [April 1969]: 375, [June 1969]: 622–23 and [July 1969]: 740). An article by Noel Mander, "Restoring Old Organs," (cx [April 1969]: 420–21), sparked more letters and replies (cx [July 1969]: 740–41 and [August 1969], 834) and Susi Jeans's article, "The 'baroquizing' of English organs," cx (August 1969): 870–71. The editor of *The Musical Times* closed the correspondence on the Great Packington organ with a letter by Paul Kenyon (cx [September 1969]: 934), while on the same page there was a letter about Jeans's "baroquizing" article, which generated further correspondence in the October, November, and December issues. Additional unpublished correspondence, much of it from the time of the controversy in the late 1950s, exists in the Lady Susi Jeans Centre for Organ Historiography at the University of Reading, which also holds a recording made by her at Great Packington. More on Lady Jeans will be found in Robert Judd, ed., *Aspects of Keyboard Music: Essays in Honour of Susi Jeans* (Oxford, 1992).

[19] CBS Odyssey, MB3K 45825, unfortunately without any of the interesting liner notes and photographs issued with the original long-playing records, issued by Columbia under various numbers singly and in collected sets.

20 Record 3 in the 4-record set, EMI SLS 824, also issued singly.

21 Capriccio 10 254, recorded in 1988.

at Great Packington around 1970.[20] A more recent digital recording of solo organ music, including Handel's "Six Fugues or Voluntarys" (HWV 605–610), was made there by Ton Koopman.[21] Together Handel's letter and the Great Packington organ constitute an interesting chapter in the story of Handel as an organist, as well as a fascinating case study (yet to be written) in modern attempts at the restoration and use of old instruments.

Karl Amadeus Hartmann's *Miserae* (1933–1934)

Lauriejean Reinhardt

KARL AMADEUS HARTMANN'S symphonic poem *Miserae* (1933–1934) stands as a watershed in the career of an artist for whom the political events of the early 1930s would assume major personal significance. A lifelong resident of Munich, Hartmann wrote *Miserae* to protest the establishment of the first Nazi concentration camp, which opened in the neighboring village and former artistic community of Dachau in March of 1933. He dedicated the score "to my friends, who must die one-hundred fold, who sleep for eternity—we will not forget you." The sense of moral anguish and political outrage that Hartmann expressed toward Nazism in *Miserae* and other works from the period—for example, the First String Quartet (1933), called the "Jewish Quartet" for its use of the melody "Elijahu ha-navi," or the opera *Simplicius Simplicissmus* (1934–1935) and the cantata *Friede-Anno 48* (1936–1937), both of which invoke clear parallels between Nazi repression and the Thirty Years War—led to the designation of the composer as a "confessional musician" (*Bekenntnismusiker*) and his compositions as "scores of social commitment."[1]

Hartmann himself acknowledged the importance of both *Miserae* and the year 1933 to his artistic development in a memorable passage from his "Autobiographical Sketch":

> Then came the year 1933, with its misery and hopelessness, [and] with it, that which must needs have developed logically from the idea of despotism, the most horrible of all crimes—the war. In that year, I recognized that it was necessary to make a statement, not out of despair and anxiety in the face of that power, but as an act of protest. I told myself that freedom triumphs even at those times when we are annihilated—at least, this is what I believed at that moment. During this period, I wrote my first String Quartet,

[1] Hartmann was known as a *Bekenntnismusiker* even among his contemporaries; see Max See, "Erinnerungen an Karl Amadeus Hartmann," *Neue Zeitschrift für Musik* 125 (1964): 102. Reference to Hartmann's compositions as "scores of commitment" is found in Andrew D. McCredie, *Karl Amadeus Hartmann: Thematic Catalogue of His Works* (Wilhelmshaven and New York: Edition Heinrichshofen, 1982), pp. 19 passim.

the symphonic poem "MISERAE" and my first symphony with the words of Walt Whitman, "I sit and look out upon all the sorrows of the world, and upon all oppression and shame."[2]

As Hartmann's remarks suggest, the works he composed around the time of *Miserae* signaled a self-conscious turning point in his artistic development. More specifically, this period marked the beginning of the composer's self-imposed exile from German musical life, a form of silent protest he waged against Nazism that came to be known as "inner emigration" (*innere Emigration*).[3] Although Hartmann continued to compose during the 1930s and 1940s, he disallowed all public performance of his compositions within the territorial Third Reich. Individual works were heard in neighboring free countries such as Czechoslovakia (1935), England (1938), Belgium (1938 and 1939), and Switzerland (1936 and 1940); however, with the acceleration of World War II, all public performance of Hartmann's music effectively ceased.

Miserae is notable further for the fact that the work's genesis is intimately intertwined with a figure who would have a major impact on Hartmann's socio-political *Weltanschauung*—the conductor Hermann Scherchen. Hartmann maintained a firm belief in the social responsibility of the artist throughout his life. In the 1920s, for example, he embraced the doctrines of socialism. In the 1930s, he participated actively in antifascist resistance efforts. And in the years following World War II, he contributed to the rebuilding of German social and cultural life through the series of new music concerts known as *Musica Viva*.[4] The particular course of political and artistic action he adopted in the early 1930s, however, was inspired in large measure by the model of Scherchen. Like Hartmann, Scherchen was a German of Aryan descent who chose self-exile as a means of opposing Nazism; but whereas Scherchen's protest was announced publicly, by his symbolic renunciation of Germany and withdrawal to neutral Switzerland, Hartmann's was expressed more privately, by his withdrawal into himself.

An event of singular importance to Hartmann's "inner emigration" and his desire to compose a work like *Miserae* was Scherchen's first series of contemporary music workshops, held

[2] [Dann kamm das Jahr 1933, mit seinem Elend und seiner Hoffnungslosigkeit, mit ihm dasjenige, was sich folgerichtig aus der Idee der Gewaltherrschaft entwickeln mu·te, das furchtbarste aller Verbrechen— der Krieg. In diesem Jahr erkannte ich, daß es notwendig sei, ein Bekenntnis abzulegen, nicht aus Verzweiflung und Angst vor jener Macht, sondern als Gegenaktion. Ich dachte mir, daß die Freiheit siegt, auch dann, wenn wir vernichtet werden—das glaubte ich jedenfalls damals. Ich schrieb in dieser Zeit mein erstes Streichquartett, das Poème symphonique "MISERAE" und meine 1. Symphonie mit den Worten von Walt Whitman: "Ich sitze und schaue aus auf alle Plagen der Welt und auf alle Bedrängnis und Schmach…"] "Autobiographische Skizze, 1955" in *Karl Amadeus Hartmann: Kleine Schriften*, ed. Ernst Thomas (Mainz: B. Schott's Söhne, 1965): pp. 12–13.

[3] While Hartmann is the composer most commonly associated with "inner emigration," the term was first introduced in Austro-German literary studies. On the provenance of the term and its meaning and usage in the realm of literature, see E. W. Herd and August Obermeyer, *A Glossary of German Literary Terms* (Dunedin, New Zealand: University of Otago Press, 1983), p. 107; Henry B. and Mary Garland, *Oxford Companion to German Literature* (Oxford and New York: Oxford University Press, 1986), s.v., "Innere Emigration," p. 436; Erwin Rotermund, "Exilliteratur," in *Moderne Literatur in Grundbegriffen*, ed. Dieter Borchmeyer and Viktor Žmegač (Frankfurt am Main: Athenäum Verlag, 1987), pp. 124–26; and Reinhold Grimm, "Innere Emigration als Lebensreform," in *Exil und innere Emigration*, ed. Reinhold Grimm and Jost Hermand [Third Wisconsin Workshop] (Frankfurt am Main: Athenäum Verlag, 1972), pp. 31–73, esp. pp. 34–38. Hartmann's own thoughts on the phenomenon of "inner emigration" are found in his "Gedanken zur Ausstellung 'Entartete Kunst'," published in *Kleine Schriften*, pp. 74–76.

[4] On this aspect of Hartmann's career, see McCredie, *Karl Amadeus Hartmann: Thematic Catalogue* pp. 11–12, 23–24, 42; Andreas Jaschinski, *Karl Amadeus*

Hartmann: Symphonische Tradition und ihre Auflösung (Munich and Salzburg: Musikverlag Emil Katzbichler, 1982), pp. 10–13, 18–31; and Michael Meyer, *The Politics of Music in the Third Reich* (New York/Bern/Frankfurt/Paris: Peter Lang, 1991), pp. 313–15.

5 The Strasbourg workshops are discussed further in Joachim Lucchesi, *Hermann Scherchen: Werke und Briefe*, Bd. 1 (Berlin/Bern/Frankfurt/New York/Paris/Vienna: Peter Lang, 1991), pp. 36–37; and Alexander Jemnitz, "Das Straßburger Musikfest," *Anbruch* 15/8 (1933): 120–22. For an anecdotal yet insightful account of the event, see also Elias Canetti, *The Play of the Eyes* (New York: Farrar, Straus and Giroux, 1986), p. 56 ff.

6 [...daß ich an keinem Konservatorium und an keiner Hochschule auch nur annähernd das gelernt habe, was Scherchen mir beigebracht hat, und zwar einfach deswegen, weil er aus der Praxis heraus arbeitet und das Menschliche in den Vordergrund stellt. ...alles Handwerkliche verdanke ich ihm...Ich denke dabei an seine Musiktagungen und musikdramatischen Arbeitstagungen deren bedeutendste 1933 in Straßburg stattgefunden hat.] Karl Amadeus Hartmann, "Hermann Scherchen," in *Kleine Schriften*, p. 23. Additional thoughts on Scherchen are found in Hartmann's "Autobiographische Skizze," and "Zu meinem 'Simplicius Simplicissmus,'" in *Kleine Schriften*, pp. 12 and 49, respectively.

7 On Hartmann's family background and his early career, see McCredie, *Karl Amadeus Hartmann: Thematic Catalogue*, pp. 7–10.

8 [...ich sitze hier ganz allein, mit keinem Musiker verkehre ich. Ich habe nur zwei Menschen, die mir wirklich gut gesind und die mir offen entgegentreten, das sind Sie lieber Herr Jemnitz und Dr. Scherchen.] Hartmann to Sandor Jemnitz, June 29, 1936, quoted in Andrew D. McCredie, "Karl Amadeus Hartmann and the Hungarian Music of the Early Twentieth Century," *Studia Musicologica* 33 (1991): 164.

in Strasbourg in the summer of 1933. Scherchen's decision to hold the workshops in the capital of Alsace, a region historically disputed between Germany and France, and his emphasis on composers branded by the Third Reich as "degenerate" were recognized by many participants as subversive acts of political protest.[5] In addition to facilitating a performance of Hartmann's *Concertino* for trumpet and wind ensemble, the Strasbourg workshops left an indelible mark on the composer's artistic and political outlook, which he explained as follows:

> ...I learned nothing in any conservatory or music academy that is in the least bit comparable to what Scherchen imparted to me, for the simple reason that he proceeded from a practical perspective and placed the human element in the foreground. I am indebted to him for almost all aspects of my craft...Along these lines, I think about his music festivals and music-dramatic workshops, the most important of which occurred in 1933, in Strasbourg.[6]

Hartmann composed *Miserae* shortly after the Strasbourg experience, in the winter of 1933–1934, and asked Scherchen to conduct the work's premiere in 1935.

Hartmann's retirement from German musical life around the time of *Miserae* was undoubtedly complicated by the fact that he came from a family with close ties to the Munich artistic and intellectual community. The family's activities, particularly in the realm of painting, contributed to the strongly interdisciplinary dimension of Hartmann's work; in the late 1920s, for example, he had sponsored a series of new music concerts in association with Munich's progressive *Deutscher Künstler-Verband "Die Juryfreien."*[7] Hartmann's severing of all cultural ties such as were left after the Nazi ascent to power in 1933 was apparently swift and decisive, for by 1936, he would confide to the Hungarian composer Alexander Jemnitz, "I sit here all alone, I do not interact with any musicians. I have just two people who are really loyal to me and open-minded; they are you, dear Mr. Jemnitz, and Dr. Scherchen."[8]

Hartmann's self-exile assumes all the more poignancy, given the knowledge that, by the mid-1930s, he stood on the threshold of a major international career, and the composition that had led him to this place was *Miserae*. *Miserae* was premiered to wide popular and critical acclaim at the Thirteenth International Society of Contemporary Music (ISCM) festival, held in Prague in the summer of 1935. Hartmann refrained from polemicizing the work in his notes for the festival's program booklet, but the impact of *Miserae* was felt undeniably—both from the emotional weight of the composition's musical style, and the symbolic weight it received as the opening selection of the festival.[9] Perhaps not surprisingly, *Miserae* met with an uneasy indifference in the local Munich press;[10] however, the international press praised the composition as one of the highlights of the festival and the herald of a major new talent. The critic and novelist Max Brod declared that "the premiere of this intensely emotional, original work would alone have been sufficient to bestow historical rank on this music festival."[11] A reviewer from the *Frankfurter Zeitung* wrote: "Among the many who received a forum, there was one new figure of whom one became especially aware. Karl Amadeus Hartmann threw open to discussion an orchestral work that may be regarded as technically exceptional, but above all, that far surpasses many other contemporary compositions by way of its expressive power and its spiritual potency."[12] Writing in the Berlin *Allgemeine Musikzeitung*, Kurt Oppens lavished warm praise on Hartmann and *Miserae*, in contrast to his equivocal reaction to Schoenberg's *Orchestral Variations*, op. 31 and Berg's *Lulu* Suite and his decidedly chilly response to Webern's *Konzert*, op. 24. Of Hartmann and *Miserae*, he wrote:

> As a work with a completely individual character, there was presented the symphonic poem *Miserae* by the Munich composer Karl Amadeus Hartmann. Conducted by Scherchen in the first concert, the work offered the impression of an extraordinary expressive talent that may be rooted in religiosity and that seized and moved the listeners directly.[13]

Even Scherchen, who expressed serious reservations about *Miserae* before conducting the work, came quickly to admire Hartmann and the resolve the composition represented. Shortly before the *Miserae* premiere, Scherchen confided to his

9 The impact of Miserae on the festival audience is recalled by Luigi Dallapiccola in "Meine Erinnerungen an Karl Amadeus Hartmann," *Melos* 37 (1970): 333. The musical commentary that Hartmann provided for the festival program booklet is reproduced by McCredie in his introduction to the score of *Miserae* (Mainz: B. Schott's Söhne, 1977), p. [7].

10 As reported by McCredie in "Karl Amadeus Hartmann and the Hungarian Music of the Early Twentieth Century," p. 162.

11 ["...die Uraufführung dieses stark emotionellen, originellen Werkes allein schon genügt hätte, diesem Musikfest historischen Rang zu verliehen."] *Prager Tagblatt* September 3, 1935, quoted in Andrew McCredie, *Karl Amadeus Hartmann: Sein Leben und Werk* (Wilhelmshaven: Heinrichshofen's Verlag, 1980), p. 41.

12 [Unter den vielen, die zu 'Wort' kamen, gab es einen Neuen, auf den man besonders aufmerksam wurde. Karl Amadeus Hartmann hat ein Orchesterwerk 'Miserae' zur Diskussion gestellt, das technisch ausgezeichnet genannt werden darf, aber vor allem durch seine Ausdruckskraft und seine geistige Potenz viele andere Kompositionen dieser Zeit weit übertraf.] *Frankfurter Zeitung*, September 1935, quoted in McCredie, *Karl Amadeus Hartmann: Sein Leben und Werk*, p. 42.

13 [Als ein Werk ganz eigener Prägung erschien die symphonische Dichtung "Miserae" des Münchners Karl Amadeus Hartmann. Das von Scherchen im 1. Konzert dirigierte Werk vermittelte den Eindruck einer ungewöhnlichen Ausdrucksbegabung, die im Religiösen verwurzelt sein mag und den Hörer unmittelbar anpackt und erschüttert.] "Das internationale Musikfest in Prag," *Allgemeine Musikzeitung* 62/38 (September 20, 1935): 566. Earlier in the review, Oppens had praised the "sensualism" of Schoenberg's *Orchestral Variations* and the "masterful and precipitous sound magic" of Berg's *Lulu* Suite, but only after a harsh

general indictment of twelve-tone composition. Oppens's claim that twelve-tone works relied too heavily on "artistic calculation," "ideological seriousness," and "complicated contrapuntal thematic intricacy," and that they were ultimately "unmusical...incomprehensible...and hopelessly unclear," coupled with his conspicuous avoidance of comment specifically on Webern's *Konzert*, suggests that his antipathy to twelve-tone music was directed largely toward Webern.

14 [Hartmanns Stück ist voll Begabung, aber auch voll Härte u. Ungeschicklichkeit; wir riskieren damit das Lächerlichwerden, wenn die Aufführung nicht unerhört gelingt—das wird sie jetzt aber wohl nach den errungenen Extraproben!] Scherchen to his wife, Auguste ('Gustel') Maria Jansen-Scherchen, August 31, 1935, in *Hermann Scherchen...alles hörbar machen: Briefe eines Dirigenten 1920 bis 1939* (Berlin: Henschelverlag, 1976), p. 254.

15 [Hartmann...ist der Stärkste, Begabteste, Ernsteste.] ibid., p. 257.

16 [Als ich 1935 für längere Zeit nach München zurückkehrte, fand ich Hartmann völlig gewandelt. Aus dem einstigen musikalischen enfant terrible, das sich in Burlesken und Persiflagen austobte, war ein Pathetiker geworden.] Max See, "Erinnerungen an Karl Amadeus Hartmann," *Neue Zeitschrift für Musik* 125 (1964): 101.

17 [Die Epoche der zwanziger Jahre drückte meinem Leben den Stempel auf. In München gab es im Publikum Zirkel—es waren wenige—die für neue und neueste Kunst aufgeschlossen waren. Futurismus, Dada, Jazz und anderes verschmolz ich unbekümmert in einer Reihe von Kompositionen. Ich schlug mich nacheinander zu verschiedenen Strömungen, die sich in jenen erregenden Jahren ebenso schnell an der Spitze der Moderne ablösten wie heute. Ich bediente mich der Schemata neuer Ideen, die blitzartig an den differenten Punkten der Welt auftauchten und stürzte mich in die Abenteuer des geistigen Umbruchs, vielleicht nicht ganz frei von dem selbstgefälligen Gefühl, dabei gewesen zu sein.] Hartmann, "Autobiographische Skizze," p. 12.

wife: "Hartmann's piece is full of merit, but also full of harshness and awkwardness; we run the risk of ridicule with it, if the performance does not succeed extraordinarily well—but it probably will, after squeezing in the extra rehearsals!"[14] Within a few weeks' time, however, in a discussion of Nazi racial policy and its effect on other musicians, Scherchen observed, "Hartmann...is the strongest, the most gifted, the most serious."[15]

Perhaps the most important aspect of *Miserae* is the change it represented in Hartmann's approach both toward genre and what might be called his musical "attitude." This point is best illustrated by the reminiscences of Hartmann's friend Max See, who recalled: "When I returned to Munich for a longer stay in 1935, I found Hartmann completely changed. The musician who was once an enfant terrible, who had sown his wild oats in burlesque and persiflage, had become an emotionalist."[16] Like so many composers in the 1920s, Hartmann had initially adopted a cynical, at times highly critical attitude toward the expressive impulse of German romantic music, using his compositions instead as a platform for bold musical experimentation and pithy social commentary. In keeping with the lean, economical tenor of the times, he had also turned primarily to chamber works and small dramatic projects that exploited the myriad of musical styles currently in vogue. As Hartmann himself explained:

The epoch of the 1920s left its impression on my life. In Munich, there were circles of the public—there were few—that were open to new and the latest art. I carelessly mingled Futurism, Dada, Jazz and other [trends] in a series of compositions. One after the other, I flirted with different trends, which, like today, alternated swiftly on the cutting edge of modernity in those exciting years. I helped myself to the schemata of new ideas that surfaced in a flash in different areas of the world. I plunged myself into the adventure of the spiritual revolution, perhaps not completely free from the complacent feeling of having been there.[17]

Like so many of his German contemporaries, Hartmann had also conspicuously avoided the genre of the symphony, regarding it, as Winfried Zillig has suggested, as "antiquated, conceptually loaded, hypertrophied, in short...as obsolete."[18] With the monumental shift in the moral and artistic landscape of the early 1930s, however, and with his attendant urge to use composition as a medium of personal "confession" (his own word), Hartmann invoked the German romantic heritage passed down from Beethoven to Mahler and turned to the question of the symphony. Indeed, beginning with *Miserae*, symphonic writing became Hartmann's chief métier; the eight numbered symphonies he composed during the remainder of his career are today regarded as his most important musical achievement—so much so that Hartmann has been called "the legitimate heir and most highly original reviver of the grand German symphonic tradition."[19]

As his first major symphonic essay, *Miserae* reveals many of the hallmarks of Hartmann's mature style, as well as some of the perceived flaws that caused him to revise his works with an earnestness and regularity rivaled only by Bruckner. Emblematic of the difficulty Hartmann faced in establishing a modern definition of the symphony was his reticence about applying the designation to his compositions. *Miserae* he referred to alternately as an *Orchesterwerk*, a *Symphonische Dichtung* and its French equivalent, a *Poème Symphonique*, his Symphony No. 1, and *Symphonie Miserae* until 1950, when he withdrew the work for major revisions that were never carried out.[20] Other of the early symphonic works suffered a similar fate. Concomitant with Hartmann's diffidence about generic designation was his inability to accept his symphonic works as complete. This situation manifested itself in a number of ways. Nearly all of his symphonic compositions were subject to reworking in one form or another. In a number of instances, early works or parts of works became the basis for later compositions. And like *Miserae*, many of the early symphonic compositions were retracted as "unofficial" beginning in the late 1940s, when Hartmann first confronted the possibility that the highly personal musical "confessions" he composed under the cloak of self-exile might reach the very public arena of print.[21]

Among the more practical reasons underlying Hartmann's *Problematik* with the symphony may have been the inconsistency he apparently sensed between the rhapsodical

[18] Winfried Zillig, "Hartmanns sinfonische Bekentnisse," *Melos* 26 (1959): 287.

[19] [...legitime Erbe und höchst originelle Erneuerer der großen deutschen symphonischen Tradition.] Zillig, quoted in Heinz-Klaus Metzger and Rainer Riehn, eds., *Karl Amadeus Hartmann-Zyklus Nordrhein-Westfalen 1989/1990* (Munich: edition text + kritik, 1989), p. 3.

[20] On the later history of *Miserae*, see also McCredie, *Thematic Catalogue*, p. 121, and Jaschinski, *Karl Amadeus Hartmann*, p. 14. Miserae was published posthumously in 1977 by Schott, the firm that became the composer's sole publisher beginning in 1954.

[21] On the larger problem of revision, retraction, and cross-fertilization in Hartmann's symphonic works, see also Jaschinski, *Karl Amadeus Hartmann*, pp. 13–17, 31–32; John Warnaby, "Karl Amadeus Hartmann's 'Klagegesang' and the Re-emergence of His Early Music," *Tempo* 180 (March 1992): 6–12; and McCredie, "The Role of Sources and Antecedents in the Compositional Process of Karl Amadeus Hartmann," *Miscellanea Musicologica-Adelaide Studies in Musicology* 10 (1979): 166–212.

22 *Moderne Music 1945–1965: Voraussetzungen, Verlauf Material* (Munich: R. Piper & Co. Verlag, 1966), p. 69.

impulse of his symphonic language and the collagelike nature of his "confessional" style on the one hand, and the conventions of architectonicism and organicism that were understood as synonymous with the German symphonic tradition on the other hand. Hartmann's symphonic works are often cited for their Brucknerian breadth and their Mahlerian inclusiveness of vision, yet they are equally notable for their loose, often unruly approach to form and thematic procedure, a feature Ulrich Dibelius has likened to "interior monologue."[22] Like *Miserae*, many of Hartmann's symphonic compositions are expansive, multisectional works based on independently conceived passages of highly diverse contents and characters. By Hartmann's own account, *Miserae* may be understood in terms of: a slow introduction, the exposition and development sections of a sonata movement (Tempo I, Allegro agitato e vivace), an interpolated slow movement (Tempo II, Lento), the recapitulation of the sonata movement, a coda based on the slow movement, and a short Presto conclusion. The largely independent nature and character of the various sections reflects not only Hartmann's all-embracing view of the symphony, but also his strong reliance on quotation as a means of defining and treating themes.

23 E.g., Warnaby, op. cit.

While recent analysts have noted important parallels between this aspect of Hartmann's musical language and the language of postmodernism,[23] Hartmann's interest in quotation stems more directly from his desire to "confess" his support for those composers and musical styles banned under National Socialism. In a sense, his symphonic works can be understood as highly personal coded messages, which draw on the vocabularies of composers (e.g., Schoenberg, Berg, Bartók, Kodály, Stravinsky, Hindemith), musical traditions (e.g., catholic liturgy, Jewish ritual) and musical idioms (e.g., atonality, *Sprechgesang*, and the twelve-tone method) repressed by the Third Reich.

Not surprisingly, the music of *Miserae* features prominently the monodic incantational style of Jewish folk melody, such as the *espressivo* bassoon theme at the opening of the slow movement shown here. Yet the work also embraces the rhythmic verve and fondness for woodwind sonorities commonly associated with Stravinsky, the saturated chromaticism of early

Schoenberg, and the military *topoi* and rich timbral palette favored by Mahler. Even more specifically, Hartmann's first sonata theme, an extended marchlike passage set low in the cellos and basses, directly recalls the apocalyptic funeral march at the opening of Mahler's Second Symphony ("Resurrection"). While such an approach yields works of a certain semantic richness and complexity, the manner and extent to which quotation is used pose unique problems with regard to the structural conventions and type of thematic integration traditionally associated with the symphony.

It was Hartmann's desire to discuss compositional problems of an even more basic nature that led him to seek guidance in the early 1940s from Anton Webern. Over the years, Hartmann had become acquainted with Webern and his music through a variety of channels. In addition to their mutual friendship with Scherchen, Hartmann and Webern had both had works performed at the ISCM festivals of 1935 and 1938.[24] In 1937, Hartmann submitted his cantata *Friede-Anno 48*, by then retitled *In Memoriam Alban Berg*, for a competition in memory of former Universal Edition director Emil Hertzka. The jurors for the competition, which included Webern, did not award Hartmann the highest prize, but they did offer him a commendation and strong words of encouragement. In 1941, Hartmann approached Webern about the possibility of having his works published by Universal Edition. While this effort did not meet with success, it did launch a cordial friendship between the two composers, and it led to the series of tutorials Hartmann took with Webern in the winter of 1941–1942.[25]

Hartmann's decision to study with Webern was undoubtedly motivated by practicality, since Webern was one of the few composers whose music he respected and who still resided within the Third Reich; but it also suggests a keen understanding of his current situation. Lessons with Webern—a composer known for both his intellectual rigor and his special skills in the areas of formal construction, thematic manipulation, and counterpoint—promised to yield important benefits for a young composer given to loose, somewhat undisciplined instrumental writing who desired to make a mark as a symphonist. Tellingly, among the works the two composers "discussed thoroughly" in terms of "the

[24] As noted earlier, the 1935 ISCM festival held in Prague saw the premieres of Hartmann's *Miserae* and Webern's *Konzert*, op. 24. The 1938 ISCM festival held in London hosted performances of Hartmann's First String Quartet ("Carillon") and the premiere of Webern's *Das Augenlicht*, op. 26. Of the two composers, only Hartmann was in attendance at both events.

[25] The details of Hartmann's early acquaintance with Webern are recorded in Hans and Rosaleen Moldenhauer, *Anton von Webern: A Chronicle of His Life and Work* (New York: Alfred A. Knopf, 1979), pp. 539–40 and 687, n. 6; and McCredie, "The Role of Sources and Antecedents," pp. 189–90, 198, nn. 27 and 28; and *Thematic Catalogue*, pp. 17–18.

[26] Hartmann's remarks on his studies with Webern are found in his "Autobiographische Skizze," but above all, in his letters to his wife published as "Lektionen bei Webern: Briefe an meine Frau," in *Kleine Schriften*, pp. 26–32; partial English translation in Moldenhauer, *Anton von Webern*, pp. 539–43. The "First Symphony" to which Hartmann refers in his second letter ("Lektionen," p. 28) is doubtless *Miserae*. The work that eventually became his official Symphony No. 1 was known alternately as *Cantata, Lamento, Sinfonie: Versuch eines Requiems—Nach Texten von Walt Whitman* and *Symphonische Fragmente* until 1955. In short, Hartmann referred to the latter work as his "First Symphony" only after *Miserae* had been withdrawn.

[27] The Moldenhauer Archives at the Library of Congress preserves communications from Hartmann to Moldenhauer dating from the years 1958 to 1963. In the first two letters, dated December 24, 1958, and August 4, 1959, respectively, Hartmann discusses the genesis and political background of *Miserae* and his anti-Fascist activities during the period in which he composed the work. (Excerpts from these letters may be found in Jaschinski, *Karl Amadeus Hartmann*, pp. 12, 18; and McCredie, *Karl Amadeus Hartmann: Sein Lebeb und Werk*, p. 169.) For further details on Hartmann's relationship with Hans Moldenhauer, see also Moldenhauer, *Anton von Webern*, pp. 449 passim, and McCredie, op. cit., pp. 181–82.

[28] *Karl Amadeus Hartmann: Thematic Catalogue*, pp. 39, 177.

smallest ramifications of form and thematic content" was *Miserae*.[26]

The presence of the *Miserae* autograph in Moldenhauer's Collection speaks to the friendship that arose between the two men beginning in the late 1950s. Moldenhauer approached Hartmann in 1958 for a manuscript to be included in his growing archival collection.[27] Hartmann responded with the original (and only) score for the yet unpublished *Miserae*, thereby initiating a cordial relationship with the Mainz-born musicologist. In 1962, Moldenhauer arranged for Hartmann to receive an honorary doctorate from the Spokane Conservatory, which Moldenhauer had founded twenty years earlier. According to McCredie,[28] among the additional materials Hartmann made available to Moldenhauer during these years were the sketches for his final, incomplete work, the *Gesangsszene* for baritone and orchestra. This work, based on Jean Giradoux's drama *Sodome et Gomorrhe* (1943) and dedicated to Moldenhauer, was published posthumously in 1965.

Josef Matthias Hauer's
Melischer Entwurf

Lauriejean Reinhardt

HISTORY HAS RELEGATED Josef Matthias Hauer (1883–1959)
to the rank of *Kleinmeister* and his twelve-tone works to a
position subordinate to that held by the Schoenberg circle. His
highly idiosyncratic compositions and theoretical writings
exerted little influence on later generations, and they were
regarded as inconsequential, if not somewhat eccentric, by
many of his contemporaries. Nevertheless, Hauer remains a
notable and colorful figure, and his works constitute a likely
barometer of the cultural and intellectual climate of Vienna
after World War I. Much of his oeuvre remains unpublished
and awaits serious study.

Hauer's extravagant metaphysical views on music and his
prickly personality placed him outside the Viennese musical
mainstream, yet he associated with some of the leading figures
of the day, most notably the Christian existentialist philosopher
Ferdinand Ebner (1882–1931) and the Bauhaus artist Johannes
Itten (1888–1967). The writings of both men reveal Hauer's
influence. He is chiefly remembered, however, as a rival of
Schoenberg, having developed his own twelve-tone method
and begun to publish his findings around 1919, slightly ahead
of Schoenberg—a fact that proved particularly irksome to the
more well-known composer.

The two men were on friendly terms briefly in the 1920s.
During this time, Hauer dedicated his two-volume *Etüden für
Klavier* (1922–1923) and his aesthetic treatise *Vom Melos zur
Pauke* (1925) to Schoenberg. His compositions were performed
by Schoenberg's *Verein für musikalische Privataufführungen*, and
the two composers even considered collaborating on a book
and a school for twelve-tone composition, neither of which
were ever realized. Hauer also recalled that during a private
conversation Schoenberg admitted "We have both found one

[1] Schoenberg sagte zu mir: "Wir haben beide einen und denselben Brillanten gefunden, Sie schauen ihn von der einen Seite an und ich von der entgegengesetzten." Ich antwortete ihm: "Und so können noch viele, viele den Brillanten von allen Seiten betrachten," quoted in Walter Szmolyan, *J. M. Hauer* (Wien: Verlag Elisabeth Lafite, 1965), p. 49.

[2] "Das atonale Melos...ist das A und O des geistigen Menschen...ist 'da' vom Anfang bis zum Ende aller Zeiten," Josef Matthias Hauer, "Melos und Rhythmus," *Melos* 3 (1922): 186.

[3] "Eine atonale Melodie kann nich erfunden, sondern nur 'gehört' werden. Der atonale Musiker ist kein Musikmacher, kein Musikant...kein 'Originalgenie,' sondern ein 'Hörender,' einer, der das Unveränderliche, Unantastbare, Ewige im Wesen der Dinge ('Tao') vernimmt," "Melos und Rhythmus," p. 186.

and the same diamond, you look at it from one side and I from the opposite side," to which Hauer replied, "And so can many, many others view it from all sides."[1] In later years both composers grew increasingly less magnanimous, each stubbornly asserting his primacy in discovering the idea of composing with twelve tones.

The "melodic sketch" shown here dates from Hauer's final period (roughly 1939–1959) and illustrates the basic features of his mature compositional method. This leaf shows preliminary ideas for a *Zwölftonspiel*, meaning both, in general, "twelve-tone composition" and, more literally, "twelve-tone game." The particular work, a string quartet written in 1954, was dedicated to the German conductor Hans Rosbaud; the dedication can be seen on the upper-right-hand corner of this sketch. The Moldenhauer Archives at the Library of Congress also contains the autograph score of the unpublished quartet and a letter from Rosbaud to Hauer, inquiring about a possible performance.

As suggested by the heading *Melischer Entwurf*, the essence of Hauer's approach to composition lay in melody, for which he used the Greek term *Melos*. Far outweighing elements such as rhythm or harmony, *Melos* was, for Hauer, both the true substance of music and the root of spiritual existence, the "Alpha and Omega of discerning man...it 'exists' from the beginning to the end of all time."[2] (The word was also adopted as the name for the journal here quoted and reflected the ideas of the Schoenberg circle.) Hauer's concept of *Melos* was influenced by the writings of ancient China, which he claimed represented the purest culture of *Melos*, and his aesthetic philosophy was strongly informed by Taoism and the *I Ching*. According to Hauer, atonal (i.e., twelve-tone) music was not invented (*erfunden*) but rather "perceived" ("*gehört*"). The atonal musician was not an active agent—neither a music maker (*Musikmacher*) nor a performer (*Musikant*) or "original genius" ("*Originalgenie*")—but a passive "hearer" ("*Hörender*"), one who "perceives that which is unchanging, intangible, the eternal in the essence of things ("*Tao*")."[3] Compositions were regarded as a *Sphärenmusik* that provided a path to self-discovery, and the creative process was likened to a cosmic game, with certain elements left to chance. In his later years,

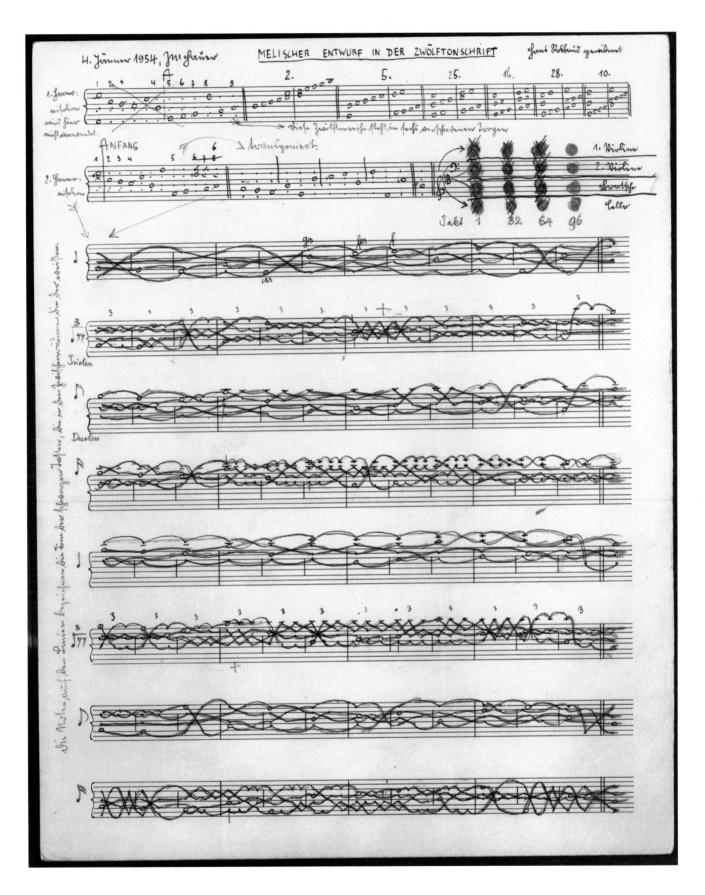

Hauer abandoned the use of opus numbers and descriptive titles, designating each of over one thousand works simply as a *Zwölftonspiel,* and distinguishing one from another by way of date and performance medium.

The resources Hauer required in order to realize his *Zwölftonspiel* are charted in this manuscript. One of the more peculiar features of the manuscript (and Hauer's sketches in general) is his unique notational system, essentially a keyboard system founded on the principle of equal temperament and a belief in the equivalence of the twelve chromatic pitches. In order to represent these pitches equitably and without the hierarchical values implied by accidentals, Hauer devised a new staff, one that eliminated the need for accidentals and approximated the design of a piano keyboard.

On Hauer's eight-line staff, all lines represent the black keys of the keyboard while spaces represent the white keys. This is explained in the left-hand margin of the manuscript: "Die Noten auf den Linien bezeichnen die Töne der schwarzen Tasten, die in den Zwischenräumen die der weißen." Traditional clefs are retained, but they are used in a nontraditional way. Treble and bass clefs no longer indicate the pitches G and F, respectively; rather, they define an octave, both indicating the pitch class G#/Ab. The "C" clef rests in the middle space, dividing the octave symmetrically at the tritone, D-natural. The wider spacing between lines 3–4 and 5–6 allows for the writing of two separate noteheads, E-F and B-C, the semitones of the piano keyboard that are represented by consecutive white notes. The lower of each pair of notes rests on the lower line, the higher pitch hangs from the line above. This neutralized notational system, first described in *Vom Wesen des Musikalischen* (1920), is used consistently in Hauer's *Melische Entwürfe.* For ease of performance, however, he generally reverted to conventional notation for full and published scores.

Fundamental to Hauer's method of composition is the trope, indirectly analogous to Schoenberg's twelve-tone row. Each new work is based on one of twelve universal trope tables, each table being oriented around a different pitch level in the chromatic scale. For each table, the basic trope consists of the simple chromatic scale, followed by forty-three systematic permutations for a total of forty-four possible tropes. (Hauer's system of tropes, tentatively announced in various articles from the early 1920s, is most thoroughly explained in his *Zwölftontechnik* of 1926. He revised his trope tables in 1948; this composition is based on the later version of the tables.)

The operative element in Hauer's method was not the total chromatic scale, however, but the hexachord. This is shown in the present manuscript. For this composition, based on the trope table oriented around C#, Hauer has chosen to use tropes 2, 5, 25, 16, 28, and 10. These are copied on the top staff and subdivided into their respective hexachords. The alignment of these hexachords as stacks of pitches rather than strict linear orderings reflects a fundamental difference between Hauer's and Schoenberg's methods; it likewise represents an aspect of Hauer's approach that was influenced by Chinese philosophy and that incorporated an element of chance.

Hauer viewed his hexachords as pitch fields or *Konstellationen*: while the pitch content of tropes and their hexachords was determined systematically, by means of interval relationships, the ordering of pitches within each hexachord was indeterminate. Like the hexagrams of the *I Ching*, Hauer's hexachords were aggregate symbols that, while clearly defined, could be internally reconfigured and were subject to a wide variety of interpretations.

> Twelve-tone compositions (*Zwölftonspiele*) embody functions of the galaxy system, [they] are the kinetic formation-center of organic processes. The twelve-tone 'game' (*Zwölfton-'spiel'*) is also similar to the oracle 'game,' as it has been handed down in the ancient Chinese book of wisdom, the *I Ching*.[4]

Pitch ordering was consequently not fixed as in Schoenberg's method, for this would inhibit the "hearing" composer's ability to divine "musical truths" from the symbology of the hexachords. In practical terms, this meant that within a given hexachord, pitches could occur in any order and recur or be reiterated freely, without violating the integrity of that hexachord. The primal law of the total chromatic scale, what Hauer called the *Urgesetz* or *Nomos*, obtained on a deep structural level, in the continuous circulation of the twelve

4 "Zwölftonspiele beinhalten Funktionen der Milchstraßensysteme, die motorische Formungszentren organischer Prozesse sind. Das Zwölfton-'spiel' ist auch gleichzeitig ein Orakel-'spiel,' wie es in dem uralten Weisheitsbuch der Chinesen, im Iging, überliefert ist." Josef Matthias Hauer, *Zwölftonspiel (8 Juli 1957) für Klavier zu vier Händen* (Wien: Fortissimo Musikverlag, 1957).

chromatic pitches; surface patterning did not contradict or negate this fundamental law.

While he did not admit so openly, Hauer appears to have been influenced likewise by the unique organizational properties of Eastern music. His *Zwölftonspiele* are ultimately not "closed" compositions based on the purposeful working out of pregnant themes and motifs, but rather highly sectional, "open cycle" compositions based on schematic repetitions of hexachord pitches. Tellingly, in his many aesthetic and theoretical writings, Hauer studiously avoided concrete terms such as *Thema* or *Motiv* opting instead for the vague and all-embracing *Melos*. He also chose the passive term *Entfaltung* (unfolding) to describe the interaction of musical ideas rather than active, teleologically charged terms like *Entwicklung*, *Durchführung*, or *Variation*.

In his attempt to appropriate ancient Chinese thought for his twelve-tone method, Hauer was neither comprehensive nor entirely consistent. To cite just one example: nowhere in his exhaustive literature on the subject does he spell out exactly how chance enters into his creative process. (Schoenberg criticized Hauer's frequent invocation of mystical and oriental philosophy as a smoke screen, intended to disguise what he saw as serious flaws in the musical foundation of Hauer's method. However, Schoenberg himself claimed "divine guidance" in the formulation of his own twelve-tone method.) Hauer also acknowledged his indebtedness to a miscellany of more traditional influences including Goethe's *Zur Farbenlehre* and medieval and ancient Greek philosophy. And while, like Schoenberg, Hauer was musically self-trained, his compositions reveal a thorough knowledge of conventional theory, as evidenced, for example, by the permutational sequence of his trope tables, the selections of tropes for a given composition, and his reliance on basic contrapuntal procedures.

Nonetheless, Hauer's interest in Oriental philosophy and its relevance to contemporary composition forms a distinctive and highly significant part of his musical aesthetic. It is indicative as well of a larger intellectual current that swept the former Hapsburg Empire after the First World War, one preoccupied with a redefinition of Western culture that embraced a variety of non-Western ideas and witnessed a resurgent interest in Taoism. Equally significant, although Hauer's work had little influence on later composers, his attempt to integrate the element of chance into the creative process and his view of composition as a musical "game" prefigure the work of John Cage, Karlheinz Stockhausen, and Pierre Boulez.

Sketches on the upper left side of the present manuscript show ideas for a *Zwölftonreihe*, the one element for which Hauer did establish a definitive pitch ordering (hence his use of the linear term *Reihe* rather than the more amorphous *Trope*). The row was the first newly composed element of a *Zwölftonspiel* and it functioned somewhat like a cantus firmus. While not outwardly thematic, this row recurred unchanged throughout the composition, its pitches embedded within the figures of individual phrases. The significance of a twelve-tone "row" as opposed to a trope was threefold: it provided a harmonic underpinning as well as a structural foundation for the composition, and its linear reiteration of the complete overtone series (German: *Obertonreihe*) symbolized the constancy and totality of the cosmos or "the Continuum" (*Das Kontinuum*).

This particular row is derived from a hexachordal division of trope 2. The basic hexachords of this trope are first reconfigured (staves 1 and 2, left), and the row is then transferred to begin on the second pitch, E-natural (stave 2, left). Hauer confirms this new beginning with a vertical line and the word *Anfang*. The new row is transferred down a perfect fourth to begin on B-natural (stave 2, center), and it is this version that provides the basis for the composition.

The analogy between row and *cantus firmus* is especially strong in this early stage of sketching, for the piece is built polyphonically around this single, independent line. The row is typically the only pitched element in Hauer's *Melische Entwürfe*. Black noteheads seen throughout the manuscript surrounding each row statement are essentially place holders, suggesting how the row is to be "harmonized." It is from this proposed harmonization, always sketched in four parts, that individual "melodies" are later created, based on the chosen tropes. (Hauer interpreted the term *Melos* rather loosely; while his *Zwölftonspiele* are essentially polyphonic compositions,

·255·

piano works occasionally employ chordal accompaniments.)
The row is distinguished further from these inchoate melodies
by the use of augmented white-note values. This too is an
abstraction; in the final composition, these row pitches will be
incorporated into musical lines which use faster values.

The colored dots on the upper right corner of the manuscript
constitute a *Vierweg* (four-way), a self-perpetuating matrix
similar to a Magic Square. Also created anew for each
composition, this matrix provides the *Spielregel* or "rule of the
game" which governs how the piece will unfold. On a more
practical level, the *Vierweg* serves as a voice-leading graph, its
colored dots plotting a general course for musical ideas to be
determined at a later stage of sketching. The *Vierweg* could be
implemented on any number of levels and in a variety of ways;
however, it did not automatically dictate decisions on details
such as number of measures, choice of trope, instrumentation,
or the number and constitution of musical ideas.

Hauer's related concepts of row and *Vierweg* were rooted in a
neo-Pythagorean belief that music reflects the eternal and
absolute laws of the cosmos, "the Continuum," and that each
Zwölftonspiel offers a brief glimpse of this Continuum. The
linear representation of the cosmos offered by the row is
rendered two-dimensional in the *Vierweg*, a relationship
underscored by his description of the latter as *das vierstimmige
harmonische Band: Das Kontinuum* (the four-voiced harmonic
thread: the Continuum).

For Hauer, each *Vierweg* offered a "specific external linking of
the Continuum, providing the basis for the building of the
most varied musical forms (*Spielformen*)." The *Vierweg's* union
of horizontal and vertical dimensions and its boundless
potential to generate musical ideas transcended the constraints
of time and place, thus elevating the resulting *Zwölftonspiel* to a
higher level of reality. As explained by Hauer's student, Viktor
Sokolowski:

> The system of the pitch world encloses itself into a unity:
> twelve-tone cycle, four-way and overtones enjoin in the
> *Zwölftonspiel* to a recognizable law of the fourth dimension,

the reality of time and place. Time and place are in equilibrium.[5]

The glimpse of the continuum afforded by this particular matrix is sketched in greater detail on the bottom of the manuscript. The ideas on staves 3–10 provide a near-complete picture of how the quartet will be put together; indeed, the entire quartet is plotted on these eight staves. This particular composition is extremely concise, and it divides neatly into four distinct blocks, each block comprising four separate polyphonic lines. Lines are exchanged at the same, regularly recurring distance of thirty-two measures (i.e., at measures 32, 64, and 96), so that blocks are perfectly synchronized. In this instance, then, the correspondence between *Vierweg* and composition is quite literal: each colored dot represents a single musical line, and each instrument of the quartet articulates exactly one statement of each line. The *Vierweg* thus represents a skeletal picture of the entire composition.

The course of the first block is mapped on the lower eight staves. Beginning with stave 3, each staff contains a single, four-measure phrase which is defined by a complete row statement and characterized by a distinctive rhythmic value. Hauer notes these values in the margin to the left. These rhythmic values serve as a general guideline and help to shape the basic rhythmic profile of the phrase. A succession of phrases characterized first by quarter notes, then eighth-note triplets, eighth notes, and finally sixteenth notes is stated twice, with a different harmonization for the second statement (i.e., staves 7–10).

These eight staves consequently chart the course of one complete thirty-two-measure block. But since the lines of this block wander throughout the composition and are simply relayered in subsequent blocks (following the pattern of the *Vierweg*), the remainder of the composition is embodied here as well. Hauer's "melodic sketch," in essence a contrapuntal graph from which the musical substance of the piece will be generated, thus also serves a purpose similar to a short score.

5 "Das System der Tonwelt schließt sich zu einem Ganzen: Zwölftonzyklus, Vierklänge und Obertöne vereinen sich im Zwölftonspiel zum erkennbaren Gesetz der vierten Dimension, der raumzeitlichkeiten Wirklichkeit. Raum und Zeit sind im Gleichgewicht." "Über das Zwölftonspiel," Viktor Sokolowski [untitled exhibition catalog], (Vienna: R. Schäffer, [n.d.]).

Paul Hindemith's *Hérodiade*

Jürgen Thym

PAUL HINDEMITH (1895–1963) had leapt onto the musical scene in the 1920s as an enfant terrible and musical revolutionary. Even though at the end of the decade his compositional style was increasingly informed by a striving for comprehensibility and by ethical considerations, the unrestrained modernity and shock character of some of his early works haunted him when the Nazis came to power in his homeland. Despite the support of many friends, the official view of Hindemith's music as "degenerate" prevailed, making it impossible for him to continue his career in Germany. Three journeys to North America in the late 1930s opened up contacts for Hindemith as violist, conductor, composer, and teacher, and shortly after the outbreak of World War II he emigrated to the United States, accepting within a year a professorship for music theory and composition at the Yale School of Music where he taught from 1940 to 1953.

The work under discussion is one of the few ballet scores composed by Hindemith. It is based on Stéphane Mallarmé's dialogue poem *Hérodiade* and consists of eleven movements, which are to be performed without major breaks. Hindemith, however, specified short pauses after movements 3, 7, and 9, thereby grouping the entire work into four larger sections. The ballet is scored for a chamber ensemble of flute, oboe, clarinet, bassoon, and horn—woodwind quintet—plus piano and strings. The music for the textual portions of the nurse in the poem is given to the strings, while the emotionally high-strung lines of Hérodiade are represented through the colorful instruments of the winds as well as the piano.

Several factors contributed to the genesis of *Hérodiade*. Since the late 1920s Hindemith had known Elizabeth Sprague Coolidge (1864–1953), the famous patron of the arts, who had commissioned from him the *Concert Music for Piano, Brass, and Two Harps*, op. 49 (premiered in Chicago in 1930) and who had been interested in drawing the composer to the United States. During the first of Hindemith's exploratory tours of North America in 1937 contacts between them were reestablished,[1] and when he settled in the United States, Coolidge supported the composer by commissioning him to write a work for Martha Graham (1893–1991), one of the leading figures of contemporary dance.[2] The inspiration to use a poem by Stéphane Mallarmé (1842–1898) as a pretext for a composition—one readily associates Debussy or Boulez with the French symbolist poet, but not necessarily Hindemith—seems to have come from the composer's wife, Gertrud Hindemith (1900–1967)[3]. During the mid-1940s she had enrolled in the graduate program in French philology at Yale University, completing her MA degree in 1945, and it is likely that she familiarized her husband with Mallarmé's famous paean of 1869.[4]

Since teaching obligations at Yale required a considerable time commitment during semesters, Hindemith had to relegate creative work mainly to the summer months. *Hérodiade* was completed in two weeks in June 1944 in New Haven.[5] Some correspondence concerning the publication of the score and piano reduction with American Music Publishers was conducted from the Hindemiths' summer quarters in Maine.[6] The premiere took place at the Library of Congress on November 30, 1944, with Martha Graham dancing the role of Hérodiade.

Hindemith always composed fast—some critics would say "dangerously fast"[7]—and *Hérodiade* seems to have been no exception. What surprises, however, is the extensive number of sketches and drafts that were part of the compositional process. Hindemith experimented in *Hérodiade* with a compositional technique of reciting the poem in the instruments, using the poem's phrases, rhythms, and cadences as *cantus firmus* for his music, thereby also following its poetic ideas and expressive gestures. (Hence the subtitle of the work: *Récitation orchestrale.*) In a way, by following the rhythm of the French language, Hindemith was able to avoid relying on his usual motoric rhythms and perpetual motions for musical continuity. It was perhaps the absence of the text as a vocal line, or rather the poem's peculiar presence in the melodic line of various

[1] Paul Hindemith, *"Das private Logbuch": Briefe an seine Frau Gertrud*, ed. Friederike Becker and Giselher Schubert (Mainz: Schott, 1995), pp. 164–67, 171; also *Selected Letters of Paul Hindemith*, ed. and tr. Geoffrey Skelton (New Haven and London: Yale University Press, 1995), pp. 100–102.

[2] Wayne D. Shirley, "Ballets for Martha," *Performing Arts Annual 1988*, Washington: Library of Congress, 1989, pp. 26–59.

[3] Conversation with Giselher Schubert, May 22, 1996.

[4] Luther Noss, *Paul Hindemith in the United States* (Urbana and Chicago: University of Illinois Press, 1989), p. 162.

[5] Ibid., p. 122.

[6] Skelton, p. 185.

[7] Ludwig Finscher, "Der Späte Hindemith," *Hindemith-Jahrbuch XIII* (1984) (Mainz: Schott, 1985), p. 11.

instruments (encompassing the entire range from the lowest to the highest registers) that led Hindemith to shape the composition through more than fifty pages of sketches and drafts.

While it cannot be the function of this commentary to provide a detailed source study of the autograph, a few general remarks may be permitted. The gathering of twenty-seven leaves (fifty-four pages), bound in cardboard with spine reinforced, falls clearly into three layers (as indicated through Hindemith's pagination) which, by and large, are also representative of different stages in the compositional process.

Layer A. Preliminary sketches, some of them so vague that it is difficult to attribute them with certainty to any one section; some can be identified because of fragments of the Mallarmé poem appearing in the score; and some of them already show the contours of the final version. (The preliminary sketches are contained on pages numbered 17 through 31 in the second half of the autograph as well as a few unnumbered pages at the beginning of the gathering.)

Layer B. Fair copy of the work in the form of a particell (mostly on two staves, but occasionally expanded to three and four staves). This compositional stage is notated on the verso of the pages numbered 1 through 17 of layer A; because of its content, an unnumbered page belongs to this group as well. These pages contain all the movements of *Hérodiade* except for the prelude and movement 8 (fair copies of these sections are intermingled with the layer of sketches described above). The movements (excluding the prelude) are numbered consecutively in Roman numerals I through X. Mallarmé's text appears not only as incipit in the titles of the various movements but also throughout the score, especially in the lengthier movements, in the form of textual fragments written (and later printed) as rubrics above a given passage. These function as "bookmarks" for the reader, much in the way they provided Hindemith with orientation during the compositional process. The fair copy is further characterized by frequent corrections and sections crossed out, indicative of the still fluid stage in the compositional process, and also by occasional listings of instruments. Hindemith wrote out a tonality chart for the entire work (again excluding the prelude) at the end of movement 7 (which he counted here as VI). We can assume that he used this section of the autograph for writing the final copy of the score.

Layer C. The fair copy of the piano reduction is notated on pages located in the first half of the gathering; they are numbered 1 through 16 and thereby designated as a unit. Moreover, Hindemith also writes "Auszug" (reduction) on the first of these pages. This layer contains the piano reduction of all the movements, except for the slow sections which are the framing sections for the prelude. (Movement 8 appears out of order before movement 2.) No references to Mallarmé's text appear in this layer of the autograph, neither as titles nor as bookmarks, suggesting that the compositional process had been completed by this time; moreover, some movements (2–7) already appear with the final numbering (counting the prelude as no. 1), indicating a late or final stage in the conception of the work. We can assume that Hindemith used these pages to write out the final copy of the piano reduction for publication.

Three facsimiles from the third movement ("Reculez") may illustrate the different stages of the compositional process:

1) Facsimile of Frame 107 (Sketch for "Reculez" at rehearsal letter A)
2) Facsimile of Frame 124 (Fair copy of beginning of "Reculez")
3) Facsimile of Frame 113 (Piano reduction of "Reculez," beginning)

In the last years of his life Hindemith returned to *Hérodiade*, not to revise it along the standards of *Unterweisung im Tonsatz* (*The Craft of Musical Composition*) as he had done with some of his earlier works, but to supply the score with a detailed scenario, written up as a trope commenting on the various movements, for performance as a ballet. He always had a special fondness for the work: "Es kommt aus der besten Kiste" ("It is something out of the top drawer"), he wrote to his publisher Ludwig Strecker in 1948.[8] The composition had been performed frequently after World War II in Europe, but

8 Skelton, p. 204.

Facsimile of Frame 107 (Sketch for "Reculez"
at rehearsal letter A)
Moldenhauer Archives, Paul Sacher Foundation,
Basel

Facsimile of Frame 124 (Fair copy of beginning of
"Reculez")
Moldenhauer Archives, Paul Sacher Foundation,
Basel

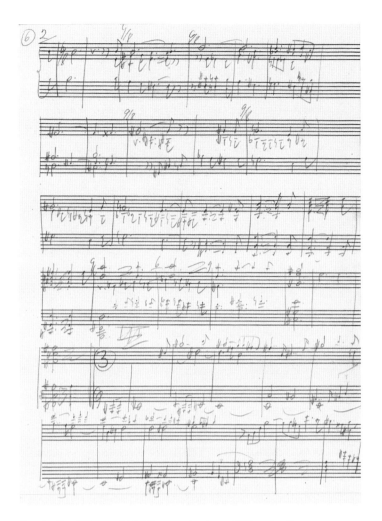

Facsimile of Frame 113 (Piano reduction of "Reculez,"
beginning)
Moldenhauer Archives, Paul Sacher Foundation,
Basel

Hindemith HÉRODIADE
Copyright 1949 by Schott & Co. Ltd., London
Copyright renewed
All Rights Reserved
Used by permission of European American Music
Distributors Corporation, sole U.S. and Canadian agent for
Schott & Co. Ltd., London

Reproduced by permission of the
Paul Hindemith-Institut

9 Andres Briner, *Paul Hindemith* (Zurich: Atlantis, 1971), p. 162.

10 Ibid.

11 Andres Briner, Dieter Rexroth, and Giselher Schubert, *Paul Hindemith: Leben und Werk in Bild und Text* (Zurich: Atlantis, 1988), pp. 180–81.

12 Skelton, p. 204.

13 Geoffrey Skelton, *Paul Hindemith: The Man Behind the Music* (London: Victor Gollancz, Ltd., 1975), p. 212. "These people are my friends. What can I say to them? Let them do it."

never with dancers. The publication of Mallarmé's poems in a German translation by Carl Fischer in 1957 as well as the prospect of having the piece performed, for the first time since its premiere, as a ballet in Mannheim and Rome during the 1961–1962 season may have inspired the composer to provide a helping hand for what he considered one of his better pieces.[9] Hindemith did not attend the 1944 Washington premiere, but, according to the recollections of Martha Graham after Hindemith's death, his wife, who attended, may have been critical of Graham's rather abstract dance forms set in counterpoint to the orchestral declamation.[10] Hindemith's handwritten instructions for the "Aufführung als Tanzstück"[11] clearly are directed against an "abstract" performance and point toward very concrete, albeit stylized, scenarios as backdrop for the dancers and similarly concrete, though restrained, expressive gestures and movements. The subtle psychological nuances of Mallarmé's enigmatic poem are translated here into a *ballet d'action*.

Not only is Hindemith's *Hérodiade* a work based on an enigmatic poem that resists immediate intelligibility, it is also a composition that reinforces the enigmatic character of the poem by rendering it in two wordless media: instrumental music and dance. By doing so, Hindemith hoped to find an equivalent for "Mallarmé's wonderfully exalted but likewise polished, brittle, and artificial creation" (preface to the piano reduction). But he undoubtedly was aware that performances of the work would face communication problems for musicians, dancers, and audience. "The whole thing is admittedly a very esoteric affair," he wrote to Strecker in 1948. "To read the text and listen to the music at one and the same time is an impossibility even for experienced connoisseurs, and one cannot demand from ordinary listeners a study of each single factor and the way they interact."[12] In order to facilitate communication, some conductors (Robert Craft and, most recently, Werner Andreas Albert) have recorded the work with a speaker reciting the text. But there is something tautological about such renditions; moreover, Hindemith expressly opposed performances with spoken recitation, and only reluctantly permitted Craft to record it with Vera Zorika's recitation.[13] "AMP [Schott's American representative] should rent the material only if the text is not to be spoken."[14] And he concludes his note to Karl Bauer: "Getanzt werden darf natürlich" ("Dancing, of course, is permitted"). Perhaps it is imperative for performers to take the "Anweisungen zur Aufführung als Tanzstück" (Hindemith-Institut, Frankfurt/Main) seriously; they seem to be Hindemith's last word on one of his most idiosyncratic yet musically appealing works.

14 Noss, p. 122.

Arthur Honegger's "Les Ombres": Fragment of a Lost Film Score

Fred Steiner

ARTHUR HONEGGER (1892–1955), French composer of Swiss parentage, wrote symphonies, concertos, chamber works, and ballets; probably his best-known compositions are the "dramatic psalm" *Le Roi David* and the "mouvement symphonique" *Pacific 231*. But Honegger also wrote music for more than forty motion pictures (some in collaboration with other composers), and that aspect of his career spanned both the silent and sound film eras. Many other French concert hall composers, e.g., Jean Françaix, Jacques Ibert, André Jolivet, Eric Satie, Henri Sauguet, as well as Honegger's confreres in *Les Six*[1]—Georges Auric, Louis Durey, Darius Milhaud, Francis Poulenc, Germaine Tailleferre—all composed for silent or sound films, or both.[2] In fact, what is presumed to be the first original film score was also composed by a Frenchman, Camille Saint-Saëns, for *L'Assassinat du Duc de Guise*, in 1908.

Composers in other European countries whose names were normally associated with the concert hall occasionally crossed over into films, e.g., Paul Dessau, Hanns Eisler, Sergei Prokofiev, Dmitri Shostakovich, Ralph Vaughan-Williams, and William Walton. Many of them regarded composing for the films as a challenge. Moreover, some of them wrote valuable essays about their experiences and the unique problems they faced in this kind of work.

"Les Ombres" is a segment of the music that Honegger composed for one of the most celebrated motion pictures of the silent era: *Napoléon vu par Abel Gance* was a giant epic, a motion picture conceived and produced on what was probably the grandest scale of any film before its time in France. The name of its writer and director, Abel Gance, was legendary in the cinema, and for him Honegger had composed and compiled music for the film *La Roue* in 1923. The premiere of

[1] The group of young French composers in the 1920s who rejected Wagnerism and Impressionism and sought to derive inspiration from the urban and witty worlds of music hall, jazz, and the circus.

[2] For filmographies of Honegger and other French composers see Alain Lacombe, *Des compositeurs pour l'image (Cinéma et Télévision)*, with a preface by Jean-Loup Tournier (Neuilly-sur-Seine: Musique et promotion, 1982).

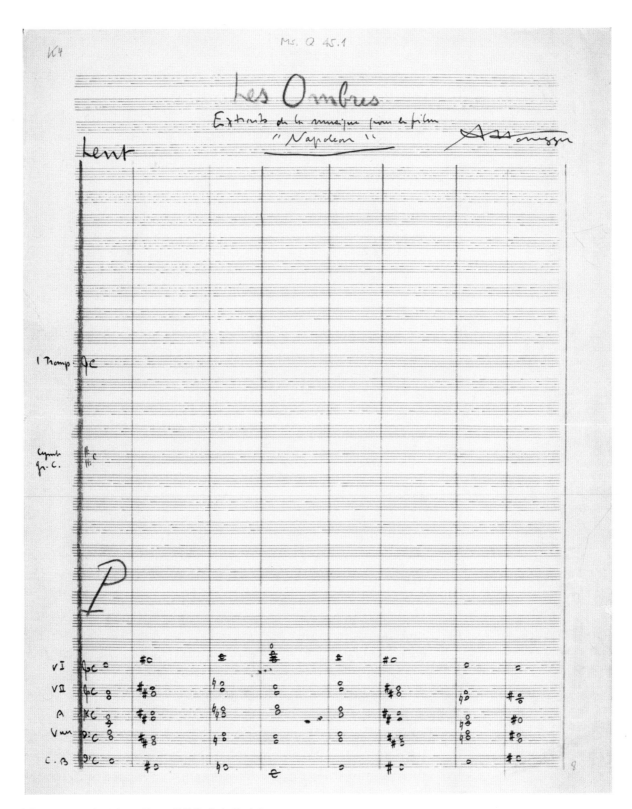

Napoléon was at the Théâtre National de l'Opéra in Paris on April 7, 1927, where it was so successful that it was repeated nine times.

Despite its initial success, the history of the film *Napoléon* is a sad and confusing tale. Gance's rough cut ran nine hours, but even if he had had the film ready in time for the premiere, such an extraordinary length was not acceptable to the exhibitors, and Gance was forced to cut it down to three hours and forty minutes.[3] A month after the premiere, a "definitive" version, lasting nine hours, was screened privately, using some of Honegger's music and excerpts from the classics. Since then, however, exhibitors and distributors have cut and changed the film so many times that it is doubtful if it has ever been seen again in its "definitive" form. In its final, "official" edit (completed in 1928), *Napoléon* ran six and a half hours. Gance himself produced a much-shortened sound version in 1935, but not with Honegger's music. It was not until 1980 that a version was exhibited that probably came closest to Gance's original concept. It was assembled and edited by the British filmmaker and historian Kevin Brownlow, but the score, composed and compiled by Carl Davis, used only one piece of Honegger's music.[4]

The fate of Honegger's score has been sadder still. Not only has his original manuscript disappeared, but to this day the cue sheet has not been found (if one ever existed). Without it or a similar music list, there is no way of knowing exactly what the score contained. Of one thing we can be certain: even had Honegger been able to compose a completely original score of nine hours duration,[5] he soon would have had to abandon any such idea because Gance was constantly reediting the film. We can therefore safely assume that a large part of the music that accompanied *Napoléon* consisted of the common silent film fare of arrangements from the classics, popular songs, and some stock music that Honegger wrote for other purposes (possibly for newsreels). We do know that for Gance's earlier *La Roue*, the composer drew on preexisting music.[6] Of course, Honegger would have been able to write new music for any scenes from *Napoléon* that the director left intact, but we do not know how much he wrote or how much of it was actually used at the screening (but see note 11 below).

3 See Kevin Brownlow, *Napoleon: Abel Gance's Classic Film* (New York: Alfred A. Knopf, 1983), pp. 150, 299, n. 3.

4 A second, somewhat longer version, also the work of Brownlow, was shown in 1982, again with Davis's score.

5 Remember that musical accompaniment was perforce continuous throughout the showing of a silent film.

6 See Harry Halbreich, *Arthur Honegger: Un musicien dans la cité des hommes* (Paris: Fayard/SACEM, 1992), p. 463; Marcel F. G. Delannoy, *Honegger*, Nouvelle édition augmentée du catalogue des oeuvres de A. Honegger par G. K. Spratt, with prefaces by Maurice Schumann and Arthur Honegger (Genève-Paris: Editions Slatkine, 1986), p. 156. Adriano, in his liner notes for *Honegger: Film Music* (see note 10 below), states that Honegger had composed music for the Pathé-Journal newsreels.

Things did not go well on the afternoon of the premiere; Gance continued to make changes in the film up to the last minute. In fact, on that very day, Gance was still so far behind that the laboratory had not yet finished printing some of the reels.[7] It is easy to imagine the composer's frustration and the exhausted orchestra's impatience at the growing impossibility of the task. The last straw fell when at five o'clock in the afternoon, after the musicians had been rehearsing since nine in the morning without a lunch break, Gance changed the editing once more. At that point, according to Arthur Hoérée, Honegger's collaborator, the composer left the pit in disgust and walked out of the theater.[8] The podium was taken over thereafter by J. E. Szyfer, the conductor of the Opéra orchestra.

Needless to say, trying to produce and perform a suitable musical accompaniment for a lengthy motion picture that was continuously being changed, with an orchestra almost totally drained of its energy, could only have had dismal results. That some critics bitterly attacked the music is not surprising; what is surprising is that Abel Gance himself criticized "the general standard of the music"[9] when, after all, he was mostly to blame for the fiasco.

Although most of the original scores composed for silent films—both here and abroad—have vanished, at least some of Honegger's music for *Napoléon* has survived. A concert suite, comprising eight pieces extracted and arranged by the composer, was published by Éditions Francis Salabert in Paris in 1927.[10] Thus it is possible to compare the printed version of "Les Ombres" with a manuscript score in the Moldenhauer Archives. The title page of the latter says, in longhand, "Extraits de la musique pour le film 'Napoléon'." It contains no descriptions of screen images or action nor any conductor cues such as would be commonly found in the majority of silent film scores or conductor parts. All this, in addition to the fact that Honegger's score has the same number of measures and musical content as the printed version, would indicate that this score was not designed for use in the film, but for the Salabert concert suite. Unfortunately, lacking a cue sheet, one thing we do not know—and probably never shall—is whether "Les Ombres," as it appears here, corresponds to the version that was performed at the premiere of the film (or if in fact it was performed at all).[11]

7 Brownlow, p. 152.

8 Hoérée, cited in op. cit., pp. 150–51.

9 Brownlow, p. 157.

10 There is a copy of the Salabert publication in the Library of Congress. The entire suite has been recorded by Adriano, conducting the CSR Symphony Orchestra, and is available on the Marco Polo CD 8.223134. It includes helpful liner notes.

11 Brownlow is of the opinion that all of the eight pieces were performed at the premiere, and furthermore that they comprised the extent of the original music. (Letter to the author, August 3, 1994.)

The "Les Ombres" manuscript comprises eight pages of orchestral score, containing forty measures. The tempo indication is "Lent" (slow); Honegger's instrumentation is very sparse, consisting only of strings, one trumpet, bass drum, and suspended cymbal. The piece commences with a series of quiet, eerie, widely spread whole-note chords in divided strings. The trumpet (muted) enters softly in the ninth measure with a statement of what is presumably Napoleon's theme, a martial tune that appears in a full orchestral setting in another piece found in the suite, and entitled "Napoléon."[12]

[12] The full orchestration of the presentation of the theme in this piece suggests that it might have served for the film's Main Title.

Under normal circumstances, the lack of a cue sheet would make it difficult if not impossible to determine for which scene this music was composed. But luckily, the answer can be found in Kevin Brownlow's *Napoleon*. Among the many stills in the book there is a frame enlargement captioned "Les Ombres."[13] This shows the ghostly forms of five figures from the French Revolution, superimposed, by double exposure, over a background shot of a phantom mob inside the walls of the Convention that ruled France during the awful days of the Reign of Terror and that saw Napoleon's rise to prominence. In his synopsis of the scenario, Brownlow describes the scene as Napoleon enters the hall of the Convention:

[13] Brownlow, p. 149.

> [Napoleon] climbs the rostrum and gazes at the empty seats. Gradually the hall becomes peopled with phantoms. Fearing this hallucination, he tries to leave, but the gigantic figure of Danton rises from the closed door and advances.[14]

[14] Ibid., p. 283.

The scene continues as Danton and the others address Napoleon, challenging him to become the leader of the Revolution, at the same time warning him not to "give way to the temptation of power." According to Brownlow, Abel Gance considered this to be the best sequence in the picture.[15] The mysterious, somber mood induced by Honegger's music seems to match perfectly the setting shown in the frame enlargement and the procession of images described by Brownlow.

[15] Ibid., p. 149.

For a film composer or film music historian, this manuscript holds special interest, not so much because it is an autograph score by a great composer (important though that may be), but because it is a piece of movie music that saw its way to publication for use in the concert hall. It is further significant that the suite from *Napoléon* was published or at least copyrighted for publication the same year as the premiere of the film itself (1927). The manuscript is in the Zentralbibliothek Zürich.

Transformation and Adaptation: The Evolution of Charles Ives's Song "From 'Paracelsus'"

Felix Meyer

ONE OF THE MOST FASCINATING aspects of the work of Charles Ives is his untiring activity as arranger of his own pieces. It went beyond the normal measure not only with respect to quantity, but above all with respect to quality, for Ives often transformed works to the extent that more or less independent new ones resulted. In some cases a strict separation between "work" and "arrangement" is therefore as impossible as a clear delimitation of the single work: "it becomes difficult to say just where one work ends and another begins."[1] Moreover, this recycling of earlier music was hardly ever motivated by external circumstances. Since Ives worked in almost complete artistic isolation for several decades, neither critical responses from colleagues nor performance prospects had much influence upon his creativity. It was not until the 1920s that some of his works began to come to the attention of a broader musical public. Yet by this time Ives had practically stopped composing.

Thus Ives's working method had little to do with the wish to reach a larger audience, nor was the composer concerned with "perfecting" a work which had been in unsatisfactory shape. His practice of arranging was primarily the expression of a philosophy of art indebted to nineteenth-century New England Transcendentalism, which in turn was rooted in English Romanticism and German Idealism. This inheritance can most easily be seen in Ives's adaptation of the neo-Platonic dichotomy of "Idea" and "Gestalt," fundamental to Romantic theory, which is reinterpreted in his writings as an opposition of "substance" and "manner."[2] While there are important differences between the two pairs of concepts,"[3] both suggest that any fixed expression of a musical thought is merely an imperfect approach toward what is intended, and that,

[1] Robert P. Morgan, "Ives and Mahler: Mutual Responses at the End of an Era," *19th Century Music*, vol. 2, no. 1 (1978): 71-81, esp. 78.

[2] Cf. especially Wolfgang Rathert, *The Seen and Unseen: Studien zum Werk von Charles Ives* (Berliner musikwissenschaftliche Arbeiten, 38) (Munich/Salzburg: Musikverlag E. Katzbichler, 1991), Part I ("Geistesgeschichtliche und ästhetische Grundlagen"), pp. 15-122.

[3] In particular, Ives's version of the dichotomy shows a moral accentuation not found in the older concepts. "Manner" here is extended to mean not only "external appearance" but "superficiality"; it thus functions as the negative counterpart of the spiritual values embodied by "substance." See especially the Epilogue of Ives's *Essays Before a Sonata*, reprinted in Charles Ives, *Essays Before a Sonata and Other Writings*, 3rd ed., ed. Howard Boatwright (London: Calder & Boyars, 1969), pp. 70-102.

FROM: NINETEEN SONGS
© 1935 Merion Music, Inc.
Reprinted by Permission of the Publisher

conversely, what is intended will become the more clearly perceptible the more persistently it is viewed from different angles. Hence the work of art is considered an "array of possibilities" rather than a tightly constructed, self-contained whole; it is not exhausted within a definite form but represents a potential which the artist seeks to "actualize" in ever new specific, tangible shapes.

In Ives's music, such a concept of creativity has found expression in several concurrently developing "works in progress," and it applies even to some of the elaborations on earlier pieces which the composer produced in the 1920s and early 1930s. The most striking example here would be the four *Emerson Transcriptions* (based on material from the first movement of the *Concord Sonata*), about which Ives remarked in 1932: "Some of the passages now played haven't been written out…and I don't know as I ever shall write them out, as it may take away the daily pleasure of playing this music and seeing it grow and feeling that it is not finished."[4] At the same time we can recognize in these years, when Ives's music gradually began to assume a role in public musical life, a category of more limited, pragmatically motivated arrangements, which the composer made with a view toward performances or publication projects offered to him. Most of his later reworkings in fact belong to this second category. That they represent minor adaptations rather than substantial transformations is due just as much to their practical function as to the general decline in the composer's creative activity.

In the following, both types of arrangement—the "actualization" of a given work, essentially motivated by an aesthetic impulse, as well as the adaptation oriented toward practical use—will be examined in the example of the song "From 'Paracelsus'," No. 30 of the collection *114 Songs*. The immediate reason is the existence of an annotated print of the *114 Songs* which formerly belonged to Nicolas Slonimsky and is now part of the Moldenhauer Archives at the Library of Congress. This document illustrates only the second type of Ives's arrangements, since the composer merely entered instrumentation suggestions for a planned performance but did not alter the musical substance of the piece. However, the collection of *114 Songs* itself guides us back to Ives's earlier

[4] Charles E. Ives, *Memos*, ed. John Kirkpatrick (New York: Norton, 1972), pp. 79f.

practice of "recomposition," for the volume, published in 1922 by the composer, is to a large extent based on earlier instrumental pieces which were substantially transformed and fitted to verbal texts. (The collection *114 Songs* is neither an "original composition" nor a volume of arrangements therefore; it is an encyclopedic, potentially expandable "Kunstbuch" in roughly reverse chronological order, in which Ives, at a critical moment in his life, took stock of his entire creative output up to that time.[5]) One of the most striking examples for such a transformation is the song "From 'Paracelsus'," whose reworking from an orchestral work was subjected to especially radical alterations.

"From 'Paracelsus'" (arranged in 1921, according to a note in the edition of *114 Songs*) is largely based on the *Robert Browning Overture* for large orchestra. Dating from the period 1908–1912, this was the only completed portion of a projected series to be entitled *Men of Literature*.[6] It is obvious that Ives could use only a fraction of the 394 measures from the orchestral work for a three-page song numbering a mere twenty measures. Yet the manner in which he proceeded is most remarkable, for it exemplifies with drastic clarity his view of how freely preexisting music could be used. In making the arrangement, Ives placed brief fragments from the *Browning Overture* as follows:[7]

Robert Browning Overture	"From 'Paracelsus'"
Mm. 42–45	Mm. 1–3
Mm. 47–53	Mm. 4–8
Mm. 54 (–55)	Mm. 9 (–10)
Mm. 27 (–28) [woodwinds]	Mm. 11–12 [piano]
Mm. 38–40 (41)	M. 13
Mm. 26–29 (31, 33) [string chords]	M. 15, beginning [piano chords]
Mm. 7–8 [violin/viola]	M. 17, end—M. 18, beginning [piano]
Mm. 10/12 [violin/viola]	M. 19, beginning [piano]
Mm. 9/11 [violin/viola]	M. 20, beginning [piano]

This table shows, first, that all revised material is drawn from the loosely structured beginning of the Overture (Adagio and Allegro, up to measure 54), while the ensuing March was not used, probably because its interlocking ostinati resisted isolation of individual passages. Second, Ives transplanted the

[5] A survey of the pieces from which the *114 Songs* were derived is given in *Memos* (see note 4), pp. 167-77. In 1918 Ives suffered a serious collapse, as a consequence of which he felt compelled to reduce, and finally give up, both his business activities and his activities as a composer. This memento mori seems to have prompted him to strike an artistic balance and to resume contact with the public, so long renounced, by publishing the *114 Songs*, as he had already done with the *Concord Sonata* and the *Essays Before a Sonata* (1920, under the composer's imprint). Insofar as Ives compiled the *114 Songs* with a view toward publication—choosing, by no means accidentally, the readily "accessible" medium of the song with piano accompaniment—his revision was therefore guided by practical considerations. Just as important, however, was Ives's autobiographical motivation for compiling the collection, i.e., the wish to represent his life's work within a "single" composition, as is suggested both by the special sequence and the textual substance of the songs. The order and content of the *114 Songs* are discussed by H. Wiley Hitchcock, "Charles Ives's Book of *114 Songs*," in *A Musical Offering: Essays in Honor of Martin Bernstein*, ed. Edward H. Clinksdale and Claire Brook (New York: Pendragon Press, 1977), pp. 127-35; and Dietrich Kämper, "Die *114 Songs* von Charles E. Ives," in *Amerikanische Musik seit Charles Ives: Interpretationen, Quellentexte, Komponistenmonographien*, ed. Hermann Danuser, Dietrich Kämper, and Paul Terse (Laaber: Laaber-Verlag, 1987), pp. 135-48. For an interpretation of the *114 Songs* as an "autobiographical act" (based mainly on the song texts), see Stuart Feder, *Charles Ives: "My Father's Song," A Psychoanalytical Biography* (New Haven/London: Yale University Press, 1992), pp. 309–22.

[6] Cf. *Memos* (see note 4). The dating is based upon "A Temporary Mimeographed Catalogue of the Music Manuscripts and Related Materials of Charles Edward Ives, 1874–1954," comp. John Kirkpatrick (New Haven 1960), p. 32. Aside from the *Browning Overture* (published 1959 by Peer International), works dealing with Matthew Arnold, Henry Ward Beecher, Ralph Waldo Emerson, Walt Whitman, and John Greenleaf Whittier had been planned.

Sparse sketches made for these were again used by Ives for the collection of the *114 Songs*.

7 Cf. the table given by Rathert, *The Seen and Unseen* (see note 2), p. 251, as well as the (rather imprecise) survey in John McLain Rinehart, "Ives' Compositional Idioms: An Investigation of Selected Short Compositions as Microcosms of His Musical Language," (Ph.D. diss., Ohio State University, 1970), p. 186.

8 Slight deviations from Browning's text occur in the following places: measure 13 (reiteration of "I gazed on power"), measure 15 (omission of "for man" [after "I sought"]), measure 17 ("in man's right constitution" instead of "In his right constitution" and "Always preceding power" instead of "love preceding Power"), and measure 20 (repetition of "always").

9 The first sketches date from the year 1908 and might be taken to reflect Ives's creative response to reading the edition of *Paracelsus* which his wife Harmony had given him for his thirty-fourth birthday; cf. David Wooldridge, *Charles Ives: A Portrait* (London: Faber and Faber, 1975), p. 280. Ives's first acquaintance with Browning probably dates back to his studies with the Browning enthusiast William Lyon Phelps at Yale; cf. J. Peter Burkholder, *Charles Ives: The Ideas Behind the Music* (New Haven/London, 1985), pp. 72–76.

10 Larry Starr speaks in this connection of "stylistic simplification." From the *114 Songs* he lists "Majority" (No. 1), "Down East" (No. 55), and "Old Home Day" (No. 52), and contrasts their type of development with one more rarely occurring in Ives's work—one aiming at "stylistic complexifying" (for instance, "Maple Leaves" [No. 23] and "Remembrance" [No. 12]); cf. Larry Starr, *A Union of Diversities: Style in the Music of Charles Ives* (New York: Schirmer, 1992), pp. 132–43.

fragments from the Overture roughly in reverse order so that the beginning of the song corresponds to the last measures of the Overture segment (measures 42–54), whereas the song's ending is related to the opening section of the Overture (measures 7–12). Ives also chose fragments of greatly differing lengths, some of which reproduce the original texture more or less completely, others only partially. Thus the song starts with sections of the orchestral score only slightly altered, while its later portions refer only obliquely to the earlier work. This marks a gradual departure from the model, which begins precisely where Ives added a new part: the voice. (Nevertheless, various places in the vocal part are derived from the Overture as well: measures 8 and 13 from the trumpet part, measure 11 from the flute and oboe parts, and measure 16 from the clarinet and bassoon parts.) For the vocal part, Ives selected a text from the fifth (and last) book of the dramatic poem *Paracelsus* (1835) by Robert Browning. However, he did not use a continuous excerpt from this source but compiled several portions of it—a procedure very much like his arrangement of the (preexisting) music, though the general sequence of verses (Browning's verses 804–807, 846–847, 854, 856–858) remains unchanged.8

Although both the music and text of the song are closely related to the *Browning Overture* (for the orchestral work as well seems to have been inspired by the poem *Paracelsus* 9), the later work is clearly differentiated from the earlier one both by the highly individual compilation of reused material and by the newly composed music. Above all, the large structural gesture is virtually reversed: whereas in the Overture a restrained beginning leads to growing intensification, in the song the fragments are integrated in a development leading from tension to relaxation, from complex polyphony to chordal homophony, and from a chromatic and atonal sphere to a diatonic and tonal one. This process, typical of a number of works by Ives,10 seems in this case to have been directly motivated by Browning's text, for in the verses used the dying Paracelsus describes the course of his life from boundless presumption ("For God is glorified in man,/ And to man's glory vowed I soul and limb") to self-knowledge and resignation ("I learned my deep error...And what proportion love should hold with power/In man's right constitution").

At the same time, new structural constellations appear, especially through the pitch organization of the newly composed material, and these lend the song a stronger coherence than we find in the corresponding portion of the *Browning Overture*.[11] We might mention, for example, the structure by fifths on which the principal pitches of the voice part in the first section are based[12] and which continues in the harmonic polarity of the second section (measures 16–20, beginning in G Major and ending in D Major).[13]

In spite of its dependence upon the *Robert Browning Overture*, the song therefore takes on a life of its own. This can be seen not least in the piano part's external appearance, which changes gradually from a "reduction" of an orchestral score, extremely dense and almost unplayable on the keyboard, to a more idiomatic pianistic texture. Yet, as has been mentioned, Ives did not consider this version of the *Robert Browning* material as definitive either and made another arrangement some years later. This is documented through two annotated prints of the *114 Songs*: first, the incomplete copy from the possession of Nicolas Slonimsky (discussed below) which went to the Moldenhauer Archives in 1961 and is now preserved in the Library of Congress; and second, the so-called Copy E (incomplete as well) preserved in the Ives Collection of the Yale University Library, one of eight to which Ives added extensive annotations.[14] While most of these copies show different kinds of annotations (details of instrumentation, verbal comments, as well as corrections of the musical text, many of which went into the partial collections from the *114 Songs* published in the 1930s),[15] the Slonimsky copy, save for minimal changes, contains only instrumentation directions;[16] and whereas some of the songs bearing annotations in the Slonimsky volume show additional corrections and entries in the other copies, "From 'Paracelsus'" is marked only with directions for instrumentation almost entirely matching those in Copy E. Within the revision process of the *114 Songs*, this work—unchanged in its essential substance and merely fitted out in an instrumental garb—therefore represents a special case, the background of which shall be briefly investigated in the following.

While the three editions published by Ives himself—the

11 Nevertheless, the breaks and discontinuities in the musical surface should not be readily dismissed. There are obvious caesuras, for instance, between measures 12 and 13, at the end of measure 13 (between "grew" and "blind"), and especially in the transition from measure 15 to measure 16, which latter clearly divides the song into two sections. Concerning the questions of discontinuity and continuity in Ives's work, see Lloyd Whitesell, "Reckless Form, Uncertain Audiences: Responding to Ives," *American Music*, vol. 12, no. 3 (1994): 304–19.

12 Cf. for instance the relationship of the beginning and ending tones in measures 7 and 15 (b'-flat) to that of the final tones in measures 12 and 13 (e'-flat) or to that of the final tone of the second verse in measure 10 (f'); also the distance between the first tones in measures 13 and 14 (f'-sharp and c"-sharp).

13 A detailed analysis of "From 'Paracelsus'" appears in Rathert, op. cit. (see note 2), pp. 252–56. The discussion, rightly, contains a criticism of the superficial and misdirected analysis by Henry Cowell (first published in 1955) as both misdirected and superficial; cf. Henry and Sidney Cowell, *Charles Ives: The Man and His Music* (New York: Oxford University Press, 1955), 2nd enl. ed. (New York: Oxford University Press, 1969) (reprint: with a new foreword, and an updated list of works, bibliography, and discography, New York: Da Capo, 1983), pp. 182–90.

14 These copies of the *114 Songs* were inventoried in 1973 by Cathy Lacny, James Sinclair, and Kenneth Singleton, and were marked with a series of letters from A to H. They are in an incomplete state because Ives removed single pages when he turned to the work, or part of a work, for rearranging or other purposes. Since 1977 the Ives Collection of the Yale Music Library has also included Aaron Copland's dedication copy of the *114 Songs*. Copland's autograph entries, however, do not go beyond verbal notes and directions for Ives's copyist Emil Hanke.

15 A survey of these and later published collections drawn from the original volume of the *114 Songs* is given by John

Kirkpatrick in *Memos* (see note 4), pp. 167–77.

[16] Together with "From 'Paracelsus'," the following songs bear annotations: "Evening" (No. 2), "At Sea" (No. 4), "The Rainbow" (No. 8), "Charlie Rutlage" (No. 10), "Remembrance" (No. 12), "The Swimmers" (No. 27), "Walt Whitman" (No. 31), "Afterglow" (No. 39), "Mists" (No. 57), and "West London" (No. 105). In addition, Copy E contains instrumentation directions for some other songs; above all, however, many of the annotated songs are marked with corrections which to a considerable extent went into the partial collection of *34 Songs* published 1933.

[17] See the reaction of the composer and violinist Henry Eichheim, related in a letter by Elizabeth Sprague Coolidge to Harmony Ives, in *Memos* (see note 4), pp. 99f, note 7.

[18] Cf. Nicolas Slonimsky, *Perfect Pitch: A Life Story* (Oxford/New York: Oxford University Press, 1988), pp. 118ff.

[19] Boston: Birchard, 1935. The original version, for large orchestra, was not published until 1976.

[20] For details on these performances and on Slonimsky's writings on Ives, see Geoffrey Block, *Charles Ives: A Bio-Bibliography*, foreword by J. Peter Burkholder (New York/Westport, Conn./London: Greenwood Press, 1988).

[21] These and the following passages from the Ives-Slonimsky correspondence are quoted with the kind permission of the American Academy of Arts and Letters.

Concord Sonata, the *Essays Before a Sonata* and the *114 Songs*—were either ignored or heavily criticized in conservative circles,[17] they met with interest, and in some cases even with admiration, on the part of some representatives of contemporary music. Among the most important musicians who acknowledged the composer in the 1920s were the pianist Elie Robert Schmitz, the composer Henry Cowell, and the conductors Eugene Goossens and Nicolas Slonimsky. The last came in contact with Ives through Cowell in 1928. As director of the Boston Chamber Orchestra, Slonimsky was anxious to incorporate some of Ives's work in his programs.[18] Ives suggested *Three Places in New England* and offered to make an arrangement for chamber orchestra. This version of *Three Places in New England* was performed in various American and European cities by Slonimsky, after his premiere of the work on January 10, 1931, in New York. In every case, as well as in the publication that followed,[19] he was able to rely on financial support from the composer. Slonimsky also championed other works by Ives. In his brief career as a conductor, which after 1934 gave way more and more to his activities as a writer and lexicographer, he premiered "Washington's Birthday" in 1931 and "The Fourth of July" in 1932 (both from the cycle *New England Holidays*). In addition, on several occasions beginning in 1932, he conducted "In the Cage" and "In the Night" (from the *Set for Theatre Orchestra*, and the *Set for Chamber Orchestra*, respectively), and on April 15, 1934 (in New York), he gave performances of the songs "The New River" and "December" (Nos. 6 and 37 from the *114 Songs*) in a version for choir and instrumental ensemble, together with "In the Night."[20]

The plan which guided the latter concert, namely to present single numbers from the song volume as "Songs with Instruments," dated back to 1930. Apparently upon Slonimsky's request, Ives had promised to enter the necessary directions into a copy of the *114 Songs*—a promise he confirmed twice in his letters: "Will send along the suggested songs as soon as I can get to it" (April 28, 1930); and: "I hope to get off [the copy of the *114 Songs*] to you with the suggested orchestration within a few days" (May 27, 1930).[21] It is possible that, in the course of making this arrangement, Ives went through one of the copies he owned before arriving at a choice for Slonimsky; this is suggested through the fact that all songs annotated in Slonimsky's copy bear similar instructions in Copy E.[22] In any event, on June 8, 1930, Ives summarized the result of his labors in the following words: "Have just gone through the book of songs and will mail it today. Some of the pages are gone. I can't seem to find any more whole copies." However, Slonimsky did not at first find the time to write out a score, as is apparent from Ives's remarks in his letter of September 6, 1930: "Don't let the arranging of the Songs take up any time you need for other work—do it entirely at your convenience—there is no hurry!" The project was indeed put off, for as late as November 7, 1932, Harmony Ives wrote to Dorothy and Nicolas Slonimsky: "Forgot to tell you that Mr. Ives asked me to say not to bother about orchestrating any songs until after you meet again."

The reason that Ives—who at that time had already been in Europe with his wife for several months—now postponed the project himself was due to the fact that just before his departure (May 1932) he had again come across the original versions for orchestra which had formed the basis for some of the songs. This "discovery," mentioned by Harmony Ives in the November 7, 1932, letter quoted above, was discussed by the composer half a year later, in an undated letter sent in May 1933, as follows:

> Am not sure, but think before leaving I told you that in cleaning house preparatory to being away so long, I found several of the old scores, etc.—from which some of the songs were taken—I had forgotten some of them or thought they were not kept—So before arranging any songs it would be better to wait until we can get together again & look over these old manuscripts.

And, with subtle self-disparagement, he added, "In looking these over, I was impressed with this—that I now have good advice for young composers—'If you write anything you think is good, copy it out in ink—if you write anything you think is no good, copy it out in ink!'"

Ives, who had not lost track of his manuscripts for the first time, thus considered—especially now in retrospect—the instrumentation directions contained in Slonimsky's copy

[22] It seems that Ives had envisaged an instrumentation of pieces from the *114 Songs* even earlier, for the following "Suggested song-groups and instruments" were listed in a memorandum on the business stationery of Ives & Myrick with the address "38 Nassau Street" (which was valid only until 1923): "Three Poets & Human Nature" (three songs, among them "From 'Paracelsus'"), "The Other Side of Pioneering" or "Side Lights on American Enterprise" (four songs), "From the Side Hill" (four songs), and "Water Colors" (four songs). The complete wording appears in Kirkpatrick, *Catalogue* (see note 6, pp. 52f). The listed songs, however, correspond almost exactly to the ones marked in the Slonimsky copy and in Copy E, so that a connection with the project here described seems possible; cf. also Ives's remarks (though somewhat ambiguous) in the *Memos* (see note 4), pp. 117f.

23 Cf. Harmony Ives's statement in *Memos* (see note 4), p. 279: "he came downstairs one day [in 1926] with tears in his eyes, and said he couldn't seem to compose any more—nothing went well, nothing sounded right."

merely as a stop-gap measure. On the one hand, in comparison with scored instrumental "Urtext," they must have seemed too sketchy and hastily made to render a clear impression of what he intended. On the other hand, Ives's attitude suggests a certain lack of confidence; it almost appears as if he had some doubt whether he, not having written anything substantial for some time, would be able to solve even a "simple" task such as the instrumentation of songs in a satisfactory manner.[23]

In no event, however, did Ives want the new postponement to distance him from the project jointly envisaged. The other projects undertaken with Slonimsky clearly show the considerable engagement with which he pursued and furthered all performances of his works (he played a much more active role in propagating his work during the first years of his physically imposed "retirement" than has been generally assumed). And indeed, when he had returned from Europe in July 1933, Ives submitted, as announced, his "old scores" to Slonimsky; this is evident from the latter's message of October 26, 1933, to Ives: "I am having a great time looking over your fragments, and putting things together in your orchestrations of the songs." Ultimately, however, these efforts did not lead to a performance of the songs originally chosen, but rather to the above-mentioned New York concert of April 15, 1934, in which "The New River" and "December" were presented in versions for chorus and instrumental ensemble, along with "In the Night" for chamber orchestra. No performance of the instrumentations sketched in Slonimsky's copy of the *114 Songs* is known, nor do we have fully executed orchestral scores for them.

Nevertheless, the instrumentation directions in Slonimsky's copy of the print and in Copy E deserve our attention, for there is more involved in Ives's later efforts than merely "retroactive realizations" of songs originally derived from ensemble or orchestral works. (Especially in the case of "From 'Paracelsus'," which while being arranged was to a large extent newly composed, such a reuse of an earlier orchestral score would not even have been possible.) Despite their sketchy notation, the new arrangements in fact represent more or less fully valid "alternative versions" which go beyond the "original" instrumental scores as well as the songs with piano accompaniment derived from them. This may not be evident from the beginning of "From 'Paracelsus'" (drawn almost exclusively from the *Robert Browning Overture*), where a comparison of the entries in the Slonimsky volume and in Copy E with the Overture shows only slight departures in instrumentation. The opening measures, for instance, are orchestrated in the three sources as follows:

	Slonimsky Copy	Copy E	Overture
M.1	"starting full"	"starting with full orchestra"	full orchestra fl. w. starting
M.2,1.h.	"brass"	—	horns 1–4
M.5	"brass dies out"	"brass dies out"	horns 3–4
			trbs. 1–2 and
			trpts. 1–2 omitted
M.6	"only strings +	"some piano?"	Bassn. 1–2, horns 1–2 and strings
	"some piano"	"piano with low strings"	

(Such concordances do not necessarily suggest that Ives may have had the Overture score at hand when he annotated the two editions of *114 Songs*, since certain figures or the general tendency toward relaxation beginning in measure 5 seem virtually to require a particular orchestration.[24])

The special quality of the instrumentation directions in Slonimsky's copy and in Copy E becomes apparent when we look at the newly composed sections of the song, for here they seem to indicate that Ives was not just trying to provide coloristic variety, but to clarify the music's formal design. This can be seen especially in the treatment of the vocal part. While in the passages taken over from the Overture (measures 8 and 13) it is assigned to the same instrument as before, namely the trumpet (in fortissimo passages always doubled at the octave by one or several trombones[25]), it moves to other instruments in the second (newly composed) section of the song. The following four "tone colors" are used, resulting in a timbral "decrescendo" which corresponds to the general decrease in dynamics:

Trb./Trpt. (Mm. 8/13)	Trpt. (Mm. 11–12/ 14–15)	Eng. horn (M. 16)	Flute[26] (End M. 17)

[24] This conjecture is most readily confirmed by the slight changes in measure 4, left hand (marked "see sketch"), which in fact go back to the *Browning Overture*. Yet they may have been later, at the time Ives had found the "old scores" again.

[25] In Slonimsky 's copy both measures 7 and 13 are marked with the plural form "Trombones," whereas in Copy E only the singular form "Trombone" is used.

[26] The precise indication in the Slonimsky copy reads: "flute or some light wood that will stand out through strings." Copy E cannot be used for comparison here, as the third page of the song (p. 73 of the song collection) is missing.

The most striking feature of this instrumental arrangement, however, is that is is unclear whether the vocal part is *supplanted* by the wind instruments or merely *supported* by them; the direction "Trumpet only on Tune" in measure 10 suggests the former, whereas the notation "Tr. & Trombone in octs. with voices" in measure 8 of the Slonimsky volume points to the latter. Apparently it was Ives's intention to leave the exact designation of the vocal part open, and thus to take up his earlier practice as described by him in *Memos*: "I got to making short pieces as songs, but played by two, three, or more instruments—with the idea of giving the listener or audience the words, and letting them put them in, or follow along with them, as the solo instrument played (a kind of 'songs without voices')."[27] Even within the limited scope of this later arrangement, therefore, Ives adhered to the "open-ended" conception of his work which, in a more radical form, had governed the change from the original orchestral composition to a song with piano accompaniment. "Open-endedness" no longer manifests itself here in the sense that a given work exists in various forms of composition; the concept is reduced to the choice of alternative scorings. Yet it is remarkable enough that one of the possibilities envisaged is an instrumental version with an implicit text, merely to be imagined by the listener in a "song without voice." For such a conception not only illustrates once again the typically Ivesian interaction of instrumental and vocal music, it also shows the extent to which Ives viewed his works as fundamentally "unfinished" and in want of the listener's active participation.

[27] *Memos* (see note 4), p. 117. The wording "optional voice," contained in some of the editions of these arrangements published since, is based upon this remark; see, for instance, Kenneth Singleton's editions of "Charlie Rutlage" (New York, 1983) and "Remember" (New York, 1977), which, however, are based on some older sources as well as on the Slonimsky copy and Copy E of the *114 Songs*.

The Kerver *Missale Romanum*

Denise P. Gallo

ON JANUARY 2, 1564, the Parisian printer and bookseller
Jacques Kerver had a stroke of good fortune. He was given
exclusive rights for ten years to publish all the works which
reflected the reforms of the Council of Trent. This privilege,
granted by King Charles IX of France, gave Kerver a veritable
monopoly on the required texts, such as breviaries and missals,
essential to the process of standardizing the liturgy according
to the Roman rite.[1] One of the books which he printed under
this agreement was the *Missale Romanum*, a copy of which is
now in the Moldenhauer Archives at the Library of Congress.

While in Barcelona in the summer of 1970, Rosaleen
Moldenhauer located the book, then tattered, in an antiquarian
shop. Subsequently, it was sent to London to be restored;
bound in fine black leather, it is now in good condition. Some
of its pages, however, particularly in the section of the
Common of the Mass, tell a tale of heavy usage, for their
corners and edges have been worn thin—and in places were
reinforced—by the priests who turned them daily during
countless celebrations of the Mass.

In the thirteenth century, missals replaced the older
sacramentaries in liturgical use. Containing all the texts (and
some music) for the preparation and celebration of the liturgy,
missals initially were compiled according to numerous local
rites. The reforms of Pope Innocent III saw the creation of a
missal according to the usage in Rome, which, along with the
breviary, was adopted and disseminated by Franciscan
missionaries. Indeed, the first *Missale Romanum* (Milan, 1474)
was printed under the Franciscan Pope Sixtus IV. A century
later, a call for the suppression of all rites save that of Rome
was issued during the Council of Trent, begun under Pope
Paul III in 1542. The exclusive use of the *Missale Romanum*
was decreed later in a Bull by Pope Pius V, published in the
preliminary pages of the missal itself, the first edition of which

[1] Philippe Renouard, *Imprimeurs & Libraires
Parisiens du XVIe siècle, Fascicule Cavellat*
(Paris: Bibliothèque Nationale, 1986),
p. 176.

St. Luke is depicted painting the portrait of the Madonna and Child which hangs in St. Mary Major in Rome.

2 A fuller discussion of the illustrations in the Kerver *Missale Romanum* can be found in volume 2 of *Harvard College Library Department of Printing and Graphic Arts Catalogue of Books and Manuscripts, Part I: French 16th Century Books*, comp. Ruth Mortimer (Cambridge, Mass.: The Belknap Press of Harvard University, 1964), p. 477.

3 Jacobus de Voragine, *The Golden Legend*, trans. William Granger Ryan, vol. 1 (Princeton: Princeton University Press, 1993), p. 174. My thanks to Keith Glaeske, for calling my attention to this legend about Luke.

was printed in 1570. Only dioceses and religious orders which could demonstrate a two-hundred-year-old tradition were exempted from the transition to the Roman rite.

The Kerver edition of the *Missale Romanum* in the Moldenhauer Archives measures 28.5 by 21 cms. It is numbered by folio, with numbers beginning at the texts for the Proper of the First Sunday of Advent, the start of the liturgical year. This numbering ends with folio 233; immediately following is the Common of the Saints, which begins anew with a folio numbered 1. Some printing errors periodically confuse the sequence of folios. For example, while all the readings and prayers appear in their proper order, the numbers printed on folios 25 and 31 have been switched. Folio 150 has been misnumbered as 154, while another 154 then appears in its correct place; finally, folio 218 is misprinted as 118. Occasionally, other typographical errors occur, as when the rubric for the Fourth Sunday after Epiphany is followed by one for the Third Sunday. Here again, however, the texts are in the correct order.

Perhaps the most intriguing feature of the Kerver *Missale Romanum* is the series of particularly fine woodcuts which introduce the texts.[2] In addition to larger images such as the one of Saints Peter and Paul which graces the title page, there are intricately carved initials which not only begin the prayers and readings but also illustrate in painstaking detail aspects from the lives of the saints or themes of particular liturgies. For example, the woodcut for the feast of Francis of Assisi (October 4) recalls the saint's reception of the stigmata by representing a celestial vision of Christ crucified from whose wounds come lines to Francis's hands and feet. A particularly noteworthy woodcut accompanies the feast of St. Luke (October 18). The evangelist is depicted as an artist himself, painting a portrait of Mary and the Child Jesus. Luke's Gospel is known for its Marian elements, but this representation of the saint comes from popular legend. Luke, it was claimed, was an artist as well as a physician, and his portrait of Madonna and Child was reputedly one which hung in the Church of Santa Maria Maggiore in Rome.[3] The most fascinating woodcuts appear at the end of the missal in the section on the Mass for the Dead, wherein stark images depict the various stages of a Christian's departure from this world.

Tridentine reform also affected the church's music, as members of the papal synod attempted to abolish the secular elements which they claimed had tainted it. As K. G. Fellerer has noted, the Council was of "paramount significance" in the subsequent structuring of Catholic Church music as well as in general church usages.[4] The reformers decreed that music, as the Liturgy, would be controlled by making its performance conform to the usage of Rome; thus, the chant in the *Missale Romanum* reflects that tradition. The Kerver missal contains fifty-eight pages with music, beginning with the chants for Holy Week. Plainsong notation, often in ligatures, is printed on four-line red staves, using C and F clefs. Common eccelesiastical Latin abbreviations such as *Dñe* for *Domine* are used throughout the text.

The Kerver family's activity in the Parisian printing industry goes back to the 1490s—some twenty years after the first book was printed in the city—when Thielman Kerver Ier ran an active business in the publication of religious works, such as Books of Hours.[5] His colophon was a woodcut of two unicorns, both facing left, standing on either side of a tree which bore a shield with his crest and the initials "T K."[6] Jacques Kerver's colophon, which appears as a full-page illustration at the end of the missal, is an adaption of the former. His depicts a single unicorn, again facing left, but with its right front leg braced over a shield bearing the family crest, now initialed "I K" (Iacobus Kerver). Below the woodcut appears a quotation from verse 6 of Psalm 28: "Dilectus quemadmodum filius unicornium—greatly beloved son of unicorns." Indeed, the symbol of the unicorn was used to identify the bookseller's shop, as was the address, noted on the title page of the missal, "Via Iacobæa, Sub signo Unicornis—Rue Jacques, under the sign of the unicorn."

The title page also notes Kerver's exclusive right to print the missal as granted by the king and the pontiffs Pius V and Gregory XIII. In 1572, a group of other printers petitioned the Parisian parliament to deny Kerver a prolongation of his privilege to the Tridentine publications. Although it upheld the original agreement, in the following year the government denied Kerver the possibility of extending it past January 1,

4 K. G. Fellerer, "Church Music and the Council of Trent," *Musical Quarterly* 39 (1953): 576. This article offers a full discussion of the major issues surrounding the Tridentine musical reforms.

5 For a list of some of the early publications of Thielman Kerver, see Anatole Claudin, *Histoire de l'Imprimerie en France au XVe et au XVIe Siècle: Tables Alphabétiques* (Paris: Imprimerie Nationale, 1915; reprint, Lichtenstein: Kraus-Thomson, 1971), pp. 199–200.

6 For an illustration, see Rev. William Parr Greswell's *Annals of Parisian Typography* (London: Cadell and Davies et al., 1818), p. 180.

Two hooded figures kneel near a grave as skulls peer eerily from the ossuary in the background.

7 Renouard, loc. cit.

8 Ibid.

9 The discussion of the missal in the Harvard College Library catalog cited above notes the possibility of four editions by Kerver. The one at Harvard was printed on June 8, 1574, while the one in the Moldenhauer Archives was printed on August 21 of the same year. See the unnumbered folio at the back of the missal which exhibits the characters of the missal's typeface.

10 My thanks to Charles Downey for assistance with the Latin abbreviations.

1575.[7] Also, while adjudicating the protest of the other printers, the Parliament set the prices which Kerver could charge for the publications in question, the cost of the *Missale Romanum* to be 50 sous.[8] Kerver, however, succeeded in printing at least three editions of the *Missale Romanum*, while the printing rights still belonged to him.[9]

Where might the missal in the Moldenhauer Archives have gone after it left Kerver's shop in Paris? Annotations can be found on several pages. For example, on 123 recto, the book apparently was torn or worn to such an extent that another piece of paper was pasted onto the bottom of the damaged page and the words of the Consecration were written in again by hand. A similar patch, used to repair the following folio, offers a possible clue to the book's whereabouts: at the bottom of 124 recto, the scrap of paper pasted onto the page seems to have come from what might have been an inventory. While the ends of the phrases are illegible Latin ecclesiastical or legal abbreviations, the beginnings are quite clear; the first reads "La campana maior" and the second, "La petita campana." The language is Catalan. Another note written in the September feast calendar confirms the possibility of a Catalonian provenance. Next to September 12 is written "dedicationis ecclæ. S^{ti} Petri de Torello"—dedication of the church of St. Peter of Torello. San Pedro de Torello—or in Catalan, Sant Pere de Torelló—is a small town in the province of Barcelona, in the diocese of Vich, a city prominent enough in the sixteenth century to have sent its bishop as one of Spain's representatives to the Council of Trent. The notation of such an important local feast strongly suggests the possibility that the book at one time belonged to a church in Sant Pere.

On the title page is written what appears to be "Ec de S^{nt} Roch—Church of St. Roch."[10] The words beneath are illegible. Did the missal at one time belong to a parish dedicated to Roch, perhaps in France where the saint was honored in an active cult? During the seventeenth and eighteenth centuries, however, antipapal sentiments there encouraged the return to older French rites, resulting in the abandonment of such books as the *Missale Romanum*. A book as valuable as Kerver's missal would most likely have been sold and taken where it could be put to use, for example, over the Pyrenees to Spain. Because the ties between France and Catalonia were age-old, and particularly because Spain remained a bastion in defense of Roman Catholicism, the exchange of a missal from a French parish which no longer wanted it to a Catalan parish which needed it seems quite possible.

Another bit of marginalia deserves comment. One priest who used the missal had carefully marked the prayer which was said in preparation for Mass; attributed to St. Ambrose, the lengthy "Summe sacerdos et vere pontifex Iesu Christe" takes up three pages of the *Missale Romanum*. In later editions, the prayer was printed in seven short sections, one of which would be recited each day. The cleric made small crosses and marked off daily sections with the rubrics, "Feria 2ᵃ, Feria 3ᵃ," etc. Might this imply that the book was used in a parish which, for whatever reasons, continued to use the older version of the Roman missal even when a new edition had come out? In fact, since major liturgical changes were not made until the early twentieth century, the missal may have been employed until it was too fragile for further use. The missal's worn pages testify to years—perhaps even centuries—in the service of the Church, at least some of which appear to have been spent only fifty miles from where the book was found in Barcelona.

Franz Liszt's *Psalm XVIII*

Rena Charnin Mueller

IN THE SUMMER OF 1860, Franz Liszt still believed that he and his longtime companion, the Princess Carolyne Sayn-Wittgenstein, were to be married in the very near future. The obstacles to their union were fewer. The princess's first husband, Nicholas, had himself obtained a Protestant divorce in 1855 and remarried the following year. This did not, of course, remove the objections of the Roman Catholic Church, whose teachings concerning divorce not only threatened their daughter, the Princess Marie, with bastardy (although Marie Sayn-Wittgenstein had come of age and married, inheriting the fortune her mother had been so careful to protect for her), but threatened Princess Carolyne herself with bigamy should she marry again.[1] However, her Protestant divorce was a liberating step and, most important, Liszt was well on his way to removing himself from the stultifying and philistine atmosphere of the Weimar court.[2]

Liszt's compositions of this period are many and varied, ranging from revisions of earlier Lieder and the publication of new songs written for the Weimar soprano Emmy Genast,[3] to the superb piano transcriptions of music from *Rigoletto* and *Il Trovatore* and the first *Mephisto Waltz*. But increasingly he was turning his attention to religious texts,[4] an outward manifestation of the pull of Rome by this point and his now unmistakable and public interest in religion.[5] Some might find it remarkable that the text Liszt chose to set to music, that of *Psalm XVIII*, was picked after one of the severest blows he was ever to suffer—the death on December 13, 1859, of his only son, Daniel.[6] Yet, "Coeli enarrant gloriam Dei" reflects Liszt's steadfast faith in God. Whatever problems had beset the composer in the past months, and whatever difficulties faced him, Liszt's faith not only consoled him but gave him the strength to forge ahead with a new turn in his life's course at the age of forty-nine. Liszt believed in God's eternal plan, and looked forward to the new phase of his life with courage.

[1] See Donna di Grazia, "Liszt, The Princess, and The Vatican: New Documents Concerning the Events of 1861" (M.A. Thesis, University of California (Davis), 1986); "Liszt and Carolyne Sayn-Wittgenstein: New Documents on the Wedding that Wasn't," *19th Century Music* XII/2 (Fall 1988): 148–62; and Alan Walker, *Liszt, Carolyne, and the Vatican: The Story of a Thwarted Marriage* (Stuyvesant, N. Y.: Pendragon Press, 1991).

[2] For the circumstances surrounding Liszt's resignation from his position in Weimar, see Walker, *Franz Liszt II: The Weimar Years*, pp. 494 ff.

[3] Of particular note is Heft VII of the Kahnt *Gesammelte Lieder*, a gemlike collection of songs that were composed over the previous year, among them "Wieder möcht ich dir begegnen," "Die stille Wasserrose," and "Blume und Duft."

[4] Among the works he produced in the immediately preceding years were *Psalm XIII* (1855), the *Gran Mass* (1855), *Psalm XXIII*, and *Psalm CXXXVII* (August 1859).

[5] Liszt's religious proclivities were never far from the surface. See the discussion of his beliefs in Walker, *Franz Liszt I: The Virtuoso Years*, pp. 101, 117, 132, and 136.

[6] For the heart-rending account of Daniel's death, see Walker, *Franz Liszt II*, pp. 474 ff.

Liszt wrote *Psalm XVIII* expressly for Carolyne Sayn-Wittgenstein, who, in May 1860, had left for Rome with the avowed intention of securing a papal annulment of her first marriage—a sine qua non before a lawful marriage to Liszt was possible.[7] On the day after she left Weimar, Liszt quoted the Latin text incipit in a letter to her, lamenting movingly how she was already missed and how his life resounded with her presence.[8] It is likely that he was working this time with the manuscript now preserved in the Moldenhauer Archives, the earliest extant source for the piece. However, the evidence for this is inferential at best: writing to Agnes Street-Klindworth on August 7, 1860, Liszt noted that "For ten days I haven't budged from my room and am working on a new psalm: 'Coeli enarrant gloriam Dei,' for which the setting rushes from my heart."[9] He completed the piece August 20, 1860, according to the date inscribed on one of the later orchestral manuscripts.[10] Immediately upon finishing, Liszt described the work to the princess in detail on August 22, 1860, a letter all the more remarkable because in it he actually cites the number of measures and pages of score of the finished piece:

> While you were listening to the Psalm 'Coeli enarrant' in Sta Maria Maggiore, I was working at mine for male-voice choir. I finished it yesterday, and it seems to have turned out not at all badly. There are just over 300 bars, 30 pages of full score distinctly hieratic in character. I have made two versions, one in Latin, the other in German. I still have to arrange the instrumentation in various forms, in such a way that it may be performed with small resources, with organ alone if need be, or else with full orchestra, or furthermore in the open air, during some festival of male-voice choirs—a very frequent occurrence in Germany, Holland, and Belgium. In the latter event it needs only brass instruments, horns, trumpets, and trombones, together with a few clarinets. I hope to produce the 'Coeli enarrant' for you in these three versions.[11]

Liszt's commentary suggests that the Moldenhauer manuscript was his first draft, and that the preparation of the "three versions" (Weimar MSS WRgs B8a-c: the Latin version, and the fleshing out of the original score for various orchestral combinations and the individual vocal parts) was the work that occupied him during the summer—at least from circa July 29

7 Ibid., p. 521. Although it was not her intention at this point, she was never to return to Weimar.

8 "Vous êtes la lumière du coin de terre, où il m'est donné de vivre. Tout cette maison est remplie de votre présence, de votre amour, de vos larmes et de votre espérance. 'Coeli enarrant gloriam Dei '—et chaque pierre ici tressaille de votre souffle, et vous bénit avec moi." Claude Knepper and Pierre-Antoine Huré, eds., *Franz Liszt Correspondence* (1987), p. 405; originally in LaMara, ed., *Franz Liszt. Briefe an die Fürstin Carolyne von S.-W. V* (Leipzig: 1900), p. 5.

9 "Depuis un dizaine de jours je ne bouge pas ma chambre et travaille à un nouveau Psaume: 'Coeli enarrant gloriam Dei,' dont l'intonation m'a jailli du coeur." LaMara, ed., *Briefe an eine Freundin*, p. 128. What is particularly charming about this line is Liszt's use of the word "dizaine," to mean ten days in a row. The votive allusion of dizaine referring to a decade, or 10, "Hail Marys," five of which constitute part of the recitation of the rosary, would not have been lost on him.

10 WRgs MS B8a.

11 Paul Merrick, *Revolution and Religion in the Music of Liszt* (New York and Cambridge: Cambridge University Press, 1987), pp. 149 ff.; originally in LaMara, ed., *Franz Liszt. Briefe an die Fürstin Carolyne von S.-W. V* (Leipzig: 1900), p. 42.

[12] See Walker, *Franz Liszt II*, Appendix I, pp. 555–65; and Emmerich Karl Horvath, *Mein letzter Wille. Testament von Franz Liszt* (Eisenstadt: E. & G. Horvath, 1970). One might ask why Liszt was moved to make a will at this time. The answer is not easily reached, although his intention to leave Weimar after twelve years might have had something to do with it. Walker views Liszt's will and the similar document drawn up by Carolyne in Rome some weeks later as a prenuptial agreement. Carolyne's will was postdated October 23, 1861, the day *after* her anticipated marriage to Liszt on his fiftieth birthday, and signed "Carolyne Liszt." Of course, this will was never to be executed, but it is clear that Liszt had seen the document.

[13] Lina Ramann, *Franz Liszt als Künstler und Mensch II* (Leipzig: Kommissions-Verlag von Breitkopf & Härtel, 1887), p. 418. The parts for all of Liszt's orchestral works performed in Weimar, both sacred and secular, are slowly reappearing. Most were unavailable since the latter part of Peter Raabe's tenure as Curator of the Liszt Museum (1931–1945) up to the present day; they were stored separately from the remainder of the Liszt orchestral *Nachlass*.

[14] Georg Kinsky, ed., *Musikhistorisches Museum von Wilhelm Heyer in Cöln: Katalog IV*, pp. 699–700, particularly note 2.

[15] Liszt's letter to the conductor Herbeck concerning the projected Viennese performance is reproduced in part by Merrick, *Religion and Revolution*, pp. 149 ff. In it, Liszt stresses just how valuable the conductor is to a performance, an attitude not shared universally by his contemporaries.

[16] Heyer incorrectly gives 1874 as the date of publication by Schuberth. See note 14, above.

[17] The description by Georg Kinsky in Volume IV of the sale catalog remains the standard reference for the work, although there are several errors that will be corrected seq.

[18] The Sotheby sale description incorrectly described the last page of the manuscript as another composition, giving the German text, "Die Rechte des Herrn sind wahrhaftig," separately. See Alec Hyatt

through August 20. Three weeks later, on September 14, 1860, Liszt drew up his Last Will and Testament, appending to it a list of compositions, still in manuscript, that he wished Carolyne to oversee through publication if he should die before her. Most of the works he listed were sacred, and the unpublished *Psalm XVIII* headed the group.[12]

The first performance was given a year later by the Weimar Männergesang-Verein on June 25, 1861, in the setting for four-part men's choir and accompaniment.[13] While it was obviously Liszt's intention to publish the work quickly, this did not happen, although he sent one manuscript of the completed orchestral version to his Leipzig publisher, Kahnt Verlag, after the first performance.[14] For some reason, Kahnt never issued the score, and Liszt had to request the return of the copy held by Kahnt in 1868, in preparation for a projected performance by the Wiener Männergesang-Verein at their twenty-fifth anniversary on October 11, 1868.[15] By this time, Liszt had resubmitted the work to Schuberth, who issued it in 1871.[16]

The manuscript preserved in the Moldenhauer Archives was acquired by the Wilhelm Heyer Museum in Cologne some time after the princess's death in March 1887. It was sold in 1926 to an unknown buyer,[17] and in 1944 it was sold again at auction by Sotheby's to Heinrich Eisemann.[18] From that point until its purchase by Moldenhauer, its whereabouts were unknown.

There are no extant sketches for the work. Although only a relatively small manuscript, the Moldenhauer draft encapsulates the complexity and problematic nature of the Liszt sources, the result of the composer's restless and mercurial mind. Liszt drafted the music on paper associated with his late Weimar works: four eighteen-stave oblong leaves, 27.4 cm. by 34.8 cm.[19] The paper was intended for orchestral work, but Liszt routinely cut the original thirty-six-stave upright bifolios in half. For this piece, he assembled the document using four disjunct leaves on which he paginated only sides 1–6, writing the main body of the music between folios 1v–4r. He used a four-stave system, one tenor and one bass staff above a two-stave brace identified only as "Begleitung." On the last page of the manuscript (folio 4v), Liszt noted "Piano" in the margin of the accompaniment system. While it is generally assumed that the principal instrumental accompaniment for this work was organ, that would have been written as usual on three staves (manuals and pedal). However, at this early stage of composition, two staves would have been sufficient for Liszt's purposes. As was his habit, Liszt left space in between the staves for the inevitable corrections.

Despite his emphasis to Princess Carolyne on a version in Latin, it is clear from this manuscript that Liszt's initial setting was for a German text: "Die Himmel erzählen die Ehre Gottes." He set only verses 1–10 of the fifteen available: in verse 5, he omitted the words "er hat der Sonne eine Hütte in denselben gemacht," and in verse 7 he left out the words "Sie gehet auf an einem Ende des Himmels, und läuft um bis wieder an dasselbe Ende," perhaps because they dampened the uplifting quality of the remainder of the text. He also altered the word order of the subsequent phrase ("und bleibt nichts vor ihrer Hitze verborgen"), something that happens quite often in his works. The substantial conclusion of the piece is based on the words "Hosannah" and "Hallelujah"— neither part of the original psalm text. For the most part, the text was written above the topmost (tenor) staff in the autograph. The time signature for the work was originally C, and Liszt's first draft of the orchestration for wind ensemble (WRgs MS B8b³) is also in C, but all subsequent sources are in ₵. At some later point, after Liszt began to work on his first draft of the orchestration, he went back to the time signature of the Moldenhauer draft and changed C to ₵ in lead.

One can see immediately that Liszt wrote the music rapidly, and the score appears in many places to be incomplete. Although the general torso of the work remained unchanged, as we would expect, the reading transmitted in the Moldenhauer manuscript differs in many musical and textual ways from Liszt's final version. In his description of this manuscript for the Heyer collection sale, Kinsky pointed out several salient differences between the draft and the printed score, most notably, the four-measure introduction in the draft

King, *Some British Collectors of Music* (Cambridge: University Press, 1963), pp. 74 and 141, for material on Eisemann.

19 Paper No. 97; used primarily in 1859–1861. See Mueller, "Liszt's *Tasso* Sketchbook: Studies in Sources and Revisions" (Ph.D. diss., New York University, 1986), pp. 386 ff. Other works inscribed on this paper include Liszt's keyboard transcriptions of the choral fugue "Lob und Ehre und Preis und Gewalt" from Bach's Cantata 21 (*Ich hatte viel Bekümmernis*), *Aus tiefer Noth*, *Der Fliegende Holländer*, the *Cantico di San Francesco*, and the *Berceuse*, among others.

[20] For a full discussion of Liszt's working methods, see Mueller, op. cit., pp. 328 ff.

[21] Kinsky, *Heyer-Katalog*, pp. 699–700.

[22] Kinsky, *Heyer-Katalog*, pp. 699.

[23] See Mueller, op. cit., pp. 98 ff. for a complete discussion of the hierarchy of Liszt's methods of correction and revision.

[24] Liszt himself described the piece as "very simple and massive—like a *monolith*." See Merrick, *Religion and Revolution*, p. 150; originally in Constance Bache, trans., *Letters of Franz Liszt II* (London: H. Grevel, 1894), p. 148.

which was later expanded to seventeen measures in the printed edition. But Liszt also added much in the way of connecting material, a familiar compositional idiosyncrasy.[20] Such passages, for example at rehearsal letter B of the final version, are noticeably absent in this draft (four measures following measure 36), as are his final thoughts on the ending of the work, rehearsal letters P–R, which Liszt further extended.[21]

The choral parts underwent considerable reworking: as Kinsky pointed out, many sections originally conceived in four parts were later handled in unison, thereby highlighting the psalm text.[22] While Liszt made minor adjustments to the vocal lines, reconfiguring the tenors and basses in both sections, the most noticeable change occurs in the accompaniment. In all of his religious settings, text clarity was of prime importance to Liszt. This explains the two large revision sections found on folios 1v and 3r of the draft, both involving a shift in emphasis from the accompaniment to the vocal parts. The extent of the revisions is easily seen in the several layers of musical correction which can be differentiated by examining the writing medium, either ink or lead, that Liszt used. The first layer of musical text appears in a gold-flecked brown-black ink. Often, minor corrections were done immediately by scratching off the still wet ink (leaving a white erasure mark on the paper) or by a deletion in the same ink with a correction immediately next to the excised note or word. On a later revision of the manuscript, Liszt used his favorite correcting implement, a lead pencil, and changed the material immediately with the same pencil.[23] A third layer of correction involves a watery brown ink, found throughout *over* the darker ink and the lead.

The Moldenhauer manuscript shows clearly that Liszt proceeded almost uninterrupted in his first attempt at the composition, working section by section, verse by verse, and setting all the text up through, but not including, the last line of verse 10 in one sitting. This is evident from the composer's own pagination, which was entered in lead pencil after he had completed writing through page 4. The texture of the composition was fairly homophonic up to this point, with little or no contrapuntal activity.[24] However, in choosing to shorten the text, Liszt obviously encountered some difficulty in setting

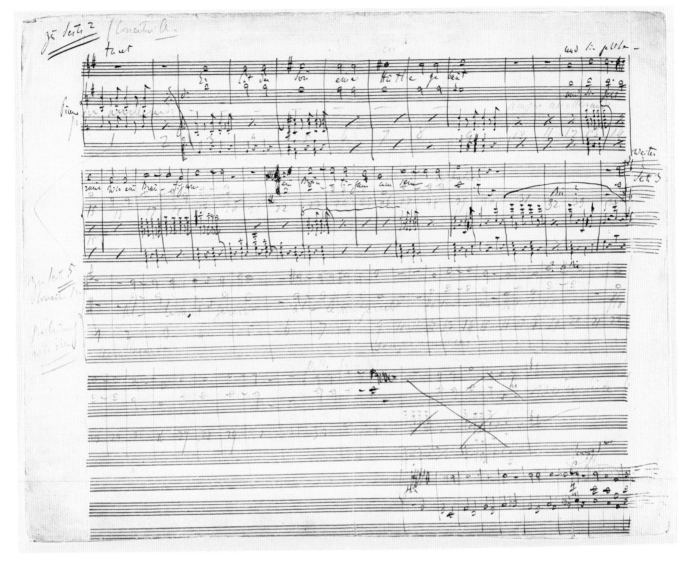

the last verse ("Die Rechte des Herrn sind wahrhaftig, allesamt gerecht"). He apparently rethought the climactic "Hosannah," which clearly called for something more special than his first layer of composition on folio 3r. It would seem that the musical ideas had evolved exponentially in his mind before he had time to write out his original thoughts on paper, hence the great variety in the readings generated in the succeeding orchestral manuscripts.[25]

Liszt began to orchestrate the work, working with a subsequent manuscript he labeled "Instrumentierung" (WRgs MS B8b³) even before he began revising the Moldenhauer

[25] There are a number of songs, for instance, in which the initial state appears to be a fully realized draft put down without any predecessors, followed by numerous revisions—both of component sections and states of the music. See Mueller, "Re-evaluating the Liszt Chronology: The Case of *Anfangs wollt ich fast verzagen*," *19th Century Music* XII/2 (1988): 132–47.

draft—specifically, before he changed the large sections on folios 1v and 3r. The evidence for this is clear: some corrections in dark ink for the accompaniment and the large-scale deletions on folios 1v and 3r of the Moldenhauer draft do not appear in this instrumental version. This was a normal occurrence for the composer, and one of the most interesting features of his musical nature: often, the very process of orchestration, or the transposition into another key (for instance, in the case of a song) resulted in a new sonority that, in turn, led to a revision in composition.[26]

[26] See Mueller, "Liszt's *Tasso* Sketchbook," pp. 128 ff., 331 ff.; and "Revising the Liszt Chronology."

Liszt then went back to the original text layer on folio 1v (measures 53 ff.), striking out the relentless quarter/two-eighths figure, opting for the more transparent quarter/eighth motif in a correction written in lead pencil and placed on the last page—up to this point, a blank one. He signaled this correction in the score on folio 1v (page 2) with a "Vide Correctur A letzte Seite": this last side (folio 4v) was still an unnumbered page at this point; the "8" was not added until later.[27] This rhythmic adjustment of the accompaniment was taken from the original musical text layer for the next large deleted section on folio 3r, the section just preceding the final "Hosannah." When he struck out this passage, he noted above the staff "Vide Correctur B, letzte Seite," entering the corrected music in lead on the last page beneath correction A. At this point, Liszt went back to put in the pagination for the third leaf, but he wrote the number "4" on folio 3r in error, mistakenly thinking that all of page 2 (folio 1v) had been deleted. When he realized his error—that several measures on page 2 were still valid—he crossed out the "4" on folio 3r and changed it to "5," and then crossed out the "5" on folio 3v and changed it to "6." The last leaf (folio 4) was never paginated, although, as we have said, in his corrections, Liszt referred to the last side as "Seite 8" (=folio 4v). Believing he had finally completed the composition, Liszt wrote the letters *DG* (*Deo Gratias*) after Correction B, letters he often used ceremonially to signal the end of a work. However, it was not the end: he further revised measures 231 ff., writing thirteen measures in the accompaniment in different brown ink *over* the *DG* in lead at the end.

[27] Number "8" in parentheses was clearly added *after* the remainder of the "Vide Correctur" notes.

Further correlation between the two large corrected sections also exists, most notably the harmonic direction in the first few bars. Satisfied with the shape of the composition, Liszt set about to prepare performing copies, using this draft as a basis. However, the layers of correction, and particularly the two revised sections whose corrections appear on folio 4v, had necessitated that Liszt keep good account of the measure numbers. To facilitate this, he had kept a running measure count, still visible in lead pencil at the bottom of each page, for example, 45 at the foot of folio 1r, 87 at the bottom of folio 1v, etc.[28] By this method he kept track for himself of the proportions of the work and, to some extent, ensured that any subsequent copy would be prepared correctly. This was not an uncommon practice for Liszt, especially given the speed with which he wrote.[29]

As we have seen, the Moldenhauer draft represents Liszt's first musical thoughts on *Psalm XVIII*, but because it played such an indispensable part in the sequence of composition, it is impossible to conclude this without describing the source array of the succeeding manuscripts. The Moldenhauer manuscript was followed by Liszt's own rough draft for wind orchestra without the vocal parts, a manuscript now found in Weimar at the Goethe-und Schiller-Archiv (WRgs MS B8b³). But Liszt's ideas on the piece were already in flux: he was changing the document even as he was orchestrating it. It would have been impossible to prepare orchestral and vocal parts from these scores, even for the most experienced copyists working with Liszt.[30] Therefore, he prepared another full score with the vocal parts including the Latin and German texts (WRgs MS B8a), incorporating the changes he had made in the Moldenhauer manuscript, and inscribed "écrit pour Carolyne / Aôut 60."[31] Choral parts (cataloged as WRgs MSS B8b¹) used for the first performance in July 1861 are quite interesting because they were based on Liszt's full score, copied by Carl Goetze[32] and then lithographically produced from Goetze's handwritten manuscript by the transfer process.[33] At a later point, the tenor parts were corrected by Liszt himself in lead pencil when he enlarged the introduction from four to seventeen measures. The next sources in the sequence are also found in Weimar: a fair copy of the complete score with German and Latin texts (WRgs MS B8b¹) in Goetze's hand.[34]

[28] When preparing the autograph for the B-Minor Sonata, for example, Liszt included a numbering sequence in the same location on the folios for a similar purpose.

[29] Before the present day, the unsophisticated analysis of the Liszt manuscripts and the layers of compositional planning they illustrate have hindered the establishment of a firm chronology for many important works in the oeuvre. See Mueller, "Liszt's *Tasso* Sketchbook," pp. 98 ff.

[30] On the function of members of the Liszt scriptorium in Weimar, see Mueller, op. cit., pp. 31 ff.

[31] It is apparent that the inscription may have been added later. This manuscript includes a line with the rubric "Clavierauszug," in addition to the organ part already in the score.

[32] Carl Goetze was one of Liszt's principal Weimar copyists and a choir director at the *Hoftheater*.

[33] On the occurrence of transfer process printing in Liszt's oeuvre, see Mueller, op. cit., pp. 171 ff.

[34] Kinsky, *Heyer-Katalog*, p. 700. This manuscript, sent to Kahnt for publication, is a unique document because it bears printers' markings for both Kahnt and Schuberth.

Goetze's copy was also used to prepare the orchestral parts (WRgs MS B8c). The final manuscript in the group is the fair copy of the version for wind orchestra alone (WRgs MS B8b^2), in the hand of an unknown scribe.

Witold Lutosławski's *Venetian Games*

Michael O'Brien

IN 1960 WITOLD LUTOSŁAWSKI (born January 25, 1913, in Warsaw) began experimenting with aleatoric techniques in *Venetian Games* (1960–1961). The piece won first prize at the Tribune Internationale des Compositeurs (May 1962) and marked Lutosławski's emergence as one of the world's leading composers. Lutosławski himself considers *Venetian Games* to demonstrate his "first maturity as a composer."[1]

The work written before *Venetian Games* was Lutosławski's *Three Postludes* (1960), a symphonic cycle for which *Venetian Games* originally was to serve as a completion. However, *Postludes* remained a torso after Lutosławski heard a 1960 radio broadcast of John Cage's *Concerto for Piano and Orchestra* (1957–1958). This piece acted as a catalyst for Lutosławski, and it was also during this time that Andrzej Markowski commissioned Lutosławski to write a piece for the Chamber Orchestra of the Cracow Philharmonic which was to participate in the Venice Biennale in 1961.

Known for his slow, meticulous working pace, Lutosławski completed only preliminary versions of the first, second, and fourth movements of *Venetian Games* for its world premiere on April 24, 1961, at the Teatro La Fenice in Venice. The fragment reproduced here is from the second movement, measures 37–55. The revised four-movement version was performed in Lutosławski's home town, Warsaw, on September 16, 1961, by the Warsaw National Philharmonic Orchestra under the direction of Witold Rowicki.

When Lutosławski wrote to Cage and acknowledged being influenced by the Piano Concerto, Cage asked him to send the full score of *Venetian Games* for publication. Cage was in the process of publishing a collection of manuscripts and presumably acquired the revised manuscript version for all four

[1] See Steve Stucky, *Lutosławski and His Music* (Cambridge: Cambridge University Press, 1981), p. 133.

movements.[2] Meanwhile the conceptual diagrams and preliminary score fragments from the first, second, and fourth movements which were premiered in Venice were being held by the Hermann Moeck Verlag in Celle, Germany.[3] Moeck published the final version of *Venetian Games* in 1962, and in June 1963, letters from Herbert Höntsch of Moeck and Lutosławski confirmed that Moldenhauer had acquired the preliminary fragments.[4] There are six conceptual diagrams for portions of the second and fourth movements (two are unidentified) and nine score fragments from preliminary versions of the first, second, and fourth movements. The majority of the diagrams and fragments reflect revisions made in the final movement.

The title *Venetian Games* pays homage to both Venice, the city of its premiere, and to the freedom of play and interpretation which occurs during performance. Many details of sound realization are left to chance. However, unlike John Cage's indeterminate works, open form is not a predominant feature in *Venetian Games*. Instead, a more formal organization prevails. For a successful realization of the work, all elements of chance must yield to Lutosławski's structural framework.

Lutosławski uses the term *aleatory counterpoint* to define the loose rhythmic structure between simultaneously sounding instruments and groups of instruments.[5] In the aleatoric portions of *Venetian Games*, individual parts have no identical time organization or common pulse; each part is independent in time. Players perform as if off by themselves. In this way a complicated-sounding performance is achieved through the simultaneous combination of different rhythms, tempi, and agogic nuances.[6] However, there is no room for improvisation in *Venetian Games*, and no pitches are left to chance. A conductor guides the players through Lutosławski's uncompromising form, and, in the end, "the composer remains the directing force."[7]

Not only does Lutosławski explore the fascinating prospects in the development of sound organization through techniques of controlled chance, but he also arranges his ideas according to harmonic relationships. "The fundamental unity of which I make use in my latest pieces is a vertical aggregation of all the

[2] See Bálint András Varga, *Lutosławski Profile: Witold Lutosławski in Conversation with Bálint András Varga* (London: Chester Music, 1976), p. 13.

[3] See the letter of June 11, 1963, from Herbert Höntsch of Hermann Moeck Verlag to Hans Moldenhauer.

[4] See the letters from Herbert Höntsch and Lutosławski to Moldenhauer of June 11 and June 20, 1963.

[5] See *Lutosławski*, ed. Ove Nordwall (Stockholm: Nordiska Musikförlaget, 1968), p. 17.

[6] See Jean-Paul Couchoud, *La musique polonaise et Witold Lutosławski* (Paris: Stock Plus Musique, 1981), p. 99.

[7] See *Funeral Music—Venetian Games* (Phillips PHS 900.159, 1967), record jacket information by the composer.

8 *Lutosławski*, op. cit., p. 145.

9 Ibid., p. 146.

notes in the scale—a phenomenon of harmonic nature."[8] In *Venetian Games* he builds specific twelve-note chords which have a characteristic color. He assigns groups of instruments to particular notes of the chord and then explores the interplay between the contrasting chords. However, he denies any connection with serial music except for the fact that there is a "chromatic whole." Rather than professing a kinship with the Viennese school, Lutosławski is linked in his work to Debussy, Stravinsky, Bartók and Varese.[9]

Gustav Mahler Sketches in the Moldenhauer Archives

Edward R. Reilly

THE SKETCHES IN THE Moldenhauer Archives for Mahler's Seventh Symphony (with one leaf also representing the Sixth) are only one part of a considerable body of important manuscripts of that composer's works in the collection. Manuscripts connected with the Second,[1] Fourth, Ninth, and Tenth Symphonies and with several songs, to say nothing of letters and other documents, make the Archives a major source for scholars interested in Mahler's evolution as a composer and in his development as a person. This particular group of sketches is characteristic in its richness and complexity. The five leaves allow students to trace certain aspects of the creation of both the Sixth and the Seventh Symphonies. At the same time they raise many questions which may be ultimately impossible to answer.

In 1924, probably at the time when a facsimile of the principal manuscripts of the Tenth Symphony was being prepared, Alma Mahler asked Alban Berg to go through her collection of the composer's sketches, probably with a view to sorting them out and identifying their contents. Berg's description of this particular group is found with them on a separate bifolio of music paper used as a cover folder for the leaves.[2] It still proves a good general introduction to their contents.

> 5 lose Blätter/ größtenteils Skizzen zur VII. Symph./(letzter Satz u./ 1 Nachtmusik/ Dazu [?]/ 1 Blatt enthält <u>außerdem</u> ein wörtliches/ Zitat aus der VI. Symphonie/ auf der Rückseite mit Tinte[.]/ 3 andere Blätter auch viel Unbekanntes!/(auch in der X. Symph./ <u>nicht</u> Verwertetes.)/ 1 [das letzte (mit "Blech" überschriebene)]/ eine ganz unbekannte 20 taktige/ Partie, wovon nur 1–2 Takte auf eine / Verwandtschaft mit der VII. schließen lassen./ Berg 9/7/24

[1] The Archives include a solo piano reduction of the symphony. The hand in the manuscript does not appear to be Mahler's, but views differ on this point. If the arrangement is not by Mahler, its author remains uncertain.

[2] Similar comments by Berg are found with at least three other manuscripts, one in the Wiener Stadt- und Landesbibliothek, and two in the Pierpont Morgan Library in New York. The first is dated July 7, 1924, the other two July 9, 1924, the same day indicated in the Moldenhauer manuscript. All are reproduced and transcribed in Gustav Mahler, *Symphonische Entwürfe, Faksimile nach den Skizzen aus der Wiener Stadt- und Landesbibliothek und der Pierpont Morgan Library New York*, ed. by Renate Hilmar-Voit (Tutzing: Hans Schneider, 1991).

5 loose [i.e. separate] leaves/ for the most part sketches for the Seventh Symphony (last movement and/ 1 Nachtmusik/ In addition/ 1 leaf also contains a literal citation from the Sixth Symphony/ on its reverse in ink. 3 other leaves also [contain] much that is unknown!/ (also not made use of/ in the Tenth Symphony.)/ 1 [leaf] [the last (superscribed "brass")]/ an entirely unknown 20-bar/ passage, of which only 1–2 bars/permit [one] to conclude a relationship with the Seventh./ Berg 9 July 1924.

Before considering the contents of these leaves in more detail, a few aspects of their makeup should be noted. In addition to the five leaves with sketches, a single leaf of blank music paper is preserved with the group. Like four of the sketch pages, it bears the colophon "J. E. & Co." (i.e. Josef Eberle & Co., a Viennese firm),[3] although the colophon itself shows a somewhat different configuration when compared with that in the other leaves.

Berg identified the works represented in the sketches with a simple Roman numeral for the symphony and his name (i. e. "VII Berg") in the upper right-hand corner of the leaf, but he did not number them. In close proximity to Berg's notes, an unidentified later owner or librarian did add page numbers, however, using the pattern VII-1, VII-2, etc. Probably the same person also provided identifications of the work, and in some cases the movement—not always accurately—in the right margins. Although the numbering of the pages probably has little to do with the order in which the sketches were written down, it is used here as a matter of convenience in identifying on which leaves specific sketches are found. The side of the leaf on which the colophon appears is identified as the recto, although Mahler may have used the verso first.

None of the sketches is dated, but from other sources it is possible to estimate very roughly when they were composed. Relatively few details have been preserved about Mahler's progress in composing his middle-period symphonies, but some points are relatively clear. Judging from Mahler's letters, he had written much of the first three movements of the Sixth Symphony in the summer of 1903,[4] with the second and third closer to being finished than the first, and had perhaps at least

3 The third leaf has no colophon and is clearly the work of a different manufacturer.

4 In a letter of July 11, 1904, Mahler wrote to Alma asking her to bring the manuscripts of the second and third movements of the Sixth with her to Maiernigg, since he had forgotten to take them himself. Thus those movements were certainly composed the preceding summer. Presumably he had brought material for the outer movements with him, but we do not know how far work on them had already advanced. See *Ein Glück ohne Ruh'. Die Briefe Gustav Mahlers an Alma*, ed., with commentary, by Henry-Louis de La Grange, Günther Weiss, and Knud Martner (Berlin: Siedler Verlag, 1995), p. 215. See also H.-L. de La Grange, *Gustav Mahler: Chronique d'une vie, II, L'age d'or de Vienne (1900–1907)* (Paris: Fayard, 1983), pp. 360–361, 1155.

sketched some of the last movement. The following summer, he completed the enormous finale of the Sixth, and also composed the second and fourth movements, both labeled *Nachtmusik*, of the Seventh. The remaining movements were completed the following year, 1905, in the period after mid-June to mid-August.[5] The draft full score of the first movement, which Mahler completed last, bears the inscription "Maiernigg 15 August 1905/ *Septima* finita." Thus, although it is always possible that Mahler drew on sketch material that he had jotted down earlier, more probably all of the sketches considered here belong within the period from the summer of 1903 to that of 1905, and the majority of those for the Seventh in 1904 and 1905. We can then narrow the dates of some of the specific sketches. The sketches for the theme used in the first movement of the Sixth Symphony may go back to 1903, but the movement itself was completed in 1904.[6] In the latter year the first of the *Nachtmusik* movements was also completed, thus the sketch for it in the Moldenhauer Archives may well belong to the same time. The first, third, and fifth movements of the Seventh were completed in 1905, and the sketches for them most probably belong either to 1904 or 1905.

The sketches for the Seventh Symphony preserved in this group fall chronologically between some important earlier ones for the first and fifth movements found in a manuscript labeled Mahler's "last sketchbook" in the Theatermuseum of the Nationalbibliothek in Vienna[7] (together with two leaves torn from another sketchbook,[8] in the Bibliothèque musicale Gustav Mahler in Paris), and a later and more advanced preliminary draft of a portion of the third movement in the Bruno Walter Collection of the New York Public Library for the Performing Arts. The only other manuscript currently known that precedes the fair copy belonging to the Royal Concertgebouw Orchestra in Amsterdam is the dated orchestral draft of the first movement noted earlier, also in the Bruno Walter Collection.[9]

By the time these sketches were made, Mahler had developed the habit, while working on one composition, of saving notations of other musical ideas for possible future use.[10] What quickly stands out in examining these pages is the large number of unused sketches. In studying the entire series of

5 In a frequently cited letter of June 8, 1910, Mahler recalled his difficulties in resuming work on the Seventh in the summer of 1905. See Gustav Mahler, *Facsimile Edition of the Seventh Symphony, Commentary* volume by Donald Mitchell and Edward R. Reilly (Amsterdam: Rosbeek Publishers, 1995), especially the "Chronology" by Mitchell, pp. 19–29. See also *Ein Glück ohne Ruh'*, pp. 218, 414.

6 Alma Mahler speaks of Mahler completing the draft of the first movement of the Sixth in the summer of 1904, and reports: "After he had drafted the first movement he came down from the wood to tell me he had tried to express me in a theme. 'Whether I've succeeded, I don't know; but you'll have to put up with it.' This is the great soaring theme of the first movement of the Sixth." This is the very theme found on the recto of the first leaf of the Moldenhauer sketches. See Alma Mahler, *Gustav Mahler, Memories and Letters*, 4th ed., trans. Basil Creighton, ed. Donald Mitchell and Knud Martner (London: Cardinal Books, 1990), p. 70, and *Gustav Mahler, Erinnerungen und Briefe* (Amsterdam: Bermann-Fischer Verlag, 1949), p. 92. This passage leaves open the possibility that the sketch may belong to the summer of 1904 rather than 1903. We do not know how far Mahler had gotten with work on the first movement in 1903.

7 See Stephen Hefling, "'*Ihm in die Lieder zu blicken*': Mahler's Seventh Symphony Sketchbook," in *Mahler Studies*, ed. S. Hefling (Cambridge: Cambridge University Press, 1997), pp. 169–216, for a detailed study of the Seventh Symphony material, with facsimiles and transcriptions, in this sketchbook. The title of the volume comes from a note by Anna Bahr-Mildenburg, accompanying the volume, to the effect that Mahler's father-in-law, the painter Karl Moll, found it on Mahler's breast when he died. Hefling raises serious questions about the validity of the story. Two pages from the volume are also reproduced in the *Commentary* volume for the *Facsimile Edition of the Seventh Symphony*, p. 76.

8 The fact that these two pages have nine staves on each page, as compared with six in the Vienna sketchbook, confirms the existence of two different volumes.

9 Pages from all of these manuscripts are also illustrated in my study, "The Manuscripts of the Seventh Symphony" in the *Commentary* volume of the *Facsimile Edition of the Seventh Symphony*, pp. 75–95.

10 See Hefling, "Mahler's Seventh Symphony sketchbook," pp. 172–183, for a review of what is known of Mahler's use of sketchbooks. He seems to have begun saving musical ideas unconnected with the work that he was currently composing from about the summer of 1901.

pages, the material may be divided into three groups: those sketches clearly connected with completed compositions, in this case the Sixth and Seventh Symphonies; those which have some similarity to themes in the Seventh but still differ in significant ways from the forms found in the symphony; and finally, those sketches which have no overt connection with the symphonies and which remained unused. About the last, quite substantial group we can only conjecture as to whether Mahler at some point considered incorporating at least some of the material in one of these symphonies, or was saving it for possible use in a later work (see below, discussion of the Third Group, for one interesting connection).

First Group

The material Mahler used in the Sixth and Seventh Symphonies may be identified as follows:

1. A two-bar sketch in ink for a theme from the first movement of the Sixth Symphony, equivalent to measures 77–78 in the published score, but in G Major rather than F (leaf 1, recto). As noted earlier (in note 6) this theme is in fact the one which Alma Mahler indicates as her husband's musical embodiment of her. All but one of the remaining sketches on this page show a variety of different brief elaborations of this theme. The final sketch, four bars in pencil, is connected with a passage in bars 2–5 of the next-to-last system on the verso of this leaf (see 2a in the third group of sketches discussed below).

2. Essentially one continuous sketch (leaf 5, recto) of the material equivalent to measures 83–105 in the second movement of the completed score of the Seventh Symphony, the first *Nachtmusik*. "As" (A-flat) is indicated as the key in the upper left-hand corner, and the meter is clearly 4/4. "Trio" appears above the first system, and this passage is indeed from the first trio of the movement.

3a. Illustration 1 (leaf 1, verso). Forty measures of sketches for material that extends from measures 7–26 in the fifth movement of the Seventh Symphony. The illustration shows the work in progress at a formative stage in which the gradual

Illustration 1 (leaf 1, verso)

Moldenhauer-Sammlungen in der
Bayerischen Staatsbibliothek München
Mus. ms. 22741

development of the order of the musical ideas and the tonal
pattern is still being worked out. The material, however, is not
found in its final sequence, and brief gaps, variants, and some
unused bars are apparent. The first two systems were originally
in B-flat Major, but the first 8 bars of the second are circled,
and "C-dur" is marked above the first bar (to indicate the
needed transposition), as well as "Original" above the fourth
(to indicate that it is to remain as notated). This second system
is an early form of bars 15–21 (with the two final measures
differing from their final shape). Mahler then writes out a
variant of the whole passage from 15–20, beginning in C, in the
third system following the double bar. The equivalent of
measures 23–26, with a different four-bar continuation, appears
on the first system of the page. The fourth and fifth systems

show two variants of the equivalents of bars 7–13, with two further bars that differ from the published score in the lower system. The material following the ninth measure and the bar line in ink in the fifth system belongs to the sketch on the lower systems of the page. Thus, the order of the material on the page is the reverse of that found in the completed work. System 1 shows measures 23–26, with an unused continuation; system 2, measures 15–21, with a different continuation; system 3, measures 15–20; systems 4 and 5, variants of measures 7–13. This sketch page also provides an extended example of unused material. It is cited as 2a in the third group below. Before the last full measure on the page one finds a late example of a "doodle" by Mahler, perhaps designed to fill a measure that Mahler had left blank with a view to providing a connection between the bars on either side.

3b. Seventeen bars of material used in the finale (leaf 3, verso). The sketches appear on the first two systems (of three staves each), with a one-bar insert following an entirely different three-bar sketch in the third system. The first system includes the equivalents of bars 7 and 8, the main fanfare combination (presenting two motives in counterpoint) of the movement. Four unused bars elaborating variants of the fanfare lead to the equivalent of measures 43–46. The second system preserves bars 38–43 (or their later equivalent in measures 566–70), with an insert of bar 41 indicated in the third system. The whole passage is circled, with a line pointing to the earlier bars 43–46 in the first system. The uncircled last three bars in the second system remained in this form unused in the symphony. The remaining sketches on this page are identified below (group 2, no. 2 and group 3, no. 5).

3c. Illustration 2 (leaf 2, verso). This sketch is the most extended in the entire group, and one of the most fascinating. Unlike the passage shown in Illustration 1 (see 3a above), it is more or less continuous, presented in five systems, all but one in four staves, the other in three, rather than the two or three found in the earlier sketch. These features suggest a somewhat more advanced stage in the composition of the movement. The passage shown is toward the end of the fifth movement (not the first, as indicated in Berg's identification at the right margin), and is roughly equivalent to measures 446–511, with some variants included of specific bars or brief passages. The material largely appears a semitone lower than in the final version. Thus Mahler was in the process of arriving at a tonal scheme for the movement. A key signature for D-flat is marked in the left corner of the page. The very light annotation in red pencil at the top of the page indicates that the music is to be transposed "1/2 [Ton] höher," and "C-moll" at the end of the second system indicates the specific key, after "H-moll" had been considered. The passage shows the contrapuntal combination of several of the most important themes of the movement, and most strikingly, the cyclical return of the main theme of the first movement. The theme that appears in the uppermost staff of the first two bars, interestingly, is the same one found in the "last sketchbook"[11] and also in the sketch pages in the Bibliothèque musicale Gustav Mahler. The specific musical content of each system may be identified as follows:

[11] See Hefling, "Mahler's Seventh Symphony Sketchbook," p. 198, and the *Commentary* volume of the *Facsimile Edition of the Seventh Symphony*, p. 76, for reproductions of the page in question.

1. 17 bars, equivalent to measures 446–61, with one canceled measure.

2. 16 bars, equivalent to measures 462–77. Alternative possibilities are indicated in the staves below bars 473–76. The eighth-note theme found in the last two bars of this system, as well as the first of the next, was later eliminated.

3. 6 bars, equivalent to bars 478–83. The original fourth and fifth bars were replaced by the alternatives below them.

4. 14 bars, equivalent to measures 481–99, thus incorporating the alternate forms of the measures inserted below the preceding system.

The letters B and A, in both ink and red pencil, above the insert sign at the end of the fifth bar suggest two sketches so labeled that are now missing, and probably supplied bars 486–91, not found in this manuscript. The material in the additional staff above the system was not used.

5. 13 bars, equivalent to measures 500–11. The three bars

following the first circled measure were not used in the
final form of the movement and were later replaced by the
equivalent of the two measures 504–5.

Second Group

These sketches are similar in some respects to material used in
the Seventh Symphony, but not identical to the parallel
themes in the completed work.

1. An eight-bar sketch in C-sharp Minor with two alternative or
additional measures (leaf 5, verso, bottom of the page) shows

Illustration 2 (leaf 2, verso)

Moldenhauer-Sammlungen in der
Bayerischen Staatsbibliothek München
Mus. ms. 22741

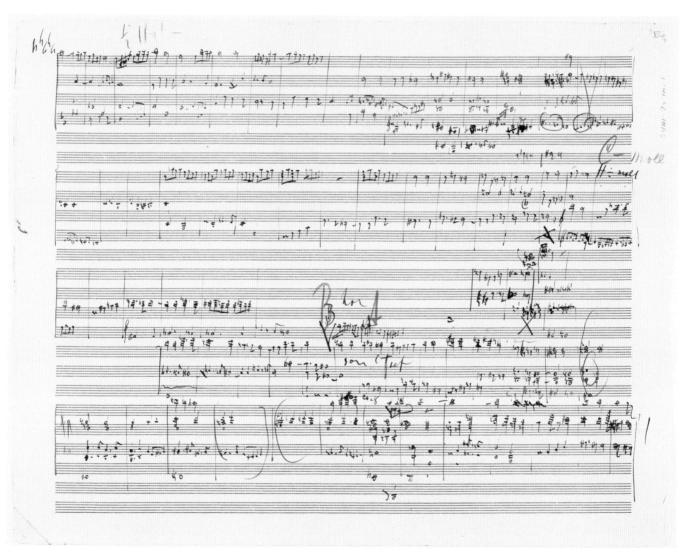

some features of the intervallic and rhythmic structure of the principal Allegro theme in the first movement of the Seventh Symphony (see measures 50–52). Significant differences are also apparent, however, and the material was not used in this form or key. Thus, the connection with the symphony cannot be regarded as conclusive.

2. Sketches of three and two bars (leaf 3, verso, third and fourth systems) of a motive similar in its opening beats to one first found in bar 56 of the fourth movement of the Seventh Symphony. The key is apparently C, and the meter 4/4. Leaf 5, verso, first system, preserves two bars of the same motive, written in time values twice as long as the preceding.

3. A continuous twenty-one-bar sketch beginning and ending in F Major, with the superscription "Blech" (Brass), which seems, because of its nearly constant triplet motion, to have a scherzolike character similar to that of the third movement of the Seventh Symphony. The thematic material, other than the scale patterns, however, differs, and the brass are not called for in the equivalent passages in that movement. "VII ?" in what appears to be Berg's hand, with an arrow pointing down to the fourth bar, draws attention to the quarter-note figure C F E D. A similar figure E-flat A-flat G F also appears as a variant in the third bar of the sketch of the Trio for the second movement of the symphony (leaf 5, recto, first system), but the surrounding music is entirely different. The question mark after the VII suggests that Berg may have had doubts about the attribution, and the connection is very tenuous. If this passage was at some point thought of as potentially usuable in the symphony, Mahler later abandoned the idea.

Third Group

This group of sketches shows even less overt thematic connection with either the Sixth or the Seventh Symphonies, or, with one important exception, with other known works of Mahler.

1. See Illustration 3. A fifty-one-bar sketch in A Major and in 2/4 time (leaf 2, recto, upper 3 systems). Although laid out in

Illustration 3 (leaf 2, recto)

three-stave Particell format, the larger part of the sketch offers only the upper melodic line. Supporting harmony and melodic variants or counterpoints are indicated in just a few bars.

2a. See Illustration 1, bottom three systems. An approximately thirty-six-bar sketch, in three two-stave systems on the lower half of the page (leaf 1, verso), beginning in C Major and in 4/4 time. A number of variants appear in the staves above the last six measures of the first system. Mahler has written "?Es-dur probiren?" (try E-flat Major) in ink above the second and third bars of the second system. On the recto side of this leaf, on a system in pencil below the sketches in ink for the Sixth Symphony, the composer has written an alternative version for bars 2–5 of this brace. As noted earlier, a curious "doodle" in ink by Mahler (many such figures appear in his early manuscripts, but few at this time) is found one and one-half measures before the end of the sketch.

2b. See Illustration 3. A twenty-four-bar sketch beginning in C and in 4/4 time (leaf 2, recto), in two lower systems (the fourth and fifth on the page) of four staves each (with variants in bars below the second system). This sketch shows an elaboration of that in 2a. A double bar appears at the end of the ninth measure, and these initial nine bars have a cancellation line drawn through them. Quite astonishingly, above the first three bars of the soprano line, Mahler has added a counterpoint that anticipates the opening of the principal melody for the first movement of the Ninth Symphony (the pitches are E D-E D-E G, one step lower than in the symphony, and the rhythm similar to measures 7–9 in the second violin part). Thus while the main melody of the sketch was not used, and this passage was actually canceled, Mahler anticipated a portion of the theme of the later work. Did Mahler consciously or unconsciously remember the theme when he came to write the Ninth? We will never be absolutely certain. Bars 15 and 16 are also canceled, but susbstitute measures are provided beneath the lower brace. Two inserts, again under the lower brace, are marked between measures 22 and 23. A counterpoint and an alternative to the upper line are also indicated above the fourth system for bars 1–3 and 10–12.

3. Three sketches, of 21, 8, and 33 bars, in G Major, G Minor and C Major (leaf 3 recto, the entire page). The first and last are in duple time (4/4 or 2/2) and the second is in 3/2. As in the first sketch of this group, although the material is laid out in 3- and 2-stave systems, the principal melody is only intermittently filled out with supporting lines. Although a one-bar gap is found between the first and second sketches, and a system and a half between the second and third, the first and third are related in their material and all three seem to be part of a larger whole.

4. A thirty-bar sketch in C Major and in 2/4 time, on the second and third systems of the page (leaf 5, verso). Variants and additions appear above the first system and below the second. An incomplete bar, with upbeat, appears immediately

below the third system, and seems to be related to the beginning of the sketch. Below this bar, a brief sketch (apparently two and a half bars) in very light pencil shows the opening of an entirely different melody in what seems to be 6/8 time.

5. A four-bar sketch, with an alternative upper part in the last two measures, apparently in G Major (leaf 3, verso, the system at the bottom of the page). No meter is indicated. The first and last bars have four beats, the second and third, three.

Felix Mendelssohn-Bartholdy: Overture to *Elijah*, Arrangement for Piano Duet (1847)

R. Larry Todd

FEW WORKS BY MENDELSSOHN have reflected the composer's shifting critical reception as compellingly as the oratorio *Elijah*. Hailed after its English premieres in 1846 and 1847 as a seminal masterpiece, *Elijah* remained a popular cornerstone in the oratorio repertory, though it withstood a later assault as the work of a composer whose polished, impeccable craftsmanship was somehow not consonant with newer directions in musical culture.

After the first performance in the Birmingham Town Hall on August 26, 1846, a critic in the *Times* reported unabashedly, "Never was there a more complete triumph—never a more thorough and speedy recognition of a great work of art."[1] And when the revised version of the oratorio, on which Mendelssohn labored intensively for several months, was performed in Exeter Hall, London, in April 1847, the scrupulous music critic Henry Fothergill Chorley went so far as to claim that "*Elijah* is not only *the* sacred work of our time, we dare fearlessly to assert, but it is a work 'for our children and for our children's children.'"[2] Perhaps the most remarkable tribute came from Prince Albert (the oratorio was performed before the prince and Queen Victoria), for whom Mendelssohn stood as a prophetic figure contending with the worshippers of false art: "To the Noble Artist, who, surrounded by the Baal-worship of debased art, has been able, by his genius and science, to preserve faithfully, like another Elijah, the worship of true art, and once more to accustom our ear, amid the whirl of empty, frivolous sounds, to the pure tones of sympathetic feeling and legitimate harmony: to the Great Master, who makes us conscious of the unity of his conception, through the whole maze of his creation, from the soft whispering to the mighty raging of the elements."[3]

[1] Quoted in Jack Werner, *Mendelssohn's "Elijah"* (London: Chappell, 1965), p. 16.

[2] Ibid., p. 28.

[3] For a facsimile of the original testimonial, in German, see Werner, op. cit., p. 31; the English translation is by Baron Christian Bunsen, the Prussian ambassador in London who collaborated on what would have been Mendelssohn's third oratorio, *Christus*, some fragments of which appeared posthumously as op. 97.

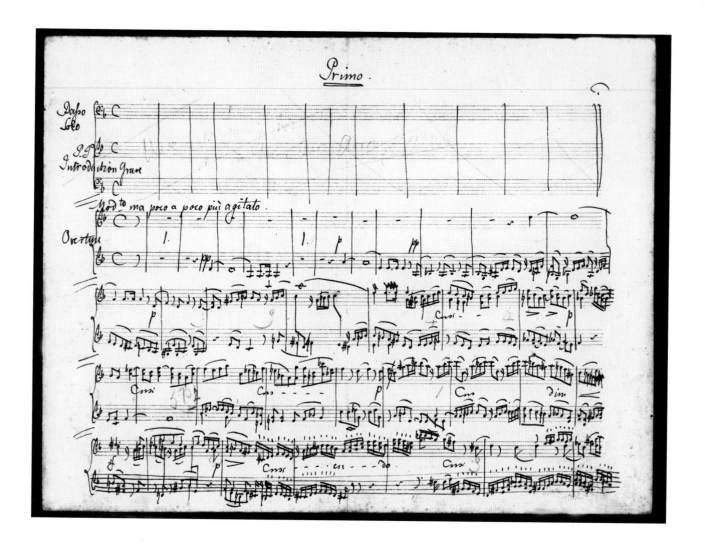

Only a few months later, in November 1847, the musical world was shocked by Mendelssohn's death at the age of thirty-eight. A type of hero worship took root, especially in Leipzig and Berlin, where much of the composer's German career had unfolded, and in England, which Mendelssohn had visited numerous times between 1829 and 1847. To English musical taste, *Elijah* offered a worthy successor to the edifying oratorios of Handel, including *Israel in Egypt* (1739) and *Messiah* (1742), both of which Mendelssohn had often performed and championed at music festivals. To German music taste, *Elijah* reflected as well the composer's abiding interest in the music of J. S. Bach. Having revived the *St. Matthew Passion* in Berlin in 1829 the twenty-year-old Mendelssohn would openly explore, in much of his music, complex contrapuntal idioms reminiscent of the Baroque splendor of Bach's works.

The second half of the nineteenth century witnessed a reaction to the composer and to *Elijah*. While Mendelssohn had been the prime mover in the nineteenth-century Bach revival, his thorough assimilation of Bach's style into his own music nevertheless left him susceptible to the charge that he had relied too heavily on historical models and that his work, especially music such as *Elijah*, was stylistically derivative (and, by implication, wanting in originality). In 1855 Franz Liszt asserted that the historical oratorio had become a more or less effete, antiquated genre, and though he did not mention *Elijah*, he certainly had the Mendelssohnian oratorio in mind.[4] Hector Berlioz, who noted in his memoirs that Mendelssohn was "a little too fond of the dead"[5] and who had little use for traditional contrapuntal writing, no doubt preferred Mendelssohn's concert overtures and the secular cantata *Die*

4 The comments appear in Liszt's article about Robert Schumann, published after Schumann's arrival at the asylum in Endenich: "[Schumann] tried to avoid stiff biblical subjects, formerly so appropriate, that Mendelssohn knew how to modernize even as their outmoded, antiquated features were becoming increasingly more perceptible." Franz Liszt, "Robert Schumann," *Neue Zeitschrift für Musik* 42/14 (1855); see the new translation in *Schumann and His World*, ed. R. Larry Todd (Princeton: Princeton University Press, 1994).

5 *The Memoirs of Hector Berlioz*, trans. David Cairns (New York: W. W. Norton, 1975), p. 294.

6 *Neue Zeitschrift für Musik* (1850): 101, 109–12.

7 *London Music in 1888–1889 As Heard By Corno di Bassetto (Later Known as Bernard Shaw) with Some Further Autobiographical Particulars* (London: Constable, 1937; 3rd ed., 1950), pp. 68ff.

8 Friedrich Nietzsche, *Beyond Good and Evil*, trans. Walter Kaufmann (New York: Vintage, 1966), p. 181 (no. 245): "It is different with Felix Mendelssohn, that halcyon master who, on account of his lighter, purer, more enchanted soul, was honored quickly and just as quickly forgotten: as the beautiful *intermezzo* of German music."

9 Leon Botstein, "The Aesthetics of Assimilation and Affirmation: Reconstructing the Career of Felix Mendelssohn," in *Mendelssohn and His World*, ed. R. Larry Todd (Princeton: Princeton University Press, 1991), p. 6.

10 "Mendelssohn," *Encyclopaedia Britannica*, 11th ed. (Cambridge, 1911), vol. 18, p. 124.

11 Wilfrid Mellers, *Man and His Music: Romanticism and the Twentieth Century* (London: Rockliff, 1957), p. 30. See further, Friedhelm Krummacher, "Composition as Accommodation? On Mendelssohn's Music in Relation to England," in *Mendelssohn Studies*, ed. R. L. Todd (Cambridge: Cambridge University Press, 1992), p. 87, and, on *Elijah*, pp. 94ff.

erste Walpurgisnacht to *Elijah*. In 1850 Richard Wagner gave voice to a more insidious type of criticism by unleashing an anti-Semitic attack on Mendelssohn in the anonymously published article "Das Judenthum in der Musik."[6] And by the 1880s, George Bernard Shaw was criticizing Mendelssohn for his "kid glove gentility, his conventional sentimentality, and his despicable oratorio mongering." Shaw objected in particular to the "dreary fugue manufacture, with its Sunday-school sentimentalities and its Music-school ornamentalities" in such works as *Elijah* and its earlier companion oratorio *St. Paul* (1836).[7] Finally, by 1886 Friedrich Nietzsche, himself a musician and accomplished composer, summarized in *Beyond Good and Evil* Mendelssohn's position in German music as a "beautiful intermezzo" ("schöner Zwischenfall"), a kind of interlude that subsequent twentieth-century music historians located between Beethoven and Wagner.[8]

As Leon Botstein has recently argued, in the closing decades of the nineteenth century the "tenets of cultural modernism were linked to a generational revolt and a rejection of middle-class conceits of culture and art," and "[t]his triggered an aversion to Mendelssohn." So it was that Mendelssohn's music came to signify "a facile consumption of an art of optimism by educated urban classes, an art that neither questioned nor resisted the presumed smugness of bourgeois aesthetic and moral values. *Elijah*. . . [was] viewed as emblematic of a vacuous and affirmative tradition of music making, undertaken thoughtlessly within a hypocritical and exploitative world."[9] By 1911, Donald Tovey, writing a summation of Mendelssohn's position for the *Encyclopaedia Britannica*, could aver, "Mendelssohn's reputation, except as the composer of a few inexplicably beautiful and original orchestral pieces, has vanished."[10] And, in 1957, Wilfrid Mellers concluded that Mendelssohn's music essentially had accommodated a "middle-class public that then, as now, feared change."[11]

Nevertheless, through all the shifting tides of the history of Mendelssohn's reception, *Elijah* has remained an incontrovertibly popular work. Indeed, in 1965, Jack Werner began his monograph on the oratorio by stating outright that alongside *Messiah*, Mendelssohn's *Elijah* was the most popular choral work in England. Recent efforts in Mendelssohn scholarship have begun to focus on reevaluating Mendelssohn's music and historical position, so that "freed of the quite arbitrary aesthetic and implicitly ideological (in the political sense) assumptions that have been applied to Mendelssohn's music since the middle of the nineteenth century, the audience at the end of our century might be able to recognize once again the invention, depth, significance, and emotional power of practically all of Mendelssohn's music."[12] Unquestionably, *Elijah* will occupy a central position in this endeavor. The complex history of the oratorio's creation is well-enough known and requires no review here.[13] But new light on the publication history of *Elijah* is shed by a little-known manuscript in the Moldenhauer collection at the Library of Congress, the composer's autograph arrangement of the overture for piano duet. A bit of musicological sleuthing enables us to establish that the arrangement, though undated, was completed in February 1847, at the height of Mendelssohn's preparations for seeing the oratorio through the press.

Soon after the Birmingham premiere of *Elijah* in August 1847 Mendelssohn began to undertake extensive revisions, in keeping with his typically hypercritical view of his music (indeed, none of Mendelssohn's major works escaped substantial reworking). In revising *Elijah* he was motivated by two particular goals: to complete an improved version of the oratorio in time for the London premiere, in April 1847, and to prepare the work in as timely a manner as possible for simultaneous publication in Germany by Simrock and in England by Ewer and Co. The composer's correspondence with these two firms in the early months of 1847 reveals in detail just how laborious and tedious a process Mendelssohn's was.[14] The publishers' interest in bringing out *Elijah* as quickly as possible was underscored as early as November 10, 1846, when Edward Buxton, the director of Ewer and Company, admonished Mendelssohn in these terms: "There is moreover some danger in keeping the work too long out of print, as there is the possibility of some of the single pieces being copied out and getting into the hands of any of the music sellers here, who would be unprincipled enough to publish them before I could enroll my copyright, which I can only do when it is all in print. I know there are several looking out for it and who have

[12] Botstein, op. cit., p. 9.

[13] See further Werner's monograph and the earlier work on which it draws, F. G. Edwards, *The History of Mendelssohn's Oratorio "Elijah"* (London and New York: Novello, 1896), and A. Kurzhals-Reuter, *Die Oratorien Felix Mendelssohn Bartholdys: Untersuchungen zur Quellenlage, Entstehung, Gestaltung und Überlieferung* (Tutzing: H. Schneider, 1978).

[14] For Mendelssohn's letters to Simrock, see Felix Mendelssohn Bartholdy, *Briefe an deutsche Verleger*, ed. Rudolf Elvers (Berlin, 1968), pp. 252ff. On Mendelssohn's relations with Edward Buxton, see Peter Ward Jones, "Mendelssohn and His English Publishers," in *Mendelssohn Studies*, pp. 254–55. Several of Mendelssohn's letters to Buxton are in the Library of Congress; some are cited in Werner, *passim*, and in "Mendelssohn and His English Publisher: Some Unpublished Letters," *The Musical Times* 46 (1905): 20–23.

15 Letter of November 10, 1846, from Edward Buxton to Mendelssohn, in the Bodleian Library, Oxford, Margaret Deneke Mendelssohn Collection, Green Books, XXIV, No. 130.

16 *Elias. Ein Oratorium nach Worten des alten Testaments componirt von Felix Mendelssohn-Bartholdy, Op. 70. Klavierauszug.*

17 *Elias. Ein Oratorium nach Worten des alten Testaments componirt von Felix Mendelssohn-Bartholdy, Op. 70. Partitur.*

18 *Elijah. An oratorio. The words selected from the Old Testament. The English version by Bartholomew Esqu. The music composed by Felix Mendelssohn Bartholdy, Op. 70. Piano-forte arrangement by the author.*

19 Autograph letter in the Library of Congress.

20 On that day Mendelssohn sent the piano reduction of the Introduction, Overture, and first five numbers to Simrock. See *Briefe an deutsche Verleger*, p. 254.

expressed their determination to print the songs if they could get hold of them."[15]

Not until the middle of January 1847 was Mendelssohn able to start sending parts of the oratorio to Simrock in Bonn. He dispatched first the choral parts for Part I of *Elijah*, and by the beginning of February the piano reduction for the piano-vocal score began to follow in installments. On February 8, the orchestral parts for Part I were ready, except for the Widow's Aria (No. 8), which was still undergoing revision. Mendelssohn sent explicit instructions that the aria was not yet ready to be engraved. By March, Mendelssohn was feverishly working on Part II, and in early April, just days before his departure for England, he was struggling to finish the piano-vocal score of Part II, even as he was correcting proofs for Part I, and writing frequent letters to Buxton, who, in turn, was maintaining an active correspondence with Simrock. But despite the composer's best efforts, the publication of the oratorio was delayed until June 1847, several weeks after he returned in May from England to Germany. Mendelssohn acknowledged receiving an exemplar of the piano-vocal score from Simrock in July 1847[16]; not until October, only days before the composer's death, was Simrock ready to send copies of the full score.[17] The English piano-vocal score[18] appeared simultaneously with the Simrock prints; Mendelssohn's letter of February 25, 1847, to Buxton makes it clear that this was, as he put it, a *"conditio sine que non."*[19]

Not surprisingly, Buxton's piano-vocal score essentially replicates the Simrock *Klavierauszug*, owing to the considerable efforts made to coordinate the simultaneous publication of the oratorio in England and Germany. Nevertheless, in one respect Buxton surpassed Simrock, for he was able to issue two English piano-vocal scores (one folio and one octavo) with two versions of the overture. The folio volume contained the arrangement of the overture for piano solo found in Simrock's *Klavierauszug*, which Mendelssohn finished by February 1, 1847.[20] The octavo volume, on the other hand, transmitted the overture arranged for piano duet, as found in Mendelssohn's autograph now in the Moldenhauer Archives. We may date this arrangement before February 17, 1847, for on that date Mendelssohn sent it, along with the revision of the Widow's

Aria and a newly finished orchestration of the hymn *Hear My Prayer*, to Buxton, with this apologetic explanation: "I am sorry to hear the no. 8 was already engraved, but I cannot help asking you not to mind these plates and to have it engraved, *as it stands here*. I assure you it is an improvement and must *stand* thus! And in order that you may not be too angry with me, I send today (via Simrock) the Ouverture à 4 mains and an Orchestra-Score of my Hymn, which I hope will reconcile you to the trouble you had for me and my alterations sake."[21]

21 Autograph letter (in English) of February 17, 1847, to Edward Buxton, in the Library of Congress.

The Moldenhauer autograph was thus made expressly for Buxton. The composer laid out the duet on facing pages for the *primo* and *secondo* parts, and he took the trouble to rule the twelve bars for the introductory recitative, preceding the overture, in which Elijah announces the seven-year draught. Then, as if to save some precious time, Mendelssohn canceled these bars and added a comment in English: "these 12 bars with the Voice as in the other Arrangement" (i.e., the previously dispatched installment of the opening numbers for the piano-vocal score with the overture for piano solo).

Mendelssohn's autograph presents a relatively clean copy with only occasional corrections. In the main, these concern minor details, such as the direction of note stems, that clarify the voice leading of the parts (e.g., bar 4 of the *secondo*). Occasionally, the alterations reflect practical concerns, such as the division of the music between the two pianists. Thus the original version of bar 10 produced an awkward encounter between the left hand of the first pianist and the right hand of the second pianist, and Mendelssohn was obliged to rearrange the distribution of the parts to simplify their execution. Apart from the notation and corrections in Mendelssohn's hand the only other markings in the manuscript were entered by the engraver, who recorded a series of numbers concerned with the layout of the overture (that is, determining the distribution of the music on each system of the printed version).

Mendelssohn's letter to Buxton suggests that the duet arrangement was intended as a special gift to his English publisher. But the letter does not reveal the composer's entire motivation. In arranging the overture as a duet, he was actually following a practice already established with his earlier oratorio,

22 *Paulus. Oratorium nach Worten der heiligen Schrift, componirt von Felix Mendelssohn-Bartholdy, Opus 36* (Bonn: Simrock); *St. Paul. An oratorio. The words selected from the Holy Scriptures (the English version adapted by Wm. Ball). The music composed by Felix Mendelssohn Bartholdy. The piano forte accompaniment arranged by the composer* (London: J. Alfred Novello).

23 Letter (in English) from Mendelssohn to Edward Buxton in the Bodleian Library, Oxford, M. Deneke Mendelssohn Collection, C42, ff. 81–82.

24 Mendelssohn originally intended to have no overture for *Elijah* but was convinced to write one by William Bartholomew, who provided the English translation of the German libretto; the overture was finished only some two weeks before the premiere in August 1846. See Werner, op. cit., pp. 44–45, 77.

St. Paul, of which the first edition of the piano-vocal score had appeared from Simrock in 1836, with the overture arranged for piano duet.[22] As in *Elijah*, the overture to *St. Paul* was conceived as a fugue, and the contrapuntal complexity of the music may have encouraged Mendelssohn to undertake the duet arrangements in 1836 and 1847 to facilitate the performance of the overtures. After all, two pianists could offer at the keyboard a more complete and convincing rendition of a four-part orchestral fugue than could a single pianist.

But one final question remains: why did Mendelssohn offer the duet arrangement for *Elijah* only to Buxton and not to Simrock? The answer may be found, perhaps, in a particular request Buxton had made of Mendelssohn, as we learn in the composer's letter to Buxton of December 30, 1846: "I did what I could to reconcile myself to the idea of adding a few bars to the Overture to make it a separate piece and give it a conclusion, but I assure you, it is *impossible*. I tried hard to do what you want, in order to show my good will—but I could not find an end, and I am sure there is *none* to be found."[23] With a publisher's shrewd sense of marketing, Buxton had evidently asked Mendelssohn to provide a concert ending for the overture, so that it could be sold and performed as a separate piece, as a kind of programmatic concert overture. But Mendelssohn conceived the overture as an instrumental depiction of the draught and famine that led through a dramatic crescendo directly into the imploration of the first chorus, "Help Lord! Wilt Thou quite destroy us?"[24] The composer was unable to separate the instrumental depiction of the famine from the vocal entreaty, the dramatic consequence of the overture, and thus could not oblige Buxton's request. In sum, the meticulously crafted duet arrangement that Mendelssohn produced in February 1847 may have been intended in part to compensate Buxton for this disappointment.

A Letter by Pietro Metastasio

Denise P. Gallo

DURING PIETRO METASTASIO'S YEARS as court poet for the Habsburgs in Vienna, people of talent—real or perceived— solicited him for opinions of their work. Women as well as men wrote to him, requesting his endorsement or, more directly, his aid in ameliorating their artistic situations. As Charles Burney noted in his memoirs of Metastasio, the poet did not appear to seek the post of judge for writers and musicians of his day, yet he always answered their inquiries, and particularly those from women "with due politeness and gallantry."[1] In one such case, Metastasio not only responded but willingly interceded in defense of a young Roman composer, Maria Rosa Coccia, whose artistic reputation had come under attack. His correspondence reveals the amicable respect in which they held one another, even though they were never to meet.

Early editions of biographical dictionaries and encyclopedias contained entries on Coccia; she was eliminated from the revised editions of some of these reference works, however, most likely to make space for more contemporary or more prolific composers. Thanks to the recent surge of research on women composers and musicians, Coccia's life has been documented again.[2] Many current sources record her birth date in Rome as January 4, 1759; however, in the Latin inscription beneath her portrait in the *Elogio storico della signora Maria Rosa Coccia Romana* (Rome, 1780) written in her defense, the date appears as June 4.[3] The latter date is substantiated by Alberto Cametti's article on Coccia which cites records from the Church of San Lorenzo in Damaso.[4]

Coccia exhibited precocious musical talent and, at 13, she composed not only an oratorio, *Daniello nel lago dei leoni*, but also a setting of Metastasio's *L'isola disabitata*. Her parents placed her under the tutelage of Sante Pesci, maestro of the Basilica Liberiana, with whom she studied counterpoint. On November 28, 1774, she was tested by members of the

[1] Charles Burney, *Memoirs of the Life and Writings of the Abate Metastasio*, vol. 3 (London: G.C. and J. Robinson, 1796; reprint, New York: Da Capo Press, 1971), p. 52.

[2] For a bibliography of sources on Maria Rosa Coccia, see Aaron Cohen, *International Encyclopedia of Women Composers*, 2nd ed. (New York: R.R. Bowker and Co., 1987), p. 157.

[3] The pertinent portion of the inscription reads: "Maria Rosa Coccia, Rom. nat. 4 Iun.an.1759" or "Maria Rosa Coccia Romana, nata 4 Iunius, annus 1759."

[4] Alberto Cametti, "Altre notizie su Maria Rosa Coccia," *Gazzetta musicale di Milano* 55 (June 21, 1900): 343.

Congregazione dei signori musici di S. Cecilia (later the Accademia di Santa Cecilia), and based on the results of this examination—a fugue on a cantus firmus, the antiphon "Hic vir despiciens mundum"—she was granted the title of Maestra di Cappella. Subsequently, the examination piece was presented to the members of the Accademia Filarmonica in Bologna, who named her Maestra pubblica di Cappella on October 13, 1779. Her examination is preserved in the Biblioteca of the Accademia in Bologna, as is that of Mozart who had earned the title of Maestro di Cappella nine years earlier.

Embellished with poetic comment, an edition of Coccia's fugue was published in 1775. Her work, however, came under the attack of Francesco Capalti, Maestro di Cappella of the Cathedral of Narni, who claimed that the fugal answer did not conform to the rules of counterpoint. His criticism clearly called into question her examination process; Coccia should never have been appointed Maestra, he maintained, assigning the blame to Pesci. To make matters worse, two of the original examiners, buckling under the pressure of having their judgment questioned, moved into Capalti's camp, stating that Coccia had been passed not on her talent but out of respect for her gender. Indeed, they had never imagined that her examination would be made public.[5] Scathing attacks flew between the two sides: Capalti and his followers versus those who defended Coccia's name and that of their maligned colleague Pesci. In order to silence the charges, her allies set about gathering letters of support from knowledgeable and respected persons. Copies of her music were sent to Giovanni Battista Martini, Carlo Broschi (the castrato Farinelli) and Metastasio. Comments were also elicited from those who knew the young composer's work firsthand, such as representatives from the courts of Naples and Portugal, and Angela Benucci, abbess of the monastery of Montealboddo, for whom Coccia had composed music to the text "Veni Creator Spiritus" in the convent's Pentecost service. The responses were compiled by Abbot Michele Mallio and published in the aforementioned *Elogio*.

Metastasio's first act in Coccia's campaign was to respond to Andrea Ratti, Archbishop of Adrianopoli, who had sent the

5 C. Lozzi, "Una govinetta romana maestra di musica ammirata dal Martini e dal Metastasio," *Gazzetta musicale di Milano* 55 (May 31, 1900): 297–98.

poet a letter of recommendation on the composer's behalf. About a week later, on December 29, 1777, Metastasio wrote directly to Coccia, acknowledging receipt of a packet containing samples of her work; therein, he admitted that he himself had not felt competent to judge her music, so he had sought the aid of someone qualified, who, in his presence, examined the material and assured him that the pieces "were not only correctly but masterfully written."[6] With this testimony in hand, Coccia might well have ended the correspondence, yet Metastasio had left the issue open, stating that he would await word as to what he was to do with her music. His next letter to her (February 12, 1778) suggests that she had responded by making it a present to him:

> The generous gift which you would make to me of your skillfully done manuscript (for which I am most grateful) will be transformed by me into a sacred deposit...and meanwhile will be guarded over jealously so as to be returned again to you when you need to put it to better use.

His third letter, dated January 15, 1779, refers again to this "sacred deposit" which had fulfilled its commission of demonstrating her talents to him.[7] Urging her to compose more such works, he expressed to Coccia, "the brave Trevia shepherdess," his wish that in some way he might be the "instrument to correct the injustice which you have until now suffered from Fate." He assured her that, if occasion should arise, he would do whatever he could to help her: "believe me truthfully," he concluded.

This third letter is now part of the Moldenhauer Archives at the Library of Congress. The stationery, without envelope, had been merely folded over and addressed on the back to "Mademoiselle Marie Rose Coccia—Rome." The letter is well-preserved, its red wax seal still intact. Together with another two of Metastasio's letters (to other recipients), also in the Moldenhauer Archives, it serves to demonstrate the court poet's fine, careful penmanship, while its text is an expression of his gentle, benevolent nature. In a fourth letter, dated February 14, 1780, Metastasio wrote to thank Coccia for sending him her portrait which, he told her, helped him to form an idea not only of her talent but also of her person. It

6 All of Metastasio's letters cited herein can be found in volume 5 of Bruno Brunelli's edition of the poet's ouevre, *Tutte le opere di Pietro Metastasio* (Verona, Italy: Arnoldo Mondadori, 1954).

7 While the month is missing from the original letter, one may assume, as does Brunelli in his edition of Metastasio's letters, that the poet was writing on the fifteenth day of the year 1779.

Vienna 15. del 779.

La gentile attenzione della valorosa Pastorella Trevia
negli augurj che mi porge, a seconda dell'universale
ufficioso costume, mi riconcilia con questa incomoda
e per lo più vana cerimonia; assicurandomi dell'
onorato loco, ch'io tuttavia conservo nella memo-
ria di persona così distinta e meritevole. Io gliene
rendo il dovuto contraccambio, e sarei glorioso
se potessi in qualche modo servir d'istrumento
per correggere l'ingiustizie ch'Ella fin ora soffre
dalla Fortuna. Il sacro deposito che si trova tuttavia appresso di me, à perfettam.te eseguita la commis-
sione d'informarmi della meravigliosa abilità
dell'ingegno che l'à prodotto. Vorrei che le produ-
cesse altri più sensibili frutti: et io sarò pronto
ad impiegarlo a tale oggetto, se mi si scoprisse oca-
sione di farlo utilm.te; o di farlo ritornare intatto alla
sua sorgente, se mai potesse costì esser meno infruttuo-
so alla illustre sua Produttrice. Mi conservi intanto
l'invidiabile sua parzialità; e mi creda veracem.te

Dmo Obb.mo Serv.re
Pietro Metastasio.

Sig.ra
S.ra Maria Rosa Coccia [Roma]

·324·

appeared, like the previous three, in Mallio's *Elogio* as witness to Coccia's musical ability and to her character.

Coccia sought Metastasio's assistance even after the publication of the *Elogio*. In the last of the five extant letters, dated September 6, 1781, Metastasio gently corrected Coccia's opinion that he frequented Court and therefore would be present there to recommend her work to the Grand Duke and Duchess of Russia who were to visit Vienna at the end of that year.[8] Metastasio patiently explained that, because of his advanced age (eighty-three), he left home only "to satisfy the duties of religion, and then not always." Since the nobles were on the way to Italy, he suggested, would it not be better to seek them in person when they arrived in Rome? He concluded by expressing his regrets that he could do no more than confirm once again his good and true wishes in her regard.

Metastasio died some seven months after this last letter. Yet the attacks on Coccia's work continued, even as long as four years after the publication of the *Elogio*.[9] It seems likely that she was merely a pawn in a larger, more personal struggle between Capalti and the opposition, and she seems to have been all but forgotten by her protectors. She did practice her art, however. In the archives of the Accademia di Santa Cecilia, Cametti discovered a petition, dated December 18, 1832, for financial assistance which Coccia, then seventy-three, had submitted. In it, she stated that she had spent her life "composing and teaching," but because she was alone, advanced in age and ill, she needed a subsidy to help provide for her necessities. She had never been able to save even "a small fund" for her old age as she had been the sole support of her elderly parents and sister before they had died. In reply, she was granted a meager pension.[10] She died some days before November 21, 1833, the date on a receipt for four Masses said for her soul at the parish of San Carlo a Catinari, headquarters of the Congregazione di Santa Cecilia. No special services marked her passing; in fact, the Masses were not even said for her alone but included the name of another deceased parishioner.[11]

If Coccia indeed spent her life composing, much of her music must have been destroyed or lost.[12] While most of her

8 Brunelli's note to this letter in *Tutte le opere*, vol. 5, *Lettere*, p. 817.

9 Lozzi, op. cit., p. 298.

10 Cametti, op. cit., pp. 343–44.

11 Ibid., p. 344.

12 For a list of Coccia's known compositions, see Barbara Garvey Jackson, *"Say Can You Deny Me": A Guide to Surviving Music by Women from the 16th Through the 18th Centuries* (Fayetteville, Arkansas, 1994).

biographical data comes directly from Mallio's *Elogio*, much about her character and personality can be deduced from Metastasio's correspondence. Coccia could count on little more than the use of his name during what amounted to a public trial of her artistry, but when others later deserted her cause the memory of his friendship must have provided her some small comfort.

Wolfgang Amadè Mozart's Allegro and Andante ("Fantasy") in F Minor for Mechanical Organ, K. 608

Neal Zaslaw

ANYONE VISITING EUROPE'S PALACES, stately homes and
museums is likely to notice the musical automata. These often
exquisitely made creations range in size from costly toys that
can be held in one hand to organs filling whole walls. But their
most common manifestations are in the form of large tabletop
clocks that contain small pipe organs, and the best of them are
serious instruments, which served those who could afford
them, just as electronic means of reproduction serve us, with
music on demand. Automata were "programmed" by pinning a
rotating barrel in such a way that the pins struck the teeth of a
comb (as in today's children's music boxes) or opened the
valves of organ pipes at precisely the right moments. The
repertory usually comprised arrangements of popular songs and
dances, although on larger instruments extended works were
sometimes undertaken, and occasionally original compositions.
C. P. E. Bach, Haydn, Mozart, and Beethoven were among the
composers who wrote for such instruments.

The earliest sign of Mozart's involvement with musical
automata is found in his letter of October 3, 1790, written from
Frankfurt to his wife, Constanze, in Vienna:

> I have now made up my mind to compose at once the
> Adagio for the clockmaker and then to slip a few ducats into
> the hand of my dear wife. And this I have done; but as it is a
> kind of composition which I detest, I have unfortunately not
> been able to finish it. I compose a bit of it every day—but I
> have to break off now and then, as I get bored. And indeed I
> would give the whole thing up, if I had not such an
> important *reason to go on with it*. But I still hope that I shall
> be able to force myself gradually to finish it. If it were for a

large clock and would sound like an organ, then I might get some fun out of it. But, as it is, the works [of the instrument] consist solely of shrill little pipes, which sound too high-pitched and too childish for my taste.

In the chronological thematic catalog of his works which Mozart kept from 1784 until his death (*Verzeichnüß aller meiner Werke*), he entered three relevant items, the second of which is the work preserved in the manuscript under consideration:

> 1) "A piece for an organ in a clock" [musical incipit of the Adagio and Allegro in F Minor, K. 594 entered in Mozart's catalog under December 1790]
> 2) "An organ piece for a clock" [musical incipit of the Allegro and Andante in F Minor, K. 608, dated in the catalog March 3, 1791]
> 3) "Andante for a cylinder in a small organ" [musical incipit of the Andante in F Major, K. 616, dated in the catalog May 4, 1791].

We shall return to the question of which, if any, of these three works is the one with which Mozart was struggling in Frankfurt.

The identity of "the clockmaker" mentioned in Mozart's letter may have been clarified by Otto Biba, who discovered in the Gesellschaft der Musikfreunde, of which he is the librarian, a letter dated January 18, 1813, from Ignaz von Seyfried to an unidentified "Hofrat" (privy councillor)—possibly Friedrich Rochlitz, editor of the *Allgemeine musikalische Zeitung* (*AmZ*). Seyfried had recently completed an orchestration of K. 608, which was about to be published in Leipzig by Breitkopf & Härtel, whose publication the *AmZ* was. His letter contains the following remarks:

> Mozart's Fantasy in F minor, composed here in Vienna for the late Father Primitiv, is (as far as I am aware) little known, and nevertheless deserves, I feel, one of the first places among the immortal's masterpieces. I still recall from my youth the lively sensation that repeated—oft repeated—hearings of this ingenious production ineradicably impressed upon my memory. A thousand varying emotions were

Das, zum Andenken des großen Feldmarchals Freyheren GIDEON ERNEST V. LOUDON durch Herrn Joseph Müller errich-
tete MAUSOLE, welches in der Himelpfortgaße Nᵒ 1355. in des Hᵉⁿ Baumeisters Gerl Hauße aufgestellet u: täglich beleichteter zu sehen ist.

aroused by that (I might almost call it) terrifying Allegro, with its artful fugue subject in the strict style. The listener is startled at the violent modulation to F sharp minor, and imagines the ground shaking beneath him. The lovely, so tenderly expressed Adagio [*recte* Andante] in A flat major is music of the spheres; it elicits tears—salutary tears of longing for heaven. The repeat of the opening Allegro catapults us back into troubled human existence. The two mutually belligerent fugue subjects impart a striking, serious, powerful image of the battle of the passions. Only at the end is there calm. Power is exhausted, human nature has died, and the soul escapes the body. The end signifies the life to come.

Father Primitivus Niemecz, librarian at Esterháza Palace, was a pupil and friend of Haydn's. He built several clock-organs which play music that Haydn wrote or arranged especially for them; some of these survive in working order and their eighteenth-century sounds may be heard on modern recordings. Wolfgang Plath doubted that Mozart would have referred to a learned man and priest like Niemecz by what he considers the disrespectful appellation "the clockmaker," yet readers of Mozart's correspondence will readily call to mind disrespectful remarks about various other persons.

In any case, although the nature of the relationship between Mozart and Niemecz is unknown, the commission that linked them was intended not for a palace or stately home but rather for a private Viennese art gallery and waxworks collection. This gallery was the creation of one Joseph Nepomuk Franz de Paula, Baron Deym von Stržitéž, who operated under the alias Müller after having had to flee from his post as an officer in the Austrian army following an illegal duel. Müller's Gallery, operated by Deym at various locations in Vienna between circa 1780 and 1804 and then by his widow until 1819, contained curious works of art, plaster-cast copies of ancient sculptures, and handsomely clad wax statues of famous living personages, among them the Austrian military hero, Field Marshal Ernst Gideon, Baron von Laudon (or Loudon; he is the also man to whom Haydn dedicated his Symphony No. 69). After Laudon died on July 14, 1790, Deym decided to construct a monument in which the Field Marshal's effigy could be viewed in a glass coffin. This was announced in the *Wiener Zeitung* for March 26, 1791:

> On March 23rd Herr Müller, who has become generally known through his art collection on the Stock-im-Eisen-Platz, No. 610, first floor, opened the Mausoleum erected by him, which he has at great expense created in memory of the unforgettable and world-famous Field Marshal Baron von Laudon, in the Himmelpfortgasse over against the Mint, in the house of Herr Gerl, master-builder (No. 1355). Here on the ground floor this remarkable monument may be seen in a setting especially designed for it, splendidly illuminated from 8 o'clock in the morning till 10 o'clock at night; access to it is by the large door up three steps of the main staircase.

The distributed advertisements as well as the posters have given some description of it, but since to describe the whole with sufficient vividness is impossible, the sight of it will not fail to surprise everyone who visits this Mausoleum and thereby renews the memory of this great and meritorious man. Herr Müller has caused it to be engraved in copper, and colored prints will shortly be available at the entrance. The seats are arranged in the best possible way, and each person pays 1 fl. for a first place and 30 kr. for a second; upon the stroke of each hour a Funeral Musique will be heard, and will be different every week. This week the composition is by Herr Kapellmeister Mozart.

Perhaps as stated above, originally the music of different composers was heard weekly, but within months only Mozart's music was presented, according to two documents: a notice in the *Wiener Zeitung* of August 17, 1791 ("choice funeral music composed by the famous Herr Capellmeister Mozart, which is wholly appropriate to the purpose for which it has been written") and a descriptive guide published in 1797 ("Every hour a suitable funeral music, especially written for the purpose by the unforgettable composer Mozart, is to be heard, which lasts eight minutes and in precision and purity surpasses anything that was ever attempted to be suitably applied to this kind of artistic work.")

It has traditionally been supposed that the commission on which Mozart was working in Frankfurt in order to "slip a few ducats into the hand of [his] dear wife" was a piece for the mechanical organ hidden in Laudon's Mausoleum, but (as Ludwig Misch and Wolfgang Plath have pointed out) this must be wrong. In Frankfurt Mozart complained of the high pitch of the instrument for which he had to compose, so he must have been working on a piece like the delicate K. 616, notated in Mozart's autograph on three treble staves and with a range of only three octaves from the f a fifth below middle c.

K. 594 and 608, on the contrary, come down to us (in the Berlin and Vienna manuscripts discussed below and the *Neue Mozart-Ausgabe* based on them) notated on three treble staves plus a bass staff and requiring an instrument with a range of three-and-a-half octaves extending a fourth lower in the bass than the instrument for which K. 616 was intended. K. 594 and 608—both in F Minor, in a heavy style, in *A-B-A* form, lasting eight or nine minutes, and entitled "Fantasy"—must have been written for the Mausoleum. Seyfried's overheated account of the music fits K. 608—the work found in the Library of Congress manuscript—which must have become permanently associated with the Mausoleum to the exclusion of K. 594.

Contrary to Seyfried's peculiar assertion that K. 608 was "little known," however, there is evidence of its dissemination in the half-century after Mozart's death in print and manuscript arrangements for piano two- or four-hands, flute duet, string quartet, and orchestra—this at a time when K. 594 was virtually unknown. And a review of the first edition of K. 608 in the *AmZ* in September 1799 begins, "This Fantasy is the organ piece, well known in Vienna, . . . which Mozart composed for the mechanical instrument in the splendid Müller's Art Gallery in that very city." The anonymous reviewer (Friedrich Rochlitz?), who said he had "in front of him a manuscript copy of this Fantasy just as Mozart composed it for the organ," enumerated, with musical examples, some of the contradictions between the first edition and his manuscript. So even in its very early dissemination, the text of K. 608 had become confused. And the work's enthusiastic reception was accurately foretold by the *AmZ* reviewer, who found it to be "one of the most consumate works of [Mozart's] inexhaustible genius."

Of Mozart's three completed pieces for mechanical instruments, an autograph manuscript survives only for K. 616 (in the Mozarteum in Salzburg). Neither it nor the autographs of K. 594 and 608 were in Mozart's possession at his death, and when the publisher Johann Anton André, who bought most of Mozart's manuscripts from his widow Constanze in 1799, wrote to her asking about them, she replied on May 31, 1800, that "these belong to the Royal Imperial Chamberlain Count von Deym here in Vienna, who is the proprietor of the Art Gallery formerly called by him Müller's Art Gallery." As there is no autograph extant for K. 608, to establish its text we are dependent on early copies of various provenance.

This brings us to the manuscript of K. 608 found at the Library of Congress. It is written on six pages or three leaves. Two of these leaves form a single bifolium (a folio folded once to make four pages) on which is written an Allegro, comprising a prelude in the style of a French overture plus a massive fugue, along with the reworked reprise of both. Inserted into the bifolium is the third leaf, of a different type of paper, slightly smaller than the bifolium; the separate leaf contains on its two pages the Andante ("that in every regard deserves to be called *heavenly*"—*AmZ*), which forms the central section of the composition. Both papers are types commonly found in Viennese musical manuscripts: the bifolium has a watermark with the extremely common three-crescent-moon pattern on one half and a helmet device with the initials "AM" on the other. This is similar to, but not identical with, Alan Tyson's watermark 86, a kind of paper that Mozart used in the years 1786–1791. The bifolium is in oblong format and ruled with fourteen staves per page, with a "total span" (the distance from the top line of the top staff to the bottom line of the bottom staff) of approximately 183 mm. The inserted leaf reveals only a bit of its watermark, which is similar to the chevron pattern seen in Tyson's watermark 106A, quadrant 3a, briefly used by Mozart in 1791. It is also in oblong format, but with only eight staves per page and a total span of approximately 175 mm. Unfortunately, in our current state of knowledge this information is insufficient to date the manuscript.

The hand of the Library of Congress manuscript's copyist and its paper types suggest possible Viennese origins, but Dexter Edge, an expert on Viennese manuscripts of the period, has not been able to associate the hand with any known copyist from Mozart's or his widow's circle (personal communication). The copyist was an experienced musician (his hand is fluent and legible even though crowded) but probably not a professional copyist, who most likely would have spread the music out to occupy more space and give the work a heading. The manuscript is, in any case, not a fair copy but a working document, with a number of corrections and the occasional passage that seems not entirely complete.

As already mentioned, the two principal manuscript copies of K. 608 are on four staves; one is in the Staatsbibliothek

Preußischer Kulturbesitz, Berlin, the other in the library of the Gesellschaft der Musikfreunde, Vienna. The four-staff version of the work in both manuscripts and in the *Neue Mozart-Ausgabe* can without further ado be played four-hands, even though it has not been specifically arranged for that purpose, which would have involved at the very least extending the mock-tutti chords of the opening and similar passages to exploit the full five-octave range of Mozart's fortepiano. A version arranged for piano four-hands did appear in the first edition (Vienna: Johann Traeg, 1799), in the so-called *Oeuvres complettes* (1800), as well as in the old complete edition of Mozart's works (1883); it can also be found in most practical editions of Mozart's four-hand music.

The Library of Congress manuscript, however, contains neither of these but rather an unpublished version on two staves, which appears to be for a single player. This version, while

keeping the top note at d''' and thus never reaching up the additional minor third to top f''' on the fortepiano of Mozart's day, does extend in the bass to make use of the available notes down to the bottom F_1. The tutti chords of the four-staff version are densely packed with notes in all octaves, presumably as a result of the relatively limited range of Deym's automaton and Mozart's judgment about effective voicing of chords on that instrument. The Library of Congress's two-staff version displays spacing more normal for piano writing, with larger intervals in the bass and smaller ones in the treble.

The spacing is more normal perhaps, but not entirely normal, for if one sits down to play this two-hand version of K. 608, some surprises are in store. To be sure, the rapid turns in thirds, which are such a prominent feature of the beginning of the Allegro and are entirely manageable for four hands, have been simplified in the two-staff version by removing the lower voice. But aside from this simple acknowledgment of human limitations, in other passages this two-staff transcription is patently awkward, often requiring reaching for notes in a way never expected in even the most brilliant eighteenth-century keyboard music. The problems of reaching grow sporadically worse as the piece progresses until, beginning in measure 118, one finds passages that cannot be played by two hands. This must mean either that the Library of Congress version was scored on two staves for purposes of study rather than performance, or that it was intended for an instrument with a pedal board—that is, if not an organ, a fortepiano such as the one Mozart owned, which, in addition to its normal five-octave range, had some number of additional bass notes (the precise details are unknown) in a second instrument with a pedal board on the floor, upon which the fortepiano stood. The presence of the indications *fp* in the Allegro and crescendo and diminuendo in the Andante means that the arranger had a fortepiano with a pedal in mind, not an organ. With a pedal for the lowest line, the work becomes playable by a single player, even though a few passages remain unidiomatically conceived for a keyboard instrument of any kind. (It should also be mentioned that in the Andante between measures 137 and 138 and again between measures 158 and 159 there is an extra measure of music not found in published versions of this piece.)

This two-staff version brings to mind an account by Johann Wenzel Tomaschek of a visit to Prague by the pianist Joseph Wölffl in March 1799, in which we read:

> Wölffl played a concerto of his own composition with unparalleled clarity and precision, which—on account of the immense stretch of his hands—no one else could perform. Then he played Mozart's *Fantasia in F minor* published in Breitkopf's edition for four hands, exactly as it is printed without leaving out a single note. Nor in any way, in his execution, did he shorten the value of the notes as the so-called romantics of our times love to do, who then imagine that they can smooth everything out again by making an appalling confusion of sounds by raising the dampers. As I said, he played this piece of music without any mishaps.

And Constanze Mozart mentioned in a letter of February 27, 1800, that "A fantasia for fortepiano in F minor should be in the hands of a certain Mr. [Franz] Leitl in Prague," referring to a flutist and oboist who played in the first performance of *Don Giovanni* and was a collector of Mozart's music. (Of course, Leitl may have had K. 594 rather than K. 608.) Hence versions of K. 608 for one player were circulating in manuscript before 1805, when Clementi published a two-hand arrangement (Vienna: Artaria).

The question naturally arises whether Mozart himself may have had a hand in the creation of the two-staff version of K. 608 found in the Library of Congress manuscript. On the basis of the unidiomatic solo keyboard writing, we should very much doubt it. When Mozart made keyboard versions of larger scorings, for instance in his marvelous rendering of the overture for *Die Entführung aus dem Serail,* he did not try to crowd in all possible notes but instead rewrote the piece to invent effects analogous to, but different from, the orchestral effects they replaced.

The early history of the manuscript of K. 608 found at the Library of Congress cannot be traced. Its first recorded appearance occurred when Johannes Wolf, music librarian of the Prussian State Library, examined it in 1928; comparing it to that Library's manuscript of K. 608, which had once belonged to Beethoven and was erroneously considered an autograph, he thought the two manuscripts were written in "obviously the same hand." In 1936 the Library of Congress manuscript was at the H. Hinterberger Antiquariat (Vienna), where it was examined by Alfred Einstein as he prepared the third edition of the Köchel Catalog. In 1951 it was sold by Hinterberger to the Otto Haas Antiquariat (London) and then to the musicologist Paul Nettl, from whom it was later acquired by Hans Moldenhauer.

An expert evaluation by the Viennese musicologist Robert Haas for the Hinterberger firm opined that the manuscript may have stemmed from Maximilian Stadler or Franz Xaver Süßmayr working under Mozart's supervision and may contain corrections in the composer's hand. (In 1791 Süßmayr acted as Mozart's amanuensis for *Die Zauberflöte* and *La clemenza di Tito* and after Mozart's death completed the Requiem and the D-Major horn concerto, K. 412; Stadler helped Constanze to inventory her husband's musical estate and completed some keyboard pieces that Mozart had left incomplete.) Haas's suggestion was, however, merely wishful thinking intended to place the manuscript's origins closer to Mozart and his circle, increasing its putative authenticity and, not incidentally, its musical and commercial value. The manuscript cannot be convincingly identified as in Stadler's or Süßmayr's hand, and the corrections appear to be in the same ink and same hand as the rest.

Since we have neither Mozart's score of K. 608 nor the mechanical instrument that played it, we must rely on manuscripts and early editions preserving conflicting versions made for reasons, under circumstances, and by persons unknown. That being so, we cannot assume prima facie that unique readings in the Library of Congress manuscript necessarily represent mistakes or high-handed alterations. As long as the autograph manuscript remains missing, the Library of Congress manuscript must be taken into account in any conscientious attempt to study, edit, or perform this extraordinary piece of music.

As Wolfgang Plath has pointed out, the influence of Mozart's Fantasy in F minor, K. 608 was considerable in the nineteenth century. Aside from the editions, manuscripts, and arrangements already mentioned, many public performances can be documented. Beethoven owned the work and made his own arrangement of the fugue. Schubert's F Minor Fantasy for piano four-hands, op. 103 (D. 940, 1828), suggests his reaction to the whole of Mozart's piece, whereas Franz Lachner's Wind Octet in B flat, op. 156 (1859) demonstrates his reception of the Andante. Given the loss of the mechanical instrument for which K. 608 was intended, we should probably join the musicians of the first half of the nineteenth century in accepting a wide variety of performance possibilities ranging from a single keyboard player to a full classical orchestra, in order to restore Mozart's inspired mourning music to a sounding condition.

[*Allgemeine musikalische Zeitung,* I (Sept. 1799), cols. 876–79:]

Fantaisie à quatre mains pour le Pianoforte, composée par W. A. Mozart. à Vienne, chez Jean Traeg dans la Singerstrasse. (22 Gr.)

This Fantasy is the organ piece, well-known in Vienna, for two keyboard instruments, which Mozart composed for the mechanical instrument in the splendid Müller's Art Gallery in that very city. Accordingly, the title should more correctly read: *Fantaisie etc. composée par W. A. Mozart, arangée pour le Pianoforte, etc.* As short as this piece is—it consists of a brief Allegro in F Minor, an Andante in A-flat major and a concluding tempo primo again in F Minor, which together last hardly nine minutes— that is how rich it is in intrinsic merit. Right in the first movement, following a few admittedly rather small ideas, which however in power and expression are so much the more copious and great and which serve as [twelve] measures of (as it were) prophetic introduction, the work begins with the following very beautiful, tasteful, and gently melancholic, elevated theme, which seems even more so after the power and (one might almost say) degree of stridency of the introduction:

After an extremely diligent contrapuntal elaboration of this theme, artful but at the same time always very pleasing to the ear, it moves suddenly and unexpectedly from C Minor [really E-flat major] to F-sharp Minor. The reviewer, who has in front of him a manuscript copy of this Fantasy just as Mozart originally composed it for the [mechanical] organ, finds, through comparison with this manuscript, that this abrupt transition must, like the [title at the] beginning [of the edition under review], be an incidental printing error. Unfortunately, a couple of wrong notes are also found in the manuscript in exactly this spot. The reviewer can affirm with certainty at least this

much, that the passage must be altered either like this:

or even more probably like this:

After a formal close in F-sharp Minor there occurs a passage, which is similar to the beginning but which owing to the felicitously daring and rapid modulation is even incomparably stronger; this passage modulates back to F Minor and to its major dominant chord and then breaks off abruptly. Now the Andante in A-flat Major begins—an Andante that in every regard deserves to be called *heavenly.* It is impossible to name a *single* beauty because it is *all* beauty—and all equally beautiful. Here the reviewer cannot refrain from communicating to his readers at least the beginning of this masterpiece:

By way of conclusion the work sinks back to a tempo primo parallel to the first Allegro, in which the theme quoted at the beginning of the review is combined with this counter subject

and worked out contrapuntally in a manner worthy of J. S. Bach, whom the reviewer holds in the very highest regard.

In this last movement too is once more found, right at the beginning in the third measure, a difference with the manuscript, which reads:

The reviewer, who (parenthetically speaking) cherishes absolutely the ability to be uncommonly concise, considers this (alas!) only too brief product of the Mozartian spirit to be one of the most consummate works of his inexhaustible genius. Since to play this piece on one instrument with two hands is in some passages extraordinarily difficult, in other passages only possible with very long fingers and despite this, however, a few passages must be altered; since for many who perhaps might like to hear it, traveling to Vienna to have it played there may really not be easily practicable; finally, since it is also not very common to find two keyboard instruments tuned perfectly purely and exactly the same, which would allow this work to be conveniently played; so this very successful arrangement for four hands on one instrument must be a very agreeable publication for every admirer of Mozart and of excellent music. Now and then, for example at the end of page 2 and page 10 from the 14th measure, it would be a rather good idea to add a sort of basso continuo. Also, in consideration of the inpenetrability of bodies and likewise of hands, a few passages have to be altered. (In the original version for organ this piece did not go above [d♭‴] or below [c].) The reviewer can only disapprove of the unnecessary dismemberment of a principal idea, for instance on page 14, measures 4 and 5.

May a great many things of this and similar sorts by Mozart continue to appear.

The Coronation Scene from Modest Musorgsky's *Boris Godunov* in Rimsky-Korsakov's Edition

Kevin LaVine

THE GROUP OF RUSSIAN COMPOSERS who began to assemble after 1857, consisting of Mily Balakirev, César Cui, Modest Musorgsky, Nikolai Rimsky-Korsakov, and Alexander Borodin, came to be known as the *moguchaia kuchka* (literally, "the mighty little heap," traditionally rendered in English as "the Mighty Handful," or simply "The Five"), after this term first appeared in the Russian press in 1867 to describe this loose configuration of composers. Unified by aesthetic ideas based on the rejection of Western musical forms and the creation of an indigenous Russian music, they were inspired by, and drew upon, the country's rich cultural heritage—an aesthetic derived directly from that established by Mikhail Glinka several decades before.

Since the most readily applicable component of this cultural heritage to the creation of a nationalist music was found in folk song, it is not surprising that the creative impulse of each member of The Five found its most natural and powerful expression in the medium of vocal music, the vocal tradition in Russia being especially strong due to the traditional exclusion of musical instruments in the services of the Russian Orthodox church.

The two most independent thinkers of The Five, Musorgsky and Rimsky-Korsakov, were the first to break away from the rigid principles of nationalism in music as espoused by the strong-willed Balakirev. However, besides sharing a common independence of thought, the lives, personalities, and music of these two composers followed totally divergent paths.

Modest Musorgsky's lifelong fascination with social issues is reflected in his music by several innovative techniques developed to convey a sense of psychological depth in his portrayal of the common man. These techniques were most fully realized in *Boris Godunov*, where formal musical structures and orchestration became more improvisatory and less restrictive in nature, serving to underscore the nuances of thought, feelings, and personalities of characters in the opera. Extraneous musical effects not functioning to advance the plot's dramatic action or to provide closer insight into a character's psychology were avoided. Inspired by the examples of both Glinka (who introduced Russian elements into Italian operatic models forty years earlier) and Alexander Dargomyzhsky (who advocated an original yet restrictive "translation" into music of the intonations of the spoken Russian language), Musorgsky envisioned the creation of "an artistic reproduction of human speech in all its finest shades, that is, *the sounds of human speech*, as the external manifestations of thought and feeling..."[1] This was the composer's musical ideal: the reproduction of speech as it was actually spoken by the peasant, the drunkard, the old woman, the child, the nobleman; in other words, the perfect realization of "living prose in music"[2] and the attainment of "the language of humanity"[3] as it would most vividly depict a character's psychological state. The contours, rhythm, and general nature of such musical material would ideally convey the attributes and personality of each character. In order to reflect the work's innate "Russianness," this musical material incorporated elements derived from folk song, rather than direct quotations from folk material, in shaping melody.

In 1868, at a gathering at the home of Liudmila Shestakova (Glinka's sister), and in the midst of his work on an experimental opera based on Nikolai Gogol's *The Marriage*, Musorgsky met Vladimir Nikolsky, a Russian literature professor and an authority on the work of Pushkin. Nikolsky suggested to the composer that he might consider Pushkin's *Boris Godunov* as a possible subject for an opera. Musorgsky's imagination seized upon the idea at once; he abandoned his work on *The Marriage* (completed only through the first act), and for the next year his inspiration poured forth material at a feverish pitch for what eventually would be molded into a universally acknowledged masterwork.

[1] Letter to Liudmila Shestakova of July 30, 1868; see *The Musorgsky Reader*, ed. and trans. Jay Leyda and Sergei Bertensson (New York: Da Capo Press, 1970), p. 112.

[2] Ibid.

[3] Ibid.

Pushkin's drama, written in 1824 during a period of political exile, was influenced, like much of Pushkin's work, by nationalistic as much as by classical Western ideals, the former influence in this case being a work of the Russian writer and poet Nikolai Karamzin. His *History of the Russian State* consists of twelve volumes which appeared between 1816 and 1826. It was here that Pushkin found the story of the medieval Russian ruler Boris Godunov. Musorgsky removed the difficulty of staging Pushkin's twenty-two separate scenes by reducing their number to seven. At first these seven independent scenes seem rather disjointed; upon closer examination, however, one realizes that the dramatic element which is sacrificed through compression is more than compensated for by the dramatic impact created by the subtle accumulation of details about the lives and personalities of the characters, and especially those of Tsar Boris himself. The complex personality of Boris Godunov is revealed in glimpses, eventually creating a vividly complete picture of a multifaceted personality. (Musorgsky's technique of building up layers of impressions in order to flesh out characters made a strong impression upon later composers: Claude Debussy's *Pelléas et Mélisande* and Alban Berg's *Wozzeck* were both influenced by Musorgsky's example.)

The opera, completed in December 1869, was submitted by Musorgsky to the reviewing board of the Imperial Opera in St. Petersburg and, after a year's delay, was rejected, the board finding it "too unconventional" and "too modern"; it was, as Richard Anthony Leonard phrases it, "the typical reaction of small minds coming into collision with a great though unfamiliar art."[4] Undaunted, Musorgsky began to make revisions in the work. It was at about this time—August 1871—when Musorgsky took lodgings with his friend and colleague from The Five, Rimsky-Korsakov, who was himself at work on an opera of his own, *Pskovitianka* (The Maid of Pskov), based upon the historical character Ivan the Terrible. For two such unlike personalities, both in the process of writing important works, to end up living in the same room, sharing the same piano and writing table—and also musical advice, plans, and ideas—is the stuff of which artistic legends are made. Despite their differing aesthetic viewpoints, a deep mutual respect and friendship developed between the two composers both artistically (Rimsky-Korsakov's *Pskovitianka* exhibits a strong

4 Richard Anthony Leonard, *A History of Russian Music* (New York: Macmillan, 1957), p. 103.

5 Nikolai Rimsky-Korsakov, *My Musical Life*, translated from the Russian by Judah A. Joffe (London: Eulenburg, 1974), p. 17.

6 Ibid., pp. 116–117.

7 Ibid., p. 119.

Musorgskian influence in its subject matter and generally somber orchestral color) and personally (Rimsky-Korsakov chose Musorgsky to be the best man at his wedding in 1872).

While Musorgsky's musical training was at best barely adequate and always haphazard, that of Rimsky-Korsakov was, like the man himself, highly structured, precise, and methodical. Where Musorgsky relied on raw talent and a penetrating psychological and artistic insight, Rimsky-Korsakov relied on a traditional education gained, however late in life, through an almost obsessive pursuit of knowledge. In 1871, in the wake of his public success as a composer, Rimsky-Korsakov was appointed to the staff of the St. Petersburg Conservatory despite his self-professed ignorance of even rudimentary musical theory ("I had no idea of counterpoint; in harmony I did not know even...the names of the chords"[5]; "I was a dilettante and knew nothing"[6]; "Having been unreservedly accepted at the Conservatory as a professor, I soon became one of its best and possibly its very best *pupil*"[7]). At the core of this self-education was a humility and a selflessness that also led him to use his talents to promote works of his fellow composers, preparing new performing versions of the operas of his revered Glinka, assisting Cui in orchestrating his opera *William Ratcliff*, twice undertaking the task of orchestrating Dargomyzhsky's *Stone Guest*, and completing and reorchestrating Borodin's *Prince Igor*, which was left in a state of chaos upon the latter's death in 1886.

A task for which he has been criticized, however, has been his editing of nearly all of Musorgsky's musical output after Musorgsky's early death. Musorgsky frequently undertook the composition of one work without finishing the work which preceded it, and Rimsky-Korsakov's formidable labors on behalf of his friend can only be taken as a mark of respect and affection. Yet the revisions Rimsky-Korsakov made to *Boris Godunov* (not once, but twice, in versions of 1896 and 1908) were of an exceptionally large scope and are those for which he drew the most severe criticism. He approached the task with typically meticulous zeal, never hesitating to "correct" every detail which did not meet his rigid academic standards. Musorgsky's precise rendering of the intonations of speech, frequently characterized by unusual intervals, were freely altered to facilitate singing; and his bold and original use of dissonant harmonies and nontraditional modulations were smoothed over to make them more palatable to public tastes. In short, as Richard Taruskin writes, Rimsky-Korsakov took "Musorgsky's most potently original ideas and turn[ed] them back into the very clichés which Musorgsky must have striven to avoid."[8] However, at his death in 1881, Musorgsky's neglected genius was on the brink of falling into obscurity. A large part of his musical output was left incomplete, and his largest completed work, *Boris Godunov*, was withdrawn from production after only fifteen performances due to continued public controversy regarding its perceived lack of musical merit. Although Rimsky-Korsakov's tastes were too grounded in the traditional to be able to permit him fully to understand Musorgsky's musical language, he undoubtedly felt that the work's merit could be preserved in a more conventional musical medium. Ironically, it was through Rimsky-Korsakov's versions that many of Musorgsky's works became known outside Russia, eventually leading to their acceptance as works of genius. The original versions of Musorgsky's works eventually came to be rediscovered as recognition of their importance increased. In the case of *Boris Godunov*, in recent years, with the appearance of David Lloyd Jones's 1975 critical edition, Musorgsky's original version of the opera has begun to supplant Rimsky-Korsakov's 1908 performing version, which more than one hundred years after the composer's death is still the version with which the public and even most musicians are most familiar.

The manuscript which forms part of the Moldenhauer Archives at the Library of Congress consists of thirty-four measures (including one silent measure and one deleted measure) in six pages in Rimsky-Korsakov's hand of his reworking of the second scene of the Prologue (the Coronation Scene). According to supporting documentation, Moldenhauer obtained the manuscript (perhaps towards 1960) from Broude Brothers Music Publishers in New York. This firm had obtained it from the Russian-born conductor Emil Cooper (1877–1960) who, among his many notable achievements, conducted the premiere of Rimsky-Korsakov's opera *The Golden Cockerel* in 1909, as well as the first performance of *Boris Godunov* outside Russia, in May 1908 in Paris for Serge

8 Richard Taruskin, *Musorgsky: Eight Essays and an Epilogue* (Princeton: Princeton University Press, 1993), p. 104.

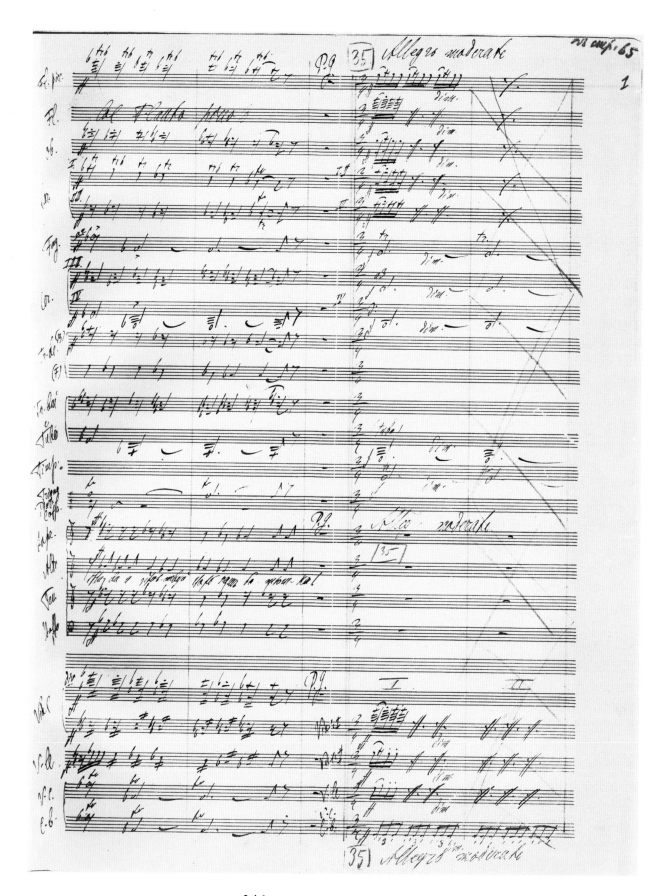

Diaghilev. A 1960 letter from Irving Broude of Broude Brothers included with the documentation, states that Cooper obtained the manuscript directly from the Rimsky-Korsakov family.

This manuscript most likely predates Rimsky-Korsakov's 1908 version, in that it differs from the published score of the second version, yet still retains features of the first, 1896 version. In some cases, the voicings and instrumentation exhibited in this manuscript differ significantly from the 1908 version. In measure 8 of the Moldenhauer manuscript, for example, the static triplet figure in the lower strings, which has been repeated from the first measure of that section, suddenly begins to double the bass voice lines of the chorus; in both the 1896 and 1908 published scores, however, the motion of this triplet figure becomes contrapuntally chromatic. Parts included in the 1908 published score for the harp, piano, and expanded percussion section are not represented in this manuscript. Other elements (dynamic markings, metronome markings, stage directions) are used inconsistently if they appear at all.

According to Rimsky-Korsakov's notation, this manuscript contains the section of the score beginning two measures before rehearsal number 35. In the composer's 1908 published score, however, this section is labeled *35bis* ("35-A," or "alternate number 35"). Rimsky-Korsakov was not mistaken: there are actually two rehearsal numbers "35" since the portion of the score contained in the manuscript is one which immediately follows an optional cut of sixteen measures (the reprise of the "pealing of bells" material with which the scene begins, added to the score at the time of Diaghilev's 1908 Paris production). Were the cut to be taken, this section would indeed conform to the content of the Moldenhauer manuscript; in modern editions of this work, however, it is standard practice to publish all musical options, hence the published edition's *35bis*.

Rimsky-Korsakov's revisions of *Boris Godunov* began in 1892 with a reworking of the Coronation Scene; these revisions eventually extended to the entire opera, and they were completed only several years later, in May 1896. This (first) version, given its premiere at the St. Petersburg Conservatory on November 28 of that year, contained numerous cuts as well as the notoriously extensive reworking of Musorgsky's original material. The Coronation Scene was expanded, adding five measures to the original one hundred and eighty-four in the process. Musorgsky had originally used a transparent orchestration style in order to express the insincerity of the Russian people's celebration of their new tsar, Boris Godunov; Rimsky-Korsakov reworked this material into weightier and contrapuntally more complex textures, with an enlarged orchestral complement (to Musorgsky's original instrumentation Rimsky-Korsakov added a third clarinet, trumpet, and trombone, as well as a harp and additional percussion). By transforming the tone of the scene from one of resigned acceptance on the part of both Boris and the crowd to one of a spectacularly brilliant civic celebration, Rimsky-Korsakov effectively shifted the focus of the entire opera from the plight of the Russian people as a whole to the workings of destiny upon a single individual. This procedure not only stood in total opposition to the way in which Musorgsky originally envisioned the work, but also served to diminish our psychological insight into the characters' personalities and motivations, and to undermine the dramatic impact of the entire opera.

In 1906 Rimsky-Korsakov returned to this first version and restored the cuts he had made, apparently going to the opposite extreme by composing new material to add to the score. For Diaghilev's 1908 Paris production, Rimsky-Korsakov added even more material to the opera, and especially to the Coronation Scene, which he still felt lacked sufficient drama and power. He inserted another forty measures before Boris's monologue at the center of the scene, and sixteen measures after it. This new material was included in the full score of Rimsky-Korsakov's second version of *Boris Godunov*, published by V. Bessel in 1908. About this second version Rimsky-Korsakov commented, with characteristic humility and lucidity, "Having arranged the new version of *Boris Godunov* I had not destroyed its original form, had not painted out the old frescoes forever. If ever the conclusion is arrived at that the original is better, worthier than my revision, then mine will be discarded and *Boris Godunov* will be performed according to the original score."[9]

[9] Rimsky-Korsakov, *My Musical Life*, p. 407.

One can find in Musorgsky's original version of the Coronation Scene all the essential elements of the composer's aesthetic principles—elements which retain their originality and brilliance even in Rimsky-Korsakov's versions. Musorgsky's novel harmonies are represented by his use of chords based on the augmented fourth to depict the pealing of the Kremlin bells at the beginning of the scene. The dramatic conflict present in the entire opera may also be embodied in the augmented fourth's harmonic ambiguity and instability. The episode is interrupted at its height by Prince Shuisky instructing the crowd to "glorify" their new tsar. The chorus's "Slava!" ["Glory!"], solidly in the key of C Major, is interrupted at the height of its celebration by Boris's soliloquy, suddenly shifting to the key of C Minor, a shift that effectively indicates the duality present in Boris's personality and that provides us with a first glimpse into his psyche, revealed more fully in the course of the opera. The C-Minor modality of this episode eventually modulates to the relative major key, E-flat, as Boris's perspective shifts from that of the individual —embodied in his own terror-filled premonitions—to that of his subjects, the Russian people, to whom he expresses his hopes for a happier future. A return to the C-Major "Slava!" chorus (the Moldenhauer manuscript reflects this point in Rimsky-Korsakov's score) ends the scene. Thus the Coronation Scene, composed of two episodes of an extrovert nature focusing on the people, and framing an individual's introvert monologue, sets up the basic conflicts on which rests the dramatic development of the entire opera: the individual versus a collective personality, and the individual facing his own moral conscience.

Krzysztof Penderecki's *Polymorphia* and *Fluorescences*

Peggy Monastra

DURING THE NAZI OCCUPATION of Poland, Hitler's forces razed the major concert halls and conservatories, burned most of the existing scores, and imprisoned or murdered numerous musicians. The period immediately following the devastation of World War II was characterized by a new intensity of governmental support for the arts. Musical education was revived with a new vigor, as concert halls and conservatories were quickly built to replace the rubble left behind. However, along with the regrowth came the restrictive censorship of Stalinist communism which commanded that artistic works embody social realism and praise of the proletariat. Few works of any lasting merit were produced during this time, and those that were often met with cultural banishment, as was the case with Lutosławski's First Symphony (1947). All of this changed in 1956 with the overthrow of the Stalinist regime in Poland. Out of the Stalinist demise was born a new spirit of adventure, individualism, and freedom. Krzysztof Penderecki (b. 1933) is of the generation that benefited most from these changing currents.

Penderecki's compositions *Polymorphia* for strings (1961) and *Fluorescences* for large orchestra (1962) are often considered jointly as the culmination of sonic and technical experimentation which characterize Penderecki's first acknowledged style period. These two works are virtual reference catalogs of Penderecki's accumulated effects and gestures which populate the sound fabric of many of his later, more "traditional" works and which have subsequently become standardized notational and technical practices in the second half of the twentieth century. While both compositions embody Penderecki's early principle of exploring "noise as sound as music," *Fluorescences* goes one step further than *Polymorphia* in the use of much larger and more varied instrumentation and the inclusion of additional nontraditional performance practices. These works and their scores are not only significant as markers of Penderecki's stylistic development, but also as the embodiment of many of the distinguishing characteristics of the early so-called "Polish school."[1] Moreover, they represent the more general midcentury tendency toward sonic experimentation apparent in the works of other internationally recognized composers such as Boulez, Lutosławski, Stockhausen, Varèse, and Xenakis.

The manuscript sketches for both *Polymorphia* (thirty-three pages) and *Fluorescences* (eighty pages) are ordered and numbered in reverse chronology, with the completed drafts in full score appearing first. These sketches are quite impressive visually, both for the aggressive use of color and for the dominating presence of Penderecki's innovative graphic notation. The completed scores are followed by incomplete sketches which grow progressively more fragmented and graphically abstract. Both sets of sketches are notated primarily in multicolored ink, with some brief passages in felt-tip markers and pencil. Performance directions and other text written in Penderecki's hand are in either Polish or German.

Polymorphia is scored for forty-eight strings: twenty-four violins and eight each of violas, cellos, and basses. It was composed in 1961 in fulfillment of a commission from North German Radio Hamburg and premiered on April 6, 1962, in a Hamburg performance conducted by Andrzej Markowski. Other works by Penderecki premiered in 1962 were String Quartet No. 1, Canon for strings and tape, and *Fluorescences*. 1962 was also the year in which Penderecki completed the composition of his *Stabat Mater*, a work which would later gain greater significance as a movement of his highly acclaimed *St. Luke Passion*.[2]

Somewhat ironically, the title *Polymorphia* (literally "of many forms") does not refer to the structure of the piece. The form of *Polymorphia* is a fairly straightforward ABA' with three segments of roughly equal duration lasting three minutes. Penderecki's biographer Wolfram Schwinger associates the title with "the broadly deployed scale of sound ... the exchange and simultaneous penetration of sound and noise, the contrast and

[1] For example, Wolfram Schwinger, Penderecki's primary biographer to date, cites the "Polish predilection for strings" shared by Penderecki, Gorecki, Lutosławski and Serocki. Wolfram Schwinger, *Krzysztof Penderecki: His Life and Work*, trans. William Mann (London: Schott, 1989).

[2] 1962 was also the year in which Penderecki first met Otto Tomek, who soon after became the program director at the annual Donaueschingen music festival, at which Penderecki's works were often performed. Discussions initiated at this first meeting resulted in Tomek's commissioning of the *St. Luke Passion*.

interflow of soft and hard sounds."[3] The work is notated in a framework of a nonmetrical system in which segments of specific, yet fluctuating duration are marked off in seconds and read by the performers at a speed proportional to the overall performance time.

The timbre and texture of continuous linear sound in the two outer sections of *Polymorphia*, composed primarily of bands of microtonal clusters, contrasts greatly with the middle section, which is characterized as "a catalogue of punctual and percussive sounds."[4] The piece closes with a sustained C-Major triad deployed throughout all four string sections. This anachronistic-sounding triad functions to release the climactic tension of the previous microtonal material and can be regarded as the coda to the overall ABA' form.[5] In a 1977 interview with *Composer* magazine, Penderecki claims that this chord was the seed from which the entire composition grew. His use of this most basic element of common-practice harmony "has nothing to do with tonality" but rather the role it can play in the underlying interplay of "tension and release."

The complete score in this set of sketches for *Polymorphia* is probably the final draft, as there are no significant discrepancies between this version and the edition published in 1963 by Moeck, Celle. It is notated in red, green, blue, and black ballpoint ink, with some musical segments, numbering, and most corrections in lead pencil. Blue and black felt markers were used to draw in the solid bands of sustained clusters and "encephalographic" pitch notation, one of the most visually distinctive aspects of this work. This notation, used to signify a sound mass of unbroken sliding pitches, is based on actual electroencephalograms (i.e., representations of brain waves) recorded at the Krakow Medical Center, where Penderecki was working as a volunteer. Penderecki was inspired by the electroencephalograms recorded as patients listened to a recording of his earlier and best-known composition, *Threnody for the Victims of Hiroshima*.

In the compositional method employed during this experimental period, Penderecki begins a composition by translating his aural concepts into abstract graphic drawings. Through the transformation and manipulation of the drawings,

3 Schwinger, op. cit., p. 131.

4 Michael Tomaszewski, liner notes to *Krzysztof Penderecki, Volume 1*, Krakow Philharmonic Orchestra/Henryk Czyz (Muza PNCD 017 A/B, 1989).

5 Other Penderecki compositions with similar tension-releasing major chord finales are the *Stabat Mater* (1963) and the *St. Luke Passion* (1966).

he formulates the pitch material and formal structure of the composition. These drawings then give way to what he described as a "shorthand" notation which, in turn, is either adapted to signify an articulatory performance directive or is allied to specific pitches which sonically illustrate the corresponding graphic figure.

The sketches for *Polymorphia* include more than a few examples of this graphic shorthand. The most striking and illustrative is a full-page plan of the entire piece as it evolves through various levels of development.

Fluorescences for orchestra was commissioned by the Southwest German Radio for the annual festival at Donaueschingen where it was premiered on October 21, 1962, under the baton of Hans Rosbaud, the work's dedicatee.

Penderecki described *Fluorescences* as the "terminal balance sheet"[6] of his experimental period and as "a culminating point from which it was difficult to progress."[7] Works composed in the time period immediately following *Fluorescences* are characterized by a turn toward the past for inspiration from more traditional styles and forms and a more light-handed use of the experimental sonorities common to his works from the late 1950s to early 1960s. Wolfram Schwinger describes *Fluorescences* as "the direct continuation" of *Polymorphia*: "what he had achieved there, on strings only, must now be braved with the full complement of the symphony orchestra."[8] Penderecki's first work to include winds (in quadruple forces, no less: four each of flutes, clarinets, oboes, and bassoons), *Fluorescences* is also scored for a full complement of strings, pianoforte, and six differing percussion sections. The score, published by Moeck in 1962, contains a more extensive list of symbols and abbreviations for special effects than any of Penderecki's works, before or since. The most distinctive timbres contributing to the sonic fabric of this work are the eerie voices of the flexaton, siren, sega, and a typewriter, included as members of the sixth percussion battery. The aural effects heard in *Fluorescences* go well beyond the percussive and glissandolike gestures of *Polymorphia*; performers are instructed to hum while they play, to saw wood or iron with a hand saw, to rub percussion instruments vigorously with a metal file, and to

6 Schwinger, op. cit., p. 140.

7 Ates Orga, "Krzysztof Penderecki," *Music and Musicians* 22 (October 1973): 39.

8 Schwinger, op. cit., p. 140.

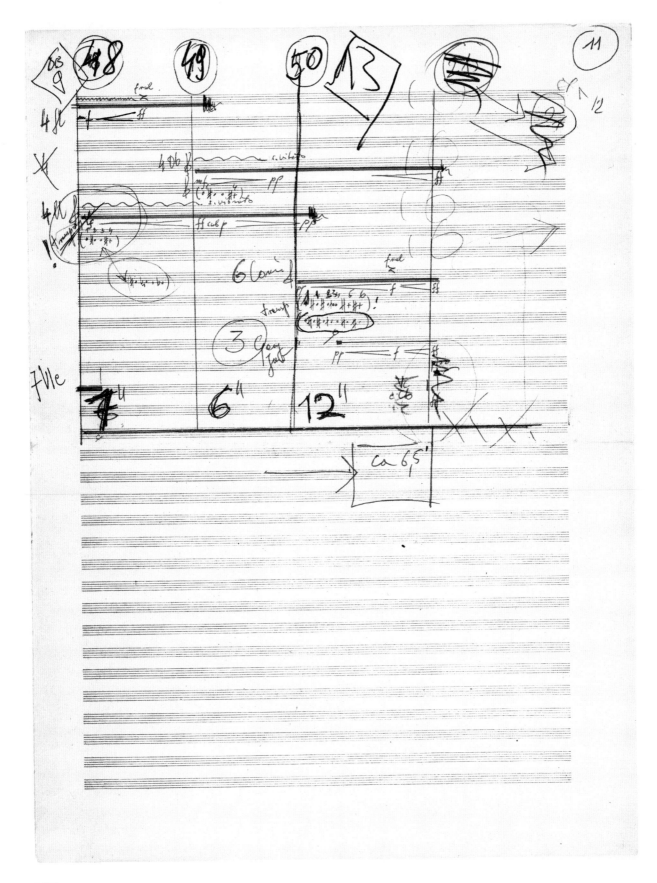

rub the soundboard of the string instruments with an open hand. For each of these new gestures, Penderecki created graphic symbols, all of which are derived from the initial conceptual graphic outline for the composition.

The structure of *Fluorescences* does not correspond with any preestablished musical forms but most closely resembles an ABA' pattern. As suggested by Schwinger, it can be best understood as a musical translation of the significance of its title as "the acoustical emergence of unusually articulated manifestations of sound" amidst a landscape of "fluent transitions … from soft to hard timbres, from translucent to opaque noises … reinvestigated through fields of contrast, adjacent and overlapping, in such a way as to achieve formal correspondence to passages resumed and audibly reversed."[9] In the first section, distinct sonic textures are individually illuminated in sequence. The B section or "invention on one note" as it is sometimes referred to, is a timbral and rhythmic study of the pitch C. The final third of the work reintroduces the previously presented timbres and textures in combinations of greater dynamic and textural intensity which contribute to a continually heightening degree of tension. This tension is relieved in the closing moment as each instrument by a downward glissando passes through the pitch C and fades to silence.

The additional material for *Fluorescences* includes a draft of the complete score, two pages of performance instructions written out in German, and forty-eight pages of sketches which grow progressively more fragmented and notationally abstract. Recorded upon these pages are two different dates and locations: "Wien, 7.VI.61" on page 59 and "Stockholm 27.XI.61" on page 41.[10] Other points of interest include a careful mapping out of the specific instrumentation for the six differing percussion batteries and a full-page graphic outline for another composition, drawn in five colors and labeled *Penetrazioni*.

These sketches, substantially more so than those of *Polymorphia*, reveal a composition which greatly challenged its composer and his ability to give voice and logical form to his sonic abstractions. The complete manuscript score, unlike that

[9] Ibid., p. 141

[10] Schwinger notes that Penderecki was in Vienna at this time for the premiere of the second version of his *Dimensions of Time and Silence*, performed by the RIAS Chamber Choir, Ensemble die riehe and conducted by Friedrich Cerha at the 35th ISCM Festival. Reconsideration of this composition while composing *Fluorescences* is reflected in several compositional similarities between the two works. These similarities, the most striking of which were edited out before the final copy, are quite evident in these sketches. A more detailed study comparing these two works would most likely reveal more extensive similarities. Penderecki travelled to Stockholm in July for a performance of *Threnody* under Michael Gielen in the Nudika Musik series of concerts (Schwinger, op. cit., p. 28).

of *Polymorphia*, reflects a work in progress and not the final version found in the published edition.[11]

The innovative developments in sonic exploration and the accompanying experimental notation achieved during Penderecki's first period of professional and stylistic evolution reached their zenith in the composition of *Polymorphia* and *Fluorescences*. *Polymorphia* carried out the search for new sonic possibilities in the string family initiated with the composition of *Anaklasis*. *Fluorescences* joined these innovations with the forces of percussion and the full orchestra to elevate Penderecki's early musical language to its highest point.

[11] The most striking difference between the score contained in these sketches and the published edition is that of six "measures," numbered 19–24 in the sketches, which do not appear in the published score and total approximately one minute in length. This sketch segment recalls the style of choral writing found in the chamber work *Dimensions of Time and Silence* (1959/1960). In this earlier work, the chorus adds to the texture of the "noise-spectrum" vocalizing nonpitched, systematized sequences of "acutely pronounced" consonants with sung vowels interspersed on sustained and specified pitches.

A Fragment from Act II of Giacomo Puccini's *La Bohème*

Linda B. Fairtile

GIACOMO PUCCINI'S FOURTH OPERA, *La Bohème*, is the work which reflects his reaching full compositional maturity. After the completion of *Manon Lescaut* in 1892, Puccini considered setting either Giovanni Verga's short story, *La Lupa*, or Henry Murger's novel, *Scènes de la Vie de Bohème*. For a time, it appears that he favored the Verga work, and even visited the author in Catania to observe Sicilian culture firsthand. However, in July of 1894, Puccini expressed his doubts about the suitability of *La Lupa* to his publisher, Giulio Ricordi, and turned his attention exclusively to *Scènes de la Vie de Bohème*.[1]

However, the librettist and composer Ruggero Leoncavallo had also discovered Murger's novel. Amid charges and countercharges of literary theft, the two composers set to work. Puccini's trips to supervise productions of *Manon Lescaut*, as well as his relentless, if often expedient, interference with the efforts of his librettists for *La Bohème*, Giuseppe Giacosa and Luigi Illica, delayed the completion of the libretto until August 1894. Puccini then began a compositional draft, notating complete vocal lines and a sketch of the accompaniment material.[2] Drawing upon previous compositions, such as his *Capriccio sinfonico* and sketches for *La Lupa*, in addition to creating new material, Puccini's progress at this stage was rapid. Still, constant revision of the libretto caused many delays. A note in the autograph full score of the opera, now at the Ricordi Archive in Milan, reveals that the composer refined and orchestrated Act I from January 21 to June 6, 1895; he dated Acts II to IV July 19, September 18, and December 10, 1895, respectively. Although in no apparent hurry, Puccini finished his *La Bohème* fifteen months ahead of Leoncavallo.

Many critics attending the premiere of Puccini's *La Bohème* on February 1, 1896, compared it unfavorably with the

[1] According to Mosco Carner, *Puccini: A Critical Biography*, 3rd ed. (London: Duckworth, 1992), p. 77, it was Contessa Blandine Gravina, Cosima Wagner's daughter by her first marriage to Hans von Bülow, who, during a chance meeting with Puccini, may have convinced the composer of the inappropriateness of an operatic *La Lupa*.

[2] Arthur Groos and Roger Parker, *Giacomo Puccini: "La Bohème"* (Cambridge: Cambridge University Press, 1986), pp. 102–14, contains a detailed discussion of the composer's work habits.

phenomenally successful *Manon Lescaut*. In the *Gazzetta Piemontese*, the critic Carlo Bersezio termed the work "a momentary error" and "a brief deviation from the path of art."[3] Alfredo Colombani, of the *Corriere della Sera*, offered a more prescient opinion:

> the improvement in workmanship is most noticeable. The melodic material displays the same origin, but here one finds it purified, made noble. Violence and brutality are diminished, perorations and bombastic phrases are less frequent, the search for effects is better camouflaged, and the music flows, swift and agile, now sprightly, now anguished…[4]

Today, Puccini's *La Bohème* is one of the most beloved works in the operatic repertory. At the Metropolitan Opera, it ranks second in number of performances behind Verdi's *Aida*. Leoncavallo's version of *La Bohème*, completed in 1897, is all but forgotten.

This manuscript transmits ten measures from the so-called "Sextet" in the opera's second act, corresponding to pages 207 (measure 2) through 210 (measure 1) of the current published orchestral score. The passage forms part of the middle section of a tripartite structure that begins and ends with the renowned "Musetta's Waltz" ("Quando m'en vo"). At this point in the plot, the inhabitants of Paris's Latin Quarter, gathering to celebrate Christmas Eve at the Cafe Momus, witness the spectacle of Musetta's successful attempt to win back her lover. The section as a whole presented a problem for Puccini's librettists, who had to reconcile its function as the old-fashioned, static set piece of the act with the composer's demands for picturesque "episodes" to aid characterization. Such problems were indicative of this collaboration, with the seasoned dramatist (Illica) and the sensitive poet (Giacosa) on the one hand, and Puccini, the demanding composer, on the other.

The manuscript is an earlier version of pages 77–78 of the autograph full score of *La Bohème*, Act II. It is on the same type of paper that Puccini used for pages 1–14 and 67–106 of the second act, containing twenty-two staves with preprinted

3 "l'errore di un momento"; "un breve traviamento dal cammino dell'arte" cited by Eugenio Gara, ed., *Carteggi Pucciniani* (Milan: G. Ricordi & C., 1958), p. 141.

4 il miglioramento nella fattura è sensibilissimo. Il materiale melodico risente della medesima origine, ma si ritrova qui purificato, nobilizzato. Sono diminuite la violenza e la brutalità, sono meno frequenti le perorazioni e le frasi ampollose, più mascherate le ricerche di effetto, e la musica corre lesta e agile, ora briosa, ora straziante…Cited by Eugenio Gara, op. cit., p. 141.

instrumental designations and six unlabeled vocal staves. There is, however, no evidence that the composer tore this manuscript page from the autograph. Puccini sent his scores to Ricordi in sections, often only a few gatherings at a time, and some time later, Ricordi employees bound the gatherings into volumes. It seems likely that Puccini replaced this manuscript page with the current pages 77–78 of the autograph score before sending the materials to Ricordi.

A secondary document suggests a continuation of the story. Included with the manuscript is a small fragment of the same type of music paper, which transmits three inscriptions. The first, "Villa del Castellaccio-Pescia," in an unknown hand, refers to the estate where Puccini had been a guest from June through November of 1895, orchestrating Acts II to IV of *La Bohème*. The second inscription, in a different hand, identifies the manuscript's contents as "Sestetto / della Bohême / quartier latino," and begins an incomplete statement of location and date, "Villa del Castellaccio a." This second inscription also includes the cryptic phrase "Scapaccione sul Collo," literally, a smack on the neck such as one might give a disobedient child.[5] Finally, Puccini himself completed the date statement with "di 4. 7. 95 / Ore di notte / mezza id" and drew a vertical line to separate the "Sestetto" and "Scapaccione" inscriptions. The date July 4, 1895, places the note within the time that Puccini worked on the orchestration of the opera's second act. The identification of music and geographical location suggests that Puccini presented the rejected page to someone at the villa, possibly his host, Count Bartolini. However, if the composer did consider the manuscript and accompanying note to be mementos, it is curious that neither bears his signature.

The manuscript reveals aspects of Puccini's compositional practice. During the orchestration phase, he apparently copied complete vocal lines from the draft, polished them, and only then wove the orchestral fabric from the sketched accompaniment. Evidence of this procedure surfaces in measure seven of the manuscript, where rhythmic figures in the vocal parts show heavy revision, while similar material appears, accurate and unedited, in the orchestral accompaniment.

5 Manlio Cortelazzo and Paolo Zolli, eds., *Dizionario etimologico della lingua italiana*, vol. 5 (Bologna: Zanichelli, 1988), p. 1143, transmit an 1836 definition of the word "scapaccione": "blow delivered with the open hand to the back of the head" ("colpo dato con la mano aperta sulla parte posteriore del capo"). Giacomo Devoto and Gian Carlo Oli, eds., *Il dizionario della lingua italiana* (Florence: Felice Le Monnier, 1990), p. 1706, add a disciplinary aspect: "slap delivered between the head and neck, usually as a means of paternal punishment" ("schiaffo dato tra capo e collo, di solito come provvedimento di punizione paterna").

On the first page of the manuscript, Puccini labeled the blank vocal staves in descending order of range, with the names "Musetta" (soprano), "Mimi" (soprano), "Rodolfo" (tenor), and "Colline" (bass). Ending with Colline, the bass of the ensemble, suggests that the composer had originally specified only four voices on this page. He then changed "Colline" to "Alcindoro," a higher bass role, before adding the baritone "Sch[aunard]," and replacing Colline at the bottom of the now six-part vocal texture. Page 2 of the manuscript presents a different situation, while providing a clue to Puccini's notational practice. After designating staves for Musetta, Mimi, and Rodolfo, the composer again inserted Alcindoro, this time just beneath Musetta. The parts for Mimi and Rodolfo were then shifted down a line, followed by those for Schaunard and Colline. However, it appears that Puccini also obliterated one measure of Mimi's vocal line to free her staff for Alcindoro. This suggests that the composer wrote out at least partial vocal lines before he had laid out the entire texture. The treatment of Alcindoro on both of the manuscript pages implies that his presence may have been a late decision, not covered in vocal drafts of the passage.

In addition, Puccini appears to have altered both the text and music of several vocal lines in the manuscript. Although by this time the composer had a completed libretto in hand, measures 5 through 8 of Musetta's line reveal drastic textual revisions, from the visible fragments "sarà mio, è vinto / ah...è vinto" to "So ben le angoscie tue / e non le vuoi dir! / ah...ma ti senti morir." It may have been these changes in text, disrupting both syllabification and rhyme scheme, which demanded a complete rewriting of the vocal line on collettes pasted over measures 5 and 8. Rodolfo's "E' fiacco amore" in measure 5 has become "E' fiacco amor quel che le," and it is possible that Puccini changed the two eighth notes to four sixteenths to accommodate the addition of syllables.[6] By contrast, in measures 7 and 8, Colline's text changed from "Chi fa quel che avverrà" (which rhymed with Schaunard's "Marcello cederà") to "Mi piaccion assai più," a variant of his text in measure 5, with no resultant change to the vocal line.

Two vocal revisions notated on the manuscript pages seem to reinforce musical and dramatic distinctions between the

6 Clearly, the omission of the syllable "of–" at the end of the measure 5 was an oversight, since the following measure (the first of page two) begins with the word's concluding syllables, "-fese."

7 Since Henry Murger's novel, *Scènes de la vie de Bohème*, trans. Elizabeth Ward Hugus, introd. D. B. Wyndham Lewis (New York: Dodd Mead and Co., 1930), portrays Musetta and Mimi as virtually interchangeable, with Musetta perhaps receiving the more sympathetic characterization, Puccini's attempts to distinguish them are all the more significant.

opera's female roles. The removal of Mimi's octave leap in the first measure, a minor third below Musetta's, strengthens each character's individuality, while the suppression of vocal material for Musetta two measures later (traces of which are visible through a collette) leaves Mimi as the lone female voice in that phrase.[7]

Still other alterations affect text setting. Puccini changed the rhythm of Colline's "cieco" in measure 3 from a jarring eighth-quarter to a smoother quarter-quarter pattern. Rather than improve the text setting, the change to Schaunard's and Colline's vocal lines in measure 5 accents insignificant syllables: "stupenda è *la* commedia" and "ma piaccion mi *as*sai più." Deleted notes in the following measure suggest that Puccini may have planned to relieve this awkwardness by assigning still higher pitches to the more appropriately stressed syllables "-me-" and "più." However, since his original choice of high E was not consonant with Musetta's vocal line, the composer substituted lower pitches for Schaunard and Colline, relying on downbeat emphasis alone to highlight the proper syllables.

Corresponding pages of the autograph score of *La Bohème* reveal that Puccini rewrote vocal lines after he rejected this manuscript. Rodolfo's music underwent the greatest change: in measure 3, the response "Mimi" replaced his "T'amo" in unison with Mimi. In addition, Musetta's "non le vuoi dir" (measure 6) now has a characteristically coquettish setting, complete with grace notes. Other alterations are minor: Mimi's "T'amo" (measure 3) ends on an eighth note rather than a quarter to make room for Rodolfo's new entrance, her text in measure 6 is distributed more smoothly over the existing rhythmic structure, and Musetta's first note in measure 5 has become an eighth note rather than a sixteenth.

Certain changes in the orchestral portions of the manuscript reflect alterations in the vocal lines. Collets pasted over the parts of the flutes and oboes in measure 5 reflect changes in Musetta's part, as do the rewritten viola and cello lines in measure 6 and the new clarinet figure inserted on the trombone line in measure 8. Other modifications reinforce the original orchestration. In the first two measures, Puccini rewrote the downbeat eighth notes in the viola and cello parts so that they now double the harp line. In measure five, a doubling of the clarinet line covers up the original horn material, while in the following bar Puccini appears to have rewritten horns two through four to conform with the rhythm of the first horn. Octave doubling in the first violins (measures 7 and 8) has disappeared, so that the entire section plays in unison. Puccini's revoicing of the parallel triads in measure 2 reflects a more daring alternative: originally, flutes and oboes each played both the third and the fifth of the triad, while the clarinets covered the root and third. In Puccini's revision, the oboes play in parallel fifths instead.

In measure 4, the second oboe and second clarinet now join the violins and violas in shadowing the vocal line, while the harp and violas have been modified to provide support a sixth below. The manuscript contains a single instance of orchestrational reduction: the elimination of the horn and bassoon chord that had doubled the harp and lower strings on the final beat of measure 4. Other changes include octave transposition (flute, measures 1 and 6).

The orchestral portions of the autograph score differ from this manuscript chiefly in terms of heavier orchestration and in reflecting changes made in the vocal lines. In the autograph score, the bass clarinet ("clarone") plays throughout the passage, save measures 7 and 8.[8] The horns in measure 1 are given a complete triad, rather than a single note, although its duration is now a full beat shorter than the original. The composer added piccolo to measures 5 and 6, while altering the flutes to conform with Musetta's new vocal line. Timpani strokes now appear in measures 4, 6, and 8, and numerous errors in English horn transposition (measures 1, 3, 4, and 8) have been corrected.

The manuscript is less detailed than the autograph score in terms of dynamics and articulation markings. However, it was customary for Puccini to add the bulk of these markings at an even later stage, on the page proofs of the published score. Compared to the first published orchestral score of *La Bohème* (plate number 99010, dated 1898), this manuscript is inconsistent in its notation of dynamic indications,

[8] In the manuscript, the bass clarinet is apparently pitched in B-flat, while in the autograph it is in A.

articulations, and phrase markings. Most tempo-related markings that appear in the published score are not present in the manuscript: "poco rall." in measures 4 and 7 (although a "poco allargando" does appear over the vocal lines in this bar), "a tempo" in measures 5 and 8, and "a tempo cres. ed incalz. un poco" in measure 9 are all missing.

It is likely that Puccini rejected this manuscript page because of its appearance. Corresponding pages in the autograph, often equally disorderly, reveal that the composer had several changes of heart after the preparation of this manuscript. He may have decided that the heavily edited page could not support further modification, and turned instead to a fresh sheet of paper. However, the presence of collets on the manuscript suggests that Puccini probably had, at one point, considered it a fair copy.

George Rochberg's *Fifth Symphony*: A Commentary by the Composer

OF THE SIX SYMPHONIES I have produced, the fifth is the most terse—some twenty-two minutes in playing time—because it is the most compressed, and its compression determines its single, large-scale, uninterrupted movement form.

Terseness and compression are the outward signs of an internal essence which I can only describe as high emotional intensity. The unrestrained nature of the opening burning statement —the core of the work—is a kind of musical sun flare, a high energy release. From here the work unfolds as a spiraling form in ever widening turns, each turn marking a new section, gathering up ideas and materials until at the Finale everything is brought together and unified.

There are seven sections in all: Opening statement, Episode 1, Development 1, Episode 2, Development 2, Episode 3, and Finale. The challenge for me was to provide the work with maximum heterogeneity of gesture while still producing a sense of strong, inevitable organic growth, that sense that even the most seemingly diverse levels of expression are ultimately variant forms of a basic idea emanating from and traceable back to an originating source according to the maxim: as in nature, so in art.

The character of the three episodes, therefore, differs dramatically from that of the two developments. Each episode is an exploration of widely changing gestures, orchestral groupings, and colors. Each development is a further probe and penetration—high voltage as in the opening—into what has taken place up to that point in the music.

I think my favorite section is the second episode. There the horns of the orchestra call to each other in a kind of magical time and space creating a long, four-part recitative whose unspoken, but underlying subtext is the ancient tale of the

fatally wounded Roland, blowing his horn with his last ounce of strength to call back his king, Charlemagne.

This medieval image has always had special meaning for me. There are times when it suddenly seems very clear that we, humankind, are Roland—and that Charlemagne is too far away to hear our desperate cries for help.

The function of art is to show us—as in a mirror—ourselves in all our shifting, changing states of uncertain existence. Perhaps art can ameliorate; but mostly I do not think so. I see art, rather than as an escape from the fires of reality, as another way —different from religion or science or psychology or philosophy—a way to pour out music, not wildly and uncontrollably, but in a disciplined and centered way, generously, passionately, like the sun from which we and our earth derive the energy of life itself.

Gioachino Rossini's *Moïse*

Philip Gossett

IT WAS TO THE THÉÂTRE ITALIEN that Gioachino Rossini first turned his attention when he began his official activities in Paris in 1824, mounting productions of his major Italian works, some of which were unknown in France. Few doubted, however, that among his goals was to compose operas in French for the primary theater of the capital, the Académie Royale de Musique, commonly known as the Théâtre de l'Opéra. He prepared his way carefully, becoming comfortable with the French language, courting government favor (his opera *Il viaggio a Reims* was written for the coronation of Charles X, in 1825) and developing a new generation of French singers proficient with Italian vocal style.

Rossini's earliest efforts at the Opéra reflect a deliberate plan. Instead of beginning immediately with a new opera in French, he adapted two of his finest Italian serious operas, works whose emphasis on theatrical spectacle made them particularly congenial to the traditions of French dramaturgy. Both operas, in fact, had been written for the Teatro San Carlo of Naples, where Rossini had functioned as music director between 1815 and 1822. Of all Italian cities, Naples was the one most influenced by French culture, a legacy of the reign of Murat during the Napoleonic era, and the operas of Gluck and Spontini were frequently seen there. It was no surprise, then, that Rossini should choose to revise two Neapolitan operas as his calling cards at the Opéra.

Le Siège de Corinthe, a French adaptation of *Maometto II* (Naples, Teatro San Carlo, December 3, 1820), had its premiere at the Opéra on October 9, 1826; *Moïse*, a French adaptation of *Mosè in Egitto* (Naples, Teatro San Carlo, March 5, 1818), followed on March 26, 1827. In each case the libretto was prepared jointly by an Italian poet, Luigi Balocchi, who worked closely with Rossini between 1825 and 1829,[1] and a French poet (Alexandre Soumet for *Le Siège de Corinthe* and Étienne de Jouy

[1] Balocchi also wrote the libretto of *Il viaggio a Reims* in 1825 and, in 1829, prepared a singing translation of Rossini's *Guillaume Tell* (Paris, Théâtre de l'Opéra, August 3, 1829), the composer's first completely original opera in French. It was also the last theatrical work to issue from his pen.

for *Moïse*). Their job was to help Rossini transform works conceived for the Italian stage into French operas, to translate into French those compositions that were to be reused in whole or in part, and to prepare new text for the added sections and numbers.

Together with his librettists, Rossini decided which compositions to preserve essentially intact, which to omit altogether, and which to present with revisions (of varying magnitude). He also composed directly the new music introduced into these operas, whose transformation to the French stage required a considerable expansion in their length, the addition of ballet movements absent in the original, and the further development of the role of the chorus. Finally, all the recitative, completely recast in French, needed to be newly prepared.

Rossini did not create a completely new autograph manuscript of *Moïse*, nor did he cannibalize the autograph of the Italian *Mosè in Egitto*, which he left intact.[2] Instead, the complete manuscript of *Moïse*, used by Eugène Troupenas (Rossini's publisher) to prepare the printed full score he issued in 1827, consisted of several different kinds of sources. Because Troupenas later disassembled this manuscript and apparently gave away sections to a number of associates, it is impossible to reconstruct the entire process, but some principles are relatively clear. For entirely new musical numbers, Rossini wrote out new autograph scores.[3] For numbers borrowed intact from *Mosè in Egitto*, but with the vocal lines now set to a French text, Rossini apparently wrote out new manuscripts of the vocal lines alone.[4] For a number partly identical with the original Italian but involving some revisions, Rossini had a copyist prepare a manuscript of the piece and entered his corrections directly in the source.[5]

Rossini apparently wrote all the recitatives anew, and the autograph manuscripts of a number of these recitatives are still known to exist.[6] The Library of Congress manuscript from the Moldenhauer Archives is such a source. It presents the recitative "Dopo il Ballo" from the second act, which follows the entire Divertissement (three Airs de Danse) and precedes the second-act Finale. Most of the Finale is newly written for

[2] It is preserved today in the collection of the Conservatoire at the Bibliothèque Nationale in Paris, Département de la Musique, MSS 1326 and 1327.

[3] Surviving are the autographs of two Airs de danse and the new Air for Anaï in the last act. The autographs of the former are in the collection of the Conservatoire, MSS 2437 and 2438. The autograph of the Air for Anaï is at present inaccessible, part of a private collection in Basel.

[4] Only one such manuscript is known to exist, autograph vocal parts for the second-act Duo between Aménophis and Pharaon, "Moment fatal! que faire?" The piece is otherwise identical to its model in *Mosè in Egitto*. Rossini's manuscript is in the Memorial Library of Music at Stanford University.

[5] The only surviving source in this form is the Finale of the third act of the opera, "Quel bruit," in part derived from *Mosè in Egitto*. The manuscript is in the Conservatoire collection, MS 2435, ff. 48–65.

[6] Previously known autograph manuscripts for recitatives in *Moïse* are found in the Conservatoire collection in Paris and in the Pierpont Morgan Library in New York.

Moïse, but no autograph manuscript is known to survive.[7] The Moldenhauer autograph consists of two folios, but is not complete: of the forty-three measures in the recitative "Dopo il Ballo," the manuscript includes measures 1–18 (on folios 1r and 1v) and 36–43 (on folio 2r); the layout of these pages suggests that an intervening single folio, notated on both sides, is missing. There is an autograph sketch on folio 2v, which will be discussed below.

In the absence of a complete set of autograph manuscripts for the newly written sections of *Moïse*, the Moldenhauer autograph (along with the other surviving autograph sources) is an important indication of the editorial practices of Troupenas. It helps us gauge the extent to which Troupenas's edition reliably reflects the *missing* originals. In fact, Troupenas's editorial policy seems to have been to remain as close as possible to Rossini's autograph manuscript.[8] For the most part, there are no significant divergencies between folio 1r of the autograph, here reproduced, and the Troupenas edition for which it was the direct source.[9] Even in seemingly insignificant details Troupenas follows the autograph: thus, following Rossini, Troupenas employs a half rest for the strings on the last two beats of the third measure, but two quarter rests in the fourth measure. The printed edition reproduces precisely the position of dynamic markings and articulation, rarely extending them to other parts. It even fails to add the tie, missing in Rossini's autograph, that must join the last whole note in the bass on folio 1r and the first whole note on folio 1v.[10]

On the other hand, from the autograph we learn that Rossini's tempo indication at the beginning of this recitative was originally "Allo Maestoso." An editorial hand changed the "Allo" above the staff to "Ande" and added the same indication above the bass staff. Who authorized this change and when? And is it clear that the revised sign should be simply "Ande" or rather "Ande Maestoso"? Research into performing materials of *Moïse* at the Bibliothèque de l'Opéra in Paris might help resolve these and many other questions pertaining to the work.

Perhaps the most fascinating element in this manuscript, however, is the sketch Rossini notated on folio 2v. This is one of the few Rossini sketches known to survive. It pertains to the

[7] There is a surviving autograph manuscript of "Strumentini" (instrumental parts that would not fit into Rossini's principal autograph) in the Conservatoire collection, MS 2435, ff. 38–39 and 40, but even this manuscript is fragmentary.

[8] A facsimile of the Troupenas score is published in the series *Early Romantic Opera*, ed. Philip Gossett and Charles Rosen (Garland Publishing, Inc., 1980). See pp. 390–92.

[9] Notice the numbers "1" through "5" on five staves after the third measure on the first system and the numbers "6" through "10" after the fourth measure on the second system: these are marks specifying the organization of the printed page. The first three measures fill one system (the first five staves on p. 390) and the next four measures fill the next system (the sixth through tenth staves on the same page). For purposes of the printed score, Troupenas has ignored the blank staves in the autograph.

[10] There are occasional mistakes. In the twelfth and eighteenth measures of this recitative, for example, the Troupenas edition mistranscribes Rossini's rhythmically correct notation in the string parts.

Finale of the second act, directly following the recitative. The relevant passage begins on page 402 of the Troupenas edition, where Osiride and Moïse invoke their respective gods, "Ser[apis]" and "[Jehova]," each addressed as "Dieu de la lumière." The sketch covers eighteen measures, providing a few hints of the orchestral material and an incomplete vocal part. At the start it is identical with the final version (although there are fascinating differences in details of declamation), but the resemblance begins to fade toward the end.

That the sketch starts in the middle of a section suggests that Rossini did not systematically work out the entire Finale in this form. More likely he resorted to sketching when faced with a problematic passage in the course of composing the Finale directly in what would become his full score. The presence of this sketch on the verso of the preceding recitative,

furthermore, implies that Rossini had completed the recitative before composing at least this part of the Finale, and perhaps before beginning the Finale at all. Further study of the surviving autograph passages from *Moïse* might well help to resolve these questions.

At the top of folio 1r, the publisher has written "offert à M. Desnoyers / E. Troupenas." This Desnoyers was almost certainly Louis Desnoyers, critic of the Parisian *Le Siècle* and author of a volume entitled *De l'Opéra en 1847, à propos de Robert Bruce* (Paris, 1847), a defense of the production that year at the Opéra of *Robert Bruce*, an adaptation of Rossini's *La donna del lago*. It may have been on that occasion that a grateful Troupenas, publisher of the full score of *Robert Bruce*, made his gift to Desnoyers. Troupenas's casual disposition of this recitative and the dispersion of other parts of the original score does not augur well for a likelihood that it will ever be possible to reassemble the entire manuscript. Each individual item in Rossini's hand, then, will continue to have special significance for our understanding of the work. Hence the importance of the Moldenhauer manuscript.

Arnold Schoenberg's
Adagio for Strings and Harp

Claudio Spies

THIS COMPLETE, SINGLE-MOVEMENT, lovely little piece in
A-flat, for an unusual combination of solo violin, small string
ensemble and harp—twelve players in all—immediately brings
to mind the slow movement of Brahms's F-Minor Piano
Quintet (whose tempo indication, by the way, is Andante, un
poco Adagio), though the resemblances are subtle rather than
blatant. Perhaps the connection is implied through an initial
melodic span of thirds—tonic to third in Schoenberg; third to
fifth in Brahms—and stepwise motion, up and down within
that span, which is gradually expanded. Perhaps it is the
indirect rhythmic kinship between them; or maybe it is just
the registrally central, reiterative middle C in both melodies
that suggests some "subliminal" recollection working in
Schoenberg's mind, for surely his familiarity with the chamber
music of Brahms must have gone back to the time when he
composed this Adagio.

Fifty measures long, straightforward in design, the piece
unfolds by gradual registral expansion and a modicum of
harmonic development abetted by the consecutive
appearances of the violin's solo line and the harp's
arpeggiations, each underlining both the dynamics' increase
and a growing textural density, and all of it subsiding at the
close—though the violin, appropriately, has the final ascent to
its previously established highest A-flat. While the piece would
be memorable for its eloquent tunefulness, its smoothly drawn
lines, and the skill shown in its instrumental writing, as
characteristic of a very remarkably accomplished young
composer, that composer's unmistakable identity is made
manifest by the manuscript itself, for not only is the
handwriting immediately recognizable, but a number of
features on those three pages add up to a view of the twenty-
three or twenty-four-year-old Schoenberg for whom the

massive achievement of *Verklärte Nacht*, composed no more than a year or two later, in some ways seems more plausible than it did before we knew of the existence of the Adagio. The very fact of a string ensemble of more than four parts suggests technical resources, necessities, and availabilities that his several experiences of the time in composing for string quartet had largely excluded, and that therefore lay bare a convincing connection to the future String Sextet, op. 4. One need but consider the prevalence of octave duplication of melodic strands—as in measures 29–35 (Vl.I and Vcl., with Vl. solo adding the highest octave in measure 35); measures 25–28 (Vl. solo and Vl.II); and measures 35–36 (Vl. solo, Vl.I., Vla.—also octave tripled).

The manuscript remained unknown and unmentioned until very recently, when its existence in the Moldenhauer Archive was disclosed. The only printed notice about it appeared in a one-page article in the *Österreichische MusikZeitschrift*[1] along with a reproduction of the first page and an altogether preposterous assumption that the year of composition was 1904 (i.e., *after Verklärte Nacht*, much of *Gurrelieder*, *Pelleas und Melisande*, and several of the Lieder, op. 6!).

Enhancing the delight in reading and playing through the score, there are a few tantalizing crossings-out, penciled additions, and changes in this manuscript that call for some scrutiny.[2] To begin with, the tempo indication, which had first been Andante (in a calligraphic writing similar to the one used for the instrumental accolade), was crossed out and substituted by the more "informally" written Adagio. Thereby, however, the rather crowded indication for Adagio in measure 43 becomes redundant; it can be understood only as an afterthought that preceded the change from Andante at the outset: for the forty-two measures before Adagio, the tempo had been Andante, and the change at measure 43 had been taken in terms of a slower peroration. One of several indications that the little work was not performed at the time of its composition is, surely, that this second Adagio was not crossed out. (An insinuation that this second Adagio might mean a *return* to the original tempo, after some uncalled-for and noisome heating and speeding-up—say, from letter B, measure 17, on—would seem unjustified by the music itself.

[1] Günther Weiss, "Fünfzig Unbekannte Takte," op. cit., 48/3–4 (March–April 1993).

[2] I am much obliged to Jon Newsom for confirming and identifying markings in pencil (rather than pen and ink), and for corroborating that these were made with one sort of pencil only; i.e., not with differently colored crayons.

·377·

·379·

Moreover, in the event of such change, the designations *a tempo* or *Tempo 1°* would have been more appropriate.) Yet, on the other hand, there is some evidence on these pages that a performance might have been planned: the penciled numbers between the instruments of the initial accolade may or may not be in Schoenberg's hand, but they certainly specify 2 + 2 for the divided violins, 3 (= 2 + 1) for the divided violas, one each for the divided cellos and a single bass. (It is conjecturable that these specifications stem from the performance mentioned in the *Österreichische MusikZeitschrift*, but it is improbable for me to envision the *original manuscript* being marked up by Moldenhauer—rather than a Xerox copy of it. Further, the penciled *senza sord.* at letter B, over the entering solo violin—corroborating Schoenberg's distinctly recognizable, handwritten diminutive *sine* (or *ohne?*) *sord.* beneath—is in a characteristically German hand, though slanted leftward, as Schoenberg's is not, and has a final *d* unlike his more habitually Latinate lettering. Finally, the most tell-tale pencil marking on this page is the large diminuendo hairpin intended for the bass's staff, but mistakenly placed between both silent harp staves—an instance of notational slovenliness to which Schoenberg would be far less prone than to the inadvertent omission of parallel diminuendo hairpins for the other string parts in the same place. The dynamic on the downbeat of the measure at B being piano for everybody, and having been forte in measure 15, Schoenberg obviously intended that diminuendo for the strings.) Likewise, the four rehearsal letters (in pencil) may have been written by Schoenberg, but their placement, either superimposed on a staff already occupied by notational symbols (A and B) or cutting into notation—C cuts into a slur; D virtually obliterates the high F at the beginning of measure 37—would belie Schoenberg's scrupulous, customary neatness.

On page 2, one measure after letter C, the arco indication is missing in the bass part; its unintended omission, coupled with a mistakenly notated A-flat eighth note at the end of measure 30, both support my assumption that the piece was never performed in Schoenberg's presence. He would undoubtedly have made these necessary corrections in the score used at the time. In measure 34, the last sixteenth note is confirmed by the almost vertical *as* (meaning the pitch A-flat) written alongside. (The question, "Why *there*, if not elsewhere?" could be answered in terms of the very neatness already cited: because that final A-flat barely misses hitting the lowest staff line of the harp part notated directly above.) The erasure —with razor blade or knife, as was necessary for pen-and-ink copying—in measure 28 left a blank which should have been filled with eighth rests, and the subsequent E-flats in the cellos and bass were mistakenly made into *dotted* quarters because the erased notes were evidently of that value.

Everywhere is Schoenberg's notational care, nevertheless, markedly in evidence. The conscientious fingerings given the cellos in measures 19–20 are practically "autobiographical"; the *unis.* for the last eighth note on page 2 is made unnecessary by the double-stemmed notation, but he wants to leave no possible doubt about it; the *I°* before the last D-flat in measure 36 is made superfluous by the eighth rest beneath this upward-stemmed note, but, again, he wants to be sure it is unmistakable, just as the ensuing *divisi* at letter D is included by way of insurance.

The harp part, which begins at letter B by octave-doubling the bass as it enters at the same place, comes into its own at the forte restatement of the melody (measure 29), arpeggiating harmonic changes in groups of thirty-second sextolets, septolets, or octolets, with occasional melodic duplication (mainly for the right hand) in measures 33–36. The boundary notes of these arpeggiations are of interest; they embody Schoenberg's concern for making the harp's top line rise very gradually, as well as exemplifying his diminution technique in having that top line imitate the melody (at one eighth-note's remove) in the measures preceding the aforementioned duplication, from measure 33 on. Seeing the accented F on the first quarter's afterbeat of measure 31 makes one wonder at his not having placed a (possibly accented) C on the last eighth, rather than the repeated F. He could have done so easily enough by making the immediately preceding septolet end on A-flat rather than C, and he consequently missed an opportunity for a cross-referential F-C, in anticipation of the (*accented*) B-flat-F in measure 31.

On the third page of this manuscript, several corrections and emendations confirm this very young composer's linear bent and certify his proven deftness in writing tonal music. The evident erasures at the end of measure 39 and at the downbeat of measure 40 show that the last eighth notes in Vl.I and II had been D and F (respectively), and that the ensuing downbeat would then have read C and A-flat in those parts. By changing these segments to B-flat-A-flat (Vl.I) and B-flat-C (Vl.II), Schoenberg "reserves" the higher C's slot for the harp, on the downbeat of measure 41, and thereupon allows the violin solo's *two* high Cs during the second quarter of that measure, as well as the syncopated one in measure 42, to make the two-octave downshift to the last occurrence of the melody in measure 43 both smoother and more meaningful. The same holds for the emendation in the harp part at the final eighth of measure 39. Originally, the upward arpeggio had ended on high D (duplicating Vl.I before it was changed), but Schoenberg realized that the occurrence of B-flat as the upper boundary of the arpeggios in measures 37–38 made a longer-range link between that B-flat and the subsequent high C of measure 41's downbeat possible. (Leaving out that C within the last eighth of measure 40 was crucial; had it been left in, the arpeggio would have ended on a senseless high E-flat, thus obliterating the connection to the repeated B-flats in measures 37–38, and spoiling the aforementioned pitch-class link to the melody's "familiar" middle C beginning.)

The correction that most eloquently proves Schoenberg's mastery is the elimination of the composition's third-last measure. Had that measure remained in place, the "rhetoric" of the ending would have become uncharacteristically redundant—even orotund. Considering the solo violin's rising line—without, for the moment, taking any of the other instrumental parts into account—it is clear that Schoenberg wanted each rising segment to begin on pitch-class B-flat: the first below middle C, the next one(s) an octave higher. The fact of the second rise starting on the second sixteenth of the measure (as did the first), would have conditioned the third (eliminated) rise to start at the same metrical point, but then the second rise would merely have been duplicated, inasmuch as a rise yet a further octave higher would have been absurd. Such a repetition would have been pointless, vacuous, and odious to the composer. The alternative was, then, to delay the rise's third entrance, by allowing for an eighth rest at the beginning of the measure; it could in that way have contributed to a natural sense of slowing toward the close. But we can discern from the crossed-out measure that this rise would, in this metrical garb, have entailed either of two intolerable features. As we see in measures 47–48, the arpeggiated rises eliminated none of their four constituent elements of this harmony, but in the crossed-out measure there is no A-flat. While that might contribute to the slowdown (by dividing the rise into two three-note segments before reaching its goal, rather than four-note ones reaching across barlines), the skip between F-flat and B-flat is jolting, especially in a *final* trajectory toward the high A-flat. On the other hand, the inclusion of the missing A-flat *within* this rise would have required a skip from D-flat, at the end of that measure, to the high A-flat, which would have been even more awkward. The alternatives would have improved nothing: neither beginning on D-flat (rather than the "accustomed" B-flat) nor beginning after a sixteenth rest would (for the reasons given) have been satisfactory. If we note, further, that the higher octave location of the harp chord in the crossed-out measure would have been senseless without some precedent, and that that, exactly, is provided by the palpable erasure in measure 47 (especially of the top staff!), with its subsequent emendation—obviously undertaken after the crossing-out of the offending measure— we understand the lack of pertinence in shifting the harp's register at all, for there is no reason for any such shift between the chord in measure 43 (bottom staff) and those in the two final measures. Lastly, a rhythmic-metric inconsistency was avoided: the isolated eighth-note articulation of the harmony on the last eighth of the eliminated measure would have had no metric connection to the preceding *triple* articulation of the same harmony in measures 47–48; nor would the syncopations in both violin parts have had any direct rhythmic bearing on the single-eighth-note chord, and the connection between that and the iterated tonic harmony of the last two measures would have been arbitrary, at best.

By canceling what would have been the third-last measure, then, Schoenberg made for a smoothly rising, consistent solo violin part, and he also made sure that the motivically syncopated harmonic articulations in measures 47–48 found a consistent consequence in the triply articulated, nonsyncopated tonic harmonies, metrically placed so as to give prominence to the violin's arrival on its high A-flat and designed to close this sweet piece, with all due gentleness, on a sonority very similar to the one with which it opened.

Two Leaves of Sketches for Arnold Schoenberg's Concerto for String Quartet and Orchestra

Claudio Spies

THE FOUR PAGES OF SKETCH material pertaining to movements III and IV of this Concerto aptly fill in those gaps in the otherwise mostly uninterrupted sequence of sketches cited and discussed in the complete edition of Schoenberg's works.[1] Although it is to be noted that these gaps were never editorially acknowledged, their existence would have been impossible to ignore by anyone seriously studying this material, unfolding as it does in so remarkably consecutive a fashion. Their being now so neatly filled in by the contents of these four pages is at the same time a cause for celebration and dismay, for it is very difficult to understand that whatever was to be found among Alma Mahler's papers should have been left unexamined and unexplored by editors engaged in research toward the publication of Schoenberg's *Gesamtausgabe*. To put it another way, one might justly shudder at such manifest negligence, and yet take pleasure and satisfaction from these particular results of the Moldenhauers' ardent pursuit of interesting musical materials, bequeathed to, and now made generally accessible through, the Library of Congress. In due time, it may be sensible to hope that these additional sketches, as well as anything further that may turn up, will be discussed in a supplementary volume of the *Gesamtausgabe*, Series B.

For present purposes, the gaps filled in by the four pages of sketch material will be identified by the measure numbering found in Schoenberg's published Concerto,[2] as follows:

1. Movement III

a. between measures 171 and 177;

[1] Arnold Schoenberg, *Sämtliche Werke, Abteilung VII: Bearbeitungen; Reihe B, Band 27, Teil 2* (Mainz: B. Schott's Söhne and Wien: Universal Edition AG, 1987), pp. 109–99.

[2] Ibid. *Reihe A, Band 27* (1976), pp. 101–220.

b. between measures 248 and 253: a sketch for measures 251 to 256;

c. between measures 261 and 268: a sketch for measures 264 to 268;

d. between measure 274 and the end of movement III at measure 291:

five sketches encompassing measures 275 to 291.

2. Movement IV

e. between measures 295 and 322: sketches for an elaborated version of measure 297, and for measure 314, besides a continuity sketch for top line melodic material in measures 292 to 327.

The sketch material itself ranges from hastily written *aides-mémoire* to fully detailed, practically fair-copy passages. In very few instances is there any pronounced change between these annotations, or working drafts, and the final score. From this point of view, the sketches confirm Schoenberg's prevalently rapid working habits; segments being elaborated seldom needed the kind of painstaking, laborious process of refinement that we associate with Beethoven's sketch material, where it is sometimes difficult to believe the degree of transformation a piece of musical material might have to undergo before reaching its final, acceptable shape. In some instances, a significant difference between a sketch and the final form goes no further than a change in transposition level: on one page, two versions of measures 170–174 and 175–176 appear at the minor seventh above—with a large cautionary *Verschiebung wie anfangs* (transposed as at the outset). Yet the change here may bespeak Schoenberg's decision—perhaps *gradually* taken—to transpose movement III from the original B-flat to D Major, in order to alleviate Handel's persistent emphasis on B-flat. (In the Largo—movement II—no such change was needed, since Handel's movement is also in G Minor.) The overall key-scheme of Schoenberg's arrangement (or rather, *recomposition*) of the Concerto is therefore: B-flat–g–D–B-flat, which could be interpreted as a symmetry of thirds surrounding the tonic B-flat, even if we allow for the tonally necessary difference between the

constituent major and minor thirds. (A different version of an all-encompassing relation by thirds was suggested to me by Paul Zukofsky, who conducted a most memorable performance of this work in 1985 with the Juilliard School's Contemporary Music Ensemble and the Juilliard String Quartet. It will be discussed further on.)

A sketch for the return from the first ending in movement IV, with measures numbered as in Handel (yet "off" by one measure) reveals a very elaborate, rather overloaded version of measure 297, garlanded with imitative sixteenth-note figures, and with an inversion of the hornpipe tune in the bass. The sketch breaks off at the subsequent measure, where Schoenberg scribbles *ohne 16tel* (without sixteenths), realizing that these would clutter up the texture—while in the score, he saves them for measures 310ff. But since it would be unlikely for Schoenberg to give up on having the tune appear prominently in inversion, it is a delightful confirmation to find it, unmistakably and clearly presented in the bassline of measures 350–351, to be answered by the string quartet's four-octave-doubled *rectus*, two measures later. It is, as always, of great interest to observe how quickly a wrong turn was avoided for measure 297, where that inversion might have been mired in textural overabundance!

Curiously enough, the contents of one leaf's two "upright" pages seem more concerned with the working out of textural details, whereas the stress in the other's is on general continuity. In particular, the opening of the hornpipe is given a good deal of space, featuring a tentative continuity draft up to the original repeat sign (as in Handel), after a corresponding number of measures, yet including Schoenberg's second ending at measure 327. A fascinating aspect of this draft is that, except for some octave displacements, it is almost the same as measures 292–299 in the solo string quartet's first violin, measures 300–303 in violin II, and after that, intermittently, until measure 308, as in the finished score. However, the layout of this hornpipe tune is intensely changed in the finished work: instead of Handel's twenty-six measures until the repeat sign to end the first strain, Schoenberg's elaboration is of a markedly different design: the repeated music is between measures 10 and 35,[3] and there is no repeated second strain. Schoenberg's decision to expand and transform the movement as he did may in part be explained by a marginal note, written as a memo to himself, around the right and bottom edge of the page; it is by far the most revealing—and puzzling—notation on these leaves. A translation follows the cited text, for whose transcription I am indebted to Andrea Castillo Herreshoff, Research Assistant at the Arnold Schoenberg Institute; her kind assistance allowed a recalcitrant phrase to be finally deciphered.

> Ich versuche herauszufinden, was der Sinn in diesem Stück sein könnte, und mit dessen ins Auge fallende Eigenthümlichkeit ich zunächts nichts anzufangen weiss: dass das in den ersten 4–5 oder 6 Takten angegebene "Thema" niemals wiederauftritt, aber trotzdem der erste Teil (ebenso der II.) als Ganzes wiederholt werden soll.

[3] i.e., measures 301 and 326 in the score.

Während also dem Thema selbst *keine* besondere Bedeutung beigelegt wird, soll der ganze Teil sich einprägen—das ist doch der Sinn der Wiederholung; nicht etwa blosse Verlängerung: Wasser in den Wein hineingiessen—wobei aber die Einprägsamkeit des ganzen auf der der kleinen und kleinsten Teile beruht und diese gefördert wird durch die Wiederholung!—Es scheint die technische Absicht zu bestehen, allmählich neue Figuren aus den Anfangsgestalten zu gewinnen und diese nicht oder selten zu wiederholen (z.B. Takt 6, 8, 16, 17, 24 etc.)—Ferner scheint eine rythmische Entwicklung zu folgendem zu bestehen: Takt 1 hat 3 8tel, Takt 2: 2 X 2, Takt 3 u 4, 3 X 2, T 5 lauter 8tel —nur nimmt es wieder ab.—Regelmässig ist das zwar nicht, aber "irgendwie" ist es so gehandhabt. In meiner Verbesserung habe ich getrachtet diese Methode nicht zu verleugnen, habe aber ganz leere Figuren, wie Takt 11 u 12 ausgelassen. Das ist ja gar nichts.

I am trying to make out the sense of this piece; for the moment I am at a loss as to how I might deal with its obvious peculiarity, where a "theme" is stated in the first 4–5 or 6 measures and never reappears; yet the first part (as well as the second) is supposed to be repeated. In other words, while no particular significance is attached to that theme, the entire part (or strain) is nevertheless expected to impress itself on the listener—that being, after all, the purpose of repetition; rather than a mere lengthening, which would be like pouring water into wine—but the impressibility of the whole thing is based on the smaller, and even the smallest, of its component elements, and that is enhanced by such repetition!—There seems to be an intent to structure by gradually gaining new figures derived from the initial configurations, and of not repeating these, or at least of rarely doing so (for instance in measures 6, 8, 16, 17, 24, etc.)—There appears, furthermore, to be a rhythmic progression, as follows: measure 1 contains 3 eighths; measure 2, 2 X 2; measure 3 and 4, 3 X 2*; measure 5, eighths throughout—only it diminishes after that. Although not regular, it seems "somehow" to be handled in that way. In my improvement I have endeavored not to deny this method, but I have omitted altogether empty figures, as in measures 11 and 12. Those represent nothing.

*The increase is reversed: measure 3 contains 4 x 2; measure 4 only 3 x 2. Schoenberg asserts this indirectly in his next sentence.

Schoenberg's trouble with this hornpipe is hard to understand. Inasmuch as it is the only music in Handel's Concerto Grosso that successfully avoids a rigidly periodized continuity, one would naturally conclude that Schoenberg might have felt particularly drawn to it; so much so, that it would not be far-fetched to imagine that he chose *this* composition (out of the twelve) by reason of the lively hornpipe. As one reads his marginal comment, moreover, it seems as if he had neglected to recognize that the piece's binary construction and the repetition of both strains is simply part of the game played by such a dance tune. The implied disappearance of the "theme," after its initial statement, is what brings about the pleasant unpredictability of the music's unfolding. Schoenberg's protestation appears contrary to his own habits, his own compositional predilections, and his firm belief that unwarranted repetition without some perceptible change in what is repeated is contrary to good sense in any music of interest—and certainly in his own works. The issue here, however, seems to be not so much the lack of the "theme's" reappearance, as the "unsatisfactory" way in which motivic material is dealt with (or "Handel'd"), so that a slightly helter-skelter mode of construction could be inferred to threaten coherence and continuity. By way of an answer to his charge—and in keeping with the *Verbesserung* (which could be taken as "correction," as well as the gentler "improvement") of which he speaks, Schoenberg's recomposition includes plenty of thematic recurrences that are recognizable as such, despite their incorporated changes, and a much expanded, far more venturesome, yet equally comely construction. His remark, in fact, is put into some slight doubt by that extraordinarily imaginative reworking; it is as if the composer were freeing the teacher from the strictures of his very convention-bound, utterly "traditional" method of instructing his composition students—as indeed it was experienced by them *all*—and as though, rather than Schoenberg's having in the process become Handelian, he had instead persuaded the stout Mr. Handel to be Schoenbergian, for a change!

Lastly, the matter of the Concerto's overall key scheme, as brought to my attention by a remark from Paul Zukofsky: instead of a "central" B-flat and its more or less symmetrical upper and lower thirds (i.e., g and D), Schoenberg's inclination was to test a greater degree of equidistance, as between B-flat, D, and F-sharp. How about an emphasis "somewhere" on F-sharp? That place was thereupon readily found to be in the hornpipe, at measure 358, where a deceptive cadence turns into a surprising, if brief, "sojourn"—still, long enough to linger—on F-sharp. Yet no notation for this tantalizing spot is to be seen on the four sketch pages at hand.

Of Songs and Cycles: A Franz Schubert Bifolio

Morten Solvik

[1] The theologian and writer Kosegarten lived in Pomerania, a region at that time controlled by Sweden. Probably the best biography on Kosegarten to this day is H. Franck, *Gotthard Ludwig Kosegarten. Ein Lebensbild* (Halle: Verlag der Buchhandlung des Waisenhauses, 1887).

[2] Schubert also wrote abundantly in other genres that year; his output included four stage works—*Fernando* (D220, completed in July), *Der vierjährige Posten* (D190, completed August), *Claudine von Villa Bella* (D239, probably completed in the summer or early fall), *Die Freunde von Salamanka* (D326, completed December)—two symphonies (Nos. 2 and 3), dozens of piano pieces (including the sonatas in E Major, D157 and C Major, D279), and numerous choral compositions (including the Magnificat in C, D486, and the Masses in G, D167 and in B-flat, D324).

[3] Schubert's 20 Kosegarten settings of 1815 are short strophic works varying in length between 7 and 31 measures and averaging 18 measures in length. Though included in this figure, one of the Kosegarten settings ("Das Abendrot" D236) is, properly speaking, not a lied but a vocal trio; Schubert set only one further Kosegarten text in his life, "An die untergehende Sonne" D457, completed in May 1817. Schubert probably took all of these poems from the collection *L. T. Kosegarten's Poesieen. Neueste Auflage*, 3 vols. (Berlin: n.p., 1803); note that Kosegarten also used the name "Ludwig Theobul."

[4] The number "1" was added to the title later.

FRANZ SCHUBERT WAS BY ANY standard a prolific composer. With well over six hundred lieder, scores of chamber and solo instrumental works, symphonies, music for the stage, and various vocal ensembles to his name, Schubert possessed an extraordinary capacity for musical composition. The legacy of this artistic productivity is documented in its most immediate form in the manuscripts that have survived to the present day. While we have hundreds of such manuscripts, each, with its myriad details and often unsolved problems, has a fascinating tale to tell.

The Schubert bifolio in the Moldenhauer Archives serves as a particularly interesting case in point. Written in 1815, the manuscript contains four lieder to texts by Gotthard Ludwig Kosegarten (1758–1818)[1]—"Nachtgesang" (D314), "An Rosa 1" (D315), "An Rosa 2" (D316), and "Idens Schwanenlied" (D317). Neither the author nor any of these songs is well known, yet the document holds important clues to a puzzling fact about Schubert's most prolific year of song production: of the approximately 140 poems that Schubert set as lieder in 1815,[2] no author save Goethe was set more often than Kosegarten. Why did Schubert dedicate such concentrated effort to this obscure north-German poet?[3] Manuscript evidence as well as details in the text settings and musical construction suggest that Schubert composed a cycle of twenty songs to Kosegarten texts meant to be performed as a set.

Inscriptions in the Moldenhauer bifolio also point to this conclusion. To take an example, let us look at "An Rosa 1" on folio 1 verso. Schubert provides the title[4] and date of composition ("19. Oct[ober] 1815") at the top as well as an author attribution with a note regarding how many verses should be added to the strophic setting ("Kosegarten dazu 4

Strophen") after the ending of the song. The score is fairly clean, though not without corrections. The Schubert Thematic Catalog refers to this document and hundreds more like it as an "erste Niederschrift,"[5] a term that roughly translates to "first written version." While many such manuscripts may represent first attempts by Schubert to write full versions of a work, many others were no doubt preceded by some form of sketch.

Musical details are vital to an understanding of Schubert's method of composition, yet those inscriptions on this page that do *not* stem from the composer are just as important in piecing together the Kosegarten cycle. Note the marginal annotations to the left, right, and underneath the score as well as various numberings and markings in the corners and to the left of the title. Virtually all of these stem from a certain Johann Wolf, a minor composer who lived in Vienna towards the latter half of the nineteenth century. Around 1860, Wolf was given the task of cataloging Schubert documents stored in the archives of the Viennese publisher C. A. Spina and identifying works that might be suitable for publication.[6] It is clear from Wolf's inscriptions that he sorted through dozens, perhaps hundreds, of manuscripts, ordering them as far as possible by date of composition and other criteria. He also cross-indexed each song with other songs bearing a similar title, noting the text author, their location in his files and, if applicable, details regarding their publication and first

5 Otto Erich Deutsch, *Franz Schubert. Thematisches Verzeichnis seiner Werke in chronologischer Folge*, rev. ed. (Kassel: Bärenreiter, 1978), p. 189.

6 It should be noted that Wolf worked in archives collected by Anton Diabelli. By the time Diabelli died in 1858, his firm, Diabelli & Co., had been passed on to C. A. Spina (in 1852). See the introduction to Alexander Weinmann, *Verlagsverzeichnis Anton Diabelli & Co (1824 bis 1840)* (Vienna: L. Krenn, 1985).

7 In this particular case, Wolf also noted the author of the text at the top of the page underneath the title. Though "Kosegarten" appears in Schubert's hand in the lower right system, the reference at the top made identification more convenient when sorting such autographs.

8 *Franz Schuberts Werke. Kritisch durchgesehene Gesamtausgabe*, ser. 20, vol. 3 (Leipzig: Breitkopf & Härtel, 1895), p. 145.

performance. This is the information scribbled in the right and left margins of this and many other Schubert manuscripts.[7]

At the bottom of the page Wolf provided detailed information regarding any other manuscript versions of the same lied, noting type of manuscript, catalog number, and any significant features:

> "Eine Copie (respect. Reinschrift) von Fr. Schuberts Hand vide № 19 Abth[eilung] IV; diese Copie hat aber einige Veränderungen u[nd] ist in der Begleitung vollstim̄iger gehalten"

> ["A copy (or rather fair copy) in Fr. Schubert's hand see No. 19 Group IV; this copy has, however, several changes and has a fuller texture in the accompaniment"]

Wolf alerts us to a second version of the song in fair copy that varies slightly from the present version. This is note-worthy, since the Thematic Catalog of Schubert's works does not recognize two distinct versions of this lied. The document in question, identified by Wolf's siglum: "Nr.19, Group IV," is in private possession today and thus not available for scholarly investigation. We can, however, examine the pub-lished version of the lied in the first complete edition of Schubert's works[8] to confirm that the document in the Moldenhauer Archives distinguishes itself from the later fair copy in the writing for the left hand and above all in the final measures.

Probably the most useful information provided by these marginal notes can be found in the lower left-hand corner in black ink: namely, Wolf's manuscript numbering. The number given here, "30," is part of a continuous sequence that can be found on every page of the bifolio. "Nachtgesang" on folio 1r is numbered 29, with each following lied numbered in sequential order through 32 ("Idens Schwanenlied"). We know from the marginal note referring to "An Rosa 2" that the present set is part of a sequence known collectively as "Group II." By numbering these pages and listing further manuscripts that relate to each of the pieces at hand, Wolf leads us to consider the significant question of how the manuscript fits into some larger pattern. To approach this issue we must look at Kosegarten settings not included in the bifolio.

Schubert's manuscript datings tell us that the twenty Kosegarten settings of 1815 were written in two concentrated bouts of creative inspiration: thirteen in June and July and seven all notated on the same day in October. The Moldenhauer bifolio constitutes the middle section of what was once a continuous autograph containing all seven of these later settings. Shortly thereafter, Schubert prepared a fair copy of all twenty lieder in what may also have been a continuous autograph: each of the lieder in what Wolf designated "Group IV" is a Kosegarten setting; what is more, Wolf numbered these fair copies as a group consecutively from "1" to "20," implying a purposeful gathering of these songs. Recall that "An Rosa 1" was number 19 in the series known as "Group IV." Note, too, that elsewhere Wolf refers to "Group IV" as a collection of songs that belonged to Franz Schubert's brother, Ferdinand. Thus, the manuscript evidence suggests that Schubert compiled an extensive series of Kosegarten songs in 1815.

To figure out why the composer did this, we should look at the songs in the order suggested by Wolf's numbering. Most remarkable about these fair copies is their arrangement and the musical affinities that emerge between them when grouped together. Rather than copy out the songs in the order of their composition, Schubert placed them in a new sequence; what is more, the resulting succession of song texts reveals strongly narrative tendencies. The story that emerges centers on a male protagonist whose amorous attentions flit from one woman to the next. The feelings of the adventurer
—Wilhelm—and two of his broken-hearted mistresses—Ida and Luisa—are presented in short strophic songs set within the typical Romantic conceits of longing and bliss. Wilhelm stands at the center of the collection with twelve settings presented from his perspective. His songs, excepting the last two, are all characterized by boundless enthusiasm and passionate, though fleeting, devotion. The women (Ida—6 settings, Luisa—2) present a very different character. Hesitant and pessimistic, their soliloquies bespeak angst, self-sacrifice, even tragic

Kosegarten Fair Copies Arranged by Wolf Catalog Number[9]

Wolf No.: IV/...	D.	Title
1	240	Huldigung
2	241	Alles um Liebe
3	228	Von Ida
4	229	Die Erscheinung
5	219	Das Finden
6	227	Idens Nachtgesang
7	313	Die Sterne
8	314	Nachtgesang
9	230	Die Täuschung
[10]	231	Das Sehnen
11	238	Die Mondnacht
12	237	Abends unter der Linde
13	236	Das Abendrot [SSB]
14	233	Geist der Liebe
15	221	Der Abend
16	317	Idens Schwanenlied
17	318	Schwangesang
18	319	Luisens Antwort
19	315	An Rosa 1
20	316	An Rosa 2

pathos. This contrast between male and female points of view surfaces repeatedly in the characters' reactions to nature: to take but one example, Wilhelm finds solace in the night, while Ida cannot help feeling dire foreboding of the future when surrounded by darkness. Finally, one of the settings ("Abendroth") includes all three characters singing a trio in praise of the evening and the sunset, a time of day that recurs throughout the set reflecting the transition from day to night, from hope to despair. In the end, the fickle Wilhelm does not escape this fate either, for in the last song we find him pining for yet another woman (Rosa) who is no longer his—and mourning over her death.

Many aspects of the individual songs support the sense of cohesion implied by this dramatic continuity. To take but one musical example, three pivotal songs sung by Wilhelm all bear an undeniable likeness.

Alles um Liebe, mm. 11-15

Die Täuschung, mm. 6-10

Geist der Liebe, mm. 8-12

There are also numerous examples of consecutive songs linked by a common motive or texture. "Idens Schwanenlied," for instance, clearly points to the following "Schwangesang." Note the repeated Cs in the voice line of "Idens Schwanenlied," also repeated in the middle voice of the piano right hand in "Schwangesang." Likewise, the descending motion in the piano from A-flat to E-natural up to F in "Idens Schwanenlied" appears again in the left hand opening of "Schwangesang."

Wie___ schaust du aus dem Ne - bel-flor,

Musical Similarly Linking Consecutive Songs

Opening measures of "Idens Schwanenlied"

End - lich steh'n die Pfor - ten of - fen.

Opening measures of "Schwangesang"

Especially important in this context is the diminished chord resolving to F Minor (at "Nebelflor" and "offen," respectively), a sonority not only in both of the passages above but also a prominent feature of the closing of "Idens Schwanenlied." This sonority takes on even greater

·397·

prominence in the song as preserved in the Moldenhauer bifolio (on folio 2v), where the music ends rather abruptly on oscillating chords. Astonishingly, this version of the song has never been published; it appears here for the first time. Much more can be said about the codecological, musical, and textual elements that point to a unified conception of Schubert's Kosegarten lieder.[10] That Schubert had already constructed a large-scale, cyclical collection of songs in 1815 will no doubt cause us to rethink certain aspects of his development as a composer and, indeed, the development of the genre itself. Thus, the Moldenhauer bifolio is a part of a

[10] A more thorough discussion of the points discussed here be found in "Lieder im geselligen Spiel—Schuberts neu entdeckter Kosegarten-Zyklus von 1815" in *Österreichische Musik-Zeitschrift* 53/1 (January 1997), 31–9.

First version of "Idens Schwanenlied," first publication

much larger complex. An examination of its contents demonstrates what riches of information a musical manuscript may contain and what implications they may have for our understanding of composers and their works.

Gunther Schuller on Edward Steuermann and Schuller's *Symphony for Brass*

Interview with Jon Newsom

GS: This is reaching back into my life fifty years.

JN: You were a student of Steuermann's?

GS: No, I was not actually a student of his, but my wife-to-be, Marjorie Black, was.

JN: As a pianist?

GS: Yes, as a pianist. We met in Cincinnati, when I played principal horn there in the orchestra, and we were both seventeen. She was studying voice and piano at the conservatory, and when I met her I was so smitten that I started courting her, and we were together most of those two years, 1943 and 1944. But as young men sometimes do, I had one little fling with another lady, and toward the end of that second year in Cincinnati I rather abandoned Marjorie for a little while, which I later very much regretted.

I went back to New York in the late spring of 1945, having been engaged to go to the Metropolitan Opera in the fall. Marjorie wanted to continue studying with her teacher, a singer from Vienna, Lotte Lenya, who was a protégé of Bruno Walter. She had a reputation as a singer and teacher, was a refugee from Nazi Germany and was quite well known in the high-level German-Austrian musical circles in America. When Marjorie found out that she was going to be at a summer camp in Gambier, Ohio, at Kenyon College, she decided to continue studying with her during the summer.

Now, in the early weeks of the summer, my guilty conscience

about having abandoned her led to a tremendous conversion, and against the wishes of my parents, I pilgrimaged out to Gambier, to be with her. That "camp" was in fact a Summer Institute, at which, if you were going to attend, you had to pay a fee or tuition to be enrolled. Well, I didn't know that; in my excitement that never occurred to me. I just got on a train and went via Cincinnati and Columbus to Gambier, and I presented myself at the front door of the Institute. They all said, who are you, you're not enrolled here as a student (mind you, I was nineteen years old), and I said I am looking for Marjorie Black, she is studying with Lotte Lenya. I had taken my French horn with me, and Fritz Cohn—who was the director of the Institute, figuring that maybe they could make use of me as a player in their chamber music concerts, and maybe because I had expressed my great admiration for Alban Berg's music and Schoenberg's *Pierrot Lunaire*—took pity on me and let me stay at the Institute. But they didn't have any dormitory room for me, no bed was free, and so I had to sleep on a mattress in some dank basement in one of the distant unoccupied campus buildings.

At the Institute, apart from my wife-to-be and Lotte Lenya, there were Rudolf Kolisch and Edward Steuermann and, in fact, the American Schoenberg circle, except for Schoenberg himself. There were Sessions, Křenek, Graudan, Jalowetz, mostly German and Austrian refugees, who had gathered to celebrate and study and perform the music of the Second Viennese School, since at that time such music was almost completely unperformed and unrecognized in the United States. Also, at that time even Mahler was still virtually unperformed in the United States, except occasionally for the First and Second Symphonies. So that summer they played a lot of Mahler's music, not with orchestra (they had no such means), but on two pianos, with Steuermann as one of the pianists. That was the first time I heard the Third, Fifth, and Seventh Symphonies, which were all as yet unrecorded at the time. So during those weeks I got to know Steuermann and Kolisch. I was also already incredibly enamored of the Berg Violin Concerto and was beginning to understand that there was a whole school of music that at that time (the 1940s) was not only not performed and not heard in the United States, but was actually boycotted by the reigning Neoclassic camp.

JN: The Boulanger students?

GS: Yes, the whole Copland-Stravinsky school, to whom Schoenberg and his school were absolute anathema. But the Berg Violin Concerto had already come out on a beautiful recording with Louis Krasner, Rodzinski, and the Cleveland Symphony. I was in love with that piece, and, by the way, it changed my life and put the final capper on the idea that I was going to be a composer and, as it turned out, a twelve-tone composer.

So here I met these great people that I had heard about, but had never met or thought I would meet. I didn't even know they were all in the United States. Rudolf Kolisch (whom I later brought to Boston, to the New England Conservatory) was the one for whom Schoenberg wrote all of his violin music, and Steuermann was the one for whom Schoenberg wrote all of his piano music. Steuermann took part in the famous *Pierrot Lunaire* performance in Berlin in 1912 and premiered many other important Schoenberg and Webern works. And both had played on the famous 1942 *Pierrot Lunaire* recording (which, by the way, Mayor LaGuardia banned from the radio in New York in 1942). So here I was, meeting these giants of music, and the next thing I knew, Rudolf and Edward were scheduled to do a chamber concert, and since I had my horn with me, they asked me to play the Brahms Horn Trio with them. I was not only meeting these people, I was playing with them, I was working with them! And of course, being barely nineteen, that was an incredible experience for me, rehearsing and playing with these great musicians. There were many other interesting concerts of modern music at Gambier that summer, including some fine chamber music and songs by Křenek, music which, as I say, at that time was totally neglected and unknown in the United States. I also met Sessions there. He was working on his opera *Montezuma* at the time.

JN: Yes, I remember looking at the sketches here at the Library of Congress. Had he written his Violin Concerto as yet?

GS: Yes, he had written that. I didn't know the Violin Concerto at the time, but I later conducted the first recording of it.

JN: Yes, and the only one, in fact, so far.

GS: Really? Sessions sort of picked my brains about the horn parts in *Montezuma*, about whether this was possible, or that was possible, and I gave him what advice I could. (I thought he was using much too much hand-stopping instead of plain muting, and I told him so.) But many years later, when I studied *Montezuma*, I realized he had not really taken much of my advice.

But the main joy of being at Kenyon that summer was working with Steuermann and Kolisch. And Margie was of course doing her studies with Lotte Lenya, but then she also became enthralled with Steuermann's piano playing. (She had just played the Liszt A-Major Concerto for her graduation in Cincinnati, so she was no amateur; the A-Major Concerto is some technical achievement.) She decided that she would leave Cincinnati and move to New York with me, and then of course, she had the idea that she would study with Steuermann. He was rather little known in America at that time, working only as a private teacher. The poor man was completely ignored as a composer—he was a first-rate composer, by the way—and had to make his living teaching, and taught—I don't know what—twelve hours a day at the time; it was a brutal schedule. He was always looking for more students because that was his only possible income, and he also took Marjorie on.

By that time I was so taken both with him and with what he stood for musically, that I practically wanted to study with him myself, which, in an informal way, I sort of did, by going to all of Marjorie's piano lessons and sitting quietly in the corner listening to Steuermann teach. And as we got to know each other we became close friends; he lent me some of his precious scores which I photostatted, and I built up a library of rare music that no one else had. Also, I worked with Steuermann and Kolisch and played the Brahms Horn Trio at Town Hall, around 1946. Some of the correspondence you have at the Library of Congress, I believe, includes mention of me as being a very talented, enterprising young musician, with words to the effect that maybe Gunther Schuller can do something for our cause.

JN: Indeed, we have Steuermann's own archives and

Schoenberg's complete correspondence as well. I am sure both include many references to you.

GS: Steuermann also began to show me his own compositions. Some were written in Vienna and Berlin, before he had come to this country. I can't recall now whether he was working on the Brecht lieder at that time or whether he just showed them to me, but he was very keen about those songs. I don't know whether it was some great admiration for Brecht he had, or whether it was that these were just pieces that he felt were a particularly good or representative product of his work. I remember I was quite impressed not only by those songs, but by others as well. They were hardly ever for soprano, usually for bass or baritone, which, as you must know, in the whole history of the vocal literature, is rather rare. It includes a lot for soprano, and quite a bit for tenor, but there is hardly anything in the way of lieder for bass or baritone. Steuermann would ask me who could sing these songs, thinking of some people at the Met, I suppose. At that time, there was a dearth of singers who could sing atonal music. Mind you, this was before Bethany Beardslee, Phyllis Bryn-Julson, Elsa Charlston, or Paul Sperry. Poor Steuermann could never find musicians or singers to play or sing his music, and so he hoped that I, being in the thick of contemporary music performance in New York (I was, for example, involved with the International Society of Contemporary Music (ISCM), various times as President, Secretary, Treasurer, Program Maker, with Milton Babbitt and Elliott Carter), could get him performances. Steuermann was very fond of his chamber orchestra pieces. There was a trio which we finally programmed (I think Erich Itor Kahn played it). But I do remember that the Brecht lieder were his own favorite. I think he thought that that was the best thing he had ever written.

JN: Did Schoenberg write his bass solo in the Serenade op. 24 with a particular singer in mind? Is that why he chose that range—and was there any connection between that and Steuermann?

GS: Not that I know of, except perhaps by some kind of a general influence. The Serenade is a great bass-baritone piece, which Steuermann certainly knew and had in fact been involved with. But I think (this is conjectural) that Steuermann had an attitude about male voices that was related to his inclination to do things in music that were not the common practice, whether it was performance on the piano, or whether it was composing. He was in so many ways a typical Pole. First of all, he spoke five languages, as most educated Poles did at that time; he felt they were as persecuted as the Jews, and, of course, Steuermann was both a Pole and a Jew. In self-defense, Polish intellectuals developed an unbelievable sense of humor, an incredible wittiness, which Steuermann had, too. He could say the most sardonically funny things with such an absolutely straight face that you didn't know whether he was serious or not. He felt he was an outsider, neglected and rejected, like Schoenberg, and that the musical establishment was never going to recognize him, help him. And I think, almost as a kind of defiance, that (like his mentor Schoenberg) he did things that someone more centered in the musical mainstream wouldn't have done, including writing songs not for soprano but for bass. I suppose Ned Rorem and all those people, like David Diamond, Theodore Chanler, Richard Hageman, who were reigning song composers at that time, wrote for soprano because that is how they would get performances immediately. I think that Steuermann's writing for bass was part of a strange obstinacy and a feeling of neglect, an I-am-going-to-go-my-own-way-and-to-hell-with-everybody attitude, but always in his super-polite Viennese way, never harsh or bitter except in the sarcastic-humorous way. He once told me that Artur Rubinstein was the same way, that under that famous public veneer he had an incredible wit, with all this Polish dark humor.

But eventually, Steuermann did gain some recognition and respect and got a job teaching piano at the Juilliard School. Here was one of the great pedagogues of that time, and he was for many years simply ignored. It took the efforts of many other musicians finally to get him into Juilliard where he became famous as a teacher and pedagogue.

JN: What was the resistance?

GS: Well, look, if you were connected with Schoenberg in those days, you were automatically ostracized, you were rejected or ignored.

·405·

JN: Was there a political feeling that these people were somehow musically subversive?

GS: Even that—although that was more during the McCarthy era. No, mostly it was that they were considered irrelevant, incompetent, or ridiculous. Why did they write all that dissonant, ugly, harsh music? Why did they write twelve-tone music? The Schoenberg bashing goes on even now, as we speak, but way back then it was out of a great deal of ignorance and because no one really knew (or wanted to know) the music.

JN: And even more, because one could not purchase the music.

GS: Yes, and the interesting thing about that is that when the Nazis invaded Austria in 1938, Universal Edition, the major publisher of Schoenberg, Berg, and Webern, had taken all the plates of the music that Hitler had banned and buried them secretly in the hills outside of Vienna, with the result that for almost a decade the music could not be printed. When I wanted to buy the score of the Violin Concerto by Berg in 1943, it wasn't available anywhere. So there was a great deal of ignorance and prejudice. Again, to put it simply, if you were associated with Schoenberg and his circle in New York, you were pretty much ostracized.

I know that from my own experience, because once I became associated with Steuermann and Kolisch and the ISCM, and word got around that I was one of those "Schoenberg disciples," I had the same problems getting my music played. I had almost no performances as a young composer because Copland and his group reigned supreme in New York and pretty much controlled the musical life of the time, as far as modern music went. And they thought of me as a traitor to their cause. That was ironic because I was as much an admirer of Stravinsky as I was of Schoenberg. They were both great composers to me.

JN: Now, where did Sessions stand? Sessions was involved with Minna Lederman, and the *Modern Music* group, was he not?

GS: Well, yes. He was the first to study Schoenberg's music and to teach it, talk about it—at Princeton. And out of that influence came Milton Babbitt and some of the other atonal and twelve-tone composers. That is why Sessions was at Kenyon that summer. I don't think his association with *Modern Music* helped him much, either, in the greater musical establishment. At least Roger had his position at Princeton, which couldn't be taken away. But for a young composer like me, it was really very difficult. And the *New York Times*, as the major newspaper, with Olin Downes as music critic, was also involved and was no friend of the Schoenberg circle. Steuermann often talked about it, saying he should really go out to Los Angeles, to be with Schoenberg, Thomas Mann, Eisler, and Brecht. They were all out there, and he felt isolated in New York.

Then later, when Dimitri Mitropoulos became music director of the New York Philharmonic, everything changed. We owe it to him that for the first time we heard the Webern Symphony, op. 21, or the Schoenberg Variations, op. 31, and many other great works. All those pieces were not recorded, so they simply did not exist. And then Mitropoulos stepped in and changed all that, and of course it also cost him his job.

JN: It killed him.[1]

GS: Yes, just about! People like Steuermann, and Krasner and Kolisch all benefited from Mitropoulos's presence in New York. They all got to do performances, at first just at Juilliard, then at Town Hall, and later even at Carnegie Hall and, of course, at the ISCM concerts. By the early 1950s, the previous, stultified, solely "Neoclassic" programming was beginning to loosen up. Then of course came the ultimate blow to the Neoclassic camp, when in 1952 Stravinsky himself abandoned Neoclassicism and became a twelve-tone composer. That threw the Boulangerie, as it was called then, into a state of shock and consternation from which it didn't recover for a long time.

So in the 1950s, Steuermann and Kolisch and their circle became much more accepted and respected. I was too, by the way. But earlier, when I returned to New York from Cincinnati

[1] On November 2, 1960, Mitropoulos was in Milan to conduct Mahler's Third Symphony with the orchestra of La Scala. "They reached bar No. 80, where the trombones make a big entrance. A few seconds later, Mitropoulos stopped conducting and sat back down on his high stool. The orchestra fell silent, anticipating further instructions. Instead, his face froze and he slowly began to pitch forward...His head crashed into the music stand...Dimitri Mitropoulos was dead." See William R. Trotter, *Priest of Music: The Life of Dimitri Mitropoulos* (Portland, Oregon: Amadeus Press, 1995), p. 439.

in 1945 and realized that my first calling was that of a composer, the impression which we young composers got was that the Schoenberg and the Stravinsky camps were feuding with each other, and that we were expected to join one camp or the other. No one said that in so many words, but that was the implication. Of course, the further implication was that if you wanted to have your music performed, given the almost monopolistic hold the Neoclassic camp had on the music scene, you had better join the Stravinsky-Copland axis. But people like myself—other young composers of my generation—said this is rank nonsense. Stravinsky and Schoenberg are both great masters, and we did not have to choose between the two, we could learn from both of them. And to this day, I think, one can hear in my music the profound influence of both composers.

JN: Did Steuermann ever get any performances of his music?

GS: Very few, hardly any at all. And he died very sad and unhappy about it. He was really frustrated about this. If you read through his letters to his nephew, Michael Gielen, you feel all the constant agonizing, the frustration over not being able to hear his music. In a way, he was pigeonholed, typecast, as a teacher, a mere pedagogue, and very few people who could have made a difference even knew that he composed, or they just rejected his kind of composing. He was seen, if at all, as a kind of orthodox Schoenberg epigone. Little did people realize that some of his best music is as great as Schoenberg's. Anyway, he was pretty bitter about all this, and he died a broken man.

JN: May we turn to a piece of yours in the Moldenhauer Archives?

GS: Yes, the *Symphony for Brass*?

JN: Yes, and maybe in some way connect your discussion of Steuermann with it and describe what place it has in your own career?

GS: I can't relate it so much to Steuermann, except in the general way—as we've described it—of my being introduced

(Opposite page)
Edward Steuermann, *Drei Brecht Lieder*, no. III, "Gedanken über die Dauer des Exils"

Reproduced by permission of Rachel Steuermann

to twelve-tone music at Kenyon; and the *Brass Symphony* is one of my first twelve-tone pieces. But it was certainly my first big success piece, my debut as a composer. It does relate in part to my time in Cincinnati, because when I was there in the orchestra, the bass trombone player led a student brass ensemble. It was one of the very early brass ensembles in a major music school in the United States. They didn't have those things in the 1940s. They had bands and orchestras, but they didn't really have brass ensembles as they do nowadays. Anyway, this fellow, Ernie Glover, and I became very close friends, and in 1948 or 1949 he called me from Cincinnati (I was then back in New York playing at the Met) and he asked me if I would write a piece for his brass group, a rather unusual, almost radical idea at the time. I immediately said yes, partly also because, as a major brass player in New York and surrounded by amazing colleagues (trombone, trumpet, tuba players) in the Met, in the New York Philharmonic, the NBC Symphony, who had extraordinary technical capabilities but who were musically frustrated because there was no or very little challenging music for them to play, I was really inspired to write for them. (You realize, of course that most of us composers, even when we are asked to compose something for a specific group of players, we generally write for some ideal or idealized players.) For these players, the the most exciting, the most challenging thing, was Wagner's *Götterdämmerung*, or Strauss's *Salome*, or once in a blue moon, Stavinsky's *Rite of Spring*. In those days nobody even performed pieces by Bartók, for example. The *Concerto for Orchestra* just came around at that time, but pieces like *The Miraculous Mandarin*, which is a brass player's feast, were never performed. Now you hear it almost every week. Also, there weren't any pieces for brass quintet in those days. That all came later in the 1960s.

So this young crop of brass players in New York, but also the ones that were coming out of Juilliard and the Manhattan School, Eastman and the other major conservatories, had nothing challenging to play. In those days, nobody even played the early brass music, say, of Gabrieli or Pezel, which is now so commonplace and has spawned dozens of brass quintet groups, for example. Anyway, I conceived of writing a whole four-movement Symphony for brass, which no one had ever done before. I said to myself, I am not going to write one of those little cute bagatelles that were coming out of the Paris Conservatory every three minutes, but a really serious, no-nonsense work, except that it would not be for orchestra but for a large brass ensemble. I sent the work to Glover in Cincinnati in 1949, and he performed the first three movements. It turned out that the fourth movement was too much for his students, too technically demanding, so actually the so-called premiere was not really a full premiere.

At that time I became close to Leon Barzin, who was at the time the director of the National Orchestral Association and a very much admired and respected, but also feared, conductor. This orchestra was a training orchestra. As in the case of Tanglewood, half the New York Philharmonic and half the Boston Symphony and other major orchestras had come out of Barzin's training orchestra, which I think he had started in 1935. They gave monthly concerts in Carnegie Hall. Barzin rehearsed three times a week in the building that used to be called the Mecca Temple in New York, where the city opera started, where Bernstein had his concerts in the 1950s, and where now the ballet companies perform in New York.

Besides going to Steuermann's lessons, I went to Barzin's rehearsals. I just sat there quietly in the corner, a "fly on the wall" watching him rehearse; and it was fantastic. I learned so much from both of these series of lessons. Somehow Barzin got wind of my *Brass Symphony*—some of his brass player coaches must have told him about it. And so it came about that he did the real premiere for one of the ISCM concerts (I think it was in 1950 or 1951). I got together my best brass player friends and colleagues, for whom, in my own mind, I had really written the piece. I handpicked these great players, and Barzin rehearsed the work. It was quite a considerable struggle, even for those great players, but we did perform the complete piece. I must say, even though it is now considered a sort of national anthem for brass players, the piece remains difficult to this day. It was really difficult then, in 1950. Nowadays people in colleges and universities play it more easily.

It turned out to be a breakthrough piece for me. Eventually,

Mitropoulos heard about it and, in 1956, he did an extraordinary thing, something unprecedented in the history of the New York Philharmonic. He presented a young composer (me) not in one performance that season, but in two. One was my *Dramatic Overture*, which I had written in 1951, and the other was this *Symphony for Brass*. The Philharmonic had quite a struggle with it, but it came off as a fine performance.

And then two things happened. I got letters (I was still working at the Met, of course, and still living in New York) from Aaron Copland, Samuel Barber, and William Schumann and others. They had heard the broadcast (in those days the weekly New York Philharmonic concerts were broadcast every Sunday afternoon) and they wrote me these laudatory letters about my piece. I remember Copland including in his letter something about how he was terrified about brass writing and brass players. He was always afraid to write music that might be too difficult. My piece had overwhelmed him, because here there was a level of brass virtuosity that he hadn't realized was possible. I had made it a point in the piece to have brass players do what most people thought only violins or cellos or woodwinds could do. I recall that, many times, people hearing the third movement would say, that sounds like clarinets, like woodwinds, or like strings (the movement is almost entirely for muted trumpets).

I was, of course, very flattered by all this sudden attention. And I suppose as a result, Mitropoulos made the recording for Columbia records in 1956, again with handpicked players, mostly the same players I had used earlier with Barzin. It is by now a legendary brass recording, and has been reissued—finally—on CD. It was for many years a rare collector's item and never reissued, because it was recorded in the earliest days of stereo, and—so I was told—the stereo equipment had broken down in the middle of the third movement. The story was that Columbia refused to reissue it because they could not put out something that was half stereo and half mono. The piece has been recorded by others since 1956, but that first recording is still for me the definitive one. I myself rehearsed and coached the piece with all those great players, and Mitropoulos came in for the kill, so to speak, and did the final two rehearsals and the recording, and put his stamp on it.

Tremendous!

JN: It is interesting to note the relative lack of respect for the brass ensemble in this country, as compared to Europe and particularly Britain. There is our great Midwestern wind or brass tradition, but it is not what Frederick Fennell tried to do with the Eastman Wind Ensemble.

GS: No, not exactly. Fennell has had a considerable success with his Wind Ensemble. But you are right, the big musical establishments, the operatic, the symphonic establishment, haven't really recognized wind or brass ensembles at all. The CBDNA [College Band Directors National Association] people have for years put up a good fight for it, but it simply is not considered on the level of other things like the symphony orchestra or chamber music. And I don't suppose it will ever change, regardless of the fact that people like Frank Battisti at the New England Conservatory, Ravelli and Bob Reynolds at Michigan, and Fennell and others do extraordinary work. The best young players are attracted to these ensembles, because it gives them an outlet for playing some things, which, with the standard symphonic literature, they would rarely get a chance to do. So my *Brass Symphony* was this kind of a breakthrough, bellwether piece at the time. And I am very proud of it. Because I was a horn player, I had a certain intimate knowledge of the brass instruments, which I suppose someone like Copland couldn't quite have had. When Sam Barber wrote *Vanessa*, I was still at the Met, and he came to me several times to ask questions about the brass instruments. Many of these ideas he incorporated in *Vanessa*.

JN: I doubt whether there is anyone whose views of music in the last half of this century are as informed as yours are by personal experience—regarding which we have not even begun to draw on your close relationship with the world of jazz. For the present, many thanks for your perspectives on an important and still controversial period in music history.

Robert Schumann's *Burla* in G Minor

John Daverio

[1] The term is Linda Correll Roesner's. See her "Studies in Schumann Manuscripts: With Particular Reference to Sources Transmitting Instrumental Works in the Large Forms" (Ph.D. diss., New York University, 1973), vol. I, pp. 18–19.

[2] Boetticher, op. cit., *Teil II*, p. 259.

[3] Ibid., p. 260.

APART FROM OCCASIONAL FORAYS into chamber and orchestral music, Robert Schumann devoted his attention during the 1830s mainly to works for piano. In addition to publishing over a dozen collections of keyboard miniatures, three sonatas, and the C-Major *Fantasie*, op. 17, he left a number of manuscript fragments ranging from the briefest of idea sketches[1] to almost fully elaborated drafts. The *Burla* in G Minor, preserved on a sketch leaf now in the Moldenhauer Archives, is closer to the latter category.

This document is of special significance, not only because it makes a small but interesting addition to our understanding of Schumann's path toward artistic maturity, but also because it was originally part of a larger group of sketches whose whereabouts have been unknown for the past forty years. Described by Wolfgang Boetticher (who was working from a microfilm made sometime before 1954) in his comprehensive *Robert Schumanns Klavierwerke: Neue biographische und textkritische Untersuchungen, Teil II*, op. 7–13 (Wilhelmshaven: Heinrichshofen's Verlag, 1984), the manuscript was part of a private collection in Berlin until 1944, and for the next decade remained in private hands in Munich.[2] Although it consists largely of sketches and more complete drafts for portions of the *Symphonische Etüden*, op. 13 (first version)—and is to date the only known sketchbook devoted primarily to that work—the manuscript also includes materials for other projected keyboard works: sketches for *Henri Herz. Fragment satyrique*; a fifty-four-measure draft for No. 5 of the *6 Konzert-Etüden nach Capricen von Paganini*, op. 10; a fifty-six-measure sketch for No. 11 of the *Impromptus über ein Thema von Clara Wieck*, op. 5 (earlier version); and, on its ninth and last page, a *Burla* in G Minor.[3]

The manuscript consists of a single leaf of upright format

Burla.

4 For his piano music of the 1830s, Schumann tended to use paper of oblong format with somewhat greater frequency than paper of upright format. When he did use paper of the latter type, it generally measured 23 cm. by 30 cm. See Roesner, op. cit., vol. 1, pp. 63–64.

5 The preliminary compositional material for op. 5, No. 11 (preserved in the same sketchbook of which the Moldenhauer leaf originally formed a part) likewise exemplifies this tendency. Its first thirty-two measures conform closely to the finished version of the movement, while the ensuing measures assume a more sketchlike profile. See Boetticher, op. cit., *Teil II*, p. 260.

measuring 28 cm. by 31 cm., and hence is a bit larger than the sheets of this format that Schumann typically used for sketches during his early period.[4] Following his customary practice, Schumann wrote on commercially manufactured paper, in this case with fourteen staves that the composer grouped into seven braces. The barlines, placed at roughly equal distances, were hand-drawn with a pen of finer point than that used for the body of the musical text, committed by Schumann to paper probably at a slightly later time. The crowding in brace 4, measures 7–8 supports the notion of such a two-stage process.

Like many of the other manuscript fragments from Schumann's early creative period, the G-Minor *Burla*—comprising sixty-one measures of music in 2/4 meter—occupies an intermediary position between sketch and draft.[5] As it stands, the piece consists of an opening section (A) in G Minor (measures 1–24), a contrasting section (B) in the parallel major mode (measures 24–43), and the beginnings of a varied return (A') of the initial music (measures 44–61), presumably in G Minor, though Schumann did not notate the change from the original key signature. Thus it falls into the kind of sectional or tripartite shape frequently encountered in Schumann's early keyboard music. But while section A and the opening phrases of section B are quite fully elaborated, it is difficult to imagine that Schumann would have left the ever-widening textural gap between melody and bass of measures 37–43 as it is without adding something for an inner voice or voices. In addition, Schumann had not yet determined how to negotiate the juncture between the B and A' sections; only a single measure (or, to be precise, three eighth notes for the beginning of measure 44) would be needed to fill out the last four-bar phrase of the B section. As for the A' section, its two-voice texture also seems to require further working out.

In short, what begins as a draft gradually approximates the appearance of a sketch. Schumann customarily went through his manuscripts several times for the purpose of adding expressive marks, articulations, performance directives, and the like. The relative density of these types of indications in the A section—rests, slurs, accents, staccati, an *all'ottava* marking, though curiously, no dynamics—lends further weight to the supposition that Schumann had completed the piece in its broad outlines and subsequently returned to the beginning to add details. The middle voice in measures 11–12 (which duplicates the inner line of measures 7–8 at the upper octave) may have been the result of such a process of amplification. In addition, Schumann took some care to ensure the accuracy of the accidentals in the opening portion of the piece; only one emendation is necessary, an E in the lowest voice, first eighth, of measure 12 (so that the passage echoes, an octave higher, the music of measure 8).[6] The more skeletal B and A' sections, in contrast, have almost no articulative or expressive marks, contain many crossed-out notes, and omit many accidentals. For reasons unknown, Schumann seems to have lost interest in the little piece.

It is not possible to date the G-Minor *Burla* with absolute certainty. Nonetheless, it is likely that the fragment was conceived late in 1832. Although Boetticher assigns a fall 1834 date to most of the material from the sketchbook in which *Burla* originally appeared,[7] some of its contents can be dated earlier. The idea sketch for *Henri Herz. Fragment satyrique*, for instance, can be assigned to spring or summer 1832 on the basis of an entry in Schumann's dairy for May 14 of that year: "The idea for a satirical Fantasy after Herz is not bad at all."[8] Furthermore, the title *Burla* (meaning "joke," "hoax," or "jest") figures often in Schumann's correspondence, diaries, and musical manuscripts during the early 1830s. In a letter of November 1832 to Breitkopf and Härtel, Schumann tentatively offered for publication a set of "XII Burlesken (Burle) after the manner of the *Papillons*"[9] which had appeared as op. 2 under Kistner's imprint the year before. While the companion volume was never published—nor has it come to light in manuscript sources—there is a good chance that individual *Burle* found their way into later collections such as the *Albumblätter*, op. 124 (published 1854, but consisting mainly of pieces written between 1832 and 1839), the twelfth number of which is a little F-Minor piece in duple meter actually entitled *Burla* and dated 1832. Schumann's nearly complete overview of the makeup of the "XII Burlesken" provides further evidence for this supposition: the entry for *Burla 5* includes the additional designation "F min. 2/4."[10] The G-Minor *Burla*, however, was probably not intended for this set. We can infer from the letter to Breitkopf and Härtel that the "XII Burlesken" were

6 Boetticher transcribes portions of the *Burla* (measures 1–15 and 45–52) in Boetticher, op. cit., pp. 260–61, but incorrectly renders the lowest voice in measure 12 as E flat-E.

7 Ibid., p. 260.

8 "Die Idee zur satyrischen Fantaisie von Herz ist so übel nicht..." See Robert Schumann, *Tagebücher*, Band I, 1827–1838, ed. Georg Eismann (Basel and Frankfurt: Stroemfeld/Roter Stern, 1971), p. 389.

9 See Gustav Jansen, *Die Davidsbündler: Aus Robert Schumanns Sturm- und Drangperiode* (Leipzig: Breitkopf and Härtel, 1883), p. 153.

10 The overview—now part of the largest single group of the composer's early sketches, in the Wiede Collection—contains entries for *Burle 1* through *9* and *Burla 12*. See Boetticher, op. cit., *Teil I*, op. 1–6 (1976), p. 101. Two other *Burle* can be provisionally coordinated with pieces from the *Albumblätter*. "*Burla 6* F maj. 6/8" with op. 124, No. 3 (Scherzino) and "*Burla 8*. As [A-flat] maj. 12/8" with op. 124, No. 13 (Larghetto).

[11] Schumann, *Tagebücher*, vol. 1, p. 413. *Papillons* and *Burle*, butterflies and jests, freely commingled in Schumann's youthful world of fanciful images. One of the sketches for the *Papillons*, op. 2, is titled "Papillon sive Burla"; see Boetticher, op. cit., *Teil I*, p. 59.

[12] See Boetticher, op. cit., *Teil I*, p. 146, and *Teil II*, p. 96.

[13] For a discussion of Schumann's contrapuntal sketches from this period, see Roesner, op. cit., pp. 27–28.

practically ready for publication, whereas the G-Minor *Burla* clearly was not. Moreover, none of the *Burle* in the overview are assigned a G-Minor key. But a list of works completed and works-in-progress from a diary entry of August 1832 includes not only "*Papillons, Liv.2*" [a probable reference to the "XII Burlesken"], but also "*2 Burle.*"[11] The G-Minor *Burla* may well have been one of the latter two. *Burla* surfaces twice more as a title in the immediately following years: first, in connection with a sketch for an unpublished work built on the bass theme of the *Impromptus*, op. 5 (first version, 1833); and second, on a draft for the piece from *Carnaval*, op. 9 (1833–1835), that was ultimately titled *Arlequin*.[12] Thereafter it disappears from Schumann's repertory of imaginative designations.

Internal evidence likewise supports a late summer 1832 date for the G-Minor *Burla*. Beginning on July 12, 1831, Schumann undertook an intense course of study in thoroughbass and counterpoint under the tutelage of Heinrich Dorn.[13] After his lessons with Dorn were suspended in April 1832, Schumann continued to hone his contrapuntal skills using Friedrich Wilhelm Marpurg's *Abhandlung von der Fuge* (1753–1754) and J. S. Bach's *Das wohltemperirte Clavier* as his guides. The G-Minor *Burla* shows the extent to which this academic approach to counterpoint was put to creative use. The A section of the piece unfolds as a series of contrapuntal variations based on the four-note motive in eighths (E flat-D-B flat-G) announced at the outset. In the first phrase (measures 1–4) the motif gives rise to a three-voice stretto pattern, while in the second phrase (measures 4–12) a varied form of the motif (extended to two bars) meets with chromatic countermelodies. The third phrase (measures 12–16) features a combination of the original motif with its inversion, the former being smoothed out into a conjunct figure in the fourth phrase (measures 16–24). Although the B section begins with an apparently new melody in the parallel major over a *Trommelbass* and a G pedal, the inner voice clearly derives from the conjunct figure (measures 16ff.) of the A section. And just as the B section is subtly linked with the previous music, so it also foreshadows the restoration of the original motif in the following section: in measures 33ff., the inner-voice line gradually evolves into the extended variant from measures 4–12. What survives of the A' section introduces one last contrapuntal variation, the original motif serving as an undulating foil to a new, cantus-firmuslike idea in the bass.[14]

Thus, within a very short space indeed Schumann manages to employ an impressive array of sophisticated compositional devices: stretto, inversion, motivic evolution and combination, and cantus-firmus technique. Yet at no point does the composer's erudition call attention to itself. Indeed, we are reminded of Schumann's own words from a review of 1837: "the best fugue is always the one that the public almost takes for a Strauss waltz."[15] Or in the case of our sketch leaf: the best kind of contrapuntal artifice is that which dissolves into a *burla*, a jest. Schumann may not have finished this diminutive piece, but it nonetheless speaks to an important juncture in the evolution of his style. In the G-Minor *Burla* we already sense the move away from the light-hearted, improvisational dance idiom of the *Papillons* and toward the rich, subliminally contrapuntal textures of the great poetic cycles of 1838, the *Kreisleriana*, op. 16, and the *Novelletten*, op. 21.

[14] Boetticher views this idea as a prefiguration of the theme for the *Symphonische Etüden*, whose sketches and drafts occupy the greater part of the nine-page sketchbook that once included the G-Minor *Burla*; see Boetticher, op. cit., *Teil II*, p. 261. Boetticher's claim, however, is not entirely convincing. Though both themes outline descending triadic lines, opus 13 begins with scale steps 8-5-3-1 in (C-sharp) Minor, whereas the quasi-cantus-firmus in the *Burla* traces steps 3-1-5-1 in (B-flat) Major. More compelling than the tenuous melodic resemblance between the themes is the similar use to which they are put. Etudes I, II, and VII of op. 13 all feature the triadic head-motif as a kind of cantus firmus. Hence it is the employment of this contrapuntal technique in the *Symphonische Etüden*, more so than its theme, that resonates with Schumann's practice in the G-Minor *Burla*.

[15] Review of Mendelssohn's Six Preludes and Fugues for Piano, op. 35, in Robert Schumann, *Gesammelte Schriften über Musik und Musiker*, 5th ed., ed. Martin Kreisig (Leipzig: Breitkopf and Härtel, 1914), vol. 1, p. 253.

Igor Stravinsky's *Threni*: Conducting Details

Claudio Spies

[1] Igor Stravinsky, *Threni, id est Lamentations Jeremiae Prophetae* (Boosey & Hawkes, 1958).

THIS SET OF UNDATED PRINTER'S proofs for *Threni*[1] was submitted to Stravinsky's attention in three separate missives (pages 1–27, 28–51, and 52–70, as shown on the initial pages of each) by his London publisher, Boosey & Hawkes. Clearly identified on each successive sheet as first proof, it reveals the corresponding first stage of corrections. Subsequent stages include not only second proofs (which the publisher normally supplied for each work, as evidenced by those I have seen for the *Fanfare for a New Theater*, *Introitus*, and *Requiem Canticles*, the last of which I was asked to correct under the composer's supervision, with his express permission for every correction suggested), but a second edition of the score, printed nearly seven years after the first, in May 1965, incorporating a great many changes in barring and eliminating some errors. Although the present set of proofs contains the scribbled, underlined indication "IS's final corrections" on the top left-hand corner of the first page, such are nowhere to be found—at least, not in Stravinsky's handwriting. All corrections on these proof sheets are in one handwriting only, and I assume it to be that of Leopold Spinner, a composer who worked for Boosey & Hawkes during those years. (I had some correspondence with him over the *Requiem Canticles* proofs in 1966–1967; his small, spare writing can be recognized from the markings on *those* proofs as well as from his signature.) I do not believe it would have been unusual for Stravinsky to have left the correction of proofs to others; he was understandably impatient with the often thoughtless errors found in all proofs and therefore sought to spare himself the concomitant annoyance. The proofs at hand certainly show an abundance of such errors; they are in this sense not out of the ordinary. Among their more distinctive traits, however, is the frequent instruction for omitting staves, if their only occupants are measures of rests. (See pages 11 and 15 of the score, for instance; all but three of the staves on the lower system of page 11 are eliminated. On the proof sheet of page 15, the proofreader's instruction concerning the numerical indication for measure 124 is to leave it "exactly where it is in glorious isolation"; it is surrounded by a "hole" left by three omitted staves.) When Stravinsky's scores began to exhibit such typographical empty spaces—i.e., all his orchestral scores from *Threni* on—it was supposed that he had taken his cue from certain graphemically quirky scores of Stockhausen, published by Universal Edition. Perhaps; but Stravinsky's working manuscripts had almost always been written on unlined paper for which he provided whatever number of staves he needed, and only wherever he needed them, by means of a staff-line-drawing implement of his own design.[2]

Threni stands out among Stravinsky's compositions of the late 1950s by virtue of its elaborate interweaving of small formal schemes, adding up to large, continuous movements, as well as its predominance of unaccompanied choral and solo vocal music, and—in that connection—its frequent canonic writing. There is no way in which the publication, in 1957, of Ernst Křenek's *Lamentatio Jeremiae Prophetae*[3] (written in 1941 for mixed chorus—in up to nine parts—a cappella) could have remained unnoticed by Stravinsky; he was evidently stimulated by Křenek's piece to try his own hand at setting parts of *Lamentations* in Vulgate Latin, to employ canonic means of continuity, to use unaccompanied voices and—not least—to use an "antiquarian" type of vocal notation without bar lines and in large note values. Yet it must be emphasized that any notion of direct influence by Křenek's work ends at the merest surface. Both pieces may share, above all, certain graphemic features in notation, but their musical identities are unmistakably distinct and utterly different from one another. (Even the device of hexachordal transposition-rotation, employed in characteristic ways by Stravinsky from *Threni* on, is illustrated by Křenek in his prefatory remarks, but employed for totally dissimilar purposes in his *Lamentatio*, as though it were an offshoot of Renaissance modality.)

The peculiarity of unbarred notation of large note values in *Threni* (as found, for example, in the *Canon a 4, duplex*, from measure 189 on page 25 to the end of page 27) had a certain

[2] See Vera Stravinsky and Robert Craft, *Stravinsky in Pictures and Documents* (New York: Simon and Schuster, 1978): pl. 12, 22, and 24, following p. 400.

[3] Bärenreiter-Ausgabe 3648.

precedent in Stravinsky's reduction for two pianos of a segment of *Agon*,[4] in which he assigns different metrical designs to each instrument: the "Bransle Double" is notated in 3/2 in Piano I, and in 8/4 (3+2+3) in Piano II between measures 336 and 352, and again between measures 365 and 372. Bar lines are shared equidistantly, inasmuch as the polymetric design remains constant; yet in the corresponding "Bransle de Poitou" of the orchestral score, all the music in those passages is written in 3/2, in accordance with the demands of sheer practicability in performance. The difference between the two modes of notation highlights the illusory aspect of the many places that were notated without barring in *Threni*. Even before the first performance, conducted in Venice by Stravinsky, on September 23, 1958, the practical necessities of rehearsing the chorus and six soloists would have compelled him to realize that beating only the *tactus* (i.e., successive downbeats) in unbarred passages would make it virtually impossible for singers to count reliably, as well as for the chorus (and orchestra) to make correct entrances. Whether before or during the preparations for the Venetian premiere, or after it, the fact is that by January 1959, in time for the rehearsals, performance, and recording sessions in New York, Stravinsky had written in bar lines for almost all previously unbarred places (the sole exception being the "Monodia" in the first section of the *Querimonia*: pages 20–21; measures 167, 169, and 172). Robert Craft, who conducted and prepared that performance, took these new barrings into account. I transferred them into my own score while attending rehearsals and the performance at the time; they correspond for the most part to the barrings incorporated into the second edition of 1965—except for several markings made in my score by the composer, and therefore not generally known.

Since the first printing of the score is dated September 1958, it is easy to conjecture that it was, by the time of the premiere, simply too late to undertake the changes required by the practical considerations described above. Ideally, the first edition's plates should then have been scrapped, and an entirely new engraving would consequently have made a more presentably correct, ultimate edition feasible. Even after the seven-odd years it took the publisher to issue the second edition, the now included dotted bar lines and the almost invisibly added parenthetic time signatures are neither very clear nor sufficiently well-spaced, and no provision was ever made for the obvious need to renumber measures. (The amount of time needlessly wasted during rehearsals, in specifying which of the segments defined by dotted bar lines and pertaining to one "mega-measure" might be meant would probably be equal to having to rehearse each "mega-measure" *entirely* each time a particular note or brief passage should require some work!) It is useless, however, to speculate as to the decent-looking, practical edition that might have been—or, indeed, on the number of good performances this particularly unnoticed composition might consequently have enjoyed. We shall have to continue to make do with the poor one at hand— and with its never corrected, wrongly aligned attacks in measure 392, which should be located halfway through the spoken sixteenth-note quintolet, after the final syllable of the word "Domine."

Stravinsky's markings in my score are concerned with conducting. Of the two that are not reflected in the dotted-line barrings added in the second edition, the one on page 52 indicates the division of the 10/8 bars: into 4/8 + 3/4 (measures 323–326). But the markings on page 16, over measures 130–131, are especially curious.

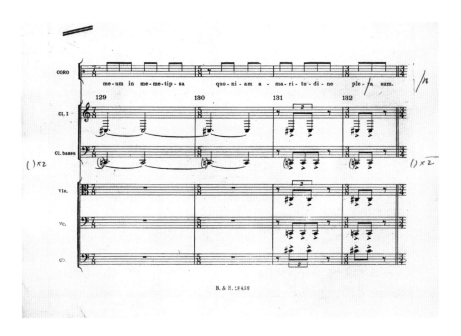

For measure 130, the 1 + 4 bespeaks the rhythm of the parlando chorus, although it contradicts the 3 + 2 in the clarinet's and bass clarinet's notation. The next bar's similar indication is in keeping with the instrumental rhythms, ensuring a cleanly accented attack on the second eighth; yet it contradicts the 2 + 3 in the choral rhythm. The square horizontal brackets starting over the 4s in Stravinsky's markings signify the right hand. The preceding 1s are to be beaten with the left (!)—which is bound to remind one of the story about a "famous" conductor who, when confronted by the second movement of Tchaikovsky's *Pathétique*, decided he would beat it this way. Absurd though this may seem, I recall quite clearly that Stravinsky told me, with a big grin, that it really works very well. (Unfortunately, I did not attend the recording sessions to see him demonstrate that assurance.)

The other conducting marks in my score, which I copied from Stravinsky's, refer to subdivisions of measures and to beating units that are frequently diminutions of the metronomic. The opening measure of the piece is of particular interest in this regard, in view of its rhythmic-metric makeup. If beaten in "straight" 4, the danger seemed to consist in the final eighth-note dyads not to be articulated with the same dynamics as the two previous ones, on account of the metric displacement. Stravinsky's instruction reads that the measure be beaten as 2/4 + 4/8. (My suggestion, in a letter written a few weeks later to a former student and colleague,[5] was that the measure be divided into two 3s, with the first one beaten as quarter-quarter-eighth and the second simply as 3/8. The advantage— or, as I see it now, the danger—is that the last F-sharp will be given a down-beat. The danger would lie in its being thereby more accented than the previous F-sharp.)

Indications pertaining to conventional divisions of 5s and 7s need not here be detailed—they are notated merely in order to avoid conducting slips. It is of some interest, in that connection, that the metronomics (i.e., counting units) are frequently subdivided: at measures 73 and 80, for instance, the tempo is given as quarter=60, yet the conducting indication is for eighth=120. Moreover, the triplet rhythm at the end of measure 81 is provided with a little triangular reminder marking (although the equivalence of triplet eighths to three

[5] Michael Senturia, conductor of the University Orchestra and member of the Faculty in the Department of Music at the University of California at Berkeley from 1962 to 1992.

eighth notes across the bar line is neither arcane nor difficult); but it is perhaps there because of the increased instrumentation (compared to the similar equivalence between measures 75 and 76).

Stravinsky's metric indications for the "Monodia" (measure 167) are confined to pinpointing built-in units of 3/8. He described these recurring interpolations as "joints."

De
ELEGIA TERTIA
1. QUERIMONIA

The unbarred heading for *De Elegia Quinta*, measure 384, is to be conducted in two large measures: 7/4 and 9/4, respectively, divided into 4 + 3, and 3 + 3 + 3.

The included metric indications for measure 178 et seq. are elucidated by Stravinsky in my score as follows: the measure at 178 (2/4 + 1/8) is to be beaten in 3; the next two measures of 5/4 are both 2 + 3. The telling admonition here was that larger triplets are never to be beaten as triplets, but always in the context (as here) of the prevailing quarter unit (i.e., = circa 56; see measure 166), or of the half-note unit, as in the continuation of the "Canon duplex" on pages 26–27 (measures 191 et seq.). The seeming contradiction between the nonbeaten triplets of these passages and the little triangular instruction in measure 81 is soon resolved, obviously.

The opening of *Sensus Spei*, measure 194, is preceded by Stravinsky's recommendation of three preparatory quarter beats; measure 194 is then taken as the fourth quarter of an imagined 4/4 measure in the new tempo. The reason for this is found in the necessity both of alerting the performers to oncoming eighth-note motion, and of avoiding a longer pause between sections of *De Elegia Tertia*. Soon after this, the measure of 20/8 (measure 197) is fanciful in accommodating the presence of double whole notes, but insufficiently clear in its notation for the conductor. Perhaps because of this, Stravinsky beat it as two bars in 4, after the model of measure 196 (which is notated, and beaten as, 3 + 2 + 3 + 2). Here, however, the 4 beats correspond to one bar of 11/8 and another of 9/8. Robert Craft preferred to treat measure 197 as 5/8 + 8/8 + 7/8, while observing the notated groupings. In keeping with the instruction concerning the large triplet in measure 178, the time signature in measure 200 means: beat 3 (i.e., 3/8 + 2/4), so that the triplet will fall neatly into a submeasure.

My score contains a purely ad hoc correction (or emendation) by Stravinsky for the little canon for sopranos and altos in measures 247–248: the composer first wanted the sopranos to double altos on their initial middle D, for needed emphasis. The repeated syllable, as well as the ensuing octave leap (which would likely have caused excessive stress on the upper D) then prompted Hugh Ross, the chorus's conductor, to suggest that the tenors be enlisted to articulate the opening middle D eighth note, and so it was done. As for the canon's ending, with its *più f* and accents, Stravinsky had the altos iterate their F-F-sharp, and extend the word's third syllable in order to coincide on the sopranos' final notes. (This evidently represents the kind of local touch-up that should not be equated to a change in the score.)

Unlike the 10/8 and 20/8 of measure 196–197, and in view of the metronomic notated by Stravinsky (i.e., eighth-note = 180), measures 323–324 are beaten as 4/8 + 3/4—a design that supports the clarinets' accented attacks and that does not interfere with the vocal phrasing; the syncopations are not lost.

Lastly, the *sul ponticello* required for the string chords at measures 322, 328, 336, 344, 348, 353, 359, 367–368, and 377 elicited Milton Babbitt's and my suggestion that they be played so that the attacks would be as specified, but that immediately after those attacks the bows would all be moved nearer the fingerboard, so as to allow the simultaneities to resonate properly. Otherwise, these simultaneities would sound indeterminate, squeaky, or like unintentional harmonics. Our suggestion, happily, was taken.

The detailed list compiled above was taken from rehearsals and a performance—all of it now almost forty years ago. A conclusion to be drawn from virtually every item mentioned on that list is that during those intervening four decades the nature of orchestral capability has undergone remarkable changes in this country. (I am referring, naturally, to those still relatively few orchestras that have been given a modicum of opportunity by their conductors to become acquainted, at least,—if not yet really familiar—with the kind of twentieth-century repertoire of which *Threni* might be classed as an instance.) It is obvious, therefore, that the precautionary nature of many of Stravinsky's conducting indications and admonitions was called for by the circumstances surrounding short-order performances (i.e., with a very small number of scheduled rehearsals, and with a pickup ensemble of orchestral players) at the time. Yet it is no less evident that, given a marked increase in the level of orchestral capability, such conducting requirements no longer obtain, or no longer apply to the same degree. Stravinsky's notion, for example, of actually beating eighth notes in a rapid 3/8 (as in measure 29) seems, now, quite unnecessary, possibly even confusing, and it harks back to an earlier age in which a change (no matter how temporary) in counting units from quarters to eighth notes *was* novel. (Stravinsky's conducting habits go back farther in this regard than even *Jeu de Cartes* (1936) whose 3/8 interpolations (at rehearsal number 9, for instance, or at 1 measure before 10) I clearly remember him always to have conducted as a very rapid, tiny 3 — at eighth-note=216!) So, if quarters (rather than eighth notes) are beaten in the 4/8 measures preceding measure 29, then that measure is surely to be beaten in 1. Similarly, the carefully marked triplet triangle in the second half of measure 81 would not in the least need to be beaten out; it would simply be the second beat of a 2/4 bar, and the attendant equivalence across the succeeding bar line would be inferred easily enough to enable the conductor to beat the 3/8 measure in 1, by the same token, rather than in Stravinsky's 3. I would think, in fact, that the proper preparation of a performance of *Threni* would, for the orchestra, nowadays take a third—or certainly half—the time it took in 1959, and it is very likely that the appended performance would be a good deal better into the bargain.

Germaine Tailleferre's
Concerto pour Piano et 12 Instruments

Michael O'Brien

GERMAINE TAILLEFERRE (1892–1983), distinguished not merely as the only woman in the circle of composers known as *Les Six*, but as a twentieth-century French composer who "builds a bridge between the contemporary mode and classical tradition,"[1] dedicated her "Concerto pour Piano et 12 Instruments" to the great Parisian patroness of avant-garde music, Princess Edmond of Polignac, whose husband was a composer of some note. Tailleferre participated in the musical evenings at the salon of the princess where one could hear the pianist Artur Rubinstein and the music of Igor Stravinsky. On various occasions she performed piano reductions of Stravinsky's *Petrushka*, *Rite of Spring*, and *Firebird*.

At the end of 1923 the princess commissioned Tailleferre to write the concerto. The composition was begun at the Polignac's family residence and completed on January 26, 1924, in Bouzaréah, Algeria. Premiered on December 3, 1924, in London by the British Women's Symphony Orchestra under the direction of Gwynneth Kimpton, with Alfred Cortot as soloist, the concerto was well received, and Tailleferre, who was present at the premiere, was hailed as progressive by the critics. Subsequent performances were directed by Serge Koussevitzky.

The manuscript consists of seventy-nine pages (seventy-seven pages of music), each measuring 24 cm. by 32 cm. The dedication to Princess Edmond of Polignac appears on the second page. On the cover of the manuscript is the remark "pour Monsieur Cortot," written in Tailleferre's hand. It is certain that the manuscript was once part of the Alfred Cortot collection. In fact, a letter from Tailleferre to Cortot states that the concerto was being sent to him via the publisher Heugel. Cortot's green monogram is stamped throughout the manuscript.

[1] Claude Rostand, *La musique française contemporaine* (Paris: Presses Universitaires de France, 1952), p. 43.

[2] See Albi Rosenthal, "Alfred Cortot as Collector of Music," *Music and Bibliography: Essays in Honour of Alec Hyatt King*, ed. Oliver Neighbour (New York: K. G. Saur, 1980), pp. 206–14.

[3] "'C'est de la musique honnête!' Une telle appréciation, venant de lui qui détestait la musique des autres, constituait un encouragement fabuleux." See Brigitta Duhme-Hildebrand, *Die französische Musikerin Germaine Tailleferre (1892–1983): Leben und Werk unter dem Aspekt des Vergnügens an der Musik* (Ph.D. diss., University of Köln, 1991), p. 53.

Cortot was a champion of the new French piano music of his day, as well as a systematic collector. He meticulously cataloged his substantial musical library. The autograph manuscripts in the collection were acquired by Robert Owen Lehman in the spring of 1962.[2] Many of these were placed on deposit at the Pierpont Morgan Library in New York. Tailleferre's concerto was subsequently sold for Lehman by the manuscript dealer J. A. Stargardt. Ultimately the piece found its home in the Moldenhauer Archives.

In her memoirs Tailleferre included the following comment by Stravinsky concerning the concerto: "It is virtuous music!" Tailleferre added that his evaluation was extraordinary praise, considering it came from a person who abhorred the music of others.[3]

Aurelio de la Vega's
The Magic Labyrinth:
Reminiscences of the Composer

"YOUR MUSIC IS PROGRESSIVELY turning into painting,"
exclaimed Hans Burkhardt, the Swiss-born painter who lived
in Los Angeles for many decades until his death, and who in
his old age received the honors, the glories and the
international recognition and critical acclaim due him many
years before. The times were the early 1970s, and the artist
was looking through some of my scores from 1965 to 1972.

What he said was true: painting being my second artistic
devotion, and having even exhibited in my youth some of my
cubistlike renditions of forms and colors as I saw them in Cuba,
my native land, I was well aware that my aural perceptions were
being influenced by geometric designs in the placing of entries
of instruments, or in the way densities were handled, or even in
the manner a particular musical phrase was shaped.

In 1974 I decided to go a step further, and created (painted?) a
score totally conceived from a pictorial point of view. The
design consisted of a single page where several musical
fragments—some totally delineated as to pitches, rhythmic
configuration phrasing, and dynamics, others merely suggested
as areas of improvisation, with multiple directional
possibilities—created a satisfactory pictorial image, playable,
but at the same time capable of projecting its own visual
architecture. To complete the validity of the adventure, the
score was then colored by hand. The musical rendering of the
piece was of undetermined length, and the instrumental and
vocal forces to be employed were also not specified. Both
parameters were to be determined by the performer, or
conductor, offering a different version of the work with each
performance. On the other hand, standing on its own artistic
merits, the score could be matted, framed, and hung on a wall
to be enjoyed as a work of art, as a true visual expression, as a
real rendition of shapes, colors, and forms.

I created six other scores based on the same idea between the end of 1974 and early 1977. Thus, I achieved the transition from music to painting, and vice versa. Before returning to the "normal" writing of music, I attempted one more level of exploration. While staying on two occasions at the Cranbrook Academy of Art as composer-in-residence for visits of three weeks each, I created three silk screens, called *The Cranbrook Triptych*, which, although using various pentagrams as links between several visual elements, were not "playable" anymore. The visual had totally taken over the aural.

It was time to return home. 1977 saw the composition of *Adiós*, for large orchestra—a regular musical work of vast proportions with no more evident visual elements, no more colors and no more philosophic considerations beyond the rendition of the spectrum of pure sound.

The Magic Labyrinth—composed in 1975, commissioned by the sculptress and art patron Gloria Morris—is the fourth of the seven graphic scores mentioned above. It has been interpreted many times, and, as far as I know, seventeen instrumental versions of it, two vocal-instrumental ones and one purely vocal one have been played and sung. The number of instruments and vocalists involved in these versions ranged from one to eight.

I met Hans and Rosaleen Moldenhauer for the first time in the autumn of 1969, after two years of phones calls and correspondence. Over subsequent years our friendship grew. Hans soon asked for some of my manuscripts, letters, and musical sketches, to be included in the Moldenhauer Collection, later the Moldenhauer Archives.

The Moldenhauers were also lovers of art. Among other things, I recall an impressive oil by Hildegard Jone—Webern's ever present muse—which hung on one of the walls of the family room in their home in Spokane; and I will always remember the meticulous descriptions of the various paintings and sculptures in my own art collection which Rosaleen recited for Hans so that he could "see" them.

In early 1978, I sent a complete hand-painted set of my seven

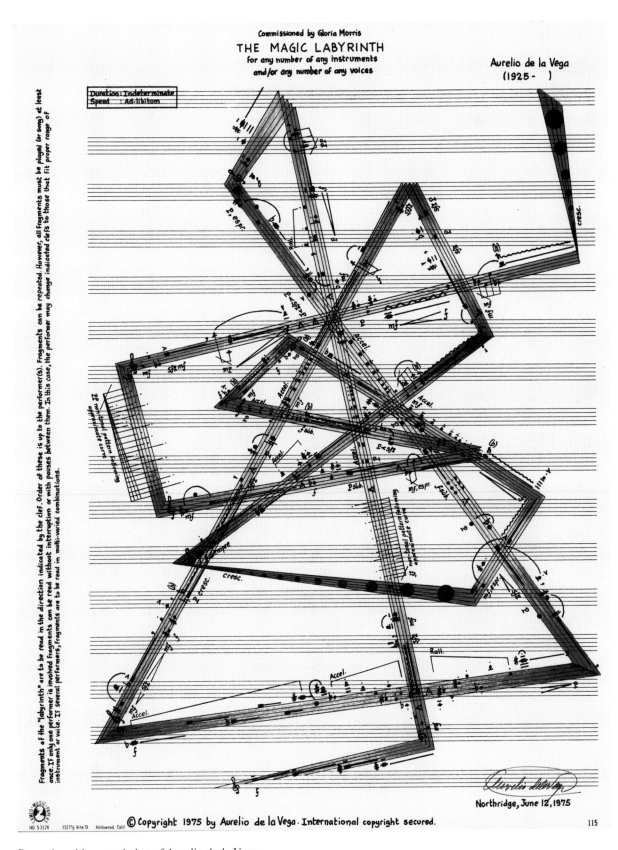

·433·

graphic scores to Spokane. Rosaleen was particularly fond of *The Magic Labyrinth*. She loved the intricacies of this "painted composition," as she called it, and the way the shapes and colors intervened in the conceptual canvas of *this* labyrinth, and she asked me about the ways this particular work could be musically rendered. I explained how at first whoever decided to play the piece had to determine what instruments or human voices were to be employed, and how a "map" had to be prepared—which usually consisted of a series of pages depicting where the parameters of time and dynamics of fragments from the score were to be realized (and in what direction), and where areas of improvisation would appear, as well as indicating the approximate curves that the instruments or human voices should follow. The "map" pages would also contain arrows for entrances and for the gestures of the conductor, as well as for the duration of the sections and the whole piece. I told them how this type of music was in danger of becoming a mere chaotic stupidity, or at best a circus act, in the hands of an uncreative conductor, or when played by instrumentalists or sung by singers who were not respectful of the philosophy behind the aleatoric musical semantics. Finally, I also conveyed to them that in my own experience when putting together and conducting a given version of one of the seven works comprising my graphic adventure, I had observed that good musical results were obtained by using one or two instrumentalists or singers, and optimum ones when employing four to seven interpreters, but that anarchy would occur when ten or more were used. These were pieces involving form, counterpoint, vertical coincidences, and instrumental color that were to be shaped in the same manner that a sculptor contours his clay, chisels a stone, or welds metals together. Therefore, besides seriousness of purpose among those taking part in the playing of the visual forms, close communication through eye contact and through the gestures of the conductor's hands was needed among all participants—intimacy being lost when big groups attempted to interpret the graphics musically.

One year before Rosaleen's death I presented to the Moldenhauers a small monoprint with watercolor touches by Hans Burkhardt, an item which I believe has become part of the Archives. The cycle was now complete: two dear friends, both with "Hans" as a given name, witnessed the evolution of my musical graphology which produced the graphic scores of the 1970s, both were deeply interested in my music, both shared with me some world premieres of works of mine and both very much enjoyed *The Magic Labyrinth*.

Giuseppe Verdi's *Attila*

Philip Gossett

IN MAY OF 1830 TWO YOUNG Russian musicians appeared in Milan: they were the composer Mikhail Ivanovich Glinka and the twenty-year-old tenor Nicolai Ivanov. They soon developed connections to musicians throughout the city (including the composers Bellini and Donizetti and the publisher Ricordi); later they traveled south, to Rome and ultimately Naples. By 1833, however, Glinka felt that he had absorbed what Italy could offer and left the country, first for a season of instruction in counterpoint with Siegfried Dehn in Berlin, then for his homeland and his future role as the father of Russian opera.

Ivanov, on the other hand, remained. Italianizing his name as Nicola Ivanoff, he made his debut at the Teatro San Carlo of Naples on July 6, 1832, as Percy in Donizetti's *Anna Bolena*, part of a cast that included Giuseppina Ronzi De Begnis as Anna and Luigi Lablache as Enrico. Ivanoff may well have returned to Milan later that summer, but by the end of the year he was back in Naples, where he participated in performances of operas by Pacini and Bellini (alternating with Giovanni David as Elvino in *La sonnambula*). Most important, it was Ivanoff who sang the role of Arnoldo in Rossini's *Guillaume Tell* when it had its first Neapolitan performances, beginning on April 7, 1833.[1]

It is not certain when Gioachino Rossini first met Ivanoff, but it was perhaps later in 1833, when the tenor took the part of Giannetto in a performance of *La gazza ladra* at the Théâtre Italien of Paris. During the next few years he sang frequently in Paris and London. He portrayed the Gondoliere in the premiere of Donizetti's *Marino Falliero* at the Théâtre Italien (March 12, 1835). Indeed, along with Labalache and the great tenor Giovanni Rubini, he was one of the soloists in the funeral service for Bellini on October 2, 1835, at Les Invalides. Rossini remained in Paris until November 1836, when, with his

[1] The spring season of 1833 in Naples also featured singers such as Maria Malibran, Domenico Reina, and Luigi Lablache.

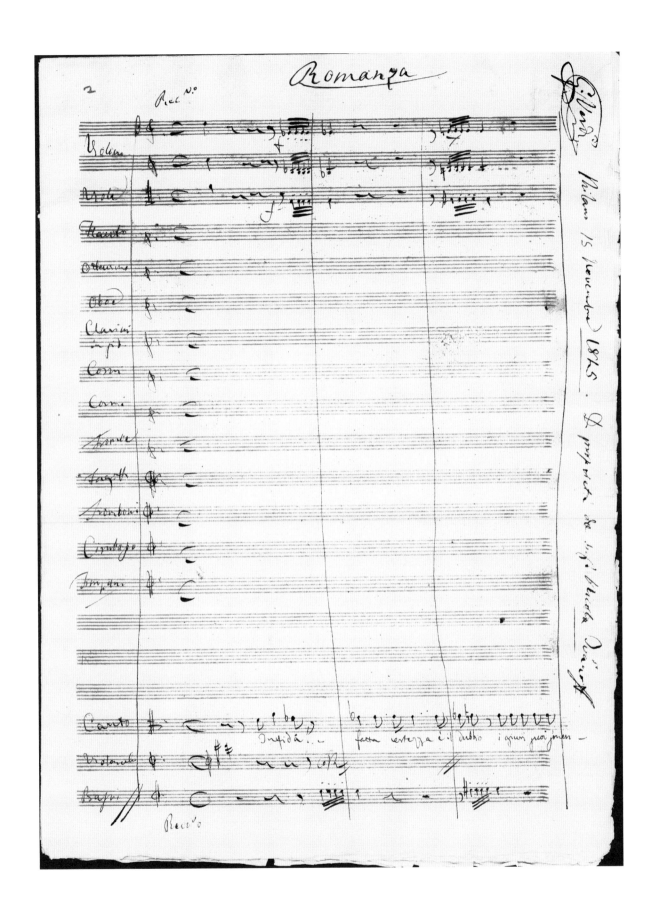

Romanza

·437·

2 In a letter to Felice Romani of December 3, 1846, Rossini wrote: "Dearest friend: Ivanoff, whom I love like a son, will be the bearer of this letter." See *Lettere di G. Rossini, raccolte e annotate*, ed. G. Mazzatinti and F. and G. Manis (Florence, 1902), p. 162.

3 *Lettere di G. Rossini*, pp. 96–97. The cabaletta was probably written for a duet, as we learn from Rossini's letter, which begins: "Dearest friend: With this same post you will find the cabaletta I received from Mercadante, which seems to me very sentimental; if the duet does not feel too long it would even be possible to repeat it." Rossini apparently also asked Mercadante to reorchestrate a romanza: see his letter to Mercadante of March 16, 1840, ibid., p. 97.

4 For further information about this commission, see the introduction to *Ernani*, ed. Claudio Gallico, in *The Works of Giuseppe Verdi*, ser. I, vol. 5 (Chicago and Milan, 1985), p. xxii. The original letter is in *Carteggi verdiani*, 4 vols, ed. Alessandro Luzio (Rome, 1935–47), vol. IV, pp. 32–33. The translation is from Gallico.

pension from the French government finally assured, he returned to Bologna.

By the time Ivanoff made his way back to Italy in 1840, there was already a very close, even quasipaternal relationship between Rossini and the singer.[2] One of the principal ways Rossini favored his protégé was by inviting composers to prepare new music for Ivanoff to insert into revivals of their operas. There is already evidence for such activity early in 1840, when Ivanoff sang as "primo tenore" at the Teatro alla Pergola of Florence. He took part in performances of Mercadante's *I due illustri rivali* (March 20, 1840), and for that occasion Rossini obtained from Mercadante a new cabaletta for Ivanoff, which Rossini sent to the singer with a letter of March 3, 1840.[3] Rossini also arranged for Ivanoff to take the role of Arnoldo when *Guillaume Tell* was given first in Bologna on October 3, 1840, as *Rodolfo di Sterlinga*, and it was to Ivanoff that Rossini turned when the first Italian performance of his *Stabat Mater* took place in the same city, directed by Donizetti, on March 18, 1842.

Mercadante was not the only composer Rossini approached on behalf of Ivanoff. In 1844 the Russian tenor was scheduled to sing the title role in Verdi's *Ernani* to open the forthcoming carnival season at the Teatro Ducale of Parma. On that occasion (December 26, 1844) he unveiled a major aria for Ernani, with chorus, "Odi il voto, o grande Iddio," replacing the original duet finale of the second act. The new composition was prepared for Ivanoff by Verdi himself, at Rossini's instigation. In a letter of November 28, 1844, Rossini sent Verdi the poetry for this new scene, which he had commissioned from Francesco Maria Piave, the original librettist of *Ernani*, adding:[4]

> In accordance with our agreement I enclose the poetry Piave has written for *Ernani*. You are so talented that I am sure you can adorn it with beautiful music and thus make my good Ivanoff happy ... My dear Verdi, please steal a few minutes from *Giovanna* to bring joy to Ivanoff.

Verdi went to work and apparently completed the commission in about a week's time.

Ivanoff actually sought the composer's advice about performing the aria, paying him a visit early in December in Milan, where Verdi was engaged in preparing his *Giovanna d'Arco* (which was to have its premiere at the Teatro alla Scala on February 15, 1845). The public success of the new aria was everything Ivanoff had hoped, and on December 26, 1844, Rossini wrote to thank Verdi and to pay him for his labors:[5]

> I was unable to write you before today to thank you enormously for what you have done for my friend Ivanoff. He is delighted to possess the beautiful piece by you that obtained for him such a brilliant success in Parma.
>
> I enclose here a check for 1,500 Austrian lire, which you should consider not a payment for your piece, which deserves so much more, but rather a simple token of Ivanoff's gratitude. I am very much obliged to you, whom I esteem and love.

This aria is, in fact, one of the most elaborate of the so-called "nondefinitive revisions" in the early operas of Verdi.[6]

It was not the last time Rossini turned to Verdi on behalf of Ivanoff. Verdi's *Attila* had its first performance at the Teatro La Fenice of Venice on March 17, 1846. When Ivanoff contracted to sing the tenor role of Foresto in a performance of the work in Trieste during the autumn of that same year, Rossini wrote from Bologna to his younger colleague on July 21, 1846, again begging a favor for his friend, who carried the letter directly to Verdi:[7]

> Just as the enamored touch of the first kiss of his lovely hand calls for a second, so Ivanoff, bearer of this letter, remembering the first precious embrace you gave him by composing for him a magnificent aria, which brought him such honor, has come to ask you for a second embrace, that is, a second piece, which will certainly bring him supreme gratification. I was the mediator for the first meeting, and I am pleased to be so now. I beg you to accede to the wishes of my good friend, who merits all your compliance, just as I too, for the love and esteem I bear you, merit something. To work, then, my illustrious colleague, and gain new rights to the gratitude of Rossini.

[5] *Carteggi verdiani*, vol. II, p. 346. The translation is from Gallico, op. cit., p. xxii. The autograph of the new Aria is preserved in the Mary Flagler Cary Music Collection at the Pierpont Morgan Library, New York.

[6] See David Lawton and David Rosen, "Verdi's Non-definitive Revisions: The Early Operas," in *Atti del III° congresso internazionale di studi verdiani (Milano, Piccola Scala, 12–17 giugno 1972)* (Parma, 1974), pp. 189–237.

[7] *Carteggi verdiani*, vol. IV, p. 33.

[8] The original text is printed in Lawton and Rosen, op. cit., pp. 236–37. This translation is based on theirs (see pp. 206–7).

[9] Emanuele Muzio, Verdi's student, in a letter of September 10, 1846, to the composer's father-in-law, Antonio Barezzi, reports: "*Attila* is being given in Trieste; I don't know whether you are aware that the Maestro, at the behest of Rossini, has prepared an aria for Ivanoff to insert into Attila. If you don't know, I'm informing you, and the aria has already been written and sent to Bologna, and perhaps within the week Rossini will send a payment." *Giuseppe Verdi nelle lettere di Emanuele Muzio ad Antonio Barezzi*, ed. Luigi Agostino Garibaldi (Milan, 1931), p. 269.

[10] The text of the new Romanza does not appear in the libretto printed for the Trieste performances. See Lawton and Rosen, op. cit., p. 207; the libretto text from Turin is reproduced on p. 234.

By this time, Verdi was losing patience with requests of this kind. It would not be long before he refused them altogether as a matter of course. But he did not yet feel that he could refuse Rossini, and so Verdi, in turn, penned this wonderful note from Milan to his librettist Francesco Maria Piave on August 10:[8]

> I need a favor: a Romanza with recitative and two quatrains; the subject will be a lover who is moaning about the infidelity of his beloved (old hat!). Write me 5 or 6 lines of recitative, then two quatrains of *ottonari*; there should be a masculine ending every other line, because it's easier to set that way…

> Make sure they're pathetic and tearful: have that imbecile of a lover say that he would have given up his share of paradise and that she rewarded him with… Horns… Long live those horns: bless them!… If I could, I'd like to give them out myself all the time!

By early September Ivanoff had his Romanza, and the opera was a great success when performed in Trieste that autumn.[9]

Ivanoff sang the Romanza several times. The last documented occasion was at the Teatro Regio of Turin in 1849, for which the text, "Sventurato! alla mia vita / Sol conforto era l'amor," actually appears in the printed libretto.[10] No edition of the music was ever printed, however, and after 1849 all contemporary references to this piece cease.

Not until the 1960s did the autograph manuscript of Verdi's Romanza resurface. At that time it was in the hands of the London manuscript dealer Albi Rosenthal, who was unwilling either to discuss its provenance or to make it available to scholars. He, in turn, sold the manuscript to Hans and Rosaleen Moldenhauer, from whose collection it has now passed to the Library of Congress. The "lost" Romanza for Ivanoff has finally reappeared, and its reappearance is a major gain for Verdi scholars and Verdi performers.

The manuscript consists of a fascicle of four bifolios in upright format (24 cm. by 32 cm.), notated on folios 1 through 8r (folio

8v is blank). At the top of the first page Verdi entitled the piece "Romanza," and in the right margin he signed and dated the manuscript: "G. Verdi. Milano 15 Novembre 1845 [*sic*]. Di proprietà da Sig. Nicola Ivanoff." The dating of this dedication is peculiar. It could not have been written during the composition of the Romanza, which was completed between the end of August and the beginning of September 1846. More likely, Verdi did not originally write a dedication on the Romanza;[11] Ivanoff, returning to Milan after the conclusion of the Trieste season, must have asked the composer to add one on November 15, 1846. The "1845" indication, which seems quite clear in the autograph, was surely a slip of the pen.

The Romanza begins with a short scene that picks up in measure 35 of the original scene for Foresto at the opening of Act III of *Attila*. (The first chord in this manuscript, a D-Major chord in first inversion, is identical with the parallel chord in the original scene.) Foresto's text, which is slightly different from the text printed in the Turin libretto, reads as follows:[12]

Infida!…

Fatta certezza è il dubbio…
I giuri suoi smentiva!… oh tradimento!
Straziata dal dolor l'alma mi sento!…
Sventurato! alla mia vita
Sol conforto era l'amor!
Sventurato! or disparita
Ogni gioia è dal mio cor!
Ah!.. perché le diede il cielo
Tanto fiore di beltà;
Se ad un cor dovea far velo
Nido reo d'infedeltà.

Piave's verses follow Verdi's request with precision, both in terms of their structure (two quatrains of *ottonari*, with a masculine ending every other line) and their poetic content ("pathetic and tearful: have that imbecile of a lover say that he would have given up his share of paradise and that she rewarded him with... Horns").

The layout of the score and orchestration is typical of Verdi's work in the mid-1840s and is perfectly consistent with the

[11] Or, more important, had not granted "proprietà" to Ivanoff, that is, exclusive rights to the Romanza. This exclusivity meant that Ivanoff alone had the right to sing the piece or use it as he saw fit.

[12] Punctuation, which is lacking for the most part in Verdi's autograph, has been integrated where necessary from the Turin libretto (see Lawton and Rosen, op. cit., p. 234). The most important differences in text between the printed libretto and the autograph are the following: 1) the words "I giuri suoi smentiva!" are not included in the Turin libretto; 2) the phrase "Nido reo" used by Verdi as the last verse becomes "Alma rea" in the Turin libretto.

remainder of *Attila*. On the twenty-stave paper the lowest three staves are occupied by "Canto" (i.e., Foresto), cellos, and double basses. The upper three staves are reserved for the violins and violas, followed by one flute, one piccolo, two oboes, two clarinets in B-flat, two pairs of horns, two trumpets, two bassoons, three trombones, cimbasso, and timpani.[13] While the scena and the beginning of the Romanza are scored for strings, the entire orchestra gradually joins the texture as the music approaches its climax, then leaves the strings alone as the sound dies away ("morendo") at the conclusion.

The masterful Romanza, an Andante in triple meter, begins in A-flat Minor with a beautiful legato phrase over a simple staccato and pizzicato accompaniment in the strings. As the

[13] Verdi specifies the tuning of the pairs of horns (in E-flat and A-flat), the trumpets (in E-flat), and timpani (in A-flat) on folio 2v, at the beginning of the Romanza proper.

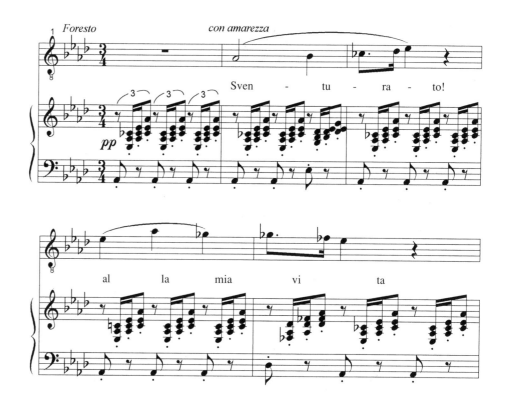

first quatrain concludes, Verdi brings the music to the relative major, then addresses the tonic again, now in major, as Foresto begins the second quatrain.

The line continues to swell as the voice ascends to a high B flat before descending for the conclusion of the phrase. Verdi

repeats this phrase, but he reorchestrates it (introducing, in particular, a pizzicato figure for the cellos) and syncopates the ascent to B flat. The voice concludes, fortissimo, on the high A flat, but the note must be held for three measures, "diminuendo" and then "morendo," while the orchestra falls away, leading to a reprise of the opening string figuration, with "morendo" chords in the first horn and the bassoons. It is a lovely effect, and daunting to any but a first-rate singer.

Ivanoff must have been delighted.

Anton Webern's Six Pieces for Orchestra, op. 6, Arrangement for Chamber Ensemble

Felix Meyer

ARNOLD SCHOENBERG FIRST DISCLOSED his plan for a private society devoted to the performance of contemporary music on June 30, 1918, at a meeting with friends and students in his Mödling home. The project, whose immediate incentive had been a series of public rehearsals of Schoenberg's *Chamber Symphony* op. 9 (in June 1918), took shape very rapidly; it led to the foundation of the Society for Private Musical Performances (*Verein für musikalische Privataufführungen*) less than half a year later, on December 6, 1918. This quick establishment of an organization which in many ways stood in stark opposition to Vienna's "official" concert life was due in large part to the clarity of Schoenberg's vision. It is equally clear, however, that Schoenberg would not have been able to put his plan into practice so expediently without the firm support of his friends.

Like Alban Berg, who wrote a detailed report about Schoenberg's "wonderful idea" immediately after the Mödling meeting,[1] Anton Webern enthusiastically endorsed Schoenberg's plan from the outset. This is documented in a letter to his friend Heinrich Jalowetz of November 9, 1918 (thus, before the official founding of the society). Since this letter, so far unpublished, contains a detailed description of the aims, the anticipated repertoire, and the organizational design of the society, it deserves to be quoted at length:

> Something magnificent is in the offing now: the establishment of a society for private performances of modern music (beginning with, and including Mahler). An evening every week, *only* for members…Not always a completely new program. Repeats. Purpose: a genuine acquaintance with modern music. Composers: any one, except candidates obviously not qualified. Thus even

[1] Letter from Alban to Helene Berg of July 1, 1918; published in *Alban Berg: Briefe an seine Frau* (Munich: Albert Langen and Georg Müller, 1965), pp. 363f.

Schmidt or Prohaska. Mahler, Schoenberg, Zemlinsky, Reger, as well as Strauss, Pfitzner, Schrecker [sic], Berg, myself. Also Marx, further Debussy, Ravel, Scriabin, Bartók, the Czechs (Suk, etc.), and so forth. The programs will not be announced until just before the performance, in order to forestall absences of those who would not wish to hear this or that, etc....*Top authority: Schoenberg. Vortragsmeister* [coach]: I am supposed to be the first (with an honorarium), then Berg, Steuermann (possibly also Bachrich, Weirich). *Performers*: only *virtuosos* if possible. At first performance with piano (arrangements and original works), songs, as soon as possible arrangements for piano and *Orgelharmonium.* Chamber music in original versions or arrangements... Needless to say, Schoenberg desires model performances presented with the greatest care. Not just modern music, but performances of the utmost clarity and accuracy... Something really grand could possibly come out of this society. It would mean a practical assignment for me (and what a noble one) as well as a small income. Yet I should not dwell on this, but rather upon the great scope of Schoenberg's idea. Instructive in innumerable ways: for composers, performers, and audience. Unlimited in purity, clarity, and self-denial. Qualifications for the coming League of Nations.[2]

[2] Letter to Heinrich Jalowetz of Nov. 9, 1918; Heinrich Jalowetz Collection, Paul Sacher Foundation.

In retrospect, we may safely say that the program outlined here did materialize in all essential points; the Association for Private Musical Performances did develop into "something really grand." For in the course of its 117 concerts, starting from December 29, 1918, no fewer than 154 modern works were heard, many of them more than once. Moreover, owing to the regular participation of leading instrumentalists such as Eduard Steuermann, Rudolf Kolisch, and Rudolf Serkin, as well as to the scrupulous supervision of the performances by first-rank representatives of the Schoenberg circle, new standards for technically polished and analytically founded performances of new music were set. And last but not least, important impulses emanated from the Society: the Viennese group served as a model for many new music organizations formed in the 1920s and 1930s both in Europe and America. These results are all the more impressive given the fact that the *Verein* was faced with serious financial problems from the

3 Regarding the history and impact of the *Verein*, see Judith Karen Melbach, "Schoenberg's 'Society for Musical Private Performances,' Vienna 1918–1922: A Documentary Study" (Ph.D. diss. University of Pittsburgh, 1984); Joan Allen Smith, *Schoenberg and His Circle: A Viennese Portrait* (New York: Schirmer, 1986), pp. 81–102; and "Schoenberg's Verein für musikalische Privataufführungen" in *Musik-Koncepte* 36, ed. Heinz-Klaus Metzger and Rainer Riehn (Munich: Edition Text u. Kritik, 1984). All three publications contain complete concert programs.

4 Letter to Heinrich Jalowetz, December 23, 1919; Heinrich Jalowetz Collection, Paul Sacher Foundation.

5 Ibid.

outset, which as early as three years later—in 1921—forced it out of existence.3

Webern's "practical assignment" consisted first and foremost of the artistic supervision of performances—a task at first shared with Schoenberg, Berg, Steuermann, and Benno Sachs, and later also with Erwin Stein and Rudolf Kolisch. In a letter of December 23, 1919, again to Heinrich Jalowetz, he commented on this activity as follows:

> Imagine what I have coached over the course of a year, what I have rehearsed, some of the most difficult and most modern works, totalling about thirty, for whose rendition I alone was responsible. With how much more confidence I now approach the performance of a new work! How intensely I have worked with singers, down to the last last [sic] detail. The enormous amount I have learned in doing this!4

Working as a *Vortragsmeister* did not, however, earn Webern the recognition for which he had hoped. Though he was gratified to see that he had succeeded in conveying his musical intention by purely verbal direction ("without the direct physical expression on which a conductor can rely"), Webern was dissatisfied with acting almost exclusively "behind the scenes," and he therefore came to the conclusion: "To continue working for the rest of my life in such a limited environment —limited with regard to our programs (piano, chamber music, songs)—is a prospect which I do not find attractive enough.... The rehearsing is wonderful, but ultimately the people perform on their own (a serious problem.)"5

When the *Verein* was able to include performances by larger instrumental ensembles and chamber orchestra, it looked for some time as if this "problem" was going to be solved for Webern. (The *Verein*'s expansion, envisioned right from the beginning, was to lead eventually to large orchestral concerts, but it did not reach that point.) He was finally given a chance to conduct two of his own works, namely the Orchestral Pieces, op. 10 (then still numbered op. 7, No. 4) and op. 6, which he presented in versions for chamber ensemble in 1920 and 1921, respectively. Once again, however, this was not nearly as much as he had expected (and desperately needed for a reliable income), and thus he was obliged to look elsewhere for work as a conductor. His efforts were successful, though short-lived, when he obtained his third engagement at the German Opera in Prague (from late August to early October 1920).[6]

Webern's third duty in the *Verein* (besides working as *Vortragsmeister* and conductor) resulted from the above-mentioned attempt to present works for larger ensembles: he arranged orchestral works, reducing the original scores to whatever smaller instrumental ensembles were available. Originally, orchestral works had been presented in piano reductions only: it was this practice that had led Webern to write a six-hand piano transcription of his Passacaglia, op. 1, which, apart from a few fragments, has not survived.[7] After February 1920, however, pieces for orchestra were performed more and more in versions specially arranged for chamber ensembles by members of the *Verein*. Webern undertook at least five such chamber arrangements, two of them of works by himself, the other three of works by Arnold Schoenberg and Johann Strauss.[8]

[6] Cf. Hans and Rosaleen Moldenhauer, *Anton von Webern: A Chronicle of His Life and Work* (New York: Knopf, 1979), p. 235.

[7] This piano transcription, made in 1918, was performed in the *Verein* on February 16, 1919.

[8] In addition, Webern had been asked during the fall of 1921, a short time before the *Verein* went out of existence, to arrange Mahler's *Lied von der Erde* and Debussy's *Prélude à l'après-midi d'un faune*. Cf. his letter of September 22, 1921, to Heinrich Jalowetz: Heinrich Jalowetz Collection, Paul Sacher Foundation. However, the Mahler arrangement was finally begun (but not completed) by Arnold Schoenberg, while the chamber version of Debussy's piece was carried out by Benno Sachs.

Composer/Work	Arrangement		
	Scoring	Year of Composition	Date of *Verein* Performance
Anton Webern: Five Pieces for Orchestra, op. 10	String trio, harmonium piano	1919	Jan. 30, March 13 (in Prague), and June 11, 1920
Anton Webern: Six Pieces for large Orchestra, op. 6	Flute, oboe, clarinet, string quintet, percussion, harmonium, piano	1920	Jan. 23/31, and May 12/23, 1921
Johann Strauss: *Schatzwalzer*	String quartet, harmonium, piano	1921	May 27, 1921
Arnold Schoenberg: *Die glückliche Hand*, op. 18	Chamber orchestra	1921	—
Arnold Schoenberg: Four Songs, op. 22	Chamber orchestra	1921	—

9 Until very recently, the surviving source material had not been collected and identified systematically, and not even all the concert programs of the *Verein* were known with certainty. Thus, for example, Hans Moldenhauer could not provide any information as to whether the chamber version of Webern's op. 6 was ever performed or how much work Webern had actually done on his arrangement of Schoenberg's Four Songs, op. 22 (see Moldenhauer, *Anton von Webern* [cf. note 6], pp. 129 and 229). The former question has meanwhile been solved (see above), while all we can say about the latter is that Webern completed the arrangement of at least the first of the Schoenberg songs, as can be seen from his letter to Heinrich Jalowetz of September 22, 1921 (Heinrich Jalowetz Collection, Paul Sacher Foundation).

10 This is indicated in Haugan's letter of November 9, 1993, to this writer. The score published by Universal Edition (UE 14778, with a copyright date of 1977) does not give an editor's name.

11 Cues are to be found in measure 18 of No. 2 (in the parts for oboe and clarinet), in measure 4 of No. 3 (in the part for drum), and in measure 11 of No. 5 (in the parts for flute, harmonium, and piano). It was Friedrich Cerha, the conductor of the ensemble *die reihe*, who provided Universal Edition with a reconstructed double bass part (conversation with Friedrich Cerha, March 7, 1994).

12 The repeated eighth notes are here given to the drum part.

Only two of these chamber versions, the arrangement of Strauss's Schatzwalzer and that of Webern's own op. 6, are known today—a fact which can be attributed not only to the private character of the *Verein* venture, but also to its belated historical appraisal.9 The two surviving Webern arrangements are therefore all the more valuable, as will be seen in the following discussion of the chamber version of op. 6. Three aspects will be singled out here for consideration: the unusual form in which this arrangement has been preserved, the aesthetics of its sound, and its relationship to the two orchestral versions, i.e., the original one of 1909 and the revised version of 1929.

The chamber version of Webern's op. 6 has survived only in a set of parts, which, after the composer's death, was in the possession of Amalie Waller (Webern's eldest daughter) and later found its way to Hans Moldenhauer's Webern Archive in Spokane (in 1961), and then to the Paul Sacher Foundation in Basel (in 1984). This set of parts—for flute (also piccolo), oboe, clarinet (also bass clarinet), percussion, harmonium, piano, violin I, violin II, and viola—is not quite complete; marked cues suggest that the scoring also included cello and double bass. The full score therefore had to be reconstructed—a task that was first undertaken, in 1968, by Edwin Haugan, Hans Moldenhauer's long-time assistant. Haugan's version, a copy of which is preserved in the Webern Collection of the Paul Sacher Foundation, was used, together with the original set of parts, both for a performance by the ensemble *die reihe* in 1970 and for the printed edition issued by Universal Edition.10 Neither score is entirely reliable, however: in Haugan's reconstruction the double bass was omitted,11 and in the published version the reference to this instrument in measures 18–19 of No. 2 was overlooked.12 In addition to this problematic documentation—doubly problematic since the manuscript score (or annotated print of the original orchestral version) from which the performance material was extracted is also lost—the parts were written by several scribes. Only the ones for the first and second piece appear throughout in Webern's hand, while those for the other pieces were to a large extent written either by Alban Berg (No. 5), or by two unidentified copyists (Nos. 3, 4, and 6). Moreover, all parts are marked with pencil corrections and performance directions, entered by the players in the course of rehearsals. Thus, we are confronted with a highly heterogeneous source, which, even in its outward appearance, bears witness to the joint efforts characteristic of the *Verein* concerts. Still, the authenticity of the musical text as such is not problematic (minor discrepancies between the parts notwithstanding),[13] since Webern supervised both the production of parts and the rehearsals, and since he conducted—though apparently not to his full satisfaction—all four performances of this version (on January 23 and 31, and on May 12 and 13, 1921).[14]

With his arrangement of the Six Pieces for Orchestra, Webern returned to a work that he had composed in 1909 and published privately four years later.[15] Shortly after publication, the composition received its premiere in the famous "Skandalkonzert" on March 31, 1913, which also included pieces by Alexander Zemlinsky, Arnold Schoenberg, Alban Berg, and Gustav Mahler.[16] The Six Pieces feature a larger scoring than the composer had ever used before or would ever use again: 4 flutes (also 2 piccolo flutes and 1 alto flute), 2 oboes, 2 English horns, 3 clarinets (also 1 clarinet in E-flat), 2 bass clarinets, 2 bassoons (also 1 contrabassoon), 6 horns, 6 trumpets, 6 trombones, 1 bass tuba, 2 harps, celesta, timpani, and other percussion instruments, and a large string group which is often subdivided. It is clear, therefore, that the chamber arrangement called for drastic changes in scoring, only three of which of the most common types will be briefly considered here.

First, Webern attempted to replace the solo instruments that were no longer available (mostly wind instruments) with the most suitable substitutes, i.e., with instruments of similar sonority; this meant, on the one hand, wind and stringed instruments of like register, and, on the other, either harmonium (for wind instruments), or piano (for celesta, harp or percussion). A particularly striking example of this kind of reinstrumentation is the beginning of the first piece, whose opening phrase (consisting of a rising or descending line in sixteenth notes, followed by a high or low pedal tone, together with "punctuating" four-part chords) was changed as follows:

1909: Fl. - Trp. - Cel. / Fl. - Hrn. - Stgs.
1920: Fl. - *Harm.* - *Piano* / Fl. - *Harm.* - Stgs.

[13] These are marked in Haugan's reconstructed score.

[14] In his letter of September 21, 1921, Webern wrote to Heinrich Jalowetz, "I cannot help thinking that my conducting of the Orchestral Pieces, which you saw and heard this year, has not made a very favorable impression upon you. Doubtless you are right!" (Heinrich Jalowetz Collection, Paul Sacher Foundation.)

[15] The full title of this first edition reads: "Sechs Stücke/für grosses Orchester/von/Anton von Webern/Op. 4/Im Selbstverlag des Komponisten" [Vienna, 1913]. In 1961 it became available as a study score issued by Universal Edition (Philharmonia Scores No. 433). The work was not given its final designation "op. 6" until 1920.

[16] See the recent article by Gösta Neuwirth, with extensive press documentation, "Kehraus des schönen Wahns," in *Aufbruch in unsere Welt: Essays zu Kunst, Musik, Literatur und Architektur* (Vienna: Löcker, 1993), pp. 60–97.

The result is a timbral reduction: whereas there is a succession of five distinct tone colors in the original version, there are only three different sonorities in the chamber version.

Second, Webern tried to preserve the many "homogeneous" chords of the full orchestra version (4 trumpets, 6 trombones, etc.) by assigning them either to the "multivoiced" instruments, i.e., harmonium or piano, or to the strings. While the sonorous integrity of the individual chords is thus retained, the timbral variety is limited to three types of sonority. In addition, the few heterogeneous sonorities of the original version were unified. This can be seen, for example, in the originally "blended" chord in measure 17 of the fifth piece (clarinet, contrabassoon, 4 horns, and strings) which, in the chamber version, is reduced to pure string sound enriched by a single tone of the harmonium.

Third, Webern often removed the doublings characteristic of the version for full orchestra. Thus, in the chord just mentioned, the original version doubles five of the seven tones heard (c in double bass and contrabassoon, f in viola II and horn IV, d in violin I and horn II, a in violin II [b] and horn I, e-flat in violin II [a] and clarinet), whereas in the chamber version—as far as can be seen in the parts—no doubling occurs.[17]

Even though a more detailed comparison shows that Webern subtly varied these techniques of reinstrumentation according to the musical context,[18] the impression may still arise that the chamber version of op. 6 represents merely a necessary expedient rather than a fully valid alternate version. However, we should bear in mind that Webern was responding just as much to some general aesthetic tendencies of the time as to the limited performing conditions of the *Verein*. In particular, his arrangement of op. 6 is indebted to the principle of "soloistic instrumentation," which the members of the Second Viennese School had increasingly adopted ever since Schoenberg's *Chamber Symphony* of 1906. Schoenberg himself had raised this principle to the status of an independent category of instrumentation in an unpublished note of April 16, 1917, contrasting it with a (Romantic) "organ-like (registration) instrumentation,"[19] and in a letter to Alexander Zemlinsky of

[17] In the Universal Edition print, the cello c of the orchestral version is given to the double bass, the result being a doubling with the c in the piano part.

[18] See the analysis by Nicolaus A. Huber, "Zu Weberns Kammerorchesterbearbeitung seiner Sechs Stücke für Orchester op. 6 für den *Verein für musikalische Privataufführungen*" in *Schönbergs Verein für musikalische Privataufführungen* (see note 3), pp. 65–85.

[19] "Unfinished Theoretical Works," No. 10, Arnold Schoenberg Center, Vienna.

February 20, 1918, he had even applied the term to certain passages in one of his early works, the Symphonic Poem *Pelleas and Melisande*.[20] (This does not mean, of course, that "soloistic instrumentation," was invented by Schoenberg, even though some of his pieces served as models for many later composers of the Second Viennese School as well as for others.)[21] And Webern too had turned to "soloistic instrumentation" as early as 1911 (in the orchestral pieces that were later published as op. 10)—a tendency he exhibited more and more in his subsequent works such as the Trakl and Rosegger songs (opp. 14 and 15, begun in 1917). It is no surprise, then, to find in his letters the following remark on the arranging practice of the *Verein*: "I take much pleasure in these arrangements. If you think of my most recent scores—which are essentially for chamber orchestra (nothing but solo parts)—you will understand how close this is to my heart."[22]

Arranging orchestral scores for the *Verein* was thus not simply a matter of necessity; it was also a matter of subjecting the original works to a new instrumental interpretation and, in the process, of probing their substance. Such a critical undertaking is aptly described in the following words of Alban Berg, which imply that instrumental "color" was no longer considered to be a primary, formative element (as in the years before the First World War), but merely served to *clarify* musical structure:

> In this manner [i.e., by using transcriptions of orchestral scores] it is possible to hear and judge a modern orchestral work divested of all the sound-effects and other sensuous aids that only an orchestra can furnish. Thus the old approach is robbed of its force—that this music owes its power to its more or less opulent and effective instrumentation and lacks the qualities that were hitherto considered characteristic of good music—melody, richness of harmony, polyphony, perfection of form, architecture, etc.[23]

It must be kept in mind, however, that when Berg spoke of renouncing *all* "sensuous aids" he meant the earlier *Verein* practice of piano transcription. In contrast, the transcription for chamber ensemble involved merely a *reduction* of such aids, one that managed to present the essence of a work by different means, but with similar explicitness. An example from the

[20] Arnold Schoenberg, letter to Alexander Zemlinsky of February 20, 1918; *Zemlinskys Briefwechsel mit Schönberg, Webern, Berg und Schreker* (Briefwechsel der Wiener Schule, 1), ed. Horst Weber, Darmstadt: Wissenschaftliche Buchgesell-schaft 1995, p. 187.

[21] In the domain of *transcriptions* (i.e. "soloistic" arrangements of large orchestral textures), a precedent can be found in Richard Wagner's *Siegfried-Idyll* for thirteen instruments (1870), the musical material of which was largely taken from the third act of his opera *Siegfried*; cf., with reference to the "soloistic instrumentation," Egon Wellesz, *Die neue Instrumentation* (Berlin: Max Hesse, 1928/9), vol. I, p. 32 and vol. II, p. 149.

[22] Letter to Heinrich Jalowetz of September 22, 1921, Heinrich Jalowetz Collection, Paul Sacher Foundation.

[23] Statement of aims of the *Verein für musikalische Privataufführungen*, February 1919; quoted from Joan Allen Smith, *Schoenberg and His Circle* (see note 3), p. 245.

chamber orchestra version of op. 6—the succession of chords in measures 9–12 of the fourth piece—illustrates this:

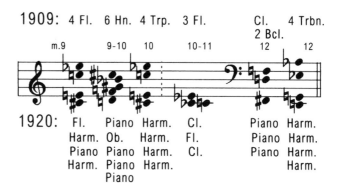

The full orchestral version, whose succession of homogenous sonorities (4 flutes, 6 horns, 4 trumpets, etc.) is indebted to an older type of "organ-like" orchestration,[24] reflects the compositional structure in two ways. On the one hand, the grouping of 3 + 3 chords (separated by a change of registers) is suggested by the similarity of two timbral processes that move from woodwinds to brass (each starting with the flutes). On the other hand, the contrasting internal structure of the two chord groups—the first being symmetrical and circular,[25] the second progressive and forward-directed[26]—is expressed through different shadings in the timbral processes, especially since the trumpet timbre of the third chord, pianissimo, is closely related to the low flute timbre,[27] whereas the timbres of clarinet and trombone in the fifth and sixth chords gradually depart from it. In the arrangement, Webern could not render these timbral progressions through successions of homogenously colored chords because he had only three unified "chord colors" at his disposal (harmonium, piano, strings) instead of the original five. He therefore aimed at a *mixture* which, in its own way, would produce a fivefold gradation. In the process, a timbral "assonance" between chords one and four moves to chords three and six (the individual mixtures of chords one and three are "homogenized" in the succeeding chords and resolved to the pure harmonium sound of chords three and six); yet the chord groupings (3+3) are still suggested in the new instrumentation, in that the harmonium is heard in chords one and three of the first group, whereas there is no such repetition of sonority in the second. Thus an analogous result is obtained

[24] In other places, however, we find clear indications of a "soloistic" type of instrumentation.

[25] The second chord arises through contraction of the outer parts and addition of the central tone g-sharp; the third chord, reached by corresponding expansion of the outer voices, is identical with the first.

[26] The general downward motion contributes as much to this as to the widening of the ambitus, the move from three-part to four-part writing, and the gradual introduction of new pitch classes. For a discussion of this passage of op. 6, No. 4, see Paul Kabbash, "Form and Rhythm in Webern's Atonal Works" (Ph.D. diss., Yale University, 1983), pp. 98ff.

[27] Cf. Nikolay Rimsky-Korsakov, *Principles of Orchestration*, ed. Maximilian Steinberg, English trans. Edward Agate (New York: Dover, 1964), p. 35: "the flute…in its lowest register, recalls the pianissimo trumpet tone."

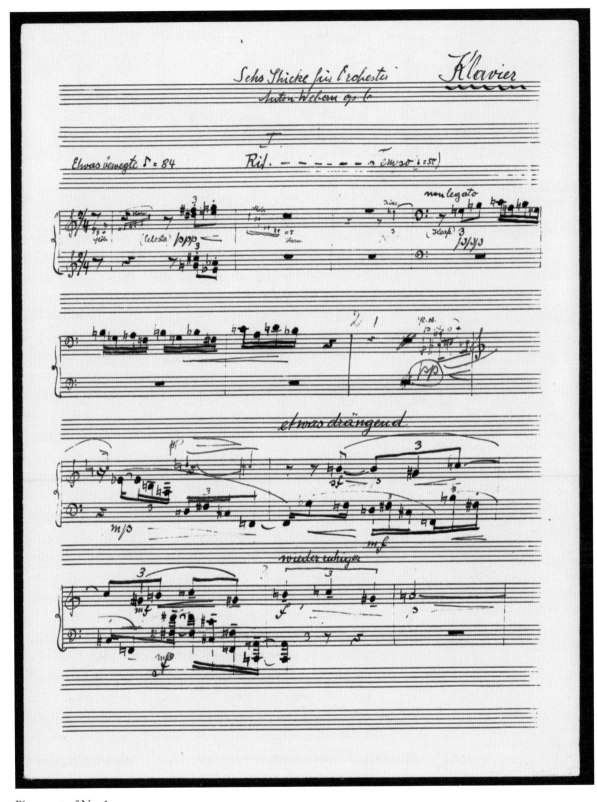

Piano part of No. 1

·453·

[28] Cf. Reinhold Brinkmann. "Die George-Lieder 1908/9 und 1919/23 - ein Kapitel Webern-Philologie," in *Beiträge der Österreichische Gesellschaft für Musik '72/'73: Webern-Kongress* (Kassel, 1973), pp. 43–50; Felix Meyer, "Im Zeichen der Reduktion: Quellenkritische und analytische Anmerkungen zu Anton Weberns Rilke-Liedern Op. 8," in *Quellenstudien I: Gustav Mahler-Igor Strawinsky-Anton Webern-Frank Martin* (Veröffentlichungen der Paul Sacher Stiftung, 2), ed. Hans Oesch (Winterthur: Amadeus, 1991), pp. 53–100; Felix Meyer/Anne Shreffler, "Webern's Revisions: Some Analytical Implications," in Music Analysis 12/3 (1993): 355–79.

[29] The revised version has been available in a pocket score since 1956 (Philharmonia Scores No. 394). Even before this version had been produced (in the summer of 1928), Webern apparently undertook a new reorchestration for a planned performance under Hermann Scherchen; cf. Erich Wolfgang Partsch, "Ergänzungen zur Verbreitungsgeschichte von Weberns *Sechs Orchesterstücken op. 6*," in *40,000 Musikerbriefe auf Knopfdruck: Methoden der Verschlagwortung anhand des UE-Briefwechsels-Untersuchungen-Detailergebnisse*, ed. Ernst Hilmar (Tutzing: H. Schneider, 1989), pp. 55–62.

[30] Cf. Webern's notation to this effect in a program book from the year 1933, quoted by Moldenhauer, *Anton von Webern* (see note 6), p. 128.

[31] Due to the shortening mentioned, the revised version's measure numbers differ from those of the original version by one.

by totally different means: the mixture caused by "soloistic instrumentation" serves to highlight the same compositional features as the changes of sonority in the orchestral version.

A final aspect of the chamber version of op. 6 involves its place in the general revision history of Webern's works. We should remember here that Webern—like Berg, but unlike Schoenberg—was not able to publish his music under regular publishing agreements until the 1920s. All his earlier attempts to find a publisher had failed, so that practically his entire early output, except for the Six Pieces for Orchestra (and a few single numbers from larger work cycles), remained at first unpublished. Having reached a contractual agreement with Universal Edition in the summer of 1920, the composer therefore subjected his entire oeuvre to a general review, not only selecting and regrouping works for publication, but also revising them thoroughly.[28]

Although their "Urfassung," exceptionally, had been published, this applies also to the Six Pieces, op. 6, which Webern republished in 1928 in a revised version.[29] This new version, in which Webern reduced the orchestral scoring (by 2 flutes, 1 clarinet, 1 bass clarinet, 2 horns, 2 trumpets, 1 harp as well as the "Rute" [a rod to be used on the bass drum]) and which he considered to be the only valid one,[30] differs from the original orchestral setting in many details; in particular we can observe a considerable thinning out of the texture (which goes beyond the removal of doublings), a shortening of the fourth and sixth pieces by one measure each, and a tightening of the correlation between instrumentation and structural design. The middle section of the fourth piece can illustrate the latter. The passage in measures 12 to 31 (or 11 to 30)[31] is conceived as a succession of four instrumental solos with chordal accompaniment. In the revised version these four solos are recast in such a way that they recall the succession of timbres of the work's first three chords (whose instrumentation remains very close to the original score): 2 flutes/2 clarinets—4 horns—4 trumpets. They thus establish a correspondence of colors which is not present in either the original or the chamber versions (see also the musical example above):

	Chords, mm. 9–10 (8–9)	Solos, mm. 12 (11), 20 (19), 21 (20), 24 (23)
1909	4 Fl. - 6 Hrns.- 4 Tpts	E-fl.Clar. - G.Fl. - Hrn. - Tpt.
1920	(Fl.) Ob. (Clar.) Pno. - Harm. (Harm.)	E-fl.Clar. - Harm. - Vc. - E-fl.Clar.
1928	(2 Fl.) 4 Hrns.- 4 Tpts. (2 Clar.)	Picc. - Clar. - Hrn. - Trpt.

Inasmuch as this form-articulating role of instrumentation appears only in the revision of 1928, the second orchestral version clearly stands apart from both the original and chamber versions. Or, to put it differently: in spite of its drastic instrumental reduction, the *Verein* version is closer to the original score, not only in time, but also with regard to its "dramaturgy of color," than the version of 1928. It is equally clear, however, that already in the chamber version Webern aimed toward the same ideal of greater economy in the use of expressive means as in the 1928 orchestral version, about which he commented: "Everything extravagant is now cut (alto flute, six trombones for a few measures, and so on). Now I can represent all this much more simply."[32] For example, both in the chamber version and in the revised orchestral version, Webern reduced the scoring (especially by omitting unusual instruments). He also abandoned some playing techniques which alter the original sound (e.g., *col legno, am Steg, Flatterzunge*), and did away with characteristic expression marks (e.g., "höchst ausdrucksvoll," "äusserst zart,").[33] Thus the chamber version of op. 6 marks an important intermediate stage between the original versions of Webern's works and the revised ones of the 1920s. It suggests that the latter profited from his work in the *Verein*, particularly from his experience with "soloistic instrumentation" and his renouncing of "sensuous aids." Webern's artistic evolution was characterized, among other things, by an aesthetic shift from an "expressionistic" concept of sonority toward one determined by the "classicist" ideal of *Fasslichkeit*.[34] It is not least with regard to this aspect of his evolution that the chamber version of Webern's Six Pieces, op. 6, deserves our attention.

[32] Letter to Arnold Schoenberg of August 20, 1928, quoted after Moldenhauer, *Anton von Webern* (see note 6), p. 128.

[33] Mention should also be made here of Webern's later reservation with regard to the programmatic dimension of his music, as can be seen from the way he described his music. For example, while in a letter of January 13, 1913, to Arnold Schoenberg, Webern refers extensively to the autobiographical background of the Six Pieces—the funeral of his mother in 1906—in the program note of 1933 mentioned above (see note 30), he limits himself to the following cues: "expectation of a catastrophe" (No. 1), "certainty of its fulfillment" (No. 2), "the most tender contrast" (No. 3), "funeral march" (No. 4), "remembrance" (No. 5), "resignation" (No. 6); quoted after Moldenhauer, *Anton von Webern* (see note 6), p. 128.

[34] Cf. Joachim Noller, "Fasslichkeit-eine kulturhistorische Studie zur Ästhetik Weberns," in *Archiv für Musikwissenschaft* 43/3 (1986): 169–80. It was by no means accidental that Webern remarked that the revised orchestral version, as distinct from the original version, looked "like an old Haydn score." (Letter of August 20, 1928, to Alban Berg: quoted from Moldenhauer, *Anton von Webern* [see note 6], p. 129).

Anton Webern's "Mein Weg geht jetzt vorüber," op. 15, No. 4

Lauriejean Reinhardt

DURING THE YEARS FROM 1915 to 1925, Webern was preoccupied almost exclusively with the composition of *Lieder*. Totalling over forty settings (complete and fragmentary) of Latin liturgical texts, pious folk texts and poems by George Trakl, these songs chronicle his continued experimentation with atonal writing and gradual adoption of the twelve-tone method. "Mein Weg geht jetzt vorüber," composed in 1922 and published as No. 4 of *Fünf geistliche Lieder*, op. 15, is the earliest-known composition documenting Webern's awareness of this method.

Sketches for this song, now at the Paul Sacher Stiftung (published in part in Moldenhauer's Webern biography),[1] reveal the formation of a prime form with its basic permutations (retrograde, inversion, and retrograde inversion), followed by the tritone transposition with its permutations. The language of the final setting, however, may best be described as protoserial. Only the opening vocal line articulates a complete row (the melody through "dein" in measure 4 presents a statement of the untransposed prime form). The remainder of the song is based on motivic pitch cells that are related to, but not systematically derived from, the basic set. Stylistically, the setting resembles earlier works like the Trakl *Lieder*, op. 14 (1917–1921), which feature jagged, irregular rhythms and an expressionistic predilection for registral extremes and atomized gestures.

This manuscript preserves an intermediate stage of composition. A fair copy in ink of the first poetic stanza (recto and top of verso) is followed by pencil sketches for the second and last stanza (bottom of verso). The music for stanza one is virtually identical to that of the published score. The most

[1] For a black-and-white facsimile of these sketches, see Hans and Rosaleen Moldenhauer, *Anton von Webern: A Chronicle of His Life and Work* (New York: Alfred A. Knopf, 1979), p. 310. A color facsimile is found in Hans Oesch, "Webern und das SATOR-Palindrom," in *Quellenstudien I: Gustav Mahler—Igor Stravinsky—Anton Webern—Frank Martin*, ed. Hans Oesch (Winterthur: Amadeus, 1991), pp. 114–15.

significant differences include: the removal of the descriptive instructions "espress." from measures 3, 4, and 6 and "zart" from measure 7; rhythmic revisions to the vocal line (e.g., "ist mir" in measure 5 is sketched with a syncopated rhythm on the blank staff above); and additional refinements of phrasing, articulation, and dynamics.

Pencil sketches beginning in measure 8 complete the setting but indicate as well that Webern reconsidered ideas for the second stanza. He apparently began this manuscript in ink, intending for it to serve as a complete fair copy (he generally reserved ink for this stage of composition) and then switched to pencil in order to revise the second stanza. A later, more definitive fair copy of the setting in ink is now preserved in the Robert Owen Lehman Collection of the Pierpont Morgan Library.

The sudden dearth of indications for phrasing, articulation, and dynamics, and the disappearance of textual underlay at this point in the setting suggest that Webern became absorbed with elements like pitch and rhythm. Indeed, the rhythmic declamation for the final two phrases of the poem (measures 11–13, "in Gottes Fried und Gnaden / fahr' ich mit Freud' dahin.") is completely recast, with halfnotes changed to quarter notes and vice versa.

Equally important changes are made regarding the ordering, registration, and voicing of pitches. While the pitch content of successive phrases remains consistent, individual gestures are recast, with pitches reordered and exchanged between parts. In measure 9, for example, the melodic figure "beladen" is revised from F-sharp–A–F to F–A–F-sharp. This redefines the relationship between flute and voice, so that the vocal line now echoes rather than mirrors the preceding flute figure. Sketches for measure 10 on staves 5–9 show that while each musical line is recomposed, the actual pitch content of the measure is literally preserved. This precise yet flexible approach to pitch suggests a musical language based on well-defined note fields rather than a strict serial ordering.

The larger significance of this setting concerns chronology. Webern composed "Mein Weg geht jetzt vorüber" in July

2 Moldenhauer, op. cit., p. 310. On the circumstances surrounding this meeting, see Joan Allen Smith, *Schoenberg and His Circle: A Viennese Portrait* (New York: Schirmer Books, 1986), pp. 183–219.

3 On the dating and evolution of Schoenberg's Sonett movement, see Jan Maegaard, *Studien zur Entwicklung des dodekaphonen Satzes bei Arnold Schoenberg* (Copenhagen: Wilhelm Hansen Musik-Forlag, 1972), vol. I, pp. 24, 104–5, and Ethan Haimo, *Schoenberg's Serial Odyssey: The Evolution of His Twelve-tone Method, 1914–1928* (Oxford: Clarendon Press, 1990), pp. 78, 90–93.

4 "Anton Webern: *Klangfarbenmelodie* (1951)," in *Style and Idea: Selected Writings of Arnold Schoenberg*, ed. Leonard Stein, trans. Leo Black (Berkeley and Los Angeles: University of California Press, 1975), p. 484.

5 "Composition with Twelve-Tones (2) c. 1948," *Style and Idea*, p. 247. These letters, many still unpublished, are currently housed in the Schoenberg Collection at the Library of Congress and the *Wiener Stadt- und Landesbibliothek, Musiksammlung.*

1922, when he and Schoenberg were vacationing in Traunkirchen. As Moldenhauer observed, this setting—which began with a deliberate charting of rows and permutations and opens with a complete row statement—thus predates Schoenberg's now famous meeting of February 1923, when he formally explained the twelve-tone method.[2] Webern's attempt to compose with a twelve-tone row is all the more noteworthy, given that Schoenberg himself did not devise a linearly ordered, chromatically complete row until October 1922, in the sketches for the Sonett movement of the *Serenade*, op. 24.[3] Schoenberg also claimed that until his official announcement in 1923, he had intentionally withheld information on the twelve-tone method from Webern:

> He [Webern] kept secret everything "new" he had tried in his compositions. I, on the other hand, immediately and exhaustively explained to him each of my ideas (with the exception of the method of composition with twelve-tones—that I long kept secret, because, as I said to Erwin Stein, Webern immediately uses everything I do, plan or say, so that—I remember my words—"By now I haven't the slightest idea who I am."[4]

Schoenberg's sensitivity regarding his authorship of the twelve-tone method led him to issue a number of highly polemical and potentially misleading statements about this period. He may well have withheld information from Webern at some point; however, strong evidence suggests that Webern did, in fact, have access to Schoenberg's latest ideas at various times during the crucial period, from 1915 to 1923.

Correspondence dating from 1915 to 1917 preserves detailed discussions on the theoretical and philosophical basis of Schoenberg's earliest protoserial work, *Die Jakobsleiter*, and Webern's own stage project, *Tot*. Included in these letters is discussion of a twelve-tone theme that Schoenberg had drafted for an instrumental scherzo. (Schoenberg later acknowledged this exchange of information with Webern, wryly predicting, "An historian will probably some day find in the exchange of letters between Webern and me how enthusiastic we were about this.")[5] In December 1922, Webern informed Berg of a recent conversation with Schoenberg, in which their mutual

lie - ber da muß ich fah-ren ein

es press.

des

nicht zu fest ba-la-den

6 "Dein Werk ist wunderbar!... Ich glaube, was Dir hier gelungen ist, ist epochal: auf Grund dieser Thematik (Melodik und Harmonik) eine *dramatische* Musik zu schreiben: eine Musik, welche die vom Drama geforderte 'Faßlichkeit' (nach Schoenberg) aufs höchste und reinste erfüllt...Er (Schoe) stimmte mir sogleich zu und formulierte gleich, ausgehend von seinen Ideen über den 'Zusammenhang,' über 'Faßlichkeit'." Letter from Webern to Berg, December 25, 1992, WSLB/MS.

7 "Unterrichtet habe ich das wohl noch nicht, weil ich es noch durch einige Kompositionen erproben und in einigen Richtungen erweitern muss. Aber im Vorunterricht der Schüler verwende ich zur Definierung der Formen und Formelemente, und insbesondere zur Erläuterung der musikalischen Technik, sehr viel davon seit einigen Jahren." Letter from Schoenberg to Hauer, December 1, 1923, in Erwin Stein, ed., *Arnold Schoenberg: Ausgewählte Briefe* (Mainz: B. Schott's Söhne, 1958), p. 109.

8 See Elliott Antokoletz, "A Survivor of the Vienna Schoenberg Circle: An Interview with Paul A. Pisk," *Tempo* 154 (1985): 18.

9 Reminiscences of Marcel Dick, cited in Joan Allen Smith, op. cit., p. 181. More recently, Anne Shreffler has proposed that even if Webern did not receive direct information from Schoenberg, he may have gotten second-hand reports from other members of Schoenberg's "inner circle," including Josef Rufer and Erwin Stein. (Conversation with the author, November 10, 1991.)

10 See H. H. Stuckenschmidt, *Schoenberg: His Life, World and Work*, trans. Humphrey Searle (London: John Calder, 1977), pp. 279–84, and Moldenhauer, *Anton von Webern*, pp. 247–49.

11 For a chronological and analytical account of Schoenberg's works leading up to this period, see Haimo, op. cit., pp. 69–105.

admiration for *Wozzeck* led to a discussion of *Zusammenhang* (unity) and *Fasslichkeit* (comprehensibility), concepts fundamental to Schoenberg's formulation of the twelve-tone method:

> Your work [*Wozzeck*] is wonderful! I believe what you have accomplished is epoch-making: to compose *dramatic* music on the basis of this theme (melodic and harmonic); a music in which the "comprehensibility" (according to Schoenberg) demanded by the drama is realized to the highest and purest... He (Schoenberg) instantly agreed with me and theorized further, proceeding from his ideas on "coherence," on "comprehensibility."[6]

Schoenberg also acknowledged to Josef Matthias Hauer in December 1923, that while he had not yet formally taught his new method, he had been refining his ideas in preliminary studies with pupils "for a few years."[7] This was later confirmed independently by Schoenberg's student, Paul A. Pisk.[8] Regarded as one of Schoenberg's chief "sentinels" during these years, when he guarded his ideas so carefully,[9] Webern very likely also numbered among these "pupils."

Perhaps most significantly, Webern joined Schoenberg at Traunkirchen on July 17, 1922, and remained there until mid-September. The two composers had been engaged in various professional activities during the course of the year, and their summer retreat to Traunkirchen provided a much anticipated opportunity to renew their friendship and focus more directly on composition.[10] Webern began drafting "Mein Weg geht jetzt vorüber" on July 26. By this point in the summer of 1922, Schoenberg had experimented with many of the ideas that would come to define the twelve-tone method, but he had not yet composed a chromatically complete row, nor had he assimilated his recent ideas into a single composition.[11] In July he resumed work on *Die Jakobsleiter*, but eventually abandoned the project and turned to the Sonett sketches early in October.

Webern's twelve-tone experimentation in the sketches for "Mein Weg geht jetzt vorüber" and his uneasy handling of the row in the final setting may well reflect his desire to realize musically the ideas that Schoenberg was on the verge of solidifying. This would explain Schoenberg's hard feelings toward Webern and his later attempt to deny any foreknowledge of the twelve-tone method on Webern's part. Webern may, in fact, have alluded to this setting during the February 1923 meeting, for as Schoenberg would later recall, "Curiously, when I had shown the four basic forms, Webern confessed that he had written also something in twelve tones (probably suggested by the Scherzo of my symphony of 1915), and he said: 'I never knew what to do after the twelve tones'."[12]

Webern's revisions for the second stanza of "Mein Weg geht jetzt vorüber," as seen in this manuscript, clearly suggest that he did not yet comprehend the full potential of the row. The uneven marriage of twelve-tone resources and atonal motivic procedures in this setting is particularly instructive; indeed, the song is extremely valuable as one of Webern's few truly transitional compositions in which elements of both musical languages can be seen to coexist.[13]

[12] Stuckenschmidt, *Schoenberg*, pp. 443–44.

[13] For a more detailed examination of "Mein Weg geht jetzt voruber," the source materials for the song, and the special place it holds in the evolution of Webern's twelve-tone style, see Anne C. Shreffler's fine article, "'Mein Weg geht jetzt voruber': The Vocal Origins of Webern's Twelve-Tone Composition," in *Journal of the American Musicological Association*, Vol. 47, no. 2 (summer 1994): 275–339, which appeared after this essay was written.

Anton Webern's *Zwei Lieder für gemischten Chor,* op. 19

Lauriejean Reinhardt

ANTON WEBERN'S *Zwei Lieder für gemischten Chor,* op. 19 (1925–1926) remains one of his least-known compositions, yet it occupies an extremely important position in his oeuvre. Not only is this Webern's first twelve-tone work on a comparatively large scale, it also marks the first time he organized constituent movements around the same row. His previous experiments with twelve-tone composition had treated the row rather as an isolated device and emphasized solo lieder accompanied by two to three instruments. Beginning with op. 19, however, and continuing with the instrumental works of opp. 20–22, Webern embarked on a series of multimovement compositions that featured an increasingly more sophisticated handling of the row and expanded performing forces as well as extended forms.[1] The choral lieder of op. 19 thus seem to signal the composer's readiness to test his twelve-tone skills on a larger, more expanded scale.[2]

The op. 19 choruses are notable additionally for the fact that their texts are drawn from the writings of Johann Wolfgang von Goethe. Goethe's influence on Webern's aesthetic outlook remains undisputed, and he was equally important to Webern as a composer: sketches on ten separate Goethe poems exist from every stage of Webern's career. Yet only three Goethe settings were completed and published by Webern: the two choral movements of op. 19 and an earlier, piano-vocal setting of the poem "Gleich und Gleich" (1917), which Webern included in his *Vier Lieder,* op. 12, No. 4.[3]

By a curious coincidence, Goethe's *Chinesisch-deutsche Jahres- und Tageszeiten,* Webern's literary source for op. 19, occupies a similarly important yet often undervalued position in Goethe's oeuvre. Written during the summer of 1827, these fourteen short poems blending Chinese and German themes constitute

[1] Also common to this group of works is the fact that they were all planned in three movements, but in each case the third movement was not completed.

[2] Perhaps not coincidentally, a similar pattern of experimentation with texted compositions followed by a consolidation of technique in instrumental works can be seen around 1908–1909, in Webern's early atonal works.

[3] A youthful setting of the poem "Blummengruss" (1903) was not published by Webern, but was instead made available posthumously by Rudolph Ganz in *Eight Early Songs* (New York: C. Fischer, 1965).

Goethe's final lyric cycle. The larger theme of the work concerns aging and the onset of maturity, represented, as the cycle's title suggests, by the metaphor of the changing seasons and the passing of time. The nature imagery that permeates the poems invokes the rich heritage of German pastoral poetry, while the aged Mandarin-poet at the center of the cycle harks back to the rococo era and its fascination with chinoiserie. The depth of wisdom the Mandarin personifies and the larger philosophical meaning that underlies much of Goethe's symbolism have, on the other hand, led some to suggest a more poignantly autobiographical level of interpretation.[4]

Webern's interest in this late Goethe cycle is remarkable for a number of reasons. Not only do the *Tageszeiten* poems stand outside the canon of Goethe texts traditionally set by lieder composers, they were also dismissed as vague in intent and design and even retrogressive until very recently.[5] In addition to the two poems Webern set as op. 19, he turned to the *Tageszeiten* lyrics once again in 1929 and began sketches on "Nun weiß man erst, was Rosenknospe sei," a pivotal poem from the end of the cycle that relates directly to the two poems he had set earlier as op. 19.[6]

Recent studies that evaluate the *Tageszeiten* cycle more favorably have identified characteristics that may help to explain Webern's interest in the poems. Among these characteristics are Goethe's exceptionally graphic representation of the natural world and his strong emphasis on visual perception and color imagery, both of which recall his *Zur Farbenlehre*, a work with special significance for Webern during the twelve-tone period. Also significant are Goethe's elliptical mode of diction and his aphoristic approach to cyclical structure, which have been compared to the style exploited by the Expressionist writers of Webern's day. In addition, the Oriental mysticism that threads its way through Goethe's cycle may also have been attractive to Webern. The Mandarin's ascetic detachment from the outside world, his advocacy of rapturous contemplation (*Begeisterung*) over intellectual instruction (*Belehrung*), and the Eastern concept of time implied by the larger cycle are all themes with an obvious appeal to a generation of Viennese artists who had long been fascinated by Eastern philosophy. Webern himself counted

4 On the meaning of Goethe's *Tageszeiten* cycle and the qualities associated with his later lyric style, see: Meredith Lee, *Studies in Goethe's Lyric Cycles* (Chapel Hill: University of North Carolina Press, 1978), pp. 129–47; Wolfgang Preisendanz, "Goethe's 'Chinesisch-deutsche Jahres- und Tageszeiten'," in *Jahrbuch der deutschen Schillergesellschaft* 8 (1964): 137–52; Friedrich Burkhardt, "Goethe's 'Chinesisch-deutsche Jahres- und Tageszeiten': Eine Ergänzung zur Entdeckung des biographischen Hintergrundes durch Wolfgang Preisendanz," in *Jahrbuch der deutschen Schillergesellschaft* 13 (1969): 180–95; Alfred Zastrau, ed., *Goethe Handbuch: Goethe, seine Welt und Zeit in Werk und Wirkung*, 2nd rev. ed. (Stuttgart: J.B. Metzlersche Verlagsbuchhandlung, 1961), see esp. Erich Trunz, "Alterslyrik," Bd. 1., pp. 171–73, and "Altersstil," Bd. 1, pp. 179–80; and Erich Trunz, "Goethe's späte Lyrik," *Deutsche Vierteljahrsschrift für Literaturwissenschaft und Geistesgeschichte* 23 (1949): 419–22, 427–28.

5 See Lee, op. cit., pp. 131–33, and Preisendanz, op. cit., pp. 137–38.

6 Webern's incomplete sketches on "Nun weiß man erst," begun as a choral work and then changed to a setting for voice and piano, are reproduced in *Anton von Webern Sketches (1926–1945): Facsimile Reproductions from the Composer's Autograph Sketchbooks in the Moldenhauer Archive* (New York: Carl Fischer, Inc., 1968), pl. 13–14. On the significance of this particular poem within the larger Goethe cycle, see: Lee, op. cit., p. 133; Preisendanz, op. cit., pp. 140–41, and Trunz, "Altersstil," p. 180, and "Goethes späte Lyrik," pp. 420–22.

Mahler's *Das Lied von der Erde*, a work based on Hans Bethge's German adaptations of Chinese verse, among his favorite compositions, and he had recently attempted a number of his own Bethge settings.

For the present composition, Webern chose a pair of *Vorfrühlingsgedichte* from the opening section of Goethe's cycle. "Weiß wie Lilien" and "Ziehn die Schafe von der Weise," poems II and III in Goethe's ordering, locate the aged Mandarin in the idyllic, isolated setting where he has chosen to live out his final days, having retreated from the burdens of "the North." The poems portray this setting alternately as a paradise garden and a verdant shepherd's meadow; they are further related through the use of parallel color imagery[7] and the shared theme of a heightened anticipation of spring in full bloom.[8] The thematic connections that bind the two poems may also have contributed to Webern's decision to unify his songs around a single row.

Webern responded to both of these themes in his musical settings, as we can see here. Goethe's vivid color imagery is matched by an admirably colorful instrumentation. The shimmering quality of the celesta and guitar is contrasted by a trio of more traditional orchestral timbres comprising violin, clarinet, and bass clarinet. The celesta was a favorite instrument of Webern's, and it features prominently in a number of his scores, but he composed rarely for guitar, perhaps because of the instrument's association with folk and popular music. He may have used the guitar in this context to complement the sound quality of the celesta, but also to evoke the *Volkslied* roots of Goethe's images.[9]

The second theme common to both texts, the Mandarin poet's anxious anticipation of the brilliant spring foliage to come, is conveyed by a luminous and dynamic musical surface. As our manuscript reveals, the songs are characterized by rapidly shifting layers of sound determined largely by performing forces and deployed in passages of homophony, polyphony, and heterophony. Webern's approach to the row results in a peculiar echoing and doubling effect that contributes further to the perception of shifting musical layers. In both songs, the trio of violin, clarinet, and bass clarinet "accompanies" the voices by

7 The colors found in Webern's first text (i.e., the white of the narcissus bed, as compared to lilies, candles, and stars, and the red glow of anticipation in which these images are enveloped) are mirrored subtly in the second poem by the white implicit in the images of sheep and clouds, and the red glow of the sun.

8 i.e., the closing lines of Webern's first text, "Mögen wohl die Guten wissen,/wenn sie so spaliert erwarten." (How well the good ones may know,/when thus they await the display.), and those of his second text, "Wunscherfühllung, Sonnenfeier,/Wolkentheilung bring' uns Glück!" (Wish fulfillment, sunburst,/parting clouds bring us luck!).

9 Webern had also written for guitar in his recently completed *Drei Lieder*, op. 18 (1925). This opus includes a folk text in Austrian dialect ("Schatzerl klein") and another taken from *Des Knaben Wunderhorn* ("Erlösung"). The only other composition in which he wrote for the guitar is the *Fünf Stücke für Orchester*, op. 10 (1911–1913), a work that was conceived programmatically and that at one time included a setting of his own folkish nature poem, "O sanftes Glühn der Berge."

presenting the same row as one or more of the vocal parts. While the instruments occasionally double the voices in a clear and audible fashion, more often their pitches are arranged so that the instrumental lines do not directly duplicate those of the voices.

This curious "accompanimental" effect can be seen in measures 23–25. Together, the soprano, alto, and tenor present the untransposed prime form for the phrase "Mögen wohl die," while the same row is given simultaneously in the three lower instruments. But while the bass clarinet literally duplicates the tenor line, the violin and clarinet perform a sort of *Stimmtausch*, revoicing the row pitches from the soprano and alto parts. The sonic effect is at once both lively and highly resonant, but the exact nature of this resonance remains somewhat obscured. The repeated-note figures seen herein, which are peculiar to Webern's early twelve-tone style, further blur these pitch correspondences and they create a lively rhythmic backdrop that contributes to the busy quality of the score. The resulting admixture of patterns, textures, and colors beautifully captures the vitality and sensuous pleasure of the Mandarin's garden paradise and his increased expectation of spring blossoms.

The manuscript shows an intermediate stage in the genesis of Webern's choral lieder. It appears to preserve his first attempt to write out the songs in a full, fair-copy score, proceeding from the sketches and done before a cleaner manuscript that was used as an engraver's copy.[10] Measures 21–26 are from the first song, "Weiß wie Lilien." The extensive amount of revision evident here and elsewhere in the manuscript does not constitute recomposition per se, but rather a refinement of details such as dynamics, phrasing, tempo, and articulation. Many of these details are either additions to, or revisions of, instructions already found in the sketches, and they reflect the special weight and importance Webern imparted to each musical gesture.

The most substantial compositional change in the manuscript is that seen in measures 25–26. The text for the passage, "Mögen wohl die Guten wissen,/wenn sie so spaliert erwarten." ("How well the good ones may know,/when thus they await the display,") follows a concise, objective

[10] The sketches for op. 19 extend from Webern's first sketchbook, now in the Robert Owen Lehman Collection at the Pierpont Morgan Library, to his second sketchbook, now located at CH Paul Sacher Stiftung. The cleaner fair copy, once owned by Webern's publisher, Universal Edition, is also found in the Lehman Collection at the Pierpont Morgan Library.

description of a white narcissus bed, and it ends the poem on a conditional note, in keeping with the theme of the expectation of spring. The manuscript shows that Webern revised his musical interpretation of the word "wissen" in measure 25, creating a tentative, "hocket" effect by syncopating the vocal parts, shortening their note values, and suspending them within the context of a triplet beat. This creates a slight hesitation at the end of the conditional phrase "How well the good ones may know," undermining in particular the cadential authority of the verb "to know." The dynamic level of the ensuing measure is then changed from piano decrescendo to forte. This sudden dynamic shift, coupled with the equally sudden shift to a more ecstatic style of declamation and a more active, polyphonic texture, adds to the instability of the passage, thereby heightening the Mandarin's anxious anticipation of the brilliant spring foliage to come.

One of the most intriguing aspects of the manuscript concerns Webern's approach to the use of clefs. Three of the four vocal parts (soprano, alto, and tenor) employ their respective transposable C-clefs. Practically speaking, this use of C-clefs would have been unusual for Webern's day, and it would most likely have been considered anachronistic and even somewhat mannered. The symbolic significance the clefs may hold becomes obscured when the poems are removed from the context of Goethe's original cycle. Webern may have intended the clefs to suggest an antique appearance, in keeping with both the character of the aged Mandarin who inhabits the garden world of the two poems and the theme of old age that the larger cycle addresses. That these musical symbols were employed deliberately is confirmed by Webern's sketches. Both the tenor and alto parts are notated from the very outset in their respective C-clefs; however, the soprano part was originally notated using a traditional treble clef.[11] Rather than revise the tenor and alto parts to conform to modern practice in the present manuscript, Webern intentionally recopied the soprano part using the anachronistic C-clef. The published score destroys this symbolism by adopting a conventional format featuring treble clefs for the three upper voices.

Webern's cover page for the manuscript is revealing in two ways. First, it indicates that he considered but later rejected an

[11] Webern's approach in the sketches can be observed most readily in the published sketches for an abandoned third movement, based on the poem "Auf Bergen in der reinsten Höhe" from Goethe's *Gott, Gemüt und Welt;* see Moldenhauer, *Anton von Webern Sketches,* pl. 2–3.

instruction suggesting that the songs might be performed by a solo quartet as well as a full, SATB choir. Second, it attests to the composer's fidelity to his literary source. Not only does he identify his poetic source in the title of the score, he also places Goethe's name above his own. A similarly comprehensive title accompanies the later fair copy manuscript that Webern submitted to Universal Edition.[12] The published title page omits any reference to Goethe or the *Tageszeiten* cycle, however, and it identifies the work simply as *Zwei Lieder für gemischten Chor*. Webern's red pencil revisions to the present title page follow the layout and contents of the published title page, and they were most likely made during or after 1928, when the work was published.

[12] The second title page reads: "Anton Webern/Zwei Lieder/aus/'Chinesisch-deutsche Jahres- und Tageszeiten'/von Goethe/für/gemischten Chor/Celesta, Gitarre, Geige, Klarinette und Bassklarinette/op. 19/Partitur."

Anton Webern's Jone Poems

Lauriejean Reinhardt

ON THE EVENING OF NOVEMBER 29, 1944, at the
Archbishop's Palace in Vienna, there occurred a poetry reading
devoted to the works of Hildegard Jone. The evening was
sponsored by Dr. Otto Mauer, a priest, professor, and patron of
modern art who was also a personal friend of Jone's. The
poetry reading was one of many such events that Mauer
organized during the latter days of World War II, for the
cultural and spiritual edification of his parishioners.[1] The same
poetry reading occasioned the elegant manuscript at hand, a
manuscript prepared by Anton Webern that contains all of the
Jone texts he set to music.[2]

The evening's program was planned from the very outset
around the poems Webern had set to music. Jone envisioned
Webern as reciter, and she also specifically requested a copy of
the texts in Webern's hand. On April 25, 1944, she wrote to
Webern:

> Please, dear Anton, write out the texts for me *sometime in the
> future,* in your own hand, in the correct sequence: I would
> like so very much to have them, perhaps as well with the
> indication that they are your texts.

Webern acknowledged Jone's request shortly thereafter and
completed the manuscript by June 2, 1944.[3]

The question of who would serve as the evening's reciter
proved considerably more problematic. In her attempt to
persuade Webern to assume the role, Jone argued:

> Regarding the recitation by you, that would frankly be the
> only satisfactory solution. Professional actors are, in a very
> large sense, dilettantes. Somehow, a word spoken by you
> truly is already entirely the music that you perceive in it:
> really your music.

[1] On Mauer's career and his patronage of modern art, see Inge Podbrecky, ed., *Sammlung Otto Mauer: Zum zehnten Todestag* (Vienna: Österreichische Bundesverlag, 1983). The Jone poetry reading is discussed briefly in Hans and Rosaleen Moldenhauer, *Anton von Webern: A Chronicle of His Life and Work* (New York: Alfred A. Knopf, 1979), pp. 596–97.

[2] Webern's manuscript contains only the texts for completed compositions (i.e., opp. 23, 25, 26, 29, and 31), not those for abandoned or incomplete projects.

[3] See his letters to Jone dated April 30, 1944, and June 2, 1944, in Josef Polnauer, ed., *Anton Webern: Briefe an Hildegard Jone und Josef Humplik* (Vienna: Universal Edition, 1959), pp. 56 and 58, respectively.

4 Webern to Jone, April 22, 1944 *(ÖNB/HIS, Webern Briefe,* 431/1–284).

5 Riemerschmid would play a far more significant role in the days immediately following World War II; i.e., that of safeguarding the Webern family home in Maria Enzersdorf.

6 Problems with the singer and the requested honorarium were discussed in a flurry of letters between Webern and Jone early in October 1944. Neither of the proposed singers is identified in the letters.

7 Although he did not specify the Mozart fantasia he had in mind, Webern referred to the work as "eine selten gespielte 'Fantasie'." (See his letter to Jone on November 25, 1944, in Polnauer, *Briefe,* p. 61). Since the C-Minor Fantasia, K. 475, was by this point a concert favorite, the work he had in mind must be either the Fantasia in D Minor, K. 397, or the earlier C-Minor Fantasia, K. 396.

This was apparently not the first time Jone had mentioned her desire for Webern to recite the poems. In an earlier letter, the composer had remarked that he was "pleased" (*glücklich*) and "fascinated!" (*fasziniert!*) with the idea of reciting the poems, but in such matters he was "unfortunately a dilettante" (hence Jone's later remark that professional actors were true dilettantes), adding "between the two of us, I regret this!"[4] Webern, in turn, tried his best to convince Jone that she should recite the poems.

> *but the reading, the reading,* dear Hilde, only *you yourself* should do it! What an *impressive rendering* you recently gave of your own poems and one of Goethe's. Recall how my wife reacted to it! Believe me, you must decide to do it! Consider the idea! What an experience it could be for an audience, *attendant* upon you in the *highest anticipation!!!* Think of that!

In the end, neither artist proved successful in convincing the other, and the task of reciting the poems ultimately fell to Werner Riemerschmid, a former neighbor of Webern's and a poet in his own right.[5]

As the date for the poetry reading approached, Webern became increasingly involved in the event's organization. In addition to Jone's poems, the evening was scheduled to include performances of the composer's *Drei Gesänge aus "Viae inviae" von Hildegard Jone,* op. 23, and the *Drei Lieder;* op. 25. The songs were eventually sacrificed when the original singer left Vienna for her native Sweden, and the "exceptional" singer Webern secured as a replacement demanded an honorarium.[6] Had the songs been performed, it would have marked the first and only time the composer heard a live public performance of any of his Jone settings.

When a performance of the songs became impossible, Webern proposed as alternative musical selections his *Variationen für Klavier,* op. 27 and Berg's *Sonata für Klavier,* op. 1. At the last minute, however, and for reasons largely of programming, Webern substituted for his own work one of Mozart's lesser-known *Fantasien.*[7] The change came about when Mauer asked for a musical selection to open the program. Since the audience was to consist of musical laymen (primarily church officials and

Drei Lieder, op. 25

I.

Wie bin ich froh!
noch einmal wird mir alles grün
und leuchtet so!
noch überblühn

die Blumen mir die Welt!
noch einmal bin ich ganz ins Werden
hingestellt
und bin auf Erden.

II.

Des Herzens Purpurvogel fliegt durch Nacht.
Der Augen Falter, die im Hellen gaukeln,
sind ihm voraus, wenn sie im Tage schaukeln.
Und doch ist er's, der sie ans Ziel gebracht.
Sie ruhen oft, die bald sich neu erheben
zu neuem Flug. Doch rastet endlich er
am Ast des Todes, müd und flügelschwer,
dann müssen sie zum letzten Blick verbeben.

III.

Sterne, Ihr silbernen Bienen der Nacht
um die Blume der Liebe!
Wahrlich der Honig aus ihr hängt schimmernd an Euch.
Lasset ihn tropfen ins Herz, in die goldene Wabe,
Füllet sie an bis zum Rand. Ach schon tropfet sie über
selig und bis ans Ende mit ewiger Süße durchtränkt.

Drei Gesänge, op. 23

2

Aus „Viae inviae"

I.

Das dunkle Herz, das in sich lauscht, erschaut den Frühling
nicht nur am Hauch und Duft, der in das Leuchten blüht.
es fühlt ihn an dem dunklen Wurzelreich, das an die Totenführt:
Was wird, legt sich mit zarten Wurzeln an das Wartende im
Dunkel,
trinkt Kraft und Stille aus der Nacht, eh' sich's dem Tage
schenkt,
eh' es als Liebeskelch zum Himmel duftet
und eh' aus ihm zu ihm ein goldnes Flattern Leben trägt:

Ich bin nicht mein.
Die Quellen meiner Seele,
sie sprudeln in die Wiesen dessen, der mich liebt,
und machen seine Blumen blühen und sind sein.

Du bist nicht dein.
Die Flüsse deiner Seele,
du Mensch, von mir geliebt,
sie strömen in das Meine, dass es nicht verdorre.

Wir sind nicht unser,
ich und du und alle.

II.

Es stürzt aus Höhen Frische, die uns leben macht:
das Herzblut ist die Feuchte uns geliehen,
die Träne ist die Kühle uns gegeben:
sie fließt zum Strom der Gnade wunderbar zurück.

parishioners), Webern decided that the evening should begin with a classical composition. Although Jone strenuously objected to the change, Webern argued that his own work might prove "problematic" and lead to "an occasion for head shaking and so on." The musical selections for the evening were ultimately limited to Berg's *Sonata* and the Mozart *Fantasia*, both performed by Olga Novacovic.[8]

Webern took an equally strong interest in the literary portion of the program. Using the manuscript he had prepared, the composer coached Riemerschmid to ensure that the latter's spoken renditions might approach his own musical interpretations. He further advised Riemerschmid to allow for "decided pauses" (*ausdrückliche Trennungen*) between individual works. In addition, Webern was apparently responsible for revising the sequence of poems for the evening's program. Although he had copied the poems according to his own opus numbers, beginning with the texts for the *Drei Gesänge*, op. 23, Webern reordered the manuscript to begin with the poems for the *Drei Lieder*, op. 25. This change is revealed by the repagination on the pages shown herein. The original page numbers, written in red pencil, had positioned the texts for the *Drei Gesänge* as pages 1–2, followed by the texts for the *Drei Lieder* as page 3. The original page numbers have been written over in lead pencil, so that the lieder texts now precede those for the *Gesänge*.

Webern's motivation for the revision may have been one of pacing. He may have felt that the short, lyric nature poems he had set as op. 25 would be more appropriate to commence the poetry portion of the program, as opposed to the texts for op. 23, which are longer, elegiac, and more deeply spiritual in nature. Then too, the texts for the *Gesänge*, op. 23 and *Das Augenlicht*, op. 26 are all taken from Jone's cycle "Viae inviae"; the revised manuscript ordering thus places the "Viae inviae" texts together.

Another program change concerns the addition of Jone's "Lumen" cycle to conclude the program. Webern had recently turned to the opening lines of the cycle ("Das Sonnenlicht spricht") in sketching a project left incomplete upon his death.[9] While he and Jone had earlier entertained the idea of

[8] Webern's decision to withdraw the *Variationen* is explained in letters to Jone dated November 25, 1944, and December 8, 1944 (see Polnauer, *Briefe*, pp. 61 and 62, respectively) and a letter to Riemerschmid dated November 25, 1944. Jone's disappointment about the sacrifice of Webern's work is expressed in letters to the composer dated November 22, 1944, and December 11, 1944.

[9] The "Lumen" sketches, initially conceived as part of an instrumental concerto, are reproduced in Hans Moldenhauer, *Anton von Webern Sketches (1926–1945): Facsimile Reproductions from the Composer's Autograph Sketchbooks in the Moldenhauer Archives* (New York: Carl Fischer, Inc., 1968), pl. 41–47.

[10] Webern informed Jone of Riemerschmid's request on November 18, 1944.

[11] Webern reports this development to Jone in a letter dated November 6, 1944 (*ÖNB/HIS Webern Briefe*, 431/1–301).

including the "Lumen" poems on the program, the decision to add them was not made until mid-November, just days before the event and largely at Riemerschmid's urging.[10] Since they were added at the last minute, the "Lumen" poems were read from a separate Jone autograph. It is also possible that selections from Jone's *Selige Augen* (Freiburg im Breisgau: Herder Verlag, 1938) were read, as Webern lent a copy of the volume to Riemerschmid before their final coaching session, when the evening's program was to be determined.[11]

One curious feature of Webern's poetry manuscript concerns the presence of Jone's handwriting on the back of one leaf. In preparing the manuscript, Webern wrote almost exclusively on the recto sides of pages; however, the verso of page 7 contains the poem "Schöpfen aus Brunnen," written in Jone's hand. Webern set this poem as the third movement of his *Kantate*, op. 31. He used the reverse side of Jone's page to copy out "Schweigt auch die Welt," the text for op. 31, movement I, which he indicated as page 7. He then pasted a separate sheet over Jone's poem and copied the text for "Sehr tiefverhalten innerst Leben singt," the poem he set as op. 31, movement II; this page is indicated as page 8. "Schöpfen aus Brunnen" was then recopied on a fresh page, which now follows as facing page 9. It is unclear why Webern broke his pattern of writing on recto sides only when he came to these texts, why he intentionally obscured Jone's original poem, or why he incorporated Jone's autograph leaf into the manuscript at all.

Frank Wedekind:
Stock Poster with His Autograph
Prologue to *Der Erdgeist*

Lauriejean Reinhardt

DURING THE WINTER AND SPRING of 1898, a dramatic
ensemble known as the Ibsen Theater and sponsored by the
Leipziger literarische Gesellschaft toured northern Germany,
Silesia, and Austria. The ensemble's program was devoted
almost exclusively to works by the playwright for whom it was
named, Henrik Ibsen, but in this, their final season, they also
included premiere performances of Frank Wedekind's Lulu
play *Der Erdgeist* (1895). Known to the *Gesellschaft* chiefly as a
poet, Wedekind accompanied the tour as a "dramaturgical
secretary," but he also performed incidental parts in various
Ibsen plays and interpreted the role of Dr. Schön in his own
work under the stage name Heinrich Kammerer. The tour
opened in Leipzig late in February, with three performances of
Der Erdgeist. The ensemble then traveled to Halle, Braunschweig,
Hamburg, Stettin, Breslau, and Vienna, returning to
Leipzig late in June for additional performances under the
sponsorship of the ensemble's director, Dr. Carl Heine.[1]

The stock poster used for the tour showed details concerning
the specific play, cast, date, and location, which were printed
for each performance in the framed area to the left.[2] The poster
was designed by Brynolf Wennerberg (1866–1950), a Swedish
artist who was active in Munich and who, like Wedekind,
contributed to the satiric journal *Simplizissimus.* Wennerberg's
elaborate illustration—with its sinuous lines, energetic surface
patterns, asymmetrical perspective, and sensuous interplay of
serpents, waves, and the female form—is a characteristic
example of turn-of-the-century *Jugendstil.* To the left, peering
over the empty frame, is a bust of Ibsen. To the right is a
likeness of "The Woman from the Sea" ("Die Frau vom
Meer"), a character from Ibsen's play by the same title that was
performed on the tour. Other Ibsen works performed by the

[1] On the circumstances surrounding the
Ibsen Theater tour and the first
performances of *Der Erdgeist*, see Kurt
Martens, *Schonungslose Lebenschronik
1870–1900* (Vienna: Rikola-Verlag, 1921),
pp. 206–7, 216–18; Artur Kutscher, *Frank
Wedekind: Sein Leben und seine Werke* (Munich
and Leipzig: Georg Müller Verlag, 1922;
repr., New York: AMS Press, 1970), Bd., 1,
pp. 395–97; Frank Seehaus, *Frank Wedekind
und das Theater 1898–1959* (Munich:
Laokoon-Verlag, 1964), pp. 132 passim, see
esp. pp. 339–48, and Seehaus, *Frank
Wedekind in Selbstzeugnissen und
Bilddokumenten* (Reinbeck bei Hamburg:
Rowohlt Verlag, 1974), pp. 78–81; and
Joachim Friedenthal, ed., *Das Wedekindbuch*
(Munich and Leipzig: Georg Müller Verlag,
1914), see esp. Joachim Friedenthal,
"Frank Wedekind. Sein Leben und sein
Werk. Eine Monographie," pp. 16–18, and
Max Liebermann, "Wie ich Wedekind
kennen lernte," pp. 212–23.

[2] For reproductions of the stock poster that
include details for actual performances, see
Hans-Jochen Irmer, *Der Theaterdichter Frank
Wedekind: Werk und Wirkung* (Berlin:
Henschelverlag, 1979), pl. 23, and Seehaus,
Frank Wedekind in Selbstzeugnissen, p. 80.

Hereinspaziert in die Menagerie,
Ihr stolzen Herren, ihr lebenslust'gen Frauen,
Mit heißer Wollust und mit kaltem Grauen
Die unbeseelte Kreatur zu schauen,
Gebändigt durch das menschliche Genie!
Hereinspaziert, die Vorstellung beginnt,
Auf zwei Personen kommt umsonst ein Kind.

Hier kämpfen Mensch und Tier in engen Gittern,
Wo dieser seine Peitsche höhnend schwingt
Und jenes mit Gebrüll wie Inge'weiher
Dem Menschen mörderisch an die Kehle springt,
Wo bald der Starke, bald der Klüg're siegt,
Bald Tier, bald Mensch geduckt am Estrich liegt,
Schirrmi das Tier, der Mensch auf allen Vieren —
Ein eisig kalter Herrscherblick,
Die Bestie beugt entwürdigt das Genick
Und läßt sich fromm die Ferse drauf postieren.

Schlecht sind die Zeiten. All die Herrn und Damen,
Die einst vor meinem Käfig sich gescharrt,
Bechren Jason, Posse, Ehen, Dramen
Mit ihrer hochgeschätzten Gegenwart.
Für meine Schandler fehlte mir das Futter,
Hätt' ein Turnvereinsverein nicht, sieggewürdert,
Mich hin und wieder eine Schwiegermutter
Mächtlicher Weile in den Sommer geführt.
Ja welch ein Abstand zwischen dem Theater
Und der Menagerie im Wiener Prater!

Was aber zeigt in Lust und Trauerspielen?
Haustiere, die so wohlerzogen fühlen,
Ja ihren Schmerz so wildlich kühlen
Und schwelgen in behaglichem Geplärre
Wie jene andern Tiere im Parterre.
Den Helden hört man an der Welt verzagen,
Ihr! Arie hört man ihn darüber klagen,
Und niemand, der den Gnadenstoß ihm gibt.
Das wilde Tier, das schöne, wahre Tier,
Das, meine Damen, sehn Sie nur bei mir.
Hereinspaziert! Es krielt nicht das Leben,
Und wem es fehlt, dem wird's bei mir gegeben.

Sie sehn den Tiger, der gewöhnheitsmäßig
Was in den Weg ihm läuft hinunterschlingt,
Den Bären, der von Anbeginn gefräßig
Sich durch ein spätes Mahl ums Leben bringt;
Sie sehn den kleinen amüsanten Affen
Aus Langeweile seine Kraft verpassen;
Er hat Talent, doch fehlt die wahre Größe,
Drum kokettiert er frech mit seiner Blöße;
Sie sehn in meinem Zelte, meiner Seele,
Sogar gleich hinterm Vorhang ein Kameel;
Und sanft schmiegt das Vieh sich mir zu Füßen,
Wenn donnernd kommernd mein — Revolver knallt;
Es bebt die Creatur, ich bleibe kalt
Und bleibe kalt, Sie ehrfurchtsvoll zu grüßen!
Hereinspaziert! Sie trau'n sich nicht herein?

Vernöhnlen, sie wollen selber Richter sein:
Ich hab auch das Gewürm aus allen Poren,
Chamäleone, Schlangen, Krokodile,
Drachen und Molche, die in Sümpfen wohnen;
Gewiss, ich weiß, Sie lächeln in der Stille
Und glauben mir nicht eine Sylbe mehr.
He, August, bring mir meine Schlange her!
Sie ward geschaffen, Unheil anzustiften,
Zu locken, zu verführen, zu vergiften,
Zu morden, ohne dass es einer spürt.
Ihr, liebes Tier, ihr doch nichts so gerührt!
Es ist jetzt nichts besondres draußen sehen,
Doch warten Sie, was drinnen wird geschehen,

Mit starkem Druck umringelt sie den Tiger,
Er stöhnt und heult; wer bleibt am Ende Sieger?
Hopp, August, marsch! Trag sie an ihren Platz,
Die süße Unschuld, meinen größten Schatz.

Und nun ist mir noch das Beste zu erwähnen:
Mein Schädel zwischen eines Raubtiers Zähnen;
Hereinspaziert, das Schauspiel ist nicht neu,
Doch seine Freude hat man oft dabei.
Ich wag' es ihm den Rachen aufzureißen,
Und diese Bestie wagt nicht dreinzubeißen;
So schön sie ist, so wild, und buntgefleckt,
Vor meinem Schädel hat das Tier Respect.
Getrost leg ich mein Haupt ihm in den Rachen;
Ein Biß, und meine beiden Schläfen krachen;
Dabei verspiel ich auf des Auges Blitz,
Mein Leben setze ich gegen einen Witz;
Die Peitsche werf ich fort und diese Waffen,
Und geh, mich kümmert, wie mich Gott geschaffen,
Will ihr den Namen, den die Raubtierin führt?
Verehrtes Publicum — hereinspaziert!

Es schwillt das Fieber meinen Pensionären
So dass sie gegenseitig sich verzehren.
Wie gottlob geht's halt zum Theater ein Schwein!
Des Henkers wird seinen Sorgen sich nicht stiller,
Sei auch der Hunger ein ganz fürchterlicher
Und des Directors Magen noch so leer.
Doch will man Großes in der Kunst erreichen
Darf man Verdienst nicht mit dem Glück vergleichen.

Was sucht man denn in Lust- und Trauerspielen ...

3 *Der Erdgeist: Eine Tragödie in vier Aufzügen* (Paris/ Leipzig/Munich: Albert Langen Verlag, 1895). Wedekind would later incorporate much of the excised material into a companion play, *Die Büchse der Pandora: Tragödie in drei Aufzügen* (Berlin: Bruno Cassirer, 1904). On the complex evolution and publication history of the Lulu dramas, see Manfred Hahn, ed., *Frank Wedekind: Werke in drei Bänden* (Berlin and Weimar: Aufbau-Verlag, 1969), Bd. 1., pp. 704–8; Kutchser, op. cit., pp. 337–56; and Seehaus, *Frank Wedekind und das Theater*, pp. 339–40.

4 As recounted by Martens, op. cit., p. 205, later cited in Kutscher, op. cit., p. 396. Some confusion exists about the version of Wedekind's Lulu drama that was performed by the Ibsen Theater. Taking his cue perhaps from Marten's claim that the work was performed "vollständig und ungestrichen," Jack Stein maintained that is was the original, five-act "Monstre-tragödie" that was premiered in 1898; see "Lulu: Alban Berg's Adaptation of Wedekind," *Comparative Literature* 26 (1974): 323. Upon closer inspection, this appears not to be the case. Martens clearly refers to the play by the revised, published title, *Erdgeist*. Moreover, the stock posters cited in n. 2 above establish that the play performed was in four and not five acts.

5 See Seehaus, *Frank Wedekind und das Theater*, p. 132, and Kutscher, op. cit., p. 397.

6 [Das für Morgen durch die Ibsen-Gesellschaft im Carltheater zur Aufführung bestimmte Stück "Erdgeist" ist bekanntlich verboten worden. Das Stück ist nicht, wie etwa der Titel "Erdgeist" vermuthen lassen könnte, aus irgend einem religiösen oder socio-politischen Grunde untersagt worden; die Behörde macht geltend, daß das Werk vom sittlichen Standpunkte aus anstößig sei...Einem Berichterstatter gegenüber, welcher heute den Verfasser des verbotenen Stückes, Herrn Frank Wedekind, und den Director des Ibsen-Ensembles, Dr. Heine, besuchte, sprachen diese ihr größtes Erstaunen über das Censurverbot aus...] *Neue Freie Presse* (Wien: Samstag, 11 Juni 1898), "Theater-und Kunstnachrichten" p. 8. Before this date, *Erdgeist* had been announced on the theater pages of the *Presse* for performances on June 3, 5, 8, 10, 11, and 12.

ensemble included *Nora, Ein Volksfeind, Die Wildente, Hedda Gabler, Rosmersholm, and Gespenster.*

Adding *Der Erdgeist* to the tour schedule was a bold and risky venture. At best, the play provided an uneasy counterpoint to the naturalistic works of Ibsen. Wedekind's original Lulu tale, a five-act play entitled *Die Büchse der Pandora: Eine Monstretragödie* (1892–1894), had initially been rejected by the Leipzig publisher Albert Langen as too controversial. The version ultimately published by Langen and premiered by the Ibsen Theater was revised and condensed into four acts, with a new third act and without the sensational fifth act where Lulu is brutally murdered by Jack the Ripper.[3] Even with these changes, the play had been rejected for public performance by Otto Brahm's progressive *Freie Bühne* after a series of private readings in Berlin, and it was only added to the Ibsen Theater tour after "much pestering" by Wedekind.[4]

Reservations about the work proved well-founded. The initial Leipzig performances registered as a qualified success, after which time the play's fate rapidly declined. The Stettin performance was cancelled after a near scandal in Hamburg.[5] The play was announced for performance in Vienna no less than five times in the *Neue Freie Presse;* however, it was not performed in that city, due to a ban by the local censor. The evening edition of the *Presse* on June 10 included a short announcement of the ban, with a full account of the situation appearing in the "Theater-und Kunstnachrichten" section the following day.

> The Ibsen Theater Company's performance of *Erdgeist* scheduled for tomorrow at the Carl Theater has, as you know, been forbidden. The work has not been prohibited on any particular religious or sociopolitical grounds, as might be imagined from the title *Erdgeist;* the authorities maintain that the work is offensive from a moral standpoint....The author of the forbidden work, Mr. Frank Wedekind, and the director of the Ibsen Ensemble, Dr. Carl Heine, expressed the greatest surprise over the prohibition to a reporter who visited them today....[6]

With a Vienna performance out of the question, Wedekind and

Heine seized the opportunity to propagandize on behalf of the play. In the notice quoted above, the reporter went on to present details of the strenuous objections voiced by Heine and Wedekind regarding both the ban of *Der Erdgeist* and the stifling conditions currently plaguing the German-speaking theater. Even more significantly, however, while the last-minute cancellation of *Der Erdgeist* was undoubtedly a personal disappointment for Wedekind, the prospect of performances in the Austro-Hungarian capital had yielded a tangible result—the celebrated Prologue for the play.

The original version of the Prologue, little known in the Wedekind literature, was drafted on the verso of the Ibsen Theater poster shown here. The circumstances surrounding the creation of the Prologue are recounted in an informal memoir by Hilde Auerbach, daughter of the theatrical agent Berthold Auerbach who accompanied the Ibsen Theater on the 1898 tour. The essential facts of Hilde Auerbach's memoir, which accompanies the stock poster in the Moldenhauer Archives at the Library of Congress, are reproduced below.

> My father's story [of] how Wedekind came to write this Prologue is as follows: Just before the first performance of the *Erdgeist* in Vienna (late summer of 1898) [sic], Dr. Heine, Wedekind and my father were sitting in a Cafe in Vienna and Dr. Heine remarked to Wedekind that the Vienna public would not understand his play without a prologue. There and then, Wedekind snatched the huge poster of the Ibsen Theater from my father. (These posters announcing the various Ibsen Theater plays and the casts all showed on one side Ibsen's head and on the other the naked "Frau vom Meer" [woman of the sea].) On the back of it, Wedekind wrote in one go, leaning on the Cafe house table, the first version of his famous Prologue to the Lulu-Tragedy. He spoke it himself in the first night of the play in Vienna [*sic*] because he himself played the part of the Circus Director, and my father was fond of imitating him as he stood before the curtain, pistol in one hand, whip in the other, speaking the words of the prologue with his harsh voice rolling his Rs and suddenly firing the pistol in the air, thus frightening the ladies.

Since the play was not performed in Vienna, Berthold

7 [PROLOGUE ZUM ERDGEIST /
TRAGOEDIE IN VIER AKTEN VON
FRANK WEDEKIND / GESPROCHEN
GELEGENTLICH DER ZEHNTEN
AUFFUEHRUNG DES "ERDGEIST"
DURCH DAS IBSEN-THEATER (DIR:
DR. CARL HEINE) IM KRYSTALL-
PALAST IN LEIPZIG. 24. JUNI 1898.]
Die Insel 6 (March 1901), 315.

Auerbach's recollection that the Prologue was presented in that city must be mistaken. The earliest-known performance of the play to include the Prologue occurred later the same month, in Leipzig. This information accompanies the Prologue as it appeared in a revised, near-final version, published in 1901 in the journal *Die Insel*. The heading for the revised Prologue text reads as follows: "PROLOGUE TO ERDGEIST / TRAGEDY IN FOUR ACTS BY FRANK WEDEKIND / SPOKEN ON THE OCCASION OF THE TENTH PERFORMANCE OF 'ERDGEIST' BY THE IBSEN THEATER (DIRECTED BY DR. CARL HEINE) IN THE CRYSTAL PALACE IN LEIPZIG, 24 JUNE 1898."[7] Long misinterpreted to mean that the Prologue was written for the tenth, Leipzig performance of *Der Erdgeist*, this heading should be interpreted more literally, as a report of the Prologue's first delivery.

While some of Berthold Auerbach's details may be inaccurate, his tale of the Prologue's genesis is substantiated by the original text, for among the many variants between autograph and published versions is a passage directed specifically toward a Viennese audience. In the original third stanza (lines 22–27), the Animal Trainer who narrates the Prologue laments the fact that the crowds have abandoned his menagerie for more genteel forms of entertainment, ironically listing among their new interests "Ibsen" and "plays." He concludes with an acerbic outburst, comparing the poverty of life in the theater (represented by his menagerie) with the comfortable complacency of the Viennese bourgeois, known for leisurely promenades through the city's famous park, the Prater: "Ha, welch ein Abstand zwischen dem Theater/Und der Menagerie im Wiener Prater!" [Ha, what a difference between the theater/and the menagerie in the Vienna Prater!]

This local reference was one of the many passages changed or deleted when the Prologue was later adapted for a general audience. Wedekind's revision can be seen here in pencil. The latter portion of the third stanza has been crossed out and marked "F" for *fortlassen* or "omit." The replacement lines, drafted across to the right, expand the stanza and focus more generally on the poverty of theatrical life. Like the original, the revised stanza concludes with a comparison, but one of a more universal, moralistic tone in which true art is distinguished from financial success: "Doch will man Großes in der Kunst erreichen/Darf man Verdienst nicht mit dem Glück vergleichen." [But if one wants to achieve greatness in art/one should not equate earnings with success.]

Wedekind's other revisions range from minor adjustments involving syntax and word choice to more substantial alterations of meaning. One of the more illuminating revisions is found in stanza four. The original version of lines 29–30 ("Haustiere, die so wohlerzogen fühlen/An blassen Theorien ihr Mütchen kühlen") [House pets who think they're so well-bred/vent their rage on pale theories] was later changed to "Haustiere, die so wohlgesittet fühlen,/An blasser Pflanzenkost ihr Mütchen kühlen." [House pets who think they're so well-mannered/vent their rage on a pale vegetarian meal.] The key expression "blassen Theorien" [pale theories] recalls a famous passage from one of the opening scenes of Goethe's *Faust* (I:2038). At this point in the poem, Mephistopheles, disguised as Faust, instructs a novice on the difference between theory and practice, privileging the latter by claiming "Grau, teurer Freund, ist alle Theorie." [Gray, dear friend, is all theory.] Wedekind's original Faustian reference may well have been aimed at his presumed Viennese audience; more specifically, the young aesthetes who patronized Vienna's famed coffeehouses and cultivated an urbane and highly literate or "wohlerzogen" [well-bred] image. The substituted phrase "blasser Pflanzenkost" [pale vegetarian meal] refers more generally to the international class of young European aesthetes, many of whom were avowed vegetarians.

Collectively, Wedekind's revisions yield a more polished result that is finely attuned to the events and characters of the ensuing drama. He would ultimately add a number of stage directions, including an introductory paragraph that sets the scene and calls for specific costumes and sound effects. By way of contrast, the impression offered by the original version shown here is one of an improvisation that had been noted down, as Auerbach recalled, on the spur of the moment. The few in-process ink changes shown on the manuscript suggest that Wedekind's ideas flowed freely as he drafted the text. His passion for the circus and intimate acquaintance with the rhetoric of the circus barker served him particularly well in this regard. Wedekind borrowed a variety of stock phrases from the circus world for his Prologue—most notably the invitation "Hereinspaziert!" [Step right up!]—using them as a scaffolding around which to structure his original lines. His experience as a lyric poet and cabaret *recitateur* is likewise evident in the Prologue, for even the unedited version possesses a genuine musical quality, revealing in particular a keen sensitivity to rhythm and meter.

Moldenhauer's interest in the Wedekind manuscript was undoubtedly influenced by Alban Berg's memorable setting of the Prologue in *Lulu*, his operatic adaptation of Wedekind's two Lulu plays. In all likelihood, Berg did not know the original version of the Prologue. Moldenhauer's acquisition of the Wedekind manuscript attests rather to his interest in the broader spectrum of musical history and the sister arts.

Inventory

Abeille, Ludwig, 1761–1838
Library of Congress
(Box 1)
A. L. S.: to Breitkopf & Härtel. Stuttgart, 24 Nov.
 1809. 1p., German

Abert, Hermann, 1871–1927
Library of Congress
(Box 1)
A. Card S.: 1 Dec. 1926. 1p., German

Abert, Johann Joseph, 1832–1915
Library of Congress
(Box 1)
A. Mus. Quot. S.: *Ekkehard*, Act II, scene 2, Stuttgart,
 Mar. 1887

Abt, Franz Wilhelm, 1819–1885
Library of Congress
(Box 1)
A. Mus. ms. S.: *Es klinget so lieblich im grünen Hain*, op.
 131, No. 2. 2p., 28x34cm. Complete score
A. Mus. ms. S.: *Leise rauscht's im Lindenbaume*, 29 June
 1870. 3p., 35x22cm. Complete score
A. Mus. ms. S.: *Mein Lieb ist fortgezogen*, op. 131,
 No. 1. 2p., 28x34cm. Complete score
A. Mus. ms. S.: *Schifferständchen*, op. 176. 3p., 27x34cm.
 Full score
Mus. ms. cop.: [Two songs with piano
 accompaniment]. 4p.
3 A. L. S.: Braunschweig, 12 Dec. 1854, 5 Sept. 1862,
 11 June 1875. 5p., German
7 A. L. S.: [to Bartolf Senff]. Braunschweig,
 1857–1878; Suderode, 1882. 10p., German

Accorimboni [Accoramboni, Accorimbeni, Accorrimboni], Agostino, 1739–1818
Library of Congress
(Box 1)
A. Mus. ms. S.: *Litanies de la Ste Vierge*. 8p., 22x29cm.
 Full score
A. Mus. ms. S.: *Veni sponsa Christi*. 8p., 22x28cm. Full score

Achron, Joseph, 1886–1943
Library of Congress
(Box 79, unless noted)
A. Mus. ms. S.: *Hebrew Dance for Orchestra*, op. 35, No.
 1, St. Petersburg, Russia, Aug. 1912, orchestrated
 1913. 44p., 38x26cm. Full score
Mus. ms. arr.: *Children's Suite*, op. 57, 1923, transcribed
 for large orchestra by David Tamkin, 1942. 94p.
Mus. ms. cop.: *Sextet*, op. 73, 1938. 8p. Bassoon part
Mus. ms. Repro.: *Elegy for String Quartet (or String
 Orchestra)*, op. 62. 8p.
Mus. ms. Repro.: *Sextet*, op. 73, 1938, in *New Music*,
 July 1942. 32p.
Pri. Sco.: *Statuettes*, 1930, in *New Music*, Oct. 1931. 16p.
Port. Phot.: by Maurice Toldberg (Box 110)

Adair, Loren W., b. 1904
Harvard University
SUMMARY OF PRINCIPAL HOLDINGS:
Mus. ms.: *Blessed Jesus, We Are Here*
2 Port.

Adam, Adolphe, 1803–1856
Library of Congress
(Box 1, unless noted)
A. Mus. ms. S.: *Marche de la jolie...*, 12 July 1842. 1p.,
 32x27cm. Piano score
A. L. S.: to Pacini. ?, 1 Oct.[?] 1842. 1p., French.
 Mounted with portrait lithograph, by Aubert (Box
 110)
A. L. S.: to David. Paris, 24 Mar. 1851. 3p., French
Port. Lith.: see letter above (Box 110)

Adler, Guido, 1855–1941
Wiener Stadt- u. Landesbibliothek
L.: to Karl Weigl. Vienna, 28 June 1918

Alary, Jules Eugène Abraham, 1814–1891
Library of Congress
(Box 1)
A. L. S.: Haymarket, 2 July 1871. 1p., French

Albani [Lajeunesse], Dame Emma, 1847–1930
Harvard University
6 L.
Port.: several portraits

Northwestern University
L.: to Mulde. London, 25 June 1881
L.: to Mrs. Eliot. London, 29 May 1892
4 L.
Doc.: Recital announcement. [1905]. With portrait
    reproduced
3 Port.

Albéniz, Isaac, 1860–1909
Library of Congress
(Box 1)
A. L. S.: to Kufferath. Nice, 28 Mar. 1904. 4p., French.
    Regarding *Pepita*
Pri. Sco. S.: *Mazurka*, Madrid: Antonio Romero, to
    Madame Berthe —[?], London, 18 May 1889. 8p.

Albergati, Pirro, 1663–1735
Library of Congress
(Box 1)
A. L. S.: to Count Silvio Albergati (uncle). Bologna,
    6 Jan. 1693. 2p., Italian

d'Albert, Eugen [Eugène], 1864–1932
Library of Congress
(Box 1)
A. Mus. ms. S.: *Caprice et Fuge* in C Minor for the
    Pianoforte, 6 June 1876. 8p., 30x24cm., ink.
    Complete score. Bound with manuscript below

A. Mus. ms. S.: [Fugue in A-flat Major for Organ],
    16 Jan. 1879. 12p., 29x23cm. Complete score. Bound
    with manuscript above
A. Mus. ms. S.: *Rosmarien (aus Des Knaben Wunderhorn)*.
    2p., 35x26cm., ink. Song with piano accompaniment
A. L. S.: to a conductor. Lausanne, 29 Feb. 1884. 1p.,
    German
A. L. S.: Berlin, 3 Nov. 1904. 2p., German
A. L. S.: Lago Maggiore, 12 June 1905. 1p., German
6 A. L. S.: 1912–1918. 16p., German
A. L. S.: to Universal Edition. Ventimiglia, 19 Apr.
    1928. 4p., German. Detailed correction list for *Die
    schwarze Orchidee*
P. card: with address for Hilde d'Albert
Doc. S.: Certificate. Membership at Wiener
    Tonkünstler-Verein for Marta Frank, signed by
    d'Albert as President. Vienna, 5 Oct. 1913. 1p.,
    German

Alboni, Marietta [Maria Anne Marzia], 1826–1894
Library of Congress
(Box 1)
A. L. S.: London, 14 Dec. 1870. 1p., Italian
A. L. S.: to Countess Tuaffe. n.p., n.d. 1p., Italian
A. Mus. Quot. S.: *Cenerentola* by Rossini. Paris, 29 Nov.
    1871
See Grisi, Giulia

Alessandrescu, Alfred, 1893–1959
Library of Congress
(Box 110)
Port. Phot. S.: to Boaz Piller, Bucharest, Apr. 1938

Allende, Pedro Humberto, 1885–1959
Harvard University
Mus. ms.: *Estudio*

Allitsen [Bumpus], Mary Francis, 1849–1912
Northwestern University
L.: to George Cecil. London, 22 Jan. 1902

Alpaerts, Flor, 1876–1954
Washington State University
L.: to Solomon Pimsleur. Antwerp, 29 July 1929

Altmann, Wilhelm, 1862–1951
Library of Congress
(Box 1)
A. L. S.: Berlin, 30 July 1924. 1p., German. Mentions
    Busoni

Altwegg, Raffaele, b. 1938
Zentralbibliothek Zürich
SUMMARY OF PRINCIPAL HOLDINGS:
Mus. ms.: *Meditazione*. Complete score
    4 L.: to Hans Moldenhauer. 1956–1974
Mus. Quot.: *Magrapresad*, to Hans Moldenhauer, 1956
Port. Phot.

Alwyn, William, 1905–1985
Northwestern University
L.: to Alan Rawsthorne. Speedwell, 6 Dec. 1954
L.: to Edward Clark. London, 1 Feb. 1956

Amadé, August, 1867–1930
Library of Congress
(Box 1)
A. Mus. ms. S.: *Klavier-Etude*, op. 52, No. 5, to Ella
    Panera. 5p., 34x27cm.

Amar, Licco, 1891–1959
Washington State University
See Rosbaud, Hans

Ambros, August Wilhelm, 1816–1876
Library of Congress
(Box 1)
A. Mus. ms. S.: Benedictus, for men's voices, 8 Jan.
    1875. 1p., 24x19cm.

Ambrosi, Gustinus, 1893–1975
Library of Congress
(Box 1)
P. card S.: to Karl Weigl. Vienna, 22 Jan. 1924. German.
    With photograph of his sculpture
See Weigl, Karl

Amengual, René, 1911–1954
Harvard University
Mus. ms.: *Cantar Chileno*, to Olga Coelho, Santiago,
    8 Aug. 1945

Amy, Gilbert, b. 1936
Washington State University
See Rosbaud, Hans

Ander, Aloys, 1817–1864
Library of Congress
(Box 1)
A. L. S.: Vienna, 20 Mar. 1839. 1p., German
A. L. S.: Salzbrunn, 4 July 1839. 1p., German

Anderson, George Frederick, 1793–1876
Northwestern University
3 L.: to Spencer Ponsonby. London, 19 May 1865,
    27 Mar. 1868, 26 Feb. 1870
L.: from Lucy Anderson (wife). London, 12 May 1865

Anderson, Thomas Jefferson, b. 1928
Harvard University
SUMMARY OF PRINCIPAL HOLDINGS:
Mus. ms.: *Squares, An Essay for Orchestra*, Sept. 1965.
    Complete score
Mus. ms. Repro.: *Personals*. Facsimile

André, Johann [Jean], 1741–1799
Northwestern University
Doc.: Theoretical treatise

André, Johann Anton, 1775–1842
Library of Congress
(Box 1)
A. Mus. ms. S.: *Missa*, No. 2. 52p., 21x34cm., German.
    Full score. Bound. With autograph title page, and
    1p. "Vorbericht" on inside cover

Andreae, Volkmar, 1879–1962
Washington State University
See Rosbaud, Hans

Zentralbibliothek Zürich
L.: Zurich, July 1920
Pri. Sco.: *Sinfonische Fantasie*

Andriessen, Hendrik, 1892–1981
Library of Congress
(Box 1)
A. Mus. ms. S.: *Symphonie II*, Fantasia, 1937. 1p.
  (opening page), 36x24cm.
A. L. S.: to Hans Moldenhauer. The Hague, 31 May
  1959. 1p., English
L. S.: to Hans Moldenhauer, from Caecilia Andriessen.
  The Hague, 27 June 1956. 1p., English
Call. c. S.

Andriessen, Jurriaan, 1925–1996
Library of Congress
(Box 1)
A. Mus. ms. S.: *Concerto per due pianoforte*, 1944. 27p.,
  34x27cm.
2 T. L. S.: to Hans Moldenhauer. The Hague,
  30, 31 Oct. 1959. 2p., English

Angyal, László, b. 1900
Library of Congress
(Box 1)
A. Doc. S.: Testimonial. Gustav Mahler's period of
  activity in Hungary. 1p., German
T. Doc.: Biography. 3p., German

Anne Cecile, Sister S.N.J.M., b. 1908
Harvard University
Mus. ms.: *Concerto for Violin and Orchestra*
L.
Prog.

Anonymous
Library of Congress
(Box 2, unless noted)
A. Mus. ms.: [Songs], "dedié à Made. de B—," 1775.
  6p., 22x30cm., French. For voice, solo and duet,
  with figured bass acccompaniment
Doc.: Dictionary. [post–1780]. 15 leaves, Italian, ink.
  Covering composers G-Q

Mus. ms.: [Neumes]. Vellum leaf, richly illuminated in
  black, red, blue, with gold, 22x17cm., Latin. The
  first four lines (of eighteen) with musical notation
  for the text passage beginning with "O culpa"
  (Shelf)
Mus. ms.: [Organ Tablature]. 32x20cm., German, ink.
  8p. Excerpt. The cover is a floral patterned marbled
  paper (Shelf)
Doc.: Historical essay. *Liutomonografia*, on violin
  making and violin builders in Italy. [1872]. 52p. + 3
  leaves inserted + 5p. clippings (German), 23x18cm.,
  Italian. Bound. On inside cover, "Bart. Poda, Pietro
  Bagatella, Pavia"

Ansermet, Ernest, 1883–1969
Washington State University
See Rosbaud, Hans

Zentralbibliothek Zürich
L.: to Rudolph Ganz. Geneva, 22 Apr. 1952
Port. Phot.: 1949
See Martin, Frank

Ansorge, Conrad, 1862–1930
Library of Congress
(Box 2)
A. L. S.: to Schrader. Irvington-on-the-Hudson,
  8 Sept. 1888. 4p., German
Draw. Repro.: Ansorge at the piano

Anthes, Georg, b. 1863
Library of Congress
(Box 2)
A. Alb. l. S.: Dresden, May 1889

Apostel, Hans Erich, 1901–1972
Library of Congress
(Box 103, unless noted)
A. Mus. ms. S.: *Cello Sonate*, op. 35. 2p., 30x21cm.
  Sketches
A. Mus. ms. S.: *Haydn Variationen*, op. 17. 1p.,
  44x34cm. Full score. With autograph note on verso
A. Mus. ms. S.: *Rondo rítmico für grosses Orchester*, op.
  27. 9p., 34x27cm. Sketches
A. Mus. ms. S.: *Zwei Gesänge*, op. 40, No. 1. 3p.,
  34x27cm.

P. card S.: to Julius Schloss. Vienna, 13 Nov. 1935.
German. Also signed by Steuermann, Felix Galimir,
Novakovic, Polnauer, Leopold Spinner, Jakob
Gimpel, Zenk and others. Card announces program
for the Verein für Neue Musik
P. card S.: to Paul Sanders. Recco, 24 May 1939.
German. Quotes a phrase from *Wozzeck*
T. L. S.: to Hans Moldenhauer. Vienna, 5 July 1965.
1p., German
A. Mus. Quot. S.: *Der Sechziger dankt für die Wünsche*, to
Polnauer, 2 Feb. 1961. 1p.
Mus. ms. Repro. S.: *Ode*, op. 36, to Hans Moldenhauer,
Vienna, July 1970. 52p. + 2p. typed text signed.
Blueprint score
Pri. Sco. S.: *Kammersymphonie*, op. 41, Vienna:
Universal, c1969, to Hans Moldenhauer, 1970. 68p.
Prog.: *Kammersymphonie*, op. 41, to Hans Moldenhauer,
4 June 1968. With accompanying printed invitation
to the premiere, to Hans Moldenhauer, and musical
quotation
Port. Phot. S.: Vienna, 1971. By Bellingrath (Box 110)
See Füssl, Karl Heinz

Wiener Stadt- u. Landesbibliothek
SUMMARY OF PRINCIPAL HOLDINGS:
Doc.: Typescript. "Kontroverse mit Helene Berg"

d'Arányi, Jelly, 1895–1966
Library of Congress
(Box 2)
A. L. S.: n.p., n.d. 2p., English. Fragment

d'Archambeau, Iwan, 1879–1955
Harvard University
See Flonzaley Quartet

Arditi, Luigi, 1822–1903
Library of Congress
(Box 2, unless noted)
A. Mus. ms. S.: *Il desio, duetto fantastico per soprano e
contralto*, to Carlotta and Barbara Marchisio, London,
5 Sept. 1862. 12p., 25x31cm. With cadenzas.
Complete score
A. Mus. Quot. S.: *Margherita*, Cincinnati, 6 Feb. 1883.
1p.
Port. Phot. S. Repro. (Box 110)

Areán, Juan Carlos, b. 1961
Harvard University
L.: to Aurelio de la Vega. 1983

Arensky, Anton Stepanovitch, 1861–1906
Library of Congress
(Box 110)
Port. Phot. S.: With accompanying musical quotation,
[Piano trio in D Minor]

Argentina, La, [Antonia Mercé], 1888–1936
Library of Congress
(Box 110, unless noted)
Port. Phot. S.: to Boaz Piller. Boston, Nov. 1929
Bk.: *La Argentina*, by Carlos Manso (Shelf)

Argento, Dominick, b. 1927
Harvard University
Mus. ms.: *The Voyage of Edgar Allan Poe*, 1973–1975
L.: to Hans Moldenhauer. Minneapolis, 25 Oct. 1976
Doc.: Program booklet. With invitation, 24 Apr. 1976

Arkan, Muzaffer, b. 1923
Library of Congress
(Box 2)
3 T. L. S.: to Hans Moldenhauer. Ankara, 6 Dec. 1959,
1 May, 1 Sept. 1960. 3p., German
L. Repro.: Ankara, 22 Oct. 1961. 1p., German
T. Doc.: Biographical sketch. 1 May 1960. 1p., German
Mus. ms. Repro. S.: *Suite*, op. 14, No. 2. 13p.

Arlen, Walter, b. 1925
Harvard University
L.: to Aurelio de la Vega. Los Angeles, 31 May 1984

Armes, Philip, 1836–1908
Northwestern University
L.: to Stainer. 12 Nov. 1894. With musical quotation

Arnold, Samuel, 1740–1802
Library of Congress
(Box 110)
A. L. S.: Duke St., 20 Apr. 1802. 1p., English. With
    accompanying portrait engraving, by Vernor & Hood

Arrau, Claudio, 1903–1991
Harvard University
Port.

Arregui Garay, Vicente, 1871–1925
Library of Congress
(Box 2)
A. Mus. ms. S.: *Sonata en fa menor para piano*, Paris,
    1902. 17p., 27x34cm.

Artôt, Désirée, 1835–1907
Library of Congress
(Box 2)
A. L. S.: to Abt. Karlsruhe, 21 Aug. 1867. 4p., French
A. L. S.: Cologne, 8 Oct. 1869. 3p., French

Asencio, Vicent, 1903–1979
Library of Congress
(Box 2)
A. Mus. ms. S.: *Foc de festa*, to Ricardo Viñes, San
    Sebastian, 8 Sept. 1938. 11p., 31x22cm. Ballet
    arranged for piano solo
Mus. ms. Repro. S.: *Albada y danza*, to the
    Moldenhauer Archives, Valencia, 31 May 1970. 6p.
Mus. ms. Repro. S.: *Danza*, Valencia, 31 May 1970. 4p.
    Blueprint score
Mus. ms. Repro. S.: *Danza V*, Valencia, 31 May 1970.
    3p. Blueprint score
Mus. ms. Repro. S.: *Desespero*, Valencia, 31 May 1970.
    3p. Blueprint score
Mus. ms. Repro. S.: *Roda la mola*. 3p. Blueprint score
Pri. Sco. S.: *Pièces originales pour guitare, Sonatina*,
    Brussels: Schott, c1964, to the Moldenhauer
    Archives, Valencia, 31 May 1970. 3p.
Pri. Sco. S.: *Pièces originales pour guitare, Tango de la
    Casada Infiel*, Brussels: Schott, c1964, to the
    Moldenhauer Archives, Valencia, 31 May 1970. 3p.

Askenase, Stefan, 1896–1985
Library of Congress
(Box 2)
A. L. S.: to [Edward] Clark. Brussels, 7 Mar. 1933. 2p.,
    German

Asuar, José Vicente, b. 1933
Harvard University
L.: to Aurelio de la Vega. Santiago, 29 Dec. 1963

Attenhofer, Carl, 1837–1914
Zentralbibliothek Zürich
L.: to Zweifel-Weber. Zurich, 21 Dec. 1900

Attwood, Thomas, 1765–1838
Northwestern University
L.: to Susan Taylor. Norwood, 24 Sept. 1829
11 Pri. Sco.

Auber, Daniel-François-Esprit, 1782–1871
Library of Congress
(Box 2, unless noted)
A. L. S.: to Eugène Scribe. n.p., Friday, 22 June. 1p.,
    French. Mentions Meyerbeer
A. L. S.: n.p., n.d. 1p., French
A. L. S.: n.p., n.d. 1p., French. Outlining concert
    program
Port. Engr.: by Walter (Box 110)
Port. Lith.: with biographical sketch. French (Box 110)

Audsley, George Ashdown, 1838–1925
Northwestern University
L.: to Charles W. Pearce. Chiswick, 11 Dec. 1889

[signature]

Auer, Leopold, 1845–1930
Library of Congress
(Box 2)
A. Mus. ms. arr. S.: *Two Caprices* by Dont. 6p.,
    33x26cm. Concert arrangement by Auer for violin
    with piano accompaniment
A. Mus. ms. S.: [Violin exercises]. 101p., 35x27cm. +
    various sizes. With accompanying 5p. autograph
    document
A. L. S.: St. Petersburg, 14 Dec. 1902. 2p., French,
    with typed translation
A. L. S.: [to Bruno Eisner]. St. Petersburg, 13 June
    1905. 2p., German

Augener, George, 1830–1915
Northwestern University
L.: to Werther. London, 29 July 1879

[signature]

Auric, Georges, 1899–1983
Library of Congress
(Box 2)
A. Mus. ms. Rev.: *Les Enchantements d'Alcine*, for piano
    solo, Paris, 21 May 1929. 20p., 35x27cm., ink, pencil.
    Tableaux I, II (incomplete), and III ("Danse des
    jeunes hommes et des jeunes femmes")
A. L. S.: Clavary Auribeau, n.d. 1p., French

Austin, Ernest, 1874–1947
Northwestern University
SUMMARY OF PRINCIPAL HOLDINGS:
L.: to Ernest Newman. Wallington, Surrey, 5 Oct. 1908
4 L.: to Glazebrook. Wallington, Surrey, 1923, n.d.

Avshalomov, Jacob, b. 1919
Harvard University
Mus. ms.: *Make a Joyful Noise unto the Lord*
Mus. ms.: *Raptures*, 1975

L.: to Hans Moldenhauer. Portland, Oregon, 18 Jan.
    1982
Doc.: Brochure. With portrait reproduced and work list

Ayala Pérez, Daniel, 1906–1975
Harvard University
Pri. Sco.: *Radiograma*, inscribed Mexico, 1941

Babin, Victor, 1908–1972
Harvard University
L.: to Paul Sanders. Paris, 20 June 1933
Doc.: Biographical information and work list
Port. Phot.: 3 Feb. 1949

Bach, Albert, 1844–1912
Northwestern University
2 L.: Edinburgh, 7 Oct. 1910; n.p., n.d.
L.: to Edwards, from Margaret Bach. Meran, 26 Oct.
    1903

[signature]

Bach, Carl Philipp Emanuel, 1714–1788
Library of Congress
(Box 3)
A. L. S.: [to Breitkopf]. Hamburg, 27 Dec. 1783. 1p.,
    German. New Year's letter; refers to songs, changes
    in his chorales

Bach, Johann Christian, 1735–1782
Library of Congress
(Box 3)
See Bach, Johann Sebastian

[signature]

Bach, Johann Sebastian, 1685–1750
Library of Congress
(Box 3)
A. Rcpt. S.: Leipzig, 26 Oct. 1746, 25 Oct. 1747, 27
    Oct. 1748, n.d. 1 leaf (2p.), 16x10cm., German, ink.
    Fourth receipt in the hand of Johann Christian Bach

Bachmann, Alberto Abraham, 1875–1963
Zentralbibliothek Zürich
2 L.: Paris, 23 Mar., 4 Sept. 1911
2 Mus. Quot.: Second Concerto; Fourth Concert
Mazurka
2 Port.

Bachrich, Sigmund [Sigismund], 1841–1913
Library of Congress
(Box 3)
A. L. S.: 1p., German

Backhaus, Wilhelm, 1884–1969
Library of Congress
(Box 3)
T. L. S.: to Bruno Eisner. Lugano, 29 June 1954. 1p.,
German
P. card S.: Lugano, June 1954. German. With portrait
photograph of Backhaus in Tokyo

Washington State University
See Rosbaud, Hans

Bacon, Ernst, 1898–1990
Harvard University
Mus. ms.: *From Blank to Blank*, 1950

Bader, Karl Adam, 1789–1870
Library of Congress
(Box 3)
A. L. S.: to J. E. Elszler. Munich, 18 Aug. 1838. 3p.,
German. Reports on a journey from Salzburg to
Munich, and details of a performance of
Meyerbeer's *Les Huguenots*
Doc.: Concert invitation. Berlin, 31 Apr. 1823. 1p.,
German

Badings, Henk, 1907–1987
Library of Congress
(Box 3)
A. Mus. ms. S.: *Concerto for Two Violins and Orchestra*,
1954. 2p., 31x24cm. Sketches from the first and
second movements
A. Mus. ms. S.: *Piano Sonata III*, Lento. 1945. 2p.,
34x26cm. Sketches

T. L. S.: to Hans Moldenhauer. Bilthoven, 29 July
1956. 1p., English
T. L. S.: to Aurelio de la Vega. Utrecht, 15 May 1963.
1p., English

Bagge, Selmar, 1823–1896
Library of Congress
(Box 13)
See Chrysander, Friedrich

Zentralbibliothek Zürich
SUMMARY OF PRINCIPAL HOLDINGS:
L.: Vienna, 22 Apr. 1861
L.: to Nottebohm. Leipzig, 30 Dec. 1862

Bailey, William Horace, 1910–1977
Washington State University
SUMMARY OF PRINCIPAL HOLDINGS:
Mus. ms.: *Album Leaf*
Mus. ms.: *Badinage*
Mus. ms.: *Birth of a Giant*, 1950
Mus. ms.: Children's Piano Pieces
Mus. ms.: *A Christmas Greeting*, op. 28, 1937
Mus. ms.: *An Easter Carol*
Mus. ms.: *Fanfare for Six Brass Instruments*, op. 25
Mus. ms.: *Legende*, op. 7
Mus. ms.: *The Lover's Lament*, op. 17
Mus. ms.: *Luminescence 1*, for orchestra
Mus. ms.: *A Wedding Wish*
Doc.: Biographical information, notes regarding
compositions and performances, photographs

Bailly, Louis, 1882–1974
Harvard University
See Flonzaley Quartet

Balfe, Michael William, 1808–1870
Library of Congress
(Box 3, unless noted)
A. Mus. ms. S.: *Lo! The Early Beam of Morning*. 9p.,
23x31cm., English, ink. Vocal quartet with piano
accompaniment

L.: to Lady Morgan. n.p., 13 Feb. 1839[?]. 1p., English
2 A. L. S.: to Simpson. n.p., 19 July 1860, 12 July 1862.
  3p., English
A. L. S.: Seven Oaks, Kent, 18 Aug. 1864. 1p., English
Port. Phot. (Box 110)

Bantock, Sir Granville, 1868–1946
Northwestern University
Mus. ms.: *Old English Suite*. Proof sheets
Mus. Quot.: *Omar Khayyám*. With accompanying letter,
  15 Oct. 1912
Mus. Quot.: *The Time Spirit*
Port. Phot.

Barber, Samuel, 1910–1981
Harvard University
L.: to Boaz Piller. Mt. Kisco, 22 Nov. 1943

Barbi, Alice, 1862–1948
Library of Congress
(Box 3)
A. L. S.: to a conductor, [Louis Lüstner?]. Karlsruhe,
  29 Oct. 1892. 1p., German. With program for a
  Wiesbaden concert

Barbirolli, Sir John [Giovanni Battista], 1899–1970
Northwestern University
2 L.: to Olga Eisner. 2 Apr. 1938; New York, 1940[?]
L.: to Alma Mahler, written by Evelyn (wife)

Barchet, Siegfried, b. 1918
Library of Congress
(Box 3)
A. Mus. ms. S.: *Duo für Violine und Cello in A Moll*, op.
  7. May 1942. 20p., 32x24cm.
A. Mus. ms. S.: *Images de Menton*. 8p., various sizes.
  Sketches
A. Mus. ms. S.: *Streichersinfonie*. 7p., various sizes.
  Sketches
6 A. L. S.: to Hans Moldenhauer. Stuttgart, 1956–1960,
  1976. 16p., German
Call. c. Annot.: to Hans Moldenhauer. German
Call. c.
Sig.

Pri. Sco.: *Duo in A Moll für Violine und Violoncello*,
  Stuttgart: Schultheiss, n.d. 16p. + 7p. (parts)
Pri. Sco. S.: *Sieben Gedichte*, Stuttgart: Schultheiss, n.d.,
  to Hans Moldenhauer, 16 Sept. 1956. 24p.

Bargiel, Woldemar, 1828–1897
Library of Congress
(Box 3)
A. L. S.: to Selmar Bagge. Rotterdam, 28 Nov. 1867.
  4p., German
2 A. L. S.: to Breitkopf & Härtel. Berlin, 12 May 1878,
  2 Aug. 1879. 7p., German

Barnay, Ludwig, 1842–1924
Library of Congress
(Box 3)
A. L. S.: Berlin, 11 Apr. 1891. 1p., German

Barnby, Sir Joseph, 1838–1896
Library of Congress
(Box 3)
A. Mus. ms. S.: *Sweet 'n Low*. 2p., 30x24cm., English
2 A. L. S.: to Miss Stephenson. London, 24 June 1875,
  3 Dec. 1895. 4p., English
2 Obit.

Barnett, John, 1802–1890
Northwestern University
Mus. ms.: *The Two Seconds*, 1827. Full score
L.: to Nicolas Mori. n.p., n.d.

Barnett, John Francis, 1837–1916
Northwestern University
L.: to J. Gill. St. John's Wood, 19 June 1885
Pri. Sco.: *The Harvest Festival*

Baron, Maurice, 1889–1964
Harvard University
Pri. Sco.: *Ode to Democracy*. Excerpt
Pri. Sco.: *Quatre Airs romantiques*
Doc.: Brochure

Barraqué, Jean, 1928–1973
Library of Congress
(Box 103)
A. Mus. ms.: *...au delà du hasard, pour quatre formations instrumentales et une formation vocale*, Section XIII, D'une pensée sans nuit. 3p. (pp.120–122), 44x31cm., French. Full score. Also printed score, c1967
2 T. L. S.: to Hans Moldenhauer. Paris, 7 June 1961; Trélévern, 17 Sept. 1961. 2p., English
Doc. A. Annot.: Brochure. 1969. 6p., English. With reviews for *Chant après chant*; *Temps restitué*

Barth, Richard, 1850–1923
Library of Congress
(Box 4)
A. L. S.: to a pianist. Hamburg, 12 Feb. 1906. 2p., German

Bartók, Béla, 1881–1945
Harvard University
See Serly, Tibor

Library of Congress
(Box 4, unless noted)
Pri. Sco. A. Rev.: Second Violin Concerto, 1937–1938. 132p., 36x25cm. First proofs (London: Hawkes & Son, c1945) with autograph corrections and - annotations
A. L. S.: Pozsony, 26 Dec. 1904. 3p., Hungarian. Regarding desire to give lessons; mentions Mahler, Strauss
A. L.: to Jelly d'Arányi. Budapest, 7 Dec. 1921. 2p., Hungarian, with English translation. Close of letter is missing
A. L. S.: to Rudolph Ganz. Budapest, 17 Apr. 1923. 4p., German. Mentions Busoni, Dohnányi, Leichtentritt, Ravel

A. L. S.: to the Budapest Radio, Foreign Department. Budapest, 4 May 1936. 1p., Hungarian, with German translation. Regarding a musical folklore lecture
A. L. S.: to Paul F. Sanders. London, 10 Feb. 1937. 1p., German
P. card S.: to Hanna Schwarz. Budapest, 13 Feb. 1938. German
Mus. ms. Repro.: [Two Cadenzas]. 8p. Written by Bartók for Mozart's Concerto in E-flat Major for Two Pianos
L. Repro.: to Bartók, from Hans Rosbaud. Curaglia (Ticino), 18 July 1935. 2p., German
Port. Phot. S.: to Boaz Piller, New York, 10 Jan. 1945
(Box 110)

Washington State University
See Rosbaud, Hans

Barye Document, 1878
Northwestern University
Doc.: Petition. Signed by 22 artists. Musicians endorsing the petition include Bazin, Delaborde, Gounod, Reber, Reyer

Battiferri, Luigi, 1600/10-after 1682
Library of Congress
(Box 4)
Rcpt.: 12 June 1662. 1p., Italian

Bauer, Harold, 1873–1951
Harvard University
Mus. ms.: "Come Unto Me"
L.: to Karl Weigl. New York, 14 May 1929
L.: to Carl Deis. New York, 29 Jan. 1936
2 L.: to Boaz Piller. New York, 30 Apr. 1940, 5 Mar. 1941
L.: to Rudolph Ganz. Miami, 20 Jan. 1945

Bauer, Marion, 1897–1955
Harvard University
Summary of Principal Holdings:
Mus. ms.: *Anagrams*, op. 48, 1950
Mus. ms.: *Ertödt uns durch dein Güte*
Mus. ms.: *To Losers*
Mus. ms.: *Moods*, op. 46, 1950–1954

Mus. ms.: *An Open Secret*
Mus. ms.: *Pan and Syrinx*, op. 28. Full score, parts
Mus. ms.: *Rainbow and Flame*
Mus. ms.: *Six Little Fugues*
Mus. ms.: Sonata for Violin and Piano, op. 17
Mus. ms.: *Ein ungefärbt Gemüthe*
Mus. ms. Repro.: *Dusk*. Blueprint score
Mus. ms. Repro. Annot.: *Patterns*, op. 41, 1946. Blueprint score

Baur, Jürg, b. 1918
Library of Congress
(Box 3)
T. L. S.: to Aurelio de la Vega. Vienna, 3 Apr. 1951. 1p., English

Baussnern [Bausznern], Waldemar von, 1866–1931
Library of Congress
(Box 103)
A. Mus. ms. S.: *Gebet*, Chorus for Four Women's Voices, 10 Jan. 1901. 2p., 47x35cm.
A. L. S.: to Eugen Lindner. Weimar, 28 Feb. 1901[?]. 1p., German
A. L. S.: to ?. Charlottenburg, 4 May 1923. 3p., German
A. L. S.: to ?. 20 Oct. 1925. 4p., German
Doc. Annot.: Brochure. *Waldemar von Bausznern 1866–1931: Verzeichnis des gesamten musikalischen Nachlasses*. 8p.

Bax, Sir Arnold, 1883–1953
Northwestern University
L.: to Ernest Newman. London, Sunday, n.d.
Pri. Sco.: String Quartet in G Major, inscribed 10 Apr. 1921

Bayer, Joseph, 1852–1913
Library of Congress
(Box 4)
A. Mus. Quot. S.: *Die Puppenfee*, Vienna, Oct. 1909

Bayer, Michael Joseph, b. 1947
Harvard University
SUMMARY OF PRINCIPAL HOLDINGS:
Mus. ms.: *Aurora–Morning Redness in the Sky*

Mus. ms.: *Burr*, 1974
Mus. ms.: *Daddy*. With additional blueprint score, and sound recording
2 Mus. mss.: *Five Dog Night;* Concerto
Mus. ms.: *Mephisto Waltz*, 1973
Mus. ms.: [Musical example, given by Bruno Maderna, continued by Bayer]
Mus. ms.: Variations for Piano, 1968
L.: to Hans Moldenhauer. Seattle, 15 June 1977

Bazin, François, 1816–1878
Northwestern University
Mus. Quot.: *Le Voyage en Chine*
See Barye Document

Beach, John Parsons, 1877–1953
Harvard University
2 L.: to Adolph Weiss. Asolo Veneto, n.d.
Port. Phot.

Beale, James H., b. 1924
Washington State University
Mus. ms.: String Quartet
Mus. ms. Repro.: Seventh Piano Sonata, op. 20. Facsimile
L.: to Hans Moldenhauer. Seattle, 16 Aug. 1958

Beauplan, Amédée Rousseau de, 1790–1853
Library of Congress
(Box 4)
A. Mus. ms. S.: *Le pardon*, Romance. 3p., 20x30cm., French. Song with piano accompaniment. With poem, *Le voyage*, and drawings (by Louis Delâtre)
Doc.: Biographical sketch. French

Beck, Conrad, 1901–1989
Washington State University
See Rosbaud, Hans

Zentralbibliothek Zürich
Mus. ms.: *Aeneas-Silvius-Symphonie*
4 L.: to Hans Moldenhauer. Basel, 1953–1961
L.: to Boaz Piller. Basel, 12 Dec. 1954

Mus. Quot.: Concertino for Clarinet and Orchestra, 1954
Port. Phot.: to Boaz Piller

Beck, Joseph Nepomuk, 1827–1904
Library of Congress
(Box 4)
A. L. S.: Vienna, 26 June 1856. 3p., German

Beck-Weixebaum, Frieda, 1814–1890
Library of Congress
(Box 4)
5 A. L. S.: 1859–1874. 21p., German

Becker, Hugo, 1863–1941
Library of Congress
(Box 4, unless noted)
A. Doc. S.: Letter fragment with signature
A. Mus. Quot. S.: Andante, Nov. 1903. On postcard with silhouette of cellist
Port. Phot. S. Repro. (Box 110)

Becker, Jean, 1833–1884
Library of Congress
(Box 4)
A. L. S.: Brünn, 2 Jan. 1870. 1p., German

Becker, John J., 1886–1961
Harvard University
Summary of Principal Holdings:
Mus. ms.: *Dierdre of the Sorrows*
4 L.: Wilmette, 15 Dec. 1958, 4, 31 Mar., 13 Apr. 1959
2 L.: to Adolph Weiss. n.p., n.d.

Becker, Reinhold, 1842–1924
Library of Congress
(Box 4, unless noted)
A. Mus. ms. S.: *Ich sah deine Lippen blühen*, op. 91. 3p., 24x27cm.
A. Doc. S.: Aphorisms on music. 1p., German
Port. Phot. S. (Box 110)

Becker, Valentin Eduard, 1814–1890
Library of Congress
(Box 4)
A. Mus. ms. S.: *Liebeshelfer*, op. 120, No. 4, 12 Mar. 1886. 2p., 27x21cm., German

Beer, Wilhelm, 1797–1850
Library of Congress
(Box 4)
A. L. S.: to the editor of a newspaper. Berlin, 5 Nov. 1846. 1p., German. Beer is the brother of Giacomo Meyerbeer

Beer-Walbrunn, Anton, 1864–1929
Bayerische Staatsbibliothek
Mus. ms.: *String Quartet in C Major*, 1891. Score, parts
2 L.: to Widmann. Munich, 9 Feb., 17 Dec. 1925

Beeson, Jack, b. 1921
Harvard University
Mus. ms.: *Sketches in Black and White*, 1958
2 L.: to Gloria Coates. New York, 14 July 1975, 14 Nov.

Beeth, Lola, 1862–1940
Library of Congress
(Box 4)
Call. c. Annot.: to Kugel. n.p., n.d. 2p., German. Regarding a concert in Pest

Beethoven, Caspar Anton Carl, 1774–1815
Library of Congress
(Box 5)
Pri. Rcpt. S.: Tax receipt. Vienna, 7 Mar. 1807. 1p.

Beethoven, Ludwig van, 1770–1827
Bayerische Staatsbibliothek
See Bülow, Hans von

Library of Congress
(Box 5)
A. Mus. ms.: [*Don Giovanni* by Mozart]. 23p.,
  23x32cm., German, ink. Beethoven's autograph
  copy, containing nos. 16 (Terzett) and 20 (Sextett),
  of the second act. Complete score of the vocal parts,
  with sketches of orchestral parts
A. Mus. ms.: [Piano Sonata in A Major, op. 101,
  Allegro, 1816?]. 2p., 23x29cm., ink. Sketch. On
  recto, unidentified sketches in D Minor and
  sketches for the canon "Das Schweigen," WoO 168
A. Mus. ms.: [Piano Sonata in D Major, op. 28,
  Andante, 1801?]. 2p., 22x30cm., ink. Continuity
  draft. With cover of authentication inscribed by
  Ignaz Sauer
L. S.: to Johannes Andreas Streicher. Vienna, 16 Sept.
  1824. 1p., German. Letter in secretarial hand,
  possibly of his nephew Karl, but place, date, and
  signature in Beethoven's autograph. Regarding the
  Missa solemnis
Mus. ms. Repro.: *Sonate* "Appassionata," op. 57, Paris:
  Piazza. 42p. Facsimile. With accompanying facsimile
  note by Baillot
See Lecocq, Charles

Begnis, Giuseppe de, 1793–1849
Library of Congress
(Box 5)
A. L. S.: to Ayrton. n.p., n.d. 3p., French

Bellaigue, Camille, 1858–1930
Northwestern University
L.: to Massenet. Paris, 8 Oct. 1889
L.: to Mme. Massenet. n.p., n.d.

Bellermann, Heinrich, 1832–1903
Library of Congress
(Box 5)
A. L. S.: to Chrysander. Berlin, 21 June 1874. 2p.,
  German. Regarding Spitta

Belletti, Giovanni Battista, 1813–1890
Library of Congress
(Box 5)
2 A. L. S.: to J. Oliver Mason. London, 30 June, 1
  Sept. 1852. 3p., French

Bellini, Vincenzo, 1801–1835
Library of Congress
(Box 5, unless noted)
A. Mus. ms. S.: *Tantum ergo*, for Soprano, Tenor, Alto,
  Bass, and Orchestra, in E Major. 4p. (33m.),
  24x29cm., ink. Incomplete. Bound
L. S.: to Tomarro of Florence. n.p., 12 Mar. 1813. 3p.,
  Italian
Mus. ms. Repro.: *Norma*, Rome: Reale Accademia
  d'Italia, 1935. (2 vols.), 148p. + 104p. Facsimile
  (Shelf)
Mus. ms. Repro.: *Composizioni giovanili inedite*, Rome:
  Reale Accademia d'Italia, 1941 (Shelf)

Belyayev, Viktor Mikhaylovich, 1888–1968
Library of Congress
(Box 110)
Port. Phot. S.: to Mrs. Pisk

Benavente, Manuel José, b. 1903
Library of Congress
(Box 5)
A. Mus. ms. S. Rev.: *"Quenas" (Evocaciones Indígenas)*,
  para piano, to Ricardo Viñes, Buenos Aires, 24 July
  1924. 5p., 33x26cm.

Benda, Franz, 1709–1786
Library of Congress
(Box 5)
A. L. S.: to Carl [son]. Potsdam, 14 Aug. 1781. 1p.,
  German

Bendel, Franz, 1833–1874
Library of Congress
(Box 5, unless noted)
A. L. S.: to Erler. n.p., n.d. 3p., German
Port. Phot. Repro. (Box 110)

Bender, Paul, 1875–1947
Library of Congress
(Box 5)
A. L. S.: to Tischer. Vienna, 13 Mar. 1929. 2p., German

Bendix, Victor, 1851–1926
Library of Congress
(Box 5)
A. L. S.: Leipzig, 28 Mar. 1883. 1p., German

Benedict, Sir Julius, 1804–1885
Northwestern University
Mus. Alb. l.: "By the sad sea-waves I listen...,"
    London, 7 Jan. 1878
L.: to Felix. n.p., 21 Sept. 1853
L.: to Lockey. London, 29 Nov. 1855
L.: to Ponsonby. London, 11 Feb. 1860
L.: to Sydney. London, 5 Apr. 1871
Doc.: Railway notice. Regarding a performance, 1872
Clip.
3 Port.

Benelli, Antonio, 1771–1830
Library of Congress
(Box 5)
A. L. S.: to J. B. Benelli. Dresden, 10 Dec. 1818. 3p.,
    Italian

Benelli, Luigi
Library of Congress
(Box 5)
A. L. S.: to Jean Baptiste Benelli. Forl, 14 June 1817.
    2p., Italian

Benelli, Vittorio
Library of Congress
(Box 5)
A. L. S.: to his "carissimo fratello." Rome, 17 [Dec.?]
    1817. 1p., Italian

Benguerel, Xavier, b. 1931
Library of Congress
(Box 104)
Mus. ms. Repro. A. Annot.: *Joc*, to Hans Moldenhauer,
    Barcelona, June 1970. 13p.

Benigni, Tommaso, 1547–1616
Library of Congress
(Box 5)
A. Rcpt. S.: 16 Apr. 1596. 2p., Italian

Bennett, Robert Russell, 1894–1981
Harvard University
Mus. ms.: *Musical Autogram*, for piano solo
3 L.: to Charles Haubiel. New York, 28 June, 11,
    26 July 1952. With copy of Haubiel's reply
4 L.: to Hans Moldenhauer. New York, 5 Dec. 1978,
    20 Mar., 3 Apr., 4 Dec. 1979

Bennett, Sir William Sterndale, 1816–1875
Northwestern University
Mus. ms.: [Song for voice and piano], 6 Sept. 1855
L.: to a singer. London, 6 Feb. [1842?]
L.: to Lockey. London, 11 June 1848
L.: to Jules Benedict. London, 18 Nov. 1858
L.: to Chorley. London, 3 Jan. 1859
L.: to Chadwick. n.p., 7 May 1868
Doc.: Ticket. For a piano recital, 1856. With
    accompanying note
2 Port.

Benoit, Peter, 1843–1901
Library of Congress
(Box 5, unless noted)
A. Mus. Quot. S.: [Agnes motive, 8m.], Antwerp, 29
    Oct. 1897
A. Mus. Quot. S.: *Concerto*, op. 36, to Braun, Brussels,
    4 Apr. 1866
A. Mus. Quot. S.: Te Deum Laudamus, to ?, Brussels,
    4 Apr. 1866. Latin, French
Port. Phot. S. Repro. (Box 110)

Northwestern University
See d'Indy, Vincent

Benshoof, Kenneth, b. 1933
Washington State University
Mus. ms.: Piano Trio, for violin, viola, and piano, 1956.
   With additional blueprint score
Mus. ms.: [Untitled work for viola and piano]. With
   additional blueprint score
L.: to Hans and Rosaleen Moldenhauer. n.p., 14 Sept.
   1958

Benvenuti, Tomaso, 1838–1906
Library of Congress
(Box 5)
A. Mus. Quot. S.: *Canzonetta scherzo*, 24 Aug. 1887

Berg, Alban, 1885–1935
Bayerische Staatsbibliothek
SUMMARY OF PRINCIPAL HOLDINGS:
A. Mus. ms.: *Kontrapunktstudien*, ca. 1905. 7p.,
   34.5x26cm.
A. Mus. ms. S.: *Lulu*, Act I, scene 3, to Schloss, Oct.
   1931. 3p., 35x27cm., pencil. Particell fragment.
   See libretto below
A. Mus. ms.: [same]. 1 leaf, 25x10cm., black ink,
   pencil. Draft of the ragtime music, measures
   1007–1021; plus rhythmic sketch of opening,
   measures 991–93
Mus. ms.: *Ein Orchesterlied*, op. 4, No. 5, arranged for
   piano, harmonium, violin, and violoncello, Mar.
   1917, to Alma Mahler
Mus. ms.: *7 frühe Lieder*. The complete cycle which
   served for the preparation of the printed edition.
   No. 5, *Im Zimmer*, is entirely in Berg's autograph.
   The other songs are partly in his handwriting, and
   all bear his markings
Mus. ms.: *7 frühe Lieder, Im Zimmer*. Transposed by
   Berg
Mus. ms.: *Viel Träume*, op. 7, No. 2, ca. 1902
Mus. ms.: *Der Wein*. Particell. 18p.
3 L.: to Hildegard Jone. 1923, 1932, 1935
50 L.: to Otto Jokl. 1926–1935. Includes letter
   addressed to Jokl, Apostel, and Schloss, 1934. With
   many corrections, musical illustrations
10 L.: to Norbert Schwarzmann. 1925
L.: to Webern. 1925
L.: to Knudsen. 3 Mar. 1926
L.: to Mrs. Stiedry
14 L.: to Ruzena Herlinger. 1927–1935
L.: to Ludwig Karpath. Vienna, 11 Dec. 1928

10 L.: to Josef Humplik. 1928–1930
L.: to Fritz Mahler. Vienna, 27 May 1930
2 L.: to Paul Sanders. Vienna, 14 Oct. 1930, Mar. 1933
5 L.: to Adolph Weiss. 1931, 1934
L.: to Fritz Stiedry. 28 May 1932
L.: to Werner Reinhart. June 1932
L.: to Paul A. Pisk. 13 July 1932
L.: to Hans Heinsheimer. 22 June 1934. On a copy of a
   letter to Berg, from Fitelberg
2 L.: to Arnold Schoenberg. Drafts, 1933, [1934]. Also
   draft to Gertrud Schoenberg, 1934
2 L.: to Pollak. 8 Aug. 1934, 15 Aug. 1935
L.: to Johan Franco. Vienna, 24 Apr. 1935
L.: to Peter Jirak. 18 Oct. 1935
L.: to Josef Polnauer. Vienna, n.d.
9 L.: to Willi Reich. With two additional notes to
   Reich, news clippings, and the proposal for the
   Wozzeck cigarette
138 L.: to Julius Schloss. With additional invitations,
   copies of letters
8 L.: including letters to the BBC
Doc.: Correspondence. Regarding the first production
   of *Wozzeck*, including letters and cards from Fritz
   Busch, Johanna Klemperer, Ernst Lert, Richard
   Lert, Otto Lohse, Franz Schalk, Bernhard Schuster,
   Waldheim-Eberle AG, and others
Doc.: Critique. By Julius Korngold, and reply by Berg
Doc.: Outline. Berg's ideal for a *Wozzeck* cast
Doc.: Typescript. Lecture on *Wozzeck*, with annotations
   by Berg, Reich
Doc.: Additional autograph documents include notes,
   drafts, annotations on clippings, radio programs,
   printed scores, programs
Lib. A. Annot.: *Lulu*. Typescript with autograph
   annotations, pp.1–19, 51 only. On bottom of the
   page and on verso, Berg writes an outline of
   symphonic excerpts from *Lulu*, including
   designation of musical forms, and text of "Lied der
   Lulu"
Pri. Sco. A. Rev.: *Der Wein*. Piano-vocal score. Proofs,
   with autograph corrections. With additional copy of
   first printed edition, including coaching directions
   by Webern, and annotations by Berg
Pri. Sco. A. Annot.: *Wozzeck*. Piano-vocal score. First
   edition, with numerous autograph annotations
Engr.: Berg's birthplace
Port. Phot. S.: several, including one to Julius Schloss
   (May 1928) with musical quotation
Port. Paint.: by Hildegard Jone
2 Port. Draw.: by Hildegard Jone

Library of Congress
See Schoenberg, Arnold
See Webern, Anton

Wiener Stadt- u. Landesbibliothek
Mus. ms.: *Chamber Symphony*, op. 9 by Arnold
   Schoenberg, arranged by Berg for piano. 1p.
L.: to Ludwig Karpath. Vienna, 13 Apr. 1915
L.: to Julius Schloss. n.p., n.d.
See Mahler, Gustav

Berg, Helene, 1885–1976
Bayerische Staatsbibliothek
L.: to Mrs. Zemlinsky. Vienna, 25 June 1923
2 L.: to Ruzena Herlinger. 1932, 1936
L.: to Julius Schloss. Hof-Gastein, 11 Feb. 1936
9 L.: to Otto Jokl. 1938, 1946–1949
L.: to Fritz Mahler. Vienna, 14 Oct. 1955
9 L.: to Alma Mahler. 1957–1959
12 L.: to Hanna Schwarz. Vienna, Veldon, 1967–1973
L.: to Hans Moldenhauer
Doc.: Typescript. Vienna, 15 July 1970. Describing
   Berg's last illness, personally given to Hans
   Moldenhauer. Unpublished

Library of Congress
See Schoenberg, Arnold
See Webern, Anton

Berger, Arthur, b. 1912
Harvard University
Mus. ms.: String Quartet, 1958. Excerpt
2 L.: to Hans Moldenhauer
Doc.: Brochure. With portrait reproduced and work list

Berger, Jean, b. 1909
Library of Congress
(Box 5)
A. Mus. ms. S.: *Ne joue pas avec mon coeur*. 2p.,
   23x10cm.

Beringer, Oscar, 1844–1922
Northwestern University
Mus. Quot.: *Presto*

Berio, Luciano, b. 1925
Library of Congress
(Box 104)
A. Mus. ms. S.: *Quaderni per orchestra (I)*. 22p.,
   47x32cm., pencil. Draft in full score
2 T. L. S.: to Hans Moldenhauer. Oakland, 25 Mar.
   1962, 23 Nov. 1963. 2p., English
L.: to Hans Moldenhauer, from Cathy Berio. Milan,
   10 Dec. 1961. 1p., English

Washington State University
See Rosbaud, Hans

Bériot, Charles-Auguste de, 1802–1870
Library of Congress
(Box 5, unless noted)
2 A. L. S.: to Vivenot. Vienna, 4 June 1826, 27 Jan.
   1840. 3p., French
A. L. S.: to the Mayor. Brussels, 11 Jan. 1843. 1p.,
   French. Mentions Sigismond Thalberg
A. L. S.: to Jules Benedict. Paris, 8 Apr. 2p., French
Port. Engr. S. Repro. (Box 110)

Bériot, Charles-Wilfride, 1833–1914
Library of Congress
(Box 5)
A. Mus. ms. S.[?]: *Sérénité*, for piano solo. 4p., 35x27cm.

Berlioz, Hector, 1803–1869
Library of Congress
(Box 5, unless noted)
A. Mus. ms. S.: *Scènes d'Alceste*, [*Alceste*, by Christoph
   Willibald Gluck]. 75p., 35x27cm., French, ink.
   Written out by Berlioz for Pauline Viardot-García.
Six scenes in full score, the role of Alceste, prepared for
   the Opéra performance in 1861. Contains authen-
   tication and provenance by Alfred Cortot (Shelf)
A. L. S.: to Morel. London, 5 Jan. 1848. 3p., French

Northwestern University
L.: to Bloque. Paris, 12 Feb. 1836
L.: to Travies. n.p., 15 Dec. 1844
L.: to Rosenhaem. n.p., n.d.
Port.

Bernaola, Carmelo, b. 1929
Library of Congress
(Box 109)
A. Mus. ms. S.: *Superficie*, No. 3, Madrid, 12 Mar. 1963.
   7p., 20x27cm. Complete draft
Mus. ms. Repro. A. Rev. S.: *Superficie*. 4p. + 2p.
   (autograph instructions). Blueprint score
2 Doc. Repro.: Biographical notes. 2p., Spanish

Bernhard, Christoph, 1628–1692
Library of Congress
(Box 5)
A. Rcpt. S.: Receipt for services. Dresden, 28 Dec.
   1687. 1p., German. With accompanying
   authentication and biographical information, by
   Aloys Fuchs (1846)

Bernstein, Leonard, 1918–1990
Harvard University
Mus. ms.: *Fancy Free*, 1944, inscribed New York City,
   10 Sept. 1944. Sketch, "V—after 1st ending."
   Condensed score
L.: to Charles Haubiel. New York, 2 Nov. 1943
L.: to Solomon Pimsleur. New York, 5 Apr. 1944
L.: to Rudolph Ganz. New York, 13 July 1944
Port. Phot.: New York, 1946
Mus. Quot.: "a two-gun bit from the new ballet,"
   Stockbridge, 1946. On verso, melody with text

Bertram, Theodor, 1869–1907
Library of Congress
(Box 5)
A. L. S.: [Stuttgart?], n.d. 1p., German

Berwald, Franz, 1796–1868
Library of Congress
(Box 5)
2 A. L. S.: to Julius Rietz. Stockholm, 10 May 1862,
   28 Apr. 1863. 2p., German, Swedish
Obit.: 1p., Swedish

Berwald, Johan Fredrik, 1787–1861
Library of Congress
(Box 5)
A. L. S.: to ?. Stockholm, 19 Aug. 1834. 2p., German

**Bessel & Co. [founded by Vasily Vasil'yevich
Bessel, 1843–1907]**
Library of Congress
(Box 5)
A. L. S.: Bad Wildungen, 9 Aug. 2p., German

Betti, Adolfo, 1873–1950
Harvard University
See Flonzaley Quartet

Library of Congress
(Box 5)
2 A. L. S.: to Solomon Pimsleur. New York City,
   31 Dec.; Bologna, 22 June. 6p., English

Betz, Franz, 1835–1900
Library of Congress
(Box 5)
A. L. S.: to Bassin. B[erlin], 17 Nov. 1876. 1p., German
A. Alb. l. Sig.

Beyer, Frank Michael, b. 1928
Library of Congress
(Box 5)
2 A. Mus. Quot. S.: to Gloria [Coates]

Bianchi, Bianca [Bertha Schwarz], 1855–1947
Library of Congress
(Box 6)
A. L. S.: to Kugel. Salzburg, 9 Feb. 1888. 3p., German
Call. c. Annot.: 2p., German

Biggs, E. Power, 1906–1977
Washington State University
L.: to Solomon Pimsleur. Cambridge, 5 June 1947

Billingsley, William A., b. 1922
Harvard University
SUMMARY OF PRINCIPAL HOLDINGS:
Mus. ms.: *Brass Quartet*, 1961
Mus. ms.: *Fantasy for Woodwind Quintet*, 1967
Mus. ms.: *Fugue*, 1961
Mus. ms.: *The Paradox*, 1974
Mus. ms.: *The Starry Night*, 1978
2 L.: to Hans Moldenhauer. Moscow, Idaho, 10 Aug.,
    6 Sept. 1983
L.: to Hans and Mary Moldenhauer, from Doris
    Billingsley. Moscow, Idaho, 28 Aug. 1983
Mus. ms. Repro.: *Landscape Sketches*, 1983. Photocopy

Billroth, Theodor, 1829–1894
Library of Congress
(Box 117)
P. card S.: to Wetzlar. Wien, Nov. 1888. German

Binder, Abraham Wolfe, 1895–1966
Harvard University
SUMMARY OF PRINCIPAL HOLDINGS:
Mus. ms.: *The Heart of America*, 3–10 July 1953

Binet, Jean, 1893–1960
Zentralbibliothek Zürich
Mus. ms.: *Petit Concert*, 1950. Complete piano-clarinet
    score

L.: to Rudolph Ganz. 8 Jan. 1960. On verso of a
    Christmas card drawn by Denise Binet
Doc.: Work list
Mus. ms. Repro.: *L'Or Perdu*. Facsimile

Bing, Sir Rudolf, 1902–1997
Harvard University
2 L.: to Alma Mahler

Bird, Henry Richard, 1842–1915
Northwestern University
L.: to Miss Stewart Wood. 28 Jan. 1904

Bisetzka, M. de
Library of Congress
(Box 6)
A. Mus. ms. S.: *Les Fileuses*. 8p., 35x27cm.

Bishop, Sir Henry Rowley, 1786–1855
Northwestern University
Mus. ms.: *May Morning*, 1834. With additional printed
    score
L.: to the Duchess of St. Albans. London, 19 Mar.
    1834
L.: to Green. London, 31 May 1845
L.: to Lockey. London, 28 June 1853
L.: to J. Wallack. n.p., n.d.

Bistevins, Olgerts
Library of Congress
(Box 6)
A. L. S.: to Aurelio de la Vega. Argentina, 22 Mar.
    1951[?]. 2p., English

Bittermann, Karl Friedrich
Library of Congress
(Box 6)
A. Mus. ms. S.: *Walzer mit VIII Variationen für das
    Clavier oder Piano-Forte*. 8p., 24x30cm.

Bittner, Julius, 1874–1939
Library of Congress
(Box 6)
P. card S.: to Otto Jokl. Vienna, 29 Apr. 1917. German

Northwestern University
2 Mus. mss.: *An einen Boten; Stille Sicherheit*
Mus. ms.: "O Himmel! Was seh ich?"
Mus. ms.: [Piano composition in C Major]
Mus. ms.: *Schwäbische Kunde*
Mus. ms.: [String Quartet in D Minor]. Fragment
L.: to Karl Weigl. Wolfpassing, 14 July [?]

Wiener Stadt- u. Landesbibliothek
2 L.: to Hanna Schwarz. Vienna, 24 Feb. 1932, 20 Feb. 1934

Bizet, Georges, 1838–1875
Library of Congress
(Box 6)
A. Mus. ms. arr.: *Scènes de bal, Entrée des masques*, op. 17 by Jules Massenet. Piano solo arrangement, written by Bizet in 1865[?]. 1p., 35x26cm., ink
A. L. S.: n.p., n.d. 2p., French. On verso, note by the addressee

Blacher, Boris, 1903–1975
Bayerische Staatsbibliothek
See Hartmann, Karl Amadeus

Library of Congress
(Box 6)
A. Mus. ms.: *Music for Cleveland*, for orchestra. 20p., 34x27cm., pencil. Complete sketches. With two typed letters to Hans Moldenhauer, from Bote & Bock (Berlin, 1958), about manuscript
L. Repro.: to Hans Moldenhauer. Berlin, 25 Nov. 1957. 1p., German
See Hartmann, Karl Amadeus

Black, Frank, 1894–1968
Harvard University
5 L.: to Charles Haubiel. New York, 25 Sept., 7 Oct. 1940, 28 Nov. 1944, 11 June (on verso, letter by Haubiel), 11 July 1945

Blackburn, John, b. 1923
Harvard University
L.: to Aurelio de la Vega. n.p., 19 Oct. 1984

Blagrove, Henry, 1811–1872
Northwestern University
L.: to Mme. Sola. London, 26 Apr. 1859

Blagrove, Richard, 1827[?]–1895
Northwestern University
L.: to Mme. Sola. London, 21 Apr. 1889

Blanchet, Émile, 1877–1943
Zentralbibliothek Zürich
Mus. ms.: *Bourrée pour deux pianos*, Paris, Jan. 1939
Mus. ms.: *Canon sur le principe de la symétrie dans le clavier*, 1938
Mus. ms.: *Fugue symétrique*, 1938
Mus. ms.: *Marche funèbre*, 1937
Mus. ms.: *Mouvement de Sonate*, 1940
Mus. ms.: *Suite for Piano Solo*, 1938
L.: to Rudolph Ganz. Zermatt, n.d.

Blank, Allan, b. 1925
Harvard University
SUMMARY OF PRINCIPAL HOLDINGS:
Mus. ms.: *Aria da capo*, 1958–1960
Mus. ms.: *Around the Clock*
Mus. ms.: *Being: Three Vignettes for Soprano and Clarinet*, 1972–1973
Mus. ms.: *Bicinium*, 1974
Mus. ms.: *Ceremonies for Trumpet and Percussion*, 1977
Mus. ms.: *Coalitions*, 1975
Mus. ms.: *Coalitions II*, 1976
Mus. ms.: *Concert Duo*, 1977
Mus. ms.: *Concert Piece for Band*, 1961–1964

Mus. ms.: *Dance Images*, 1975
Mus. ms.: *Diversions*, New York, Dec. 1972
Mus. ms.: *Divertimento for Solo Tuba and Symphonic Band*, 1979
Mus. ms.: *Esther's Monologue*, 1970
Mus. ms.: *Four Dream Poems*, 1975–1976
Mus. ms.: *Knock-on-Wood*, 1972
Mus. ms.: *Kreutzer March*, 1981
Mus. ms.: *Moments in Time*, 1968
Mus. ms.: *Music for Orchestra*, 1964–1967
Mus. ms.: *Music for Solo Cello*, 1982
Mus. ms.: *Music for Tubas*, 1976
Mus. ms.: *Paganini Caprice*, Ossining, New York, July 1974
Mus. ms.: *Poem*, 1963
Mus. ms.: *Psalm V*, 1975
Mus. ms.: *Sicilienne*, 1981
Mus. ms.: *Six Miniatures and a Fantasia*
Mus. ms.: *Six Significant Landscapes*, 1972–1974
Mus. ms.: *Some Funnies and Poems*, 1982
Mus. ms.: *Some Thank-You Notes*, New York, 1970
Mus. ms.: *A Song of Ascents*, 1967
Mus. ms.: String Quartet, 1981
Mus. ms.: *Thirteen Ways of Looking at a Blackbird*, 1964–1965
Mus. ms.: *Three Novelties*, 1971
Mus. ms.: *Three One-Noters*, 1974–1975
Mus. ms.: *Three Pieces for Clarinet Trio*, 1976
Mus. ms.: *Three Pieces for Solo Trumpet*, 1971
Mus. ms.: *Trio for Flute, Cello, and Piano*, 1983
Mus. ms.: *Two Parables by Franz Kafka*, 1964
Mus. ms.: *Two Studies for Brass Quintet*, 1969–1970
Mus. ms.: *Utterances*, 1984–1985
Mus. ms. Repro.: *The Legs*. Blueprint score
Mus. ms. Repro.: *In Memoriam*, 1985. Blueprint score
Mus. ms. Repro. Annot.: *Music for Violin*, 1961. Blueprint score
Port. Phot.

Blech, Leo, 1871–1958
Library of Congress
(Box 6, unless noted)
A. Mus. ms. S.: *Schön Rothraut*, for four women's voices with piano. 2p., 35x27cm.
A. L. S.: to Bruno Eisner. Berlin, 1935. 1p., German. With musical notation
A. L. S.: to Fritz Steinbach. Berlin, 30 Aug. 2p., German
Port. Phot. Repro. S. (Box 110)

Bleyle, Karl, 1880–1969
Library of Congress
(Box 6, unless noted)
A. Mus. ms. S.: *Christ's Descent into Hell*, op. 17. 1p., 18x23cm. Excerpt
A. L. S.: Munich, 6 July 1911. 4p., German
Port. Phot. S.: by Hartmann (Box 110)

Bliss, Sir Arthur, 1891–1975
Northwestern University
L.: to Edward Clark. London, 23 Oct. 1952
L.: to Sir Herbert Read. London, 14 July 1963
L.: to Aurelio de la Vega. Somerset, 22 Sept.
Mus. Quot.: *Checkmate*
Port. Phot.: Boston, 5 Dec. 1939

Blitzstein, Marc, 1905–1964
Harvard University
L.: to Charles Haubiel. n.p., 10 Feb. 1936

Bloch, Ernest, 1880–1959
Library of Congress
(Box 79)
A. Mus. ms. Annot. S.: *Schelomo*, Geneva, Jan.–Feb. 1916, to Alexandre and Catherine Barjansky. 63p., 40x31cm., blue ink, pencil, black, brown, blue and orange crayon. Full score. Acquired in tribute to Rabbi Salomon Weil, his son Abraham Weil, and his eldest daughter Thekla Weil. A Christian, she married Richard Moldenhauer and became the mother of Hans Moldenhauer
A. L. S.: to Aurelio de la Vega. Agate Beach, 1 Feb. 1958. 2p., English

Northwestern University
SUMMARY OF PRINCIPAL HOLDINGS:
Mus. ms.: *Abodah (God's Worship): A Yom Kippur Melody for Violin with Piano Accompaniment*, San Francisco, 4 Dec. 1928. Full score, with violin part
2 Mus. mss.: *Baal Shem, Vidui; Simchas Torah*
Mus. ms.: *Enfantines (Ten Pieces for Children for the Piano)*, 1923. Complete score
Mus. ms.: *Helvetia*. Sketches

Mus. ms.: *Sinfonia breve*. Thematic material for the finale. With accompanying notes by Suzanne Bloch

14 L.: to Boaz Piller. New York, San Francisco, Berkeley, 1923–1941

L.: to Gustav Saenger. 3 Jan. 1929

L.: to Paul A. Pisk. Berkeley, 26 Feb. 1942

L.: to Friderike Zweig. Agate Beach, Oregon, 19 Mar. 1946

L.: to Aurelio de la Vega. Agate Beach, Oregon, 1 Oct. 1953

L.: to Hans Moldenhauer. Agate Beach, Oregon, 28 Sept. 1955

Mus. Quot.: *America*, 1929

Mus. Quot.: *Schelomo*

2 Mus. mss. Repro.: *Quartet No. II*, 1945. "First sketches." Photostat

3 Port. Phot.: 1925, 1928, n.d.

Bloch, Suzanne, b. 1907
Harvard University

Mus. ms.: "Basso Ostinato, Myxolidian Mode," from Ernest Bloch's counterpoint book vol. IX, transcribed and adapted for lute by Suzanne Bloch

3 L.: to Hans Moldenhauer. New York, 17 Apr. 1960, 22 Sept., 3 Oct. 1961

L.: to Mary Sanks. 10 Aug.

Northwestern University
See Bloch, Ernest

Blomdahl, Karl-Birger, 1916–1968
Library of Congress
(Box 6)

A. Mus. ms. S.: *Five Songs for Mezzo and Piano*, 1954. 7p., 29x22cm., Italian, pencil. Stage music. Sketches

A. Mus. ms. S.: *De Trogna*, 1954. 5 leaves (9p.), 31x24cm., pencil. Sketches. Stage music for a Masefield drama

A. L. S.: to Hans Moldenhauer. Sweden, 9 Mar. 1960. 1p., English

Blow, John, 1649–1708
Northwestern University
See Walter, John

Blumenthal, Jakob, 1829–1908
Library of Congress
(Box 6)

A. Mus. ms. S.: *A Twilight Song*, to Tennant, 4 May 1863. 5p., 22x30cm. Exhibited at the Victorian Era Exhibition, London, 1897

2 A. L. S.: to Silas. Montreaux, 15 Dec. 1850; Kensington Gore, 18 Mar. 1872. 5p., French, English

A. L. S.: to Lady Mary. London, 1 May 1856. 2p., German

A. L. S.: to a student. London, 1863. 3p.

3 A. L. S.: to Miss Stephenson. Kensington Gore, 1873–1876. 7p., English

A. Card S.: to Mrs. Eliot. Kensington Gore, 15 Feb. 1892. 2p., English

A. L. S.: to Mrs. Eliot. Kensington Gore, 16 Jan. 1894. 4p., English

A. Doc. S.: Autograph title. *She Is No More.* 1p.

Boatwright, Howard, b. 1918
Harvard University

Mus. ms.: *Nunc sancte nobis Spiritus*. With additional printed score

Mus. ms.: Quartet, for violin, clarinet, viola, and cello, 1958

L.: [to Paul A. Pisk?]

Doc.: Student assignment. Notes and materials from a classroom project given by Paul Hindemith at Yale University in 1945. Included is a sketch by Hindemith, as well as corrections by Hindemith

Bochkoltz-Falconi, Anna, 1820–1870
Library of Congress
(Box 17)

4 A. L. S.: Gotha, Coburg, 1854. 7p., German

Bochsa, Nicolas Charles, 1789–1856
Northwestern University

L.: [United States], 29 Jan. 1853

Bodanzky, Artur, 1877–1939
Harvard University
2 L.: to Zemlinsky. Mannheim, 17 Sept. 1911; Dorset, 22 Aug. 1939
L.: to Berthold Nener. Cortina d'Ampezzo, 4 July 1922
L.: to Malkin. New York, 19 Oct. 1938
See Zemlinsky, Alexander

Boehe, Ernst, 1880–1938
Library of Congress
(Box 6)
Call. c. Annot.: German
A. Mus. Quot. S.: *Odysseus*, to Schey, Munich, 14 Nov. 1905

Böhme, Franz Magnus, 1827–1898
Library of Congress
(Box 6)
A. L. S.: [to A. W. Gottschalg]. Dresden, 22 Aug. 1862. 1p., German

Böhme, Walther, 1884–1952
Library of Congress
(Box 6)
A. Mus. ms. S.: *Jugend*, op. 3, No. 3. 3p., 34x27cm. Full score

Böhner, Ludwig [Louis], 1787–1860
Library of Congress
(Box 6)
A. Mus. ms. Annot.: *Pianoforte Conzert*, Allegro con brio, 1844. 19p., 21x34cm. Draft in condensed and full score. Bound

Boelke, Walter R., 1905–1987
Library of Congress
(Box 79)
Obit.

Boguslawski, Moissaye, 1887–1944
Washington State University
3 L.: to Solomon Pimsleur. Chicago, 23 July, 26 Sept. 1940, 15 Oct. 1941
Doc.: Announcement. Regarding Solomon Pimsleur

Boieldieu, Adrien, 1775–1834
Library of Congress
(Box 6)
A. L. S.: to Castil-Blaze. n.p., n.d. 2p., French. With draft of "Air de Victor au 1er acte" from *La Dame blanche*

Boito, Arrigo [Enrico], 1842–1918
Northwestern University
L.: Milan, 12 Dec. 1894
Port. Phot.: mounted with musical quotation
Port.

Bolcom, William, b. 1938
Harvard University
SUMMARY OF PRINCIPAL HOLDINGS:
Mus. ms.: *Ah*, 1963
Mus. ms.: *Décalage*, 1961–1962
Mus. ms.: *Dynamite Tonight*, 1960–1963
Mus. ms.: *Fantasy-Sonata*, 1960–1962
Mus. ms.: *Octet*, 1962
Mus. ms.: *Oracles*, 1964
Mus. ms.: *Pastoral*, 1962
Mus. ms.: *Study*
Mus. ms.: *Three Studies for Piano*, 1963. Excerpt

Bónis, Ferenc, b. 1932
Library of Congress
(Box 6)
5 T. L. S.: to Hans Moldenhauer. Budapest, 1986–1987. 5p., English, German
2 L.: to Bónis. n.p., 1986–1987. 2p., English

Bonn, Ferdinand, 1861–1933
Library of Congress
(Box 110)
Port. Repro. S.

Bonnet, Joseph, 1884–1944
Library of Congress
(Box 110)
Port. Phot. S.: to Boaz Piller, Boston, 22 Dec. 1918

Boone, Charles, b. 1939
Harvard University
Mus. ms. Repro. Annot.: *Suite for Violoncello Solo*, 1963.
    Facsimile

Borbolla, Carlo [Carlos], 1902–1990
Harvard University
2 Mus. mss.: *El Esbelto Talle de S...* ; on verso, *El
    Abufar*
Mus. ms.: *Estudio No. 17*, June 1976
Mus. ms.: *Son No. 34*, op. 386
2 L.: to Aurelio de la Vega. Cuba, 22 Jan. 1974. With
    musical illustration
L.: to Hans Moldenhauer. Cuba, 13 Aug. 1980. With
    translation
L.: from Aurelio de la Vega. Northridge, 2 Jan. 1980
L.: to Aurelio de la Vega. Cotorro, 3 Nov. 1984. With
    letter regarding Cuban music, to Hans
    Moldenhauer, from Aurelio de la Vega
Doc.: Biographical information
Port. Phot.

Borch, Gaston Louis Christopher, 1871–1926
Library of Congress
(Box 6)
A. Mus. ms. S.: *Romance sans paroles*, op. 69, No. 2, for
    piano. 4p., 34x26cm.
L. S.: to Hans Moldenhauer, from Gerald Borch.
    Bellevue, Washington, 19 Sept. 1964. 1p., English

Borghi-Mamo, Adelaide, 1826–1901
Library of Congress
(Box 6)
A. L. S.: ?, 1 Oct. 1860. 1p., Italian

Bornschein, Franz Carl, 1879–1948
Harvard University
Mus. ms. Repro. Annot.: *The Mission Road*. Blueprint
    score, with typescript

Borowski, Felix, 1872–1956
Harvard University
L.: to Charles Haubiel. Chicago, 30 Nov. 1935
L.: to Karl Weigl. Chicago, 13 Sept. 1945

Borwick, Leonard, 1868–1925
Northwestern University
6 L.
Doc.: Address panel [to Downall?]
Obit.

Bostelmann, Otto, 1907–1981
Harvard University
Summary of Principal Holdings:
Mus. ms.: *Concerto for Organ and Flute*, op. 45
Mus. ms.: *Nonet*, op. 38
Mus. ms.: *Prelude XI*, op. 61
Mus. ms.: *Sierra Suite*, op. 23, Crescendo II ("Among
    the Giants"), 1953
Mus. ms.: *String Quartet No. 4*, op. 66
Mus. ms.: *String Trio No. 4*, op. 80
Mus. ms.: *String Trio No. 5*, op. 81
Mus. ms.: *Symphony No. 2*, op. 20, 1950
Mus. ms.: *Woodwind Quartet*, op. 25, 1955
Mus. ms.: *Woodwind Trio*, op. 53
Port. Phot.

Bote & Bock, est. 1838, Berlin
Library of Congress
(Box 6)
A. L. S.: to ?. Berlin, 25 Apr. 1872. 2p., German

Boulanger, Nadia, 1887–1979
Harvard University
See Koussevitzky, Serge

Library of Congress
(Box 6)
2 A. L. S.: to Boaz Piller. Boston, 23 Oct., 25 Dec.
    1945. 2p., French
A. L. S.: Paris, n.d. 1p., English

Boulez, Pierre, b. 1925
Library of Congress
(Box 6)
A. Mus. ms.: [*Le Marteau sans maître*, Cantata for Contralto, Flute, Viola, Guitar, Vibraphone, and Percussion, 1953–1955]. 5p., 20–28x34cm., pencil, colored pencil. Sketches
A. Mus. ms.: [Third Sonata for Piano], Formant I. 1p., 35x27cm., ink. First draft
A. L. S.: to Hans Moldenhauer. Baden, 9 Feb. 1960. 1p., French
T. L. S.: to Hans Moldenhauer. Baden, 14 Sept. 1962. 1p., French
Pri. Sco. S.: *Le Soleil des eaux*, 31 Oct. 1948, Paris: Heugel, c1959, to Karl Amadeus Hartmann. 44p.

Paul Sacher Stiftung
A. Mus. ms.: *Le Marteau sans maître*. Full score. With additional copy containing inscriptions by Boulez and Hans Rosbaud

Washington State University
See Rosbaud, Hans

Boult, Sir Adrian, 1889–1983
Northwestern University
L.: to Mrs. Morland. London, 29 July 1963
Doc.: Essay. In tribute to Edward Clark

Bour, Ernest, b. 1913
Washington State University
See Rosbaud, Hans

Bourgault-Ducoudray, Louis, 1840–1910
Library of Congress
(Box 6, unless noted)
A. Mus. Quot. S.: *Thamara*, Largo Amoroso, Act II
Port. Phot.: by Henri Manuel (Box 110)

Bozza, Eugène, 1905–1991
Library of Congress
(Box 110)
Port. Phot. S.: to Hans Moldenhauer, 1954

Braham, John, 1774–1856
Northwestern University
L.: Hyde Park Gardens, 6 July 1848
4 L.

Brahms, Johannes, 1833–1897
Library of Congress
(Box 6, unless noted)
A. Mus. ms. Rev.: *Rinaldo v. Göthe* [*Rinaldo*, op. 50, Cantata for Tenor solo, Men's Chorus, and Orchestra, 1868]. 162p., 23x35cm. + 26x33cm., ink, black and colored pencils. Full orchestral-vocal score. In original cardboard folder (Shelf)
A. Mus. ms.: [*Vier Lieder für Singstimme und Klavier*, op. 46, No. 1, *Die Kränze*], Baden-Baden, 26 June 1865. 4p., 25x33cm., ink. With documentation of provenance
Pri. Sco. A. Annot.: *Neue Liebeslieder Walzer*, op. 65a, [1877]. 38p. + 6 leaves (separated after conservation), ink, pencil, blue pencil. Full score of the version for piano four hands, with autograph additions and annotations. Basing his arrangement on the proofs of the original setting for vocal quartet with piano duet accompaniment, Brahms makes all appropriate changes, many glued into the proofs. The closing section, *Zum Schluss* (text by Goethe), is fully written out as a separate autograph (1 leaf, 25x34cm.) (Shelf)
A. L. S.: to Philipp Spitta. Vienna, Jan. 1874. 3p., German. Musical topics; Nottebohm, Bach biography
A. L. S.: [to Dr. Max Abraham at C. F. Peters]. [Vienna, 3 Oct. 1881]. 3p., German. Expressing thanks for honorarium; mentions von Bülow, Julius Stockhausen, Franz Wüllner, Adolph Schulze
A. L. S.: [20 Nov. 1881]. Regarding laurel twigs; *Nänie*

A. L. S.: Ischl, 18 June 1882. 2p., German. Refers to marital differences between Joseph and Amalie Joachim; Riedel, Hanslick. Engraved portrait of Hans von Bülow on stationery

A. L. S.: [Ischl], [11 Aug. 1896?]. 3p., German. Sarcastic letter to a friend about literary matters; illness

A. L. S.: to Rudolf von der Leyden. Vienna, 1887. 1p., German. Comments about a difficult situation

A. L. S.: to Ferdinand Vetter. n.p., [Sept. 1896]. 3p., German

A. L. S.: to a copyist. n.p., n.d. 1p., German

Port. Phot. Gr.: May 1896, after the funeral of Clara Schumann (Box 110)

Brand, Max, 1896–1980
Wiener Stadt- u. Landesbibliothek

Mus. ms. Repro.: *The Gate*. Blueprint score of manuscript piano reduction. Also, copy of typed libretto, with autograph corrections

Brandt, Marianne [Bischoff, Marie], 1842–1921
Library of Congress
(Box 7)

4 A. L. S.: to ?. Aug. 1869–Sept. 1871. 10p., German

Brandt, William Edward, b. 1920
Harvard University

L.: to Hans Moldenhauer. Pullman, 25 Sept. 1980

Washington State University
SUMMARY OF PRINCIPAL HOLDINGS:

Mus. ms.: *Divertimento for Flute, Clarinet, Bassoon*, 1959
Mus. ms.: *The Lark*
Mus. ms.: *Sonata for Clarinet and Piano*
Mus. ms.: *Toccata for Piano*, 1973. With additional copy
4 L.: to Hans Moldenhauer. Pullman, 1960, 1975

Brandts Buys, Jan Willem Frans, 1868–1939
Library of Congress
(Box 7)

A. Mus. ms. S.[?]: *A.E.I.O.U.*, op. 48. 22p., 26x35cm. Full score

Braunfels, Walter, 1882–1954
Library of Congress
(Box 7)

A. L. S.: to Tischer. Munich, 27 Jan. 1925. 2p., German

Washington State University
See Rosbaud, Hans

Brazil, 1985. VI. Bienal Brasileira de Música Contemporánea
Harvard University

Doc.: Festival program book. Signed by many participating composers

Bresgen, Cesar, 1913–1988
Library of Congress
(Box 7, unless noted)

A. Mus. ms. S.: *Advent*, 22 Nov. 1966. 2p., 32x24cm., German. Text by Hans Moldenhauer

A. Mus. ms. S.: *Drei Gesänge nach Hans Moldenhauer für Bariton und Streichquartett*, 31 July 1972. 14p., 34x27cm.

A. Mus. ms. S. Rev.: *Drei Gesänge...*, July 1972. 10p., 34x27cm. Sketches

A. Mus. ms. S.: *Ester, ("Der Engel von Prag")*, [1977]. 16p., 17x23cm. Notebook of first sketches to Act III, scene 2

A. Mus. ms. S.: [same], July 1977. 14p., 34x27cm. Piano-vocal score

A. Mus. ms. S.: *Requiem für Webern*, [1945], revised 1972. 42p., 32x25cm. Complete draft and sketches

A. Mus. ms.: *Trio*, Aug. 1972. 15p., 34x27cm. + various sizes

Mus. ms. Repro.: *Advent*, 22 Nov. 1966. 2p., 32x23cm., German. Text by Hans Moldenhauer

Mus. ms. Repro. S.: *Requiem für Webern*, Sept. 1945, revised July 1972. 68p., 34x25cm., Latin. Autograph title page

Pri. Sco. S.: *Balkanstudien*, vols. 1 and 2, Frankfurt: Litolff's, c1964, to Rosaleen Moldenhauer, Grossgmain, 1965. 18p. (vol. 1) + 16p. (vol. 2)

Pri. Sco. S.: *Bilder des Todes*, Vienna: Doblinger, c1973, to Hans Moldenhauer. 44p.

2 Pri. Sco. S.: *Klaviertrio*, Vienna: Doblinger, c1974, to Hans Moldenhauer, 1975. 20p. + 7p. + 4p.

Pri. Sco.: *Requiem für Anton Webern*, Cologne: Gerig, c1976. 51p., Latin
2 Clip.: 27 Oct. 1975. German
2 Port. Phot. S.: by Alfred Pittertschatscher (Box 110)
Port. Phot. S.: by Carl Pospesch (Box 110)
Bk. S.: *Europäische Liebeslieder aus acht Jahrhunderten.* München: Heimeran, c1978, to Hans Moldenhauer, 19 Aug. 1978. 360p. (Shelf)
Bk. S.: *Trariro*, Zurich: Gemeinschaft, n.d., to Hans Moldenhauer, Grossgmain, 1 Aug. 1965. 44p., German (Shelf)

Washington State University
See Rosbaud, Hans

Breunung, Ferdinand, 1830–1883
Library of Congress
(Box 7)
A. L. S.: Aachen, 13 Feb. 1877. 1p., German

Brewer, Sir Herbert, 1865–1928
Northwestern University
3 L.

Bricken, Carl Ernest, 1898–1971
Harvard University
Mus. ms.: *Daniel Boone*, 1951
Mus. ms.: *Edward*
Mus. ms.: *Etchings*
Mus. ms.: *Lord Randal*
Mus. ms.: *Making of a River*
Mus. ms.: [Orchestral score, pp.4, 16]
Mus. ms.: *The Prairie Years*, 1952
Mus. ms.: *Quartett I in C Minor*
Mus. ms.: *Sonata No. 1*
Mus. ms.: *Sonata No. 2*
Mus. ms.: *Sonata for Violin and Piano*, 1944
Mus. ms.: *Symphony No. 3*, 1949
Mus. ms. Repro. Annot.: *For the Time Being: A Christmas Oratorio.* Blueprint score
Mus. ms. Repro. Annot.: *The Travelled Sea*, 1955
Mus. ms. Repro.: *The Trojan Women*, 1960. Incidental music

Bridge, Frank, 1879–1941
Northwestern University
L.: to Edward Clark. Kensington, 31 Mar. 1936

Bridge, Sir Frederick, 1844–1924
Northwestern University
4 L.: The Cloisters, Westminster Abbey, n.d.
L.: fragment
Obit.

Bringuet-Idiartborde, A., 1898–1971
Harvard University
Pri. Sco. Annot.: *Páginas argentinas.* Proofs

Brisman, Heskel, b. 1923
Library of Congress
(Boxes 8–10)
A. Mus. ms. S.: *Cantata: "Don't Listen to the Wind"* for Chorus, 4 Soloists, Wind Ensemble, Percussion, 1978. 195p., 34x27cm. Piano reduction
A. Mus. ms. S.: *Chaconne and Allegro for Double Bass Solo.* 6p., 34x27cm. With reproduction of same, signed
A. Mus. ms. S.: *Concerted Music for Piano and Percussion Ensemble,* to Paul Price and Elizabeth Marshall. 50p., 34x27cm. Draft
A. Mus. ms. S.: *Concerto for French Horn and Orchestra,* 1982. 43p., 32x24cm.
A. Mus. ms. S.: *Menagerie Suite for Piano (Eight Character Sketches of Diverse Animals)*, 1968. 17p., 32x24cm.
A. Mus. ms. S.: *Serenata for Flute, Viola, and Harp,* 1985. 23p., 32x24cm.
A. Mus. ms. S.: *Sonata II.* 25p., 32x23cm. With reproduction of same
A. Mus. ms. S.: *Trio for Flute, Cello, and Piano,* 1980. 42p., 32x24cm.
A. Mus. ms. S.: *Trio Sonata for Violin, Viola, and Cello,* 1955, revised May 1979. 24p., 34x26cm.
T. L. S.: to Mary Moldenhauer. Teaneck, 14 June 1989. 1p., English
A. L. S.: to Mary Moldenhauer. n.p., 16 Aug. 1989. 1p., English

L. S.: to Brisman, from Lukas Foss. 10 Oct. 1980. 1p., English

L. Repro.: to Brisman, from Paul Doktor. New York, 9 Dec. 1984. 2p.

Mus. ms. Repro. S.: *Andante Sostenuto*, transcription of the 2nd movement from *String Quartet I*, 1983. 15p., 32x21cm. With autograph inscription by Lukas Foss

Mus. ms. Repro. S.: *Cantata: "Don't Listen to the Wind."* 188p., 28x21cm. Accompanying program and flyer for the premiere

Mus. ms. Repro.: *Canto I*, 1959. 6p.

Mus. ms. Repro.: *Canto III*. 4p.

Mus. ms. Repro. A. Annot. S.: *Cinemuse*, 1987. 85p. Blueprint score

Mus. ms. Repro. A. Rev. S.: *Concerted Music for Piano and Percussion Ensemble*, 1975. 50p. Blueprint score. With program of the premiere New York City performance

Mus. ms. Repro. A. Rev. S.: *Concerto for French Horn and Orchestra*, 126p. (see letter above, from Lukas Foss)

Mus. ms. Repro.: *Dithyrambic Ode*. 2p.

Mus. ms. Repro.: *Interplay*, 1974. 16p.

Mus. ms. Repro. S.: *Profiles*, 1987. 37p.

Mus. ms. Repro.: *Serenata*, 1985. 25p.

Mus. ms. Repro. A. Rev.: *String Quartet I*, 1951, revised 1982. 40p.

Mus. ms. Repro.: *Woodwind Trio I*, 1986. 19p.

Mus. ms. Repro.: *Woodwind Trio II*, 1986. 15p.

S. rec.: *Dithyrambic Ode*. Solo flute

Britain, Radie, 1899–1994
Harvard University
Summary of Principal Holdings:
Mus. ms.: *Awake to Life*
Mus. ms.: *In the Beginning*
Mus. ms.: *Cactus Rhapsody*
Mus. ms.: *Kuthara (The Scythe)*
Mus. ms.: *Little Per Cent*, 1963
Mus. ms.: *Lullaby of the Bells*, 1964
Mus. ms.: *Nebula*. Excerpt
Mus. ms.: *Nisan*
Mus. ms.: *Rhumbando*, 1975
Mus. ms.: *Southern Symphony*. Excerpt
Mus. ms.: *Withered Flowers*. Corrections
Mus. ms.: *The World Does Not Wish for Beauty*

L.: to Charles Haubiel. Hollywood, 6 Sept. 1956. With copy of Haubiel's reply

2 L.: to Hans Moldenhauer. Hollywood, 25 May 1976, 10 Apr. 1979

Mus. ms. Repro.: *Lament (Prison)*

Mus. ms. Repro.: *Pastorale*. Blueprint score. With additional copy

Bk.: *Composer's Corner*

Britten, Benjamin, 1913–1976
Northwestern University
3 L.: to Alma Mahler. Stratford Festival, 30 Aug. 1957; Aldeburg, 1 May 1959; Season's Greetings, n.d.

Mus. Quot.: *Albert Herring*, 13 Aug. 1964

Port.

Washington State University
See Rosbaud, Hans

Brod, Max, 1884–1968
Library of Congress
(Box 11, unless noted)
A. L. S.: to Alma Mahler. Tel-Aviv, 2 Apr. 1959. 2p., German

Pri. Sco. S.: *Vier Lieder*, Vienna: Universal, to Alma Mahler Werfel, 25 Dec. 1950. 22p.

Port. Phot.: of Brod and Hans Pfitzner, Apr. 1928 (Box 110)

Bronsart von Schellendorf, Hans [Hans von Bronsart], 1830–1913
Library of Congress
(Box 11)
15 A. L. S.: to Eugen Lindner. 1896–1913. 50p., German. Critical commentaries on cultural life and composers

Call. c. Annot.: to Eugen Lindner. New Year's greetings. German. Satiric poem in which Bronsart refers to Reger, Pfitzner, and Strauss. Illustrated with musical quotations

Broqua, Alfonso, 1876–1946
Harvard University
Mus. ms.: *Evocaciones criollas: Vidala*

Brosig, Moritz, 1815–1887
Library of Congress
(Box 11)
A. L. S.: Breslau, 21 Oct. 1874. 2p., German

Bruch, Max, 1838–1920
Library of Congress
(Box 11)
3 A. L. S.: to Karl Krebs. Friedenau [Berlin], 23 Mar.
  1907, 5, 7 Apr. 1910. 15p., German. Expresses
  outrage over a newspaper article
A. L. S.: to Bruch, with response to Radecke.
  Friedenau, 24, 26 Apr. 1906. 2p., German

Northwestern University
Mus. ms.: *Moses*, op. 67. Full score
Mus. Alb. l.: *Romanze*, 14 June 1854
L.: to Miss Florence. Bonn, 30 July 1880
L.: to a Paris music society. Breslau, 26 Jan. 1884
L.: Breslau, 20 Jan. 1889
Mus. Quot.: *The Lay of the Bell*, Birmingham, 27 Aug.
  1879
Pri. Sco.: *Frithjof*, scene 5

Bruckner, Anton, 1824–1896
Library of Congress
(Box 11)
A. L. S.: to a friend. Vienna, 13 Nov. 1883. 2p.,
  German
A. L. S.: to Baron von Perfall. Vienna, 27 Feb. 1885.
  4p., German. Regarding the Richard Wagner
  Society; Munich and *Seventh Symphony*, asking Levi
  for special rehearsals
Draw. Repro.: "Gedenkblatt zum Zyklus der 9
  Symphonien in der Aula der Universität zu
  München 1946/1947." 1p., 32x22cm., pencil.
  Rosbaud conducted the cycle

Brüll, Ignaz, 1846–1907
Library of Congress
(Box 11)
A. Mus. ms. S.: *Nachtwandler*. 4p., 34x26cm., German.
  Complete score
A. L. S.: Voslau, 28 Sept. 1875. 2p., German
A. L. S.: [to Carl Reinecke?]. Vienna, 16 Dec. 1896.
  2p., German
A. L. S.: Vienna, 12 Nov. 1897. 2p., German
A. L. S.: Unterach, 30 May 1903. 1p., German

Brün, Herbert, b. 1918
Harvard University
L.: to Aurelio de la Vega. Urbana, Illinois, 8 Dec. 1983

Bruneau, Alfred, 1857–1934
Library of Congress
(Box 11)
A. Mus. ms. S.: *Ballade de l'Amie bien belle*. 4p.,
  35x27cm., French. Complete score
A. L. S.: to Manheim. Paris, 2 May 1882. 1p., French
A. Card S.: n.p., 4 Jan. 1897. 2p.

Brunswick, Mark, 1902–1971
Harvard University
SUMMARY OF PRINCIPAL HOLDINGS:
Mus. ms.: *Viola Fantasia*
L.: to Paul F. Sanders. New York, 9 May 1947

Bruyck, Karl Debrois van, 1828–1902
Wiener Stadt- u. Landesbibliothek
4 L.: to Selmar Bagge. Vienna, 26 May 1860, New
  Year's Eve 1862; Penzing, 8 Sept. 1866; Vienna,
  13 July 1868

Buck, Dudley, 1839–1909
Harvard University
2 L.: to Flora Klickmann. Brooklyn, 1, 17 May 1899

Budd, Harold, b. 1936
Harvard University
L.: to Donivan Johnson. Valencia, California, 17 Jan.
1975
L.: to Aurelio de la Vega. n.p., n.d.
Clip.

Büchtger, Fritz, 1903–1978
Bayerische Staatsbibliothek
SUMMARY OF PRINCIPAL HOLDINGS:
Mus. ms.: *Weihnachtsoratorium, Drei Könige,* 1959
11 L.: Munich, 1959–1962
Port.

Bülow, Cosima Liszt von, 1837–1930
Library of Congress
See Wagner, Cosima

Bülow, Hans von, 1830–1894
Bayerische Staatsbibliothek
Mus. ms.: *Militärmarsch* by Beethoven, arranged by
von Bülow for piano solo
L.: Berlin, 31 Oct. 1858

Library of Congress
(Box 11, unless noted)
A. Mus. ms. arr. S.: *Sechs Menuetten von L. v. Beethoven,*
für das Pianoforte. 7p., 27x34cm. Complete score
A. L. S.: to Steyl. Meiningen, 8 Dec. 1884. 1p.,
German
A. L. S.: to Leopold Marxsen. Hamburg, 21 Nov. 1887.
2p., German, with translation
Obit.: With portrait photograph. England, Mar. 1894.
English
Port. Phot.: 1884 (Box 110)
See Brahms, Johannes

Bülow, Marie Schanzer von
Library of Congress
(Box 11)
A. L. S.: to Miss Eisenach. Florence, 15 Feb. 1897.
3p., German

P. card S.: to Bruno and Olga Eisner. Charlottenburg,
13 Mar. 1932. 2p., German
A. Doc. S.: Attestation. For Olga Eisner. Berlin,
14 July 1938. 1p., German

Bukofzer, Manfred F., 1910–1955
Harvard University
L.: Berkeley, 8 May 1947

Bull, Ole, 1810–1880
Library of Congress
(Box 110)
Port. Phot.: 1870. By Warren. With accompanying
album leaf signed, Boston, 29 Apr. 1877

Bulss, Paul, 1847–1902
Library of Congress
(Box 11)
2 A. L. S.: to Senff. Dresden, 8 Jan., 10 Nov. 1877.
2p., German

Bungert, August, 1845–1915
Library of Congress
(Box 11)
A. Mus. ms.: [Corrections for a vocal composition].
1p., 25x20cm.

Buonamente, Giovanni Battista, d. 1642
Library of Congress
(Box 11)
6 A. L. S.: to Prince Cesare Gonzaga in Mantua.
Vienna, Prague, 1627. 6p., Italian
L. Repro.: 3 Dec. 1627. 1p., Italian

Buonamici, Giuseppe, 1846–1914
Library of Congress
(Box 11)
2 A. L. S.: to Murdoch. ?, 10 Oct. 1884; 1901[?].
2p., English, Italian

Burge, David, b. 1930
Harvard University
SUMMARY OF PRINCIPAL HOLDINGS:
Mus. ms.: *Blood Wedding*
Mus. ms.: *Intervals*
Mus. ms.: *Second Piano Sonata*, 1958. With additional
facsimile
Mus. ms.: [Sketchbook, 1958]
Mus. ms.: *Variations on a Well-Known Tune*, 1958
Mus. ms. Repro.: *Six Piano Pieces*. Facsimile
Mus. ms. Repro.: *Third Piano Sonata*. Facsimile

Burkhard, Heinrich, 1888–1950
Washington State University
See Rosbaud, Hans

Burkhard, Paul, 1911–1977
Washington State University
See Rosbaud, Hans

Burkhard, Willy, 1900–1955
Washington State University
See Rosbaud, Hans

Zentralbibliothek Zürich
Mus. ms.: *Cantique de notre Terre*, op. 67, 1942–1943
Mus. ms.: *Concerto for Two Flutes, Cembalo, and String
Orchestra*, op. 94, 1954. On verso, sketches to a vocal
work
Mus. ms.: [Chorale melodies]
Mus. ms.: *Konzert für Bratsche und Orchester*, op. 93,
1953
Mus. ms.: *Lobet im Himmel den Herrn*, op. 96, 1954
Mus. ms.: *Messe*, op. 85, 1951
Mus. ms.: *Neun Lieder nach Gedichten von Christian
Morgenstern*, op. 70, 1943–1944
Mus. ms.: *Die schwarze Spinne*, 1947–1948
Mus. ms.: *Sinfonie in einem Satz*, op. 73, 1944
Mus. ms.: *Die Sintflut*, op. 97, 1954–1955

Mus. ms.: [Sketches to three movements of a
symphony], Nov. 1921
Mus. ms.: *Till Ulenspiegel*, op. 24, 1929
Mus. ms.: *Toccata*, op. 55, 1939
Mus. ms. Repro. Annot.: *Sinfonie in einem Satz*, op. 73,
1944. Blueprint score

Burkhardt, Hans, 1904–1994
Harvard University
L.: to Aurelio de la Vega. 1983

Burleigh, Cecil, 1885–1980
Harvard University
Mus. ms.: *Four Small Concert Pieces*, op. 21
L.: to Rudolph Ganz. Madison, 28 May 1942

Burmester, Carl Adolph Wilhelm, 1869–1933
Library of Congress
(Box 11)
A. L. S.: to Eugen Lindner. Bayhill on Sea, 5 Mar.
1927. 1p., German

Burney, Charles, 1726–1814
Library of Congress
(Box 11)
A. L. S.: to Samuel Wesley. n.p., [ca. 15 July 1810]. 1p.,
English. With authentication of letter and short
history written on letter by Vincent Novello
L.: to Rev. Dr. Burney [Charles Parr Burney,
grandson]. Kent, 13 Feb. 1829. 4p., English. With
newspaper clipping in which Percy Scholes asks for
available letters about Burney. Also response letter
(from the previous owner of this letter) to Scholes

Bury, Agnes, 1831–1902
Library of Congress
(Box 11)
A. L. S.: to a theater director in Bremen. Leipzig,
8 Oct. 1855. 4p., German

A. L. S.: to a Kapellmeister. Berlin, 27 Sept. 1858. 1p., German

A. L. S.: to a patron. Zehlendorf, n.d. 2p., German

Busch, Adolf, 1891–1952
Library of Congress
(Box 11)
A. L. S.: to Karl Weigl. Basel, 3 July 1928. 4p., German

Bush, Alan, 1900–1995
Northwestern University
L.: to Mrs. Morland. Radlett, Hertfordshire, 12 Sept. 1963

Busoni, Ferruccio, 1866–1924
Library of Congress
(Box 11, unless noted)
3 A. L. S.: to Rüppel. Leipzig, 5 Feb., 15 Feb., 12 Apr. 1887. 3p., German
9 A. L. S.: to Rudolph Ganz. 1899–1908. 20p., French, German
A. L. S.: to Rudolph Ganz. Weimar, 16 July 1900. 2p., German. With self-caricature
Pri. Sco. S.: *Concerto*, op. 39, Breitkopf & Härtel, c1906, to Rudolph Ganz, 1906. 328p. First edition (Shelf)
Doc.: Essay. "An Unknown Essay by Busoni: Critique of Beethoven's Last String Quartets," by Hans Moldenhauer, in *Neue Zeitschrift für Musik*, Dec. 1960. 2p., German
Doc. Repro.: Critical discussion of Beethoven. Neuchatel, 15 Nov. 1917. 8p.
See Palmgren, Selim

Washington State University
See Rosbaud, Hans

Bussotti, Sylvano, b. 1931
Library of Congress
(Box 11)
A. Mus. ms. S.: *Breve*; *Due voci*, 1958. 1p., 30x30cm. Sketches

A. Mus. ms. S.: *Sonate pour clavier, aprés Pièces de chair II*, Florence, 27 Apr. 1960. 1p., 20x27cm.
A. Mus. ms. S.: [*Torso*], Milan, 22 Nov. 1960. 2p., 66x16cm. First version
2 A. L. S.: to Hans Moldenhauer. Venice, 20 Apr. 1963; Florence, 21 Sept. 1963. 3p., Italian
Mus. ms. Repro. A. Rev.: *Torso III*, 1963. 1p.

Caba, Eduardo, 1890–1953
Harvard University
Mus. ms.: *Aires indios de Bolivia*, No. 5

Cadman, Charles Wakefield, 1881–1946
Harvard University
Mus. ms.: *Down in the Deep Void Tank*
Mus. ms.: *Wild Geese Flew to the South Last Night*, 1944
Mus. ms. Repro.: *As the Crow Flies*. Blueprint score
Mus. ms. Repro.: *The Enchanted Flute*. Blueprint score

Cage, John, 1912–1992
Harvard University
SUMMARY OF PRINCIPAL HOLDINGS:
19 L.: to Adolph Weiss. [student years–1966, n.d.]
Doc. Annot.: Typescript. "Adolph Weiss: Reminiscences"

Library of Congress
(Box 79)
A. Mus. ms. S.: *The Wonderful Widow of Eighteen Springs*, for voice and piano, New York, Nov. 1942. 6p. (2p. of music), 33x26cm., ink. On transparent sheets (used for publication by Peters)
A. L. S.: to Adolph Weiss. Urbana, Illinois, 28 Oct. 1966. 2p., English
Doc.: Brochure. KPFA radio station, Berkeley, California, 1965. 4p., English

Callcott, William Hutchins, 1807–1882
Northwestern University
2 L.: 1844; n.d.

Calusdian, George, b. 1949
Harvard University
Mus. ms.: *Piano Piece No. 1*, 1978
L.: to Hans Moldenhauer. n.p., n.d.

Calvocoressi, Michel-Dimitri, 1877–1944
Northwestern University
L.: to Edward Clark. n.p., 30 July

Campana, Fabio, 1819–1882
Library of Congress
(Box 11)
A. L. S.: London, 2 Feb. 1882. 2p., French
A. L. S.: to Mrs. Graham. London, n.d. 3p., French

Campos Parsi, Héctor, b. 1922
Harvard University
L.: to Aurelio de la Vega. Santurce, 6 Apr. 1983

Canneti, Francesco, 1807–1884
Library of Congress
(Box 11)
A. L. S.: to Marchese Gherado Bevilacqua in Ferrara.
  Bologna. May ?. 3p., Italian

Capoul, Victor, 1839–1924
Library of Congress
(Box 11)
A. Mus. ms. S.: *Demain*. 3p., 34x26cm., French.
  Complete score
A. Mus. ms. S.: [same]. 4p., 30x24cm., French. Fair
  copy

Carafa, Michele [Michel], 1787–1872
Library of Congress
(Box 11, unless noted)
A. Mus. ms. S.: *Abufar*. 6p., 26x32cm., French. Duet in
  piano-vocal score
A. L. S.: to Schieker. Paris, 19 Feb. 1847. 1p., French
A. L. S.: to a colonel. Paris, 21 June 1850. 2p., French
A. Mus. Quot. S.: *O caro...*, to Adele di Lopigerane,
  Milan, Autumn, 1817. Italian
Obit.: from *Le Figaro*, Paris, 29 July 1872. French
Port. Lith. S. Repro. (Box 110)

Carelli, Vicente
Library of Congress
(Box 11)
A. Mus. ms. S.: *Danza vida porteña*, to Ricardo Viñes.
  8p., 36x26cm.

Carpenter, Charles Wayne, b. 1942
Washington State University
Mus. ms.: *String Quartet No. 1*

Carpenter, John Alden, 1876–1951
Harvard University
L.: to Carl Deis. Chicago, 17 June 1936
L.: to Boaz Piller. Chicago, 14 Dec. 1937
L.: to Rudolph Ganz. Chicago, 12 Apr. 1947
Mus. Quot.: *Violin Concerto*
Port. Phot.
See Koussevitzky, Serge

Carré, Michel, 1822–1872
Library of Congress
(Box 11)
A. L. S.: n.p., n.d. 1p., French

Carreño, Teresa, 1853–1917
Harvard University
L.: 14 June 1905

Carte, Richard D'Oyly, 1844–1901
Northwestern University
L.: London, 1 Jan. 1894

Carter, Elliott, b. 1908
Harvard University
Mus. ms.: *Second String Quartet*. Master sheets,
  pp.30–31

Washington State University
See Rosbaud, Hans

Carter, Thomas, ca. 1740–1804
Library of Congress
(Box 12)

A. L. S.: to a theater director. London, 29 Dec. 1802.
2p., English

Caruso, Enrico, 1873–1921
Library of Congress
(Box 110)
Port. Caric. S.: 1916

Casadesus, Robert, 1899–1972
Library of Congress
(Box 110)
Port. Phot. S.: to Boaz Piller, 1938. By Hrand

[signature]

Casals, Pablo [Pau], 1876–1973
Library of Congress
(Box 12, unless noted)
A. L. S.: to Boaz Piller. Prades, 6 May 1940. 2p.,
French. Discusses the conditions in Europe as a
result of the Hitler regime. With clipping regarding
letter
12 A. L. S.: to Boaz Piller. 1918–1951. 19p., French,
English
A. L. S.: to Karl Weigl. Vienna, 30 Mar. 1927. 2p.,
French
A. L. S.: to Guido Adler. Vienna, 12 Mar. 1928. 2p.,
French
P. card S.: to Karl Weigl. Barcelona, 3 June 1935.
French
23 P. cards S.: to Boaz Piller. 1936–1957. French,
English
P. card S.: to Vally Weigl. Prades, 8 May 1951. French
T. L. S.: to Boaz Piller. Puerto Rico, 20 Feb. 1958. 1p.,
English
Port. Gr.: at the organ with Schweitzer (Box 110)
Bk. S.: *Gespräche mit Casals*, by J. MA. Corredor, Bern:
Alfred Scherz, c1954. 328p.
Bk. S.: *Pablo Casals*, by Bernard Gavoty, Geneva: René
Kister, c1955, to Hans Moldenhauer. 31p.
See Weigl, Karl

Zentralbibliothek Zürich
See Tobel, Rudolf von

Casanova, André, b. 1919
Washington State University
Mus. ms. Repro.: *Notturno*, op. 13. Blueprint score

Cascarino, Romeo, b. 1922
Harvard University
Mus. ms.: *The Acadian Land*, 1954
4 L.

[signature: Casella]

Casella, Alfredo, 1883–1947
Library of Congress
(Box 12, unless noted)
53 L. S.: to Boaz Piller. 1927–1946. 65p., French. Five
letters are from his wife, Yvonne, who writes on his
behalf
3 T. L. S.: to Paul Sanders. n.p., 18 May 1931; Rome,
4 Oct. 1931; Siena, 15 Sept. 1933. 5p., French.
Regarding the ISCM; Pijper
2 A. L. S.: to Hanna Schwarz. Jassy, 16 Apr. 1937;
Egypt, 12 Jan. 1938. 2p., French
2 A. L. S.: to Ružena Herlinger. Siena, 15 Feb. 1938;
Rome, 23 Mar. 1938
T. L. S.: to Ružena Herlinger. Dahlem, n.d.
T. Doc. A. Rev.: Essay. On the development of the
modern orchestra. 3p., French
A. Mus. Quot. S.: *Concerto*, 1924, 14 Feb. 1927
Pri. Sco. S.: *Tre canzoni trecentesche*, Ricordi, to Ružena
Herlinger, Vienna, 20 Dec. [1911?]. 16p.
Port. Phot. S.: to Boaz Piller, Boston, 12 Jan. 1927.
By de Gueldre (Box 110)

Caspary, Clodomiro
Harvard University
L.: to Hans Moldenhauer. Porto Alegre, 18 Mar. 1986
Doc.: Theoretical treatise. "Seríalísmo integral
parámetros," Porto Alegre, 18 Mar. 1986

Cassadó, Gaspar, 1897–1966
Library of Congress
(Box 12)
A. L. S.: to Bruno Eisner. Venice, 22 July 1934. 2p.,
French

Mario Castelnuovo-Tedesco [signature]

Castelnuovo-Tedesco, Mario, 1895–1968
Library of Congress
(Box no./Folder no.)

A. Mus. ms. S.: *Alborada del gracioso for Cello and Piano* by Ravel, Beverly Hills, 20 Oct. 1944. 17p., 33x24cm. (80/1)

A. Mus. ms. S.: [*Amours de Ronsard*, op. 197], Beverly Hills, 30 July 1961. 1p., 33x27cm. (80/1)

A. Mus. ms. S.: *The Book of Esther*, op. 200, to Hans Moldenhauer, Beverly Hills, July 1962. 1p., 24x31cm. Sketches (80/2)

A. Mus. ms. S.: [same], Beverly Hills, 10–23 Sept. 1962. 3p. (pp.42, 244–245), various sizes. Discarded master sheets (80/2)

A. Mus. ms. S.: *Capriccio*, op. 133, Beverly Hills, 21 May 1947. 9p., 32x25cm. (80/3)

A. Mus. ms. S.: "Cherubino," from *The Marriage of Figaro* by Mozart, Beverly Hills, 1944. 21p., 31x24cm. (80/3)

A. Mus. ms. S.: *Le Columbe*, 6 May 1946. 4p., 36x27cm. (80/3)

A. Mus. ms. S.: *Concerto for Guitar and Orchestra*, to Andrés Segovia, Florence, 1938–1939. 67p., 32x23cm. (80/4)

A. Mus. ms. Rev. S.: [*Concerto for Two Guitars and Orchestra*], Beverly Hills, 10 July 1962. 10p., 24x33cm. + 35x28cm. Sketches and discarded pages (80/5)

A. Mus. ms. S.: *Dodici studi dodecafonici*. 5p., 33x25cm. (80/6)

A. Mus. ms. S.: *2. Quintetto per due violini, viola, violoncello, e pianoforte*, 28 Feb. 1934. 3p., 33x24cm. Draft (80/6)

A. Mus. ms.: *Exotica*, [1934]. 8p., 33x24cm. Violin part (80/6)

A. Mus. ms. S.: *Fantasia Napolitana, for Two Pianos*, 19–21 Mar. 1945. 15p., 31x25cm. (80/6)

A. Mus. ms. S.: *La figlia del reggimento*, op. 110, to Jascha Heifetz, Hollywood, May 1941. 56p., 32x24cm. Full score (80/7)

A. Mus. ms. S.: [*Greeting Card*], "Preparations" for Nos. 18, 19, to Hans and Rosaleen Moldenhauer, Beverly Hills, Mar. 1959. 1p., 24x33cm. Sketches (80/8)

A. Mus. ms. S.: [*Greeting Card*], *Choral-Prelude*, op. 170, No. 18, on the name Albert Schweitzer, Beverly Hills, 1 Mar. 1959. 4p., 33x24cm. Draft (80/8)

A. Mus. ms. S.: [*Greeting Card*], *Duo-Pianism, Impromptu for Two Pianos*, op. 170, No. 19, on the names Hans and Rosaleen Moldenhauer, Beverly Hills, Mar. 10, 1959. 10p., 33x27cm. Master sheets (80/8)

A. Mus. ms. S.: [*Greeting Card*], *Suite 508*, op. 170, No. 21, to Hans Moldenhauer, Beverly Hills, 24 Mar. 1960. 1p., 24x33cm. (81/1)

A. Mus. ms. S.: [*Greeting Card*], [*Ein Quartett-Satz*], op. 170, No. 28, Beverly Hills, 18–19 Sept. 1960. 1p., 33x27cm. Closing page (81/1)

A. Mus. ms. S.: [*Greeting Card*], *Arabesque*, op. 170, No. 29, on the name Roger Taylor, 1961. 1p., 33x24cm. Master sheet. With accompanying note to Hans Moldenhauer (81/1)

A. Mus. ms. S.: [*Greeting Card*], *Ballatella*, op. 170, No. 34, on the name Chris Parkening, Beverly Hills, 10 Nov. 1963. 1p., 36x28cm. Master sheet (81/1)

A. Mus. ms.: [*Greeting Card*], [*Fanfare*], on the name E. Power Biggs. 2p., 22–36x30cm. Sketches (81/1)

A. Mus. ms. S.: *Les Guitares bien tempérées*, op. 199, Nos. 2, 21–24, Beverly Hills, 6 Apr. 1962. 3p., various sizes. Sketches (81/1)

A. Mus. ms. S.: *Hommage à Paderewsky*, Hollywood, 21–23 Mar. 1941. 9p., 31x24cm. (81/2)

A. Mus. ms. S.: *The Importance of Being Earnest*. 7p. (pp.1–6), 34x27cm. Master sheets (81/2)

A. Mus. ms. S.: *The Importance of Being Earnest*, to Hans Moldenhauer, Beverly Hills, 26 Dec. 1961. 3p., 33x27cm. (81/2)

A. Mus. ms. S.: *Jeux d'Eau* by Ravel, Beverly Hills, 14 Oct. 1944. 18p., 31x24cm. Transcribed for violin and piano (81/3)

A. Mus. ms.: *Die Kraniche des Ibykus*, op. 193, No. 1. 1p., 34x27cm. (81/4)

A. Mus. ms.: *Lament of David*, op. 169. 2p., 35x31cm. Sketch of opening (81/4)

A. Mus. ms. S.: *Minstrels* by Debussy, 30 June 1951. 3p., 32x24cm. Transcribed for guitar (81/4)

A. Mus. ms.: [*Naaritz'cho*]. 2p., 36x31cm. Draft of ending (81/4)

A. Mus. ms. S.: *The Octoroon Ball*, op. 136. 14p., 30x24cm. Beginning of the piano score (81/4)

A. Mus. ms. S.: *Ozymandias*, op. 124, for voice and piano, Beverly Hills, 8 June 1944. 5p., 36x27cm. Unpublished. Based on the poem by Shelley. Inspired by the reading of the poem when Raymond Gram Swing announced the downfall of Mussolini over the radio. See letter below to Hans Moldenhauer, 6 Feb. 1959 (81/4)

A. Mus. ms. S.: *Pavane pour une infante défunte* by Ravel, Beverly Hills, 28 July 1946. 9p., 32x24cm. Arranged for two pianos, four hands (81/5)

A. Mus. ms. S.: *Platero y yo*, op. 190, Beverly Hills, 18 July 1960. 2p., 33x24cm. With accompanying work sheet, containing four themes and the composer's comments, to Hans Moldenhauer, 26 Dec. 1960 (81/5)

A. Mus. ms.: *I Profeti*. 7p., 32x23cm. Piano-violin version. Draft of introduction (81/5)

A. Mus. ms.: *The Queen of Sheba*, op. 161. 1p., 36x30cm. Draft of opening (81/5)

A. Mus. ms.: *Rondo*, op. 129. 5p., 36x27cm. Sketches (81/6)

A. Mus. ms. S.: "*Rosina*," from *The Barber of Seville* by Rossini, Beverly Hills, 30 Sept. 1944. 11p. (full score) + 4p. (parts), 31x24cm. (81/6)

A. Mus. ms. S.: *Saul*, op. 191, 1 Aug.–12 Sept. 1960. 1p., 43x29cm. (81/7)

A. Mus. ms. S.: *The Seventh Day*, 1963. 2p., 33x27cm. Formerly called "The Peace of the Sabbath." Master sheets (81/7)

A. Mus. ms. S.: *The Shadow*, Beverly Hills, 14 June 1944. 4p., 36x27cm. (81/7)

A. Mus. ms. S.: "Shakespeare Overtures," ca. 1932. 3p., 33x24cm. Thematic sketches to *As You Like It*, *Othello*, *Romeo and Juliet*, *Antony and Cleopatra*, *All's Well That Ends Well* (81/7)

A. Mus. ms. S.: *Shakespeare Sonnets*, Sonnet No. LVII, "What is your substance whereof you are made," 22 Sept. 1945. 5p., 31x24cm. Full score (81/8)

A. Mus. ms. S.: *Shakespeare Sonnets*, Sonnet No. XXX, op. 125, to Aldo, Beverly Hills, 3 July 1944. 4p., 32x24cm. (81/8)

A. Mus. ms. S.: *Shakespeare Sonnets*, Sonnet No. XCIV, op. 125, 11 Oct. 1945. 10p., 31x26cm. (81/8)

A. Mus. ms. S.: *Shakespeare Sonnets*, Sonnet No. CLIV, op. 125, Beverly Hills, 21 Sept. 1945. 6p., 31x24cm. (81/8)

A. Mus. ms. S.: [*Six Keats Settings*, op. 157], 30 Dec. 1952. 2p., 36x30cm. Drafts of opening and closing pages (81/8)

A. Mus. ms. S.: *16 Préludes* by Chopin, Beverly Hills, 23 Nov. 1944. 36p. (piano score) + 16p. (violin part). 32x25cm. Markings by Heifetz (81/9)

A. Mus. ms.: [Sketches]. 4p., various sizes. Includes *Divertimento*, op. 119; *Suite nello Stile Italiano*, op. 138; *Sonatina*, op. 130; *Serenade*; *Second Concerto* (81/10)

A. Mus. ms.: *Sonata*, op. 208, 1967, to Hans Moldenhauer, 1967. 48p., 38x28cm. (81/10)

A. Mus. ms.: *Sonata for Oboe and Piano*, op. 146. 2p., 38x28cm. (81/10)

A. Mus. ms. S.: *Sonatina for Flute and Guitar*, op. 205, 2 Aug. 1965. 3p. (pp.9, 15, 16), 36x28cm. Master sheets (81/10)

A. Mus. ms.: *Songs of the Shulamite*, op. 163. 1p., 31x24cm. Opening page (81/10)

A. Mus. ms. S.: "Susanna," from *The Marriage of Figaro* by Mozart. 2p., 31x24cm. Violin part (81/10)

A. Mus. ms. S.: *Three Sephardic Songs*, to Bracha Zefire, Beverly Hills, 14–15 Sept. 1949. 9p. + 1p. (of themes), various sizes. Transcribed and harmonized with piano or harp accompaniment (82/1)

A. Mus. ms.: *Tobias and the Angel*. 8p., various sizes. Includes an omitted aria, p.31 (piano-vocal score), p.73 (orchestral score), pp.77–81 (full score), and 1p. (master sheets) (82/1)

A. Mus. ms. S.: *La Vallée des Cloches* by Ravel, Beverly Hills, 16 Oct. 1944. 6p., 31x24cm. Arranged for cello and piano (82/1)

A. Mus. ms. S.: *Variazioni sinfoniche*, part I, 1928. 18p., 33x24cm. Draft of full score (82/2)

A. Mus. ms.: *24 caprichos de Goya*, op. 195, Nos. X, XIX, XXII, Mar. 1961. 7p., 33x24cm. Master sheets (82/2)

A. Mus. ms. S.: "Violetta," from *La Traviata* by Verdi, Beverly Hills, 30 Sept. 1944. 4p., 32x24cm. (82/2)

A. L. S.: to Andrés Segovia. Pisa, 22 Sept. 1948. 2p., French. Containing musical illustrations (Box 118)

4 A. L. S.: to Andrés Segovia. Beverly Hills, 10 Mar., 3 June 1951, 18 July 1955, 20 June 1956. 8p., French. Discussing compositions and Segovia's performances (Box 118)

134 A. L. S.: to Hans Moldenhauer. 1958–1967. 261p. Much detail about his works, some cards and post cards; includes notes from his wife Clara (Box 118)

A. L. S.: to Andrés Segovia. n.p., n.d. 1p., French. Fragment, containing musical illustrations (Box 118)

Card S.: to Hans and Rosaleen Moldenhauer, from Lisbeth, wife of Castelnuovo-Tedesco's son Pietro. Los Angeles, 1960. English (Box 118)

Card: Birth announcement for Diana Clara Castelnuovo-Tedesco. 22 June 1960 (Box 118)

2 L. S.: to Hans Moldenhauer, from Clara Castelnuovo-Tedesco. Beverly Hills, 8 Mar. 1980. 2p., with two clippings and application forms for the Castelnuovo-Tedesco Society (Box 118)

A. Lib. S.: *The Importance of Being Earnest*. 41p. (Box 118)

T. Doc.: Biographical data with accompanying catalog of works. 8p., English (Box 118)

A. T. p.: *The Merchant of Venice*, also titled *"Sem"* (82/2)

Mus. ms. Repro. S.: *Amours de Ronsard*, op. 197, 1961. 29p. (I) + 33p. (II). Blueprint score (82/3)

Mus. ms. Repro. S.: *Appunti, Ritmi*, 1967–1968, to Hans and Rosaleen Moldenhauer, 2 Feb. 1968. 34p. (I) + 29p. (II). Blueprint score (82/4)

Mus. ms. Repro. S.: *Appunti, Intervalli*, 1967, to Hans and Rosaleen Moldenhauer, 28 Nov. 1967. 34p. Blueprint score (82/4)

Mus. ms. Repro. Annot. S.: *Il bestiario*, op. 188, 1960. 45p. Blueprint score (82/5)

Mus. ms. Repro. S.: *Bitter Lemons*, 1960. 3p. Blueprint score (82/5)

Mus. ms. Repro. S.: *The Book of Esther: A Biblical Oratorio*, op. 200, 1962, to Hans and Rosaleen Moldenhauer, 4 Dec. 1962. 144p. Blueprint score (82/6)

Mus. ms. Repro.: [*Tobias and the Angel*], *The Book of Tobit*, op. 204, 1964–1965, to Hans Moldenhauer, 1964/1965. 83p. (I) + 125p. (II) + 33p. (III). Blueprint score (83/1)

Mus. ms. Repro. S.: *Candide*, op. 123, 1944. 50p. Blueprint score (83/2)

Mus. ms. Repro. S.: *Cherry Ripe*, 1955. 6p. Blueprint score (83/2)

Mus. ms. Repro. S.: *5 Poesie Romanesche*, op. 131, 1946. 13p. Blueprint score (83/2)

Mus. ms. Repro. S.: *Concerto for Two Guitars and Orchestra*, op. 201, 1962. 132p. (orchestral score) + 57p. (two guitars and piano). Blueprint score (83/3)

Mus. ms. Repro. S.: *The Divan of Moses-Ibn-Ezra*, op. 207, 1966, to Hans and Rosaleen Moldenhauer, 22 July 1966. 59p. Blueprint score (84/1)

Mus. ms. Repro. S.: *2 Canti Greci*, 1916. 16p. Blueprint score (84/2)

Mus. ms. Repro. S.: *Eclogues*, op. 206, 1966, to Hans and Rosaleen Moldenhauer, 15 June 1966. 25p. Blueprint score (84/2)

Mus. ms. Repro. S. Rev.: *11 Preludes* by Chopin, May 1946. 25p. Arranged for violin and piano. Blueprint score (84/2)

Mus. ms. Repro. S.: *Exotica (A Rhapsody of the South Seas)*, 1943, to Hans Moldenhauer, 1964. 23p. (parts). Blueprint score (84/3)

Mus. ms. Repro. S.: *Fantaisie impromptu* by Chopin, 1947. 11p. Arranged for violin and piano. Blueprint score (84/3)

Mus. ms. Repro. S.: *The Fiery Furnace*, op. 183, 1958, to Joseph Leonard. 30p. Blueprint score (84/4)

Mus. ms. Repro. Rev. S.: *La figlia del reggimento*, op. 110, 1941, to Hans Moldenhauer, 9 Apr. 1964. 54p. Arranged for violin and piano. Blueprint score (84/5)

Mus. ms. Repro. S.: [same]. 44p., missing pp.23–32. Arranged for violin and piano. Blueprint score (84/5)

Mus. ms. Repro. S.: *Fuga elegiaca*, 1967, to Hans and Rosaleen Moldenhauer, 3 Nov. 1967. 8p. Blueprint score (84/6)

Mus. ms. Repro. Annot.: [*Greeting Card*], *Tango*, op. 170, No. 1, on the name André Previn, 1953. 5p. Blueprint score (85/1)

Mus. ms. Repro. Annot. S.: [*Greeting Card*], *Serenatella*, op. 170, No. 2, on the name Jascha Heifetz, 1954. 12p. Blueprint score (85/1)

Mus. ms. Repro. S.: [*Greeting Card*], *Valse*, op. 170, No. 3, on the name Gregor Piatigorsky, 1954. 14p. Blueprint score (85/1)

Mus. ms. Repro. Annot. S.: [*Greeting Card*], *Mirages*, op. 170, No. 4, on the name Gieseking. 7p. Blueprint score (85/1)

Mus. ms. Repro. Annot. S.: [*Greeting Card*], *Tonadilla*, op. 170, No. 5, on the name Andrés Segovia, 1954. 6p. With autograph fingerings by Segovia. Blueprint score (85/1)

Mus. ms. Repro.: [same]. Blueprint score (85/1)

Mus. ms. Repro.: [*Greeting Card*], *Rondel*, op. 170, No. 6, on the name Siegfried Behrend, 1954. 8p. Blueprint score (85/1)

Mus. ms. Repro.: [*Greeting Card*], *Preludio*, op. 170, No. 7, on the name Bruno Tonazzi, 1954. 5p. Blueprint score (85/1)

Mus. ms. Repro. S.: [*Greeting Card*], *Humoresque*, op. 170, No. 8, on the name Tossy Spivakovsky, 1954. 12p. Blueprint score (85/1)

Mus. ms. Repro. S.: [*Greeting Card*], *Fandango*, op. 170, No. 9, on the name Amparo Iturbi, 1954. 8p. Blueprint score (85/1)

Mus. ms. Repro.: [*Greeting Card*], *Tanka*, op. 170, No. 10, on the name Isao Takahashi, 1955. 5p. Blueprint score (85/2)

Mus. ms. Repro.: [*Greeting Card*], *Étude*, op. 170, No. 11, on the name Jakob Gimpel, 1955. 8p. Blueprint score (85/2)

Mus. ms. Repro. S.: [*Greeting Card*], *Für Erna*, op. 170, No. 12, 1956. 3p. (85/2)

Mus. ms. Repro.: [*Greeting Card*], *A Canon for Robin*, op. 170, No. 13, on the name Robin Escovado, 1956. 4p. Blueprint score (85/2)

Mus. ms. Repro.: [*Greeting Card*], *A Lullaby for Eugene*, op. 170, No. 14, to Eugene Robin Escovado, 1957. 4p. Blueprint score (85/2)

Mus. ms. Repro.: [*Greeting Card*], *A Fandango for Escovado*, op. 170, No. 16, to Robin Escovado, on the name Robin Escovado, 1958. 5p. Blueprint score (85/2)

Mus. ms. Repro.: [*Greeting Card*], *Ricercare*, op. 170, No. 17, on the name Luigi Dallapiccola, 1958. 8p. Blueprint score (85/2)

Mus. ms. Repro.: [*Greeting Card*], *Choral-Prelude*, op. 170, No. 18, on the name Albert Schweitzer, 1959. 7p. Blueprint score (85/2)

Mus. ms. Repro. S.: [*Greeting Card*], *Duo-Pianism*, op. 170, No. 19, to Hans and Rosaleen Moldenhauer, 10 Mar. 1959. 10p. each. Two copies. Blueprint scores (85/2)

Mus. ms. Repro. S.: [*Greeting Card*], *Little March*, op. 170, No. 20, on the name Scott Harrison, 1960. 2p. each. Two copies. Blueprint scores (85/3)

Mus. ms. Repro. S.: [*Greeting Card*], *Suite 508*, op. 170, No. 21, on the name Walter Hodgson, 1960. 31p. (score) + 15p. (parts). Blueprint score (85/3)

Mus. ms. Repro. S.: [*Greeting Card*], *Slow—with Variations*, op. 170, No. 22, 1960. 9p. Blueprint score (85/3)

Mus. ms. Repro. S.: [*Greeting Card*], *Intermezzo*, op. 170, No. 23, on the name Harvey Siegel, 1960. 8p. + 3p. (insert). Blueprint score (85/3)

Mus. ms. Repro. S.: [*Greeting Card*], *Valse-Bluette*, op. 170, No. 24, on the name Eric Friedman, 1960. 6p. + 2p. (insert). Blueprint score (85/3)

Mus. ms. Repro.: [*Greeting Card*], *Hungarian Serenade*, op. 170, No. 25, on the name Miklós Rózsa, 1960. 8p. Two copies. Blueprint scores (85/4)

Mus. ms. Repro.: [*Greeting Card*], *La torre del diavolo*, op. 170, No. 26, on the name Gisela Selden-Goth, 1960. 12p. Blueprint score (85/4)

Mus. ms. Repro.: [*Greeting Card*], *Angelus*, op. 170, No. 27, on the name Nino Rota Rinaldi, 1960. 5p. Blueprint score (85/4)

Mus. ms. Repro.: [*Greeting Card*], *Ein Quartett-Satz*, op. 170, No. 28, on the name Walter Arlen, 1960. 14p. (full score) + 19p. (parts). Blueprint score (85/4)

Mus. ms. Repro.: [*Greeting Card*], *Arabesque*, op. 170, No. 29, on the name Roger Taylor, 1961. 7p. Blueprint score (85/4)

Mus. ms. Repro. S.: [*Greeting Card*], *Melodia (o Tema?...)*, op. 170, No. 30, on the name Claudio Sartori, 1961. 6p. Blueprint score (85/5)

Mus. ms. Repro. S.: [*Greeting Card*], *Prelude and Fugue*, op. 170, No. 31, on the name Gerhard Albersheim, 1962. 7p. Blueprint score (85/5)

Mus. ms. Repro. S.: [*Greeting Card*], *Toccata*, op. 170, No. 32, to Hugh Mullins. 10p. Blueprint score (85/5)

Mus. ms. Repro.: [*Greeting Card*], *Canzone Siciliana*, op. 170, No. 33, on the name Mario Gangi, 1962. 4p. Blueprint score (85/5)

Mus. ms. Repro. S.: [*Greeting Card*], *Ballatella*, op. 170, No. 34, on the name Christopher Parkening, 1963, to Hans Moldenhauer, 18 Nov. 1963. 4p. Blueprint score (85/5)

Mus. ms. Repro.: [*Greeting Card*], *Sarabande*, op. 170, No. 36, on the name Rey de la Torre, 1964. 3p. Blueprint score (85/5)

Mus. ms. Repro.: [*Greeting Card*], *Romanza*, op. 170, No. 37, on the name Oscar Ghiglia, Beverly Hills, 1964. 4p. Blueprint score (85/5)

Mus. ms. Repro. S.: [*Greeting Card*], *Homage to Purcell*, op. 170, No. 38, on the names Ronald, and Henry Purcell, 1966, to Hans Moldenhauer, 22 July 1966. 7p. Blueprint score (85/5)

Mus. ms. Repro.: [*Greeting Card*], *Canción Venezuela*, op. 170, No. 40, on the name Alirio Díaz, 1966. 4p. Blueprint score (85/6)

Mus. ms. Repro. S.: [*Greeting Card*], *Canción Venezolana*, op. 170, No. 40, on the name Alirio Díaz, to Hans Moldenhauer, 1966. 4p. Blueprint score (85/6)

Mus. ms. Repro. S.: [*Greeting Card*], *Canción Argentina*, op. 170, No. 41, on the name Ernesto Bitetti, 1966, to Hans Moldenhauer, 22 July 1966. 4p. Blueprint score (85/6)

Mus. ms. Repro. S.: [*Greeting Card*], *Estudio*, op. 170, No. 42, on the name Manuel López Ramos, 1966, to Hans Moldenhauer, 22 July 1966. 4p. Blueprint score (85/6)

Mus. ms. Repro. S.: [*Greeting Card*], op. 170, No. 43, on the name Ruggero Chiesa, 1967, to Hans and Rosaleen Moldenhauer, 1967. 3p. Blueprint score (85/6)

Mus. ms. Repro. S.: [*Greeting Card*], op. 170, No. 44, on the name Laurindo Almeida, 1967, to Hans and Rosaleen Moldenhauer, 1967. 4p. Blueprint score (85/6)

Mus. ms. Repro. S.: [*Greeting Card*], op. 170, No. 45, on the name Pearl Chertok, 1967, to Hans and Rosaleen Moldenhauer, 1967. 4p. Blueprint score (85/6)

Mus. ms. Repro. S.: [*Greeting Card*], op. 170, No. 46, on the name Jiro Matsudo, 1967, to Hans and Rosaleen Moldenhauer, 1967. 5p. Blueprint score (85/6)

Mus. ms. Repro. S.: [*Greeting Card*], op. 170, No. 47, on the name Angelo Gilardino, 1967, to Hans and Rosaleen Moldenhauer, 1967. 6p. Blueprint score (85/6)

Mus. ms. Repro. S.: [*Greeting Card*], op. 170, No. 48, on the name Ernest Calabria, 1967, to Hans and Rosaleen Moldenhauer, 1967. 4p. Blueprint score (85/6)

Mus. ms. Repro. S.: [*Greeting Card*], op. 170, No. 49, on the name Frederick Tulan, 1967, to Hans and Rosaleen Moldenhauer, 1967. 4p. Blueprint score (85/6)

Mus. ms. Repro. S.: [*Greeting Card*], op. 170, No. 50, on the name Eugene DiNovi, 1967, to Hans and Rosaleen Moldenhauer, 1967. 6p. Blueprint score (85/6)

Mus. ms. Repro.: *La guarda cuidadosa*, 1955. 5p. Blueprint score (86/1)

Mus. ms. Repro. S.: *Les Guitares bien tempérées*, op. 199, to Hans and Rosaleen Moldenhauer, 1962. 4 vols.: 53p. (I) + 51p. (II) + 48p. (III) + 50p. (IV). Blueprint score (86/2)

Mus. ms. Repro. S.: *Der Handschuh*, op. 193, No. 2, 1961. 13p. each. Two copies (86/3)

Mus. ms. Repro. S.: *The Importance of Being Earnest*, 1961–1962, to Hans and Rosaleen Moldenhauer, 1962. 123p. (I) + 146p. (II) + 94p. (III). Full score. Blueprint score (87/1–3)

Mus. ms. Repro. A. Rev. S.: *Keats's Songs, On the Grasshopper and the Cricket*, op. 113, No. 4, to Walter Kramer, 1951. 6p. With accompanying letter from Kramer. Blueprint score (88/1)

Mus. ms. Repro. S.: *Die Kraniche des Ibykus*, op. 193, No. 1. 37p. (score) + 7p. (parts). Two copies. Blueprint score (88/1)

Mus. ms. Repro.: *Lauda—In honore Sanctæ Birgittæ*, op. 189A, 1960. 5p. each. Two copies. Blueprint score (88/2)

Mus. ms. Repro. S.: *Liberty, Mother of Exiles*, to A. Walter Kramer, 1944. 19p. Blueprint score (88/2)

Mus. ms. Repro. S.: *Memorial Service for the Departed*, op. 192, 1960. 10p. Blueprint score (88/2)

Mus. ms. Repro.: *The Merchant of Venice*, 99p. (I) + 120p. (II) + 131p. (III). Blueprint score (88/3–5)

Mus. ms. Repro. S.: *The Mermaid Tavern*, opera 113A and 113B, 1942. 6p. (A) +10p. (B). Blueprint score (89/1)

Mus. ms. Repro. S.: *Nocturne in Hollywood*, 1941. 9p. Blueprint score (89/1)

Mus. ms. Repro. S.: *I Nottambuli*, 1960. 93p. Blueprint score (89/2)

Mus. ms. Repro.: *Notturno*, 1960. 19p. each. Two copies. Blueprint scores (89/3)

Mus. ms. Repro.: *Ozymandias*, 1944. 4p. Blueprint score (89/3)

Mus. ms. Repro. S.: *Partita in B Minor* by J. S. Bach, to Hans Moldenhauer, April 1964. 35p. Arranged for string orchestra. Blueprint score (89/4)

Mus. ms. Repro. Annot. S.: *Pastorale and Rondo*, op. 185, 1958. 35p. Blueprint score (89/5)

Mus. ms. Repro. S.: *Platero y yo*, op. 190, 1960. 35p. (I) + 30p. (II) + 36p. (III) + 39p. (IV). Blueprint score (89/6)

Mus. ms. Repro.: *Poesia Svedese*, op. 189, 1960. 67p. Blueprint score (90/1)

Mus. ms. Repro. S.: *Prayers My Grandfather Wrote*, 1962, to Hans and Rosaleen Moldenhauer, 4 Dec. 1962. 18p. Blueprint score (90/2)

Mus. ms. Repro.: *Primavera Fiorentina*, 1911, 1967. 28p. Blueprint score (90/2)

Mus. ms. Repro.: *The Proverbs of Solomon*, op. 168, *Go to the Ant; Hear, Ye Children; There Be Six Things; The Foolish Woman Is Clamorous; Who Hath Woe?*, to Hermann Stein; *A Virtuous Woman Who Can Find*, 1953. 45p. Blueprint score (90/3)

Mus. ms. Repro. S.: *Psyche*, op. 113, No. 5, 1951. 10p. Blueprint score (90/3)

Mus. ms. Repro. S.: *The Queen of Sheba*, op. 161, 1953. 32p. Blueprint score (90/3)

Mus. ms. Repro. S.: *Sacred Service*, op. 122, 1943. 54p. Blueprint score (90/4)

Mus. ms. Repro. A. Rev. S.: *Serenade*, op. 118, 1942–1943. 48p. + 13p. (guitar part, revised). Blueprint score (90/5)

Mus. ms. Repro. S.: *The Seventh Day*, op. 202, 1963, to Hans Moldenhauer, 18 Nov. 1963. 16p. Blueprint score (90/6)

Mus. ms. Repro. S.: *Shakespeare Sonnets*, Nos. XXXV, XL (to Hans Moldenhauer), XLVII, LXXI, 1963. 17p. Blueprint score (90/6)

Mus. ms. Repro. S.: *La Sirenetta e il pesce Turchino*. 28p. each. Two copies. Blueprint scores (90/6)

Mus. ms. Repro.: *Sonatina canonica*, op. 196. 23p. Blueprint score (90/7)

Mus. ms. Repro. S.: *Sonatina for Bassoon and Piano*, to Adolph Weiss, 1946. 39p. Blueprint score (90/7)

Mus. ms. Repro. S.: *Sonatina for Flute and Guitar*, op. 205, 1965, to Hans and Rosaleen Moldenhauer, 14 Feb. 1966. 30p. Blueprint score (91/1)

Mus. ms. Repro. S.: *Sonatina zoologica*, op. 187, 1960. 18p. Blueprint score (91/1)

Mus. ms. Repro. S.: *The Song of Songs*, op. 172, 1954, to Hans Moldenhauer. 200p. With autograph Italian text. Blueprint score (91/2)

Mus. ms. Repro.: *Songs of the Oceanides*, 1954. 25p. each. Two copies. Blueprint scores (91/3)

Mus. ms. Repro. A. Rev. S.: *Songs of the Shulamite*, op. 163, 1953. 66p. Blueprint score (91/4)

Mus. ms. Repro. S.: *Stars*, op. 104, 1940. 86p. Blueprint score (91/4)

Mus. ms. Repro. S.: *3rd String Quartet*, op. 203, to Bernard Berenson, Beverly Hills, 1964, also inscribed to Hans Moldenhauer, 13 May 1965. 57p. + 58p. (parts). Blueprint score (91/5)

Mus. ms. Repro. S.: *Three Sephardic Songs*, 1960. 43p. Blueprint score (92/1)

Mus. ms. Repro. S.: *Three Shelley Songs*, op. 173, to A. Walter Kramer, 1955. 21p. Blueprint score (92/2)

Mus. ms. Repro. S.: *Tre preludi al Circeo*, 1961. 11p. Blueprint score (92/2)

Mus. ms. Repro. S.: *Tre preludi Mediterranei*, op. 176, 1955. 13p. Blueprint score (92/2)

Mus. ms. Repro. S.: *Two Motets*, op. 174, 1955. 18p. Blueprint score (92/2)

Mus. ms. Repro. S.: *Two Sonatas*, op. 179, 1955. 95p. Blueprint score (92/3)

Mus. ms. Repro. S.: *24 caprichos de Goya*, op. 195, 1961. 30p. (I) + 29p. (II) + 29p. (III) + 29p. (IV). Blueprint score (92/4)

Mus. ms. Repro. S.: *Vogelweide*, op. 186, 1958, to Hans and Rosaleen Moldenhauer, 26 Feb. 1959. 54p. Blueprint score (92/5)

Mus. ms. Repro. S.: *Le Voyage*, 1959, to Hans and Rosaleen Moldenhauer. 4p. Blueprint score (93/1)

Mus. ms. Repro.: *Le Voyage*, 1959. 4p. Blueprint score (93/1)

Doc. Repro. S.: "Complete Bibliography (up to 1962)." Compiled by Robert Taylor, for the University of California, Los Angeles, to Hans Moldenhauer, 1 Oct. 1963. 30p. (Box 118)

Doc. Repro.: List of lectures. 1p., English (Box 118)

Doc. Repro.: News release. Michigan State University, Oct. 25 (Box 118)

Doc. Repro.: Text. *Aucassin et Nicolette*. 18p., English (Box 118)

Pri. Sco.: *Appunti*, I and III, Milan: Zerboni, c1968. 31p. (93/1)

Pri. Sco. S.: *Aria of Ruth*, New York: Mills Music, c1950, to Irene Hanna, 7 Jan. 1952. 4p. (93/2)

Pri. Sco.: *La barba bianca*, in *Il giornalino della Domenica*, Milan, 26 Dec. 1920. 4p. (93/2)

Pri. Sco. S.: *Endymion*, New York: Marks Music, c1960, to Hans and Rosaleen Moldenhauer, 9 Mar. 1960. 20p. (93/2)

Pri. Sco. S.: *English Suite*, New York: Mills Music, c1962, to Hans and Rosaleen Moldenhauer, 31 Jan. 1962. 11p. (93/2)

Pri. Sco. Rev. S.: *Evangelion*, op. 141, 1949, Florence: Forlivesi, c1958. 77p. (93/3)

Pri. Sco. S.: *The Fiery Furnace*, New York: Ricordi, c1959, to Hans and Rosaleen Moldenhauer, Dec. 1959. 36p. (93/4)

Pri. Sco.: *Girotondo dei Golosi*, in *Il giornalino della Domenica*, Florence, 31 Jan. 1924. 4p. (93/4)

Pri. Sco. S.: *Homer*, Los Angeles: Delkas, c1944, to Irene Hanna, 13 Aug. 1944. 4p. (93/4)

Pri. Sco. S.: *The Nightingale*, New York: Galaxy, c1944, to Irene Hanna, 7 June 1944. 4p. (93/4)

Pri. Sco.: *Passacaglia*, op. 180, Milan: Edizioni Musicali, c1970. 11p. (93/5)

Pri. Sco.: *Platero y yo*, op. 190, Milan: Edizioni Musicali, c1972. 38p. (93/5)

Pri. Sco.: *The Shadow*, New York: Carl Fischer, c1945. 5p. (93/5)

Pri. Sco.: *Sonatina canonica*, Paris: Max Eschig, c1971. 17p. (93/5)

Pri. Sco. S.: *Songs of the Oceanides*, New York: Franco Colombo, c1963, to Hans and Rosaleen Moldenhauer, 15 Mar. 1963. 40p. (93/6)

Pri. Lib. A. Rev.: *The Merchant of Venice*. 17p. (93/6)

Pri. Lib. S.: *The Merchant of Venice*, Milan: Ricordi, to Hans Moldenhauer, 25 May 1961. 70p. (93/6)

Pri. Sco.: *24 caprichos de Goya*, op. 195, Nos. 13–18, *Milan:* Edizioni Musicali, c1971. 34p. (93/6)

2 Prog.: Undicesimo Concerto, Florence, 1959 (Box 118)

Prog.: 6 Oct. 1959 (Box 118)

Prog.: Michigan State University, 13 Nov. 1959 (Box 118)

Prog.: San Francisco Symphony, 3–6 Feb. 1960 (Box 118)

Prog.: University of Southern California, 30 Apr. 1961 (Box 118)

Prog.: *The Merchant of Venice*, 1961. 23p. Synopsis in Italian, French, English, German (Box 118)

Prog. S.: *The Song of Songs*, to Hans and Rosaleen Moldenhauer, 7–8 Aug. 1963. With clipping regarding world premiere (Box 118)

2 Clip.: Los Angeles, Apr. 1966. English (Box 118)

Port. Phot. Draw.: Sept. 1964, by Pablo Ghiglia, inscribed 7 Apr. 1965 (Box 110)
Phot. Draw.: sketch of the set of *The Merchant of Venice*, by Attilio Colonnello (Box 110)
3 Port. Phot. S.: 1958, 1961 (Box 110)
Port. Gr. (Box 110)
S. rec.: *The Merchant of Venice* (1961); *Song of Songs* (1963); *Sonnets* (1964) (RXA 6747, 6748–6752, 6754)
See Segovia, Andrés

Castiglioni, Niccolò, 1932–1996
Library of Congress
(Box 12)
A. Mus. ms. S.: *Quodlibet at the Year's Corner, Wie schön leuchtet der Morgenstern*, 1968–1969. 20p., 31x24cm.

Washington State University
See Rosbaud, Hans

Castillo, Manuel, b. 1930
Library of Congress
(Box 12)
A. Mus. ms. S.: *Cuatro invenciones para cuarteto de cuerda*, Sevilla, May 1967. 14p., 36x27cm. Full score
A. Mus. ms. S. Rev.: *Sonata para violín y piano*, Sevilla, 1961–1962. 26p., 36x26cm. Full score

Castro, José María, 1892–1964
Harvard University
Mus. ms.: *Preludio*

Castro, Juan José, 1895–1968
Harvard University
Mus. ms.: *Danza*, for piano, 1919

Caudella, Eduard, 1841–1924
Library of Congress
(Box 12)
A. L. S.: Jassy, 4 May 1909. 2p., French
P. card S.: to Georges Bainton. Jassy, 12 May 1909. French
Call. c.
A. Mus. Quot. S.: *Chant de la race latine*, Jassy, 12 May 1909. 1p., French

Cellier, Alfred, 1844–1891
Northwestern University
2 L.: to Ponsonby. London, 30 Apr.; Cheshire, n.d.

Cerha, Friedrich, b. 1926
Library of Congress
(Box 109)
A. Mus. ms.: [*Enjambements*, for six players, 1959]. 3p., 44x59cm. + 44x56cm. Sketches
A. Mus. ms.: [*Lanbegger Nachtmusik*, II, for orchestra, 1969–1970]. 12p., various sizes. Sketches on master sheets
3 T. L. S.: Vienna, 12 Mar. 1970, 19 Dec. 1971. 3p., German; Maria Langegg, 19 July 1973. 1p., German
Pri. Sco. S.: *Enjambements*, Universal Edition, 1959, to Hans Moldenhauer, 1975

Cervetti, Sergio, b. 1941
Harvard University
L.: to Aurelio de la Vega. Brooklyn, 9 Dec. 1984

Chabrier, Emmanuel, 1841–1894
Library of Congress
(Box 12, unless noted)
A. Mus. ms. S.: [Piano composition in E Major], to Boaz Piller. 1p., 25x32cm., ink. Incomplete, in 9/8 time. Mounted with portrait photograph
A. L. S.: to "Maman" [Mme. Chabrier]. Paris, 1887. 1p., French
Port. Phot.: mounted with music manuscript above
Port. Phot.: by Benoue (Box 110)

Northwestern University
See d'Indy, Vincent

Chadwick, George Whitefield, 1854–1931
Harvard University
Mus. ms.: [Sketch in G Minor]
Port. Phot.: Boston, 1929

Chaminade, Cécile, 1857–1944
Library of Congress
(Box 12)
A. L. S.: to ?. Marseille, 5 Mar. 2p., French. On
   musical matters
A. Mus. Quot. S.: *Au Pays bleu*, Côte d'Azur, Feb. 1914.
   French. On picture postcard

Champein, Stanislas, 1753–1830
Library of Congress
(Box 12)
A. L. S.: Theater Feydeau, [8 Mar. 1813]. 1p., French

Chapí, Ruperto, 1851–1909
Library of Congress
(Box 12)
A. Mus. ms. S.: *Las hijas del Zebedeo, Carceleras.* 7p.,
   35x27cm. Complete score

Charpentier, Gustave, 1860–1956
Northwestern University
2 L.: to Hermann Zucker. Paris, 19 May 1928; n.d.
L.: n.p., n.d.
Mus. Quot.: *Louise*, 1908
Mus. Quot.: mounted with portrait photograph
Port.

Chase, Gilbert, 1906–1992
Harvard University
4 L.: to Aurelio de la Vega. New Orleans, 8 Apr.,
   16 July, 11 Nov. 1963, 20 June 1964

Chasins, Abram, 1903–1987
Harvard University
L.: to Aurelio de la Vega. n.p., 26 June 1985

Chatterton, Julia, 1886[?]–1936
Northwestern University
Mus. ms.: *Valse tragique.* Full score, with additional
   copies, parts, and reduced score

Mus. ms.: [French folk song, melody only]
L.: to the Manager of the Pavlova Memorial Concert.
   London, 10 Feb. 1931
Doc.: Scrapbook. Regarding her activities with the folk
   songs of Yugoslavia and Egypt

Chaulieu, Charles, 1788–1849
Library of Congress
(Box 12)
A. L. S.: to Noqford. London, n.d. 2p., French
A. L. S.: London. 1p., French, English

Chávez, Carlos, 1899–1978
Harvard University
SUMMARY OF PRINCIPAL HOLDINGS:
A. Mus. ms.: *Sinfonía No. 6.* 4p., 34x27cm., pencil.
   Sketches in full score. Commissioned by the New
   York Philharmonic in celebration of its opening
   season in the Lincoln Center for the Performing
   Arts, 1961–1962
2 Port.

Chelard [Chélard], Hippolyte-André-Baptiste, 1789–1861
Library of Congress
(Box 12)
A. Mus. Quot. S.: *Die Seekadetten*, Andantino, to
   Schlösser, Darmstadt, 28 Aug. 1848. German

Cherubini, Luigi, 1760–1842
Library of Congress
(Box 12, unless noted)
A. Mus. ms.: *Sujet de fugue, traiter avec deux contre-sujets
   seulement...*, "(concours de 1838)." 1p. (12m.), ink.
   With authentication by Dancla
A. L. S.: to Breitkopf & Härtel. Paris, 10 Dec. 1833.
   2p., French. Regarding *Ali Baba*
A. L. S.: to Levasseur. n.p., Monday, the 19th. 1p.,
   French

2 A. Doc. S.: Certificates of admission. For
conservatory classes, to Charles Dancla. 22 Apr.
1828, 7 Sept. 1829. 2p., French
Port. Lith. S. Repro.: Mounted on page of *Allgemeine
Musikalische Zeitung*, 1833 (Box 110)

Northwestern University
L.: to Dragonetti. Paris, 10 Oct. 1825

Chevillard, Camille, 1859–1923
Library of Congress
(Box 12, unless noted)
A. L. S.: Paris, 18 June 1910. 2p., French. Mentions
conducting Elgar's *Gerontius*. On verso, 8m.
autograph musical quotation from Gounod's *Mireille*
Port. Phot. S.: 1910 (Box 110)
Port. Phot. Repro. (Box 110)

Chiapusso, Jan, 1890–1969
Harvard University
L.: to Verne Kelsey. Kansas, 4 Feb. 1955

Chisholm, Erik, 1904–1965
Washington State University
See Rosbaud, Hans

**Chopin, Fryderyk Franciszek [Frédéric François],
1810–1849**
Library of Congress
(Box 13, unless noted)
A. Mus. ms. S.: [*Prelude in A-flat Major*, op. posth.],
for piano solo, to P[ierre] Wolff, 10[?] July 1834. 2p.,
16x24cm., ink. Complete score. With letter of
authentication reproduced, from Arthur Hedley
Mus. ms. Repro.: *Nocturne*, op. 62, No. 1. 4p. Sketch.
Mounted on board (Box 109)
Mus. ms. Repro.: *Tarantelle*, op. 43, Paris: Catlin, 1930.
8p. Facsimile

Chorley, Henry F., 1808–1872
Northwestern University
L.: to Charles Lockey. London, n.d.

Chou Wen-chung, b. 1923
Harvard University
Pri. Sco.: *And the Fallen Petals*, inscribed

Christen, Ernest, b. 1873
Zentralbibliothek Zürich
Doc.: Excerpt. Zermatt, 31 Aug. 1956. From his book
on Casals. With photograph
Call. c. Annot.

Chrysander, Friedrich, 1826–1901
Library of Congress
(Box 13)
A. L. S.: to Selmar Bagge. Berne, 28 Feb. 1876. 4p.,
German. Includes a second letter to Selmar Bagge,
from Karl Opitz (24 Feb. 1876)
A. L. S.: to Elise. London, n.d. 3p., German

Chung, Woo-Hyen
Library of Congress
(Box 94)
A. Mus. ms. S.: *Quartett*, to Adolph Weiss, 23 May
1955. 12p., 39x27cm.

Cilea, Francesco, 1866–1950
Library of Congress
(Box 13)
T. L. S.: to Baron Angelo d'Eisner. Naples, 16 May
1930. 2p., Italian
A. Mus. Quot. S.: *Adriana*, Naples, 17 Jan. 1930. 1p.

Cimarosa, Domenico, 1749–1801
Library of Congress
(Box 13)
A. Mus. ms.: [*Il marito disperato*], "Come gli animali,"
premiered Naples, 1785. 8p., 22x29cm. 17 measures
of the prelude to the aria, and the first 26 measures

of the aria itself, "Voi siete un amoroso galante francesino"

Ciortea, Tudor, 1903–1982
Library of Congress
(Box 13)
A. Mus. ms. Annot. S.: *Variatiuni.* 52p., 35x25cm. Full
    score

Clark, Edward, 1888–1962
Northwestern University
Doc.: Files include correspondence, diaries, essays,
    lectures, newspaper clippings, photographs,
    programs. Also, materials for organizations such as
    the Association of British Musicians, the North
    Eastern Regional Orchestra, and the ISCM

Clark, Richard, 1780–1856
Northwestern University
L.: to Sir Henry Bishop. Westminster, 18 Apr. 1844
L.: The Cloisters, Westminster, 10 Dec. 1850

Clarke, Henry Leland, 1907–1992
Harvard University
SUMMARY OF PRINCIPAL HOLDINGS:
Mus. ms.: [Canon]. Composed for the composition
    class of Gustav Holst at Harvard University, 8 Mar.
    1932. With accompanying correspondence, and a
    copy of a letter to Ralph Vaughan Williams, from
    Gustav Holst
Mus. ms.: *Three Clerihews*

Clarke-Whitfeld [Clarke], John, 1770–1836
Northwestern University
L.: to Hedgley. Hereford, 16 Nov. 1825

Clauss-Szarvady, Wilhelmine, 1834–1907
Library of Congress
(Box 13)
A. L. S.: to Fischer. n.p., n.d. 3p., French
A. L. S.: [London], 30 Jan. 1871. 2p., French
Obit.: for Frederick Szarvady (husband). 1p., English.
    Transcribed from *World,* 8 Mar. 1882

Clay, Frederic, 1838–1889
Northwestern University
Mus. ms.: [Musical dedication to Edward Lloyd],
    20 Feb. 1877
L.: to a poet. n.p., 17 June 1867
L.: to Miss Helen. n.p., 23 Mar. 1872
Doc.: Biographical information

Clementi, Muzio, 1752–1832
Library of Congress
(Box 13)
A. L. S.: to Viotti. 20 Jan. 1813. 3p., French, English.
    Letter written by Viotti in French, with reply
    written in English by Clementi
A. L. S.: London, 17 Apr. 1823. 1p., English
Pri. Sco. S.: *Sonata for the Pianoforte or Harpsichord,*
    op. 26, London: Preston. 10p. Also signed by
    Margaret Abernethie

Coates, Albert, 1882–1953
Northwestern University
L.: to Adolph Weiss. Laveno, Lago Maggiore, 20 June
    1931

Coates, Eric, 1886–1957
Northwestern University
L.: to Alma Mahler, from Phyllis (widow). Eastbourne,
    22 Mar. 1959

Coates, Gloria, b. 1938
Harvard University
Mus. ms.: *Five Poems of Emily Dickinson*
Mus. ms.: *Music on Open Strings*
Mus. ms.: *String Quartet No. 3*
26 L.: to Alexandra (daughter). 1982–1983
15 Prog.
Port. Phot.: 1966

Library of Congress
See Otte, Hans

Coates, John, 1865–1941
Northwestern University
2 L.: London, 27 July 1907; fragment
Port.

Cocteau, Jean, 1889–1963
Library of Congress
See Stravinsky, Igor

Coelho, Olga Praguer, b. 1909
Harvard University
SUMMARY OF PRINCIPAL HOLDINGS:
Mus. ms.: [Songs for voice and piano or guitar]
Mus. ms.: [Music manuscripts, mostly for voice and
    piano, by the following composers: Estela Bringuer,
    Jesus Calvino de Castro, S. Cardillo, Bravilio de
    Carbalho, Lia Cimaglia Espinosa, Luys Milan,
    Mercedes Orrego de Ugarte, Cesar de Sá, Pedro
    Silva, J. Osvaldo Sosa Cordero, Clara Souviron, O.
    Spadaro, Juan Vega, Gabriela Vidal Tagle; other
    printed scores]
Phot.

Library of Congress
(Shelf)
SUMMARY OF PRINCIPAL HOLDINGS:
Mus. ms.: [Music manuscripts, mostly for voice and
    piano or guitar]
Doc.: Files containing correspondence, photographs,
    printed scores
See Segovia, Andrés

Coerne, Louis, 1870–1922
Harvard University
Mus. ms.: *Zenobia*, op. 66, 1900

Cohen, Jerome Daniel, b. 1936
Harvard University
Mus. ms.: *Concert Overture No. 1*, 1959
Mus. ms.: *Concerto for Flute and Orchestra*, 1957
Mus. ms.: *Preludes*, 1958
L.

Cohn, Arthur, b. 1910
Harvard University
55 L.: to Solomon Pimsleur. 1929–1943
Prog.

Coleridge-Taylor, Samuel [Taylor, Samuel
Coleridge], 1875–1912
Northwestern University
L.: to Miss Johnson. With musical illustration
Doc.: Biographical information. 1898
Port.

Colgrass, Michael, b. 1932
Harvard University
SUMMARY OF PRINCIPAL HOLDINGS:
Mus. ms.: *Image of Man*
L.: to Hans Moldenhauer. Toronto, 7 Aug. 1974

Colles, H. [Harry] C., 1879–1943
Northwestern University
L.: to Brewer. Hereford, 9 Sept.

Collins, Anthony, 1893–1963
Northwestern University
Mus. ms. Repro. Annot.

Colonne, Edouard [Judas], 1838–1910
Library of Congress
(Box 13)
A. L. S.: to Fischer. Paris, 19 Aug. 1877. 1p., French.
    Regarding a concerto by Lalo

Comes, Liviu, b. 1918
Library of Congress
(Box 13)
Pri. Sco.: *Melopee*, Cluj: Conservatorul de Muzică,
    c1970. 5p.
Pri. Sco.: *Sonata pentru pian*, Cluj: Conservatorul de
    Muzica, c1970. 32p.

Commer, Franz, 1813–1887
Library of Congress
(Box 13)
A. L. S.: B[erlin], 27 Jan. 1848. 1p., German

Constantinescu, Dan, b. 1931
Library of Congress
(Box 13)
A. Mus. ms. S.: *Strukturi I, II*, pentru pian. 8p.,
33x25cm.

Constantinides, Constantine Demetrios [Dinos], b. 1929
Harvard University
SUMMARY OF PRINCIPAL HOLDINGS:
Mus. ms.: *Antitheses*, 1977
Mus. ms.: *Chorale Prelude on a Byzantine Hymn*, 1966
Mus. ms.: *Composition for Flute, Harp, and Percussion*, 1973
Mus. ms.: *Composition for String Orchestra*, 1968
Mus. ms.: [Composition for strings], 1968
Mus. ms.: *Dedications*, 1974
Mus. ms.: *Designs for Strings*, 1971
Mus. ms.: *Designs for Women's Chorus*, 1975. Incomplete
Mus. ms.: *Diakos, Preludio*, 1961
Mus. ms.: [Duos for two violins], 1970
Mus. ms.: *Eight Miniatures*, 1978
Mus. ms.: *Evangeline*, 1976
Mus. ms.: *Exploding Parallels*, 1972
Mus. ms.: *Fantasy*, 1978
Mus. ms.: *La Folia*, 1965
Mus. ms.: *Four Greek Songs in the Old Manner*
Mus. ms.: *Fugue for Two Voices*, 1975
Mus. ms.: *Homecoming*, 1968
Mus. ms.: *Impressions*, 1975
Mus. ms.: *Improvisation*, 1971
Mus. ms.: *Kaleidoscope*, 1974
Mus. ms.: *Kaleidoscope Fantasy*, 1979
Mus. ms.: *Lament of Antigone*, 1976
Mus. ms.: "Miscellaneous Studies and Sketches on the Modes"
2 Mus. mss.: *Mutability I, II, and III*, 1979
Mus. ms.: *I Never Saw a Moor*
Mus. ms.: *Pentatonic*, 1971
Mus. ms.: [Piece for solo flute], 1979
Mus. ms.: *Preludi and Dance*, 1965
Mus. ms.: *Rhapsody*, 1977

Mus. ms.: *Sonata*, 1971
Mus. ms.: *Sonata*, 1976
Mus. ms.: *Sonata*, 1977
Mus. ms.: *Sonata No. 1*, 1968
Mus. ms.: *String Quartet No. 1*
Mus. ms.: *Study for Brass*, 1970
Mus. ms.: *Study for Brass Ensemble*, 1971
Mus. ms.: *Symphony*, 1967
Mus. ms.: *Symphony No. 1*, 1967
Mus. ms.: *Theme and Variations on a Greek Theme*, 1965
Mus. ms.: [Trio for flute, viola, and guitar], 1970
Mus. ms.: *Trio No. 1*, 1966
Mus. ms.: *Trio No. 2*, 1976
Mus. ms.: *Triple Concerto*, 1968
Mus. ms.: *Woodwind Quintet*, 1978
L.: to Hans Moldenhauer. Pittsford, New York, 6 Aug. 1979
4 L.: to Hans and Rosaleen Moldenhauer. Baton Rouge, New York City, 1979
L.: to Rosaleen Moldenhauer. Baton Rouge, 20 July 1981
Mus. ms. Repro.: *Antigone*, scene 4. Blueprint score
Mus. ms. Repro. Annot.: *Dedications for Woodwind Quintet*, 1975. Blueprint score
Mus. ms. Repro.: *Marcha de Glavez*, 1976. Blueprint score

Cooke, Thomas Simpson [Tom], 1782–1848
Northwestern University
L.: to Crouch. London, 20 Jan. 1841
L.: n.p., n.d.

Cooper, Emil, 1877–1960
Harvard University
L.: Baton Rouge, 23 Sept. 1960

Library of Congress
(Box 94)
Doc. S. Repro.: Schedule. Baton Rouge Civic Symphony Association. 23 Sept. 1960. 2p., English Obit.

Cooper, George, 1820–1876
Northwestern University
L.: London, n.d.

Cope, David, b. 1941
Harvard University
SUMMARY OF PRINCIPAL HOLDINGS:
Mus. ms.: *Arena*, 1974
Mus. ms.: *Clone*
Mus. ms.: *FMS*
Mus. ms.: *Or*
Mus. ms.: *Rituals*
Mus. ms.: *Spirals*
Mus. ms.: *Vectors IV*
2 L.: to Hans Moldenhauer. Oxford, Ohio, 22 Apr.
   1975, 12 Dec. 1976
Doc.: Biographical information
Port. Phot.

Copland, Aaron, 1900–1990
Harvard University
L.: to Paul Sanders. New York, 19 May 1933
L.: to Charles Haubiel. n.p., 4 Dec. 1937
L.: to Rudolph Ganz. Los Angeles, 22 May 1943
4 L.: to Hans Moldenhauer. Ossining, New York, 1956,
   30 Apr. 1958, 6 Jan., 10 Feb. 1960
Doc. A. Annot.: Essay. "Liszt as Pioneer"
Mus. Quot.: *El Salón Mexico*
Mus. ms. Repro.: *Letter from Home*. Facsimile of full score
Mus. ms. Repro. Annot.: *Piano Quartet*, 1950. Facsimile
Port. Phot.

Cordero, Roque, b. 1917
Harvard University
Mus. ms.: *Duo*, 1954. With additional facsimile and
   printed scores
8 L.: to Aurelio de la Vega. 1962–1985
L.: to Hans Moldenhauer

Cornelius, Peter, 1824–1874
Northwestern University
3 Mus. mss. cop.: [Three volumes of manuscript
   copies from the works of Beethoven and Mozart,
   with some original sketches]
L.: to Milde. ?, 17 Jan. 1859

Cornet, Julius, 1793–1860
Wiener Stadt- u. Landesbibliothek
L.: to Eduard Genast. Braunschweig, 5 Nov. 1834
2 L.: n.p., 12 Sept.; n.p., n.d.

Cortolezis, Fritz, 1878–1934
Library of Congress
(Box 13)
A. L. S.: to Alexander Zemlinsky. Karlsruhe, 2 Mar.
   1924. 1p., German

Cortot, Alfred, 1877–1962
Library of Congress
(Box 13, unless noted)
A. L. S.: [to Boaz Piller]. 14 Feb. 1929. 2p., French
A. L. S.: [to Boaz Piller]. 12 May 1938. 1p., French
Port. Phot. S.: to Boaz Piller, 1921 (Box 110)
Port. Phot. Repro. S.: to Boaz Piller, Boston, 1918
   (Box 110)

Washington State University
See Rosbaud, Hans

Cossmann, Bernhard, 1822–1910
Library of Congress
(Box 13)
A. L. S.: Weimar, 22 Feb. 1860. 1p., German
See Tchaikovsky, Pyotr Ilyich

**Costa, Sir Michael [Michele Andrea Agniello],
1808–1884**
Northwestern University
L.: to Zélia Trebelli. London, 25 Dec. 1878
2 Doc.: Contracts. For performances with Dragonetti,
   1841, 1844
Port.

Cottrau, Giulio, 1831–1916
Library of Congress
(Box 13)
A. Mus. Quot. S.: *Addio di Griselda*. Italian

Courtois, P.
Library of Congress
(Box 13)
A. Mus. ms. S.: *Le Tambour major amoreaux*. 3p.,
   35x27cm., French

Courvoisier, Walter, 1875–1931
Northwestern University
Mus. ms.: *Totenfeier*, op. 26, Munich, 1915

Coussemaker, Charles-Edmond-Henri de, 1805–1876
Library of Congress
(Box 13)
A. L. S.: Dunkirk, 3 Feb. 1857. 6p., French
A. L. S.: [to Schneider?]. Lille, 6 Dec. 1875. 3p., French

Cowell, Henry, 1897–1965
Harvard University
SUMMARY OF PRINCIPAL HOLDINGS:
Mus. ms.: *Concerto for Piano*, 1930. Excerpt
Mus. ms.: *Symphony No. 4*. Excerpt
Mus. ms.: *Symphony No. 13*. Excerpt
17 L.: to Adolph Weiss. 1932–1959
L.: to Paul A. Pisk. [1962]
L.: to Rudolph Ganz. San Francisco, n.d.
Port. Draw. Repro.: 20 Feb. 1956

Cowell, John, b. 1912
Washington State University
SUMMARY OF PRINCIPAL HOLDINGS:
Mus. ms.: *Moses*. Excerpt
Mus. ms.: *Rhapsody*. With additional copy
3 L.: to Hans Moldenhauer. Longbranch, 6 June, 27 July 1961; Paris, 4 July

Cowen, Sir Frederic Hymen [Hymen Frederick], 1852–1935
Northwestern University
L.: London, 31 Dec. 1895
L.: to a librettist. London, 6 Oct.
Pri. Sco.: *Harold*, inscribed June 1895

Craft, Robert, b. 1923
Washington State University
See Rosbaud, Hans

Cramer, Johann [John] Baptist, 1771–1858
Library of Congress
(Box 13)
A. L. S.: to Charles Ashley. London, 12 Jan. 1814. 1p., English
A. L. S.: to Costa. n.p., 24 Feb. 1856. 1p., French
A. Mus. Quot. S.: *Piccolo canone*, to J. Dessauer, Paris, 17 Aug. 1833

Northwestern University
L.: to Dragonetti. London, 15 June 1835

Crawford, Ruth Porter, 1901–1953
Harvard University
SUMMARY OF PRINCIPAL HOLDINGS:
4 L.: to Adolph Weiss. 1931, n.d.

Crescentini, Girolamo, 1762–1846
Library of Congress
(Box 13)
A. L. S.: n.p., 15 Apr. 1807[?]. 1p., Italian
A. L.: to Irene Ricciardi. n.p., Wednesday, 9 Sept. 1p., Italian

Creston, Paul [Guttoveggio, Giuseppe], 1906–1985
Harvard University
SUMMARY OF PRINCIPAL HOLDINGS:
Mus. ms.: *Second Symphony*. Excerpt
L.: to Ganz
L.: to Hans Moldenhauer
Mus. ms. Repro.: *Partita*. Facsimile, with additional printed score
Mus. ms. Repro.: *Suite for Saxophone and Piano*. Facsimile
Mus. ms. Repro.: *The Youth of America*

Crossley, Ada, 1874–1929
Northwestern University
L.: to Cecil. London, 4 Apr. 1902
Port.

Crotch, William, 1775–1847
Northwestern University
L.: to Sir George Smart. London, 22 Feb. 1816

Crouch, Frederick Nicolls, 1808–1896
Northwestern University
L.: to a publisher. 6 Sept. 1845
L.: to Mrs. Barnett. Baltimore, 15 Feb. 1889
L.: to Henry Phillips. 4 Apr.
2 Doc.: Contract; Program, 28 Apr. 1843

Crumb, George, b. 1929
Harvard University
Mus. ms.: *Variations on Time and the Sea*. Excerpt. With
accompanying letter (Philadelphia, 6 Nov. 1972)

Cruvelli [Crüwell], Friederike Marie, 1824–1868
Library of Congress
(Box 13)
A. L. S.: to Escudier. n.p., n.d. 4p., French

Cruvelli [Crüwell], Jeanne Sophie Charlotte, 1826–1907
Library of Congress
(Box 13)
3 A. L. S.: to Fiorentino. n.p., n.d. 9p., French

Cui, César [Kyui, Tsezar Antonovich], 1835–1918
Library of Congress
(Box 13, unless noted)
A. L. S.: to Heugel. n.p., 28 Apr. 1887. 1p., French
A. L. S.: [to von Schuch]. Petersburg, 24 Oct. 1898.
3p., French. Mentioning Dresden concerts
A. Mus. Quot. Repro.: see portrait reproduced below
(Box 110)
Port. S. Repro.: with musical quotation reproduced,
1888. By A. de Wit (Box 110)

Cummings, W. H., 1831–1915
Northwestern University
Mus. ms.: *Domine, Domine, dirige nos*, 20 Sept. 1906.
Excerpt
5 L.: Hastings, 17 Aug. 1870; London, 1900–1910
Port.
See Grove, Sir George
See Manns, Sir August

Curschmann, Karl Friedrich, 1805–1841
Library of Congress
(Box 13)
A. Mus. ms. S.: "Im Walde geh' ich wohlgemuth,"
Berlin, to ?, 26 Sept. 1834. 3p. 22x27cm.

Curwen, John Spencer, 1847–1916
Northwestern University
L.: to W. T. Freemantle. London, 31 July 1911. With
reply

Cushing, Charles, b. 1905
Harvard University
L.: to Mary Clement Sanks. Berkeley, 4 Feb. 1950

Cusins, Sir William, 1833–1893
Northwestern University
2 L.: to Ponsonby. London, 5 Aug. 1867, 24 Feb. 1870

Czartoryski, C. [Casimir, Adam ?]
Wiener Stadt- u. Landesbibliothek
5 L.: to Selmar Bagge. Vienna, 1855
7 L.: to Selmar Bagge. ?, 1858–1862

Czerny, Carl, 1791–1857
Library of Congress
(Box 13, unless noted)
A. L. S.: to Breitkopf & Härtel. Vienna, 16 Mar. 1836.
1p., German
A. L. S.: to R. de Vivenot. n.p., 29 Mar. 1846. 1p.,
German
A. L. S.: to Robert Cocks. Vienna, 5 Nov. 1853. 3p.,
English. Regarding his works, ensemble settings
Port. Engr. (Box 110)
Port. Engr. (Box 125)

Dahl, Ingolf, 1912–1970
Harvard University
SUMMARY OF PRINCIPAL HOLDINGS:
Mus. ms.: *Fanfares*. With additional facsimile score
containing annotations

Mus. ms.: *Sonata Seria*. Excerpt
3 L.: to Adolph Weiss. 1942, 1949, 1965
4 L.: to Aurelio de la Vega. Los Angeles, 1961–1966
L.: to Hans Moldenhauer
Mus. ms. Repro.: *Allegro and Arioso*, 1942. Blueprint
score. Annotations in the hand of Adolph Weiss

Library of Congress
(Box 94)
Mus. ms. Repro.: *A Christmas Canon for Five Voices*,
Dec. 1949. 1p., English

Dahl, Viking, 1895–1945
Library of Congress
(Box 14)
A. Mus. ms. S.: *Pluie*, op. 2, No. 1, to Ricardo Viñes.
4p., 35x27cm.

Dalberg, Johann Friedrich Hugo von, 1760–1812
Library of Congress
(Box 14)
A. L. S.: to Bellermann. ?, 8 Jan. 1802. 1p., German
A. L. S.: to ?. ?, 5 Jan. 1807. 1p., German

Dallapiccola, Luigi, 1904–1975
Library of Congress
(Box 14)
A. Mus. ms. S.: [*Ulisse*], "*Calypso*," to Richard
Hartmann, München, 27 Jan. 1961–Firenze, 3 Feb.
1961. 4p., 22x31cm., red and black ink, pencil. For
voice with accompaniment. Sketch, with vocal line
beginning "Son soli..."
A. L. S.: to Hanna Schwarz. Florence, 14 Dec. 1934.
1p., German
T. L. S.: to Hans Moldenhauer. Flushing, 12 June
1957. 1p., French
T. L. S.: to Paul A. Pisk. Florence, 19 July 1962. 1p.,
French
T. L. S.: to Aurelio de la Vega. Florence, 28 June 1964.
1p., French
A. L. S.: to Mario Castelnuovo-Tedesco. Florence, 30
Mar. 1965. 1p., French
L. S.: to Hans Moldenhauer, from Laura Dallapiccola.
Flushing, 22 Apr. 1957. 2p., French

Northwestern University
2 L.: to Edward Clark. Florence, 16 June 1954; Lucca,
13 July 1955

Paul Sacher Stiftung
A. Mus. ms.: *Concerto per la notte di Natale dell'anno
1956*, for soprano and chamber orchestra.
Workbook containing preparatory studies

Washington State University
Mus. ms. Repro.: *Requiescant*, inscribed 9 Dec. 1960.
Facsimile
See Rosbaud, Hans

Damrosch, Frank, 1859–1937
Harvard University
Port.

Damrosch, Leopold, 1832–1885
Harvard University
L.: to a publisher. n.p., n.d.

Damrosch, Walter, 1862–1950
Harvard University
L.: to Solomon Pimsleur. Bar Harbor, Maine, 13 Aug.
1926

Dancla, Charles, 1817–1907
Library of Congress
See Cherubini, Luigi

Daniels, Mabel W., 1878–1971
Harvard University
See Koussevitzky, Serge

Dannreuther, Edward, 1844–1905
Northwestern University
L.: to Mrs. Boyd. London, 2 June 1880

Da Ponte, Lorenzo, 1749–1838
Library of Congress
(Box 117)
A. L. S.: to Fortunato Stella. New York, 29 Mar. 1832.
1p., Italian, with typed transcription, and with

English translation by Albi Rosenthal. Reflects activities as writer, poet, and bookseller

Northwestern University
Rcpt.: London, 30 June 1796. For refreshments at a Dragonetti concert

Darreg, Ivor, 1917–1994
Harvard University
Mus. ms.: *Fugue in E Minor*
L.: to Adolph Weiss
Mus. ms. Repro.: *Caprice*, op. 38, arranged for piano. Blueprint score

Darzins, Volfgangs, 1906–1962
Harvard University
SUMMARY OF PRINCIPAL HOLDINGS:
Mus. ms.: *Petite Suite No. 6*, 1960
2 L.: to Hans Moldenhauer
3 Port.

David, Félicien, 1810–1876
Northwestern University
Mus. ms.: *Le Sommeil de Paris*
Mus. ms.: *Souvenir d'Orient*. Full score
L.: to Gerard. n.p., n.d.
L.: to Ferdinand Laub. n.p., n.d.
Port.

David, Ferdinand, 1810–1873
Library of Congress
(Box 14, unless noted)
A. L. S.: [to Julius Rietz?]. Leipzig, 25 Nov. 1850. 1p., German
A. L. S.: to Julius [Rietz]. Leipzig, 27 Feb. 1866. 3p., German
Port. Engr.: by Weger & Singer (Box 110)

David, Johann Nepomuk, 1895–1977
Library of Congress
(Box 14)
A. Mus. ms.: *Requiem chorale*, 31 Jan.–7 Feb. 1956. 58p., 34x27cm., ink, pencil
2 L.: to Hans Moldenhauer. 5 Oct. 1956, 22 July 1967. 2p., German
Port. Phot. S.: 1956

Washington State University
See Rosbaud, Hans

Davidovsky, Mario, b. 1934
Harvard University
L.: to Aurelio de la Vega. New York, 1963

Washington State University
See Rosbaud, Hans

Davies, Ben, 1858–1943
Northwestern University
L.: to Lord Lathom. London, 23 June 1897
L.: to Ole Bull. London, 30 Jan. 1938
L.: fragment

Davies, Sir Walford, 1869–1941
Northwestern University
L.: to Henderson. Wales, n.d. With musical illustration
L.: Newtown, 12 Mar. 1923

Davisson, Walther, b. 1885
Washington State University
See Rosbaud, Hans

Dawson, Frederick, 1868–1940
Northwestern University
L.: to Mme. Graham. Delf View, 17 Jan. 1918
Prog.: 1920

Deakin, Andrew, 1822–1903
Northwestern University
2 L.: to Middleton. London, 3 Sept. 1894; Birmingham, 15 July 1900

Debussy, Claude, 1862–1918
Library of Congress
(Box 14)
A. L. S.: to Vincent d'Indy. 10, rue Gustave Doré, [ca.

July 1893]. 1p., French. Offering friendship, refers to *La Damoiselle élue*. Attached to portrait below

A. L. S.: to Ernest Bloch. Paris, 3 May 1910. 1p., French

A. L. S.: to André Caplet. 5 May 1913. 1p., French. Mentions *Nocturnes*

A. Mus. Quot. S.: "Je vous la souhaite...," based on the song *Mandoline*, [Jan. 1883]. 2p., French. 12 measures complete score for voice and piano. New Year's musical greeting, for Mme. Vasnier. With dedication

Port. Phot.: with attached letter above, to d'Indy. By Otto

Defauw, Désiré, 1885–1960
Library of Congress
(Box 14, unless noted)

T. L. S.: to Rudolph Ganz. Chicago, 20 Mar. 1944. 1p., English

A. Mus. Quot. S.: *Symphony in D Minor* by Franck, Brussels, 12 Dec. 1932

Port. Phot. S.: to Boaz Piller, Boston, 2 Dec. 1940 (Box 110)

Deiters, Hermann, 1833–1907
Library of Congress
(Box 14)

3 A. L. S.: to Selmar Bagge. Bonn, 8 Sept. 1867, 6 Mar. 1868; Düren, 14 Dec. 1873. 10p., German

De Koven, Reginald, 1859–1920
Harvard University
L.: to McNutt

Delaborde, Elie, 1839–1913
Northwestern University
See Barye Document

Delibes, Léo, 1836–1891
Library of Congress
(Box 14, unless noted)

A. Mus. ms. S.: *Fanfares composées pour la distribution des récompenses à l'Exposition Universelle de 1889*, to Paul Blondot, Sept. 1889. 4p., 27x35cm., ink. Reduced piano score from original for brass band and orchestra

A. L. S.: to the Director of the National Theater at Pest. n.p., 20 May 1881. 4p., French. Regarding *Jean de Nivelle*

A. L. S.: to Bandon. 54 Chateau d'Eau, n.d. 3p., French. With musical illustration

A. L. S.: to Pougin. n.p., Monday, 31 May. 3p., French

A. Card S.: n.p., 19 June. 1p., French

Port. Lith.: with biographical sketch. French (Box 110)

Delius, Frederick, 1862–1934
Library of Congress
(Box 14, unless noted)

A. Mus. ms. Rev. S.[?]: [*Five Piano Pieces*], *Valse*, No. III, for piano solo. 2p., 35x27cm., ink, pencil. First draft, sketches on verso

A. Mus. ms. S.: *Zwei braune Augen*, song with piano accompaniment, text by H. C. Andersen, 1885. 2p., 34x27cm., German, ink, pencil

Port. Phot. (Box 110)

Dello Joio, Norman, b. 1913
Harvard University

Mus. ms.: *Variations and Capriccio*, Wilton, Connecticut, 1 June–9 Aug. 1948. Full score, parts

L.

Mus. Quot.: *The Lamentation of Saul*, 1954

Port. Phot.

De Lone, Richard Peter, b. ca. 1929
Harvard University
SUMMARY OF PRINCIPAL HOLDINGS:
Mus. ms.: *Second Piano Sonata*. Complete score

Demantius [Demant], Christoph, 1567–1643
Library of Congress
(Box 14)

A. Doc.: *Psalmus 98*, Freiburg, 19 Nov. 1615. 1p.,

Latin. Dedicatory page of Demantius's setting for sixteen voices (distributed over four choruses) on the occasion of the fifth birthday of the Saxon heir to the electorate, Hared, and dedicated to his parents Johann George and Magdalena Sybil

Dent, Edward J., 1876–1957
Northwestern University
6 L.: to Edward Clark. London, 1936–1952

Denza, Luigi, 1846–1922
Library of Congress
(Box 14)
A. L. S.: to Mrs. Custace. n.p., 27 Apr. 1887. 1p., Italian
A. Mus. Quot. S.: "Hush a-bye, dearie, hush-a-bye low," London, Oct. 1891
Clip.: 1p., English. See portrait photograph below
Port. Phot. Repro.: attached to clipping above. Portrait photograph of B. Tours on verso

Dessau, Bernhard, 1861–1923
Library of Congress
(Box 14)
A. L. S.: to Bruno Eisner. Charlottenburg, 16 Apr. 1909. 2p., German

Dessau, Paul, 1894–1979
Bayerische Staatsbibliothek
See Hartmann, Karl Amadeus

Library of Congress
(Box 14)
A. Mus. ms. S.: *Beruhigung*, from *2 Gesänge von O. J. Bierbaum*, to Mrs. Lattermann, Schleswig, 23 Oct. 1917. 3p., 35x27cm. Arranged for voice and piano
A. Mus. ms. S.: *Verkündigung von Richard Dehmel*, to Dälberg, Hamburg, 1914. 2p., 35x27cm.
T. L. S.: to Bruno Eisner. Zeuthen, 14 Dec. 1973. 1p., German
A. L. S.: to K. A. Hartmann. n.p., 29 July 1961. 1p., German

Mus. ms. Repro.: *Two Canons*. 8p.
Pri. Sco. S.: *Kinderkantate*, to Bruno Eisner, 6 Dec. 1932. 34p.
See Hartmann, Karl Amadeus

Dessauer, Josef [Joseph], 1798–1876
Library of Congress
(Box 14)
A. Mus. ms. S.: *"Du willst nicht mit zum Tanze gehn?"*. 4p., 29x22cm., German
A. L. S.: to ?. Ischl, Oct. 1855. 3p., German

Destin, Tomaso Loewe
Library of Congress
(Box 14)
A. L. S.: Bergamo, 19 Sept. 1875. 1p., Italian

Destouches, Franz Seraph von, 1772–1844
Bayerische Staatsbibliothek
L.: Weimar, 27 Jan. 1808

Deutsch, Otto Erich, 1883–1967
Library of Congress
(Box 14)
P. card: to Hans Moldenhauer. Vienna, 29 Sept. 1956. English
Doc. S.: Essay. "Mozart und die Wiener Logen," Vienna: Wiener Freimaurer-Zeitung, 1932, to Hans Moldenhauer, Vienna, Aug. 1956. 35p., German
Call. c. Annot.

Devčić, Natko, b. 1914
Harvard University
L.: to Aurelio de la Vega. n.p., Dec. 1984

Library of Congress
(Box 14)
2 A. Cards S.: to Aurelio de la Vega. Season's Greetings 1970, 1983. English

DeVoto, Mark, b. 1940
Harvard University
Summary of Principal Holdings:
Mus. ms.: *Concerto No. 4*, 1983

2 L.: to Hans and Rosaleen Moldenhauer. Dover, New Hampshire, 12 Dec. 1981, 7 Feb. 1982

3 L.: to Hans Moldenhauer. Medford, Massachusetts, 13 May 1984, 25 July 1985, 17 Feb. 1986

Doc.: Errors. In the published scores of *Les Noces*, Feb. 1986. Second list

Doc.: Essay. "Alban Berg's Picture Postcard Songs," 13 Apr. 1984

Doc.: Lecture. "Arnold Schoenberg as Musician and Jew"

Devrient, Eduard, 1801–1877
Library of Congress
(Box 14)
A. L. S.: to Richard Pohl. Karlsruhe, 27 Jan. 1864. 2p., German
A. L. S.: to an editor. Karlsruhe, 3 Oct. 1864. 1p., German

Dianda, Hilda, b. 1925
Harvard University
L.: to Aurelio de la Vega. Havana, 29 Sept. 1984

Diémer, Louis [Joseph-Louis], 1843–1919
Library of Congress
(Box 14)
A. L. S.: to Adolphe. n.p., 14 Feb. 1878. 4p., French
A. Card S.: to Leguy. 21 Nov. 1894. 2p., French
A. Card S.: 22 Mar. 1906. 2p., French

Diez, Ernst, 1878–1961
Paul Sacher Stiftung
SUMMARY OF PRINCIPAL HOLDINGS:
DOC.: Files include articles, books, correspondence, diaries, notebooks, photographs
See Webern, Anton

Diez [née Hartmann], Sophie, 1820–1887
Library of Congress
(Box 14)
4 A. L. S.: 1855–1870. 9p., German

Dittersdorf, Carl Ditters von [Ditters, Carl], 1739–1799
Library of Congress
(Box 14)
A. Mus. ms. S.: *Menuet, pour le clavecin*, Breslau, 16 Nov. 1779. 2p., 10x31cm., ink. Complete score

Döhler, Theodor, 1814–1856
Library of Congress
(Box 15)
A. L. S.: Hôtel de Paris, n.d. 1p., French
See Thalberg, Sigismond

Dohnányi, Ernö [Ernst von], 1877–1960
Library of Congress
(Box 15, unless noted)
T. L. S.: to Hans Moldenhauer. Tallahassee, 18 June 1955. 1p., English
A. Mus. Quot. S.: [*Der Schleier der Pierrette*], "Pierrot," 27 Jan. 1910
A. Mus. Quot. S.: [*Variations on a Nursery Song*]. 6m. Full score
Pri. Sco. S.: *A Dedication*, op. 13, No. 1, New York: Marks Music, c1938. 3p.
Pri. Sco. S.: *Rhapsody*, op. 11, No. 4, New York: Marks Music, c1930. 10p.
Pri. Sco. S.: *Rhapsody (C Major)*, op. 11, No. 3, New York: Marks Music, c1935. 13p.
Port. Phot. S. (Box 110)

Doktor, Paul, 1919–1989
Library of Congress
See Brisman, Heskel

Dommer, Arrey von, 1828–1905
Library of Congress
(Box 15)
3 A. L. S.: [to Selmar Bagge?]. Reudnitz, 14 Dec. 1860;
  Lauenburg, 21 July 1864; Altona, 25 Sept. 1864.
  9p., German

Donalda [Lightstone], Pauline, 1882–1970
Harvard University
L.: to Cecil. London, 10 May 1906

Donizetti, Gaetano, 1797–1848
Northwestern University
SUMMARY OF PRINCIPAL HOLDINGS:
Mus. ms.: *Di gioia di pace la dolce speranza*, 1813. 4p.,
  with sketches
L.: to the Conte Giulio Palle. Venice, 20 Feb. 1837
24 L.: to the Countess Taaffe. n.p., n.d.
Port.

Donovan, Richard Frank, 1891–1970
Harvard University
SUMMARY OF PRINCIPAL HOLDINGS:
2 L.: to the American Composers Alliance. New York,
  3 Mar., 12 Apr. 1965
5 L.: to Adolph Weiss. New Haven, n.d.

Donzelli, Domenico, 1790–1873
Library of Congress
(Box 15)
A. L. S.: n.p., 6 June 1833. 1p., French

Door, Anton, 1833–1919
Wiener Stadt- u. Landesbibliothek
L.: to Karl Weigl. Bad Gastein, 22 June 1902

Door, Carl
Library of Congress
(Box 15)
A. L. S.: to Alexander Zemlinsky. Vienna, 13 Aug.
  1924. 1p., German

Doppler, Franz [Ferenc], 1821–1883
Wiener Stadt- u. Landesbibliothek
L.: to a publisher. Vienna, 26 June 1874

Dorati, Antal, 1906–1988
Washington State University
See Rosbaud, Hans

Doreste, Víctor
Library of Congress
(Box 15)
A. Mus. ms. S.: *Suite canaria. Folía.* 5p., 33x26cm.

Dorn, Heinrich Ludwig Egmont, 1804–1892
Library of Congress
(Box 15)
A. L. S.: [to Robert Seitz]. Berlin, 17 Feb. 1881.
  1p., German

Dorn, Otto, 1848–1931
Library of Congress
(Box 15, unless noted)
A. Mus. ms. S.: *Frühlingslied*, op. 34, No. 1. 1p.
  (opening page), 31x27cm., English, German.
  Fragment
A. Doc. S.: Aphorisms. 1p., German
Call. c. Annot.: Wiesbaden, 11 Feb. 1911
Port. Caric. Repro.: with autograph note mentioning
  Ferdinand Hiller (Box 110)

Dotzauer, Friedrich, 1783–1860
Library of Congress
(Box 15)
A. L. S.: [to the director of the Dresden Orchestra?].
  Leipzig, 21 Jan. 1811. 2p., German

Downes, Olin, 1886–1955
Harvard University
L.: to Solomon Pimsleur. n.p., 6 Oct. 1933
L.: to David Tamkin. New York, 16 Nov. 1937

Draeseke, Felix, 1835–1913
Library of Congress
(Box 15)
A. Mus. ms. S.: [*Symphony in F Major*], Presto. 2p., 28x18cm. Sketch. With attached autograph letter signed, Coburg, 22 June 1876. 4p., German
A. L. S.: n.p., n.d. 1p., German
A. L. S.: see manuscript above
A. Doc. S.: Biographical information. Outline of his studies and professional career with a list of his published works. 1p., German
Clip.: Biographical information with portrait. English

Dragonetti, Domenico, 1763–1846
Northwestern University
Mus. ms.: "Corelli's Favorite Solo in A, op. 5, No. 9, with a Bass Accompaniment"
L.: to Signora Terrazza. Amsterdam, 14 May 1814
L.: to Mrs. Paploe. London, 27 Aug. 1816
L.: to Watts. n.p., 1817
2 L.: to Rossini. London, 12 Jan., 20 July 1827
2 L.: to Calvi. London, 12 Feb., 24 Aug. 1829
2 L.: to Romanin. London, 15 Nov. 1830, 2 Aug. 1839
L.: to Signora Moeser. London, 12 July 1838
L.: to the Academy of Saint Cecilia in Rome. London, 13 Mar. 1839
L.: [to Calvi?]. London, 6 Aug.
L.: to the Edinburgh Festival. London, n.d.
3 Rcpt.: 5 Apr. 1830, 10 June 1837, n.d.
Doc.: Agreement. 1832
Doc.: Contract
Doc.: File. Materials include biographical information, letters, manuscripts, portraits
See Costa, Sir Michael
See Esterházy, Prince Pál Anton
See Novello, Vincent

Dresden, Sem, 1881–1957
Library of Congress
(Box 15)
A. Mus. ms.: *Hor ai dolor*, for piano, 1950. 2p., 36x27cm.
A. Mus. ms.: *Psalm 84*, for Chorus, Soprano, Tenor, and Orchestra, 1953–1954. 1p., 21x29cm. Sketch of work plan
T. L. S.: to Hans Moldenhauer. Bussum, 10 July 1956. 1p., English

T. L.: to Hans Moldenhauer, from A. Annegard, Librarian. The Hague, 3 Mar. 1958. 1p., English
3 T. L.: to Hans Moldenhauer, from Anton Dresden (son). Bussum, 1957–1958. 4p., English
Obit.: Dutch

Drew, James, b. 1929
Harvard University
Mus. ms.: *Symphonies*, 1967–1968

Dreyer, Johann Melchior, 1747–1824
Library of Congress
(Box 15)
2 A. Mus. mss. S.: *Die Geduld*; *Ich danke Gott.* 2p. (1 leaf), 24x31cm.

Dreyschock, Alexander, 1818–1869
Library of Congress
(Box 15)
2 A. Mus. mss. S.: [*Fugue in E-flat Major*], to Schlösser, Darmstadt, 29 Nov. 1843. On verso, fragment of an [Allegro for string quartet], Darmstadt, 29 Mar. 1858. 3p., 28x22cm.
A. L. S.: Berlin, 26 Feb. 1860. 1p., German
Doc.: Work list, to op. 27. 1p.

Dron, Marthe Nancy, 1878–1960
Library of Congress
(Box 15, unless noted)
T. Doc.: Documentation. 1p., English. Association material to César Franck's *Prélude, choral, et fugue*
T. Doc.: Biographical information. 5p., French
Port. Phot. Gr.: Marthe Dron and Andrée Parent (Box 110)
See Franck, César

Drouet, Louis, 1792–1873
Library of Congress
(Box 15)
A. L. S.: Frankfurt, 8 Jan. 1860. 1p., French. Regarding his pianist son

Dubinsky, Vladimir, 1876–1938
Harvard University
L.: to Solomon Pimsleur. New York, 26 May 1935

Dubois, Théodore, 1837–1924
Library of Congress
(Box 15)
Pri. Sco. S.: *2. Concerto pour piano et orchestra*, Paris:
Heugel, 1897, to E. Colonne. 58p. Transcription for
two pianos. With copy of same

**Dubuque [Dyubyuk], Alexander Ivanovich,
1812–1898**
Library of Congress
See Tchaikovsky, Pyotr Ilyich

Dukas, Paul, 1865–1935
Library of Congress
(Box 15, unless noted)
2 A. L. S.: to Servières. Paris, 8 Jan. 1901, 17 June
1923. 3p., French
Port. Phot. Gr.: with pupils, including Marguerite
Long. By Joaillier (Box 110)
Port. Phot. Repro.: with biographical sketch (Box 110)

Duparc [Fouques Duparc], Henri, 1848–1933
Library of Congress
(Box 15)
A. L. S.: Tarbes, 29 Apr. 1917. 2p., French. Concerning
Franck's *Paris*

Dupont, [Pierre?, 1821–1870]
Library of Congress
(Box 15)
A. Mus. Quot. S.: Andante, 1866

Dupré, Marcel, 1886–1971
Library of Congress
(Box 15)
Pri. Sco. S.: *Cortège et litanie*, for organ, Paris: Leduc,
1924, inscribed 15 Dec. 1925. 23p.

Duprez, Gilbert, 1806–1896
Library of Congress
(Box 15)
A. Alb. l. S.: to Chorley. n.p., n.d. 1p., English

Durand, Marie Auguste, 1830–1909
Library of Congress
(Box 15)
A. L. S.: to Schott. London, Paris, 30 June 1879.
1p., French

Dustmann-Meyer, Luise, 1831–1899
Wiener Stadt- u. Landesbibliothek
L.: to an author. Vienna, 28 July 1861
L.: to an artist. Vienna, 18 Mar. 1872
L.: Vienna, 18 Nov. 1872

Dutilleux, Henri, b. 1916
Washington State University
See Rosbaud, Hans

Dvořák, Antonín, 1841–1904
Library of Congress
(Box 15)
A. L. S.: Vysoká, Sunday at 5 o'clock in the morning,
July 1885. 4p., English. Mentions *Ludmilla*
A. L. S.: Prague, 14 Dec. 1886. 4p., English. Mentions
Ludmilla
Pri. Sco. S.: *Stabat Mater*, op. 58, for Soloists, Chorus,
and Orchestra, London: Novello, Ewer, 1876/1877,
1880. 104p. Signed at Cambridge, 15 June 1891,
when Dvořák received the Doctor of Music degree.
From the Edward Lloyd Library

Ebdon, Thomas, 1738–1811
Library of Congress
(Box 16)
A. Mus. ms. S.: *Glee 3 Voices the Acrostick*, "to a
celebrated composer," Durham, 1795. 3p.,
24x30cm., English, ink. Full score

Ebert, Carl [Charles], 1887–1980
Library of Congress
(Box 16)
A. Card S.: to Alma Mahler. Berlin, Apr. 1959. 1p.,
German
See Rosbaud, Hans

Wolffgangum Ebner

Ebner, Wolfgang, 1612–1665
Library of Congress
(Box 16)
A. Mus. ms. S.[?]: [Unidentified composition in
condensed score, ca. 1655]. 2p., 13x23cm., ink. With
facsimile signatures of Ebner, A. Poglietti, and G.
Paganelli. Authentication by Aloys Fuchs

Eckert, Karl, 1820–1879
Library of Congress
(Box 16)
A. L. S.: Stuttgart, 8 Mar. 1865. 2p., German
6 Clip.: 1879–1880. German. With biographical
information

Edlund, Lars, b. 1922
Library of Congress
(Box 16)
Mus. ms. Repro. A. Annot. S.: *Elegi*, 23 Aug. 1971, to
Alan Stout. 30p. Blueprint score

Edwards, Clara, 1887–1974
Harvard University
L.: to Carl Deis. Paris, 15 Oct.

Eeden, Jan [Jean-Baptiste] van den, 1842–1917
Library of Congress
(Box 16, unless noted)
A. Mus. ms. S.: *Rhéna*, 1912. 1p., 29x22cm. Fragment
from introduction to Act III, with poem
Port. Phot. Repro. (Box 110)

Egk, Werner, 1901–1983
Bayerische Staatsbibliothek
Summary of Principal Holdings:
Mus. ms.: *Irische Legende*
L.: to Hans Moldenhauer. 22 Feb. 1960
Port.

Ehlert, Louis, 1825–1884
Library of Congress
(Box 16)
A. Card S.: [Vienna], 27 Nov. 1p., German

Ehrlich, Heinrich, 1822–1899
Library of Congress
(Box 16)
A. L. S.: n.p., n.d. 3p., German

Einem, Gottfried von, 1918–1996
Harvard University
See Mitropoulos, Dimitri

Library of Congress
(Box 16)
A. Mus. ms. S.: [*Prinzessin*] *Turandot*, op. 1, Finale,
1944. 2p., 34x27cm., ink, pencil. Sketch. Only
portion to have survived the burning of Berlin
A. L. S.: Vienna, 19 Dec. 1958. 3p., German.
Christmas greetings
A. L. S.: Vienna, 8 Oct. 1969. 2p., German
A. L. S.: to Alma Mahler. n.p., n.d. 2p., English,
German. Christmas greetings
A. Doc. S.: Synopsis. For the Los Angeles premiere of
Hexameron. 1p., German

Einstein, Alfred, 1880–1952
Harvard University
L.: to Paul Sanders. Berlin, 3 July 1933
L.: to Bruno Eisner. Northampton, Massachusetts, 2 June 1942

Library of Congress
See Mozart, Wolfgang Amadeus

Eisikovits, Max, b. 1908
Library of Congress
(Box 16)
Pri. Sco.: *Cîntece Stinse Maramureşene*, Cluj: Conservatorul de Muzică, c1969. 6p.
Pri. Sco.: *Patru Schiţe*, Cluj: Conservatorul de Muzică, c1970. 13p.

Eisler, Hanns, 1898–1962
Library of Congress
(Box 16)
Mus. ms. Annot. Repro.: *Divertimento für Bläserquintett*, op. 4. 15p. Blueprint score

Eisner, Bruno, 1884–1978
Harvard University
SUMMARY OF PRINCIPAL HOLDINGS:
4 L.: to Hans Moldenhauer. New York, 1956, 1973, 1977
Doc.: Diary. "Engelberg Tagebuch," 1972
Doc.: Essay. "Comparing Weber and Mozart"
Doc.: Essay. Nov. 1973
Doc. Repro.: Memoirs. *Gedenken und Gedanken aus dem Leben eines Musikers*
Port. Phot.: to Hans Moldenhauer, Mar. 1971

Library of Congress
See Orlik, Emil

Eisner-Eyn, Stella, 1889-ca. 1972
Harvard University
SUMMARY OF PRINCIPAL HOLDINGS:
2 L.: to Hans Moldenhauer. New York, 29 Nov. 1966; 17 Nov.
L.: to Paul Nettl. n.d.
L. cop.: Eisner-Eyn's copy of a Schoenberg letter dated 16 Sept. 1949

Doc.: Memoirs
Doc. cop.: Poem. "Der grösste Deutsche aller Zeiten," by Franz Werfel, Sept. 1938

Eitner, Robert, 1832–1905
Library of Congress
(Box 16)
P. card S.: to Friedrich Chrysander. Templin, 19 Apr. 1896. German
2 P. cards S.: to Gerhard Tischer. Templin, 22 Nov. 1903, 27 Jan. 1904. German

Elgar, Sir Edward, 1857–1934
Northwestern University
Mus. ms.: *Owls*, op. 53, No. 4. Full score
L.: to Mrs. Manns. Malvern, 21 Oct. 1902
Port.

Ella, John, 1802–1888
Northwestern University
L.: to Rudolph Ganz. London, Easter Sunday, 1881

Ellington, Duke [Edward Kennedy], 1899–1974
Harvard University
Alb. l.: to Hans and Rosaleen Moldenhauer, Hurricane Night Club, Manhattan, 1943

Elman, Mischa, 1891–1967
Harvard University
Port.

Elmendorff, Karl, 1891–1962
Library of Congress
See Rosbaud, Hans

Elston, Arnold, 1907–1971
Harvard University
SUMMARY OF PRINCIPAL HOLDINGS:
Mus. ms.: *The Ecstatic*, Dec. 1970–Jan. 1971
Mus. ms.: *Spring Omnipotent Goddess*, 1971
3 L.: Berkeley, 25 Sept. 1961, 11 Jan., 6 Feb. 1962
4 L.: to Hans Moldenhauer. Berkeley, 1969–1971

Library of Congress
See Webern, Anton

Elvey, Sir **George**, 1816–1893
Northwestern University
L.: to Lockey. Windsor, 2 Dec. 1850
L.: Windsor, 5 Mar. 1863
Clip.
3 Port.

Elwell, Herbert, 1898–1974
Harvard University
Mus. ms. Repro.: *Pliant*
2 L.

Emborg, Jens Laurson, 1876–1957
Library of Congress
(Box 16)
A. L. S.: to Rheinische Musik-und Theater-Zeitung.
   Vordingborg bei Kopenhagen, 14 June 1929. 1p.,
   German

Enescu, George [Enesco, Georges], 1881–1955
Library of Congress
(Box 16, unless noted)
A. L. S.: to Fritz Mahler. New York, 20 Apr. 1948.
   1p., German
Pri. Sco. Annot. S.: *Trois rhapsodies routtaines*, op. 11,
   Paris: Enoch, n.d., to Fritz Mahler, 1948. 89p.
Port. Phot. S.: to Boaz Piller, Boston, 1938. By Toppo
   (Box 110)

Engelmann, Theodore
Library of Congress
(Box 16)
A. L. S.: to A. W. Gottschalg. Leipzig, 7 May 1862.
   1p., German. Penned on stationery of Wilhelm
   Engelmann

Enríquez, Manuel, 1926–1994
Harvard University
SUMMARY OF PRINCIPAL HOLDINGS:
Mus. ms.: *1x4*, Mar. 1975
Mus. ms.: *Monólogo*, Barcelona, May 1971
2 L.: to Aurelio de la Vega. Paris, 11 July 1976;
   Mexico, 14 Oct. 1983

Epstein, David M., b. 1930
Harvard University
SUMMARY OF PRINCIPAL HOLDINGS:
Mus. ms.: *Fantasy Variations for Solo Violin*, 1963
Mus. ms.: *Piano Variations*, 1961
Mus. ms.: *Symphony No. 1*
Mus. ms. Repro.: *Symphonic Prelude for Orchestra*.
   Blueprint score

Epstein, Julius, 1832–1926
Library of Congress
(Box 16)
A. L. S.: to Karl Weigl. Vienna, 28 Jan. 1911. 2p.,
   German
Call. c. Annot.: Baden, 2 Sept. 1919. 2p., German

Erbse, Heimo, b. 1924
Library of Congress
(Box 104)
A. Mus. ms.: *Klavierkonzert*, op. 21, 1964. 142p., various
   sizes. Sketches in reduced score. Includes sketches
   for *Drei Lieder von Texten nach Celan*
A. Mus. ms.: *Mörike-Lieder*, op. 17, Nos. 1, 2. 22p.,
   34x27cm. Sketches
A. Mus. ms.: *Ruth*, op. 16. 67p., 33x24cm. Sketches of
   piano score
P. card S.: to Hans Moldenhauer. Wilder Kaiser, Tyrol,
   20 Sept. 1960. German
4 T. L. S.: Taxenbach, Jan.–Oct. 1960. 4p., German
Mus. ms. Repro.: *Julietta*, Act IV. 1p. Facsimile
   photograph from the full score
Doc.: Two Articles. "Über das Schaffen von Heimo
   Erbse," by Karl Heinz Füssl; "Julietta...," by Rudolf
   Lück, in *Musik Nachrichten 1*, Frankfurt: Peters, n.d.
   16p., German

Washington State University
See Rosbaud, Hans

Erdmann, Eduard, 1896–1958
Library of Congress
(Box 16)
A. L. S.: to Bruno Eisner. Langballigau, 19 June 1932.
 2p., German

Erlanger, Camille, 1863–1919
Northwestern University
11 L.: to Louis Schneider. Paris, 1897–1907
2 Call. c. Annot.: 1904–1906

Ernst, Heinrich Wilhelm, 1814–1865
Library of Congress
(Box 16)
A. L. S.: to Chorley. n.p., n.d. 1p., French
A. L. S.: n.p., 11 Apr. 2p., French
A. Mus. Quot. S.: Hamburg, 18 June 1843, inscribed.
 German
A. Mus. Quot. S.: London, 24 July 1843

Eröd, Iván, b. 1936
Library of Congress
(Box 16)
A. Mus. ms.: *Die Seidenraupen.* 4p., 34x27cm. Sketches
 in condensed score

Erskine, John, 1879–1951
Harvard University
L.: to Rudolph Ganz. New York, 23 Mar. 1931
L.: to Charles Haubiel. New York, 26 May 1939

Escudier, Marie-Pierre-Yves, 1819–1880
Library of Congress
(Box 16)
A. L. S.: Paris, 3 Feb. 1861. 2p., French

Espagne [d'Espagne], Franz, 1828–1878
Library of Congress
(Box 16)
A. L. S.: [to Selmar Bagge?]. Berlin, 12 Nov. 1863.
 3p., German

Espinosa, Guillermo, 1905–1990
Harvard University
2 L.: to Aurelio de la Vega. Washington, D.C., 18 Feb.,
 26 Aug. 1955

Esplá, Oscar, 1886–1976
Library of Congress
(Box 16)
A. Mus. ms. S.: *Evocaciones. Cantos de Vendimia,* [op.
 16], No. III, Madrid. 18p., 36x26. With fingerings
 by Ricardo Viñes

Essipoff, Anna, 1851–1914
Library of Congress
(Box 110)
A. Alb. l. S.: to Papbram. Vienna, 2 Jan. 1874.
 Mounted with portrait photograph

Esterházy, Prince Pál Anton, 1786–1866
Northwestern University
Doc.: Passport. For Dragonetti, to travel from London
 to Paris, 12 Aug. 1820

Estrada, Carlos, 1909–1970
Harvard University
Mus. ms.: *Interludios I-II-III*, 1933–1934

Etler, Alvin, 1913–1973
Harvard University
Mus. ms. Repro.: *Concerto for String Quartet and
 Orchestra*, 1961. Facsimile
Phot.

Evans, Edwin, Jr., 1874–1945
Northwestern University
2 L.: to Edward Clark. London, 19 July 1938, 1 Apr.
 1943
L.: to Oliver Buridge. London, 11 June 1940

Eysler [Eisler], Edmund, 1874–1949
Wiener Stadt- u. Landesbibliothek
Mus. Quot.: Jan. 1917. With portrait photograph on
 verso

Fahrbach, Joseph, 1804–1883
Library of Congress
See Parish Alvars, Elias

Falke, Gustav, 1853–1916
Library of Congress
(Box 117)
A. L. S.: Hamburg, 1 Feb. 1902. 2p., German

Falkenstein, Claire, b. 1908
Harvard University
L.: to Aurelio de la Vega. 27 Jan. 1978

Fall, Leo, 1873–1925
Northwestern University
Mus. ms.: *Der süsse Kavalier*. Includes complete
orchestral score, piano-vocal score, and sketches

Falla, Manuel de, 1876–1946
Library of Congress
(Box 17, unless noted)
A. Mus. ms.: [*Concerto* for Harpsichord or Piano, Flute,
Oboe, Clarinet, Violin, and Cello, 1923–1926]. 1 leaf,
35x27cm., pencil. Preliminary draft of p.3, containing
alternate versions, and 11 measures incorporated in
the printed edition of the full score. Formal
presentation from the Archdiocese of Granada to
Hans Moldenhauer, in Latin. With accompanying
document concerning the manuscript. On verso,
authentication tracing the manuscript to composer's
secretary and friend, Valentín Ruiz Aznar
A. L. S.: to Ricardo Viñes. Paris, 13 Oct. 1907. 2p.,
Spanish
A. L. S.: to Calvocoressi. Paris, 16 Apr. 1908. 1p.,
French
A. Mus. Quot. S.: *El retablo*, Lento. 2m. thematic
quotation
Mus. ms. cop. A. Rev.[?]: *El corregidor y la molinera*. 8p.
Arranged for piano solo. Probably copyist's
manuscript, possibly revised by Falla
Port. Phot. S.: to Boaz Piller, Granada, 1929. By Eschig
(Box 111)

Farberman, Harold, b. 1929
Harvard University
SUMMARY OF PRINCIPAL HOLDINGS:
Mus. ms.: *Evolution, Music for Percussion*, 1957. Full
score (with annotations by Leopold Stokowski)

Fauré, Gabriel, 1845–1924
Library of Congress
(Box 17)
A. Mus. ms. S.: *Arpège*, op. 76, No. ?, 6 Sept. 1897. 6p.,
34x27cm., French, ink. Song with piano
accompaniment, text by Albert Samain. Full score
A. L. S.: [to Loeffler?]. Paris, 16 Apr. 1922. 1p.,
French. Regarding new works, health
A. L. S.: to a conductor. Rue des Vignes, 7 Mar. 1923.
1p., French. Regarding doubling the role of
Penelope

Fautch, Magdalen, Sister S.N.J.M., b. 1916
Washington State University
Mus. ms.: *Irsomnia II*. Excerpt
Mus. ms.: *Troi Melodies dans la nuit*
5 L.: to Hans Moldenhauer. Seattle, 1958–1960

Feinhals, Fritz, 1869–1940
Library of Congress
(Box 17)
A. L. S.: Munich, 29 Mar. 1906. 2p., German

Fernandes, Armando José, 1906–1983
Library of Congress
(Box 17)
A. Mus. ms. S.: *Fandango*, for piano solo, 1937. 7p.,
29x21cm.
A. Mus. ms. S.: *Homenagem a Fauré (Nocturno)*, for
piano solo, 1938. 9p., 29x21cm.

Fernández, Oscar Lorenzo, 1897–1948
Harvard University
Pri. Sco.: *Dentro da noite*, Rio de Janeiro, Nov. 1947

Fernaud, Ana
Harvard University
L.: to Aurelio de la Vega. 1983

Ferrari, Gabrielle, 1851–1921
Library of Congress
(Box 111)
Port. Phot.

Fétis, Edouard, 1812–1909
Library of Congress
(Box 17)
A. L. S.: Brussels, 29 Dec. 1881. 1p., French

Fétis, François-Joseph, 1784–1871
Library of Congress
(Box 17)
A. L. S.: to Benedict. Brussels, 30 May 1842. 1p.,
    French

Feuermann, Emanuel, 1902–1942
Library of Congress
(Box 17, unless noted)
A. L. S.: to Boaz Piller. [Cleveland?], 18 Nov. 1939.
    1p., German
Port. Phot. S.: to Boaz Piller, Apr. 1940 (Box 111)

Février, Henry, 1875–1957
Library of Congress
(Box 17)
A. Mus. Quot. S.: *Monna Vanna*, inscribed. French

Ficher, Jacobo, 1896–1978
Harvard University
Mus. ms. cop.: *Dos poemas de Tagore*, op. 10, No. 1

Ficker, Ludwig von, 1880–1967
Library of Congress
(Box 111)
Port. Phot. S.: to Josef Humplik and Hildegard Jone,
    12 Aug. 1926

Fiedler, Arthur, 1894–1979
Harvard University
L.: to Charles Haubiel. Boston, 16 Nov. 1937

Fiedler, Max, 1859–1939
Library of Congress
(Box 94)
A. Mus. ms. Rev. S.: *Praeludium und Fuge mit Choral
    "Nun danket alle Gott."* 42p., 33x26cm. Full score.
    Bound

Washington State University
See Rosbaud, Hans

Field, John, 1782–1837
Northwestern University
Mus. Alb. l.: "Beef Cabbage," 12 Aug. 1835

Fielitz, Alexander von, 1860–1930
Library of Congress
(Box 17, unless noted)
A. Mus. ms. S.: *Vom Berge*, op. 55, No. 2. 2p., 36x27cm.,
    German, English
A. L. S.: Berlin, 31 Jan. 1909. 1p., German
Port. Phot. (Box 111)

Finke, Fidelio Friedrich, 1891–1968
Library of Congress
(Box 17)
A. Mus. ms. S.: *Sonate für Bratsche und Klavier*, 1952.
    28p., 34x27cm. + 32x24cm. Complete sketches, with
    sketch on last page for large orchestra and solo
Mus. ms. cop.: *Sonatine*, 1945. 12p.
Pri. Sco. S.: *Konzert für zwei Klaviere*, Leipzig: Peters,
    c1959, to Hans Moldenhauer, Dresden, 21 Dec.
    1959. 38p.

Finkes, Dominik
Library of Congress
(Box 17)
A. Mus. ms. cop. S.: *Graduale in B Dur (In Sanae)*, "*Die Nacht der Musik*," für Chor und Orchester, 1828. 27p., 29x24cm., Latin. Leopold Hauser, copyist, 25 Aug. 1892. Full score

Finney, Ross Lee, 1906–1997
Harvard University
SUMMARY OF PRINCIPAL HOLDINGS:
Mus. ms.: *Second Sonata in C Major*, 1950.
Mus. ms. Repro. Annot.: *Sixth String Quartet*. Facsimile

Firkušný, Rudolf, 1912–1994
Harvard University
L.: to Boaz Piller
Port. Phot.: 1947

Fischer, Adolphe, 1847–1891
Library of Congress
(Box 17)
Pri. Sco. S.: *Etude*, op. 25, No. 7 by Chopin, transcribed by Fischer, to Servais, Mar. 1879, Leipzig: Breitkopf & Härtel, n.d. 6p.

Fischer, Christian Wilhelm, 1786[?]–1859
Library of Congress
(Box 17)
6 A. L. S.: to Remie. Berlin, Magdeburg, Leipzig, Apr.–June, 1829. 25p., German

Fischer, Edwin, 1886–1960
Washington State University
See Rosbaud, Hans

Fischhof, Joseph, 1804–1857
Wiener Stadt- u. Landesbibliothek
L.: to Otto v. Prechtler. n.p., 16 July 1852

Fischhof, Robert, 1856–1918
Wiener Stadt- u. Landesbibliothek
L.: n.p., 20 Jan. With musical illustrations

Fitzwilliam, Edward Francis, 1824–1857
Northwestern University
L.

Flesch, Carl, 1873–1944
Library of Congress
(Box 17)
T. L. S.: [to Bruno Eisner]. Berlin-Wilmersdorf, 19 Dec. 1916. 2p., German
T. L. S.: to a lady. n.p., 24 Nov. 1920. 2p., German
T. L. S.: to Bruno [Eisner]. Baden-Baden, 20 June 1935. 1p., German

Flonzaley Quartet
Harvard University
Port. Gr.: New York, Mar. 1921. Signed by Adolfo Betti, Alfred Pochon, Louis Bailly, and Iwan d'Archambeau

Flood, W. H. Grattan, 1859–1928
Northwestern University
L.: to Edwards. Ireland, 7 Nov. 1908

Flothuis, Marius, b. 1914
Library of Congress
(Box 17, unless noted)
A. Mus. ms. S.: *Round, for Eight Part Mixed Choir*, op. 50, 3 July 1953. 9p., 34x25cm., English, ink. Based on words of Orlando Gibbons
A. Mus. ms. S.: *Love and Strife*, Cantata, 1947. 12p., 35x27cm., English, pencil. Sketches
A. L. S.: to Hans Moldenhauer. ?, 24 July 1956. 1p., German
T. L. S.: to Hans Moldenhauer. Amsterdam, 7 Jan. 1977. 1p., English
Port. Phot. Gr. S.: Flothuis with Rosaleen Moldenhauer (Box 111)
See Rosbaud, Hans

Washington State University
See Rosbaud, Hans

Flotow, Friedrich, 1812–1883
Library of Congress
(Box 17, unless noted)
A. Mus. ms. S.: *Dorf-Messe, für Männerchor (Messe villageoise)*, Kyrie, Gloria, Laudamus te, Credo, Incarnatus, Sanctus, Agnus dei. 37p., 33x26cm., ink. Full score. Bound. According to a newspaper clipping glued to inside back cover, the mass was originally composed for men's chorus, soli, and organ. First performed by the Darmstadt men's chorus on 27 Nov. 1882 (Shelf)
A. L. S.: [to a theater director in Berlin]. n.p., 4 Aug. 1859. 3p., German
A. L. S.: n.p., n.d. 4p., French
A. Mus. Quot. S.: *Indra*, Act II, Berlin, Apr. 1853, 1p.

Floyd, Carlisle, b. 1926
Harvard University
Mus. ms.: *Wuthering Heights*. Excerpt

Foerster, Adolph Martin, 1854–1927
Harvard University
Mus. ms. Repro.: *To the Beloved*

Foerster [Förster], Josef Bohuslav, 1859–1951
Library of Congress
(Box 111)
Port. Phot. S.: by Schiestl & Wolf

Förster, Sophie, 1831–1899
Library of Congress
(Box 17)
A. L. S.: to Müller. Dresden, 10 Oct. 1861. 2p., German
A. L. S.: to [Julius] Schloss. Dresden, 8 May 1862. 1p., German

Foldes [Földes], Andor, 1913–1992
Washington State University
See Rosbaud, Hans

Foli [Foley], A. J., 1835–1899
Northwestern University
L.: London, 13 May

Foote, Arthur, 1853–1937
Harvard University
Mus. ms.: *Song of the Forge*, 5 July 1895. Excerpt

Formes, Karl Johann, 1816–1889
Library of Congress
(Box 17)
A. L. S.: London, 24 Jan. 1861. 2p., German

Formes, Theodor, 1826–1875
Library of Congress
(Box 17)
11 A. L. S.: to Bartolf Senff. Berlin, London, Magdeburg, 1853–1869. 29p., German

Forsyth, Cecil, 1870–1941
Harvard University
Mus. ms.: *The Last Supper*, New York, 1915

Forte, Vicente, b. 1888
Harvard University
Mus. ms.: *Cuadros argentinos: Las noches en la enramada*

Forti, Anton, 1790–1859
Library of Congress
(Box 17)
A. L. S.: to Remie at the Royal Court Opera, Dresden. Vienna, 20 Mar. 1829. 2p., German

Fortner, Wolfgang, 1907–1987
Library of Congress
(Box 17)
A. Mus. ms. S.: *Streichtrio*, Andante con moto, [1952]. 2p., 31x27cm., ink. First draft

T. L. S.: to Hans Moldenhauer. Heidelberg, 16 Jan. 1956. 1p., German

Washington State University
See Rosbaud, Hans

Foss [Fuchs], Lukas, b. 1922
Harvard University
Mus. ms.: *Psalms*, 1956
Mus. ms.: *Time Cycle*, 1959–1960. Full score, and piano-vocal score. With additional materials, including a facsimile score containing annotations, notes on instrumentation, text insert, sketches
2 L.: to Aurelio de la Vega. Buffalo, 8 Apr. 1964, 17 June 1967
L.: to Hans Moldenhauer

Library of Congress
See Brisman, Heskel

Washington State University
See Rosbaud, Hans

Fournier, Pierre, 1906–1985
Washington State University
See Rosbaud, Hans

Fradkin, Fredric, 1892–1963
Library of Congress
See Rabaud, Henri

Fraenkel, Wolfgang, 1897–1983
Bayerische Staatsbibliothek
SUMMARY OF PRINCIPAL HOLDINGS:
The following music manuscripts may consist of and include additional items such as condensed sketches, scores, parts, transparencies, drafts, printed scores, sound recordings, or other materials
Mus. ms.: *Die 82. Sure des Koran*, 1936
Mus. ms.: *Aphoristische Symphonie*, 1970
Mus. ms.: *Ballade in C-Moll*, 1923
Mus. ms.: *Blaue Stunde*, 1919
Mus. ms.: *Der Brennende Dornbusch*, 1928
Mus. ms.: *Burleske*, 1922
Mus. ms.: *Cantata brevis*, 1933
Mus. ms.: *Chanson*, 1935
Mus. ms.: *Chinese Song*, [ca. 1960]

Mus. ms.: *Divertimentum Canonicum*, 1935. Excerpt
Mus. ms.: [Drafts and sketches for 14 early songs]
Mus. ms.: *Drei Gesänge*, 1924
Mus. ms.: *3 Klavierstücke*, 1913
Mus. ms.: *3 Lieder nach chinesischen Dichtern für Altstimme und Orchester*, 1941
Mus. ms.: *13 Lieder*, 1919
Mus. ms.: *Dritte Symphonie*, 1940
Mus. ms.: *Duo für Geige und Bratsche*, 1917
Mus. ms.: *Filippo and his Flute*, 1948
Mus. ms.: *An eine Fremde, Dunkele Frau*, 1921
Mus. ms.: *Frühe Klavierwerke*, 1919–1923
Mus. ms.: *5 Lieder*, 1914
Mus. ms.: *5 Lieder*, 1915
Mus. ms.: *5 Lieder*, 1921
Mus. ms.: *Fünf Lieder nach Gedichten von Christian Morgenstern*, 1928
Mus. ms.: *Fünf Stücke von Frescobaldi, bearbeitet für Orchester*, 1958
Mus. ms.: *Im Garten des Serails*, 1921
Mus. ms.: *Gavotte und Musette aus der Englischen Suite in G-Moll* by Bach, 1939
Mus. ms.: *Gesellschaft im Herbst*, 1962
Mus. ms.: *Die Heimkehr*, 1915
Mus. ms.: *In himmelblauer Ferne*, 1919
Mus. ms.: *Hölle, Weg, Erde*, 1944
Mus. ms.: *Impromptu in As-Dur*, 1919
Mus. ms.: *Impromptu in Es-Dur*, 1918
Mus. ms.: *Impromptu in D-Dur*, 1921
Mus. ms.: *Impromptu in D-Moll*, 1919
Mus. ms.: *Impromptu in F-Dur*, 1919
Mus. ms.: *Invention*, 1951
Mus. ms.: *Jazz*, 1927
Mus. ms.: *Des Jungen Joseph-Osarsiph wundersamer Abendsegen und Sterbespruch*, 1968
Mus. ms.: [Kadenzen, to Mozart's *Serenades*, K. 204, K. 250; *Konzert in G-Dur für Flöte und Orchester*, 1933]
Mus. ms.: *Klavierstück*, 1964
Mus. ms.: *Klavierwerke*, 1925–1964
Mus. ms.: *Konzert für Flöte und Orchester*, 1930
Mus. ms.: *Konzert für Violoncello und Orchester*, 1935
Mus. ms.: *Kyrie*, 1921
Mus. ms.: *Langsamer Satz* by Webern
Mus. ms.: *Liebesgedichte*, 1919
Mus. ms.: *Meeressrand*, 1913
Mus. ms.: *Mein Sterbelied*, 1921
Mus. ms.: *Missa aphoristica*, 1973. With additional blueprint score
Mus. ms.: *Mitternacht*, 1919
Mus. ms.: *Motette*

Mus. ms.: *Musik zum Faust*, [ca. 1908–1910]

Mus. ms.: *Musik für Orchester (Symphonie)*, 1948, 1949

Mus. ms.: *Musik für Violine allein*, 1954

Mus. ms.: *Musik (Sonate) für Cello allein*, 1933

2 Mus. mss.: *One Step*, 1919, 1927

Mus. ms.: *Passacaglia in Fis-Moll*, 1923

Mus. ms.: *Passacaglia in G-Moll* by Handel, 1939

Mus. ms.: *Pontius Pilatus*. With additional typescript of libretto

Mus. ms.: *Portrait of an American Town*, 1957

Mus. ms.: *Preludium und Fuge in C-Moll*, 1933

Mus. ms.: *Priester-Chor*, 1912

Mus. ms.: *Pythia*, 1921

Mus. ms.: *Quartette*, 1919

Mus. ms.: *Requiem*, 1915

Mus. ms.: *Resurrexit*, 1913

Mus. ms.: *Ritter Olaf*, 1915

Mus. ms.: *Romanze*, 1915

Mus. ms.: *Scherz, List, und Rache*, 1918

Mus. ms.: *6 frühe Lieder*, 1914–1921

Mus. ms.: *6 Lieder*, 1922

Mus. ms.: *Sérénade amoureuse*, 1918

Mus. ms.: *Serenade in F-Dur*, 1920

Mus. ms.: *7 Lieder*, 1920

Mus. ms.: *7 Preludes*, 1921

Mus. ms.: *Sinfonia*, 1956

Mus. ms.: *Sommerduft*, 1919

Mus. ms.: *Sonate*, 1911

Mus. ms.: *Sonate für Bratsche allein*, 1929

Mus. ms.: *Sonate für Bratsche und Pianoforte*, 1963

Mus. ms.: *Sonate für Cello und Klavier*, 1934

Mus. ms.: *Sonate für Pianoforte Solo, (Musik für Pianoforte, No. 2)*, 1930

Mus. ms.: *Sonate für Violine und Klavier*, 1935

Mus. ms.: *Sonate in C-Dur*, 1921

Mus. ms.: *Sonate in D-Moll*, 1916

Mus. ms.: *Sonate in D-Moll*, 1919

Mus. ms.: *Sonate in Es-Dur*, 1920

Mus. ms.: *Sonate in G-Moll*, 1915

Mus. ms.: *Sonatine für Klavier*, 1925

Mus. ms.: *Sonne und Fleisch*, 1949. Excerpt

Mus. ms.: *Streichquartett*, 1949

Mus. ms.: *Streichquartett*, 1960

Mus. ms.: *Streichquartett in F-Dur*, 1923

Mus. ms.: *Streichquartett in Fis-Moll*, 1924

Mus. ms.: *Streichquintett*, 1976

Mus. ms.: *Suite*, 1924

Mus. ms.: *Suite in G-Moll*, 1918

Mus. ms.: *Symphonie*, 1962

Mus. ms.: *Symphonie in D-Moll*, 1920

Mus. ms.: *Symphonische Aphorismen*, 1959

Mus. ms.: *Toccata für Orgel*, 1934

Mus. ms.: *Tor und Tod*, 1916

Mus. ms.: *Trio-Sonate für Orgel in G-Dur* by Bach, 1936

Mus. ms.: *Valse*, 1918

Mus. ms.: *Variationen in C-Dur*, 1918

Mus. ms.: *Variationen und Fantasien über ein Thema von Arnold Schoenberg*, 1954

Mus. ms.: *4 Lieder*, 1913

Mus. ms.: *4 Lieder*, 1919

Mus. ms.: *IV. Symphonie*, 1943

Mus. ms.: *4 Totenlieder*, 1915

Mus. ms.: *Der Wegweiser*, 1931

Mus. ms.: *Auf Wiedersehen*, 1921

Mus. ms.: *Der Wingwurz*, 1924

Mus. ms.: *2 Lieder*, 1913

Mus. ms.: *2 Lieder*, 1919

Mus. ms.: *Zwei Lieder*, 1934

Mus. ms.: *2 Sonaten*, 1918

Mus. ms.: *Zweite Symphonie*, 1937

Mus. ms. Repro.: *3 Orchesterlieder*, 1941

Mus. ms. Repro.: *4 Klavierstücke*, 1937

Library of Congress
(Box 94)

A. Mus. ms. S.: *Streich-Quintett*, 1975–1976. 22p., 31x24cm.

A. Mus. ms.: *Streich-Quintett*, 1975–1976. 10p., 28x21cm.

T. Doc. A. Rev.: Bermerkungen. 2p. 2 copies

2 Prog.: 14 Apr. 1978, 24 Feb. 1987. 7p., English. Signed by performers

Washington State University
See Rosbaud, Hans

Fraenzl, Ferdinand, 1767–1833
Bayerische Staatsbibliothek
L.: to Johann André. Moscow, 30 May/11 June 1804

2 L.: Munich, 18 June 1815, 11 May 1822

Françaix, Jean, 1912–1997
Harvard University
See Koussevitzky, Serge

Francescatti, Zino [René], 1902–1991
Library of Congress
(Box 111)
Port. Phot. S.: to Boaz Piller, 1944

Franck, César, 1822–1890
Library of Congress
(Box 17, unless noted)
A. Mus. ms. S.: *Paris*, patriotic ode, for tenor and
    orchestra. 28p., 35x27cm., ink. Full score
A. Mus. ms. S.: *Prélude, choral et fugue*, for piano solo, to
    Marie Poitevin. 21p., 35x27cm. Bound in white
    vellum. The original manuscript used for the first
    performance by Marie Poitevin. With reproduction
    of same (Shelf)
A. L. S.: ?, 1884. 1p., French
A. L. S.: n.p., n.d. 1p., French
Port. Paint. Repro. (Box 111)
See Dron, Marthe
See Duparc, Henri

Franco, Johan, 1908–1988
Harvard University
SUMMARY OF PRINCIPAL HOLDINGS:
Mus. ms.: *Concerto Lirico No. 5*, 1971
Mus. ms.: *Sinfonia*, 1932
Mus. ms.: *Theme and Twelve Variations*, 1944
Mus. ms.: *Two Pieces*, 1948
3 L.: to Hans Moldenhauer. n.p., 18 Aug. 1979;
    Virginia Beach, Virginia, 18, 28 Nov. 1982
L.: to Hans and Rosaleen Moldenhauer.
    Lüdinghausen, 5 Sept. 1979
2 S. recs.: *Incidental Music for Productions by the
    Everyman Players*; *Seven Biblical Sketches*, 24 Nov.
    1980

Library of Congress
See Lier, Bertus van

Northwestern University
SUMMARY OF PRINCIPAL HOLDINGS:
Mus. ms.: *Alla Marcia, Intermezzo for Piano*, 1939
Mus. ms.: *Concerto Lyrico No. 1*, 1937
Mus. ms.: *Fantasia for Organ*, 1935
Mus. ms.: *Old Tune*, 1939
Mus. ms.: *Peripetie, Symphonic Poem*, 1935
Mus. ms.: *Seven Epigrams*, 1932
Mus. ms.: *Sonata II for Pianoforte*, 1933–1934
Mus. ms.: *Sonata a tre (II)*, 1935
Mus. ms.: *Symphony No. 2*, 1939
6 Port. Phot.: 1938–1971

Frank, Ernst, 1847–1889
Bayerische Staatsbibliothek
5 L.: to Franz von Holstein. Mannhein, 1875. With
    musical illustrations

Frank, Maurits, 1892–1959
Washington State University
Doc.: Death announcement

Frank, René, 1910–1965
Harvard University
SUMMARY OF PRINCIPAL HOLDINGS:
Mus. ms.: *The Great Invitation*, op. 18-C
Mus. ms.: *Six Hymn Preludes*, Nos. 4, 6

Frankenstein, Alfred, 1906–1981
Harvard University
Clip. Annot.: "Webern's Legacy"

Franz [Knauth], Robert, 1815–1892
Library of Congress
(Box 18)
A. Mus. ms.: *Für Einen*, op. 1, No. 8. 4p. (pp.5–8),
    24x33cm.
3 A. L. S.: Halle, 24 Jan. 1859, 18 May 1881, 7 Nov.
    1885. 6p., German
A. L. S.: to Schäfler. Halle, 7 Mar. 1869. 3p., German
4 A. L. S.: [to Carl Reinecke?]. Halle, 26 Sept., 14, 25,
    30 Nov. 1884. 15p., German. With musical notation
A. L. S.: to Carl Reinecke. Halle, 16 Dec. 3p., German
A. L. S.: to Meier. n.p., n.d. 1p., German

A. Doc.: Musical notation. Annotations concerning Mozart's music. 4p., German
A. Mus. Quot. S.: Halle, 14 Sept. 1885, inscribed

Frege [née Gerhard], Livia, 1818–1891
Library of Congress
(Box 18)
2 A. L. S.: to Molli[?]. Leipzig, 11 Dec. 1833, ? Apr. 6p., German
A. Card: to Molli Zölzel[?]. Vienna, 13 May 1874. German

Frickenhaus, Fanny, 1849–1913
Northwestern University
L.

Fricker, Peter Racine, 1920–1990
Harvard University
L.: to Aurelio de la Vega. Santa Barbara, 12 May 1986

Friedberg, Carl, 1872–1955
Library of Congress
(Box 18)
3 A. L. S.: to Bruno Eisner. Blue Hill, Maine, 5 Aug. 1940; New York, 17 Mar., 22 Apr. 1945. 8p., German

Washington State University
L.: to Solomon Pimsleur. Baden-Baden, 4 Sept. 1929

Friedheim, Arthur, 1859–1932
Library of Congress
(Box 18)
A. L. S.: Leipzig, 14 Apr. 1884. 2p., German

Friedlaender [Friedländer], Max, 1852–1934
Library of Congress
(Box 18, unless noted)
A. L. S.: Misdroy[?], 25 Aug. 1898. 3p., German
P. card S.: to Eugen Lindner. Berlin, 21 May 1904. 1p., German. About Brahms
P. card S.: to Gusti Tick. Bad Reichenhall, 28 Aug. 1910[?]. German
T. L. S.: to Karl Weigl. Berlin, 14 Oct. 1912. 2p., German

P. card S.: to Robert F. Arnold. Meran, ?. German
Obit.: German
T. Doc. S.: Attestation. For Olga Eisner as singer and teacher. Berlin, 1 May 1933. 1p., German
T. Doc.: Biography with portrait photograph reproduced. German
Port. Phot. S.: to Olga Eisner. By Scherl (Box 111)

Friedman, Ignaz, 1882–1948
Northwestern University
Mus. ms. arr.: *Die Schönbrunner* by Lanner. Complete score
5 L.: to Karl Weigl. 1928–1937

Frimmel, Theodor von, 1853–1928
Wiener Stadt- u. Landesbibliothek
2 L.: to Ernst Weizmann. Vienna, 20 June, 20 July 1927
L.: Vienna, 23 Nov. 1927

Fritzsch, Ernst Wilhelm, 1840–1902
Library of Congress
(Box 18)
A. L. S.: to A. W. Gottschalg. Leipzig, 29 Nov. 1885. 1p., German. Regarding a Liszt manuscript

Fuchs, Robert, 1847–1927
Wiener Stadt- u. Landesbibliothek
Mus. ms.: *Mondaufgang*
2 L.: to Karl Weigl. Vienna, 6 Oct. 1902, 9 Feb. 1910

Führer, Robert, 1807–1861
Library of Congress
(Box 18)
Mus. ms. cop.: *Vier Trauergesänge für vier Singstimmen.* 32p., 26x33cm.

Fürstner, Adolph, 1833–1908
Library of Congress
(Box 18)

A. L. S.: to A. W. Gottschalg. Berlin, 8 Feb. 1871. 2p., German. Mentions Liszt manuscripts, Schubert, Weber

Fuerstner, Carl, 1912–1994
Harvard University
2 L.: to Aurelio de la Vega. Provo, 7 Jan. 1955; n.p., 25 Mar. 1963

Füssl, Karl Heinz, 1924–1992
Library of Congress
(Box 18)
A. Mus. ms. S.: *Celestina*, Oct. 1975, to the Moldenhauer Archives. 44p. + 13p. (sketches), 21x27cm.
A. Mus. ms. S.: *Dybuk*, Act II. 2p., 32x25cm.
A. Mus. ms. S.: *Dybuk*, Act III, to Stravinsky for his 80th birthday. 4p., 32x25cm.
A. Mus. ms. S.: [Choral composition written for Hans Erich Apostel's 70th birthday], 1971. 1p., 21x27cm.
A. L. S.: to Hans Moldenhauer. Vienna, 11 May 1976. 1p., German
T. Doc. A. Rev.: Program notes and chart of tone rows for *Dybuk*. 6p., German
T. Doc. A. Rev.: Typed synopsis of the three acts of the opera, *Dybuk*. 2p., German
T. Doc. A. Rev. S.: Work list. 2p.
2 T. Lib. A. Rev. S.: *Dybuk*, Act III. 21p., German
Mus. ms. Repro. S.: *Dialogue in Praise of the Owl and the Cuckoo*, 1948, revised 1966, to the Moldenhauer Archives, Oct. 1975. 33p.
Mus. ms. Repro. A. Rev.: *Le Rhinocéros*, 1966. 55p. Also three copies of the text (English, German, French), and 1p. accompanying document
Pri. Sco. S.: *Epitaph und Antistrophe*, Vienna: Universal, c1965, to the Moldenhauer Archives, 1975. 29p.
Pri. Sco. S.: *Refrains für Klavier und Orchester*, Vienna: Universal, c1972, to the Moldenhauer Archives, Oct. 1975. 55p.
Pri. Lib. A. Rev. S.: *Dybuk*, Vienna: Universal, c1968, 26 Sept. 1970. 48p., German
Pri. Lib. A. Rev. S.: *Dybuk*. 23p., German
Pri. Lib. S.: *Dybuk*, Vienna: Universal, c1968. 48p., German
2 Docs. S.: Brochure. *Dybuk*, to the Moldenhauer Archives. 6p. each
Prog. S.: *Celestina*, to the Moldenhauer Archives. With two additional copies

2 Docs. Repro. S.: Articles on Füssl. 2p.
See Erbse, Heimo

Fugère, Lucien, 1848–1935
Library of Congress
(Box 18, unless noted)
A. L. S.: n.p., 1893. 1p., French
Port. Phot.: Paris, [1884]. Fugère in *Joli Gilles*. By Chalot (Box 111)
Port. Phot.: Paris, [1884]. Fugère with Mme. Molé-Truffier in *Joli Gilles*. By Chalot (Box 111)

Fuleihan, Anis, 1900–1970
Harvard University
Summary of Principal Holdings:
Mus. ms.: *Fugue*

Library of Congress
(Box 111)
Port. Phot. S.: to Hans Rosbaud, Frankfurt, 1932. By Sudak

Fuller Maitland, J. A., 1856–1936
Northwestern University
L.: to Miss Stephenson. London, 10 May

Furtwängler, Wilhelm, 1886–1954
Library of Congress
(Box 18)
A. L. S.: to Bekker. Frankfurt, 17 May 1921. 1p., German
A. L. S.: to Tischer. Leipzig, 15 Mar. 1925. 2p., German
T. L. S.: to Tischer. St. Moritz, 14 Sept. 1926. 1p., German
A. L. S.: to Karl Weigl. Leipzig, 3 Feb. 1927. 1p., German
T. L. S.: to Karl Weigl. Berlin, 27 May 1931. 1p., German
T. L. S.: to Zemlinsky. Berlin, 16 Jan. 1934, 1p., German. With sketches on verso

T. L. S.: to Bruno Eisner. Vienna, 8 Jan. 1936. 1p.,
  German
See Orlik, Emil

Washington State University
L.: to Lothan Goldschmidt. Luzern, 21 Aug. 1947
See Rosbaud, Hans

Futterer, Carl, 1873–1927
Zentralbibliothek Zürich
2 Docs.: Texts on Futterer
S. rec.: *Goethelieder*

Gabriel, Mary Ann Virginia, 1825–1877
Northwestern University
3 L.

Gabrieli, Giovanni, ca. 1553/6–1612
Library of Congress
A. Doc. S.: Entry in a guest book. 16 Nov. 1596. 1p.,
  16x10cm. Gives full signature, title, date, and
  autograph of Henricus Julius, Duke of Brunswick,
  1595

Gabrilowitsch, Ossip, 1878–1936
Harvard University
Mus. Quot.: inscribed 21 Nov. 1913. Mounted on
  portrait photograph
Port. Phot. Annot.

Gade, Niels, 1817–1890
Library of Congress
(Box 19)
A. L. S.: to Reinecke. Copenhagen, 16 Jan. 1875. 3p.,
  Danish

Northwestern University
Mus. ms.: *Symphony No. 3*, 1808. Excerpt
L.: n.p., 5 Mar. 1853
Mus. Quot.: On G-A-D-E, Copenhagen, May 1886
Mus. Quot.: *Violin Sonata*, op. 6, Leipzig, Dec. 1843
Obit.

Gänsbacher, Johann, 1778–1844
Library of Congress
(Box 19)
A. Mus. ms. S.: *Serenade*, Innsbruck, 8 Mar. 1823. 8p.,
  22x32cm.

Gagnebin, Henri, 1886–1977
Zentralbibliothek Zürich
Doc.: Address. "Hommage à Andrés Segovia," 5 Dec.
  1956
See Rosbaud, Hans

Gál [Gal], Hans, 1890–1987
Library of Congress
(Box 19)
A. Mus. ms. S.: *Three Preludes for Pianoforte*, op. 65.
  14p., 24x30cm.

Galán, Natalio, b. 1917
Harvard University
L.: to Aurelio de la Vega. n.p., 28 Dec. 1982

Galimir, Felix, 1910–1999
Library of Congress
See Apostel, Hans Erich

Galimir String Quartet
Wiener Stadt- u. Landesbibliothek
L.: to Otto Jokl. Vienna, 4 June 1934

Galindo-Dimas, Blas, 1910–1993
Harvard University
Mus. ms.: *Sexteto de alientos*
3 L.: to Aurelio de la Vega. Mexico, 7 Apr. 1958,
  24 May 1963, 4 Oct. 1974
Doc.: Outline. Curriculum at National Conservatory
  of Music, Mexico City

Gall, Rudolf, 1907–1962
Washington State University
See Rosbaud, Hans

Galpin, Francis W., 1858–1945
Northwestern University
L.: to Peter Epstein. Witham, Essex, 25 Jan. 1933
L.: to Bull. Richmond, 1 May 1937
L.: to a museum director. n.p., n.d.
L.: to Galpin, from Standfield
Doc.: Essay. "Frederick the Great's English Harpsichords." Preparatory notes and drafts

Ganz, Rudolph, 1877–1972
Harvard University
See Griffes, Charles T.

Washington State University
See Rosbaud, Hans

Zentralbibliothek Zürich
Summary of Principal Holdings:
Mus. ms.: *After Midnight*, op. 27, No. 1
Mus. ms.: *Oh, Beautiful Month of May*, 1932
Mus. ms.: *Le Four*, 1906
Mus. ms.: *Le Jour des morts*, 1906
Mus. ms.: *Les Noix*, 1906
Mus. ms.: *Percussional Mélée*, 1941
Mus. ms.: *Piano Concerto in E-flat Major*, to Hans Moldenhauer. Excerpt
Mus. ms.: *Sports and Games*
Mus. ms.: *Twenty Animal Pictures*, 1931–1932
Mus. ms.: *Two Voice Inventions*, op. 38, No. 1
Mus. ms.: *Woody Scherzo*, 1944
139 L.: to Hans and Rosaleen Moldenhauer. 1951–1966. Including letters from Esther Ganz
L. Repro.: to Ganz, from Ravel. 9 Feb. 1908
L. Repro.: to Ganz, from Bartók. Budapest, 17 Apr. 1923
L. Repro.: to Ganz, from Schweitzer. Chicago, July 1949
Doc. Annot.: Article. "Music in Europe," by Hans Moldenhauer, with autograph corrections by Ganz
Doc.: Introductory remarks. Given before a recital, 1962
Mus. ms. Repro. A. Annot.: *Laughter...yet Love*
2 Port. Phot.

Ganz, Wilhelm, 1833–1914
Library of Congress
(Box 19)
A. Card S.: to Munday. [London], 9 Mar. 1888. 2p., English

A. L. S.: to Routlege. [London], 18 May 1898. 4p., English. With musical illustration. Regarding Enrico Tamberlik

García, Manuel, 1805–1906
Library of Congress
(Box 19)
A. L. S.: Manchester Square, 25 Mar. 1871. 2p., French
A. L. S.: n.p., n.d. 1p., Italian
Clip.: 18 Mar. 1905. 2p., English

Gardoni, Italo, 1821–1882
Library of Congress
(Box 19, unless noted)
A. L. S.: n.p., n.d. 1p., French
Port. Phot. S.: 28 July 1861. By Caldesi (Box 111)

Gastinel, Léon-Gustave-Cyprien, 1823–1906
Library of Congress
(Box 19)
A. Mus. Quot. S.: *Le Miroir*, Andante, to Achille Vogue[?], 23 June 1884. 1p., French. Part of an autograph letter signed, mailed from Antony, Seine

Gatty, Nicholas Comyn, 1874–1946
Northwestern University
L.: to Colles. London, 28 Aug.

Gaul, Alfred, 1837–1913
Northwestern University
L.: fragment

Gebhard, Hans, 1882–1947
Library of Congress
(Box 19)
A. Mus. ms. S.: *5 Christian-Wagner Lieder I*, 1924. 12p., 34x27cm.
A. Mus. ms. S.: *Christian-Wagner Lieder II*, 1925. 9p., 34x27cm.

Geiringer, Karl, 1899–1989
Harvard University
2 L.: to Hans and Rosaleen Moldenhauer. Boston,
  8 Dec. 1961; Santa Barbara, 1962
Doc.: Lecture. "Symbolism in the Music of Bach"

Library of Congress
See Haydn, Joseph

Genée, Richard, 1823–1895
Wiener Stadt- u. Landesbibliothek
Mus. ms.: *Entreacte*, Thorn, 24 July 1856
Clip.

Genzmer, Harald, b. 1909
Bayerische Staatsbibliothek
SUMMARY OF PRINCIPAL HOLDINGS:
Mus. ms.: *Concerto for Violin and Small Orchestra*, 1959.
  Sketches
Mus. ms.: *Prolog*, 1959. Sketches
4 L.: to Hans Moldenhauer. Munich, 1959, 1960

Gérardy, Jean, 1877–1929
Library of Congress
(Box 19)
A. Mus. Quot. S.: *Cello Concerto* by Saint-Saëns, 5 Mar.
  1906

Gerber, Ernst Ludwig, 1746–1819
Northwestern University
Mus. ms.: [Music notebook], including *Cantate di Rolle*;
  Five arias with bass accompaniment; *An die höchste
  Landesherrschaft...*; *Die Genügsamkeit von Pantalon und
  Telemann...*; *Cantata dell Sig. C. E. Graun*; "Das
  allerbeste Weib..."
L.: to Waag-Amtmann. Sondershausen, 23 Feb. 1799

Gerber, Heinrich Nikolaus, 1702–1775
Library of Congress
(Box 19)
A. Mus. ms. S.: "*Freu dich sehr o meine Seele, cum 12*

Variationibus di Johann Pachelbel," Apr. 1716. 14p.,
  32x19cm., ink. Complete score. This work is one in a
  series published in 1683. A copy of this publication
  has not been located, although a number of pieces
  contained therein are extant in manuscript form

Gerber Library, Liedersammlung
Northwestern University
Mus. ms.: [Manuscript collection]. Over 100 lieder
  with figured bass accompaniment, including
  compositions by Fleischer, Neefe, Graun, and
  Breitkopf

Gerhard, Roberto, 1896–1970
Library of Congress
(Box 94)
A. Mus. ms.: *Concerto for Orchestra*. 1p. (p.85),
  47x32cm., ink
31 L. S.: to Adolph Weiss. 1927–1956. 71p., German.
  Many letters signed jointly by Gerhard's wife, Poldi.
  Some postscripts by Kolisch, Wladimir Vogel.
  Details Schoenberg circle at Berlin. Includes
  autograph letters, typed letters, and postcards
T. Doc.: Lecture. "On Webern." 4p., English. With
  autograph title
L. Repro.: to Poldi Gerhard, from Dr. H. A. Fleming,
  Cambridge, 5 Jan. 1970. 1p., English
2 Pri. Sco.: *Libra; Leo*, London: Oxford University
  Press, c1970, to Hans and Rosaleen Moldenhauer.
  122p. + 115p. Inscribed by Poldi Gerhard
4 Pri. Sco.: opera 20, 22, 27, 28, by Webern. With
  analyses by Gerhard
3 Clip.: Reviews. 1966, 1973
Bk.: *The Complete Instrumental and Chamber Music of Arnold
  Schoenberg and Roberto Gerhard*, London: Sinfonietta
  Production, 1973, to Hans and Rosaleen Moldenhauer.
  180p., English. Inscribed by Poldi Gerhard

Northwestern University
2 L.: to Mrs. Morland. Cambridge, 16 July, 16 Sept.
  1963

Washington State University
See Rosbaud, Hans

Gericke, Wilhelm, 1845–1925
Library of Congress
(Box 19, unless noted)
A. Card S.: Vienna, 1 Feb. 1p., German
A. Mus. Quot. S.: Allegretto, Boston, 27 Oct. 1899. On Gericke's letterhead as conductor, Boston Symphony Orchestra. Mounted with portrait photograph below (Box 111)
Port. Phot.: Mounted with musical quotation above. By Chickering (Box 111)

German, Sir Edward [Jones, German Edward], 1862–1936
Northwestern University
L.: London, 24 Feb. 1910

German Reed, Thomas, 1817–1888
Northwestern University
2 L.: to Spencer Ponsonby. London, 19 Jan. 1861; n.p., 12 May 1863

Gernsheim, Friedrich, 1839–1916
Library of Congress
(Box 19)
P. card S.: to Chrysander. Berlin, 12 Apr. 1900. German
A. L. S.: ?, 2 Feb. 1909. 2p., German
Call. c. Annot.: Berlin, 24 Feb. 1898. German

Gernsheim, Willi, b. 1899
Library of Congress
(Box 19)
A. Mus. ms. S.: *Maikäferlied*, Mannheim, 12 Feb. 1927. 3p., 34x27cm.

Gershwin, George, 1898–1937
Harvard University
Mus. ms.: *Porgy and Bess*, Act II, scene 1, incomplete
Mus. ms. cop.: *Summertime.* Full score, parts for thirteen instruments, in the hand of Jorge Whiteman (São Paulo, 1944), and autograph title page
2 L.: to Boaz Piller. New York, 4 May 1929, 9 June 1931

Library of Congress
(Box 95)
A. Mus. ms. S.: [*Jascha, Mischa, Sascha, Toscha*], Boston, 31 Dec. 1929. 1p., 21x25cm., ink. Four-part song written for a party at the home of Koussevitzky. Unpublished
A. Mus. ms.: [*Porgy and Bess*]. 1p., 33x26cm., pencil. Sketches in condensed score, including text, marked "Robbins, Page 3"
Doc.: Text. "*Jascha, Mischa, Sascha, Toscha.*" Text by Ira Gershwin, to music by George Gershwin, written out by Nicolas Slonimsky. 1p., English, 23x15cm.
A. L. S.: to Boaz Piller. New York, 3 Feb. 1930. 1p., English
L.: to Hans Moldenhauer, from Boaz Piller. Brookline, Massachusetts, 25 May. 1p., English. Regarding "*Jascha...*"
2 Sig.
See Ravel, Maurice

Gerstberger, Karl, 1892–1955
Northwestern University
Mus. ms.: *String Quartet in C Minor*, op. 11, 20 May 1925. Full score

Gervinus, Georg Gottfried, 1805–1871
Library of Congress
(Box 19)
A. L. S.: to Selmar Bagge. Heidelberg, 18 Oct. 1863. 3p., German

Geselschap, Marie, b. 1874
Library of Congress
(Box 19)
Doc. S.: Publicity brochure. Weimar, Aug. 1900, inscribed. 11p., German and English

Gevaert, François-Auguste, 1828–1908
Library of Congress
(Box 19)
A. L. S.: to Duvernoy. n.p., 6 Sept. 1859. 1p., French
A. L. S.: to Gustave. Paris, n.d. 3p., French. On musical life in Paris
A. L. S.: Paris, 8 Mar. 1864. 1p., French

Geyer, Stefi, 1888–1956
Zentralbibliothek Zürich
L.: to Hindermann. Budapest, 25 Oct. 1908
L.: to Trude Levaitlant. Budapest, 19 June 1909

Ghil, René, 1862–1925
Northwestern University
4 L.: to Massenet. Paris, 1893–1895. With
transcription, by Demar Irvine

Ghircoiaşiu, Romeo, b. 1919
Library of Congress
(Box 19)
Pri. Sco.: *Rondo*, Cluj: Conservatorul de Muzică, to
Hans Moldenhauer, c1970. 5p.

Giardini [Degiardino], Felice, 1716–1796
Library of Congress
(Box 19)
A.[?] Mus. ms. S.: *Chorus's to the Stabat Mater*, "O quam
tristis," "Fac ut ardeat cor meum," "Amen."
Arranged for solo voices, chorus, and instruments.
36p. + 16p. (parts), 24x30cm.

Gibert, Vicente María de, 1879–1939
Library of Congress
(Box 19)
A. Mus. ms. S.: *Tres cants extrets del cicle*, "De la primera
jornada." 18p., 31x21cm.

Giehne, Heinrich
Library of Congress
(Box 19)
2 A. L. S.: [to Selmar Bagge?]. Karlsruhe, Nov. 1860,
5 Aug. 1862. 10p., German

Gieseking, Walter, 1895–1956
Library of Congress
(Box 19, unless noted)
A. L. S.: to Marion Bauer. n.p., n.d. 1p., French

Port. Phot. S.: to Boaz Piller, Boston, 4 Mar. 1928. By
Lucas-Kanarian (Box 111)

Gigli, Beniamino, 1890–1957
Library of Congress
(Box 19)
T. L. S.: to Ramón Palacio. New York, 1 Dec. 1928.
1p., Italian

Gil, José, 1886–1947
Library of Congress
(Box 19)
A. Mus. ms. S.: *Valse*, para piano, to Ricardo Viñes. 4p.,
37x27cm.

Gilardi, Gilardo, 1889–1963
Harvard University
Mus. ms. cop.: *Serie argentina*, No. 4

Gilbert, Henry F., 1868–1928
Harvard University
Mus. ms.: *The Treasures of the Wise Man*, Cambridge,
4 Feb. 1940
Doc.: Poem. "All hail to thee, America..."
Port.

Gilbert, Pia, b. 1921
Harvard University
SUMMARY OF PRINCIPAL HOLDINGS:
Mus. ms.: *Metamorphoses*, 1966
Mus. ms.: *Orders (of the sea, of the land, of the air)*, 1966
2 L.: to Aurelio de la Vega. 1983, 1985
S. rec.: *Transmutations; Interrupted Suite*

Gilbert, Sir William Schwenck, 1836–1911
Northwestern University
2 L.: to Miss Stephenson. London, 27 Feb. 1891,
21 Dec. 1895

Gilmore, Patrick S., 1829–1892
Harvard University
Mus. Quot.: Maestoso, 13 May 1885
Port.: with poem

Gilson, Paul, 1865–1942
Library of Congress
(Box 19)
P. card: Brussels, Coventry, 1910[?]. French

Gimpel, Jakob, 1906–1989
Harvard University
L.: to Aurelio de la Vega. Los Angeles, Dec. 1984

Library of Congress
See Apostel, Hans Erich

Ginastera, Alberto, 1916–1983
Harvard University
Summary of Principal Holdings:
Mus. ms.: Second String Quartet, third movement
   ("Presto magico"). 8p. Complete draft

Giordano, Umberto, 1867–1948
Library of Congress
(Box 19)
A. Mus. ms. S.: *Esercizii*, 15 July 1917. 1p., 33x27cm.,
   pencil

Giuglini, Antonio, 1827–1865
Library of Congress
(Box 19, unless noted)
3 Sig.
Port. Phot. (Box 111)

Giuliani, Michel, 1801–1867
Library of Congress
(Box 19)
A. L. S.: to Diabelli. Florence, 29 Jan. 1825. 3p.,
   German

Glaz, Herta, b. 1908
Harvard University
L.: to Aurelio de la Vega. New York, 18 June 1954
L.: to Otto Jokl. n.p., n.d.

Glazunov, Alexander Konstantinovich, 1865–1936
Library of Congress
(Box 20)
A. L. S.: to Taneyev. 8 Sept. 1915. 1p., Russian
A. Mus. ms. Quot. S.: *Concerto pour Violon*, Boston, Jan.
   1930

Glinka, Mikhail Ivanovich, 1804–1857
Library of Congress
(Box 20)
A. L. S.: to a publisher. Varese, 30 Oct. 1p., French

Globokar, Vinko, b. 1934
Library of Congress
(Box 20)
2 A. L. S.: to Aurelio de la Vega. Paris, 31 Aug.,
   31 Dec. 1979. 2p., English

Gluck, Alexander Johannes, 1683–1743
Library of Congress
(Box 20)
A. Doc. S.: Chemnitz, 31 July 1723. 1p., German.
   Regarding a supply of wood

Gluck, Christoph Willibald, 1714–1787
Library of Congress
(Box 20, unless noted)
A. Mus. ms.: [*Le feste d'Apollo*, Act II, *Aristeo*], Primo
   coro nel Aristeo che ancora si balla. The opera was
   performed at Parma in 1769 for the wedding of the
   Infante Don Ferdinando to Maria Amalia. 7p.,
   22x30cm., ink. Full score of the first chorus. Text by

C. I. Frugoni. The leaves bear Gluck's original pagination, 27–30. After the manuscript was broken up, this section was repaginated 1–8. Inscribed with provenance and text by Felix von Bamberg to whom Aloys Fuchs transferred the manuscript on 27 May 1842 at Vienna (Shelf)

Mus. ms. Repro.: *Alceste*. 1p. Facsimile. Previously framed with portrait engraving below

Port. Engr. (Box 111)

See Berlioz, Hector

See Walter, Bruno

Godard, Benjamin, 1849–1895
Library of Congress
(Box 20, unless noted)
A. L. S.: to his editor. Cannes, 12 Oct. 1894. 1p., French
Port. Engr.: by Kiss (Box 111)

Goddard, Arabella, 1836–1922
Northwestern University
L.: to Lord Sydney. Hampstead, 13 May 1863
Port.: with obituary

Godefroid, Félix, 1818–1897
Library of Congress
(Box 20)
Pri. Sco. S.: *La Fille de Saul*, Air de Saul, to Madame Lafleur, Durdilly, Paris. 10p., French

Godfrey, Dan, 1831–1903
Northwestern University
3 L.
Port.: with accompanying newspaper clippings

[signature]

Godowsky, Leopold, 1870–1938
Library of Congress
(Box 95)
A. Mus. ms. S.: *Two Cadenzas to Mozart's Concerto in E-flat for Two Pianos*, K. 365, Carl Fischer, Los Angeles, Sept. 1920. 7p., 33x26cm.

P. card S.: to B. Neuer. Tampa, Florida, 14 Mar. 1916. English

Pri. Sco. S.: *Fréderic Chopin: Selected Studies for Pianoforte, Arranged for Left Hand by Leopold Godowsky*, op. 10, No. 1, G. Schirmer, 1899, to Florence Ziegfeld, Chicago, 2 June 1900. 7p.

Goehr, Rudolph, 1906–1981
Library of Congress
(Box 20)
Mus. ms. Repro. S.: *Chatteries*, 1957. 22p. Blueprint score
Mus. ms. Repro. S.: *Concerto cancrizante*. 12p. Blueprint score
Pri. Sco. S.: *Concerto cancrizante*, New York: Rongwen Music, c1956. 25p. (parts)

Goepfart, Karl Eduard, 1859–1942
Library of Congress
See Lindner, Eugen

Goetz, Hermann, 1840–1876
Zentralbibliothek Zürich
L.: [to Franz von Holstein]. Hottingen bei Zürich, 19 Oct. 1874

Götze, Emil, 1856–1901
Library of Congress
(Box 20)
A. Alb. l. S.: Leipzig, 1 Nov. 1890

Golde, Walter, 1887–1963
Harvard University
Mus. ms.: *Chick Lorimer (Gone)*, 1959
Mus. ms.: *A Lover Sings to His Garden*, 1924
L.

[signature]

Goldmark, Karl [Carl; Károly], 1830–1915
Library of Congress
(Box 20, unless noted)

A. Mus. ms.: [*Die Königin von Saba*]. 4p., 33x25cm. Fragment from the full score, containing the "Chor der Jungfrauen"

3 A. L. S.: Gmunden, 17 June 1887[?], 22 Aug. 1899, 4 June 1900. 9p., German

A. L. S.: to Schittenhelm. Gmunden, 25 May 1900. 3p., German. On page three, sixteen singers have signed their names certifying that they have read the letter

A. L. S.: to Frau von Müller. Vienna, 23 May 1912[?]. 2p., German

Call. c. S.: Gmunden, 10 Sept. 1901. German

A. Mus. Quot. S.: see portrait photograph below

Port. Phot. S.: May 1898. On verso, accompanying autograph musical quotation. By Löwy (Box 111)

Port. Phot. S.: to Francis Young (Box 111)

Port. Gr. S. (Box 111)

Goldmark, Rubin, 1872–1936
Washington State University

2 L.: to Solomon Pimsleur. New York, 9 Oct. 1923, 16 Oct. 1933

Goldschmidt, Otto, 1829–1907
Library of Congress
(Box 20, unless noted)

A. L. S.: to Lockey. London, 25 Nov. 1859. 4p., English

A. L. S.: to Mrs. Wright. London, 23 May 1871. 1p., English. On verso is pasted a newspaper obituary of Goldschmidt

A. L. S.: to Sebastian Veit. London, 21 July 1871. 4p., German

A. L. S.: to Benson Rathbone. London, 22 Apr. 1873. 1p., English

A. L. S.: [1876?]. 2p., English. Fragment

A. L. S.: to [Mary] Wurm. London, 13 May 1889. 2p., English

A. L. S.: to the firm of Novello. London, 8, 13 Oct. 1903. 2p., English. Reply on verso

Port. Caric. S.: Dec. 1879. 1p., 10x8cm. Original pencil drawing portraying a violinist (Box 111)

Golinelli, Stefano, 1818–1891
Library of Congress
(Box 20)

A. L. S.: n.p., n.d. 1p., Italian

Golschmann, Vladimir, 1893–1972
Harvard University

2 L.: to Solomon Pimsleur. Paris, 15 May 1935; New York, 25 Oct. 1937

L.: to Rudolph Ganz. St. Louis, 8 Dec. 1951

Goossens, Sir Eugene, 1893–1962
Northwestern University

Mus. ms.: *Judith*, Boston, inscribed Jan. 1930. Excerpt

L.: to Charles Haubiel. Cincinnati, 13 Feb. 1947. With Haubiel's letter

Port. Phot.: Boston, 25 Jan. 1930

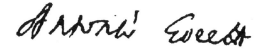

Goretti, Antonio, ca. 1570–1649
Library of Congress
(Box 20)

A. L. S.: to Marchesa Bentivoglio in Ferrara. Parma, 1629. 1p., Italian

Gorter, Albert, 1862–1936
Library of Congress
(Box 20)

A. Mus. ms. S.: *Frühling ohne Ende*. 7p., 34x27cm.

A. Mus. ms. S.: *Herbst*, 26 Aug. 1908. 2p., 35x27cm.

A. Mus. ms. Rev. S.: *Ich schreite gottheitstrunken*. 3p., 32x25cm.

A. L. S.: to Hans Moldenhauer, from Alberta Gorter. n.p., 1 Feb. 1964, 2p., German

A. Card S.: to Hans Moldenhauer, from Alberta Gorter. n.p., n.d. 1p., German

Doc.: Brochure. "Den deutschen Männergesangvereinen," Essen: Rheinischer. 19p., German

A. Doc.: Draft of an opera libretto, *Friedemann Bach*. 13p.

Mus. ms. cop.: *Der Gruss*. 8p.

Mus. ms. cop.: *Sie müssen sich's gefallen la'n*. 4p.

15 Pri. sco.: *Das Glück von Edenhall*; *Drei heitere Lieder*; *Drei Gesänge*; *Fünf Lieder*; *Sie müssen sich's gefallen la'n*; *Stimmungsbilder*, *Acht Clavierstücke*, op. 17, No. 6

Goss, Sir John, 1800–1880
Northwestern University
SUMMARY OF PRINCIPAL HOLDINGS:
L.: to Pettit. London, 5 Oct. 1825

Gossec, François-Joseph, 1734–1829
Library of Congress
(Box 20)
A. L. S.: n.p., 11 June 1791. 1p., French

Gottschalg, Alexander Wilhelm, 1827–1908
Library of Congress
(Box 20)
6 A. L. S.: to Bartolf Senff. Weimar, 1856–1867, n.d.
18p., German
2 P. cards S.: to Bartolf Senff. Weimar, 1 Mar. 1898,
1 July 1905. 2p., German
Doc.: Page from a journal. Advertising new books.
1866. 1p. German

Gould, Morton, 1913–1996
Harvard University
Mus. ms.: *American Salute*
Mus. ms.: *Jekyll and Hyde*
Mus. Quot.: [4m., for string orchestra, E-flat Major]
2 L.: 25 Apr. 1960; n.d.
3 Port.

Gounod, Charles, 1818–1893
Library of Congress
(Box 20, unless noted)
A. Mus. ms. Rev.: *Sapho*, [1878]. 46p., French. Duet
between Sapho and Glycère, with accompaniment
of the orchestra. (Shelf)
A. L. S.: to Ullmann. n.p., 30 May 1882. 2p., French

Northwestern University
Mus. ms.: *Dodelinette (Berceuse)*, for orchestra, Paris,
14 Mar. 1876. Full score
Mus. ms.: *La Reine de Saba*. Excerpt. Full score
Mus. ms.: *Scherzo*, for orchestra. Incomplete
L.: n.p., 9 Feb. 1866

L.: to Chappell. Saint-Cloud, 25 Aug. 1876
L.: to Henri de Régnier. Nieuport, 1 May 1881
L.: to Lebeau. n.p., 22 Feb. 188[?]
L.: Paris, n.d.
Port. Phot.: 1887
Port.
See Barye Document

Gouvy, Louis Théodore, 1819–1898
Library of Congress
(Box 20)
A. L. S.: to a conductor. Oberhomburg, 22 Oct. 1890.
4p., German. Regarding *Variations symphoniques*

Gow, Nathaniel, 1766–1831
Northwestern University
Doc.: Receipt and agreement. Between Gow and
Robert Purdie for "two sheets of tunes"

Gradenwitz, Peter, b. 1910
Library of Congress
(Box 21)
2 T. L. S.: to Aurelio de la Vega. Israel, 16 Feb.,
23 May 1954. 2p., English

Grädener, Carl, 1812–1883
Library of Congress
(Box 21)
6 A. L. S.: to Selmar Bagge. Vienna, 1862–1865. 18p.,
German
A. L. S.: to Selmar Bagge, from Wilhelmine Grädener.
Vienna, Aug. 1862. 3p., German. 1p. postscript by
Carl Grädener

Grädener, Hermann, 1844–1929
Library of Congress
(Box 21, unless noted)
A. Mus. ms. S.: *Horch auf, mein Lieb*, op. 27, No. 3. 1p.,
36x26cm.
A. L. S.: Vienna, 14 July 1886. 2p., German
A. L. S.: Vienna, 8 Apr. 1911. 3p., German. Regarding
manuscript above
A. Doc. S.: Autobiographical sketch. 2p., German
Port. Phot. S.: by Scolik (Box 111)
Port. Phot. Repro. (Box 111)

Graener, Paul, 1872–1944
Library of Congress
(Box 21)
P. card S.: to Scheel. Steinebach, 31 Aug. 1921.
 German

Graham, G. F. [George Farquhar], 1789–1867
Northwestern University
2 L.: to Dragonetti. Edinburgh, 8 Aug. 1815, 9 Feb.
 1816
Doc.: Minutes. From a meeting of the Edinburgh
Musical Festival, 1815–1816

Grainger, Percy, 1882–1961
Library of Congress
(Box 21)
A. Mus. ms. S.: *My Robin is to the Greenwood gone*, to
 George Bainton, 20 May 1912. 2p., 30x23cm., ink.
 For piano solo. Incomplete
T. L.: White Plains, 7 May 1932. 3p., English. Round
 robin letter sent to Marion Bauer, Martin Bernstein,
 Charles Haubiel, Gustave Reese, Philip James, and
 Jacques Pillois. Expressing his views on
 compositions being written and played in America.
 With reply, 7 June 1932, from Charles Haubiel
8 A. L. S.: to Charles Haubiel. 1932–1942. 16p.,
 English. The letter of 15 Apr. 1942 is a manifesto of
 his artistic beliefs; why he does not like to write for
 solo piano, his performance abilities, thoughts on
 composition and art
T. L.: to Percy Grainger, from Charles Haubiel. n.p.,
 7 June 1932. 4p., English
2 A. L. S.: to Carl Deis. Boston, 5 Mar. 1931;
 Segeltorp, near Stockholm, 4 July 1932. 4p., English
A. L. S.: to Leon Theremin. Melbourne, 12 Sept.
 1938. 1p., English
A. L. S.: to Rudolph Ganz. "In the Train," 28 Nov.
 1945. 2p., English
T. L.: to Lois Marshall. White Plains, 8 June 1948. 1p.,
 English

Grammann, Karl, 1844–1897
Library of Congress
(Box 21)
A. L. S.: to Eugen Lindner. Dresden, 19 Oct. 1889.
 3p., German

Granada Manuscript
Library of Congress
(Shelf)
Mus. ms. cop.: In festo.... Possibly dating from the
 sixteenth century, before the Council of Trent, with
 the reformed text added later, ca. late seventeenth
 century. 65p., 41x28cm., black, red, ornate violet
 ink, crayon[?]. Bound in brown leather, ornately
 embossed in gold on front and back covers as well
 as on the spine. Bound into front of the volume are
 eight additional pages in a later hand. The front
 cover shows the Cross, surmounting the legend
 "IHS," surrounded by an oval design of flowers and
 leaves. Antiphoner and gradual are combined. Much
 of the text conforms to the Dominican rite

Granados, Enrique, 1867–1916
Library of Congress
(Box 21, unless noted)
A. Mus. ms.: [Music notebook], [1887–1889]. 81
 leaves, some blank, 2 leaves laid in. Used jointly by
 Granados and Viñes and others during student years
 in Paris (1887–1889). Student exercises fill the bulk
 of the volume, as well as sketches, incipits to
 various compositions, two movements to a
 symphony in D Minor, and pencil drawings which
 adorn inside covers (Shelf)
A. L. S.: to Ricardo Viñes. Barcelona, 12 Mar. 1910,
 2p., Spanish
T. Doc.: Biographical information. French, Spanish
See Segovia, Andrés

Grandjany, Marcel, 1891–1975
Harvard University
L.: to Charles Haubiel. New York, 5 July 1954

Grau, Agustí, 1893–1964
Library of Congress
(Box 21)
Mus. ms. cop. S.: *"Tamarit," barcarola*, to Ricardo
Viñes, Barcelona, June 1928. 15p., 32x22cm.
Mus. ms. cop.: *"Sardana de Concert,"* per a piano. 18p.,
34x26cm.

Gray, Alan, 1855–1935
Northwestern University
L.: to Miss Ann. Cambridge, 4 Feb.
L.: to Pearce. Cambridge, 25 Oct.

Grayson, Richard, b. 1951
Harvard University
L.: to Aurelio de la Vega. Occidental College, 7 Jan.
1985

Grechaninov, Alexandr Tikhonovich, 1864–1956
Library of Congress
(Box 21, unless noted)
A. Mus. ms. S.: *Etudes progressives pour piano à 4 mains*,
op. 144, to the Spokane Conservatory, New York,
12 June 1955. 17p., 35x27cm., ink. Full score. With
accompanying autograph letter signed to Hans
Moldenhauer
T. L. S.: New York, 7 Sept. 1955. 1p., English
A. Doc. S.: Biographical information. New York, 1929.
4p., French
2 Pri. Sco. S.: *Holidays*; *Mommy*
Prog.: 28 Apr. 1955
2 Port. Draw. Repro. S.: 1944, 1955, to the Spokane
Conservatory (Box 111)

Greef, Arthur de, 1862–1940
Library of Congress
(Box 21)
Prog. S.: Southport, 28 Mar. 1915. 19p., English

Gregorian Chant
Library of Congress
(Box 104)
Mus. ms.: Containing portions of the Liturgy. 1 vellum
leaf, 2p., 32x23cm.
Pri. Mus. ms.: 1 leaf, 19x8cm. Mounted on card
Pri. Mus. ms.: 3 leaves, 6p., 44x28cm.

Greissle, Felix, 1894–1982
Harvard University
L.: to Charles Haubiel. New York, 7 July 1965

Library of Congress
See Rosbaud, Hans
See Webern, Anton

Paul Sacher Stiftung
See Webern, Anton

Grell, Eduard, 1800–1886
Library of Congress
(Box 21)
A. L. S.: to W. Brose. Berlin, 16 Dec. 1862. 2p.,
German

Grétry, André-Ernest-Modeste, 1741–1813
Library of Congress
(Box 21, unless noted)
Mus. ms.: *Le Rival confident*, 1788, complete piano-
vocal score (reduction marked for clavecin) by
Starck (Vicaire de la Metropole de Mayence), 1790.
78p. (pages numbered to 28), 31x22cm., French,
red, black ink. Inscribed by Starck. Bound in
decorative vellum (Shelf)
A. L. S.: to Bossenge, *père*. Paris, 19 Sept. 1810. 2p.,
French
T. p. S.: *Les deux Avares*, Paris. French
Port. Engr. (Box 111)

Grieg, Edvard, 1843–1907
Library of Congress
(Box 21, unless noted)
A. L. S.: Copenhagen, 16 Mar. 1891. 4p., German, with
   English translation. Regarding a Milan appearance
A. Card S.: to Levysohn. Copenhagen, 23 Apr. 1896.
   1p., Norwegian
P. card S.: to Martin R. Henriques. Troldhaugen,
   22 Dec. 1901
A. L. S.: to Lola Artôt de Padillha. Cristiania, 14 Feb.
   1906. 3p., German
A. Card S.: n.p., n.d. Norwegian
A. Doc. S.: Petition. For August Winding.
   Copenhagen, 5 Dec. 1899. 2p., Norwegian.
   Cosigned by Angul Hammerich, Jens Wilhelm
   Hansen, Christian Frederik Emil Horneman,
   Gottfred Matthison-Hansen
A. Mus. Quot. S.: Allegro Moderato
A. Mus. Quot. S.: Andante. With sketch on verso
3 Clip.: 1907, 1923. English
Port. Gr. S.: Edvard and his wife, Nina (Box 111)
Port. Phot.: by Christiansen (Box 111)

Griepenkerl, Wolfgang Robert, 1810–1868
Library of Congress
(Box 21)
A. L. S.: 22 Jan. 1859. 2p., German

Griffes, Charles T., 1884–1920
Harvard University
L.: to Marion Bauer
Mus. ms. Repro.: *The White Peacock*. With annotations
   by Rudolph Ganz

Griffis, Elliot, 1893–1967
Harvard University
Mus. ms.: *Port of Pleasure*. Excerpt
Mus. ms. cop. Annot.: *Sonata for Violin and Piano*
Mus. ms.: *Suite for Trio*, Pastorale
Mus. ms.: *Transmutations*
Mus. ms. Repro.: *Playa Laguna*. Facsimile
Mus. ms. Repro. Annot.: *Sonata in G Major*

Pri. Sco.: *Sunlight and Shadow*. With autograph
   Prologue

Grimm, Julius Otto, 1827–1903
Library of Congress
(Box 21)
2 A. L. S.: to Selmar Bagge. Münster, Easter Sunday,
   1867, 1 Dec. 1867. 7p., German

Grimminger, Adolf, 1827–1909
Library of Congress
(Box 21)
A. L. S.: to Eugen Lindner. Stuttgart, 10 June 1891.
   2p., German

Grisi, Giulia, 1811–1869
Library of Congress
(Box 21, unless noted)
A. L. S.: to Willert Beale. n.p., 20 June 1860. 3p.,
   Italian
A. L. S.: to Madame Graham. n.p., 11 [May 1866]. 4p.,
   Italian
A. L. S.: to Creyke. Morrison's Hotel, 19 Sept. 3p.,
   Italian
A. Alb. l.: London, 8 July 1847. 1p., Italian. Cosigned
   by Marietta Alboni, Giovanni Mario, and Antonio
   Tamburini
A. Doc.: Biographical notes. 4p., English
2 Port. Engr. (Box 111)
2 Port. Phot. (Box 111)
Port. Phot. Repro. (Box 111)
Port. Paint. Repro. (Box 111)

Grofé, Ferde [Ferdinand], 1892–1972
Harvard University
Mus. ms.: *Hudson River Suite*, No. 2, Hendrik Hudson
Call. c.
Port.

Gropius, Walter, 1883–1969
Library of Congress
(Box 117)
T. L. S.: to Hans Dollinger. The Architects
   Collaborative, Cambridge, Massachusetts, 1 Nov.
   1960. 1p., English. Regarding French manifesto

Gross, Robert, 1914–1983
Harvard University
Mus. ms.: [Sketchbook]
Mus. ms.: *Sonatina for Solo Viola*. With additional
facsimile score
L.: to Aurelio de la Vega, 15 Oct. 1974
Mus. ms. Repro.: *Brief Introduction to the Problems of Philosophy*
Mus. ms. Repro.: *String Quartet No. 5*

Grove, Sir George, 1820–1900
Northwestern University
L.: to Lockey. London, 6 May 1856
73 L.: to W. H. Cummings. London, 1866–1898
3 L.: London, 13, 30 Dec. 1882, 29 Oct. 1887
L.: to C. Krebs. London, 29 Mar. 1893
Clip.

Grün, Friederike, 1836–1917
Library of Congress
(Box 21)
4 A. L. S.: to Senff. Berlin, Prague, ?, 1869–1873. 10p.,
German

Grünbaum, Johann Christoff, 1785–1870
Library of Congress
(Box 21)
A. L. S.: to ?. Darmstadt, 20 June 1831. 2p., German
A. L. S.: n.p., n.d. 2p., German. Fragment
See Meyerbeer, Giacomo

Grünbaum [Müller], Therese, 1791–1876
Wiener Stadt- u. Landesbibliothek
Doc.: Aphorisms

Gruenberg, Louis, 1884–1964
Harvard University
L.: to Rudolph Ganz. 30 Oct. 1935

Grünfeld, Alfred, 1852–1924
Wiener Stadt- u. Landesbibliothek
L.: Vienna, 15 Dec. 1879
Call. c. Annot.: to Bruno Eisner. Vienna, 8 Mar. 1897
Mus. Quot.: Budapest, 25 Jan. 1890

Grünfeld, Heinrich, 1855–1931
Wiener Stadt- u. Landesbibliothek
2 L.: to Mary Wurm. Berlin, 4 Apr. 1891, 18 May 1897
L.: to Bruno Eisner. 2 Jan. 1912

Grützmacher, Friedrich, 1832–1903
Library of Congress
(Box 21)
A. L. S.: ?, n.d. 1p., German

Guarnieri, Camargo, 1907–1993
Harvard University
SUMMARY OF PRINCIPAL HOLDINGS:
Mus. ms. cop.: *Quebra o coco, menina*
Mus. ms.: *Sai Aruê*
Mus. ms.: *Tanta coisa a dizer-te*, Paris, 21 Aug. 1942
Mus. ms. cop.: *Tocata for piano*, 1935
Mus. ms.: *Tostão de chuva*
Mus. ms. Repro.: *Concerto No. 2*, 1946
Mus. ms. Repro. Annot.: *Estudo No. 2*, 1949. Blueprint
score

Gudehus, Heinrich, 1845–1909
Library of Congress
(Box 21)
4 A. L. S.: ?, 1886–1889. 7p., German

Gugler, Bernhard
Library of Congress
(Box 21)
3 A. L. S.: [to Selmar Bagge?]. Stuttgart, 1865–1868.
9p., German. With musical illustrations

Guilbert, Yvette, 1865–1944
Library of Congress
(Box 21, unless noted)
A. L. S.: to Lacour. Nîmes, n.d. 4p., French. Outlining
a concert program
Port. Phot. S.: Inscribed to Clarkson le coiffeur. By
Ellis & Walery (Box 111)

Guilmant, Alexandre, 1837–1911
Northwestern University
Mus. ms.: *24. Psaume* by Louis Spohr, transcribed for
  organ by Guilmant
Mus. Alb. l.: Adagio, 5 Sept. 1893
L.: to Fétis. Boulogne sur Mer, 13 Oct. 1869
L.: to Bridge. Meudon, 30 Nov. 1898
Doc.: Contract. Sheffield, 22 Jan. 1875
Clip.
Port. Phot.: Meudon, 18 May 1907

Guinjoán, Juan, b. 1931
Library of Congress
(Box 21)
2 A. L. S.: to Aurelio de la Vega. Barcelona, 9 Jan., 11
  Dec. 1980. 3p., Spanish
A. L. S.: n.p., n.d. 2p.

Guiraud, Ernest, 1837–1892
Library of Congress
(Box 21)
A. L. S.: n.p., n.d. 3p., French

Gumprecht, Otto, 1823–1900
Library of Congress
(Box 21)
3 A. L. S.: to Selmar Bagge. Berlin, 9 Oct. 1861, 22
  Dec. 1865; n.p., n.d. 8p., German

Gunz, Gustav, 1831–1894
Library of Congress
(Box 21)
6 A. L. S.: to Schloss. Hamburg, Hannover, 1865–1873.
  8p., German. With brief typewritten explanation.
  On various musical performances

Gura, Eugen, 1842–1906
Library of Congress
(Box 21)
A. Alb. l. S.: to Johann S. Schmidt. Zwickau, 25 Mar.
  1879. 1p., German
2 A. L. S.: Leipzig, 20 Nov. 1872, 11 Nov. 1874. 2p.,
  German
A. L. S.: Hamburg, 12 Oct. 1877. 3p., German

A. L. S.: to Franz von Holstein. Hamburg, 16 Oct.
  1877. 4p., German
2 A. L. S.: to Eugen Lindner. Munich, 3 Mar. 1895,
  19 Oct. 1901. 4p., German

Gurlitt, Wilibald, 1889–1963
Washington State University
See Rosbaud, Hans

Gutheil, Gustav, 1868–1914
Library of Congress
(Box 21)
A. L. S.: to Eugen Lindner. Strassburg, 28 Oct. 1896.
  8p., German
See Lindner, Eugen

Gutheil-Schoder, Maria, 1874–1935
Library of Congress
(Box 21)
A. L. S.: to Eugen Lindner. n.p., 19 May. 4p., German
See Schoenberg, Arnold

Gyring, Elizabeth, 1909–1970
Washington State University
Summary of Principal Holdings:
Mus. ms.: *Adagio*
Mus. ms.: *Allegro*
Mus. ms.: *Andante*
Mus. ms.: *Andante cantabile*
Mus. ms.: *Beloved Land*, 1941
Mus. ms.: *O Boys! O Boys!*
Mus. ms.: *Capriccio*
Mus. ms.: *Concert Piece*, for clarinet and piano
Mus. ms.: *Concert Piece*, for piano
Mus. ms.: *Concertino*
Mus. ms.: *Concerto*, for oboe and string orchestra
Mus. ms.: *Daffodils*
Mus. ms.: *Divertimento No. 1*
Mus. ms.: *Divertimento No. 2*
Mus. ms.: *Duo No. 2*
Mus. ms.: *The Eagle*
Mus. ms.: *Enoch*
Mus. ms.: *Fable*
Mus. ms.: *Fantasy*, 1959
Mus. ms.: *Fantasy* [Nos. 1–15]

Mus. ms.: *Four Orchestral Pieces*
Mus. ms.: *Fugue in the Old Style*
Mus. ms.: *Fugue* [Nos. 1–16]
Mus. ms.: *Happy Birthday, a joke on a familiar theme*
Mus. ms.: *Heresy for a Classroom*
Mus. ms.: *Hymn*
Mus. ms.: *A Hymn of Gratitude*, 1948
Mus. ms.: *Introduction and Fugue*
Mus. ms.: *Kyrie, Gloria, Sanctus, and Agnus Dei*, 1955
Mus. ms.: *Larghetto*, 1944
Mus. ms.: *Larghetto*
Mus. ms.: *Largo*
Mus. ms.: *Little Serenade*
Mus. ms.: *Little Woodwind Quartet*
Mus. ms.: *My Country: A Symphonic Cantata*
Mus. ms.: *New York*
Mus. ms.: *Nonett*
Mus. ms.: *Oktett*
Mus. ms.: *Prelude and Fugue* [Nos. 1–3]
Mus. ms.: *Prelude*, for organ
Mus. ms.: *Quartett in C-Moll*
Mus. ms.: *Quintett*
Mus. ms.: *The Reign of Violence Is Over*, 1943
Mus. ms.: *Rondo*, 1942
Mus. ms.: *Rondo giocoso*
Mus. ms.: *Scherzo No. 1*. With additional blueprint
  score
Mus. ms.: *Sextett*
Mus. ms.: *Sinfonietta No. 1*, 1948
Mus. ms.: *Sinfonietta No. 2*, 1948
Mus. ms.: *Sonata für Klavier*
Mus. ms.: *Sonata No. 1*, for clarinet and piano
Mus. ms.: *Sonata No. 1*, for organ
Mus. ms.: *Sonata No. 1*, for piano
Mus. ms.: *Sonata No. 2*, for piano
Mus. ms.: *Song from Henry the Eighth*
Mus. ms.: *Suite*, 1942
Mus. ms.: *Symphony*
Mus. ms.: *Symphony No. 2*
Mus. ms.: *Ten Canons for Woodwind Instruments*
Mus. ms.: *Thema con Variazioni*
Mus. ms.: *Theme and Variations*
Mus. ms.: *Trio*
Mus. ms.: *Two Marches*
Mus. ms.: *Two Military Marches*
Mus. ms.: *Two Piano Pieces*
Mus. ms.: *Two Psalms*
Mus. ms.: *Variations and Fugue*
Mus. ms.: *Violinkonzert*

Mus. ms.: *Waltz*
Mus. ms.: *We Take Those Things We Gave Away*
Mus. ms. Repro.: *Night at Sea and Day in Court.*
  Blueprint score
Mus. ms. Repro.: *Canons*. Blueprint score
Mus. ms. Repro.: *Clarinet Solo*, 1952. Blueprint score
Mus. ms. Repro.: *Concerto for Oboe and Strings*, Adagio
  and Rondo. Blueprint score
Mus. ms. Repro.: *Four Orchestral Pieces*. Blueprint score
Mus. ms. Repro.: *Quintett*, 1961. Blueprint score
Mus. ms. Repro.: *Trio Fantasy*, 1954. Blueprint score
Mus. ms. Repro.: *Two Pieces for Orchestra*. Blueprint
  score
S. rec.: *The American Flag*
S. rec.: *In that Blissful Eden*
S. rec.: *Blissful Evening*
S. rec.: *The Coasters; Beloved Land*
S. rec.: *At the Hacienda*
S. rec.: *Woodwind Quartet No. 1*

Gyrowetz [Gyrowez, Gürowetz], Adalbert, 1763–1850
Library of Congress
(Box 21)
A. Mus. ms. S.: *Romanze*. 2p., 31x23cm.

Haas, Joseph, 1879–1960
Bayerische Staatsbibliothek
Mus. ms.: *Nachtwandler*, op. 102, 1950. Includes draft
  in condensed score, piano part, and typescript
L.: to Paul A. Pisk. Munich, 25 Nov. 1925
L.: to Tischer. Munich, 20 Dec. 1926
L.: to Hans Moldenhauer. Munich, 7 Mar. 1958
L.: Munich, 18 Apr. 1959. On verso, portrait
  reproduction, to Hans Moldenhauer

Library of Congress
(Box 22, unless noted)
3 P. cards S.: to Hanna Schwarz. Munich, 1932–1934.
  German. See portrait photograph below
Call. c. Annot. S.: to Hanna Schwarz. German
Port. Phot. Repro.: with accompanying card signed, to
  Hanna Schwarz, 7 Dec. 1932 (Box 112)

Washington State University
See Rosbaud, Hans

Haas, Robert, 1886–1960
Library of Congress
See Mozart, Wolfgang Amadeus

Hába, Alois, 1893–1973
Library of Congress
(Box 22, unless noted)
P. card S.: to Hanna Schwarz. Prague, 27 Sept. 1937.
  German
2 A. L. S.: [to Hans Moldenhauer]. Prague, 21 Dec.
  1959, 5 Nov. 1960. 8p., German. Regarding his
  work; Gershwin, Joachim, others
P. card S.: to Hans Moldenhauer. Baden-Baden, 1 Aug.
  1960. German
T. Doc. A. Annot.: Biography and work list. 6p.
A. Mus. Quot. S.: *XII. Streichquartett im Vierteltonsystem*,
  op. 90, Allegro energico, 30 Sept. 1959. Full score
A. Mus. Quot. S.: *XIII. Streichquartette*, op. 92,
  Andante, 1961. Full score
Mus. ms. Repro. S.: *Duo*, op. 49, 27 Feb. 1937. 15p.
Mus. ms. Repro.: *Ukázky ze skladeb Aloise Háby*
Port. Phot. S.: Prague, 12 Sept. 1960. Showing Hába at
  the quartertone piano (Box 112)
Port. Phot. S.: to Hans Moldenhauer, Prague, 1960
  (Box 112)

Hába, Karel, 1898–1972
Wiener Stadt- u. Landesbibliothek
Mus. ms. Repro.: *Stara Historie*, op. 20, inscribed
  Prague, 5 June 1962. Facsimile of piano-vocal score

Hadley, Patrick, 1899–1973
Northwestern University
2 L.: to Edward Clark. n.p., 4 July 1937; Cambridge,
  5 Dec. 1952

Hänsel, Peter, 1770–1831
Library of Congress
(Box 22)
2 A. L. S.: to Johann André. Vienna, 31 Dec. 1798,
  21 Aug. 1799. 2p., German

Härtel, Gottfried Christoph, 1763–1827
Library of Congress
(Box 22)

A. L. S.: to Wilhelm Speyer. Cotta, 16 July 1822. 2p.,
  German
See Koch, Heinrich Christoph

Härtel, Hermann, 1803–1875
Library of Congress
(Box 22)
5 L. S.: to A. W. Gottschalg. Leipzig, 1857–1862. 12p.,
  German. Copious references to Liszt
2 L. S.: to Selmar Bagge, for Breitkopf & Härtel.
  Leipzig, 18, 30 June 1863. 4p., German
A. L. S.: to Selmar Bagge, for Breitkopf & Härtel. n.p.,
  n.d. 1p., German

Hahn, Reynaldo, 1875–1947
Library of Congress
(Box 22, unless noted)
A. Mus. ms. Rev. S.: *Lydé*. 4p., 35x27cm., French, ink,
  pencil revisions. Complete score
2 A. L. S.: n.p., n.d. 4p., French. See musical quotation
  below
A. Mus. Quot. S.: *L'Heure exquise*. With accompanying
  autograph letter signed, and portrait photograph
  (Box 112)
Port. Phot. Repro.: with newspaper clipping. French
  (Box 112)
Port. Phot.: see musical quotation above (Box 112)

Haieff, Alexei, 1914–1994
Harvard University
Mus. ms.: [Six complete melodies to be set by
  Frederic Tausend], New York City, 1955

Haigh, Thomas, 1769–1808[?]
Northwestern University
Mus. ms. Repro.: *Three Sonatas for the Pianoforte*

Haizinger [Haitzinger], Anton, 1796–1869
Library of Congress
(Box 22)

A. L. S.: to Chelard. Karlsruhe, 13 Mar. 1833. 2p.,
German. Arrangements for a concert tour

A. L. S.: to a theater director. Karlsruhe, 28 Feb. 1828.
1p., German

Halévy, Fromental [Fromentin], 1799–1862
Library of Congress
(Box 22, unless noted)
A. L. S.: to Heinrich Panofka. n.p., 7 Jan. 1847. 1p.,
French
A. L. S.: to Guyoz[?]. Paris, n.d. 1p., French
A. L. S.: to a conductor. n.p., n.d. 1p., French
A. L. S.: [to a poet, Goethe?]. n.p., n.d. 1p., French
A. L. S.: n.p., n.d. 1p., French
Obit.: 1p., German
Port. Lith.: with biographical sketch (Box 112)
Port. Lith. S.: by Grégoire et Deneux (Box 112)
See Scribe, Eugène

Halffter, Cristobal, b. 1930
Library of Congress
(Box 109)
A. Mus. ms. S.: *Fibonaciana*, 1960. 1p., 49x32cm.
Sketches in full score
A. Mus. ms. S.: *Secuencias*, 1964. 2p., 49x34cm.
Sketches in full score
A. Mus. ms. S.: *Sinfonía para tres grupos instrumentales*,
1962. 4p. (pp.19, 20, 23, 24), 52x31cm.
A. Mus. ms. S.: *Symposion*, 1965. 2p., 49x34cm.
T. L. S.: to Aurelio de la Vega. Madrid, 8 July 1976.
1p., Spanish
A. Card S.: to Aurelio de la Vega. Madrid, 11 Apr.
1977. 2p., Spanish

Halffter, Rodolfo, 1900–1987
Harvard University
SUMMARY OF PRINCIPAL HOLDINGS:
Mus. ms.: *Tres piezas*, op. 23
3 L.: to Aurelio de la Vega. Mexico, 11 Nov. 1976,
1 July 1977, 11 Aug. 1983
L.: to Hans Moldenhauer. 15 Feb. 1977
Port. Phot.: Feb. 1977

Halíř, Karel [Halir, Karl], 1859–1909
Library of Congress
(Box 22)
P. card S.: to Eugen Lindner. Berlin, 25 Aug. 1894.
German. With drawings
3 A. L. S.: to Eugen Lindner. Berlin, 23 Mar. 1897,
3 July; Charlottenburg, 16 Sept. 1901. 10p., German.
On many musical matters
A. L. S.: to Eugen Lindner, from Anna Helene Halir.
Weimar, 16 Feb. 1905. 3p., German. Mentions Liszt

Hallé, Sir Charles, 1819–1895
Northwestern University
L.: to Lockey. Manchester, 30 Oct. 1856
L.: to W. Finlayson. Edinburgh, 15 Feb. 1880
L.: n.p., 12 July 1893
Clip.
2 Port.

Hallock, Peter R., b. 1924
Washington State University
Mus. ms.: *Ye Choirs of New Jerusalem*, op. 32
2 L.: to Hans Moldenhauer. Seattle, 8 May, 22 Aug.
1960

Hamilton, Iain, b. 1922
Northwestern University
Mus. ms.: *Sinfonia for Two Orchestras*, 1959
L.: to Edward Clark. London, 7 Nov. 1960
L.

Hammerich, Angul, 1848–1931
Library of Congress
See Grieg, Edvard

Handel, George Frideric, 1685–1759
Library of Congress
(Box 95, unless noted)
A. L. S.: [to Charles Jennens]. London, 30 Sept. 1749.
3p., English. Giving specifications for an organ to be
newly built by Mr. Bridge

Mus. ms. Repro.: *The Choice of Hercules.* 3p. Facsimile. Was mistakenly listed in Albrecht's *A Census...* as an original manuscript

Mus. ms. Repro.: *Messiah.* 1p. Facsimile of the last page, with accompanying typed document describing the facsimile, and lithograph from the *Musical Gem*, London, edited by N. Mori and W. Ball, 1831

Port. Engr. (Box 112)

Hanfstängel [née Schröder], Marie, 1846–1917
Library of Congress
(Box 22)
A. L. S.: to Claar. Frankfurt, 30 Sept. 1882. 3p., German
A. L. S.: Frankfurt, 24 Nov. 1886. 4p., German

Hansen, Jens Wilhelm, 1821–1904
Library of Congress
See Grieg, Edvard

Hanslick, Eduard, 1825–1904
Library of Congress
(Box 22)
A. L. S.: to Dessauer. Vienna, 2 Jan. 1865. 2p., German. Regarding Glinka
3 A. L. S.: to Bruckmann, a publisher. Marienbad, 13 Aug. 1871; Vienna, 7 Jan. 1878; Marienbad, 16 Mar. 1880. 7p., German
A. L. S.: to Gabriele Joel. Vienna, 1 Sept. 1p., German

Wiener Stadt- u. Landesbibliothek
2 L.: to a publisher. Marienbad, 13 July 1872; Vienna, 16 July 1873

Hanson, Howard, 1896–1981
Harvard University
SUMMARY OF PRINCIPAL HOLDINGS:
Mus. Quot.: *Symphony No. 2* ("Romantic")
Mus. Quot.: *Symphony No. 3*
L.: to Adolph Weiss. Rochester, 31 Oct. 1933

8 L.: to Solomon Pimsleur. Rochester, 1933–1943
L.: to Charles Haubiel. Rochester, 2 Nov. 1959
2 Port. Phot.

Hanssens, Charles-Louis, 1802–1871
Library of Congress
(Box 22)
A. L. S.: to Jules Dugniole. Gand, 6 Oct. 1843. 1p., French

Harriers [née Wippern], Luise, 1830–1878
Library of Congress
(Box 22)
A. L. S.: Berlin, 4 Jan. 1858. 1p., German
A. L. S.: to Schloss. Dresden, 2 June 1862. 1p., German
A. L. S.: to Baron Reven. Mannheim, 6 Sept. 1873. 2p., German

Harriet Mary, Sister S.N.J.M., b 1916
Washington State University
SUMMARY OF PRINCIPAL HOLDINGS:
Mus. ms.: *Trois mélodies dans la nuit.* Complete score. Also worksheets to *Insomnia II*

Harris, Johana, 1912–1995
Harvard University
L.: to Aurelio de la Vega. Los Angeles, California, 15 May 1984

Harris, Roy, 1898–1979
Harvard University
SUMMARY OF PRINCIPAL HOLDINGS:
Mus. ms.: *Blow the Man Down.* Excerpts. Full score and reduced score
Mus. ms.: *Theme Music for N.Y.A.* [National Youth Administration]
Mus. ms.: *Third Symphony*, Oct. 1939. Excerpt
L.: to Rudolph Ganz. Colorado Springs, 30 Aug. 1945, 3 Dec. 1945
L.: to Paul Pisk. Season's Greetings, n.d.
2 Port.: 1939,1955
See Koussevitzky, Serge

Harrison, William, 1813–1868
Northwestern University
L.

Harsányi, Tibor, 1898–1954
Northwestern University
Mus. ms.: *Nonette*, Paris, Mar.–July 1927

Hart, Joseph Binns, 1794–1844
Northwestern University
L.: Hastings, 3 Dec. 1843

Hartmann, Karl Amadeus, 1905–1963
Bayerische Staatsbibliothek
SUMMARY OF PRINCIPAL HOLDINGS:
Mus. ms.: *Anno 48-Friede*, 1936. Includes libretto,
  corrections, and other documents
Mus. ms.: *Gesangsszene*, to Hans Moldenhauer.
  Sketches and complete draft
Mus. ms.: [Sketches]: *Concerto funebre, Konzert für
  Bratsche und Klavier, Simplicius Simplicissimus,*
  [Symphonies, including Nos. 1, 5, 6, 7], *Symphonische
  Ouverture,* and many more unidentified sketches
Mus. ms.: *Streichquartett,* "Carillon," 1934. Full score,
  with accompanying newspaper clippings
Mus. ms.: *Suite for Violin Solo.* Unpublished
See Stravinsky, Igor

Library of Congress
(Box 105, unless noted)
A. Mus. ms. Annot. S.: *Miserae,* Symphonische
  Dichtung für Orchester, 1933–1934, also dated at
  end Aug. 1934. 59p., 41x32cm., ink, colored pencils.
  Annotations by Scherchen. Full score. Bound
  (Shelf)
16 T. L. S.: to Hans Moldenhauer. Munich,
  1958–1963. 19p., German
12 A. L. S.: to Hans Moldenhauer. Munich,
  1959–1963. 15p. German
T. L.: to Paul Dessau. 14 July 1961
3 A. Cards S.: to Hans Moldenhauer. 1961–1963. 7p.,
  German

Tlgm.: to Hans Moldenhauer. 24 Dec. 1962. German
T. L.: to Friedrich Wildgans. 9 Jan. 1963. 2p., German
T. L.: to Amalie Waller. Dessau, 2 Feb. 1963
2 P. cards S.: to Hans Moldenhauer. German
2 L. S.: to Hans Moldenhauer, from Elisabeth
  Hartmann. Munich, 1962. 4p., German
L. S.: to Hartmann, from Amalie Waller Webern.
  8 Mar. 1963
Call. c. S.: to Hans Moldenhauer
2 Doc.: Biographical outline. 2p. each, German
Pri. Sco. S.: *Miserae,* Mainz: Schott's, c1977. 85p.
Pri. Sco. S.: *Simplicius Simplicissimus,* Mainz: Schott's,
  c1957, to Hans Moldenhauer, 10 Oct. 1962. 378p.
  (Shelf)
Bk.: *Epitaph,* Richard P. Hartmann Bibliothek, Band 1,
  5 Dec. 1963. No. 232 (Shelf)
Obit.: Death announcement. 5 Dec. 1963. German
S. rec.: *Jüdische Chronik.* Also composed by Boris
  Blacher, Paul Dessau, and Hans Werner Henze
  (Shelf)
See Stuckenschmidt, Hans Heinz

Washington State University
See Rosbaud, Hans

Harty, Sir Hamilton, 1879–1941
Northwestern University
L.: to Helen Fraser. St. John's Wood, 6 July 1919
L.: to an editor. London, 24 July 1920. With musical
  quotation, from *Sea Wrack*
2 L.: from Agnes (wife). Home Park, 10, 19 Oct. 1917

Haskil, Clara, 1895–1960
Washington State University
See Rosbaud, Hans

Haslinger, Tobias, 1787–1842
Library of Congress
(Box 22)
A. L. S.: to a composer. Vienna, 12 Dec. 1830. 1p.,
  French

Northwestern University
Doc.: Contract. Regarding publishing rights to works
  by Hummel

Hatton, John Liptrot, 1808–1886
Northwestern University
L.: to his family. Vienna, 24 Dec. 1843
L.: to Giovanni Mario. London, 10 Oct. 1859
L.: to Lockey. Margate, 30 Aug.

Hatze, Josip, 1879–1959
Library of Congress
(Box 22)
A. Mus. ms. S.: "Cvati, cvati ružice...". 3p., 32x24cm., Croatian
A. Mus. ms. S.: *Noć na Uni*, 1902. 7p., 35x25cm.
A. Mus. ms. S.: *"Večernje zvono (Impresija)."* 6p., 32x23cm.
T. Doc. A. Annot.: Biographical data. 1p., Italian
Doc.: Brochure on Hatze. "Josip Hatze, O Pedesetgodivsnjici umjetnickog I Nacijonalnog rada...." 1948. 45p., Croatian
Pri. Sco.: *Uvelo lišće, Sjećanje, Handžaru, Ala j'lep, Jutrom*
Pri. Sco.: *Skladbe, Ljuven sanak.* 7p.

Haubenstock-Ramati, Roman, 1919–1994
Washington State University
SUMMARY OF PRINCIPAL HOLDINGS:
Mus. ms. Repro. Annot.: *Credentials.* Blueprint score. With conductorial markings of Hans Rosbaud
See Rosbaud, Hans

Haubiel [Pratt], Charles Trowbridge, 1892–1978
Library of Congress
See Grainger, Percy

Washington State University
The materials encompass 104 music manuscripts and 174 documents, including blueprint scores with autograph annotations, a bronze bust, clippings, correspondence (1924–1960), lectures, printed scores, programs, reference materials, sound recordings, student compositions, and additional items from the Composers Press
SUMMARY OF PRINCIPAL HOLDINGS:
Mus. ms.: *1865 A.D., Symphonic Saga*
Mus. ms.: *From Ancient Greece*, 1944. Excerpts
Mus. ms.: *Brigands Preferred*, "Love Song"
Mus. ms.: [Canons for Women's Voices]
Mus. ms.: *The Cosmic Christ*

Mus. ms.: *Cryptics*
Mus. ms.: *Ecchi classici*
Mus. ms.: *Elegy for Piano*
Mus. ms.: *Flight into Egypt*
Mus. ms.: *Gothic Variations for Violin and Orchestra*
Mus. ms.: *Heroic Elegy for Symphony Orchestra*
Mus. ms.: *Of Human Destiny*
Mus. ms.: *Miniatures*
Mus. ms.: *Mississippi Story for Symphony Orchestra*
Mus. ms.: *Pastoral Trio for Flute, Cello, and Piano or Harp*
Mus. ms.: *Portals*
Mus. ms.: *Portraits*
Mus. ms.: *Preludes for Harp*
Mus. ms.: *Requiescat for Women's Chorus with String Quartet and String Orchestra*
Mus. ms.: *Scherzo for Piano Solo*
Mus. ms.: *Solari*, 1933–1936
Mus. ms.: *Songs: For Christmas, Consecration*
Mus. ms.: *Suite for Flute and Cello*
Mus. ms.: *Suite for Bassoon Quartet*
Mus. ms.: *Suite in C Minor*
Mus. ms.: *Suite Passacaille*
Mus. ms.: *Suwanee River Variations*
Mus. ms.: *Symphony No. 1 in the Form of Variations*, 1937
Mus. ms.: *Trio in D minor*
Mus. ms.: *Vision of Saint Joan*
Mus. ms.: *Vox Cathedralis*
Mus. ms.: *What Wondrous Sacrifice Is This*
Doc.: Lectures. Topics include the following: Carl Philipp Emanuel Bach, Johann Christoph Friedrich Bach, Bach Chamber Music and Orchestral Works, Bach Clavier Works, Bach—Choral Works, Bach—Organ Works, Wilhelm Friedemann Bach, Balakirev, Bellini, Berlioz, Bizet, Borodin, Brahms, Mendelssohn, Meyerbeer, Mussorgsky, Mozart—Orchestra, Mozart Piano Pieces, Mozart Vocal Works, Paganini, Palestrina, Pergolesi, Pergolesi—Haydn—Mozart, Peri, Pugnani, Rameau, Rimsky-Korsakov, Rossini, Anton Rubinstein, Saint-Saëns, Domenico Scarlatti, Schubert—Chamber Music, Schubert—Orchestral Works, Schubert—Piano Music, Schubert—Songs
Mus. ms. Repro.: *Duoforms*
Mus. ms. Repro.: *Father Abraham.* Blueprint score
Mus. ms. Repro.: *Five Etudes for Two Harps*
Mus. ms. Repro.: *Gay Dances.* Negative photostat
Mus. ms. Repro.: *Pioneers, A Symphonic Saga of Ohio*, 1946. Blueprint score

Mus. ms. Repro.: *In Praise of Dance*. Blueprint score
Mus. ms. Repro.: *Sea Wind*. Facsimile
Mus. ms. Repro.: *Sonata in E Minor for Oboe and Piano*. Blueprint score
Mus. ms. Repro.: *Suite for Flute and Cello*. Blueprint parts
Mus. ms. Repro.: *Sunday Costs Five Pesos*. Blueprint score
Mus. ms. Repro.: *A Threnody for Love*. Blueprint score
Mus. ms. Repro.: *You 48 States*. Blueprint score
Port.

Hauer, Josef Matthias, 1883–1959
Library of Congress
(Box 22)
A. Mus. ms. S.: [Trope, in four colors], Vienna, 3 May 1949. 1p., 35x27cm. With the following inscription, as translated: "Josef Matthias Hauer, the intellectual originator and, despite many poor imitators, regrettably still the sole expert and craftsman of twelve-tone music."
A. Mus. ms. S.: *Melischer Entwurf in der Zwölftonschrift*, to Hans Rosbaud, 4 Jan. 1954. 1p., 34x27cm., ink, pencil, in 4 colors
A. Mus. ms. S.: [same], 29 Jan. 1955. 1p., 34x27cm., ink, pencil, in 4 colors
A. Mus. ms. S.: *Zwölftonspiel für Orchester*, Mar. 1955. 36p., 34x27cm. Full score
A. Mus. ms. S.: *Zwölftonspiel für Streichquartett*, to Hans Rosbaud, Vienna, 12 Jan. 1954. 11p., 34x27cm. Full score
A. L. S.: to Rudolph Réti. Vienna, 5 Feb. 1924. 4p., German. Discussion of Hauer's system of "tropes," illustrated with four musical examples
A. L. S.: [to Paul A. Pisk]. Vienna, 11 Jan. 1935. 1p., German. Comments about Berg
A. L. S.: to Hans Rosbaud. Vienna, 31 Dec. 1953. 1p., German
T. Doc.: Critical comparison of twelve-tone system. *Josef Matthias Hauer und Arnold Schoenberg*, to Hans Moldenhauer, from Victor Sokolowski, Mar. 1981. 1p., German

L. Repro.: to Hauer, from Rosbaud. 5 Apr. 1954. 1p., German
Doc.: Brochure. Josef Matthias Hauer. 18p., German
Doc.: Text. *Tropentafel von Josef Matthias Hauer*, 1948. 2p. On verso, a facsimile quotation from Hauer's credo (1947), with autograph dedication to Hans Moldenhauer, from Victor Sokolowski
Doc.: Commentary. *Das Zwölftonspiel*, by Hauer. 2p., German
Obit.: Vienna, 22 Sept. 1959. 1p., German

Hauk, Minnie [Hauck, Amalia Mignon], 1851–1929
Northwestern University
35 L.: to Bartolf Senff. 1875–1891
L.: to ?. Baden-Baden, 24 July
3 Call. c.

Haupt, Karl August, 1810–1891
Library of Congress
(Box 22)
A. L. S.: Berlin, 26 Aug. 1856. 1p., German

Hauptmann, Moritz, 1792–1868
Library of Congress
(Box 22)
A. Mus. ms. S.: *Album-Canons*, 3 Apr. 1865, to S. Jadassohn, from Suzette Hauptmann, signed and dated at Leipzig, Apr. 1868. 12p., 26x33cm. Bound
A. Mus. ms. S.: *Sonata*, to Julius Rietz, 6 Aug. 1835. 25p., 24x33cm. Bound
A. L. S.: to A. Bott. Leipzig, 29 Oct. 1843. 2p., German
A. L. S.: to a concertmaster. Leipzig, 20 Dec. 1863. 4p., German

Hausegger, Siegmund von, 1872–1948
Bayerische Staatsbibliothek
L.: to Karl Weigl. Munich, 13 June 1928

Hauser, Franz, 1794–1870
Wiener Stadt- u. Landesbibliothek
2 L.: to Selmar Bagge. Munich, 1 Oct. 1856; Freiburg i. Br., 22 Mar. 1868

Hausmann, Robert, 1852–1909
Library of Congress
(Box 23)
P. card S.: to Louis Lüstner. Berlin, 6 Jan. 1890.
    German

Hawes, Maria, 1816–1886
Northwestern University
L.: to Lockey. n.p., 23 May 1846

Haydn, Michael, 1737–1806
Library of Congress
(Box 23, unless noted)
A. Mus. ms. S.: *Canone à 8*, Vienna, 16 Oct. 1798. 1p.,
    19x12cm., Latin
Mus. ms. cop.: *Graduale*, for Soprano, Alto, Violin, and
    Organ, Allegretto. 3p., 30x23cm. Full score
Mus. ms. cop.: *Missa in G Dur*. 156p., 30x23cm. Full
    score (Shelf)

Hayes, Catherine, 1825–1861
Northwestern University
L.: to Lockey

Hayes, Roland, 1887–1976
Harvard University
L.: to Boaz Piller. 30 Jan. 1929
Port. Phot.: inscribed 11 Nov. 1928

Headley, Hubert Klyne, b. 1906
Harvard University
SUMMARY OF PRINCIPAL HOLDINGS:
Mus. ms.: *Piano Quintet*, 1957
Mus. ms.: *Prelude to Man*, 1950
Mus. ms.: *Sonata ibérica*, 1954
Port. Phot.

Hegar, Friedrich, 1841–1927
Zentralbibliothek Zürich
2 L.: Zürich, 21 Oct. 1903, 31 May 1907
L.: to F. Georg Hübscher. Zürich, 29 May 1917

Heger, Robert, 1886–1978
Washington State University
See Rosbaud, Hans

Heiden, Bernhard, b. 1910
Harvard University
SUMMARY OF PRINCIPAL HOLDINGS:
Mus. ms.: *The Darkened City*
Mus. ms.: *Memorial*, 1955
Mus. ms.: *Trio*, 1956

Heifetz, Jascha, 1901–1987
Harvard University
L.: to Boaz Piller. Beverly Hills, 22 July 1944

Library of Congress
See Castelnuovo-Tedesco, Mario

Heinefetter, Sabine, 1809–1872
Library of Congress
(Box 23)
3 A. L. S.: Leipzig, Munich, 1830–1845. 6p., German

Heinrich, Anthony Philip [Anton Philipp],
1781–1861
Harvard University
L.: n.p., Saturday, n.d.

Heinsheimer, Hans, 1900–1993
Harvard University
L.: to Norbert Schwarzmann. Vienna, 31 Mar. 1925

Heiss, Hermann, 1897–1966
Library of Congress
(Box 105, unless noted)
A. Mus. ms. S.: *Calamites, Schachtelgesänge*, for soprano,
    tenor, and small orchestra, Aug. 1962. 2p., 34x27cm.
    Multicolored sketches
A. Mus. ms.: *Zuordnung Vier*. 3p., includes two
    diagrams + 1p. analysis
3 T. L. S.: to Hans Moldenhauer. Darmstadt, 27 Jan.
    1960, 17 May, 11 Mar. 1963. 4p., German

T. Doc. S.: Conceptual idea for *Zuordnung Vier*. Darmstadt, Nov. 1961. German

T. Doc. S.: Graph of time conception. *Composition for Three Pianos*. With description. 2p., German

T. Doc. S.: Idea for a composition. 1p., German. With autograph note

2 Docs.: Work list. Wiesbaden: Breitkopf & Härtel, 29 Dec. 1897. 6p., German

Mus. ms. Repro.: *Conception for Three Pianos*. Photographic reproduction

Mus. ms. Repro.: *Configurationen I*, Mainz: Schotts, n.d. 78p. (Shelf)

Mus. ms. Repro.: *Zuordnung Drei*, for light, dance, and electronic music. Photographic reproduction

See Xenakis, Iannis

Heller, Stephen [István], 1813–1888
Library of Congress
(Box 23, unless noted)

A. Mus. ms. S.: *Trois Eglogues*, op. 92, to E. L. Corning, Paris, 23 Apr. 1881. 23p., 26x34cm. Also inscribed to Felix le Couppey

A. L. S.: to Georges Kastner. 18 Nov. 1842. 1p., French

A. L. S.: Paris, 27 June 1857. 3p., French

Port. Lith. Repro. (Box 112)

Hellmesberger, Georg, Jr., 1830–1852
Wiener Stadt- u. Landesbibliothek
L.: to a poet. Vienna, n.d.

Hellmesberger, Joseph [Pepi], Jr., 1855–1907
Wiener Stadt- u. Landesbibliothek
L.: n.p., n.d.

Hellmesberger, Joseph [Sr.], 1828–1893
Wiener Stadt- u. Landesbibliothek
L.: to Richard Heuberger. n.p., Wednesday, 1877

L.: to an official at Klosterneuburg. Vienna, 7 Sept. 1882

Hempel, Frieda, 1885–1955
Library of Congress
(Box 23)

A. L. S.: to an editor. Berlin, 23 Oct. 1912. 2p., German

Henkemans, Hans, 1913–1995
Library of Congress
(Box 23)

A. Mus. ms. S.: *Cello Sonate*, 30 Mar. 1936. 15p., 34x27cm. Complete draft

A. Mus. ms. S.: *Vioolconcert*, 1948, 1950. 49p., 35x27cm. Complete draft

Henschel, Sir George [Georg], 1850–1934
Northwestern University
Mus. ms.: *There Were Shepherds*, op. 66

Mus. Quot.: *Morning Hymn*, Nov. 1905

Mus. Quot.: *Polonaise in G Major*, 28 Aug. 1879

Port. Phot.: inscribed 10/11 Oct. 1930

Henselt [Hänselt], Adolf [Adolph], 1814–1889
Library of Congress
(Box 23)

A. Mus. ms. S.: *Normanns Gesäng*. 2p., 26x33cm.

A. Mus. ms. S.: [Piano composition in G Major], to Hauser. 4p., 24x32cm.

A. Mus. ms. S.: [Piano composition in B Major]. 2p., 17x24cm.

A. L. S.: n.p., 1882. 4p., German. Mentions Chopin, Hummel

Henze, Hans Werner, b. 1926
Bayerische Staatsbibliothek
See Hartmann, Karl Amadeus

Library of Congress
(Box 23)

A. Mus. ms. S.: *Sinfonische Etüden*, for orchestra, 1955, to Hans Moldenhauer, Naples, 16 Mar. 1958. 36p., 34x23cm., pencil, colored pencils. Sketches

T. L. S.: to Hans Moldenhauer. Naples, 16 Mar. 1958. 1p., German

See Hartmann, Karl Amadeus

Washington State University
See Rosbaud, Hans

Herbeck, Johann Ritter von, 1831–1877
Library of Congress
(Box 23)

A. L. S.: [to Selmar Bagge]. Vienna, 15 Apr. 1862. 2p., German

A. L. S.: to a conductor. Vienna, 18 June 1870. 2p., German

Herbert, Victor, 1859–1924
Harvard University
Mus. ms.: *Faust, Fantasie* by Gounod, parts orchestrated by Herbert
L.: to Lux
Port. Phot.: inscribed Oct. 1887

Herbst, Gottfried, 1877–1944
Whitworth College
SUMMARY OF PRINCIPAL HOLDINGS:
Doc.: Collection of personal and professional documents relating to his career and that his wife, Ina Wright Herbst

Herfurth, Rudolf
Library of Congress
(Box 23)
A. L. S.: Rudolstadt, 10 June 1894. 4p., German

Herlinger [née Schwartz], Ružena, 1890–1978
Library of Congress
(Box 23, unless noted)
22 A. L. S.: to Hans and Rosaleen Moldenhauer. 1962–1965. 47p., German, English. Mentions Berg, Webern
P. card S.: to Hans and Rosaleen Moldenhauer. Indian Rocks Beach, Florida, 28 Aug. 1964. English
2 Tlgms.: to Hans and Rosaleen Moldenhauer. 12, 13 Sept. 1964. 3p., English
T. L. S.: to Hans and Rosaleen Moldenhauer. Montreal, 15 Mar. 1965. 1p., English
L. S. Repro.: to a conductor. n.p., 23 Mar. 1964. 1p., French
2 Docs. A. Rev.: Brochure
Doc.: Flyer with program. 1928–1929. 2p., German
Doc.: Invitation. 23 Apr. 1961. 2p., French.
Port. Phot. S.: to Hans Moldenhauer, June 1964. By Hulley (Box 112)

Herman, Vasile, b. 1929
Library of Congress
(Box 23)
Pri. Sco.: *Sonata II-a*, Cluj: Conservatorul de Muzică, c1971. 25p.

Hermann, Hans, 1870–1931
Library of Congress
(Box 23, unless noted)
A. L. S.: Berlin, n.d. 4p., German. With biographical information
Port. Phot. S.: 1910 (Box 112)

Hérold, Ferdinand, 1791–1833
Library of Congress
(Box 23)
A. L. S.: [to Ferdinando Paër]. n.p., n.d. 1p., French

Hertel, Johann Wilhelm, 1727–1789
Library of Congress
(Box 23)
A. Mus. ms. S.: *Der 100. Psalm, in Zwey Choeren auf den Hohen Geburts-Tag des Durchlauchtigsten Herzogs Friedrich zu Meklenburg Schwerin*, Schwerin, 9 Nov. 1780. 33p. 34x40cm., German, ink

Hervé, [Ronger, Florimond], 1825–1892
Library of Congress
(Box 23)
T. p. S.: *Aladdin the Second*, to his daughter Louise, London, 7 Mar. 1871. 1p., French

Herz, Henri [Heinrich], 1803–1888
Library of Congress
(Box 23)
A. L. S.: to Gait. n.p., n.d. 1p., French, with translation. On p.4, note in another hand, with reference to Pacini and Ponchard

Herzog, Johann Georg, 1822–1909
Library of Congress
(Box 23)
A. L. S.: to Selmar Bagge. Erlangen, 12 Oct. 1865. 2p., German

Hess, Dame Myra, 1890–1965
Northwestern University
Port. Phot.: inscribed Boston, 1927

Hesse, Adolf Friedrich, 1809–1863
Library of Congress
(Box 24)
7 A. L. S.: to Aloys Fuchs, Friedrich Kühmstadt, C. F.
   Peters, and others. Breslau, 1832–1861. 19p.,
   German
Doc.: [Receipt?]. To A. Hesse. Breslau. 1p., German
A. Mus. Quot. S.: *Sixth Symphony*, Dresden, 14 Jan.
   1845

Hessen, Alexander Friedrich, Landgraf von,
1863–1945
Washington State University
SUMMARY OF PRINCIPAL HOLDINGS:
Mus. ms.: *Klavierkonzert*, op. 23, 1922. Full score

Hessenberg, Kurt, 1908–1994
Library of Congress
(Box 24)
A. Mus. ms. S.: *Vom Wesen und Vergehen*, op. 45. 20p.,
   23x34cm. Sketches
3 T. L. S.: to Hans Moldenhauer. Frankfurt, Sept.-
   Nov. 1958. 3p., German

Washington State University
See Rosbaud, Hans

Heussenstamm, George, b. 1926
Harvard University
SUMMARY OF PRINCIPAL HOLDINGS:
8 L.: to Charles Haubiel. Pasadena, 1972–1973
2 L.: to Aurelio de la Vega. Pasadena, 19 Apr. 1977;
   La Crescenta, n.d.

Hey, Julius, 1832–1909
Library of Congress
(Box 24)
A. L. S.: to Bartolf Senff. Munich, 23 Sept. 1887. 1p.,
   German
A. L. S.: to Eugen Lindner. Berlin, 5 May 1898, 3p.,
   German

Hibbard, William, 1939–1989
Library of Congress
See Webern, Anton

Hildreth, Daisy Wood, b. 1894
Washington State University
SUMMARY OF PRINCIPAL HOLDINGS:
3 Mus. mss.: *Rest*; *Midnight*; *Carmel*

Hill, Arthur Frederick, 1860–1939
Northwestern University
Doc.: Inquiry. Regarding Dragonetti's stringed
   instruments. London, 12 June 1915

Hill, Edward Burlingame, 1872–1960
Harvard University
Mus. Quot.: Cambridge, 5 Feb. 1938. Mounted with
   portrait photograph
See Koussevitzky, Serge

Hill, Karl, 1831–1893
Library of Congress
(Box 24)
11 A. L. S.: to Bartolf Senff. 1866–1881. 25p., German.
   Letters detail singer's successes; Wagner

Hiller, Ferdinand, 1811–1885
Library of Congress
(Box 24, unless noted)
2 A. L. S.: n.p., n.d. 4p., English, German
A. Doc. S.: Poem. *Bald verlässt du die Ufer*, 29 Nov.
   1869. 1p., German
Port. Phot. Repro. (Box 112)

Hiller, Johann Adam, 1728–1804
Library of Congress
(Box 24)
A. Mus. ms. S.: *Cantata*. 45p., 23x31cm., German. Full
   score

Himmel, Friedrich Heinrich, 1765–1814
Library of Congress
(Box 24)

A. L. S.: to Kühnel. Berlin, 18 Oct. 1809. 1p., German

Pri. Sco.: *Die Sendung*, No. 4, arranged by Westenbolz, Berlin: Stechbahn. 2p.

Hindemith, Gertrud, 1900–1967
Washington State University
See Rosbaud, Hans

Paul Hindemith [signature]

Hindemith, Paul, 1895–1963
Harvard University
See Boatwright, Howard
See Slonimsky, Nicolas

Library of Congress
(Box 24, unless noted)

A. Mus. ms. S.: *Bratschensonate mit Klavier*, Tucson, Hutchinson, 1/2 April 1939, to Boaz Piller, Boston, Apr. 1939. 12p., 17x13cm., pencil. Excerpt (14m. + 65m.) from second and third movements

A. L. S.: to a Geheimrat. Berlin, 1 Mar. 1934. 1p., German

A. Card S.: Season's Greetings, 1946–1947. German. Created by Hindemith

A. Card S.: Season's Greetings, 1950–1951. German. Created by Hindemith, signed by Hindemith and wife Gertrud

2 Cards: Season's Greetings, 1954–1955; n.d. German. Created by Hindemith

A. L. S.: to Boaz Piller. n.p., n.d. 1p., English

T. L. S.: [to Boaz Piller]. Yale Music School, New Haven, Connecticut, 9 Nov. 1p., English

T. Doc. A. Rev. S.: Typescript. *Vorschläge für den Aufbau des türkischen Musiklebens*, 1937. 32p., German. Bound in cardboard

A. Mus. Quot. S.: *Der Schwanendreher*, Boston, Apr. 1937. Three thematic quotations

Doc.: Brochure. Printed by Schott at Hindemith's death. German. With portrait reproduced

Doc.: Memoranda. "Commemoratio brevis," 1948. From Hindemith's classes at Yale. 11p., English. 3 copies

Doc.: Reprint, "Alla Battaglia." For the Paul Hindemith Commemoration, Yale University, 1964, reproduced from the Collegium Concert, Yale University, 21 May 1951. Includes cover with Hindemith's drawing; music. 4p.

Doc. Repro. Rev.: Typescript. "My Teacher, Paul Hindemith," by Silvia Kind, 26 Sept. 1965. 5p. each, English. Two copies. With letter to Hans Moldenhauer, from Kind, 1965

Pri. Sco. S.: *Let's Build a Town*, Mainz: Schott, c1931. 15p., English

Pri. Sco. S.: *Lied*, Mainz: Schott, c1927. 5p.

Pri. Sco. A. Rev.: *Der Schwanendreher*, Mainz: Schott, c1937

Pri. Sco. S.: *Sonate, Flöte und Klavier*, Mainz: Schott, c1937. 27p. (piano score)

Pri. Sco. S.: *String Quartet in E-flat*, 1943, to Eugene Weigel, Nov. 1944. 59p. Pocket score. Also signed by Weigel. With pencil notes

3 Clip.: 5, 10, 12, Jan. 1964. 3p., English

Port. Phot. S.: to Boaz Piller, Boston, 25 Feb. 1938 (Box 112)

Bk. S.: *A Composer's World*, Cambridge, Massachusetts: Harvard University Press, 1952. 221p. (Shelf)

Bk. S.: *Traditional Harmony*, New York: Associated Music Publishers, c1944. 125p. (Shelf)

Paul Sacher Stiftung

A. Mus. ms.: *Hérodiade*, for chamber orchestra, June 1944, to Karl Amadeus Hartmann. 54p. First draft in condensed score, of the work commissioned by the Elizabeth Sprague Coolidge Foundation in the Library of Congress

Washington State University
Port. Phot.
See Rosbaud, Hans

Hinkel, Karl
Library of Congress
(Box 24)
A. Mus. ms. S.: *Rundgesang*. 2p. 20x32cm.

Hirsch, Karl Jacob, 1892–1952
Library of Congress
(Box 24, unless noted)
A. Mus. ms. S.: *Wenn der erste Frühlingsatem über die Erde geht*. 2p., 34x27cm. Incomplete

A. L. S.: Heilbronn, 8 Apr. 1908. 1p., German.
Attached to above
Port. Phot. S. (Box 112)

Hirsch, Paul, 1881–1951
Library of Congress
(Box 24)
T. L. S.: to Aurelio de la Vega. Cambridge, 16 Nov.
1950. 1p., English
A. L. S.: Cambridge, 2 Mar. 1951. 1p., German

Hobbs, John William, 1799–1877
Northwestern University
L.: to Charles Lockey. Bloomsburg, 15 May 1846

Höller, Karl, 1907–1987
Bayerische Staatsbibliothek
Mus. ms.: *Sweelinck-Variationen für Orchester*, op. 56
2 L.: to Hans Moldenhauer. Munich, New York,
27 Apr. 1959, 29 Feb. 1961

Hoffmann, Richard, b. 1925
Washington State University
Mus. ms. Repro.: *Concerto for Piano and Orchestra*, 1954,
to Hans Rosbaud, 1954

Hofmann, Heinrich, 1842–1902
Library of Congress
(Box 24)
A. Doc. S.: Note. Certification that manuscripts are
authentic. Berlin, n.d. 1p., German, with English
translation

Hofmann, Josef [Józef Kazimierz; Dvorsky, Michel], 1876–1957
Harvard University
L.: to Adolph Weiss. Philadelphia, 26 Aug. 1931
L.: to Rudolph Ganz. Hollywood, 7 Apr. 1941
L.: to Harold C. Schonberg. Long Beach, California,
22 Nov. 1955
3 Port. Phot.: 1888, 1938, 1940

Hofmeister, Friedrich, 1782–1864
Library of Congress
(Box 24)
A. L. S.: to Hippolyte Chelard. Leipzig, 2 Nov. 1840.
2p., German

Hokanson, Dorothy Cadzow, b. 1916
Washington State University
Mus. ms.: *Cow Town*, 1945. Excerpt
Mus. ms.: *Prelude*, 1944
2 L.: to Hans Moldenhauer. Seattle, 1958

Holbrooke, Joseph [Josef], 1878–1958
Northwestern University
Mus. ms.: *The Bells*, op. 50. Proof sheets with
corrections
Mus. ms.: *Queen Mab*. Proofs with annotations and
corrections
Bk.: *The Bells*. With notes, corrections

Holde, Artur, 1885–1962
Library of Congress
(Box 24)
T. L.: to Alma Mahler. Connecticut, 13 Nov. 1958. 1p.,
German. Fragment, with annotations on verso
P. card S.: to Alma Mahler. Connecticut, n.d. German

Holenia, Hanns, b. 1890
Washington State University
See Rosbaud, Hans

Hollaender, Alexis, 1840–1924
Library of Congress
(Box 24)
2 A. L. S.: Berlin, 9, 31 Jan. 1889. 2p., German

Hollaender, Gustav, 1855–1915
Library of Congress
(Box 24, unless noted)
A. Mus. Quot. S.: *Violinkonzert*, op. 52
Port. Phot. S.: 1905. By Meyer (Box 112)

Hollaender [Holländer], Victor [Tolveno, Arricha del], 1866–1940
Library of Congress
(Box 24, unless noted)
A. Mus. ms. S.: *Schaukel-Walzer*. 1p., 19x26cm.
A. L. S.: to George Bainton. Bad Ischl, 18 July 1909. 2p., German, English
Port. Phot. S. Repro. (Box 112)

Holle, Ludwig
Library of Congress
(Box 24)
A. L. S.: to A. W. Gottschalg. Wolfenbüttel, 11 July 1858. 1p., German

Holliger, Heinz, b. 1939
Zentralbibliothek Zürich
Mus. ms.: *Elis*. Corrections for No. II
Mus. ms.: *Mobile*. Corrections

Holmès, Augusta, 1847–1903
Library of Congress
(Box 24)
A. L. S.: to a journalist. Paris, 15 Oct. 1901. 1p., French

Holst, Imogen, 1907–1984
Northwestern University
L.: to Oswald Jonas. London, 6 May 1938

Holstein, Franz von, 1826–1878
Northwestern University
Mus. ms.: *Francesca von Rimini*, 16 Feb. 1855. Overture. Full score
Mus. ms.: *Morgenglocken*. Full score
L.: to Bernhard. Leipzig, 3 Sept.
Doc.: List. Performance dates for various operas

Holzmann, Rudolf [Rodolfo], 1910–1992
Harvard University
Mus. ms.: *Divertimento pour Quintett à Vent*, Lima, Peru, 1936
L.: to Aurelio de la Vega. Lima, Peru, 21 Feb. 1966

Honegger, Arthur, 1892–1955
Zentralbibliothek Zürich
Summary of Principal Holdings:
A. Mus. ms.: *Napoléon, extraits de la musique...*, "Les Ombres." Excerpt, 40m. Full score. 8p., 35x27cm., ink
Mus. ms.: *Pacific 231*, Moderé. 1p. (3m.). Full score
5 L.: to Boaz Piller. 1930–1948, n.d.
5 L.: to Boaz Piller, from Vaura Honegger. 1947, n.d.
Port. Phot.: to Boaz Piller, Boston, 1929

Hoogstraten, Willem van, 1884–1965
Library of Congress
(Box 24)
T. L. S.: to Solomon Pimsleur. New York City, 29 July 1938. 1p., English

Jascha

Horenstein, Jascha, 1899–1973
Library of Congress
(Box 24)
T. L. S.: New York, 26 Apr. 1943. 1p., English
P. card S.: to Alma M. Werfel, also signed by Trudy and Jascha. Athens, 30 Aug. 1957. German
2 A. L. S.: to Alma Mahler Werfel. Nice, 21 June 1959; London, n.d. 6p., German
A. L. S.: to Vally Weigl. Lausanne-Pully, 9 June 1971. 1p., English

Horn, Camillo, 1860–1941
Library of Congress
(Box 112)
Port. Phot. S.: to Hans Rosbaud, Vienna, 21 Jan. 1936

Horn, Charles Edward, 1786–1849
Northwestern University
L.: to d'Almain. New York, 22 June 1838
Port.

Horneman, Christian Frederik Emil, 1840–1906
Library of Congress
See Grieg, Edvard

Horowitz, Vladimir, 1904–1989
Harvard University
L.: North Conway, New Hampshire, n.d.
L.: from Wanda Toscanini Horowitz. Jackson, New
Hampshire, n.d.

Horsley, Charles Edward, 1822–1876
Northwestern University
L.: to Lockey. London, 22 Mar. 1849
3 L.: to Costa. London, 26–28 May 1854

Horsley, William, 1774–1858
Northwestern University
L.: to Lockey. London, 9 May 1844

Horszowski, Mieczyslaw, 1892–1993
Harvard University
SUMMARY OF PRINCIPAL HOLDINGS:
L.: to Hans Moldenhauer. Philadelphia, 12 May 1972
Doc.: List. Works by Guarnieri, Copland

Washington State University
See Rosbaud, Hans

Horwitz, Karl, 1884–1925
Library of Congress
See Webern, Anton

Hovhaness [Hovaness], Alan [Chakmakjian, Alan Hovhaness], b. 1911
Harvard University
Mus. ms.: *Concerto No. 2*
Mus. ms.: *Glory to God*, op. 124
L.: New York, 3 Apr. 1959

Hřímalý, Jan, 1844–1915
Library of Congress
See Tchaikovsky, Pyotr Ilyich

Hrisanide, Alexandru, b. 1936
Library of Congress
(Box 25, unless noted)
A. Mus. ms. S.: *Duett für Flöte und Oboe, Chanson sous
les étoiles*. 4p., 28x21cm. Sketches
A. Mus. ms. S.: *First Piano Sonata*, 1955–1956. 57p.,
34x25cm. Complete score
A. Mus. ms. S.: *Sonnets*, 1972–1973. 12 leaves + 43p.,
30x22cm. Preliminary drafts in two spiral notebooks
2 T. L. S.: to Aurelio de la Vega. Los Angeles, 5 Jan.
1973; Oregon, 23 Feb. 1973. 2p., English
T. L. S.: to Hans Moldenhauer. Eugene, 1 June 1973.
2p., German
T. L. S.: to Hans Moldenhauer. New York, 30 July
1973. 3p., German
A. L. S.: to Hans Moldenhauer. Harleem, 28 Dec.
1973. 1p., German
4 T. L. S.: to Hans Moldenhauer. Haarlem, 1974–1978.
4p., English
P. card S.: to Aurelio de la Vega. Greece, 18 July 1976.
English
Card S.: to Aurelio de la Vega. Oregon, Season's
Greetings 1976. 1p., English
Mus. ms. Repro.: *Directions*, Cologne: Gerig, c1971.
32p. (Box 109)
Mus. ms. Repro.: *I-Ro-La-Hai für Orchester*, Cologne:
Gerig, c1972. 26p. (Box 109)
Mus. ms. Repro.: *Mers-tefs per violino solo*, Cologne:
Gerig, c1971. 6p. Blueprint score (Box 109)
Mus. ms. Repro.: *Musik für mehrere Violinen*, Cologne:
Gerig, c1973. 21p. Blueprint score (Box 109)
Mus. ms. Repro.: *"À la recherche de la verticale,"*
Cologne: Gerig, c1970. 12p. With accompanying
biographical information
Mus. ms. Repro.: *Soliloquium x II, Streichquartett*.
Cologne: Gerig, c1971. 16p. Blueprint score (Box
109)
Mus. ms. Repro.: *Sonata for Clarinet and Piano*,
Bucharest: Editura Muzicală, c1969. 24p.
Mus. ms. Repro.: *Sonata for Viola and Piano*, c1965 by
Hrisanide. 12p.
Mus. ms. Repro.: *Sonata for Violin and Piano*,
Bucharest: c1968 by Hrisanide. 36p.
Mus. ms. Repro.: *Sonata Nr. 1*, Bucharest: Editura
Muzicală, c1966. 49p.

2 Mus. mss. Repro.: *Sonnets, Concerto per Clavicembalo e orchestra*, Cologne: Gerig, c1973. 10p., 31p. Blueprint score (Box 109)

Mus. ms. Repro.: *Third Piano Sonata*, Bucharest: c1968 by Hrisanide. 16p.

Mus. ms. Repro.: *Trio for Violin, Viola, and Bassoon*, c1968 by Hrisanide, to Hans Moldenhauer, Eugene, Oregon, 1 June 1973. 14p.

Mus. ms. Repro.: *UNDA*, Paris: Salabert, c1969. 10p.

Mus. ms. Repro.: *Volumes, Inventions*, Bucharest: Editura Muzicala, 1963. 14p. With biographical information

Doc. Repro. Annot.: Biographical information. Includes curriculum vitae, articles, letters of recommendation, work list

Hubay, Jenő, 1858–1937
Library of Congress
(Box 26, unless noted)
A. L. S.: to Hugo Neuburger. Zurich, 15 Oct. 1919. 3p., German
Port. Phot. S.: to Heinrich Grünfeld, Berlin, 29 Jan. 1903 (Box 112)

Huber, Hans, 1852–1921
Zentralbibliothek Zürich
L.: to Selmar Bagge. Wesserling, 1 Feb. 1877

Huber, Klaus, b. 1924
Washington State University
See Rosbaud, Hans

Huberman, Bronislaw, 1882–1947
Library of Congress
(Box 26, unless noted)
T. L. S.: to Karl Weigl. Ascona, 20 Oct. 1927. 1p., German
A. L. S.: Jerusalem, n.d. 1p., German
Port. Gr. S. Repro.: Tel-Aviv, 20[?] Dec. 1938[?]. Photograph and facsimile signatures of Huberman and Toscanini and the Palestine Orchestra on the occasion of the orchestra's first concert (Box 112)

Hübner, Herbert, b. 1903
Washington State University
See Rosbaud, Hans

Hüttenbrenner, Anselm, 1794–1868
Northwestern University
Mus. ms.: *Festcantate*, Graz, 29 Jan. 1851

Hüttenbrenner, Josef, 1797–1882
Library of Congress
(Box 26)
A. L. S.: Vienna, 7 Oct. 1869. 1p., German

Hughes, Edwin, 1884–1965
Harvard University
L.: to Solomon Pimsleur. New York, 23 Mar. 1959

Huhn, Charlotte, 1865–1925
Library of Congress
(Box 26)
2 A. L. S.: to Bartolf Senff. Westerland auf Sylt, 6 Aug. 1893; Lüneburg, 22 Aug. 1893. 7p., German
Rcpt.: Cologne, 8 Dec. 1898. 1p., German
Clip. Annot.: *Neue Musik-Zeitung*, XIV, 1893. 2p. (p.185–186), German. With photograph reproduced

Hullah, John, 1812–1884
Northwestern University
L.: to the University of Edinburgh. Westminster, 7 Mar. 1876
Sig.

Hummel, Johann Nepomuk, 1778–1837
Northwestern University
Mus. ms.: *Nah und fern im treuen Bunde...*
L.: Weimar, 1 June 1826
L.: to an editor. Weimar, 22 June 1826
L.: to Tobias Haslinger. Weimar, 21 Dec. 1834
2 Ports.
See Haslinger, Tobias

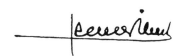

Humperdinck, Engelbert, 1854–1921
Library of Congress
(Box 26, unless noted)
A. Mus. ms. S.: *Rosmarin*, for voice and piano,
  Grünenwald, 1 Mar. 1908[?]. 2p., 27x34cm.,
  German, ink. Complete score
2 P. cards S.: to Edward Speyer. Frankfurt, 2 May
  1892; Strassburg, 10 Nov. 1894. German
A. L. S.: 2 July 1897. 2p., German
A. L. S.: 24 May 1907. 1p., German
P. card S.: to Kirchhoff. Berlin, 25 June 1907. German
P. card S.: to Mary Wurm. Berlin-Wannsee, 25 Oct.
  1915. German
A. Mus. Quot. S.: *Gaudeamus*, "Hoch der Jugend! Tod
  den Philistern!", Berlin-Wannesee, 24 Jan. 1919
Port. Phot. (Box 112)

Huré, Jean, 1877–1930
Library of Congress
(Box 26)
A. Mus. ms. S.: *Le petit Cordonnier*. 7p., 32x25cm.,
  French
2 A. L. S.: Paris, 17 Oct., 15 Nov. 1910. 2p., French

Hůrka, Friedrich Franz [Franciscus Wencsslaus], 1762–1805
Library of Congress
(Box 26)
A. L. S.: Berlin, 7 Apr. 1801. 1p., German

Husa, Karel, b. 1921
Harvard University
3 L.: to Aurelio de la Vega. Ithaca, New York, 27 Oct.
  1982, 12 Jan. 1984; Roanoke, Virginia, 15 July 1984

Hutcheson, Ernest, 1871–1951
Washington State University
L.: to Solomon Pimsleur. 12 Apr. 1928

Ibert, Jacques, 1890–1962
Library of Congress
(Box 112)
Port. Phot. S.: to Hans Moldenhauer, Rome, 11 Mar.
  1954
Port. Phot.

Imbrie, Andrew Welsh, b. 1921
Harvard University
SUMMARY OF PRINCIPAL HOLDINGS:
Mus. ms.: *On the Beach at Night*, 1948
S. rec.: *Violin Concerto*. Tape of premiere

d'Indy, Vincent, 1851–1931
Library of Congress
(Box 26)
A. L. S.: n.p., 22 Mar. 1914. 2p., French. Regarding
  Parsifal
A. L. S.: to a singer. n.p., n.d. 3p., French
A. L. S.: n.p., n.d. 2p., French. Discusses the rehearsal
  of a work of Brahms and one of his own

Northwestern University
Mus. ms.: *Sonata for Piano and Violin*, op. 59, to
  Armand Parent, 1904. Complete draft. Also,
  complete second proofs, with corrections; and with
  additional fair copy of the violin part, including
  annotations by Armand Parent
3 L.: to Boaz Piller. Cincinnati, 21 Oct. 1921; Paris,
  14 May, 8 June 1922
L.: n.p., n.d.
Call. c.: to Armand Parent
Mus. Quot.: *Wallenstein*, Boston, 9 Dec. 1921
Port. Phot.: to Madame Ch. Loeffler
Port. Phot.: to Boaz Piller, 1922
Phot. Gr.: with Benoit, Chabrier, and others

Washington State University
L.: to Solomon Pimsleur. Paris, 2 June 1929

Ingenhoven, Jan, 1876–1951
Northwestern University
Mus. ms.: *Drei Stücke*. Full score, parts

Ingham, Michael, b. 1944
Harvard University
L.: to Aurelio de la Vega. Santa Barbara, California,
13 Apr. 1983

Inghelbrecht, D. E., 1880–1965
Library of Congress
(Box 26, unless noted)
A. Mus. ms. S.: *"La Nursery."* 1p., 31x23cm. For piano,
four hands. Excerpt
Port. Phot. S.: by Liard (Box 112)

Inglés, Joan A.
Library of Congress
(Box 26)
Mus. ms. arr. cop.: *Paris-Lleyda*, for band, arr. by
Ribera, 10 May 1908. 11p. Full score

Iradier, Sebastián, 1809–1865
Library of Congress
(Box 78)
A. L. S.: Madrid, 16 Sept. 1858. 2p., Spanish

Ireland, John, 1879–1962
Northwestern University
L.: to Edward Clark. Banbury, 19 Oct. 1942

Irvine, Demar, 1908–1995
Washington State University
Summary of Principal Holdings:
Mus. ms.: *Reynard the Fox*. With typescript
Pri. Sco.: *Sonatina*, to Hans Moldenhauer, 10 July 1958

Isamitt, Carlos, 1887–1974
Harvard University
Summary of Principal Holdings:
Mus. ms.: *Estudios para piano*

Iturbi, José, 1895–1980
Harvard University
L.: to Solomon Pimsleur. New York, 1 May 1935

Ives, Charles E., 1874–1954
Harvard University
Summary of Principal Holdings:
2 L.: to Nicolas Slonimsky. New York, 1934, with
comments by Slonimsky; London, 1934
2 L.: to Adolph Weiss, from Edie Ives. West Redding,
n.d.
Mus. ms. Repro.: *Orchestral Set No. 2*. Blueprint score
Mus. ms. Repro.: *Sonata No. 1*. Blueprint score
Mus. ms. Repro.: *Three Places in New England,
Orchestral Set No. 1*. Blueprint score
Mus. ms. Repro.: *Washington's Birthday*. Facsimile.
With handwritten titles
Pri. Sco.: *4th of July*

Library of Congress
(Box 95, unless noted)
Pri. Sco. A. Annot.: *114 Songs*, 1884–1921. 258p. (the
first page missing) (Shelf)
A. L. S.: to NS Pa [Nicolas Slonimsky]. New York,
[1934]. 2p., English
A. L. S.: to Weiss. W. Redding, Connecticut, n.d. 2p.,
English
L. S.: to Mrs. Weiss, from Harmony Ives. Taormina,
21 Jan. 4p., English

d'Ivry, Paul Xavier Désiré, Marquis, 1829–1903
Library of Congress
(Box 26)
A. L. S.: Coraboeuf, 27 Dec. 1869. 8p., French.
Mentions Verdi, others

Jackson, Hanley, b. 1939
Harvard University
L.: to Aurelio de la Vega. 4 Dec. 1984

Jackson, William [Jackson of Exeter], 1730–1803
Northwestern University
Mus. ms.: *Concerto a 7*, 1749. Full score
L.: n.p., n.d.

Jacobi, Frederick, 1891–1952
Harvard University
Mus. ms.: *Circe*
Mus. ms.: *And a Lovely Little Movie Actress*
Mus. ms.: *Prelude*
L.: to Charles Haubiel. Riverdale, 29 June 1945
L.: to Aurelio de la Vega. Gstaad, 12 Mar. 1951

Jaëll, Alfred, 1832–1882
Library of Congress
(Box 26, unless noted)
A. L. S.: Grand Hotel, 26 Apr. 3p., French
Port. Phot. Repro. (Box 112)

Jahn, Otto, 1813–1869
Library of Congress
(Box 26)
A. L. S.: to Carl Georg Grädener. Leipzig, 23 Feb.
    1853. 1p., German
A. L. S.: Leipzig, 22 Feb. 1855. 1p., German
A. L. S.: to Becker. Bonn, 11 Feb. 1856. 1p., German
A. L. S.: to ?. Bonn, 14 Mar. 1856. 1p., German
A. L. S.: Bonn, 30 Oct. 1858. 1p., German
4 A. L. S.: to Selmar Bagge. Bonn, 1861–1868. 4p.,
    German
A. L. S.: to André. Bonn, 7 Apr. 1867. 1p., German.
    With musical quotation

Jalowetz, Heinrich, 1882–1946
Library of Congress
(Box 26)
A. L. S.: [to Alexander Zemlinsky]. n.p., 28 Feb. 2p.,
    German

Janácek, Leos [Leo Eugen], 1854–1928
Library of Congress
(Box 26)
P. card S.: to Frau Kretschmerová. Hukvaldy, 14 June
    1927. Czech., with typed translation in German

Janssen, Werner, 1899–1990
Harvard University
L.: to Charles Haubiel. 16 Apr. 1935

Jaques-Dalcroze, Emile, 1865–1950
Northwestern University
Mus. ms.: *Chansons romandes*
L.: n.p., 12 Dec. 1887
Port.

Jarecki, Tadeusz, 1889–1955
Library of Congress
(Box 26)
A. Mus. ms. S.: *Aria*, op. 28. 7p., 31x24cm. (full score),
    18x23cm. (violin)
Mus. ms. Repro.: *Concerto-Suite*, op. 27. 34p. Facsimile

Jarnach, Philipp, 1892–1982
Library of Congress
(Box 26)
A. Mus. ms. S.: *Kleine Rhapsodie für Klavier*. 5p.,
    34x24cm., ink
A. Mus. ms. S.: *Zwei Humoresken für Klavier*, I. *Kleine
    Rhapsodie*, II. *Giga*. 11p., 34x27cm. Complete score.
    With sketch on verso and 1p. crossed out
Pri. Sco.: *Zwei Humoresken für Klavier*, Starnberg:
    Tischer & Jagenberg, n.d. 11p.

Washington State University
See Rosbaud, Hans

Jehin-Prume, Frantz [François], 1839–1899
Library of Congress
(Box 26)
A. L. S.: to Léon de Chier de Lirgé. Spa, 7 Dec. 1871.
    2p., French

Jelinek [Elin], Hanns, 1901–1969
Library of Congress
(Box 26)
A. Mus. ms. Rev. S.: *Three Blue Sketches*, op. 25, Vienna,
    1 May 1956, to Hans Moldenhauer, Vienna, Sept.
    1963. 22p., 34x27cm.
A. Mus. ms. S.: *Zwölftonwerk*, *Vier Tokkaten*, op. 15,
    No. 4, Vienna, Jan.–Feb. 1948. 12p., 34x27cm.

T. L. S.: to Aurelio de la Vega. Vienna, 25 Nov. 1964.
  1p., German
L. S.: to Hans Moldenhauer, from Grete Steingruber.
  Vienna, 17 Apr. 1969. 2p., German
Obit.
2 Clip.: 30 Jan., 2 Feb. 1969. German

Jemnitz, Sándor [Alexander], 1890–1963
Library of Congress
(Box 26)
T. L. S.: [to Paul Sanders]. Budapest, 15 Oct. 1931.
  1p., German

Jenkins, Cyril, b. 1885
Northwestern University
L.: London, 6 Dec. 1921

Jeppesen, Knud, 1892–1974
Library of Congress
(Box 26)
A. L. S.: [to Alfred Mann]. Denmark, 8 Nov. 1938. 2p.,
  German

Jewson, Frederick Bowen, 1823–1891
Northwestern University
Mus. Alb. l.: *Prelude*, 31 Jan. 1879

Jirák, K. B., 1891–1972
Library of Congress
(Box 26)
A. Mus. ms. S.: *Quartet*, op. 82, No. 7, 5 Feb. 1960. 2p.,
  34x27cm.
A. L. S.: to Hans Moldenhauer. Chicago, 12 Nov. 1960.
  1p., English
T. Doc.: Biographical information. 1p., English
Mus. ms. Repro. S.: *Symphony No. 5*, op. 60. 1p.
  Photographic reproduction

Joachim [née Schneeweiss], Amalie, 1839–1899
Library of Congress
(Box 26)

A. Alb. l. S.: New York, May 1892. 1p., German
A. L. S.: [to Dr. Hildebrand?]. Westerland auf Sylt,
  5 Sept. 1895. 8p., German
A. Card S.: Dessau, 1 Jan. 1896. 1p., German
A. Doc.: Address panel. To Frau Prof. Michaelis.
  Hamburg

Joachim, Joseph, 1831–1907
Library of Congress
(Box 26, unless noted)
A. L. S.: to Volkland. Berlin, 10 Sept. 1888. 3p.,
  German
A. L. S.: n.p., 20 Mar. 1895. 1p., English
A. L. S.: to Chorley. Bayswater, n.d. 1p., English
A. L. S.: to Hermann Levi. Moos, 16 Aug. 2p.,
  German. Regarding a letter to Brahms; Munich trip;
  suggests they meet
A. L. S.: n.p., n.d. 2p., German
2 L. S.: to Miss Graham, from Edith Joachim. Glasgow,
  N. B., 19 Feb. 1910, 16 Oct. 1912. 4p., English
A. Mus. Quot. S.: [*3. Sonata*, Fuga, BWV 1005 by J. S.
  Bach]
Obit.: 15 Aug. 1907. 2p., English
Port. Phot. Repro.: attached to an envelope addressed
  to Michaelis (Box 112)

Jochum, Eugen, 1902–1987
Washington State University
See Rosbaud, Hans

Johnson, Donivan, b. 1949
Moldenhauer Archives, Spokane, Washington
SUMMARY OF PRINCIPAL HOLDINGS:
Doc.: Collection includes music manuscripts and other
  documents

Johnson, Edward [Di Giovanni, Eduardo], 1878–1959
Harvard University
L.: to Rudolph Ganz. New York, 22 June 1945

Johnson, Lockrem, 1924–1977
Washington State University
Mus. ms.: *A Letter to Emily*

Johnson, Thor, 1913–1975
Harvard University
L.: to Rudolph Ganz. Cincinnati, 7 Apr. 1950
L.: to Charles Haubiel. Cincinnati, 15 Apr. 1953

Jokl, Otto, 1891–1963
Bayerische Staatsbibliothek
SUMMARY OF PRINCIPAL HOLDINGS:
Mus. ms.: *Abend*
Mus. ms.: *Abseits*, op. 17
Mus. ms.: *Beauty*
Mus. ms.: *Die Braut spricht*
Mus. ms.: *The Brothers*
2 Mus. mss.: *Chartless; Autumn Sky*
Mus. ms.: *Dance of the Puppets*
Mus. ms.: *The Day of an American Baby*
Mus. ms.: *Drei Chöre*, op. 18
Mus. ms.: *8 Minute Symphony*
Mus. ms.: *Einblick*
Mus. ms.: *Einsamkeit*
Mus. ms.: *In the Evening*
Mus. ms.: *Five Dance Pieces*
Mus. ms.: [*Five Fugues*]
Mus. ms.: [*Five Piano Pieces*]
Mus. ms.: *Four Tame Satires*
Mus. ms.: [*Fourth String Quartet*]
Mus. ms.: *Die frühe Stunde*
Mus. ms.: *Grosses Klaviertrio*, op. 10
Mus. ms.: *Heimliche Liebschaft*
Mus. ms.: *Heitere Suite*, op. 24. Full score, parts,
   sketches, blueprint score
Mus. ms.: *Immerfort*
Mus. ms.: *Jazzvariationen*
Mus. ms.: *An ein Kind*
Mus. ms.: *Lebenstraum*, 1908
Mus. ms.: *Zur Lebensweisheit*
Mus. ms.: *Liebesdrang*
Mus. ms.: *Lied der Stimmen in uns*
Mus. ms.: *Light a Candle in the Chapel*, arranged by J.
   Mason
Mus. ms.: *Love, Life, and After*
Mus. ms.: *Lulu Suite* by Berg. Piano reduction
Mus. ms.: *Eine Nacht*
Mus. ms.: *Nachtbild*

Mus. ms.: *Nachtstille*
Mus. ms.: *Neurotic Songs*
Mus. ms.: *Orchester-Suite*, op. 26
Mus. ms.: *Phantastische Improvisation*, 1911
Mus. ms.: *Präludium und Fuge*, op. 7
Mus. ms.: *Praeludium und Fuge* by Bach, arranged by
   Max Reger
Mus. ms.: *Reigen*
Mus. ms.: *The Reply*
Mus. ms.: *S'ist no net lang*
Mus. ms.: *Scherzo bizzarro*
Mus. ms.: *Schicksal*
Mus. ms.: *Second Suite for Orchestra*
Mus. ms.: *Selbstgefällig*
Mus. ms.: *Seven Songs and Ballads*
Mus. ms.: *Sinfonietta for String Orchestra*
Mus. ms.: *Sinfonietta seria*, op. 27
Mus. ms.: *So nimm denn meine Hände*
Mus. ms.: *Sonate*, op. 13, 1926
Mus. ms.: *Sonate*, op. 29
Mus. ms.: *Sonate für Klavier*, op. 14
Mus. ms.: *Sonatine*, op. 11
Mus. ms.: *Das Sterben Jesu*
Mus. ms.: *Streichduo*, 1925
Mus. ms.: *String Quartet*, op. 25
Mus. ms.: *Stück für Streichduo*, 1927
Mus. ms.: *Stück für Streichquartett*
Mus. ms.: *Suite on Yugoslavian Folk Melodies*
Mus. ms.: *Suite aus C. M. von Webers* Euryanthe
Mus. ms.: *Summer Is*
Mus. ms.: *Ein Talisman*
Mus. ms.: *Third String Quartet*
Mus. ms.: *Trauermarsch*, 1922
Mus. ms.: *Einer Verlassenen*
Mus. ms.: *Weine nur nicht*
Mus. ms.: *When You Return*
Mus. ms.: *Wir wähnten lange recht zu leben*, op. 20,
   No. 2
Mus. ms.: [*Woodwind Quartet*]
Mus. ms.: [*Woodwind Trio*]
Mus. ms.: *A Wreath of Meyerbeerian Melodies*
Mus. ms.: *Zwei Stücke für Streichorchester*, op. 12
Mus. ms.: *Zweites Streichquartett*, op. 28
Mus. ms. Repro.: *Slavic Folk Tune Suite*
S. rec.: *String Quartet No. 2*
See Berg, Alban

Library of Congress
See Mohaupt, Richard

Jolivet, André, 1905–1974
Library of Congress
See Rosbaud, Hans

Washington State University
See Rosbaud, Hans

Jommelli [Jomelli], Nicolò [Niccolò], 1714–1774
Northwestern University
Mus. ms.: *Così spaventa il tuono.* Full score

Jonás, Alberto, 1868–1943
Library of Congress
(Box 26)
A. Mus. ms. S.: *Vision.* 3p., 32x24cm.

Jonas, Oswald, 1897–1978
Library of Congress
(Box 27)
A. Doc.: Lecture. "The Genius and His
    Contemporaries," Berkeley, Spring 1940. 30p.
Doc.: Announcement. Jonas lecture series. 1p.,
    English

Jone, Hildegard, 1891–1963
Library of Congress
(Box 27)
A. Doc. S.: Program. "Zum ersten internationalen
    Webern-Fest, in Zuneigung." German
See Webern, Anton

Paul Sacher Stiftung
SUMMARY OF PRINCIPAL HOLDINGS:
Doc.: Files include articles, notebooks, poems (many
    about Webern, or set to music by Webern),
    photographs, prose
See Webern, Anton

Jones, David
Harvard University
2 L.: to Aurelio de la Vega. 1983; Middlesex, Dec.
    1984

Jongen, Joseph, 1873–1953
Library of Congress
(Box 27)
A. L. S.: Brussels, n.d. 2p., French, English
A. Mus. Quot. S.: *Concerto for Piano,* op. 127

Jordan, Sverre, 1889–1972
Northwestern University
Mus. ms.: *Holbergsilhuetter,* op. 39. Full score, with
    preface in Norwegian, German, and English
Mus. ms.: *Second Sonata for Violin and Piano in D
    Minor,* op. 43. Full score

Josten, Werner, 1885–1963
Harvard University
Mus. ms.: *Sonata for Cello and Piano,* 1938
L.

Journet, Marcel, 1867–1933
Library of Congress
(Box 27)
A. L. S.: London, 9 June 1906. 2p., French

Judson, Arthur, 1881–1975
Harvard University
3 L.: to Adolph Weiss. New York, Philadelphia, 1930

Jullien, Louis, 1812–1860
Library of Congress
(Box 27, unless noted)
A. L. S.: n.p., 18 Mar. 1p., English
Obit.: 1860
Clip.: 5 July 1845. English
Port. Caric. Repro.: 21 Nov. 1846 (Box 112)

Kàan, Jindrich z Albestu, 1852–1926
Library of Congress
(Box 27)
A. Mus. Quot. S.: *Germinal*, Overture, Prague, 15 Feb.
1909

Kabalevsky, Dmitri, 1904–1987
Library of Congress
(Box 27, unless noted)
A. Mus. ms. S.: *Concerto for Violoncello and Orchestra*, op.
49, 1948–1949, to the Spokane Conservatory,
Moscow, 10 Dec. 1955. 1p., 37x25cm. Full score.
First eighteen measures of the Allegro movement
T. L. S.: to Hans Moldenhauer. Moscow, 12 Dec 1955.
1p., Russian
Port. Phot. S.: to Hans Moldenhauer, Moscow, 12 Dec.
1955 (Box 112)

Kadosa, Pál, 1903–1983
Library of Congress
(Box 27)
2 A. L. S.: to Paul F. Sanders. Budapest, 18 Apr.,
15 June 1933. 2p., German

Kämpf, Karl, 1874–1950
Library of Congress
(Box 27, unless noted)
A. Mus. ms. S.: *Idyllen für Pianoforte*, op. 35, No. 2. 3p.,
34x27cm.
A. L. S.: Berlin, 9 June 1912. 4p., German. With work
list
Port. Phot. S. Repro.: to George Bainton, Berlin,
9 June 1912 (Box 112)

Kahn, Erich Itor, 1905–1956
Harvard University
Summary of Principal Holdings:
Mus. ms.: *Invention*, Paris, 7 Jan. 1938
L.: to René Leibowitz. New York, 16 Oct. 1949
L.: from Frida Kahn (wife)

Library of Congress
(Box 95)
A. L. S.: to Evarts. New York, 23 Dec. 1945. 1p.,
English

Kahn, Otto, 1867–1934
Library of Congress
(Box 95)
T. L. S.: to James Pond. New York, 24 Oct. 1919. 1p.,
English

Kahn, Robert, 1865–1951
Library of Congress
(Box 27, unless noted)
A. Mus. ms. S.: *Morgenfrühe*. 2p., 23x33cm., German.
On verso, complete draft of another song
A. Card S.: Berlin, 5 Mar. 1p., German
Port. Phot. S. Repro. (Box 112)

Kahnt, Christian Friedrich, 1823–1897
Library of Congress
(Box 27)
3 A. L. S.: to A. W. Gottschalg. Leipzig, 27 Oct. 1860,
12 Aug. 1861, 4 July 1873. 4p., German. References
to Liszt
3 A. L. S.: to A. W. Gottschalg, from Paulina Kahnt.
Leipzig, 1898; n.p., n.d. 18p., German

Kalbeck, Max, 1850–1921
Library of Congress
(Box 27)
A. L. S.: Vienna, 26 May 1883. 2p., German

**Kalkbrenner, Frédéric [Friedrich Wilhelm
Michael], 1785–1849**
Wiener Stadt- u. Landesbibliothek
Mus. ms.: *Vivace sempre legato*, 29 Jan. 1824. Complete
score
L.: to Mayer. Paris, 6 Aug. 1832
L.: to a publisher. Paris, 10 Dec. 1844
Port.

Kálmán, Imre [Emmerich], 1882–1953
Library of Congress
(Box 27)
T. L. S.: to Paul F. Sanders. New York, 28 Feb. 1947.
1p., German
A. Mus. Quot. S.: [Waltz melody], 1941

Kanitz, Ernest [Ernst], 1894–1978
Harvard University
Mus. ms.: *The Lucky Dollar*
Mus. ms.: *Notturno*
L.: to Aurelio de la Vega. California, 13 Aug. 1951,
1 Dec. 1970
10 L.: to Hans Moldenhauer. Van Nuys, California,
1960, 1961

Karauschek [Karasek], Wendelino, ?–1789
Library of Congress
(Box 27)
A. Mus. ms. S.: *Sonata à violoncello solo con basso*. 6p.,
31x27cm.

Karg-Elert [Karg], Sigfrid, 1877–1933
Northwestern University
SUMMARY OF PRINCIPAL HOLDINGS:
Mus. ms.: *Kanzone und Tokkata*, op. 85, Aug. 1910
See Sceats, Godfrey

Karkoschka, Erhard, b. 1923
Library of Congress
(Box 96)
A. Mus. ms. S.: *"Szene im Schlagzeug,"* to Michael
Ranta. 6p., 30x42cm., German. Complete draft,
sketches
3 T. L. S.: to Hans Moldenhauer. Stuttgart, 26 Apr.
1971, 1 Apr. 1972, n.d. 3p., German
L. S.: to Karkoschka, from Duczek. Stuttgart, 20 Apr.
1971. 1p., German
T. Doc.: List. Works given to the Moldenhauer
Archives. 1p., German
Mus. ms. Repro.: *Antinomie*, 1968. 16p. Blueprint score

Mus. ms. Repro.: *Bewegungs-Strukturen*, 1961. 27p.
Facsimile
Mus. ms. Repro. Rev. S.: *Omnia ad Maiorem Dei Gloria*,
1963. 88p. Facsimile. With typed document
regarding manuscript
Mus. ms. Repro.: [*Psylex*], 1968. 7p. Incomplete
Mus. ms. Repro. Rev. S.: *Quattrologe*, 1966. 46p.
Blueprint score
Mus. ms. Repro. S.: *Sechs Konstellationen*, 1962. 27p.
Facsimile
Mus. ms. Repro.: *Undarum continuum für Orchester*,
1960. 69p. Facsimile. With typed document
regarding manuscript

Karr-Bertoli, Julius, b. 1920
Washington State University
See Rosbaud, Hans

Kasemets, Udo, b. 1919
Harvard University
L.: to Aurelio de la Vega. Toronto, 28 Nov. 1963

Kashkin, Nicolai Dmitrievich, 1839–1920
Library of Congress
See Tchaikovsky, Pyotr Ilyich

Kashperov, Vladmir Nikitich, 1826–1894
Library of Congress
See Tchaikovsky, Pyotr Ilyich

Katwijk, Paul van, 1885–1974
Harvard University
L.: to Boaz Piller. Dallas, 7 Oct. 1961

Kauder, Hugo, 1888–1972
Wiener Stadt- u. Landesbibliothek
L.: to Mrs. Kisch-Arndt. n.p., n.d.
Mus. ms. Repro.: *Second Sonata for Violin and Piano*,
1939, inscribed 8 Sept. 1945. Blueprint score

Kaufman, Louis, 1905–1994
Harvard University
SUMMARY OF PRINCIPAL HOLDINGS:
L.: to Aurelio de la Vega. Los Angeles, 7 Feb. 1961

3 S. recs.: *Second Violin Concerto* and *Concertino de Printemps* by Milhaud; *Sonata for Violin and Piano* by Poulenc; *Duo concertant* by Stravinsky, inscribed to the Moldenhauers

2 S. recs.: *Twelve Concerti Grossi*, op. 8 by Torelli; *Three Sonates Concertantes* by Spohr, to the Moldenhauers

Kaufmann, Walter, 1907–1984
Harvard University
SUMMARY OF PRINCIPAL HOLDINGS:
Mus. ms.: *The Coat*, 1962
Mus. ms.: *Concerto for Violin and Orchestra No. 3*, 1943
Mus. ms. cop.: *Concerto for Violin and String Orchestra*
Mus. ms.: *Configuration*, 1946
Mus. ms.: *Dirge*, 1946
Mus. ms.: *III. Sinfonie für grosses Orchester*
Mus. ms.: *George from Paradise*
Mus. ms.: *Der Hammel bringt es an den Tag*, 1933
Mus. ms.: *Kalif Stork*, 1944
Mus. ms.: *Klaviertrio*, op. 40, 1936
Mus. ms.: *Konzert für Klavier und Orchester*
Mus. ms.: *Paracelsus*
Mus. ms.: *Pembina Road*, 1949
Mus. ms.: *Piano Trio*, 1958
Mus. ms.: *Picture Book for Katherine*, 1946
Mus. ms.: *Prag*, 1932
Mus. ms.: *The Scarlet Letter*
Mus. ms.: *Sextet*, 1964
Mus. ms.: *Spanish Folk Song*
Mus. ms.: *Streichquartett No. 3*, 1935
Mus. ms.: *String Quartet*, 1951
Mus. ms.: *Symphonie für Streicher*, 1937
Mus. ms.: *Symphony No. 4*, 1938
Mus. ms.: *Tripelfuge*, 1927
Mus. ms.: *Vier Lieder*
Mus. ms. Repro.: *Arabesques*, 1963. Blueprint score
Mus. ms. cop. Repro.: *Caprice*, 1950
Mus. ms. Repro.: *Eight Pieces for Twelve Instruments*, 1966. Photocopy
Mus. ms. Repro.: *Faces in the Dark*, 1954. Blueprint score
Mus. ms. Repro.: *Four Essays*, 1956. Blueprint score
Mus. ms. Repro.: *Sechs Lieder*. Blueprint score
Mus. ms. Repro.: *Sinfonietta*. Photoreduction
Mus. ms. Repro.: *Sinfonietta No. 2*, 1959. Spirit master print
Mus. ms. Repro.: *Sonata*, for piano, 1960. Photo-offset
.Mus. ms. Repro.: *Sonata*, for three violas. Blueprint score

Mus. ms. Repro.: *String Quartet*, 1972. Photocopy
Mus. ms. cop. Repro.: *Swanee River Variations*, 1949
Mus. ms. Repro.: *Symphony No. 6*, 1956. Photocopy
Mus. ms. cop. Repro.: *Timpani Concertino*. Blueprint score
Mus. ms. Repro.: *Variations for Strings*. Blueprint score
7 L.: to Hans Moldenhauer. 1973, 1979–1980
2 Port. Phot.: inscribed

Kaun, Hugo, 1863–1932
Library of Congress
(Box 27)
A. L. S.: [to Römmisch?]. Berlin, 2 Feb. 1903. 1p., German
A. L. S.: to Eugen Lindner. Berlin, 3 Oct. 1907. 4p., German
3 A. L. S.: to Gerhard Tischer. Zehlendorf, 26 Jan. 1925, 1 Sept. 1928; ?, 22 Sept. 1928. 3p., German
A. L. S.: to Huch. Zehlendorf, 4 Feb. 1927. 1p., German

Kay, Ulysses, 1917–1995
Harvard University
Mus. ms.: *Suite for Orchestra*, 1945
L.: to Hans Moldenhauer. New York, 14 Nov. 1968

Kechley, Gerald R., b. 1919
Washington State University
Mus. ms.: *The Golden Lion*
2 L.: to Hans Moldenhauer. Seattle, 31 Aug. 1960, 20 Mar. 1962

Keilberth, Joseph, 1908–1968
Washington State University
See Rosbaud, Hans

Kelemen, Milko, b. 1924
Library of Congress
(Box 97, unless noted)
A. Mus. ms. S.: *Mageia, for Orchestra and Laser Beams*, 1977. 3p., 21x30cm., ink, pencil, colored pencils. Graph
Doc. Repro. S.: *Opera Bestial*, inscribed to the

Moldenhauer Archives, Stuttgart, 8 June 1977.
Blueprint of the complete plan of opera. Scroll
Doc. S.: Typescript. Giving description for *Opera
Bestial*. 4p.
2 Docs. S.: Brochures
2 Pri. Sco. S.: *Surprise*, 1966, Frankfurt: Peters, c1967;
SubRosa, 1964, Frankfurt: Peters, c1972
S. rec.: *Changeant*; *Composé*; *Floréal*; *Hommage à Heinrich
Schütz*; *Surprise* (Shelf)

Keller, Homer, 1915–1996
Harvard University
Mus. ms.: *Duo for Violin and Harpsichord*
L.: to Hans Moldenhauer. Eugene, 24 Aug. 1962

Keller, Max, 1770–1855
Northwestern University
Mus. ms.: *Cantata*, op. 99, Altötting, 11 Feb. 1824
Mus. ms.: *Deutsche Messe für 4 Singstimmen*, Altötting,
15 Apr. 1834
Mus. ms.: *Duetto*, Altötting, 22 Feb. 1850
Mus. ms.: *Auf dem Gottesacker*, Altötting, 12 May 1847.
On verso, sketch in another hand
Mus. ms.: *6 Deutsche Tänze*
Mus. ms. cop.: *Hymnus in Resurrectione Domini a 4
Voci...*
Mus. ms. cop.: *Ignazi Walzer*
Mus. ms. cop.: *Klage*
Mus. ms. cop.: *Der untröstliche Wittwer*
Mus. ms. cop.: *Wiegenlied*
4 Pri. Sco.: *120 Cadenzen und Vorspiele*, vol. 2; *Die
Wunder der Tonkunst*; *Zechlied von J. B. Reck in Musik
gesetzt von C. Lochner*; *24 leichte Orgel-Compositionen
zum gottesdienstlichen Gebrauche* (all first editions)

Kelsey, Verne, b. 1897
Harvard University
SUMMARY OF PRINCIPAL HOLDINGS:
Mus. ms.: *The Beatitudes*
Mus. ms. arr.: *Bourrée-Rigaudon*
Mus. ms.: *Capriccio*
Mus. ms.: *Chorale Preludes*
Mus. ms.: *Etude for Pedals*
Mus. ms.: *Etude for Two Pianos on Themes of Chopin*
Mus. ms.: *Fantasie for Four Clarinets*
Mus. ms.: *Festival-Postlude*

Mus. ms.: *Five Songs*
Mus. ms.: *Hymn Anthem Duet*, 1971
Mus. ms.: *Introduction and Passacaglia for Organ on a
Modal Theme*
Mus. ms.: *Konzertstück*, 1960
Mus. ms.: *Mass*
Mus. ms.: [*Notebook*], includes *Hursley, Regent Square,
Hymn Anthem*
Mus. ms.: *Pastorale*
Mus. ms.: *Prelude*
Mus. ms.: *Psalm*
Mus. ms.: *Psalm LXXXVI*
Mus. ms.: *Requiem*
Mus. ms.: *Scherzo for Tuba with Piano*
Mus. ms.: *Sonata No. 2*
Mus. ms.: *Sonata for Cello and Piano*
Mus. ms.: *Sonata for Clarinet and Piano*
Mus. ms.: *Sonata for Trombone and Piano*
Mus. ms.: *Sonata for Violin and Piano in a Minor Key*
Mus. ms.: *String Quartet*
Mus. ms.: *String Trio*
Mus. ms.: *Theme and Variations*
Mus. ms.: *Three Fragments for a Medium Voice*
Mus. ms.: *'Tis Morning*
Mus. ms.: *Toccata*
Mus. ms.: *Trio*, 1960
Mus. ms.: *Valse* by Ravel, arranged by Kelsey for two
pianos
Mus. ms.: *Variations on a Theme of Paganini*
2 L.: to Hans Moldenhauer. Hendersonville, n.d.; n.p.,
1 Apr. 1970
68 L.

Kemp, Joseph, 1778–1824
Northwestern University
L.: London, 30 Nov. 1810

Kennan, Kent, b. 1913
Harvard University
Mus. ms.: *Night Soliloquy*, 1936
L.: to Hans Moldenhauer. 10 Sept. 1962

Kerr, Harrison, 1897–1978
Harvard University
Mus. ms. Repro.: *Etude for Violoncello*. Facsimile

Kessner, Daniel, b. 1946
Harvard University
Mus. ms.: *Chamber Concerto*, 1972. With additional
blueprint score and sound recording
L.: to Hans Moldenhauer. n.p., 8 Aug. 1979
2 L.: to Aurelio de la Vega. Perugia, 25 Nov. 1982;
Villefranche-sur-mer, 27 Oct. 1982
Doc.: Work list

Keussler, Gerhard von, 1874–1949
Library of Congress
(Box 27)
7 A. L. S.: to Alexander Zemlinsky. Vienna, Prague,
1913–1917. 19p., German
A. L.: to Keussler, from the Deutscher Männergesang-
Verein. Prague, 5 Jan. 1916. 2p., German. Draft of a
reply
T. L.: to the Deutscher Männergesang-Verein. Vienna,
9 Jan. 1916. 2p., German. Carbon copy

Khuner, Felix, b. 1906
Library of Congress
(Box 27, unless noted)
4 T. L. S.: to Adolph Weiss. Vienna, Berkeley,
May–Aug. 1937. 5p., German
P. card S.: to Adolph Weiss. Maine, 21 Aug. 1956.
English
Phot. Gr.: Khuner's children (Box 112)
See Schoenberg, Arnold

Kiel, Friedrich, 1821–1885
Library of Congress
(Box 27)
A. Mus. ms.: [*9 Ländler*]. 9p., 33x27cm.
A. L. S.: to ?. Berlin, 17 Apr. 1848. 3p., German

Kienzl, Wilhelm, 1857–1941
Library of Congress
(Box 27)
A. L. S.: Graz, 1 Feb. 1889. 3p., German

Wiener Stadt- u. Landesbibliothek
SUMMARY OF PRINCIPAL HOLDINGS:
Mus. ms. cop.: *Alt Wien*, op. 21, Heft III
Mus. ms.: *Rieke im Manöver singt*
2 L.: to Karl Weigl. Bad Aussee, 17 Aug. 1932, 26 Sept.
1936
L.: to Tischer. Vienna, 19 June 1935

Kiesewetter, Raphael Georg, 1773–1850
Library of Congress
(Box 27)
A. L. S.: to Baron von Hammer-Purgstall.
Neuwaldegg, 29 Sept. 1840. 4p., German. Discusses
Die Musik der Araber
L.: to Hans Moldenhauer, from Demar Irvine.
Denmark, 27 Oct. 1960. 1p., English

Kilenyi, Edward, Jr., b. 1910
Harvard University
L.: to Verne Kelsey. Tallahassee, 19 June 1955

Kilpatrick, Jack Frederick, 1915–1967
Library of Congress
SUMMARY OF PRINCIPAL HOLDINGS:
(Box 140)
A. Mus. ms. S.: *Forked Deep River*, op. 1. 10p.,
32x25cm., ink
A. Mus. ms. S.: *Four Ozark Dances*, op. 10, Oklahoma,
1940. 20p., 43x28cm., ink
A. Mus. ms. S.: *Invocation and Ritual*, op. 30,
Washington, D.C., Apr. 1944. 33p., 34x28cm., ink
A. Mus. ms. S.: *The Land*, 1 Sept. 1955. 8p., 36x27cm.,
ink
A. Mus. ms. S.: *Three Cherokee Cosmogonic Legends*,
Oklahoma, 1940. 28p., 43x28cm., ink

Kindermann, August, 1817–1891
Library of Congress
(Box 27)
2 A. L. S.: to Julius Schloss. Munich, 23 Feb., 3 Mar.
1869. 3p., German

Kindler, Hans, 1892–1949
Harvard University
L.: to Solomon Pimsleur. Washington, D.C., 30 Jan.
1934

Kinkeldey, Otto, 1878–1966
Harvard University
Summary of Principal Holdings:
L.: to Hans Moldenhauer. South Orange, New Jersey, 26 June 1958

Kirchner, Leon, b. 1919
Harvard University
Mus. ms.: *Second String Quartet*, 1958
2 L.: 6 Mar. 1958, 23 Jan. 1959
Doc.: Brochure. Includes portrait reproduced and work list

Washington State University
See Rosbaud, Hans

Kirchner, Theodor Fürchtegott, 1823–1903
Northwestern University
Mus. ms.: [Collection includes 56 complete compositions and numerous sketches]

Kirkpatrick, John, 1905–1991
Harvard University
Mus. ms.: *Improvisation* by Eugene Weigel
Doc. Repro.: Catalog. Manuscripts of Charles Ives

Kirnberger [Kernberg], Johann Philipp, 1721–1783
Library of Congress
(Box 97)
2 A. Mus. mss.: *Aria vivace*; [Studies in figured bass]. 4p. + 10p., 19x24cm., ink
A. L. S.: [to Johann Nikolaus Forkel]. Berlin, 4 Sept. 1779. 2p., German. Refusing to enter into a literary controversy; mentions Reichardt, Royal Princess, others

Northwestern University
See Zelter, Carl Friedrich

Kistler, Cyrill, 1848–1907
Northwestern University
Mus. ms.: *Meditation, Erinnerung an Franz Lachner*
Port.

Klatte, Wilhelm, 1870–1930
Library of Congress
(Box 27)
A. L. S.: to Eugen Lindner. Berlin, 8 June 1899. 2p., German
A. L. S.: to Bruno Eisner. Berlin, 13 Aug. 1917. 4p., German
A. L. S.: to Bruno Eisner, from Clara Klatte. Berlin, 10 Oct. 1931. 1p., German

Klaus, Kenneth Blanchard, 1923–1980
Harvard University
Summary of Principal Holdings:
Mus. ms.: *Symphony No. 5*, 1977. Excerpt
2 L.: to Hans Moldenhauer. Baton Rouge, 4 Aug., 12 Sept. 1977
Mus. ms. Repro.: *Fugato Concertato for Percussion and Orchestra*. Facsimile
Mus. ms. Repro.: *Quartet No. 3*. Facsimile

Klemperer, Otto, 1885–1973
Bayerische Staatsbibliothek
See Berg, Alban

Library of Congress
(Box 97, unless noted)
A. Mus. ms. S.: *Der König in Thule (aus Goethes Faust)*, for voice and piano, ca. 1915, signed 1973. 1p., 34x27cm., pencil, crayon
A. Mus. ms. S.: [Sketches], June 1968, signed again by Klemperer in 1970[?]. 19p., 12x20cm.
L. S.: to Hans Moldenhauer, from Lotte Klemperer. Zurich, 20 Mar. 1973. 1p., German
Doc. S.: Article. On Klemperer's music, by Ernst Hoff. 1p., German
Mus. ms. Repro.: *Der König in Thule*, Mainz: Schott, n.d. 1p. + 3p. (catalog list)
Mus. ms. Repro. A. Annot.: *Merry Valse; One Step*, 1963. 19p. + 14p.
Pri. Sco.: *Symphony in Two Movements*, Peters, c1962. 58p.
Pri. Sco.: *Symphony No. 2*, Hinrichsen, c1970. 67p.
Port. Phot. (Box 112)
Port. Phot. S.: 1973 (Box 112)
Bk.: *Conversations with Klemperer*, edited by Peter Heyworth, London: Victor Gollancz, c1973. 128p., English (Shelf)
S. rec.: *Merry Waltz*. Conducted by Klemperer with the Philharmonia Orchestra

Washington State University
See Rosbaud, Hans

Klenau, Paul von, 1883–1946
Library of Congress
(Box 27)
A. L. S.: to Latzcko. Berlin, 15 Jan. 1920. 1p., German.
    Regarding *Sulamith*
P. card S.: to Alexander Zemlinsky. Munich, 22 Apr.
    1924. German
A. L. S.: [to Marta Pisk]. Vienna, 28 Apr. 19[29?]. 2p.,
    German. Mentions Alma Mahler

Klengel, Paul, 1854–1935
Library of Congress
(Box 27)
A. L. S.: to Mary Wurm. Leipzig, 21 Dec. 1914. 3p.,
    German
Call. c.

Klindworth, Karl, 1830–1916
Library of Congress
See Tchaikovsky, Pyotr Ilyich

Klingler, Karl, 1879–1971
Library of Congress
(Box 27)
A. L. S.: Charlottenburg, 30 Mar. 1919. 2p., German

Klughardt, August, 1847–1902
Library of Congress
(Box 27)
P. card S.: Carlos Droste. Dessau, 14 Apr. 1899. 1p.,
    German

Klussmann, Ernst Gernot, b. 1901
Northwestern University
Mus. ms.: *Musik zu einem Gesang*

Knab, Armin, 1881–1951
Library of Congress
(Box 27)

A. L. S.: to Tischer. Würzburg, 2 Apr. 1928. 1p.,
    German

Knorr, Ernst-Lothar von, 1896–1973
Library of Congress
(Box 27)
2 T. L. S.: to Adolph Weiss. Berlin, 24 Sept. 1931,
    18 Jan. 1932. 2p., German

Knorr, Iwan, 1853–1916
Library of Congress
(Box 27, unless noted)
A. L. S.: Frankfurt, 17 Nov. 1908. 2p., German. Giving
    biographical information
A. Mus. Quot. S.: *Dunja*, Overture
Port. Phot. Repro. (Box 112)

Koch, Heinrich Christoph, 1749–1816
Library of Congress
(Box 27)
5 A. L. S.: [to Johann Friedrich Rochlitz]. Rudolstadt,
    1807–1810. 14p., German. Submitting reviews. Also
    with signed note by Gottfried Christoph Härtel,
    8 Jan. 1809

Kochański, Paweł, 1887–1934
Washington State University
L.: to Solomon Pimsleur. New York, 11 Apr. 1930
Port. Phot.: to Boaz Piller, New York, 1928

Koczalski, Raoul [Raul], 1884–1948
Library of Congress
(Box 27, unless noted)
A. Mus. ms. S.: *Ne li occhi porta la mia donna amore*, op.
    110, No. 1, to Frau G. Tischer, Christmas 1932. 3p.,
    34x27cm.
Port. Phot. S.: to ?, Lausanne, 30 Dec. 1900. With
    musical quotation (Box 112)

Kodály, Zoltán, 1882–1967
Harvard University
See Serly, Tibor

Library of Congress
(Box 27)
A. L. S.: [to Ricordi]. Budapest, 5 July [1924?]. 3p., French. Inquiring about folklore in Italy; improvised funeral songs
A. L. S.: to the Director [of Universal Edition]. Budapest, 1 Dec. 1935. 2p., German. Includes musical example. Regarding corrections to his op. 8; Casals, Piatigorsky, Cassado

Koechlin, Charles, 1867–1950
Library of Congress
(Box 27)
A. Mus. ms.: *Chanson de Nuit dans la Jungle*, for Chorus and Orchestra. 18p., 35x27cm., ink. Based on words by Kipling. Includes: score for "Contralto ou Mezzo soprano; Baryton ou Tenor" with orchestra (7p., condensed); score for choral conductor (4p., voice parts only); score for piano accompaniment (7p., with voice part)

Köhler, Ernst, 1799–1847
Library of Congress
(Box 27)
A. Mus. Quot. S.: *Lebe wohl*, 15 Dec. 1838. German

Koenig, Gottfried Michael, b. 1926
Library of Congress
(Box 27)
4 T. L. S.: to Aurelio de la Vega. Utrecht, 8 Dec. 1965, 8 Apr., 12 Aug. 1970, 17 Mar. 1971. 4p., English
A. Card S.: to Aurelio de la Vega. Utrecht, 1979. English

Koering, René, b. 1940
Library of Congress
(Box 106, unless noted)
A. Mus. ms. S.: *Cantate pour ensemble du chambre*, Barcelona 1959-Strasbourg 1960, inscribed to the Moldenhauer Archives. 8p., 42x32cm. + various sizes. Section B. Sketches in full score (Shelf)
A. Mus. ms. S.: *Ein Garten für Orpheus*, 1963, inscribed

to Hans Moldenhauer, 1964. 38p., 32x43cm. Full score. With accompanying 4p. typed instructions and instrumentation
A. Mus. ms.: *Triple et trajectoires*, 1963. 21p., 42x30cm. + 50x33cm. Full score
A. L. S.: to Hans Moldenhauer. 6 Nov. 1961. 1p., German
T. L. S.: to Hans Moldenhauer. Strasbourg, 13 Dec. 1962. 1p., French
A. Doc. S.: Outline. *Ci-gît*. Titles for the movements. 1p.
Doc.: Biography. "René Koering *Combat T 3 N*," in *Bulletin for the S.I.M.C.*, Madrid, 28 May 1965. 1p.
Pri. Sco.: *Ci-gît*. 11p.
Pri. Sco.: *Combat T 3 N*, Berlin: Ahn & Simrock. 22p.
2 Pri. Sco.: *Musique pour une Passion*, Berlin: Ahn & Simrock. 24p. each (Shelf)
Pri. Sco.: *Trauma*, Berlin: Ahn & Simrock. 14p.
2 Pri. Sco. A. Annot.: *Triple et trajectoires*, Ahn & Simrock, Berlin. 43p. each. One copy with autograph corrections
3 Prog.: *Triple et trajectoires*, 24 June 1965, International Strasbourger Festspiele. 4p. each, German

Kohn, Karl, b. 1926
Harvard University
4 L.: to Aurelio de la Vega. Claremont, 27 Jan. 1964, 1970; n.p., 8, 28 Feb. 1984

Kohs, Ellis, b. 1916
Harvard University
Mus. ms.: *Symphony No. 1*
5 L.: to Aurelio de la Vega. Los Angeles, 31 Mar. 1975, 1983, 9 Nov., 24 Dec. 1984, Dec. 1985
2 L.: to Hans Moldenhauer. Los Angeles, California, 31 Jan., 24 Mar. 1982
Mus. ms. Repro.: *Concerto for Violin and Orchestra*, 1980. Photocopy
Mus. ms. Repro.: *Duo for Violin and Cello*, 1971

Rudolph Kolisch

Kolisch, Rudolf, 1896–1978
Library of Congress
(Box 28, unless noted)

P. card S.: to Adolph Weiss. Southhampton, 17 May 1935. German

A. L. S.: to Paul A. Pisk. Los Angeles, 24 July 1962. 1p., English, German

P. card S.: to Adolph Weiss, from Henriette Kolisch. Venice, ?. German

Port. Gr.: to Frau Adolph Weiss, 1978 (Box 112)

See Gerhard, Roberto

See Schoenberg, Arnold

See Webern, Anton

Kollmann, Augustus Frederic Christopher, 1756–1829
Northwestern University
Doc.: Biographical information. With annotations by J. H. Sainsbury

Komauer, Edwin, 1869–1944
Paul Sacher Stiftung
Port. Phot.
See Webern, Anton

Komzák, Karel, 1850–1905
Library of Congress
(Box 112)
A. Mus. Quot. S.: *Märchen*, St. Louis, 3 Nov. 1904. Mounted with portrait photograph signed, to G. Steward, St. Louis, 1 Dec. 1904

Kopsch, Julius, 1887–1970
Library of Congress
(Box 28)
A. Mus. ms. S.: *Erinnern*, to Maria, Berlin-Grunewald, 2 Mar. 1958. 3p., 29x21cm. Complete score for piano solo

Korbay, Francis Alexander, 1846–1913
Library of Congress
(Box 28)
A. Mus. ms. S.: "O lieb' so lang du lieben kannst." 1p., 25x24cm. Fragment

Kornauth, Egon, 1891–1959
Library of Congress
(Box 28, unless noted)

12 A. L. S.: Henndorf, 1956–1959. 27p.

2 T. L. S.: to Hans Moldenhauer. 10 Nov. 1957, 10 Feb. 1958. 3p., German

3 P. cards S.: July 1959. 6p.

2 A. L. S.: to Hans Moldenhauer, from Hertha Kornauth. Henndorf, 6 Nov. 1959; Augsburg, 23 Jan. 1962. 4p., German

5 T. L. S.: to Hans Moldenhauer, from Hertha Kornauth. Vienna, Henndorf, 1959–1961. 6p., German

P. card S.: to Hans Moldenhauer, from Hertha Kornauth. [Vienna?], 23 July 1962. German

Doc. S.: Article. "Theorie und Praxis," in *Wissenschaft und Praxis, Festschrift für Bernhard Paumgartner*, Atlantis, 1958, to Hans Moldenhauer, 7 Apr. 1958. pp.127–134, German

Pri. Sco. S.: *Drei Canons*, Vienna: Österreichischer Bundesverlag, c1951, to Hans Moldenhauer, 1958. 2p.

Pri. Sco. S.: *Sechs Lieder*, op. 1, Vienna: Doblinger, c1913, to Hans Moldenhauer, 3 Mar. 1958. 4p., German

Pri. Sco. S.: *Trio*, op. 27, Leipzig: Peters, n.d., to Hans Moldenhauer, 10 July 1957. 39p. + 16p. (parts)

Obit.: 30 Oct. 1959

Obit.: for Kornauth's mother, 1957

Port. Phot. S.: to Hans Moldenhauer, 1956 (Box 112)

See Schoenberg, Arnold

Wiener Stadt- u. Landesbibliothek
SUMMARY OF PRINCIPAL HOLDINGS:
Mus. ms.: *Elegie (auf den Tod eines Freundes)*. Incomplete

Mus. ms.: *Kammermusik*, op. 31. Sketches

Mus. ms.: *Nonett*, op. 31a

L.: to Marthe Frank. Vienna, 7 June 1917

Port. Phot.: June 1959

2 Port.: with work lists

Korngold, Erich Wolfgang, 1897–1957
Wiener Stadt- u. Landesbibliothek
Mus. ms.: *Cello Concerto*. Draft

Mus. ms. cop.: *Welt ist stille eingeschlafen*, to Hanna Schwarz

P. card: to Regine Zwira. Vienna, Dec. 1916. With musical quotation. Mounted on portrait photograph

L.: to Melanie Gutmann Rice. Vienna, 9 Dec. 1930

5 L.: to Alma Mahler, from Luise Korngold. Hollywood, 1957–1959

L.: to Bruno Eisner, from Luise Korngold. Hollywood, 16 June 1958

Mus. Quot.: Karlsbad, 17 July 1914[?]. Penned on verso of a calling card of Oskar Paior

Mus. Quot.: to Siegfried Keiler, Apr. 1922

Port. Phot.: see postcard above

Korngold, Julius, 1860–1945
Bayerische Staatsbibliothek
See Berg, Alban

Wiener Stadt- u. Landesbibliothek
L.: to Robert Müller-Hartmann. Vienna, 27 Apr. 1912
L.: Vienna, 17 July 1920. With musical illustration
L.: to Zemlinsky. Vienna, n.d.

Koschat, Thomas, 1845–1914
Library of Congress
(Box 28)
A. L. S.: Vienna, 26 May 1903. 2p., German
2 P. cards: of Koschat and the Koschat-Museum in Klagenfurt
A. Mus. Quot. S.: *Verlassen*, op. 4, Linz, 16 Nov. 1901
Doc.: Brochure. "Das Koschatmuseum in Klagenfurt." 12p., German
Doc.: Exhibition checklist. "Führer durch das Koschatmuseum in Klagenfurt." 52p., German

Kounadis, Arghyris, b. 1924
Library of Congress
(Box 97, unless noted)
A. Mus. ms. S.: *Heterophonika Idiomela*, Freiburg, 1967. 8p. + 1p. (explanation), various sizes. Sketches (Shelf)
A. Mus. ms. S.: *Teresias*, "Die Stadt," 1971. 39p., various sizes. Sketches. With additional blueprint score (18p.), and outline (1p.)
T. L. S.: to Hans Moldenhauer. Freiburg, 15 Oct. 1975. 1p., German

Koussevitzky, Serge, 1874–1951
Harvard University
Port. Gr.: with Nadia Boulanger, John Alden Carpenter, Mabel Daniels, Jean Françaix, Roy Harris, Edward Burlingame Hill, and Walter Piston

Kowalski, Max, 1882–1956
Washington State University
See Rosbaud, Hans

Kozinski, David B., 1917–1986
Whitworth College
SUMMARY OF PRINCIPAL HOLDINGS:
Mus. ms.: *Polish Fantasy*, for two violins, cello, and piano, 1975. Commissioned by AMPOL, Wilmington, Delaware. Full score

Kozinski, Stefan, b. 1953
Library of Congress
(Box 28)
A. Mus. ms. S.: *Bloomsday Odyssey*, Commissioned by the Spokane Symphony Orchestra for the Washington State Centennial Celebration Dedicated to Bruce Ferden...." 106p., 43x28cm., pencil, ink. With additional sketches and alternate pages

Whitworth College
SUMMARY OF PRINCIPAL HOLDINGS:
Mus. ms.: *Birthday Greetings*, for piano, to Dr. Hans Moldenhauer, 1986

Kraft, William, b. 1923
Harvard University
SUMMARY OF PRINCIPAL HOLDINGS:
Mus. ms.: *Andirivieni*
Mus. ms.: *Cadenze*, 1971
Mus. ms.: *Contextures*
Mus. ms.: *Games*
Mus. ms.: *I Will Go Cry with the Woman*, 1972
Mus. ms.: *Jazz Quartet*
Mus. ms.: *In Memoriam Igor Stravinsky*, 1972–1974
Mus. ms.: *Momentum*, 1966
Mus. ms.: *Transluscences*, 1979
Mus. ms.: *Triangles*, 1968
L.: to Hans Moldenhauer. Los Angeles, 11 Jan. 1978, 29 July 1983
Mus. ms. Repro.: *Encounters V*, 1975. Blueprint score

Krane, Sherman M., b. 1927
Harvard University
SUMMARY OF PRINCIPAL HOLDINGS:
Mus. ms.: *Sinfonia*

Krantz, Eugen, 1844–1898
Library of Congress
(Box 28)
Doc. S.: Report. On Edyth Walker's study at the
Royal Conservatory of Music in Dresden. Dresden,
19 Apr. 1893. 2p., German

Krastel, Fritz, 1839–1908
Library of Congress
(Box 28, unless noted)
A. L. S.: [to Ferdinand Löwe]. Vienna, 19 Oct. 1899.
2p., German
Port. Engr. S. (Box 112)

Kraus, Felix von, 1870–1937
Library of Congress
(Box 28)
2 A. L. S.: to Eugen Lindner. Vienna, 5, 11 May 1898.
16p., German

Krauss, Gabrielle, 1842–1906
Wiener Stadt- u. Landesbibliothek
2 L.: n.p., n.d.; Paris, 30 Nov.

Krebs, Carl, 1857–1937
Library of Congress
(Box 28)
A. L. S.: to Chrysander. Berlin, 14 Jan. 1893. 2p.,
German

Krebs [Miedcke], Karl August, 1804–1880
Library of Congress
(Box 28)
A. L. S.: to Brünner. Freiburg, 31 Dec. 1842. 1p.,
German

Krebs, Marie, 1851–1900
Library of Congress
(Box 28, unless noted)
A. Mus. Quot. S.: *Alla Polacca*, op. 89, Vivace by
Beethoven, [to a friend, Minnie?], London, 22 May
1875
Port. Phot. (Box 112)

Kreisler, Fritz, 1875–1962
Harvard University
L.: to Alexander Lászlo. 1927

Kremser, Eduard, 1838–1914
Wiener Stadt- u. Landesbibliothek
SUMMARY OF PRINCIPAL HOLDINGS:
Rcpt.: by Haslinger, for op. 6

Křenek, Ernst, 1900–1991
Harvard University
SUMMARY OF PRINCIPAL HOLDINGS:
Mus. ms.: *Basler Massarbeit*
Mus. ms.: *Doppelt beflügeltes Band*, op. 207, 1969–1970
Mus. ms.: *The Holy Ghost's Ark*, op. 91a, 1941
Mus. ms.: *Horizon Circled*, op. 196, 1967
Mus. ms.: *Instant Remembered*. With accompanying
letter to Hans Moldenhauer, 16 Sept. 1968
Mus. ms.: *Jonny spielt auf.* Excerpt
Mus. ms.: *Kleine Symphonie*, op. 58, Andante Sostenuto.
Excerpt. Mounted with portrait photograph
Mus. ms.: *Konzert für Klavier und Orchester in Fis-Dur*,
op. 18, Berlin, 21 Apr. 1923
Mus. ms.: *De Lamentatione Jeremiae Prophetae*,
1941–1942
Mus. ms.: *Miniature*
Mus. ms.: *Pallas Athene weint*, op. 144, 1952–1955. With
libretto
Mus. ms.: *Six for Two*
Mus. ms.: *Sonata*, op. 92, San Clemente, California,
5 Sept. 1941
Mus. ms.: *String Quartet No. 6*, 1935
Mus. ms.: *Twenty Miniatures*
Mus. ms.: *Vier Stücke*, op. 193, 1966
4 L.: to Paul Sanders. 1933, 1937
5 L.: to Aurelio de la Vega. Palm Springs, 21 Mar.
1971, 20 Nov. 1979, 1 Apr., 22 Nov. 1984, 7 May
1986
7 L.: to Hans Moldenhauer. 1982–1985
L.: to Nicolas Slonimsky
52 L.: to Helene Berg, Otto Jokl, Verne Kelsey, Boaz
Piller, others
Lib.: *Chrysomallos*, op. 186. English
2 Doc.: Lectures. On Webern, 1957, 1960
Doc. Repro.: Synopsis. *Der Zauberspiegel*, op. 192, 1966
2 Port. Phot.: see manuscript above
Paint.: 18 Aug. 1966. Watercolor, with dedication
S. rec.: *4 Hopkins Songs, 2 Zeitlieder, 3 Verhaeren Songs*

S. rec.: *Gesänge des späten Jahres*, op. 71
S. rec.: *Santa Fe Timetable, O Lacrymosa, Tape and Double, Accordion Toccata*
S. rec.: *Spätlese*, op. 218, *Drei Gesänge*, op. 56
See Slonimsky, Nicolas

Washington State University
See Rosbaud, Hans

Kretschmer, Edmund, 1830–1908
Library of Congress
(Box 28, unless noted)
A. L. S.: Dresden, 26 June 1878. 1p., German
A. L. S.: Dresden, 11 Apr. 1885. 1p., German
A. L. S.: to a theater director. Dresden, 22 Aug. 1898. 1p., German
A. Mus Quot. S.: *Heinrich der Löwe*, "Heinrichs Erzählung," Dresden, 23 Mar. 1876. German
Port. Phot. Repro. (Box 112)

Kretzschmar, Hermann, 1848–1924
Library of Congress
(Box 28)
P. card S.: to Otto Sonne. Leipzig, 15 Feb. 1897. 1p., German

Kreutzer [Kreuzer], Conradin [Conrad], 1780–1849
Wiener Stadt- u. Landesbibliothek
Mus. ms.: *Vengeance*
L.: to Diabelli. Vienna, 5 June 1835
L.: to Bäuerle. n.p., [1846]
Port. Engr.

Kreutzer, Leonid, 1884–1953
Library of Congress
(Box 28, unless noted)
A. L. S.: to Ferdinand Löwe. 5 Sept. 1908. 1p., German. Concerning the *Piano Concerto*, op. 30 by Rimsky-Korsakov
Port. Phot. Repro.: with accompanying biographical information (Box 112)

Kreutzer, Rodolphe, 1766–1831
Library of Congress
(Box 28)
A. L. S.: to Plantade. Paris, 6 Dec. 1806. 2p., French. Recommending a colleague; mentioning Cherubini

Krolop, Franz, 1839–1897
Library of Congress
(Box 28)
3 A. L. S.: to Schloss. Dresden, 10 May, 19 Dec. 1872; n.d. 5p., German

Krommer, Franz [Kramář, František Vincenc], 1759–1831
Library of Congress
(Box 28)
A. Mus. ms. S.: *Quartetto I*, [22 Nov.?] 1808. 38p., 14x32cm.

Krueger, Karl, 1894–1979
Harvard University
L.: to Charles Haubiel. Detroit, 28 May 1947. With copy of Haubiel's letter

Krzyżanowski, Rudolph, 1862–1911
Wiener Stadt- u. Landesbibliothek
L.: to Eugen Lindner. Hamburg, n.d.

Kubelík, Jan, 1880–1940
Library of Congress
(Box 28, unless noted)
A. Mus. Quot. S.: for Baron Fritz Schey, 12 Nov. 1906. 3m.
Port. Phot. S.: to Miss Reyburn. With clipping attached on verso, 26 Sept. 1921. English (Box 112)

Kubelík, Rafael, 1914–1996
Washington State University
See Rosbaud, Hans

Kubik, Gail, 1914–1984
Harvard University
L.: to Aurelio de la Vega. MacDowell Colony,
Petersboro, 10 Mar. 1960

Kücken, Friedrich Wilhelm, 1810–1882
Library of Congress
(Box 28)
A. Mus. ms. S.: *Die jungen Musikanten*, op. 36, Heft II,
Berlin. 2p., 24x30cm., German
3 A. L. S.: to Robert Cocks. 1850–1853. 11p., German.
With musical illustration
A. L. S.: to ?. Schwerin, 16 Feb. 1879. 3p., German
Clip.: Köln: *Neue Musik-Zeitung*, No. 9, 1 May 1882. 2p.
Biographical account, with portrait reproduced

Kuhe, Wilhelm, 1823–1912
Library of Congress
(Box 28)
A. Mus. Quot. S.: 18 Aug. 1872
A. Mus. Quot. S.: 31 Mar. 1896

Kurzmann-Leuchter, Rita [Henriette], 1900–1942
Library of Congress
(Box 28)
A. L. S.: to Otto Jokl. Heyst, Belgium, 1 Oct. 1931.
2p., German

Labarre [Berry], Théodore, 1805–1870
Library of Congress
(Box 28)
A. L. S.: to Olivier, of the publishing firm Mori and
Lavenu. Brighton, 4 Oct. [ca. 1837]. 1p., French

Labey, Marcel, 1875–1968
Library of Congress
(Box 113)
Port. Phot. S.: By Mathieu-Deroche

Lachner, Franz Paul, 1803–1890
Bayerische Staatsbibliothek
Mus. ms.: *Fugue in Three Voices on "Lachner,"* Munich,
Apr. 1841

2 L.: to Carl Reinecke. Munich, 5 Nov. 1871, 30 Nov.
1884

Lachner, Ignaz, 1807–1895
Bayerische Staatsbibliothek
L.: to the court conductor Lampert. Hamburg, 28 Mar.
1858
Doc.: Biographical information

Lachner, Vincenz, 1811–1893
Library of Congress
(Box 28)
A. L. S.: Karlsruhe, 18 Nov. 1875. 3p., German

Lack, Théodore, 1846–1921
Library of Congress
(Box 28, unless noted)
A. Mus. ms. S.: *Cavatine*. 3p., 35x27cm. For piano
A. L. S.: Paris, 13 June 1910. 1p., French
A. Doc. S.: Work list and artistic credo. Paris, 1910. 2p.,
French
Port. Phot. S. (Box 113)

Lackner, Stephan, b. 1910
Harvard University
SUMMARY OF PRINCIPAL HOLDINGS:
Mus. ms.: *Divertimento*
Mus. ms.: *Fantasia No. 2*, 1935
Mus. ms.: *A Legend*, 1956
Mus. ms.: *The Pied Piper*, 23 July 1958
Mus. ms.: *The Wayfarer*, op. 9
Mus. ms. Repro.: *Empfindungen*
Mus. ms. Repro.: *First Symphony*. Blueprint score
Mus. ms. Repro.: *Happy Birthday Variations*
Mus. ms. Repro.: *Music, When Soft Voices Die*. Blueprint
score
Mus. ms. Repro.: *Nostalgic Suite*. Facsimile
Mus. ms. Repro.: *Ein Paar Lieder*
Mus. ms. Repro.: *Passacaglia*
Mus. ms. Repro.: *Prisms*, op. 7
Mus. ms. Repro.: *Requiem for Falling Leaves*. Blueprint
score
Mus. ms. Repro.: *Romantic Overture*, op. 10
Mus. ms. Repro.: *The Tolling Bell*. Blueprint score
Port. Gr.: with Thomas Mann, 1935

Lacombe, Paul, 1837–1927
Library of Congress
(Box 113)
Port. Phot. S.: By Bernon

La Fage, Adrien de, 1805–1862
Library of Congress
(Box 28)
2 A. L. S.: n.p., 1 July [?], 13 Oct. 1858. 2p., French

Lafite, Karl, 1872–1945
Library of Congress
(Box 28)
Mus. ms. Repro. S.: *Vier Marienlieder*, June 1934, to
    Hanna Schwarz. 10p., 34x7cm., German. Blueprint
    score

La Forge, Frank, 1879–1953
Harvard University
Mus. ms.: *Retreat*

La Grange, Henry-Louis de, b. 1924
Library of Congress
(Box 28)
A. L. S.: to Alma Mahler. Vienna, 18 June 1959. 2p.,
    English
P. card S.: to Alma Mahler. n.p., n.d. French

Laires, Fernando, b. 1925
Library of Congress
(Box 28)
A. Card S.: to Aurelio de la Vega. [1983]. English

Lalo, Edouard, 1823–1892
Library of Congress
(Box 28)
A. Mus. ms. S.: *O Salutaris*, pour 3 voix de femmes,
    harmonium, et quintette à cordes, arranged by Lalo,

written "especially for my friend Lemoine," 4 Jan.
    1885. 8p., 34x27cm., ink
A. L. S.: to a friend. n.p., Monday, 23 Mar. 1p., French

Lamond, Frederic, 1868–1948
Northwestern University
L.: to Louis Lüstner. Frankfurt, 30 Jan. 1894

Lanao, Ulises
Harvard University
Mus. ms.: *Anda caminante*, Lima, Peru, 3 Sept. 1941
Mus. ms.: *Nostalgias del Perú*

Lang, Hans, 1897–1968
Library of Congress
(Box 29)
A. Mus. ms. S.: *Drei Männerchöre*, op. 11, *Nachtzauber*,
    Abendständchen, Nachtmusikanten. 16p.
A. Mus. ms. S.: *Gebet*. 2p., 34x25cm., German.
    Complete score
A. Mus. ms. S.: *Nachtzauber*. 5p., 35x28cm.

Lang, Max, b. 1917
Zentralbibliothek Zürich
Summary of Principal Holdings:
Mus. ms.: *David singt vor Saul*
Mus. ms.: *Kirke*
2 L.: to Hans Moldenhauer. St. Gallen, 16 Oct. 1957,
    17 Dec. 1958

Lang, Walter, 1896–1966
Zentralbibliothek Zürich
Mus. ms.: *Bulgarische Volksweisen*, op. 18, 1947

Lange, Francisco [Franz] Curt [Kurt], 1903–1997
Harvard University
L.: to Aurelio de la Vega. New Orleans, 26 Oct. 1965
2 L.

Lange, Samuel de, 1840–1911
Library of Congress
(Box 29)
A. L. S.: Köln, 27 Nov. 1883. 1p., German
P. card S.: to Isidor Seiss. The Hague, 30 Sept. 1886.
German
A. L. S.: The Hague, 19 Mar. 1887. 1p., German
2 A. L. S.: Stuttgart, 10 Dec. 1894, 25 Sept. 1907. 2p.,
German

Lantz, Christopher, b. 1936
Harvard University
Mus. ms.: *Sextet*, for woodwinds
Mus. ms.: *Suite for Piano*

Laparra, Raoul, 1876–1943
Library of Congress
(Box 29)
A. Mus. ms. S.: *Sépulture d'un poète maudit*, for voice
and piano, 8 Sept. 1924. 3p., 28x22cm.

**Laroche [Larosh, German Augustovich],
Hermann, 1845–1904**
Library of Congress
See Tchaikovsky, Pyotr Ilyich

Lassen, Eduard, 1830–1904
Library of Congress
(Box 29, unless noted)
A. Mus. ms. S.: *Den Frauen und Mädchen des
Künstlervereins zur Erinnerung*, Weimar, 20 Apr./12
June 1900. 2p., 34x25cm.
2 A. L. S.: to Eugen Lindner. Wilhelmshöhe, 13 Dec.
1885; Weimar, 2 Nov. 1903. 7p., German
A. Card S.: Weimar, 16 Apr. 1903. 2p., German
Port. Phot. Repro. S.: on postcard, to Matthias, 15 Apr.
1898. German (Box 113)
See Lindner, Eugen

Latrobe [La Trobe], Christian Ignatius, 1758–1836
Northwestern University
Pri. Sco.: *Three Sonatas for the Pianoforte*. Signed, first
edition

Laub, Ferdinand, 1832–1875
Library of Congress
See Tchaikovsky, Pyotr Ilyich

Laugs, Richard, b. 1907
Washington State University
See Rosbaud, Hans

Lauska, Franz, 1764–1825
Library of Congress
(Box 29)
A. L. S.: to a benefactor. Schleswig, [early 1790s]. 3p.,
German
A. L. S.: to a publisher [Peters?]. Berlin, 1 Mar. [1814].
2p., German
A. L. S.: to C. F. Peters. Berlin, 21 Jan. [1825]. 2p.,
German
A. L. S.: to Klosz. Berlin, n.d. 4p., German
A. L. S.: n.p., n.d. 1p., German

La Violette, Wesley, 1894–1978
Harvard University
L.: to Adolph Weiss. Chicago, 2 June 1930

Lavista, Mario, b. 1943
Harvard University
3 L.: to Aurelio de la Vega. Iztapalapa, 30 Nov. 1982;
Mexico, 2 Jan., 10 Apr. 1985

Leborne, Fernand, 1862–1929
Library of Congress
(Box 29)
A. L. S.: Ain, France, n.d. 4p., French
A. L. S.: n.p., 2 Jan. 1917. 1p., French

Lecocq, Charles, 1832–1918
Library of Congress
(Box 29, unless noted)
A. Mus. ms. Rev.: ["Jupiter tonans"]. 19p., 27x35cm.,
black ink, blue crayon, pencil, French. Undated.
Full score. Operatic aria for bass and orchestra
A. Mus. ms. S. arr.: String Quartets by Beethoven,
opera 59, 74, 95, 127, 130, 131, 132, ca. 1906–8.

223p., 27x35cm., brown ink, pencil. Score for piano, two hands
A. L. S.: 28 Dec. 1871. 1p., French
A. L. S.: Paris, 14 Mar. 1882. 1p., French
A. Mus. Quot. S.: *La Fille de Madame Angot*. 11m. For voice and piano
Port. Engr. (Box 113)

Lederer, Felix, 1877–1957
Northwestern University
Mus. ms. arr.: *Perpetuum mobile* by Paganini, op. 11, 11 July 1932. Full score

Leginska [Liggins], Ethel, 1886–1970
Northwestern University
Port. Phot.: to Boaz Piller, Boston, 1928

Legrenzi, Giovanni, 1626–1690
Library of Congress
(Box 29)
A. L. S.: to Count Albergati. Venice, 13 Oct. 1683. 1p., Italian. Discusses Torelli

Lehár, Franz [Ferencz], 1870–1948
Library of Congress
(Box 29, unless noted)
A. Mus. ms.: *Strohwitwe sein*. 2p., 34x26cm., pencil. Full score. Last 9m. of draft
P. card S.: to Leo Heller. Budapest, 21 Feb. 1912. German
A. L. S.: Vienna, 21 Apr. 1920. 1p., German
P. card S.: to Hilb[?]. Berlin, 27 Mar. 1926. German
A. L. S.: Vienna, 21 June 1928. 1p., German
A. Mus. Quot. S.: *Der Rastelbinder*, Vienna, 3 Feb. 1905
A. Mus. Quot. S.: with portrait photograph below
Port. Phot. S.: with autograph musical quotation, *Das Fürstenkind* (Box 113)
Port. Phot. S.: to Alexander Zemlinsky, 1918 (Box 113)

Lehmann, Hans Ulrich, b. 1937
Zentralbibliothek Zürich
Mus. ms.: *Monodie*, für ein Blasinstrument. With additional blueprint score
Mus. ms.: *Quanti I*
Mus. ms.: *Spiele für Oboe und Harfe*, 1965. With additional facsimile
2 L.: to Hans Moldenhauer. Basel, 7 Nov. 1970, 12 Apr. 1971
Doc.: Biographical information and work list

Lehmann, Lilli, 1848–1929
Library of Congress
(Box 29, unless noted)
A. L. S.: to Lola Artôt de Padilla. Berlin, 19 June 1909. 2p., German
A. L. S.: to Ellis. n.p., n.d. 2p., English
T. p.: *Meine Gesangskunst*. Berlin, 1909
Port. Phot. Gr.: (Box 113)
Port. S. Repro.: 1909 (Box 113)

Lehmann, Liza [Elizabeth], 1862–1918
Northwestern University
L.: to Mrs. Head. Wimbledon, Tuesday, n.d.

Leibowitz, René, 1913–1972
Library of Congress
(Box 29, unless noted)
A. Mus. ms. S.: *Concertino for Piano Four Hands*, op. 47, Paris and Darmstadt, Sept.–Oct. 1958. 12p., 35x27cm., ink, pencil. Complete score, first draft
A. L. S.: to Erich Itor Kahn. Paris, 20 Oct. 1949. 1p., French
2 T. L. S.: to Aurelio de la Vega. Paris, 15 May 1957, 20 May 1959. 2p., English
3 A. L. S.: to Aurelio de la Vega. Paris, 28 May 1957, 4 Mar. 1958; Madrid, 17 Aug. 1959. 3p., English
6 A. L. S.: to Hans Moldenhauer. Paris, Ljubljana, 1960–1962. 7p., English

A. L. S.: to Paul A. Pisk. Paris, 2 Apr. 1962. 1p.,
English
2 Mus. mss. Repro. S.: *Concertino for Piano Four Hands.*
20p. each
Doc.: Article. "Hommage à René Leibowitz," by
Pierre Chan, Max Deutsch, Claude Helffer, Michel
Leiris, Maurice Le Roux, Jean-Marie Move, Michel
Philippot, in *Musique de tous les temps,* Feb.–Mar.
1973. 30p., French. Inscribed by Mary Jo Leibowitz
Prog. S.: "Hommage à Arnold Schoenberg," program
booklet for the Festival International de Musique
de Chambre Contemporaine, to the Moldenhauers,
29 Jan. 1947. 22p., French. Inscribed by René and
Mary Jo Leibowitz
Prog.: "Mödlinger Schoenberg-Tage," Oct. 1982. 10p.,
German
Port. Phot.: to Hans Moldenhauer, 28 Oct. 1982.
Inscribed by Mary Jo Leibowitz (Box 113)
Bk. S.: *Erich Itor Kahn: un grand répresentant de la
musique contemporaine,* by René Leibowitz and
Konrad Wolff, Paris: Buchet, 1958. 182p., French.
Inscribed by René and Mary Jo Leibowitz, 29 Oct.
1982

Leichtentritt, Hugo, 1874–1951
Harvard University
L.: to Paul Sanders. Berlin, 30 Nov. 1932
L.: to Bruno Eisner. Cambridge, 18 Nov. 1943
Doc. Repro.: Recommendation. For Olga Eisner

Leinsdorf [Landauer], Erich, 1912–1993
Harvard University
L.: to Solomon Pimsleur. n.p., 1 Oct. 1943

Lemmens [née Sherrington], Helen, 1834–1906
Northwestern University
L.

Léner, Jenő, 1894–1948
Library of Congress
See Schoenberg, Arnold

Léonard, Adolph
Library of Congress
(Box 29)
A. Mus. Quot. S.: [Melodic line, 4m.]. Château de
Bomal, 26 Feb. 1866

Leoncavallo, Ruggero, 1857–1919
Library of Congress
(Box 30)
A. Mus. Quot. S.: *La Bohème,* Vienna, 27 May 1897

Leroux, Xavier, 1863–1919
Northwestern University
L.: to Massenet. n.p., 1908

Lert, Ernst Josef Maria, 1883–1955
Bayerische Staatsbibliothek
See Berg, Alban

Lert, Richard Johannes, 1885–1980
Bayerische Staatsbibliothek
See Berg, Alban

**Leschetizky, Theodor [Leszetycki, Teodor],
1830–1915**
Library of Congress
(Box 30)
A. L. S.: to Frau Mankiewicz. Vienna, 20 July 1903.
3p., German

Le Senne, Camille, 1851–1931
Northwestern University
L.: to Massenet. Paris, n.d.

Leslie, Henry, 1822–1896
Northwestern University
2 L.: to Miss Stephenson. Llansaintffraid, Apr. 1874;
London, 22 Apr. 1874
L.: to Sir Spenser. Montgomeryshire, 20 Nov. 1885

L'Espée, Roland de
Library of Congress
(Box 30)
2 A. L. S.: Saint Germain en Laye, 6 Friday, 1919; 30
    July 1936. 3p., French
T. L. S.: Paris, 23 May 1935. 1p., French
T. Doc. Rev.: Draft. Suggested concerts for the "Week
    of French Music." 1p., French
Doc.: Flyer announcing concert series. "Semaine
    Debussy 1935," Saint Germaine en Laye. 1p.,
    French
T. Doc.: List of names. 1p.
T. Doc. Annot.: List of sponsor names. 1p., with
    additional copy

Le Sueur [Lesueur], Jean-François, 1760–1837
Library of Congress
(Box 30)
A. L. S.: to Baron ?. n.p., 15 Sept.[?] 1821. 1p., French

Lesur, Daniel Jean Yves, b. 1908
Washington State University
See Rosbaud, Hans

Letelier, Alfonso, 1912–1994
Harvard University
5 L.: to Aurelio de la Vega. Aculce Rangue, 22 July
    1963; 11 Dec. 1983; 1983, from Carmen Letelier;
    Santiago, 26 Apr., 14 Nov. 1985

Lettvin, Theodore, b. 1926
Harvard University
L.: to Ed Costello. Cleveland, 11 Apr. 1936

Levi, Hermann, 1839–1900
Bayerische Staatsbibliothek
Mus. ms. cop.: *Falstafferel*, ca. 1870
L.: Munich, [31 Dec. 1873]

Library of Congress
(Box 30)
A. L. S.: Bayreuth, 7 July 1896. 1p., German

Levitzki, Mischa, 1898–1941
Library of Congress
(Box 113)
Port. Phot. S.: to Boaz Piller, Boston, 1 Mar. 1921

Lewis, Malcolm, b. 1925
Harvard University
Mus. ms.: *Children's Petite Suite*
Mus. ms.: *Hobby Horse*
Mus. ms.: *Lycanthropy*
Mus. ms.: *Trio for Violin, Cello and Piano*
L.

Lewis, Robert Hall, b. 1926
Harvard University
2 L.: to Aurelio de la Vega. Baltimore, 17 Sept. 1983,
    21 Jan. 1984

Lhévinne, Rosina, 1880–1976
Harvard University
Port. Gr.: with Josef Lhévinne, 1951

Liebermann, Rolf, b. 1910
Washington State University
See Rosbaud, Hans

Zentralbibliothek Zürich
SUMMARY OF PRINCIPAL HOLDINGS:
Mus. ms.: *Furioso*
5 L.: to Hans Moldenhauer. Hamburg, Küssnacht,
    1956–1964
Doc.: Article. "Music in Europe." With annotations by
    Hans Moldenhauer
2 Port. Phot.

Lienau, Emil Robert, 1838–1920
Library of Congress
(Box 30)
A. L. S.: to A. W. Gottschalg. Berlin, 9 June 1870. 1p.,
    German

Lier, Bertus van, 1906–1972
Library of Congress
(Box 55)
A. Mus. ms. Rev.: "In Memoriam," by Johan Franco, 1933, piano reduction of "Elegy" by van Lier. 3p., 34x26cm. Music in the autograph of van Lier, annotations at the top of the first page by Franco
Doc. Repro.: Article on van Lier. "The Song of Songs," by Johan Franco, in *Rosicurcian Digest*, Mar. 1955. 2p.
Pri. Sco. S.: *In Memoriam*, for String Orchestra, Composers Press: New York, 1939. 5p.
Pri. Sco. S.: *Kleine Suite*, to Wolfgang Fraenkel, Amsterdam: Broekmans & Van Poppel, 1935

Lifschitz, Max, b. 1948
Harvard University
L.: to Aurelio de la Vega. New York, 2 Nov. 1983

Ligeti, György, b. 1923
Library of Congress
(Box 107, unless noted)
A. Mus. ms. S.: *Apparitions*, [1958–1959]. 9p., 42x30cm., pencil. Full score
A. Mus. ms.: [*Atmosphères*, 1961]. 5p., 34x27cm., blue, red ink, pencil. Sketches in full score (Box 109)
2 T. L. S.: to Aurelio de la Vega. Vienna, 8 June 1963, 17 July 1966. 2p., English
P. card S.: to Gloria Coates. Berlin, 4 Nov. 1972. 2p., English

Limbert, Frank L., 1866–1938
Library of Congress
(Box 30, unless noted)
A. L. S.: Frankfurt, 22 May 1912. 2p., German. Giving autobiographical details
A. Mus. Quot. S.: *Johannes*, op. 18. German
Port. Phot. S.: by Luck (Box 113)

Lincke, Paul, 1866–1946
Library of Congress
(Box 30)
A. Mus. Quot. S.: London, 21 Feb. 1911

Lind [Lind-Goldschmidt], Jenny [Johanna Maria], 1820–1887
Library of Congress
(Box 30, unless noted)
A. L. S.: to Balfe. n.p., [1846?]. 3p., French, with translation
A. L. S.: to Madame Gonne. n.p., n.d. 3p., German, with English translation. Fragment
Clip.: 6 Oct. 1920. 1p., English
2 Obit.: English
Port. Engr.: with attached clipping (Box 113)

Lindblad, Rune
Library of Congress
(Box 30)
2 T. L. S.: to Aurelio de la Vega. Gothenburg, 28 Feb. 1970; Västra Frölunda, 14 June 1972. 2p., English

Lindner, Eugen, 1858–1915
Library of Congress
(Box 30)
A. L. S.: to colleagues. Weimar, 20 May 1899. 4p., German. Also signed by Gustav Gutheil, Karl Goepfart, Eduard Lassen, Rosel, and others

Lindpaintner, Peter J. von, 1791–1856
Bayerische Staatsbibliothek
Mus. ms.: *Des Todtengräbers Liebeslied*, 1838
2 L.: Stuttgart, 14 May 1842; 31 May 1850

Lipínski, Karol Józef, 1790–1861
Northwestern University
L.: to Dragonetti. Dresden, 15 Sept. 1840

Lipsius, Marie [La Mara], 1837–1927
Library of Congress
(Box 30)
2 A. L. S.: Ischl, 9, 19 Aug. 1895. 7p., German

Liszt, Franz [Ferenc], 1811–1886
Library of Congress
(Box 30, unless noted)
A. Mus. ms.: [*Psalm XVIII*], *Die Himmel erzählen die Ehre Gottes*, for Tenor, Bass, and Accompaniment, [1860]. 8p., 27x35cm., ink, pencil. Draft in condensed score
A. Mus. ms. S.: *Le Triomphe funèbre du Tasso*, for piano duet, St. Elizabeth, 19 Nov. 1866. 11p., 31x24cm., brown, red ink. Unpublished
A. L. S.: 22 July 1844. 3p., French
A. L. S.: to an editor, [von Bülow?]. Weimar, 6 Aug. 1850. 3p., French
A. L. S.: to Eduard von Liszt. Vienna, 30 Apr. 1869. 3p., German
A. L. S.: n.p., 9 May 1874. 1p., German
A. L. S.: [to a Berlin conductor]. Budapest, 24 Jan. 1881. 1p., German
A. L. S.: 11 May [1881?]. 1p., German
A. L. S.: Weimar, 7 May 1884. 2p., German
A. L. S.: to Louis de Serres. Budapest, 29 Jan. 1885. 1p., French
A. L. S.: n.p., Friday morning, n.d. 2p., French
A. L. S.: n.p., Friday, n.d. 4p., French. Referring to a visit with the Schumanns
2 L. Repro.: to Franz Liszt, by "Ossiana" and "Sorella." 4p., French
Pri. Sco. S.: *Ungarischer Marsch*, Leipzig: Schuberth, 1867, to Anton Faulwetter, Budapest, Mar. 1885. 31p. Faulwetter did the instrumentation of the march. First autograph purchase by Hans Moldenhauer
Port. Lith. (Box 113)
Port. Phot. (Box 113)

Port. Repro.: of Liszt, inscribed to Webern, from Schoenberg, Jan. 1911 (Box 113)
Port. Repro. (Box 113)
See Webern, Anton

Litolff, Henry, 1818–1891
Library of Congress
(Box 30)
A. Mus. S.: "Mein Lieb! Flieht ein Tag," to Heinrich Schlesinger, Dresden, 1844. 4p., 17x25cm.
3 A. L. S.: Wiesbaden, 20 June, 6 July, 23 July 1860. 8p., French, German
2 A. L. S.: Ilsenberg, 5, 8 Sept. 1860. 4p., French, German

Lloyd, Charles Harford, 1849–1919
Northwestern University
L.: to Miss Stephenson. Windsor, 19 Dec. 1897

Lloyd, Edward, 1845–1927
Northwestern University
L.: to Charles Hallé. London, 9 May

Lockey, Charles, 1820–1901
Northwestern University
L.: to Elise. London, 11 Dec. 1879
L.: from Martha (wife). Hastings, n.d.

Lockwood, Normand, b. 1906
Harvard University
2 L.: to Eugene Weigel. Keene Valley, 13 Aug. 1948; Middlebury, n.d.
L.: to Solomon Pimsleur. New York, 9 July 1951

Loeffler, Charles Martin, 1861–1935
Library of Congress
(Box 98, unless noted)
A. Mus. ms. S.: [*Bolero triste, Chansons d'amant*], to Povla Frijsh, Medfield, Massachusetts, Summer 1900. 4p., 33x26cm., ink. Text by Gustave Kahn.

With accompanying letter, to Hans Moldenhauer, from Ellen Knight, 27 Feb. 1985
A. L. S.: to Piller. Medfield, Massachusetts. 1p., French
Port. Phot. (Box 113)

Loesser, Arthur, 1894–1969
Harvard University
2 Port. Phot.: one with Beryl Rubinstein

Loevensohn, Marix, 1880–1943
Library of Congress
(Box 30)
A. L. S.: to Paul F. Sanders. Amsterdam, 27 July 1932. 6p., French

Loewe, Carl, 1796–1869
Library of Congress
(Box 30)
A. Mus. ms.: *Die Elfenkönigin.* 3p., 33x20cm., German. Complete score

Löwe, Ferdinand, 1865–1925
Wiener Stadt- u. Landesbibliothek
L.: [after 1910]

Loewe, Sophie, 1812–1866
Library of Congress
(Box 30)
A. L. S.: to ?. n.p., n.d. 3p., Italian
A. L. S.: to ?. n.p., n.d. 4p., Italian

Logothetis, Anestis, 1921–1994
Library of Congress
(Box 107)
A Mus. ms. S.: *Anastasis,* 1969. 15p., various sizes. With additional 4p. typescript, and 11p. facsimile
A. Mus. ms. S.: *Mensuren,* 19 May 1969. 1p., 33x46cm.
A. Mus. ms. S.: *Odyssee,* 27 Mar. 1963. 1p., 49x37cm. Complete score. With additional printed score

A. Mus. ms. S.: *Styx,* 17–18 Dec. 1968. 2p., 43x33cm. Draft, sketches. With additional blueprint score signed, copy of same, and sound recording
Mus. ms. Repro.: *Erwosis; Diffusion; Kentra; Orbitals, Oscillations.* 6p., photoreproduction of scores
Doc.: Booklet. "Zeichen als Aggregatzustand der Musik," Vienna: Jugend und Volk, c1974
S. rec.: *Kentra,* 1965

Lohse, Otto, 1858–1925
Bayerische Staatsbibliothek
See Berg, Alban

London, Edwin, b. 1929
Harvard University
L.: to Aurelio de la Vega. Cleveland, Ohio, 8 Sept. 1982

Long, Marguerite, 1874–1966
Library of Congress
See Dukas, Paul

Lopatnikoff, Nikolai, 1903–1976
Harvard University
2 L.: to Aurelio de la Vega. Pittsburgh, 26 May, 29 Oct. 1950
L.: to Bruno and Olga Eisner, from Mrs. Lopatnikoff. Finland, 26 June 1933
Mus. Quot.: *String Quartet No. 3.* With accompanying letter to Aurelio de la Vega, Pittsburgh, 1 Apr. 1958
Port. Repro.: with work list

López-Chávarri, Eduardo, 1875–1970
Library of Congress
(Box 12)
A. Mus. ms. S.: *Danza Valenciana,* to Ricardo Viñes. 4p., 36x26cm.

Loriod, Yvonne, b. 1924
Washington State University
See Rosbaud, Hans

Lortzing, Albert, 1801–1851
Library of Congress
(Box 98, unless noted)
A. L. S.: ?, 2 June 1838. 1p., German
A. Quot. S.: *Hans Sachs*, to Ernst Streben
Port. Engr. (Box 113)

Louis Ferdinand [Friedrich Christian Ludwig], Prince of Prussia, 1772–1806
Library of Congress
(Box 30)
A. L. S.: to Captain von Schweder. n.p., n.d. 1p., German

Lucca, Pauline, 1841–1908
Library of Congress
(Box 30)
A. L. S.: Hotel zum Kronprinzen, 4 Feb. 1864. 3p., German
A. L. S.: to an opera director in Leipzig. Vienna, 28 Aug. 1871. 1p., German
A. L. S.: to Sendersky[?]. n.p., 4 Mar. 1875. 3p., German
A. L. S.: Berlin, n.d. 2p., German

Lübeck, Ernst, 1829–1876
Library of Congress
(Box 30)
A. Mus. ms. S.: *Scherzo pour piano*, to Adelma Bournos[?] de Godoy, Mexico, Mar. 1854. 9p., 35x27cm.
A. L. S.: to Miss Stephenson. Paris, 13 May 1875. 3p., English
A. L. S.: Westbourne Park Crescent, Friday, n.d. 2p., French
Obit.: *The Times*, 1876

Luening, Otto, 1900–1996
Harvard University
Summary of Principal Holdings:

Mus. ms.: *Fantasia Brevis for Flute and Piano*, 1929
L.: to Adolph Weiss. 1931–1935
L.: to Eugene Weigel. New York, 20 Oct. 1949
8 L.: to Gloria Coates. 1971–1976

Lully, Jean-Louis, 1667–1688
Library of Congress
(Box 30)
Doc. S.: [Receipt?]. Paris, 2 Apr. 1687

Luna, Adolfo Victorio, 1889–1942
Library of Congress
(Box 30)
A. Mus. ms. S.: *Procesión de los Allis (Tradición Riojana), para piano*. 4p., 34x27cm.

Lunn, Charles, 1838–1906
Northwestern University
L.: to William Cummings. n.p., n.d.

Lussan, Zélie de, 1862–1949
Harvard University
L.: to George Cecil. London, 7 May
L.

Lutosławski, Witold, 1913–1994
Library of Congress
(Box 107)
A. Mus. ms.: [*Jeux vénitiens*], 7 Mar. 1961. 7 leaves, various sizes + 7p. (pp.9–17, 46x35cm.), pencil, colored pencils. See letter below
T. L. S.: to Hans Moldenhauer. Warsaw, 20 June 1963. 1p., English
L.: to Hans Moldenhauer, from Herbert Höntsch at Moeck Verlag. 11 June 1963. 1p., German. Regarding manuscript above
Prog.: *Jeux vénitiens*, 11 Jan. 1963. German. Musica Viva program listing

Lutyens, Elisabeth, 1906–1983
Northwestern University
Mus. ms.: *Symphonies for Solo Piano, Wind, Harps, and Percussion*, op. 45, 1961. With additional printed score
See Clark, Edward

Lutzer, Jenny, 1816–1877
Wiener Stadt- u. Landesbibliothek
3 L.: n.p., n.d.

Lux, Friedrich, 1820–1895
Library of Congress
(Box 30)
P. card S.: to Enzian. Mainz, 11 May 1885. 1p., German

L'vov, Alexei Feodorovich, 1798–1870
Library of Congress
(Box 30)
A. L. S.: to Schlesinger. St. Petersburg, 21 Feb., 5 Mar. 1845. 4p., French. Refers to his new opera; Viardot, Meyerbeer, others

MacCunn, Hamish, 1868–1916
Northwestern University
L.: to August Manns. London, n.d.

MacDowell [McDowell], Edward, 1860–1908
Harvard University
L.: to Arthur Schmidt. Boston, 22 Dec. 1891
L.: New York, 24 Oct. 1896
L.: to Story. Peterboro, 14 Sept. 1898
L.: to Barton. Boston, n.d.
Port. Phot.: 24 Dec. 1907
See MacDowell, Marian

MacDowell, Marian, 1857–1956
Harvard University
37 L.: to Charles Haubiel. 1934–1956
L.: to Rudolph Ganz. Peterborough, 9 Oct. 1945

Macfarren, Sir George, 1813–1887
Northwestern University
L.: to Ignaz Moscheles. London, 7 Oct. 1850
L.: to Lockey. London, 20 Apr.
L.: London, 29 Mar.
Obit.
Port.

Macfarren, Walter, 1826–1905
Northwestern University
Mus. ms.: *Symphony in B-flat*, 1879. Full score. With performance listing

Mach, Ernst, 1838–1916
Wiener Stadt- u. Landesbibliothek
2 L.: to Bruno Eisner. Vienna, 9 Oct. 1902, 7 Nov. 1903

Mackenzie, Sir Alexander, 1847–1935
Northwestern University
Mus. Alb. l.: *Twelfth Night*, Florence, 2 Feb. 1888. Excerpt
L.: to Otto Goldschmidt. London, 21 Mar. 1894
10 L.: to Baron Angelo Eisner von Eisenhof. 1910–1933

Mader, Jerry, b. 1944
Harvard University
Mus. ms.: *The Manichees*

Mader, Raoul Maria, 1856–1940
Wiener Stadt- u. Landesbibliothek
L.: to a conductor. Vienna, 24 Sept. 1891

Maderna, Bruno, 1920–1973
Harvard University
See Bayer, Michael Joseph

[Maffon, Pietro?], 1513[?]–1575
Library of Congress
(Box 31)
A. Doc. S.: Tax declaration. Brescia, Apr. 1548. 1p., Italian

Mahler, Alma, 1879–1964
Bayerische Staatsbibliothek
SUMMARY OF PRINCIPAL HOLDINGS:
4 A. L. S.: to Norbert Schwarzmann. ca. 1924
A. L. S.: to Julius Schloss. 29 Mar. 1936
A. Card S.: to Zemlinsky. [1936].
A. L. S.: to Friederike Zweig. Beverly Hills, 14 Aug. 1950
A. L. S.: to Hans Moldenhauer. New York, 3 Mar. 1958. 2p.
A. L. S.: n.d. 1p.
A. Doc.: Autobiographical sketch. 2p. With additional typescript
Call. c. Annot.
A. Doc. S.: Facsimile. Mahler's Tenth Symphony. With Alma Mahler's autograph dedication to Zemlinsky
Doc.: File. Correspondence, writings, documents, 1956–1959. Includes letter by friends and business associates, typescripts of original writings, interviews, legal papers, photos, newspaper criticisms, and assorted notes
A. Doc. S.: Note. Description to accompany the sketches for Mahler's Tenth Symphony
Doc. A. Annot.: Poem. Carbon copy of "An Alma," by Franz Werfel, with Alma Mahler's annotation. 1p., with two portrait photographs of Franz Werfel

Mahler, Fritz, 1901–1973
Library of Congress
See Schoenberg, Arnold

Mahler, Gustav, 1860–1911
Bayerische Staatsbibliothek
SUMMARY OF PRINCIPAL HOLDINGS:
A. Mus. ms.: *Des Knaben Wunderhorn*, No. 3, "Trost im Unglück," for voice and piano. 2p., 32x25cm. First draft; No. 10, "Lob der Kritik," for voice and piano. 3p., 32x25cm.
[A?]. Mus. ms. S.: *Symphony No. 2*. 60p., 27x35cm. Piano reduction, complete manuscript
A. Mus. ms.: *Symphony No. 4*. 2p., 27x34cm. First movement, condensed score, early sketches. Recto of leaf contains measures 184–197, followed by 20 measures crossed out. Verso of leaf begins with measures 226–242 (crossed out), with 8 unidentified measures following; First movement, condensed score, early sketches (1p., 27x34cm.); Preliminary version of the final full score, including first

movement (28p.), second movement (25p.), and third movement (26p.), all 27x34cm.; Fourth movement, "'Das himmlische Leben,' aus *Des Knaben Wunderhorn*, Eine Humoreske für eine Singstimme mit Orchester, Partitur" (37p., 35x27cm.); also, piano-vocal score (13p., 35x27cm.), both manuscripts by a copyist, with numerous additions and corrections in Mahler's autograph, with cover marked "4.Satz," (33x26cm.)
A. Mus. ms.: *Symphony No. 7* and *Symphony No. 6*; additional unused sketches, ca. 1903–5. 5 single leaves (9 pages), 27x35cm., with accompanying statement by Alban Berg (9 July 1924)
A. Mus. ms.: *Symphony No. 9*: Third movement, sketches in condensed score. 2p., 35x27cm.; Fourth movement, measures 3 to 39 in condensed score; on verso, early draft for the second movement (2p., 27x34cm.)
A. Mus. ms.: *Symphony No. 10*: First movement, Adagio. Complete first draft (12p., 27x35cm.); sketch in condensed score (1p., 19 measures, 34x27cm.), with a note in the hand of Alma Mahler; sketches in condensed score (1p., 41 measures, 27x35cm.); Third movement, "Purgatorio." Sketch in condensed score. (1p., 27x34cm.); Fourth movement. Sketches in condensed score. (1p., 27x34cm.) A note accompanies the leaf, partly written by Alban Berg, partly by Alma Mahler
A. Mus ms.: "Der Tamboursgesell," for voice and orchestra. 11p., 27x35cm. Full score, containing some corrections. Also, piano-vocal score, dated at end, Maiernigg, 12 July 1901. 2p., 27x35cm. The first page contains 2 versions
A. L. S.: to Josephine Poisl. [Vienna, 18 Mar. 1880]. 4p.
A. L. S.: to Josephine Poisl. [Vienna], n.d. 7p.
A. L. S.: to Fanni Poisl. Vienna, 29 Mar. 1880. 4p.
A. L. S.: to Alma Mahler. Communications, 1901–1910. Approximately 326 items, including 225 autograph letters (totaling 580 pages), 59 postcards, 2 Bons, 34 telegrams, 6 poems (all dating from 1910, listed above). Included are the following communications to Alma Mahler: Prague, 10 Sept. 1908. 4p., opening with the motto "O selig, o selig" and expressing his exasperation over rehearsals and instrumentalists. Also asking for Pfitzner's address; Hotel Blauer Stern, Prague, 22 Sept. 1908. 2p.; Amsterdam, n.d. 3p., telling her that his symphony was a great success in Amsterdam. He had decided to present the Fourth and not the Seventh Symphony in New York

19 A. L. S.: to Carl and Anna Moll. 43p. The correspondence begins in Vienna during Mahler's tenure at the Court Opera and continues through his American period up to the summer of 1910 when he stayed in Toblach

A. L. S.: to Heinrich Conried. [1907]. 3p.

24 A. L. S.: to Emil Hertzka. [1909–1910]. 58p.

A. L. S.: to Gatti-Casazza. n.d. 7p.

4 L.: to Musik Edition Wien [Universal Edition]. n.d.

A. L. S.: to Prince Montenuovo. n.d. 3p.

A. L. S.: to a publisher. n.d. 4p.

A. L. S.: to Fritz Steinbach. Maiernigg, n.d. 4p. Discusses in detail the rehearsals for his Third Symphony

Tlgm. A. Annot.: from H. Fernow. Berlin. With Mahler's notes on recto

Tlgm. A. Annot.: from Sachnowsky. With draft of Mahler's response penned on verso

Tlgm.: from Ambassador Tucher. Berlin

A. T. p.: "2. Satz./(Scherzo)/(August 1901. Maiernigg beendet)." 1p., 27x35cm.

A. Doc.: Note. [ca. 1880]. 1p.

3 A. Doc.: Poems. "In der Nacht!", Sept. 1884; "Ebenso," n.d.; "für den 18. August .84." 4p.

A. Doc. S.: Poems. Letter draft, with poem stanzas, 18 Oct. 1884. 4p.

A. Doc.: Poems. Draft of 2 poems for *Lieder eines fahrenden Gesellen*: "Die zwei blauen Augen," 15 Dec. 1884; "Ich hab' ein glühend' Messer," 19 Dec. 1884. 2p.

A. Doc.: Poems. Miscellaneous drafts of poems. 5p.

A. Doc.: Poetic stanzas. 2p.

6 A. Doc.: Poems. "Meiner Holden! Immer Gegenwärtigen!," 17 Aug. 1910. 1p.; "Holdeste! Liebste! Mein Saitenspiel! Und mein Sturmlied!," n.d. 1p.; "Im faden Coupè—nach alter Gewohnheit!," n.d. 2p.; "In lichten Fernen," n.d. 2p., 12 lines of poetry. Autograph of the poem sent by telegram on Mahler's departure for the consultation with Dr. Sigmund Freud in Leiden, on verso, note to Alma Mahler; "Im Coupè auf der Rückkehr," 27 Aug. 1910. 1p.; "Du süsse Hand, die mich gebunden!," n.d. 1p.

Port. Phot.: 1884

Port. S.: Original etching by Rudolf Herrmann. Signed by the artist and by Mahler

Port. Phot. S.: Signed and dated by Mahler, 1911

Doc.: Card of admission to Mahler's funeral

3 Docs.: Posters. One promoting Mahler's First and Second Symphonies, and two others announcing the publication of the Third Symphony

Doc. S.: Second Symphony. First edition. With autograph dedication to Busoni

2 Docs.: Tenth Symphony. Full score of the Adagio and "Purgatorio" movements, edited by Otto Jokl, printed by Associated Music Publishers, New York, 1951

Mus. ms. Repro.: [same], 1924. Facsimile edition

See Mahler, Alma

Library of Congress
See Weigl, Karl

Northwestern University
Mus. ms.: *Third Symphony in D Minor*. First page of the last movement, condensed score

Paul Sacher Stiftung
A. Mus. ms.: *Symphony No. 2*, ("Resurrection"), Todtenfeier, Prague, 10 Sept. 1888. 77p., 33x24cm. Full score. The original version of the first movement. On the title page, the original heading "Symphonie in C-moll," and signed by Mahler. Dated at end, with added note "Dauer netto 20 Minuten." With many instructions to the conductor and performers in the margins. Original fitted case, folio

A. Mus. ms.: *Lieder eines fahrenden Gesellen*, for voice and orchestra, 1891–1893[?]. 58p., 34x27cm. Full score, consisting of "Wenn mein Schatz Hochzeit macht," "Ging heut' Morgen übers Feld," "Ich hab' ein glühend Messer," "Die zwei blauen Augen." Containing many differences from the published versions and the only autograph source of the full score. Notated in ink, with many erasures and corrections. Some annotations in pencil. Instructions for the players added in the margins. On flyleaf, inscription of Hermann Behn, 1895. Original cover binding

Wiener Stadt- u. Landesbibliothek
A. Mus. ms.: Sketches to an unidentified symphonic movement, with a cover page in the autograph of Alban Berg. Calling the musical material "totally unknown" ("völlig unbekannt"), Berg comments on the possible date of origin, which he ascribes to an early period. The sketches represent a scherzo-like movement in 6/8, C Major-C minor, with a projected trio in 2/4 in A-flat Major. Berg conjectures that the melodies may have been transformed by Mahler at some time, possibly as late as in the Tenth Symphony. Berg signs his name and the date July 7,

1929. A total of 10p. (1p. by Berg, 7 leaves (9p.) by Mahler), 27x34 cm.

Mus. ms.: *Symphony No. 2.* 31m. Sketches for the coda of the first movement

L.: to Carl Moll. [Vienna, 1901]

Doc.: Outline. *Das Lied von der Erde*

See Berg, Alban

See Redlich, Hans F.

Mahler, Leopoldine, 1863–1889
Bayerische Staatsbibliothek
SUMMARY OF PRINCIPAL HOLDINGS:
A. L. S.: n.d. 4p.

Mainardi, Enrico, 1897–1976
Washington State University
See Rosbaud, Hans

Malherbe, Charles, 1853–1911
Library of Congress
(Box 31)
A. L. S.: Paris, 17 Dec. 1907. 3p., French. Giving biographical data, including Edmond Malherbe

Malibran [née Garcia], Maria, 1808–1836
Library of Congress
(Box 31)
A. L. S.: to Mrs. Crouch. n.p., n.d. 1p., English

[signature: Gfrancesco Malipiero]

Malipiero, Gian Francesco, 1882–1973
Library of Congress
(Box 31, unless noted)
A. Mus. ms. S.: *L'Asino d'oro,* Preludio, Asolo, 1959. 2p., 32x24cm., black ink, pencil. For baritone and orchestra. Sketches
A. Mus. ms. S.: *Il marescalco,* Preludio II. atto, Asolo, 1960. 1 leaf, 33x24cm. On verso, sketches to Intermezzo

A. L. S.: to a conductor. Bodensdorf, 21 Sept. 1909. 3p., German
3 A. L. S.: to Paul F. Sanders. Asolo, 21 Nov. 1932, 22 May 1933, 4 Oct. 1934. 6p., French
P. card S.: to Hanna Schwarz. Asolo, 20 May 1934. 1p., German
A. L. S.: to Hanna Schwarz. Asolo, 27 July 1934. 2p., German. Regarding the ISCM and Berg
2 A. L. S.: Asolo, 18 Oct. 1957, 28 Feb. 1959. 3p., German
A. L. S.: to Hans Moldenhauer. Asolo, 9 Mar. 1960. 2p., German
2 A. L. S.: to Hans Moldenhauer. Asolo, 25 Oct. 1960, 13 Feb. 1961. 3p., German
A. L. S.: to Castelnuovo-Tedesco. n.p., n.d. 1p., Italian
A. Alb. l.: 26 Sept. 1928. 1p., Italian
A. Mus. Quot. S.: *L'esilio dell'éroe,* Asolo, 14 Dec. 1927. 1p.
Clip.: 1p., Italian
Port. Phot. S.: Asolo, Christmas 1927 (Box 113)

Washington State University
Mus. ms. Repro.: *Il Capitan Spavento.* Facsimile. With full score, piano reduction, and text (translated into German)
See Rosbaud, Hans

Malko, Nikolai, 1883–1961
Library of Congress
(Box 31, unless noted)
T. L. S.: to Edward Clark. Copenhagen, 25 Sept. 1933. 2p., English
Port. Phot. S.: to Edward Clark, London, 8 Mar. 1929 (Box 113)

Mallinger [née Lichtenegger], Mathilde, 1847–1920
Library of Congress
(Box 31)
A. Mus. Quot. S.: *The Marriage of Figaro*

Malmberg, Helga
Library of Congress
(Box 31)
A. L. S.: [to Paul A. Pisk]. Stockholm, 27 Apr. 1925. 3p., German

Malten [Müller], Therese, 1855–1930
Library of Congress
(Box 31)
6 A. L. S.: Dresden, Berlin, 1873[?]–1878. 7p., German
4 Call. c. Annot.: to Julius Rietz. 7p., German

Mana-Zucca [Zuccamana, Gizella], 1894–1981
Harvard University
2 Mus. mss.: *My Musical Calendar*, op. 181, *Mangroves*;
   El Morro

Mandl, Richard, 1859–1918
Wiener Stadt- u. Landesbibliothek
2 L.: to Karl Weigl. Vienna, 2 Apr., 10 June 1916 (with
   portrait photograph)

Mandyczewski, Eusebius [Mandicevschi,
Eusebie], 1857–1929
Library of Congress
(Box 31)
Mus. ms. cop. S.: *Zwölf Lieder*, for voice and piano, to
   the Kirchl sisters. 39p., 34x27cm., German

Wiener Stadt- u. Landesbibliothek
Mus. ms.: *Ave Maria*, 1884
L.: Vienna, 28 Nov. 1926

Mann, Alfred, b. 1917
Bayerische Staatsbibliothek
See Strauss, Richard

Mann, Arthur Henry, 1850–1929
Northwestern University
L.: to Middleton. Cambridge, 30 Jan. 1919

Mann, Robert, b. 1920
Washington State University
See Rosbaud, Hans

Mannes, David, 1866–1959
Harvard University
2 L.: to Charles Haubiel. Edgartown, Massachusetts,
   13 Aug. 1946; n.p., [1952?]

Mannes, Leopold Damrosch, 1899–1964
Harvard University
5 L.: to Charles Haubiel. 1926–1956

Manns, Sir August, 1825–1907
Northwestern University
36 L.: to W. H. Cummings. London, 1865–1905

Manschinger, Kurt, 1902–1968
Weiner Stadt- u. Landesbibliothek
SUMMARY OF PRINCIPAL HOLDINGS:
Mus. ms.: *Cupid and Psyche*
Mus. ms.: *Grand Slam*
Mus. ms.: *Der Talisman*
Mus. ms.: *The Triumph of Punch*
Doc.: File contains correspondence, personal items,
   photographs, scrapbooks, scores, sound recordings,
   typescripts

Mantius, Eduard, 1806–1874
Library of Congress
(Box 31)
A. L. S.: to Bolten. Berlin, 12 Mar. 1842. 3p., German
A. L. S.: [to Kierneff?]. Berlin, 13 Apr. 1843. 1p.,
   German

Mapleson, James Henry, 1830–1901
Northwestern University
L.: to Michael Costa. Osborne, Dec. 1881. With
   accompanying clipping

Marchesi, Blanche, 1863–1940
Northwestern University
L.: to Cecil. Kilburn Priory, n.d.
L.: to Gore. Kilburn Priory, n.d.

Marchesi [née Graumann], Mathilde, 1821–1913
Library of Congress
(Box 31, unless noted)
A. Mus. ms. S.: [*L'Art du Chant*], *12 Etudes de style*, op.
   7. 34p., 32x24cm. + 24x32cm.
A. Mus. ms. S.: *L'Art du Chant*, *Huit Vocalises à trois
   voix*, op. 22, to her three daughters, Teresa, Stella,
   Bianca, Vienna, 14 Mar. 1877. 15p., 33x25cm.

A. Card S.: 31 Mar. 1901. 2p., French
Clip.: 5p., English. About her wedding and career
Port. Gr. Repro.: London, 3 May 1902, with her
  husband (Box 113)
Port. Phot. Repro. (Box 113)

Marco, Tomás, b. 1942
Library of Congress
(Box 31)
A. Mus. ms. S.: *Ultramarina*, 1975. 17p., 31x21cm.
  Accompanying typed document on the notation
  used in the work
T. L. S.: to Aurelio de la Vega. Madrid, 19 Mar. 1977.
  1p., Spanish
T. L. S.: to Hans Moldenhauer. Madrid, 24 Oct. 1977.
  1p., English

Mario, Giovanni Matteo, 1810–1883
Library of Congress
(Box 31, unless noted)
A. L. S.: to Gye. n.p., n.d. 1p., French
Call. c. S.: with address
Doc.: Biographical notes. 1910. 4p., English
Port. Draw. Repro. (Box 113)
Port. Paint. Repro. (Box 113)
See Grisi, Giulia

Marpurg, Friedrich, 1825–1884
Library of Congress
(Box 31)
A. L. S.: to Peters. Mainz, 24 Nov. 1862. 1p., German

Marquard, Paul, b. 1836
Zentralbibliothek Zürich
2 L.: to Selmar Bagge. Holland, 23 Sept., 4 Nov. 1862

Marschner, Heinrich August, 1795–1861
Library of Congress
(Box 31, unless noted)
A. Mus. ms. S.: *Unsre Zeit*, for quartet of men's voices,
  2 June 1850. 2p., 31x24cm., German, ink. Full score

A. L. S.: Hanover, 20 Nov. 1845. 2p., German
A. L. S.: Hanover, 17 Feb. 1854. 1p., German
Port. Engr. S. Repro. (Box 113)

Marteau, Henri, 1874–1934
Library of Congress
(Box 31, unless noted)
A. L. S.: [to Zemlinsky?]. n.p., n.d. 2p., German
A. Card S.: n.d. 2p., French
A. Mus. Quot. S.: to Baron Friedrich Schey. Vienna,
  18 Jan. 1906. With proverb
Port. Phot. (Box 113)

Martí, F. Riba
Library of Congress
(Box 31)
A. Mus. ms. S.: *Pastorale*, 1918. 3p., 30x23cm.

Martí Llorca, José, 1853–1903
Library of Congress
(Box 31)
A. Mus. ms. S.: *Espontaneidad*, to Ricardo Viñes. 2p.,
  34x22cm.
A. Mus. ms. S.: *Del llano a la sierra*, to Ricardo Viñes.
  2p., 32x22cm.
A. Mus. ms. S.: *Petite Berceuse*, to Ricardo Viñes. 3p.,
  34x22cm.

Martín, Edgardo, b. 1915
Harvard University
L.: to Aurelio de la Vega. Habana, 30 Dec. 1965

Martin, Frank, 1890–1974
Zentralbibliothek Zürich
Mus. ms.: *Ouverture en Rondeau*, to the Spokane
  Conservatory, 1958
L.: to Rudolph Ganz. Geneva, 12 Apr. 1939
L.: to Hans Moldenhauer. Naarden, 15 Feb. 1960
Mus. Quot.: *Der Sturm*
Pri. Sco.: *Der Sturm*, inscribed, and also signed by
  Ernest Ansermet
Port.: Aug. 1956

Martinet, Jean-Louis, b. 1912
Washington State University
See Rosbaud, Hans

Martínez Torner, Eduardo, 1888–1955
Library of Congress
(Box 55)
Pri. Sco. S.: *Cancionero musical Español*, compiled by
Torner, London: George Harrap, c1948, to Olga
Coelho, London, Nov. 1951. 64p.

**Martini, Padre Giovanni Battista [Giambattista],
1706–1784**
Northwestern University
SUMMARY OF PRINCIPAL HOLDINGS:
Mus. ms.: *Confitebor tibi, Domine*. Full score. With
performance listing

Martinů, Bohuslav, 1890–1959
Library of Congress
(Box 31)
A. Mus. ms.: [Various sketches for instrumental
combinations, including a score for two saxophones,
and a jazz tune for piano]. 3p., 35x27cm., ink
A. Mus. ms.: [Sketches for piano and instrumental
ensemble]. 4p., 35x27cm., ink
Obit.: Pratteln. Basel, Switzerland. French

Northwestern University
Mus. ms.: *Concerto No. 1 for Violin and Orchestra*. Full
score, with performance instructions. 1 leaf
Mus. ms.: *Scherzo Caprice*, for violin and orchestra
Mus. ms.: *What Men Live By*. Full score. Excerpt (p.13),
first version
3 L.: to Boaz Piller. Paris, 18 May 1937; n.p., 20 Nov.
1941; 26 Nov.[?], 1942
L.: from Charlotte (wife)
Mus. Quot.: *Inventions for Orchestra*. Full score
Port. Phot.: to Boaz Piller, Paris, 1937
Port. Phot.

Martín y Soler, Vicente, 1754–1806
Library of Congress
(Shelf)

Mus. ms. cop.: *Una cosa rara*, overtura per il
clavicembalo. 199p., 21x30cm. Vocal score of the
opera

Martucci, Giuseppe, 1856–1909
Library of Congress
(Box 31)
A. Mus. Quot. S.: *Trio*, op. 62, Naples, 20 Mar. 1885

Marx, Adolf Bernhard, 1795[?]–1866
Library of Congress
(Box 31)
A. Mus. ms. S.: *Hinaus mein Lied*. 4p., 26x33cm.
Bound. German
A. Mus. ms.: [Vocal composition in A Major]. 2p.
(143m.), 27x33cm., German, ink. Sketches
A. L. S.: 3 Feb. 1855. 1p., German
A. L. S.: to Zopf. n.p., n.d. 2p., German

Marx, Joseph, 1882–1964
Library of Congress
(Box 31, unless noted)
A. Card S.: to Karl Weigl. ?. 1p., German
Call. c.
Doc.: Work list and life sketch. 1p., German
Pri. Sco. S.: *Quartetto in modo antico*, Vienna: Doblinger,
n.d., to Hans Moldenhauer, Vienna, 1956. 40p.
Prog. S.: to Hans Moldenhauer, Vienna, June 1956.
2p., German
Port. Phot. S.: to Hans Moldenhauer, 1956. On verso,
typed letter (Box 113)

Mary Teresine, Sister S.N.J.M., **1897–1988**
Harvard University
Mus. ms.: *Six Pieces for Organ*

[signature: P. Mascagni]

Mascagni, Pietro, 1863–1945
Library of Congress
(Box 31, unless noted)
A. L. S.: Rome, 5 June 1890. 1p., Italian
Call. c.: to Jacchia. Rome, 13 Nov. 1901. 1p., Italian
A. Doc. S.: Fragment. Italian
Port. S.: on postcard, signed by Mascagni and others
(Box 113)

Mason, Daniel Gregory, 1873–1953
Harvard University
Mus. ms.: _Songs of the Countryside_, op. 23. With
accompanying documents
L.: to Charles Haubiel. New York, 30 Nov. 1935
Mus. ms. Repro.: _Preludes for Piano_, op. 33

Massa, Juan Bautista, 1885–1938
Northwestern University
Mus. ms.: _Tres canciones indígenas_. Full score, parts, and
piano-vocal score

Massé, Victor [Felix-Marie], 1822–1884
Library of Congress
(Box 31)
A. L. S.: n.p., 1 Mar. 1879. 3p., French
A. Mus. Quot. S.: _Paul et Virginie_, Andante cantabile,
June 1870

[signature: J. Massenet]

Massenet, Jules, 1842–1912
Library of Congress
(Box 31, unless noted)
A. L. S.: 14 Apr. 1876. 1p., French. Mentions Gaston
Schefer
A. L. S.: to Renaud. En voyage, 2 Sept. 1898. 3p.,
French

A. L. S.: to ?. 16 May 1910. 1p., French
Call. c.
Doc.: Dissertation. _Massenet_, by Demar Irvine, 1974
(Shelf)
See Bizet, Georges

Northwestern University
Mus. ms.: _Espada_. Complete piano score, with
choreographic instructions
Mus. ms.: _Gavotte chantée et dansée_. Full score
Mus. Quot.: _Manon_. Mounted on portrait photograph
72 L.: to Henri Heugel. 1877–1912. Transcript of
letters, with annotations, by Demar Irvine
L.: Marseille, 3 Apr. 1884
43 L.
Port. Phot.: see musical quotation above

Matecscu, Patricia
Library of Congress
(Box 32)
Card S.: to Aurelio de la Vega. Season's Greetings,
1983
Phot.

Materna, Amalie, 1844–1918
Library of Congress
(Box 32)
A. L. S.: to ?. n.p., [26 May 1870]. 1p., German
A. Doc. S.: Poem. Frankfurt, 7 Aug. 1870. 1p., German

[signature: Yoritsuné Matsudaira]

Matsudaira, Yoritsuné, b. 1907
Library of Congress
(Box 32)
A. L. S.: to Aurelio de la Vega. Tokyo, 23 Aug. 1965.
3p., French

Mattei, Stanislao, 1750–1825
Library of Congress
(Box 32, unless noted)
A. L. S.: to ?. Bologna, 1823. 1p., Italian
Port. Engr. (Box 113)

Mattei, Tito, 1841–1914
Library of Congress
(Box 32)
A. L. S.: to Mary Dallas. London, 21 Sept. 1882. 2p.,
    English. With two clippings
A. L. S.: to Fernandez. London, 12 Mar. 1897. 1p.,
    English
A. L. S.: to Fernandez. 1p., English. Fragment

Matthison-Hansen, Gottfred, 1832–1909
Library of Congress
See Grieg, Edvard

Mauke, Wilhelm, 1867–1930
Bayerische Staatsbibliothek
L.: to Löwe. 20 Aug. 1910

**Mayr [Mayer], Simon [Giovanni Simone],
1763–1845**
Library of Congress
(Box 32)
A. L. S.: [to Tischer?]. Rome, 30 Jan. 1808. 2p., Italian

McArthur, Edwin, 1907–1987
Harvard University
L.: to Fenton. New York, 6 Oct. 1951
L.: to Charles Haubiel. New York, 18 Jan. 1966

McBride, Robert, b. 1911
Harvard University
Mus. ms. Repro.: *Serenade to Country Music*. Facsimile
Mus. ms. Repro.: *Variations on Various Popularisms*.
    Facsimile

McIntyre, Paul, b. 1931
Harvard University
Summary of Principal Holdings:
Mus. ms.: *Concerto for Piano and Orchestra*
Mus. ms.: *Judith*
3 Mus. mss.: [Notebooks]
Mus. ms.: *Quartet Movement in A Minor*
Mus. ms.: *The Rivals*

Mus. ms.: *Song of Autumn*
Mus. ms.: *Symphonia Sacra*
L.: to Aurelio de la Vega. Alaska, 19 Sept. 1963
Port. Phot.

McKay, George Frederick, 1899–1970
Washington State University
Summary of Principal Holdings:
Mus. ms.: *Folksong Variants, Three Pieces for Band*
Mus. ms.: *Sonata No. 2*, for organ, 1940
L.: to Adolph Weiss. Seattle, 7 Jan. 1931
3 L.: to Hans Moldenhauer. Seattle, 26 Jan., 21 Feb.,
    4 Mar. 1956
Mus. ms. Repro.: *Six Pieces on Winter Moods and
    Patterns*
Port. Phot.: 1956

McKenzie, Wallace, b. 1928
Harvard University
Summary of Principal Holdings:
Mus. ms.: *Exhortatic*. With sound recording
Mus. ms.: *Tagelied*, 1964
Mus. ms. Repro.: *The Palm Branches*

Medtner, Nicolai, 1880–1951
Library of Congress
(Box 32)
A. Mus. ms. S.: [*Seven Songs, Elegy*], op. 52, No. 3. 4p.,
    35x27cm. With miscellaneous sketches

Mehta, Mehli, b. 1908
Harvard University
L.: to Charles Haubiel. Los Angeles, 15 Oct. 1966

Mehta, Zubin, b. 1936
Harvard University
See Vega, Aurelio de la

Méhul, Etienne-Nicolas, 1763–1817
Library of Congress
(Box 32)
A. L. S.: to a conductor. n.p., n.d. 1p., French

Meisl, Karl, 1775–1853
Library of Congress
(Box 32)
A. L. S.: to [Anton] Diabelli. n.p., 22 Nov. 1827. 1p.,
German

Melba, Dame Nellie [Mitchell, Helen Porter],
1861–1931
Northwestern University
Port. Phot.

Melichar, Alois, 1896–1976
Bayerische Staatsbibliothek
SUMMARY OF PRINCIPAL HOLDINGS:
Mus. ms.: *In tyrannos*, Berlin, 1940–1942. With typed
synopsis
2 L.: to Hans Moldenhauer. Munich, 8 Dec. 1959,
23 Mar. 1960

Library of Congress
(Box 32)
A. L. S.: to Hans Moldenhauer. Dorfgastein, 31 Jan.
1960. 2p., German
4 T. L. S.: to Hans Moldenhauer. Munich,
Dorfgastein, 1960–1962. 4p., German
P. card S.: to Hans Moldenhauer. Munich, 24 Nov.
1962. German

Menasce, Jacques de, 1905–1960
Library of Congress
(Box 32)
A. L. S.: [to Paul A. Pisk]. New York, 11 Mar. 1950.
1p., English
Mus. ms. cop.: *Abend*, autograph inscription to Hanna
Schwarz, Vienna, May 1936. 3p., German
Mus. ms. cop.: *Frühlingslied*. 7p., German
Mus. ms. cop.: *Juli*. 2p., German

Mus. ms. cop.: *Sommermorgen*. 2p., German
Mus. ms. cop.: *Vorm Himmelstor*. 3p.

Mendelssohn, Alexander, 1797–1871
Library of Congress
(Box 32)
A. L. S.: to Frau Berend. ?, 17 June 1871. 2p., German

Mendelssohn, Arnold, 1855–1933
Library of Congress
(Box 32)
P. card S.: to Edith Weiss-Mann. Darmstadt, 3 Feb.
1920. German

Mendelssohn, Cécile Charlotte Sophia
Jeanrenaud, 1817–1853
Library of Congress
(Box 98)
A. L. S.: to a music teacher. 3 Dec. 2p., German
A. L. S.: to Ries. 2p., German

Mendelssohn, Felix, 1809–1847
Library of Congress
(Box 98, unless noted)
A. Mus. ms. S.: *Canone*, Leipzig, 19 Feb. 1846. 1p.
(8m.), 12x32cm., ink
A. Mus. ms.: [*Elijah*, 1847], "Introduction" and
"Overture," arranged for piano duet. 6p., 24x32cm.,
ink
A. Mus. ms. S.: [*Abschied der Zugvögel*], *Herbstlied der
Zugvögel*, op. 63, No. 2, to Livia Frege, London,
20 May 1844. 2p., 30x23cm., German, ink. For vocal
duet with piano accompaniment. Full score. Poem
by August Heinrich Hoffmann von Fallersleben
A. Mus. ms. A. Rev.: [*Three English Church Pieces*, for
Solo Voices and Chorus, op. 69], *Jubilate Deo,
Magnificat, Nunc dimittis*, [London, 1847]. 24p. + 2p.
oblong, 30x22cm., ink. With many corrections and a
passage omitted from the published version. English
language texts as suggested by Vincent Novello
(1781–1861). Bound, red morocco gilt (Shelf)

A. Mus. ms.: [*Vier Männerchöre*], *Jagdlied*, op. 120, No. 1, [1847]. 2p., 30x24cm., ink. Marked "Tenore 2nd Solo." 42 bars of music and three strophes of the text, by Sir Walter Scott, in German translation. On verso, "Im Süden," op. 120, No. 3, 2nd tenor part of chorus "Auf dem Meere," 13m. with 3 strophes of text underlying the music

A. L. S.: to Pierre Baillot. n.p., 29 Dec. 1831. 1p., French

A. L. S.: to Madam. London, 2 May [1832?]. 1p., English

A. L. S.: to Seeburg. Berlin, 14 Oct. 1842. 1p., German. Regarding Bach monument

A. L. S.: [to Karl Klingemann]. Leipzig, 23 Nov. 1842. 8p., German. Details his audience with King Friedrich Wilhelm IV, and negotiations with the King of Saxony; mentions *Antigone*, *A Midsummer Night's Dream*

A. L. S.: [to a Count]. Leipzig, 20 Nov. 1843. 3p., German

A. L. S.: to E. Clare. Hobart Place, Eaton Square, 17 May 1844. 2p., English

A. L. S.: to Goodwin. Hobart Place, Eaton Square, 5 June 1844. 2p., English

A. L. S.: to [Niels] Gade. Leipzig, 19 Mar. 1846. 1p., German

A. L. S.: to Jenny Lind. Leipzig, 23 July 1846. 4p., German. Regarding *Elijah*

A. L. S.: to R. Friese. Leipzig, 26 Oct. 1846. 1p., German

Prog.: *Paulus*, Schwerin, 18 June 1840

A. Draw. S.: by Mendelssohn. Landscape of the cliffs at Amalfi. Signature on mounting paper. 15x21cm., ink. With photograph of same

Port. Engr.: after the painting by L. Vogel (Box 113)

Mendelssohn, Paul, 1813–1874
Library of Congress
(Box 98)
A. L. S.: to [Henry] Chorley. Berlin, 11 July 1864. 6p., French. With many corrections for the new volume of correspondence

Mendes, Gilberto, b. 1922
Harvard University
SUMMARY OF PRINCIPAL HOLDINGS:
Mus. ms.: *Saudades do Hotel Parque Balneário*, 1980

L.: to Aurelio de la Vega. Santos, 2 Dec. 1985
L.: to Hans Moldenhauer. Santos, 25 Jan. 1986

Mengelberg, Willem, 1871–1951
Library of Congress
(Box 32)
A. Mus. Quot. S.: *A Hero's Life* by Richard Strauss, London, 19 Feb. 19[??]. On verso, musical quotation signed by Albert Sammons, Cadenza for a concerto by Brahms, 8 Mar. 1919

Washington State University
L.: to Solomon Pimsleur. New York, 2 Nov. 1928

Menotti, Gian Carlo, 1911–1993
Harvard University
2 L.: to Otto Jokl. Mount Kisco, New York, 17 Jan. 1949; n.p., n.d.
Clip.

Menuhin, Yehudi, b. 1916
Harvard University
L.: to Adolph Weiss. Seattle, 7 Jan. 1931
L.: to Greta Manschinger. London, 5 Nov. 1968
2 Port. Phot.

Washington State University
See Rosbaud, Hans

Mercadante, Saverio, 1795–1870
Library of Congress
(Box 32)
A. Mus. ms. S.: [Trio, for men's voices], Naples, 12 July 1843. 3p., 19x15cm., Italian
A. Mus.: [Melody in C Minor]. 1p. (9 measures), 24x31cm., Italian

A. L. S.: to Carlo Lombardi. Novarra, 22 Feb. 1835.
1p., Italian

A. L. S.: to Isabella Tadini. 6 Feb. 1843. 3p., Italian

Merino, Luis, b. 1924
Harvard University
L.: to Aurelio de la Vega. 1983

Méry, Joseph, 1797–1865
Library of Congress
(Box 117)
A. L. S.: to Rossini. Paris, 6 Nov. 1852. 4p., French

Messager, André, 1853–1929
Library of Congress
(Box 32)
A. L. S.: to Lucy Vauthrin. Paris, 11 Sept. 1922. 1p.,
French

Messemaeckers, Louis, 1809–1862[?]
Library of Congress
(Box 32)
A. Mus. Quot. S.: Cantabile Moderato, to Stern, Paris,
15 Mar. 1846

Messiaen, Olivier, 1908–1992
Washington State University
Doc.: Catalog. "Olivier Messiaen, Oiseaux exotiques."
Bird songs used in his work, and their natural
habitat
See Rosbaud, Hans

Mestres-Quadreny, Josep, b. 1929
Library of Congress
Summary of Principal Holdings:
(Box 32, unless noted)
A. Mus. ms. S.: *Digodal*, to Cristòfor Taltabull, July
1964. 30p., 22x31cm. Accompanying 1p. typed
document describing the three movements

3 A. Mus. ms. S.: *Digodal*. 29p. total, 31x22cm.
Sketches; complete draft; score for strings
(completed July 1964)

A. Mus. ms. S.: *Divertiment "La Ricarda."* 9p.,
31x22cm. Sketches

A. Mus. ms. S.: *Duo per a Manolo*. 6p., 31x22cm.
Complete draft

A. Mus. ms. S.: *Homenatge a Joan Prats*, Barcelona,
1972. 73p., 39x27cm. + 35x25cm. Complete score
(Box 98)

A. Mus. ms. S.: *Música per a Anna*. 13p., 38x28cm.
Sketches

A. Mus. ms. S.: *Roba i ossos*. 37p., 38x28cm. Full score

A. Mus. ms. S.: *Roba i ossos*. 15p., various sizes.
Sketches

A. Mus. ms. S.: *Soliloqui per flauta*, Mar. 1963. 2p.,
31x22cm.

A. Mus. ms. S.: *Sonata No. 1*, Sept. 1957. 4p., 36x26cm.

A. Mus. ms. S.: *Sonata orgue*, Dec. 1959. 9p., 31x21cm.
Complete draft. Accompanying 2p. autograph
document listing organ registrations

A. Mus. ms. S.: *Tramesa a Tàpies*, Aug. 1961. 14p.,
31x21cm. Complete draft

A. Mus. ms. S.: *Tres piezas para violoncelo y piano*, Jan.
1962. 7p., 31x22cm. Complete draft

2 T. L. S.: to Hans Moldenhauer. Barcelona, 27 June
1972, 7 Feb. 1973. 2p., French

T. Doc. A. Rev.: Work list. 4p.

Doc.: Brochure. On composers, with two copies of
biographical information. French

Doc.: Work list. Includes other composers

**Metastasio, Pietro [Trapassi, Antonio Domenico
Bonaventura], 1698–1782**
Library of Congress
(Box 117)
A. L. S.: [to Adami]. Vienna, 29 April 1757. 3p., Italian
A. L. S.: to Pietro Buontempi. Vienna, 13 Aug. 1768.
1p., Italian
A. L. S.: to Marie Rose Coccia. Vienna, 15 [Jan.] 1779.
1p., Italian

Metdepenninghen, Gabriel
Library of Congress
(Box 33)
Pri. Sco. S.: *Sonatine*, op. 61, Gent: Cnuddle, c1939, to
    René Vaunes, 25 Mar. 1940. 7p.

Methfessel, Albert Gottlieb, 1785–1869
Library of Congress
(Box 33)
A. L. S.: to Schwarz. n.p., 3 Oct. 1816. 1p., German
A. L. S.: [to Carl Reinecke?]. Braunschweig, 20 Jan.
    1850. 4p., German. Mentions L. Hahn

Meyer, G. M., [1846–1927?]
Zentralbibliothek Zürich
L.: to Selmar Bagge. Halle, 31 Mar. 1869

Meyer, Jenny, 1834–1894
Library of Congress
(Box 33)
A. L. S.: to ?. Leipzig, 31 Dec. 1857. 1p., German
A. L. S.: [to Lederer?]. Berlin, 7 Nov. 1871. 1p.,
    German
2 A. L. S.: Berlin, 29 Dec. 1888, 31 Mar. 1889. 2p.,
    German. Stationery lists Jenny Meyer as Director of
    Conservatorium

Meyer, Leopold von, 1816–1883
Library of Congress
(Box 33)
Doc. S.: Selling the right of publication. New York,
    Sept. 1867, Jan. 1868. 1p., German

Meyer-Baer [née Meyer], Kathi, b. 1892
Library of Congress
(Box 33)
A. L. S.: to Ernest Eiseman. New Rochelle, New York,
    6 Jan. 1959. 2p., German

**Meyerbeer [Meyer Beer], Giacomo [Jakob
Liebmann], 1791–1864**
Library of Congress
(Box 33, unless noted)
A. L. S.: [to F. W. Jähns]. n.p., 25 Mar. 1845. 2p.,
    German
A. L. S.: to ?. Nice, 13 Dec. 1857. 2p., French
A. L. S.: to Kastner. ?, n.d. 3p., German
A. Doc.: *Roberto el diablo*, Acto 4. 22p., Spanish
Lib. S.: 1p., German. Half page in Meyerbeer's
    autograph and half page in J. C. Grünbaum's
    autograph
A. Mus. Quot.: Mounted with 1p. autograph letter
    signed, n.d., French
Port. Engr.: by Pound (Box 113)

Meyer-Helmund, Erik, 1861–1932
Library of Congress
(Box 33)
A. L. S.: to a doctor. Berlin, 26 June 1886. 3p., German

Meyerowitz, Jan, b. 1913
Harvard University
SUMMARY OF PRINCIPAL HOLDINGS:
Mus. ms.: *The Glory Around His Head*
Mus. ms.: *Hommage à Jérome Bosch*

Miaskovsky, Nikolai, 1881–1950
Library of Congress
(Box 33, unless noted)
A. Mus. ms. Quot. S.: *Symphony No. 17*, op. 41, to Boaz
    Piller, 23 May 1937
Port. Phot. S.: Moscow, 23 May 1937 (Box 113)

Mignone, Francisco, 1897–1986
Harvard University
SUMMARY OF PRINCIPAL HOLDINGS:
Pri. Sco. Annot.: *Quando una flor desabrocha*

Mihalovici, Marcel, 1898–1985
Library of Congress
(Shelf)
5 Pri. Sco. S.: *Sinfonia variata*; *Ritournelles*; *Scènes de
Thésée*; *III. Quatour*; *Ouverture tragique*, to Karl
Amadeus Hartmann

Washington State University
See Rosbaud, Hans

Milanollo, Teresa, 1827–1904
Library of Congress
(Box 33)
2 Sigs.: Cosigned by her sister, Maria (1832–1848)

Milde, Hans von, 1821–1899
Library of Congress
(Box 33)
2 A. L. S.: to a conductor. Weimar, 31 Jan. 1834, 8 Mar.
1860. 2p., German

Miles, Frank T., 1869–1953
Washington State University
SUMMARY OF PRINCIPAL HOLDINGS:
Mus. ms.: *Concert Waltz*

Milhaud, Darius, 1892–1974
Library of Congress
(Box 33, unless noted)
A. Mus. ms. S.: *Ne me console pas*, for Voice and Piano,
5 May 1911. 2p., 35x27cm., French, ink. Complete
score
A. Mus. ms. S.: *Traversée*, (Paul Verlaine), choeur mixte
à capella, Paris, 10–12 Nov. 1961. 6p., 38x27cm.,
black marker. Master sheets. Written for the

Seventh International Choral Festival at Cork,
Ireland
A. L. S.: to the Director of Universal Edition. Paris,
26 May 1928. 1p., French
A. L. S.: to Hans Moldenhauer. Paris, 6 Nov. 1957. 1p.,
English
A. L. S.: to Hans Moldenhauer. Oakland, California,
6 Feb. 1963. 1p., English
A. L. S.: [to K. A. Hartmann]. Oakland, California,
16 Mar. [1963?]. 1p., French
P. card S.: to Hans Moldenhauer. Oakland, California,
14 May 1963. English
2 A. L. S.: to Hans Moldenhauer. Oakland, California,
31 May, 10 June 1963
A. Card S.: to Aurelio de la Vega. France, 1964. 1p.,
French
T. L. S.: [to Rudolph Ganz]. California, 3 Oct. 1p.,
French
P. card S.: Hans Moldenhauer. Oakland, California,
8 May. English
A. L. S.: to Hans Moldenhauer. Oakland, n.d. 1p.,
English
A. L. S.: [to Boaz Piller]. Paris, 27 Nov. 1p., French
3 A. L. S.: [to Paul Sanders]. Paris, n.d. 3p., French
A. L. S.: Paris. 1p., French
L. S.: to Hans Moldenhauer, from Madeline Milhaud.
Oakland, California, 31 May 1963. 2p., English
L. S.: to K. A. Hartmann and wife, from Madeline
Milhaud. Oakland, California, n.d. 1p., English
3 A. L. S.: to Hans Moldenhauer, from Daniel
Milhaud. Florence, [Mar. 1963], 30 May, 25 June
1963. 7p., English. With 2 art gallery brochures
T. Doc. A. Rev.: Biographical information. 1p., English
A. Mus. Quot. S.: *Second Symphony*
Pri. Sco. A. Rev.: *Pastorale*, for Oboe, Clarinet, and
Bassoon. 6p. (parts)
Pri. Sco. S.: *Aspen-Serenade*, Paris: Heugel, to Karl
Amadeus Hartmann, 1957. 56p.
L. Repro.: Paris, 16 Sept. 1955. 1p., English. Letter of
recommendation for Walter Kaufmann
Port. Phot. S.: to Kirschstein, 29 Oct. 1965. With
melodic quotation from *Agamemnon* (Box 113)
Port. Phot. S.: to Hans and Rosaleen Moldenhauer,
1947 (Box 113)
Port. Phot. S.: to Boaz Piller, 1947 (Box 113)
Port. Phot. (Box 113)

Washington State University
See Rosbaud, Hans

Milliet, Paul, b. 1858
Northwestern University
2 L.: to Massenet. n.p., 6, 21 July 1900

Millöcker, Carl, 1842–1899
Library of Congress
(Box 33)
A. L. S.: Vienna, 28 Feb. 1884. 1p., German
A. L. S.: to a librettist. ?, n.d. 3p.
A. Mus. Quot. S.: *Gasparone*, to Häflinger, Vienna, 18 Sept. 1885
A. Mus. Quot. S.: *Gasparone*, Vienna, 2 May 1886
A. Mus. Quot. S.: "Ich knüpfte manche zarte Bande, studierte die Pariserin," Vienna, 14 Feb. 1891

Miró, Francisco
Library of Congress
(Box 33)
A. Mus. ms. S.: *Murcia*, to Ricardo Viñes. 10p., 34x27cm.

Missale Romanum, 1574
Library of Congress
(Shelf)
Bk.: Published by Iacobus Kerver, 21 Aug. 1574. The volume is printed in several sections, some paginated with roman numerals, others unnumbered. Bound in black leather. 29x21cm.

Mitropoulos, Dimitri, 1896–1960
Harvard University
SUMMARY OF PRINCIPAL HOLDINGS:
L.: to Boaz Piller. 1937–1953
2 L.: to Alma Mahler. n.p., 19 Feb.; n.p., n.d. Also signed by Trudy Goth, and with a postscript by Gottfried von Einem
Port. Phot.: 29 Jan. 1936

Washington State University
L.: to Solomon Pimsleur. n.p., 22 Dec. 1951
L.: to Ashley Vernon. n.p., 17 June 1952
Doc.: Recommendation. 31 Dec. 1951

Möser, Karl, 1774–1851
Library of Congress
(Box 33)
3 A. L. S.: to Hubert Ries. n.p., Nov. 1829; Berlin, 13 Nov. 1831, 18 Oct. 1843. 3p., German

Mohaupt, Richard, 1904–1957
Library of Congress
(Box 98)
Mus. ms. Repro.: *Concerto for Violin and Orchestra*, reduced for violin and piano, New York: Associated Music Publishers, n.d. 54p.
Mus. ms. Repro.: *Lysistrata*, New York: Associated Music Publishers, 1946. 60p.
Pri. Sco. S.: *Double Trouble*, New York: Associated Music Publishers, c1954, to Otto Jokl, Oct. 1954. 213p. With annotations and signed by Jokl

Mohler, Philipp, b. 1908
Library of Congress
(Box 33)
A. Mus. ms. S.: *Konzertante Sonate für Viola und Klavier*, II, op. 31. 2p., 34x27cm. With accompanying letter to Hans Moldenhauer, from A. Klostermann (Frankfurt, 13 Oct. 1959), regarding manuscript
A. Mus. ms.: *Sinfonisches Capriccio*, op. 40. 20p., various sizes. Complete sketches
T. L. S.: to Hans Moldenhauer. Frankfurt, 9 Apr. 1959. 1p., German
Card S.: 1960. 1p., German
Doc.: Article. "Philipp Mohler," by Willy Fröhlich, in *Festblätter*, Aug. 1956. 2p., German
Pri. Sco.: *Konzertante Sonate*, op. 31, Mainz: Schott. 44p.
Pri. Sco.: *Sinfonisches Capriccio für Orchester*, op. 40, Hamburg: Sikorski. 85p.
Prog.: 11 July 1959. 2p.

Moiseiwitsch, Benno, 1890–1963
Library of Congress
(Box 113)
Port. Phot. S.: Mar. 1921

Mokrejs, John, 1875–1968
Harvard University
SUMMARY OF PRINCIPAL HOLDINGS:
Mus. ms.: *June*
Mus. ms.: op. 66

Moldovan, Mihai, 1937–1981
Library of Congress
(Box 33)
A. Mus. ms. S.: *Muzica pentru un pianist*, to Alexandru
Hrisanide. 3p., 35x25cm.

Molinari, Bernardino, 1880–1952
Zentralbibliothek Zürich
Prog.: St. Gallen, 20 May 1925

Molique, Bernhard, 1802–1869
Library of Congress
(Box 33)
A. Mus. ms. S.: *Flying Leaves, Six Pieces for Flute and
Pianoforte*, for W. S. Broadwood, London, 26 Dec.
1851. 4p., 27x33cm., ink. Fair copy. Exhibited in
London, 1897, contributed by W. H. Cummings
A. L. S.: to [Henry] Chorley. Stuttgart, 1 Mar. 1835.
3p., English. Mentions Abert; Anna's (daughter)
concert
A. L. S.: to [Henry] Chorley. London, 17 May 1864.
1p., English
L. S.: to [W. H.] Cummings, from Anna Molique.
Trickenham, 18 Aug. 4p., English

Mompou, Federico, 1893–1987
Library of Congress
(Box 34, unless noted)
A. Mus. ms. S.: *Aquesta nit un mateix vent*, No. 2, cant i
piano, 1946. 4p., 32x22cm. With separate copy of
text by poet J. Janés (in Catalan), and its
translations, in Mompou's autograph, into Spanish
and French
A. Mus. ms. Rev. S.: [same], Dec. 1946. 5p., 32x22cm.,
ink, pencil

A. Mus. ms. Rev. S.: [same], Dec. 1946. 2p. of
beginning + 2p. title page
A. Mus. ms. S.: *Cançó i dansa (populars)* [No. 1]. 4p.,
36x26cm.
A. Mus. ms. S.: *Canción y Danza*, No. 1, para piano,
revised 1948. 5p., 32x22cm.
A. Mus. ms. S.: *Cançó i dansa*, II, 1924. 4p., 35x27cm.
Sketches
A. Mus. ms. S.: *Cançó i dansa*, III, 1926. 5p., 35x27cm.
A. Mus. ms. S.: *Cançó i dansa*, III, 1926. 6p., 35x27cm.
A. Mus. ms. S.: *4. Cançó i dansa*, Paris, 1928. 4p.,
35x27cm.
A. Mus. ms. S.: *Canción y danza*, No. VI, to Arthur
Rubinstein. 3p., 32x26cm.
A. Mus. ms. S.: *Canción y danza*, No. VII, 1945. 4p.,
32x22cm.
A. Mus. ms. S.: *Canción y danza*, No. 8, para piano. 5p.,
32x22cm.
A. Mus. ms. S.: *Canción y danza*, No. 9. 4p., 35x27cm.
A. Mus. ms. S.: *Canción y danza*, No. IX, to Gonzalo
Soriano. 7p., 32x26cm.
A. Mus. ms. S.: *Canción y danza*, No. X. 2p., 32x26cm.
A. Mus. ms. S.: *Cançó i dansa*, No. 12, Nov. 1953. 6p.,
35x27cm.
A. Mus. ms. S.: *Cantar del Alma*. 11p., 32x22cm.
A. Mus. ms. S.: *Damunt de tu, només les flors*. 6p.,
35x27cm. First version
A. Mus. ms. S.: *Fêtes Lointaines*, 1920, to Paul Huvelin.
9p., 35x27cm.
A. Mus. ms. S.: *Impropères*. 10p., various sizes (Box 98)
A. Mus. ms. S.: *Jo et pressentia com la mar*, cant i piano,
Aug. 1948. 5p.
A. Mus. ms. S.: *Música callada*, Nos. 22–28. 12p.,
32x26cm. Drafts
A. Mus. ms. S.: *La música callada, la soledad sonora*,
1943, 20 Aug. 1951. 19p., 18x14cm., ink, pencil.
Missing No. 8. With accompanying 4p. autograph
document describing the title, the work, and the
composer's intentions. French and Spanish
A. Mus. ms. S.: *Sant Martí*, cant i piano. 6p., 35x27cm.
A. Mus. ms. S.: *Scenes d'Enfants*. 15p., 36x26cm.
A. Mus. ms. S.: *Sonet, jo et pressentia com la mar*. 4p. +
1p. sketch, 32x22cm. First version
2 A. Mus. ms. S.: *Sonet*. 5p. each
A. Mus. ms. Annot. S.: *Variations sur un Thème de
Chopin*, cant i piano. 80p., 35x25cm. Sketches
2 A. L. S.: to Hans Moldenhauer. Barcelona, 11 Dec.
1957, 9 May 1958. 2p., Spanish, French
A. L. S.: to Hans Moldenhauer. Barcelona, 19 Feb.
1973. 1p., French

T. L. S.: to Hans Moldenhauer. Barcelona, 12 May 1973. 1p., French

L.: [to Mompou, from Hans Moldenhauer]. n.p., 27 July 1984. 1p., French

Doc.: Brochure. With picture and work list. 12p., French

2 Pri. Sco.: 8p. Printer's proofs

Port. Phot. Gr.: with Arthur Rubinstein, 1970 (Box 113)

2 Port. Phot. S.: to the Moldenhauer Archives (Box 113)

Port. Gr.: with Rosa Sabater (Box 113)

Port. Draw. Repro. (Box 113)

Monsigny, Pierre-Alexandre, 1729–1817
Library of Congress
(Box 35)
A. L. S.: Paris, 22 Aug. 1763. 3p., French. Regarding the story of Troy as an operatic subject

Montemezzi, Italo, 1875–1952
Library of Congress
(Box 113)
Port. Phot. S.: to Boaz Piller, Boston, 3 Apr. 1941

Monteux, Pierre, 1875–1964
Harvard University
4 L.: to Rogers. 1922–1931
L.: to Henry Cowell. San Francisco, 11 Mar. 1936
2 L.: to Adolph Weiss. San Francisco, 1 Feb., 18 June 1937
L.: to Charles Haubiel. San Francisco, 24 Nov. 1944
L.: to Rudolph Ganz. Hancock, 25 Sept. 1951

Moodie, Alma, 1900–1943
Zentralbibliothek Zürich
Prog.: St. Gallen, 16 Dec. 1926

Moór, Emanuel, 1863–1931
Library of Congress
(Box 35, unless noted)
A. Mus. ms. S.: *Thestilis*. 1p., 27x21cm. Song with piano accompaniment. Excerpt
A. L. S.: Lausanne, 11 Oct. 1910. 1p., English

A. Mus. Quot. S.: *Symphony in Memoriam L. Kossuth*. With signed note from Anita Moór (Florence, 19 Feb. 1863)

Port. Phot. Repro. S. (Box 113)

Moore, Douglas S., 1893–1969
Harvard University
Mus. ms.: *Dedication*
Mus. ms.: *Six Pieces for Piano*
L.: to Solomon Pimsleur. New York, 16 Nov. 1934
L.: to Eugene Weigel. New York, 24 Sept. 1948
L.: to Charles Haubiel. New York, 11 Jan. 1955

Moore, Francis Silvey, b. 1877
Harvard University
SUMMARY OF PRINCIPAL HOLDINGS:
Mus. ms.: *Music Box*
Mus. ms.: *The Walk to Jerusalem*, arranged for two pianos
Port. Phot.

Moore, Thomas, 1779–1852
Library of Congress
(Box 35)
A. L. S.: ?, 25 Dec. 1841. 1p., English

Moran, Robert, b. 1937
Harvard University
L.: to Aurelio de la Vega. San Francisco, 27 Dec. 1965

Moran-Olden [Tappenhorn], Fanny, 1855–1905
Library of Congress
(Box 35)
A. L. S.: Frankfurt, 13 Oct. [1880?]. 2p., German
Doc. S.: Contract for a guest appearance. 24 Mar. 1892. 2p., German

Morel, Auguste-François, 1809–1881
Library of Congress
(Box 35)
A. Mus. ms. S.: *La Fille de l'Hôtesse*, to Julius Stern. 2p., 23x28cm., French

Morin, Gösta, b. 1900
Library of Congress
(Box 35)
2 T. L. S.: to Hans Moldenhauer. Stockholm, 2 Dec.
   1959; 12 Apr. 1960. 2p., German
Doc. A. Rev. S.: Essay. "Music Libraries and
   Collections." 1p.
Doc. S.: Essay. "Wolfgang Amadeus Mozart,"
   Stockholm: Swedish Royal Library, 1956, Vienna,
   1956. 10p.

Morlacchi, Francesco, 1784–1841
Library of Congress
(Box 35)
A. L. S.: Genoa, 14 May 1828. 1p., Italian

Morris, Harold, 1890–1964
Harvard University
3 L.: to Charles Haubiel. New York, 30 June, 21 July,
   5 Aug. 1955. With copies of Haubiel's replies

Mortari, Virgilio, 1902–1993
Northwestern University
L.: to Edward Clark. Rome, 26 Apr. 1949

Morton, Lawrence, 1904–1987
Harvard University
L.: to Aurelio de la Vega. Marina del Rey, 3 July 1984

Moscheles, Ignaz, 1794–1870
Northwestern University
2 Mus. mss.: *Hommage à Weber*, op. 102, sketch; on
   verso, *Romance et Tarantella brillante pour le Piano*,
   op. 101, draft of beginning
L.: 2 Feb. 1841
L.: to Taubert. Leipzig, 8 Oct. 1849
L.: to Carl Reinecke. Leipzig, 13 Mar. 1850
L.: to C. Haslinger. Leipzig, 21 May 1862
Mus. Quot.: *Andantino*, to Miss Dance, 6 Jan. 1833
Port.

Mosel, Ignaz Franz von, 1772–1844
Library of Congress
(Box 35)
A. L.: n.p., n.d. 2p., German. Draft of a letter.
   Discusses Lulli, Rameau, vocal style

Moser, Gustav von, 1825–1903
Library of Congress
(Box 35)
A. L. S.: Gürlitz, 25 Oct. 1894. 1p., German. With
   portrait photograph reproduced
A. L. S.: n.p., n.d. 3p., German. On aesthetic and
   philosophical views

Moser, Hans Joachim, 1889–1967
Library of Congress
(Box 35)
A. L. S.: Charlottenburg, 18 Mar. 1937. 1p., German
P. card S.: to Hans Moldenhauer. Berlin, 1 Mar. 1958.
   1p., German
A. Doc.: Name and address

Moss, Lawrence K., b. 1927
Harvard University
L.: to Aurelio de la Vega. New Haven, 26 Mar. 1963

Moszkowski, Moritz, 1854–1925
Library of Congress
(Box 35, unless noted)
A. L. S.: to Hugo Courat. Paris, 16 June 1902. 2p.,
   German
A. L. S.: to Rosenberg. n.p., n.d. 2p., German
A. L. S.: n.p., n.d. 1p., German, with translation
Port. Phot. S.: Berlin, 13 Sept. 1890. By Brasch
   (Box 113)

Mottl, Felix, 1856–1911
Bayerische Staatsbibliothek
L.: to a publisher. n.p., 16 Sept. 1888
L.: to Eugen Lindner. Munich, 28 June 1906
L.: Munich, 9 Mar. 1910
Doc.: Statement regarding Mozart. Munich, 4 Jan.
   1906
Port.

Library of Congress
See Wagner, Siegfried

Mounsey, Elizabeth, 1819–1905
Northwestern University
L.: to W. Edwards. n.p., 6 Sept. 1897

Mozart, Franz Xaver Wolfgang, 1791–1844
Library of Congress
(Box 99)
Pri. Sco. S.: *Fest-Chor*, "zur Enthüllung des Mozart
   Denkmals in Salzburg, aus Compositionen des
   Gefeierten, zusammengestellt, instrumentiert, und
   mit einem passenden Texte versehen von dessen
   Sohne W. A. Mozart," Vienna: Artaria, n.d., to
   Madame Ungher-Sabatier. 31p., 25x33cm.

Mozart, Leopold, 1719–1787
Library of Congress
(Box 99)
A. Mus. ms.: *Cadenze per il Clavicembalo*, Concerto in
   D, K. 624A-B [Cadenzas for J. C. Bach, *Klavier
   Conzerte*, K. 107]. 1 leaf (2p.), 17x23cm., ink.
   Consists of two cadenzas. With authentication,
   Salzburg, 24 July 1835

[signature]

Mozart, Wolfgang Amadeus, 1756–1791
Library of Congress
(Box 99, unless noted)
A. Mus. ms. S.: *6 Menuette*, K. 164, Nos. 1, 2, Salzburg,
   1772. 2p., 23x30cm., ink. Full score
A. Mus. ms.: *Anfang einer Fuge* [Fragment of Fugue in
   C Minor, K. 626b/27]. 1p. (27m.), 12x27cm., ink.
   Inscribed by Georg Nissen
Pri. Sco.: *Don Giovanni*, arranged by Carlo Zulehner,
   Mainz: Schott, n.d. 207p. Signed by Zulehner. First
   edition, piano-violin arrangement. Containing the
   incipits of rearrangement into various movements of
   a mass (Shelf)

Mus. ms. cop. Rev.: [Allegro and Andante ("Fantasy")
   in F Minor for Mechanical Organ, K. 608], 1791. 6p.,
   22x29cm. Two-staff version. With accompanying
   document from Robert Haas, and letter to Nettl,
   from Alfred Einstein (19 Oct. 1951) regarding the
   manuscript
A. Doc.: Diary entries. [24 May 1780]. 1 leaf (3 lines +
   3 lines on verso), German. Fragment, from the diary
   of Nannerl and Wolfgang Mozart. Verified by
   Mozart's widow, Salzburg, 1829. With letter on
   provenance to Hans Moldenhauer, from Fibiger,
   6 Oct. 1961
Mus. ms. Repro.: *Fantasia* in F Minor, K. 608, for
   piano solo, as revised and edited by John Cowell
   from the original. 14p. Blueprint score
Mus. ms. Repro.: *Das Veilchen*, to the Spokane
   Conservatory, from Ferdinand C. O. Speyer,
   London, Apr. 1958. 2p. Facsimile, with 4p.
   document by Alfred Einstein, Wien: Reichner, 1936
   (Shelf)
Mus. ms. Repro.: "Fragmens d'une Sonate à quatre
   mains en Re majeur." Facsimile
Prog.: *Die Zauberflöte*, Bayreuth, 18 Apr. 1817
Port. Lith.: by Johann Neidl, after Posch, ca. 1800
   (Box 113)
Port.: Enamelled miniature portrait on white cross.
   Insignia of the Masonic Lodge at Leipzig, "Mozart
   zur Bruderkette" (Box 124)
Medal: Mozart medal. Bronze, 7". By A. Hartig,
   coined by Mozarteum, Salzburg (Box 124)
See Beethoven, Ludwig van

Mubarak, Eduardo
Harvard University
L.: to Aurelio de la Vega. 1983

[signature]

Muck, Carl, 1859–1940
Library of Congress
(Box 35, unless noted)
A. L. S.: Berlin, 7 Nov. 1895. 2p., German
2 A. L. S.: to Rogers. Munich, 11 Aug. 1921; Hamburg,
   31 May 1924. 6p., English. Private and musical
   matters

A. L. S.: to Sigmund Herzog. New York, n.d. 1p.,
   German
A. L. S.: to Sauerquell. n.p., n.d. 2p., German
Sig.: Berlin, 9 Mar. 1912
2 Port. Phot. (Box 113)
See Wagner, Siegfried

Müller, August Eberhard, 1767–1817
Library of Congress
(Box 35)
A. L. S.: to Schrader. Weimar, 21 Dec. 1810. 1p.,
   German, with translation

Müller, Iwan, 1786–1854
Bayerische Staatsbibliothek
Mus. ms.: *Duo de l'Opera d'Armide* by Rossini. Parts

Müller, Karl Ludwig, b. 1875
Library of Congress
(Box 35)
5 A. Mus. mss. S.: [Five Songs to Poems by Herta
   Kanner], *Ein Requiem, Ritornelle, Die Bajadere,
   Vergessene Liebe, Abschied.* 18p., 34x27cm.

Müller, Wilhelm, 1794–1827
Library of Congress
(Box 117)
A. L. S.: to L. Spohr. Dessau, 8 Jan. 1827. 2p., German

Müller-Hermann, Johanna, 1878–1941
Library of Congress
(Box 35)
A. L. S.: to Zemlinsky. Vienna, 31 Mar. 1914. 3p.,
   German

Müller-Reuter, Theodor, 1858–1919
Library of Congress
(Box 35)
A. L. S.: to M. A. Middleton, a bookseller. Krefeld, 28
   Nov. 1908. 3p., English

Müthel, Johann Gottfried, 1728–1788
Library of Congress
(Box 35)
A. Doc. S.: Title page and thematic incipit. In two
   staves (2m.) for a *Concerto à cembalo obligato, violino
   primo, violino secondo, viola con violon e violoncello del.
   Sigr. Graun.* 1p., 31x20cm., ink

Mumma, Gordon, b. 1935
Harvard University
4 L.: to Aurelio de la Vega. Ann Arbor, 1963–1966

Munck, Ernest, Chevalier de, 1840–1915
Library of Congress
(Box 14)
A. L. S.: to Ries. Vienna, 25 Dec. 1878. 3p., French

Murcía de Toledano, Hildade
Library of Congress
(Box 54)
A. Mus. ms. S.: *Rapsodia Ruffeña*, to Ricardo Viñes. 5p.,
   31x24cm.

**Musorgsky [Mussorgsky], Modest Petrovich,
1839–1881**
Library of Congress
See Rimsky-Korsakov, Nikolai Andreevich

Mysz-Gmeiner, Lula, 1876–1948
Library of Congress
(Box 35)
A. L. S.: Berlin, 10 Dec. 1902. 3p., German
A. Card S.: Berlin, n.d. 2p., German

Nachbaur, Franz, 1835–1902
Library of Congress
(Box 36)
2 A. L. S.: to Giessen. Friedrichshafen, 6 May 1859
   (includes repertoire list); Darmstadt, 14 May 1867.
   4p., German

Nachèz, Tivadar, 1859–1930
Library of Congress
(Box 36)
A. L. S.: to Mrs. Elliot. London, 3 Jan. 1893. 4p.,
   English
2 A. L. S.: to Mrs. Tweedale[?]. London, 15, 25 July
   1903. 8p., English
Pri. Sco. S.: *Concerto pour violon et piano* by Vivaldi,
   Mainz: Schott, c1921, to Ernest Newmann, 1923.
   20p.

Nadalovitch, Jean, 1875–1966
Library of Congress
See Reznicek, E. N. von

Nápravník, Eduard, 1839–1916
Library of Congress
(Box 36)
A. L. S.: Petersburg, 16 Apr. 1879. 2p., German

Nardini, Pietro, 1722–1793
Library of Congress
(Box 36)
A. L. S.: to Joseph Otter. Florence, 13 July 1790. 2p.,
   Italian

Naudin, Emilio, 1823–1890
Library of Congress
(Box 36)
A. L. S.: London, 2 June 1871. 1p., Italian
See Paganini, Nicolò

Naumann, Emil, 1827–1888
Library of Congress
(Box 36)
A. L. S.: to Selmar Bagge. Dresden, 27 June 1879. 4p.,
   German

Naumann, Johann Gottlieb, 1741–1801
Library of Congress
(Box 36)
A. Mus. ms. S.: [Allegro movement, second horn part].
   2p., 22x29cm.

Naumann, Otto, 1871–1932
Library of Congress
(Box 36)
A. Mus. ms. S.: [Three songs], op. 12, Nos. 1, 2, 3,
   Mutterglück, Gondelliedchen, Der erste Schritt, Dresden,
   30 July 1912, 4 Aug. 1911, 26 July 1912. 10p. total,
   35x27cm., German
A. Doc.: Text. [Three songs]. 5p., German

Naylor, John, 1838–1897
Northwestern University
L.: York, 13 May 1887

Neefe, Christian Gottlob, 1748–1798
Northwestern University
See Gerber Library

Neitzel, Otto, 1852–1920
Library of Congress
(Box 36)
T. L. S.: to Bruno Eisner. Cologne, 21 Dec. 1916. 1p.,
   German
Doc. S.: Article. "Der Rubinstein-Preis 1905," by
   Neitzel. Cologne. 2p., German

Neruda, Wilma [Lady Hallé], [1838?]–1911
Northwestern University
2 L.
Obit.

Nessler, Viktor E., 1841–1890
Library of Congress
(Box 36)
A. L. S.: [to Eugen Lindner]. [Strassburg], 30 July
   1889. 3p., German
A. Rcpt. S.: Strassburg, 16 Feb. 1889. 1p., German
Pri. Rcpt. S.: Leipzig, 6 June 1882. 1p., German
Sig.: from letter fragment

Nešvera, Josef, 1842–1914
Library of Congress
(Box 36, unless noted)
A. L. S.: Olmütz, 27 May 1898. 2p., German
Port. Phot. S.: by Atelier (Box 113)

Nettl, Paul, 1889–1972
Library of Congress
SUMMARY OF PRINCIPAL HOLDINGS:
(Box 36, unless noted)
A. Doc. S.: Essay. "Über ein Manuskript
    volkstümlicher österreichischer Barockmusik." 21p.
    German. With musical examples
Bk. S.: includes various signed copies of his books
    (Shelf)
See Mozart, Wolfgang Amadeus

Neukomm, Sigismund Ritter von, **1778–1858**
Library of Congress
(Box 36)
L.: n.p., 2 Apr. 1831. 1p., French. Written in third
    person. Neukomm accepts an invitation of Sir Gore
    Ouseley

Northwestern University
L.: to Paccini. n.p., 12 May 1836
L.: n.p., n.d.
Port.

Neumann, Angelo, 1838–1910
Wiener Stadt- u. Landesbibliothek
L.: to Franz von Holstein. Leipzig, 10 Feb. 1877

Nevin, Ethelbert, 1862–1901
Harvard University
L.: to Hale. Boston, 18 Dec. 1890
Port. Phot.

Ney, Elly, 1882–1968
Washington State University
Port. Phot.: with accompanying note on verso
See Rosbaud, Hans

Ney, Jenny, 1824–1886
Library of Congress
(Box 11)
6 A. L. S.: n.p., 1853–1861. 16p., German. With
    accompanying typed explanation of letters

Nicholls, Agnes, 1877–1959
Northwestern University
L.: to Cecil. London, 23 Mar. 1905

Nicodé, Jean Louis, 1853–1919
Library of Congress
(Box 36, unless noted)
P. card S.: to ?. Marienbad, 5 July 1886. German
P. card S.: to Kramer. Langebrück, 7 Sept. 1900.
    German
P. card S.: to George Bainton. Langebrück, Dresen,
    13 Feb. 1911. German
A. Card S.: Langebrück, 6 Sept. 1912. 1p., German
Port. Phot. S. Repro. (Box 113)
Port. Phot. Repro. (Box 113)

Nicolai, Otto, 1810–1849
Library of Congress
(Box 36)
A. L. S.: to Raymond Härtel, Breitkopf & Härtel.
    Munich, 18 Dec. 1833. 3p., German. With eight
    musical examples, metronome markings, directions
    for engraving his *Weihnachtsouvertüre*
A. L. S.: to Schmidt. n.p., 13 Jan. 1846. 1p., German
A. L. S.: to R. de Vivenot. n.p., 7 May 1847. 1p.,
    German
Mus. ms. Repro.: *Duettino*. 4p., German

Nicolini [Nicolas], Ernest, 1834–1898
Library of Congress
(Box 36)
A. L. S.: to Cusins. n.p., 25 June 1883. 4p., French.
    Regarding a performance with Patti
A. L. S.: to Benedict. n.p., 22 Sept. 1880. 2p., French

Niedermeyer, Louis, 1802–1861
Zentralbibliothek Zürich
L.: St. German, 17 May 1839

Nielsen, Carl, 1865–1931
Library of Congress
(Box 36)
Pri. Sco. S.: *Thema med Variationer*, op. 40,
    Copenhagen: Hansen, c1920, to Bruno Eisner,
    Copenhagen, 20 Dec. 1922. 27p.

Niemann, Albert, 1831–1917
Library of Congress
(Box 36)
A. L. S.: to Franz Abt. Hanover, 15 Mar. 1814. 1p.,
    German

Niemann, Walter, 1876–1953
Library of Congress
(Box 36, unless noted)
A. L. S.: [to Dr. Felix Huch]. Leipzig, 16 Oct. 1941.
    3p., German
A. Card S.: n.p., n.d. 2p., German. Fragment
Port. Phot. Repro. S.: to ?. Leipzig, 16 Oct. 1941
    (Box 113)

Nikisch, Arthur, 1855–1922
Library of Congress
(Box 36)
P. card S.: Eugen Lindner. Weimar, 11 Nov. 1896.
    German
A. L. S.: [to Eugen Lindner]. Ostende, 18 July 1904.
    2p., German
A. L. S.: [to Eugen Lindner]. Leipzig, 3 Nov. 1905.
    1p., German

Nilsson, Bo, b. 1937
Washington State University
See Rosbaud, Hans

Nilsson, Christine [Kristina], 1843–1921
Library of Congress
(Box 36, unless noted)
A. L. S.: to Cusins. London, 1 June. 2p., French
A. L. S.: to a Royal Highness. London, 15 Mar. 1886.
    4p., French
Obit.
Port. Phot. (Box 113)
Port. Phot. Repro. (Box 113)

Nin, Joaquín, 1879–1949
Library of Congress
(Box 36)
A. Mus. ms. S.: *Paño Murciano, canto e piano*. 4p. + title
    page + 1p. giving text, 33x24cm., black, blue ink
Pri. Sco. A. Rev. S.: *Vingt Chants populaires espagnols*,
    Paris: Eschig, c1923, to Ruzena Herlinger, Paris,
    1924. 39p. (vol. 1)

Nin-Culmell, Joaquín, b. 1908
Harvard University
Summary of Principal Holdings:
Mus. ms.: [Spanish Christmas Carol]. Complete score
Mus. ms.: *Tonadas*
L.: to Aurelio de la Vega. Barcelona, 19 Feb. 1958

Nissen, Georg Nikolaus, 1761–1826
Library of Congress
See Mozart, Wolfgang Amadeus

Nissen, Henriette, 1819–1879
Library of Congress
(Box 36)
2 A. L. S.: to Bartolf Senff. Frankfurt, 11 June 1850;
    n.p., n.d. 4p., German

Noble, T. Tertius, 1867–1953
Harvard University
Mus. ms.: *Fierce Was the Wild Billow*, Feb. 1899

Nobre, Marlos, b. 1939
Harvard University
SUMMARY OF PRINCIPAL HOLDINGS:
4 L.: to Aurelio de la Vega. Rio, 1983–1985

Nohl, Karl Friedrich Ludwig, 1831–1885
Library of Congress
(Box 36)
A. L. S.: Oldenburg, 7 Mar. 1868. 1p., German

Nono, Luigi, 1924–1990
Library of Congress
(Box 107)
A. Mus. ms. S.: [*Intolleranza 1960*], to Richard
    Hartmann, Venice, 21 May 1963. 4p., 47x32cm.,
    pencil, colored pencils, black marker. Draft of Act I,
    the Revolutionary Chorus. Also signed by Hartmann

Washington State University
See Rosbaud, Hans

Nordenstrom, Gladys, b. 1924
Harvard University
SUMMARY OF PRINCIPAL HOLDINGS:
Mus. ms.: *Elegy for Robert F. Kennedy*, June 1968
Mus. ms.: *Orchestra Piece No. 3*, 1974–1975
Pri. Sco.: *Rondo*, 19 Feb. 1964

Nordoff, Paul, 1909–1977
Harvard University
Mus. ms.: *Mr. Fortune.* Excerpt
L.

Norman, Ludvig, 1831–1885
Northwestern University
39 L.: to Bargiel. Leipzig, Stockholm, 1849–1877

Notari, Angelo, 1566–1663
Library of Congress
(Box 36)
A. Rcpt. S.: n.p., 19 Oct. 1618. 1p., English

Nottebohm, Gustav, 1817–1882
Library of Congress
(Box 36)
2 A. L. S.: [to Selmar Bagge]. Vienna, 11 July 1872,
    16 Sept. 1873. 7p., German

Novello, Clara, 1818–1908
Northwestern University
L.: to Dragonetti. n.p., 1 May
Obit.

Novello, Mary Victoria, 1809–1898
Northwestern University
L.: to Dragonetti. Soho, 22 Nov. 1837

Novello, Vincent, 1781–1861
Northwestern University
Mus. ms. arr.: "Select Airs from Mozart's *Così fan tutte*"
L.: to William Watts. Lincoln's Inn, 9 Oct. 1828
L.: to Dragonetti. n.p., 26 Aug. 1835
L.: to Flowers. n.p., 13 Feb. 1843
3 L.: to Henry Phillips. Bayswater, 21 Mar. 1844; n.p.,
    6 July, 3 Aug. 1846
L.: to Bridgetower. Bayswater, 6 July 1846
Doc.: Contract. London, 16 Aug. 1839. On behalf of
    Dragonetti
Port.

Nystroem, Gösta, 1890–1966
Library of Congress
(Boxes 37–38)
A. Mus. ms. S.: *Bön*, Särö, 1927. 4p., 35x27cm., ink.
    Song with piano accompaniment
A. Mus. ms. A. Rev. S.: *Concerto für Altviolin och
    Orkester, Hommage à la France.* 111p., 35x27cm.,
    pencil. Full score

A. Mus. ms. S.: *"Regrets," 6 pièces pour piano*, Paris, Särö, St. Leonard, 1923–1924. 13p. 35x27cm., ink. Complete score

A. Mus. ms. S.: *Som ett blommande Mandelträd*. 3p., 36x27cm., ink

A. Mus. ms. S.: *Teatersvit Nr. 4, Köpmannen i Venedig, Burlesque*, 1936. 28p., 35x27cm., pencil. Full score, second section

3 A. L. S.: to Hans Moldenhauer. Särö, 6 June, 18 July, 26 Dec 1961. 5p., English

L.: to Hans Moldenhauer, from Theodore Seder, Fleisher Music Collection. Philadelphia, 24 July 1961. 1p., English

Mus. ms. Repro. A. Rev. S.: *Concerto, für Viola och Orkester*, 1944. With autograph dedication and program, June 1960. 99p. Blueprint score

Mus. ms. Repro.: *Concerto Nr. 2*, Stockholm: Nordiska, c1960. 55p.

Mus. ms. Repro. A. Rev.: *Concerto per violino ed orchestra*. 115p. Blueprint score

Doc.: Dissertation abstract. "The Orchestral Works of Gösta Nystroem...," by P. Louis Christensen, Ann Arbor: University Microfilms, 1961. 3p., English

Pri. Sco.: *Sinfonia breve*, Stockholm: Nordiska, c1949. 97p.

Pri. Sco. S.: *Sinfonia concertante*, Stockholm: Nordiska, c1949, to Louis Christensen, 1959. 43p.

Pri. Sco.: *Sinfonia del mare*, Stockholm: Nordiska, c1950. 149p. each. Two copies

Pri. Sco. S.: *Sinfonia espressiva*, Stockholm: Nordiska, c1956. 133p. each. Two copies, one is inscribed to Hans Moldenhauer

Draw. S.: 1921, 28x21cm.

Oakeley, Sir Herbert, 1830–1903
Northwestern University

L.: to Sir Alexander. n.p., 23 Aug. 1876

L.: to Mrs. Boyd. n.p., 14 Nov. 1878

L.: to Mrs. M. Duncan. Edinburgh, 22 Dec. 1888

L.: to Bumpus. Dover, 24 Jan. 1902

Clip.

Oberthür, Charles [Karl], 1819–1895
Library of Congress
(Box 39)

A. L. S.: to Rudolf Herfurth. London, 21 Oct. 1894. 3p., German

Obradovíc, Aleksandar, b. 1927
Library of Congress
(Box 39)

2 A. Card S.: to Aurelio de la Vega. [Belgrade], [Christmas 1979], n.d.

Obrist, Alois, 1867–1910
Library of Congress
(Box 39)

A. L. S.: to Eugen Lindner. Stuttgart, 21 Oct. 1895. 3p., German

Očadlík, Mirko, 1904–1964
Library of Congress
(Box 39)

A. L. S.: [to Paul A. Pisk]. Prague, 16 Dec. 1929. 2p., German

Ochs, Siegfried, 1858–1929
Library of Congress
(Box 39)

A. L. S.: to Schmidt. Berlin, 5 Oct. 1909. 1p., German

A. L. S.: to Karl Weigl. Vienna, 3 Apr. 1914. 4p., German

T. L. S.: to Karl Weigl. Berlin, 20 May 1914. 2p., German

Odnoposoff, Ricardo, b. 1914
Washington State University
See Rosbaud, Hans

Offenbach, Jacques [Jacob], 1819–1880
Library of Congress
(Box 39, unless noted)

A. Mus. ms.: Begleitung Barcarole C Dur. 2p., 23x29cm., ink. Sketch. Accompaniment for a Barcarolle in C major. On verso, sketches of a refrain

2 A. Mus. mss.: *Chanson of Valeria*, with orchestral accompaniment. Full score; on p4., Fanfare for brass instruments. Sketch in full score. 4p., 23x31cm., ink

A. Mus. ms.: *Ermite*, "Je suis l'Ermite le vieux
    devin...." 4p., 27x35cm., ink. Draft of the voice line
    with text and sketches for the accompaniment
A. Mus. ms.: *Les Trois Baisers du diable*, [1857]. 62p.,
    27x35cm., ink. Initialed. Overture in full score, and
    orchestral drafts of various scenes, with figurative
    drawings. Bound with slip case and gold embossing
    (Shelf)
A. L. S.: to the organ builder Alexandre. June. 2p.,
    French
A. L. S.: n.p., n.d. 1p., French
A. Doc.: Invitation. To the Offenbach family, 26 Aug.
    1864. 1p., French. Invitation with a musical
    quotation to the words "Je suis Alsacienne,"
    mounted with portrait engraving (Box 114)
Port. Engr.: see document above (Box 114)

O'Hara, Geoffrey, 1882–1967
Harvard University
L.: [to Randolph Hanson?]. Brooklyn, 20 Sept. 1938

O'Leary, Arthur, 1834–1919
Northwestern University
18 L.: to W. H. Cummings, including one letter from
    Rosetta O'Leary
Doc.: Invitation

Olitzka, Rosa, 1873–1949
Library of Congress
(Box 39)
A. L. S.: London, 8 July 1901. 1p., French

Oliveira, Jocy de, b. 1936
Harvard University
SUMMARY OF PRINCIPAL HOLDINGS:
Mus. ms.: *Mobius sonorum*, 1983

d'Ollone, Max, 1875–1959
Library of Congress
(Box 39)
A. L. S.: n.p., 18 Sept. 1910. 3p., French
2 A. Mus. Quot. S.: Both on 1p., excerpts from *In
    Memoriam*, "Sombre Maison," and "Le Son du vent
    qui passe..."

Olmeda, Federico, 1865–1909
Library of Congress
(Box 39)
A. Mus. ms. S.: *Escenas Nocturnes*, rima 19, No. 1. 4p.,
    21x31cm.
A. Mus. ms. S.: *Rima 4a*. 4p., 22x13cm.
A. Mus. ms. S.: *Sonata en la menor*. 12p., 22x31cm.

Olsen, Poul Rovsing [Rovsing Olsen, Poul], 1922–1982
Library of Congress
(Box 39)
A. Mus. ms. S.: [*Images*, op. 51], 1964–1965. 11p.,
    35x26cm. Sketches
A. Mus. ms.: *Improvisation*, [1965], for Svara Mandala.
    2p., 35x26cm.
A. Mus. ms.: *A l'inconnu*, 11 July 1962. 25p., 35x28cm.
A. Mus. ms.: *A l'inconnu*. 11p., 35x28cm. Sketches in
    condensed score
Mus. ms. Repro. S.: *Images*, op. 51, 1964–1965. 11p.
    Blueprint score
Mus. ms. Repro. S.: *A l'inconnu*, op. 48, June–Aug.
    1962. 26p.

O'Mara, Joseph, 1861–1927
Northwestern University
L.: to Cecil

Ondříček, František, 1857–1922
Library of Congress
(Box 39)
A. Mus. Quot. S.: *Concerto* by Brahms, for Baron Fritz
    Schey, Vienna, 17–18 Feb. 1905

Onslow, Georges, 1784–1853
Library of Congress
(Box 39)
A. Mus. ms. S.: *Minuetto moderato*, for String Quartet,
    1834. 3p., 35x26cm. Full score, fragment (without
    Trio section). Title page in copyist's hand
A. L. S.: Paris, 23 Nov. 1842. 2p., French

Oppo, Franco, b. 1935
Library of Congress
(Box 39)
T. L. S.: to Aurelio de la Vega. Cagliari, 15 Apr. 1981.
1p., Italian

Orel, Alfred, 1889–1967
Wiener Stadt- u. Landesbibliothek
L.: to Paul Pisk. Vienna, 7 Oct. 1925

Orff, Carl, 1895–1982
Bayerische Staatsbibliothek
SUMMARY OF PRINCIPAL HOLDINGS:
Mus. ms.: *Oedipus*
5 L.: to Hans Moldenhauer. 1955–1959
Port.

Washington State University
See Rosbaud, Hans

Orgeni, Aglaja [Görger St. Jörgen, Anna Maria von], 1841–1926
Library of Congress
(Box 39)
A. Doc. S.: Certificate. Recommendation for Edith Walker. Dresden, 15 Apr. 1893. 2p., English

Orlik, Emil, 1870–1932
Library of Congress
(Box 117, unless noted)
A. L. S.: to Hanna Schwarz. n.p., n.d. 2p., German. With drawing
A. L. S.: to Eisner. See portrait drawing below
Port. Draw.: to Bruno Eisner, 4 Apr. 1932. Pencil drawing of Wilhelm Furtwängler, Bruno Eisner, Bertram, and Franz Joachim Osborn. Drawn on the occasion of a performance under Furtwängler
Port. Draw. S.: Bruno Eisner seated at the piano. Ink (Box 114)
Port. Draw.: Bruno Eisner (head), with autograph letter signed, to Eisner. Ink (Box 114)

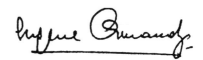

Ormandy, Eugene [Blau, Jenő], 1899–1985
Harvard University
L.: to Solomon Pimsleur. Minneapolis, 23 Oct. 1934
L.: to Charles Haubiel. Philadelphia, 28 Nov. 1944
27 L.: to Hans Moldenhauer. Philadelphia, 1961–1975
Port. Phot.: to Segovia, Philadelphia, 1956

Library of Congress
(Box 99)
3 T. L. S.: to Alfred Mann. Philadelphia, 9 Dec. 1975, 28 Nov. 1979, 16 Nov. 1982. 3p., English
A. L. S.: to Alfred Mann. Philadelphia, 11 Dec. 1976. 1p., English
See Schoenberg, Arnold
See Webern, Anton

Ornstein, Leo, b. 1892
Harvard University
Mus. ms.: [Sketches]
2 L.: to Hans Moldenhauer, from Paulina Ornstein. Brownsville, Texas, 14 Dec., 29 Dec. 1976
L.: to Rudolph Ganz. n.p., n.d.
2 Port. Phot.

Orrego-Salas, Juan, b. 1919
Harvard University
Mus. ms.: *Concerto for Wind Orchestra*, op. 53, 1964
Mus. ms.: *Sonata a quattro*, op. 55, 1964
Mus. ms.: *3 Alboradas*, op. 5, 1964
Mus. ms.: *Trio*, op. 58, 1965
Mus. ms.: *The Tumbler's Player*, op. 48, 1960
2 L.: to Aurelio de la Vega. Bloomington, 15 Oct. 1962; 1983
L.

Osborn, Franz, 1903–1933
Library of Congress
See Orlik, Emil

Othegraven, August von, 1864–1946
Northwestern University
Mus. ms.: *Ein Marienleben*. Complete piano-vocal score

Otte, Hans, b. 1926
Library of Congress
(Box 39)
T. L. S.: to Gloria Coates. Bremen, 4 Apr. 1974. 1p.,
  English. Also signed by Gloria Coates

Ouseley, Sir Frederick Arthur Gore, 1825–1889
Northwestern University
L.: to the Dean of Rochester. Tenbury, 2 June 1876

Pablo, Luís de, b. 1930
Library of Congress
(Box 99, unless noted)
A. Mus. ms. S.: *Imaginario II*, para orquesta, Apr.–Aug.
  1967, 2nd revision 11 Nov. 1967. 23p., 82x64cm.
  With accompanying 1p. decorative design in
  multicolors, (29 Apr. 1967, 21x115cm.), and 7p.
  typed document with autograph annotations
  (Spanish, French) (Shelf)
A. Mus. ms. S.: *Portrait imaginé*, 1974–1975. 156p.,
  28x21cm. Complete sketches
A. Mus. ms. S.: *Vielleicht*, para 6 percusionistas, 1973.
  24p., 39x27cm.
20 A. L. S.: to Aurelio de la Vega. 1966–1983. 25p.,
  Spanish, French
T. L.: to Lawrence Schoenberg. Buenos Aires, 7 July
  1971. 1p., English. Letter requesting permission to
  publish parts of Schoenberg's music. See letter
  reproduced below
T. L. S.: to Aurelio de la Vega. Madrid, 13 Feb. 1973.
  1p., Spanish, French. Cosigned by Horacio Vaggione
  (composer, Argentina)
A. L. S.: to Hans Moldenhauer. Madrid, 19 May 1973.
  1p., French. Regarding *Imaginario II*
A. Card S.: to Aurelio de la Vega. Loyola, n.d. 1p.,
  Spanish
L.: to Hans Moldenhauer, from Aurelio de la Vega.
  Northridge, California, 3 Aug. 1977. 1p., English.
  Regarding a letter received by de la Vega from Luis
  de Pablo
L. Repro.: to Lawrence Schoenberg. Madrid, 2 Apr.
  1972. 1p., French

2 Docs.: Autograph; Work list, [1977], 15p., with
  portrait reproduced
S. rec.: *Imaginario II*, 1967

Pabst, Paul, 1854–1897
Library of Congress
See Ries, Hubert

Pachelbel, Johann, 1653–1706
Library of Congress
See Gerber, Heinrich Nikolaus

V. de Pachmann

Pachman [Pachmann], Vladimir de, 1848–1933
Library of Congress
(Box 39)
Prog. S.: St. Gallen, 15 Mar. 1928. Flyer for a Chopin
  recital

Pacini, Giovanni, 1796–1867
Northwestern University
Mus. ms.: *Giuditta*. Complete score, with additional
  printed libretto
2 L.: to Dragonetti. Paris, 1 May 1839, 1842
L.: to ?. 1 May 1862

J. Paderewski

Paderewski, Ignacy Jan, 1860–1941
Library of Congress
(Box 39, unless noted)
A. L. S.: to Kneisel. Paris, n.d. 1p., German
Port. Phot. S. (Box 114)

Paër, Ferdinando, 1771–1839
Library of Congress
(Box 39, unless noted)
A. L. S.: to Rosa Movandi. Paris, 15 Sept. 1813. 3p.,
  Italian

A. L. S.: to Bériot. Paris, 14 Jan. 1832. 1p., French
A. L. S.: to Schlesinger. Paris, 23 July 1834. 1p.,
    French
Port. Engr.: by Bettoni (Box 114)

**Paganelli, Giuseppe [Gioseffo] Antonio, 1710–ca.
1763**
Library of Congress
See Ebner, Wolfgang

Paganini, Nicolò, 1782–1840
Library of Congress
(Box 39, unless noted)
A. Mus. ms.: *Dolci d'amor parole*, for voice and violin
    obligato with accompaniment. 12p., 22x29cm., ink.
    Particell. Unpublished. Exhibited at Genova, 1940
A. L. S.: to Francesco Morlacchi, at the court of
    Dresden. Frankfurt, 19 Feb. 1830. 1p., Italian.
    Regarding a Signor Scutezzi, for travel
    companionship and handling musical matters
Port. Draw.: to Armand Parent. By Naudin. 35x22cm.,
    black, brown watercolors (Box 114)

Northwestern University
L.: Dublin, 17 Sept. 1831
L.: to Dragonetti. n.p., n.d.
L.: to Bote & Bock, from Achilles Paganini (son).
    Parma, 15 May 1884
Prog.: Dublin, 17 July 1833
Port.

Paisiello, Giovanni, 1740–1816
Library of Congress
(Box 39)
A. L. S.: to Gregoire. Naples, 23 Mar. 1812. 2p.,
    Italian. Refers to pension endowed by Napoléon
    upon his departure from Paris; his *Stabat Mater*, Le
    Sueur

Paladilhe, Emile, 1844–1926
Library of Congress
(Box 39)
A. Mus. Quot. S.: *Patrie*, Act IV, "Pauvre martyr
    obscur"

Palmer, Christian David Friedrich von, 1811–1875
Library of Congress
(Box 39)
3 A. L. S.: [to Selmar Bagge]. Tübingen, 18 Jan. 1866,
    9 June, 19 Nov. 1867. 8p., German

Palmgren, Selim, 1878–1951
Library of Congress
(Box 39)
P. card S.: to the Szántó family. Weimar, 11 July 1901.
    Also signed by Busoni, Petri, and others
A. Mus. Quot. S.: *May Night*

Panofka, Heinrich, 1807–1887
Library of Congress
(Box 39)
8 A. L. S.: to Fétis. London, Paris, 1850–1865. 15p.,
    French
A. L. S.: to a doctor. Paris, 5 Feb. 1864. 1p., French

Panseron, Auguste, 1796–1859
Library of Congress
(Box 39)
A. Mus. Quot. S.: *Canon enigmatique à 2 parties*, with
    text "Bonjour bon au Henry Berton Montan"

Papier Paumgartner, Rosa, 1858–1932
Library of Congress
(Box 40)
A. Alb. l. S.: Leipzig, 7 Nov. 1885. 1p

Wiener Stadt- u. Landesbibliothek
L.: Vienna, 13 Oct. 1889
L.: to Ignaz Kugel. Weiden, 17 Apr. 1890
L.: n.p., 21 Nov. 1923
L.: n.p., n.d.

Papini, Guido, 1847–1912
Library of Congress
(Box 40)
A. L. S.: to Baering. Lausanne, 18 [Dec.?] 1876. 3p., French
Pri. Sco. S.: *"Le Mécanisme du Jeune Violiniste," A Complete and Progressive Course of Instruction for the Violin in Four Parts*, London: Chanot, to Constance and Rob Bell, Dublin, 7 Jan. 1888. 100p.

Parent, Armand, 1863–1934
Library of Congress
(Box 40, unless noted)
A. Mus. ms.: "Asseyons-nous tous deux près du chemin sur le vieux banc...," song with piano accompaniment. 4p., 33x25cm. Complete score
T. Doc. Rev.: Article. "Armand Parent," by Laurent Ceillier, in *Le Monde Musical*. 6p., French
T. Doc.: Typescript. "La Sonate de Franck," from Parent's *Souvenirs et Anecdotes*. 3p., French
Port. Paint.: 1906. By Rouault. Paint, colored chalks (Box 114)
See Redon, Odilon
See Utrillo, Maurice

Northwestern University
See Indy, Vincent d'

Parish Alvars, Elias [Parish, Eli], 1808–1849
Library of Congress
(Box 40)
A. Mus. ms. S.: *Fantasie sur le dernier pensé musicale de Bellini*, pour flûte et harpe. 19p., 33x25cm. By Parish Alvars and Joseph Fahrbach

Parratt, Sir Walter, 1841–1924
Northwestern University
6 L.: Windsor Castle, 1897–1921
Clip.

Parry, John, 1776–1851
Northwestern University
3 L.: London, 11, 12 May, 15 June

Parry, Sir Hubert, 1848–1918
Northwestern University
L.: to Harding. Gloucester, 23 Oct. 1899
L.: to Miss Stephenson. Gt. Berkhampstead, Thursday
Clip.

Partch, Harry, 1901–1976
Harvard University
SUMMARY OF PRINCIPAL HOLDINGS:
Mus. ms.: *Barstow*
3 L.: to Adolph Weiss. New York, 1933

Pascual-Ayllón, Fernando, b. 1893
Library of Congress
(Box 40)
Mus. ms. cop. Rev. S.: *Lugareñas*, Buenos Aires, July 1926, to Ricardo Viñes. 11p., 37x27cm.

Pasdeloup, Jules Etienne, 1819–1887
Library of Congress
(Box 40, unless noted)
A. L. S.: 8 Dec. 1p., French
A. L. S.: [to Massenet?]. n.p., n.d. 1p., French. Mentions Lalo
Port. Phot. S.: to ?. By Marion (Box 114)

Pasta [née Negri], Giuditta, 1798–1865
Library of Congress
(Box 40, unless noted)
A. L. S.: to ?. [Italy], 28 Sept. 1826. 1p., Italian
Port. Engr.: by Armytage (Box 114)

Patti, Adelina [Adela], 1843–1919
Library of Congress
(Box 40, unless noted)
A. L. S.: to Emily. Breconshire, South Wales, 12 Oct. 1899. 4p., English
L. S.: from Patti's husband. 20 May 1868
L. S.: to Spencer Consanby, from Patti's husband (the Marquis de Caux). London. French

A. Alb. l. S.: London, 26 July 1876
2 Clip.
2 Port. Phot. Repro. (Box 114)

Paul, Ada
Washington State University
Mus. ms.: *Musikalisches Akrostichon*, for piano. Based on
  Hans Rosbaud's name. 14p.

Pauer, Ernst, 1826–1905
Library of Congress
(Box 40)
A. L. S.: to ?. London, 20 May 1876. 2p., English. On
  verso, obituary

Paumgartner, Bernhard, 1887–1971
Washington State University
Doc.: Certificate. Salzburg, 24 June 1932

Wiener Stadt- u. Landesbibliothek
L.: to Paul Pisk. Salzburg, 12 Apr. 1924
Port.: Salzburg, 21 Mar. 1958

Paur, Emil, 1855–1932
Wiener Stadt- u. Landesbibliothek
L.: to a composer. New York, 8 Mar.

Paz, Erberto
Harvard University
Mus. ms.: Sonatina en forma libre, for piano solo, to
  Ricardo Viñes, 1924

Paz, Juan Carlos, 1901–1972
Library of Congress
(Box 99)
A. Mus. ms. S.: *Dos baladas*, op. 7, Nos. 3, 5, Buenos
  Aires, Dec. 1927. 9p., 36x26cm.

Pedrell, Carlos, 1878–1941
Harvard University
Mus. ms.: *A orillas del Duero (Sur les bords du Duoro)*

Pellicari, Giovanni, 18th century
Northwestern University
Mus. ms.: [Manuscript collection of Italian keyboard
  music], 1764. Contains keyboard music of Giovanni
  Battista Patoni, and Paolo Francesco Gordini

Pembaur, Joseph, Jr., 1875–1950
Library of Congress
(Box 40)
A. L. S.: [to Eugen Lindner]. Leipzig, 9 Nov. 1908.
  4p., German

Washington State University
See Rosbaud, Hans

Pembaur, Joseph, Sr., 1848–1923
Library of Congress
(Box 40, unless noted)
A. Mus. ms. S.: *Hildegundens Lied*, Leipzig. 1p.,
  34x26cm.
A. L. S.: [to the director of the Musician's Association
  in Vienna]. Innsbruck, 6 Sept. 1899. 3p., German
A. L. S.: Innsbruck, 22 Mar. 1911. 1p., German
Call. c. Annot.: German
Port. Phot. S. (Box 114)
2 Port. Phot. Repro. (Box 114)

Pénavaire, Jean Grégoire, 1840–1906
Library of Congress
(Box 40)
Pri. Sco. S.: *Ninette et Ninon*, Paris: Chatot, Feb. 1881.
  88p.

Penderecki, Kryzstof, b. 1933
Library of Congress
(Box 107, unless noted)
A. Mus. ms. S.: *Fluorescences*, for Orchestra, Vienna,
  Stockholm, 1961–1962. 80p., 45x34cm., some
  19x35cm., multicolored ink, felt-tip markers, pencil.
  Performance instructions in German and Polish.
  Sketches, complete draft in full score, and

incomplete sketches. Includes outline for
Penetrazioni (full page, multicolored)
A. Mus. ms.: *Polymorphia*, for 48 String Instruments,
1961. 33p., 45x34cm., multicolored ink, felt-tip
markers, pencil. Performance instructions in Polish.
Complete draft in full score, and incomplete
sketches
Doc.: Review. 1p., English
2 Port. Phot.: Donaueschingen Festival, 1962. One
with Hans Rosbaud (Box 114)

Pentland, Barbara, b. 1912
Harvard University
Mus. ms.: *Symphony for Ten Parts*
L.

Pepping, Ernst, 1901–1981
Library of Congress
(Box 40)
A. Mus. ms. S.: *Zwei Orchesterstücke über eine Chanson des
Binchois*, 1958. 119p., 33x27cm. Full score
T. L. S.: to Hans Moldenhauer. Berlin, 7 Nov. 1960.
1p., German

Pepusch, Johann Christoph, 1667–1752
Northwestern University
Mus. ms.: [Manuscript volume, ca. 1700]. The volume
contains a theoretical discourse and sixteen sonatas
for violin and figured bass

Perabo, Ernst, 1845–1920
Harvard University
10 L.: to Bargiel. Leipzig, Boston, Wilton, 1878–1893

Pergolesi, Giovanni Battista, 1710–1736
Library of Congress
See Giardini, Felice

Peri, Achille, 1812–1880
Library of Congress
(Box 40)
A. L. S.: ?, 19 May 1844. 3p., Italian. Includes response
A. L. S.: ?, 22 Aug. 1844. 2p., Italian

Perle, George, b. 1915
Harvard University
Mus. ms.: *Quintet for Strings*
L.

Perron, Karl, 1858–1928
Library of Congress
(Box 40)
A. L. S.: to a concert director. Leipzig, 2 Sept. 1885.
3p., German
A. Card S.: Leipzig, 26 Jan. 1885. 1p., German

Persichetti, Vincent, 1915–1987
Harvard University
SUMMARY OF PRINCIPAL HOLDINGS:
Mus. ms.: *The Little Piano Book, Masque*
L.: to Charles Haubiel. Philadelphia, 12 Feb. 1970
Mus. ms. Repro.: *Second String Quartet*
2 Port. Phot.

Peschka-Leutner, Minna, 1839–1890
Library of Congress
(Box 40)
25 A. L. S.: to ?. 1868–1889. 50p., German
2 A. Card S.: Köln, 1885; Leipzig, 2 Nov. 1876. 3p.,
German
Call. c. Annot. S.: German, 2p.
2 Clip.: German

Pessard, Emile, 1843–1917
Northwestern University
2 L.: to Massenet. n.p., 24 Nov. 1887, 16 Mar. 1896
L.: to Madame Massenet. Paris, 16 Jan. 1909

Goffredo Petrassi

Petrassi, Goffredo, b. 1904
Library of Congress
(Box 40)
A. Mus. ms. S.: *Suoni notturni*, per chitarra, Rome,
1959. 8p., 32x23cm., ink. Complete score
A. L. S.: to Aurelio de la Vega. Rome, [6 Feb. 1984?].
1p., Italian
Call. c. Annot.: to the Webern Society

Petrella, Errico, 1813–1877
Library of Congress
(Box 40)
A. L. S.: Milan, 18 Dec. 1862. 1p., Italian

Petri, Egon, 1881–1962
Library of Congress
(Box 114)
Port. Phot. S.: to Hans and Rosaleen Moldenhauer, Oakland, California, Dec. 1947
See Palmgren, Selim

Petrobelli, Pierluigi, b. 1832
Library of Congress
See Verdi, Giuseppe

Petyrek, Felix, 1892–1951
Library of Congress
(Box 40)
A. L. S.: to Paul A. Pisk. 22 Nov. 1924. 2p., German

Pfitzner, Hans, 1869–1949
Bayerische Staatsbibliothek
SUMMARY OF PRINCIPAL HOLDINGS:
L.: 9 June 1916
4 L.: to Hans Rosbaud. 1941, 1946, n.d.
L.: to Alfred Mann. [1945]
L.: to Leonhard, Office of Military Government for Bavaria. Munich, 31 July 1946
L.: to Gutmann. n.d.

Library of Congress
See Brod, Max

Philipp, Isidor, 1863–1958
Library of Congress
(Box 40, unless noted)
P. card S.: to Bruno Eisner. Paris, 1932. French
A. L. S.: to Solomon Pimsleur. New York, 18 Aug. 1934. 1p., English

A. L. S.: [to Rudolph Ganz]. New York, 16 May 1952. 1p., French
7 A. L. S.: to Boaz Piller. New York, 1952. 7p., French
4 A. L. S.: to Charles Haubiel. New York, 3, 11, 24 Oct., 15 Nov. 4p., English
A. Mus. Quot. S.: *Fuggevole*, to Boaz Piller, Paris. Mounted with portrait photograph signed (Box 114)
Port. Phot. S.: mounted with musical quotation above (Box 114)

Phillips, Burrill, 1907–1988
Harvard University
SUMMARY OF PRINCIPAL HOLDINGS:
Mus. ms.: *The Age of Song*. Excerpt
Port.

Phillips, Henry, 1801–1876
Northwestern University
L.: to Lockey. Cornwall, 3 Dec. 1849

Piatigorsky, Gregor, 1903–1976
Harvard University
L.: to Hans Moldenhauer. 1 May 1970
2 Port. Phot.: 1970

Piatti, Alfredo, 1822–1901
Library of Congress
(Box 114)
A. L. S.: to Clara. Notting Hill, n.d. 1p., Italian. Mounted with portrait photograph

Picasso, Pablo, 1881–1973
Library of Congress
See Stravinsky, Igor

Piccinni, Louis Alexandre [Luigi Alessandro; Lodovico Alessandro], 1779–1850
Library of Congress
(Box 41)
A. L. S.: Paris, 8 Germinal An 11. 1p., French

Piccinni [Piccini], Niccolò [Nicola], 1728–1800
Library of Congress
(Box 41)
Rcpt. S.: Paris, 31 Mar. 1779. For royalties covering
1778–1780

Piccolomini, Marietta, 1834–1899
Library of Congress
(Box 41, unless noted)
Sig.
Port. Phot. (Box 114)

Pierné, Gabriel, 1863–1937
Library of Congress
(Box 41, unless noted)
A. L. S.: to Charles Lefebvre. Naples, 5 Jan. 1924. 1p.,
French
A. L. S.: [to Ravel?]. n.p., n.d. 1p., French. Mounted
with portrait photograph (Box 114)
Prog. S.: to Boaz Piller. Boston, 27 Jan. 1922. 2p. With
thematic quotation from *Ramuntcho*
Port. Phot.: mounted with letter above. By Lipnitzki
(Box 114)

**Pierson [Pearson], Henry Hugo [Hugh],
1815–1873**
Northwestern University
L.: to Lord Tennyson. Würzburg, 28 May 1859

Pijper, Willem, 1894–1947
Library of Congress
(Box 41, unless noted)
Mus. ms.: [*Merlijn*]. 1 leaf (pp.101–102), 35x27cm. Full
score of his unfinished opera. With accompanying
letter to Hans Moldenhauer, from L. Bolleman
(Amersfoort, 23 Mar. 1959)
Sig. Repro.
Port. Phot. S. (Box 114)
2 Port. Repro. S. (Box 114)
Port. Draw. Repro. Annot. S. (Box 114)

Pillney, Karl Hermann, b. 1896
Northwestern University
Mus. ms.: *Divertimento*, op. 2, 1928

Pimsleur, Solomon, 1900–1962
Washington State University
Materials include the complete estate of music
manuscripts (which may include drafts, blueprint
scores, printed scores, and sketches) and scrapbooks
(which contain clippings, correspondence, programs,
etc.)
SUMMARY OF PRINCIPAL HOLDINGS:
Mus. ms.: *Beethovenesque Sonata for String Quartet*
Mus. ms.: *Behold Our Bodies*
Mus. ms.: *Contemporary Verse and Prose*
Mus. ms.: *Contrapuntal Etudes*, op. 4, No. 1
Mus. ms.: *Cycle of Self-Castigation*, op. 52, 1943–1944
Mus. ms.: *Duos: Three Versions of Archaic Suite*
Mus. ms.: *Elegy in Memory of My Father*, op. 61, No. 2,
1948
Mus. ms.: *Eloquent Sonata for String Quartet*, 1944–1945
Mus. ms.: *Exalted Ballade*
Mus. ms.: *Fiery Sonata for Trio*
Mus. ms.: *First Drama in a Cycle of Symphonies*. Excerpt
Mus. ms.: *Four Introspective Poems*
Mus. ms.: *Four Madrigals*
Mus. ms.: *Fourth Drama in a Cycle of Symphonies*
Mus. ms.: *Heart Rending Sonata for String Sextet*
Mus. ms.: *Imaginative Sonata for String Quartet*
Mus. ms.: *Impetuous Sonata*, 1921–1935
Mus. ms.: *Impetuous Toccata*
Mus. ms.: *Impulsive Sonata*
Mus. ms.: *Solemn Prelude and Labyrinth Fugue*
Mus. ms.: *Light and Beauty*
Mus. ms.: *Lofty Sonata for String Quartet*, op. 12
Mus. ms.: *Lucy Cycle*, op. 62, 1948
Mus. ms.: *Meditative Nocturne*, 1924
Mus. ms.: *Melancholy Sonata for String Quartet*, 1946
Mus. ms.: *The Miracle of Life and the Mystery of Death*,
op. 32
Mus. ms.: *Moody Sonata*
Mus. ms.: *La Morte da la Poete*
Mus. ms.: *Mournful Prelude*, op. 9, No. 1
Mus. ms.: *Narrative Ballade*
Mus. ms.: *Neo-Classic Overture*
Mus. ms.: *Overture to the Martyrdom of Anne Frank*
Mus. ms.: *Pageant of War Sonnets*

Mus. ms.: *Partita for String Orchestra*
Mus. ms.: *Philosophical Sonata for String Quartet*
Mus. ms.: *Poetical Symphony for Orchestra*
Mus. ms.: *Poignant Sonata for String Quartet*, op. 13
Mus. ms.: *Preamble: To the Charter of the United Nations*, op. 75, 1951
Mus. ms.: *Rapturous Dialogue Concertante*, op. 60, 1947–1948
Mus. ms.: *Reflective Sonata*
Mus. ms.: *Reign of Terror*
Mus. ms.: *Rhapsodic Suite*
Mus. ms.: *Sardonic Humor*
Mus. ms.: *Second Drama in a Cycle of Symphonies*
Mus. ms.: *Six Proletarian Songs*
Mus. ms.: [Sketchbooks]
Mus. ms.: [Sketches], 1956
Mus. ms.: *Soaring Sonata*
Mus. ms.: *Song Cycle of Ten Modern Hebrew Sonnets*
Mus. ms.: *Sonnet Tableau*
Mus. ms.: *Soulful Sonata*
Mus. ms.: *Splendid Sonata*, op. 59
Mus. ms.: *Statuesque Sonata*, op. 47
Mus. ms.: *Suite of Transformations*, op. 18, 1924
Mus. ms.: *Symphonic Ode and Peroration*, op. 35
Mus. ms.: *Symphonic Suite for Orchestra*
Mus. ms.: *Symphony to Disillusionment*, op. 25, 1928
Mus. ms.: *Symphony to Terror and Despair*
Mus. ms.: *Third Drama in a Cycle of Symphonies*
Mus. ms.: *Tranquil Sonata*. Excerpt
Mus. ms.: *Twelve Songs to the Poetry of P. B. Shelley*
Mus. ms.: *Valse Melancholique*
Mus. ms.: *Virile Sonata*, op. 2
Mus. ms.: *Vocal Sonnets*
Doc.: Essay. "Musical Trends, Personalities and Tendencies in Israel During the Past Quarter Century." Incomplete
Doc.: Sonnets
Mus. ms. Repro.: *Poem for May First*. Blueprint score
Port.
Paint.
Bk.: *Sonnets*, by Pimsleur, privately printed, 1963
55 S. recs.
See Paumgartner, Bernhard

Pincherle, Marc, 1888–1974
Library of Congress
See Rosbaud, Hans

Pinsuti, Ciro, 1829–1888
Library of Congress
(Box 41)
A. L. S.: to Miss Stepheson. n.p., n.d. 1p. English. On verso, obituary
Doc.: Biographical essay. 2p., English

Pisk, Paul A., 1893–1990
Harvard University
SUMMARY OF PRINCIPAL HOLDINGS:
Manuscripts may include additional notes, sketches, printed scores, and sound recordings
Mus. ms.: *Ballade*
Mus. ms.: *Brass Quintet*, 1977
Mus. ms.: *British Songs*, 1975
Mus. ms.: *Campanella*, op. 28
Mus. ms.: *Dialogue for Clarinet and Piano*, op. 102, No. 2
Mus. ms.: *Drums*, op. 48, No. 6
Mus. ms.: *Envoy*, op. 104
Mus. ms.: *Epigramm*
Mus. ms.: *Four Memorial Songs*, op. 126, 1981
Mus. ms.: *Four Pieces for Cello Solo*, op. 130, 1983
Mus. ms.: *Five Songs*, op. 122a, 1977
Mus. ms.: *5 Lieder*
Mus. ms.: *George Lieder*, op. 6, 1920
Mus. ms.: *Gesang vom Rundfunk*, 1929
Mus. ms.: *Geschichten aus dem Wienerwald* by Johann Strauss, arranged by Pisk for piano, string quartet, and voice
Mus. ms.: *God Is Light*, op. 123, 1977
Mus. ms.: *Konzertarie*, op. 20
Mus. ms.: *Ein lustiges Pfingstkinderlied*
Mus. ms.: *Die neue Stadt*, 1926
Mus. ms.: *Not Now*, op. 124a, No. 3, 1978
Mus. ms.: *Partita für Orchester*, op. 10
Mus. ms.: *Piano Variations*, op. 107
Mus. ms.: *Prayer for Tenor or Baritone Solo, Mixed Chorus, and Organ*
Mus. ms.: *Proud Maisie*, op. 124, 1978
Mus. ms.: *Rose-Leaves, A Kiss, A Greek Gift, Uraeus Exit*
Mus. ms.: *Shakespeare Chorus*, op. 105
Mus. ms.: [Sketches, opera 93-96, 98–100, 1958, 1960]
Mus. ms.: *So Long*, op. 124a, No. 2, 1978
Mus. ms.: *So war's einmal*
Mus. ms.: *Spruch*, 1983
Mus. ms.: *Suite III*, op. 129, 1982
Mus. ms.: *Things Will Go*, op. 124a, No. 4
Mus. ms.: *Three Biblical Chorales*, op. 127

Mus. ms.: *Three Movements for Violin and Piano*, op. 124, 1978

Mus. ms.: *Three Sandburg Choruses*, op. 108

Mus. ms.: *Three Sea Poems*, op. 78

Mus. ms.: *Three Sisters*, 1982

Mus. ms.: *Trail of Life*, op. 88

Mus. ms.: *Trio for Oboe, Clarinet, and Bassoon*, op. 125, 1979

Mus. ms.: *Twilight*

Mus. ms.: *Two Sonnets*, op. 103

Mus. ms.: *Vier Orchesterlieder*, op. 4

Mus. ms.: *Vom Winter*

Mus. ms.: *A Youth*, op. 75, No. 1

Mus. ms.: *Zwischendeck*, op. 23c, 1930

L.: to Paul Sanders. Vienna, 28 June 1933

L.: to Solomon Pimsleur. Los Angeles, 11 July 1957

L.: to Hans Moldenhauer. Several hundred pieces of correspondence

Doc.: Essay. Untitled, for inclusion in *The Death of Webern* by Hans Moldenhauer

Doc.: Lecture. "Bach in Our Time"

Doc.: Lecture. "The Life and Works of Heinrich Schütz"

Doc.: Lecture. "Musicology"

Doc.: Lecture. "Musikwissenschaft hier und drüben"

Doc.: Lecture. "The Serious American Composer and the Piano Student"

Doc.: Lecture. "Symphony"

Doc.: Lecture. "Webern's String Quartet (1905)"

Doc.: Lecture notes. "Church Music"

Doc.: Lecture notes. "Figaro"

Doc.: Lecture notes. "Formal Analysis as Aid to Interpretation"

Doc.: Lectures. Including the following topics: Berg the Creative Artist, Bizets Meisteroper "Carmen" und ihr Schicksal, Die blamierten Kritiker, Brahms, Campanella the Philosopher and Reformer, Development of a Musical Audience Achieved by Worker's Musical Education in Vienna, Early Music Through College Performance, Das Ende der Tonalität, Gallus the Austrian Palestrina, Die Harmonie der Sphaeren, Hindemith's Ludus Tonalis, Historical and Sociological Background of Opera in Europe, Honegger, Vom Lied zum Song, The Melodic Structure in the Non-Stylized Dance Movements of the Late Baroque German Keyboard Music, Method of Composition with 12 Tones and Its Influence on Contemporary Composers, Modern Music in Texas, Mozart's and Beethoven's Compositions for Mechanical Instruments, Music

Historical Speculations in Kircher's *Musurgia*, Mozartaufführung und -Studien in den Vereinigten Staaten, Music Pioneering in California, Musikalische Volksbildung im demokratischen Wien, Musicology and the Composer, Musikwissenschaft in Oesterreich bis 1938, The Pianist's Repertoire, Problems of the Music Library in the Small Liberal Arts College, Psychology of Music, Recent Mozart Literature, Regers Klavierstil, The Road to Modern Music, Romanticism in Music and Schumann's Piano Works, Zur Soziologie der Musik, Some Analytical Remarks for Schumann's *Carnaval*, Structural Analysis as Aid to Musical Interpretation, Subdivision of Tones, Symposium in Texas, Tchaikovsky, Telemann's Menuet Collection of 1728, The Triumph of Tchaikovsky, Wagner auf den Barrikaden, Wagner's Influence on Twentieth Century Music, Western Outposts of Musical Culture, Wie gelangt der Hoerer zum Verstaendnis moderner Musik

Doc.: Reports. "Ehrenbeleidigungsklage." Regarding the dispute between Pisk and Karl Kraus

Doc.: Review. *Anton Webern—Troubled Genius*

Doc.: Review. *Dansk Aarbog for Musikforskning*

Doc.: Review. *The Music Forum*, vol. III, edited by William Mitchell and Felix Salzer

Doc.: Review. *Music Notation*, by Gardner Read

Doc.: Review. *Musical Form*, by Robert E. Tyndall

Doc.: Review. *Nineteenth Century Romanticism in Music*, by Rey Longyear

Doc.: Typescript. "Anton Webern: Profile of a Composer." Draft

Doc.: Typescript. "Anton Webern's Early Orchestral Works"

Doc.: Typescript. "Arnold Schoenberg, 1874–1951"

Doc.: Typescript. "Arnold Schoenberg as Teacher"

Doc.: Typescript. "Dreams of Death and Life, A Study of Two Songs by Johannes Brahms"

Doc.: Typescript. "The Early ISCM." Draft

Doc.: Typescript. "Elements of Impressionism and Atonality in Liszt's Last Piano Pieces"

Doc.: Typescript. [On Max Reger]

Doc.: Typescript. "Memories of Arnold Schoenberg"

Doc.: Typescript. "Mozart." Draft

Doc.: Typescript. "The Music Library in the Liberal Arts College"

Doc.: Typescript. "New Music in Austria during the 1920s"

Doc.: Typescript. "From Titelouze to Tournemire, 300 Years of French Organ Music." Draft

Doc.: Typescript. "Urtext and Other Editions of
    Familiar Piano Music." Draft
Doc.: Typescript. "The Viennese Triumvirate
    Remembered"
Mus. ms. Repro.: *Trio for Oboe, Clarinet, and Bassoon,*
    op. 100. Facsimile
Mus. ms. Repro.: *Trio for Violin, Viola, and Cello*
Port.
S. rec.: *The Works of Paul Pisk*

Library of Congress
See Webern, Anton

Piston, Walter, 1894–1976
Harvard University
L.: to Verne Kelsey. Cambridge, 7 Jan. 1949
L.: to Eugene Weigel. South Woodstock, Vermont, n.d.
Mus. Quot.: *The Incredible Flutist*, inscribed Boston,
    10 Feb. 1939. Mounted on portrait
Mus. ms. Repro.: *Three Pieces*. With blueprint score,
    and additional printed score
Port.
See Koussevitzky, Serge

Pittrich, George Washington, 1870–1934
Library of Congress
(Box 41, unless noted)
A. L. S.: Dresden, 27 June 1909. 1p., German
A. Mus. Quot. S.: *Gomera*. German
Port. Phot. S.: Dresden, 1907. By Herzfeld (Box 114)

Pixis, Johann Peter, 1788–1874
Library of Congress
(Box 41)
A. L. S.: to Vivenot. Paris, 4 Nov. 1826. 1p., German

**Pizzetti, Ildebrando [Parma, Ildebrando da],
1880–1968**
Library of Congress
(Box 41)
A. L. S.: to Mario Castelnuovo-Tedesco. Rome,
    13 Sept. 1950. 3p., Italian

Planquette, Robert, 1848–1903
Library of Congress
(Box 41)
A. Card S.: n.p., n.d. 1p., French

Planté, Francis, 1839–1934
Library of Congress
(Box 41)
A. L. S.: to a conductor. n.p., 12 Feb. 3p., French
A. L. S.: to Dulan. n.p., 29 Apr. 1909. 2p., French
Call. c. S.: Brussels, 5 Apr. 1891

Pleyel, Ignace Joseph, 1757–1831
Library of Congress
(Box 41)
A. L. S.: to Artaria. Paris, 21 May 1796. 4p., French.
    Discussing a series of compositions

Plotnikov, Eugene, 1877–1951
Library of Congress
(Box 41)
T. L. S.: to Solomon Pimsleur. New York, 3 Sept. 1934.
    1p., English

Plüddemann, Martin, 1854–1897
Library of Congress
(Box 41)
P. card S.: to Gattel. Betellt, 30 Mar. 1896. 1p., German
A. Mus. Quot. S.: *Der Taucher* by Schiller, to Fritz
    Wittek, Vienna, 17 Feb. 1894. German

Pochon, Alfred, 1878–1959
Harvard University
See Flonzaley Quartet

**Poglietti, Alessandro [Boglietti, Alexander de],
early 17th century–1683**
Library of Congress
See Ebner, Wolfgang

Pohl, Richard, 1826–1896
Library of Congress
(Box 41)
A. Mus. ms. S.: *Warum?*. 2p., 33x24cm., German

Poise, Ferdinand, 1828–1892
Northwestern University
L.: to Massenet. n.p., n.d.

Polko, Elise, 1822–1899
Library of Congress
(Box 41)
A. Card S.: n.p., n.d. 1p., German
See Taubert, Wilhelm

Ponce, Manuel, 1882–1948
Harvard University
SUMMARY OF PRINCIPAL HOLDINGS:
Mus. ms. cop.: *Palomita*

Library of Congress
See Segovia, Andrés

Poné, Gundaris, 1932–1994
Harvard University
SUMMARY OF PRINCIPAL HOLDINGS:
Mus. ms.: *Reaktionen: Punkt-Gruppe-Feld*
Mus. ms.: *Serie-Alea, Dodici Proposizioni*, op. 32

Poniatowski, Józef Michal Ksawery Franciszek
Jan, 1816–1873
Library of Congress
(Box 41)
A. L. S.: n.p., n.d. 1p., French. With musical quotation
   (Italian text)

Popper, David, 1843–1913
Library of Congress
(Box 41)
A. L. S.: London, 22 June 1866. 2p., English
A. L. S.: Budapest, 12 Nov. 1877. 11p., German
A. L. S.: Budapest, 19 Jan. 1888. 4p., German

Porter, Cole, 1891–1964
Library of Congress
(Box 99)
Mus. ms. cop. S.: *Night and Day*. 5p., 32x24cm. Albert
   Sirmay, copyist

Porter, Quincy, 1897–1966
Harvard University
L.: to Eugene Weigel. New Haven, 22 Sept. 1948

Posselt, Ruth, b. 1914
Harvard University
Port. Phot.: Boston, 1933

Potocka [née Komar], Delphine, 1807–1877
Library of Congress
(Box 41)
A. L. S.: to Mikuli. n.p., n.d. 1p., Polish

Potter, Cipriani [Hambley], 1792–1871
Northwestern University
L.: London, 13 May 1833

Poulenc, Francis, 1899–1963
Library of Congress
(Box 41)
A. L. S.: to René Koering. ?, 15 Dec. 1961. 2p.,
   French. Mentions Berg, Boulez, Milhaud,
   Schoenberg, Webern
Tlgm.: to René Koering. Paris, 8 Jan. 1962. French
A. Mus. Quot. S.: *Les Mamelles de Tirésias*, "Envolez-
   vous oiseaux de ma faiblesse," Noizay, 1947. 2p.
   (8m.). Voice and piano
Pri. Sco. S.: *Stabat Mater*, Paris: Rouart-Lerolle, 1951,
   to Karl Amadeus Hartmann, Paris, 1952. 68p.

Pousseur, Henri, b. 1929
Library of Congress
(Box 41)
A. Mus. ms. Annot.: *Mobiles*. 16p., 28x34cm. Complete
sketches
A. Mus. ms.: *Trois Chants sacrés, pour voix de soprano et
trio à cordes*. 9p., 37x27cm.
A. L. S.: to Hans Moldenhauer. Brussels, 14 Jan. 1960.
3p., German
T. L. S.: to Hans Moldenhauer. n.p., [8 Oct. 1962]. 1p.,
German
T. L. S.: to Hans Moldenhauer. Buffalo, 1 Feb. 1966.
1p., English
Card: to Hans Moldenhauer. 2 Feb. 1966. 1p., French

Washington State University
L.: to Aurelio de la Vega. Buffalo, 31 Jan. 1966

Powell, Mel, 1923–1998
Harvard University
Mus. ms.: *Haiku Settings*. Excerpt
L.

Pradher, Louis Barthelemy, 1781–1843
Library of Congress
(Box 41)
A. L. S.: n.p., Monday, 13 Mar. 1p., French

Praeger, Ferdinand, 1815–1891
Northwestern University
SUMMARY OF PRINCIPAL HOLDINGS:
Mus. ms.: *Am See*
Mus. ms.: *Der Kampf um's Leben*
Mus. ms.: *Fifth Sonata in A Major*
Mus. ms.: *First Grand Sonata in C Minor*
Mus. ms.: *Fleeting Thoughts*
Mus. ms.: *Fourth Sonata in F Major*
Mus. ms.: *Funeral March*
2 Mus. mss.: *Gondoliera*; on verso, *Procession*
Mus. ms.: *Gretchen's Gebete*
Mus. ms.: *Lullaby*
Mus. ms.: *Lullaby No. 3*
Mus. ms.: *Second Symphonic Poem in F Major*

Mus. ms. cop.: *Second Symphony in F Major*
Mus. ms.: *Seventeenth Sonata in F-sharp Major*
22 Mus. mss.: [Including "Slow movements" for
piano]
Mus. ms.: *Spanish Romance*
4 Mus. mss.: *String Quartet* [Nos. 11, 16, 21, 22]
Mus. ms.: *Thirtieth Sonata in C Major*
Doc.: Doctoral dissertation. *The Musical and Literary
Manuscripts of Ferdinand Praeger in the Moldenhauer
Archives*, by M. Clare Lucille Hutchinson, Indiana
University, 1969
Doc.: Essay. "Guide pratique pour la composition."
With musical illustrations
13 Docs.: Poems
Doc.: Typescript. "Wagner as I Knew Him"
Mus. ms. Repro.: *Festival Overture in E Major*

Prater, Jeffrey, b. 1947
Harvard University
SUMMARY OF PRINCIPAL HOLDINGS:
Mus. ms.: *And on Earth, Peace*, 1982
Mus. ms.: *Interfusions*, 1980
Mus. ms.: *Intrada, Chorale, and Postludium*, 1984
Mus. ms.: *Three Motets from Psalm 24*, 1979
Mus. ms.: *Three Reflexives*, 1978
Mus. ms. Repro.: *Vier Geburtstagszueignungen*,
1968–1980. Photocopy
2 L.: to Hans and Mary Moldenhauer. Ames, Iowa,
27 Jan. 1981, 27 Apr. 1984

Predieri, Giacomo Cesare, 1671–1753
Library of Congress
(Box 41)
Rcpt. S.: 6 Apr. 1743. 1p., Italian. Regarding an
oratorio

Predieri, Luca Antonio, 1688–1767
Library of Congress
(Box 41)
3 A. L. S.: to Lodovico Preti. 1761–1766. 6p., Italian.
With biographical account

Preussner, Eberhard, 1899–1964
Washington State University
See Rosbaud, Hans

Primrose, William, 1903–1982
Washington State University
See Rosbaud, Hans

Proch, Heinrich, 1809–1878
Wiener Stadt- u. Landesbibliothek
L.: to Lehmann. San Gustav, 30 Mar. 1858

Prohaska, Felix, 1912–1987
Washington State University
See Rosbaud, Hans

Prohaska, Karl, 1869–1927
Library of Congress
(Box 41)
A. L. S.: to Hans Moldenhauer, from Margarete
  Prohaska (wife). Vienna, 29 Dec. 1959. 2p., German

Wiener Stadt- u. Landesbibliothek
Mus. ms.: *Madeleine Guinard*. With additional blueprint
  of the libretto
Doc.: Work list
Clip.

Svrge Prokofieff (signature)

Prokofieff, Sergei, 1891–1953
Harvard University
See Slonimsky, Nicolas

Library of Congress
(Box 41, unless noted)
A. Mus. Quot. S.: [*The Giant*, 1897], inscribed 1938. 1p.
  In piano score. With authentication by Nicolas
  Slonimsky
A. Card S.: to Boaz Piller. Moscow, 23 May 1937. 2p.,
  French
A. Mus. Quot. S.: *Second Concerto*, op. 16, Boston, 1930
Port. Phot. (Box 114)

Prout, Ebenezer, 1835–1909
Northwestern University
L.: to Bennett. London, 19 Mar. 1886
L.: to Middleton. London, 7 Dec. 1895

L.: to Miss E. Wheeler. London, 15 Feb. 1897

Prudent, Emile, 1817–1863
Library of Congress
(Box 41)
A. Mus. ms. S.: *Fantaisie sur Un ballo in maschera, opéra
  de Verdi*, op. 63, Sept. 1861. 14 leaves + 2 leaves
  sewn together + one unattached leaf, with many
  paste-overs, ink, pencil

Prüwer, Julius, 1874–1943
Library of Congress
(Box 41)
A. L. S.: [to Bruno Eisner]. n.p., 12 Jan. 1941. 1p.,
  German

Prunières, Henry, 1886–1942
Library of Congress
(Box 41)
3 T. L. S.: to Paul F. Sanders. Paris, 29 Mar.,
  24, 28 Apr. 1933. 4p., French
2 P. cards S.: to Paul F. Sanders. Paris, 18, 26 Apr. 1933.
  2p., French
2 A. L. S.: [to Ruzena Herlinger]. Paris, 25 Mar. 1938;
  n.d. 3p., French
T. L. Repro. S.: to Paul F. Sanders. Paris, 3 Apr. 1933.
  1p., French

G. Puccini (signature)

Puccini, Giacomo, 1858–1924
Library of Congress
(Box 107)
A. Mus. ms. A. Rev.: [*La Bohème*, Act II, Sextet], 1 leaf
  (2p. with four paste-overs), 46x32cm., ink.
  Full score
P. card S.: to Gatteschi. Milan, 31 Mar. 1894. Italian.
  Receiving illustrations for *La Bohème*
P. card S.: to ?. 29 June 1913. Italian. With portrait
  photograph, inscribed
A. L. S.: to Antonio Bettolacci. Torre del Lago,
  12 Sept. 1916. 1p., Italian. About financial matters

A. L. S.: to Carlo Chiusuri of Ricordi. Viareggio, 4 Mar. 1918. 1p., Italian. Requesting corrections

A. L. S.: to Raoul Gunsbourg. Torre del Lago, 26 Apr. 1919. 1p., Italian, with English translation

Port. Phot.: see postcard above

Pucitta [Puccitta], Vincenzo, 1778–1861
Library of Congress
(Box 41)
Rcpt. S.: 16 Aug. 1811. 1p., English

Pugno, Raoul, 1852–1914
Library of Congress
(Box 41, unless noted)
A. L. S.: Paris, 2 July 1907. 2p., French

T. L. S.: to Louis Schneider. Paris, 28 Oct. 1907. 1p., French

2 A. L. S.: to Louis Schneider. Paris, 12 Oct. 1911; n.p., n.d. 4p., French

A. L. S.: to Baron Larrey. n.p., n.d. 1p., French

A. L. S.: to Leuven[?]. n.p., n.d. 1p., French

A. L. S.: n.p., n.d. 1p. + 1p. (notes), French

A. L. S.: n.p., n.d. 1p., French

Call. c. S.: Madame Pugno's calling card, with autograph note by Pugno. French

A. Mus. Quot. S.: *Piano Concerto*, Allegro vivo by Schumann, to Stenzel, Breslau, 5 Jan. 1910

Port. Phot.: by Reutlinger (Box 114)

Purdie, Robert, fl. 1809–ca. 1837
Northwestern University
See Gow, Nathaniel

Pyne, Louisa, 1832–1904
Northwestern University
L.: to Lockey
2 L.: from [Zoi?] Pyne

Rabaud, Henri, 1873–1949
Library of Congress
(Box 42, unless noted)
A. L. S.: to Jacques de la Presle. 9 June 1922. 1p., French

10 A. L. S.: to Boaz Piller. 1922–1947. 17p., French

4 P. cards S.: to Boaz Piller. 1922–1947. 4p., French

A. Card S.: to Boaz Piller. n.p., n.d. 1p., French

Doc. S.: Menu. Copley Plaza, 29 Apr. 1919. 2p. For a testimonial dinner in honor of Rabaud. Also signed by Fredric Fradkin, Georges Laurent, Boaz Piller, and others

A. Mus. Quot. S.: *Roland et le mauvais garçon*, to Boaz Piller. 1p., mounted with portrait photograph signed, to Boaz Piller (Box 114)

Port. Phot.: see musical quotation above. By Harcourt (Box 114)

Rabinof, Benno, 1908–1975
Harvard University
4 L.: to Charles Haubiel, from Sylvia Smith Rabinof (wife). 1965–1972

Rachmaninoff, Sergei, 1873–1943
Library of Congress
(Box 42, unless noted)
T. L. S.: to Rudolph Ganz. New York, 23 Feb. 1922. 1p., English

Port. Phot.: Rachmaninoff's hands (Box 114)

Port. Draw. Repro.: by Juley (1935) (Box 114)

Radecke, Robert, 1830–1911
Library of Congress
(Box 42, unless noted)
A. Mus. Quot.: Berlin, 10 Jan. 1911. Mounted with clipping, and portrait photograph reproduced (Box 114)

Pri. Sco. S.: *Zwei Fantasiestücke*, op. 5, Leipzig: Breitkopf & Härtel, Berlin, to ?, 15 Jan. 1860. 19p.

See Bruch, Max

Radica, Ruben, b. 1931
Library of Congress
(Box 42, unless noted)
A. Mus. ms. S.: *Trois Mélodies pour voix de soprano et piano*, op. 7, Paris, Feb. 1961. 8p., 35x27cm.

2 A. Card S.: to Hans Moldenhauer. Split, 1963. Italian, French

7 T. L. S.: to Hans Moldenhauer. Split, 1961–1965.
  7p., German, Italian
2 T. Docs.: Biographical information. 2p., Italian,
  French
Mus. ms. Repro.: *Dva Komada za Klavir*, op. 6, 1961.
  7p.
Mus. ms. Repro.: *Variations lyriques*, op. 8, 1961. 22p.
Pri. Sco.: *4 Dramatska Epigram*, Kompozitora
  Jugoslavije. 32p.
Port. Phot. S.: at Split (Box 114)

Raff, Joseph Joachim, 1822–1882
Bayerische Staatsbibliothek
L.: [to Carl Reinecke?]. Wiesbaden, 25 Oct. 1867
L.: Wiesbaden, 20 June 1877
Rcpt.: 29 Sept. 1880

Ramin, Günther, 1898–1956
Library of Congress
(Box 42)
T. L. S.: to Karl Weigl. Leipzig, 8 May 1934. 1p.,
  German

Ramrath, Konrad, b. 1880
Library of Congress
(Box 42)
A. Mus. ms. S.: *In der Kirschenblüt*, op. 19, No. 3, 2 July
  1910. 4p., 34x26cm., German

Randegger, Alberto, 1832–1911
Northwestern University
Mus. Quot.: *Peacefully Slumber*, 23 June 1880

Rangström, Ture, 1884–1947
Library of Congress
(Box 42)
A. Mus. Quot. S.: Stockholm, 1933

Raphael, Günter, 1903–1960
Library of Congress
(Box 42)
A. Mus. ms. S.: *Christ the Son of Righteousness*, 1956. 4p.,
  29x21cm.
2 A. L. S.: to Hans Moldenhauer. Cologne, 16 Jan.,
  18 Apr. 1959. 6p., German
Doc.: Death announcement. 19 Oct. 1960. 1p.

Rasch, Kurt, b. 1902
Washington State University
See Rosbaud, Hans

Rasmadse, Alex. S., 1845–1896
Library of Congress
See Tchaikovsky, Pyotr Ilyich

Rasnovanu, Alexandru, b. 1937
Library of Congress
(Box 42)
A. Mus. ms. S.: *[Klaviermusik I]*, *Bridges Above
  Emptiness*, *4 Pieces for Piano*, 1967. 4p., 35x25cm.
  With biographical information

Rathaus, Karol, 1895–1954
Harvard University
SUMMARY OF PRINCIPAL HOLDINGS:
Mus. ms.: *Cross Talk*
Mus. ms.: *Fourth String Quartet*, op. 59
L.: to Karl Weigl. Flushing, 10 June 1946
L.: to Herbert Murrill. Flushing, 9 Apr. 1951. Draft
2 L.: to Hans Moldenhauer, from Gerta Rathaus. 1961

Rațiu, Adrian, b. 1928
Library of Congress
(Box 42)
A. Mus. ms. S.: *Constellations*, to Alexandru Hrisanide.
  4p., 35x25cm., multicolored inks

Ratz, Erwin, 1898–1973
Library of Congress
(Box 42)
T. L. S.: to Alma Mahler Werfel. Vienna, 27 May 1958.
  1p., German. Reports on a Mahler performance

Rauch, Joseph, b. 1904
Bayerische Staatsbibliothek
Mus. ms.: *Quintet*, op. 12, 1941

Maurice Ravel

Ravel, Maurice, 1875–1937
Library of Congress
(Box 42, unless noted)
A. L. S.: to Léon Vallas. Paris, 31 Dec. 1905. 4p.,
    French
A. L. S.: Paris, 6 Feb. 1909. 2p., French
A. L. S.: to Boaz Piller. n.p., 2 May 1918. 1p., French.
    Mounted with group portrait below
2 A. L. S.: [to Alma Mahler?]. Montfort, 14 Jan.,
    23 July 1922. 8p., French. Mentions his *Sonata for
    Violin and Cello, La Valse*, Salzburg Festival
A. L. S.: to Guido Gatti. Brussels, 16 May 1926. 3p.,
    French
A. L. S.: to Boaz Piller. n.p., 17 May 1930. 1p., French
A. Card S.: [to Paul Sanders]. Monfort, 7 June 1933.
    1p., French
A. Mus. Quot. S.: *Ma Mère l'Oye*, Boston, 11 Jan. 1928.
    1p. (16m.)
Port. Gr.: with autograph note by Gershwin. Photo
    shows Ravel with Gershwin in the company of
    friends (Box 114)
Port. Phot. S.: to Boaz Piller, 11 Jan. 1928. By Manuel
    (Box 114)
Port. Phot. (Box 114)

Rawsthorne, Alan, 1905–1971
Northwestern University
L.: to Mrs. Morland. Essex, 17 July 1963
Doc.: Manifesto. British Musical Association

Read, Gardner, b. 1913
Harvard University
Summary of Principal Holdings:
Mus. ms.: *Partita for Small Orchestra*, op. 70
Mus. ms.: *Suite for Organ*, op. 81
Mus. ms.: *Symphony No. 1*, op. 30
2 L.: to Aurelio de la Vega. Boston, 5 Sept. 1974, 6 July
    1984

Reber, Henri, 1807–1880
Northwestern University
See Barye Document

Rech, Géza, 1910–1992
Library of Congress
See Rosbaud, Hans

Redlich, Hans F., 1903–1968
Wiener Stadt- u. Landesbibliothek
L.: to Albi Rosenthal. Edinburgh, 15 Oct. 1956.
    Regarding Mahler
See Mahler, Gustav

Redon, Odilon, 1840–1916
Library of Congress
(Box 125)
Port. Draw. S.: of Armand Parent, inscribed to Armand
    Parent, 1913. 42x36cm. Showing the violinist's head
    in profile

Reed, H. Owen, b. 1910
Harvard University
Mus. ms.: *Concerto for Cello and Orchestra*
3 L.: to Charles Haubiel. East Lansing, 27 Dec. 1963,
    11, 29 July 1966
Mus. ms. Repro.: *The Passing of John Blackfeather*.
    Facsimile

Reeves, Sims, 1818–1900
Northwestern University
6 L.: to Chorley, Lockey, others. London, 1860–1889
L.: from Emma (wife). London, 11 Sept.
Doc.: Article
2 Port.

Max Reger

Reger, Max, 1873–1916
Bayerische Staatsbibliothek
Summary of Principal Holdings:
Mus. ms.: *Zwei Gesänge für gemischten Chor mit Orchester*

L.: to E. Decsey. Munich, postmarked May 1905
L.: Leipzig, 28 April 1907
L.: to E. Kramer. Leipzig, 14 April 1910
L.: to Wendel. Meiningen, 10 June 1912
L.: to Franz Nachbaur. Meiningen, 21 June 1914
L.: to Hans Rosbaud. Weimar, 13 Dec.
Port. Phot.

Library of Congress
See Bronsart von Schellendorf, Hans

Reich, Willi, 1898–1980
Bayerische Staatsbibliothek
See Berg, Alban

Library of Congress
(Box 42)
A. Mus. ms. S.: *Notenbeispiele zum "Wozzeckführer" von Willi Reich.* 1p., 34x26cm. Musical examples to Reich's essay, "Alban Bergs Oper *Wozzeck*." See document below
13 T. L. S.: to Adolph Weiss. Vienna, New York, 1930–1933. 15p., German
P. card S.: to Julius Schloss. Vienna, 11 Feb. 1931. German
3 P. cards S.: to [Adolph and Mary] Weiss. Vienna, 19 June 1931, 5 June 1934, 24 Dec. 1935. German
T. L. S.: [to Alma Mahler]. Zürich, 18 Dec. 1958. 1p., German
2 T. L. S.: to Hans Moldenhauer. Zurich, 31 July 1963, 28 Sept. 1965. 2p., German
2 P. cards S.: to Hans Moldenhauer. Zurich, 15 Jan., 17 Oct. 1965. German
T. Doc. S.: Essay. "Alban Berg." 2p., German
T. Doc.: Disposition. "Disposition für ein Lehrbuch des Kontrapunkts auf neuer Grundlage." 1p., German
T. Doc. S.: Typescript. "Alban Bergs Oper *Wozzeck*." 16p., German. Carbon copy
See Schoenberg, Arnold

Reichardt, Gustav, 1797–1884
Library of Congress
(Box 42)
A. Mus. ms. S.: *An den König*, op. 20. 1p., 20x28cm. On verso, text in Italian

A. Doc. S.: Poem. "Vor Kaulbach's Carton am Jahrestag der Schlacht des 25. IX. 480 v. Ch.," Munich, 23 Sept. 1860. 1p., German

Reichardt, Johann Friedrich, 1752–1814
Library of Congress
(Box 42)
A. L. S.: [to a friend in Altona]. n.p., 1 Oct. 1782. 4p., German. Regarding personal and financial matters

Reicher-Kindermann, Hedwig, 1853–1883
Library of Congress
(Box 42)
A. L. S.: Vienna, 7 Apr. 1878. 1p., German

Reichmann, Theodor, 1849–1903
Library of Congress
(Box 42)
A. L. S.: Cologne, 14 Mar. 1872. 2p., German

Reinecke, Carl, 1824–1910
Library of Congress
(Box 42, unless noted)
A. L. S.: to Schloss. Barmen, 24 May 1858. 2p., German
A. L. S.: to a conductor. Leipzig, 4 Oct. 1863. 1p., German
10 A. L. S.: to Brassin, Fischer, and others. Leipzig, 1863–1893. 21p., French, German
A. L. S.: n.p., 27 Nov. 1883. 2p., German
A. L. S.: Leipzig, 10 Oct. 1894, 1p., German
A. L. S.: Leipzig, 2 Apr. 1904. 1p., German
A. Mus. Quot. S.: *Fughetta*, Leipzig, 4 Aug. 1848. 11m. in piano score. With inscription
Port. Phot. (Box 114)
Port. Lith. Repro. (Box 114)

Reiner, Fritz, 1888–1963
Harvard University
Summary of Principal Holdings:
L.: to Solomon Pimsleur. New York, 22 Feb. 1938

L.: to Charles Haubiel. Westport, 28 June 1939
L.: to Rudolph Ganz. New York, 12 Dec. 1952

Washington State University
See Rosbaud, Hans

**Reinhardt, Gottfried (son of Max Reinhardt
[Goldmann]), 1873–1943**
Library of Congress
(Box 42)
A. L. S.: to Bruno Eisner. New York, 20 Nov. 1943.
  1p., German

Wiener Stadt- u. Landesbibliothek
L.: to Bruno Eisner. Santa Monica, 2 June 1933

Reinhardt, Heinrich, 1865–1922
Wiener Stadt- u. Landesbibliothek
Mus. ms.: *The Spring Maid, We'll Seek a Haven of
  Flowers and Trees*
L.: Mondsee, 15 Aug. 1911

Reinhold, Hugo, 1854–1935
Wiener Stadt- u. Landesbibliothek
Port. Phot.

Reinthaler, Karl, 1822–1896
Library of Congress
(Box 42)
A. L. S.: Bremen, 8 Sept. 1875. 1p., German

Reiss, Karl, 1829–1908
Library of Congress
(Box 42)
2 A. L. S.: ?, 27 Dec. 1876, 10 Jan. 1877. 3p., German

Reissiger, Karl Gottlieb, 1798–1859
Library of Congress
(Box 42)
A. L. S.: to a concertmaster. n.p., n.d. 1p., German
A. L. S.: to H. Dorn. n.p., n.d. 2p., German. Discusses
  the theater at Leipzig

A. Doc. S.: Text. "Musica Sacra, Fragment aus den
  Psalmen Davids," describing orchestration and
  giving the text of the three sections. 1p., German
T. Doc.: Biographical information and work list

Rellstab, Ludwig, 1799–1860
Library of Congress
See Taubert, Wilhelm

Reményi [Hoffmann], Ede [Eduard], 1828–1898
Library of Congress
(Box 42)
A. Mus. Quot. S.: New York, 6 Jan. 1879

Respighi, Ottorino, 1879–1936
Library of Congress
(Box 42, unless noted)
A. Mus. ms.: [Closing page of an instrumental
  composition]. 1p., 31x21cm., ink. On verso, pencil
  sketches for a vocal composition. With
  accompanying note from Boaz Piller
A. L. S.: to Boaz Piller. Rome, 3 June 1923. 3p.,
  French. Regarding Boston performances
A. Mus. Quot. S.: *Fontane di Roma*, Rome, 27 Feb.
  1922. Mounted with portrait photograph below
Port. Phot. S.: to Boaz Piller. New York, 10 Feb. 1926.
  Mounted with musical quotation (Box 114)
See Piller, Boaz
See Stravinsky, Igor

Réti, Rudolph [Rudolf], 1885–1957
Library of Congress
(Box 42, unless noted)
A. Mus. ms. S.: *The Dead Mourn the Living...*, 6 Oct.
  1961. 4p. (pp.10–13), 34x28cm., English. With
  autograph commentary by Jean Réti (6 Oct. 1961)
A. Mus. ms. S.: *"Der grosse Elefant."* 4p., 34x27cm.
A. Mus. ms. Rev. S.: *Irmchen, Schirmchen und ein
  Stückchen Sonnenschein.* 6p., 34x27cm.
T. Doc.: Typescript. "The Origin of the I.S.C.M.,"
  [Jan. 1957]. 9p., English. With autograph
  commentary by Jean Réti (6 Oct. 1961)

Mus. ms. Repro.: *Die Geige.* 5p. + 12p. (parts). Facsimile

Mus. ms. Repro. S.: *Vier Lieder nach Kindertexten von Christian Morgenstern*, to Hanna Schwarz, Vienna, 10 Apr. 1937. 12p. Blueprint score

Port. Phot.: by Hoeller (Box 114)

Réti-Forbes [née Sahlmark], Jean, 1911–1972
Library of Congress
(Box 42)

3 A. L. S.: to Hans Moldenhauer. Munich, 24 Feb. 1961; Regina, 30 Aug. 1962; Paris, 28 May 1963. 14p., English

T. L. S.: to Hans Moldenhauer. Regina, 13 June 1961. 1p., English

Doc.: Lecture announcement. Royal Academy of Music, London, 7, 9 May 1963.

Doc.: Program announcement

Prog.: Munich, 20 Feb. 1961. 2p., German

See Réti, Rudolph

Reuter, Florizel von, 1890–1985
Harvard University
Port.: 1910

Reutter, Hermann, 1900–1985
Library of Congress
(Box 43)

A. Mus. ms. S.: *Chanson variée (Ein Füllen ward geboren).* 7p., 34x27cm., German

A. Mus. ms. S.: *Drei altägyptische Gedichte*, 1962. 17p., 34x27cm., German. Draft

A. Mus. ms.: *Epitaph für einen Dichter*, 1962. 8p., 34x27cm., German. Draft

A. Mus. ms. S.: *Der Lübecker Totentanz*, op. 35. 15p., 33x26cm., German. Complete piano-vocal score

A. Mus. ms. S.: *Saul*, op. 33. 39p., 34x27cm., German. Complete piano-vocal score

A. L. S.: to Hans Moldenhauer. Stuttgart, 26 Dec. 1959. 1p., German

6 T. L. S.: to Hans Moldenhauer. Stuttgart, 1959–1963. 6p., German. With work list

T. Lib.: *Der Lübecker Totentanz.* 3p., German

Doc.: Brochure with work list. German

Doc.: Announcement of classes. English

Mus. ms. Repro.: *Brücke von San Luis Rey.* 136p. With autograph title page

Washington State University
See Rosbaud, Hans

Revueltas, Silvestre, 1899–1940
Harvard University
SUMMARY OF PRINCIPAL HOLDINGS:
Mus. ms.: *3 pequeñas piezas serias*
Mus. ms. Repro.: *Esquinas.* Photostat

Rey, Cemal Reşit, 1904–1985
Library of Congress
(Box 43)

A. Mus. ms. S.: *Paysages de Soleil*, Istanbul, 1928. 33p., 34x25cm. Piano score

A. Mus. ms. S.: [same]. Istanbul, Mar.–May 1931. 42p., 34x27cm. Full score, reduced orchestra

Rey, Jean-Baptiste, 1734–1810
Library of Congress
(Box 43)

A. Rcpt. S.: 1778. 1p., French. Fees for two operatic productions

Reyer [Rey], Ernest, 1823–1909
Northwestern University

L.: Paris, [1890?]

L.: to Filippi. n.p., n.d.

L.: n.p., n.d.

Call. c. Annot.

Mus. Quot.: *Lors des...*

Port. Phot.

See Barye Document

Reznicek, Emil Nikolaus von, 1860–1945
Library of Congress
(Box 107, unless noted)

2 A. L. S.: to his wife. Berlin, 1, 26 June 1933. 4p., German. Mentioning personal and political matters; *Donna Diana*

T. L. S.: to Hans Moldenhauer, from Felicitas von Reznicek (daughter). Engelberg, 27 Apr. 1970. 1p., German

2 Docs.: Eulogy. Offprint in *Deutsche Kultur*, Berlin: Eckstein, n.d. 3p. each, German. Bound, embossed in gold

Clip.: "Brahms, Grillparzer, Strauss, Mahler," by Reznicek, in *Stuttgarter Tageblatt*, 17 Oct. 1931. 2p., German

Port. Phot. S.: 1906. By Wertheim (Box 125)

Port. Gr.: Reznicek and his wife. 1920 (Box 125)

Port. Gr.: Reznicek and his daughter. 1935 (Box 125)

Port. Phot.: [1935]. By Schneider (Box 125)

Port. Paint. Phot.: Orlik's oil portrait of Reznicek (Box 125)

Port. Phot. Repro. S.: of Hans [Jean] Nadalovitch, inscribed to Reznicek, Berlin, 1905–1910 (Box 125)

Paul Sacher Stiftung

A. Mus. ms.: *Tragic Symphony*, Wilderswyl, 11 Aug. 1902. 118p. Full score

Wiener Stadt- u. Landesbibliothek

2 L.: to an editor. Rostock, 6 Oct. 1925; n.p., 11 Nov. 1930

Rheinberger, Josef Gabriel, 1839–1901
Bayerische Staatsbibliothek

3 L.: Munich, 17 Oct. 1872, 24 Nov. 1887, 2 Mar. 1895
Port.

Ricci, Federico, 1809–1877
Library of Congress
(Box 43)
A. L. S.: to Dessauer. n.p., n.d. 1p., Italian

Richards, Brinley, 1819–1885
Northwestern University
L.: to Charles Lockey. London, n.d.

Richardson, Vaughan, ca. 1670–1729
Northwestern University
Mus. ms.: *O Come Hither and Hearken*, 1727. Full score

Richter, Hans, 1843–1916
Bayerische Staatsbibliothek
L.: London, 25 Apr. 1877
L.: to L. Engel. Vienna, 4 Sept. 1882
L.: to Louis Diener. Vienna, 1 Oct. 1892

Library of Congress
(Box 43, unless noted)
A. L. S.: n.p., 26 May 1879. 3p., German
A. L. S.: London, 28 May 1885. 3p., German
2 A. L. S.: to Astruc. Baracs, 27 Sept. 1908; Bowdon, Cheshire, received 1 Nov. 1908. 3p., French
Port. Phot. S.: Vienna, 14 Mar. 1882. By London Stereoscopic (Box 114)

Riedel, Carl, 1827–1888
Library of Congress
(Box 43)
2 A. L. S.: Leipzig, 5 May 1877, 14 May [1877?]. 7p., German
A. Mus. Quot. S.: [Canon, 6m.]. Leipzig, 9 Oct. 1874

Riedel, Hermann, 1847–1913
Library of Congress
(Box 43)
A. L. S.: to a lawyer. Braunschweig, 13 Mar. 1882. 1p., German
Call. c. Annot.: n.p., n.d. German

Rieger, Fritz, 1910–1978
Washington State University
See Rosbaud, Hans

Riegger, Wallingford, 1885–1961
Harvard University
Mus. ms.: *Consummation*, 1939
Mus. ms.: [Notebook]
Mus. ms.: [Sketchbook]
2 L.: to Eugene Weigel. New York, 26 Sept. 1949, 23 Sept.
3 L.: to Richard Yardumian. New York, 1955, 1961
L.: to David Burge. New York, 21 Apr. 1956
2 L.: to Hans Moldenhauer. New York, 18 Nov., 26 Dec. 1957
Doc. Annot.: Work list. With timings of dance works

Mus. ms. Repro.: *String Quartet*. Photostat, with
additional blueprint score

Mus. ms. Repro.: *Three Canons*. Blueprint score, with
additional printed score

Library of Congress
(Box 99)

A. Mus. ms. Rev. S.: [*Consummation*, Piece for
Orchestra, 1939]. 64p. 35x27cm., ink, pencil. Full
score

A. L. S.: to David Burge. New York, 21 Apr. 1956. 2p.,
English. Contains corrections for *New and Old*

2 T. L. S.: to Hans Moldenhauer. New York, 18 Nov.,
26 Dec. 1957. 4p., English

Ries, Ferdinand, 1784–1838
Northwestern University

Mus. ms.: *Grande Simphonie à Grande Orchestre*, 1809

L.: to C. F. Peters. Frankfurt, 20 Sept. 1833

L.: to H. F. Chorley. Frankfurt, 10 Nov. 1835
Port.

Ries, Franz, 1755–1846
Library of Congress
(Box 43)

A. L. S.: to an author. Berlin, 15 Nov. ?. 1p., German.
With musical illustration

A. L. S.: to Artaria of Vienna. Bonn, 28 Nov. 1809. 1p.,
German

Ries, Hubert, 1802–1886
Library of Congress
(Box 43)

A. Mus. Quot. S.: *Chant pour Violin*, op. 19, 24 Dec.
1884. 2p. On verso, autograph musical quotation by
Paul Pabst, Moscow, 1 Dec. 1886

Rieter-Biedermann, Jakob Melchior, 1811–1876
Zentralbibliothek Zürich

2 L.: to A. W. Gottschalg. Leipzig, 16 Nov. 1866;
Winterthur, 9 Mar. 1867

Rieti, Vittorio, 1898–1994
Harvard University

Mus. ms.: *Symphony No. 5*

L.: to Rudolph Ganz. New York, 24 Mar. 1956

2 L.: to Hans Moldenhauer. New York, 3 Jan. 1957,
17 Jan. 1959

Rietz, Julius, 1812–1877
Library of Congress
(Box 43)

A. L. S.: to ?. Dresden, 28 Oct. 1860. 3p., German

A. L. S.: [to Reinecke?]. Dresden, 8 Mar. 1868. 1p.,
German

A. Card S.: to Carl Reinecke. Dresden, 24 Oct. 1876.
2p., German

Rihm, Wolfgang, b. 1952
Library of Congress
(Box 43)

A. Mus. ms.: *Sinfonia da requiem*, Darmstadt, 1972. 2p.,
34x27cm. Sketches, and "fun notes," written in
conversation with Gloria Coates

Prog. S.: Basel, 24 Apr. 1986. 1p. With address

Rimsky-Korsakov, Nikolai, 1844–1908
Library of Congress
(Box 107)

A. Mus. ms.: [*Boris Godunov*, "Coronation scene,"
Prologue, scene 2, by Musorgsky, ca. 1907]. 6p.
(34m.), 36x27cm. Orchestrated by Rimsky-Korsakov
for mixed chorus and orchestra. Fragment, full
score. With letter of authentication and letter of
provenance

A. L. S.: to Carré. St. Petersburg, 29 Oct. 1907. 2p.,
French. Regarding *Snow Maiden*; Russian and
French music publishers

Risler, Edouard, 1873–1929
Library of Congress
(Box 43)

A. L. S.: Reichenberg, n.d. 1p., French

Ritter, Alexander [Sascha], 1833–1896
Library of Congress
(Box 43, unless noted)
A. L. S.: to Steyl. Munich, 10 Mar. 1892. 4p., German.
  With postscript dated 15 Mar. 1892
Port. Phot. Repro. (Box 114)

Ritter, August Gottfried, 1811–1885
Library of Congress
(Box 43)
A. L. S.: to A. W. Bach. Erfurt, 25 Mar. 1838. 1p.,
  German
A. L. S.: to Müller. Erfurt, 6 Aug. 1842. 1p., German
A. L. S.: to Brendel. Magdeburg, 11 July 1850. 2p.,
  German
A. L. S.: to Lippert. Magdeburg, 23 July 1857. 1p.,
  German
A. L. S.: to Moritz Fürstenau. Magdeburg, 24 Nov.
  1857. 1p., German
A. L. S.: Magdeburg. 9 Nov. 187[9?]. 2p., German

Ritter, Frédéric Louis, 1834–1891
Harvard University
L.: to John Weidemeyer. 26 Mar. 1891

Ritter [Bennet], Théodore, 1841–1886
Library of Congress
(Box 43)
A. L. S.: n.p., Thursday, n.d. 2p., French

Rivier, Jean, 1896–1987
Library of Congress
(Box 43)
Call. c. Annot. S.: [to Hans Rosbaud]. Paris, 8 Dec.
  French

Robertson, Sir Hugh Stevenson, 1874–1952
Northwestern University
L.: Glasgow, 11 Dec. 1922

Robinson, Michael F., b. 1933
Northwestern University
Doc.: Proofs for *Opera before Mozart*

Rochberg, George, b. 1918
Harvard University
SUMMARY OF PRINCIPAL HOLDINGS:
A. Mus. ms.: *Symphony No. 5*, Newtown Square,
  10 Oct. 1984. 140p., 28x38cm., pencil. Sketches.
  With additional sketches
Mus. ms.: *Cheltenham Concerto*. Full score, reduced
  score, sketches
Mus. ms.: *Concerto for Oboe and Orchestra*, 1983
Mus. ms.: *Partita Variations*, 1976
Mus. ms.: *Second String Quartet with Voice*, 1961
Mus. ms.: *Symphony No. 1*
Mus. ms.: *Symphony No. 4*, 1976
Mus. ms.: *Third String Quartet*, 1972
Mus. ms. Repro.: *Phaedra*. Blueprint score
Mus. ms. Repro.: *Waltz Serenade*, 1957
6 L.: to Aurelio de la Vega. Philadelphia, 1961–1984
4 L.: to Hans Moldenhauer. Philadelphia, 5 Dec. 1976,
  8, 19 Dec. 1984, 22 Jan. 1985

Rochlitz, Friedrich, 1769–1842
Library of Congress
(Box 43)
A. L. S.: to Johann Heinrich Voss. Leipzig, 1794. 1p.,
  German

Rockstro [Rackstraw], William, 1823–1895
Northwestern University
5 L.: to Miss Strode. Torquay, 1889–1890, n.d.

Rodrigo, Joaquín, b. 1901–1999
Library of Congress
(Box 44)
Mus. ms. cop. S.: *Berceuse*, for piano, 13 Dec. 1923. 3p.,
  31x22cm. Initialed
Mus. ms. cop.: *Cantiga*, song with piano
  accompaniment, 8 Sept. 1925. 9p., 31x22cm.
Mus. ms. cop.: *Plegaria de la Infanta de Castilla*, for
  piano solo. 4p., 35x27cm.

2 L. S.: to Aurelio de la Vega. Madrid, 12 May 1956,
   15 [May?] 1976. 2p., Spanish. Written by his wife,
   Victoria
L.: to Aurelio de la Vega. n.p., 1972. Spanish. Written
   by his wife, Victoria
P. card: to Aurelio de la Vega. Madrid, 8 Apr. 1973.
   Spanish. Written by his wife, Victoria
T. L.: to Aurelio de la Vega. Madrid, 12 June 1977. 1p.,
   Spanish. Signed "J. Rodrigo" by his wife, Victoria
2 T.L.: to Andrés Segovia. 4p., Spanish
See Coelho, Olga Praguer
See Segovia, Andrés

Rodriguez, Ricardo, 1879–1951
Library of Congress
(Box 44)
A. Mus. ms. S.: *Paisage*. 5p., 36x26cm.

Rodzinski, Artur, 1892–1958
Harvard University
2 L.: to Charles Haubiel. Cleveland, 11 Oct. 1937;
   New York, 25 Nov. 1944. With copy of letter by
   Haubiel
L.: to Solomon Pimsleur. New York, 17 Sept. 1943

Röder, Georg Vincenz, 1780–1848
Library of Congress
(Box 43)
A. L. S.: to Chelard. Altötting in Oberbayern, 28 Sept.
   1843. 1p., German

Roger-Ducasse, Jean, 1873–1954
Library of Congress
(Box 44)
A. L. S.: Le Caillan, n.d. 2p., French

Roldán, Amadeo, 1900–1939
Harvard University
L.: to Adolph Weiss. Havana, 8 Dec. 1933
L.: to Henry Cowell. Havana, 27 Feb. 1934
Pri. Sco.: *Motivos de son*

Rolla, Alessandro, 1757–1841
Northwestern University
Mus. ms.: *Divertimento*

Rolland, Romain, 1866–1944
Library of Congress
(Box 117)
A. L. S.: [to Paul Sanders]. n.p., 22 Feb. 1916. 3p.,
   French
A. Doc. S.: Address. "An Beethoven. Dankgesang," to
   Dr. Guido Adler, 28 Mar. 1927. 17p., French.
   Original manuscript of the address given in 1927 for
   the Musical Congress in Vienna. Unpublished in
   original French

Romaniello, Luigi, 1860–1916
Harvard University
L.

Library of Congress
(Box 44)
T. Doc.: Biographical information. 2p.
Call. c. Annot.

Romberg, Bernhard, 1767–1841
Library of Congress
(Box 44, unless noted)
A. L. S.: to Madame Franck in Wilna. Vienna, 24 Jan.
   1812. 2p., German
A. L. S.: Rathbone Place, London, n.d. 1p., German
Port. Lith. (Box 114)

Ronald [Russell], Sir Landon, 1873–1938
Northwestern University
L.: Feb. 1921
L.: to Middleton. London, 22 July 1922
L.: to Cecil. London, n.d.

**Ropartz, Joseph Guy [Guy-Ropartz, Joseph],
1864–1955**
Library of Congress

(Box 44, unless noted)
A. Mus. ms. S.: *Symphonie en la, sur un choral Breton*, to
   Alfred Cortot, 1894–1895. 45p. 35x27cm., ink,
   pencil. Condensed score
2 A. L. S.: 28 Jan. 1908, 21 Apr. 1920. 2p., French
Port. Phot. S. Repro. (Box 114)

Rorem, Ned, b. 1923
Harvard University
SUMMARY OF PRINCIPAL HOLDINGS:
Mus. ms.: *Little Elegy*, 1949
3 L.: to Hans Moldenhauer. New York, 21 Dec. 1976,
   Jan. 1977
Port. Phot.: 1 Jan. 1977

Rosbaud, Hans, 1895–1962
Library of Congress
(Box 44, unless noted)
A. L. S.: to André Jolivet. n.p., n.d. 2p., French. Draft
A. Alb. l. S.: Aix-en-Provence, 24 July 1953. 2p. On
   same leaf, inscriptions by Ebert, Elmendorff,
   Flothuis, Greissle, Pincherle, Rech, and Sauguet
Doc. Repro.: Testimony. To Hans Moldenhauer,
   Munich, 7 Nov. 1946. 1p., German. Copy of
   Rosbaud's "Zeugnis"
Clip.: *Chicago Sun Times*, 5 Jan. 1959. 1p., English
3 Obit.: 6 Jan. 1963. German
3 Port. Phot. (Box 114)
See Bartók, Béla
See Hauer, Josef Matthias
See Penderecki, Kryzstof
See Roussel, Albert
See Walter, Bruno

Washington State University
In addition to the listing below, the collection includes
books and scores belonging to Rosbaud's library
(numerous printed scores with conductorial markings
and inscriptions), articles, awards, correspondence,
engravings, photographs, recordings, watercolors
SUMMARY OF PRINCIPAL HOLDINGS:
Mus. ms. arr.: *Agrippina*, Overture by Handel
Mus. ms. arr.: *Ariadne auf Naxos* by Haydn
Mus. ms.: [Chorale settings]

Mus. ms.: [Compositions by Medieval and
   Renaissance composers]
Mus. ms.: [Counterpoint exercises]
Mus. ms.: *Einladung zum Schlaf*
Mus. ms.: *Fughette für Fagotte*
Mus. ms.: "Heil Dir, du treue Magd"
Mus. ms.: *Kleines Volksliedspiel*. Full score
Mus. ms.: *Konzertstück*, for solo violin and orchestra,
   4 Dec. 1918. Full score
Mus. ms.: *Konzertstück für Basstuba und Orchester*, 1936
Mus. ms.: *Novelletten*
Mus. ms.: Ouverture zu Franz Grillparzers *Des Meeres
   und der liebe Wellen*
Mus. ms.: *Passacaglia für grosses Orchester*
Mus. ms.: [Piano compositions]
Mus. ms.: *Serenade für 5 Blasinstrumente*
Mus. ms.: *Serenade für Streichtrio*
Mus. ms. arr.: *Sinfonie No. IV* by Schumann
Mus. ms.: [Sketches]
Mus. ms.: *Das Spiel von der Zeit*. Excerpt
Mus. ms.: *Thema mit Variationen*
Mus. ms.: [Variations]
L.: Correspondence between Rosbaud and the
   following: Licco Amar, Gilbert Amy, Volkmar
   Andreae, Ernest Ansermet, Wilhelm Backhaus, Béla
   Bartók, Conrad Beck, Luciano Berio, Pierre Boulez,
   Ernest Bour, Walter Braunfels, Cesar Bresgen,
   Benjamin Britten, Heinrich Burkhard, Paul
   Burkhard, Willy Burkhard, Gerda Sjostrand Busoni,
   Elliott Carter, Niccolò Castiglioni, Erik Chisholm,
   Alfred Cortot, Robert Craft, Luigi Dallapiccola,
   Johann Nepomuk David, Mario Davidovsky,
   Walther Davisson, Antal Dorati, Henri Dutilleux,
   Heimo Erbse, Max Fiedler, Edwin Fischer, Marius
   Flothuis, Andor Foldes, Wolfgang Fortner, Lukas
   Foss, Pierre Fournier, Wolfgang Fraenkel, Wilhelm
   Furtwängler, Henri Gagnebin, Rudolf Gall,
   Rudolph Ganz, Roberto Gerhard, Charles T. Griffes,
   Wilibald Gurlitt, Joseph Haas, Karl Amadeus
   Hartmann, Clara Haskil, Roman Haubenstock-
   Ramati, Robert Heger, Hans Werner Henze, Kurt
   Hessenberg, Gertrud Hindemith, Paul Hindemith,
   Hanns Holenia, Madame Arthur Honegger,
   Mieczyslaw Horszowski, Klaus Huber, Herbert
   Hübner, Philipp Jarnach, Eugen Jochum, André
   Jolivet, Julius Karr-Bertoli, Joseph Keilberth,
   Wilhelm Kempff, Leon Kirchner, Otto Klemperer,
   Egon Kornauth, Max Kowalski, Ernst Křenek,
   Rafael Kubelík, Emil Landolt, Richard Laugs, Yrsa
   von Leistner, Daniel Lesur, Rolf Liebermann,

Yvonne Loriod, Enrico Mainardi, Gian Francesco
Malipiero, Robert Mann, Jean-Louis Martinet,
Yehudi Menuhin, Olivier Messiaen, Marcel
Mihalovici, Darius Milhaud, Hans Moldenhauer,
Elly Ney, Bo Nilsson, Luigi Nono, Ricardo
Odnoposoff, Carl Orff, Joseph Pembaur, Jr.,
Eberhard Preussner, William Primrose, Felix
Prohaska, Radiotelevisione Italiana, Kurt Rasch,
Alice Rau, Fritz Reiner, Hermann Reutter, Fritz
Rieger, Edel Rosbaud, Lazare Saminsky, Herbert
Ludwig Sandberg, Hermann Scherchen, Armin
Schibler, Erich Schmid, Heinrich Kaspar Schmid,
Hans Schmidt-Isserstedt, Paul Schmitz, Othmar
Schoeck, Georg Schoenberg, Gertrud Schoenberg,
Franz Schreker, Carl Schuricht, Albert Schweitzer,
Mátyás Seiber, Bernhard Sekles, Roger Sessions,
Alphons Silbermann, Emmerich Smola, Karlheinz
Stockhausen, Igor Stravinsky, Willy Strecker,
Heinrich Strobel, Hans Heinz Stuckenschmidt,
Heinrich Sutermeister, Joseph Szigeti, Alexander
Tcherepnin, Ernst Toch, Henri Tomasi, Wladimir
Vogel, Wieland Wagner, Wolfgang Wagner, Rudolf
Wagner-Régeny, Felix Weingartner, Julius
Weismann, Jacques Wildberger, Felix Woyrsch,
Iannis Xenakis, Winfried Zillig, Bernd Alois
Zimmermann, Friderike Zweig
Doc.: [File of personal documents]. Includes
    appointment and address books, clippings, family
    documents, lectures, passport
Doc.: [Notebooks]. Materials include notes on
    composers and music history, outlines for
    conducting, programs, schedules
Port.
S. rec.: including some of Rosbaud's compositions
Marble cast of Rosbaud's hands
See Haubenstock-Ramati, Roman
See Schoenberg, Gertrud
See Stravinsky, Igor

Rosé, Arnold, 1863–1946
Wiener Stadt- u. Landesbibliothek
Mus. Quot.: 23 Oct. 1917

Rosen, Charles, b. 1927
Harvard University
L.: to Charles Haubiel. n.p., 18 Nov. 1965

Rosenberg, Hilding, 1892–1985
Library of Congress
(Box 44)
A. Mus. ms.: [*Sonata for Solo Clarinet*], *Clarinet Solo*,
    Andante. 3p., 37x25cm. Sketches
Mus. ms. Repro.: *Sonata for Solo Clarinet*, 1960. 6p.

Rosenstock, Joseph, 1895–1985
Harvard University
L.: to Gerhard Tischer. Wiesbaden, 27 Mar. 1928
4 L.: to David Tamkin. New York, 21 May, 2 Aug.,
    13 Sept. 1954, 19 Apr. 1962

Rosenthal, Albi, b. 1914
Library of Congress
(Box 44)
Doc. S.: Essay. "Franz Anton und Carl Maria von
    Weber in der Frühgeschichte der Lithographie,"
    Tutzing: Hans Schneider, 1985, to Hans and Mary
    Moldenhauer, Sils-Maria, 26 Sept. 1985. 9p.,
    German
See Da Ponte, Lorenzo

Rosenthal, Manuel, b. 1904
Library of Congress
(Box 44)
A. Mus. ms. S.: *Missa Deo Gratia*. 19p., 35x27cm. Full
    score
A. L. S.: [to Paul Sanders]. Le Haye, Holland, 12 Apr.
    1946. 1p., French

Rosenthal, Moriz, 1862–1946
Library of Congress
(Box 44, unless noted)
A. L. S.: to Madame Neuer. New York, 27 Jan. 1925.
    1p., English
Doc.: "Mahleriana." 9p., German. In the hand of Mrs.
    Rosenthal. Describes various encounters with
    Mahler
A. Mus. Quot. S.: Sostenuto, to Francesco Berger, June
    1899
Port. Phot. S.: to Bruno Eisner, Cap d'Ail, 31 Dec.
    1932. On verso, message by Hedwig Rosenthal-
    Kammer. By Foyer (Box 114)
Port. Phot. (Box 114)

Rossi, Lauro, 1812–1885
Northwestern University
L.: to Costa. Milan, 12 Apr. 1857

G. Rossini (signature)

Rossini, Gioachino, 1792–1868
Library of Congress
(Box 44, unless noted)
A. Mus. ms.: *Moïse*. 3p. + 1p. sketches to Finale, 26x34cm., ink. French version. Section of the ensemble beginning with the words of Moses, "Je réclame la foi promise Pharaon," marked "Dopo il Ballo." Full score
A. L. S.: to Angelo Mignani. Florence, 21 Apr. 1849. 1p., Italian
A. L. S.: to Pacini. Paris, 29 Nov. 1861. 1p., Italian
A. L. S.: from Olympie Desguilliers Rossini. ?, 17 Oct. 4p., French
A. L. S.: [to Balzac?], from Olympie Desguilliers Rossini. n.p., n.d. 4p., French
Mus. ms. Repro.: *Liceo Musicale Rossini in Pesaro*. 3p. Facsimile of an unpublished autograph manuscript. Bound
Port. Engr.: by Woolnoth (Box 114)

Rota [Rinaldi], Nino, 1911–1979
Library of Congress
(Box 44)
A. Mus. ms.: *Messa per coro e organo*, 16 Mar. 1960. 30p., 33x24cm., pencil. Complete draft of the full score

Roters, Ernst, 1892–1961
Library of Congress
(Shelf)
Mus. ms. cop. S.: *Musik zu Ein Sommernachtstraum (Shakespeare)*, op. 14I. 86p., 33x26cm. Piano reduction. Bound

Roth, Feri, 1899–1969
Harvard University
L.: to Charles Haubiel. Los Angeles, 25 Apr. 1965

Rothmüller, Marko, 1908–1993
Harvard University
2 Mus. mss.: *Sonata Movement*, 1958; *Symphonic Movement*, sketch
L.: to Hans Moldenhauer. Bloomington, 22 Sept. 1958
L.: to David Tamkin. Bloomington, 8 Apr. 1964

Rouault, Georges, 1871–1958
Library of Congress
See Parent, Armand

Roussel, Albert, 1869–1937
Library of Congress
(Box 44, unless noted)
A. L. S.: n.p., 12 Aug. 1910. 2p., French
A. L. S.: to a conductor. Paris, 5 Dec. 1936. 1p., French
L.: Draft of a letter to Mrs. Roussel, from Hans Rosbaud. Also, a draft to André Améller. 2p.
A. Mus. Quot. S.: *Symphonie in Sol*, Boston, 22 Oct. 1930. Themes from each movement
Port. Phot. S.: to Boaz Piller, Boston, 21 Oct. 1930. By Lipnitzki (Box 114)
Port. Phot. Repro. Annot. S.: to Hans Rosbaud, n.p., 12 Nov. [1949?]. 2p., French. Composer at the piano (Box 114)

Rózsa, Miklós, 1907–1995
Harvard University
SUMMARY OF PRINCIPAL HOLDINGS:
Mus. ms.: *Beasts of Burden*
Mus. ms.: *Concerto for Violin and Orchestra*, op. 24
Mus. ms.: *Un Jardin dans la nuit*
L.: to Aurelio de la Vega. Los Angeles, 23 June 1985

Rubin, Marcel, 1905–1995
Library of Congress
(Box 44)
A. Mus. ms. S.: *Konzert für Kontrabass und Orchester*, 19 Jan. 1970. 17p., 34x27cm. Sketches
A. Mus. ms. S.: *Quatre Poëmes de Rimbaud*, 28 Feb. 1937, to Hanna Schwarz, Oct. 1937. 17p., 35x27cm.

Pri. Sco. S.: *Quatre Poëmes de Rimbaud*, 1937, to Hanna Schwarz, 4 Apr. 1937. 15p.

Pri. Sco. S.: *Troisième Sonate*, Paris, 1928, to Stefan Auber, Vienna, May 1934. 24p.

Rubinstein, Anton, 1829–1894
Library of Congress
(Box 44, unless noted)

A. Mus. ms. S.: *Zwölf Lieder*, op. 78, for Voice and Piano, *Hebräische Melodie, Lied, Der Engel, Der Sturm, Klage, Der Gefangene, Neugriechisches Lied, Elegie, Lied, Sinngedicht, Lied, Scene aus "Der Zigeuner."* 17p., 38x26cm., ink, pencil. Based on poems by Pushkin and others, translated into German. The manuscript was used for publication by B. Senff, Leipzig

A. Doc.: Texts. 15p., German. For thirteen poems, with correction for *Der Morgen*

A. Doc.: Printing instructions. 1p.

2 Docs.: Music covers. [Musical Evenings, copy books 9, 10]. Russian

Port. Paint. Repro. (Box 114)

Northwestern University
Mus. ms.: *Sonate pour le Piano*, op. 100
L.: to Chorley. n.p., 23 June 1868
L.: n.p., 28 Nov. 1871
Mus. Quot.: *Melody in F*, Frankfurt, 18 May 1883
Port. Phot.

Rubinstein, Beryl, 1898–1952
Harvard University
L.: to Hans Moldenhauer. Cleveland, 19 May 1949
Port. Phot.
See Loesser, Arthur

Rubinstein, Nikolai, 1835–1881
Library of Congress
(Box 44)
A. L. S.: to Reinecke. n.p., n.d. 1p., German
See Tchaikovsky, Pyotr Ilyich

Rudersdorff, Hermine, 1822–1882
Library of Congress
(Box 44)
A. L. S.: [to Lockey]. London, 1 Apr. 1856. 1p., English
A. L. S.: to Creythe. ?, 25 Oct. 1860. 1p., English
A. L. S.: [London]. 1p., French

Rudhyar, Dane [Chennevière, Daniel], 1895–1985
Harvard University
SUMMARY OF PRINCIPAL HOLDINGS:
10 L.: to Nicolas Slonimsky. 1972–1977
2 L.: to Adolph Weiss. Brookline, Carmel, n.d.
Doc.: Recommendation. Signed by Slonimsky, 10 May 1975

Rudolph, Archduke of Austria, 1788–1831
Library of Congress
(Box 44)
L. S.: to Cardinal Pallotta. Vienna, 24 Dec. 1827. 1p., Italian

Rüdinger, Gottfried, 1886–1946
Bayerische Staatsbibliothek
Mus. ms.: *6 Deutsche Tänze*, op. 122

Rufer, Josef, 1893–1985
Library of Congress
(Box 44)
5 A. L. S.: to Adolph Weiss. Berlin, 1927–1933. 12p., German
4 T. L. S.: to Adolph Weiss. Berlin, 1931–1934. 7p., German
2 L. S.: to Adolph Weiss, from Rufer's father, Joseph. Vienna, 31 July, 24 Oct. 1931. 4p., German
T. Doc. A. Rev. S.: Essay. "Das Problem der modernen Oper." 5p., German

Rugeles, Ana Mercedes A., b. 1914
Harvard University
L.: to Aurelio de la Vega. 19 Dec. 1983. Also signed by Alfredo (son, b. 1949)
2 L.: to Aurelio de la Vega, from Alfredo Rugeles (son). Caracas, 29 Jan. 1985, 15 Apr. 1986

Ruger, Morris Hutchins, 1902–1974
Harvard University
Mus. ms.: *Quintet for Winds and Horn*, July 1941

Ruggles, Carl [Charles], 1876–1971
Harvard University
SUMMARY OF PRINCIPAL HOLDINGS:
5 L.: to Adolph Weiss. Arlington, Vermont, 1929–1933
Port. Phot.: Jan. 1932

Ruiz Aznar, Valentín, 1902–1972
Library of Congress
(Box 44)
A. Mus. ms. S.: *Nana*, Granada, to Hans Moldenhauer,
    15 Sept. 1971. 3p., 30x21cm.
Pri. Sco. S.: *Cinco canciones para soprano y
    acompañamiento de piano*, Granada, 1962, to Hans
    Moldenhauer, Granada, 14 Sept. 1971. 17p.
Prog.: Granada, 6 July 1970. 16p., Spanish. Booklet of
    testimonial ceremony. Also contains a reproduction
    of *Solea* by Ruiz Aznar

Ruiz García-Jalón, Sabino
Library of Congress
(Box 19)
Mus. ms. cop. A. Rev. S.: *Danza de diablillos*, to
    Ernesto Halffter, Bilbao, Mar. 1925. 8p. Title was
    originally *Danza grotesca*
Mus. ms. cop. A. Rev.: *Humoresca*, Bilbao, 1925. 9p.

Rumford, Kennerley, 1870–1957
Northwestern University
L.: to Miss Stewart Wood. Dublin, 27 Apr. 190[3?]
L.: to Mrs. Eliot. South Hampstead, n.d.
L.: to Miss Wood. Portrush, n.d.

Ryterband, Roman, 1914–1979
Harvard University
SUMMARY OF PRINCIPAL HOLDINGS:
Mus. ms.: *Alexander's Ragtime Band*, 1940
Mus. ms.: *Ballade*, 1954
Mus. ms.: *Ballett Studie nach Chopin*
Mus. ms.: *Bouquet of Musical Flowers from Broadway to
    Hollywood*
Mus. ms.: *Capriccio gavottuoso*, 1940

Mus. ms.: *Chagrin d'Amour*, 1944
Mus. ms.: *A Christmas Processional*
Mus. ms.: *Concerto*
Mus. ms.: *Deux Sonnets*, 1955
Mus. ms.: *Dialogue for Two Flutes*, 1952
Mus. ms.: *Dolly*
Mus. ms.: *Fantômes rebelles*, 1943
Mus. ms.: *Heracles and the Argonauts*, 1978
Mus. ms.: *Ich weiss es nicht*, 1953
Mus. ms.: *Jubilate Deo*, 1953
Mus. ms.: *Kol nidre*
Mus. ms.: *Let's Praise the Lord*
Mus. ms.: *Lob des Liedes*, 1954
Mus. ms.: *Memories of Broadway*
Mus. ms.: *The Men of Delta U*
Mus. ms.: *A Musical Bouquet*
Mus. ms.: *Nocturne*, 1941
Mus. ms.: *Pater Noster*, 1963
Mus. ms.: *Phantasie on Polish Folk Melodies*, 1959
Mus. ms.: *Pray for the Peace of Jerusalem*, 1970
Mus. ms.: *Psalm 97*, 1952
Mus. ms.: *Quintet*
Mus. ms.: *Raise Your Heads O Gates*, 1977
Mus. ms.: *Rhapsodia Helvetica*, 1948
Mus. ms.: *Róze i Sen*
Mus. ms.: *Russian Rhapsody*, 1962
Mus. ms.: *Seu O Granadzie*, 1939
Mus. ms.: *Seven Songs for High Voice and Piano*
Mus. ms.: *Sonata breve*, 1961
Mus. ms.: *Sonata for Piano Solo*, 1951
Mus. ms.: *Sonata for Two Flutes and Harp*
Mus. ms.: *Souvenir d'un Bal*
Mus. ms.: *Spring of Love*, 1958
Mus. ms.: *Suite International for Piano Solo*
Mus. ms.: *Suite polonaise*, 1944
Mus. ms.: *Three Hebrew Songs*
Mus. ms.: *Three Negro Spirituals*
Mus. ms.: *Three Preludes*, 1944
Mus. ms.: *Three Songs*, 1949
Mus. ms.: *Toccata*
Mus. ms.: *Der Tod*
Mus. ms.: *Triptyque contemporain*, 1944
Mus. ms.: *Trois Ballades Hebraiques*, 1943
Mus. ms.: *Two Desert Scenes*
Mus. ms.: *Two Images*, 1942
Mus. ms.: *Two Italian Romances*
Mus. ms.: *Two Sonnets*, 1965
Mus. ms.: *Under Your Star*
Mus. ms.: *Vida heróica*
Mus. ms.: *We Are the People*

Mus. ms. Repro.: *Fanfare for a Christmas Festival.*
  Blueprint score

Saar, Louis Victor, 1868–1937
Library of Congress
(Box 44)
A. L. S.: to Franko. Cincinnati, 21 [June?] 1917. 1p.,
  German

Sachse-Hofmeister, Anna, 1853–1904
Library of Congress
(Box 44)
A. L. S.: to a conductor. Frankfurt, 30 Oct. 1874. 2p.,
  German
A. L. S.: to Eichberger. Dresden, 1 Apr. 1878. 1p.,
  German
A. L. S.: to Director von Platten. Dresden, 3 Apr. 1878.
  1p., German. With note in the hand of Count
  Platten

Sadero, Geni, 1886–1961
Harvard University
Mus. ms.: *Curi, Curuszu*
Mus. ms.: *Stornella Romagnolo*

Saint-Foix, Georges, 1874–1954
Library of Congress
(Box 44)
A. L. S.: [to Felix Huch?]. Aix-en-Provence, 16 June
  1947. 2p., French

Saint-Luban, Léon de, 1805–1850
Library of Congress
(Box 44)
3 A. L. S.: to Rudolph de Vivenot. Berlin, 1830–1843.
  8p., German
A. Doc. S.: Address. Vienna, 14 [June? 1839?]

Sainton-Dolby, Charlotte, 1821–1885
Northwestern University
3 L.: London, 3 Oct. 1849, 25 Mar. 1884, n.d. One
  letter also signed by Prosper Sainton
Clip.

Saint-Saëns, Camille, 1835–1921
Library of Congress
(Box 44)
A. Mus. Alb. l. S.: *Danse macabre*, 1 Nov. 1877, for
  piano. 13m., ink, with engraved borders
A. L. S.: to a pianist. [Rue de Longchamp 17?],
  24 Sept. 1907. 3p., French. Regarding concert
  activities; Beethoven, Mozart, Chopin arrangement

Northwestern University
L.: Monte Carlo, 6 Mar. 1906
L.: Paris, 4 July 1912
L.: n.p., 2 Aug. 1920
2 L.: n.p., n.d.
Mus. Quot.: Birmingham, 26 Aug. 1879
3 Port. Phot.: 1906, 1915, n.d.
See Sousa, John Philip

Salaman, Charles, 1814–1901
Northwestern University
L.: n.p., n.d.

Salazar, Adolfo, 1890–1958
Library of Congress
(Box 45)
A. Mus. ms. S.: *Trois Prèludes, pour le piano*, Madrid,
  Apr. 1916. 9p., 35x27cm., ink. Complete score.
  Bound in leather and cloth, embossed

Salieri, Antonio, 1750–1825
Northwestern University
Mus. ms.: "Son le donne poverine di buon core,"
  Vienna, 1774
L.: n.p., 17 Jan. 1809

Salmhofer, Franz, 1900–1975
Wiener Stadt- u. Landesbibliothek
L.: to Paul Pisk. Kierling, 31 July 1924

Salomon, Johann Peter, 1745–1815
Library of Congress
(Box 115)
Port. Engr.

Salsman, Joel, b. 1941
Harvard University
Mus. ms.: [Piece for piano]. With letter on verso, Paris,
27 Mar. 1964

Salvador, Matilde, b. 1918
Library of Congress
(Box 45)
A. Mus. ms. S.: *Desvelo, de la madre*, 1947. 3p.,
31x22cm.
A. Mus. ms. S.: *En donde tejemos la ronda*, Apr. 1952.
4p., 31x21cm.
A. Mus. ms. S.: *Una enredadera*, 15 Jan. 1956. 4p.,
31x21cm.
A. Mus. ms. S.: *Mayo*, Valencia, 1951. 3p., 31x21cm.
A. Mus. ms. S.: *Nana, de la Virgen*, 1947. 3p., 31x22cm.
A. Mus. ms. S.: *Si algún día vols cantar*, to the
Moldenhauer Archives, Valencia, 1963. 2p.,
31x21cm.
3 Mus. mss. Repro.: *Rapto*; *Presentimento*; *Cancioncilla*.
11p. Blueprint score
Mus. ms. Repro. S.: *El río feliz*. 2p. Blueprint score
Mus. ms. Repro. S.: *Tres nanas*. 6p. Blueprint score
Pri. Sco.: *Canción de Vela*, 1946. 2p.
Pri. Sco.: *Canciónes de nana y desvelo*, Madrid: Unión
Musical Española, c1960. 17p.

Samaras, Spyridon, 1863[?]–1917
Library of Congress
(Box 45)
A. Mus. Quot. S.: "La Martire," Milan, 12 Jan. 1895.
1p., Italian

Samaroff [née Hickenlooper], Olga, 1882–1948
Harvard University
L.: to Adolph Weiss. New York, 26 Nov. 1930

Samazeuilh, Gustave, 1877–1967
Library of Congress
(Box 45)
A. Mus. ms. S.: *Trois Poèmes, pour piano*, I, II, 1917. 8p.,
35x27cm.

Saminsky, Lazare, 1882–1959
Harvard University
Mus. ms.: *Two Poems for Piano*, op. 41, No. 2, *Grass*,
1934
2 L.: to Paul Sanders, and one to the International Jury
of the ISCM. New York, 21 Nov. 1932
3 L.: to Paul Sanders. New York, 16 Sept.; Jamaica,
5 Apr.

Washington State University
See Rosbaud, Hans

Sammons, Albert, 1886–1957
Library of Congress
See Mengelberg, Willem

Northwestern University
L.: London, 9 Jan. 1922

Samuel, Gerhard, b. 1924
Harvard University
2 L.: to Aurelio de la Vega. n.p., 7 June, 17 July 1977

Sandberg, Herbert Ludwig, 1902–1966
Washington State University
See Rosbaud, Hans

Sandberger, Adolf, 1864–1943
Bayerische Staatsbibliothek
5 L.: to Widmann. Munich, 1921–1937

Library of Congress
(Box 45)
Call. c. Annot.: to Hans Rosbaud. 9 July 1937

Sander, Constantin, 1826–1905
Library of Congress
(Box 45)
7 A. L. S.: [to A. W. Gottschalg]. Leipzig, 1890–1902.
   23p., German. Writing as Director of the publishing
   firm of Leuckart

Sanderson, Lillian, b. 1867
Harvard University
L.: to Eugen Lindner. Berlin, 10 Dec. 1895

Sanderson, Sibyl, 1865–1903
Harvard University
L.: n.p., n.d.

Sanjuán, Pedro, 1886–1976
Harvard University
L.: to Adolph Weiss. Habana, 24 Mar. 1921

Santa Cruz, Domingo, 1899–1987
Harvard University
3 L.: to Aurelio de la Vega. San Diego, 1957–1962

Santini, Fortunato, 1778–1861
Library of Congress
(Box 45)
A. L. S.: to Chelard. Munich, 11 Apr. 1836. 1p., French

Santley, Sir Charles, 1834–1922
Northwestern University
L.: to Benedict. London, 20 Mar. 1880
L.: to Chorley. London, 19 Mar. 1891
L.: to Miss Alderson. London, 20 May 1892
Clip.
4 Port.

Santoro, Cláudio, 1919–1989
Harvard University
SUMMARY OF PRINCIPAL HOLDINGS:
Mus. ms.: *Agrupamento à 10*, for chamber ensemble,
   1966
Mus. ms.: *Cello Concerto*, 1961

Mus. ms.: *Duo*, for violin and piano
Mus. ms.: *Mutationen X*, for oboe solo
5 L.: to Aurelio de la Vega. 1965–1976, n.d.
2 L.: Schriesheim, 25 Aug., 29 Oct. 1976
Doc.: Biographical information and work list
Port.

Saran, August, 1836–1922
Zentralbibliothek Zürich
5 L.: to Selmar Bagge. Halle, Königsberg, Lyck,
   1861–1862

Sarasate, Pablo de, 1844–1908
Library of Congress
(Box 45, unless noted)
A. Mus. Quot. S.: to Florence Rathbone. Liverpool,
   6 Dec. 1879
Port. Phot. S.: New York, 1875. By Gurney (Box 115)

Sass, Marie Constance, 1834–1907
Library of Congress
(Box 45)
A. L. S.: n.p., 28 July 18[63?]. 1p., French

Satie, Erik [Eric], 1866–1925
Library of Congress
(Box 45, unless noted)
A. L. S.: to Jean Cocteau. Paris, 11 Jan. 1920. 2p.,
   French
Port. Phot. (Box 115)

Sato, Keijiro, b. 1927
Library of Congress
(Box 107)

A. Mus. ms. S.: *Calligraphie, pour piano*, 1957–1960.
7p., 29x33cm. On verso of title page, detailed
instructions for its performance (1960, German), to
Selma Epstein and Midori Tanbe (1962)

5 A. L. S.: to Selma Epstein. Tokyo, 1962–1963. 22p.,
English. Regarding composing; *Calligraphie*. With
letter from Tatsuo Sato (brother)

3 A. L. S.: to Hans Moldenhauer. Tokyo, 18 Oct. 1963,
15 Feb., 25 Apr. 1964. 6p., English

A. Doc. S.: Program notes. On "Calligraphy, for
piano." 6p., English

A. Doc.: Work list. 1p., English

L. Repro.: to Selma Epstein, from Thomas Merton.
Kentucky, 18 Dec. 1962. 1p., English

Pri. Sco.: *Calligraphy*, for piano, Tokyo: Ongaku no
Tomo, c1964. 12p.

Sauer, Emil von, 1862–1942
Library of Congress
(Box 45, unless noted)
A. L. S.: Budapest, 16 Feb. 1891. 1p., German
A. Mus. Quot. S.: Allegro non troppo, to Francesco
Berger, London, 26 Mar. 1903. 1p.
Port. Phot. S.: to Henrich Grünfeld, 1 Mar. 1885. By
Risse (Box 115)

Sauguet [Poupard], Henri, 1901–1989
Library of Congress
See Rosbaud, Hans

Sauret, Emile, 1852–1920
Library of Congress
(Box 45)
A. Mus. Quot. S.: Lento, Prague, May 1886

Sax, Adolphe [Antoine-Joseph], 1814–1894
Library of Congress
(Box 45)
A. L. S.: n.p., 30 Aug. 1862. 1p., French

Scalero, Rosario, 1870–1954
Harvard University
3 L.: to Charles Haubiel. New York, 1 Mar. 1928;
Philadelphia, 1946; Alps (fragment)
L. Repro.: to Scalero, from Haubiel

Scaria, Emil, 1838–1886
Library of Congress
(Box 45)
14 A. L. S.: to B[artolf] Senff. Vienna, Leipzig,
Dresden, Weimar, 1867–1873. 21p., German

Sceats, Godfrey
Northwestern University
L.: to Glazebrook. Orpington, 5 Oct. 1950
Port.
Phot.: portrait of Karg-Elert. Inscribed by Sceats

Schaedler, Rudolf, b. 1903
Zentralbibliothek Zürich
Mus. ms.: *Der Berg*, 1939. Poem by Hans Moldenhauer
Mus. ms.: *Gesang der Bergwanderer*, 1962. Three songs
on texts by Hans Moldenhauer. With additional
sound recording
Mus. ms.: *Traumlied*. With additional copy
4 L.: to Hans Moldenhauer. Gaflei, 1934
18 L.: to Hans Moldenhauer and Greta Irvine.
1960–1962

Schäffer, Bogusław, b. 1929
Library of Congress
(Box 45)
2 A. L. S.: to Gloria Coates. Poland, 19 Mar., 23 June
1976. 5p., English

Schalk, Franz, 1863–1931
Bayerische Staatsbibliothek
See Berg, Alban

Library of Congress
(Box 45)
A. Card S.: to Baroness Henriette von Schey. Vienna,
22 Feb. 1904. 2p., German
A. L. S.: [to Zemlinsky]. Brinoi, 28 Apr. 1922. 3p.,
German

Wiener Stadt- u. Landesbibliothek
L.: to Bistron. Vienna, 15 Dec. 1929

Scharwenka, Xaver, 1850–1924
Library of Congress
(Box 45, unless noted)
A. L. S.: Berlin, 1885. 1p., German
A. L. S.: Schlachtensee, 21 July 1891. 1p., German
A. L. S.: Berlin, 25 May 1906. 2p., German
Port. Phot.: 1889 (Box 115)
Port. Repro. (Box 115)

Schat, Peter, b. 1935
Washington State University
Mus. ms. Repro.: *Entelechie I*. Facsimile

Schebest, Agnes, 1813–1870
Library of Congress
(Box 45)
A. L. S.: to a physician. n.p., 31 Aug. 2p., German
A. L. S.: to von Heidetoff. ?, Nov. 1841. 1p., German

Scheffler, Siegfried, 1892–1969
Library of Congress
(Box 45)
A. Mus. ms. S.: [Ten Songs]. 24p. + 8p. (vocal score), 34x26cm., German

Scheidemantel, Karl, 1859–1923
Library of Congress
(Box 45)
5 A. L. S.: [to Heyer]. Dresden, 1896–1900. 6p., German

Scheinpflug, Paul, 1875–1937
Library of Congress
(Box 45)
A. L. S.: [to Tischer]. Duisburg, 28 Nov. 1925. 2p., German. Mentions Hindemith

Schelling, Ernest, 1876–1939
Harvard University
L.: to Carl Deis. n.p., [1931?]

Mus. Quot.: Boston, 1924. Mounted with portrait photograph

Schelper, Otto, 1840–1906
Library of Congress
(Box 45)
4 A. L. S.: to Fritzsch, Lindner, and others. Leipzig, 1877–1900. 6p., German. With musical illustration

Schenker, Heinrich, 1868–1935
Wiener Stadt- u. Landesbibliothek
4 L.: to Karl Weigl. Vienna, 22 Oct. 1927; Ilz, Styria, 4 Aug. 1933; Vienna, 10 Apr., 29 Oct. 1934

Scherchen, Hermann, 1891–1966
Library of Congress
(Box 45)
T. L. S.: to Adolph Weiss. Gravesano, 23 Dec. 1954. 1p., German
See Hartmann, Karl Amadeus

Paul Sacher Stiftung
See Webern, Anton

Washington State University
See Rosbaud, Hans

Scheunemann, Max, 1881–1965
Northwestern University
Mus. ms.: *Piano Quartet in E Major*. Full score

Schibler, Armin, 1920–1986
Washington State University
See Rosbaud, Hans

Schicht, Johann Gottfried, 1753–1823
Library of Congress
(Box 45)
A. L. S.: to Christian Friedrich Uber. Leipzig, 24 Apr. 1818. 1p., German

Schiff de Labarque, Otto, 1869–1948
Library of Congress
(Box 28)
A.[?] Mus. ms. S.: *Les Histoires de Jésus*, Paris, 16 Mar.
1937. 6p.
A. Mus. ms. S.: *En Mémoire d'un Chef Hindou; Amaryllis;*
Vielle Ronde Française; Christiane, 1916, 1917. 8p.,
30x23cm. + 35x27cm.
A. Mus. ms. S.: *Prelude 11*, 13 Sept. 1904. 2p.,
35x27cm.
A. Mus. ms. S.: *Prelude 19*, 3 Oct. ?. 3p., 35x27cm.
(Box 45)
[A?]. Mus. ms. S.: *Prelude 22*, 16 Oct. 1904. 2p.,
35x27cm.

Schillings, Max von, 1868–1933
Bayerische Staatsbibliothek
2 L.: Gürzenich, 19 July 1912; Stuttgart, 20 May 1913
L.: to Zemlinsky. Berlin, 10 July 1923
Mus. Quot.: *Hexenlied*
Sig.

Schindler, Anton Felix, 1795–1864
Library of Congress
(Box 45)
A. L. S.: to Karl August André. Frankfurt, 14 Oct.
[ca. 1850]. 1p., German

Schiske, Karl, 1916–1969
Wiener Stadt- u. Landesbibliothek
Mus. ms.: *Thema, 8 Variationen und Doppelfuge*, op. 2,
Vienna, Christmas 1935/Jan. 1936. Complete score
L.: to Aurelio de la Vega. Vienna, 5 Dec. 1951

Schjelderup, Gerhard, 1859–1933
Northwestern University
Mus. ms.: *Frühlingsreigen*, 30 May 1930. Full score
Mus. ms.: *Kleine norwegische Suite*, 31 Mar. 1930. Full
score

Schleb, Josef, b. 1894
Washington State University
Mus. ms. Repro.: *Symphonia apocaliptica*, 1955.
Blueprint score

Schloss, Julius, 1902–1972
Bayerische Staatsbibliothek
See Berg, Alban

Library of Congress
(Box 100)
A. Mus. ms. S.: "Happy Birthday to You...," 10 Sept.
1949. 1p., English. Birthday canon for Schoenberg's
75th birthday. See autograph document below
A. Mus. ms. S.: "Heil! Alban Berg!". 1p., German.
Birthday canon for Berg's 46th birthday
A. Mus. ms. S.: *Requiem*, 1932. Full score. 6p.,
34x27cm.
P. card S.: to Otto Jokl. Vienna, 31 Mar. 1930. German.
Details about the reception given after the
performance of *Wozzeck*
8 T. L. S.: to Hans Moldenhauer. Belleville, New
Jersey, 1963–1971. 8p., German, English. Many
details regarding his work; Berg, Webern,
Schoenberg
A. Card S.: to Hans Moldenhauer. Newark, 21 Dec.
1965. English
P. card S.: to Hans Moldenhauer. Montreal, 26 Oct.
1966. English
T. L. S.: to Hans Moldenhauer. Belleville, 6 Oct. 1969.
1p., English
A. Doc. S.: Sketch. Birthday card for Schoenberg's
75th birthday, with sketch of canon on verso.
10 Sept. 1949. 2p. See manuscript above
Mus. ms. Repro.: *Impressions*, 1964, c1967 by Julius
Schloss. 15p.
2 Mus. mss. Repro.: *Sonata for Piano*, c1963 by Julius
Schloss. 37p. each
Mus. ms. Repro.: *Sonate für Klavier*, 1928–1929. 31p.
Blueprint score
Mus. ms. Repro.: *Symphony*, c1969 by Julius Schloss.
35p.
Mus. ms. Repro.: *Twelve-Tone Suite for the Young Pianist*,
c1967 by Julius Schloss. 14p.
Mus. ms. Repro.: *23rd Psalm, for Chorus and Organ*,
c1971 by Julius Schloss. 24p. Blueprint score
L. Repro.: to Schloss, from Alban Berg. Vienna,
23 June 1930. 1p., German
L. Repro.: from Arnold Schoenberg. Los Angeles,
28 Sept. 1947. 1p., German
L. Repro.: from Arnold Schoenberg. Los Angeles,
18 Dec. 1948. 1p., English. Recommending Schloss
Pri. Sco. Repro.: *Brass Octet*, c1950 by Julius Schloss.
11p.

Pri. Sco. Repro.: *4 Songs for Soprano and Piano after poems by Alfred Mombert*, c1966 by Julius Schloss. 12p.

Pri. Sco. S.: *Requiem*, c1962 by Julius Schloss. 13p.

2 Pri. Sco.: *Twenty-three Pieces, For Children in Twelve-Tone Style*, New York: Peer, c1958, 1965. Two volumes, each set

2 Prog.: 1966, 1973

3 Clip.: Nov. 1966, German; *Toronto Gazette*, 16 June 1962

See Schoenberg, Arnold

Schmid, Erich, b. 1907
Washington State University
See Rosbaud, Hans

Schmid, Heinrich Kaspar, 1874–1953
Bayerische Staatsbibliothek
Mus. ms.: *Ringelreihen*, op. 15, Munich, 26 Jan. 1913

Washington State University
See Rosbaud, Hans

Schmidt, Franz, 1874–1939
Library of Congress
(Box 45)
A. Mus. ms.: [*Fredigundis*]. 3p., 33x26cm., ink. Excerpt, full score
A. Card S.: to Karl Weigl. Perchtoldsdorf, 27 Dec. 1934. 1p., German
Call. c.

Schmidt, Gustav, 1816–1882
Library of Congress
(Box 45)
A. L. S.: [to Franz von Holstein]. Leipzig, 18 Aug. 1875. 4p., German

Schmidt-Garre, Helmut, b. 1907
Bayerische Staatsbibliothek
Mus. ms.: *Fünf Klavierstücke*, No. 1, 1929
Mus. ms.: *Sonate für Klavier*, 1929. Complete score

Schmidt-Isserstedt, Hans, 1900–1973
Washington State University
See Rosbaud, Hans

Schmitt, Alőys, 1788–1866
Library of Congress
(Box 45)
A. L. S.: to Diabelli. Frankfurt, 5 Jan. 1834. 1p., German

Schmitt, Florent, 1870–1958
Library of Congress
(Box 45)
A. L. S.: St. Cloud, 3 Dec. 1927. 4p., French
A. L. S.: St. Cloud, n.d. 1p., French

Schmitz, Paul, b. 1898
Washington State University
See Rosbaud, Hans

Schnabel, Artur, 1882–1951
Library of Congress
(Box 100, unless noted)
2 P. cards S.: to Bruno Eisner. Berlin, 2 May 1907; Forte dei Marmi, 26 Aug. 1929. 3p., German. Also signed by others
A. L. S.: to Bruno Eisner. New York, 5 Nov. 1940. 1p., German
Mus. ms. Repro. S.: [*Sonata for Violin and Piano*], to Bruno Eisner, 1944. 42p. + 16p. (parts). Blueprint score
Port. Phot. S.: to Boaz Piller. Boston, 13 Mar. 1939 (Box 115)

Schneider, Friedrich, 1786–1853
Library of Congress
(Box 45)
A. L. S.: to Ole Bull. Dessau, 20 Dec. 1840. 3p.,
German
A. L. S.: Dessau, 3 Feb. 1843. 3p., German
A. L. S.: to Eberius. Dessau, 19 Feb. 1845. 2p.,
German

Schnerich, Alfred, 1859–1944
Wiener Stadt- u. Landesbibliothek
4 L.: Wilhelm Widmann. Vienna, 3, 26 Jan. 1937,
4 Dec. 1938, 9 June 1939

Schoberlechner, Sophie Dell'Occa, 1807–1864
Library of Congress
(Box 45)
A. L. S.: to Baron de Vivenot. n.p., 14 Sept. 1842. 1p.,
French

Schoeck, Othmar, 1886–1957
Washington State University
See Rosbaud, Hans

Zentralbibliothek Zürich
Mus. ms.: *Massimilla Doni*. Excerpt
Mus. ms.: *Septembermorgen*
Mus. ms.: *Widmung*
L.: n.p., [Feb. 1923?]
Doc. Repro.: Biographical information

Arnoldfolxenbe

Schoenberg [Schönberg], Arnold, 1874–1951
Harvard University
See Schoenberg, Gertrud
See Zemlinsky, Alexander

Library of Congress
(Box no./Folder no.)
A. Mus. ms.: *Adagio*, for string orchestra and harp,
[before 1897]. 3p., 35x27cm., pencil. Full score.
Unpublished. Originally titled, "Andante" (46/1)

A. Mus. ms.: [*Concerto for String Quartet and Orchestra*,
adapted from Handel's *Concerto Grosso*, op. 6, No. 7,
to Alma Mahler, 1933]. 2 leaves, 35x27, 27x35cm.
ink, red pencil. Sketches. With a description of his
method and purpose for the transcription, in
German (46/1)
A. Mus. ms. S.: *Gavotte und Musette (im alten Style), für
Streich-Orchester*, [1897]. 7p., 35x27cm., ink. Full
score (46/2)
A. Mus. ms.: *Im Korn*, song for soprano and piano by
Zemlinsky. 2p., 25x30cm., German. Text by Evers.
Signed by Zemlinsky. With Zemlinsky's dedication
to Mela (46/2)
A. Mus. ms.: *Der Tag wird kühl*, song for soprano and
piano, by Zemlinsky, to Melanie Guttmann Rice.
3p., 34x26cm., German. Fair copy in Schoenberg's
autograph. Also inscribed by Melanie Guttmann
(46/2)
Mus. ms. cop.: *Quintett für Flöte, Oboe, Klarinette, Horn
and Bassoon* [sic], op. 26, 1924. 39p. (parts
incomplete). With "Klarinette in A" (46/3)
Mus. ms. cop.: *String Trio*, op. 45, 1946. Incomplete.
17p. (46/3)
P. card S.: to William C. Rice Jr., from Ed.
F[riedmann?]. Vienna, 2 Dec. 1898. English. Joint
greetings by "companions" Schoenberg, Oskar
Friedmann, Wassermann, and other musicians,
authors (Box 119)
P. card S.: to [Anton] Webern. Berlin-Zehlendorf,
8 Nov. 1912. 1p., German. Penned on verso of his
own portrait photograph (Box 115)
P. card S.: to Roberto Gerhard. Mödling, 19 Feb. 1924.
German. Text addresses Wieser (Box 119)
P. card S.: to Melanie Rice. Prague, 9 June 1924. 2p.,
German. Cosigners include Berg, Helene Berg,
Trudi Greissle, Gutheil-Schoder, Steuermann,
Martha Ullmann, Webern, Zemlinsky, and others
(Box 119)
T. L. S.: to Julius Schloss. Mödling, 6 Nov. 1924. 1p.,
German (Box 119)
T. L. S.: to Schloss. Beaulieu sur Mer, 10 Feb. 1925.
1p., German (Box 119)
24 L.: to Adolph Weiss. 1925–1937. 24 leaves, German.
Translating *Harmonielehre* (Box 119)
A. L. S.: to Alban Berg. Pörtschach, 9 Aug. 1927. 1p.,
German. Mentions *Lyric Suite*; Hertzka (Box 119)
A. L. S.: to Berg and Webern. Roquebrune, 25 Aug.
1928. 2p., German (Box 119)

A. L. S.: to Dr. Norbert Schwarzmann. Roquebrune-Cap Martin, 31 Oct. 1928. 2p., German. About Webern's illness (Box 119)

A. L.: to Berg and Webern. Monte Carlo, 12 Feb. 1929. 2p., German (Box 119)

T. L. S.: to Paul Pisk. Charlottenburg, 22 Oct. 1929. 1p., German (Box 119)

A. Card S.: to Melanie Guttmann Rice. [Boston], 23 Dec. 1933. German. Includes note from Gertrud Schoenberg (Box 119)

A. L. S.: to Paul Pisk. Brookline, Massachusetts, 4 Mar. 1934. 1p., German (Box 119)

P. card S.: to Melanie [Guttmann] Rice. Chautauqua, 21 July 1934. German. Includes note from Gertrud Schoenberg (Box 119)

P. card S.: to Universal Edition. Chautauqua, 15 Sept. 1934. German (Box 119)

L. S. A. Annot.: to Kurt Manschinger. Los Angeles, 3 Oct. 1944. 1p., English (Box 119)

5 T. L. S.: to Fritz Mahler. 1947–1949. 7 leaves, English. Included are an additional five carbon copy letters to Schoenberg, from Fritz Mahler, 1949; a letter to Fritz Mahler, from Richard Hoffmann; and an invoice for *Moses und Aron*, "Dance around the Golden Calf," with autograph annotations, 1949 (Box 119)

6 L. S.: to Friderike Zweig. Los Angeles, Feb. 1950-May 1951. 7p., German, English (Box 119)

A. L. S.: [to Melanie Guttmann Rice]. Vienna, n.d. 1p., German (Box 119)

A. L. S.: to Carl Hagemann. Kopenhagen, n.d. 1p., German (Box 119)

Doc.: "Fehlerliste." Corrections for *Variationen*, op. 31, 29 Jan. 1933. Marked "Neue Liste." Corrections for 90 measures, including musical examples and annotations. 3 leaves, ink, colored pencils. Stamped with address (46/4)

T. Doc.: Dedication. To [Alexander] Zemlinsky, for *Pierrot Lunaire* score. 1p., German (Box 119)

T. Doc. A. Rev.: Lecture. On Brahms, delivered over the radio, 12 Feb. 1933, for the centenary of the birth of Brahms. Carbon copy of original typescript with musical examples. Revised in 1947 for *Style and Idea* (1975) under the title "Brahms the Progressive." 28p., German (46/4)

A. Doc. S.: Poem. "Wer mit der Welt laufen will...," to Dr. David Joseph Bach, 24 Mar. 1926. 1p. (9 lines) (46/5)

Doc.: Text. "Choral-Bearbeitung," ca. 1930. 1p., German (46/5)

Doc.: Announcement. For Schoenberg lecture, "Stil und Gedanke...," Vienna, 15 Feb. 1933. 1p., German. With newspaper report (46/5)

Doc.: Birth announcement. Los Angeles, 26 May 1937. 1p., English. For Rudolf Ronald Schoenberg (46/5)

T. Doc.: Essay. "Arnold Schönbergs neue Männerchöre," [by Willi Reich?]. 4p., German (46/5)

T. Lib. A. Rev. S.: *Moses und Aron*. 46p., German (46/6)

3 A. Mus. Quot. S.: *Pelleas und Melisande*, op. 5, Boston, 9 Jan. 1934. 1p. (10m.). Three thematic quotations: Melisande (Andante), Golaud (Moderato), Pelleas (Vivace). Mounted with portrait photograph, to Piller, 30 Dec. 1921 (46/6)

Mus. ms. Repro.: *Gurre-Lieder*. 179p., German. First edition, facsimile. Autograph annotations by Polnauer. Bound (Box 101)

Mus. ms. Repro.: *Von Heute auf Morgen*, 1929. 149p. First edition, facsimile, of piano reduction, with annotations concerning staging in the hand of Willi Reich. Bound (Box 101)

Mus. ms. Repro.: *Die Jacobsleiter*. 39p., German. Facsimile of original manuscript. Stamped by Schoenberg, Los Angeles (46/7)

Mus. ms. Repro. S.: [*Moses und Aron*], "Der Tanz um das goldene Kalb," Vienna: Scherchen, c1951 to Adolph Weiss, 1952. Facsimile of piano-vocal score. 198p. (Box 120)

Mus. ms. Repro.: [*Moses und Aron*], to Fritz Mahler. pp.103–178 (mm. 166-976). Photostat of autograph in full score (46/8)

Mus. ms. Repro. S.: *Ode to Napoleon Buonaparte*, to Adolph Weiss, Christmas, 1944. 36p., English. Blueprint score (Box 101)

Mus. ms. Repro.: *Ode to Napoleon Buonaparte*, [Los Angeles]. 8p., German. Facsimile of melodic line. Stamped by Schoenberg (46/9)

Mus. ms. Repro.: *String Trio*, op. 45, New York: Boelke-Bomart, c1950. 23p. First edition (46/9)

Mus. ms. Repro. S.: [*2.*] *Streich-Quartett*, op. 10, Vienna: Schoenberg, n.d., to Alexander Zemlinsky, 18 Feb. 1909. 47p., German. Facsimile (46/10)

77 L. Repro.: to Alexander Zemlinsky. 1911–1927. 82 leaves, German. Drafts of letters, typed transcripts of letters and postcards (Box 119)

12 L. S. Repro.: to Rudolph and Nina Goehr. 1933–1949. 16 leaves, German (Box 119)

2 L. Repro.: to [Julius] Schloss. Los Angeles, 28 Sept. 1947, 18 Dec. 1948. 2p., German (Box 119)

L. Repro.: Los Angeles, 18 Dec. 1948. 1p., German. Letter of recommendation for [Julius] Schloss by Schoenberg (Box 119)

Doc. Repro.: Excerpt. [*Moses und Aron*], "Moses zieht Aron zur Verantwortung." 1p., German. From autograph libretto (47/1)

Doc. Repro.: Specifications. *Moses und Aron.* 5p. Photostat of Schoenberg's handwritten specifications for orchestration, annotations on many aspects of the opera, and drawing (47/1)

Pri. Sco. S.: *Concerto for Piano and Orchestra*, op. 42, New York: G. Schirmer, c1944, to Adolph Weiss with inscription, 12–13 Sept. 1944. 99p. First edition, reduction for 2nd piano by Steuermann (47/2)

Pri. Sco.: *Dreimal tausend Jahre*, op. 50a, Mainz: Schott's, c1955 by Mrs. Arnold Schoenberg. 3p. each, German, English. With signature by the poet of the text, Dagobert D. Runes. Two copies, with embossed stamp of Mrs. Schoenberg (47/3)

Pri. Sco. S.: *Fünf Orchesterstücke*, op. 16, Leipzig: Peters, c1912. First printing, with an inserted errata list, 1922. Signed on title page, and with several notations in the score. The cover contains the rubber stamp of Rudolph Ganz, who received the score from the composer. The score was used by Schoenberg when he conducted the work with the Chicago Symphony Orchestra (8 Feb. 1934) (48/6)

Pri. Sco. S.: *Erwartung*, op. 17, Vienna: Universal Edition, c1922, to Josef Polnauer, Prague, June 1924. 47p., German. First edition, piano-vocal score. Also signed by Marie Pappenheim, Alexander Zemlinsky, and Marie Gutheil-Schoder (47/3)

Pri. Sco. S.: *Gurre-Lieder*, No. 49, of the special edition, Büttenpapier, c1912. 238p. Piano-vocal score by Alban Berg (Box 101)

Pri. Sco.: *Von Heute auf Morgen*, Berlin: Schoenberg, c1930. 140p. Second edition, piano reduction (47/4)

Pri. Sco.: *Klavierstueck*, 1932, in *New Music*, San Francisco, Apr. 1932. 7p. (47/5)

Pri. Sco.: [*Moses und Aron*], "Der Tanz um das goldene Kalb," Vienna: Ars Viva Hermann Scherchen, c1951. Signed by Gertrud Schoenberg, to Adolph Weiss, 12 Sept. 1952 (Box 101)

Pri. Sco. S.: *Pelleas und Melisande*, op. 5, Vienna: Universal Edition, c1911, to Josef Polnauer, 29 Feb. 1912 (mentions leap year). 131p. Three lines of text by Schoenberg. Signed by Alexander Zemlinsky, 2 June 1920 (47/6)

Pri. Sco. Annot.: *Pierrot Lunaire*, op. 21, Vienna: Universal Edition, c1914, to Hans Moldenhauer, from E. Stiedry, 22 Mar. 1972. 78p., German. Schoenberg coached Stiedry for the first recording of the work (47/7)

Pri. Sco.: *Quartett*, Berlin: Dreililien, n.d. 80p. (48/1)

Pri. Sco.: *Quintett für Flöte, Oboe, Klarinette, Horn und Fagott*, op. 26, [Vienna]: Universal Edition, c1925. 111p. (parts). All bear Schoenberg stamp except flute part (Douglas Craig) (48/2)

10 Pri. Sco. S.: [Songs], Leipzig: Dreililien. 35p., German. Ten individual printings of songs from Schoenberg's opera 2 and 3 (48/3)

Pri. Sco.: *Der Tanz um das Goldene Kalb*, Vienna: Ars Viva Hermann Scherchen, c1951. Signed by Gertrud Schoenberg, to Adolph Weiss, 12 Sept. 1952 (Box 120)

Pri. Sco. S.: *Variationen für Orchester*, op. 31, Vienna: Universal Edition, c1929, to Adolph Weiss, 13 Sept. 1936. 80p. (48/4)

Prog. A. Annot.: Vienna, 2 May 1924. 2p., German (48/5)

Prog.: Vienna, 19 Sept. 1927. 3p. The program covers two concerts for the world premiere, sponsored by Mrs. Elizabeth Sprague Coolidge (48/5)

Prog.: Vienna, 26 Feb. 1928. 2 leaves. Song recital given by Margot Hinnenberg-Lefèbre (48/5)

Prog. S.: to Adolph Weiss, University of California, Los Angeles, 4–8 Jan. 1937. 4p. Autograph messages by Arnold Schoenberg, Gertrud Schoenberg, and the four quartet members: Rudolf Kolisch, Felix Khuner, Jenö Léner, Benar Heifetz (48/5)

Prog.: University of California, Los Angeles, 27 Mar. 4p., English. Signed by Irene Hanna (48/5)

A. Paint.: [*Die glückliche Hand*]. 20x24cm., in dark hues. Schoenberg's own stage design. Given to Webern (48/5)

Port. Paint.: Arnold Schoenberg, by Hildegard Jone. Oil, 59x47cm. Framed by artist (Shelf)

4 Draw.: Arnold Schoenberg, by Hildegard Jone. Original charcoal drawings, three with poetic inscription. Initialed (Box 115)

Port. Caric.: of Schoenberg and Zemlinsky, by E. Weiss. Prague, [6 June 1924] (Box 115)

Port. Phot. S.: to Boaz Piller, 30 Dec. 1921. Mounted with musical quotation above (Box 115)

Port. Phot. S.: to [Edward] Clark, Mödling, 19 Aug. 1925 (Box 115)

Port. Phot. S.: to [Adolph] and Mrs. Weiss, New York, 29 Mar. 1934 (Box 115)

Port. Phot. S.: to Fritz and Erika Stiedry, [Christmas] 1950. German (Box 115)

Phot.: [Photo of the plaque on the house in Barcelona], installed in 1955 (Box 115)

Port. Gr.: with Schoenberg (Box 115)

Port. Phot. (Box 115)

Port. Phot.: on postcard to Webern (Box 115)

Port. Draw. Repro.: 1917. From a drawing by Egon Schiele (Box 115)

Bk.: *Arnold Schoenberg*, Munich: R. Piper, 1912. 90p., German. First edition (Box 120)

Bk.: [*Arnold Schoenberg, Gedenkausstellung 1974*], Vienna: Universal Edition, c1974, edited by Ernst Hilmar, inscribed to Hans Moldenhauer, from Hilmar, Vienna, 7 Oct. 1974. 386p. (Box 120)

Bk.: *Arnold Schoenberg zum 60. Geburtstag 13. September 1934*, Vienna: Universal Edition, 1934. 75p., German (Box 120)

Bk.: *Harmonielehre*, Leipzig-Vienna: Universal Edition, 1911. Signed in 1911 by T. E. Clark. 476p., German. Bound in linen. Page proofs were used for Clark's private instruction by Schoenberg. Detailed annotations and analysis, in red, blue, and black pencil, including musical examples (Box 120)

Bk.: [same], 1922. 516p., German. Third edition (Box 120)

Bk.: *Schoenberg-Gespräch*, Vienna: Hochschule für angewandte Kunst in Wien, [1984]. 77p., 32p. ill., German. Illustrated book dealing with Schoenberg's paintings (Box 120)

S. rec.: *Quintet for Flute, Oboe, Clarinet, Horn and Bassoon*, op. 26, LWO 23682 A5–6: B6–9: B11–12, tape 40 (Shelf)

S. rec.: [Heinrich Strobel-Arnold Schoenberg], LWO 23682 A2–3, tape 40, 3 Mar. 1931 (Shelf)

S. rec. S.: [Discussion with Heinrich Strobel and Eberhard Preussner], Berlin, 30 Mar. 1931. On verso, "Tanzscene" from *Serenade for 7 Instruments*, to Adolph Weiss, Christmas 1937 (Shelf)

S. rec.: Schoenberg lecture, K. B. Klaus, [Louisiana State University, 1942?] (Shelf)

S. rec.: *Theme and Variations*, op. 43b, LWO 23682 B5: B1–4, tape (Shelf)

S. rec.: [Unidentified student work], LWO 23682 A6, tape 41, 1933[?] (Shelf)

Medal: *Arnold Schönberg 1874–1951*. [Original model of the Schoenberg medal], designed by Josef Humplik. Awarded by the Arnold Schoenberg Kuratorium. Bronze, 17cm. (Box 124)

Medal: [The Schoenberg medal]. Awarded to Edward Clark in 1951. 7cm. Engraved on verso (Box 124)

Baton: with calling card and note to Hans Rosbaud, from Gertrud Schoenberg (Shelf)

See Liszt, Franz

See Schloss, Julius

See Schoenberg, Gertrud

See Webern, Anton

See Weigl, Karl

Paul Sacher Stiftung
See Webern, Anton

Wiener Stadt- u. Landesbibliothek
Mus. ms.: *Das verlassene Mädchen*

Doc.: Instrumentation list. *Gurre-Lieder*

Schoenberg, Georg
Washington State University
See Rosbaud, Hans

Schoenberg, Gertrud, 1924–1967
Library of Congress
(Box 119)

7 L. S.: to Mrs. Adolph Weiss (Mary). Feb. 1934-July 1935. 7p., German. Three of the letters contain autograph postscripts signed by Arnold Schoenberg

A. L. S.: to Friderike Zweig. Los Angeles, 18 July 1950. 1p., German

7 L. S.: to Alma Mahler. Los Angeles, Apr. 1957–Feb. 1959. 11p., German. Musical and personal topics

See Schoenberg, Arnold

Washington State University
SUMMARY OF PRINCIPAL HOLDINGS:

Doc.: Wedding announcement. For Nuria Schoenberg and Luigi Nono. Los Angeles, 8 Aug. 1955

Phot.

See Rosbaud, Hans

Schoenberg, Nuria, b. 1932
Library of Congress
(Box 48)

Card S.: to Alma Mahler. [Vienna?, Christmas, 1958]. 1p., English

Schonberg, Harold C., b. 1915
Harvard University
SUMMARY OF PRINCIPAL HOLDINGS:
L.: Includes a group of season's greeting cards with
   reproductions of original drawings

Schott, Anton, 1846–1913
Library of Congress
(Box 49)
A. L. S.: Schwerin, 10 Oct. 1891. 1p., German

Schreck, Gustav, 1849–1918
Library of Congress
(Box 49)
A. L. S.: Leipzig, 19 Mar. 1911. 2p., German
Port. Phot. Repro. (Box 115)

Schreiner, Alexander, 1901–1987
Harvard University
L.: Salt Lake City, 9 Jan. 1957

Schreker, Franz, 1878–1934
Library of Congress
(Box 49, unless noted)
A. L. S.: to Universal Edition. n.p., received 4 Oct.
   1922. 1p., German
A. L. S.: to Tischer. Cologne, 18 Mar. 1924. 1p.,
   German
A. Mus. Quot. S.: Salzburg, 5 Mar. 1920
Port. Phot. S.: to Paul Pisk. Christmas 1912. By Bänder
   (Box 115)
Port. Phot.: Vienna, 1919. By Löwy (Box 115)

Washington State University
See Rosbaud, Hans

Wiener Stadt- u. Landesbibliothek
2 L.: to Otto Jokl. Vienna, 2 Apr. 1913; Reichenau,
   5 Aug. 1916
2 L.: to Alma Mahler, from Maria Schreker. Berlin,
   10, 25 July 1958

Schröder-Devrient, Wilhelmine, 1804–1860
Library of Congress
(Box 49)
A. L. S.: to [Charlotte] Pfeiffer. n.p., 1824. 2p.,
   German

Schubert, Ferdinand, 1794–1859
Wiener Stadt- u. Landesbibliothek
Mus. ms.: *Verjüngung*, Vienna, 17 Apr. 1839. Full score

Schubert, Franz, 1797–1828
Library of Congress
(Box 49, unless noted)
A. Mus. ms. S.: *An den Mond in einer Herbstnacht*, Apr.
   1818. 11p., 22x30cm., ink. Song with piano
   accompaniment. Based on a poem by Aloys Wilhelm
   Schreiber (1761–1841). Complete score
A. Mus. ms.: [Four Songs], *Nachtgesang, An Rosa I, An
   Rosa II, Idens Schwanenlied*, 1815. 4p., 24x32cm., ink
A. Mus. ms. S.: *Das Mädchen aus der Fremde*, 16 Oct.
   1814. 4p., 25x33cm., ink. Song with piano
   accompaniment, first version. Schubert wrote this
   song on the day of the first performance of his first
   mass. He again set the poem (Schiller) on 12 Aug.
   1815
Doc.: Death Announcement. "Schullehrer in der
   Rossau." Vienna, 20 Nov. 1828. 1p., German
Mus. ms. Repro.: *Drei Symphonie-Fragmente*, Kassel:
   Bärenreiter, 1978, to Hans and Rosaleen
   Moldenhauer, from Ernst Hilmar, 1 May 1979.
   31p. Fascimile (Shelf)
Mus. ms. Repro.: *Symphony in B Minor* ("Unfinished"),
   London: Cockerell, Willis & Belliere, 1943, to Hans
   Rosbaud, from ?. 77p. Fascimile (Shelf)

Schubert, Heinz, 1908–1945
Library of Congress
(Box 49)
A. Mus. ms. S.: *Hymnus nach dem Persischen des
   Zarathustra*. 38p., 34x27cm. Piano score

Schubert, Joseph, 1757–1837
Library of Congress
(Box 49)
A. L. S.: Dresden, 8 Apr. 1803. 4p., German

Schuberth, Julius, 1804–1875
Library of Congress
(Box 49)
8 A. L. S.: to A. W. Gottschalg. Leipzig, 1870–1884.
9p., German. Writing on behalf of Schuberth & Co.,
numerous references to Liszt

Schuch-Proska [née Procházka], Clementine, 1850–1932
Library of Congress
(Box 49)
A. L. S.: to Eugen Lindner. Kötzschenbroda bei
Dresden, 11 Nov. 1890. 3p., German
3 A. L. S.: [to Garr?]. Dresden, 13 May 1875, 10 Dec.
1877, 28 Dec. 1879. 7p., German
A. L. S.: to a theater official in Coburg. Dresden, n.d.
3p., German

Schütt, Eduard, 1856–1933
Wiener Stadt- u. Landesbibliothek
L.: Vienna, 26 Mar. 1900
L.: to Schlösser. Vienna, 26 Mar. 1901

Schulhoff, Ervín, 1894–1942
Library of Congress
(Box 49)
4 P. cards S.: to Paul Sanders. Prague, 23 Sept., 28
Oct., 5, 11 Nov. 1931. 4p., German
6 T. L. S.: to Paul Sanders. Prague, Sept.–Dec. 1931.
11p., German
A. L. S.: to Paul Sanders. Prague, 9 July 1932. 2p.,
German. Politics; the opera, *Flammen*
T. Doc.: Typescript. Text with specifications of
setting, *H.M.S. Royal Oak, Ein Jazz Oratorium von
Otto Rombach und Erwin Schulhoff.* 7p., German.
Carbon copy

Schulhoff, Julius, 1825–1898
Library of Congress
(Box 49)
A. Card: to Louis Lüstner. n.p., n.d. 2p., German

Schuller, Gunther, b. 1925
Harvard University
Mus. ms.: *Symphony for Brass and Percussion.* First draft
in full score, including alternate Scherzo ending
2 L.: to Hans Moldenhauer. 23 Apr. 1961; Season's
Greetings
Prog.: to Hans Moldenhauer, Spokane, 9 Mar. 1982
Port. Phot.: to the Moldenhauer Archives

Schulz-Beuthen, Heinrich, 1838–1915
Library of Congress
(Box 49, unless noted)
A. Mus. ms. S.: *Des Enkelkindes Schlummerlied.* 2p.,
35x27cm.
A. Mus. ms. S.: *Koenig Lear.* 1p., 35x27cm. Excerpt,
full score
A. Mus. ms. S.: [*Suite for Piano Solo*]. 12p., 34x27cm.
Port. Phot. S.: Dresden, 19 Apr. 1908 (Box 115)

Schuman, William, 1910–1992
Harvard University
L.: to Charles Haubiel. New York, 29 Aug. 1945
L.: to Rudolph Ganz. New York, 25 June 1946
L.: to Aurelio de la Vega. New York, 1 Oct. 1963
Mus. Quot.: inscribed, and mounted with portrait
photograph

Schumann [née Wieck], Clara, 1819–1896
Library of Congress
(Box 49, unless noted)
A. L. S.: to Black. n.p., 4 June 1859. 2p., English.
Regarding a concert rehearsal
A. L. S.: to a conductor in Edinburgh. London,
13 Feb. 1867. 4p., German. Regarding *Carnaval*
P. card S.: to Julie Deichmann. Frankfurt, 15 Feb.
1881. German
A. Card S.: Frankfurt, 16 Oct. 188[3?]. 2p., German
A. L. S.: to Speyer. London, 9 Apr. 1886. 2p., German
A. Mus. Quot. S.: *Ad Libitum*, inscribed Frankfurt, Mar.
1890

Doc.: Address panel. To Marie Michaelis, 3 June 1876
Call. c. Annot.: German
Port. Engr.: with biographical sketch from *The Graphic*
    (Box 115)
Port. Engr. (Box 115)

Schumann, Elisabeth, 1888–1952
Harvard University
L.: to Karl Weigl. Sheffield, 19 Nov. 1937
L.: Westport, 3 July 1939

Schumann, Georg, 1866–1952
Northwestern University
Mus. ms.: *Sonate Cis Moll für Clavier und Violine*, op. 13,
    Harzburg, 16 Sept. 1893

Schumann, Robert, 1810–1856
Library of Congress
(Box 49, unless noted)
A. Mus. ms.: *Burla*, for piano solo in G Minor, [ca.
    1832]. 1p. (61 measures), 28x31cm., ink.
    Unpublished
A. L. S.: [to Spohr]. Leipzig, 9 Feb. 1838. 2p.,
    German. Regarding Spohr, Mendelssohn
A. L. S.: to Whistling. Dresden, 23 June 1846. 2p.,
    German. Details publishing Bach fugues; ill health
A. L. S.: to Pauline. Dresden, 22 Apr. 1849. 2p.,
    German
A. L. S.: to French horn virtuoso Levy. [Dresden?],
    5 May 1849. 1p., German
A. L. S.: to a singer. [Düsseldorf], n.d. 1p., German
Port. Engr. (Box 115)

**Schumann-Heink [née Rössler], Ernestine,
1861–1936**
Harvard University
L.: Dresden, 29 Dec. 1882
L.: Hamburg, 11 Mar. 1887
Port.

Schuncke, Hugo
Library of Congress
(Box 49)
A. Mus. ms. S.: *Bavaria, Hymne für grosses Orchester*,
    4 May 1906. 15p. + 18p., 32x25cm. Arranged for two
    pianos. Piano I in Schuncke's autograph, Piano II in
    the hand of a copyist

Schuricht, Carl, 1880–1967
Washington State University
See Rosbaud, Hans

Schuster, Bernhard, 1870–1934
Bayerische Staatsbibliothek
See Berg, Alban

Schwartz, Paul, b. 1907
Harvard University
Mus. ms.: *Serenade*. Full score
6 L.: to Hans Moldenhauer. 1957–1960
Mus. ms. Repro.: *Chamber Concerto*, op. 18. Facsimile

Schweitzer, Albert, 1875–1965
Library of Congress
See Casals, Pablo

Washington State University
Port. Phot.: 1961
See Rosbaud, Hans

Sciortino, Edouard, 1893–1979
Library of Congress
(Box 49)
2 Mus. mss. cop.: *Ibère*; *Berbère*, to Henry de
    Montherlant. 22p., 35x27cm.

Scontrino, Antonio, 1850–1922
Library of Congress
(Box 49)
A. Mus. Quot. S.: *Quartetto per archi in do maggiore*, to
    Glas, Florence, 31 Dec. 1906

Scott, Cyril, 1879–1970
Northwestern University
Mus. ms.: [Manuscript fragment]. In organ score, 13m.
Pri. Sco.: *Poems*, inscribed to Bain

Scott, Lady **John Douglas, 1810–1900**
Northwestern University
L.: to Emily. n.p., 17 Apr. 1897
Obit.

Scribe, Eugène, 1791–1861
Library of Congress
(Box 117)
A. L. S.: London, 30 May. 1p., French. Cosigned by F. Halèvy

Search, Frederick Preston, 1889–1959
Harvard University
SUMMARY OF PRINCIPAL HOLDINGS:
Mus. ms.: *Cello Concerto in A Minor*
Mus. ms.: *The Dream of McKorkle*, 1936
Mus. ms.: *Exhilaration*
Mus. ms. Repro.: *Sinfonietta*. Blueprint score

Searle, Humphrey, 1915–1982
Library of Congress
(Box 49)
A. Mus. ms. S.: *Symphony No. 5*, op. 43, "In Memory of Anton Webern," London, June–Sept. 1964. 25p., 37x27cm., ink, pencil. Complete condensed score

Northwestern University
Mus. ms. arr.: *Fugue I in F Minor, Voluntary IV in G Minor, Fugue III in F Minor* by Roseingrave, arranged for string orchestra, 1939. Parts

Sechter, Simon, 1788–1867
Library of Congress
(Box 49)
A. Mus. ms. S.: *Thema von Mozart, weiter bearbeitet von Simon Sechter*, 9 Nov. 1858. 4p., 26x33cm. Contains

three fragmentary themes (C Minor, F Major, G Major) by Mozart, worked out by Sechter
A. Doc. S.: Autobiographical and aesthetical manifesto. Setting forth his credo as a composer, theoretician, and pedagogue, to August Schmidt. 2p., German

Seeger, Ruth, 1901–1953
Library of Congress
See Crawford, Ruth Porter

Segovia, Andrés, 1893–1987
Harvard University
See Villa-Lobos, Heitor

Library of Congress
SUMMARY OF PRINCIPAL HOLDINGS:
(Box 49, unless noted)
A. Mus. ms. S.: *La Maja de Goya, Tonadilla* by Granados, to Olga Coelho, 1949. 6p., 30x23cm., ink
A. Mus. ms.: *Canciones arcaícas* by Manuel Ponce. 4p., 32x21cm.
A. Mus. ms.: *Casinha pequenina*. 2p. + 4p. sketches, 27x18cm.
A. Mus. ms. S.: *Easy Lesson No. 5*, to Olga Coelho, New York, 2 Apr. 1948. 3p., 32x24cm.
A. Mus. ms. S.: *Estudio (invocación a Schumann)*, New York, 11 Apr. 1949. 4p., 34x27cm.
A. Mus. ms. S.: *Estudio en b menor*, Naples, 20 Dec. 1949. 4p., 33x24cm.
A. Mus. ms. S.: *Improvisación para guittara*, Montevideo, 25 Oct. 4p., 33x23cm.
A. Mus. ms. S.: *Lección 17*, New York, 6 Apr. 1950. 2p., 34x27cm.
A. Mus. ms. S.: *Lección 21*, New York, 30 Apr. 1950. 3p. + 1p. sketches, 30x23cm.
A. Mus. ms.: *Lección fácil*, 28 Mar. 1950. 1p., 32x24cm.
A. Mus. ms.: *Ojos morenicos* by Escobar. 1p. + 1p. sketches, 32x24cm.
A. Mus. ms. S.: *Platero y yo, Angelus* by Castelnuovo-Tedesco. 4p., 34x25cm. Guitar score with fingerings by Segovia
A. Mus. ms. S.: *Platero y yo, Melancolía* by Castelnuovo-Tedesco. 5p., 34x25cm. Guitar score with fingerings by Segovia, text in the hand of Castelnuovo-Tedesco

A. Mus. ms. S.: *Preludio*, Montevideo, 1944. 3p., 33x23cm.

A. Mus. ms.: *Preludio* by Manuel Ponce. 6p., 27x17cm.

A. Mus. ms. S.: *Preludio en mi menor*, Washington, 9 Dec. 1946. 4p., 32x24cm. Manuscript in pencil, crossed out in ink

A. Mus. ms. S.: *Siciliana (lección no. 16 para el método)*, New York, 16 Aug. 1949. 3p. + 1p. sketches, 34x27cm.

A. Mus. ms.: [Sketch of four chords, some text]. 1p., 34x27cm.

A. Mus. ms. S.: *Tempo I*, to Olga Coelho. 2p., 27x16cm.

A. Mus. ms. S.: [Untitled composition for guitar]. 4p., 32x21cm.

A. Mus. ms.: [Chaconne for guitar solo]. 3p., 35x27cm., ink

A. L. S.: to Boaz Piller. Detroit, 26 Feb. 1929. 1p., French

A. L. S.: to Frank La Forge. Rochester, 18 Mar. 1947. 3p., French

Tlgm. Annot.: 8 Mar. 1956

2 T.L.: from Joaquin Rodrigo. 12 July, 13 Aug. 1956. 2p., Spanish (Box 129)

2 T. L. Annot.: one to Segovia, the other written on his behalf. 14, 21 Aug. 1956. 2p., French. Regarding concerts in Paris

T. Doc. Annot.: "La guitarra y yo". First chapter of autobiography. 10p. (Box 128)

T. Doc.: List of classical guitars

Doc.: Booklet. Outlining Segovia's Italian tour Dec. 1955. 10p.

Doc.: Signatures and photographs. Segovia's 50th birthday party. 2p.

Doc.: File, ca. 1950s. Financial documents; visa applications; passport

Mus. ms. Repro.: *Estudio (invocación a Schumann)*, New York, 11 Apr. 1949. 3p.

Mus. ms. Repro.: *Oración*, New York, May 1949. 2p.

Mus. ms. Repro.: *Palomita*, arranged by Manuel Ponce. 2p., 32x24cm.

Pri. Sco.: *Canciones mexicanas*, by Manuel Ponce, Leipzig: Breitkopf, 1917, to Segovia, from Ponce. 4p.

2 Prog.: 7 Mar. 1948 (Box 128)

Prog. Annot.: 17 Oct. 1955

3 Prog.: Sept. 1956 (Box 128)

Prog.: Sunday, 20 Nov. Brighton Philharmonic Society

2 Port. Phot. S.: to Olga Coelho, New York, Dec. 1943 (Box 115)

Port. Phot.: Segovia's hands (Box 115)

3 Port. Gr. (Box 115)

9 Port. Phot. (Box 115)

12 Phot.: (Box 129)

17 Phot.: (Box 130)

Port. Phot. Repro.: presentation to Segovia (Box 115)

Twelve-carat gold guitar strings

See Castelnuovo-Tedesco, Mario

See Coelho, Olga Praguer

See Rodrigo, Joaquín

Sehlbach, Erich, b. 1898
Northwestern University

Mus. ms.: *Baal*, scene 4. With accompanying libretto

Mus. ms.: *Concertino*, 1940. Full score

Mus. ms.: *Konzertante Partita*, op. 55, 8 Oct. 1946

Mus. ms.: *Orchester-Fantasie I in D*, 1938. Full score

Mus. ms.: *Quartett*, op. 92, 2 Feb. 1917

Mus. ms.: *Vorspiel für Orchester*, 1935. Full score

Mus. ms.: *Zum neuen Jahre Glück und Heil...*

17 L.: to Hans Moldenhauer. Essen-Werden, 1958–1961

L.: from Sehlbach's wife. Essen-Werden, 11 Mar. 1960

Doc.: Pamphlet

Seiber, Mátyás, 1905–1960
Washington State University
See Rosbaud, Hans

Seiffert, Henri
Library of Congress
(Box 50)

A. Mus. ms. S.: *Prière, (on G. B. S.)*, to G.B.S. [George Bernard Shaw], Sweden, Jan. 1911. 3p., 33x25cm. Full score

Sekles, Bernhard, 1872–1934
Washington State University
See Rosbaud, Hans

Selden-Goth, Gisela, 1884–1975
Harvard University
SUMMARY OF PRINCIPAL HOLDINGS:

Mus. ms.: *Praeludium und Fuge*

Mus. ms.: *Streichtrio No. 2*. Excerpt

Sembrich, Marcella [Kochańska, Prakseda
Marcelina], 1858–1935
Harvard University
L.: Dresden, 1880

Sendrey, Albert Richard, b. 1911
Harvard University
Mus. ms.: *Essay for Woodwinds*

Senff, Bartolf Wilhelm, 1815–1900
Library of Congress
(Box 50)
A. Alb. l. S.: Leipzig, 15 Oct. 1851. 1p., German. Poem

Serkin, Rudolf, 1903–1991
Harvard University
L.: to Hans Moldenhauer. Marlboro, 5 Sept. 1968
L.: to Hans Rosbaud. Zurich, n.d.

Library of Congress
(Box 50)
4 A. L. S.: to Alfred Mann. Vermont, 1986–1989. 4p.,
    German
T. L. S.: to Alfred Mann. Vermont, 5 Apr. 1988. 1p.,
    German

Serly, Tibor, 1901–1978
Harvard University
SUMMARY OF PRINCIPAL HOLDINGS:
Mus. ms.: *Music for Four Harps and String Orchestra*,
    1976–1977
Mus. ms.: *The Pleiades*, 1975
4 L.: to Nicolas Slonimsky. Longview, 1974–1975
10 L.: to Hans Moldenhauer. Longview, 1977–1978
Port. Gr.: with Bartók, 1942. On verso, description by
    Serly
Port. Gr.: with Kodály, Mrs. Kodály, and Mrs. Ivan
    Engel, 1961

Serocki, Kazimierz, 1922–1981
Library of Congress
(Box 50)
Mus. ms. Repro. S.: *A piacere, propositions for piano*. 4p.
    Facsimile. With autograph page of instructions

Servais, Adrien François, 1807–1866
Library of Congress
(Box 50, unless noted)
A. L. S.: to Matis. Gotha, 23 Feb. 1854. 1p., French
Doc.: Biographical sketch
Port. Phot. S. Repro. (Box 115)

Sessions, Roger, 1896–1985
Harvard University
SUMMARY OF PRINCIPAL HOLDINGS:
L.: to Paul Sanders. Berlin, n.d.

Washington State University
See Rosbaud, Hans

Séverac, Déodat de, 1872–1921
Library of Congress
(Box 50, unless noted)
6 A. L. S.: to Lucy Vauthrin. Béziers, Pyrenees,
    Toulouse, 1912–1914. 7p., French
Tlgm.: to Lucy Vauthrin. Paris, 15 May 1913. French
P. card S.: to Lucy Vauthrin. Pyrenees, 25 Aug. 1913.
    French
Clip.: with portrait photograph reproduced. French
    (Box 115)
Port. Phot. S.: by Delon (Box 115)

Severn, Edmund, 1862–1942
Library of Congress
(Box 50)
A. Mus. ms. S.: [*String Quartet in A-flat*, Andante]. 12p.
    (parts), 34x27cm.

Sevitzky [Koussevitzky], Fabien, 1891–1967
Harvard University
2 L.: to Charles Haubiel. Indianapolis, 26 Dec. 1944,
    30 Apr. 1947

Seyfried, Ignaz von, Ritter, 1776–1841
Library of Congress
(Box 50)
A. L. S.: to publisher Peters. Vienna, 9 May 1821. 1p.,
    German, with typed translation and biographical
    information, in English

Sgambati, Giovanni, 1841–1914
Library of Congress
(Box 50)
A. L. S.: Rome, 10 Nov. 1884. 4p., Italian. Mentions
Liszt

Shaporin, Yuri, 1887–1966
Library of Congress
(Box 115)
Port. Phot. S.: to Boaz Piller, 1937. With musical
quotation

Shepherd, Arthur, 1880–1958
Harvard University
L.: to Adolph Weiss

Shield, William, 1748–1829
Northwestern University
L.: to Charles Hatchett. London, ? Nov. 1828

Short, Greg, b. 1938
Whitworth College
SUMMARY OF PRINCIPAL HOLDINGS:
Mus. ms.: "A Cradle Hymn," for double mixed chorus,
soloists, and organ, 1965. Full score
Mus. ms.: "The Pilgrim," song cycle for soprano,
piano, and percussion, 1972
Mus. ms.: Third Piano Sonata, to Francis Puttman,
1972. Pencil draft
Mus. ms.: "Welcome Carol," 1970. Sketches, with
additional sketches
Mus. ms.: Woodwind Quintet, 1972, rev. 1981. Pencil
sketches

Shostakovich, Dmitri, 1906–1975
Library of Congress
(Box 50, unless noted)
A. Mus. Quot. S.: to Boaz Piller, Boston, 14 Nov. 1959.
Russian

Pri. Sco. S.: *Sonate pour piano*, op. 12, Moscow: State
Music Publishers, 1927, to Fritz Stiedry, Leningrad,
23 Nov. 1927. 21p. First edition
Pri. Sco. S.: *Trio for Piano, Violin, and Violoncello*, op. 67,
printed in Russia, 1945, to Fritz Stiedry, Moscow,
18 Feb. 1946. Piano (62p.) + violin (19p.) + cello
(19p.). Also signed by Stiedry, New York City
Pri. Sco. S.: [*Twenty-four Preludes*], op. 34, Moscow:
State Publishing House of the Soviet Union, 1935,
to Fritz Stiedry, Leningrad, 4 June 1936. 43p.,
Russian
Port. Phot.: Youthful photo, mounted with note,
signed (Box 115)
S. rec.: *Aus jüdischer Volkspoesie*, op. 79

Steinberg, Maximilian Oseyevich, 1883–1946
Library of Congress
(Box 51)
A. L. S.: to Boaz Piller. Leningrad, 23 June 1929. 1p.,
English

Sibelius, Jean [Johan], 1865–1957
Library of Congress
(Box 50, unless noted)
A. Mus. ms. S.: *Affettuoso*, for piano, op. 76, [No. 7].
3p., 36x27cm., ink
A. L. S.: to an author. Järvenpää, 26 Dec. 1915. 1p.,
German
Port. Draw. Repro.: by Lupas (Box 115)
Port. Phot. S. Repro. (Box 115)

Siebold, Agathe Schütte von, 1835–1909
Library of Congress
(Box 50)
A. Card S.: to Joachim (son of Joseph Joachim).
Göttingen, 6 Aug. 1907. 2p., German

Siegmeister, Elie, 1909–1991
Harvard University
SUMMARY OF PRINCIPAL HOLDINGS:
32 L.: to Nicolas Slonimsky. Great Neck, New York,
1968–1979

T. Doc.: List. Songs by Siegmeister, with timings and annotations

Silas, Edouard, 1827–1909
Northwestern University
L.: London, 21 May 1885

Silbermann, Alphons, b. 1909
Washington State University
See Rosbaud, Hans

Silcher, Friedrich, 1789–1860
Library of Congress
(Box 50)
2 A. Mus. mss.: *Heimlicher Liebe Pein*. 2p., 17x21cm., German. On verso, *Schnaderhüpfeln*, with verification of manuscript by Carl Lachenmann, Silcher-Museum, Schnait, 22 Nov. 1971, 19 Jan. 1972
A. L. S.: Tübingen, 29 Apr. 1852. 3p., German
T. L.: to Hans Moldenhauer, from Walther Gephardt. Tübingen, 24 Nov. 1971. 1p., German
Clip.: Biographical sketch. 1p., English

Siloti, Alexander, 1863–1945
Library of Congress
(Box 50, unless noted)
A. Mus. ms. S.: *Adagio* from the *Sonata for Piano and Violin in F Minor* by Bach, transcribed by Siloti for piano solo. 4p., 34x27cm.
A. Mus. ms. S.: *Partita, in E Minor* by Bach. 14p. (full score) + 4p. (violin), 33x26cm.
A. Mus. ms. S.: *Sonia's Song*. 4p., 32x24cm. Transcribed for voice or piano solo from an old Russian folk song from the Ukraine
A. L. S.: New York, 23 Mar. 1922. 1p., French, with English translation
Obit.: 10 Dec. 1945. 1p., English
Port. Phot. S.: Boston, 7 Apr. 1922 (Box 115)
See Tchaikovsky, Pyotr Ilyich

Silva, Alfonso de, 1903–1937
Library of Congress
(Box 50)
A. Mus. ms. S.: *Preludio, para piano*, to Ricardo Viñes, Sept. 1928. 3p., 35x27cm.

Simmons, Homer, 1900–1971
Harvard University
2 L.: to Charles Haubiel. Sunland, California, 7, 15 Feb. 1961

Simonetti, Achille, 1857–1928
Northwestern University
L.: to Louis Lüstner. London, 16 Oct. 1896

Simons, Rainer, 1869–1934
Library of Congress
(Box 50)
A. L. S.: to Zemlinsky. Tegernsee, 9 July 190[8?]. 3p., German

Simrock, Peter Joseph, 1792–1868
Library of Congress
(Box 50)
A. L. S.: to Heinrich Cramer. Bonn, 16 June 1846. 2p., German

Sinigaglia, Leone, 1868–1944
Library of Congress
(Box 50)
P. card S.: to Achille Simonetti. Ceresole Reale, 3 Sept. 1903. Italian
2 A. L. S.: to Karl Weigl. Rome, 21 Apr. 1934; [Torino?], 12 Nov. 1934. 2p., German. Suggestions regarding compositions; Toscanini

Sittard, Alfred, 1878–1942
Library of Congress
(Box 50)
A. L. S.: to Tischer. Hamburg, 27 Feb. 1930. 1p., German

Sivori, Camillo, 1815–1894
Library of Congress
(Box 50, unless noted)
A. Mus. Quot. S.: Andante, Leeds, 30 Sept. 1855. With text (English) on verso
Port. Phot. (Box 115)

Sjögren, Emil, 1853–1918
Library of Congress
(Box 50)
A. Mus. Quot. S.

Skalkottas [Scalcotas], Nikolaos [Nikos, Nicos], 1904–1949
Library of Congress
(Box 50)
Mus. ms. Repro.: [*Kretikos*]. 3p.
Mus. ms. Repro. A. Rev.: *Second Little Suite*, for Solo
    Violin and Piano, c1953. 11p. Blueprint score
Mus. ms. Repro.: [*Sonatine*]. 4p.

Skapski, George Joseph, 1920–1996
Harvard University
2 L.: to Donivan Johnson. California, 1976, n.d.

Slevogt, Max, 1868–1932
Library of Congress
(Box 117)
P. card S.: to Bruno Eisner. Neukastel, 14 Oct. 1927.
    German. With ink drawing
A. Card S.: [to Bruno Eisner]. Neukastel, 1928.
    German. With drawing on verso
A. L. S.: to Bruno Eisner. Neukastel, 22 Oct. 1931. 2p.,
    German. With typescript of letter
A. L. S.: to Bruno Eisner. n.p., n.d. 1p., German. With
    ink drawing
See Mozart, Wolfgang Amadeus

Slonimsky, Nicolas, 1894–1995
Harvard University
SUMMARY OF PRINCIPAL HOLDINGS:
2 Mus. mss.: *Bitonal Arpeggios*; *Aufschwung/Abschwung*
2 Mus. mss.: *Bitonal Scales*; "Fragment from an
    unwritten piano concerto"
Mus. ms.: *Déjà vu*
Mus. ms.: *Dodekaphonische Träumerei*
Mus. ms.: *Fantasy in Black and White*
Mus. ms.: *Happy Birthday!*
Mus. ms.: *Minitudes*, including *Anabolism, Bach x
    2=Debussy, Bach in Fluid Tonality, A Bad Egg Polka,
    Blitzpartie, Borborygmus, Boustrophedon, Cabbage
    Waltz, Casanova in Casa Nueva, Catabolism, Déjà
    entendu, Dodecaphilia, Felinity, Oligophrenia,*
*Omphaloskepsis, Palindrome I-III, Quaquaversal
    Quarks, Quodlibet (La Putaine), 3 Blind Mice,
    Triskaidecaphobia*
Mus. ms.: *Multiple Scales*
Mus. ms.: *Orion*
Mus. ms.: *Pandiatonic and Panpentatonic Clusters*
Mus. ms.: *Pervicacious Dodecaphilia*
Mus. ms.: *Pièce enfantine*
Mus. ms.: *Polytetrachord*
Mus. ms.: *Studies in Black and White*
Mus. ms.: *Thesaurus of Scales and Melodic Patterns,
    Dodecaphonic Patterns*
Mus. ms.: [same], *Pandiatonic Cadences*
L.: to Adolph Weiss. n.p., 11 Dec. 1931
L.: to Solomon Pimsleur. Boston, 11 Dec. 1959
L.: to Charles Haubiel. New York, 7 Feb. 1970
L.: to Aurelio de la Vega. 28 July 1983
Doc.: Essay. "Sex and the Music Librarian"
Doc. Repro.: Guest book entry. Hindemith, Krenek,
    Prokofieff
Port. Phot.: 1978
3 S. recs.
See Gershwin, George
See Ives, Charles E.
See Rudhyar, Dane

Library of Congress
See Gershwin, George

Smart, Sir George, 1776–1867
Northwestern University
5 L.: to Charles Lockey
Doc.: Ticket. Royal Musical Festival
Port.

Smetana, Bedřich [Friedrich], 1824–1884
Library of Congress
(Box 50)
Mus. ms. S. Repro.: *IV Symfonická báseň*, [symphonic
    poems, No. 4, From Bohemia's Woods and Fields].
    5p. Photographic reproduction of excerpt
A. L. S.: [to the Association of Singers of the
    Typographers in Prague]. Gabjenice, 14 Feb. 1878.
    1p., Czechoslovakian

Smit, Leo, b. 1921
Harvard University
Mus. ms.: *Channel Firing*, 1970
2 L.: to Hans Moldenhauer. Buffalo, 7 Aug., 6 Dec. 1977

Smith, Carleton Sprague, 1905–1994
Harvard University
L.: to Aurelio de la Vega. New York, 16 Feb. 1959

Smith, Leland C., b. 1925
Harvard University
Summary of Principal Holdings:
Mus. ms.: *Intermezzo and Capriccio*
Mus. ms.: *Sonata for Heckelphone*, 1954
Mus. ms.: *Three Pacifist Songs*, No. 2

Smith, Robert Archibald, 1780–1829
Northwestern University
L.: to Purdie. 28 Feb. 1826

Smola, Emmerich, b. 1922
Washington State University
See Rosbaud, Hans

Smyth, Dame Ethel, 1858–1944
Northwestern University
L.: to Miss Graham. 1 Oct. 1920
L.: fragment
3 Clip.

Sollberger, Harvey, b. 1938
Harvard University
L.: to Gloria Coates. Cherry Valley, New York, n.d.

Somervell, Sir Arthur, 1863–1937
Northwestern University
L.: to Mrs. Eliot. London, 16 July 1912
L.: fragment

Sontag [Sonntag], Henriette, 1806–1854
Library of Congress
(Box 50)
A. L. S.: Frankfurt, 20 Mar. 1838. 4p., French

Sontheim, Heinrich, 1820–1912
Library of Congress
(Box 50)
A. Alb. l. S.: Stuttgart, 23 Oct. 1866. 1p., German

Souberbielle [Léon Souberbiele, éditeur?]
Library of Congress
(Box 51)
Mus. ms. cop. S.: *Jeux d'Enfants*, to Ricardo Viñes. 19p.

Sousa, John Philip, 1854–1932
Northwestern University
Mus. Quot.: [2m. melody], New York, 30 Jan. 1895
Mus. Quot.: [3m.], Portland, 1897. Mounted with portrait photograph of Sousa and Saint-Saëns at the San Francisco Exposition, 1915

Sowerby, Leo, 1895–1968
Harvard University
Mus. ms.: *And They Drew Nigh*. Complete score, drafts, proofs

Spagnoletti, Paolo, 1768–1834
Library of Congress
(Box 51)
A. L. S.: to Lord Burghersh. Brompton Square, 4 Aug. 1825. 1p., English

Spalding, Albert, 1888–1953
Harvard University
L.: to Rudolph Ganz. Murray Bay, 3 Aug.
L.: to Solomon Pimsleur. Great Barrington, Massachusetts, n.d.

Spark, William, 1823–1897
Northwestern University
L.: Leeds, 13 Feb. 1870
Doc.: Autobiographical information

Spazier, Johann Gottlieb Karl, 1761–1805
Library of Congress
(Box 51)
3 A. L. S.: 20 Feb. 1791, 4 Aug. 1802, 14 Aug. 1804.
  4p., German
T. Doc.: Biographical data. 2p., German

Spazierer, Michaelis
Library of Congress
(Box 51)
Mus. ms. cop.: *Missa da Requiem, à 4 vocibus.* 17p.,
  34x22cm. Full score. Marked "227, Director of
  Choir, St. Michael in Vienna"

Specht, Richard, 1870–1932
Wiener Stadt- u. Landesbibliothek
L.: [Vienna], 21 May 1907

Spena, Lita, 1904–1989
Library of Congress
(Box 51)
Mus. ms. cop.: *Suite para piano.* 18p.

Speyer [Speier], Wilhelm, 1790–1878
Library of Congress
See Spohr, Louis

Spies, Adolf, b. 1890
Library of Congress
(Box 51)
A. Mus. ms. S.: *Rosen,* Cologne, 28 Feb. 1920. 3p.,
  34x27cm. German

Spies, Hermine, 1857–1893
Library of Congress
(Box 51)
3 A. L. S.: to ?. Wiesbaden, 1 Jan. 1871, 18 Dec. 1883;
  n.p. n.d. 9p., German

Spindler, Fritz, 1817–1905
Library of Congress
(Box 51)

A. L. S.: to ?. [Niederlössnitz bei Dresden?], 8 June
  1885. 2p., German

Spinner, Leopold, 1906–1980
Library of Congress
(Box 51)
Mus. ms. Repro.: *Concerto for Piano and Orchestra,* op.
  4, 1947. 41p. Full score. Blueprint score
See Apostel, Hans Erich

Spitta, Julius August Philipp, 1841–1894
Library of Congress
(Box 51)
P. card S.: to Friedrich Chrysander. Berlin, 2 Aug.
  1893. German

Spivakovsky, Tossy, b. 1907
Harvard University
L.: to Ed Costello. Westport, Connecticut, 29 Apr.
  1963

Spohr, Louis [Ludewig, Ludwig], 1784–1859
Library of Congress
(Box 51)
A. L. S.: to Fr. Schmidt. Cassel, 27 Apr. 1826. 1p.,
  German
A. L. S.: to Johann Simon Hermstedt. Cassel, 17 June
  1836. 1p., German
Mus. ms. Repro.: *Vater unser von Klopstock.* 46p.,
  German. Signature of ownership by W. Speyer

Northwestern University
Mus. Alb. l.: Allegro, London, 22 July 1847
L.: to Ignaz Moscheles. Breslau, 8 July 1850
L.: to a conductor. Kassel, 7 Feb. 1855
2 Port.

Spontini, Gaspare, 1774–1851
Northwestern University
Mus. ms.: *Alcidor*. Excerpt, in full orchestral score
Mus. ms.: *Fernand Cortez*, 1817. Second version, reworking of the engraved first edition
L.: n.p., 17 Oct. 1814
L.: [to the Prussian Crown Prince?]. 18 Feb. 1838
L.: to Banck. Berlin, 12 Oct. 1840
L.: to Georges Bousquet. Berlin, 7 July 1841
L.: to Boieldieu. n.p., n.d.
L.: n.p., n.d.
Doc.: Copies of letters. To Spontini, from Frederic Guillaume (copied by Spontini)
2 Port.

Spring, Glenn Ernest, Jr., b. 1939
Washington State University
SUMMARY OF PRINCIPAL HOLDINGS:
Mus. ms.: *Missa Brevis*, 1968, 1972. With additional text
L.: to Hans Moldenhauer. College Place, Washington, 22 July 1977

Stadlen, Peter, 1910–1996
Library of Congress
(Box 51)
T. L. S.: [to Paul Sanders]. London, 5 July 1958. 1p., German
2 Docs. S.

Stadler, Albert, 1794–1888
Library of Congress
(Box 117)
A. Doc. S.: *Lieb Minna*, 27 [June?] 1815. 2p., German. Set to music by Schubert

Stahl, Hermann Wilhelm, 1872–1954
Library of Congress
(Box 51)
A. Mus. ms. S.: *A Piece for String Quartet*, [1943?]. 5p. (parts), 32x24cm.

Stainer, Sir John, 1840–1901
Northwestern University
Mus. ms.: *Amen (After Consecration Prayer and after the Blessing)*
3 L.: London, 23 Apr. 1873; Oxford, 6 Mar. 1892; n.p., 11 Feb.
L.: to William McNaught. Oxford, 19 Dec. 1893
Clip.
2 Port.

Stanford, Sir Charles Villiers, 1852–1924
Northwestern University
Mus. ms.: *Rondo*, 1869
Mus. ms.: *Symphony in B-flat Major*, Cambridge, 1876
L.: to Miss Stephenson. Malvern, 7 Sept. 1896
L.: Windsor, n.d.
Mus. Quot.: *Songs of the Fleet*
Clip.
Port. Phot.

Starck [Ingeborg?]
Library of Congress
See Grétry, André-Ernest-Modeste

Stavenhagen, Bernhard, 1862–1914
Library of Congress
(Box 51, unless noted)
A. L. S.: to Lindner. [Philadelphia?], 16 Feb. 1895. 4p., German
A. Mus. Quot. S.: *Heilige Elisabeth* by Liszt. Weimar, 31 May 1902
Clip.: with portrait engraving and biographical information (Box 115)

Stefan [Stefan-Grünfeldt], Paul, 1879–1943
Wiener Stadt- u. Landesbibliothek
2 L.: to Paul Pisk. Salzburg, 13 Aug. 1939; Vienna, n.d.

Steggall, Charles, 1826–1905
Northwestern University
L.: to the Bach Society. London, 13 June 1857
2 L.: to Mrs. Edwards. London, 3 Oct., 13 Nov. 1896

Stein, Erwin, 1885–1958
Wiener Stadt- u. Landesbibliothek
L.: to Adolph Weiss. Vienna, 11 Jan. 1932
L.: to Alma Mahler. Kensington, 10 Dec. 1957
Doc.: Excerpts and synopses. From Schoenberg
letters, for use in publication

Steinbach, Fritz, 1855–1916
Library of Congress
(Box 51)
P. card S.: to Carlos Droste. Meiningen, 9 Feb. 1901.
German

Steinberg, William [Wilhelm], 1899–1978
Harvard University
6 L.: to Charles Haubiel. 1939–1945
2 L.: to Bruno Eisner. New Rochelle, 20 Dec. 1943;
Pittsburgh, 12 Apr. 1958
L.: Pittsburgh, 17 Apr. 1962
L.: to Hans Moldenhauer. Pittsburgh, 6 Oct. 1962
L. Repro.: to Steinberg, from Haubiel
Port. Phot.: to Hans Moldenhauer

Stekel, Eric-Paul, b. 1898
Library of Congress
(Box 51)
A. L. S.: [to Alma Mahler]. Grenoble, 14 Jan. 1958.
2p., German

Stenz, Arthur
Library of Congress
(Box 51)
A. L. S.: to Miss A. Cumberland. Dresden, 18 Nov.
1884. 1p., German. On verso, listings of music in
another hand

Stephan, Rudi, 1887–1915
Library of Congress
(Box 51)
P. card S.: to Wilhelm Scheele. Munich, Theresicentr.
1381I. German
Pri. Sco. A. Rev.: *Lieder* [Ten songs]. 20p. First proofs
3 Clip.: Reports on the debut concert in Munich
which featured Stephan's opera 2, 3, and 4. German

Steuermann, Edward [Eduard], 1892–1964
Library of Congress
(Box 102, unless noted)
A. Mus. ms. S.: [*Drei Brecht Lieder*, No. III, "Gedanken
über die Dauer des Exils," for Voice and Piano,
1945], dated at end, 19 June ?. 4p., 34x17cm.
Complete score
A. L. S.: to Julius Schloss. New York, 17 Nov. 1949.
1p., German
P. card S.: to Hans Moldenhauer. New York, 30 Sept.
1964. 1p., German
T. Card: to the Moldenhauers. New York, 11 Nov.
1964. 1p. Death announcement
Prog.: Flyer. Announcing two Steuermann concerts,
with portrait photograph reproduced, 1964
2 Clip.: 4p.
Port. Phot.: 1964 (Box 115)
See Apostel, Hans Erich
See Schoenberg, Arnold

Stevens, Halsey, 1908–1989
Harvard University
SUMMARY OF PRINCIPAL HOLDINGS:
Mus. ms.: *Sonata for Trumpet and Piano*, 1953–1956

Stevens, Richard John Samuel, 1757–1837
Northwestern University
L.: to William Horsley. Charterhouse, 22 Dec. 1835

Stevenson, Robert M., b. 1916
Harvard University
SUMMARY OF PRINCIPAL HOLDINGS:
3 L.: to Aurelio de la Vega. Lisbon, 16 Feb. 1966; Los
Angeles, 10 Sept. 1984, 11 July 1985

Stiedry, Fritz, 1883–1968
Library of Congress
(Box 102)
A. L. S.: to Bruno Eisner. New York, 30 Mar. 1945. 2p.,
German

A. L. S.: to Alma Mahler. Zurich, Easter Monday 1959.
6p., German. Comments on his three-act opera;
Wozzeck

A. L. S.: to Alma Mahler. Zurich, 25 June 1959. 2p.,
German. Lists three corrections in musical notation;
Klemperer; *Wozzeck*

See Berg, Alban

See Shostakovich, Dmitry

Still, William Grant, 1895–1978
Harvard University
SUMMARY OF PRINCIPAL HOLDINGS:
Mus. ms.: *Wood Notes.* Sketch of the original themes
for *Singing River* and *Whippoorwill's Shoes*
Mus. ms.: [Unidentified sketch, with typewritten
note]

Stock, Frederick [Friedrich August], 1872–1942
Harvard University
2 L.: to Charles Haubiel. Chicago, 4 Apr., 15 Sept.
1935. With copy of Haubiel's replies
L.: to Rudolph Ganz. Chicago, 15 Sept. 1935
L.: to Haubiel, from Stock's secretary

Stockhausen, Julius, 1826–1906
Library of Congress
(Box 51)
A. L. S.: to Sir George Grove. Frankfurt, 27 June 1884.
4p., English

Stockhausen, Karlheinz, b. 1928
Library of Congress
(Box 51)
A. Mus. ms.: *Klavierstücke VIII*, 1954. 3p., 33x25cm. +
26x26cm., pencil. Complete draft and sketches
T. L. S.: to Hans Moldenhauer. Locust Valley, New
York, 5 Feb. 1963. 2p., English
T. Doc.: Lecture notes. For Stockhausen lecture at
Washington State University, 3 Dec. 1958. With
typed biographical notes and introduction by Hans
Moldenhauer. 3p., English
3 Docs. S.: Brochures. 1958

Doc. S.: Brochure, from *Die Reihe*. 1958. 9p., English
Mus. ms. Repro.: *Sonatine für Klavier und Violine*, 1950.
11p.
3 Clip.: 23 Nov., 6 Dec. 1958, n.d. English

Washington State University
L.: to Heinrich Strobel. Koeln, 20 Dec. 1957
See Rosbaud, Hans

Stojowski, Sigismund [Zygmunt], 1870–1946
Harvard University
L.: to Solomon Pimsleur. New York, 17 May 1938

Northwestern University
Mus. ms.: *Concerto for Piano and Orchestra*, op. 3, 1890.
With two additional printed scores

Stokowski, Leopold, 1882–1977
Harvard University
3 L.: to Adolph Weiss. Philadelphia, 1931; New York,
1938
L.: to Charles Haubiel. Hollywood, 10 Sept. 1945
2 L.: to Nicolas Slonimsky. New York, 20, 27 Jan. 1965
See Farberman, Harold

Stoltz, Rosine [Noël, Victoire], 1815–1903
Library of Congress
(Box 52)
A. L. S.: to ?. n.p., 22 Sept. 1860[?]. 2p., French

Stout, Alan B., b. 1932
Harvard University
Mus. ms.: *Christmas Poem*, op. 67
Mus. ms.: op. 29, No. 1
Mus. ms.: op. 68
L.: to Hans Moldenhauer

Stout, Kemble, b. 1916
Washington State University
Mus. ms.: *Andante for Orchestra*

Strässer, Ewald, 1867–1933
Northwestern University
Mus. ms.: *Quintett*, op. 18. With accompanying
performance list

Mus. ms.: *Sinfonie für grosses Orchester*, op. 22. Full score, first three movements only. With accompanying analysis by the composer
L.: to Gutmann. Cológne, 9 Sept. 1910. With score corrections

Strang, Gerald, 1908–1983
Harvard University
Mus. ms.: *Variations for Four Instruments*
L.: to Adolph Weiss. Los Angeles, 27 Mar. 1937
L.: to Aurelio de la Vega. Murray Hill, New Jersey, 16 July 1963
L.: to Hans Moldenhauer

Straube, Karl, 1873–1950
Library of Congress
(Box 52)
3 A. L. S.: to Karl Weigl. Bad Gastein, 4 Mar., 27 June 1926; Leipzig, 20 Sept. 1928. 5p., German
P. card: to Karl Weigl, from Straube's wife. Leipzig, 17 Mar. 1934. German

Straus, Oscar, 1870–1954
Wiener Stadt- u. Landesbibliothek
L.: to Emil Steinbach. 29 June 1898

Strauss, Eduard, 1835–1916
Wiener Stadt- u. Landesbibliothek
L.: Vienna, 17 May 1883
L.: Mannheim, 24 Aug. 1889
Prog.: Leipzig, 10 Apr. 1880

Strauss, Johann, 1804–1849
Wiener Stadt- u. Landesbibliothek
L.: to an impressario. [Vienna, Oct. ?]
L.: to Maurice Schlesinger. Vienna, 20 Apr. 1839
Port.

Strauss, Johann, 1825–1899
Wiener Stadt- u. Landesbibliothek
L.: to Hanna Weiss. Vienna, 5 Apr. 1898. On verso, engraved portrait
L.: n.p., n.d.
Port.

Strauss, Richard, 1864–1949
Bayerische Staatsbibliothek
SUMMARY OF PRINCIPAL HOLDINGS:
Mus. ms.: *Einleitung und Walzer Rosenkavalier I und II*, Erste Walzerfolge, 18 Dec. 1945. 37p.
Mus. ms.: *Albumblatt für Pianoforte*, to Bertha Schüssel, 31 Mar. 1882
L.: to Otto Lessmann. Meiningen, 26 Feb. 1886
L.: to Vincent d'Indy. Munich, 25 Sept. 1897
L.: to Eugen Lindner. Charlottenburg, 28 Sept. 1901
L.: Marquartstein, 7 June 1904
L.: to Frau Raminger. Garmisch, 24 Nov. [1924]
L.: to Wymetal. Garmisch, 13 Sept. 1928
4 L.: to Paul Bekker. 1929
L.: to Karl Böhm. Garmisch, 27 Apr. 1945 (See document below, 28 May 1945)
L.: to Hans Rosbaud. Palace Hotel, 11 Feb. 1948
L.: to Gustave Samazeuilh. Garmisch, 3 June 1949
Doc.: Artistic Testament. "Memorandum über Wesen und Bedeutung der Oper und ihre Zukunft", Garmisch, 28 May 1945
Doc.: List of names. May 1945. Strauss suggests Hartmann, Höllreiser, Krauss, and Wetzelsberger as qualified in the reconstruction of musical life in Germany after the collapse. Includes letter from Alfred Mann, [1945]
Mus. Quot.: with portrait photograph
Mus. ms. Repro.: *Oboe Concerto*, 1945. Photostat
Port. Phot.: with musical quotation above

Harvard University
See Zemlinsky, Alexander

Library of Congress
See Bronsart von Schellendorf, Hans

Stravinsky, Igor, 1882–1971
Bayerische Staatsbibliothek
L.S.: Letter of testimony. Hollywood, Mar. 1958. English, German. Citing the importance of *Musica viva;* includes a note to K. A. Hartmann

Mus. Quot. Phot. S.: to K. A. Hartmann, Hollywood, Jan. 1952. Mounted with note in Hartmann's hand stating that the musical quotation (3 measures in score of 3 and 4 staves) is from Hartmann's Third Symphony (p. 76 of the printed score)

Library of Congress
(Box 52, unless noted)
Pri. Sco. Rev.: *Threni, id est lamentationes Jeremiae prophetae*, for Six Solo Voices, Chorus, and Orchestra. 70p. folio, 35x26cm. Undated printer's proofs (Boosey & Hawkes) incorporating corrections in the hand of Leopold Spinner from first proofs through final corrections for the second edition
A. L. S.: to Edward Clark. Paris, 17 May 1927. 2p., French
A. L. S.: to Boaz Piller. Los Angeles, 21 Dec. 1939. 1p., English
A. L. S.: to Edward Clark. n.p., n.d. 2p., French
L.: to Hans Moldenhauer, from Lillian Libman. New York, 25 Jan. 1962. 1p., English
Call. c. Annot.: to Hans Moldenhauer. Hollywood, 10 May 1961. English. With typed document by Stravinsky regarding *The Death of Anton Webern*
A. Mus. Quot. S.: [*The Firebird*], to Boaz Piller, Paris, 10 June 1922. 1p. On verso, musical quotation from *Fontane di Roma* by Respighi, to Piller, 20 June 1922
A. Mus. Quot. S.: "Nul, nul...," Boston, 15 Mar. 1935
A. Mus. Quot. S.: [*Pétrouchka*], London
Pri. Sco. S.: *Scherzo à la Russe*, New York: Associated Music Publishers, c1945. 34p.
Pri. Sco. S.: *Sonata for Two Pianos*, New York: Associated Music Publishers, c1945. 48p.
Prog.: 15–16 Mar. 1935. U.S. premieres of *Fireworks* and *Perséphone*, with the Cecilia Society Chorus and Arthur Fiedler
Doc.: Brochure from Broadcast Music, Inc.
Port. Draw. Gr. Repro. S.: Caricature of Stravinsky and Picasso, by Jean Cocteau, to Boaz Piller, Providence, 28 Nov. 1939. With musical quotations from *The Rite of Spring* and *The Barber of Seville* (Box 115)
Port. Phot. S.: to Boaz Piller, 15 Mar. 1935. Conducting the Los Angeles Philharmonic (Box 115)
Port. Phot. S.: to the Spokane Conservatory, 1955 (Box 115)
Port. Draw. Repro. S.: to Boaz Piller, Boston, Nov. 1939. Drawing by Picasso, 31 Dec. 1920 (Box 115)
Bk. S.: *Chroniques de ma vie*, Paris: Denoël et Steele, 1935, to Piller, Boston, 1939 (Shelf)

Bk. S.: *Poetics of Music*, Cambridge, Massachusetts: Harvard University Press, 1947 (Shelf)

Washington State University
Doc.: Affidavit. On behalf of Hans Rosbaud, Paris, Sept. 1936
Doc.: Instructions. Giving Rosbaud directives for conducting
Mus. ms. Repro.: *Movements for Piano and Orchestra*, 1958–1959
Port.: includes photograph of Stravinsky's hands
See Rosbaud, Hans

Strecker, Willy, 1884–1958
Washington State University
See Rosbaud, Hans

Streicher, Nanette, 1769–1833
Library of Congress
(Box 52)
A. L. S.: to ?. Vienna, 1 June 1823. 3p., German

Strickland [Anderson], Lily, 1887–1958
Harvard University
Mus. ms.: *To Arms, America!*

Strobel, Heinrich, 1898–1970
Washington State University
See Rosbaud, Hans

Stroe, Aurel, b. 1932
Library of Congress
(Box 52)
A. Card S.: to Aurelio de la Vega. 1969. 1p., English

Stuckenschmidt, Hans Heinz, 1901–1988
Library of Congress
(Box 52)
T. L. S.: to Adolph Weiss. Berlin, 3 Sept. 1930. 1p., German
T. L. S.: to Hans Moldenhauer. Berlin, 13 Apr. 1960. 1p., German. Regarding Karl Amadeus Hartmann

Washington State University
See Rosbaud, Hans

Such, Percy, 1878–1959
Harvard University
L.: to Solomon Pimsleur. New York, 20 Feb. 1936

Sucher [née Hasselbeck], Rosa, 1849–1927
Library of Congress
(Box 52)
2 A. L. S.: to Fustigrath. Hamburg, 2, 17 May 1887.
   6p., German

Suk, Josef, 1874–1935
Library of Congress
(Box 52)
P. card S.: to Mrs. Dvořák. Nice, 15 Mar. 1898. 1p.,
   German. With accompanying letter to Hans
   Moldenhauer, from Josef Suk (grandson), 20 Mar.
   1975
A. Alb. l. S.: also signed by members of the Bohemian
   String Quartet. St. Gallen, 29 Oct. 1920

Sulzer, Salomon, 1804–1890
Wiener Stadt- u. Landesbibliothek
L.: Vienna, [8?] Mar. 1866
Port. Engr.

Suppé, Franz, 1819–1895
Library of Congress
(Box 52)
A. L. S.: to André. n.p., 11 Mar. 1882. 2p., German.
   Regarding unauthorized arrangements of his works

Wiener Stadt- u. Landesbibliothek
L.: n.p., 27 Dec. 1869

Surinach, Carlos, 1915–1997
Harvard University
Mus. ms. Repro.: *Sinfonietta flamenca.* Facsimile

Suter, Hermann, 1870–1926
Zentralbibliothek Zürich
L.: to Neuburger. Basel, 12 July 1913

Sutermeister, Heinrich, 1910–1995
Washington State University
See Rosbaud, Hans

Zentralbibliothek Zürich
Mus. ms.: *Concerto for Cello and Orchestra*
Mus. ms.: *Second Concerto for Piano and Orchestra*
11 L.: to Hans Moldenhauer. Vaux-sur-Morges,
   1958–1963

Sutro, Ottilie, 1872–1970
Harvard University
L.: to Charles Haubiel. Baltimore, 25 Aug. 1959

Svendsen, Johan, 1840–1911
Northwestern University
Mus. Quot.: *Og Vaar og Sommerskal kom*, Copenhagen,
   Mar. 1893
Mus. Quot.: [Melodic line], 9 Oct. 1898
2 Port. Phot.

Swarowsky, Hans, 1899–1975
Library of Congress
(Box 52)
A. L. S.: [to Klara Kwartin]. Vienna, 15 Nov. 1924. 2p.,
   German. Relates news of musical life in Vienna;
   Webern

Swert, Jules de, 1843–1891
Library of Congress
(Box 14, unless noted)
A. L. S.: to E. Spegl. Vienna, 5 Oct. 1878. 2p.,
   German. With attached clipping regarding *Die
   Albigenser*
Port. Phot. S. Repro. (Box 110)

Swift, Richard, b. 1927
Harvard University
Mus. ms.: *Concerto*, op. 26, 1961
Mus. ms.: *Concerto for Violin and Chamber Orchestra*, 1968
Mus. ms.: *Extravaganza*, op. 28, 1962
Mus. ms.: *Stravaganza IV*, op. 25, 1961
Mus. ms.: *Summer Notes*, 1965
5 L.: Davis, 1966
L.: to Hans Moldenhauer. Davis, California, 4 Aug. 1982

Swoboda, Henry, 1897–1990
Harvard University
2 L.: to Aurelio de la Vega. Stockholm, 28 Mar. 1957; Copenhagen, 2 June 1957

Szell, George [Georg], 1897–1970
Harvard University
Port. Phot.: New York, Feb. 1945

Szigeti, Joseph, 1892–1973
Library of Congress
(Box 52)
A. L. S.: to Rudolph Ganz. Palos Verdes, 29 Jan. 1958. 1p., English

Washington State University
See Rosbaud, Hans

Szymanowski, Karol, 1882–1937
Library of Congress
(Box 52, unless noted)
A. L. S.: to Stein. Warsaw, n.d. 3p., German. Regarding score changes
3 Clip.: 3p., German. With biographical information (Box 115)
2 Port. Phot. Repro. (Box 115)

Tacuchian, Ricardo, b. 1939
Harvard University
Mus. ms.: *Cárceres*, 1979
Mus. ms.: *Mitos*, 1971

Tada Paz, Herberto di, b. 1903
Harvard University
Mus. ms.: *Sonatina en forma libre*, Buenos Aires, 27 Nov. 1924

Täglichsbeck, Thomas, 1799–1867
Library of Congress
(Box 52)
A. L. S.: [to Hubert Lind?]. Löwenburg, 20 Jan. 1857. 2p., German

Tailleferre, Germaine, 1892–1983
Library of Congress
(Box 52)
A. Mus. ms. Rev. S.: *Concerto pour piano et 12 instruments*, to Princess Édmond de Polignac, for Alfred Cortot, 26 Jan. 1924. 77p., 24x32cm., inks, pencil, crayon. Full score
A. Mus. ms. Rev. S.: *Hommage à Debussy*, 2 Oct. 1920. 3p., 31x24cm., ink, pencil
A. L. S.: [to Alfred Cortot]. n.p., n.d. Lundi, n.d. 2p., French

Tamburini, Antonio, 1800–1876
Library of Congress
See Grisi, Giulia

Tamkin, David, 1906–1975
Harvard University
SUMMARY OF PRINCIPAL HOLDINGS:
Mus. ms.: *The Blue Plum Tree*. With copy of libretto, signed by A. Tamkin, to the Moldenhauers, 1977
Mus. ms.: *The Dybbuk*
Mus. ms.: *The Hebraic Sketches*, op. 4
2 L.: to Hans Moldenhauer. Los Angeles, 8 Nov., 13 Dec. 1974

4 Draw.: by Tamkin. Characters in *The Dybbuk*
2 Port. Phot.: 1951, 1974

Library of Congress
See Achron, Joseph

Taneyev, Sergei, 1856–1915
Library of Congress
(Box 52)
A. L. S.: to Schaeffer. Moscow, 13 Oct. 1901. 1p.,
   German

Tansman, Alexandre [Aleksander], 1897–1986
Library of Congress
(Box 53, unless noted)
A. Mus. ms. S.: *Musica a Cinque*, Paris, Sept.–Nov.
   1956. 12p., 35x27cm., ink. Complete sketches
A. Mus. Quot. S.: *Musica a Cinque*, 1955. 1p.
Port. Phot. S.: to Boaz Piller, Jan. 1928. By Eschig
   (Box 115)
Port. Phot. S.: to the Spokane Conservatory, Paris, Jan.
   1956 (Box 115)

Tăranu, Cornel, b. 1934
Library of Congress
(Box 53)
Mus. ms. A. Rev.: *Dialogues II*, 1966–1967. 20p.
Pri. Sco.: *Piano Concerto*, Cluj: Conservatorul de
   Muzica, c1972. 37p.

Taubert, Wilhelm, 1811–1891
Library of Congress
(Box 53)
A. Mus. ms. S.: *Gruss*, Berlin, 4 Apr. 1847. 1p.,
   29x33cm. Mounted on verso, three letters to
   Ludwig Rellstab, signed by Elise Polko, Robert
   Prütz, and Johanna Schopenhauer

A. L. S.: to Vivenot. Berlin, 2 [June?] 1846. 3p.,
   German
A. L. S.: Berlin, 9 June 1856. 2p., German
A. L. S.: ?, 4 Feb. 1858. 1p., German
A. L. S.: 17 Nov. 1875. 1p., German
2 Pri. Sco. S.: *12 Lieder*, op. 17, Berlin: Schlesinger, n.d.,
   to Sophie Jacobson, Berlin, Feb. 1843. 10p. each

Tausig, Carl [Karol], 1841–1871
Library of Congress
(Box 53)
A. L. S.: to Spiegl. Vienna, 13 Apr. 1864. 3p., German
L.: to Spiegl, from Tausig's wife. n.p., n.d. 3p., German

Taylor, Fred, b. 1954
Whitworth College
Mus. ms.: *Flutterby's Waltz*, for jazz instruments, 1976.
   With recording

Tchaikovsky, Pyotr Ilyich, 1840–1893
Library of Congress
(Box 53, unless noted)
A. L. S.: [to publisher Pavel Jurgenson]. Kamenka,
   Ukraine, 13 May (O.S.) 1880. 1p., Russian Mounted
   with portrait photograph below
A. L. S.: [to Felix Mackar]. Klin, 13/25 Feb. 1889. 4p.,
   French
A. L. S.: to Mania [Hermann Laroche]. 21 July [1890].
   4p., Russian. With letter of authentication by
   William Lichtenwanger, Library of Congress
   (18 May 1971)
Doc. S.: [The Cossmann Testimonial]. Moscow,
   [between 1868–1874]. 3p., German. Also signed by
   Nikolai Rubinstein, Ferdinand Laub, Nikolai
   Kashkin, Hermann Laroche, Eduard Langer,
   Alexander Ivanovich Dubuque, Vladimir Kashperov,
   Alex. S. Rasmadse, Johann Hřimalý, Karl
   Klindworth. Presented to Bernhard Cossmann on
   his retirement from the Moscow Conservatory,
   recalls his teaching skills
A. Mus. Quot. S.: *Tscharodeika*, to L. A. Vizentini, St.
   Petersburg, 23 Oct. 1887. 7m. in piano score,
   beginning of the Overture

Port. Gr.: with Siloti. Signed by Siloti (mounted with letter above, and note, Boston, 17 Feb. 1898) (Box 115)

Tcherepnin, Alexander, 1899–1977
Library of Congress
(Box 53, unless noted)
A. Mus. ms.: [*Elegie*], for violin and piano. 5p. (full score) + 2p. (parts), 33x27cm., ink. Fair copy
A. Mus. ms. S.: *La Quatrième*, for piano solo, 5–6 Feb. 1949, to Hans Moldenhauer, 28 Sept. 1955. 4p., 34x28cm., pencil. Fair copy
2 A. L. S.: to Hans Moldenhauer. San Francisco, 29 Aug. 1955; Chicago, 28 Sept. 1955. 5p., English. Details life, compositional process
T. L. S.: to Hans Moldenhauer. Chicago, 2 Nov. 1955. 1p., English
Pri. Sco. S.: *Sonate en Fa Majeur pour violon et piano*, Paris: Durand, n.d., to Emanuel Zeltin, 14 Sept. 1926. 25p. (piano-violin score)
Pri. Sco. S.: *Symphonie en Mi pour Orchestre*, op. 42, Paris: Durand, c1929, to Rudolph Ganz, Chicago, 17 Sept. 1948. 80p.
3 Docs.: Brochures
Port. Phot. S.: to Hans Moldenhauer, Chicago, 28 Sept. 1955. By Harcourt (Box 115)

Washington State University
See Rosbaud, Hans

Telemann, Georg Philipp, 1681–1767
Library of Congress
(Box 53)
A. Mus. ms. S.: *Drama per musica composta di Melante*, 1711. 1 leaf (30m.), 29x20cm., ink. Draft of the beginning of the Overture, in four parts. Includes authentication of the manuscript by Aloys Fuchs and explanation of Telemann's use of the pseudonym "Melante"

Temianka, Henri, 1906–1992
Harvard University
L.: to Rudolph Ganz. Los Angeles, 26 Dec. 1952
L.: to Charles Haubiel. Los Angeles, 27 Jan. 1966

Terényi, Ede, b. 1935
Library of Congress
(Box 53)
Pri. Sco.: *Compoziție Pentru Orgă*, Cluj: Conservatorul de Musică, 1971. 26p.

Ternina [Trnina], Milka, 1863–1941
Library of Congress
(Box 53)
A. L. S.: to Mary E. L. Joline. New York, 17 Nov. 1901. 2p., English

Terrasse, Claude, 1867–1923
Library of Congress
(Box 53)
A. Mus. ms. S.: *Pantagruel*, "Bacchanale." 1p. (13m.). Fragment
A. L. S.: Paris, 14 [Dec.?] 1910. 1p., French
A. L. S.: Paris, 12 Oct. 1913. 1p., French
Doc.: Biographical sketch

Terry, Charles Sanford, 1864–1936
Northwestern University
L.: to Ernest Newman. Newport Pagnell, Buckinghamshire, n.d.
Bk. Annot.: *The Origin of the Family of Bach Musicians*

Terziari Canzonetta, ca. 1768
Library of Congress
(Box 53)
A. Mus. ms. S.: *Gratias, et Domine, a due soprani*. 5p. (score, 23x30cm.) + 5p. (parts, 24–25x19cm.)

Tetrazzini, Luisa, 1871–1940
Library of Congress
(Box 53)
A. L. S.: to Ethel Blackburn and Constance Golle. London, 17 June 1908. 1p., French

Thalberg, Sigismond, 1812–1871
Library of Congress
(Box 53)
A. Mus. ms. S.: *Souvenir de Pesth, Airs hongrois variés*,
  for piano solo, to Vincent Almasy, Paris, 1846. 6p.,
  35x27cm., ink
2 A. L. S.: to Rudolph de Vivenot. n.p., n.d.; Berlin,
  29 Jan. 1839. 3p., German
A. L. S.: Paris, 6 Apr. 1843. 1p., German
A. L. S.: to Dessauer. Ischia, 27 Sept. 1843. 3p.,
  French. With postscript by Mme. Thalberg
A. L. S.: to Willert. Naples, 17 Dec. 1866. 2p., English
A. L. S.: to Dessauer. n.p., n.d. 3p., German. Includes
  a self-caricature
A. L. S.: n.p., 29 May. 1p., German
A. Mus. Quot. S.: Allegretto, Karlsruhe, 16 Aug. 1839
A. Mus. Quot. S.: Andante in G Minor, London,
  15 July 1847
A. Mus. Quot. S.: Lento, Milan, 24 Nov. 1841
A. Mus. Quot. S.: Presto, Edinburgh, 22 Jan. 1838. On
  verso, album leaf musical quotation signed, by
  Theodor Döhler, 8 May 1840
Port. Caric.: see letter above

Thibaud, Jacques, 1880–1953
Library of Congress
(Box 54, unless noted)
A. Mus. ms. S.: *Minute Caprice* by Rodé, arranged by
  Thibaud, to Mischa Elman, New York, 26 Apr. 1920.
  4p., 35x27cm.
A. L. S.: to Carl Flesch. Paris, 28 Dec. 1907. 4p.,
  French
A. Doc. S.: Address list. 2p.
Port. Phot. S.: to Boaz Piller. Boston, Feb. 1921. By
  Stein (Box 115)

[signature]

Thomas, Ambroise, 1811–1896
Library of Congress
(Box 54, unless noted)
A. Mus. ms. S.: Ricercare, No. 3. 2p., 35x27cm.
  Excerpt in piano score
A. L. S.: Paris, 20 July 1857. 2p., French
A. L. S.: to ?. 8 July 1866. 1p., French
L. S.: Paris, 14 June 1890. 1p., French

Port. Caric. (Box 115)
Port. Engr. S. Repro. (Box 115)
Port. Lith.: with biographical sketch. Mounted with
  autograph letter signed, Paris, 1877. 1p., French
  (Box 115)
2 Port. Phot. Repro.: with clipping (Box 115)

Thomas, Arthur Goring, 1850–1892
Northwestern University
L.: London, n.d.

Thomas, John [Pencerdd, Gwalia], 1826–1913
Northwestern University
L.: to Mrs. Darby Griffith. [London?], 3 Apr. 1879
L.: to Mrs. Eliot. [London?], 2 July 1892

Thomas, Theodore, 1835–1905
Harvard University
Port. Phot.: Boston, 1 Mar. 1876

**Thomé, Francis [François Luc Joseph],
1850–1909**
Library of Congress
(Box 54)
A. L. S.: Paris, 16 Jan. 1890. 1p., English
A. L. S.: n.p., n.d. 2p., French

[signature]

Thompson, Dorothy, 1894–1961
Library of Congress
(Box 117)
2 T. L. S.: to Alma Mahler. Vermont, 25 Aug. 1958,
  9 Feb. 1959. 5p., English
A. L. S.: to Alma Mahler. Vermont, 16 Sept. 1958. 2p.,
  English

Thompson, Randall, 1899–1984
Harvard University
Mus. Quot.: *Symphony No. II*
Port. Phot.: Boston, 7 Apr. 1945

Thomson, Virgil, 1896–1989
Harvard University
Mus. ms.: *Portrait of Florine Stettheimer*
Mus. ms.: *Portrait of Nicolas de Chatelain*
L.: to Hans Moldenhauer

Thulean, Donald, b. 1929
Harvard University
L.: to Aurelio de la Vega. Washington, D.C., 29 May 1984

Tichatschek, Josef, 1807–1886
Library of Congress
(Box 54)
A. L. S.: to Pellet. Vienna, 24 Oct. 1837. 3p., German
A. L. S.: to a theater director. n.p., 22 Dec. 1838. 1p., German
A. L. S.: to the Chairman of the North German Music Festival. Dresden, 11 Apr. 1843. 1p., German
A. L. S.: to a court councillor. Hamburg, 23 Mar. 1846. 1p., German
A. Mus. Quot. S.: "Heil euch," from Wagner's *Rienzi*, Dresden, Aug. 1846

Tietjens, Therese, 1831–1887
Library of Congress
(Box 54)
A. L. S.: to Luigi. London, 20 May 1873. 1p., Italian
A. L. S.: to a physician. [London], n.d. 1p., German

Tinel, Edgar, 1854–1912
Library of Congress
(Box 54)
A. L. S.: Brussels, 22 Oct. 1909. 1p., French

Tischler, Hans, b. 1915
Harvard University
Doc.: Analyses. Mozart's piano concertos

Tobel, Rudolf von, b. 1903
Zentralbibliothek Zürich
Mus. ms. arr. Repro.: *El pessebre, Les rois majes* by Casals. Facsimile

L.: to Hans Moldenhauer. Trössingen, 18 Nov. 1956
Port. Gr.: Zermatt, 31 Aug. 1956. With Pablo Casals

Toch, Ernst, 1887–1964
Library of Congress
(Box 54, unless noted)
A. Mus. ms.: [*Fourth Symphony*]. 4p., 34x27cm., pencil. Sketches
A. Mus. ms. S.: *Tanz-Suite*, op. 30, 1923, 1924. 42p., 34x27cm., ink. The cover lists the date of composition as 1923, while the title page lists it as 1924
2 A. L. S.: to Otto Jokl. Mannheim, 27 June 1923; 12 July 1923. 2p., German
T. L. S.: to Otto Jokl. Mannheim, 20 July 1923. 1p., German
P. card S.: to Otto Jokl. Mannheim, 30 Oct. 1923. German
T. L. S.: to Otto Jokl. Berlin, 18 July 1930. 1p., German
P. card S.: to Paul Pisk. Pacific Palisades, 4 Nov. 1937. German
3 T. L. S.: to Aurelio de la Vega. Santa Monica, 24 Apr. 1947; 28 Nov. 1948; 15 Jan. 1963. 3p., English
A. L. S.: to Aurelio de la Vega. Santa Monica, 20 Oct. 1948. 1p., English
P. card S.: to Adolph Weiss. Cathedral City, California, 29 Mar. 1949. English
6 T. L. S.: to Hans Moldenhauer. Santa Monica, 1955–1960. 6p., English, German
P. card S.: to Aurelio de la Vega. Santa Monica, 31 Mar. 1962. English
2 A. Mus. Quot. S.: *First Piano Concerto*, op. 38. Quotations differ in time signature. See portrait photograph below
Mus. ms. Repro. A. Rev.: *Zweite Symphonie*, op. 73. 152p.
2 Docs.: Brochures. With portrait photograph, work list, and biographical information. English
Prog.: Vienna, 11 Jan. 1952
Clip.: "Toch to Record Chamber Works for CR." 1p., English
Pri. Sco. S.: *Burlesken für Klavier*, op. 31, Mainz: Schott, 1924, to Hans Moldenhauer, Los Angeles, 24 Oct. 1955. 16p. Also signed by Hans Moldenhauer

Pri. Sco. S.: *Der Jongleur*, Mainz: Schott, 1955

2 Pri. Sco. S.: *10 Concert Studies I, II*, Mainz: Schott, 1931

Pri. Sco. S.: *10 Easy Studies*, Mainz: Schott, 1931

2 Pri. Sco. S.: *10 Recital Studies I, II*, Mainz: Schott, 1931

Pri. Sco. S.: *10 Studies for Beginners*, Mainz: Schott, 1931

2 Pri. Sco. S.: *10 Studies of Medium Difficulty I, II*, Mainz: Schott, 1931

Port. Phot. S.: to Hans Moldenhauer, Nov. 1955. By Fayer (Box 115)

Port. Phot. S.: Boston, 25 Mar. 1932. With autograph musical quotation above (Box 115)

Washington State University
See Rosbaud, Hans

Tomaschek, Wenzel Johann, 1774–1850
Library of Congress
(Box 54)

A. L. S.: [to a publisher]. Prague, 31 Mar. 1842. 2p., German. Announcing a new song; views on artistic and human affairs

A. L. S.: to C. C. Kraukling. Dresden, 22 July 1846. 1p., German

A. L. S.: [to a composer in Frankfurt]. Prague, 12 Jan. 1848. 2p., German. Comments on his own artistic independence; musical conditions in Prague

Rcpt. S.: 29 Dec. 1849. German

Tomasi, Henri, 1901–1971
Library of Congress
(Box 115)
Port. Phot. S.: to Hans Moldenhauer

Washington State University
See Rosbaud, Hans

Tosar, Héctor, b. 1923
Harvard University
L.: to Aurelio de la Vega. San Juan, 8 Oct. 1974

[signature]

Toscanini, Arturo, 1867–1957
Library of Congress
(Box 55)
Sig.
See Huberman, Bronislaw

Tosti, Sir Paolo, 1846–1916
Library of Congress
(Box 55, unless noted)

A. Card S.: n.p., 28 Dec. 1885. 1p., Italian

A. L. S.: London, 11 May. 1p., Italian

A. L. S.: London, 19 June. 3p., French

A. L. S.: French. Fragment

A. Alb. l. S.: Villa d'Este, Sept. 1880

2 Pri. Sco. S.: *A Greyswood*; *La serenata*, to Mrs. Goodall, Sept. 1899. 5p., 15p.

Clip.: showing portrait. English (Box 115)

Tours, Berthold, 1838–1897
Library of Congress
(Box 55)
A. Mus. ms. S.: *A Passing Cloud*. 6p., 30x24cm., English
See Denza, Luigi

Tovey, Sir Donald, 1875–1940
Northwestern University
Mus. ms.: [Transcriptions of Austrian yodelling tunes], *Der Zeller-Staritzer*, *Der Stuhlecker Juchzer*, *Schladminger Dreidudler*. On verso, sketches, and "Pentatonic-Diatonic," an original rondel
Mus. Quot.

Traiger, Laurence
Harvard University
Mus. ms. Repro.: *Ein altes Blatt*. Photocopy
Mus. ms. Repro.: *Duets for Two Violins*, 1974, 1979. Blueprint score
Mus. ms. Repro.: *Five Yiddish Folk Songs*, 1979. Blueprint score
Mus. ms. Repro.: *String Quartet No. 2*, 1980. Photocopy
Mus. ms. Repro.: *Three Pieces*, 1977. Blueprint score

Mus. ms. Repro.: *Touches*, 1981. Blueprint score
Mus. ms. Repro.: *Tre Poesie di Giuseppe Ungaretti*, 1977. Blueprint score
L.: to Hans and Rosaleen Moldenhauer. Paris, 12 Sept. 1981

Travnicek, Josef, d. 1975
Library of Congress
(Box 55)
T. L. S.: [to Paul A. Pisk]. [Vienna], 29 Apr. 1973. 2p., German. Details the Arnold Schoenberg Society

Trebelli, Zélia [Gillebert, Gloria Caroline], 1838–1892
Library of Congress
(Box 55)
2 A. L. S.: Liverpool, 12 Nov.; London, n.d. 4p., French
Sig.

Treitschke, Friedrich, 1776–1842
Library of Congress
(Box 117)
A. L. S.: to Gottlieb Benedikt Bierey. Vienna, 3 Nov. 1821. 2p., German

Tremblay, George Amedée, 1911–1982
Harvard University
Mus. ms.: *First Piano Sonata*, op. 8
2 L.: to Aurelio de la Vega. 18 July 1963, 30 Nov. 1970
Mus. ms. Repro.: *Wind Quintet*, 1950. Blueprint score, parts

Trunk, Richard, 1879–1968
Northwestern University
Mus. ms.: *Abendgang*, op. 27, No. 1
Mus. ms.: *Drei Männerchöre*, op. 52
Mus. ms.: *Froher Tag; Gegen Abend*
Mus. ms.: *Unter Blüten*, op. 27, No. 2
Mus. ms.: *Zwei Männerchöre*, op. 53, No. 1

Tuczek-Ehrenburg, Leopoldine, 1821–1883
Library of Congress
(Box 55)
2 A. L. S.: Berlin, 23 Feb. 1843, 7 Dec. 1854. 3p., German
A. L. S.: to L. Hahn. n.p., 27 Jan. 1855. 1p., German

Tufts, Paul, b. 1924
Washington State University
Mus. ms.: *Sonata for Cello and Piano*, 1959
L.: to Hans Moldenhauer. Seattle, 14 Oct. 1963

Turina, Joaquín, 1882–1949
Library of Congress
(Box 55)
A. Mus. ms. S.: *Rima, para canto y piano*, to Henri Collet, Sevilla, Oct. 1908. 7p., 35x27cm., Spanish, ink, with additional text (French) in pencil. Text by Becquer. Complete score. Signed twice

Turner, Godfrey, 1913–1948
Northwestern University
2 L.: to Adolph Weiss. San Francisco, 4 May 1937; New York, 13 May

Turner, Thomas G., b. 1937
Harvard University
SUMMARY OF PRINCIPAL HOLDINGS:
Mus. ms.: *Six Variations*, 1962. With sound recording

Tuthill, Burnet, 1888–1982
Harvard University
Mus. Quot.: *Bethlehem*, op. 6
Pri. Sco.: *Concerto for Clarinet and Orchestra*, inscribed
Port. Phot.

Tyson, Alan, b. 1926
Library of Congress
See Beethoven, Ludwig van

Ugarte, Floro M., 1884–1975
Harvard University
SUMMARY OF PRINCIPAL HOLDINGS:
Mus. ms.: *De mi tierra*

Uhl, Alfred, 1909–1992
Library of Congress
(Box 55, unless noted)
A. Mus. ms. S.: *Kleine Suite für Viola*. 4p., 34x24cm.
   Complete draft
T. L. S.: to Hans Moldenhauer. Vienna, 30 Dec. 1975.
   1p., German
Doc. Repro.: Work list. 2p., German
Port. Phot. S.: by Fayer (Box 116)

Unger, Hermann, 1886–1958
Northwestern University
Mus. ms.: *Weihnachts-Musik in drei Sätzen nach alten
   Weisen*, op. 59. Full score

**Unger [Ungher], Karoline [Caroline, Carolina,
Carlotta], 1803–1877**
Library of Congress
(Box 55)
A. L. S.: to Robert. Turin, 22 July 1829. 1p., French
2 A. L. S.: 9 Feb. 1829, 1877[?]. 6p., German
A. L. S.: to Schober. Paris, 8 Jan.[?] 1844. 3p., German

Urspruch, Anton, 1850–1907
Library of Congress
(Box 55)
P. card S.: to Carlos Droste. Frankfurt, 7 Mar. 1901.
   German

Utrillo, Maurice, 1883–1955
Library of Congress
(Box 55)
Paint. S.: [Paris street scene]. Vignette, painted by the
   artist, for a Christmas dinner given by him in 1921,
   to Armand Parent, 1921. Menu is in Utrillo's hand.
   21x13cm. Signed on the painting

Valcárcel, Edgar, b. 1932
Harvard University
L.: to Aurelio de la Vega. Feb. 1985

Vaňhal [Wanhal], Johann Baptist, 1739–1813
Library of Congress
(Box 57)
A. L. S.: Vienna, 11 Feb. 1789. 2p., German. Stipulates
   fees for specified compositions

Van Slyck, Nicholas, 1922–1983
Harvard University
SUMMARY OF PRINCIPAL HOLDINGS:
Doc.: Biographical information and work list
3 S. recs.: "Cadenzas"; *Judgment in Salem*; *La Tomba di
   Scarlatti*

Varèse, Edgard [Edgar], 1883–1965
Harvard University
SUMMARY OF PRINCIPAL HOLDINGS:
3 L.: to Paul Sanders. New York, 17 Apr. 1957; at sea,
   postmarked Rotterdam, 2 Sept. 1957; Eindhoven,
   19 Sept. 1957
4 L.: to Adolph Weiss. Antibes, 18 May [1931?]; Paris,
   Dec. 1931, 16 Jan. 1933; Holland, 20 Mar. 1958
Doc.: Typescript. "The Liberation of Sound," 20 Mar.
   1957. With autograph musical illustration

Paul Sacher Stiftung
A. Mus. ms.: *Intégrales*, 1924–1925. Full score. 48p.,
   31x24cm.

Vaughan Williams, Ralph, 1872–1958
Northwestern University
L.: to Miss Scott. Dorking, 8 Aug.
Pri. Sco.: *A Sea Symphony*
2 Port.

Vega, Aurelio de la, b. 1925
Harvard University
SUMMARY OF PRINCIPAL HOLDINGS:
A. Mus. ms. S.: *The Magic Labyrinth*, for any number of

any instruments and/or any number of any voices, Northridge, 12 June 1975. 1p., 28x36cm., multicolored. With additional blueprint of the graphic score

Mus. ms.: *Adiós*, 1977. With program of the premiere, signed jointly by de la Vega and Zubin Mehta

Mus. ms.: *Adramante*, 1985

Mus. ms.: *Analigus*, 1965

Mus. ms.: *Asonante*, 1985

Mus. ms.: *Astralis*, 1977

Mus. ms.: *Cantata for Two Sopranos, Alto, and Chamber Orchestra*, 1958. Excerpt

Mus. ms.: *Corda*, 1977

Mus. ms.: *Exametron*, 1965. Excerpt

Mus. ms.: *Exospheres*, 1966

Mus. ms.: *Galandiacoa*, 1982

Mus. ms.: *Happy Birthday Nicolas*, 1984

Mus. ms.: *The Infinite Square*, 1975

Mus. ms.: *Inflorescence*, 1976

Mus. ms.: *Interpolation*, 1965

Mus. ms.: *Intrata*, 1972

Mus. ms.: *Labdanum*, 1970

Mus. ms.: *Magics and Inventions*, 1986

Mus. ms.: *Nones*, 1977

Mus. ms.: *Olep ed Arudamot*

Mus. ms.: [*Revista Musical Chilena*, excerpts for illustration]

Mus. ms.: *Septicilium*, 1974

Mus. ms.: *Sound Clouds*, 1975

Mus. ms.: *Structures*, 1962. Excerpt

Mus. ms.: *Tropimapal*, 1983

Mus. ms.: *Undici colori*, Cincinnati, 9–12 Apr. 1981

Mus. ms.: *Woodwind Quintet*, 1959

L.: to Donivan Johnson (1973–1982), Hans Moldenhauer (1983–1986, some addressed jointly to Mary Moldenhauer), Hilda Dianda (13 June 1983), Sergio Fernández Barroso (28 Oct. 1989, 9 May 1991), Alicia Terzian (23 Aug. 1991), José Eduardo Martins (1991), Neal Stulberg (1 Apr. 1992), Michael Brebes (1 June 1992), Marlos Nobre (18 June 1992), Kathleen Chase (24 June 1992), George Rochberg (29 June 1992), Ricardo Tacuchian (Aug. 1992), Juan Orrego-Salas (Oct. 1992), Emilio Mendoza (Dec. 1992), Hanley Jackson (23 Jan. 1993), Mehli Mehta (9 Feb. 1993), Lalo Schifrin (5 Mar. 1993), Alice Ramsay (9 May 1993), Roque Cordero (1993, with musical quotation), Jon Newsom (1994), Goffredo Petrassi (3 Jan. 1994), Roberto Sierra (1994), Kenneth Gaburo, Luis de Pablo, Bertram Turetzky

Mus. Quot.: Christmas 1961

Mus. ms. Repro.: *Andamar-Ramadna*. Blueprint of the graphic score

Mus. ms. Repro.: *Variants*. Facsimile

Port.

Draw.: by Angel Hurtado. Watercolor and ink

Draw.: by Irving Block. Watercolor and pencil

8 Draw. Repro.

S. rec.

See Widmer, Ernst

Library of Congress

SUMMARY OF PRINCIPAL HOLDINGS:

A. Mus. ms. S.: *The Magic Labyrinth*, for any number of any instruments and/or any number of any voices, Northridge, 12 June 1975. 1p., 28x36cm., multicolored

Verdi, Giuseppe, 1813–1901

Library of Congress

(Box 55, unless noted)

A. Mus. ms. S.: [*Attila*], "Romanza," aria for tenor and orchestra, to Nicola Ivanoff, Milan, 15 Nov. 1845 [*sic*]. 16p., 24x32cm., ink. Commissioned by Rossini for Ivanoff, a new romanza for Foresto, Act III. Complete score. With letter to Albi Rosenthal, from Pierluigi Petrobelli, Istituto di Studi Verdiani, 12 July 1969

L.: to Verdi, from the Duke of Parma's parochial opera company. Busseto, 9 July 1839. 2p., Italian

A. L. S.: to Léon Escudier. Napoli, 22 Dec. 1872. 1p., Italian

A. L. S.: to a baron. Busseto, 31 Oct. 1882. 2p., Italian. Mentions *Simone Boccanegra* and *Don Carlos*

A. L. S.: to Marchesi. Sa. Agata, 22 May 1887. 1p., Italian

A. L. S.: to Zaffignara. Sa. Agata, 21 Aug. 1887. 1p., Italian

Tlgm.: to Muck. Berlin, 30 Nov. 1894. Italian. On verso of telegram, draft of response letter by Verdi. Regarding Berlin performance of *Falstaff*

Doc.: Letter[?]. To Verdi, from Maggie[?]. Milan, 20 Feb. 1870. 4p., English

Port. Engr. S. (Box 116)

3 Port. Phot. Repro. (Box 116)

Verne, Mathilde, 1865–1936
Northwestern University
L.: London, 19 Sept.

Vernon, Ashley, 1902–1968
Wiener Stadt- u. Landesbibliothek
See Manschinger, Kurt

Verrall, John, b. 1908
Washington State University
Mus. ms.: *String Quartet No. 7*
Mus. ms.: *Suite for Orchestra*
3 L.: to Hans Moldenhauer. Seattle, 14 Oct. 1958,
    24 Jan. 1959; n.p., n.d.

**Vianesi, Auguste Charles Léonard François,
1837–1908**
Northwestern University
7 L.: to Michael Costa. 1862–1866

Viardot, Pauline, 1821–1910
Library of Congress
(Box 55)
2 A. Mus. mss. S.: Andantino, 28 Aug. 1839. 4p.
    (pp.95–7), 22x29cm., ink. For piano solo. On same
    double leaf, arrangement of same by Charles
    Zeuner, for 2 violins, viola, and cello, 23 Oct. 1839,
    to Pauline Viardot-Garcia. On last page, *à la
    Libertad*, a canon, by Escudero, 2 Aug. 1839
A. Mus. ms. S.: [Polka], 17 May 1847. 1p., 34x26cm.,
    ink. Complete sketch
9 A. L. S.: to [Karl] Eckert and [Bartolf Senff]. Paris,
    Baden-Baden, 1858–1869. 20p., French
A. L. S.: to ?. London, 9 Sept. 1870. 1p., English
A. L. S.: to Miss Holden. London, 7 Jan. 1871. 1p.,
    English. On verso, clipping reviewing concerts by
    Viardot-Garcia, and Halle
A. L. S.: to Chorley. Baden, 11 June. 2p., English
A. L. S.: n.p., n.d. 3p., French
See Berlioz, Hector

Vicars [Moya], Harold
Northwestern University
Mus. ms.: *Zorayma*, Leeds, 1906. Piano-vocal score

Vidal, Paul Antonin, 1863–1931
Library of Congress
(Box 55, unless noted)
A. L. S.: Rome, n.d. 1p., French
Port. Phot. Repro.: by Manuel (Box 116)

Vidal, Pedro
Library of Congress
(Box 55)
A. Mus. ms. S.: *Capricho Español*, para piano, to
    Ricardo Viñes, Rosario, 16 Sept. 1930. 9p., 34x26cm.

Vierne, Louis, 1870–1937
Library of Congress
(Box 55)
Pri. Sco. S.: *Deux pièces pour alto*, No. 1, *Le Soir*, [to Th.
    LaBarge?], Paris: Leduc, c1895. 7p.

Vieux, Maurice, 1884–1951
Library of Congress
(Box 116)
Port. Phot. Repro. S.: to Boaz Piller, Sept. 1927

Vieuxtemps, Henry, 1820–1881
Library of Congress
(Box 55, unless noted)
A. L. S.: to Alarg. [Paris?], 13 Feb. 1863. 1p., French
Port. Lith. (Box 116)

Vignand, Henri de
Library of Congress
(Box 55)
A. L. S.: to Raoul Pugno. Roubaix, 26 Jan. 1909. 3p.,
    French

Villa-Lobos, Heitor, 1887–1959
Harvard University
A. Mus. ms. S.: *Estudio No. 7*, for guitar, to Segovia, Paris, 1929. 4p., 32x23cm., ink, pencil fingerings by Segovia
Mus. ms.: *Estudio No. 5*, for guitar, Paris, 1929
Mus. ms.: *Estudio No. 9*, for guitar, to Segovia, Paris, 1929
Mus. Quot.: *Preludio*, to Boaz Piller, Rio, 20 Mar. 1941
L.: to Boaz Piller. New York, 5 Mar. 1945
L.: to Segovia
Doc.: List. Themes used in *Guia pratico*
2 Port. Phot.: to Adolph Weiss, 1941, 1953
Port.: to Boaz Piller

Viñes, Ricardo, 1875–1943
Library of Congress
(Box 55)
A. Mus. ms. S.: *Menuet Spectral*, "a la mèmoire de Maurice Ravel," Paris, Dec. 1937–Jan. 1938. 4p., 35x27cm. Incomplete
12 Mus. mss.: [Music manuscripts, some are incomplete, most are unsigned. Includes manuscripts of Antonio Piedrahita, Rafael Romero Rinola, Ramón Seca, and Enrique Prins]
See Esplá, Oscar
See Granados, Enrique

Vinton, John, b. 1937
Harvard University
L.: to Aurelio de la Vega. Brooklyn, 2 Feb. 1985

Viotti, Giovanni Battista, 1755–1824
Library of Congress
(Box 56)
A. L. S.: Bath, 7 Apr. 1815. 1p., French. Commenting on a concert by Cherubini
See Clementi, Muzio

Virchi, Paolo, ca. 1550–1610
Library of Congress
(Box 56)
A. Doc. S.: Tax document. [Brescia?], [1588?]. 1p., Italian

Vlad, Roman, b. 1919
Library of Congress
(Box 116)
2 Cards S.: [to Alma Mahler]. n.p., 1957–1958, n.d. 2p., German. With photograph of child

Vogel, Wladimir, 1896–1984
Library of Congress
See Gerhard, Roberto

Washington State University
See Rosbaud, Hans

Zentralbibliothek Zürich
L.: to Adolph Weiss. Berlin, 3 Apr. 1930

Vogler, Georg Joseph [Abbé Vogler], 1749–1814
Library of Congress
(Box 56)
A. L. S.: Darmstadt, 7 Feb. 1810. 1p., German

Voiculescu, Dan, b. 1940
Library of Congress
(Box 56)
A. Mus. ms. S.: *Croqui*. 2p., 35x25cm.
Mus. ms. Repro. S.: *Sonate*, piesa pentru pian, Cluj: Conservatorul de Muzica, 1971. 6p.

Volbach, Fritz, 1861–1940
Library of Congress
(Box 56)
A. L. S.: Mainz, Oct. 1904. 4p., German

Volkmann, Robert, 1815–1883
Northwestern University
Mus. ms.: *Visegrad*
Mus. ms.: *Weihnacht*. Full score
L.: Pest, 2 June 1871

L.: to Carl Reinecke. Budapest, 1 Oct. 1875
L.: to Chrysander. n.p., n.d.

Wachtel, Theodor, 1823–1893
Library of Congress
(Box 56, unless noted)
A. L. S.: Vienna, 1 May 1862. 3p., German
A. L. S.: to a professor. [London], dated twice, 3 July
  1864, 1 July 1865. 3p., German
A. L. S.: Pittsburgh, 28 Jan. 1872. 1p., Italian
Port. Phot. S.: Vienna, 19 Dec. 1860. By Harmsen
  (Box 116)

Wagenseil, Georg Christoph, 1715–1777
Library of Congress
(Box 56)
A. Mus. ms.: *Responsoria. Terza Quinta in Cena Domini
  ad Matutinum*, n.d. 34p., 22x31cm., Latin. Set for
  alto and tenor solo with four-part choir, with violin
  and basso continuo accompaniment. Authenticity
  confirmed on front cover by Aloys Fuchs, 9 Sept.
  1832; on verso, Fuchs relates story about seven-year-
  old Mozart at the imperial court at Vienna

Wagner, Cosima, 1837–1930
Library of Congress
(Box 56)
A. L. S.: n.p., 25 Jan. 1866. 1p., German
A. L. S.: [to Eugen Lindner]. Bayreuth, 10 Mar. 1897.
  2p., German
P. card S.: [to Bodenstein]. Bayreuth, Dec. 1926.
  German
A. Doc.: Manifesto. Draft, concerning the resolution to
  leave the early works of Wagner unperformed and
  unpublished. 4p., German

Wagner, Eva, 1867–1942
Library of Congress
(Box 56)
A. L. S.: [to Klaar]. Florence, 10 May 1900. 3p.,
  German

Wagner, Friedelind, 1918–1991
Library of Congress
(Box 56)
T. L. S.: to Rudolph Ganz. Chicago, 12 Mar. 1948. 1p.,
  English
A. L. S.: to Alma Mahler. New York, 1956. 3p.,
  German

Wagner, Joseph F., 1900–1974
Harvard University
2 L.: to Solomon Pimsleur. Brighton, Massachusetts,
  27 May 1933

Wagner, Peter, 1865–1931
Library of Congress
(Box 56)
A. L. S.: to Wilhelm Widmann. Freiberg, 18 July 1906.
  1p., German
2 P. cards S.: to Wilhelm Widmann. Freiberg, 28 Jan.
  1916, 4 July 1919. German

Wagner, Richard, 1813–1883
Library of Congress
(Box 56, unless noted)
Mus. ms. A. Annot. S.: [*Der fliegende Holländer*],
  Overture. 1p., 32x24cm., ink with red ink. Opening
  page in full score. With fourteen-line instruction to
  engraver regarding arrangement of the
  instrumentation, initialed "R. W."
Mus. ms.: *Der Tannenbaum, Ballade für Piano*, Berlin.
  2p., 27x35cm. Complete text of poem, incomplete
  piano score. Inscribed to E. Corning, Geneva,
  4 Feb. 1883, by previous owner, Edouard Krause.
  With two letters, to Hans Moldenhauer, from the
  Pierpont Morgan Library (19 Nov. 1963), and from
  the Richard-Wagner-Archiv (13 Jan. 1964)
A. L. S.: to Theodor Uhlig. Zurich, 5 Aug. 1852. 1p.,
  German
A. L. S.: to Bourdillat. Paris, 19 Nov. 1860. 1p., French
A. L. S.: Vienna, 15 Dec. 1862. 1p., German. On
  behalf of Peter Cornelius
A. L. S.: to K. Maier. St. Petersburg, [1862]. 1p.,
  German

A. L. S.: [to E. W. Fritsch]. Lucerne, 21 Dec. 1870.
3p., German

A. L. S.: to A. Stuher, a book dealer. Bayreuth, 16 June
1872. 1p., German

3 A. L. S.: to Alois Schmitt. Bayreuth, 7 Jan., 20 Mar.
1875; Venice, 21 Sept. 1876. 11p., German

A. L. S.: to Signora Giovanni Lucca. Sorrento, 22 Oct.
1876. 4p., French. Regarding suggested cuts for
Rienzi

A. L. S.: to the Archduke of Schwerin. Bayreuth,
16 Mar. 1877. 3p., German

Mus. ms. Repro.: *Siegfried-Idyll*. Facsimile of autograph
score in Wahnfried Archive, Bayreuth, Munich,
1923. Inscription to Hans Rosbaud, from Muck
(23 Oct. 1937)

Mus. ms. Repro.: *Der Tannenbaum*, 1838. 3p. Photostat

Doc.: Catalog. "The Richard-Wagner-Museum,"
Tribschen-Luzern, 1956. 50p., German

Doc.: Catalog. "The Wagner Collection," Roundelay
Book & Music Shop. 73p.

Clip.: "Morgan to Show Rare Documents," in the *New
York Times*, 7 Oct. 1963. 1p., English

24 Phot.: Bayreuther Festspiele, 1956 (Box 116)

Port. Phot. (Box 116)

Bk.: *Richard Wagner: Life, Work, Festspielhaus*, Bayreuth:
Festspielleitung, n.d. Signed by Wolfgang Wagner,
Bayreuth, 9 Aug. 1956

Wagner, Siegfried, 1869–1930
Library of Congress
(Box 56, unless noted)

P. card S.: to Dr. Adams. Bayreuth, 29 May 1905.
English

P. card S.: to the editor of *Simplicissimus*. Halle, 25 Feb.
1910. German

P. card S.: Bayreuth, 8 Oct. 1911. 1p., German.
Fragment

P. card S.: to Bodenstein. Bayreuth, 27 Dec. 1913.
German

Sig.: on calling card of Dr. Felix Huch

Port. Gr.: Siegfried Wagner with Muck and Felix Mottl
before the Bayreuth Festival House (Box 116)

Wagner, Wieland, 1917–1966
Washington State University
See Rosbaud, Hans

Wagner, Wolfgang, b. 1919
Library of Congress
See Wagner, Richard

Washington State University
See Rosbaud, Hans

Wagner-Régeny, Rudolf, 1903–1969
Bayerische Staatsbibliothek
See Hartmann, Karl Amadeus

Library of Congress
See Blacher, Boris

Washington State University
See Rosbaud, Hans

Waldteufel [Lévy], Emile, 1837–1915
Library of Congress
(Box 116)

A. Mus. Quot. S.: *Les Violettes Valse*, Paris, 2 May 1898.
1p. Mounted with portrait lithograph, to German

Walker, Edyth, 1867[?]–1950
Harvard University

L.: from the Marshal of Crown Princess Stephanie.
Vienna, 15 Nov. 1897

Doc.: Contract

Library of Congress
See Krantz, Eugen
See Orgeni, Aglaja

Wallace, William Vincent, 1812–1865
Northwestern University

L.: to Edward Lane. Oxford, 3 May 1860

Doc.: Biographical information

Mus. Quot.: *Le Rêve*, New York, 27 Oct. 1857

Port.

Wallenstein, Alfred, 1898–1983
Harvard University
L.: to Charles Haubiel. New York, 10 Oct. 1940
L.: to Adolph Weiss. 25 Dec. 1955
Port. Phot.: 1951

Waller [née Webern], Amalie, 1911–1973
Library of Congress
(Box 116)
Port. Gr.: Weihnachten, 1970
See Webern, Anton

Walmisley, Thomas Attwood, 1814–1856
Northwestern University
L.: London, 25 Oct. 1823
L.: to Henry Philips. Cambridge, 22 June 1842
L.: to Rev. R. F. Elwin. Cambridge, 1 Aug. 1845
Doc.: Biographical information and work list

Walter, Bruno [Schlesinger, Bruno Walter], 1876–1962
Library of Congress
(Box 57, unless noted)
P. card S.: to Karl Weigl. Vienna, 21 Jan. 1909. German
2 A. L. S.: to Karl Weigl. London, 14 May 1930;
    Beverly Hills, 27 Dec. 1939. 3p., German
2 T. L. S.: to Kurt Manschinger. Vienna, 8 Nov. 1937;
    New York, 10 Mar. 1941. 2p., German
A. L. S.: to Kurt Manschinger. Paris, 30 Apr. 1939. 2p.,
    German
T. L. S.: to Charles Haubiel. New York, 26 Apr. 1941.
    1p., English
Pri. Card: New York, March 1944
T. L. S.: to Alma Mahler. Beverly Hills, 23 Sept. 1956.
    1p., German
T. L. S.: to Hans Moldenhauer. Beverly Hills, 16 Sept.
    1958. 1p., German
Tlgm.: to Alma Mahler. Beverly Hills, 14 Feb. 1959.
    1p., German
A. L. S.: to Alma Mahler. 1p., German. Letter
    fragment from Delia (wife), with postscript signed
    by Bruno Walter

A. L. S.: to Alma Mahler, from Delia (wife). Santa
    Monica, 7 Feb. 1959. 3p., German
A. Doc. S.: Recommendation. For Karl Weigl as
    composer and teacher. New York, 26 Mar. 1939. 1p.,
    English
Pri. Sco. Annot. S.: *Orpheus* by Gluck. Piano-vocal
    score. 142p. Used by Walter, containing numerous
    autograph annotations, and 14p. of manuscript
    reproduced. Also includes notes by Hans Rosbaud
Prog.: London, 24–25 Oct. 1946. 8p., English
Port. Phot. (Box 116)
Port. Phot. S.: to Hans Moldenhauer, Sept. 1958
    (Box 116)

Walter, Georg A., 1875–1952
Library of Congress
(Box 57)
A. L. S.: to Tischer. Stuttgart, 16 Oct. 1930. 2p.,
    German

Walter [Water?, Waters?], John, ca. 1660-in or after 1708
Northwestern University
Mus. ms.: *A Song for Newyears Day 168[?]*, by John
    Blow, transcribed by Walter. Text begins with
    "Arise, great monarch." 19p., 32x21cm. Full score.
    On flyleaf, note of previous ownership
Rcpt.: 10 Feb. 1700

Walton, Sir William, 1902–1983
Northwestern University
L.: to Mrs. Morland. Lisbon, 13 Aug. 1963
Doc.: Manifesto. Association of British Musicians
Doc.: Minutes. Association of British Musicians,
    16 Feb.–22 June 1940

Wanning [Waningus Campensis, Wannigk, Wannicke, Wangnick], Johannes, 1537–1603
Library of Congress
(Box 57)
A. Mus. ms. S.: "Jauchzet dem Herrn alle Welt,"
    Discantus, Tenor, Bassus. 9p., 16x22cm., German.
    Complete parts

Ward-Steinman, David, b. 1936
Harvard University
L.: to Aurelio de la Vega. n.p., 10 Feb. 1985

Peter Warlock

Warlock, Peter [Heseltine, Philip], 1894–1930
Library of Congress
(Box 57)
A. Mus. ms. Annot. S.: *Pretty Ring Time*, Eynsford, Kent, May 1926. 4p., 30x23cm., English, ink, pencil. Song with piano accompaniment, to poem by Shakespeare. Complete score

Weaver, Powell, 1890–1951
Harvard University
Mus. ms.: *Kol nidre*
Mus. ms. Repro. Annot.: *Sonata for Violin and Piano.* Facsimile

Weber, Ben, 1916–1979
Harvard University
Mus. ms.: *Ballade*
L.: to Hans Moldenhauer. New York, 2 Feb. 1959
Doc.: Brochure. With work list and portrait reproduced

Weber, Bernhard Anselm, 1764–1821
Library of Congress
(Box 57)
A. L. S.: to Christian von Mechel. Berlin, 31 Dec. 1813. 1p., German

C. M. von Weber

Weber, Carl Maria von, 1786–1826
Library of Congress
(Box 57, unless noted)
A. L. S.: to Peter Ritter. Dresden, 30 July 1818. 1p., German
A. L. S.: to Simrock. Dresden, 12 Sept. 1819. 1p., German. With two letters signed from Anton

Meysel, writing on behalf of Simrock, 21 Sept., 19 Nov. 1819
A. L. S.: to Baron von Budberg. Dresden, 20 Nov. 182[?]. 2p., German, with translation. Bound with two portrait engravings
A. L. S.: to Frau von Chezy. Dresden, 17 June 1823. 1p., German
2 Port. Engr.: see letter above. By Carl Mayer; Payne after a painting by Jügel (Box 116)

Weber, Max Maria von, 1822–1881
Library of Congress
(Box 57)
2 A. L. S.: Dresden, 8 Dec. 1864, 22 May 1870. 5p., German
A. L. S.: to ?. Berlin, 2 April 1879. 2p., German

Anton Webern

Webern, Anton, 1883–1945
Bayerische Staatsbibliothek
See Berg, Alban

Library of Congress
(Box no./Folder no.)
Unless otherwise indicated, the materials stem directly from Webern's estate, as administered by Amalie Webern Waller. Includes formerly uncataloged acquisitions (see *Anton von Webern: Perspectives*, 1966; and *Supplement*) as well as new acquisitions since 1983
A. Mus. ms. S.: [*First Cantata*, op. 29, No. 2], *Kleiner Flügel Ahornsamen...*, to Hildegard Jone, 1938. 14p., 34x27cm., German, ink. Full score. Presentation copy inscribed on title page to "Hildegard Jone von Ihrem Anton Webern" (58/1)
A. Mus. ms. Annot.: [*Five Canons on Latin Texts*, op. 16, No. 4], *Lateinische Lieder*, "Asperges me...." 2 leaves, 16x26cm., Latin, ink, pencil. Complete draft (58/2)
A. Mus. ms. S.: [*Five Sacred Songs for Voice and Instruments*, op. 15], *Mein Weg geht jetzt vorüber.* 2p., 32x25cm., German, ink, pencil. Unsigned; *Fahr' hin, o Seel'...*, to Hildegard Jone, Mödling, 25 June 1929. 2p., 28x38cm., German, ink. Full score. Presentation copy bearing the inscription, "Frau Hildegard Jone in Herzlichkeit von Ihrem A. Webern," with a small photograph of Webern pasted on the margin (58/3)

A. Mus. ms.: [*Five Songs after Poems by Richard Dehmel*], *Himmelfahrt*, 1908[?]. 4p., 34x26cm., German, ink. Dated in pencil. Number III of the cycle (58/4)

A. Mus. ms. Annot.: [*Passacaglia for Orchestra*, op. 1, 1908]. 4p., 34x26cm., ink, pencil. Full score, mm.1–56 (58/5)

A. Mus. ms.: *Quartett*, Preglhof, 25 Aug. 1905. 21p., 34x26cm., ink, pencil. Full score. On verso of title page, quotation from the writings of Jacob Böhme (58/6)

A. Mus. ms. Rev.: [*Rondo*, for string quartet], [Vienna, 1906]. 6p. 34x26cm., ink, pencil, blue pencil. First draft, mm.1–39 (m.13 is missing). Includes various sketches, some close to mm.140–141 (58/7)

A. Mus. ms. S.: *Sechs Lieder nach Gedichten von Georg Trakl, für eine Singstimme, Klarinette, Bass-Klarinette, Geige und Violoncello*, op. 14, *Klavierauszug*, Mödling, 1919, 1921, to Hugo Winter, Nov. 1938. 14p., 21x34cm., German, ink, pencil annotations (58/8)

A. Mus. ms.: *Stefan George VII. Ring*, op. 3, *Dies ist ein Lied*. 2p., 34x26cm., German, ink; *An Bachesranft*. 2p., 34x26cm., German, ink, pencil, colored pencils; *Im Morgentau*. 3p., 35x27cm., German, ink, title and text in red ink. Signed. Varying indications for opus number and placement of the song within the cycle; *Kahl reckt der Baum*. 2p., 35x26cm., German, ink (58/9)

3 A. Mus. mss.: [*Three Poems for Voice and Piano*], *Vorfrühling*, text by Ferdinand Avenarius, Klagenfurt, 12 Jan. 1900. 1p., 35x27cm., German, ink. Following the closing double bar, a setting of the phrase "Leise tritt auf" for voice, oboe, two horns in E-flat, and harp, 4m.; *Nachtgebet der Braut*, text by Richard Dehmel, Karfreitag, 1903. 4p., 34x26cm., German, ink; *Fromm*, text by Gustav Falke, Preglhof, 11 Sept. 1902. 1p., German, ink. *Vorfrühling* and *Fromm* appear on recto and verso of one leaf, and are signed; *Nachtgebet der Braut* is written on a double leaf. All manuscripts are in full score, 6p. total (58/10)

A. Mus. ms. S.: [*Three Songs*, for Voice, Clarinet and Guitar, op. 18], *Volkslied, Schatzerl klein*, Mödling, Sept. 1925. 2p., 28x38cm., German, ink. Full score. This presentation copy inscribed [to Emil Hertzka] on the occasion of the 25th anniversary of Universal Edition (58/11)

A. Mus. ms. Rev. S.: *Zwei Lieder, "Chinesisch-Deutsche Jahres-und Tageszeiten" von Goethe für gemischten Chor, Celesta, Gitarre, Geige, Klarinette und Bass-Klarinette,* op. 19, *Weiss wie Lilien; Ziehn die Schafe von der Wiese.* 10p., 34x27cm., German, ink with corrections in black, red and blue pencil. Signed on title page, and on each song. Full score (58/12)

Mus. ms. arr.: *Streichquartett*, op. 28. 6p., ink. Transcription for piano by Otto Jokl, Oct. 1959 (58/13)

A. L.: to Ernst Diez. Vienna, 28 Dec. 1902. 7p., German (58/14)

2 A. L. S.: to Alban Berg. Danzig, 25 Dec. 1910, 18 Jan. 1911. 11p., German. With letter to Amalie Webern Waller, from Helene Berg, Vienna, 8 Apr. 1965, about editing the Berg-Webern correspondence. On page 2 of this letter, the editing is assigned to Moldenhauer as of 15 July 1970 (58/14)

7 A. L. S.: to Ludwig and Teresa Zenk. Mödling, 1922–1927. 7p., German (58/14)

P. card S.: to Melanie Guttmann Rice. Alt-Aussee, 24 Aug. 1922. Also signed by Felix and Trudi Greissle, Rudolf Kolisch, Schoenberg, Georg Schönberg, Zemlinsky, and others (58/14)

A. L. S.: to Alexander Zemlinsky. Mödling, 24 Apr. 1923. 1p., German (58/16)

3 A. L. S.: to Ludwig Zenk. Mödling, Maria Enzersdorf, 14 Apr. 1923, 20 Oct. 1925, 27 Mar. 1943. 3p., German (58/16)

2 A. L. S.: [to Paul Sanders]. Mödling, Maria Enzersdorf, 17 Sept. 1930, 7 Nov. 1935. 3p., German (58/15)

2 A. L. S.: [to David Joseph Bach]. Mödling, 14 Nov. 1930, 10 May 1939. 5p., German (58/15)

T. L. S.: [to Paul Sanders]. Mödling, 14 Jan. 1934. German (58/15)

A. L. S.: [to Alban Berg]. [Maria Enzersdorf], 25 Dec. 1934. 1p., German (58/15)

5 P. cards S.: to Ludwig Zenk. Maria Enzersdorf, 1934–1936, 1943. German (58/16)

3 P. cards S.: to Otto Jokl. Maria Enzersdorf, 10 Nov. 1937, 22 Dec. 1939, 3 Feb. 1940. 6p., German (58/15)

A. L. S.: to Jella Jokl. Maria Enzersdorf, 30 Dec. 1937. 1p., German (58/15)

3 P. cards S.: to Erwin Stein. Maria Enzersdorf, 31 Jan., 1 Mar., 29 May 1939. 6p., German (58/16)

P. card S.: from Ludwig Zenk. Gürgl, 12 Aug. 1942. Picture postcard by Zenk. Greetings from Mia Zenk (58/16)

L.: to ?, from R. Tyrolt (actor). Gutenstein, 3 Oct. 1928. 3p., German. Describing Tyrolt's first meeting with Peter Rosegger (1843–1918), a favorite writer of Webern's (58/16)

L.: to Hildegard Jone, from Maria von Webern Halbich. [Mittersill], 15 Jan. 1951. 3p., German (58/17)

Card S.: to Hildegard Jone, from Otto Tomek. 1955. German. Season's Greetings from Universal Edition, which quotes a letter by Webern to Berg regarding the significance of Christmas (58/17)

L.: to Hans Moldenhauer, from Arnold Elston. Berkeley, 18 Sept. 1961. 1p., English. Relates his period of study under Webern (58/17)

L.: to Amalie Webern Waller, from Hildegard Jone. 16 Apr. 1963. Easter wishes in a two-line poem (58/17)

8 L.: to Hans Moldenhauer, from Rosa Warto (Webern's sister). 1963–1964. Includes postcards and letters, one written by Amalie Webern Waller (58/17)

P. card: to Mitzi (Maria) von Webern, signed by her Aunt Leopoldine ("Poldi"), Aunt Maria ("Mitzi"), grandmother [Mörtl], and two cousins. n.p., n.d. (58/17)

L.: to Hans Moldenhauer, from William Hibbard. Iowa City, 7 June 1984. 1p., English. Regarding *Six Bagatelles for String Quartet*, op. 9 (58/17)

Doc.: Decree of nobility. "Adels-Diplom der Familie Weber von Webern," Vienna, 15 Aug. 1731. 16p., German. Bestowed upon the brothers Johann Jacob and Joseph Antonius Weber. Bound in silk with gold embossing. With ornate coat-of-arms (58/18)

Doc.: File of documents and letters pertaining to Guido von Webern (1888–1962), the composer's first cousin (59/19)

A. Doc.: Poems. Fair copies, Webern's autograph of all poems by Hildegard Jone set to music by him, 29 Nov. 1944, and with Jone's autograph of the text for "Schöpfen aus Brunnen." 12p., German. Includes *Drei Lieder*, op. 25; *Drei Gesänge*, op. 23; *Das Augenlicht*, op. 26; *I. Kantate*, op. 29; *II. Kantate*, op. 31. Written out in recitation during an evening, 29 Nov. 1944, honoring the poetess. 20x15cm., in brocade cover (59/2)

T. Doc. S.: Speech. "A Webern Scandal (Salzburg, 1922)," Seattle, First International Webern Festival, 16 Jan. 1962. 3p., English. Originally titled "Two Scandals" (1922), personal recollections of Webern given by Ganz at the Festival (59/3)

Call. c.: of Dr. Anton Webern. Maria Enzersdorf (59/3)

Call. c.: of Ann Quartin. She gave the first performance of Webern's *Trakl-Lieder*, op. 14, in 1924 (59/3)

Mus. ms. Repro.: Drei Lieder, op. 18, c1954 (59/3)

Mus. ms. Repro.: *Im Sommerwind, Idylle für grosses Orchester*, c1961 by Hans Moldenhauer, Seattle, score dated 25 May 1962. 34p. Full score. Blueprint score. The original score from which Ormandy conducted the Philadelphia Orchestra in the work's premiere in Seattle. With autograph annotations by Ormandy (Box 102)

Mus. ms. Repro.: *Der Zigeunerbaron, Schatzwaltzer* by Johann Strauss, arranged by Webern, 1921. For piano, harmonium, and string quartet. Microfilm, from the autograph manuscript (at Wiener Stadtbibliothek) (Box 121)

Pri. Sco. S.: *Fünf Sätze für Streichquartett*, op. 5, Vienna: Universal Edition, c1922, to Amar-Hindemith Quartett, Salzburg, 8 Aug. 1922. 11p. On the occasion of the work's first performance, which resulted in a riot (59/4)

Pri. Sco.: *Fünf Sätze für Streichquartett*, op. 5, Vienna: Universal Edition, c1922, to Hans Moldenhauer, May 1962. 11p. Inscribed by Ganz, who used this score at the Salzburg Festival premiere in 1922 (59/4)

Pri. Sco. Annot.: *Konzert*, op. 24, Vienna: Universal Edition, c1948. 14p. Annotations by Rosbaud (59/5)

Pri. Sco. S.: *Passacaglia für Orkester*, op. 1, Vienna: Universal Edition, c1922, to Josef Polnauer, 17 Dec. 1922. 37p. (59/6)

Pri. Sco. A. Annot.: *Sechs Lieder nach Gedichten von Georg Trakl*, op. 14, Vienna: Universal Edition, c1924, "Juli 1924." 16p., German. Composer gives timings of each song. Annotated throughout, presumably by the composer during rehearsals and after the first performance on 20 July 1924 (59/7)

Pri. Sco. S.: *Sechs Stücke für grosses Orchester*, op. 4, Im Selbstverlag [pub. by Webern in 1913], to Heinrich Jalowetz, Semmering, 1913. 24p. (59/8)

Pri. Sco. S.: *Streichtrio*, op. 20, Philharmonia Edition, Vienna: Universal Edition, c1927, to Hildegard Jone and Josef Humplik, Christmas 1933. 20p. (59/9)

Pri. Sco. S.: *Trio*, op. 20, Vienna: Universal Edition, c1927, to Hildegard Jone and Josef Humplik, Christmas 1927. 20p. (59/9)

Pri. Sco. S.: *Variationen für Klavier*, op. 27, Vienna: Universal Edition, c1937, to Ludwig Zenk, May 1937. 11p. (59/10)

Pri. Sco. A. Annot.: *Vier Lieder*, op. 12, Vienna: Universal Edition, c1925. 9p., German. Dated 1925, with composer's own timings at the end of each song (59/10)

Pri. Sco. S.: *Zwei Lieder*, op. 19, Vienna: Universal Edition, c1928, [to Hildegard Jone and Josef Humplik], Christmas 1928. 20p., German (59/11)

Pri. Sco.: *Aus dem "Glühenden" von Alfred Mombert*, op. 2, No. 4, by Alban Berg. 2p. From Webern's library (59/11)

2 Pri. Sco.: *Lieder*, op. 7; op. 9 by Karl Horwitz, Zürich: Hüni, c1925. 16p. + 11p. Signed by Paul Pisk (59/12)

Prog. A. Annot.: Alban Berg Memorial Concert, London, 1 May 1936. 1p., German. Conducted by Webern. Red underscorings by Webern, pencil notes on verso (59/13)

Prog.: The First International Webern Festival, University of Washington School of Music, 25–28 May 1962. 24p., English (59/13)

Prog.: The Philadelphia Orchestra, with Eugene Ormandy, to Rosaleen [Moldenhauer], Seattle, 25 May 1962. 15p., English. Inscribed by Ormandy for the performance of *Im Sommerwind* (59/13)

Prog.: Monday Evening Concerts, Los Angeles, 22 Feb. 1971. 5p., English (59/13)

Obit. Card: for Peter von Webern, sent to Mr. and Mrs. Ludwig Zenk, 3 Mar. 1945. 1p., German. Webern's only son, who was killed on 14 Feb. 1945. The announcement was typeset by the monks of St. Gabriel Abbey under the supervision of Webern and his daughter-in-law Hermine, both of whom drew by hand the black cross and border lines (59/14)

Obit. Card: for Wilhelmine von Webern, Mittersill, Vienna, 31 Dec. 1949. 1p., German. The composer's widow died 29 Dec. 1949 (59/32)

Port.: Anton von Webern, 1928. Portrait bust. Plaster cast made from the original head sculptured from life, by Josef Humplik. Painted black and mounted on wooden pedestal (59/14)

Port. Draw.: *Anton von Webern vor der Todestüre*, by Hildegard Jone. 36x26cm. Preparatory drawing of Webern's head for the oil painting *Webern in der Haustüre stehend...* (Box 116)

Port. Lith.: *Anton Webern*, by Hildegard Jone. 31x22cm. Signed by Jone. Engraved below the portrait is a musical quotation of *Freundselig ist das Wort* from the *II. Kantate*, op. 31. The quotation being a facsimile of Webern's autograph and signature (59/14)

2 Port. Lith.: Mödling, 13 Feb. 1927, by Emil Stumpp (1886–1941). 50x35cm. (front view), 43x33cm. (side view). Signed by Stumpp. Drawn from life (Box 125)

12 Port. Phot.: Formal and informal portraits, individual and group. Some inscribed (Box 116)

Port. Paint.: Copy. *Anton von Webern*, by Egon Batai. 70x60cm., oil, framed. Original painted by Tom von Dreger in 1934 (Shelf)

Port. Paint.: Copy. *Webern in der Haustüre stehend, wenige Augenblicke vor seinem gewaltsamen Ende*, by Egon Batai. 69x51cm., oil, framed. Original created by Hildegard Jone (1945) (Shelf)

Bk.: *Die Ethic*, by Benedict de Spinoza, Leipzig: Alfred Kröner, [ca. 1932]. 273p., German (Box 121)

Bk.: *Gedichte*, by Friedrich Matthisson, Zurich: Johann Heinrich Füssli, 4th ed., 1797. 189p., German. Bound together with supplement, "Nachtrag." From Webern's library (Box 121)

See Gerhard, Roberto

See Jone, Hildegard

See Liszt, Franz

See Schoenberg, Arnold

See Webern, Josef Eduard von

Paul Sacher Stiftung

For a comprehensive list, see *Anton von Webern: Perspectives*, compiled by Hans Moldenhauer and Demar Irvine, and *Inventare der Paul Sacher Stiftung, 4: Anton Webern Musikmanuskripte* (1994). In addition to the inventory below, the collection includes numerous personal documents, including art objects, books, calling cards, diplomas, identity card, passport, printed scores, programs

SUMMARY OF PRINCIPAL HOLDINGS:

A. Mus. ms.: *Acht frühe Lieder*, 1901–1904. 33p.

A. Mus. ms.: *Cellosonate*, 1914. 4p.

A. Mus. ms.: *Drei Gedichte*, 1900–1903. 12p.

A. Mus. ms.: *Drei kleine Stücke*, op. 11, 1914. 6p.

A. Mus. ms.: *Drei Lieder*, 1903–1904. 13p.

A. Mus. ms.: *Drei Lieder*, 1913–1914. 22p.

A. Mus. ms.: *Drei Lieder*, op. 18, 1924[?]–1925. 14p.

A. Mus. ms.: *Entflieht auf leichten Kähnen*, op. 2, 1914. 7p.

A. Mus. ms.: *Fünf Canons*, op. 16, 1923–1924. 31p.

A. Mus. ms.: *Fünf geistliche Lieder*, op. 15, 1917–1922. 80p. + 3p. (title pages) + 1p. (in another hand)

A. Mus. ms.: *Fünf Lieder*, 1906–1908. 17p.

A. Mus. ms.: *Fünf Lieder*, op. 3, 1908–1909. 31p.

A. Mus. ms.: *Fünf Lieder*, op. 4, 1908–1909. 40p. + 2p. (title pages)

A. Mus. ms.: *Fünf Sätze*, op. 5, 1909. 21p. + 2p. (title pages)

A. Mus. ms.: [same], op. 5, 1928/1929. 22p.

A. Mus. ms.: *Fünf Stücke*, op. 10, 1911/1913. 4p.

A. Mus. ms.: *Kantate Nr. 1*, op. 29, 1938–1939. 24p. + 2p. (text)

A. Mus. ms.: *Kantate Nr. 2*, op. 31, 1941–1943. 98p.

A. Mus. ms.: *Kinderstücke*, 1924. 3p.

A. Mus. ms.: *Langsamer Satz*, 1905. 38p.

A. Mus. ms.: *Liebeslied*, 1904. 1p.

A. Mus. ms.: *Passacaglia*, op. 1, 1908. 67p.

A. Mus. ms.: *Quartett*, for two violins, viola, and violoncello, 1905. 36p.

A. Mus. ms.: *Quintett*, for two violins, viola, violoncello, and piano, 1907. 150p. With suggestions in the hand of Arnold Schoenberg

A. Mus. ms.: *Rondo*, for two violins, viola, and violoncello, 1906. 57p.

A. Mus. ms.: *Satz*, for piano, ca. 1905. 20p., including 7p. (photocopy) in the hand of F. Wildgans

A. Mus. ms.: *Satz*, for string trio, 1925. 5p.

A. Mus. ms.: *Sechs Bagatellen*, op. 9, 1911/1913. 22p.

A. Mus. ms.: *Sechs Lieder*, op. 14, 1917–1921. 72p.

A. Mus. ms.: *Sechs Stücke*, op. 6, 1909, revised 1928. 1p. Excerpt

A. Mus. ms.: [same, 1920]. 53p. Also in the hand of Berg, and two others

A. Mus. ms.: [Sketchbook 2], 1926–1930. Contains opera 19–22; *Auf Bergen in der reinsten Höhe*, 1926; Movement for orchestra, 1928; Movement for string quartet, 1927; Movement for string quartet, 1929; *Nun weiß man erst*, 1929

A. Mus. ms.: [Sketchbook 3], 1928–1934. Contains opera 22–25; *Cirrus*, 1930; Movement for woodwinds, strings, piano, 1934; Movement for clarinet quartet, 1930; *Der Spiegel sagt mir*, 1930; Piece for orchestra, 1931; *Wie kann der Tod so nah der Liebe wohnen*, 1934

A. Mus. ms.: [Sketchbook 4], 1931–1938. Contains opera 24–28

A. Mus. ms.: [Sketchbook 5], 1938–1943. Contains opera 29–31

A. Mus. ms.: [Sketchbook 6], 1941–1945[?]. Contains op. 31; *Kleiner sind Götter geworden*, op. 32, 1943–1944; Concerto, 1944–1945[?]

A. Mus. ms.: [Sketches, drafts, incomplete compositions]: *An eine Heilige*, ca. 1922–1924, 3p.; *Alladine und Palomides*, 1908. 1p.; *Dämmerstunde*,

1905[?], 2p.; *Dein Leib geht jetzt der Erde zu*, 1925, 1p.; *Drei Lieder*, 1918–1920, 15p.; *Drei Studien über einen Basso ostinato*, 1907, 16p.; *Du bist mein, Ich bin dein*, 1903[?], 1p.; Eight sketches for orchestra, 1911/1913, 6p.; Eight songs, 1915–1921, 21p.; Eighteen German chorale harmonizations, 1906, 8p.; *Elf kurze Stücke*, ca. 1904, 15p.; *Hochsommernacht*, 1904, 3p.; *Kinderstück*, 1924, 1p.; *In einer lichten Rose*, 1914, 2p.; *Meiner Mutter*, ca. 1914, 1p.; *Morgenglanz der Ewigkeit*, 1924, 3p.

A. Mus. ms.: *Im Sommerwind*, 1904. 54p.

A. Mus. ms.: *Sonatensatz (Rondo)*, ca. 1905. 18p.

A. Mus. ms.: *Stücke*, for orchestra, 1913. 18p.

A. Mus. ms.: [Two pieces, for violoncello and piano, 1899]. 10p.

A. Mus. ms.: [Unidentified, ca. 75p.]

A. Mus. ms.: [Unpublished movements, pieces]: Clarinet quartet, 1904, 2p.; Clarinet trio, 1920, 3p.; Orchestra, F Major, 1904, 3p.; Orchestra, F Major, 1904, 35p.; Orchestra, D Major, 1904, 53p.; Orchestra, B Minor, 1906, 1p.; Orchestra, E Major, 1906, 2p.; Piano, C Major, ca. 1904, 5p.; Piano, C Major, ca. 1904, 4p.; Piano, C Major, ca. 1904, 4p.; Piano, A-flat Major, ca. 1904, 3p.; Piano, A Major, ca. 1904, 6p.; Piano, A Minor, ca. 1905, 2p.; Piano, F Major, ca. 1905, 8p.; Piano, G Major, ca. 1905, 2p.; Piano, C Minor, ca. 1905, 3p.; Scherzo and Trio, A Minor, 1903[?], 8p.; *Schien mir's, als ich sah die Sonne*, 1913 or 1914, 1p.; *Schmerz immer, Blick nach oben*, 1913, 4p.; Song, 1917, 1p.; *Das Sonnenlicht spricht*, 1944–1945[?], 7p.; String quartet, E Minor, 1903, 2p.; String quartet, G Major, 1903, 1p.; String quartet, B Major, 1904, 1p.; String quartet, C Minor, 1904[?], 1p.; String quartet, C Major, 1905[?], 3p.; String quartet, D Major/D Minor, 1905, 5p.; String quartet, D Major/A Major, 1906, 8p.; String quartet, D Major, 1906, 8p.; String quartet, C Major, 1906, 3p.; String quartet, E Minor, 1906, 1p.; String quartet, D Minor, 1906, 2p.; String quartet, D Minor, 1906, 3p.; String quartet, A Major/E Major, 1906, 2p.; String quartet, A Minor, 1907, 51p.; String quartet, C Minor/C Major, 1907, 45p.; String quartet, 1914, 1p.; String quartet, 1917–1918, 7p; String quintet, G Minor, 1905, 5p.; String quintet, C Minor, 1906, 3p.; Strings, C-sharp Minor, 1903, 1p.; Strings, C Major, 1903, 6p.; Strings, D Minor, 1904, 35p.; String trio, 1925, 8p.; *In tiefster Schuld*, ca. 1916, 2p.; Two pieces for piano, ca. 1904, 11p.; Two pieces for piano, 1909–1910[?], 2p.; Two songs, 1917–1918, 5p.; Two songs, 1918–1920, 7p.; Variations for orchestra, D Major/D Minor, 1905, 28p.; Variations for piano and string quartet, A Minor, ca. 1904, 14p.; Variations for string quartet, F Major/F Minor, 1903, 6p.; Variations for string quartet, C-sharp Minor, 1907, 6p.; Variations on *Der Winter ist vergangen*, ca. 1904, 15p.; *Verderben, sterben — ich leb' ohne Trost*, 1925, 1p.; Violin and piano, E Minor, 1906, 28p.; *Vorfrühling II*, 1900, 2p.; *Wehmut*, 1901, 3p.; *Wolkennacht*, 1900, 3p.

A. Mus. ms.: *Vier Lieder*, 1908–1909. 15p.

A. Mus. ms.: *Vier Lieder*, op. 12, 1915–1917. 28p.

A. Mus. ms.: *Vier Lieder*, op. 13, 1914–1918. 94p. + 1p. (title page)

A. Mus. ms.: *Vier Stücke*, op. 7, 1910. 14p. + 2p. (title pages) + 6p. (parts, in Webern's hand, with inscriptions in another hand)

A. Mus. ms.: *Zwei Lieder*, op. 8, 1910–1921, 1925. 26p.

A. Mus. ms.: *Zwei Lieder*, op. 19, 1926. 9p.

Mus. ms. cop.: *Drei deutsche Volkslieder*, arranged by Schoenberg, 1928. 14p.

Mus. ms. cop.: *Friede auf Erden*, op. 13 by Schoenberg. 6p. With additional manuscript copied by Felix Greissle, and with annotations by Webern (1907/1911, 36p.)

Mus. ms. annot.: *Vier deutsche Volkslieder* by Schoenberg, copied by Felix Greissle, with annotations by Webern, 1929. 11p.

Mus. ms. arr.: *Arbeiterchor* by Liszt, 1924. 45p.

Mus. ms. arr.: *Du bist die Ruh'* by Schubert, 1903. 7p.

Mus. ms. arr.: *Fünf Orchesterstücke*, op. 16 by Schoenberg, 1912. 26p.

3 Mus. mss. arr.: Gedichte von Eduard Mörike: *Denk es, o Seele!*; *Der Knabe und das Immlein*; *Lebe wohl* by Hugo Wolf, 1903. 10p. + 4p. + 3p.

Mus. ms. arr.: *Gurrelieder*, Vorspiel by Schoenberg, 1909–1910. 14p.

Mus. ms. arr.: [same], *Lied der Waldtaube*, 1900–1911. 5p.

Mus. ms. arr.: *Ihr Bild* by Schubert, 1903. 5p.

Mus. ms. arr.: *Kammersymphonie* by Schoenberg, 1922–1923. 78p.

Mus. ms. arr.: *Pelleas und Melisande* by Schoenberg, 1911–1912. 4p.

Mus. ms. arr.: *Rosamunde*, Romanze by Schubert, 1903. 6p.

Mus. ms. arr.: *Die schöne Müllerin, Tränenregen* by Schubert, 1903. 5p.

Mus. ms. arr.: *Sechs Orchester-Lieder*, op. 8 by Schoenberg, 1910. 6p.

Mus. ms. arr.: *Siegfrieds Schwert* by Martin Plüddemann, 1903. 15p.

3 Mus. mss. arr.: [Three piano sonatas] by Schubert, opera 42, 122, 147, 1903. 5p. + 4p. + 8p. Incomplete

Mus. ms. arr.: *Verklärte Nacht* by Schoenberg, 1911–1912. 1p.

Mus. ms. arr.: *Die Winterreise, Der Wegweiser* by Schubert, 1903. 7p.

Mus. ms. arr.: *Zum Schluss* by Leo Blech, ca. 1903. 4p.

Mus. ms.: *Canon*, 1943, in the hand of Erich Schmid. 5p.

Mus. ms.: *Compositionen für Amalie Geer*, in the hand of Eduard Brunner, 1866. 124p.

Mus. ms.: *Impromptu*, in the hand of Edwin Komauer. 1p.

Mus. ms. cop.: *Ouvertüre zu "Hermann und Dorothea"* by Robert Schumann, 1851. 27p.

Mus. ms.: *Vor Maria Wörth*, in the hand of Edwin Komauer. 3p.

L.: [from Webern, to]: Ernst Diez (1900–1934), Wilhelmine Webern (1906–1934), Guido Adler (1910–1935), Paul Königer (1910–1913, microfilm only), Rosa and Otto Warto (1910–1945), Josef Polnauer (1914–1941), Alexander Zemlinsky (1915–1924, photocopies only), Arnold Schoenberg (1922), Egon Wellesz (1922, 1934, photocopies only), the Zenks (1922–1943, including Ludwig Zenk), Ludwig Zenk (1923–1945), David Joseph Bach (1925–1940), Emil Hertzka (1925), Ruzena Herlinger (1926–1936), Norbert Schwarzmann (ca. 1926–1931), Amalie and Maria Webern (1926), Freie Typographia (1928), Öttle (1928–1936), Christine Webern (1928), Peter Webern (1928, 1941), Paul Emerich (1930, 1933), Erika Wagner (1930, photocopy only), Adolf Weiss (1930–1934), Roberto Gerhard (1931–1936), Otto Jokl (1931–1939), Mia Zenk (1931), Yella Hertzka (1933–1934), Julius Schloss (1933), Hans Humpelstetter (1934–1945), Karl Amadeus Pisk (1934), Franz Rederer (1934–1939), Amalie Webern (1934), Gisela Bach (1935–1936), Willi Reich (1938–1944), George Robert (1938–1941), Karl Amadeus Hartmann (1941–1944), Erwin Ratz (1942), Friedrich Wildgans (1943, photocopy only), Werner Riemerschmid (1944, copies in the hand of Riemerschmid), Hermine Webern (1944–1945)

L.: [to Webern, from]: Carl von Webern (1910, 1918), Wilhelmine Webern (1910), Arnold Schoenberg (1922), Universal Edition (1922–1936), Wien. Bürgermeister (1924–1931), Alma Mahler (1933),

Ernst Diez (1936, 1939), Ralph Hawkes (1938), Erwin Stein (1938–1939), Josef Humplik (1939), Hildegard Jone (1939–1945), Alfred Kalmus (1939), C. A. Rosen (1939), Josef Marx (1942), Otto Warto (1944), Rudolf Kolisch (n.d.), Hermann Scherchen, and others (n.d.)

L.: [regarding Webern, Webern family]: to Ernst Diez, from Carl von Webern (1902); to Ernst and Beryl Diez, from Wilhelmine Webern (1917–1949); to Adolph Weiss, from Elizabeth Sprague Coolidge (1930); to Amalie Waller, from Peter Webern (1938); to the Österreichische Staatsamt, from Universal Edition (1945); to Hermine Webern, from Wilhelmine Webern (1945–1949); to Ernst Diez, from Ludwig Zenk (1946–1947); to Hans Humpelstetter, from Wilhelmine Webern (1946–1948); to Amalie Waller, from Wilhelmine Webern (1946–1949); to Josef Hueber, from Wilhelmine Webern (1947–1949, photocopies only); to Hildegard Jone, from Gisela Bach (1947); to Josef Polnauer, from Werner Riemerschmid (1947); to Wilhelmine Webern, from Hans Humpelstetter (1947); to Ludwig and Maria Zenk, from Wilhelmine Webern (1947); to Josef Polnauer, from Wilhelmine Webern (1949); to Amalie Waller, from Josef Hueber (1949); to Hans Moldenhauer, from Josef Hueber (1966); to Hans Moldenhauer, from Hermine Webern (1967)

Doc.: Analysis. *Passacaglia*, op. 1. 9 May 1922

Doc.: Catalog. "Bücher und Noten," in Webern's personal library, 1914–1929. 129p.

Doc.: Corrections. Pertaining to vocal compositions

8 Docs.: Diaries and Notebooks

A. Doc.: Family lineage. 2p.

Doc.: Instrumentation list. For Mahler's *Seventh Symphony*, *2. Nachtmusik*

Doc.: Outline. Seven different instrumental combinations to be employed in an orchestral work. With musical notation

Doc.: *Second Cantata*, op. 31. The textual source materials of the work, consisting of Hildegard Jone's poems in her autograph, Webern's annotations consisting of musical outlines, syllable counts, dates of composition, numbering of movements and signatures. 5p.

Doc.: Stage play. *Tot: Sechs Bilder für die Bühne*. 35p.

Mus. ms. Repro. A.: *Variationen für Orchester*, op. 30. Photostat of the full score. Conducting cues in the hand of Hermann Scherchen

Pri. Sco.: *Drei Lieder*, op. 25. With an original poem by Hildegard Jone

Port.: Large file of photographs and portraits of Webern, his family, study

See Diez, Ernst

See Jone, Hildegard

Wiener Stadt- u. Landesbibliothek

Mus. ms.: *Chamber Symphony*, op. 9 by Arnold Schoenberg, arranged by Webern for five instruments, 1923. 2p. Sketches

Mus. ms.: *Four Songs for Voice and Orchestra, Die Einsame*, op. 13, No. 2, 1914

L.: to Erika Wagner Stiedry. Mödling, 24 Mar. 1930

Webern, Josef Eduard von, 1778–1831
Library of Congress
(Box 121)

Port. Paint.: Miniature portrait of Webern's great-grandfather. Painted in oil on ivory, in an original frame. The name is given in Gothic script on the verso of the matting. Webern kept this picture above his work table

Port. Phot.: see Webern, Anton

Weckerlin, Jean-Baptiste, 1821–1910
Library of Congress
(Box 60)

A. L. S.: to Marchesi. Paris, Dec. 4p., French

Wedekind, Frank, 1864–1918
Library of Congress
(Shelf)

Doc.: Stock poster. [*Erdgeist*, Prologue, Vienna, June 1898]. 98 lines, 94x43cm., lithograph. Penned on the verso of a poster advertising the Ibsen Theater, of which Wedekind was a member. First draft. With a typed statement, signed by Hilde Auerbach

Wedig, Hans Josef, b. 1898
Library of Congress
(Box 60)

A. Mus. ms. S.: *Das Wessobrunner Gebet*, op. 11. 9p., 34x27cm., German

A. Mus. ms. S.: *Deutscher Psalm*, op. 4, 1927–1928. 10p., 35x28cm., German. Piano-vocal score

Weigel, Eugene J., b. 1910
Harvard University
SUMMARY OF PRINCIPAL HOLDINGS:
Mus. ms.: *The Birds*, 1937
Mus. ms.: *Fall of the Leaf*, 1944
Mus. ms.: *At 5 in 7*
Mus. ms.: *Improvisation*, 1947
Mus. ms.: *Lonely Peace*, 1933
Mus. ms.: *The Morgan Point Christmas Carol*, 1944
Mus. ms.: *Prairie Symphony*, 1953
Mus. ms.: *A Requiem Mass*, 1950
Mus. ms.: *The Sick Rose*, 1932

Weigl, Joseph, 1766–1846
Library of Congress
(Box 60)
A. L. S.: to von Lehr. Vienna, 1 Nov. 1820. 1p.,
German

Weigl, Karl, 1881–1949
Library of Congress
(Box no./Folder no.)
A. Mus. ms.: [Albums of student assignments]. Jan.
1899-Sept. 1900. 286p. (61/1)
A. Mus. ms.: *Auferstehung*. 8p., 26x34cm. Piano sketch.
With accompanying piano sketch, "Sehr langsam."
4p., 35x26cm. (61/2)
A. Mus. ms. S.: [*Cello Concerto, in G Minor*], 1934. 27p.,
27x34cm. (61/3)
A. Mus. ms. S.: *Clavierstücke zu vier Händen*, 14 May
1898. 8p., 35x26cm. (61/4)
A. Mus. ms. S.: *Konzert für Klavier, linke Hand, und
Orchester*, 1925. 38p., 27x34cm. (61/5)
A. Mus. ms. S.: *Dances from Old Vienna*, 1940. 31p.,
32x24cm., 35x27cm. Arranged for two pianos from
orchestral score (61/6)
A. Mus. ms.: [*3*] *Streichquartett in A-Dur*. 72p.,
26x34cm. Complete sketches. Beethoven prize 1910
(61/7)
A. Mus. ms.: *Esterházy Phantasy* by Schubert. 4p.,
35x27cm. For two pianos (61/8)
A. Mus. ms. S.: *In the MacDowell Woods*, to Mrs.
Edward MacDowell, Bass River, 15 Aug. 1942. 4p.,
34x28cm. (61/9)
A. Mus. ms.: *The Invisible Light*. 4p., 35x26cm. (61/10)
A. Mus. ms.: *Klavier Concerto*. 155p., 27x34cm.
Sketches (62/1)

A. Mus. ms. S.: *Komödienvorspiel*, 31 Oct. 1933. 14p.,
27x34cm. Sketches (62/2)
A. Mus. ms. S.: *Landsturm*, 8 Nov. 1914. 5p., 35x28cm.
With additional 6p. copyist's manuscript (62/3)
A. Mus. ms. S.: *Lustspiel-Overture*, Vienna, 26 May
1901. 55p., 35x27cm. Full score (62/4)
A. Mus. ms.: [Part songs]. 77p. (62/5)
A. Mus. ms.: [*The Pied Piper of Hamelin*]. 26p.,
35x27cm. Sketches (62/6)
A. Mus. ms. S.: *Quartett* [in G Major], Vienna, May
1900. 37p. (full score) + 42p. (parts) (62/7)
A. Mus. ms. S.: *Requiem für Eva (Adagio für
Streichquartett)*, 1927–1928. 42p. + 101p. (sketches),
27x34cm. (62/8)
A. Mus. ms. S.: *Rhapsodie für Klavier und Orchester*. 23p.
+ 79p. (sketches) + 102p. (piano score), 34x27cm.
(63/1)
A. Mus. ms. S.: *Der 71. Psalm*, Vienna, 28 Dec. 1901.
32p., 34x26cm. (63/2)
A. Mus. ms.: [Sketch books]: 1893–1899, 149p.;
1898–1900, 119p.; 1938, 48p.; 1940, 100p.; 1941, 29p.
(63/3–5)
A. Mus. ms.: [Sketches, identified fragments]. 318p.
(64/1–9)
A. Mus. ms.: [Sketches, unidentified]. 3,426p. (65–70)
A. Mus. ms.: [Solo songs]. 733p. (71–72)
Mus. ms. cop.: *Sonate für Klavier & Violine*, 1910[?].
10p. (parts), 35x27cm. (73/1)
A. Mus. ms. S.: *Streich-Quartett* [in C Minor], Vienna,
1903–1904. 59p., 27x34cm. (73/2)
A. Mus. ms.: [*String Quartet No. 6*]. 72p. + inserts,
34x27cm. (73/3)
A. Mus. ms.: *String Quartet in F Minor*, No. 7. 71p.,
34x26cm. Sketches (73/4)
A. Mus. ms.: [*String Quartet No. 8*]. 36p., 33x26cm.
Sketches (73/5)
A. Mus. ms. S.: *Suite in A Dur, für Streichorchester*,
16 June 1898. 5p., 26x34cm. (73/6)
A. Mus. ms. S.: *Symphonisches Vorspiel für eine Tragödie*,
Vienna, Mar. 1933. 102p., 27x33cm. Sketches (73/7)
A. Mus. ms. S.: *Symphonie in E*, 1900–1901. 162p.,
35x27cm. Full score (74/1)
A. Mus. ms.: [same]. 129p., various sizes. Sketches for
all movements, in piano score (74/2)
A. Mus. ms. S.: [same]. 60p., 35x27cm. Piano sketches
(74/3)
A. Mus. ms.: [*Symphony No. 4*]. 2p., (pp.1–2 of the full
score), 34x26cm. (74/4)
A. Mus. ms. S.: [same]. 1935. 35p., 27x34cm. Reduced
score (74/5)

A. Mus. ms.: [same]. 12p. (mvts. I, II) + 186p. (sketches for mvt. III), 27x34cm. (74/6)

A. Mus. ms.: *Symphony No. 5 in C Minor*. 1 leaf (p.67), 38x27cm. (Box 108)

A. Mus. ms. S.: [same], 1943–1944. 67p., 34x27cm. Sketches in reduced score (75/1)

A. Mus. ms. S.: [*Symphony No. 6*]. 41p. Reduced score (75/2)

A. Mus. ms. S.: *Tänzl, für Clavier*, 1898. 12p., 35x27cm. (75/3)

A. Mus. ms. S.: *Toteninsel, Phantasie für grosses Orchester*, Vienna, 4 July 1904. 50p., 35x26cm. Full score (75/4)

A. Mus. ms.: [*Two Pieces for Cello and Piano*], 1940. 16p., 35x27cm. Sketches (75/5)

A. Mus. ms. S.: [*Two Religious Choruses, Who Knows?*], New York, Dec. 1941. 1p., 36x31cm. Draft (75/6)

A. Mus. ms. S.: *Valse lente*, op. 3, 1893. 5p., 33x26cm. (75/7)

A. Mus. ms. S.: *Variationen*, Dec. 1899. 11p., 35x26cm. (75/8)

A. Mus. ms. S.: *4 Clavierfugen*, Vienna, Sept. 1899. 7p., 35x27cm. (75/9)

A. Mus. ms. S.: *The Watchman's Report*, to the Germantown Friends School, 19 Jan. 1945. 6p., 38x28cm. (75/10)

A. Mus. ms. S.: *Weltfeier, von Heinrich Hart, für Chor und grosses Orchester*, op. 17, 1910. 92p. + 2p. (text insert), 35x27cm. Sketches (75/11)

Mus. ms. cop.: *String Quartet in G Major*. 20p. First movement only (75/12)

L.: to Weigl, from Arnold Schoenberg. Berlin, 31 May 1903. 2p. With calling card annotated. Also, photograph of Schoenberg, his daughter, and Zemlinsky (Box 123)

2 A. L. S.: to Weigl, from Alexander Zemlinsky. [5 Dec. 1907?, 22 Feb. 1911?]. 2p. German (Box 123)

2 L. S.: to Weigl, from Wilhelm Furtwängler. Mannheim, 28 May 1920; Hamburg, 21 May 1922. 2p. (Box 123)

2 L. S.: to Weigl, from Alfred Einstein. Munich, 12 Dec. 1924; New York, 7 Apr. 1939. 2p. (Box 123)

P. card: to Weigl, from Eusebius Mandyczewski. Vienna, 2 Jan. 1928 (Box 123)

P. card: to Weigl, from Heinrich Schenker. Vienna, 23 Nov. 1934 (Box 123)

L. S.: to Weigl, from Wilhelm Kienzl. 15 Sept. 1935. Note on Kienzl's calling card (Box 123)

P. card: to Weigl, from Felix Weingartner. 22 Sept. 1936 (Box 123)

2 L. S.: to Weigl, from Bruno Walter. New York, 26 Mar. 1939, 23 Oct. 1943. 2p. (Box 123)

2 P. cards: to Weigl, from Julius Bittner. Vienna, ?. German (Box 123)

P. card: to Weigl, from Ignaz Friedman (Box 123)

A. L. S.: to Vally Weigl. Boston, 18 Dec. 1946. 1p., German. Giving his wife instructions regarding his last wishes (76/1)

L. S. Repro.: to Vally Weigl, from Pablo Casals. 2 Jan. 1952. 1p., French (Box 123)

2 L. S. Repro.: to Vally Weigl, from Mrs. Elizabeth Coolidge. 2, 20 Aug. 1952. 2p. (Box 123)

A. Doc.: Text. Conversations with the deaf-mute sculptor Gustinus Ambrosi (1893–1975). 15p. (76/2)

Doc.: Articles, brochures, catalog, publicity materials, programs, photographs (including one of Gustav Mahler) (76/6, 123)

Doc.: Diploma (Box 108)

Doc.: Personal materials, letters (76/3–5)

5 Pri. Sco.: *8 Frauenchöre*, op. 25; *Viola Sonata; Two Religious Choruses; Five Songs* (two copies); [*3*] *Songs for Contralto or Mezzo Soprano* (76/7–11)

Port. Draw.: [by Paunzen?], to Vally Weigl, Sept. 1925. 52x37cm. With letter to Hans Moldenhauer, from John Weigl, 1963 (Box 108)

12 Phot.: of Weigl, and Vally (wife). Some with autograph annotations (Box 116)

Phot.: including one of Gustav Mahler (Box 123)

Weigl, Vally, 1899–1982
Harvard University

SUMMARY OF PRINCIPAL HOLDINGS:
In addition to the materials below the collection also includes uncataloged manuscripts, sketches, letters, recordings

Mus. ms.: *All Day I Hear the Noise of Waters*

Mus. ms.: *The Blackbird*

Mus. ms.: *Cardinal in March*, 1975

Mus. ms.: *Children's Songs*

Mus. ms.: *Christmas Carol*

Mus. ms.: *On Christmas Eve*

Mus. ms.: *Come In*

Mus. ms.: *A Conceit of Spring*

Mus. ms.: *Conscientious Objector*, 1974

Mus. ms.: *Dear Earth: A Quintet of Poems*

Mus. ms.: *Death Snips Proud Men by the Nose*

Mus. ms.: *Dirge*

Mus. ms.: *Easter*

Mus. ms.: *Epitaph*

Mus. ms.: *Oh Fair to See*
Mus. ms.: *Four Choruses on Death and Man*, No. 1
Mus. ms.: *Friends, Will We Reach the Promised Land?*
Mus. ms.: *Gifts*
Mus. ms.: *Grace for a Child*
Mus. ms.: *Grasshopper*
Mus. ms.: *Hoffnungsschimmer*, 1939
Mus. ms.: *How Long Is the Night*
Mus. ms.: *I Have Lighted the Candles*
Mus. ms.: *Irish House Blessing*
Mus. ms.: *In Just Spring*
Mus. ms.: *Let My Country Awake*
Mus. ms.: *Let There Be Music*
Mus. ms.: *Of Life, Love, and Leaving*
Mus. ms.: *The Long Nights*
Mus. ms.: *Lyrical Suite*
Mus. ms.: *Native Island*
Mus. ms.: *Nature Moods*
Mus. ms.: *New England Suite*, No. 1
Mus. ms.: *Night of Prayer*
Mus. ms.: *The Night Will Never Stay*
Mus. ms.: *No Boundary*
Mus. ms.: *Oiseau de la Vie*
Mus. ms.: *Out of the Dark*
Mus. ms.: *The People, Yes!*
Mus. ms.: *Rain at Night*
Mus. ms.: *Regennacht*
Mus. ms.: *Requiem for Allison*
Mus. ms.: *The Rivals*
Mus. ms.: *Saint Francis*
Mus. ms.: *A Shelter for All*, 1962
Mus. ms.: *Solo for Saturday Night Guitar*
Mus. ms.: *The Song of Shadows*
Mus. ms.: *Songs for a Child*. Excerpt
Mus. ms.: *Songs of Remembrance*
Mus. ms.: *The Sorrow Dance*
Mus. ms.: *Stars, Songs, and Faces*
Mus. ms.: *Swiftly Along Flows the River*
Mus. ms.: *Take My Hand*
Mus. ms.: *Te Deum*
Mus. ms.: *Thistle, Yarlow, Clover*
Mus. ms.: *Three Choral Songs from the Southwest*, Nos. 1, 2
Mus. ms.: *We Are the Music Makers*
Mus. ms.: *What Once the Heart Has Loved*
Mus. ms.: *What Were They Like*
Mus. ms.: *When I Am Dead, My Dearest*
Mus. ms.: *When the Song of the Angels Is Stilled*
Mus. ms.: *When the Vision Dies*
Mus. ms.: *Who Goes There Through the Night?*
Mus. ms.: *Who Is at My Window*

20 L.: to Hans Moldenhauer. 1967–1977
Doc.: Poems
Mus. ms. Repro.: *April*. Blueprint score
Mus. ms. Repro.: *The Drums of War*, 1966. Facsimile
Mus. ms. Repro.: *Fog*. Photocopy
Mus. ms. Repro.: *Glimpse of Hope*. Blueprint score
Mus. ms. Repro.: *Liebster, Liebster, schläfst Du noch?*, 1916. Photocopy
Mus. ms. Repro.: *Nightfall in the Mountains*. Blueprint score
Mus. ms. Repro.: *No Loveliness Is Ever Lost*. Blueprint score
Mus. ms. Repro.: *Ode to Beauty*
Mus. ms. Repro.: *The Owl and the Pussy-Cat*
Mus. ms. Repro.: *Rainy Day Song, Billy Goats Chew*. Photocopy
Mus. ms. Repro.: *Who Bids Us Sing?*. Blueprint score

Weill, Kurt, 1900–1950
Library of Congress
(Box 102)
A. L. S.: to Universal Edition. n.p., 18 Nov. 1926. 2p., German. Confidential matters; *Der Protagonist, Der neue Orpheus*
A. Mus. Quot. S.: *Street Scene*, to Lois Spitzbart, Oct. 1948. 1p., 9x16cm.

Weinberger, Jaromir, 1896–1967
Moldenhauer Archives, Spokane, Washington
SUMMARY OF PRINCIPAL HOLDINGS:
Mus. ms.: *Czech Rhapsody*, for full orchestra, 1943
Mus. ms.: *The Outcasts of Pokerflat*, 1932
Mus. ms.: *Préludes réligieux et profanes*. Complete draft
Mus. ms.: *Symphonie aus den Alpen*, for large orchestra, 1958
Mus. ms.: *A String Quartet*. Score, parts, complete draft
Doc.: Correspondence, program notes, photographs, sketches for compositions

Weingartner, Felix, 1863–1942
Library of Congress
(Box 77, unless noted)
A. Mus. ms. Annot. S.: [Five Songs]: *Guter Rath,*
Weberlied, Schuhmacherlied, Spielmannslied, Der Liebe
Erwachen, 7–9 July 1899, to Julius Wahle, Munich,
17 Apr. 1900. 6p., 27x34cm., German, ink, pencil.
For voice and piano. Complete drafts of all songs
A. L. S.: to Eugen Lindner. Krieglach, 30 July 1890.
1p., German
A. L. S.: n.p., 20 Oct. 1895. 3p., German
A. L. S.: to the Generalintendant. Paris, 24 Feb. 1898.
2p., German
T. L. Annot. S.: [to Zemlinsky]. Darmstadt, 15 Oct.
1915. 3p., German. Regarding *Kain und Abel*
P. card S.: to Karl Weigl. Vienna, 7 Oct. 1918. German
P. card S.: to Gerhard Tischer. Basel, 29 Dec. 1928.
German
A. L. S.: Basel, 25 Apr. 1930. 1p., German
A. L. S.: [to Paul A. Pisk]. Vienna, n.d. 1p., German
Port. Phot. S.: to Carl Stasny, 1912 (Box 116)

Washington State University
See Rosbaud, Hans

Weinstock, Herbert, 1905–1971
Harvard University
Bk.: *Rossini,* to Hans Moldenhauer, New York, 4 Sept.
1968

Weis [Weiss], Karel, 1862–1944
Library of Congress
(Box 77)
A. Mus. Quot. S.: *Die Dorfmusikanten,* Polka, ?, 6 Oct.
1904. German

Weisgall, Hugo, 1912–1997
Harvard University
Summary of Principal Holdings:
Mus. ms.: *Purgatory.* Sketches, discarded pages

Weismann, Julius, 1879–1950
Library of Congress
(Box 77)
A. Mus. ms. S.: *Ein nachdenkliches Tänzlein,* to Frau D.
[Füglistaller-Schmid?], 16 July 1937. 2p., 27x34cm.
Complete score
A. Mus. ms. S.: [*Sonatine A Moll*], for two pianos, to
Hans Rosbaud. 4p. (pp.23–26), 27x34cm. Ritornell
movement only. Full score
Doc. S.: Poem. "Mozart." 2p., German. With
autograph note on verso
Mus. ms. Repro. A. Rev.: *Andantino,* 4 Jan. 1936. 2p.
On verso, *Andante con moto*
Mus. ms. Repro. Rev.: *Der Fugenbaum,* op. 150. 48p.
Incomplete. Blueprint score

Washington State University
See Rosbaud, Hans

Weiss, Adolph, 1891–1971
Harvard University
Complete estate of manuscripts may include original
or reproduced scores, correspondence, and recordings
Summary of Principal Holdings:
Mus. ms.: *American Life*
Mus. ms.: Cadenzas, to Mozart's *Bassoon Concerto*
Mus. ms.: *Chorale for Three Trombones and Tuba,* 1936
Mus. ms.: *Concerto for Bassoon and String Quartet*
Mus. ms.: *Concerto for Trumpet and Orchestra*
Mus. ms.: *Dance*
Mus. ms.: *David*
Mus. ms.: *Driftwood*
Mus. ms.: *Duos*
Mus. ms.: *Fantasies*
Mus. ms.: *Greeting*
Mus. ms.: *I Want to See a Little More of You*
Mus. ms.: *It Was a Lover and His Lass*
Mus. ms.: *Kammersymphonie,* 1926/1934
Mus. ms.: *Libation Bearers*
Mus. ms.: *Loafers*
Mus. ms.: *Das Märchen vom sicheren Mann,* 1921
Mus. ms.: *Mardi-Gras Medley*
Mus. ms.: *Nacht-Lied*
Mus. ms.: *Ode to the West Wind*
Mus. ms.: *Passacaglia for Viola and Horn,* 1942
Mus. ms.: *Petite Suite for Flute, Clarinet, and Bassoon*
Mus. ms.: *Auf Poseidons grüner Flur,* 1915
Mus. ms.: *Pulse of the Sea,* 1944
Mus. ms.: *Quartet No. II*

Mus. ms.: *Quartet for Strings*, 1923

Mus. ms.: *Quartets*, for winds

Mus. ms.: *Quintets*, for winds

Mus. ms.: *Rhapsody for Four French Horns*

Mus. ms.: *Ricerar del VII Tuono* by Gabrieli, arranged by Weiss

Mus. ms.: *Ricerar for Flute, Clarinet, and Bassoon*, 1936

Mus. ms.: *I Segreta*

Mus. ms.: *Seven Songs for Soprano and String Quartet*

Mus. ms.: [Sketches]. 825p.

Mus. ms.: *Sonata for Flute and Viola*

Mus. ms.: *Sonata for Piano*, 1932

Mus. ms.: *String Quartet*

Mus. ms.: *Stücke für Kinder*

Mus. ms.: *Suite for Large Orchestra*

Mus. ms.: *Ten Bach Chorales*, arranged by Weiss

Mus. ms.: *Theme and Variations*

Mus. ms.: *Third String Quartet*

Mus. ms.: *Tone-Poem for Brass and Percussion*

Mus. ms.: *Trio for Clarinet, Viola, and Cello*, 1949

Mus. ms.: *Trio for Flute, Violin, and Piano*

Mus. ms.: *Trios*, for winds

Mus. ms.: *Twelve Preludes*

Mus. ms.: *Wind Quintet*, 1932

Mus. ms.: *Das Wohltemperierte Klavier*, vol. I by Bach, arranged by Weiss for woodwinds and horn

L.: to Carl Ruggles

Doc.: [Personal papers]. Including essays, legal documents, letters, notebooks (with text and musical notation), photographs, poems

Mus. ms. Repro.: *Fughetta* by J. S. Bach

Mus. ms. Repro.: *Sextet*, for winds and piano. Blueprint score

Mus. ms. Repro.: *Six Songs*, for soprano, string quartet, and piano. Incomplete. Photocopy

Mus. ms. Repro.: *Sonata for Violin and Piano*, 1935. Blueprint score

Mus. ms. Repro.: *Sunday Morning for Orchestra*

Mus. ms. Repro.: *Ten Pieces for Low Instrument and Orchestra*. Blueprint score

Mus. ms. Repro.: *Two x Five Fancies*. Blueprint score

See Dahl, Ingolf

Weissmann, Frieder, b. 1893
Library of Congress

(Box 77)

L.: to Aurelio de la Vega. New York, 9 May 1952. 1p., English

Weldon, Georgina, 1837–1914
Northwestern University

L.: to Leslie Ward. n.p., n.d.

Wellesz, Egon, 1885–1974
Library of Congress

(Box 77)

A. Mus. ms. S.: *Sonata for Violin Solo*, op. 72, Oxford, 16–17 Apr. 1953, revised 24–26 Nov. 1959. 7p., 31x23cm., ink, pencil

A. Mus. ms.: [same], Adagio. 2p., 31x23cm., pencil. Sketches

A. L. S.: to Mrs. Pisk. n.p., 1 May 1925. 1p., German

2 P. cards S.: to Otto Jokl. Vienna, 29 Oct. 1935; ?. 2p., German

3 A. L. S.: to Paul Pisk. Vienna, 18 Sept. 1937; 5 Jan. 1938; 17 July 1962. 5p., German, English

3 A. L. S.: to Hans Moldenhauer. Oxford, 12 Feb. 1962; 10 July 1965; Bozen, 21 Aug. 1969. 4p., German, English

A. L. S.: to Aurelio de la Vega. Kritzendorf, 6 Aug. 1965. 1p., English

Doc. Repro.: Recital handout. 5p., German, English. Poems with translation

Pri. Sco.: *Sonata for Violin Solo*, op. 72, New York: Rongwen, c1961. 8p.

2 Prog.: "In Memoriam Egon Wellesz." 6p. each, English

Wenzel, Eberhard, 1896–1982
Library of Congress

(Box 77)

A. Mus. ms. S.: *Bauernlied*. 2p., 34x27cm., German. Full score

A. Mus. ms. S.: *Ährenlied*. 2p., 34x27cm., German. Full score

Wesendonck [Wesendonck; née Luckemeyer], Mathilde, 1828–1902
Zentralbibliothek Zürich

L.: n.p., n.d.

Wesley, Samuel Sebastian, 1810–1876
Northwestern University

L.: to Reid. 2 Dec. 1833. On verso, draft of a letter from Reid

Westrop, Henry, 1812–1879
Northwestern University
Mus. ms.: *Trio for Pianoforte, Violin, and Violoncello.*
    Score, parts

Wetz, Richard, 1875–1935
Library of Congress
(Box 77)
2 A. L. S.: to Tischer. Erfurt, 17, 26 Dec. 1929. 12p.,
    German. Discusses *Weihnachtsoratorio*
A. Card S.: [to Tischer]. Erfurt, 14 Jan. 1930. 2p.,
    German

White, Maude Valérie, 1855–1937
Northwestern University
L.: to Miss Molesworth. n.p., n.d.

White, Paul, 1895–1973
Harvard University
Port. Phot.: to Adolph Weiss

Widmer, Ernst, b. 1927
Harvard University
L.: to Hans Moldenhauer, from Aurelio de la Vega.
    Northridge, 18 Feb. 1986
Mus. ms. Repro.: *Utopia*, op. 142. Facsimile

Widor, Charles-Marie, 1844–1937
Library of Congress
(Box 77)
A. L. S.: to Fanny ?. Paris, 25 June 1886. 2p., French
2 A. L. S.: n.p., n.d. 2p., French
Doc.: Biographical sketch

Wiel, Marie, 1833–1891
Library of Congress
(Box 77)
A. L. S.: n.p., 28 [Sept.?]. 4p., German

Wieniawski, Henryk [Henri], 1835–1880
Library of Congress
(Box 77)
A. L. S.: to ?. [Salzburg?], [Aug. ?]. 1p., French

Wieniawski, Józef, 1837–1912
Library of Congress
(Box 77)
Call. c. Annot.: 17 Mar. 1880. German

Wild, Franz, 1792–1860
Library of Congress
(Box 77)
2 A. L. S.: to Tichatschek. Theater zu Graz, 16,
    23 Feb. 1837. 6p., German

Wildberger, Jacques, b. 1922
Washington State University
See Rosbaud, Hans

Wilder, Alec [Alexander], 1907–1980
Harvard University
Prog.: Washington, D.C., 10 Dec. 1971

Wilhemj, August, 1845–1908
Library of Congress
(Box 77)
P. card S.: to Rudolf Herfurth. Biebrich, 19 Dec. 1884.
    German

Williamson, John Finley, 1887–1964
Washington State University
L.: to Solomon Pimsleur. Ithaca, New York, 8 Sept.
    1931

Willner, Arthur, 1881–1959
Northwestern University
Mus. ms.: *First Symphony*

Mus. ms.: [Unidentified sketch]
Mus. ms. arr.: *String Quartet in C Major*, arranged for
  piano, four hands

Wilt, Marie, 1833–1891
Wiener Stadt- u. Landesbibliothek
Rcpt.: Vienna, 31 July 1873

Wimberger, Gerhard, b. 1923
Library of Congress
(Box 77)
A. Mus. ms. S.: *Ars amatoria*, 1967. 1p., 33x27cm.
A. Mus. ms. S.: *La Battaglia oder Der rote Federbusch*,
  1959. 2p., 34x27cm.
A. Mus. ms. S.: *Chronique*, 1969. 2p., 34x27cm.
A. Mus. ms. S.: *Dame Kobold*, 1963. 1p., 34x27cm.
A. Mus. ms.: *Drei lyrische Chansons*. 40p., 34x27cm. Full
  draft in condensed score
A. Mus. ms. S.: *Hero und Leander*, 1963. 1p., 34x27cm.
A. Mus. ms. S.: *Lebensregeln*, 1972. 2p., 34x27cm.
A. Mus. ms. S.: *Memento vivere*, 1974. 2p., 32x21cm.
A. Mus. ms. S.: *Multiplay*, 1973. 2p., 27x32cm.
A. Mus. ms. S.: *Resonance für 3 Orchester-Gruppen*, 1967.
  2p., 34x27cm.
A. Mus. ms. S.: *Signum für Orgel*, 1970. 2p., 34x27cm.
A. Mus. ms. S.: *Stories*, 1962. 2p., 36x27cm.
T. Doc. A. Rev.: Work list and biographical sketch. 2p.

Winding, August, 1835–1899
Library of Congress
See Grieg, Edvard

Winkelmann, Hermann, 1849–1912
Library of Congress
(Box 77)
A. L. S.: Hamburg, 14 Mar. 1881. 1p., German

Wirén, Dag, 1905–1986
Library of Congress
(Box 77)
Pri. Sco. S.: *Sinfonietta*, op. 7, Vienna: Universal, c1951,
  to Fritz Mahler. 105p.

Wit, Margarete
Library of Congress
(Box 116)
Port. Phot. Repro. S.

Witherspoon, Herbert, 1873–1935
Harvard University
L.: to Rudolph Ganz. New York, 8 Mar. 1935

Wittgenstein, Paul, 1887–1961
Library of Congress
(Box 77)
A. L. S.: to Karl Weigl. Scheveningen, 30 Dec. 4p.,
  German. Concerning piano concerto for the left
  hand

Wittinger, Róbert, b. 1945
Library of Congress
(Box 102, unless noted)
A. Mus. ms. S.: *Concentrazione*, op. 6, Budapest, 1965. 1
  leaf, 42x29cm. Title page and first page of full score.
  With additional printed score, c1967
A. Mus. ms.: *Divergenti*, op. 13, [June–Sept. 1969]. 2p.
  (1 leaf), 60x42cm. Sketch. With additional printed
  score, c1969
2 Docs. A. Rev.: Work list. 2p., German
Call. c.
Clip.: Jan. 1971. 1p., German. With accompanying
  photograph
Port. Phot.: see clipping above
S. rec.: opera 6, 7, 9, 10, 12, 17; *Espressioni*; *Construzioni*
  (Shelf)

Wölfl [Wölffl, Woelfl], Joseph, 1773–1812
Northwestern University
Mus. ms.: *J. Woelfl's 5th Grand Sinfonia for a Full Band*

Wohlgemuth, Justus Albert
Library of Congress
(Box 77)
A. L. S.: to A. W. Gottschalg. Berlin, 18 Mar. 1857. 2p., German

Wolf, Hugo, 1860–1903
Library of Congress
(Box 77)
2 A. Mus. mss. S.: *An* (Lenau)*, Windischgraz, 27 Apr.–8 May 1877. Song with piano accompaniment; on verso of leaf, *Morgenthau ("aus einem alten Liederbuche")*, Windischgraz, 19 June 1877. Song with piano accompaniment. 1 leaf, 35x27cm., ink, pencil. Complete scores
A. Mus. ms. S.: [*Der Corregidor*], "Ave Maria purissima." 1p. (10m.), 25x33cm., ink, pencil. Fourth act. Original draft. With accompanying letter to Hinterberger, from Ilse Kautsky (Frauenkirchen, 4 July 1956)
P. card S.: to Heinrich Potpeschnigg. Vienna, 31 May 1897. 1p., German. Regarding *Der Corregidor*
Rcpt. S.: Vienna, 7 July

Wiener Stadt- u. Landesbibliothek
Mus. ms.: [Sixty-two complete songs and three song fragments]. From the estate of the tenor Ferdinand Jäger, includes autograph and copyist's scores, corrections, proofs

Wolff, Edward, 1816–1880
Library of Congress
(Box 77)
A. Mus. ms. S.: *Marzurka*, Paris, 1 May 1846. 1p., 14x10cm.

Wolff, Werner, 1883–1961
Library of Congress
(Box 77)
A. L. S.: to Bruno Eisner. n.p., n.d. 3p., German

Wolf-Ferrari, Ermanno, 1876–1948
Bayerische Staatsbibliothek
L.: to Ernst Oppler. Munich, 27 Dec. 1912

Wolfrum, Philipp, 1854–1919
Library of Congress
(Box 78)
A. L. S.: Heidelberg, 28 Nov. 1903. 2p., German

Wolpe, Stefan, 1902–1972
Library of Congress
(Box 102)
A. Mus. ms. S.: *String Quartet*, 1951. 12p., 34x27cm. Third movement
P. card S.: to Bruno Eisner. New York, 28 Dec. 1951. 1p., English

Wolzogen, Karl August Alfred von, 1823–1883
Library of Congress
(Box 78)
2 A. L. S.: Breslau, 12 Jan. 1861; Schwerin, 5 Mar. 1871. 5p., English

Wood, William, b. 1935
Harvard University
Summary of Principal Holdings:
Mus. ms.: *Eight Music*
Mus. ms.: *Five for Six*
Mus. ms.: *Sonata for Violoncello and Piano*, 29 Aug. 1969
Mus. ms.: *Symphony in Three Movements*

Wotton, Thomas, 1862–1939
Northwestern University
L.: Bexhill-on-Sea, 22 Jan. 1920

Woyrsch, Felix, 1860–1944
Library of Congress
(Box 78, unless noted)

A. L. S.: Altona, 27 Dec. 1908. 2p., German
A. Mus. Quot. S.: "The Lord's Prayer." German,
   English
Port. Phot. S. (Box 116)

Washington State University
See Rosbaud, Hans

Wranitzky, Anton, 1761–1820
Library of Congress
(Box 78)
A. L. S.: to Anton André. Vienna, 13 Feb. 1802. 3p.,
   German

Wranitzky-Seidler, Karoline, 1790 or 1794–1872
Library of Congress
(Box 78)
A. L. S.: Berlin, 21 Jan. 1825. 3p., German
L.: to ?. Berlin, 11 June 1828. 2p., German

Wüllner, Franz, 1832–1902
Bayerische Staatsbibliothek
2 L.: Munich, 15 May 1876; Dresden, 24 Oct. 1883

Wüllner, Ludwig, 1858–1938
Library of Congress
(Box 78)
P. card S.: to Therese Lindenberg. Berlin, 1[7?] July
   1917. German

Wuerst, Richard, 1824–1881
Library of Congress
(Box 78)
A. Mus. Quot. S.: Allegretto, 29 Mar. 1846. 2p.,
   23x28cm.

Würz, Richard, 1885–1965
Library of Congress
(Box 78)
P. card S.: to Marie Geselschap. Munich, 5 Sept. 1924.
   German

Wuorinen, Charles, b. 1938
Harvard University
L.: to Gloria Coates. New York, 23 Apr. 1972

Wynne, Sarah Edith, 1842–1897
Northwestern University
L.

Xenakis, Iannis, b. 1922
Library of Congress
(Box 78, unless noted)
A. Mus. ms. S.: *Metastasis*. 1p. (p.10), 73x52cm., pencil.
   Full score (Shelf)
A. Mus. ms. S.: *Pithoprakta*, 16 Apr. 1956. 1p.,
   22x51cm., ink (Shelf)
2 A. L. S.: to Hans Moldenhauer. Paris, 4 Mar., 9 Apr.
   1963. 2p., English
T. Doc. S.: Text. "Viel sind der Wunder...." German
Prog.: Premiere, "Woche der leichten Musik Stuttgart
   1962," 22–25 Oct. 1962. Hermann Heiss documents
   inserted

Washington State University
See Rosbaud, Hans

Yardumian, Richard, 1917–1985
Harvard University
SUMMARY OF PRINCIPAL HOLDINGS:
Mus. ms.: *Cantus Animae et Cordis*
Mus. ms.: *Chorale-Prelude for Orchestra*
Mus. ms.: *Chorale-Prelude on Plainsong*
Mus. ms.: *Concerto for Piano and Orchestra*
Mus. ms.: *Symphony No. 1*
2 L.: to Wallingford Riegger. 5 Dec. 1955; draft
L.: to Hans Moldenhauer
Doc.: Essay. On theoretical system
Mus. ms. Repro.: *Chromatic Sonata*, 25 Oct. 1976.
   Blueprint score
Mus. ms. Repro.: *Symphony No. 2*. Facsimile
S. rec.: *Chorale-Prelude; Concerto for Piano and Orchestra;
   Mass; The Story of Abraham; Symphony
   No. 1; Symphony No. 2; Violin Concerto*

Yoo, Insook
Library of Congress
(Box 78)
A. Card S.: to Aurelio de la Vega. [1983]. English

Young, Michael, b. 1939
Whitworth College
SUMMARY OF PRINCIPAL HOLDINGS:
Doc.: Sketchbooks. Contains sketches and drafts,
  along with annotations and other notes, tape
  recordings, and printed programs for works dated
  1971–1988

Ysaÿe, Eugène, 1858–1931
Library of Congress
(Box 116)
A. L. S.: n.p., 20 June 1884. 1p., French. Mounted
  with portrait photograph, 1898

Zarlino, Gioseffo [Gioseffe], 1517–1590
Library of Congress
(Box 78, unless noted)
Doc. S.: Three-line attestation. To the last will of
  Vincenzo Diedo, Patriarch of Venice. Dec. 1559. 3p.,
  Italian, 30x22cm. Witnessed by several persons
  besides Zarlino
Bk.: *L'Istitutioni Harmoniche*, Venice: Francesco Senese,
  1562 (Shelf)

Zeisl, Eric, 1905–1959
Library of Congress
(Box 78)
A. L. S.: to Alma Mahler, from Trude Zeisl.
  Hollywood, n.d. 2p., German

Zelter, Carl Friedrich, 1758–1832
Northwestern University

L.: [to a royal highness]. n.p., n.d. With Zelter's copy of a
  letter from Johann Philipp Kirnberger (14 Mar. 1783)

Zemlinsky, Alexander, 1871–1942
Harvard University
SUMMARY OF PRINCIPAL HOLDINGS:
A. Mus. ms. S.: *Sechs Lieder*, op. 22, 1934. 9p.,
  35x27cm., ink, pencil. Full score
A. Mus. ms.: *Der Tag wird kühl*, to Melanie Guttmann,
  June 1897
Mus. ms. cop.: *Tod in Aehren*
Mus. ms. cop.: *Turmwächterlied*, op. 8, No. 1
Mus. ms.: *Das verlassene Mädchen*
Mus. ms.: *IV. Streichquartett*. Complete parts
4 L.: to Karl Weigl. Dresden, 5 June 1902; Gmünden,
  15 July 1905; Vienna, 15 Nov. 1923; Steinkirchen, ?
6 L.: to Melanie Guttmann. 1902–1907, n.d. Also
  signed by Schoenberg, Richard Strauss
L.: to Melanie Guttmann. Rottach-Ege, 11 Aug. 1906.
  Also signed by Schoenberg, others
14 L.: to Kramer. 1920–1924
3 L.: to Klara Kwartin. Leningrad, 30 Jan., 4 Feb.
  1928; Prague, n.d.
32 L.: to Louise Sachsel-Zemlinsky. 1928–1935
L.: to Alban Berg. Fragment. On verso, addresses in
  the hand of Alma Mahler
2 L.: to Bruno Eisner. n.p., n.d.
2 L.: to Louise Sachsel. Prague, n.d.; n.p., n.d.
L.: Vienna, 22 Dec.
14 L.: to Zemlinsky, from Universal Edition, Simrock,
  others
Doc.: Scrapbook. Contains clippings, 1893–1896
2 Call. c. Annot.
2 Pri. Sco. Annot.: *Der Kreidekreis*, 1933, 1938
Pri. Sco. Annot.: *Der 23. Psalm*, op. 14, 1922
Pri. Sco. Annot.: *Der Zwerg*, 1921
2 Port. Phot.: to Melanie Gutman, 1907, 1927
Port. Phot.: some of Zemlinsky alone, other group
  photographs with Bodanzky, Max Klein, Kramer,
  friends, family, stage settings

Library of Congress
See Schoenberg, Arnold
See Webern, Anton
See Weigl, Karl

Wiener Stadt- u. Landesbibliothek
See Schoenberg, Arnold

Zenk, Ludwig, 1900–1949
Library of Congress
(Box 78)
A. Mus. ms. S.: *Missa Pacis 1945*, Gloria, to Josef and
    Hildegard Humplik, 23 Dec. 1946. 1p.
    (mm.104–110), 34x26cm.
A. Mus. ms.: [Sketches for a song with piano
    accompaniment], 1947. 4 leaves, 13–26x34cm.
A. Mus. ms.: [Sketches for a four-part chorus with
    continuo], 1 June 1948. 5p., 34x26cm. + 32x24cm.
A. Mus. ms. cop.[?]: [*String quartet*]. 11p. (viola part),
    34x26cm.
A. Mus. ms.: *Symphonie*, 28 Apr., 14 Sept. 1935. 31p.,
    34x27cm. Sketches and draft of Adagio and another
    movement
19 A. L. S.: to Hildegard Jone and Josef Humplik.
    Vienna, 1936–1948. 42p., German. Containing
    references to Webern, his compositions, Trakl's
    poems; some bear postscript from Mia (wife)
10 P. cards S.: to Hildegard Jone and Josef Humplik.
    Vienna, Berlin, Gurgl, 1938–1945. German. Some
    postcard photos taken by Zenk
Tlgm.: to Hildegard Jone. Aug. 1946. German
A. L. S.: to Josef Humplik, from Mia Zenk. Vienna,
    19 June 1949. 1p., German
2 Mus. mss. Repro. S.: *Blumen hörte ich sterben im
    Grund*. 4p., German. Two copies, one signed
Mus. ms. Repro.: *2. Klaviersonate*. 1p. Third movement
2 Obit.: Vienna, 23 June [1949]. German. Includes
    copy
See Apostel, Hans Erich
See Webern, Anton

Zeuner, Charles, 1795–1857
Library of Congress
See Viardot, Pauline

Ziehrer, C. M., 1843–1922
Wiener Stadt- u. Landesbibliothek
L.: n.p., n.d.

Zilcher, Hermann, 1881–1948
Bayerische Staatsbibliothek
Mus. ms.: *Der Kuckuck ist ein braver Mann*, op. 10,
    No. 5
3 L.: to Fritz Steinbach. Munich, 19 Dec. 1909,
    31 May, 2 Aug. 1910

Zilcher, Paul, 1855–1943
Library of Congress
(Box 78, unless noted)
A. Mus. ms. S.: *Greetings from the Poets*, op. 63, No. 2.
    1p., 34x27cm.
A. L. S.: Frankfurt, 19 Sept. 1910. 3p., German. With
    work list
Port. Phot. S. (Box 116)

Zillig, Winfried, 1905–1963
Bayerische Staatsbibliothek
Mus. ms.: *Troilus und Cressida*, Chorus II
L.: Munich, 8 Aug. 1959

Washington State University
See Rosbaud, Hans

Zimbalist, Efrem, 1889–1985
Harvard University
L.: to Charles Haubiel. Philadelphia, 19 Sept. 1946

Zimmermann, Bernd Alois, 1918–1970
Library of Congress
(Box 78)
A. Mus. ms. S.: *Omnia tempus habent*, Rom., Oct. 1957.
    6p., 33x26cm.
P. card S.: to Hans Moldenhauer. Kampen, Sylt, 5 Apr.
    1960. German
A. L. S.: to Hans Moldenhauer. Cologne, 4 May 1960.
    1p., German

Washington State University
L.: to Heinrich Strobel. Cologne, 9 Feb. 1962
See Rosbaud, Hans

Zingarelli, Niccolò Antonio, 1752–1837
Library of Congress
(Box 78)
A. L. S.: to Pietro Polivante[?]. Civitavecchia, 14 June
    [1811?]. 1p., Italian. Written from prison where
    Zingarelli had been committed for refusing to
    conduct a concert in celebration of the birthday of
    Napoleon's son

Zöllner, Heinrich, 1854–1941
Library of Congress
(Box 78, unless noted)
A. L. S.: Antwerp, n.d. 1p., German
A. Mus. Quot. S.: *Die versunkene Glocke*, to Gerhart
  Hauptmann. Includes poem
Port. Phot. Repro. (Box 116)

Zöllner, Karl Heinrich, 1792–1836
Library of Congress
(Box 78)
A. L. S.: to Peters. Leipzig, 13 Aug. 1822. 1p., German

Zschiesche, August, 1800–1876
Library of Congress
(Box 78)
A. L. S.: Berlin, 9 Mar. 1828. 1p., German

Zuckmayer, Carl, 1896–1977
Library of Congress
(Box 117)
P. card S.: to Alma Werfel. Saas-Fee, 19 Dec. 1958.
  German. Postscript on a letter from his wife
Doc. S.: Festival address. "Das Ziel der Klasse,"
  Mainz: Philipp von Zabern, to Hans Moldenhauer,
  15 Feb. 1962 [1963]. 32p., German

Zuckmayer, Eduard, 1890–1972
Library of Congress
(Box 78, unless noted)
A. Mus. ms. S.: *Bursa Sekme*, 6 Dec. 1953. 3p.,
  34x25cm. Full score
A. Mus. ms. S.: *Gens Osman*, Nov. 1956. 2p., 34x25cm.
  Full score
A. Mus. ms. S.: *Des Herrn Verheissung an Jaakob*, 8 Sept.
  1934. 3p., 34x27cm. Draft from the unfinished
  oratorio
P. card S.: to Hans Moldenhauer. Turkey, 25 Dec.
  1959. German
T. L. S.: to Hans Moldenhauer. Ankara, 8 Feb. 1960.
  2p., German
A. L. S.: to Hans Moldenhauer. Ankara, 24 Feb. 1960.
  1p., German
Port. Phot. S.: to Hans Moldenhauer, 8 Feb. 1960 (Box
  116)

Zumpe, Herman, 1850–1903
Bayerische Staatsbibliothek
L.: n.p., n.d.

Zumsteeg [Zum Steeg], Johann Rudolf, 1760–1802
Library of Congress
(Box 78)
A. Mus. ms. S.: *Klage*. 2p., 24x30cm., ink. Song with
  accompaniment. Incomplete. On verso, draft of
  another vocal composition
A. L. S.: to a publisher. Stuttgart, 6 Dec. 1796. 1p.,
  German
Pri. Sco. S.: *Die Geisterinsel*, Overture, arrangée
  Frederic Schneider à quatre mains, Leipzig:
  Hofmeister. 8p. First edition. Autograph title page

Zweig, Friderike, 1882–1971
Library of Congress
(Box 117, unless noted)
14 P. cards S.: to Hanna Schwarz. 1934–1970. German
23 A. L. S.: to Hanna Schwarz. 1935–1971. German.
  Discusses leading writers and musicians of the time
16 A. Cards S.: to Hanna Schwarz. n.d. German.
  Holiday greeting cards with short messages
Doc.: Brochure. With portrait photograph reproduced.
  4p., English
Port. Gr.: Friderike Zweig, Hanna Schwarz, and
  others, at Stanford (Box 116)

Washington State University
See Rosbaud, Hans

Zweig, Stefan, 1881–1942
Library of Congress
(Box 117)
8 A. L. S.: to Hanna Schwarz. 1933–1938. German
8 P. cards S.: to Hanna Schwarz. 1933–1937. German
11 T. L. S.: to Hanna Schwarz. 1934–1939. German,
  English. Regarding addressee's wish to appear in
  London as a concert singer; musical society of
  England
Doc.: Announcement. Vienna, n.d. 1p., German.
  Regarding the founding of the International Stefan
  Zweig Society. With membership application
Doc. Repro.: Catalog. Vienna: Herbert Reichner, n.d.
  German. With portrait photograph reproduced,
  listing Zweig's literary output

Wiener Stadt- u. Landesbibliothek
L.: to Friderike (wife). London, 2 June 1937

Nonmusical Items

García Lorca, Federico, 1898–1936
Library of Congress
(Box 117)
A. Doc. A. Rev.: Text, original draft. Contains unpublished lines from section "The Poet in New York," from *New York (Oficina y Denuncia)*, New York, 1930. 3p., Spanish, ink, pencil

Hamsun, Knut, 1859–1952
Library of Congress
(Box 112)
Port. Phot. S.: to ?. By Walery

Hesse, Hermann, 1877–1962
Library of Congress
(Box 117)
P. card S.: to Otto Jokl. Gaienhofen, 24 July [1901?]. German
P. card S.: to Bruno Eisner. Mendrisio, 7 Oct. 1926. German. Includes rhymed messages from "Emmy" and "Ben"
Pri. Card: to Hans Moldenhauer. Zug, Switzerland, 7 Jan. 1957. German

Kotzebue, August von, 1761–1819
Library of Congress
(Box 117)
A. L. S.: to a poet in Dresden. Berlin, 28 May 1803. 2p., German
A. L. S.: to Ackermann. Mannheim, 14 Jan. 1819. 1p., German. Shortly before his assassination

Mann, Monique, 1910–1992
Library of Congress
(Box 117)
2 A. L. S.: to Bruno Eisner. Funes, 21 Sep. 1954; Kilchberg, 18 Aug. 1955. 3p., German

Nuremberg chronicle
Library of Congress
(Box 107)
Doc.: Original leaf. Paginated ccxvii. Printed on both sides. German. With five woodcut illustrations, hand-colored in many hues of watercolor. 44x30cm.

Rilke, Rainer Maria, 1875–1926
Library of Congress
(Box 117)
A. L. S.: to Professor Wilhelm Fliess. Sierre, 4 Dec. 1921 (his birthday). 3p., German

Sand, George, 1804–1876
Library of Congress
(Box 117)
A. L. S.: to Gustave Papet. n.p., n.d. 1p., French

Whymper, Edward, 1840–1911
Library of Congress
(Box 117)
A. L. S.: to Foa. London, 24 Nov. 1899. 3p., English

Wilder, Thornton, 1897–1975
Library of Congress
(Box 117)
P. card S.: to Alma Mahler. Sommering, 1 Jan. 1959. German. Also signed by others

Glossary

A.	Autograph		Paint.	Painting
Alb. l.	Album leaf		P. card	Postcard
Annot.	Annotated, annotations		Phot.	Photograph
Arr.	Arranged, arranger		Port.	Portrait
b.	born		Pri.	Printed
Bk.	Book		Prog.	Program
ca.	circa		Quot.	Quotation
Call. c.	Calling card		Rcpt.	Receipt
Caric.	Caricature		Repro.	Reproduction
Clip.	Clipping		Rev.	Revised, revisions
Comp.	Composer		S.	Signed
Cop.	Copyist		Sco.	Score
d.	died		S. rec.	Sound recording
Doc.	Document		Sig.	Signature
Doc. cop.	Document copied		T.	Typewritten
Draw.	Drawing		Tlgm.	Telegram
Engr.	Engraving		T. p.	Title page
fl.	flourished			
Gr.	Group			
L.	Letter			
L. cop.	Letter copied			
Lib.	Libretto			
Lith.	Lithograph			
Mus.	Music			
Mus. ms.	Music manuscript			
Mus. ms. arr.	Music manuscript arranged			
Mus. ms. cop.	Music manuscript copied			
Obit.	Obituary			
p.	post			

Repositories

Bayerische Staatsbibliothek
Harvard University
Library of Congress
Moldenhauer Archives, Spokane, Washington
Northwestern University
Paul Sacher Stiftung
Washington State University
Whitworth College
Wiener Stadt- u. Landesbibliothek
Zentralbibliothek Zürich

Contributors

FERENC BÓNIS, who resides in Budapest, is a musicologist and an eminent expert on Béla Bartók. He is also President of the Hungarian Kodály Society.

SUSAN CLERMONT is a Music Specialist in the Music Division at the Library of Congress.

JOHN DAVERIO is the author of *Robert Schumann: Herald of a "New Poetic Age"* (Oxford UP, 1997) and *Nineteenth-Century Music and the German Romantic Ideology* (Schirmer Books, 1993). He is currently Professor of Music and Chairman of the Musicology Department at Boston University.

JOËL-MARIE FAUQUET, Director of Musicological Research at the Centre National de la Recherche Scientifique, works on French chamber music and on the social history of music in the nineteenth century. He is currently preparing critical editions of Gluck's *Orphée* and *Alceste*, as they were edited by Berlioz, for *The New Berlioz Edition*.

LINDA B. FAIRTILE is a Music Specialist at the New York Public Library for the Performing Arts.

DOUGLAS W. FOARD, currently the Executive Secretary of Phi Beta Kappa, is an historian of modern Spain and is the author of *The Revolt of the Aesthetes: Ernesto Gimènez Caballero and the Origins of Spanish Fascism*.

DENISE P. GALLO teaches music history at Loyola University. She has also taught at the Catholic University of America and Peabody Conservatory.

DON C. GILLESPIE is a musicologist specializing in American music and is vice-president of C. F. Peters Corporation.

PHILIP GOSSETT, general editor of the *Edizione critica delle opere di Gioachino Rossini* and of *The Works of Giuseppe Verdi*, is the Robert W. Reneker Distinguished Service Professor and Dean of the Division of the Humanities at the University of Chicago.

WILLIAM D. GUDGER, Professor of Music History and Theory at the College of Charleston and Organist of the Cathedral of St. Luke and St. Paul, writes on Handelian topics and eighteenth-century British organ music in such publications as *The Musical Times*, *The Diapason*, *The American Organist*, *Current Musicology*, and the *Händel-Jahrbuch*.

PATRICIA HALL is Associate Professor of Music Theory at the University of California, Santa Barbara, and the author of *A View of Berg's* Lulu *Through the Autograph Sources*.

CAROL A. HESS is an Assistant Professor of Music at Bowling Green State University and has published on Spanish and American music (of the North and the South) and Brahms.

KEVIN LaVINE is a member of the reference staff of the Music Division at the Library of Congress.

ALFRED MANN, Professor Emeritus of Musicology at Rutgers University and at the Eastman School of Music, University of Rochester, has been connected in personal friendship with Hans Moldenhauer for over fifty years.

ROBERT L. MARSHALL is the Sacher Professor of Music at Brandeis University and the author of numerous publications on the life and music of J. S. Bach and Mozart.

FELIX MEYER, musicologist, is Curator of Music Manuscripts at the Paul Sacher Foundation.

PEGGY MONASTRA is currently working as Promotion Manager of European Catalogues for G. Schirmer, Inc. in New York.

RENA CHARNIN MUELLER's recent work on Liszt includes Henle urtext editions of the *Ballades* and the *Trois Études de Concert*, and a new edition of *Les Préludes* for Editio Musica Budapest. With Mária Eckhardt, she is preparing the new *Franz Liszt Werkverzeichnis* (Henle Verlag).

JON NEWSOM is Chief of the Music Division at the Library of Congress, where, over a span of thirty-two years, he has served as Head of the Reference Section and Assistant Chief.

MICHAEL NOTT is a freelance musicologist and full-time parent who specializes in American music.

MICHAEL O'BRIEN, who holds Master's degrees in Musicology and Library Science, is a System Administrator for the Mission Viejo Library, California.

PHILIP OLLESON is Senior Lecturer in Music, School of Continuing Education, University of Nottingham.

MASSIMO OSSI is Associate Professor in the Music Program of the University of Rochester. His primary area of research is early seventeenth-century secular music, with particular emphasis on the madrigals and theoretical writings of Claudio Monteverdi.

ROBERT PIENCIKOWSKI, a specialist in twentieth-century music, has been on the staff of the Paul Sacher Stiftung since 1990. He has published numerous articles on Boulez, Messiaen, and Stockhausen, among others.

ROBIN RAUSCH is a Music Specialist in the Music Division, Library of Congress.

EDWARD R. REILLY is the author of *Gustav Mahler and Guido Adler: Records of a Friendship* and a number of studies of Mahler's musical manuscripts.

LAURIEJEAN REINHARDT holds a Ph.D. in musicology and writes frequently on topics in twentieth- century European and American music.

GEORGE ROCHBERG, now in his eightieth year, continues writing, traveling, and helping performers prepare new and old works.

GUNTHER SCHULLER is a Pulitzer prize-winning composer, conductor, jazz historian, educator, former President of the New England Conservatory of Music in Boston, and an indefatigable presenter of new music.

WATKINS SHAW, Honorary Librarian of the Ouseley Collection at St. Michael's, Tenbury, and Keeper of the Royal College of Music Library, has published widely and served as principal editor for the publications of Novello.

WAYNE SHIRLEY is a Music Specialist in the Music Division, Library of Congress. He writes often on Gershwin but has, up until now, written about Dallapiccola only in program notes.

MORTEN SOLVIK, born in Norway and educated in the United States, currently lives in Vienna, Austria, and is a freelance musicologist researching musical and cultural topics of the nineteenth century. He is a lecturer at the Hochschule für Musik und darstellende Kunst and at the Institute of European Studies.

CLAUDIO SPIES, composer, is Professor Emeritus of Music at Princeton University, from which he recently retired after twenty-eight years of teaching.

FRED STEINER is a composer and conductor who worked for many years in the film and television studios in Hollywood. He has written and lectured extensively about the history and art of music for motion pictures.

JÜRGEN THYM, Professor and Chair of Musicology at the Eastman School of Music, has published widely on nineteenth-century German lied.

R. LARRY TODD is Professor and Chair of the Music Department at Duke University. He has written extensively about nineteenth-century music, particularly Mendelssohn's.

AURELIO DE LA VEGA, composer, was born in Cuba in 1925, became an American citizen in 1966, and is currently Distinguished Emeritus Professor at California State University, Northridge.

NEAL ZASLAW is Herbert Gussman Professor of Music at Cornell University and editor of *Der neue Köchel*.

ISBN 0-8444-0987-1

Hans Moldenhauer and Fred Gaiser
Mont Blanc (July 21, 1932)
Photograph taken by Henry Krotoschin